HANDBOOK
OF
MEDICAL SOCIOLOGY

FIFTH EDITION

Editors

CHLOE E. BIRD, *Brown University*

PETER CONRAD, *Brandeis University*

ALLEN M. FREMONT, *Harvard Medical School*

Formerly Edited by

HOWARD E. FREEMAN, LEO G. REEDER,

and SOL LEVINE

PRENTICE HALL, UPPER SADDLE RIVER, NEW JERSEY 07458

Library of Congress Cataloging-in-Publication Data

Handbook of medical sociology / edited by Chloe E. Bird, Peter Conrad, Allen M.
Fremont — 5th ed.
    p. ; cm.
  Includes bibliographical references and index.
  ISBN 0-13-014456-8
   1. Social medicine—Handbooks, manuals, etc. I. Bird, Chloe E. II. Conrad, Peter,
1945– III. Fremont, Allen M.
   [DNLM: 1. Social Medicine. 2. Sociology, Medical. WA 31 H236 2000]
  RA418.H29 2000
  362.1—dc21   99-057953

*We dedicate this edition to Sol Levine,
who would have dedicated it to Howard Freeman.*

Editorial Director: Laura Pearson
Publisher: Nancy Roberts
Managing Editor: Sharon Chambliss
Senior Marketing Manager: Christopher DeJohn
Interior Design and Project Manager: Serena Hoffman
Prepress and Manufacturing Buyer: Mary Ann Gloriande
Illustrations: Mirella Signoretto
Cover Art Director: Jayne Conte
Cover Designer: Bruce Kenselaar

Printed in the United States of America

10 9 8 7 6 5 4 3 2 1

This book was set in 10/12 Times New Roman
by Publications Development Company of Texas
and was printed and bound by Courier Companies, Inc.
The cover was printed by Courier Companies, Inc.

ISBN 0-13-014456-8

Prentice-Hall International (UK) Limited, *London*
Prentice-Hall of Australia Pty. Limited, *Sydney*
Prentice-Hall Canada Inc., *Toronto*
Prentice-Hall Hispanoamericana, S.A., *Mexico*
Prentice-Hall of India Private Limited, *New Delhi*
Prentice-Hall of Japan, Inc., *Tokyo*
Pearson Education Asia Pte. Ltd., *Singapore*
Editora Prentice-Hall do Brasil, Ltda., *Rio de Janeiro*

Prentice Hall College
Handbook of Medical Sociology
Bird/014456-8

ISBN 0-13-014456-8

90000

9 780130 144560

CONTENTS

FOREWORD

As the last surviving founder of the *Handbook of Medical Sociology*, Sol Levine had begun the task of organizing a new edition to appear at the millennium. The *Handbook* had always been important to Sol as an educator and a researcher. It was a way to present current thinking in the field of medical sociology, to explore new ideas, and to sow seeds for future research, as well as to try to influence the directions the field was taking. By the mid-1990s, Sol was aware that there were major new areas that a revised *Handbook* could explore. He contacted the present editors to work with him on an edition that would build on the past ones, but would expand to include these newer concerns.

The new edition would allow for what Sol termed "creative integrationism" of ideas not only from medical sociology, but also from the allied fields of social and medical policy. Sol hoped that this edition would examine the interaction between society and health, including the social factors that contribute to illness. Even more important, it would present ideas for improving the quality of life, sense of well-being, and functional performance for people at every level of society. These were ideas that Sol and his colleagues at the Health Institute, the Harvard School of Public Health, and Boston University had been working on for almost a decade.

Because all the original editors of the *Handbook* have now died, the work was carried forward by their colleagues—mostly younger scholars, some of them former students—who had worked directly with one or more of the three founders of the *Handbook*. Although Leo Reeder died in a tragic plane crash in 1978, Howard Freeman and Sol Levine continued his work, publishing two more editions of the *Handbook*. Howard and Sol were close collaborators and co-conspirators until Howard's sudden death in 1992. The work of all three editors informed and shaped the four previous editions, and the present edition would not be appearing without the foundation they laid. Their work will now go forward into the new century because of this new edition of the *Handbook*.

Sol Levine spent a large part of his professional life working in schools of public health and became convinced that both sociologists and their medical colleagues are enriched when they learn from one another and integrate their work. Some of Sol's most important personal and professional relationships were examples of this kind of collaboration. Quite a few of these people are contributors to this volume, while others influenced this work in ways that are not as apparent. They include S.M. Miller, Frank Reissman, Norman Scotch, Paul E. White, and Elliott Mishler. The breadth of topics covered by this new edition, as well as the fresh way in which many subjects are explored, is a testament to the intellectual vitality that interdisciplinarity can encourage.

Many critically important—and sometimes controversial—areas are covered in the chapters of this volume, mirroring the lively debates taking place in our classrooms, the media, and society at large. For example, several of the authors provide alternative viewpoints on ways of understanding and examining the pathways between social conditions and health and illness. Other authors cite examples of how ideological factors vie with the practical mandate to reduce health care costs, and they point out the irony that managed care, which began as a pragmatic attempt to improve health care delivery, is now being experienced by patients and providers alike as limiting the quality of care.

In the compelling concluding chapter, Bernice Pescosolido, Jane McLeod, and Margarita Alegría reassess traditions of medical sociology and the future of the field in both academic settings and in the field of medical care. They point out the inherent tension between academic sociologists, who assess social factors, and their medical colleagues, who focus on scientifically based physical evidence. Is the current ethos of the "marketplace of medicine" compatible with concerns about the effects of social inequality and the lack of access to affordable health care? While many authors in this volume call for more collaboration with medical colleagues, some still wonder, as Sol Levine did, whether it is possible to function as an evaluator and contributor to health policy without losing one's capacity to stand aside and offer critical commentary.

One of the great strengths of this book is that it ranges from chapters dealing with traditional medical sociological concerns, such as Sam Bloom's excellent historical account of the field and chapters on medical education and organizational change, to innovative work on the environment and health, alternative medicine, use of narrative, and bioethics. These chapters raise issues that have previously been marginalized in sociology as well as in the medical world.

Sol Levine would have been very happy with this edition. He would have been especially proud that his work and influence were going forward in this way. In 1996, Sol died suddenly, halfway through his 75th year. As Diana Chapman Walsh wrote in the obituary in *Social Science and Medicine,* "He died young, late in life . . . ." He had only accomplished part of what he hoped to leave as a legacy to the field of medical sociology. While his published work is an important contribution, it has become clear that a major legacy lay in his relationships with family, friends, colleagues, and students. Untold numbers of personal communications tell me of his deep commitment to really listening to students, of hours spent helping a colleague formulate ideas or revise a career path, always taking genuine pleasure in helping others grow, and always maintaining a twinkle in his eye.

This book, so appropriately produced by many of those Sol worked with or mentored, stands as a tribute to his thinking and life. It is a fitting legacy, one that he would be very proud of, and I am honored to write this foreword.

Alice Levine

PREFACE

When the first edition of the *Handbook of Medical Sociology* was published in 1963, medical sociology was an emergent subspecialty in the discipline of sociology. Roughly once every decade the *Handbook* was revised, reflecting changes in the knowledge and focus of medical sociology. Sol Levine and Howard Freeman were involved in editing the first four editions; sadly, both have passed on since the last edition. It has been eleven years since the fourth edition of the *Handbook* was published, and medical sociology has continued to grow and diversify.

When Sol Levine approached each of us to work on the fifth edition, he sought to assemble a new *Handbook* for the millennium that would reflect the breadth and changes in medical sociology. Sol was involved in the early stages of planning this edition, but he passed away before the whole shape of the volume could be realized. As his students, colleagues, and friends, we endeavored to capture the spirit of Sol Levine in this edition. It was Sol's intention—and it is ours—that this edition represent a broader range of sociological research than was covered in the earlier editions. All 29 chapters are new pieces especially written for this edition of the *Handbook*.

Virtually everyone we approached to write a chapter for the fifth edition agreed to contribute and was enthusiastic about the project. We presented the authors with a difficult assignment. We asked them to write the chapters as critical discussions rather than comprehensive reviews and to cover their topic in an interesting and lively fashion. Moreover, since we wanted to cover a broad array of topics, we had to limit the authors' space; we asked the authors to write chapters that were short, pithy, and tightly focused. We dialogued with all during the revision process and are delighted with the high quality of the contributions.

Several changes in this edition are noteworthy. We include some of the core areas of medical sociology that have appeared in previous editions, albeit with a different angle (e.g., professions, social factors and illness, medical education, and doctor-patient relationships). But we also include chapters on topics and areas that have emerged as critical in recent years: gender, race and ethnicity, environment, disability, the experience of illness, managed care, alternative medicine, medicalization, and bioethics. Unique to this edition is an entire section on research and perspectives from related disciplines whose work parallels that of medical sociology, including medical anthropology, health psychology, social epidemiology, and bioethics. The role and impact of social scientific studies of health and health care are changing, and it is clear that while we need to keep our feet firmly planted in sociology, our arms need to stretch out to other disciplines. It is in this spirit we organized Part VI of the book. We also have taken a few small steps toward making this book more international, including contributions by a few of our British colleagues. Finally, in the spirit of the new millennium, we have set up a web page to complement the *Handbook*. Among other features, the web page (www.brandeis.edu/conrad/handbookmedsoc) offers interested readers additional updates provided by chapter authors.

While all of the editors believe that our discipline is better defined as the Sociology of Health and Illness than as Medical Sociology, we have chosen to keep the traditional title because it lends continuity to previous editions. We hope that neophytes and established scholars alike will find resources and ideas in these pages that will enrich and challenge their own thought and work around health and illness. To the extent we have succeeded in providing this, we dedicate this edition to Sol Levine.

Chloe Bird, Peter Conrad, and Allen Fremont

CONTRIBUTORS

MARGARITA ALGERÍA, Ph.D., is a Professor of Health Services Research and the Director of the Center for Sociomedical Research and Evaluation in the School of Public Health, University of Puerto Rico.

MICHAEL BURY, B.A. M.Sc., is a Professor of Sociology and Head of the Department of Social and Political Science at Royal Holloway, University of London.

SUSAN E. BELL, Ph.D., is a Professor of Sociology in the Department of Sociology and Anthropology at Bowdoin College.

CHLOE E. BIRD, Ph.D., is an Assistant Professor of Community Health in the Center for Gerontology and Health Care Research and an Adjunct Assistant Professor in Sociology in the Department of Sociology at Brown University.

CHARLES L. BOSK, Ph.D., is a Professor of Sociology in the Department of Sociology and a Faculty Associate in the Center for Bioethics at the University of Pennsylvania.

SAMUEL W. BLOOM, Ph.D., is a Professor of Sociology and Community Medicine in the Department of Community Medicine at Mount Sinai School of Medicine and a Professor (Emeritus) of Sociology at the Graduate Center at the City University of New York.

PHIL BROWN, Ph.D., is a Professor of Sociology in the Department of Sociology at Brown University.

LAWTON R. BURNS, Ph.D., MBA, is the James Joo-Jin Kim Professor and a Professor of Health Care Systems, as well as Director of the Wharton Center for Health Management and Economics in the Wharton School at the University of Pennsylvania.

WILLIAM C. COCKERHAM, Ph.D., is a Professor of Sociology, Medicine, and Public Health, and the Chair in the Department of Sociology at the University of Alabama at Birmingham.

PETER CONRAD, Ph.D., is the Harry Coplan Professor of Social Sciences and Chair in the Department of Sociology at Brandeis University.

CARROLL ESTES, Ph.D., is a Professor in the Department of Social and Behavioral Science and the Director of the Institute of Health and Aging at the University of California at San Francisco.

EUGENE B. GALLAGHER, Ph.D., is a Professor of Medical Sociology in the Department of Behavioral Science and the Department of Sociology at the University of Kentucky.

MICHAEL S. GOLDSTEIN, Ph.D., is a Professor of Public Health and Sociology in the Department of Community Health Sciences at the University of California at Los Angeles.

BYRON J. GOOD, Ph.D., is a Professor of Medical Anthropology in the Department of Social Medicine at Harvard Medical School.

MARY-JO DELVECCHIO GOOD, Ph.D., is a Professor of Social Medicine in the Department of Social Medicine at Harvard Medical School.

ALLEN M. FREMONT, M.D., Ph.D., is a Fellow in the Division of General Internal Medicine in Brigham and Women's Hospital and the Department of Health Care Policy at Harvard Medical School.

BRADFORD H. GRAY, Ph.D., is a Professor and Director in the Division of Health and Science Policy at the New York Academy of Medicine.

FREDERIC W. HAFFERTY, Ph.D., is a Professor in the Department of Behavioral Sciences at the University of Minnesota, Duluth School of Medicine.

JAMES S. HOUSE, Ph.D., is a Professor of Sociology and Director of the Survey Research Center in the Institute for Social Research at the University of Michigan at Ann Arbor.

DEBRA LERNER, M.S., Ph.D., is a Research Scientist at the Health Institute and the Division of Clinical Care Research in the Department of Medicine at the New England Medical Center, as well as an Assistant Professor at Tufts University School of Medicine.

BRUCE G. LINK, Ph.D., is a Professor of Public Health at the Mailman School of Public Health, Columbia University.

KAREN W. LINKINS, Ph.D., is a Research Specialist in the Institute for Health and Aging in the Department of Social and Behavioral Sciences at the University of California at San Francisco.

DONALD W. LIGHT, Ph.D., is a Professor and Director in the Division of Social and Behavioral Sciences at the University of Medicine and Dentistry of New Jersey, as well as a member of the Graduate Faculty of Sociology at Rutgers University.

JOHN MIROWSKY, Ph.D., is a Professor of Sociology in the Department of Sociology at Ohio State University.

JAMES O'LEARY, Ph.D., is a Senior Consultant at the Blue Cross/Blue Shield Association.

BERNICE A. PESCOSOLIDO, Ph.D., is the Chancellors' Professor of Sociology in the Department of Sociology at Indiana University.

JO C. PHELAN, Ph.D., is an Assistant Professor of Public Health in the Mailman School of Public Health, Columbia University.

PATRICIA P. RIEKER, Ph.D., is a Professor of Sociology at Simmons College and an Associate Professor of Psychiatry at Harvard Medical School.

STEPHANIE ROBERT, M.S.W., Ph.D., is an Assistant Professor of Social Work in the School of Social Work and is affiliated with the Institute on Aging and the Institute for Research on Poverty at the University of Wisconsin at Madison.

CATHERINE E. ROSS, Ph.D., is a Professor of Sociology in the Department of Sociology at Ohio State University.

JOHN R. REYNOLDS, Ph.D., is an Assistant Professor of Sociology in the Department of Sociology at Florida State University.

SUSAN F. SHARP, Ph.D., is an Assistant Professor in the Department of Sociology at the University of Oklahoma.

ROBIN SIMON, Ph.D., is an Assistant Professor in the Department of Sociology at the University of Iowa.

CHRIS SMAJE, M.Sc, Ph.D., is a Lecturer in the Department of Sociology at the University of Surrey, Guilford, United Kingdom.

CAROLYN SCHWARTZ, Sc.D., is an Assistant Clinical Professor of Psychiatry at Harvard Medical School and Director of the Behavioral Science Research Program at Frontier Science.

THOMAS J. STEWART, Ph.D., is an Associate Professor in the Department of Psychiatry and Behavioural Sciences at the United Arab Emirates University.

TERRY STRATTON, Ph.D., teaches in the Department of Behavioral Sciences at the University of Kentucky.

S. LEONARD SYME, Ph.D., is a Professor of Epidemiology (Emeritus) in the School of Public Health at the University of California at Berkeley.

STEFAN TIMMERMANS, Ph.D., is an Assistant Professor of Sociology in the Department of Sociology at Brandeis University.

DEBRA UMBERSON, MSW, Ph.D., is a Professor in the Department of Sociology and the Population Research Center at the University of Texas at Austin.

STEVEN WALLACE, Ph.D., is in the Department of Community Health at the University of California at Los Angeles.

HOWARD WAITZKIN, M.D., Ph.D., is a Professor of Sociology and Medicine, as well as the Director in the Division of Community Medicine at the University of New Mexico.

DOUGLAS R. WHOLEY, MBA, Ph.D., is a Professor in the Division of Health Services Research, Policy, and Administration in the School of Public Health at the University of Minnesota.

KRISTI WILLIAMS, M.A., is a doctoral candidate in the Department of Sociology at the University of Texas, Austin.

IRENE H. YEN, Ph.D., M.P.H., is an Epidemiologist in the Institute for Health and Aging at the University of California at San Francisco.

PART I: Introduction and History of Medical Sociology

1 MEDICAL SOCIOLOGY AT THE MILLENNIUM

CHLOE E. BIRD, *Brown University*

PETER CONRAD, *Brandeis University*

ALLEN M. FREMONT, *Harvard Medical School*

INTRODUCTION

At the last turn of the century, the modern discipline of sociology was only beginning to emerge in the writings of Weber, Durkheim, Simmel, and Ward. Despite a few brief mentions (e.g., McIntire 1894) and a few social scientific precursors, such as the work of Engels and Virchow, medical sociology would not appear in the United States for nearly half a century. As we begin the twenty-first century, medical sociology has become a well-established, flourishing subfield. In a very real sense this book represents the status of medical sociology at the millennium. The chapters herein provide a broad understanding of what medical sociology is today and what challenges remain or are likely to emerge in the near future.

In this chapter, we briefly consider the context of medical sociology by highlighting its institutionalization, its unique contributions to health and health care, changes in the health care system, and medical sociology's present and future dilemmas.

THE INSTITUTIONALIZATION OF MEDICAL SOCIOLOGY

The history of medical sociology in the United States is well described in Chapter 2 of this handbook, so we present only an overview here. Interest in the social

Thanks to Phil Brown, Gene Gallagher, and Bernice Pescosolido for comments on an earlier draft of this chapter.

aspects of health and medicine can be traced at least as far back as the seven-volume treatise by Frank in 1798 on the "medical police" and the mid-nineteenth century writings of Engels and Virchow (Waitzkin 1981) on social inequality and health. As early as the 1920s sociologists such as Lynd and Lynd (1929, 1937), Stern (1945), and Faris and Dunham (1939) studied how social structure and culture affected health. However, it was not until the post-war period that medical sociology emerged as a specialty within the sociological discipline.

Following World War II, a growing number of sociologists entered medical settings and observed medical institutions and patient-provider relations. In contrast to the relatively congenial health care environment of today, early medical sociologists faced numerous barriers. For example, most health care providers and organizations were unfamiliar with the concepts and methodologies of sociology and were uncomfortable with outside scholars evaluating their practices. In addition, many health professionals of the time viewed sociologists as having a liberal bias that conflicted with their own more conservative beliefs.

As sociologists published increasingly on health and health care, some began identifying themselves as "medical sociologists." These early medical sociologists faced resistance from within sociology itself. Many of their sociological colleagues viewed the emerging specialty of medical sociology with disdain and suspicion, contending it was solely an applied activity, often sponsored by those being studied and lacking theoretical substance.

Sociologists' access to previously closed doors was facilitated by interested psychiatrists and other physicians who sometimes collaborated with sociologists in research (e.g., Merton, Reeder, and Kendall 1957; Hollingshead and Redlich 1958; Stanton and Schwartz 1954) and became advocates for the utility of sociological work on health. Support from within the larger discipline also grew as a number of sociology's most prominent figures contributed to the development of medical sociology, including Talcott Parsons (1951) on the sick role and Robert K. Merton (Merton et al. 1957) and Everett Hughes (Becker et al. 1961) on medical education. These individuals and others trained a whole generation of students who specialized in studying aspects of health and health care. As Samuel Bloom points out in Chapter 2, the relative availability of research and training funds from the National Institute of Mental Health and other private foundations fueled the development of sociological investigations in health and helped to shape the subdiscipline.

Despite the establishment of the subfield, a division began to emerge between those doing "sociology of medicine" and those doing "sociology in medicine" (Straus 1957). Sociology *of* medicine referred to studies that examined medicine with sociological questions in the forefront, using sociological concepts and theories and intended largely for a sociological audience. Studies of professions, socialization, and organizations typify this orientation. In contrast, sociology *in* medicine included studies that used sociological perspectives and knowledge to investigate medically oriented questions. The primary goals were to solve medical problems and improve medical care. Such research included studies on doctor-patient interaction, social factors affecting the delivery of services and obtaining medical care, and social epidemiology of disease. For many years, sociology in medicine was seen by some sociologists to be of lesser value, because it was an "applied" rather than a "pure" use of sociology. Such intellectual snobbishness has diminished, although it still persists to a limited extent.

Today most researchers eschew such distinctions and believe that first-rate sociological research on health can contribute both to the development of medical sociology and to the improvement of health and health care. In fact, in some circles the specialty is no longer called *medical sociology* but rather the *sociology of health and illness.* Although we believe this is a more accurate descriptor, for the sake of continuity in this book we continue to use the term *medical sociology.*

By the 1970s, medical sociology became a well-established specialty. Whereas through the 1960s, medical sociology courses remained rare in sociology curricula, today most departments offer medical sociology courses, and a significant number of departments emphasize medical sociology as a specialty for graduate training. Moreover, medical sociology has become a common major among undergraduates, including those planning to pursue careers in the health professions. Prior to the 1960s probably fewer than 25 sociologists held tenure positions in schools of health professions (Freeman et al. 1979); yet today sociologists are common in academic medical institutions, sometimes comprising major research groups.

Medical sociology was one of the first sections of the American Sociological Association and has for several decades been among the three largest sections. Similarly, in the United Kingdom, the Medical Sociology Group of the British Sociological Association is the largest of all the affiliate groups. In recent years, communication among medical sociologists around the world has been facilitated by the growth of the World Wide Web.

The range and quantity of medical sociology research has grown steadily. In contrast to the early days, when the literature first merited review papers (Freeman and Reeder 1957), there are now over a dozen medical sociology texts and readers, several of which are in their fifth or higher edition. The success of these texts and readers, as well as the large number and range of journals publishing medical sociology, reflects the subfield's intellectual strength and depth. Medical sociology has contributed to wider sociology and to academia in general. In fact, work by medical sociologists has been honored with two major academic prizes: the Sorokin Award presented to Eliot Freidson and the Pulitzer Prize awarded to Paul E. Starr.

UNIQUE CONTRIBUTIONS

Although several disciplines, including epidemiology, health psychology, medical anthropology, and public health, have contributed to social science research on health and health care, medical sociology has made several unique contributions. These include: (1) study of medicine as a profession, (2) study of the sick role and illness experience, (3) social construction of illness and medical knowledge, including medicalization, (4) sociological epidemiology, and (5) sociological study of health care services as organizations. In each instance, sociologists have offered a fresh perspective on understanding the issues by examining the impact of power, authority, norms, social inequality, and the distribution of resources. In the following section, we briefly describe the distinctive sociological stance on each of the aforementioned areas.

The *study of the medical profession* has long been a central area of medical sociology and has formed a basis for the general sociological study of the professions. As such, sociological concepts of the profession of medicine have provided the very definitions of professional work and the ways in which a profession obtains and maintains control of expertise. Interest in professional authority in general and medicine in particular led to extensive sociological work on medical education and socialization. Early work on the profession included Talcott Parsons's (1951) explanations of professional authority, Renée Fox's (1957) training for uncertainty, Howard Becker and colleagues' (1961) study of medical education and socialization (described in *Boys in White*), and Eliot Freidson's (1970) *Profession of Medicine.* These studies examined the power and authority physicians hold as a group, the social and economic privileges associated with the status of medicine, and the ways in which the profession has protected these privileges—both from competing occupations and from women and minorities who had faced restricted access to the profession. In addition, sociologists have examined interprofessional relations between doctors and nurses and other health professionals (including chiropractors, dentists, and psychologists). This research has focused on the roles of professionals in organizations and the competition between professions for authority and autonomy. Furthermore, sociological work has contributed to the understanding of the history of medicine as a contested terrain in which physicians first established and then fought to maintain their professional dominance. Physicians' success in these struggles has shaped health care in many areas, from doctor-patient interactions to the organization and delivery of care (Starr 1982; Abbott 1988). Sociologists have also examined the medical profession's loss of power, prestige, income, and status. They have shown how countervailing forces contribute to the deprofessionalization of medicine as a growing number of physicians become employees and as insurers use bureaucratic systems to evaluate and even limit autonomy in treatment decisions and doctor-patient communication (Haug 1976, 1988; see Chapter 14 in this volume by Light).

A second unique contribution of medical sociology has been the *study of the sick role,* which expanded into a broader study of illness experience. This area includes the social role of the patient, illness behavior, illness/patient careers, and the ways that these factors shape and are shaped by doctor-patient interaction.

Talcott Parsons's (1951) work on the sick role laid the foundation for the sociological examination of illness and the expectations placed on those who are ill. Although the breadth of the field developed in large part from criticisms of the limitations of Parsons's model, which was best suited to explaining the experience of a white, middle-class person with an acute illness, it is hard to overestimate the contribution of his work to bringing health and illness into the domain of sociology and out of the sole realm of biomedical researchers.

One fertile line of this research has been work on *illness behavior* (Mechanic 1962). Whereas medical anthropologists have long studied illness in part as a way to examine the values in a society or group in the face of uncontrollable events, sociologists brought a greater interest in the impact of role expectations, norms, and sanctions, and the accommodations or lack thereof for the needs of those with illnesses or disabilities. This work includes rich ethnographic studies of illness experiences (e.g., Roth and Conrad 1987; Charmaz 1991), as well as research on factors affecting the decision to seek care (Berkanovic, Telesky, and Reeder 1981), and patterns of health care utilization (Mechanic, Cleary, and Greenly 1982).

The women's health movement has encouraged sociological research on illness experience through the movement's criticism of medicine for devaluing women's reports of their own health and well-being and their experiences of illness and medical treatment. As a result, sociological studies of illness experience have evolved into a wide range of quantitative and qualitative work. For example, sociologists' increased emphasis on the patient's perspective fostered the development of what is now known as *patient-centered outcomes* in health services research. Moreover, medical sociologists have contributed to a rapidly growing body of work on women's experiences with reproductive technologies (e.g., Bell 1988; Riessman and Nathanson 1986). These two examples represent areas that have become truly interdisciplinary.

A third unique contribution of medical sociology has been the examination of the *social construction of illness and medical knowledge.* This area includes a range of studies from a social constructionist perspective, including those of the sociological history of diseases, medicalization, and the social meaning of illness (e.g., whether particular illnesses are stigmatized). As Judith Lorber (1997) and others have noted, "What is normal depends on whom is being compared to whom." In this body of work, sociologists have examined the ways in which new illnesses have been discovered and characterized, the attribution of new medical knowledge, and the myriad ways in which nonmedical events and experiences have entered the purview of medicine. By now we have numerous studies of the medicalization of deviance and "normal life events" (Conrad 1992; Conrad and Schneider 1992) ranging from behavioral problems such as attention deficit disorder (ADD), eating disorders, alcoholism, and other addictions, to life events such as pregnancy, childbirth, and menopause.

Sociologists have also used the constructionist perspective to examine the social processes by which certain constellations of troubles become diseases, such as hypertension, black lung disease, or PMS (see Chapter 22 by Conrad). Medicalization and the intrusion of medical concerns into everyday life encompasses an ever-expanding list of health behaviors (diet, exercise, risk prevention, preventive care compliance). This intrusion results in a growing transfer of authority over aspects of everyday life to the domain of medicine and responsibility for one's own health to the individual (see Chapter 11 by Cockerham).

The assessment and documentation of the causes and consequences of social inequality are a central concern of sociology. Although other disciplines examine social inequalities and health, the unique contribution of medical sociology involves studies of sociological factors in the development of disease and illness, especially social class, gender, and stress. For medical sociology, this research interest has developed into a *sociological epidemiology* that demonstrates the social patterning of illness (see Chapter 25 by Syme and Yen). Sociologists bring a different theoretical perspective to this research by focusing on the multiple ways in which social inequalities contribute to differences in health and by recognizing the persistence of these relationships over time despite ever-changing mechanisms that lead to poorer health among the disadvantaged (see Chapter 6 by Robert and House and Chapter 3 by Link and Phelan). The documentation of inequalities in health across class and gender has contributed to the now-flourishing field of research on stress and health (see Chapter 4 by Mirowsky, Ross, and Reynolds and Chapter 7 by Rieker and Bird). This work seeks to document the ways in which social inequality leads to unequal exposure to stressors and to unequal social and economic resources that might allow an individual to limit stress exposure or to mitigate its effects.

Interestingly, although a large number of sociologists have examined factors related to the income gradient in health (with the strongest studies typically coming from European countries) and many American sociologists conduct work documenting and assessing the social origins of gender differences in mental and physical health, far fewer have examined racial inequalities in health. In the United States, researchers have focused on Black/White differences; however, European examples offer greater insight into the complexity of racial and ethnic patterning of health and illness (see Chapter 6 by Robert and House and Chapter 8 by Smaje).

Finally, sociologists have made a unique contribution to the *understanding of health care through research on medical care organizations.* Just as medicine became the prototype for occupational research on the professions, research on hospitals, medical practices, nursing homes, and other health care organizations has shaped both our understanding of how care is provided and the power and interests that have shaped the provision of health care (see Chapter 15 by Wholey and Burns). Medical sociologists have studied hospitals and mental health institutions as complex organizations designed to meet multiple needs in society, which often involve competing agendas. These organizations are also total institutions with their own norms, roles, actors, and status hierarchies.

In addition to these unique contributions, sociology has played a leading role in the use of patient-centered surveys as a tool for the evaluation of both individual clinician and organizational practices. In collaboration with physicians and clinical researchers, sociologists have contributed to the growing movement to examine patient-centered aspects of treatment and outcomes. Consequently, outcomes research now uses functional health status and quality-of-life measures as a standard for evaluating health care interventions. Although this work has not yet contributed directly to sociology by extending sociological perspectives to health care studies, it has reshaped biomedical research and to a large extent raised the standard for evaluating care, from assessing narrowly defined biomedical success of an intervention to considering the broader effects (or lack thereof) on functional health status and the quality of life. In other words, examining whether a specific treatment improves a patient's life and role functioning across the range of mental and physical health (see Chapter 20 by Lerner and Swartz).

CHANGES IN THE HEALTH CARE SYSTEM

The contributions of medical sociology have not occurred in a social vacuum or a static society. In the 37 years since the first edition of the *Handbook* was published, probably no other major social institution has changed as much as health care. Indeed, a central theme of previous editions of the *Handbook* has been that like all other scientific and intellectual endeavors, medical sociology is inherently linked to contemporary social, political, and economic concerns, as well as to the structural and technological developments taking place at the time (Freeman, Levine, and Reeder 1979). For example, during the 1960s and 1970s, a period of relatively progressive politics and a strong economy, one of the major developments was the combination of governmental and community efforts to improve access to health care for the poor. These efforts reflected a concern for ethnic and racial equality and the emerging view of health care as a *right*. Sociologists were uniquely equipped to focus attention on and articulate concerns about these issues and played leading roles in the design of social initiatives and research.

The 1980s witnessed a shift to a more conservative political and economic environment and a dramatic change in emphasis from a focus on improving access to medical care to controlling health care costs and evaluating the effectiveness of health services. In response to the shift in interest and funding, some sociologists turned their attention to issues such as the quality of care, including assessment of patient-centered outcomes and quality of life (see Chapter 20 by Lerner and Swartz), care under different types of organizational arrangements (see Chapter 15 by Wholey and Burns), and the challenges to physicians' traditional autonomy in medical decision making (see Chapter 14 by Light). Other medical sociologists moved to entirely new areas where they could apply an interest in social inequalities in health, such as assessing the health gradient (see Chapter 6 by Robert and House), the then emerging area of stress research (see Chapter 4 by Mirowsky, Ross, and Reynolds), and to broader issues of equity such as exposure to environmental toxins (see Chapter 10 by Brown).

Reflecting on major changes and issues identified in past editions of the *Handbook* reveals the close linkage among many of these developments. The emergence of third-party payers—such as Medicare, Medicaid, and private insurance—facilitated the rise of large academic medical centers, increasing specialization and fragmentation of care, rapid adoption of new medical technologies, rising incomes for physicians, and ultimately the escalation of health care costs. These developments fueled growing criticism of physicians and the health care system, increasingly aggressive efforts to curtail medical costs, greater societal focus on issues of resource allocation, and related debates over issues of access and utilization.

Since the last edition of the *Handbook* was published in 1989, the health care system has undergone remarkable changes, some of which would have been inconceivable even a short time ago. We highlight a few of these changes here.

- Although the Clintons' effort to fundamentally restructure health care delivery failed, concerns over rising costs have culminated in a "managed care revolution," which is fundamentally changing the way virtually all aspects of health care are structured and financed. Where there were previously small to moderate size groups of independent physicians with a range of types of hospital affiliations, there are now vast for-profit and not-for-profit networks of physicians and hospitals. Clinical decisions and doctor-patient relationships that were once strictly in the physicians' domain are now closely scrutinized and regulated by payers and health care organizations. At the same time, many clinicians who previously disavowed any involvement with administrative or business concerns have become increasingly active participants in management (Hafferty and Light 1995). Whereas health care formerly centered on inpatient care in large medical centers, it has rapidly shifted to less expensive outpatient care in the community. Some health care organizations are even moving beyond the rhetoric by making concerted efforts to improve preventive care and health maintenance for their patient populations (Shortell, Gillies, and Devers 1995).

- There are unprecedented challenges to the status, power, and prestige of the medical profession. Studies demonstrating wide variation in physician practice styles, often without significant differences in outcomes, and a growing recognition that there has been remarkably little research comparing the effectiveness of different treatments and procedures have severely undermined public confidence in the rational, scientific basis of medical practice (Wennberg and Gittelsohn 1973). These revelations, coupled with the view that physicians' decisions are influenced by their desire to increase their profits rather than solely to provide cost-effective care, have greatly facilitated payers' and organizations' ability to scrutinize and restrict physicians' use of health care resources. In response, physicians have embarked on ambitious initiatives to conduct the necessary research and alter the culture of medical practice to one that is truly "evidenced based." Indeed, some sociologists have ironically suggested that the encroachments by managed care may ultimately strengthen the profession of medicine (Hafferty and Light 1995).

- The American value that high quality health care is an entitlement, at least for those who can pay, is also being challenged in fundamental ways. Unlimited access to care conflicts with the desire of health care payers and organizations to control costs. Thus, managed care organizations have devised a variety of ways to alter the behavior of patients, such as requiring co-pays for medications and doctor visits, requiring approval from a primary care physician for emergency room visits and referrals to subspecialists, and 24-hour stays for maternity patients with "uncomplicated" deliveries. Instances in which physicians have been co-opted by "gag rules" in their contracts, preventing them from discussing more expensive options for care with their patients, have led to growing concerns about patient trust and physician incentives (Mechanic 1996; see also Chapter 18 by Waitzkin). Such developments have in turn prompted a "managed care backlash" led by patient advocates, politicians, and physicians that has produced such changes as a patient bill of rights, a requirement that maternity patients be allowed 48-hour hospital stays after delivery, and even the formation of physician unions.

- Managed care companies are not alone in attempting to alter Americans' views about health and health care. Indeed, public health initiatives and increasing media coverage of developments in medicine have helped to fundamentally change perceptions of health. Now well versed in the language of risk factors for disease—such as smoking, alcohol, high-fat low-fiber diets, and sedentary or high stress lifestyles—many Americans have learned to view physical and mental health as an individual responsibility requiring personal efforts (see Chapter 11 by Cockerham). At the same time, the constantly changing recommendations regarding risk factors have to some extent bewildered the public and undermined the authority of health professionals.

- Along with growing interest in health and health care on the part of the general public has come a tremendous increase in the amount and accessibility of medical information. This includes in-depth coverage on TV, radio, newspapers, health magazines, and newsletters of nearly every interesting development relating to medicine or health. Research funding agencies and scientists have contributed to this media blitz out of a desire to publicize each study as the latest and perhaps final word, the "breakthrough." Moreover, pharmaceutical companies now direct information to consumers that previously was only available to physicians, including the results of studies favorable to their products. The emergence of the Internet and the World Wide Web are further expanding patient access to medical information and exposure to unrefereed portrayals of products and interventions.

- The increasing sophistication of consumers regarding medical matters has been accompanied by a growing recognition of the limits of conventional biomedical approaches in treating many types of mental and physical health problems. For example, recent surveys indicate that the use of alternative medicine equals or surpasses the use of conventional allopathic medicine despite the fact that most medical insurers do not pay for such treatments (Eisenberg et al. 1998; see also Chapter 19 by Goldstein). There has also been greater acknowledgement of the limits of the biomedical model within medicine itself, manifested by calls for a biopsychosocial model of care (Engel 1977), increasing research into the impact of social psychological factors on health and possible physiological pathways, and use of and referrals to alternative care approaches (e.g., biofeedback, meditation, acupuncture, chiropractic care).

- Whereas clinicians once relied exclusively on practitioner-centered outcomes based on "objective" measures (e.g., blood sugar, blood pressure, and white blood cell count), efforts to better assess the effectiveness and relative utility of care have led to the development and widespread use of a variety of measures of patient-centered outcomes, including functional health status and well being (e.g., physical and social functioning), and quality of life (e.g., health status weighted by patient preferences). Indeed, most large clinical studies now routinely include some of these measures. Increasing concerns over quality of care in this managed care era have also prompted widespread use of patient surveys ranging from questions about satisfaction with care to detailed reports on specific aspects of care salient to patients and their families (Cleary et al. 1992). The potential impact of these types of surveys is substantial, as they are now required in the accreditation process of hospitals and ambulatory care sites and are increasingly used in quality improvement efforts to assess organizational and individual provider performance.

- Advances in biomedical technology and knowledge are proceeding apace. Although the impact of biomedical approaches on the health of the population over the past 40 years is debatable, it would be a mistake to underestimate the potential for biomedical breakthroughs to significantly alter society's conception of health and disease (see Chapter 21 by Timmermans). Perhaps at no time since the development of antibiotics have the biomedical sciences been in a better position to fundamentally alter the landscape of health and illness. Advances in molecular biology and genetics in particular hold the promise for early diagnoses and treatment of many chronic and debilitating conditions that have overtaken acute diseases as the major cause of morbidity and mortality. Along with these promises of improving health come tremendous risks for further medicalization of everyday life and increased discrimination (see Chapter 22 by Conrad). Such advances may also paradoxically undermine sociologists' efforts to focus research and policy concerning the effects of social inequalities on health and well being, even as the impact of these factors on physiological processes and disease is becoming clearer.

- As the baby boomer generation approaches retirement, the societal view of aging is being redefined. However, the aging of society has affected both the demand for medical care and the frequency with which adult children are called upon to care for aging family members. As a result, research has expanded on both the provision of health care to the elderly and the consequences of the caregiver burden. Research has increasingly focused on the quality of care provided to the elderly (e.g., nursing home care and end-of-life care) and the provision of care within the community, as well as the social and economic consequences of the rising cost of medical care for older adults. The aging of society raises questions as to how to distribute resources to meet the needs of the elderly and the young as the demand for social and medical services for both groups increases (e.g., daycare services), and the extent to which social policies increase racial and gender

inequality in access to care (Meyer and Pavalko 1996; see also Chapter 9 by Estes, Wallace, and Linkins).

These rapid changes in the organization and delivery of health care are part of the reason that sociologists have found health and illness to be a fascinating area to study. In some respects the changes described above can be easily traced to previous trends and issues. Yet in other respects they represent radical departures from the health care system as sociologists have come to know it. In contrast to previous decades, when there had been apparent stability and slowly progressive changes within the health care system, the 1990s are best characterized in terms of uncertainty and turmoil, fundamental change, and continuing flux. These often unpredictable changes offer new challenges and opportunities for medical sociology as they beg for a re-examination of well-established sociological theories. Indeed, the demand and opportunities for social science research on health care may be greater than ever before. As Bernice Pescosolido and Jennie Kronenfeld (1995) have observed, it is in times of major change within the health care arena and the larger society that sociologists are most valued and can make the greatest contributions.

DILEMMAS FOR MEDICAL SOCIOLOGY

Although the prospects for medical sociology are promising, as we enter the new millennium the subfield faces a number of dilemmas. Some of these arise from medical sociology's success. Growth has brought an ever-increasing diversity in medical sociologists' research interests, methods, and intended audiences. In addition, medical sociology is not alone in the study of health and health care. Moreover, many researchers who are not sociologists are now trained in sociological research methods. Thus medical sociologists must keep up with rapidly growing literatures from a variety of related disciplines as well as the work of other medical sociologists. It has become virtually impossible to keep abreast of both the range and depth of current research within both medical sociology and related disciplines regarding one's primary areas of interest. Although medical sociology remains vibrant, it has lost ground in several areas to other disciplines, either because of a shift in policy emphasis, specialization, the emergence of new, competing disciplines, or the migration of sociological expertise to other disciplines.

Medical sociology was perhaps the first fully developed social science of health and health care. In the 1960s medical sociology had a central place at the policy table, whether the issue was about long-term health policy, medical education, utilization of services, or community mental health. When access to care was the central policy issue—how to make health care more accessible to people who need it—sociology had a great deal to offer policy deliberations (see Chapter 17 by Gray and O'Leary). However, as health care costs soared in the 1970s, cost controls became the central policy concern, and sociologists seemed to have less to contribute in this direction. Health economics came to the fore as the prime social science discipline that could address the policy concerns around health care cost controls. Thus, sociologists lost influence at the policy table.

More recently, concerns have extended beyond costs to quality and effectiveness of care. Utilization of health services used to be an active part of the medical sociological enterprise. In the past two decades, researchers (including many sociologists) have migrated to a new field called "health services research," which has become the intellectual home for research on the organization and delivery of health care. Health services research has its own journals and organizations, separate from sociology and other disciplines. Here, similar to criminology and the study of deviance, we have a field that has more or less seceded from sociology and developed as a self-sufficient and specialized area. Health services research has become the principle producer of policy-relevant research. This is a loss for medical sociology. Some sociologists still do participate in such research, but they identify themselves as health services researchers and rarely publish this work in sociology journals (see Chapter 17 by Gray and O'Leary).

In other areas, medical sociology missed an opportunity to affect medical care. For example, in the past twenty-five years, the field of bioethics has come to have great influence in medicine. Spawned in the wake of the misuse of human subjects in studies like the Tuskegee syphilis research (where African-American men were purposely left suffering from the disease so the researchers could ascertain its natural course) and nurtured by the dilemmas of increasing powers of medical technology (e.g., neonatal technology, brain death), bioethics has grown to a full-fledged discipline and has become a central part of medical education and a major force in shaping medical research and treatment. As Renée Fox and Judith Swazey (1984) note, bioethics collapses the social into individual issues and often decontextualizes medical problems. Despite early sociological critiques of medicine, bioethics has become the major discipline that medicine calls upon for advice and sometimes consent for medical actions and procedures. One might say that medical sociology has been by-passed here, in large part because sociologists usually do not see it as their place to take a stand on moral choices or decisions to be made. Sociology studies what is, rather than what should be. In recent years there has been something of a rapprochement between some sociologists and bioethicists, some of which is reviewed in Chapter 28 by Bosk.

Sociologists pioneered social epidemiological studies of health (e.g., Hollingshead and Redlich 1958; Srole et al. 1962) and have developed entire literatures around some issues (e.g., stress and social support and health). However, social epidemiological studies are now as likely to be done by public health researchers as by sociologists. The upside of this development is that social variables are taken more seriously and researched more assiduously. The downside is that studies done by epidemiologists tend to be atheoretical, treating variables such as sex, race, class, or occupation as singular attributes of individuals which affect their risk of poor health (i.e., individual "risk factors") rather than characteristics of a society or social system that put groups at risk (see Chapter 25 by Syme and Yen). This view dilutes some of the power of the analysis and gives the false impression that sociological perspectives are being considered in the research. In particular, epidemiologists frequently lack the sociological framework that contextualizes social variables and recognizes the interactions among them.

The major dilemma for medical sociology is that along with the great success of the discipline has come specialization, some migration, competition, and succession. In one sense this change can be seen as an erosion of medical sociology and a decrease in its influence. However, it can also be considered a new type of institutionalization of medical sociological concerns in other disciplines and the opportunity for sociologists to work in multidisciplinary fashion with researchers and scientists from related disciplines.

It is our belief that for medical sociology to thrive in the new millennium, it must keep its roots firmly implanted in sociology while embracing the possibilities of interdisciplinary cooperation, both with other social science disciplines and with the emergent, newer interdisciplinary fields that now are central to the social scientific study of health and health care.

REFERENCES

ABBOTT, ANDREW. 1988. *The System of Professions.* Chicago: University of Chicago Press.

BECKER, HOWARD S., BLANCHE GEER, EVERETT C. HUGHES, and ANSELM L. STRAUSS. 1961. *Boys in White: Student Culture in Medical School.* Chicago: University of Chicago Press.

BELL, SUSAN. 1988. "Becoming a Political Woman: The Reconstruction and Interpretation of Experience Through Stories." In *Gender and Discourse: The Power of Talk,* ed. Alexandra Dundas Todd and Sue Fisher. Norwood, NJ: Ablex, pp. 97–123.

BERKANOVIC, EMIL, CAROL TELESKY, and SHARON REEDER. 1981. "Structural and Social Psychological Factors in the Decision to Seek Medical Care for Symptoms." *Medical Care* 19: 693–709.

CHARMAZ, KATHY. 1991. *Good Days, Bad Days: The Self in Chronic Illness and Time.* New Brunswick, NJ: Rutgers University Press.

CLEARY, PAUL D., SUSAN EDGMAN-LEVITAN, WILLIAM MC-MULLEN, THOMAS DELBANCE. 1992. "The Relationship Between Reported Problems and Patient Summary Evaluations of Hospital Care." *Quality Review Bulletin* 18(2): 53–59.

CONRAD, PETER. 1992. "Medicalization and Social Control." *Annual Review of Sociology* 18: 209–32.

CONRAD, PETER, and JOSEPH W. SCHNEIDER. 1992. *Deviance and Medicalization: From Badness to Sickness,* Expanded Edition. Philadelphia: Temple University Press.

EISENBERG, D. M., R. B. DAVIS, S. L. ETTNER, S. APPEL, S. WILKEY, M. VAN ROMPAY, and R. C. KESSLER. 1998. "Trends in Alternative Medicine Use in the United States, 1990–1997: Results of a Follow-up National Survey." *Journal of the American Medical Association* 290: 1569–75.

ENGEL, G. L. 1977. "The Need for a New Medical Model: A Challenge for Biomedicine." *Science* 196(4286): 129–36.

FARIS, ROBERT, and WALTER DUNHAM. 1939. *Mental Disorders in Urban Areas.* Chicago: University of Chicago Press.

FOX, RENÉE C. 1957. "Training for Uncertainty" In *The Student-Physician,* ed. R. K. Merton, G. G. Reader, and P. L. Kendall. Cambridge, MA: Harvard University Press, pp. 207–241.

FOX, RENÉE C., and JUDITH P. SWAZEY. 1984. "Medical Morality Is Not Bioethics—Medical Ethics in China and the United States." *Perspectives in Biology and Medicine* 27: 336–60.

FREEMAN, HOWARD E., SOL LEVINE, and LEO G. REEDER, eds. 1963. *Handbook of Medical Sociology.* 1st ed. Englewood Cliffs, NJ: Prentice Hall.

FREEMAN, HOWARD E., SOL LEVINE, and LEO G. REEDER, eds. 1979. *Handbook of Medical Sociology.* 3rd ed. Englewood Cliffs, NJ: Prentice Hall.

FREEMAN, HOWARD E., and SOL LEVINE, eds. 1989. *Handbook of Medical Sociology.* 4th ed. Englewood Cliffs, NJ: Prentice Hall.

FREEMAN, HOWARD E., and LEO G. REEDER. 1957. "Medical Sociology: A Review of the Literature." *American Sociological Review* 22(1): 73–81.

FREIDSON, ELIOT. 1970. *Profession of Medicine.* New York: Dodd, Mead.

HAFFERTY, FREDERIC W., and DONALD W. LIGHT. 1995. "Professional Dynamics and the Changing Nature of Medical Work." *Journal of Health and Social Behavior* (extra issue): 132–53.

HAUG, MARIE R. 1976. "The Erosion of Professional Authority: A Cross-Cultural Inquiry in the Case of the Physician." *Milbank Memorial Fund Quarterly/Health and Society* 54(1): 83–106.

HAUG, MARIE R. 1988. "A Re-Examination of the Hypothesis of Physician Deprofessionalization." *Milbank Quarterly* 66(supplement 2): 48–56.

HOLLINGSHEAD, AUGUST B., and FREDRICH C. REDLICH. 1958. *Social Class and Mental Illness: A Community Study.* New York: John Wiley.

LEVINE, SOL, and S. H. CROOG. 1984. "What Constitutes Quality of Life? A Conceptualization of the Dimensions of Life Quality in Health Populations and Patients with Cardiovascular Disease." In *Assessment of Quality of Life in Clinical Trials of Cardiovascular Therapies,* ed. N. K. Wenger et al. New York: LeJacq Publishing, pp. 46–58.

LORBER, JUDITH. 1997. *Gender and the Social Construction of Illness.* Thousand Oaks, CA: Sage Publications.

LYND, ROBERT, and HELEN MERRELL LYND. 1929. *Middletown: A Study in Contemporary American Culture.* New York: Harcourt, Brace, and World.

LYND, ROBERT, and HELEN MERRELL LYND. 1937. *Middletown in Transition: A Study in Cultural Conflicts.* New York: Harcourt, Brace, and World.

MCINTIRE, CHARLES. 1894. "The Importance of the Study of Medical Sociology." *Bulletin of the American Academy of Medicine* 1: 425–34.

MECHANIC, DAVID. 1962. "The Concept of Illness Behavior." *Journal of Chronic Diseases* 15: 189–94.

MECHANIC, DAVID. 1996. "Changing Medical Organization and the Erosion of Trust." *Milbank Quarterly* 74(2): 171–89.

MECHANIC, DAVID, PAUL D. CLEARY, and J. R. GREENLEY. 1982. "Distress Syndromes in Illness Behavior, Access to Care and Medical Utilization in a Defined Population." *Medical Care* 20:361–72.

MERTON, ROBERT, LEO G. REEDER, and PATRICIA L. KENDALL, eds. 1957. *The Student-Physician: Introductory Studies in the Sociology of Medical Education.* Cambridge, MA: Harvard University Press.

MEYER, MADONNA HARRINGTON, and ELIZA K. PAVALKO. 1996. "Family, Work, and Access to Health Insurance

Among Mature Women." *Journal of Health and Social Behavior* 37(4): 311–25.

PARSONS, TALCOTT. 1951. *The Social System.* Glencoe, NY: The Free Press.

PESCOSOLIDO, BERNICE A., and JENNIE J. KRONENFELD. 1995. "Health, Illness, and Healing in an Uncertain Era: Challenges from and for Medical Sociology." *Journal of Health and Social Behavior* (extra issue): 5–33.

RIESSMAN, CATHERINE KOHLER, and CONSTANCE A. NATHANSON. 1986. "The Management of Reproduction: Social Construction of Risk and Responsibility." In *Applications of Social Science to Clinical Medicine and Health Policy,* ed. Linda Aiken and David Mechanic. Princeton, NJ: Robert Wood Johnson Foundation.

ROTH, JULIUS A., and PETER CONRAD. 1987. *The Experience and Management of Chronic Illness,* volume 6 of *Research in the Sociology of Health Care.* Greenwich, CT: JAI Press.

SHORTELL, STEPHEN, ROBIN GILLIES, and KELLY DEVERS. 1995. "Reinventing the American Hospital." *Milbank Quarterly* 73(2): 131–60.

SROLE, LEO, T. S. LANGNER, S. T. MICHAE, M. K. OPLER, and T. A. C. RENNIE. 1962. *Mental Health in the Metropolis: The Midtown Manhattan Study.* New York: McGraw-Hill.

STANTON, ALBERT H., and MORRIS S. SCHWARTZ. 1954. *The Mental Hospital.* New York: Basic Books.

STARR, PAUL. 1982. *The Social Transformation of American Medicine.* New York: Basic Books.

STERN, BERNARD J. 1945. *American Medical Practice.* New York: The Commonwealth Fund.

STRAUS, ROBERT. 1957. "The Nature and Status of Medical Sociology." *American Sociological Review* 22: 200–204.

WAITZKIN, HOWARD. 1981. "The Social Origins of Illness: A Neglected History." *International Journal of Health Services* 11: 77–103.

WENNBERG, JOHN, and ALAN GITTELSOHN. 1973. "Small Area Variations in Health Care Delivery." *Science* 182: 1102-1108.

2 THE INSTITUTIONALIZATION OF MEDICAL SOCIOLOGY IN THE UNITED STATES, 1920–1980

SAMUEL W. BLOOM, *Mount Sinai School of Medicine*

Intellectual activities like medical sociology character-istically offer two dimensions for historical study: the development of knowledge and professional or institu-tional formation. For example, Merton, in his analysis of the sociology of science, differentiates the spe-cialty's *cognitive identity,* "in the form of its intellec-tual orientations, conceptual schemes, paradigms, problematics, and tools of inquiry," and its *social iden-tity,* "in the form of its major institutional arrange-ments" (Merton 1977:5). The former is the more common in the literature of medical sociology, but the focus here will be on the social, following the steps of its institutionalization (Ben-David and Collins 1966; Shils 1970).

Medical sociology is today a field of study fully institutionalized in every sense. There is an organized demand for teaching and research; there are profes-sional associations and scholarly journals specifically devoted to the field; within the university, its main locus of activity, as well as in government and private organizations, medical sociology is supported with fi-nancial and other rewards for performance (ASA Com-mittee on Certification in Medical Sociology 1986; Wolinsky 1988). It is only since about 1950 that med-ical sociology has begun to achieve such full measure of professional status; however, as early as the mid-nineteenth century, one can trace both an approach to study and actual research activities that are remarkably close, at least in style, to their modern counterparts. Until about seventy years ago, however, such ideas and activities were episodic, linked in Europe to major events like the struggle for political and social rights of the European middle class in the 1840s, the similar struggle of the English working class later in the nine-teenth century, and in the United States, the radical technological and social changes caused by the Civil War. Such events typically heightened public feelings of social responsibility, and, in the process, stimulated early variants of the sociology of medicine (Chadwick 1842; Oberschall 1972). Just as typically, however, at least in the field of medicine, the motivating force of such intellectual activity was not sustained. It was not until the 1920s that an unbroken development of knowledge began in the sociology of medicine, and only after World War II were individuals identified as "medical sociologists."

The term itself first appeared in the United States at the turn of the century. In 1879, John Shaw Billings linked the study of hygiene with sociology (Billings 1888; Larkey 1938), and in 1894, Charlie McIntire de-fined medical sociology as:

> The science of the social phenomena of the physicians themselves as a class apart and separate; and the sci-ence which investigates the laws regulating the rela-tions between the medical profession and human society as a whole; treating of the structure of both, how the present conditions came about, what progress civilization has effected and indeed everything related to the subject. (McIntire 1894)

Elizabeth Blackwell (1902) also wrote about medical sociology, and in 1910, James Warbasse published a book called *Medical Sociology* (Rosen 1979:37). In that same year, 1910, Warbasse started the Section on Sociology of the American Public Health Association. The members of this group, however, included few so-ciologists; they were mainly social workers and physi-cians. Their deliberations reflected the belief, widely shared at that time, that "the sociological enterprise stood at the intersection of social analysis and social reform" (Roemer et al. 1997). They saw sociology as not yet entirely differentiated from economics, political science, anthropology, and social work, and "as a countervailing point of view and a moral disposition rather than as a specialized academic discipline" (Roemer et al. 1997:37). This group was derived more from social medicine in Europe and public health in the United States than it was from sociology. Even so, the time was not yet ripe for this type of specialized subfield. The Section on Sociology of the APHA was disbanded in 1921.

The decade following World War I was an important demarcation point for American sociology. The first laboratories of social research were formed in 1925 at the University of North Carolina and the University of Washington. The Social Science Research Council was created in 1923. The first large-sample public opinion polls were conducted. Studies of American life were typified by the classic *Middletown* (1929) by Robert and Helen Lynd. The first presidential commission devoted primarily to social research was appointed by Hoover in 1928 (Ogburn 1933), and the first distinctively American theories to dominate sociological scholarship internationally emerged during the 1920s. What was to be known later as medical sociology grew largely within these important developments of sociology's mainstream. This is when, following the schema of Ben-David, the first steps occurred in which there was "some differentiation in subject matter, method, and techniques from earlier disciplines" (Oberschall 1972: 4). This is also when the activities of a number of scholars formed an identifiable pattern such that they became more than individual actors. They were, in effect, the "precursors" of medical sociology as we now know it.

THE PRECURSERS

Among those who stand out as precursers of the field, some explicitly expressed their interest in creating a sociology of medicine, while others used medicine or health problems only as the empirical subject of otherwise generic sociological approaches and concerns. Michael Davis, for example, began his study of immigrant health before World War I, and Bernhard Stern, in 1927, published a doctoral research specifically concerned with the study of medicine; Henry Sigerist and Lawrence J. Henderson were physicians who forged a special identity with sociology. Others who fit in one or another of these categories include Robert E. L.

Faris, H. Warren Dunham, Harry Stack Sullivan, W. I. Thomas, and Talcott Parsons. Michael Davis stands out as a unique figure, but the others can be defined in four major trends during the period from 1920 to 1940:

- Social histories of medicine
- The social psychology of interpersonal relations in therapeutic institutions
- Social epidemiology
- The sociology of the professions

Most of the work was centered in three sociology departments, beginning with the University of Chicago, which had dominated American sociology during the first three decades of the century, and, during the '30s, at Harvard and Columbia. Sigerist inhabits his own niche in Baltimore at the Johns Hopkins School of Medicine, and Sullivan, also centered mainly in Baltimore, found his closest social science collaborators at the University of Chicago.

Michael Davis was very much a social advocate, close in work and spirit to the social medicine movement. Bernhard J. Stern and Henry Sigerist shared Davis's advocacy but were outstanding pioneers in the social history of medicine. As scholars, they were guided by theories of sociocultural determinants of social change and by historical methods. Robert Faris and Warren Dunham, in the social ecology tradition of Park and Burgess at Chicago, focused on the effects of the modern urban environment on mental illness, using methods of social epidemiology. Lawrence Henderson (1935) and Talcott Parsons (1951) were pioneers of structural-functional theory, which was to dominate American sociology for the next twenty-five years, and they used the doctor-patient dyad to demonstrate how the medical profession is a key institution of the societal social system. In contrast to the social advocacy of the historians, Henderson and Parsons, particularly, represented the effort to achieve objectivity, to demonstrate sociology's identity as a science.

Michael M. Davis

Michael M. Davis wrote his thesis (Davis 1909) at Columbia University under Franklin Giddings, the third president of the American Sociological Society (later changed in name to the American Sociological Association). Following his mentor's deep interest in urbanization, he studied problems of health to illustrate how sociological principles contributed to explaining the effects of social status, particularly with reference to the massive waves of immigrants that were then coming to the United States. His book, *Immigrant Health and the Community,* published in 1921, is one of the first monographs of modern medical sociology.

Davis was quickly drawn into a leadership role in social policy. His interest in immigrants made him aware of deficiencies in access to health care that were related to poverty. Just prior to World War I, a community health center movement was started. Beginning with a demonstration center for maternal and child health in Milwaukee in 1911, the concept of neighborhood health centers for the poor grew rapidly. By 1920, there were 72 such centers in 49 communities. By 1930, the number had grown to 1,511. Davis studied this movement and was active in its implementation. When the Committee on the Costs of Medical Care (CCMC) was created in 1927, Davis was on its executive committee (CCMC 1972). By this time, he was a functionary of a philanthropic foundation: director for medical services of the Julius Rosenwald Fund of Chicago.

THE SOCIAL HISTORIANS

Bernhard J. Stern (1894–1956), is usually omitted in the textbooks and published historical accounts of medical sociology. Even in public health and social medicine, fields in which he was better known, the "new meaning" between history and medicine that took place during the 1920s and '30s is credited mainly to Henry Sigerist. Sigerist, without question, is the outstanding medical historian of his time, and he was the major influence in the expansion of medical history from its previous focus on great men and their discoveries to include social and political phenomena (Reverby and Rosner 1979:7). However, even though Sigerist defined an element of his own history as "sociological," it was Stern who was the pioneer within the discipline of sociology and who introduced the "sociological approach" to medical history (Reverby and Rosner 1979:10).

In 1927, the year Stern received his Ph.D. degree, he published two books. The first and most important was his dissertation, published by the Columbia University Press: *Social Factors in Medical Practice* (Stern 1927a). Sigerist and Stern were friends, and they are often compared. Among their followers, there is a friendly rivalry as to who was first. Primacy seems less important, however, than the fact that both were such outstanding scholars, but there are, nevertheless, important differences. Sigerist was a physician-philologist,

trained as a medical historian under Karl Sudhoff at the University of Leipzig's Institute of the History of Medicine; Stern was primarily a sociologist, trained by Ogburn and Boas at Columbia in sociology and anthropology, developing the historical method in the service of his analysis of the role of medicine in society. Sigerist's focus tended always to be on medicine and became more so as his career proceeded. Stern focused more on the social factors, and therefore, seems most legitimately to come by the title "The Father of Medical Sociology" (Straus 1978).

Although known as the premier medical historian of his time, Henry E. Sigerist (1891–1957) outlined a field that he called "medical sociology" and saw himself as its pioneer (Fee and Brown 1997). He came to the United States in 1932 as an international authority on the history of medicine, to a chair established by William Welch at Johns Hopkins when that school was at the zenith of its prestige as the model of American medical education. Therefore, his position was the opposite of Stern's, who worked mainly for others and never with the protection of a secure academic position. Yet they shared much, both intellectually and in life experience. Sigerist, in the '30s, conceived an ambitious project in the "Sociology of Medicine." Yet, although he was an outstanding professional historian, his sociology was "a product of its time. It was an expression of the thirties, not so much as an emerging academic discipline but as a compelling, comparative, and implicitly political approach to the evolving contemporary relations between medicine and society" (Roemer et al. 1997:315). Rosen described Sigerist's sociology as "a tool . . . [and] a means of contributing to the urgent present problems of medicine and of helping to prepare the future" (Roemer et al. 1997:315). Although Stern's politics were more radical than Sigerist's, his medical sociology was less ideological. Both, however, were embraced as intellectual heroes of the social medicine movement, whereas they were much less influential in medical sociology as it developed after the second world war.

Recently, in a new book about Sigerist, several medical historians, two of them former close associates of both Stern and Sigerist, critically reassess the role of Sigerist in American medical sociology (Roemer et al. 1997). They present new data about the depth and focus of Sigerist's recognition that "medical care is not a technical problem which can be considered separately . . . [but] is much more a sociological problem" (Roemer et al. 1997:291). Sigerist taught two courses and a seminar specifically devoted to medical sociology at Johns Hopkins. He also planned and began, in 1938, a two-volume sociology of medicine, which was never completed. Roemer and his colleagues raise the question of why Sigerist's sociological ideas and actions influenced a generation of American health policy activists but not the later academic field of medical sociology. Their answer is both a bitter indictment of sociology and a striking differentiation of social medicine and medical sociology:

> Sigerist's legacy was abandoned in the course of the specialized professional evolution of the field of medical sociology. As it developed after World War II, formal medical sociology departed more and more sharply from the area of study and advocacy Sigerist had so effectively promoted in the thirties and early forties. A chasm of incomprehension began to separate those physicians and others who vividly remembered and were still inspired by Sigerist's "medical sociology" and those Ph.D.-trained academicians who developed professional careers in the emerging subdiscipline of the same name but who had never heard of Sigerist. (Roemer et al. 1997:326)

This indictment of medical sociology listed the "restricted channels" in which the mainstream of the 1950s medical sociology flowed. The research problems that are identified accurately reflect the patterns of inquiry that were followed by medical sociology, some beginning in the '30s and all developing extensively during the decades immediately following World War II (e.g., the medical utilization patterns and health care practices of various segments of the population; the professional behavior of physicians and the professionalization process of medical education; the doctor-patient relationship and the organization of health care personnel and institutions; the social epidemiology of mental illness and the internal working of psychiatric hospitals). "What all these investigations in the mainstream had in common," Roemer and his co-authors conclude, "was their attempt to achieve 'objectivity' by following the models of behavioral and/or natural science. In practice, this meant that medical sociology became increasingly 'scientific' by narrowing its focus, purifying its methodology, and restricting its interpretive goals" (Roemer et al. 1997:327).

For physicians like Roemer, and by implication, Sigerist, medical sociology as it developed devoted itself to the goals of basic science and, in the process, lost the "passion" of solving the major social problems of medicine. Certainly, this is an accurate description of the controversy that separated social medicine from medical sociology. Whether it is in fact a valid criticism is, in my opinion, not so clear.

INTERPERSONAL RELATIONS IN THERAPEUTIC SITUATIONS

This was also the time when a sociological perspective guided a radical change in the treatment of mental illness. From the work of Harry Stack Sullivan particularly, a social psychology of therapeutic situations emerged (Bloom and Zambrana 1983:78). Two papers by Sullivan, published in 1931, signaled the beginning of what became known as the "therapeutic community" movement in the hospitalization of the mentally ill (Sullivan 1931a, 1931b). During the preceding half-century, hospital care for the mentally ill was custodial, and in the best of circumstances, therapy was represented only by the brief time the patient might see a doctor. The therapeutic community provided a new focus for the "other twenty-three" hours of the patient's day.

This expanded view of hospital care turned the spotlight away from a narrow focus on the intrapsychic aspects of mental disorder and toward the inclusion of the interpersonal and inspired a generation of ethnographic studies of the mental hospital as a small society. The best known occurred after World War II (Jones 1953; Ginzberg et al. 1959; Barrabee 1951; Stanton and Schwartz 1954; Belknap 1956; Caudill 1958; Goffman 1957, 1959, 1961). However, there was earlier work directly stimulated by Sullivan (Rowland 1938, 1939; Devereux 1944).

SOCIAL EPIDEMIOLOGY

During the two decades between the World Wars, sociologists became important players in another aspect of inquiry about mental disorder, the incidence and prevalence of mental illness. Within this area of research, the social ecology research at the University of Chicago was outstanding, conducted by Faris and Dunham in the 1930s based on the theories of modern urban development by Burgess (Faris and Dunham 1939). Their work appeared at the midpoint of a developing series of studies to document and interpret the nature and scope of mental disorder. Several related propositions were at the foundation of this field:

1. There has been a substantial increase in the rate of mental illness in the United States over the past century.

2. The increase in mental illness is associated directly with increased industrialization and urbanization; therefore, it can be concluded that the

causes of serious mental disorder, in significant part, include factors of lifestyle, particularly the stress and pressure of modern society.

3. There is, beyond the increase in the rate of diagnosed cases of mental illness, a significant amount of undetected and consequently untreated mental illness in society.

The Chicago studies were critical in the study of major hypotheses about the relation between social conditions and mental disorder (Leacock 1957). These hypotheses dealt with the question of rural versus urban living, the importance of nationality and cultural factors, and the significance of socioeconomic variables. They were precursers of one of the most important categories of research conducted by medical sociologists in the post-war period.

THE SOCIOLOGY OF THE PROFESSIONS

Modern sociologists have studied the professions largely according to the conception of A. M. Carr-Saunders and P. A. Wilson (1933). They identified a set of characteristics that separated professions from other occupations and placed the existence of professionalism distinctly in modern Western society, dating from the late middle ages in association with the appearance of the university. Those individuals who represented such occupations as medicine and law in previous ages were seen not as professionals but more as craftsmen-spiritualists until the thirteenth century. This definition was the point of departure for the development of the sociology of the professions as an active field of inquiry, and medicine as the prototypical profession has been the subject of much of the modern work in this field.

Two characteristics were asserted to be, in combination, the core characteristics of a profession. The first was extended formal training required for qualification, and the second was a commitment to service to the community. A further set of attributes was derivative: The practitioners of a profession form a distinct social group, classified as such both by the practitioners themselves and by the society in which they operate. The basis of this social group was their professional activity and not some other social or economic attribute. The social group, or "community" itself (Larson 1977), was organized into an association that established formal rules and informal practices of behavior. The association disciplined its own members, maintaining an ethical standard by its own means, thus preserving the independence of its members in the practice of the profession.

Talcott Parsons, beginning in the 1930s, is usually credited with the beginnings of the sociology of medicine as a profession. His work, in turn, owes much to his colleague-mentor at Harvard, Lawrence J. Henderson, and was carried on in the post-war period by their student Robert K. Merton at Columbia University.

Lawrence Henderson was a physician-scientist who, attracted to sociology in midcareer, conceived a model of social systems that was an early variant of functionalist theory, which as developed by Talcott Parsons and Robert Merton, was to dominate sociological theory during the next thirty years. Parenthetically, it is notable that Henderson shared with Bernhard Stern the neglect of future scholars in the specialty that each was so important in founding. Otherwise, they could hardly have been more different. Whereas Henderson built his theoretical model from the dyad that he conceived to be the most fundamental type of human relationship, Stern studied society in socio-political terms, always working as a concerned intellectual in close touch with the social problems of his time and deliberately reaching for ideological expression of his inquiry. Henderson was committed to creating a social science that he believed possessed a rigor comparable to that of natural science, and in which he saw no proper place for socio-politics. Indeed, in contrast to the activist, policy-oriented Stern, Henderson epitomized the value-neutrality that many sociologists idealized as the model of all scientific endeavor.

Henderson (1878–1942) was from an old New England family, and he took very seriously his role as the Abbott and James Lawrence Professor of Chemistry at Harvard University. A graduate of Harvard Medical School in 1902, he never practiced medicine but admired clinical therapy. Functional theory, derived from the classic generalized description of physico-chemical systems by Willard Gibbs, was the point of departure for his own central achievement as a biological scientist. The Henderson-Hesselbach theorem, his scientific formulation in 1908 of the acid-base equilibrium, is still taught to medical students today (Parascandola 1992). He was fascinated with the concepts of equilibrium, of regulation, and of homeostatic mechanisms, and when a colleague introduced him to the work of Vilfredo Pareto, the Italian sociologist, Henderson converted his interests to functional analysis of social systems (Barber 1970).

Henderson's ideas were seminal in the early development of social system theory, and his famous

Pareto seminar spread further influence through its outstanding group of participants. The latter included a variety of disciplines, from business and law to psychology. The participants included sociologists Robert K. Merton, Talcott Parsons, Kingsley Davis, and George Homans, and the anthropologist Clyde Kluckhohn. The way in which this seminar influenced the early history of medical sociology is indicated by Merton:

> All you have to do is read Henderson's brilliant little book on Pareto . . . to see the analogies which he drew between or to see the use of Pareto's conceptual scheme which he applied to physician-patient relations. . . . So in that sense I am sure that was the first time that I and the rest of us were exposed to the idea of looking at the relationship between physicians and patients from a sociological standpoint, and that in turn was second nature to Henderson because of his involvement in the medical school. (Merton 1980)

Henderson himself was a relatively unknown figure among sociologists for decades after his death in 1942. The heritage of his ideas were best known through the work of Parsons, especially his 1951 book, *The Social System,* in which Chapter 10 became the blueprint for the functional analysis of medical practice (Parsons 1951). This has changed in recent years, as his full impact on sociology has been recognized (Parascandola 1992; Nichols 1992).

The story of the sociology of medicine from 1920 to 1945, even in brief outline, does not stop here. The task here, however, requires that we can only mention this part of the story, and move on to the main part of medical sociology's history, the period that followed World War II.

MEDICAL SOCIOLOGY FROM 1945 TO 1960

At the end of the war, the institutions responsible for higher education in the United States were poised for a radical transformation. The resulting situation affected both medicine and sociology. The changes appear at first to pick up and continue the pre-war trends, but they were both more fundamental and more diverse. For example, the scientific function of the medical school that Abraham Flexner had recommended in 1910 had been gradually realized during the next three decades. "The faculties in the best schools had become scientific investigators" (Stevens 1971:358). However, with support for research projects coming mainly from earmarked foundation grants, "in large part, medical

schools made no distinction between teaching and research" (Stevens 1971:358). Following the war, the research function became dominant, reflecting a structural change that altered the social environment of medical schools in a way that no one had predicted, not even the ubiquitous Flexner.

Most obvious was the replacement of private foundation grants by the federal government as the main outside source of research support, but the significance of the change went beyond that. The primary sources were the National Institutes of Health. Some trace NIH origins to 1887, when a laboratory for bacteriological studies was created within the United States Public Health Service. However, the contemporary model began only in 1930, and it was not until a congressional act in 1937 that NIH developed "specialist research programs focused on specific conditions or diseases." At first these were predominantly on-site research and training at the national capital, but gradually extramural research grants to individuals and institutions were added. The latter grew rapidly to change the balance between the medical school functions of teaching, research, and service. This process started during World War II:

> An accelerated, focused program of medical research, sponsored both by private organizations and by various governmental departments for wartime needs, led to *separate accounting for research in the schools,* and thus to *a separation of the research function* from the regular expected role of teaching. (Stevens 1971:358)

By 1948, almost all medical schools budgeted research separately, and by so doing, set off a chain of major effects. The nominally independent medical schools became dependent for their continued existence on federal research grants. Within the medical schools and the medical centers of which they were part, the role of the scientist became dominant, and inevitably, teaching and service became less important. Faculties grew in size, even when student bodies remained stable, but *the balance among functions was skewed to science* because of its contribution to the medical school budget.

While these changes were occurring in medical education, sociology followed what appeared to be a similar growth pattern, but on a much smaller scale. Until World War II, there was virtually no separation of roles between teaching and research, and sociology's main locus in the university was in the college of arts and sciences. Whatever external funding there was came almost totally from private foundations. Although individual scholars contributed to special commissions like the Ogburn Committee on Social Trends, (Ogburn

1933), sociologists played virtually no role in the inner circles of government science.

The development of medical sociology as a subspecialty began not so much within departments of its own parent discipline or with the creation of a new academic department, but as part of particular interdisciplinary programs in the university, like those in Yale's Institute of Human Relations, or by direct funding from foundations. The Russell Sage Foundation, the Milbank Memorial Fund, and the Rockefeller Foundations were the main sources of such support.

Sociologists in general, despite their extensive wartime participation in government war-related research, returned after the war to traditional university roles (Lyons 1969:122). In the universities, meanwhile, following the trend of wartime experience, research quickly took on greater importance, and like other sciences, sociology turned to the federal government for support. Medical sociology, as it grew toward full identification as an intellectual activity in its own right, epitomized this shift, no doubt speeded in this direction by a growing association with medical institutions, which always had higher priority for government support. Although private sources of support remained important, medical sociology's development at this stage was closely associated with the National Institute of Mental Health (NIMH), then the newest federal institute.

The NIMH, created in 1946, is arguably the single institution that, more than any other, was responsible for the emergence of medical sociology as we now know it. In the background, there was, of course, the post-war increase of the government's role in all of science in the United States, and the development of medical sociology was part of that process. Close examination, however, shows that Robert H. Felix, the founding director of the NIMH, and a few of his closest associates played critical roles in how medical sociology developed. The NIMH was instrumental in both the training of social scientists and the financing of research about social factors in health and illness. On the surface, it is not immediately evident that Felix himself, or any social scientists, made a special contribution beyond responding to the requests for proposals that eventually appeared. However, unpublished testimony from Robert Felix tells a very different story about his own very deep interest and the influence of sociologists like Raymond Bowers, August Hollingshead, and John Clausen. The policies that they conceived and set in motion fit the needs of the post-war university, and within it medical sociology found its place.

Created by the National Mental Health Act of 1946, the NIMH appeared to be a direct result of the war. A twenty-page memorandum by Dr. Felix, "Outline of a Comprehensive Community-Based Mental Health Program," written in 1944, became the working paper of the National Mental Health Act. At the time, Felix had just been appointed the medical officer in charge of the Federal Narcotics Hospital in Lexington, Kentucky, which was part of the Division of Mental Hygiene within the Public Health Service (Segal 1975). Prior efforts to update and reform this agency tended to be either limited to particular mental health problems, such as drug addiction, or to muckraking, consciousness-raising public campaigns to call attention to the abuses of the mentally ill. Only with the National Mental Health Act was a comprehensive approach taken by the federal government to such problems. The creation of the NIMH as the central agency for research and training was the culmination of this development.

NIMH, in the record of its first years, shows little evidence of the importance it was to place on a role for the social sciences. It was an institutional expression primarily of the recognition that psychiatry achieved during the war. It has also been described as a reaction to the public scandal that erupted after the war over the conditions in state mental hospitals (Starr 1982:346). Springing from these origins, the emphasis in the early very rapid expansion of NIMH appears to have been focused entirely on psychiatry, on the creation of medical research and training programs related to mental health and on the improvement of psychiatric clinical service.

Behind the scenes, in the staff operations of NIMH, the story was different. Social science was given an important role to play from the very beginning. What the official record of NIMH does not reveal is that Felix, before his appointment as the first director, had been converted to the importance of social science in medicine at Johns Hopkins, where he was sent by the Public Health Service (PHS) in 1941 to study public health. At the time, Felix was a medical officer in the Division of Mental Hygiene at the United States Narcotics Hospital in Lexington, Kentucky. When the PHS sent him to Johns Hopkins in 1941, he later wrote:

> I just became entranced with what I was learning about epidemiology of diseases. And they were concerned at that time about the epidemiology of so-called chronic medical conditions. From this I extrapolated that there must be something we could do to understand in the area of mental diseases. But there were no epidemiologists interested. The people who were most nearly what I was looking for were sociologists. And this is why I turned to sociologists. (Felix 1983)

During the years 1946–1949, while he was shaping the institution that was to become the NIMH, Felix maintained this interest.

Raymond V. Bowers was the first sociologist who worked with him. Bowers never thought of himself as a medical sociologist, or any other type of specialist. When asked if he was aware of a field called medical sociology at that time, he answered: "Not really, because I never had been interested in these special sociologies. I was a sociologist. And quantitatively oriented. And I still have a hard time—I gulp when I think of some of these specialties" (Bowers 1983). Despite the brief period of their association—and Bowers' own disclaimers—Bowers was ideal for Felix's purpose, to create a psychiatric epidemiologial research effort. Their combined vision was described in 1948. "The impact of the social environment on the life history," they wrote, "and the relevance of the life history to mental illness, are no longer in serious question as clinical and research findings. But, even though we have come a considerable distance in our systematic understanding of the symptomology and psycho-dynamics of mental disorders, such understanding does not extend to any extent to the role played by socio-environmental factors" (Felix and Bowers 1948).

The beginning, however, was not easy. Although Felix chose unusually talented and effective social scientists, the social climate of the country made his task difficult. His first problem was with the name. He had to deal with Congress: "I had to keep in mind that I didn't have any money if I didn't please Congress," he reported, and some members of Congress advised him to be careful about names. "When I first set up, I wanted to set up a branch on sociology, but I was advised against it because they would consider that socialism. Sociology was socialism. So I . . . dreamed up a name that I borrowed from public health, and I developed a laboratory of socio-environmental studies." As he explained further:

> As long as I was talking about environment, that went along with fodder, and sewage, and so forth. Socio-environmental. I could get by with the "socio" because I had the "environmental" in it. And that's how I got things started, and through that we developed grant programs both intramural and outside. (Felix 1983)

When asked about the term "behavioral sciences," Felix dated its creation later, "sometime in the fifties." Its origin, however, was similar, in Felix's view. It was a way to avoid the association between "social" and "socialism." In his exact words:

Behavior was something they could understand. Kids behave, and misbehave. And I'll never forget, someone was asking me about it one time, and I said, "Well, everything is behavior. Even misbehavior is behavior." And they said, "Well, I guess you're right." And I said, "So I can call anything behavioral studies." (Felix 1983)

Unfortunately, the name strategy was not enough to mute the associations with political deviationism. Congress attacked his support of specific early research grants, calling them "communistic." To deal with this issue, Felix gives credit to John Clausen.

John Clausen, trained at the University of Chicago, was an Assistant Professor of Sociology at Cornell when Felix recruited him to replace Bowers in 1948. As Social Science Consultant to the Director, he immediately launched a program of research. In 1951, when the intramural research program was founded, he became the first chief of the Laboratory of Socio-environmental Studies at NIMH, remaining in that position until 1960, when he went to the University of California at Berkeley. In Felix's opinion, Clausen made "a tremendous contribution to the program." Others have said the same (Sewell 1988:130). But the formal measure of his importance, indicated by programs and research, does not do justice to the informal advice and support for Felix, who said:

> I think it's due to him (Clausen) as much as anything else that I didn't get discouraged when I was trying to develop the whole area of medical sociology as far as mental illness was concerned. And people didn't think this was such a smart thing to do. They thought this was a lot of boondoggle. You know the path of medical sociology was not a smooth and easy one. (Felix 1983)

Explaining what he meant, Felix referred to two studies, the research on the Hutterites by Eaton and Weil (1955), and a study of "complementary needs." Both the general public and particularly some members of Congress "raised unmitigated hell with us." The Hutterite study was "viewed as trying to promote communism," and the other (complementary needs in marriage) led to the claim "that we were trying to find out how we could get laws passed so we could control who got married to who, to breed a master race" (Felix 1983). This objection to a common type of family study was, of course, absurd, but how Congress could object to the Hutterite research is even more difficult to imagine. Now considered a classic of the epidemiology of mental illness, it contained a rarely used methodology—total prevalence study—which is difficult to execute and time-consuming but ideal for the uncovering of rates of untreated illness. How Congress could have perceived it as "promoting communism" is truly a mystery, even if allowance is made for the distortions of the McCarthyism so pervasive at that time.

Fortunately, what Congress saw as boondoggle was recognized by Felix and Clausen for its research merit, and they persisted. The direction they chose, weighted toward research, also included a heavy investment in research training. Although the training programs were conceived first with psychiatrists in mind, they were actually awarded to all types of professionals who were in any way related to mental health. Such support grew slowly at first, expanded dramatically between 1956 and 1965 as Congress became more approving, stabilized in the mid-sixties, and began to decline in the late sixties (Segal 1975:11).

It is important to note that, in spite of the early priority that Felix placed on training, sociology and anthropology were not included during NIMH's first decade. Not until 1957 was the training program broadened to support them. Why this selective delay? One knows, of course, from Felix and others, that the values of the early stages of the Cold War created part of the problem. There were also questions about its academic legitimacy. When the bill to found the National Science Foundation (NSF) was brought before the Congress on July 3, 1946, the Senate voted by 46 to 26, with 24 members not voting, to exclude the social sciences (Lyons 1969:169). The reason given by Senator Thomas C. Hart, Republican of Connecticut, was that "no agreement has been reached with reference to what social science really means." Social science was also attacked because it was an "applied science," and the NSF was intended to support "pure science" (Lyons 1969:169). Like other objects of prejudice, the sociologists were attacked, as they say, "coming and going."

For Felix, when asked what he thought of the way medical sociology developed, he answered: "I thought it developed soundly and well. I was very pleased with the people I was working with, both intramurally and extramurally. They were helpful. They knew what we were trying to do. They were dedicated people. And I thought we made tremendous progress. As a matter of fact, I think we made more solid progress in the area of sociology than we did in the area of physiology, for the first ten years" (my underlining).

Hollingshead was one of the first major research sociologists to be supported by NIMH. Hollingshead's relationship with NIMH began in 1949, when, together with the psychiatrist Frederic C. Redlich, he made his first proposal for an epidemiological study of mental illness in New Haven. This was in the second year of grant support by NIMH, and the Advisory Council served as a review panel for all grant proposals. Hollingshead and Redlich were turned down on that first application, but in 1950 they reapplied and were funded (Hollingshead 1978). However, when Hollingshead sought training support from NIMH, he was turned down. He turned to private foundations and was more successful, but this experience demonstrates the selective policy of Felix to support sociology only in research and research consultation in the early years.

Among the other sociologists used as advisors were Leonard Cottrell, Jr., Kingsley Davis, H. Warren Dunham, Clifford Shaw, and Robin M. Williams, Jr. In this way, Felix quietly but consistently relied heavily on the help of sociologists in his leadership of NIMH. In his formal appointments, Felix always kept someone to represent sociology, but in the beginning, the numbers were small. Robin Williams replaced Hollingshead on the Mental Health Study Section, and in 1956, William Sewell replaced him, still the only sociologist, the others all psychiatrists and psychologists. Sewell felt that the extramural program, unlike Clausen's intramural research in the socio-environmental laboratory, did not appreciate the potential contribution of sociology to mental health. "Immediately I began advocating," wrote Sewell, "a broader definition of mental health relevance and the need for greater representation of sociology and anthropology in the study section" (Sewell 1988:130). Soon, two such members were added, and the volume of proposals from these disciplines increased. NIMH responded by creating in 1959 a Behavioral Science Study Section to review all social science proposals relevant to mental health other than those in psychiatry and experimental psychology. Sewell chaired this new group. As he reported:

> In its first year of existence, over 300 research proposals were evaluated, of which 125 were funded. These included several studies that have become classics in their fields. The section continued to be a major source of support for social science projects until the Reagan administration's insistence on a very restricted definition of mental health relevance crippled it. (Sewell 1988:130–1312)

Such development, however, could hardly have been predicted in 1949 when the first proposals were made to study mental health in its relation to social class.

NIMH was not alone in its interest in this kind of research. In the immediate aftermath of the war, there was an unusual confluence of concern among both private foundations and the government about mental illness. In 1949 and 1952, for example, the Milbank Memorial Fund conducted conferences on the epidemiology of mental disorders (Milbank 1950, 1953). In 1950, The Social Science Research Council brought together two conferences of social scientists and psychiatrists "to consider the common ground in the fields of their interest" (Leighton et al. 1957). At the same time, a longitudinal study of mental illness in Stirling county of Nova Scotia was sponsored by a consortium of government, universities, and private foundations in Canada and the United States. This was explained by the recognition that until that time, just following World War II, the amount of mental illness in the United States was usually judged from the number of persons in mental hospitals. There were almost no studies of untreated mental illness in the community. Now, in the decade 1945–55, an extraordinary research effort occurred to remedy this problem, and the NIMH made a major contribution. The Midtown Manhattan Project is one of the outstanding examples (Srole et al. 1962).

As the first decade of the National Mental Health Act ended, Congress in 1955 passed the Mental Health Study Act, authorizing $1,250,000 for "an objective, thorough nationwide analysis and reevaluation of the human and economic problems of mental illness." This was a far cry from the beginning in 1946, described earlier by Robert Felix. In 1948, after its first two years without a budget, NIMH was up and running, with 38 research grants totalling $373,226. Seven years later, the Mental Health Study Act was a strong indicator that Congress no longer was being sidetracked by questions of legitimacy, political or scientific, in its willingness to support mental health research, even when it was done by sociologists. The Joint Commission on Mental Illness, which it created, was directed by a social psychologist, Marie Jahoda. M. Brewster Smith, also a social psychologist, was one of its officers. With what was at the time a huge budget, it represented a highly significant juncture in the federal government's commitment to both mental health research and the participation of social scientists. Shortly after the Joint Commission legislation was passed, the annual NIMH budget was almost doubled, from $3,890,631 to $7,326,311 in 1957 (Williams 1972). Ten years after that, in 1967, the NIMH budget was $303,000,000.

Federal support for research training in the social sciences, however, followed a different course. The formal change occurred in 1957, but several years passed before it was actualized. In the fall of 1958, a brochure was sent to chairmen of sociology and anthropology departments, announcing the availability of grant support for two broad categories of doctoral and postdoctoral training: (1) "Training of social scientists for research in mental health areas, and (2) training of professional personnel from the mental health disciplines in the research methods of the social sciences." Twenty-two applications were received and reviewed by an ad hoc committee in the fall of 1959; four of these were awarded five-year grants with activation dates of July 1, 1960, and the three grants previously awarded as pilot programs were reclassified as regular programs (Vincent 1965).

In 1960, the first full-time administrator for the social science training program, Clark Vincent, was appointed, and the Social Sciences Subcommittee was started with six members. Within a decade, the budget for this program grew from $314,128 for 7 programs to $4,664,400 for 76 programs (Lutterman 1975). The growth of this program was extraordinary, as if they were attempting to make up for the delay before 1960. Until 1965, the concentration of this support was in sociology: 80 percent of both the monies and the doctoral trainees was for sociology and social psychology; about 11 percent was for anthropology.

The rapid growth of support for research training in the social sciences during the early 1960s coincided with manpower shortages in new and expanding universities. The annual supply of Ph.D.s in sociology and anthropology was considered too low to meet the growing demand. In 1965, Clark Vincent estimated that 185 Ph.D.s in sociology and about 70 in anthropology graduated in the United States. He regarded these numbers as "critically low to meet the demand for new and replacement faculty in existing departments of these two disciplines, much less to supply the needs of new and expanding universities" (Vincent 1965:759). The NIMH program proved to be influential on a much wider academic base than the originally planned mental health relevance. Such support, in both research and training, spilled over to other federal agencies. At the National Institute of General Medical Sciences (GMS), individual research grants with sociologists as principal investigators appeared, and some special training program grants were awarded. GMS supported a research training program at Brown University and another at the University of Michigan School of Public Health. These types of grants were reassigned to The National Center for Health Services Research (NCHSR), an agency created in 1968.

Suddenly, in 1972, the Nixon administration, in connection with the amended budgets of fiscal years 1973 and 1974, announced its decision to phase out federal support for categorical professional training programs. This included all programs, affecting the

NCHSR as well. At the same time, the Public Health Service reached the apex of reorganization that had begun during the middle 1960s. The net effect was to reduce both research and training support in the social sciences in the 1970s. There seems to be no question that the purpose of administration actions from 1972 to 1974 was to phase out federal support for much of the social science programs, especially training. Fortunately, that goal was never realized, but the levels of support that were achieved during the decade of the 1960s were gone and did not return.

THE ROLE OF PRIVATE FOUNDATIONS

Although the federal government, particularly NIMH, was instrumental in the professional development of medical sociology, private foundations prepared the way, especially in training, in introducing the social sciences into medical education, and in directly stimulating and supporting professional organization. Both before and after federal agencies became involved, private foundations continued to play a vital function. The Commonwealth Fund, the Milbank Memorial Fund, and the Rockefeller Foundations deserve special mention, but the Russell Sage Foundation played what can be considered the most singular role. Its influence set directions of research, recruited already established social scientists, and trained a cadre of sociologists who were to be among the most influential of the early medical sociologists.

Medicine was not targeted in the Russell Sage Foundation's program until Dr. Donald Young became the head of the staff in 1948. At the time, the Foundation was closely identified with social work, and Young, the executive director of the Social Science research Council and former Professor of Sociology at the University of Pennsylvania, was recruited with the assignment to give it a new and more social science research-oriented direction. Esther Lucile Brown, the first woman to get a Ph.D. in anthropology from Yale (in 1927), was at the time the only staff person doing any work related to medicine. She headed the Foundation's Division on the Professions.

From the start, however, Young asked Brown to concentrate her work on the health field (Hammock and Wheeler 1994), reportedly a strategic decision to turn away from the Foundation's former association with social work. "Although Dr. Young had respect for some practitioners in the field of social work," Hammack wrote, "he thought the field as a whole was rather soft and poorly developed. Perhaps even more important, in the prestige rankings of the professions, social work

fell far below medicine. If the Russell Sage Foundation could bring social science to bear in an important way on medical practice, the world of practitioners and scholars would sit up and listen. The same effect in social work would not be seen as such an accomplishment. And among the professions of a status higher than that of social work, medicine, unlike law, had a research tradition" (Hammock and Wheeler 1994:94). In this way, medical sociology became a major beneficiary of Young's policy.

Young and Brown were well aware that, within medicine, the most receptive fields to social science at that time were public health and psychiatry, so they started there. But Young wanted to penetrate the more standard and resistant parts of medicine as well. Esther Lucile Brown was already in contact with Harold G. Wolff, the Professor of Medicine and Neurology at Cornell University Medical College, and knew of his interest in having a social scientist join him in both research and teaching. Dr. Brown convinced both Wolff and Leo W. Simmons, an anthropologist at Yale, that they should work together. In 1949, Simmons took a leave from Yale to join Dr. Wolff at Cornell. This was the initial collaboration that resulted from Young's new approach to social science and the professions (Simmons and Wolff 1954). Others were quickly to follow. Next was a grant to Columbia University in 1949 to create a University Seminar on the Professions in Modern Society. This became the source of what eventually was to be the landmark study of the sociology of medical education directed by Robert K. Merton, Patricia Kendall, and George G. Reader (Merton et al. 1957).

These early efforts of Young and Brown almost immediately produced teaching programs at medical schools and schools of public health, as well as research. In effect, they helped to create a new academic market, setting up a demand for social scientists to work in medical institutions. To meet the demand, the Foundation created a program of Health Service Residencies for Social Scientists. The plan for these residencies was completed by 1950, and the first appointment was made. "The demand for social scientists," the Foundation wrote, "within medical centers, public health agencies, and professional associations interested in promoting medical and health services is already larger than can be met by drawing upon university faculties of the behavior sciences. There is also a need for more specialized knowledge and experience in dealing with questions of sickness and therapeutic and preventive services than now possessed by most academic social scientists if any distinctive contributions are to be made" (Russell Sage Foundation

1950–1951). Accordingly, residencies were created for young Ph.D.s to train in institutions requesting such services. The Foundation provided comparable university salaries for two-year appointments. The first appointment of this plan was Albert F. Wessen, a recent Yale Ph.D. in sociology, to work in the Department of Pediatrics of the Yale Medical School, studying the impact of the department's clinical services on the sick child and its family. With this program, Russell Sage anticipated by a full decade the training programs of NIMH.

By 1953, there were six Russell Sage cross-disciplinary residencies. Over the next ten years, a substantial number of medical sociology's future leadership was trained in this program. The Foundation also gave start-up support to the Yale Sociology Department in 1952 to create the first university training program in medical sociology which, with Commonwealth Fund financing, began in 1955, with Leonard Syme and Ray Elling among its first four graduate fellows.

The Russell Sage Foundation also played an important role in the creation of the first professional organization of medical sociologists, the Committee on Medical Sociology, which, in turn, became the Section on Medical Sociology of the American Sociological Association. In this last case, Donald Young showed how foundations need not wait for requests before acting to commit resources. Initially, A. B. Hollingshead convened a small group of medical sociologists at the 1954 Annual Meeting of the American Sociological Society (now the American Sociological Association) in order "to explore ways of exchanging experiences and better identifying common interests" (Straus 1978). When an informal committee was formed, ready to use their own meager resources, Donald Young approached them and offered a small amount of discretionary funds from Russell Sage to help them get started. In this way, the Committee on Medical Sociology began.

Space does not allow the telling of similar stories about the Commonwealth Fund and the Milbank Memorial Foundation. They also contributed in important ways to the early decades of the modern period of medical sociology. This was a time of palpable promise for sociology. There was a climate of optimism that the study of both human emotions and social relations would find a common and binding ground in a science of behavior. Medicine, already deeply committed to psychosomatic explanations for diseases like ulcerative colitis, and opening its education to psychoanalytic theory, was poised to give access in education and research to social scientists. Demand for such social scientists emerged from various sources. Individual physicians like Frederick Redlich, Thomas Rennie, Alexander Leighton, and

Ernest Gruenberg, all psychiatrists interested in psychiatric epidemiology, sought and found skilled social researchers and made them equal research partners. These efforts found support from both the private and public sectors. Schools of public health were already converts to the importance of basic knowledge from the social sciences and were ready to try experiments in teaching. For these efforts, the private foundations provided strategic support, impossible to get elsewhere. New theoretical conceptions about critical problems of the medical profession, like socialization for the profession and comprehensive care, found expression that, at the outset, was almost entirely based on support from their own universities or the private foundations, especially the Commonwealth Fund.

Very few careers in medical sociology during the post-war period were unaffected by the efforts of these three family foundations. In the earliest stage, from 1946 to 1953, they responded mainly to requests that depended on the leadership and participation of established figures. Within a short time, they were helping the youngest recruits, such as Eliot Freidson, Harvey Smith, Edmund Volkart, Renée Fox, Mary Goss, Robin Badgley, Ray Elling, Leonard Syme, and others. One can argue that the attitudes and policies of large government organizations like the NIMH did catch up with those of the foundations and might very well have ended up where they eventually did, driven by other social and political forces of the time. On the other hand, the historical fact is that the private foundations acted early to encourage and help shape the pathways of social science in medicine. Moreover, in one vital step in the institutionalization of medical sociology, the creation and advancement of professional associations and journals, it was again private foundation support that proved to be crucial.

THE ASA SECTION ON MEDICAL SOCIOLOGY

The Section on Medical Sociology of the American Sociological Association is the first and most widely known professional association for social scientists with interests in problems of health and illness. The Section was formally created by the American Sociological Society in 1959, [1] but it developed from an unaffiliated organization, the Committee on Medical Sociology,

---

[1] The name of the national organization of sociologists was changed to the American Sociological Association in 1959, the year following the addition of the by-law creating sections.

started in 1955. The Committee was founded by sociologists but included the full range of social scientists, anthropologists, social psychologists, social workers, and physicians. Even after it evolved into an official Section, it continued as a multidisciplinary group.

In 1954, Hollingshead convened a group at the annual meeting of the American Sociological Society, inviting anyone who had some interest in problems of health or illness. At the end of this first meeting, the group decided to meet more formally in 1955, to call itself the Committee on Medical Sociology and thereby became the source of what, in five years, would be a full-fledged professional organization. The style of the Committee was completely informal, that is, the customary paraphernalia of officers, by-laws etc., were sidestepped. Robert Straus, who served as Hollingshead's co-leader, reported that this meeting led to agreement on two specific goals: the designation of time on the program of the American Sociological Society annual meeting for the presentation of research papers in medical sociology, and the facilitation of communication among interested persons (Straus 1957).

The first objective was quickly achieved. The number of contributed papers that fit the definition of medical sociology was sufficient to secure a regular and important place on the annual program. Toward the second goal, Straus, then just beginning as the Chairman of the only Department of Behavioral Science at a medical school, was designated to act as the first secretary, the sole office of the organization. Absorbing the costs in his own University of Kentucky office at the time, Straus began the biannual publication of a census of individuals engaged in teaching in medical settings or in research on problems concerning health and illness. This list was the membership of the Committee. No formal requirements for membership were specified, and at no time during its history did the Committee charge dues. Straus also created a newsletter to be distributed annually to the members.

In 1957, the American Sociological Society agreed to provide its facilities for the biannual census of medical sociologists (the annual newsletter) and to underwrite the cost of its mailings. Behind the scenes, and unknown to the public, Donald Young of the Russell Sage Foundation provided the necessary funds to the ASS.

When, in 1958, the ASS approved new by-laws authorizing sections (Rhoads 1981), there were 280 participants in the Committee on Medical Sociology. Of these, 71 percent were sociologists; the remainder were anthropologists, psychologists, physicians, and social workers. The majority thought that joining the national society as a section was little more than a formalization of a relationship already in existence, and in addition a means of stabilizing the Committee's structure, both financially and professionally. When the Council of the ASS, in September 1959, voted to approve the formation of the Section on Medical Sociology, it became the second section to be created, following social psychology.

In January 1960, only four months after the Section was formed, the paid membership of the Section numbered 407. In April 1961, the membership had risen above 700. The Section continued to be one of the largest and most active in the national organization. As shown in Table 2-1, the membership continued to be large, increasing in its proportion of the ASA membership.

There were dissenters in the Committee on Medical Sociology against joining the national professional sociological organization. Although the majority of the membership were sociologists, the other members expressed concern. In time, separate professional organizations were formed to express both the desire for multidisciplinary professional identity and separate disciplinary representation. In 1970, the Association for the Behavioral Sciences and Medical Education (ABSAME) was formed, with the objective of "bringing together behavioral scientists and professionals from medicine, nursing, and other health care fields around issues of enhancing the teaching of the behavioral sciences in medical (health) education" (Hughes and Kennedy 1983). The Academy of Behavioral Medicine was also formed, with the purpose of "the integration of biological and behavioral knowledge in a multidisciplinary approach" (Holden 1980). On the other hand, new organizations were formed based on loyalty to both academic discipline and problem focus. The former found expression in organizations like the Society for Medical Anthropology (Landy 1983) and the Division of Health Psychology of the American Psychological Association[2] (Adler and Stone 1983). The Section on Mental Health was created in ASA to express a focus on problems of mental health.

The federal science establishment, increasingly, has favored the use of the more inclusive term of behavioral science. Most recently, the National Research Council published a report on biomedical and behavioral scientists, defining the latter to include "psychology, sociology, anthropology and speech and hearing sciences" (National Academy of Sciences Committee on National Needs for Biomedical and Behavioral

---

[2] More than 1,500 members were reported in 1980.

**TABLE 2–1 Membership of Medical Sociology Section
and American Sociological Association**

Year	Section Membership	ASA Membership	Section Percentage of ASA
1970	693	14,156	4.9
1971	697	14,827	4.7
1972	759	14,934	5.1
1973	843	14,398	5.8
1974	888	14,644	6.0
1975	928	14,387	6.7
1976	944	13,958	6.8
1977	969	13,755	7.0
1978	1,026	13,561	7.6
1979	1,061	13,208	8.0
1980	1,018	12,868	7.9
1981	957	12,599	7.5
1982	916	12,439	7.4
1983	885	11,600	7.6
1984	846	11,223	7.5
1985	993	11,485	8.6
1986	1,072	11,965	8.9
1987	1,120	12,370	9.0
1988	1,121	12,382	9.0
1989	1,102	12,666	8.7
1990	1,080	12,841	8.4
1991	1,166	13,021	8.9
1992	1,116	13,072	8.5
1993	1,108	13,057	8.5
1994	1,033	13,048	7.9
1995	980	13,254	7.4
1996	948	13,134	7.2
1997	970	13,108	7.4

Research Personnel 1994:52). Although this does not in any way adjudicate the issue, it bears mentioning that no separate analysis is included in the Academy report for each discipline, but only for the whole, and medical schools unanimously favor behavioral science as the name for faculty engaged in research or teaching involving psychosocial problems.

The first organizational meeting of the Section on Medical Sociology, on September 2, 1959, committed the Section to continuing the major functions of the Committee that preceded it. Once a year, a directory of members would be published, and twice a year, a newsletter. The first major issue brought before the Section concerned the criteria of identity as a medical sociologist. Should there be formalized requirements? Should a certification procedure be established? Both ideas were defeated.

At the sixth meeting of the Council of the Section, August 31, 1964, in Miami Beach, a formal proposal was made by E. Gartly Jaco, the editor and publisher of the *Journal of Health and Human Behavior,* requesting

that the Section take over the publication. At the time, no section sponsored its own journal. In fact, until 1954, there was only one official journal of the ASA, the *American Sociological Review,* created in 1936. When the American Sociological Society was founded in 1905, it took over the *American Journal of Sociology,* started in 1895 as the first sociology journal published in the United States. In 1936, the *AJS* was separated from official sponsorship and returned to the University of Chicago when the *ASR* was founded. Not until *Sociometry* was donated in 1954 by J. L. Moreno and officially published by the Association in 1956 under the editorship of Leonard S. Cottrell, Jr., was another journal added to the national organization. In 1958, the *Journal of Educational Sociology* became the third. However, none of these journals was presented to the ASA by sections. It was the policy of the ASA that no journal could be officially sponsored by a section, even though there might be, as was the case with medical sociology, a close association between a section and its related journal.

After intensive negotiations, the ASA Council and Publications Committee accepted the journal on a three-year trial basis. Vital in the success of this negotiation was a grant that the Section had won from the Milbank Memorial Fund. This grant guaranteed the financial risks undertaken by the ASA in accepting the *Journal*. Although formally the journal was not sponsored by the Section, the connections were close. In the end, the *Journal*'s success made all the questions raised by the ASA groundless. The name was changed to the *Journal of Health and Social Behavior* (JHSB). Eliot Freidson was chosen by the ASA as the first editor, and his already distinguished reputation as a sociological theorist blunted the professional reservations of the ASA's Publications Committee.

In March 1966, when the ASA began publishing the *JHSB,* there were 1,000 subscribers, 80 percent of which were institutions. By August 1967, Freidson reported a sharp increase in the number of submitted manuscripts and improved quality. In December 1967, the subscription rate was up to 1,600. Records of the ASA on its publications go back only to 1979. At that point, the *JHSB* had the third highest subscription rate of all the official journals, ranked behind *ASR* and *Contemporary Sociology*. More precisely, there were 4,203 total subscriptions, 2,339 individual members, and 1,254 nonmembers including institutions. The rank remained constant. In the stated opinion of the ASA

executive office, *JHSB* is more than self-sufficient and has been from very early in its history.

THE LEADERSHIP OF THE SECTION

In its first decade the officers of the Section were a mix of established sociologists out of the mainstream of the discipline and relatively young scholars whose achievements were more focused in medical sociology. August Hollingshead, Everett Hughes, and Edward Suchman, for example, were well-known senior professors in leading sociology departments. Although it was fitting that these trailblazers should be the first elected to the top office of the Section, younger people were not forced to wait long. As Table 2-2 shows, by 1963, when Harvey Smith from the University of North Carolina was elected chairman, the pattern shifted to the younger, though still broadly trained, medical sociologists.

Rhoads, in his official history of the ASA, described the period after 1970 as a time of troubles between Sections and the parent group. "Relations," he wrote, "between Sections and the Association were somewhat strained through a major part of the seventies. The problem centered on the amount of time allocated to Sections during the Annual Meeting and the scheduling of Section Day activities" (Rhoads 1981:70). For the Medical Sociology Section, however,

TABLE 2–2 Chairs of Section on Medical Sociology, 1960–1979

Name	Affiliation	Year
August B. Hollingshead	Yale University	1960
Odin W. Anderson	Center for Health Ad Studies, University of Chicago	1961
Everett C. Hughes	University of Chicago	1962
Harvey L. Smith	University of North Carolina	1963
Eliot Freidson	New York University	1964
Samuel W. Bloom	Downstate Med School-SUNY	1965
Edward A. Suchman	Cornell University	1966
Howard E. Freeman	Brandeis University	1967
Robert Straus	University of Kentucky School of Medicine	1968
Sol Levine	Harvard School of Public Health	1969
David Mechanic	University of Wisconsin	1970
Jerome Myers	Yale University	1971
John Clausen	University of California-Berkley	1972
Robert Wilson	University of North Carolina	1973
Rose Coser	SUNY-Stony Brook	1974
Renée Fox	University of Pennsylvania	1975
Saxon Graham	University of Buffalo	1976
Jack Ellinson	Columbia University of Public Health	1977
Peter K. New	Brandeis University	1978
Virginia Olesen	University of California, San Francisco	1979

these were not problems. Secure as the largest section, it did not need to worry about its share of the annual program for scientific papers. Also, its Section Day activities were established as an occasion when invited presentations consistently met the highest academic standards, were topical, and usually published in the best available refereed journal.

On the other hand, one important problem presented itself in 1970. The Milbank grant, which had been so important for the organization to launch its professional services, was now ended. David Mechanic, during his term as Chairman of the Section in 1970, created a development committee to deal with this problem. He wanted to break new ground. A proposal to the Carnegie Foundation was created, which marked a shift in the Section's history in the direction of public policy and health services research. The proposal, "Sociological Aspects of Health and Health Services," was funded, and the first meeting of the Carnegie Grant Steering Committee was held on December 29, 1971, at the Center for Health Administration Studies of the University of Chicago. Carnegie granted $69,000 as requested, for a three-year period to finance the activities of two new committees: the Committee on Organizational Consequences of Varying National Programs for Providing Health Services, with Odin Anderson as its chairman, and the Committee on Preventive Health and Health Maintenance, led by Sol Levine. Their work was published in a special supplement of *Medical Care* (Mechanic and Levine 1977). The report argued that, in the debate about national health insurance, a variety of issues were being neglected. The prevailing focus, they said, was on financing. More important were the organizational consequences, preventive health and health maintenance. Speaking most directly to the mission of the Carnegie grant in 1972, the Section's Public Policy Committee presented a strong statement, "Principles and Criteria for National Health Insurance," which became the subject of a special symposium at the Annual Meeting of the ASA in New Orleans. Articulated in the publications of 1977 and 1982, the Section moved strongly toward the promotion of health services and health policy research, bringing medical sociology once again in close synchrony with social medicine.

Among the Section's achievements was its participation, in 1967, in the decision by the National Board of Medical Examiners to explore the feasibility of including the behavioral sciences in their examinations. By June 1973, a Behavioral Science Test Committee was operating and responsible for including the same number of test items in Part I of the National Boards,

with equal weighting as the six other basic sciences (anatomy, biochemistry, microbiology, pathology, pharmacology, and physiology).

The first twenty years after the establishment of the Section on Medical Sociology was, for its members and for the social sciences of health, a period of rapid growth, diversification of activities, and conflict. In some ways, it was a golden age. As 1980 approached, however, there was a significant contraction in demand, reflected in both the pattern of government support and in the directions of substantive interest that affected medical sociology, and with it, the Section. The reduction of federal support was signaled by the announcement in 1973, in connection with the amended budgets of fiscal years 1973 and 1974, of the administration's decision to phase out federal support for categorical professional training programs, including all research training programs in NIH/NIMH. Strong protests from the scientific community and Congress led to the restoration of a much smaller research training program (Segal 1975:12). By 1980, even though the extreme negative view of the Nixon administration toward the social sciences had been mitigated, the policies of the government toward training and research in the social sciences were drastically reduced.

Intellectually, the changes were equally striking. When the Section began, the primary host for social science in medical education was still psychiatry, and in research this was reflected by emphasis on problems of mental health relevance. Public health and preventive medicine had much longer historical roots for the social sciences, but these roots were limited to research, and full partnership did not follow after World War II. In the 1960s, the pattern changed. The grand themes of the decade—social welfare, civil rights, equality of access to education and health care—produced the community medicine movement, and with it a special home in medical school departments of community medicine and schools of public health for medical sociologists. At the same time, new therapeutic drugs in psychiatric treatment, the so-called psychomimetic or tranquilizer drugs, began to replace and sometimes eliminate the intense interest that psychiatry had been focusing on the social factors in mental illness. But social science was not abandoned entirely by psychiatry; NIMH continued as a major source of support. In 1975, NIMH devoted 15 percent of its research funds to studies by social scientists. However, only about one-fifth of the money for the social sciences supported basic research. In actual dollars, this meant that of $11 million spent for extramural programs of social science research, $1,832,000 were spent for basic research in all of the social sciences, and $333,000 specific to sociologists.

To some extent, these patterns of changing interest and therapeutic emphasis helped to upgrade the importance of health services research. What had been a hope that social science would contribute to the theoretical understanding of mental illness, the interpersonal relations of the health professions, the social organization of its major institutions, the social ecology of illness, and other subjects of basic research shifted toward a more policy-oriented study of health care, its access, delivery organization, cost, and insurance. The Section was in the forefront of these changes in research interest, mounting a large effort in the 1970s to study and explain the questions about health services that were most urgent.

Throughout the twenty-five years of medical sociology's most intense professional growth, 1955–1980, a group of individuals played highly visible roles as leaders and workers in making the Section the central institutionalizing group of this relatively new subdiscipline. Robert Alan Day has referred to them as the "influentials" of the field, and they fall into two distinct categories (Day 1981). One outstanding group was composed of sociologists who had already achieved positions as leaders of the field more generally, and for whom studies in the sociology of medicine were incidental to the main body of their work. Talcott Parsons, for example, and Robert Merton, Everett Hughes, and August Hollingshead. All four were presidents of the American Sociological Association. Each of them used medicine as an empirical case to test their more general ideas. They were also mentors to younger people who became influential in the field. Again, however, few of the younger people trained in medical sociology; most entered the field of medical sociology after they completed their studies. As examples, one thinks of Eliot Freidson, Edmund Volkart, Sol Levine, Howard Becker, Blanche Geer, Patricia Kendall, Leo Simmons, Howard Freeman, Robert N. Wilson. A few did dissertations that studied medicine or health: Renée Fox, Robert Straus, David Mechanic, Walter Wardwell, Mary E. W. Goss, Harvey Smith, Mark Field, and Emily Mumford, but they were not part of formal training programs in medical sociology.

However they came into the field, they were active in the Section on Medical Sociology. Overall, they number about thirty individuals who were truly influential in the institutionalization of the field, as well as playing an active part in its scholarship. This was also a generation that is unique in another way.

With few exceptions, they were participants in World War II. Many came from the kind of modest origins that supplied neither the academic sociologists nor other kinds of university faculty for previous generations in the United States. They were driven to change their own lives and the world, for the most part in the most idealistic of value terms. The war, the holocaust, the Cold War, the technological and scientific revolutions of the post-war decades formed the context of their development into the leadership of this emerging intellectual field. Against such a background, public policy and the application of knowledge in the public interest were not ever far removed from view. Medicine, with its own traditions of the search for knowledge and its use in the service of public good, seemed a most reasonable partner.

But this partnership seemed to shift ground in 1980. A new era appeared at that time, when large-scale social and intellectual changes challenged everyone in the society. For medical sociology, several aspects of these changes were to be specially significant. The women's movement and its expression in academic women's studies had a profound effect. The changes in the national economy, particularly as represented in the restructuring of the health care industry, is equally if not more important.

SUMMARY

Professionally, in 1980, medical sociology appeared to be at the crest of its development (Altman 1990). The ASA Section on Medical Sociology had grown from 407 members in 1960 to 1,018, eight percent of the ASA membership and the largest of the 20 existing sections. Sociologists were on the faculties of most of the 143 medical schools of the United States and Canada, in full-time or part-time roles (Stokes 1984). Of the 228 university graduate departments of sociology, 226 were offering specialization in medical sociology (Haney et al. 1983). Sociologists were also employed by all kinds of medical and health care organizations, in health-related policy-oriented roles in government and in research positions directed toward the evaluation of the health care system (Altman 1990:iii). The attitude of the medical profession found expression in the editorial of the AMA official journal (*Journal of the American Medical Association*) of March 8, 1981:

> The question should no longer be: Should the social sciences have a role in undergraduate medical education? Rather, it should be: How can we more

effectively bring the lessons and insights of the relevant social and behavioral sciences to the students? (1981:955)

This opinion was matched by Sol Levine, probably the premier medical sociologist of the time, who said: "It is time to start thinking of sociology *with* medicine" (Levine 1987). The same view was shared by the opinion leaders of medical education. They joined in public support for the behavioral sciences in general and medical sociology specifically (AMA 1982). Moreover, these endorsements continue to the present day, gaining strength as they are repeated. The major educational report of the eighties, the so-called GPEP Report (AAMC 1984), was followed during the next decade by a series of commissions, all unanimous in the recommendation that the teaching of the social behavioral sciences should be a basic part of the education of physicians. Even the Liaison Committee for Medical Education, in its most recent certification procedures, requires that a teaching program in behavioral sciences be in place in all the medical schools of the United States.

Similar status was also evident in Europe. Thirty-two of the 34 medical schools in the United Kingdom were teaching medical sociology (Field 1988). The same was true for many other countries (Aakster 1978).

Thus, in both medical institutions and in the university, a consistent demand for medical sociology existed in 1980. Medical school faculty positions, sociology department programs, and financial support from private foundations and government agencies seemed, despite the cutbacks of certain federal agencies, to assure the structural foundations of its training and research. Professional associations and scholarly journals provided for the communication of its theoretical and research analyses. Medical sociology was an intellectual activity fully institutionalized in every way.

If we study medical sociology as a case example of the effects of increasing dependence on the fiscal policies of the federal government, we see a discipline, small but increasingly visible among university-based professions because its subject and methods are relevant to problems of health and illness. As it responded to medicine over the years, it was caught in the tides of medical manpower development, sharing the experience of institutional changes and, after startup support from private foundations, becoming almost totally dependent upon federal subsidy. In 1980, it found itself threatened with the withdrawal of those federal funds in both training and research. However, this was a threat that, under one or another changing circumstance, had happened before and would repeat itself again. Each time, medical sociology survived these challenges. In effect, it continued much as always, succeeding in the intellectual side of its activities, while institutionally adapting to the structure of the various situations in which it conducted its work. After 1980, that situation, more and more, downgraded the importance of sociological inquiry about education and professionalization, and about the social organization of the profession, demanding cost-related health services research because the dominance of medical education as the site of a research-focused medical center yielded to a form of practice organization, managed care, whose major mission was to control costs within the boundaries of commercial markets.

In this chapter, medical sociology has been shown in a wide range of functions and activities. Overall, the intellectual achievements of the sociology of health and medicine appear to be very strong. Most medical sociologists, however, have settled into institutional roles mainly outside medical settings but very actively engaged in research about problems of health and illness and the organizations that deal with them. They are essentially guests in those organizations, still outsiders. As such, their function as critical analysts has been one of the most important, as attested to by the work of Erving Goffman, Eliot Freidson, and Howard Waitzkin, to name just a few (Freidson 1970; Goffman 1961; Waitzkin 1983). At the same time, they have increased the technical skills that brought them into medical institutions in the first place, allowing them to better serve the applied aspects of their work.

The observation that, at heart, sociology is a scholarly profession and, as such, requires a work environment that protects and nurtures free, intellectual inquiry remains true today. There is a natural tension between independent intellectual analysis and the controlled knowledge enterprise of "targeted" research. The latter, increasingly, is demanded of medical sociology. The threat is that to survive in the current climate created by scarce resources for an expanded high-skill social science manpower, medical sociologists will become the "hired guns" (Britell 1980) of government agencies and special interest groups, charged with producing research results that fit preconceived policies. In the process, the traditional heart of this enterprise may be lost. Medical sociology is in equal jeopardy with medicine, both struggling to retain the independence of science, on the one hand, and of trusted service, on the other. In their histories, one hopes, the strength will be found to sustain the inherent values of a venerable contract with society to continue in mutual benefit.

REFERENCES

AAKSTER, C. W. 1978. "Medical Sociology Training for Medical Doctors." In *Teaching Medical Sociology: Retrospection and Prospection,* ed. Y. Nuyens and J. Vansteenkiste. Boston: Martinus Nijhoff, pp. 141–152.

ADLER, NANCY, and GEORGE STONE. 1983. "Psychology and the Health System." In *Advances in Medical Social Science.* Vol. I, ed. Julio Ruffini. New York: Gordon Breach Science Publishers, Inc.

ALTMAN, BARBARA M., co-editor. 1990. *Special Issue on Medical Sociology. Teaching Sociology* 18:#3.

AMERICAN MEDICAL ASSOCIATION (AMA). 1982. *Future Directions for Medical Education: A Report of the Council on Medical Education.* Chicago: American Medical Association.

ASSOCIATION OF AMERICAN MEDICAL COLLEGES (AAMC). 1984. *Physicians for the Twenty-first Century. Journal of Medical Education* 59: Part 2 (The GPEP Report).

AMERICAN SOCIOLOGICAL ASSOCIATION COMMITTEE ON CERTIFICATION IN MEDICAL SOCIOLOGY. 1986. *Guidelines for the Certification Process in Medical Sociology.* Washington, DC: American Sociological Association.

BARBER, BERNARD. 1970. *L. J. Henderson, On the Social System.* Chicago: University of Chicago Press.

BARRABEE, PAUL S. 1951. A Study of a Mental Hospital: The Effects of its Social Structure on its Function. Ph.D. Diss. Harvard University.

BELKNAP, IVAN. 1956. *Human Problems of a State Mental Hospital.* New York: McGraw-Hill Book Co.

BEN-DAVID, DAVID, and RANDALL COLLINS. 1966. "Social Factors in the Origin of a New Science." *American Sociological Review* 31:4(August): 451–65.

BILLINGS, JOHN SHAW. 1888. "The History of Medicine." *Boston Medical and Surgical Journal* 118:29.

BLACKWELL, ELIZABETH. 1902. *Essays in Medical Sociology.* 2 vols. London: Ernest Bell.

BLOOM, SAMUEL W., and RUTH E. ZAMBRANA. 1983. "Trends and Developments in the Sociology of Medicine." In *Advances in Medical Social Science* Vol I., ed. Julio Ruffini. New York: Gordon Breach, Science Publishers, Inc., pp. 73–122.

BOWERS, RAYMOND V. 1983. Telephone interview with the author, February 8.

BRITELL, JENNE K. 1980. "Hazards in Social Research." *New York Times,* September 7.

CARR-SAUNDERS, A. M., and P. A. WILSON. 1933. *The Professions.* London: Oxford University Press.

CAUDILL, WILLIAM. 1958. *The Psychiatric Hospital as a Small Society.* Cambridge, MA: Harvard University Press (for the Commonwealth Fund).

CHADWICK, EDWIN. 1842. *Report on the Sanitary Condition of the Labouring Population of Great Britain,* ed. with an introduction by M. W. Flinn. Edinburgh: University Press.

CLAUSEN, JOHN A. 1950. "Social Science Research and the National Mental Health Program." *American Sociological Review* 15(June):402–408.

COMMITTEE ON THE COSTS OF MEDICAL CARE (CCMC). [1932] 1972. *Medical Care for the American People.* New York: Arno Press.

DAVIS, MICHAEL M. 1909. *The Psychological Interpretations of Society.* New York: Columbia University Press.

DAVIS, MICHAEL M. 1971. *Immigrant Health and the Community.* Montclair, NJ: Patterson Smith.

DAY, ROBERT ALAN. 1981. Toward the Development of a Critical Sociohistorically Grounded Sociology of Sociology: The Case of Medical Sociology. Ph.D. Diss. University of Missouri.

DEVEREUX, GEORGE. 1944. "The Social Structure of a Schizophrenic Ward and Its Therapeutic Fitness." *Journal of Clinical Psychopathology* VI:231–265.

EATON, JOSEPH, and ROBERT J. WEIL. 1955. *Culture and Mental Disorders: A Comparative Study of the Hutterites and Other Populations.* Glencoe, Ill: The Free Press.

ELLING, RAY H., and MAGDALENA SOKOLOWSKA, eds. 1978. *Medical Sociologists at Work.* New Brunswick, NJ: Transaction Books.

ELLIOTT, CLARK A., and MARGARET W. ROSSITER, eds. 1992. *Science at Harvard: Historical Papers.* Bethlehem, PA: Lehigh University Press.

FARIS, ROBERT E. L., and H. WARREN DUNHAM. 1939. *Mental Disorders in Urban Areas.* Chicago: University of Chicago Press.

FEE, ELIZABETH, and THEODORE M. BROWN, eds. 1997. *Making Medical History: The Life and Times of Henry E. Sigerist.* Baltimore: The Johns Hopkins University Press.

FELIX, ROBERT H. 1983. Interview by author.

FELIX, R. H., and R. V. BOWERS. 1948. "Mental Hygiene and Socio-Environmental Factors." *Milbank Memorial Fund Quarterly* 26:125–147.

FIELD, D. 1988. "Teaching Sociology in U.K. Medical Schools." *Medical Education* 22:294–300.

FREIDSON, ELIOT. 1970. *The Profession of Medicine.* New York: Dodd, Mead and Co.

GINZBERG, ELI, J. H. MINER, J. K. ANDERSON, SOL W. GINSBURG, and JOHN I. HERMA. 1959. *The Ineffective Soldier: Breakdown and Recovery.* New York: Columbia University Press.

GOFFMAN, ERVING. 1957. "Characteristics of Total Institutions." In *Symposium on Preventive and Social Psychiatry.* Washington, D.C.: Walter Reed Army Institute of Research.

GOFFMAN, ERVING. 1959. "The Moral Career of Mental Patients." *Psychiatry* 22:123–42.

GOFFMAN, ERVING. 1961. *Asylums.* Garden City, NY: Doubleday Anchor Books.

GREENBLATT, MILTON, RICHARD H. YORK, and ESTHER LUCILE BROWN. 1955. *From Custodial to Therapeutic Care in Mental Hospitals.* New York: Russell Sage Foundation.

HAMMOCK, DAVID C., and STANTON WHEELER. 1994. *Social Sciences in the Making: Essays on the Russell Sage Foundation, 1907–1972.* New York: Russell Sage Foundation.

HANEY, C. A., M. A. ZAHN, and J. HOWARD. 1983. "Applied Medical Sociology: Learning from Within." *Teaching Sociology* 11:92–104.

HENDERSON, LAWRENCE J. 1935. "Physician and Patient as a Social System." *New England Journal of Medicine* 212:819–23.

HOLDEN, CONSTANCE. 1980. "Behavioral Medicine: An Emergent Field." *Science* 209:479–481. Cited in Charles Hughes and Donald Kennedy. 1983. "Beyond the Germ Theory." In *Advances in Medical Social Science.* Vol. I, ed. Julio Ruffini. New York: Gordon Breach Science Publishers, Inc.

HOLLINGSHEAD, AUGUST. 1978. Interview by author, August 4.

HUGHES, CHARLES C., and DONALD KENNEDY. 1983. "Beyond the Germ Theory: Reflections on Relations between Medicine and the Behavioral Sciences." In *Advances in Medical Social Science.* Vol. I, ed. Julio Ruffini. New York: Gordon Breach Science Publishers, Inc.

JONES, MAXWELL. 1953. *The Therapeutic Community.* New York: Basic Books, Inc.

JOURNAL OF THE AMERICAN MEDICAL ASSOCIATION *(JAMA).* 1981. Editorial. 245:955.

LANDY, DAVID. 1983. "Medical Anthropology: A Critical Appraisal." In *Advances in Medical Social Science.* Vol. I, ed. Julio Ruffini. New York: Gordon Breach Science Publishers, Inc.:189.

LARKEY, SANFORD V. "John Shaw Billings and the History of Medicine." *Bulletin of the History of Medicine* 6(1938):360–76.

LARSON, MARGALI SARFATTI. 1977. *The Rise of Professionalism.* Berkeley: University of California Press.

LEACOCK, ELEANOR. 1957. "Three Social Variables and the Occurrence of Mental Disorder." In *Explorations in Social Psychiatry,* ed. A. Leighton et al. New York: Basic Books.

LEIGHTON, ALEXANDER H., JOHN A. CLAUSEN, and ROBERT N. WILSON, eds. 1957. *Explorations in Social Psychiatry.* New York: Basic Books.

LEVINE, S. 1987. "The Changing Terrains in Medical Sociology: Emergent Concern with Quality of Life." *Journal of Health and Social Behavior* 28:1–6.

LUTTERMAN, KENNETH G. 1975. "Research Training from the Perspective of Government Funding." In *Social Policy and Sociology,* ed. N. J. Demerath et al. New York: Academic Press, pp. 307–20.

LYND, ROBERT S., and HELEN M. LYND. 1929. *Middletown.* New York: Harcourt, Brace.

LYONS, GENE M. 1969. *The Uneasy Partnership: Social Science and the Federal Government in the Twentieth Century.* New York: Rusell Sage Foundation.

MCINTIRE, CHARLES. 1894. "The Importance of the Study of Medical Sociology." *Bulletin of the American Academy of Medicine* 1:425–34.

MECHANIC, DAVID, and SOL LEVINE, eds. 1977. "Issues in Promoting Health: Committee Reports of the Medical Sociology Section, American Sociological Association." *Medical Care,* Supplement, vol. 15, no. 5.

MERTON, ROBERT K. 1977. "The Sociology of Science: An Episodic Memoir." In *The Sociology of Science in Europe,* ed. Robert K. Merton and Jerry Gaston. Carbondale, IL: Southern Illinois Press.

MERTON, ROBERT K. 1980. Interview by author.

MERTON, ROBERT K., GEORGE G. READER, and PATRICIA L. KENDALL, eds. 1957. *The Student-Physician: Introductory Studies in the Sociology of Medical Education.* Cambridge, MA: Harvard University Press (for the Commonwealth Fund).

MILBANK MEMORIAL FUND. 1950. Epidemiology of Mental Disorder. Papers presented at 1949 Conference of the Milbank Memorial Fund, New York.

MILBANK MEMORIAL FUND. 1953. Interrelations Between the Social Environment and Psychiatric Disorders. Papers presented at 1952 Annual Conference of the Milbank Memorial Fund, New York.

NATIONAL ACADEMY OF SCIENCES COMMITTEE ON NATIONAL NEEDS FOR BIOMEDICAL AND BEHAVIORAL RESEARCH PERSONNEL. 1994. *Meeting the Nation's Needs for Biomedical and Behavioral Scientists.* Washington, D.C.: National Academy Press.

NICHOLS, LAWRENCE T. 1992. "The Establishment of Sociology at Harvard: A Case of Organizational Ambivalence and Scientific Vulnerability." *Science at Harvard: Historical Papers,* ed. Clark Elliott and Margaret Rossiter. Bethlehem, PA: Lehigh University Press, pp. 192–222.

OBERSCHALL, ANTHONY, ed. 1972. *The Establishment of Empirical Sociology: Studies in Continuity, Discontinuity, and Institutionalization.* New York: Harper & Row.

OGBURN, WILLIAM F. 1933. *President's Commission on Social Trends: Recent Social Trends* 2 volumes. New York: McGraw-Hill.

PARASCANDOLA, JOHN. 1992. "L. J. Henderson and the Mutual Dependence of Variables: From Physical Chemistry to Pareto." In *Science at Harvard: Historical Papers,* ed. Clark Elliott and Margaret Rossiter. Bethlehem, PA: Lehigh University Press.

PARSONS, TALCOTT. 1951. *The Social System.* New York: The Free Press, pp. 428–79.

REVERBY, SUSAN, and DAVID ROSNER. 1979. "Beyond the Great Doctors." In *Health Care in America: Essays in Social History,* ed. Susan Reverby and David Rosner. Philadelphia: Temple University Press.

RHOADS, LAWRENCE J. 1981. *A History of the American Sociological Association: 1905–1980.* Washington, D.C.:

American Sociological Association, pp. 26, 37, 47, 58, 63, 70, 71.

ROEMER, MILTON I., and RAY H. ELLING. 1963. "Sociological Research Medical Care." *Journal of Health and Human Behavior* 4:49–88.

ROEMER, MILTON I., LESLIE A. FALK, and THEODORE M. BROWN. 1997. "Sociological Vision and Pedagogic Mission: Henry Sigerist's Medical Sociology." In *Making Medical History: The Life and Times of Henry E. Sigerist,* ed. Elizabeth Fee and Theodore M. Brown. Baltimore: The Johns Hopkins University Press, p. 18.

ROSEN, GEORGE. 1979. "The Evolution of Social Medicine." In *Handbook of Medical Sociology,* 3rd ed, ed. Howard Freeman, Sol Levine, and Leo Reeder. Englewood Cliffs, NJ: Prentice-Hall, Inc., p. 37.

ROWLAND, HOWARD. 1938. "Interaction Processes in a State Mental Hospital." *Psychiatry* 1 (August): 323–37.

ROWLAND, HOWARD. 1939. "Friendship Patterns in a State Mental Hospital." *Psychiatry* 2 (August): 303–73.

RUFFINI, JULIO L., ed. 1983. *Advances in Medical Social Science,* Vol I. New York: Gordon Breach Science Publishers, Inc.

RUSSELL SAGE FOUNDATION. *Annual Report: 1950–51.* New York: Russell Sage Foundation.

SEGAL, JULIUS, ed. 1975. *National Institute of Mental Health: Research in the Service of Mental Health.* Washington, DC: Department of Health, Education & Welfare (Publication ADM 72–236), p. 6.

SEWELL, WILLIAM H. 1988. "The Changing Institutional Structure of Sociology and My Career." In *Sociological Lives.* Vol. 2. Newbury Park: Sage Publications, 130n.

SHILS, EDWARD. 1970. "Tradition, Ecology and Institution in the History of Sociology." *Daedalus* 99 (#4):760–825.

SIMMONS, LEO W., and HAROLD G. WOLFF. 1954. *Social Science in Medicine.* New York: Russell Sage Foundation.

SMITH, CYRIL S., and OTTO LARSEN. 1989. "The Criterion of 'Relevance' in the Support of Research in the Social Sciences: 1965–1985." *Minerva: Review of Science, Learning and Policy* XXVII:461–82.

SROLE, LEO, THOMAS S. LANGNER, S. T. MICHAEL, M. K. OPLER, and T. A. C. RENNIE. 1962. *Mental Health in the Metropolis.* New York: McGraw-Hill.

STANTON, ALFRED H., and MORRIS S. SCHWARTZ. 1954. *The Mental Hospital.* New York: Basic Books, Inc.

STARR, PAUL. 1982. *The Social Transformation of American Medicine.* New York: Basic Books, Inc.

STERN, BERNHARD J. 1927a. *Social Factors in Medical Progress.* New York: Columbia University Press.

STERN, BERNHARD. 1927b. *Should We Be Vaccinated? A Survey of the Controversy in Its Historical and Scientific Aspects.* New York: Harper and Brothers.

STEVENS, ROSEMARY. 1971. *American Medicine and the Public Trust.* New Haven: Yale University Press.

STOKES, JOHN III, P. STRAND, and C. JAFFE. 1984. "Distribution of Behavioral Science Faculty in U.S. Medical Schools." *Social Science and Medicine* 18: 753–56.

STRAUS, ROBERT. 1957. "The Nature and Status of Medical Sociology." *American Sociological Review.* 22:200–204.

STRAUS, ROBERT. 1978. "Becoming and Being a Medical Sociologist." In *Medical Sociologists at Work,* ed. Ray Elling and Magdalena Sokolowska. New Brunswick, NJ: Transaction Books, pp. 312ff.

SULLIVAN, HARRY STACK. 1931a. "Socio-psychiatric Research: Its implications for the Schizophrenia Problem and for Mental Hygiene." *American Journal of Psychiatry* 10:977–91.

SULLIVAN, HARRY STACK. 1931b. "The Modified Psychoanalytic Treatment of Schizophrenia." *American Journal of Psychiatry* 11:519–40.

VINCENT, CLARK. 1965. "Support for Research Training in Anthropology under the National Institute of Mental Health Training Program." *American Anthropologist* 67:754–61.

WAITZKIN, HOWARD. 1983. *The Second Sickness: Contradictions of Capitalist Health Care.* New York: Free Press.

WILLIAMS, RICHARD H. 1972. "The Strategy of Sociomedical Research." In *Handbook of Medical Sociology,* 2nd ed., Howard Freeman, Sol Levine, and Leo Reeder. Englewood Cliffs, NJ: Prentice-Hall, p. 477.

WOLINSKY, FREDERIC D. 1988. *The Sociology of Health.* Belmont, CA: Wadsworth, p. 28.

3 EVALUATING THE FUNDAMENTAL CAUSE EXPLANATION FOR SOCIAL DISPARITIES IN HEALTH

BRUCE G. LINK, *Columbia University and New York State Psychiatric Institute*

JO C. PHELAN, *Columbia University*

Patterns of disease and death are shaped by social, economic, political, and cultural factors. This principle of social epidemiology has been powerfully articulated in different ways at different times. One of the founders of social medicine, Rudolf Virchow (1848), declared that "medicine is a social science and politics nothing but medicine on a grand scale." More recently Mervyn Susser et al. (1985:17) put it this way: "Societies in part create the disease they experience and, further, they materially shape the way in which diseases are to be experienced."

But the idea that social factors create and shape patterns of disease and death has not always been considered important or useful. In recent decades, for example, many have assumed that growing knowledge about individual risk factors, such as genetic factors and unhealthy lifestyles, would explain social patterns of disease according to socioeconomic status, social networks, and other social circumstances, and that these individual risk factors would take the place of social conditions as the relevant explanatory variables. The logic is simple and seemingly compelling. If, for example, socioeconomic status is related to disease, the explanation for that association must lie in factors more proximal to disease in the causal chain. It must be because people of lower socioeconomic status (SES) smoke more, exercise less, experience greater exposure to chemical pollutants, eat more fatty food, are exposed

to more hazardous occupational conditions, experience more barriers to health care, are less adherent to preventive medications, and so on. In this view, the social conditions are only important as starting points—only as clues as to which individually based risk factors might be implicated in disease causation (e.g., Potter 1992). Once adopted, such a view leads to the conclusion that social epidemiology has become irrelevant—no longer important or useful in the age of modern epidemiology. This orientation is reflected, for example, in Kenneth Rothman's *Modern Epidemiology* (1986:90) when he indicates that social class is "causally related to few if any diseases but is a correlate of many causes of disease."

At the present time, however, there is a resurgence of interest in social epidemiology. The number of articles focused on socioeconomic factors in health has increased dramatically in recent years, with a number of very influential papers appearing in journals like *Science* and *The New England Journal of Medicine* (House, Landis, and Umberson 1988; Pappas et al. 1993; Geronimus et al. 1996; Dohrenwend et al. 1992). Moreover, important new books focused on social, economic, political, and cultural factors in disease causation have appeared (e.g., Wilkinson 1996; Evans, Barer, and Marmor 1994). All of this activity implies that social epidemiologists have mobilized a vigorous response to the charge of irrelevance.

In this chapter, we present some of the evidence and ideas that are part of this new emphasis on social epidemiology. We begin with a review of some compelling findings regarding the role of social factors in

This work was supported by a Robert Wood Johnson Health Policy Investigator Award to Drs. Phelan and Link. The authors thank Chloe Bird, Steven Gortmaker, and David Mechanic for particularly helpful comments.

health. With this as background, we turn our attention to several explanations for the patterns observed. Specifically, we consider two perspectives that argue that social factors play important causal roles in creating social distributions of health—roles that cannot be dismissed as irrelevant. We refer to the first of these as the "hierarchy stress" approach and the second as the "fundamental cause" approach.

SOCIAL FACTORS AND HEALTH

Historical Changes in Life Expectancy Although there are several studies that provide compelling demonstrations of the association between environmental conditions and health, one of the most persuasive is also one of the most obvious. Life expectancy has increased dramatically over the past 150 years or so (Antonovsky 1967). For example, Michael Marmot and Fraser Mustard (1994) show that, between 1922 and 1984, life expectancy at birth increased by about 16 years for both men and women. Dramatic changes like these cannot be plausibly attributed to changes in genes or to biological or psychological attributes determined by genes. The change has been too rapid. The significance of this historical change in life expectancy is its message that environmental conditions must be powerful determinants of health conditions. Thus, as we move forward in an effort to understand why some groups experience longer and healthier lives than others, we do so with the firm knowledge that environmental changes have had an enormous impact on the health of populations.

Strategic Geographical Comparisons Some of the most compelling demonstrations of social influences on health compare people living in different geographical locations. For example, C. McCord and H. P. Freeman (1990) compared the life expectancy of African-American men in Harlem to that of men in Bangladesh. They found that men in Bangladesh had a *better chance* of surviving to age 65 than did men in Harlem. Using more recent data on mortality rates of men in Harlem, Arline Geronimus et al. (1996) found, consistent with McCord and Freeman, that an African-American male, living in Harlem, who reached the age of 15 had only a 37 percent chance of living to age 65. But Geronimus and colleagues also included strategic comparison groups. They found, for example, that African Americans living in sections of Brooklyn and Queens, just a few miles from Harlem, had mortality rates only slightly higher than the national average for whites. While racial differences in health have

sometimes been attributed to biological factors, these stunning contrasts between racially similar populations indicate that social factors play a major role in elevated rates of mortality among African Americans. More generally, these findings serve as powerful reminders of the role of social conditions in rates of disease and death.

Socioeconomic Status People who are advantaged with respect to indicators of socioeconomic status, such as education, occupational standing, and income, live longer than people who are disadvantaged in these ways (e.g., Sorlie et al. 1995; Lantz et al. 1998; Davey Smith et al. 1996; Kunst et al. 1998). The association arises at the very beginning of life, contributing to what Steven Gortmaker and P. H. Wise (1997) call "the first injustice." In this regard, G. K. Singh and S. M. Yu (1995) used data from the 1987 National Linked Birth and Infant Death data set to calculate infant mortality rates by maternal education. Mortality among infants born to women with less than a high school education was about 12.5 per 1,000 live births, whereas for college graduates the rate was 5.8 per 1,000 births. This first injustice is followed by an enduring association between socioeconomic status and the risk of death that persists throughout adult life. Age-adjusted mortality rates are two to three times as high among people at the bottom of the socioeconomic continuum compared to those of the people at the top (Sorlie et al. 1995; Lantz et al. 1998). In addition to its persistence throughout most of adult life, the association is remarkably persistent in at least three other ways.

First, as we shall see, the association between socioeconomic status and the risk of death is persistent across time; it has been evident ever since the earliest attempts to study the association. Second, the association is evident in many different countries. For example, A. E. Kunst et al. (1998) studied 11 western European countries and found that the risk of dying between ages 45 and 59 is substantially higher among men engaged in manual work than among men in nonmanual work. Third, the association persists when one seeks to explain it away. For example, Paula Lantz and colleagues (1998) wondered whether the association between income and mortality could be explained by smoking, alcohol use, sedentary life style, and relative body weight. While these potential mechanisms were indeed associated with SES, the odds ratios for low and moderate income, as compared to high income, remained significant and above 2 even when these risk factors were controlled (see also Hirdes and Forbes 1992; Hahn et al. 1987, Woodward et al. 1990; Davey

Smith 1990). The magnitude, persistence, and pervasiveness of the association between SES and mortality speak strongly to its potential importance as a social cause of inequalities in health.

Social Supports and Social Networks Another compelling demonstration of the influence of social conditions on health comes from a series of studies examining the role of social supports and social connectedness in morbidity and mortality. Lisa Berkman and Leonard Syme (1979) used baseline data on social networks collected in 1965 to predict mortality during the subsequent nine years. They found a near doubling of risk for mortality among those low on a social-network index as compared to those high on the index. Although this study controlled for many competing risks (smoking, obesity, physical activity, etc.), it did not include measures derived from a physical exam. A subsequent study by James House et al. (1988) did include a physical exam and controlled for baseline blood pressure, cholesterol levels, and other biomedical variables. These investigators found associations between social relationships and mortality that were similar to those reported by Berkman and Syme. This line of work has continued to become more and more refined. For example, Berkman and colleagues (1992) have shown that a measure of perceived support collected before the occurrence of a heart attack predicts survival following the heart attack holding constant an impressive array of biomedical and psychosocial control variables.

Social Inequality An intriguing set of studies links income inequality in populations to the health of those populations. One of the most influential studies along these lines is Richard Wilkinson's (1992). He used data from nine industrialized nations to show that life expectancy at birth is much lower in nations that provide smaller income shares to the 70 percent of the population that is least well off. Put otherwise, when a relatively large share of the income goes to the people in the top 30 percent of the distribution, life expectancy for the population as a whole is compromised. Moreover, the effect of income inequality holds after adjusting for per capita gross national product. Indeed, compared to the correlation between income inequality and life expectancy (.86) the correlation between gross national product per capita and life expectancy (.38) is modest. Following Wilkinson, a twin set of papers demonstrated much the same association for income inequality in the 50 United States (Kennedy et al. 1996; Kaplan et al. 1996). Subsequent research along these lines has sought to determine the pathways that might account for this association.

One idea is that income inequality has an adverse effect on social capital, destroying connections between people and their trust in one another. Ichiro Kawachi et al. (1997) used data from the General Social Survey conducted by the National Opinion Research Center to test the potential importance of social capital. Consistent with their hypotheses, Kawachi et al. found that, across states, the percent of people who agreed that "most people would try to take advantage of you if they got a chance" was strongly related to income inequality and to mortality rates. Moreover, once social trust was controlled, income inequality was unrelated to mortality. These findings suggest a strong medicating role for social trust in the association between inequality and mortality.

Any one of the findings we have just reviewed might be challenged as to how potent it is as a motivation for social epidemiology. However, in combination, and when buttressed by the vastly larger literature that these studies represent, it is clear that there exists a powerful set of findings upon which social epidemiology can rest. Our interest in this chapter is to move toward a more integrated explanation for this broad set of findings. Once such findings are assembled, they pose an interesting challenge for social epidemiology, one that forces researchers to go beyond declarations about the importance of social factors and to develop theoretical explanations that integrate the full array of new findings.

EXPLANATIONS FOR SOCIAL INEQUALITIES IN HEALTH

Reviews of the literature on social class and disease offer a list of possible explanations for their association including, among others, artifactual explanations and selection/drift. Artifactual explanations suggest that methodological factors produce an apparent association between socioeconomic status and mortality that is not real. Such explanations are made implausible by the cumulative results of many studies done by different investigators, in different settings, using different designs and measures. In what follows, we turn our attention to selection/drift explanations and then consider two social causation explanations that we extract from the extant literature. The causation explanations we consider are ones that are consistent with some of the intriguing findings within social epidemiology and that also provide a compelling answer as to why social epidemiology is essential in an era of "modern" risk factor epidemiology.

Social Selection Explanations

The vast majority of the literature on physical health concludes that the association between SES and health is causal (West 1991). With the exception of a few dissenters (Himsworth 1984; Illsley 1955, 1986; Stern 1983), relatively little attention has focused on social selection explanations. Selection explanations take one of two general forms. In the first, health status is considered the cause of socioeconomic status rather than vice versa. The idea here is that illness causes disability, which in turn impairs the attainment of education, high-status occupational positions, and income. This reverse causation explanation is clearly operative in some circumstances (Kitagawa and Hauser 1973), but most investigators have concluded that it does not account for a large part of the association between SES and health (Wilkinson 1986; Hahn et al. 1989). One reason is that education is often as strongly related to mortality as is income, and education is typically achieved before serious illness emerges (Hahn et al. 1989). Moreover, population-based prospective studies that ascertain years of education and income several years before mortality (presumably, in most cases, before the emergence of serious disease that might lead to downward mobility and eventual death) nevertheless find strong associations with mortality in the follow-up period (Sorlie et al. 1995; Fox et al. 1985). Finally, as Mary Hahn and her colleagues (1989) argue, there are strong associations between the health of children and wives and the SES circumstances of their fathers or husbands, between SES and mortality of retirees, and between SES and death by unintentional injury. These facts also argue against a strong role for reverse causation, because education, income, or occupational status is not likely to be strongly affected by a family member's illness or by health status after one's retirement and certainly not by meeting an untimely accidental death.

The second generic type of social selection explanation claims that pre-existing attributes or vulnerabilities determine both socioeconomic attainment and health—rendering the SES-health association spurious. While a lively debate has focused on height as a pre-existing attribute, there are many other characteristics that might also affect both mobility and health. Examples that have been considered in the literature are intelligence (Adams et al. 1998; Marmot et al. 1997), personality attributes such as hostility (Smith 1992), and conscientiousness (Friedman et al. 1993).

Unfortunately, at this time there are relatively little data assessing the association between such factors and health. One recent empirical study found intellectual efficiency to be the strongest predictor of health in a prospective study of highly educated women (Adams et al. 1998), but another concluded that intelligence measured in high school could not account for SES gradients in adult health (Marmot et al. 1997). Further research in this area might clarify the associations between intelligence, personality, health, and SES. However, at this point there is no compelling evidence to suggest that intelligence or personality can account for socioeconomic inequalities in health.

Social Causation: The Hierarchy Stress Explanation

The hierarchy stress explanation starts with the observation that the socioeconomic gradient in health simultaneously involves an association with *both* material circumstances and hierarchical position (Wilkinson 1997). Put otherwise, people of relatively low socioeconomic status might be disadvantaged with regard to health either because they are less well situated in terms of such material conditions as housing, diet, or access to health care or because their lower position in a social hierarchy is inherently stressful. The hierarchy stress perspective emphasizes the latter of these two components. According to this explanation, stress associated with lower relative position in the hierarchy has both direct and indirect ill effects on health. Indirect effects occur when stress due to relative deprivation causes people to smoke, consume too much alcohol, eat too much or too little, sleep too little, etc. Direct effects occur when stress due to hierarchical position influences biological processes in the nervous and immune systems.

But why should hierarchical position have an effect independent of the material advantages associated with that position? Why should hierarchical position per se engender "stress"? Both Roslyn Lindheim and Leonard Syme (1983) and Richard Wilkinson (1997) give primacy to the concept of relative deprivation in answering this question. The concept of relative deprivation grew out of *The American Soldier* (Stouffer et al. 1949). Stouffer and colleagues observed that soldiers' feelings of deprivation, resentment, and anger depended on whom they compared themselves to. As Stouffer et al. put it, "Becoming a soldier meant to many men a very real deprivation. But the felt sacrifice was greater for some than others, depending on their standards of comparison" (Stauffer et al. 1949:125). Stouffer et al. then used the concept throughout their analysis to help explain seemingly anomalous findings in which the soldiers' feelings of deprivation were different from what one would expect based on objective conditions. Translating this concept to the issue of hierarchical positions in modern western societies leads to the expectation that people further down in the hierarchy would feel deprived relative to others, marginalized and angry. This stressful circumstance would in turn have direct and indirect effects on health. While more recent studies have challenged the assumption of a linear association between income level and feelings of relative deprivation (e.g., Jasso and Rossi 1977; Mirowsky 1987) the idea that people further down in a hierarchy suffer as a consequence of relative deprivation remains a key foundation of the hierarchy stress formulation (Wilkinson 1997).

We believe that the hierarchy stress formulation would be strengthened by considering an additional set of social processes that are a direct consequence of hierarchical position. A relatively high position implies control or dominance over those lower down. The person on top can direct, control, and plan the activities of subordinates, whereas the person on the bottom is subject to the strictures of those above (Link et al. 1993). This social power allows one to feel in control, and feeling in control provides a sense of security and well being that is salutogenic. Conversely, the absence of such social power translates into feeling a lack of control over one's life, that one is subject to the whim of others, and that undesirable or unwanted experiences can occur at any time—a stressful set of circumstances that can have direct physiological effects (Lindheim and Syme 1983).

This notion of "control" shares with the relative deprivation approach an emphasis on the effects of hierarchy per se and the idea that hierarchical position generates stress for those lower down. It differs from the relative deprivation approach in that it does not imply social comparison of one's circumstances with those of others or the feelings of envy or resentment that may ensue. According to the control hypothesis, one would expect effects of hierarchy even in the absence of such social comparison processes. Because the notions of relative deprivation and control both focus on stress that arises from hierarchical position per se, we shall incorporate both ideas in our consideration of the hierarchy stress approach.

At least three sets of empirical facts provide a motivation for the hierarchy stress explanation. The first are the previously mentioned findings concerning the effects of income inequality on mortality in societies with advanced economies. As indicated above, Wilkinson shows that income inequality is a stronger predictor of life expectancy in industrialized nations than is per capita income. This finding leads to the conclusion that the absolute level of material resources, as measured by

per capita income, is less important than a person's relative position within a society. If only absolute levels of material resources were important, one would expect a person directly in the middle of the income distribution in a relatively wealthy society (e.g., median income $50,000 per year) to be better off than a person located in the middle of the income distribution of a society that was less wealthy (e.g., median income $25,000 per year). But as the evidence we have reviewed suggests, this is not true (Wilkinson 1992; Kennedy et al. 1996; Kaplan et al. 1996).

A second set of empirical facts comes from the Whitehall study of British civil servants (Marmot et al. 1978, 1984, 1991). None of the men in this study was extremely materially deprived, and all received medical coverage from the British National Health Service. Yet the results show a strong gradient according to the men's levels in the civil service—a finding that held not only for all cause mortality but for most major causes of death as well. In addition, there were consistent differences between men whose occupation placed them in the highest rank (administrators) and men in the next highest rank (professionals and executives). Moreover, only a portion of the differences in coronary heart disease mortality by employment grade could be explained by obesity, smoking, leisure time activity, baseline illness, blood pressure, and height. So even within one industry (civil service), and even with extensive controls on other risk factors, relatively finely graded differences in occupations were associated with differences in mortality. Because so many competing factors are held constant in the design and analysis, the evidence appears to strongly support the idea that being lower in the social hierarchy is inherently stressful.

A third set of facts derives from studies of nonhuman primates. Whether conducted in the wild (Sapolsky 1990) or in controlled circumstances (Hamm et al. 1983; Shively and Clarkson 1994; Kaplan et al. 1982), these studies show that having a lower position in the social hierarchy is associated with detrimental biological consequences. For example, T. E. Hamm et al. (1983) fed macaques a diet that mimicked the diets of humans living in the United States in terms of cholesterol content. The monkeys not only developed atherosclerosis when placed on this diet but did so differentially by social status. Subordinate animals experienced a far greater degree of occlusion than did dominant animals. Other studies have linked social status among primates to hyper secreted cortisol, blood pressure, and suppressed immune function. Moreover, in one study (Shively and Clarkson 1994) this was true even though the animals' social status was manipulated experimentally.

With these and other research findings as background, Richard Wilkinson (1997) asks the following question: "Is the health disadvantage of the least well off part of the population mainly a reflection of the direct physiological effects of lower absolute material standards (of bad housing, poor diets, inadequate heating, and air pollution), or is it more a matter of the direct and indirect effects of differences in psychosocial circumstances associated with social position—of where you stand in relation to others?" (591) Based on evidence like the evidence reported above, Wilkinson concludes that "psychosocial effects of social position account for the larger part of health inequalities" (591) and that "mortality in developed countries is affected more by relative than by absolute living standards" (592).

In addition to its coherence with a complex and intriguing set of facts, the hierarchy stress explanation provides a rationale for social epidemiology—an answer to the charge that it has become irrelevant. Because the social factor of social position has direct biological effects leading to pathogenesis, it resides on a par with more traditional epidemiological risk variables like diet and exercise that also have direct biological effects leading to pathogenesis. Moreover, the idea that being at the bottom of a hierarchy is stressful is particularly powerful when considered in tandem with the observations of the influential social epidemiologist John Cassel (1976), who pointed out that when stress induces vulnerability to disease, many disease outcomes are possible. In this way, the hierarchy stress explanation can help account for the fact that SES is associated with many disease outcomes.

Social Causation: Fundamental Social Causes

The second explanation we consider derives from our reasoning about fundamental social causes of inequalities in health (Link and Phelan 1995). In developing this concept, we shall direct attention to some facts about the persistence of the association between SES and mortality that we alluded to only briefly above. To begin, consider a pioneering study of deaths in the French city of Mulhouse during the period 1823–1834. Villerme (1840) showed dramatic evidence of an association between life expectancy and occupational position: people from the class of "managers, merchants and directors etc." could expect to live 28.2 years, whereas people from the class of factory workers could expect to live only 17.6. Since Villerme's report, studies have repeatedly demonstrated that people more favorably situated in

the socioeconomic hierarchy live longer than those who are less favorably situated (Chapin 1924; Coombs 1941; Antonovsky 1967; Pappas et al. 1993). An important recent example comes from the National Longitudinal Mortality Study (Sorlie et al. 1995), which finds that people at the bottom of the education and income distributions are at two to three times greater risk of dying than those at the top of the distributions.

When one considers the dramatic changes that have occurred in social and health conditions between the times that Villerme and Sorlie conducted their studies, the persistence of the association between socioeconomic status and mortality is remarkable. There have been dramatic changes in life expectancy, dramatic changes in the diseases afflicting human beings, and dramatic changes in health care systems. Amidst all this change, the persistence of the association between SES and mortality stands as an undeniable fact in need of explanation.

The standard approach to understanding the association is to seek to identify the risk-factor mechanisms that appear to account for the association in the current historical context. Thus, to account for the relatively recent findings of Sorlie and colleagues, one might focus attention on behavioral risk factors such as smoking, exercise, diet, and other variables likely to influence the development of cardiovascular disease and cancer—the big killers of our time. But doing so, while valuable for understanding the current situation, fails to explain the persistence of the SES association. The marked changes in health conditions over time suggest that the risk factors that explain present distributions of cardiovascular disease and cancer are very different from the risk factors that would account for past distributions of cholera and tuberculosis. The risk factor mechanisms have changed, but the SES association has persisted (Link and Phelan 1995; House et al. 1990; Williams 1990.) This finding suggests that there is something fundamental about the association between SES and mortality that causes such an association to emerge under dramatically different health conditions. What explains this persistence? Why should socioeconomic status have such an enduring association with mortality?

An important clue can be found in the classic principle of social epidemiology that we cited at the outset of this chapter. According to this principle, societies "create" and "shape" patterns of disease. These words tell us that the connections between social conditions and disease are dynamic—social forces actively create and shape patterns of disease. In explaining why this shaping and creating occurs, the fundamental cause approach brings two sets of sociological ideas to social epidemiology. The first focuses on the importance of contexts. Drawing upon classic traditions in sociology, the fundamental cause approach asserts that seemingly powerful determinants of health outcomes can be rendered inconsequential when macro level conditions change. The second focuses on social and economic advantages and on the idea that these can be used to garner benefits—including health benefits—in diverse circumstances.

In keeping with these notions, we have proposed a sociologically inspired explanation for persistent associations between SES and disease. We argue that the reason SES has been so consistently associated with disease is that it embodies resources like knowledge, money, power, and prestige that can be used in different ways in different situations to avoid risks for disease and death (Link and Phelan 1995, 1996). People who are relatively better off use their advantage to avoid risks and to adopt protective strategies that enhance health and well-being no matter what the risk and protective factors happen to be at a given point in time. Viewed through this broad historical lens, associations between SES and risk factors are dynamic—the associations change as conditions and knowledge change. When new risk factors (such as chemical pollutants) arise, when new knowledge about risk factors (such as smoking) emerges, or when new treatment technologies (such as neonatal intensive care units) develop, those who command the most resources are best able to avoid the risks and take advantage of the protective factors, resulting in the emergence of an SES gradient in these factors. According to the fundamental cause idea, the association between SES and mortality has been so persistent because of the dynamic connection between SES and risk factors.

Other social factors such as social support may also operate in this manner. Social support can effectively protect a person from risks or encourage a person to adopt protective strategies under very different circumstances and with respect to widely varying profiles of risk and protective factors. We refer to social conditions whose association with health persists even when profiles of risk and protective factors change radically as "fundamental social causes" (Link and Phelan 1995).

The fundamental cause perspective is directly antagonistic to the claims of modern risk factor epidemiologists, who assert that social epidemiology is no longer relevant. Recall that the rationale for such a claim is that once full knowledge of the intervening risk factors is available, the more distal social conditions are irrelevant

to understanding the incidence of disease and death. More proximal risk factors are easier to address via intervention, and once we have done so, the social patterns—social disparities in health—will disappear. The fundamental cause perspective suggests why this assumption is incorrect. Social factors like SES and social support are dynamically related to risk factors—as the profile of risk factors and knowledge about how to avoid them changes, people with more resources are able to attain a health advantage in the changed circumstances. This means that associations between fundamental social causes and risk factors continually re-emerge, leading to an enduring gradient between fundamental social causes and health. We needed social epidemiology to understand health circumstances in the nineteenth century, we need it to understand the patterns we now experience, and we will need it for the same reasons 100 years hence.

The fundamental cause approach is compatible with, and in fact incorporates, the hierarchy stress explanation in the sense that hierarchy-related stress is one of the many health risks that persons of higher SES can use their resources to avoid. Within a fundamental cause perspective, stress is related to disease and death, and thereby plays a role in generating social disparities in health. As with other risk factors, people with more resources use those resources to avoid stressful circumstances and to mitigate the effects of any they do encounter. This is true whether the stress is thought of as being generated from relative deprivation, from lack of control associated with low hierarchical position, or from adverse experiences associated with low SES. In the case of stress, the benefits accruing to the relatively advantaged might result from attaining a higher position and thereby avoiding hierarchy-generated stress, or they might result from the avoidance of a wide range of stress-generating events and experiences like exposure to crime, low birth weight infants, routine work, and the like. Once generated, stress can lead to many untoward health outcomes in a manner consistent with John Cassel's (1976) idea that adverse environmental conditions compromise "host resistance" and make people vulnerable not just to one disease but to many. The notion of host resistance and the idea that adverse environmental circumstances induce vulnerability to disease has endured, with new concepts like "allostatic load" specifying the biological underpinnings of these ideas. However conceptualized, these ideas cohere with the fundamental social cause approach in that once people are compromised by stress, they become vulnerable in many different circumstances that can lead to multiple negative physical and mental health effects. Thus the stress idea can help explain why social factors like SES are associated with disease across time and place.

The fundamental cause approach, however, does not share the hierarchy stress view that objective material conditions play only a minor role in explaining social disparities in disease and death in developed countries. At its core, the fundamental cause idea asks us to attend to "who gets what," and stress, important as it is, is not the only health-relevant entity that people get. In addition to stress, the fundamental cause idea asks us to be attentive to a host of other health-related matters whose distribution is shaped by access to knowledge, money, power, prestige, and social connections. The list of specific factors is enormous but includes diet, exercise, smoking, preventive health care, problem-solving abilities, health insurance, environmental and occupational exposures, quality of medical care, and so on. The hierarchy stress approach recognizes these, but attributes little importance to them in generating social disparities in health and mortality. It is on this point that we strenuously disagree. We assert that these so-called material factors are central to understanding disparities in health.

On what basis do we make such a claim? In the sections that follow we (1) provide an empirical example that illustrates the processes specified by the fundamental cause approach, (2) ask whether the fundamental cause approach is compatible with the facts that motivate and support the hierarchy stress explanation, and (3) consider facts that are compatible with the fundamental cause approach but are incompatible with the hierarchy stress explanation.

Exemplifying the Fundamental Causes Process: Screens for Cervical and Breast Cancer

To the extent that processes associated with the fundamental cause idea operate, one should be able to demonstrate that SES differentials in risk and protective factors, and in morbidity and mortality, change in ways that are favorable to higher status individuals when new diseases and risk factors, treatments, and other medical discoveries emerge.

With this in mind, it is apparent that one informative situation with regard to the fundamental cause idea is the discovery of effective screening techniques for disease. Here we consider the two primary screens for female cancers—the PAP test for cervical cancer and mammography for breast cancer. Data on the utilization of these screens are likely to be instructive for three critical reasons.

First, there is evidence suggesting that use of these screens can lead to early detection of treatable health conditions and that, when treated, these conditions are less lethal. Second, both screening procedures resulted from technological innovations. This means that, at an earlier time in history, the use of these screens could not have been related to SES, because the screens did not exist. Consequently, the screens could not have contributed to the SES gradient in mortality. Third, because these screens represent human inventions and not acts of nature, they directly illustrate how the social distribution of health advantages shape mortality trends—how the good things we create, like effective screens for deadly diseases, result in social inequalities in health when their use becomes patterned by SES.

Evidence from a series of population-based studies and from the Behavioral Risk Factor Surveys conducted under the auspices of the Centers for Disease Control shows that women of higher SES are much more likely to be screened than those of lower SES (Link et al. 1998). For example, in 1995 nearly four in five college educated women were screened via the PAP test (77.9%), whereas just over half of those with a grade school education or less (54.3%) were screened. Similarly with regard to mammography, nearly three in four women (74.4%) who were 50 or older and who had family incomes greater than $50,000 were screened, whereas fewer than half of those of the same age with family incomes below $20,000 were screened. Because these effective screens did not always exist, our results indicate that new SES-linked protective factors have been created. They have and will continue to shape mortality patterns. As such, they exemplify how human actions structure disease patterns according to socioeconomic status and other social variables. When innovations beneficial to health are developed, their implementation necessarily occurs within the context of existing inequalities in knowledge, money, power, prestige, and social connections. These inequalities shape the distribution of the health benefit, and in doing so have an impact on patterns of mortality.

The distribution of PAP tests and mammography by income and education not only points to some of the core processes of the fundamental cause idea, it also provides an example of a pattern that cannot be explained by hierarchy stress. In this instance, the benefit arising from high status has nothing to do with the inherent advantages of being at the top of a hierarchy. It is not only less stressful to be relatively advantaged, but high status also entails resources that lead to specific benefits like access to effective screens.

But recall that the hierarchy stress explanation was compatible with a set of intriguing facts concerning income inequality in nations (and in states in the United States), the Whitehall study of British civil servants, and studies of hierarchies in animals. Is the fundamental cause approach compatible with these findings? In what follows, we return to each of these sets of findings and consider whether the fundamental cause approach is consistent with them.

Is the Fundamental Cause Approach Compatible With Findings Motivating the Hierarchy Stress Explanation?

SES Differences in Mortality Within and Between Countries The first fact motivating the hierarchy stress approach is that, for modern industrialized societies, there are within-country differences in mortality according to SES but no between-country differences according to indicators of material standards of living. Proponents of the hierarchy stress view conclude that, because one's economic position relative to others within the society is more closely linked to mortality than one's absolute level of economic resources, the relevant mechanisms linking economic resources to mortality must be psychosocial rather than material. However, this conclusion neglects the important fact that one's place in the socioeconomic hierarchy has not only psychological consequences but material ones as well. Some people have more resources and others less, and having more resources relative to one's neighbors puts one at an advantage in gaining access to whatever health benefits are available within a given society. From this viewpoint, the facts on within-country versus between-country differences in mortality by SES are fully compatible with a fundamental cause approach. When people use resources of knowledge, money, power, prestige, and social connections, they do so within the context of a given system—a process that produces health inequalities within countries. This process does not generate between-country differences, because for the most part individuals do not vie for health advantages across international boundaries.

The Gradient in the SES Mortality Associations The second fact motivating the hierarchy stress model is the step-by-step SES gradient in mortality, a compelling example of which is provided by the Whitehall study of British civil servants. Proponents of the hierarchy stress model have drawn particular support from the facts that (1) none of the study subjects was

extremely poor or deprived of medical care, and (2) significant mortality differences were found between adjacent grades that do not differ dramatically in terms of economic rewards, arguing that these facts point to the importance of hierarchical position per se as opposed to material factors. Here again, however, a fundamental cause perspective is fully compatible with these findings and, in fact, predicts just such a mortality gradient.

There is no reason to assume that the hardships associated with poverty are the only material factors that affect health. Certainly, a Whitehall administrator and unskilled manual worker share health-enhancing material resources that a homeless person does not, but the administrator also has access to salutogenic resources that neither the unskilled manual worker nor the homeless person enjoys. Nor is there any reason to assume that mortality differences between adjacent grades in an employment hierarchy must be due to hierarchy stress per se. The distribution of resources can be just as finely graded as is hierarchical status. One reason is that the list of ways in which people with more resources can garner a health advantage is very, very long: getting to the best doctors, knowing about and asking for beneficial health procedures, getting better treatment from physicians, quitting smoking, living in an SES context that supports healthy life styles, living where garbage is picked up frequently, having children who bring home useful health information from good schools, wearing seat belts, eating fruits and vegetables, getting flu shots, getting screened for dangerous but treatable cancers, etc. etc. People with more resources are more likely to be advantaged with regard to all of these risk mechanisms, resulting in a mortality gradient. Thus a gradient in mortality is exactly what a fundamental cause approach would predict.

Of course, some studies have statistically controlled for risk factor mechanisms and still found an association between hierarchical position and mortality. For example, as mentioned above, after controlling risk factors for coronary heart disease, the Whitehall study explained at most only 40 percent of the association between employment grade and mortality. It has been suggested that this finding argues for a unique direct effect of hierarchical position. But there are three problems with such an inference. First, as implied above, the list of risk and protective factors is both enormously long and constantly changing. No study can possibly claim comprehensive control of all of them. Second, efforts to adjust for the risk factors are limited by the reliability and validity with which such variables are measured. To the extent that they are unreliably measured, underadjustment for their effects will occur, and an illusory residual association between grade of employment and mortality will be observed. Such a residual effect can be interpreted as a direct effect of hierarchy. Finally, the studies at issue control only for baseline assessments of risk factors and do not consider changes in those risk factors. People with more resources are more likely to identify and have the wherewithall to address risk factors *during the follow-up period.* To the extent that they do, baseline measures assessing cholesterol level, blood pressure, or a sedentary life style provide a poor representation of the level of risk actually experienced during follow-up. When baseline measures are controlled, changes in risk factors are missed, and less of a causal role is attributed to them than they deserve. If changes in risk factors are also related to SES, as a fundamental cause perspective would predict, the residual association between low status and mortality (the direct effect) will appear larger than it really is. In light of these potential problems, we think it unwise to make strong claims about the inherent effects of hierarchical position based only upon observing a residual association between positional location and mortality.

Hierarchy Is Important for the Health of Primates Studies of primates like those referred to above provide strong support for the hierarchy stress explanation. They demonstrate that, among nonhuman primates, relative position has an impact on health-related biological processes. Given that humans are also primates, these findings suggest that hierarchical position probably also matters for the health of humans.

However, although dominant monkeys have the opportunity to exert power over subordinate monkeys and thereby attain desired outcomes, we must keep in mind that their situation is much different from that of humans. The life situation of the monkeys is for the most part unfettered by the social, economic, and medical conditions of modern industrialized nations. The monkeys do not live in a world in which their comrades are rapidly developing health knowledge and technology and distributing it within a system in which people can use resources such as knowledge, money, power, prestige, and social connections to garner a health advantage. The primate studies isolate and demonstrate the effects of social hierarchy but exclude many of the social and economic forces that we point to in our fundamental cause explanation. As such, these studies support the idea that there is health-relevant stress associated with hierarchical position, but they cannot tell us how important such stress is compared to the broader array of processes implied by the fundamental cause perspective.

In sum, we find a fundamental cause explanation compatible with the facts that are used to put forward the hierarchy stress explanation. In what follows, we turn the question around and ask whether the hierarchy stress approach is compatible with the facts used to support the fundamental cause explanation.

Is the Hierarchy Stress Approach Compatible with Findings Motivating the Fundamental Cause Explanation?

The hierarchy stress explanation is compatible with many of the facts that the fundamental cause explanation also seeks to explain. However, central to the fundamental cause idea is a dynamic association between SES and risk and protective factors. As knowledge about risk factors and how to avoid them becomes available, as new protective mechanisms are discovered, the association between SES and those risk and protective factors changes. Because the association between SES and risk and protective factors is dynamic, the association between SES and diseases persists. These changing circumstances present a challenge to the hierarchy stress explanation. The hierarchy stress explanation posits a constant mechanism linking SES to illness—the stress engendered by positional location. As such, the perspective does not account for the continued association between SES and health, as the intervening processes of risk exposure and protective strategies change over time.

Consider first changes in the association between SES and health behaviors. According to the hierarchy stress approach, the untoward consequences of low position can occur through both direct and indirect effects. Indirect effects occur through so-called stress related health behaviors. Wilkinson uses smoking as an example of an indirect effect in which stress makes it more difficult for people who hold lower positions in hierarchies to stop smoking. Smoking then harms health. The problem here is that, historically, high SES persons smoked more than people of low SES (Ernster 1988; Novotny et al. 1988; Simpson 1982). Now they smoke much less. Given that the association changed in this fashion, it does not make sense to attribute the current association between SES and smoking to stress— particularly to hierarchy-related stress. It would have to be argued that higher SES persons used to experience more stress than those of lower SES, but this is incompatible with the hierarchy-stress explanation. The reason for the current association must reside with factors that caused the change from a direct association between SES and smoking to an inverse association.

Consider next the direct effects of hierarchy stress that operate on the nervous and immune systems. Here it becomes difficult to explain changing associations between SES and particular diseases. The reason is that if hierarchy stress were a potent cause one would expect relatively constant associations between SES and particular diseases. If changes occur, they would be expected to be changes having to do with the extent of inequality and thus the amount of hierarchy stress people experience. But the changing association between SES and some diseases is so dramatic that it cannot possibly be explained by increasing (or decreasing) levels of inequality.

An example is the association between SES and coronary artery disease, which has changed from a direct association to an inverse one in the past 50 years or so (Marmot and Mustard 1994). It is difficult to explain such a dramatic change from a hierarchy stress perspective. The stress of hierarchical position should have remained relatively constant over that time. Certainly there is no reason to believe that fifty years ago relatively advantaged people experienced stress because they were at the top of the hierarchy but that now the disadvantaged experience stress due to their position. Something changed to alter the SES association with coronary artery disease, and it seems far more persuasive to identify smoking, diet, exercise and access to preventive health measures (Beaglehole 1990) than to posit changes in stress associated with hierarchical position. Given that it fails to explain this change, the hierarchy stress explanation turns out to be a very poor explanation for the current inverse association between SES and coronary artery disease.

Breast cancer mortality is another example. Just a few years ago, mortality was higher among women of higher SES due to the higher incidence of disease in this group. Now, among white women, the association between SES and breast cancer mortality has largely disappeared (Heck et al. 1997). Methods of early detection and effective treatments for breast cancer appear to be benefiting higher SES women more than lower SES women (Link et al. 1998). If this trend continues, and women of higher SES continue to receive better surveillance, the association may become inverse in the time ahead. Breast cancer mortality may follow coronary artery disease mortality in shifting from a direct to an inverse relationship with SES. Such a transition will have nothing to do with the stress of hierarchical position.

AIDS is a final example. Early in the epidemic, mortality due to AIDS was not particularly strongly related to SES. However, as we learned about HIV, its modes of transmission, and how it might be prevented, the association with SES has become much stronger (Fife and Mode 1992; Hu et al. 1994). Changes in disease patterns like this are incompatible with a hierarchy stress explanation. On the other hand, because they can be explained by changes in the association between SES and risk and protective factors, they are fully compatible with a fundamental cause perspective.

It might be possible to discount any one of the foregoing examples as special circumstances—after all the hierarchy stress explanation is concerned with overall mortality and overall health, and one might accept one or two counter examples regarding specific diseases. But the examples just given are major factors in health—two big killers and an important new epidemic. A strong explanation should encompass these important diseases.

CONCLUSION

At the outset of this chapter, we cited classic statements of the principle that societies shape patterns of disease and death. Consistent with this principle are numerous recent findings from social epidemiology demonstrating dramatic variations in health and life expectancy associated with social and economic conditions. The accumulation of these findings underscores the need for social epidemiology and the need for derivative principles from that discipline that can help us understand why the social patterns emerge so consistently and so dramatically. In this regard, we focused on the association between socioeconomic status and disease and offered the fundamental cause idea as just such a derivative principle. Because of its ability to explain changes in the association between socioeconomic status and risk factors and between socioeconomic status and specific diseases, we found it to be more powerful than an explanation focused on the stress of hierarchical position, which is less versatile in explaining such changes. We end by specifying a sociologically inspired principle for social epidemiology that states that, when social factors shape patterns of disease and death, they do so in predictable ways with the result that people who are more advantaged with regard to resources of knowledge, money, power, prestige, and social connections enjoy a health advantage.

REFERENCES

ADAMS, SALLY, LILLIAN CARTWRIGHT, JOAN OSTROVE, ABIGAIL STEWART, and PAUL WINK. 1998. "Psychological Predictors of Good Health in Three Longitudinal Samples of Educated Midlife Women." *Health Psychology* 17:412–20.

ANTONOVSKY, A. 1967. "Social Class Life Expectancy and Overall Mortality." *Milbank Memorial Fund Quarterly* 45:31–73.

BEAGLEHOLE, R. 1990. "International Trends in Coronary Heart Disease Mortality, Morbidity, and Risk Factors." *Epidemiologic Reviews* 12:1–16.

BERKMAN, L., L. LEO-SUMMERS, and R. HORWITZ. 1992. "Emotional Support and Survival after Myocardial Infarction: A Prospective, Population Based Study of the Elderly." *Annals of Internal Medicine* 117:1003–1009.

BERKMAN, LISA, and LEONARD SYME. 1979. "Social Networks, Host Resistance, and Mortality: A Nine-Year Follow-Up Study of Alameda County Residents." *American Journal of Epidemiology* 109:186–204.

CASSEL, JOHN. 1976. "The Contribution of the Social Environment to Host Resistance." *American Journal of Epidemiology* 104:107–23.

CHAPIN, C. V. 1924. "Deaths among Taxpayers and Non-taxpayers Income Tax, Providence, 1865." *American Journal of Public Health* 4:647–51.

COOMBS, L. C. 1941. "Economic Differentials in Causes of Death." *Medical Care* 1:246–55.

DAVEY SMITH, G., J. NEATON, D. WENTWORTH, R. STAMLER, AND J. STAMLER. 1996. "Socioeconomic Differentials in Mortality Risk Among Men Screened for the Multiple Risk Factor Intervention Trial I. White Men." *American Journal of Public Health* 86:486–96.

DAVEY SMITH, G., M. SHIPLEY, and G. ROSE. 1990. "The Magnitude and Causes of Socioeconomic Differences in Mortality: Further Evidence from the Whitehall Study." *Journal of Epidemiology and Community Health* 44:265–70.

DOHRENWEND, BRUCE P., ITZHAK LEVAV, PATRICK SHROUT, SHARON SCHWARTZ, GUEDALIA NAVEH, BRUCE LINK, ANDREW SKODAL, and ANN STUEVE. 1992. "Socioeconomic Status and Psychiatric Disorders: The Causation Selection Issue." *Science* 255:946–51.

ERNSTER, VIRGINIA L. 1988. "Trends in Smoking, Cancer Risk and Cigarette Promotion." *Cancer* 62:1702–12.

EVANS, ROBERT, MORRIS BARER, and THEODORE MARMOR. 1994. *Why Are Some People Healthy and Others Not: The Determinants of Health of Populations.* New York: Walter De Gruyter.

FIFE, DANIEL, and CHARLES MODE. 1992. "AIDS Incidence and Income." *Journal of Acquired Immune Deficiency Syndromes* 5:1105–10.

FOX, A. J., P. O. GOLDBLATT, and D. R. JONES. 1985. "Social Class Mortality Differentials: Artefact, Selection or Life Circumstances." *Journal of Epidemiology and Community Health* 39: 1–8.

FRIEDMAN, H., J. TUCKER, C. TOMLINSON-KEASEY, J. SCHWARTZ, D. WINGARD, M. CRIQUI. 1993. "Does Childhood Personality Predict Longevity?" *Journal of Personality and Social Psychology* 66:176–85.

GERONIMUS, ARLINE, JOHN BOUND, TIMOTHY WAIDMAN, MARIANNE HILLEMEIER, and PATRICIA BURNS. 1996. "Excess Mortality Among Blacks and Whites in the United States." *New England Journal of Medicine* 335:1552–58.

GORTMAKER, STEVEN L., and P. H. WISE. 1997. "The First Injustice: Socioeconomic Disparities, Health Services Technology, and Infant Mortality." *Annual Review of Sociology* 23: 147–70.

GOTTFREDSON, LINDA. 1997. "Why g Matters: The Complexity of Everyday Life." *Intelligence* 24:79–132.

HAHN, M., H. KAPLAN, and T. CAMACHO. 1987. "Poverty and Health: Prospective Evidence from the Alameda County Study." *American Journal of Epidemiology* 125:989–98.

HAHN, MARY N., GEORGE A. KAPLAN, and S. LEONARD SYME. 1989. "Socioeconomic Status and Health: Old Observations and New Thoughts." In *Pathways to Health: The Role of Social Factors,* ed., John Bunker, Deanna S. Gomby, and Barbara H. Kehrer. Menlo Park, CA: Henry S. Kaiser Family Foundation, pp. 76–135.

HAMM, T. E. JR., J. R. KAPLAN, T. B. CLARKSON, and B. C. BULLOCK. 1983. "Effects of Gender and Social Behavior on the Development of Coronary Artery Atherosclerosis in Cynomolgus Macaques." *Atherosclerosis* 48: 221–33.

HECK, KATHERINE, DIANE WAGENER, ARTHUR SCHATZKIN, SUSAN DEVESA, and NANCY BREEN. 1997. "Socioeconomic Status and Breast Cancer Mortality, 1989 through 1993: An Analysis of Education Data From Death Certificates." *American Journal of Public Health* 87:1218–22.

HIMSWORTH, H. 1984. "Epidemiology, Genetics and Sociology." *Journal of Biosocial Science* 16: 159–76.

HIRDES, J. P., and W. F. FORBES. 1992. "The Importance of Social Relationships, Socioeconomic Status and Health Practices with Respect to Mortality Among Ontario Males." *Journal of Clinical Epidemiology* 554: 175–82.

HOUSE, JAMES S., RONALD C. KESSLER, A. R. HERZOG, R. P. MERO, A. M. KINNEY, and M. J. BRESLOW. 1990. "Age, Socioeconomic Status, and Health." *The Milbank Quarterly* 68: 383–411.

HOUSE, JAMES S., KARL R. LANDIS, and DEBRA UMBERSON. 1988. "Social Relationships and Health." *Science* 241:540–45.

HU, DALE, ROBERT FREY, SAMUAL COSTA, JOHN MASSEY, JOHN RYAN, PATRICIA FLEMMING, SALLY D'ERRICO, JOHN WARD, and JAMES BUEHLER. 1994. "Geographical AIDS Rates and Socio-Demographic Variables in the Newark New Jersey Metropolitan Area." *AIDS and Public Policy Journal* 9:20–25.

ILLSLEY, R. 1955. "Social Class Selection and Class Differences in Relation to Stillbirths." *British Medical Journal* 2: 1520–24.

ILLSLEY, R. 1986. "Occupational Class Selection, and the Production of Inequalities in Health." *Quarterly Journal of Social Affairs* 2: 151–65.

JASSO, GUILLERMINA, and PETER ROSSI. 1977. "Distributive Justice and Earned Income." *American Sociological Review* 42:639–51.

KAPLAN, G. A., E. PAMUK, J. W. LYNCH, R. D. COHEN, and J. L. BALFOUR. 1996. "Income Inequality and Mortality in the United States." *British Medical Journal* 312: 999–1003.

KAPLAN, J. R., S. B. MANUCK, T. B. CLARKSON, F. M. LUSSO, and D. M. TAUB. 1982. "Social Status, Environment, and Atherosclerosis in Cynomolgus Monkeys." *Arteriosclerosis* 2:359.

KAWACHI, ICHIRO, BRUCE P. KENNEDY, K. LOCHNER, and D. PROTHROW-STITH. 1997. "Social Capital, Income Inequality, and Mortality." *American Journal of Public Health* 87: 1491–98.

KENNEDY, BRUCE P., ICHIRO KAWACHI, and D. PROTHROW-STITH. 1996. "Income Distribution and Mortality: Cross-sectional Ecological Study of the Robin Hood Index in the United States." *British Medical Journal* 312: 1004–1007.

KITAGAWA, E. M., and P. M. HAUSER. 1973. *Differential Mortality in the United States: A Study in Socioeconomic Epidemiology.* Cambridge: Harvard University Press.

KUNST, A. E., G. FEIKJE, J. P. MACKENBACH, and the EU WORKING GROUP ON SOCIOECONOMIC INEQUALITIES IN HEALTH. 1998. "Occupational Class and Cause Specific Mortality in Middle Aged Men in 11 European Countries: Comparison of Population Based Studies." *British Medical Journal* 316: 1636–42.

LANTZ, PAULA M., JAMES S. HOUSE, J. M. LEPKOWSKI, DAVID R. WILLIAMS, R. P. MERO, and J. CHEN. 1998. "Results From a Nationally Representative Prospective Study of US Adults." *Journal of the American Medical Association* 279: 1703–1708.

LINDHEIM, ROSLYN and S. LEONARD SYME. 1983. "Environments, People and Health." *Annual Review of Public Health* 4:335–59.

LINK, BRUCE, MARY CLARE LENNON, and BRUCE P. DOHRENWEND. 1993. "Socioeconomic Status and Depression: The Role of Occupations Involving Direction Control and Planning." *American Journal of Sociology* 98:1352–87.

LINK, BRUCE G., MARY E. NORTHRIDGE, JO C. PHELAN, and MICHAEL L. GANZ. 1998. "Social Epidemiology and the Fundamental Cause Concept: On the Structuring of Effective Cancer Screens by Socioeconomic Status." *Milbank Quarterly* 76: 375–402.

LINK, BRUCE G., and JO C. PHELAN. 1995. "Social Conditions as Fundamental Causes of Disease." *Journal of Health and Social Behavior.* Extra Issue. 80–94.

LINK, BRUCE G., and JO C. PHELAN. 1996. "Understanding Sociodemographic Differences in Health—The Role of Fundamental Social Causes." *American Journal of Public Health* 86:471–73.

MARMOT, MICHAEL, and J. FRASER MUSTARD. 1994. "Coronary Heart Disease From a Population Perspective." In *Why Are Some People Healthy and Others Not: The Determinants of Health of Populations,* ed. Robert Evans, Morris Barer, and Theodore Marmor. New York: Walter De Gruyter, pp. 189–214.

MARMOT, MICHAEL, CAROL RYFF, LARRY BUMPASS, MARTIN SHIPLEY, and NADINE MARKS. 1997. "Social Inequalities in Health: Next Questions and Converging Evidence." *Social Science and Medicine* 44:901–10.

MARMOT, MICHAEL, G. DAVEY SMITH, S. STANSFELD, C. PATEL, F. NORTH, J. HEAD, I. WHITE, E. BRUNNER, and A. FEENEY. 1991. "Health Inequalities Among British Civil Servants: The Whitehall II Study." *Lancet* 337 (8754):1387–93.

MARMOT, MICHAEL, G. ROSE, M. SHIPLEY, P. HAMILTON. 1978. "Employment Grade and Coronary Heart Disease in British Civil Servants." *Journal of Epidemiology and Community Health* 32:244–49.

MARMOT, MICHAEL, M. SHIPLEY, and G. ROSE, 1984. "Inequalities in Death—Specific Explanations of a General Pattern." *Lancet* 1(8384): 1003-1006.

McCORD, C., and H. P. FREEMAN. 1990. "Excess Mortality in Harlem." *New England Journal of Medicine* 322:173–77.

MIROWSKY, JOHN. 1987. "The Psycho-Economics of Feeling Underpaid: Distributive Justice and the Earnings of Husbands and Wives." *American Journal of Sociology* 92:1404-34.

NOVOTNY, THOMAS E., KENNETH E. WARNER, JULIETTE S. KENDRICK, and PATRICK REMINGTON. 1988. "Smoking by Blacks and Whites: Socioeconomic and Demographic Differences." *American Journal of Public Health* 78:1187–89.

PAPPAS G., S. QUEEN, W. HADDEN, and G. FISHER. 1993. "The Increasing Disparity in Mortality Between Socioeconomic Groups in the United States." *New England Journal of Medicine* 329:103–109.

POTTER, JOHN D. 1992. "Reconciling the Epidemiology, Physiology, and Molecular Biology of Colon Cancer." *Journal of the American Medical Association* 268:1573–77.

ROTHMAN, KENNETH. 1986. *Modern Epidemiology.* Boston, MA: Little, Brown and Company.

SAPOLSKY, R. M. 1990. "Stress in the Wild." *Scientific American* 262: 116–23.

SHIVELY, C., and T. CLARKSON. 1994. "Social Status and Coronary Artery Atherosclerosis in Female Monkeys." *Arteriosclerosis Thrombosis* 14:721–26.

SIMPSON, O. 1982. "Trends in Major Risk Factors: Cigarette Smoking." *Postgraduate Medical Journal* 60:20–25.

SINGH, G. K., and S. M. YU. 1995. "Infant Mortality in the United States: Trends, Differentials, and Projections, 1950 through 2010." *American Journal of Public Health* 85: 957–64.

SMITH, T. 1992. "Hostility and Health: Current Status of a Psychosomatic Hypothesis." *Health Psychology* 11:139–50.

SMITH, TOM W. 1992. "A Life Events Approach to Developing an Index of Societal Well-Being." *Social Science Research* 21:353–79.

SORLIE, PAUL D., E. BACKLUND, and J. KELLER. 1995. "US Mortality by Economic, Demographic, and Social Characteristics: The National Longitudinal Mortality Study." *American Journal of Public Health* 85:949–56.

STERN J. 1983. "Social Mobility and the Interpretation of Social Class Mortality Differentials." *Journal of Social Policy* 12: 27–49.

STOUFFER, SAMUEL A., EDWARD A. SUCHMAN, LELAND C. DEVINNEY, SHIRLEY A. STAR, and ROBIN M. WILLIAMS. 1949. *The American Soldier: Adjustments During Army Life.* Vol. 1. Princeton, NJ: Princeton University Press.

SUSSER, MERVYN, WILLIAM WATSON, and KIM HOPPER. 1985. *Sociology in Medicine.* New York: Oxford University Press.

VIRCHOW, RUDOLF. 1848. "Die Offentliche Gesundheitspflege." *Medizinische Reform* 5:21–22.

VILLERME L. 1840. *Tableau d'etat physique et moral des ouvriers.* Vol. 2. Paris: Jules Renouard et Cie.

WEST, PATRICK. 1991. "Rethinking the Health Selection Explanation for Health Inequalities." *Social Science and Medicine* 32:373–84.

WILKINSON, RICHARD G. 1986. "Socio-economic Differences in Mortality: Interpreting the Data on Their Size and Trends." In *Class and Health,* ed. Richard G. Wilkinson. London: Tavistock, pp. 1–20.

WILKINSON, RICHARD G. 1992. "Income Distribution and Life Expectancy." *British Medical Journal* 304:165–68.

WILKINSON, RICHARD G. 1996. *Unhealthy Societies: The Afflictions of Inequality.* London: Routledge.

WILKINSON, RICHARD G. 1997. "Health Inequalities: Relative or Absolute Standards?" *British Medical Journal* 314: 591–95.

WILLIAMS, DAVID R. 1990. "Socioeconomic Differentials in Health: A Review and Redirection." *Social Psychology Quarterly* 53:81–99.

WOODWARD, M., M. SHEWRY, W. SMITH, and H. TUNSTALL PEDOE. 1990. "Coronary Heart Disease and Socioeconomic Factors in Edinburgh and North Glasgow." *The Statistician* 39:319–29.

4 LINKS BETWEEN SOCIAL STATUS AND HEALTH STATUS

JOHN MIROWSKY, *The Ohio State University*

CATHERINE E. ROSS, *The Ohio State University*

JOHN REYNOLDS, *Florida State University*

Inequality. Stratification. Status. Sociologists use these terms to name the gradation of opportunity, prosperity, and standing observed in human populations. Sociologists try to understand how that gradation comes to exist and what consequences it has. Higher social status and better physical and mental health generally go together. Partly they coincide because health and well-being help individuals to succeed. Mostly, though, they coincide because the opportunities, orientations, abilities, and resources that create or result from achievement also sustain health and well-being. Social standing takes form in education, employment, occupation, daily work, earnings, income, household prosperity, neighborhood poverty, and so on (Ross and Bird 1994). Differences in status mean differences in hardship and stress, in psychological resources such as the sense of control over one's own life, and in lifestyle. All of these influence health.

The review that follows has five sections. The first defines the terms *social status* and *health,* and describes a general paradigm for understanding their relationship. The second section reviews the effects on health of four important elements of social standing: education, employment, work conditions, and economic well-being. The third section analyzes the roles of two possible links between status and health: perceived control and health lifestyle. The fourth takes positions on two issues: the greater importance of behavioral prevention than of medical treatment, and the larger rather than smaller effects of resources among the disadvantaged. The fifth section calls for more research studying the status effects on health over the life course.

DEFINITION AND STUDY OF HEALTH AND SOCIAL STATUS

The impact of social inequality extends beyond differences in jobs, earnings, prestige, and power to the consequences of this inequality for individual well-being (Ross and Bird 1994). Stratification research describes and explains the unequal distribution of socially valued resources: opportunities, goods, and quality of life. Physical and mental health are valued goods. Stratification research typically focuses on outcomes such as earnings, income, and wealth. However, differences in educational, economic, and occupational status create differences in health that directly affect quality of life. Social inequality sorts people into different positions that are associated with different risks and rewards. Location in the stratification system shapes the exposure to stressors, the availability of coping resources, and lifestyle (Pearlin 1989). Social factors that affect health endure and persist, anchored in economic and social organization (Pearlin et al. 1981).

Physical and Mental Health

The World Health Organization defines health as a state of physical and mental well-being, not simply the absence of disease. This broad definition of health focuses on differences in the physical and emotional quality of people's lives, more than on differences in the rates of diagnosed illness. Physical and psychological well-being varies along a continuum (Mirowsky and Ross 1989). At one extreme people feel tired, sick, and run-down. They are physically unable to climb stairs or walk, have many short-term illnesses like colds or the flu, have ongoing problems like arthritis that interfere with activity, or feel depressed, anxious, and demoralized. At the other extreme, people feel healthy and energetic, rarely spend a day sick in bed, and feel happy and hopeful about the future. Most people fall somewhere between these two extremes. People who qualify for medical or psychiatric diagnoses tend toward the sick end of the continuum. Those who do not qualify for diagnoses tend toward the health end. Nevertheless, people who qualify for medical diagnoses differ considerably among themselves in their degree of sickness or health. So do people not qualified for diagnoses.

Physical well-being consists of feeling fit and able, unlimited by discomfort or disability. Physical distress includes feeling in poor health, spending days in bed or disabled by health problems, having acute and chronic illnesses, feeling tired and listless, having head aches or stomach aches, feeling faint or short of breath, being in pain, having difficulty with walking, lifting, carrying, bending, using stairs, seeing, hearing, and so on (Waldron and Jacobs 1989; Verbrugge 1983). The best measures of physical well-being assess it directly, rather than by reference to the use of medical services. Factors such as income, insurance, time, and inclination make doctor visits a dubious measure of health.

Emotional well-being consists of feeling happy, hopeful, and energetic, with a zest for life. Psychological distress includes moods of depression or anxiety, and physiological symptoms associated with the moods (Pearlin et al. 1981; Mirowsky and Ross 1989). Depression and anxiety often go together and afflict everyone to some degree from time to time. They correlate with other unpleasant emotions such as anger, with cognitive problems such as paranoia, and with substance abuse such as heavy drinking (Mirowsky and Ross 1989). Depression consists of feeling sad, demoralized, lonely, hopeless, worthless, wishing you were dead, having trouble concentrating, having trouble sleeping, not feeling like eating, crying, feeling everything is an effort, feeling run-down, and being unable to get going. Anxiety consists of being tense, restless, worried, irritable, afraid, and having "fight or flight" symptoms such as acid stomach, sweaty palms, and cold sweats, as well as accelerations in heartbeat, shortness of breath, or the feeling of being hot all over when not exercising or working hard.

Physical and mental health go together for several reasons (Aneshensel et al. 1984; Bruce and Leaf 1989; Mechanic and Hansell 1987; Ross and Duff 1982; Verbrugge 1986). First, the circumstances that generally promote and protect physical well-being do the same for emotional well-being. Education, for example, improves both physical and emotional health by helping individuals to acquire information and use it effectively in managing their own lives (Mirowsky and Ross 1998). Second, each type of health (or type of health problem) contributes to the other. A disability or an uncomfortable or threatening chronic disease can make a person demoralized or worried. Depression can make a person too listless and indifferent to exercise, eat right, and avoid health risks. Worry, fear, and hopelessness can drive a person to seek comfort or escape in risky behaviors such as drug abuse or promiscuity. Third, symptoms such as tiredness, shortness of breath, and heart palpitations can result from either physical disease or emotional strain. Finally, the body's endocrine and nervous systems bridge the physical and mental. Thoughts and feelings exist on the biological level as physiological processes linked directly or indirectly to all of the body's other processes. Our language distinguishes between physical and mental, but our bodies do not.

Sometimes researchers study satisfaction with health or with life in general. Satisfaction does not necessarily indicate health and well-being. Satisfaction indicates contentment with the current situation; dissatisfaction implies discontent. Often the members of groups with many problems come to expect nothing better than what they experience currently. Members of groups with few problems come to expect nothing less. For example, among people with similar jobs and incomes, those with higher levels of education report less satisfaction with the job but also greater happiness and less frequent depression and anxiety (Ross and Reskin 1992; Ross and Van Willigen 1997). Social psychologists tell an apocryphal tale to remind students what reported satisfaction means. In the story a criminologist surveyed prisoners on death row. The researcher asked the prisoners if they were satisfied with life there. They said "Yes." Satisfaction implies a convergence between expectations and prospects that may indicate resignation rather than well-being.

Social Status

Social status has four main components that can affect health: education, employment, work, and economic status. The first component, education, includes years of schooling and degrees. It indicates the knowledge, skills, values, and behaviors learned at school, as well as the credentials that structure job opportunities. The second, employment status, differentiates categories of labor, distinguishing among being employed full time, employed part time, laid off or unemployed, unable to work because of a disability, in school full time, retired, or keeping house. The third, work status, corresponds to various aspects of productive activity. It includes occupational prestige or rank and class for employed persons, and the conditions and qualities of activity for employed persons and for others. The fourth component, economic status, includes aspects of economic well-being such as personal earnings, household income, and material or economic hardship.

Research on social status and health must consider persons outside the paid labor force, as well as paid workers. Much sociological and economic research considers only persons who work for pay or earn income. Such research excludes the most disadvantaged members of society, severely truncating variation in social status. It can obscure the extent of social differences in health. Researchers studying the nation's prosperity must address the health and morale of its workers. However, not everyone who contributes work gets paid for it. Not everyone is obliged or able to work. Not everyone who would or might work does. Often people without paid jobs are the most disadvantaged in valued resources such as health.[1] Research on social status and health needs to compare paid workers with women doing unpaid domestic labor, people who have been fired or laid off, the retired elderly, people receiving welfare, and so on.

Each element of social status should be viewed as distinct, rather than as interchangeable with the others. Sometimes researchers measure general social standing by averaging together rank on a number of dimensions such as education, occupational prestige, and household income. That practice obscures two things needed for understanding the relationship of social status to health. First, it obscures the causal relationships among the different aspects of status. Education, employment, work status, and economic

[1] Much of the descriptive research on "social class" and health is British, and almost all of it equates social class with occupation (e.g., Wilkinson 1986). By one estimate 42 percent of British women aged 16 to 64 were excluded from these studies because they had "no occupation" (Carstairs and Morris 1989). This estimate of exclusion is for people under the age of 65. Everyone who is retired is also excluded in these studies. This is an especially problematic exclusion in the study of health, since the elderly have the most health problems of any age group.

resources occupy ordered positions in a causal chain. To best understand how social differences in health evolve, research should represent the connections among aspects of status, not hide them. Second, the practice of averaging ranks obscures the differences among aspects of status in their effects on health. It can be revealing to know which aspect of status produces an effect on health. Is it the lifestyle learned in school? The social standards enforced by co-workers or neighbors? The stress produced by a job, or by the lack of a job? The worries about not having the money to pay the bills or buy food, clothes, and other necessities? The inability to get medical services and treatments? Much can be gained by knowing the specifics.

Structural Analysis

How can researchers describe and talk about the complex ways that health or sickness depends on education, employment, work, and economic status? Patterns of physical and mental health, as well as the social and personal conditions that explain or modify the patterns, are shaped by the "structural arrangements in which individuals are embedded" (Pearlin 1989: 241). Observing the association between social status and health takes the first step toward specifying how social structures influence patterns of physical and mental health. Research also must clarify how the association operates: through what channels and under what circumstances. Sociologists need to *explain* the association between health and social status by using an analytic approach that can reveal and describe (1) causal relationships among the four components of social status, (2) moderators of the relationship between status and health, and (3) mediators that link components of social status to physical and psychological health.

The past two decades of research produced a general format or paradigm for thinking about and studying how such "durable, structured experiences" generate and regulate variations in well-being. The paradigm, which we call structural analysis, searches for two types of patterns: *causal chains,* where intermediate links explain patterns of well-being; and *conditional effects* (or interactions), where one element of the social context modifies the impact of another on well-being. Both provide means of explaining why and how social stratification affects well-being (Mirowsky and Ross forthcoming; Wheaton 1985). Causal-chain models divide the overall correlation between an aspect of social status and health into component links that account for the correlation. For example, education instills better health habits, which improve health. It also leads to jobs with more autonomy, which reinforce the sense of control over personal outcomes, which improves health. Conditional-effect models specify the conditions that strengthen, weaken, eliminate, or perhaps even invert an association. For example, low income accelerates the rise of physical impairment as people age. However, education moderates that effect, reducing the correlation between low income and the rise of impairment. Sometimes causal chains and conditional effects combine. In the resulting *structural amplification* an element of social context erodes the barriers that would otherwise moderate its correlation with well-being. For example, economic hardship magnifies the detrimental effect of widowhood on health. Widowhood increases the risk of the very economic hardship that magnifies its impact on health.

Causal analysis provides a conceptual toolkit that researchers can draw upon to identify the conditions that link social status and health, and to more fully specify the contexts and personal characteristics that accentuate or attenuate those links.

HEALTH AND THE ELEMENTS OF SOCIAL STANDING

The association of low social status with poor mental and physical health appears consistently in the literature. Higher social status, as indicated by education, employment, work, and income, correlates with lower frequency and intensity of depression, anxiety, physiological malaise, distress, demoralization, mistrust, paranoia, delusions, and hallucinations (Dohrenwend and Dohrenwend 1969; Kessler 1982; Kessler and Cleary 1980; Wheaton 1978; Kohn 1976; Pearlin et al. 1981; Ross and Mirowsky 1989; Ross, Mirowsky, and Cockerham 1983; Ross and Huber 1985; Ross and Van Willigen 1997). The same pattern exists for physical health. As Leonard Syme and Lisa Berkman note, "a vast body of evidence has shown consistently that those in the lower classes have higher mortality, morbidity, and disability rates." (1986: 28). Well-educated people with high incomes and good jobs experience better physical health than the poor and poorly educated, as indicated by high levels of self-reported health and physical functioning and low rates of morbidity, disability, and death. In contrast, low social status is marked by high rates of infectious and parasitic diseases, infant mortality, chronic noninfectious diseases, impairment, poor subjective health, lower life expectancy, and higher death rates (Kitagawa and Hauser

1973; Leigh 1983; Gortmaker 1979; Feldman et al. 1989; Guralnik et al. 1993; Gutzwiller et al. 1989; Kaplan, Haan, and Syme 1987; Liu et al. 1982; Morris 1990; Pappas et al. 1993; Syme and Berkman 1986; Williams 1990; Winkleby et al. 1992; Woodward et al. 1992). People of lower social status are more likely to get sick, and less likely to survive if sick.[2]

The association between health and social status results from the effect of social status on health (called "social causation") more than from the effect of health on status attainment (called "social selection"). In terms of psychological health, differences in the demands and resources of various social positions produce differences in psychological well-being and distress (Pearlin et al. 1981; Wheaton 1978). For example, Bruce Link and colleagues show that occupation has a large causal effect on depression and schizophrenia. It is not simply that people with psychological problems drift into low-level occupations (Link, Dohrenwend, and Skodol 1986; Link, Lennon, and Dohrenwend 1993). Likewise, downward mobility among persons in poor physical health does not explain most of the association of status and physical health (Doornbos and Kromhout 1990; Fox, Goldblatt, and Jones 1985; Power, Manor, Fox, and Fogelman 1990; Wilkinson 1986). Education, full-time employment, household income, and a lack of economic hardship significantly slow the decline in self-reported health and physical functioning over time (Mirowsky and Hu 1996; Ross and Wu 1995).

Higher social status protects and improves psychological and physical health. Next we examine the effects of each component of social status separately. We begin with a discussion of education and proceed down the causal chain to employment, the nature of work, and economic well-being.

Education

Education acts as the key to position in the stratification system. As the root component of social status, education shapes the likelihood of being employed, the qualities of the job a person can get, and income. Education has a fundamental influence on adult health and well-being because it generates social inequalities

---

[2] Of course these general patterns are not true in every case. For example, well-educated women have higher rates of breast cancer than the poorly educated largely because they have fewer children, which increases risk. However, well-educated women with breast cancer survive longer than poorly educated women with breast cancer (Lipworth et al. 1970).

in employment, job, and economic status. People with high levels of education experience better physical health than those with less education, as indicated by high levels of self-reported health and physical functioning and low levels of morbidity, mortality, and disability (Doornbos and Kromhout 1990; Feldman et al. 1989; Fox, Goldblatt, and Jones 1985; Guralnik et al. 1993; Kitagawa and Hauser 1973; Pappas et al. 1993; Ross and Wu 1995; Wilkinson 1986). People with high levels of education also experience better mental health, as indicated by low levels of depression and psycho-physiological malaise (Kessler 1982; Pearlin et al. 1981; Ross and Huber 1985; Ross and Van Willigen 1997; Wheaton 1980). Typically, education has one of the strongest net influences on health, a finding that affirms education's role as the root feature of social status and a central determinant of the social distribution of health and well-being.

The explanations for the presence of such a strong relationship between education and physical and psychological health fall into three categories: work and economic conditions, social-psychological resources, and health lifestyle. Well-educated people are less likely to be unemployed than the poorly educated; they are more likely to work full time, and their work is likely to be more fulfilling, more autonomous, less routine, and less dangerous. Their incomes are higher, and they experience less economic hardship. In addition, the more educated have a stronger sense of control over their own lives, healthier habits, and more social support. Each of these consequences of education may protect health, as detailed below.

Employment

For most Americans employment improves physical and psychological well-being. On the aggregate level, higher rates of unemployment coincide with higher rates of morbidity and mortality, including heart disease mortality, infant mortality, admissions to mental hospitals, and suicide (Brenner 1971; Catalano and Dooley 1983). Studies that follow individuals provide more direct tests of the effect of unemployment on health. Most find that the people who are unemployed have worse physical and mental health than others of similar background who remain employed (Kasl and Cobb 1982; Pearlin et al. 1981; Linn, Sandifer, and Stein 1985; Frese and Mohr 1987). Ronald Kessler, James House, and Blake Turner (1987) find that the unemployed have worse self-reported health and higher levels of somatization, anxiety, and depression that

cannot be explained through a selection of sicker people from the work force.

Education increases the likelihood of employment. Among persons aged 25 to 34 in 1991, 87 percent of college graduates were employed, compared to 77 percent of those with only a high school degree, and 56 percent of those with eight years of education or less (U.S. Department of Education 1992). The unemployment rate for college graduates was 3 percent, or one-fifth of the rate for persons with some high school, of whom 15 percent were unemployed. Lack of education limits employment opportunities. The poorly educated often work at low-status, poorly paid jobs and have the greatest risk of losing their jobs in an economic downturn (Elder and Liker 1982). Among the employed, education increases the likelihood of full-time employment. Part-time work typically offers lower returns to experience and fewer benefits.

Women benefit physically and mentally from paid employment, as do men. Few ever questioned that paid employment benefits men's health. However, in the 1970s Walter Gove and colleagues showed that paid work provided psychological benefits for women, too (Gove and Tudor 1973; Gove and Geerken 1977). Most research finds that employed women have less depression, anxiety, and other forms of psychological distress than do housewives (Gove and Geerken 1977; Rosenfield 1980; Ross, Mirowsky, and Ulbrich 1983; Kessler and McRae 1982; Gore and Mangione, 1983), although some research finds no significant differences between employed women and housewives. Employed women are physically healthier than nonemployed women (Bird and Fremont 1991; Lewin-Epstein 1986; Nathanson 1980; Verbrugge 1983; Marcus, Seeman, and Telesky 1983; Waldron and Jacobs 1989). Among women, the employed report the best physical health, housewives report lower health, and the unemployed (in the labor market but out of work) report the worst health (Jennings, Mazaik, and McKinlay 1984; Brenner and Levi 1987). Death rates of women in the labor force are substantially lower than those of housewives (Passannante and Nathanson 1985). Part-time female workers have worse health than full-time female workers, although their health is better than the nonemployed (Herold and Waldron 1985).

The positive effects of employment on women's health depend somewhat on preferences and household demands. One study found that in a large minority (39%) of U.S. families in the early 1980s, the wife was employed but she and her husband preferred that she not work, and that in a large majority (80%) of families in which the wife was employed her husband did not share the housework and child care equally (Ross, Mirowsky, and Huber 1983). Such conditions reduce, and sometimes reverse, the beneficial psychological impact of the wife's employment. Her employment improves well-being most when her earnings are high enough to clearly improve the family's economic well-being, she and her husband want her to be employed, and he shares the household tasks. In the ideal healthy marriage the husband and wife both earn good pay, both contribute similar amounts to the total family income, and both share the housework and child care equally.

Work Conditions

Workers doing routine, simple jobs closely controlled by management report higher levels of psychological distress compared to workers doing other types of jobs (Reynolds 1997). They also have significantly higher rates of impaired physical functioning (Lerner et al. 1994), cardiovascular disease (Karasek and Theorell 1990), and mortality (Falk et al. 1992; Moore and Hayward 1990). Workers who constantly face role overload or who persistently work overtime report significantly higher levels of psychological distress (Loscocco and Spitze 1990; Menaghan and Merves 1984), and they have higher rates of morbidity and mortality (House et al. 1986).

Education gives people access to subjectively rewarding work. Well-educated people are more likely than the poorly educated to control their own work. They often have autonomy on the job and stimulating nonroutine work, both of which increase psychological functioning, the sense of personal control, job satisfaction, and psychological well-being (Karasek and Theorell 1990; Kohn and Slomczynski 1990; Ross and Reskin 1992; Ross and Van Willigen 1997). Work done by people with a high school education or less is not as rewarding subjectively as work done by college graduates. It typically provides less intrinsic enjoyment, fewer opportunities to learn new things and develop as a person, less recognition from others, and fewer opportunities for pride in accomplishments, all of which result in poorer health (Reynolds and Ross 1998; Ross and Wu 1995). (Some researchers, however, find smaller and inconsistent health effects of intrinsic work rewards among the employed (Hibbard and Pope 1987; House et al. 1986)). Low education often leads to working at hazardous, risky, and physically noxious jobs characterized by noise, heat, fumes, cold, humidity, physical dangers, exposure to carcinogens, and so on (Leigh 1983; Link, Dohrenwend, and Skodol 1986), in addition to working at jobs that do not pay well, all of which negatively impact health.

Economic Well-Being

Studies consistently find that low income, poverty, and economic hardship erode health and well-being, raising the risk of morbidity, impairment, and death (Kessler and Cleary 1980; Kessler 1982; Pearlin et al. 1981; Mirowsky and Hu 1996; Ross and Huber 1985). Having learned this, students often assume that income buys what it takes to protect and enhance health. However, a number of observations suggest that the differences in health resulting from differences in income depend on circumstances. First, the desirable effect of additional income on health occurs only at the bottom of the income scale. In the United States, differences in income predict larger differences in health the lower one gets on that scale. Below the 20th percentile, poor health, chronic disease, physical impairment, and the risk of death increase more and more sharply as one approaches the lowest levels of income. Above the 20th percentile, higher income produces little or no effect on health. The diminishing incremental effects of income show up in international comparisons too. Increases in gross national product (GNP) per capita generally reduce infant mortality and increase life expectancy at birth. Once countries get above the per capita GNP of, say, Greece, Portugal, Taiwan, and the Czech Republic, differences in GNP account for little of the differences in life expectancy and infant mortality. Second, the effect of income on health depends on education. This occurs because difficulty paying bills or buying necessities such as food and clothes forms the main link between low income and poor health. Education reduces the association between low income and economic hardship. Education also reduces the association of economic hardship with depression, impairment, and poor subjective health (Mirowsky and Hu 1996; Ross and Huber 1985). As a result, the higher the level of education, the less health is undermined by low income. Unfortunately, low income often results from low education, in a classic example of structural amplification.

Household economic hardship explains much of the effect on depression, impairment, and poor health of low family income and loss of family income due to being laid off, fired, or downgraded (Mirowsky and Hu 1996; Pearlin et al. 1981; Ross and Huber 1985). In the household the larger social and economic order impinges on individuals, exposing them to varying degrees of hardship, frustration, and struggle. The ongoing effort to pay the bills and feed and clothe the family on an inadequate income exacts a toll in feelings of depression—in feeling run-down, tired, listless, overwhelmed, hopeless and sad, with gnawing worries that make sleep restless and drain the joy from life. Susceptibility to infectious and chronic disease increases when life becomes a weary, relentless, unending struggle to get by (Pearlin et al. 1981; Syme and Berkman 1986; Ross and Huber 1985).

Economic hardship afflicts women and children more often than men (Moen 1983; Preston 1984; Ross and Huber 1985). One reason is that women earn less than men, but typically have custody of children from a broken marriage or who were born outside marriage. Women and children in female-headed households make up a large and growing fraction of the poor in the United States. For example, the percentage of families below the poverty level increased from 10.1 percent in 1970 to 10.8 percent in 1995, but the percentage of children living in poor households increased from 14.9 percent to 20.0 percent (United States Bureau of the Census 1997). Even in the intact families, wives' responsibilities can make them more acutely aware of economic strains (Ross and Huber 1985). Traditionally the wife bears responsibility for shopping, preparing meals, taking children to the doctor, and paying bills. The traditional arrangement occurs most commonly in working class families, which have just enough money to get by and must juggle to pay the bills and still have enough money for food.

LINKS BETWEEN SOCIAL STATUS AND HEALTH

Causal analysis provides the tools needed to find out how social status protects and improves health. Although a number of people call for research on explaining the association (Pearlin 1989; Williams 1990), surprisingly little explanatory research has been done (cf. Leigh 1983; Reynolds and Ross 1998; Ross and Wu 1995). This section describes research on the explanations for the impact of social status on health, focusing on the sense of personal control and health lifestyle (smoking, exercising, heavy drinking, and so on) as primary mechanisms. (Social support is discussed in Chapter 24 of this text.)

In the explanatory model developed here, social-psychological resources and health lifestyle link structured inequality to health. Discussions often pose individual responsibility and structured inequality as rival explanations of differences in health. Some analysts say differences in health result from individual

behaviors such as exercise or smoking (Knowles 1977). Others criticize that view, arguing the differences result from a social structure that allocates resources unequally (Crawford 1986). We combine those views by arguing that stressors, hardships, beliefs, and behaviors are socially structured, not randomly distributed. Smoking, exercising, drinking, or a sense of personal control are not *alternative* explanations of the poor health associated with low education, unemployment, undesirable jobs, and economic hardships. They *link* those elements of social status to health.

Perceived Control

The sense of control over one's own life may be one of the most important determinants of psychological and physical well-being, and one of the most important links between social status and health. Melvin Seeman (1983) defined the sense of powerlessness and lack of control as the expectancy or probability, held by the individual, that his own behavior cannot determine the occurrence of the outcomes, or reinforcements, he seeks. The individual believes that he or she is powerless and at the mercy of the environment; that outcomes of situations are determined by forces external to one's own actions, such as powerful others, luck, fate, or chance. Belief in personal control, the opposite, is a learned, generalized expectation that outcomes are contingent on one's own choices and actions. The individual believes that he or she can master, control, or effectively alter the environment.

Beliefs about personal control generally represent realistic perceptions of objective conditions. An individual learns through social interaction and personal experience that his or her choices and efforts are usually likely or unlikely to affect the outcome of a situation. Failure in the face of effort leads to a sense of powerlessness, fatalism, or belief in external control, which leads to passivity and giving up. Success leads to a sense of mastery, efficacy, or belief in internal control, characterized by an active, problem-solving approach to life (Wheaton 1980, 1983; Mirowsky and Ross 1983, 1984; Ross and Mirowsky 1989).

People with low educational attainment, restricted employment opportunities, and poor economic circumstances often learn that failure is built into their lives. Through experience they come to believe that powerful others and unpredictable forces control their lives and that they cannot get ahead no matter how hard they try. In contrast, those in higher social positions tend to have a sense of control learned through a personal history of successful efforts. Higher education builds the sense of control directly and leads to the kinds of jobs and economic circumstances that reinforce it (Mirowsky and Ross 1983, 1984; Ross, Mirowsky, and Cockerham 1983; Wheaton 1980). The autonomous, substantively complex jobs available to better educated workers increase the sense of personal responsibility, control, and self-direction (Kohn 1976; Kohn and Schooler 1982; Link, Lennon, and Dohrenwend 1993). In contrast, low-status jobs often produce a sense of powerlessness because the routine, ungratifying work seems imposed and oppressive, and the limited opportunity and income provided by the job seem barriers rather than means to achievement of life goals (Wheaton 1980). Job disruptions such as being laid off, downgraded, fired, or leaving work because of illness decrease the worker's sense of mastery, partly by lowering income and increasing economic hardship (Pearlin et al. 1981). Poverty and chronic economic difficulties decrease feelings of mastery, instrumentalism, and control over one's life, and increase feelings of powerlessness (Pearlin et al. 1981). The poor have a triple burden: They have more problems to deal with; their personal histories often leave them with a distressing sense of powerlessness; and that sense of powerlessness demoralizes them and undermines the will to seek and take effective action in order to solve problems. The result for many is a multiplication of sickness and despair.

In addition to its indirect effect on the sense of personal control through labor market and economic conditions, education directly impacts perceived control (Ross and Van Willigen 1997; Mirowsky and Ross 1998). Through education individuals develop capacities on many levels that increase the sense of personal control, mastery, and self-direction. These capacities include the habits and skills of communication, including reading, writing, inquiring, discussing, looking things up, and figuring things out; and analytic skills involved in mathematics, logic, and, on a more basic level, observing, experimenting, summarizing, synthesizing, interpreting, and classifying. Because education develops one's ability to gather and interpret information and to solve problems on many levels, it increases one's potential to control events and outcomes in life. Moreover, through education one encounters and solves problems that are progressively more difficult, complex, and subtle, building problem-solving skills and confidence in the ability to solve problems. Education instills the habit of meeting problems with attention, thought, action, and persistence.

The sense of powerlessness and lack of personal control has consequences for health. It can effect psychological and physical well-being in two ways: It can be distressing in itself, and it can hamper effective problem-solving. People who believe they have little influence over the things that happen to them tend to be more distressed, whereas those who believe that what happens to them is of their own doing tend to be less distressed (Wheaton 1980). Similarly, increasing belief that "I have little control over the things that happen to me" increases distress over time, whereas increasing belief that "I can do just about anything I really set my mind to," or that "What happens to me in the future mostly depends on me" decreases distress over time (Pearlin et al. 1981).

In addition to its direct, demoralizing impact, the sense of not being in control of one's own life can diminish the will and motivation to actively solve problems. Blair Wheaton (1983) argues that fatalism decreases coping effort. Belief in the efficacy of environmental rather than personal forces makes active attempts to solve problems seem pointless: "What's the use?" The result is less motivation and less persistence in coping and, thus, less success in solving problems and adapting. Instrumental people, in contrast, are likely to search the environment for potentially distressing events and conditions, to take preventive steps, and to accumulate resources or develop skills and habits that will reduce the impact of unavoidable problems. For example, Melvin Seeman and colleagues find that people with a high sense of control are more likely to be knowledgeable about health, are more likely to initiate preventive behaviors like quitting smoking on their own, are less likely to be dependent on doctors, and have better self-rated health than those with a low sense of control (Seeman and Seeman 1983; Seeman, Seeman, and Budros 1988).[3]

In the long run, the sense of control can lead to a change in status that further reinforces a high or low sense of control. Most of the cross-sectional correlation reflects the impact of current and long-term conditions on the sense of control. However, some of it reflects the long-run impact that the sense of control has on education, job status, and earnings. People who feel powerless and fatalistic, or who are cognitively rigid, may wind up in tedious jobs that do not pay well, or may even lose their jobs. People who feel responsible, instrumental, and that they have a high sense of personal control improve their conditions with time (Dunifon and Duncan 1998; Kohn and Schooler 1982). The long-run feedback benefits some, by reinforcing

[3] Lack of personal control also affects health more directly through physiological mechanisms, because experiences of uncontrollability and the resulting demoralization are associated with suppression of the immune system (Rodin and Timko 1992; Rowe and Kahn 1987). See also Chapter 24 in this text.

moves toward responsibility and control. Unfortunately, the long-run feedback works both ways. Little success over long periods discourages and demoralizes some, leaving them fatalistic.

Health Lifestyle

Education shapes lifestyle directly, as well as indirectly, by increasing the sense of personal control. Of the four elements of social status, education acts as the most consistent predictor of healthy lifestyle. Compared to the poorly educated, well-educated people more frequently engage in proven healthy behaviors such as exercising, avoiding obesity, drinking moderately, and not smoking (Leigh 1983; Hayes and Ross 1986; Ross and Wu 1995; Berkman and Breslow 1983). The effects of education on behavior and exposure, more than on access to medical care, explain the beneficial impact of education on health (Syme and Berkman 1986). Although most research on lifestyle and health looks at physical health, lifestyle also shapes mental health. For instance, people who exercise have fewer symptoms of depression (Hayes and Ross 1986; Ross and Hayes 1988).

Smoking The well educated are less likely to take up smoking than the poorly educated, and more likely to quit if they do take it up (Helmert et al. 1989; Jacobsen and Thelle 1988; Liu et al. 1982; Matthews et al. 1989; Millar and Wigle 1986; Shea et al. 1991; Wagenknecht et al. 1990; Winkleby et al. 1992). Of all the common practices that affect health, smoking has the most extensive and dire consequences (Rogers and Powell-Griner 1991). Smoking makes people feel unhealthy and increases the risk of coronary heart disease, stroke, atherosclerosis, aneurysm, emphysema, bronchitis, pneumonia, other respiratory infections, liver disease, burns, and cancer of the lung, esophagus, pancreas, bladder, larynx, and cervix (Abbott et al. 1986; NCHS 1989; Segovia, Bartlett, and Edwards 1989; Surgeon General 1982; U.S. Preventive Services Task Force 1989). Heart disease, cancer, stroke, and emphysema alone account for about 65 percent of all deaths (NCHS 1992).

Exercise In American society, levels of physical activity increase with educational attainment (Ford et al. 1991; Helmert et al. 1989; Jacobsen and Thelle 1988; Leigh 1983; Shea et al. 1991). Compared to inactivity, any physical activity, aerobic or nonaerobic, reduces mortality (Berkman and Breslow 1983). Exercise reduces cardiovascular risk, back pain, osteoporosis, atherosclerosis, colon cancer, obesity, high blood pressure, constipation, varicose veins, and adult onset diabetes,

and it improves subjective health and psychological well-being (Berlin and Colditz 1990; Caspersen et al. 1992; Duncan, Gordon, and Scott 1991; Leon et al. 1987; Hayes and Ross 1986; Magnus, Matroos, and Strackee 1979; Paffenbarger et al. 1993; Sandvik et al. 1993; Segovia et al. 1989; U.S. Preventive Services Task Force 1989).

Drinking The well educated drink moderately more often than the poorly educated. People with lower levels of education more often either abstain from or abuse alcohol (Darrow et al. 1992; Midanik, Klatsky, and Armstrong 1990; Romelsjo and Diderichsen 1989). Research finds a U-shaped relationship between drinking and illness. Both abstainers and very heavy drinkers have higher mortality and morbidity than do those who drink moderately (Berkman and Breslow 1983; Guralnik and Kaplan 1989; Midanik et al. 1990). Moderate drinking, as compared to abstinence, is associated with lower risk of coronary heart disease, stroke, and hypertension, whereas very heavy drinking is associated with higher risk (Gaziano et al. 1993; Gill et al. 1986; Stampfer, Colditz, Willet, Speizer, and Hennekens 1988).

Heavy drinking may temporarily relieve the stresses of poverty or low-level, high-risk jobs available to those with little schooling (Shore and Pieri 1992), although evidence for the hypothesis that job-related distress causes increased drinking is mixed. Some research suggests that workers in overly demanding and stressful jobs are more likely to drink more frequently and engage in "escapist drinking" (House et al. 1986), but other studies find no evidence that job pressures and work problems lead to stress-induced drinking (Cooper, Russell, and Frone 1990; Fennell, Rodin, and Kantor 1981).

Of the leading 15 causes of death, drinking as a risk factor is implicated in only 4 (fewer than smoking or sedentary lifestyle): car accidents (one of the top 5 causes of death), cirrhosis of the liver, suicide, and homicide. Of these, only cirrhosis and injuries from car accidents affect self-reported health and physical functioning, making drinking far less ubiquitous in its health consequences than smoking or inadequate physical activity.

Health Check-ups The well educated are more likely to get preventive medical care—annual physical exams, immunizations, and screening—than are the poorly educated (Coburn and Pope 1974; Ross and Wu 1995). They are more likely to have insurance that covers check-ups and to have social networks that encourage regular check-ups. Many people believe that annual physical examinations help detect early signs of illness, thus forestalling more serious health problems. National policy reviews in both the United States and Canada find little scientific justification for the belief (Canadian Task Force on the Periodic Health Examination 1988; U.S. Preventive Services Task Force 1989).

In summary, the healthy lifestyle indicated by exercising, limiting body weight, drinking moderately, and not smoking forms much of the link between higher social status and better health. Education enables people to forge a healthy lifestyle, improving health largely by that means (Mirowsky and Ross 1998). Education encourages a healthy lifestyle both directly and indirectly by increasing the sense of control, increasing household income, and decreasing economic hardship. The sense of control forms the main link between social status and healthy lifestyle. If *efforts* seem useless, if health and sickness seem beyond one's control, what is the point of exercising, quitting smoking, or avoiding heavy drinking (Wheaton 1980)? The failure structured into the life of a person with little education creates a pervasive sense of powerlessness that undermines the motivation to live a healthy lifestyle. Unhealthy lifestyles, as well as material deprivations, account for the association between low social status and poor health.

OUTLOOKS ON SOCIAL STATUS AND HEALTH

The research reviewed above leads to several conclusions. First, higher social status protects and improves health. Second, the primary aspects of social status that improve health include education, employment, autonomous and fulfilling work, and the absence of economic hardship. Third, those aspects of social status improve health by developing and reinforcing a sense of mastery and control and by encouraging and enabling a healthy lifestyle.

Most researchers studying social status and health probably would endorse the conclusions stated above. In this section we draw conclusions about social status and health that may be more controversial. We argue that behavioral prevention rather than medical treatment accounts for most of the social status differences in health and that increments in resources have larger rather than smaller effects among the disadvantaged.

Prevention Rather Than Treatment

It probably comes as no surprise to most Americans that higher social status brings with it a healthier and longer life. Many may assume that it does so by allowing individuals to buy more medical treatments or more expensive ones. We call this the health commodity assumption. In our review we came across no evidence to support that assumption. In fact, we could find no studies questioning it. This seems odd given the many findings indirectly suggesting that the assumption is false. We now review the evidence that challenges the health commodity assumption. The evidence suggests that the purchase of treatments accounts for little of the social status differences in health.

Some individuals may think that the health and longevity of modern populations came from the development and use of increasingly sophisticated medical treatments. To those who hold that belief it makes sense that wealthier individuals buy more treatments, particularly the newest and most expensive ones, thus getting healthier than others. The inference builds on the false premise that advances in medical treatments created the health and longevity enjoyed by modern, industrialized societies. Historical scholars say that the rise of modern life expectancy cannot be attributed to the medical and surgical treatment of disease, because most of the declines in mortality rates preceded the advent of effective treatments (McKinlay and McKinlay 1977; Sagan 1987). Even today, differences among countries (in medical resources such as doctors and hospitals) explains little of the variance in infant mortality rates when one has adjusted for social and economic resources such as education and gross domestic product per capita (Kim and Moody 1992).

Going on the belief that medical treatments create healthy populations, many countries such as Great Britain instituted national health care systems providing universal access to treatment. Doing so reversed the social gradient in the use of services, making it greatest among the lower-status groups. It did not reduce the gradient in health and survival (Angell 1993; Anonymous 1994; Hollingsworth 1981; MacIntyre 1997; Marmot, Kogevinas, and Elston 1987; Morris 1990; Wagstaff, Paci, and van Doorslaer 1991). Indeed, social-status mortality differentials are stable or growing in countries with national health care systems, just as in the United States (Pamuk 1985, 1988; Pappas et al. 1993). Stable or increasing economic inequality may be responsible (Kawachi and Kennedy 1997; Wilkinson 1986, 1992, 1997).

Surprisingly few studies in the United States question the health benefits of medical insurance, despite (or maybe owing to) the recurring debates about instituting universal coverage. We found a number of studies reporting positive effects of medical insurance on outcomes for specific groups most likely to benefit, such as pregnant women (e.g., Syverson et al. 1991) or appendicitis patients (e.g., Braveman et al. 1994). We found an impressive study showing that medical insurance increases the use of medical services by elderly Americans net of health status (Hurd and McGarry 1997). We found only one questioning whether medical insurance might generally improve health. Data from the National Medical Expenditure Survey show that Americans with private medical insurance are healthier than those with no medical insurance. However, those with publicly funded insurance are *un*healthier than the uninsured, which suggests a spurious association between health and insurance (Hahn and Flood 1995).

The few studies we found comparing mortality rates across categories of insurance also suggest a largely spurious association. One must read diligently and skeptically to see this, though. One study of Americans age 25 and older finds that adults with private insurance have about half the mortality rate of those with no medical insurance (Franks, Clancy, and Gold 1993). However, adjustment for age, sex, race, and income increases the fraction to 80 percent. More importantly, the study excludes individuals with publicly funded insurance (Medicare and Medicaid). A second study of Americans age 25 through 64 finds that those with Medicare or Medicaid insurance have twice the mortality rate of those with employer-provided insurance, and *1.6 times the mortality rate of the uninsured,* adjusting for age, sex, race, and income (Sorlie et al. 1994). A forthcoming study finds the highest mortality rates among persons with government-sponsored, means-tested health insurance (Medicaid for all adult age groups, and Medicare for persons under 65)(Rogers, Hummer, and Nam forthcoming, Chapter 8). Adjustment for baseline subjective health eliminates the association between mortality and type of insurance for persons 65 and older, and greatly attenuates the association for those under 65. The seeming benefits of medical insurance probably represent the effects on health of current and past employment, occupational standing, and wealth associated with different categories of insurance.

The citation counts of the first two studies described above suggest a possible market preference for findings implying a beneficial effect of medical insurance. The first one, suggesting a benefit, appeared in the August 1993 *Journal of the American Medical Association.* It was cited 48 times as of early 1998 (Institute for Scientific Information 1998). The second one, suggesting a spurious association, appeared in the November 1994 *Archives of Internal Medicine.* It was cited twice (Institute for Scientific Information 1998). That second study also reported the following: Persons with incomes below $10,000 per year have twice the mortality rate of those with incomes above $25,000 (Sorlie et al. 1994).

If medical insurance proves to yield measurable health benefits, those benefits may come mostly from the reduction of economic hardship. Medical insurance greatly reduces the likelihood of not having the money to buy medicine or medical services considered necessary. It also greatly reduces the likelihood of not having the money to pay bills and buy necessities such as food and clothes (Mirowsky and Ross forthcoming). Apparently, medical insurance protects the household budget from the voracious demands of the medical industry, thus reducing overall economic hardship. That protection may indirectly improve health.

Despite reviews occasionally raising the issue for decades, we found no recent study questioning and testing the general proposition that consumption of medical services accounts for social status differences in health. Thirty years ago an econometric study questioned the contribution of medical expenditures to differences in mortality rates across states (Auster, Leveson, and Sarachek 1969). It found an effect, but found much larger contributions of environmental factors such as levels of education and smoking. Twenty years ago a sociological study questioned the contribution of medical resources such as physicians, specialists, and hospital beds per 1,000 population to differences in mortality and decreases in mortality across Northern U.S. counties (Miller and Stokes 1978). It found no apparent beneficial effect of differences or increases in medical resources on mortality and infant mortality rates adjusting for factors such as education. One exception was the apparent benefit of increases in the number of nurses per 1,000 population. Studies directly testing the hypothesis that medical resources and services account for status differences in health seem curiously hard to find, but consistent in their results.

A decade ago Williams reviewed the literature on U.S. socioeconomic differentials in health, and again questioned medicine's role (Williams 1990). He noted the dearth of evidence given the importance of the issue. He also noted that, despite the absence of universal medical coverage in the U.S., the use of medical services now increases as social status decreases. Lower-status persons use more medical services because they have more health problems (Aday, Andersen, and Fleming 1980) and have more favorable attitudes about the medical system and visiting the doctor (Sharp, Ross, and Cockerham 1983). Clearly, differential access to medical care cannot explain the status differences in health and survival. Williams notes that variable quality of care might yet account for those differences. Some evidence exists that uninsured patients suffer higher rates of medical injuries in hospitals than do other patients (Burstin, Lipsitz, and Brennan 1992). They may suffer more iatrogenic disease in general. The use of preventive services also seems like it might account for some of the status differences in health. Education increases behavior aimed at catching and treating disease early (called "secondary prevention") (Coburn and Pope 1974; Ross and Wu 1995). Yet the benefits to overall health of uncovering and treating disease early are uncertain (e.g., Bailar and Smith 1986). Yearly check-ups have little effect (Canadian Task Force on the Periodic Health Examination 1988; U.S. Preventive Services Task Force 1989). Screening often entails some risk, such as exposure to small amounts of radiation (Bailar 1976). The risks and side effects of treatment often outweigh the benefits for low-level disease, which may usually get better if left untreated (Deyo 1998; Deyo et al. 1991; Epstein 1996; Johansson et al. 1997; Verrilli and Welch 1996; Wennberg et al. 1996). An alternative explanation seems worth considering. Perhaps, on the whole and on balance, medical treatment does not greatly benefit health.

Based on the indirect evidence, we think it is time to hypothesize that differences in the availability, amount, cost, kind, quality, or propriety of medical services account for little or none of the social status differences in health. We call this the ineffectual commodity hypothesis. It will be interesting to see how many more decades pass before research directly addressing the hypothesis becomes easy to find.

Resources Among the Disadvantaged

Additional resources improve health the most among those who have the least. It might seem that few would argue with this. However, social scientists frequently offer interpretations that assume the opposite. For example, a sociologist might explain the lower educational attainment of persons from low-status backgrounds by arguing that education produces smaller benefits for them. A social psychologist might explain the low sense of control over life among the poor or poorly educated by arguing that greater determination and self-direction benefits them less than others. When applied to physical and emotional health such arguments often have the ring of truth, but little or no validity on testing (Mirowsky and Ross 1990).

Two elementary principles embody the differential effects of additional resources: diminishing returns and resource substitution. The effect on health of an additional unit of a resource tends to diminish with the amount of that resource already available. The effect on health of a deficit in one resource tends to diminish with the amount of other resources available.

Diminishing Effect of Greater Income Health increases with economic prosperity across countries, states, counties, and individuals (Auster, Leveson, and Sarachek 1969; Adler et al. 1994; Epelbaum 1990; Miller and Stokes 1978; Mirowsky and Hu 1996; Rogers, Hummer, and Nam forthcoming). Graphs of the association often show a steep grade in health going from the least prosperous cases to the moderately prosperous ones near the median, but little or no improvements beyond that level. For example, international data show a rise in life expectancy at birth from about 45 years among countries with a gross domestic product (GDP) per capita under $200 to about 67 years for countries with ten times that amount, or $2,000 per capita (U.S. Bureau of the Census 1997, tables 1336 and 1347). It increases to about 77 years for countries with ten times that amount, or $20,000 per capita. Thus life expectancy at birth goes up about 22 years with the first order-of-magnitude increase in wealth but only about ten years with the second order-of-magnitude increase. Among prosperous industrialized countries, such as those in the Organization for Economic Cooperation and Development (OECD), measures of income or wealth per capita have little or no correlation with age adjusted mortality rates, infant mortality rates, or life expectancies at birth (Duleep 1995; Wilkinson 1997). Individual level data show diminishing effects too. For example, rates of physical impairment and mortality correlate negatively with household income below the 30th percentile (around $25,000) but not above it (Mirowsky and Hu 1996; Rogers, Hummer, and Nam forthcoming).

The diminishing effects on health of greater income and wealth at the high end do not necessarily imply diminishing effects of other quantitative resources. In particular, we find no evidence that additional years of education have diminishing effects. Distributions of income and wealth may be distinct in that their range and variance can grow without bound. On the other hand, years of education may yet rise to a range where diminishing incremental effects become detectable.

Resource Substitution Resources other than income and wealth also protect and promote health. Education, employment, and sense of control act as health-enhancing resources too, as discussed previously. The effect of one resource often depends on the presence or amount of another. Theoretically, the interaction between resources can take two mutually exclusive forms. *Resource substitution* exists when having (more of) one resource makes the lack of another less damaging. *Resource multiplication* exists when having (more of) one resource makes the presence of another more beneficial. Sociologists often assume resource multiplication, perhaps generalizing from principles of stratification. However, health research more commonly finds resource substitution. For example, stratification research finds that men's advantage over women means, among other things, that education increases earnings more for men than for women (resource multiplication). In contrast, health research finds that education is more important to women's health than to men's, in part because women earn less than men (resource substitution)(Glenn and Weaver 1981; Kessler 1982; Kessler and McRae 1982; Reynolds and Ross 1998; Ross and Huber 1985; Ross and Van Willigen 1997). We do not claim that resource substitution acts as a universal principle in the production of health. Researchers should question and test the interactions between pairs of resources to see which pattern fits. Instances may exist of resource multiplication. However, the interactions we find typically conform to the pattern of resource substitution.

Perhaps the most important resource substitution occurs between education and economic status. Education reduces the impact of low income on physical impairment (Mirowsky and Hu 1996). One reason is that people with higher levels of education are more successful at avoiding economic strain at any given level of income (Mirowsky and Hu 1996; Ross and Huber 1985). These interactions exist even after corrections for boundary effects. A poorly educated person needs more money to fend off economic hardship than does a well-educated person, and that hardship has a more detrimental effect on the poorly educated. Education provides skills, information, a sense of mastery, and well-educated friends that help a person deal with the stresses of life, including a low income. People who have not finished high school or have barely finished high school are doubly disadvantaged because their low education translates into low earnings, and it increases the difficulties of coping with low earnings. Thus, education is particularly important for the health status of those in the lower end of the income distribution.

International data also suggest resource substitution between education and economic status. For example, the effect on life expectancy of logged GNP per capita depends on the literacy rate (Mirowsky and Hu 1996). The slope rises steeply for countries with less than 65 percent literacy, going from 45 to 65 years over a 20-fold increase in per capita GNP. The slope rises more gently for countries with greater than 65 percent literacy, rising from 65 to 75 years over a 50-fold

increase in per capita GNP. Countries with low GNP per capita but high literacy tend to have life expectancies above 65 years. Sri Lanka, with a GNP of $500 per capita but literacy of 87.1 percent, has a life expectancy at birth of 71.5 years. Whether on the national level or the individual, education apparently acts as an alternative to income.

Education's beneficial effects on health may be somewhat greater for disadvantaged groups in general. John Reynolds and Catherine Ross (1998) find that women, people whose fathers held low-status jobs, and people who are not employed full time benefit more from education than others. Being from lower social status origins, not participating full time in the paid economy, and being female do not render education less consequential to health. Instead, education may be especially important to the well-being of people with fewer alternative resources.

Resource substitution reflects the basic reality that most sickness and suffering is concentrated at the lower end of the distribution of social status. Since the components of social status are causally related, low education tends to go with unemployment, unfulfilling and overly demanding work, and lower earnings. Improvements in status and resources produce the largest health payoff among relatively disadvantaged groups, for whom such improvements are least common.

NEW DIRECTIONS FOR RESEARCH ON HEALTH AND SOCIAL STATUS

Life Course Social Status and Cumulative Health

Higher childhood social status predicts better health and lower mortality rates throughout adulthood (Elo and Preston 1992; Lynch, Kaplan, and Salonen 1997; Mare 1990; Mirowsky and Ross 1998; Reynolds and Ross 1998). To a large extent the social status of one's childhood home affects later adulthood health through educational attainment and its consequences (Mare 1990; Lynch, Kaplan, and Salonen 1997; Mirowsky and Ross 1998; Reynolds and Ross 1998). However, several studies find other effects of parental status too. People who had parents on welfare, parents with little education, or who do not know their parents' education have significantly worse health even adjusting for educational attainment and adulthood social status (Reynolds and Ross 1998). Parental education and occupational status in one's childhood affect adulthood health lifestyle (e.g., smoking, exercise, diet) net of educational attainment and adulthood status, as well as through them (Lynch,

Kaplan, and Salonen 1997; Mirowsky and Ross 1998). Some effects of childhood status on later health may result when childhood exposures harm biological development. For example, poor respiratory function shows stability from childhood on, with childhood problems predictable from atmospheric pollution (Wadsworth 1997). Finally, poverty seems to have its worst effects on health when episodes are prolonged and repeated (Brooks-Gunn 1997; Wadsworth 1997). Thus poverty throughout one's life may have effects more damaging than either recent or past poverty alone.

Some research suggests that health advantages or disadvantages increase over the life course (Dannefer 1987; O'Rand 1996). According to the hypothesis, advantages accumulate and compound, producing more heterogeneity and inequality in older ages than in younger. The general hypothesis receives support in research on careers and labor markets (Kerckhoff 1993) and income (Crystal and Shea 1990). Catherine Ross and Chia-Ling Wu (1996) test the hypothesis of cumulative advantage in health, using two large national samples. They find that the gap in self-reported health, in physical functioning, and in physical well-being between people with high and low educational attainment *increases* with age. Health advantages of income also increase with age, but household income does not explain all of education's enlarging effect. Mirowsky and Hu (1996) find compounding reciprocal effects between economic hardship and physical impairment that concentrate the two together over time. Such cumulative compounding may enlarge the effects of status origins and status attainment over time. House and colleagues also find that the socioeconomic gap in health diverges throughout most of life, but their data show a convergence in the oldest old (House et al. 1994). James House and colleagues argue that health eventually converges across social statuses because people inevitably weaken and die in old age regardless of status. The apparent convergence could represent selection. Death, disability, and demoralization might keep the sickest old persons out of the sample. If they disproportionately come from the lowest status groups then those groups will appear healthier then they really are. Whatever happens in old age, the studies all indicate one thing. Relatively small social status differences in health established in childhood and adolescence accumulate and grow throughout most of adulthood.

REFERENCES

ABBOTT, ROBERT D., YIN YIN, DWAYNE M. REED, and KATSUHILO YANO. 1986. "Risk of Stroke in Male Cigarette Smokers." *The New England Journal of Medicine* 315:717–20.

ADAY, LuANN, RONALD ANDERSEN, and GRETCHEN V. FLEMING. 1980. *Health Care in the U.S. Equitable for Whom?* Beverly Hills, CA: Sage.

ADLER, NANCY, THOMAS BOYCE, MARGARET CHESNEY, SHELDON COHEN, SUSAN FOLKMAN, ROBERT KAHN, and LEONARD SYME. 1994. "Socioeconomic Status and Health: The Challenge of the Gradient." *American Psychologist* 49(1):15–24.

ADLER, NANCY, THOMAS BOYCE, MARGARET CHESNEY, SUSAN FOLKMAN, and LEONARD SYME. 1993. "Socioeconomic Inequalities in Health: No Easy Solution." *Journal of the American Medical Association* 269(24): 3140–45.

ANESHENSEL, CAROL S., RALPH R. FRERICHS, and GEORGE J. HUBA. 1984. "Depression and Physical Illness: A Multiwave, Nonrecursive Causal Model." *Journal of Health and Social Behavior* 25: 350–71.

ANGELL, MARCIA. 1993. "Privilege and Health: What Is The Connection?" *The New England Journal of Medicine* 329:126–27.

ANONYMOUS. 1994. "The Unhealthy Poor." *The Economist* June 4th:55–56.

AUSTER, RICHARD, IRVING LEVESON, and DEBORAH SARACHEK. 1969. "The Production of Health: An Exploratory Study." *Journal of Human Resources* IV(4):411–36.

BAILAR, JOHN C. 1976. "Mammography: A Contrary View." *Annals of Internal Medicine* 84: 77–84.

BAILAR, JOHN C., and ELAINE M. SMITH. 1986. "Progress Against Cancer?" *New England Journal of Medicine* May 8: 1226–32.

BERKMAN, LISA F., and LESTER BRESLOW. 1983. *Health and Ways of Living: The Alameda County Study.* New York: Oxford University Press.

BERLIN, JESSE A., and GRAHAM A. COLDITZ. 1990. "A Meta-Analysis of Physical Activity in the Prevention of Coronary Heart Disease." *American Journal of Epidemiology* 132:612–28.

BIRD, CHLOE E., and ALLEN M. FREMONT. 1991. "Gender, Time Use, and Health." *Journal of Health and Social Behavior* 32:114–29.

BRAVEMAN, P., V.M. SCHAAF, S. EGERTER, T. BENNETT, and W. SCHECTER. 1994. "Insurance-Related Differences in the Risk of Ruptured Appendix." *New England Journal of Medicine.* 331(7):444–49.

BRENNER, M. HARVEY. 1971. "Economic Changes and Heart Disease Mortality." *American Journal of Public Health* 59:1154–68.

BRENNER, STEN-OLAF, and LENNARD LEVI. 1987. "Long-Term Unemployment Among Women in Sweden." *Social Science and Medicine* 25(2): 153–61.

Brooks-Gunn, J., and G.E. Duncan. 1997. "The Effects of Poverty on Children." *Future of Children* 7(2):55–71.

Bruce, Martha Livingston, and Philip J. Leaf. 1989. "Psychiatric Disorders and 15-Month Mortality in a Community Sample of Older Adults." *American Journal of Public Health* 79(6): 727–30.

Brunner, Eric. 1997. "Socioeconomic Determinants of Health: Stress and the Biology of Inequality." *British Journal of Medicine* 314:1472–82.

Burstin, H.R., S.R. Lipsitz, and T.A. Brennan. 1992. "Socioeconomic Status and Risk for Substandard Medical Care." *Journal of the American Medical Association* 268(17): 2383–87.

Cairns, John. 1985. "The Treatment of Diseases and the War Against Cancer." *Scientific American* 253(3): 51–59.

Canadian Task Force on the Periodic Health Examination. 1988. "The Periodic Health Examination." *Canadian Medical Association Journal* 138: 617–26.

Carstairs, Vera, and Russell Morris. 1989. "Deprivation and Mortality: An Alternative to Social Class?" *Community Medicine* 11:210–19.

Caspersen, Carl J., Bennie P.M. Bloemberg, Wim H.M. Saris, Robert K. Merritt, and Daan Kromhout. 1992. "The Prevalence of Selected Physical Activities and Their Relation With Coronary Heart Disease Risk Factors in Elderly Men: The Zutphen Study, 1985." *American Journal of Epidemiology* 133:1078–92.

Catalano, Ralph, and David Dooley. 1983. "Health Effects of Economic Instability: A Test of Economic Stress Hypothesis." *Journal of Health and Social Behavior* 24(March): 46–60.

Citro, Constance F., and Robert T. Michael, eds. 1995. *Measuring Poverty: A New Approach.* Washington, D.C.: National Academy Press.

Coburn, David, and Clyde R. Pope. 1974. "Socioeconomic Status and Preventive Health Behavior." *Journal of Health and Social Behavior* 15: 67–78.

Conger, Rand D., and Glen H. Elder. 1994. *Families in Troubled Times.* New York: Aldine de Gruyter.

Cooper, M. Lynne, Marcia Russell, and Michael R. Frone 1990. "Work Stress and Alcohol Effects: A Test of Stress-Induced Drinking." *Journal of Health and Social Behavior.* 31:260–76.

Crawford, Robert. 1986. "Individual Responsibility and Health Politics." In *The Sociology of Health and Illness,* 2d ed., ed. P. Conrad and R. Kern. New York: St. Martin's, pp. 369–77.

Crystal, Stephen, and Denis Shea. 1990. "Cumulative Advantage, Cumulative Disadvantage, and Inequality among Elderly People." *The Gerontologist* 10(4): 437–443.

Dannefer, Dale. 1987. "Aging as Intracohort Differentiation: Accentuation, the Matthew Effect, and the Life Course." *Sociological Forum* 2(2): 211–37.

Darrow, Sherri L., Marcia Russell, M. Lynne Cooper, Pamela Mudar, and Michael R. Frone. 1992. "Sociodemographic Correlates of Alcohol Consumption Among African-American and White Women." *Women and Health* 18: 35–51.

Deyo, Richard A. 1998. "Low-Back Pain." *Scientific American* 279(2): 48–53.

Deyo, Richard A., Daniel Cherkin, Douglas Conrad, and Ernest Volinn. 1991. "Cost, Controversy, Crisis: Low Back Pain and the Health of the Public." *Annual Review of Public Health* 12:141–56.

Dohrenwend, Bruce P., and Barbara S. Dohrenwend. 1969. *Social Status and Psychological Disorder: A Causal Inquiry.* New York: Wiley.

Dooley, David, Ralph Catalano, and Georgeanna Wilson. 1994. "Depression and Unemployment: Panel Findings From the Epidemiological Catchment Area Study." *American Journal of Community Psychology* 22(6): 745–765.

Doornbos, G., and D. Kromhout. 1990. "Educational Level and Mortality in a 32-Year Follow-Up Study of 18-Year-Old Men in the Netherlands." *International Journal of Epidemiology* 19: 374–79.

Downey, Geraldine, and Phyllis Moen. 1987. "Personal Efficacy, Income, and Family Transitions: A Longitudinal Study of Women Heading Households." *Journal of Health and Social Behavior* 28: 320–33.

Duleep, Harriet Orcutt. 1995. "Mortality and Income Inequality Among Economically Developed Countries." *Social Security Bulletin* 58(2): 34–50.

Duncan, Greg, Jeanne Brooks-Gunn, and Pamela Klebanov. 1994. "Economic Deprivation and Early Childhood Development." *Child Development* 65: 296–318.

Duncan, John J., Neil F. Gordon, and Chris B. Scott. 1991. "Women Walking for Health and Fitness." *Journal of the American Medical Association* 266: 3295–99.

Dunifon, Rachel, and Greg J. Duncan. 1998. "Long-Run Effects of Motivation on Labor Market Success." *Social Psychology Quarterly* 61:33–48.

Elder, Glen H., and Jeffrey K. Liker. 1982. "Hard Times in Women's Lives: Historical Influences Across Forty Years." *American Journal of Sociology* 88: 241–69.

Elo, Irma T., and Samuel H. Preston. 1992. "Effects of Early-Life Conditions on Adults' Mortality: A Review." *Population Index* 58(2): 186–212.

Elo, Irma T., and Samuel H. Preston. 1996. "Educational Differentials in Mortality: United States, 1979–85." *Social Science and Medicine* 42(1): 47–57.

Epelbaum, Michael. 1990. "Sociomonetary Patterns and Specifications." *Social Science Research* 19:32–47.

Epstein, A.M. 1996. "Use of Diagnostic Tests and Therapeutic Procedures in a Changing Health Care Environment." *Journal of the American Medical Association* 275:1197–98.

Falk, Anders, Bertil S. Hanson, Sven-Olaf Isacsson, Per-Olaf Ostergren. 1992. "Job Strain and Mortality in Elderly Men: Social Network, Support, and Influence as Buffers." *American Journal of Public Health* 82(8):1136–39.

Feldman, Jacob J., Diane M. Makuc, Joel C. Kleinman, and Joan Cornoni-Huntley. 1989. "National Trends in Educational Differentials in Mortality" *American Journal of Epidemiology* 129: 919–33.

FENNELL, MARY L., MIRIAM B. RODIN, and GLENDA K. KANTOR. "Problems in the Work Setting, Drinking, and Reasons for Drinking." *Social Forces* 1981 60(1):114–32.

FORD, EARL S., ROBERT K. MERRITT, GREGORY W. HEATH, KENNETH E. POWELL, RICHARD A. WASHBURN, ANDREA KRISKA, and GWENDOLYN HAILE. 1991. "Physical Activity Behaviors in Lower and Higher Socioeconomic Status Populations." *American Journal of Epidemiology* 133: 1246–55.

FOX, A.J., P.O. GOLDBLATT, and D.R. JONES. 1985. "Social Class Mortality Differentials: Artefact, Selection, or Life Circumstances?" *Journal of Epidemiology and Community Health* 39:1–8.

FRANKS, P., C.M. CLANCY, and M.R. GOLD. 1993. "Health Insurance and Mortality: Evidence From a National Cohort." *Journal of the American Medical Association* 270(6):737–41.

FRESE, MICHAEL, and GISELA MOHR. 1987. "Prolonged Unemployment and Depression in Older Workers: A Longitudinal Study of Intervening Variables." *Social Science and Medicine* 25(2):173–78.

GAZIANO, J. MICHAEL, JULIE E. BURRING, JAN L. BRESLOW, SAMUEL Z. GOLDHABER, BERNARD ROSNER, MARTIN VANDENBURGH, WALTER WILLETT, and CHARLES H. HENNEKENS. 1993. "Moderate Alcohol Intake, Increased Levels of High-Density Lipoprotein and Its Subfractions, and Decreased Risk of Myocardial Infarction." *The New England Journal of Medicine* 329: 1829–34.

GILL, JASWINDER S., ALEXANDER V. ZEZULKA, MARTIN J. SHIPLEY, SURINDER K. GILL, and D. GARETH BEEVERS. 1986. "Stroke and Alcohol Consumption." *The New England Journal of Medicine* 315:1041–46.

GLENN, NORVAL D., and CHARLES N. WEAVER. 1981. "Education's Effects on Psychological Well-Being." *Public Opinion Quarterly* 45: 22–39.

GORE, SUSAN S., and THOMAS W. MANGIONE. 1983. "Social Roles, Sex Roles, and Psychological Distress." *Journal of Health and Social Behavior* 24:300–312.

GORTMAKER, STEVEN L. 1979. "Poverty and Infant Mortality in the United States." *American Sociological Review* 44(2): 280–97.

GOVE, WALTER R., and MICHAEL R. GEERKEN. 1977. "The Effect of Children and Employment on the Mental Health of Married Men and Women." *Social Forces* 56:66–76.

GOVE, WALTER R., and JEANNETTE F. TUDOR. 1973. "Adult Sex Roles and Mental Illness." *American Journal of Sociology* 78 (4): 812–35.

GURALNIK, JACK M., and GEORGE A. KAPLAN. 1989. "Predictors of Healthy Aging: Prospective Evidence From the Alameda County Study." *American Journal of Public Health* 79:703–708.

GURALNIK, JACK M., KENNETH C. LAND, GERDA G. FILLENBAUM, and LAUREN G. BRANCH. 1993. "Educational Status and Active Life Expectancy Among Older

Blacks and Whites." *New England Journal of Medicine* 329:110–16.

GUTZWILLER, FELIZ, CARLO LA VECCHIA, FABIO LEVI, EVA NEGRI, and VINCENT WIETLISBACH. 1989. "Education, Disease Prevalence and Health Service Utilization in the Swiss National Health Survey" *Preventive Medicine* 18: 452–59.

HAHN, BETH, and ANN B. FLOOD. 1995. "No Insurance, Public Insurance, and Private Insurance—Do These Options Contribute to Differences in General Health?" *Journal of Health Care for the Poor and Underserved* 691:41–59.

HAYES, DIANE, and CATHERINE E. ROSS. 1986. "Body and Mind: The Effect of Exercise, Overweight, and Physical Health on Psychological Well-Being." *Journal of Health and Social Behavior* 27(4): 3874–3900.

HELMERT U., B. HERMAN, K.-H. JOECKEL, E. GREISER, and J. MADANS. 1989. "Social Class and Risk Factors for Coronary Heart Disease in the Federal Republic of Germany: Results of the Baseline Survey of the German Cardiovascular Prevention Study." *Journal of Epidemiology and Community Health* 43:37–42.

HEROLD, JOAN, and INGRID WALDRON. 1985. "Part-Time Employment and Women's Health." *Journal of Occupational Medicine* 27(6):405–12.

HIBBARD, JUDITH H., and CLYDE R. POPE. 1987. "Employment Characteristics and Health Status Among Men and Women." *Women and Health* 12:85–102.

HOUSE, JAMES S., JAMES M. LEPKOWSKI, ANN M. KINNEY, RICHARD P. MERO, RONALD C. KESSLER, and A. REGULA HERZOG. 1994. "The Social Stratification of Aging and Health" *Journal of Health and Social Behavior* 35: 213–234.

HOLLINGSWORTH, J. ROGERS. 1981. "Inequality in Levels of Health in England and Wales, 1971–1981." *Journal of Health and Social Behavior* 22: 268–83.

HOUSE, JAMES S., VICTOR STRECHER, HELEN L. METZNER, and CYNTHIA A. ROBBINS. 1986. "Occupational Stress and Health Among Men and Women in the Tecumseh Community Health Study." *Journal of Health and Social Behavior* 27:62–77.

HURD, MICHAEL D., and KATHLEEN MCGARRY. 1997. "Medical Insurance and the Use of Health Care Services by the Elderly." *Journal of Health Economics* 16(2): 129–54.

INSTITUTE FOR SCIENTIFIC INFORMATION. 1998. "ISI Citation Databases: 1992 to Present." Retrieved July 24, 1998 (http://cite.ohiolink.edu/isi.html).

JACOBSEN, BJARNE K., and DAG S. THELLE. 1988. "Risk Factors for Coronary Heart Disease and Level of Education." *American Journal of Epidemiology* 127(5): 923–32.

JENNINGS, SUSAN, CHERYL MAZAIK, and SONJA MCKINLAY. 1984. "Women and Work: An Investigation of the Association Between Health and Employment Status in Middle-Aged Women." *Social Science and Medicine* 19(4): 423–31.

JOHANSSON, JAN-ERIK, LARS HOLMBERG, SARA JOHANSSON, REINHOLD BERGSTRÖM, and HANS-OLOVO

ADAMI. 1997. "Fifteen-Year Survival in Prostate Cancer: A Prospective, Population-Based Study in Sweden." *Journal of the American Medical Association* 277(6): 467–71.

KAISER FOUNDATION HEALTH PLAN. 1976. "Health Examinations." *Planning for Health* 19: 2–3.

KAPLAN, GEORGE A., MARY N. HAAN, and S. LEONARD SYME. 1987. "Socioeconomic Status and Health." *American Journal of Preventive Medicine* 3(supp.): 125–29.

KARASEK, ROBERT A., and TORES THEORELL. 1990. *Healthy Work.* New York: Basic Books.

KASL, STANISLAV V., and SIDNEY COBB. 1982. "Variability of Stress Effects Among Men Experiencing Job Loss." In *Handbook of Stress,* ed. L. Goldberger and S. Breznitz. New York: Free Press, pp. 445–65.

KAWACHI, ICHIRO, and BRUCE P. KENNEDY. 1997. "Socioeconomic Determinants of Health: Health and Social Cohesion: Why Care About Income Inequality?" *British Journal of Medicine* 314(5):1037–40.

KERCKHOFF, ALAN C. 1993. *Diverging Pathways: Social Structure and Career Deflections.* New York: Cambridge University Press.

KESSLER, RONALD C. 1982. "A Disaggregation of the Relationship Between Socioeconomic Status and Psychological Distress." *American Sociological Review* 47:752–64.

KESSLER, RONALD C., and JAMES A. MCRAE. 1982. "The Effect of Wives' Employment on the Mental Health of Married Men and Women." *American Sociological Review* 47: 216–27.

KESSLER, RONALD C., and PAUL D. CLEARY. 1980. "Social Class and Psychological Distress." *American Sociological Review* 45: 463–78.

KESSLER, RONALD C., JAMES S. HOUSE, and J. BLAKE TURNER. 1987. "Unemployment and Health in a Community Sample." *Journal of Health and Social Behavior* 28:51–59.

KIM, K.K., and P.M. MOODY. 1992. "More Resources, Better Health: A Cross-National Perspective." *Social Science and Medicine* 34(8): 837–42.

KITAGAWA, EVELYN M., and PHILIP M. HAUSER. 1973. *Differential Mortality in the United States: A Study in Socioeconomic Epidemiology.* Cambridge, MA: Harvard University Press.

KNOWLES, JOHN H. 1977. "The Responsibility of the Individual." In *Doing Better and Feeling Worse: Health in the U.S.,* ed. J.H. Knowles. New York: W.W. Norton, pp. 57–80.

KOHN, MELVIN. 1976. "Occupational Structure and Alienation." *American Journal of Sociology* 82:111–30.

KOHN, MELVIN, and CARMI SCHOOLER. 1982. "Job Conditions and Personality: A Longitudinal Assessment of Their Reciprocal Effects." *American Journal of Sociology* 87:1257–86.

KOHN, MELVIN, and KAZIMIERZ M. SLOMCZYNSKI. 1990. *Social Structure and Self-Direction: A Comparative Analysis of the United States and Poland.* Cambridge, MA.: Blackwell.

LAROCCO, JAMES M., JAMES S. HOUSE, and JOHN R.P. FRENCH. 1980. "Social Support, Occupational Stress, and Health." *Journal of Health and Social Behavior* 3: 202–18.

LEIGH, J. PAUL. 1983. "Direct and Indirect Effects of Education on Health." *Social Science and Medicine* 17: 227–34.

LEON, ARTHUR S., JOHN CONNETT, DAVID R. JACOBS, and RAINER RAURAMAA. 1987. "Leisure-Time Physical Activity Levels and Risk of Coronary Heart Disease and Death: The Multiple Risk Factor Intervention Trial." *Journal of the American Medical Association* 258: 2388–95.

LERNER, DANIEL J., SOL LEVINE, SUE MALSPEIS, and RALPH B. D'AGOSTINO. 1994. "Job Strain and Health-Related Quality of Life in a National Sample." *American Journal of Public Health* 84(10): 1580–85.

LEWIN-EPSTEIN, NOAH. 1986. "Employment and Ill-Health Among Women in Israel." *Social Science and Medicine* 23(11): 1171–79.

LIEM, RAMSAY, and JOAN H. LIEM. 1988. "Psychological Effects of Unemployment on Workers and Their Families." *Journal of Social Issues* 44(4): 87–105.

LINK, BRUCE G., BRUCE P. DOHRENWEND, and ANDREW E. SKODOL. 1986. "Socioeconomic Status and Schizophrenia: Noisome Occupational Characteristics as a Risk Factor." *American Sociological Review* 51(April): 242–58.

LINK, BRUCE G., MARY CLARE LENNON, and BRUCE P. DOHRENWEND. 1993. "Socioeconomic Status and Depression: The Role of Occupations Involving Direction, Control, and Planning." *American Journal of Sociology* 98: 1351–87.

LINN, MARGARET W., RICHARD SANDIFER, and SHAYNA STEIN. 1985. "Effects of Unemployment on Mental and Physical Health." *American Journal of Public Health* 75:502–506.

LIPWORTH, L., T. ABELIN, and R.R. CONNELLY. 1970. "Socioeconomic Factors in the Prognosis of Cancer Patients." *Journal of Chronic Disease* 23:105–16.

LIU, KIANG, LUCILIA B. CEDRES, JEREMIAH STAMLER, ALAN DYER, ROSE STAMLER, SERAFIN NANAS, DAVID M. BERKSON, PAUL OGLESBY, MARK LEPPER, HOWARD A. LINDBERG, JOHN MARQUAR, ELIZABETH STEVENS, JAMES A. SCHOENBERGER, RICHARD B. SHEKELLE, PATRICIA COLLETTE, SUE SHEKELLE, and DAN GARDSIDE. 1982. "Relationship of Education to Major Risk Factors and Death From Coronary Heart Disease, Cardiovascular Diseases, and All Causes." *Circulation* 66:1308–14.

LOSCOCCO, KARYN A., and GLENNA SPITZE. 1990. "Working Conditions, Social Support, and the Well-Being of Female and Male Factory Workers." *Journal of Health and Social Behavior* 31:313–27.

LYNCH, J.W., G.A. KAPLAN, and J.T. SALONEN. 1997. "Why Do Poor People Behave Poorly? Variation in Adult Health Behaviors and Psychological Characteristics by Stages of the Socioeconomic Lifecourse." *Social Science and Medicine* 44(6):809–19.

MacIntyre, Sally. 1997. "The Black Report and Beyond: What Are the Issues?" *Social Science and Medicine* 44(6): 723–45.

Magnus, K., A. Matroos, and J. Strackee. 1979. "Walking, Cycling, or Gardening, With or Without Seasonal Interruptions, in Relation to Acute Coronary Events." *American Journal of Epidemiology* 110: 724–33.

Marcus, Alfred C., Teresa E. Seeman, and Carol W. Telesky. 1983. "Sex Differences in Reports of Illness and Disability: A Further Test of the Fixed Role Hypothesis." *Social Science and Medicine* 17(15): 993–1002.

Mare, Robert D. 1990. "Socioeconomic Careers and Differential Mortality Among Older Men in the United States." In *Measurement and Analysis of Mortality: New Approaches,* ed. J. Vallin, S. D'Souza, and A. Palloni. Oxford, England: Clarendon Press, pp. 362–87.

Marmot, Michael, M. Kogevinas, and M.A. Elston. 1987. "Social/Economic Status and Disease." *Annual Review of Public Health* 8:111–35.

Matthews, Karen A., Sheryl F. Kelsey, Elaine N. Meilahn, Lewis H. Kuller, and Rena R. Wing. 1989. "Educational Attainment and Behavioral and Biological Risk Factors for Coronary Heart Disease in Middle-Aged Women." *American Journal of Epidemiology* 129:1132–44.

McKinlay, John, and Sonja McKinlay. 1977. "The Questionable Contribution of Medical Measures to the Decline of Mortality in the Twentieth Century." *Milbank Memorial Fund Quarterly* 55:405–28.

Mechanic, David, and Stephen Hansell. 1987. "Adolescent Competence, Psychological Well-Being and Self-Assessed Physical Health." *Journal of Health and Social Behavior* 28(4): 364–74.

Menaghan, Elizabeth G., and Esther S. Merves. 1984. "Coping With Occupational Problems: The Limits of Individual Efforts." *Journal of Health and Social Behavior* 25:406–23.

Midanik, Lorraine T., Arthur L. Klatsky, and Mary Anne Armstrong. 1990. "Changes in Drinking Behavior: Demographic, Psychosocial, and Biomedical Factors." *International Journal of the Addictions* 25: 599–619.

Millar, Wayne J., and Donald T. Wigle. 1986. "Socioeconomic Disparities in Risk Factors for Cardiovascular Disease." *Canadian Medical Association Journal* 134:127–32.

Miller, Michael K., and C. Shannon Stokes. 1978. "Health Status, Health Resources, and Consolidated Structural Parameters: Implications for Public Health Care Policy." *Journal of Health and Social Behavior* 19:263–79.

Mirowsky, John. Forthcoming. "Analyzing Associations Between Circumstances and Mental Health." In *The Handbook of the Sociology of Mental Health,* ed. C.S. Aneshensel and J. Phelan. New York: Plenum.

Mirowsky, John, and Catherine E. Ross. 1983. "Paranoia and the Structure of Powerlessness." *American Sociological Review* 48: 228–39.

Mirowsky, John, and Catherine E. Ross. 1984. "Mexican Culture and Its Emotional Contradictions." *Journal of Health and Social Behavior* 25: 2–13.

Mirowsky, John, and Catherine E. Ross. 1989. *Social Causes of Psychological Distress.* New York: Aldine de Gruyter.

Mirowsky, John, and Catherine E. Ross. 1990. "The Consolation-Prize Theory of Alienation." *American Journal of Sociology* 95(6):1505–35.

Mirowsky, John, and Catherine E. Ross. 1996. "Fundamental Analysis in Research on Well-Being: Distress and the Sense of Control." *The Gerontologist* 36:584–94.

Mirowsky, John, and Catherine E. Ross. 1998. "Education, Personal Control, Lifestyle and Health: A Human Capital Hypothesis." *Research on Aging* 20(4): 415–49.

Mirowsky, John, and Catherine E. Ross. Forthcoming. "Economic Hardship Across the Life Course." *American Sociological Review.*

Mirowsky, John, and Paul Nongzhuang Hu. 1996. "Physical Impairment and the Diminishing Effects of Income." *Social Forces* 74(3):1073–96.

Moen, Phyllis. 1983. "Unemployment, Public Policy, and Families: Forecasts for the 1980's." *Journal of Marriage and the Family* (November): 751–60.

Moore, David E., and Mark D. Hayward. 1990. "Occupational Careers and Mortality of Elderly Men." *Demography* 27: 31–53.

Morris, J.N. 1990. "Inequalities in Health: Ten Years and Little Further On." *The Lancet* 336: 491–93.

Nathanson, Constance A. 1980. "Social Roles and Health Status Among Women: The Significance of Employment." *Social Science and Medicine* 14A: 463–71.

National Center for Health Statistics (NCHS). 1989. *Advance Report of Final Mortality Statistics, 1987.* Hyattsville, MD: Public Health Service.

National Center for Health Statistics (NCHS). 1992. *Advance Report of Final Mortality Statistics, 1989.* Hyattsville, MD: Public Health Service.

Noh, Samuel, and R. Jay Turner. 1987. "Living With Psychiatric Patients: Implications for the Mental Health of Family Members." *Social Science and Medicine* 25(3): 263–71.

O'Rand, Angela M. 1996. "The Precious and the Precocious: Understanding Cumulative Disadvantage and Cumulative Advantage Over the Life Course." *The Gerontologist* 36: 230–38.

Paffenbarger, Ralph S., Robert T. Hyde, Alvin L. Wing, I-Min Lee, Dexter L. Jung, and James B. Kampert. 1993. "The Association of Changes in Physical Activity Level and Other Lifestyle Characteristics with Mortality Among Men." *New England Journal of Medicine* 328:538–45.

Pamuk, E. 1985. "Social Class Inequality in Mortality From 1921–1972 in England and Wales." *Population Studies* 39:17–31.

PAMUK, E. 1988. "Social Class Inequality in Infant Mortality in England and Wales, 1921–1980." *European Journal of Population* 4:1–21.

PAPPAS, GREGORY, SUSAN QUEEN, WILBUR HADDEN, and GAIL FISHER. 1993. "The Increasing Disparity in Mortality Between Socioeconomic Groups in the United States, 1960 and 1986." *New England Journal of Medicine* 329:103–109.

PASSANNANTE, MARIAN R., and CONSTANCE A. NATHANSON. 1985. "Female Labor Force Participation and Female Mortality in Wisconsin, 1974–1978." *Social Science and Medicine* 21:655–65.

PEARLIN, LEONARD I. 1989. "The Sociological Study of Stress." *Journal of Health and Social Behavior* 30: 241–56.

PEARLIN, LEONARD I., and JOYCE M. JOHNSON. 1977. "Marital Status, Life Strains, and Depression." *American Sociological Review* 42:704–15.

PEARLIN, LEONARD I., MORTON A. LIEBERMAN, ELIZABETH G. MENAGHAN, and JOSEPH T. MULLAN. 1981. "The Stress Process." *Journal of Health and Social Behavior* 22: 337–56.

POWER, C., O. MANOR, A.J. FOX, and K. FOGELMAN. 1990. "Health in Childhood and Social Inequalities in Health in Young Adults." *Journal of the Royal Statistical Society* 153:17–28.

PRESTON, SAMUEL H. 1984. "Children and the Elderly in the United States." *Scientific American* 251: 44–49.

REYNOLDS, JOHN R. 1997. "The Effects of Industrial Employment Conditions on Job-Related Distress." *Journal of Health and Social Behavior* 38:105–16.

REYNOLDS, JOHN R., and CATHERINE E. ROSS. 1998. "Social Stratification and Health: Education's Benefit Beyond Economic Status and Social Origins." *Social Problems* 45:221–47.

RODIN, JUDITH, and CHRISTINE TIMKO. 1992. "Sense of Control, Aging, Health." In *Aging, Health, and Behavior,* ed. M.G. Ory, R.P. Abeles, and P.D. Lipman. Newbury Park, CA: Sage, pp. 207–36.

ROGERS, RICHARD G., and EVE POWELL-GRINER. 1991. "Life Expectancies of Cigarette Smokers and Nonsmokers in the United States." *Social Science and Medicine* 32:1151–59.

ROGERS, RICHARD G., ROBERT A. HUMMER, and CHARLES B. NAM. Forthcoming. *Living and Dying in the U.S.A.: Behavioral, Health, and Social Forces of Adult Mortality.* New York: Academic.

ROMELSJO, ANDERS, and FINN DIDERICHSEN. 1989. "Changes in Alcohol-Related Inpatient Care in Stockholm County in Relation to Socioeconomic Status During a Period of Decline in Alcohol Consumption." *American Journal of Public Health* 79:52–56.

ROSENFIELD, SARAH. 1980. "Sex Differences in Depression: Do Women Always Have Higher Rates?" *Journal of Health and Social Behavior* 21: 33–42.

ROSS, CATHERINE E., and BARBARA F. RESKIN. 1992. "Education, Control at Work, and Job Satisfaction." *Social Science Research* 21:134–48.

ROSS, CATHERINE E., and CHIA-LING WU. 1995. "The Links Between Educational Attainment and Health." *American Sociological Review* 60:719–45.

ROSS, CATHERINE E., and CHLOE E. BIRD. 1994. "Sex Stratification and Health Lifestyle: Consequences for Men's and Women's Perceived Health." *Journal of Health and Social Behavior* 35:161–78.

ROSS, CATHERINE E., and DIANE HAYES. 1988. "Exercise and Psychologic Well-Being in the Community." *American Journal of Epidemiology* 127(4): 762–71.

ROSS, CATHERINE, and JOAN HUBER. 1985. "Hardship and Depression." *Journal of Health and Social Behavior* 26:312–27.

ROSS, CATHERINE E., and JOHN MIROWSKY. 1984. "Components of Depressed Mood in Married Men and Women: The Center for Epidemiologic Studies' Depression Scale." *American Journal of Epidemiology* 119: 997–1004.

ROSS, CATHERINE E., and JOHN MIROWSKY. 1989. "Explaining the Social Patterns of Depression: Control and Problem-Solving—or Support and Talking." *Journal of Health and Social Behavior* 30: 206–19.

ROSS, CATHERINE E., and JOHN MIROWSKY. 1995. "Does Employment Affect Health?" *Journal of Health and Social Behavior* 36: 230–43.

ROSS, CATHERINE E., and MARIEKE VAN WILLIGEN. 1997. "Education and the Subjective Quality of Life." *Journal of Health and Social Behavior* 38: 275–97.

ROSS, CATHERINE E., and RAYMOND S. DUFF. 1982. "Medical Care, Living Conditions, and Children's Well-Being." *Social Forces* 61:456–74.

ROSS, CATHERINE E., JOHN MIROWSKY, and JOAN HUBER. 1983. "Dividing Work, Sharing Work, and In-Between: Marriage Patterns and Depression." *American Sociological Review* 48: 809–23.

ROSS, CATHERINE E., JOHN MIROWSKY, and PATRICIA ULBRICH. 1983. "Distress and the Traditional Female Role: A Comparison of Mexicans and Anglos." *American Journal of Sociology* 89: 670–82.

ROSS, CATHERINE E., JOHN MIROWSKY, and WILLIAM C. COCKERHAM. 1983. "Social Class, Mexican Culture, and Fatalism: Their Effects on Psychological Distress." *American Journal of Community Psychology* 11: 383–99.

ROWE, JOHN W., and ROBERT J. KAHN. 1987. "Human Aging: Usual and Successful." *Science* 143: 143–49.

SAGAN, LEONARD A. 1987. *The Health of Nations: True Causes of Sickness and Well-Being.* New York: Basic.

SANDVIK, LEIV, JAN ERIKSSEN, ERIK THAULOW, GUNNAR ERIKSSEN, REIDAR MUNDAL, and KAARE RODAHL. 1993. "Physical Fitness as a Predictor of Mortality Among Healthy, Middle-Aged Norwegian Men." *New England Journal of Medicine* 328:533–37.

SCHAFFER, CHARLES B., PATRICK T. DONLON, and ROBERT M. BITTLE. 1980. "Chronic Pain and Depression: A Clinical and Family History Survey." *American Journal of Psychiatry* 137(1):118–20.

SEEMAN, MELVIN. 1983. "Alienation Motifs in Contemporary Theorizing: The Hidden Continuity of Classic Themes." *Social Psychology Quarterly* 46: 171–84.

SEEMAN, MELVIN, and SUSAN K. LEWIS. 1995. "Powerlessness, Health, and Mortality: A Longitudinal Study of Older Men and Mature Women." *Social Science and Medicine* 41: 517–25.

SEEMAN, MELVIN, and TERESA E. SEEMAN. 1983. "Health Behavior and Personal Autonomy: A Longitudinal Study of the Sense of Control in Illness." *Journal of Health and Social Behavior* 24:144–60.

SEEMAN, MELVIN, ALICE Z. SEEMAN, and ART BUDROS. 1988. "Powerlessness, Work, and Community: A Longitudinal Study of Alienation and Alcohol Use." *Journal of Health and Social Behavior* 29:185–98.

SEGOVIA, JORGE, ROY F. BARTLETT, and ALISON C. EDWARDS. 1989. "The Association Between Self-Assessed Health Status and Individual Health Practices." *Canadian Journal of Public Health* 80: 32–37.

SHANFIELD, STEPHEN B., ELLIOTT M. HEIMAN, D. NATHAN COPE, and JOHN R. JONES. 1979. "Pain and the Marital Relationship: Psychiatric Distress." *Pain* 7: 343–51.

SHARP, KIMBERLY, CATHERINE E. ROSS, and WILLIAM C. COCKERHAM. 1983. "Symptoms, Beliefs, and the Use of Physician Services Among the Disadvantaged." *Journal of Health and Social Behavior* 24: 255–63.

SHEA, STEVEN, ARYEH D. STEIN, CHARLES E. BASCH, RAFAEL LANTINGUE, CHRISTOPHER MAYLAHN, DAVID S. STROGATZ, and LLOYD NOVICK. 1991. "Independent Associations of Educational Attainment and Ethnicity With Behavioral Risk Factors for Cardiovascular Disease." *American Journal of Epidemiology* 134: 567–82.

SHORE, ELSIE R., and SHARON A. PIERI. 1992. "Drinking Behaviors of Women in Four Occupational Groups." *Women and Health* 19: 55–64.

SORLIE, P.D., N.J. JOHNSON, E. BLACKLUND, and D.D. BRADHAM. 1994. "Mortality in the Uninsured Compared With That in Persons with Public and Private Health Insurance." *Archives of Internal Medicine* 154: 2409–16.

STAMPFER, MEIR J., GRAHAM A. COLDITZ, WALTER C. WILLETT, FRANK E. SPEIZER, and CHARLES H. HENNEKENS. 1988. "A Prospective Study of Moderate Alcohol Consumption and the Risk of Coronary Heart Disease and Stroke in Women." *New England Journal of Medicine* 319: 267–73.

SURGEON GENERAL. 1982. *The Health Consequences of Smoking.* Rockville, MD: Public Health Service.

SYME, LEONARD S., and LISA F. BERKMAN. 1986. "Social Class, Susceptibility, and Sickness." In *The Sociology of Health and Illness,* 2nd ed., ed. P. Conrad and R. Kern. New York: St. Martin's Press, pp. 28–34.

SYVERSON, C.J., W. CHAVKIN, H.K. ATRASH, R.W. ROCHAT, E.S. SHARP, and G.E. KING. 1991. "Pregnancy-Related Mortality in New York City, 1980 to 1984: Causes of Death and Associated Risk Factors." *American Journal of Obstetrics and Gynecology* 164 (2): 603–608.

U.S. BUREAU OF THE CENSUS. 1997. *Statistical Abstract of the United States 1997,* 117th ed. Washington, D.C.: Government Printing Office.

U.S. DEPARTMENT OF EDUCATION. 1992. *Digest of Education Statistics* (92–097). Washington DC: National Center for Education Statistics.

U.S. PREVENTIVE SERVICES TASK FORCE. 1989. *Guide to Clinical Preventive Services.* Baltimore, MD: Williams and Wilkins.

VERBRUGGE, LOIS M. 1983. "Multiple Roles and Physical Health of Women and Men." *Journal of Health and Social Behavior* 24:16–30.

VERBRUGGE, LOIS M. 1986. "From Sneezes to Adieux: Stage of Health for American Men and Women." *Social Science and Medicine* 22: 1195–1212.

VERRILLI, DIANA, and H. GILBERT WELCH. 1996. "The Impact of Diagnostic Testing on Therapeutic Interventions." *Journal of the American Medical Association* 275: 1189–91.

WADSWORTH, M.E.J. 1997. "Health Inequalities in the Life Course Perspective." *Social Science and Medicine* 44(6): 859–69.

WAGENKNECHT, LYNNE E., LAURA L. PERKINS, GARY R. CUTLER, STEPHEN SIDNEY, and GREGORY L. BURKE, TERI A. MANOLIA, DAVID R. JACOBS, KIANG LIU, GARY D. FRIEDMAN, GLENN H. HUGHES, and STEPHEN B. HULLEY. 1990. "Cigarette Smoking Is Strongly Related to Educational Status: The CARDIA Study." *Preventive Medicine* 19:158–69.

WAGSTAFF, ADAM, PIERELLA PACI, and EDDY VAN DOORSLAER. 1991. "On the Measurement of Inequalities in Health." *Social Science and Medicine* 3:545–57.

WALDRON, INGRID, and JERRY A. JACOBS. 1989. "Effects of Multiple Roles on Women's Health—Evidence From a National Longitudinal Study." *Women and Health* 15: 3–19.

WENNBERG, DAVIS E., MERLE A. KELLETT, JOHN D. DICKENS JR., DAVID J. MALENKA, L.M. KEILSON, and ROBERT B. KELLER. 1996. "The Association Between Local Diagnostic Testing Intensity and Invasive Cardiac Procedures." *Journal of the American Medical Association* 275:1161–64.

WHEATON, BLAIR. 1978. "The Sociogenesis of Psychological Disorder: Reexamining the Causal Issues With Longitudinal Data." *American Sociological Review* 43:383–403.

WHEATON, BLAIR. 1980. "The Sociogenesis of Psychological Disorder: An Attributional Theory." *Journal of Health and Social Behavior* 21: 100–124.

WHEATON, BLAIR. 1983. "Stress, Personal Coping Resources, and Psychiatric Symptoms: An Investigation of Interactive Models." *Journal of Health and Social Behavior* 24: 208–29.

WHEATON, BLAIR. 1985. "Models for the Stress-Buffering Functions of Coping Resources." *Journal of Health and Social Behavior* 26: 352–64.

WILKINSON, RICHARD G. 1986. *Class and Health: Research and Longitudinal Data.* London, England: Tavistock.

WILKINSON, RICHARD G. 1992. "Income Distribution and Life Expectancy." *British Medical Journal* 304:165–68.

WILKINSON, RICHARD G. 1997. "Socioeconomic Determinants of Health: Health Inequalities: Relative or Absolute Material Standards?" *British Medical Journal* 314: 591–98.

WILLIAMS, DAVID R. 1990. "Socioeconomic Differentials in Health: A Review and Redirection." *Social Psychology Quarterly* 53:81–99.

WILLIAMS, DAVID R., and CHIQUITA COLLINS. 1995. "US Socioeconomic and Racial Differences in Health: Patterns and Explanations." *Annual Review of Sociology* 21: 349–86.

WINKLEBY, MARILYN A., DARIUS E. JATULIS, ERICA FRANK, and STEPHEN P. FORTMANN. 1992. "Socioeconomic Status and Health: How Education, Income, and Occupation Contribute to Risk Factors for Cardiovascular Disease." *American Journal of Public Health* 82: 816–20.

WOODWARD, MARK, MICHAEL C. SHEWRY, W. CAIRNS, S. SMITH, and HUGH TUNSTALL-PEDOE. 1992. "Social Status and Coronary Heart Disease: Results From the Scottish Heart Health Study." *Preventive Medicine* 21:136–48.

5 THE IMPORTANCE OF CULTURE IN SOCIOLOGICAL THEORY AND RESEARCH ON STRESS AND MENTAL HEALTH: A MISSING LINK?

ROBIN W. SIMON, *The University of Iowa*

INTRODUCTION

Although structural explanations continue to be dominant in sociology, the inability of strictly structural factors such as individuals' socioeconomic status to explain social—especially social psychological—phenomena satisfactorily has resulted in a growing recognition of the importance of culture and ideology in social life. Sociologists in a number of areas (e.g., stratification, intergroup relations, social movements, gender and the family, emotion, and medical sociology) have increasingly turned their attention to the conjoint influence of structure and culture on micro-level phenomena—a core element being ideology and cultural norms, values, expectations, and beliefs (Griswold 1994).[1] An area in which cultural explanations are surprisingly absent, though, is the sociology of stress and mental health, where most theory and research focus on specifying the social (i.e., the social structural) conditions under which stressors negatively affect the emotional well-being of individuals. The predominance of structural explanations of the etiology of mental illness is especially apparent in the recent contextual approach, which attributes variation in the psychological impact of both acute and chronic stressors to variation in the social structural circumstances surrounding them. However, the failure to include structural *and* cultural factors in current explanations of the differential effects of stress on mental health has serious consequences for theory and research in this area because it results in underestimates of the importance of social conditions for the etiology of mental illness.

In this chapter, I first review existing theoretical approaches for explaining variation in the effects of life events and ongoing strains on mental health. Within sociology, the three current theoretical approaches to the issue of differential vulnerability all ignore the cultural and ideological context in which persons are embedded and in which acute and chronic stressors take place. I next consider the role of culture in the stress process. Here I draw on insights from stress researchers in several disciplines who argue (and show) that, by influencing their meaning and emotional significance, the cultural and ideological context surrounding both eventful and ongoing stressors helps account for variation in their psychological impact. In the final section of the chapter, I discuss the importance of sociocultural factors for explaining gender differences in two different components of the stress process. Although there are a number of ways in which sociocultural factors affect stress and mental illness, I focus on the role of culture and ideology for explaining gender differences in vulnerability to role-related stressors as well as for understanding gender differences in the manifestation of emotional distress. I conclude the chapter by briefly discussing how the sociocultural antecedents of mental illness can provide a missing link in our knowledge of the fundamental causes of psychological and psychiatric

---

[1] Although there are numerous definitions of both structure and culture in the sociological literature, throughout this chapter I use the term *structure* to refer to materially based elements affecting individuals—such as their relative power and status—which are based on individuals' location in the class system. In contrast, I use the term *culture* to refer to ideological and normative elements influencing persons—such as their values, expectations, and beliefs—that are rooted in deeply embedded collective systems of meaning.

disorders and shed light on some links between macro- and micro-level social phenomena.

CURRENT APPROACHES FOR EXPLAINING VARIATION IN THE MENTAL HEALTH EFFECTS OF ACUTE AND CHRONIC STRESS

Although mental health scholars have long conceptualized life events and ongoing strains as major sources of stress that inevitably result in psychiatric or psychological disorder, the culmination of years of empirical research reveals considerable variation in the mental health effects of both "acute" and "chronic" stressors. For example, epidemiological studies consistently show that even culturally undesirable life events—such as the death of a loved one and other types of loss events (e.g., divorce)—do not always have adverse emotional consequences for individuals and that there is only a weak to modest association between exposure to stressful life events and psychological or psychiatric disorder. Similarly, while there has been considerably less research on the psychological impact of chronic than of acute stressors, research nevertheless finds considerable variation in their psychological effects (Aneshensel 1992; Kessler, Price, and Wortman 1985; Pearlin and Johnson 1977; Thoits 1983, 1995).

Sociological inquiry into the underlying causes of the differential impact of stressful life experiences on mental health has resulted in three main theoretical approaches. These approaches emphasize variation in either the characteristics of the *stressor* itself (i.e., the characteristics of the life event or ongoing strain), the characteristics of the *person* experiencing the stressor (i.e., his or her coping and social support resources), or the *social context* surrounding the stressor (i.e., the immediate social circumstances in which stressful life experiences take place). Although they differ with regard to which factors moderate (i.e., *buffer* or *exacerbate*) the effects of stress on mental health, all of these approaches assume that the magnitude of the association between stress exposure and psychological or psychiatric symptoms increases when variation in the types of events and strains, the person's coping and social support resources, *or* social contexts in which events and strains occur are held constant.

The First Approach: The Characteristics of Stressors

The first theoretical approach—which, to date, has focused mainly on explaining variation in the mental health effects of eventful stressors—contends that events vary in their stressfulness and emotional consequences because of differences in *characteristics* such as their desirability, controllability, predictability, and magnitude (Thoits 1983). Research based on this approach finds that certain types of events (e.g., undesirable and uncontrollable ones) are more damaging for mental health than others (Dohrenwend 1974; Thoits 1983) and that distinguishing positive from negative events strengthens the association between event exposure and psychological or psychiatric symptoms (Dohrenwend 1974; Shrout et al., 1989).

While this approach was originally developed to explain the differential emotional consequences of eventful stressors, variation in the mental health effects of chronic stressors may also be attributable to differences in their characteristics. For example, because they involve enduring problems that characterize the overall quality of people's lives, Leonard Pearlin (1989) suggests that ambient strains (e.g., chronic financial difficulties and health problems) are likely to be more harmful for psychological well-being than role strains that are characterized by ongoing problems that are role specific (e.g., marital or work problems).

Along similar lines, life course scholars argue (and show) that characteristics of role transitions such as their timing, sequencing, expectedness, and normativeness moderate their impact and help explain variation in the psychological consequences of status (or role) transitions (George 1993). Indeed, some life course research suggests that life transitions are more harmful for mental health when they are "off-time," "out-of-sequence" (i.e., "out-of-order"), and "non-normative" (Hogan 1978, 1981; Jackson 1999; Hagan and Wheaton 1993).

The Second Approach: The Characteristics of Persons Experiencing Stressors

In contrast to the first theoretical approach, which focuses on characteristics of the event or strain itself, the second approach to the problem of the differential impact of stress on mental health focuses on characteristics of the person experiencing the stressor. According to this theoretical approach, variation in the effects of both acute and chronic stressors is a function of variation in people's response (i.e., their vulnerability or reactivity) to stressors. Indeed, a large body of research on coping and social support examines the extent to which individuals and groups vary in their possession of personal and social resources—such as mastery, self-esteem, and social support—which buffer the negative impact of eventful and ongoing stressors (Aneshensel 1992; Kessler et al., 1985; Pearlin and Schooler 1978; Thoits 1995). Overall, studies based on this approach indicate that people who possess coping resources such as high mastery, personal control, and self-esteem, and who have access to social resources such as functional, structural, and especially emotional social support are better able to weather the harmful psychological consequences of eventful and ongoing stressors than people who lack these personal and social resources.

The Third Approach: The Social Context Surrounding Stressors

More recently, a third theoretical approach has emerged that attributes variation in the mental health consequences of stressful life experiences to variation in the larger social context surrounding both acute and chronic stressors. This work developed in response to the growing recognition among scholars that stress research must take into account the *meaning* stressors have for individuals (e.g., Brown and Harris 1978, 1989; Lazarus and Folkman 1984; Pearlin 1988, 1989; Silver and Wortman 1980; Thoits 1991, 1992; Simon 1995, 1997; Wheaton 1990; Wortman, Silver, and Kessler 1993). Advocates of this approach argue that the social circumstances in which events and strains occur are crucial for explaining variation in their psychological impact because they shape the personal meaning and emotional significance of stressors. To date, the aspects of social context that have been shown to moderate the impact of life events on symptoms include individuals' socioeconomic status (Brown and Harris 1978), their level of prior stress in the role (Wheaton 1990), and their exposure to subsequent role strain (Umberson et al., 1992). For example, Blair Wheaton (1990) showed that a role loss such as a divorce is less distressing to individuals who have previously experienced a high level of marital stress than for those whose marital history is less stressful. Similarly, Deborah Umberson et al. (1992) found that widowhood is more depressing to people who experience subsequent financial and household strain than for those who do not confront these stressors. In general, research based on the contextual approach indicates that differences in the immediate social circumstances surrounding acute and chronic stressors help explain variation in their mental health effects.

By directing attention away from the characteristics of stressors and persons themselves to the more immediate social context surrounding stressors, contextually based research has begun to identify some *fundamental causes* of the differential impact of life

events and ongoing strains on psychological well-being. In contrast to individually based risk factors for major diseases, which are relatively proximal, fundamental causes of disease refer to basic social conditions, such as poverty, which are rooted in society and are more distal (Link and Phelan 1995). Research on the importance of context has also improved our understanding of mechanisms linking larger social conditions and individual well-being, or what C. Wright Mills (1959) called the "intersections of social structure and biography." Indeed, elucidating the links between these macro and micro dimensions of social life is the most central contribution sociologists can make to the study of stress and mental illness.

However, to date, studies based on the contextual approach have focused almost exclusively on structural aspects of context, such as individuals' relative position in the power and status hierarchy, and have ignored more cultural aspects of context, such as ideology and cultural norms, values, expectations, and beliefs. The lack of attention given to the various ways in which cultural systems influence the stress process in the contextual approach is ironic since the very goal of this approach is to specify the *meaning, emotional significance,* and *psychological impact* of stressors for people. The failure to incorporate culture and ideology into this (and other) theoretical approaches for explaining the differential effects of stress on mental health has serious consequences for sociological theory and research in this area because it *under*estimates the importance of *social* conditions for the etiology of mental illness.[2]

THE ROLE OF CULTURE IN SHAPING THE MEANING, EMOTIONAL SIGNIFICANCE, AND PSYCHOLOGICAL IMPACT OF STRESSORS

Stress researchers in other disciplines as well as in sociology have called attention to the more cultural and ideological contexts in which life experiences occur for understanding the meaning, emotional significance, and psychological impact of these experiences. In fact, cultural anthropologists are specifically concerned with the meanings people assign to their various experiences and the cultural contexts in which such meanings arise (e.g., Geertz 1973). With respect to the stress process, David

---

[2] In contrast to Bruce Link and Jo Phelan (1995), who define social conditions as "factors that involve a person's relationship to other people," I use the term to refer to the structural, social psychological, cultural, and ideological *constraints* and *resources* of individuals.

Jacobson (1987, 1989) claims that it is the social and cultural significance people attach to events and strains—not the events and strains themselves—that determines their consequences for mental health. Indeed, because the meaning and emotional significance of life experiences vary across different cultural contexts, Jacobson and other medical anthropologists argue (and show) that what is stressful and distressing in one cultural context is not necessarily stressful and distressing in another. For example, while divorce tends to be a stressful and depressing life event in American culture, it has another meaning and is neither stressful nor depressing in other cultures such as the Tiv of Africa (Bohannon 1971). In contrast to American culture, where the institution of marriage is perceived as a personally meaningful emotional bond between two individuals, marriage among the Tiv is perceived as an economic alliance between two larger kinship groups or families.[3]

Social historians also claim that the larger sociohistorical context in which life experiences take place influences their meaning, emotional significance, and psychological consequences. Like culturally oriented medical anthropologists, historians of emotion and mental illness argue (and document) that life events that are considered to be highly stressful and distressing during one historical period are not necessarily perceived as equally stressful and distressing during others. For instance, while the death of a child tends to be an unexpected and major traumatic life event (perceived as highly stressful and distressing) for individuals in low mortality, low fertility, modern societies, the loss of a child was an expected, routine, and less stressful and distressing event for people in high mortality, high fertility, pre-industrial societies (Aries 1962, 1981; Lofland 1985).[4]

Social psychologists have also acknowledged that culture shapes the meaning, emotional significance, and psychological impact of both eventful and chronic stressors. Although they focus on individual rather than cross-cultural or historical variation in the effects of life events and strains on mental health, psychological stress researchers (e.g., Averill 1980; Schacter and Singer 1962; Lazarus 1982; Lazarus and Folkman 1984) assert that psychological *and* sociocultural factors are important for mental health because, together, they influence the stress appraisal process. For example, according to Richard Lazarus and Susan Folkman (1984), the sociocultural context in which events and strains take place shapes the cognitive appraisal process whereby individuals evaluate whether an experience is benign or a threat, harm, loss, or challenge.

Finally, sociologists have recognized that the meaning, emotional significance, and psychological impact of acute and chronic stressors depend on the sociocultural context in which persons are embedded and in which events or strains take place. Indeed, several sociological stress researchers (e.g., Brown 1974; Brown and Harris 1978, 1989; Marris 1984; Parkes 1971) argue that the cultural and ideological context in which eventful and ongoing stressors occur plays a pivotal role in the stress process because it influences whether (and the extent to which) people perceive events and strains as stressful in the first place. For instance, in his seminal article on contextualizing the stress process, Leonard Pearlin (1989) writes that social values—which vary from one society to the next as well as across different social groups within the same society—regulate the meaning and emotional significance of acute and chronic stressors and, therefore, help explain variation in their psychological impact (also, see Pearlin 1988).

In short, stress researchers in a number of disciplines emphasize that culture provides a perceptual lens through which individuals interpret experiences and that it is the *subjective interpretation* of experiences—not the experiences per se—that is most consequential for mental health. It is clear that cultural systems—which include deeply embedded and collectively shared norms, values, expectations, and beliefs—provide an interpretive framework in which individuals assess the meaning and emotional significance of acute and chronic stressors. However, sociological theory and research on stress and mental health have, to date, overlooked this fundamentally *social* aspect of context. For the remainder of this chapter, I briefly discuss the importance of incorporating culture into sociological theory and research on stress and mental health.

---

[3] For other examples of cross-cultural variation in the effects of life events on emotional well-being, see Levy 1984; Kleinman and Kleinman 1985; Kleinman and Good 1985; LaBarre 1974; and Schweder 1985.

[4] While these findings from social history suggest that the more common, expected, or "normal" the event or strain is, the less stressful and distressing it is for individuals, this need not be the case. For example, although divorce is currently a commonly experienced life event for individuals in the United States (thus considered an expected or "normal" part of the life course), persons undergoing divorce experience it as highly stressful and distressing (Riessman 1990). It is certainly possible that demographic factors such as high rates of infant mortality and divorce influence cultural views about life events such as child death and marital dissolution (Stearns and Stearns 1985). However, I argue, as do social historians and social demographers, that the stressfulness and psychological impact of an event or strain is determined by the *meaning* it has for individuals—which may or may not be influenced by whether it is a common, expected, or normal life experience.

THE IMPORTANCE OF CULTURE FOR SOCIOLOGICAL THEORY AND RESEARCH ON STRESS AND MENTAL HEALTH: A MISSING LINK?

Although there are several ways in which sociocultural factors affect mental illness, I focus on the influence of culture and ideology—including cultural norms, values, expectations, and beliefs—on the stress process. It seems that there are at least two different, though related, reasons why it is important to incorporate culture into sociological theory and research on stress and mental health. The first reason is that the cultural and ideological context in which events and strains occur can help explain group differences in vulnerability (i.e., reactivity) to acute and chronic stressors. The second reason is that the cultural and ideological context in which persons are embedded can provide insight into group differences in the manifestation of stress and the expression of emotional disorder. While I emphasize the importance of culture for understanding gender differences in stress-reactivity and in the expression of emotional disorder, it is likely that sociocultural factors can also help explain other group (e.g., class, age, ethnic, and race) differences in the stress process, including those in exposure to both eventful and ongoing stressors.

The Social Distribution of Mental Illness

For some time, sociologists of stress and mental health have sought to document the social distribution of mental illness in the population and, in doing so, have uncovered some of the social antecedents of psychological disorder. Indeed, sociologists and epidemiologists consistently find that members of socially disadvantaged groups such as the poor, the young, ethnic minorities, and blacks have higher rates of mental illness than the well-to-do, older persons, ethnic majorities, and whites. In fact, *explaining* group differences in the prevalence of mental disorders is, perhaps, the most significant contribution sociologists have made to the study of stress and mental health over the second half of the twentieth century. To date, most sociologists attribute group differences in mental health to group differences in both exposure and vulnerability to acute and chronic stressors. Scholars argue (and show) that members of socially disadvantaged groups have higher rates of mental illness than members of socially advantage74d groups because they are both more exposed to stressful life exigencies and more vulnerable to their psychological effects (Aneshensel 1992; Kessler and Cleary 1980; McLeod and Kessler 1990; Turner, Wheaton, and Lloyd

1995; Thoits 1995). Current explanations of group differences in the impact of stressful life events and strains on mental health emphasize group differences in either the types of stressors experienced, the availability of coping and social support resources, or the structural context surrounding stressors. However, group differences in vulnerability to acute and chronic stressors can also be linked to the larger cultural and ideological context in which persons are embedded and in which these stressors take place. In particular, group differences in stress-reactivity may reflect group differences in the meaning and emotional significance people attach to their various life experiences. This point can best be illustrated in the case of gender.

Explaining Gender Differences in Vulnerability to Stressors A large body of research now indicates that there are gender differences in both exposure and vulnerability to stressful life experiences, particularly to *role-related* stressors. In general, studies show that men are more likely than women to report work and occupational events and problems, whereas women are more likely than men to report family and interpersonal events and difficulties (Kessler and McLeod 1984; Simon 1992, 1998; Turner and Avison 1989). Moreover, research indicates that men are more vulnerable than women to work and occupational stress, while women are more reactive than men to family and interpersonal stressors (Pearlin 1975; Pearlin and Lieberman 1979; Kessler and McLeod 1984; Simon 1998; Turner and Avison 1989).[5] This second finding from research that assesses gender differences in the impact of role-related events and strains on mental health strongly suggests that stressors do not have the same meaning and emotional significance for males and females. Thus, rather than simply reflecting gender differences in either the availability of coping and social support resources or the structural circumstances surrounding stressors (i.e., gender differences in socioeconomic status) as previous

---

[5] While some research indicates that there are significant male-female differences in vulnerability to role-related stressors, a few studies (e.g., Newman 1986; Umberson et al. 1996) find no gender differences in stress-reactivity. These inconsistencies across studies may be due to differences in their measures of mental health. Elsewhere, I argued that research on gender differences in emotional distress and vulnerability must include the types of mental health problems associated with both females (anxiety, depression, and generalized distress) and males (e.g., substance abuse) in order to avoid *over*estimating female's, and *under*estimating male's, psychological distress (Simon, 1998; also, see Aneshensel et al., 1991; Dohrenwend and Dohrenwend 1976; Lennon 1987). I will come back to the issue of differential expressions of distress later in this chapter when I discuss the importance of culture for understanding gender differences in the manifestation of emotional disorder.

research suggests, gender differences in vulnerability to role-related stressors can also be explained by the cultural and ideological context in which males and females are embedded and in which these stressors take place.

For example, part and parcel of American culture are collectively shared and deeply embedded norms, values, expectations, and beliefs about male and female roles and the overall importance of certain role domains for men and women. As a culture, we believe and expect that work and occupational roles (i.e., breadwinner roles) are central in the lives of men, while family roles and interpersonal relationships (i.e., nurturant roles) are central in the lives of women. Like other cultural information, individuals learn these gendered expectations and beliefs throughout the entire life course by socialization. Most importantly, males and females come to view these norms, values, expectations, and beliefs as standards for their own as well as for other people's behavior. To the extent that these gender-linked cultural norms, values, expectations, and beliefs serve as a framework through which men and women interpret the events and strains they experience, gender differences in vulnerability to role-related stressors can be attributed—at least in part—to the more cultural and ideological aspects of social context.

Although research that directly links gender differences in vulnerability to cultural norms, values, expectations, and beliefs about male and female roles is limited, there is some empirical support for this idea in the literature on gender differences in the mental health effects of both acute and chronic stressors. For example, Ronald Kessler and Jane McLeod (1984) asserted that undesirable network events (i.e., undesirable events that occur to people in one's social network) are more distressing to women than to men because women are socialized to *value* empathy. Along similar lines, I argued (and showed) that parental strains (e.g., ongoing health and behavior problems among one's children) are more distressing to women than to men because the parental identity is more salient in women's than in men's self-conceptions (Simon 1992). In other words, women are more vulnerable than men to undesirable network events and parental role strains because of the primacy of their nurturant roles and their greater empathy for other people's problems.

Given the importance attached to nurturant roles for females and occupational roles for males in American culture, it makes sense that events and strains in these role domains have different meanings, emotional significance, and psychological consequences for women and men in the United States. Together, these findings strongly suggest that gender variation in the mental health effects of role-related stressors can be traced to the cultural context in which males and females are embedded in general, and to gender-linked cultural norms, values, expectations, and beliefs about men's and women's social roles in particular. These findings also suggest that a central task for sociologists of stress and mental health in the next millennium is to elucidate the specific ways in which the cultural context surrounding persons and stressors influence this aspect of the stress process.

The Social Distribution of Types of Emotional Disorders

In addition to documenting group differences in overall rates of mental illness, as well as group differences in exposure and vulnerability to role-related stressors, sociologists and epidemiologists have also documented group (e.g., class, age, ethnic, race, *and* gender) differences in the manifestation of psychological disorder. That is, scholars find that there are group differences in the types of emotional disorders found in the general population. Here again, group differences in the manifestation of mental illness can be linked to sociocultural factors and can best be illustrated with respect to gender differences in the expression of emotional (i.e., psychological and psychiatric) disorder.

Understanding Gender Differences in the Manifestation of Mental Illness A large body of research now indicates that although males and females have similar overall rates of mental illness, males and females manifest psychological distress with different types of mental health problems. Sociological and epidemiological studies of life-time and recent prevalence rates for mental disorders consistently show that females have higher rates than males of nonspecific psychological distress such as depression and anxiety and their psychiatric corollaries of depressive and anxiety disorders. In contrast, males have higher rates than females of substance abuse-dependence and their psychiatric corollaries of antisocial personality and substance abuse-dependence disorders (Dohrenwend and Dohrenwend 1976; Dohrenwend et al. 1980; Meyers et al. 1984; Robins et al. 1984). In fact, these findings have led scholars to conclude that females are more likely than males to manifest emotional problems through internalizing disorders, whereas males are more likely than females to express emotional problems by externalizing disorders. However, rather than simply reflecting underlying physiological (including genetic and hormonal) differences between males and females, these observed gender differences in the manifestation of stress and the expression of emotional disorder may also reflect cultural norms, values, expectations, and beliefs about feeling and emotion (i.e., our *emotional culture)*, that are deeply gendered (Hochschild 1979, 1981; West and Zimmerman 1987).

In addition to containing norms, values, expectations, and beliefs about male and female roles and the importance of work and family role domains for men and women, American culture also includes collectively shared and deeply embedded norms, values, expectations, and beliefs about emotion, which include feeling and expression norms that specify appropriate feeling and expression for males and females. For instance, part of our emotional culture is the expectation and belief that males are less emotional and more rational than females, and that females are more emotional and less rational than males. Our emotional culture also includes feeling and expression norms that specify the emotions males and females should (and should not) feel and express both in general and in particular situations (Gordon 1981; Hochschild 1979, 1981; Thoits 1989; Ross and Mirowsky 1984). For example, we expect and believe that females are more prone to feelings of sadness and empathy and are more likely to cry than males. In contrast, we expect and believe that males are more likely to feel anger and are more likely to express anger in antisocial (and behaviorally outward) ways than females. We also believe that females should neither feel (nor express) anger and that males should neither feel (nor express) sadness. Similar to the way they obtain other cultural information, individuals begin to acquire gender-linked cultural knowledge about emotions in early childhood and adolescence through socialization, and this learning process continues well into adulthood.[6] Insofar as American culture includes norms, values, expectations, and beliefs about the appropriate *experience* and *expression* of emotion for males and females, sex-typical expressions of emotional disorder can be traced to our emotional culture.

Although research has not directly assessed whether (and the extent to which) gender differences in the experience and expression of emotional distress are a function of gender-linked feeling and expression norms in particular—and our emotional culture more generally—there is some evidence in the literature on male and female expressions of psychological and psychiatric disorders that supports this notion.

[6] See Leslie Brody (1985), Arlie Hochschild (1981), Steven Gordon (1981), and Robin Simon, Donna Eder, and Cathy Evans (1992) for research that examines the content and process of gender emotional socialization in childhood, adolescence, and early adulthood.

Overall, this research suggests that when males and females respond to stressful, emotion-eliciting situations, they do so with mental health problems that are consistent with expectations associated with their gender. For instance, Mary Clare Lennon (1987) showed that employed women react to stressful occupational conditions such as a lack of substantive complexity and job autonomy with depression, while employed men respond to these same stressful occupational conditions with substance abuse. Similarly, Aneshensel et al. (1991) reported that stressful life events (including network events) are more strongly associated with symptoms of depression and major depressive disorder for women and substance abuse-dependence for men. In a similar vein, I found that males and females respond to parental and work problems with sex-typical mental disorders (Simon 1998). Females respond to work and parental strains with depression, whereas males respond to these same types of stressors with alcohol problems.

Taken together, these findings strongly suggest that gender differences in the manifestation of mental illness can be traced to the cultural context in which persons are embedded in general, and to gender-linked cultural norms, values, expectations, and beliefs about the experience and expression of emotions (i.e., to our emotional culture) in particular. These findings also suggest that sociological research on stress and mental health in the twenty-first century should focus on identifying the specific ways in which our emotional culture influences the manifestation of stress and results in sex-typical expressions of emotional (including psychological and psychiatric) disorder.

CONCLUSIONS

While the sociological study of stress provides a unique opportunity to enhance our understanding of the relationships between larger social conditions and individual well-being, as well as elucidate links between macro- and micro-level phenomena, sociological research on stress and mental health has been criticized for paying insufficient attention to larger social contexts that are related to variation in the occurrence, consequences, *and* manifestation of stressful life experiences. In response to this criticism, sociologists have increasingly turned their attention away from the characteristics of persons and events and toward the social contexts surrounding stressors. However, to date, contextually based studies have focused almost exclusively on structural aspects of context (such as individuals' material circumstances and resources) and have overlooked more cultural and ideological aspects of context (such as cultural norms, values, expectations, and beliefs). In this chapter and elsewhere (Simon and Marcussen 1999), I have argued that our understanding of the relationships between social conditions and individual well-being cannot be complete unless we consider the cultural and ideological context in which persons and stressors are embedded.

In the first part of the chapter, I reviewed current theoretical approaches for explaining the differential effects of both acute and chronic stressors on mental health. To date, sociologists have attributed variation in the psychological impact of stress to variation in either the characteristics of the event or strain (i.e., its desirability, controllability, predictability, and magnitude), the characteristics of the person (i.e., one's coping and social support resources), or social structural aspects of the context in which a person is embedded (i.e., one's relative power and status). Although research based on these theoretical approaches has certainly deepened our knowledge about social factors that contribute to individual well-being, and helped us identify some specific links between macro- and micro-level phenomena, a more complete understanding of the social conditions underlying the etiology of mental illness can only be achieved with concomitant attention to the structural *and* cultural contexts surrounding persons and stressors.

In the second part of the chapter, I discussed the role of culture in shaping the stress process. Drawing on insights from stress researchers in several disciplines (including anthropologists, historians, psychologists, *and* sociologists), I argued that culture is important for understanding the differential psychological impact of events and strains because it influences the meaning and emotional significance of stressors. In this section of the chapter, I emphasized the idea that individuals attribute meaning and attach emotional significance to events and strains based on their cultural framework, and that the subjective interpretation of experiences is as, if not more, consequential than the experiences themselves for individuals' psychological well-being.

In the final section of the chapter, I discussed two reasons why it is important to incorporate culture into sociological theory and research on stress and mental health. The first reason is that the cultural and ideological context in which events and strains occur can help explain observed group (e.g., class, age, ethnic, race, and gender) differences in vulnerability to acute and chronic stressors. The second reason is that the cultural and ideological context surrounding stressors can provide insight into group (e.g., class, age, ethnic, race, and gender) differences in the manifestation of emotional disorder. I illustrated the importance of culture in these two components of the stress process by focusing on gender differences in vulnerability to role-related stressors and gender differences in the manifestation of emotional disorder, though there is undoubtedly a plethora of other ways in which culture affects the stress process and the etiology of mental illness.

Overall, while sociological research on stress and mental health during the twentieth century has made enormous inroads toward illuminating both the personal and structural antecedents of emotional disorder. However, the greatest challenge for sociologists of stress and mental health, as we approach the next millennium, is to identify the sociocultural antecedents of mental illness and to explicate the *conjoint* influence of structure *and* culture in the production of mental illness. An integrative theoretical approach in which structure and culture are front and center should help us explain a range of social conditions that are associated with the occurrence, consequences, and manifestation of psychological and psychiatric disorders. In my opinion, an approach that elucidates the links between experiences of individuals, as they are embedded in a broader sociocultural and historical context and that explicates the ways in which structure and culture operate in tandem in the etiology of mental disorders will provide a missing link in our understanding of fundamental causes of disease and connect the unique substantive concerns of stress research to broader sociological issues and themes.

REFERENCES

Aneshensel, Carol S. 1992. "Social Stress: Theory and Research." *Annual Review of Sociology* 18:15–38.

Aneshensel, Carol S., and Leonard I. Pearlin. 1987. "Structural Contexts of Sex Differences in Stress." In *Gender and Stress,* ed. Rosalind C. Barnett, Lois Biener, and Grace K. Baruch. New York: The Free Press, pp. 75–95.

Aneshensel, Carol S., Carolyn M. Rutter, and Peter A. Lachenbruch. 1991. "Social Structure, Stress, and Mental Health: Competing Conceptual and Analytic Models." *American Sociological Review* 56:166–78.

Aries, Philippe. 1962. *Centuries of Childhood: A Social History of Family Life.* New York: Random House.

ARIES, PHILIPPE. 1981. *The Hour of Death.* New York: Vintage Books.

AVERILL, JAMES R. 1980. "A Constructionist View of Emotion." In *Emotion: Theory, Research, and Experience,* ed. Robert Plitchick and Henry Kellerman. New York: Academic Press, pp. 305–39.

BOHANNAN, PAUL. 1971. "Dyad Dominance and Household Maintenance." In *Kinship and Culture,* ed. Francis L.K. Hsu. Chicago: Aldine Press, pp. 42–65.

BRODY, LESLIE. 1985. "Gender Differences in Emotional Development: A Review of Theories and Research." In *Gender and Personality: Current Perspectives on Theory and Research,* ed. Abigail J. Stewart and M. Brinton Lykes. Durham, NC: Duke University Press, pp. 14–61.

BROWN, GEORGE W. 1974. "Meaning, Measurement and Stress of Life Events." In *Stressful Life Events: Their Nature and Effects,* ed. B. S. Dohrenwend and B. P. Dohrenwend. New York: John Wiley, pp. 217–44.

BROWN, GEORGE W., and TIRRIL O. HARRIS. 1978. *The Social Origins of Depression: A Study of Psychiatric Disorder in Women.* New York: Free Press.

BROWN, GEORGE W., and TIRRIL O. HARRIS. 1989. *Life Events and Illness.* New York: Guilford.

DOHRENWEND, BRUCE P. 1974. "Problems in Defining and Sampling the Relevant Population of Stressful Life Events." In *Stressful Life Events: Their Nature and Effects,* ed. B.S. Dohrenwend and B.P. Dohrenwend. New York: Wiley, pp. 275–313.

DOHRENWEND, BRUCE P., and BARBARA S. DOHRENWEND. 1976. "Sex Differences in Psychiatric Disorders." *American Journal of Sociology* 81:1447–54.

DOHRENWEND, BRUCE P., PATRICK E. SHROUT, GLADYS EGRI, and FREDRICK S. MENDELSOHN. 1980. "Nonspecific Psychological Distress and Other Dimensions of Psychopathology." *Archives of General Psychiatry* 37:1229–36.

GEERTZ, 1973. *The Interpretation of Culture.* New York: Basic Books.

GEORGE, LINDA K. 1993. "Sociological Perspectives on Life Transitions." *Annual Review of Sociology* 19:353–73.

GORDON, STEVEN L., 1981. "The Sociology of Sentiments and Emotion." In *Social Psychology: Sociological Perspectives,* ed. Morris Rosenberg and Ralph H. Turner. New York: Basic Books, pp. 562–92.

GRISWOLD, WENDY. 1994. *Cultures and Societies in a Changing World.* Thousand Oaks, CA: Pine Forge Press.

HAGAN, JOHN, and BLAIR WHEATON. 1993. "The Search for Adolescent Role Exits and the Transition to Adulthood." *Social Forces* 71:955–80.

HOCHSCHILD, ARLIE R. 1979. "Emotion Work, Feeling Rules, and Social Structure." *American Journal of Sociology* 85:551–75.

HOCHSCHILD, ARLIE R. 1981. "Attending to, Codifying, and Managing Feelings: Sex Differences in Love." In *Feminist Frontiers: Rethinking Sex, Gender, and Society,* ed. Laurel Richardson and Verta Taylor. Reading, MA: Addison Wesley, pp. 250–62.

HOGAN, DENNIS P. 1978. "The Variable Order of Events in the Life Course." *American Sociological Review* 43:573–86.

HOGAN, DENNIS P. 1981. *Transitions and Social Change: The Early Lives of American Men.* New York: Academic.

JACKSON, PAMELA BRABOY. 1999. "Role Sequencing and Adult Mental Health." Unpublished paper.

JACOBSON, DAVID. 1987. "Models of Stress and Meanings of Unemployment: Reactions to Job Loss Among Technical Professionals." *Social Science and Medicine* 24:13–21.

JACOBSON, DAVID. 1989. "Comment: Context and the Sociological Study of Stress: An Invited Response to Pearlin." *Journal of Health and Social Behavior* 30:257–60.

KESSLER, RONALD C. 1979. "Stress, Social Status, and Psychological Distress." *Journal of Health and Social Behavior* 20:259–72.

KESSLER, RONALD C., and JANE D. MCLEOD. 1984. "Sex Differences in Vulnerability to Network Events." *American Sociological Review* 49:620–31.

KESSLER, RONALD C., and PAUL D. CLEARY. 1980. "Social Class and Psychological Distress." *American Sociological Review* 45:463–78.

KESSLER, RONALD C., RICHARD H. PRICE, and CAMILLE WORTMAN. 1985. "Social Factors in Psychopathology: Stress, Social Support, and Coping Processes." *Annual Review of Psychology* 36:531–72.

KLEINMAN, ARTHUR. 1986. *Social Origins of Distress and Disease: Depression, Neurasthenia, and Pain in Modern China.* New Haven: Yale University Press.

KLEINMAN, ARTHUR, and BYRON GOOD. 1985. *Culture and Depression: Studies in the Anthropology and Cross-Cultural Psychiatry of Affect and Disorder.* Berkeley, CA: University of California Press.

KLEINMAN, ARTHUR, and JOAN KLEINMAN. 1985. "Somatization: The Interconnections in Chinese Society Among Culture, Depressive Experiences, and the Meanings of Pain." In *Culture and Depression: Studies in the Anthropology and Cross-Cultural Psychiatry of Affect and Disorder,* ed. Arthur Kleinman and Byron Good. Berkeley, CA: University of California Press, pp. 429–90.

LABARRE, WESTON. 1947. "The Cultural Basis of Emotions and Gestures." *Journal of Personality* 16: 49–68.

LAZARUS, RICHARD S. 1982. "Thoughts on the Relations Between Emotion and Cognition." *American Psychologist* 37: 1019–24.

LAZARUS, RICHARD S., and SUSAN FOLKMAN. 1984. *Stress, Appraisal, and Coping.* New York: Springer Publishing Company.

LENNON, MARY CLARE. 1987. "Sex Differences in Distress: The Impact of Gender and Work Roles." *Journal of Health and Social Behavior* 28:290–305.

LENNON, MARY CLARE. 1989. "Comment: The Structural Contexts of Stress: An Invited Response to Pearlin." *Journal of Health and Social Behavior* 30: 257–60.

LEVY, ROBERT I. 1984. "Emotion, Knowing, and Culture." In *Culture Theory: Essays on Mind, Self, and Emotion,* ed. Richard A. Shweder and Robert Levine. Cambridge: Cambridge University Press.

LINK, BRUCE G., and JO PHELAN. 1995. "Social Conditions as Fundamental Causes of Disease." *Journal of Health and Social Behavior* (Extra Issue): 80–94.

LOCKER, DAVID. 1981. "The Construction of Definitions of Illness." In *Symptoms of Illness: The Cognitive Organization of Disorder,* ed. David Locker. England: Tavistock Publications, pp. 93–132.

LOFLAND, LYN H. 1985. "The Social Shaping of Emotion: The Case of Grief." *Symbolic Interaction* 8: 171–90.

MARRIS, PETER. 1984. *Loss and Change.* New York: Pantheon Books.

MCLEOD, JANE D., and RONALD C. KESSLER. 1990. "Economic Status Differences in Vulnerability to Undesirable Events." *Journal of Health and Social Behavior* 31:162–72.

MEYERS, JEROME K., MYRNA M. WEISSMAN, GARY L. TISHLER, CHARLES E. HOLZER, PHILIP J. LEAF, HELEN ORVASCHEL, JAMES R. ANTHONY, JEFFREY H. BOYD, JACK D. BURKE, JR., MORTON KRAMER, and ROGER STOLZMAN. 1984. "Six-Month Prevalence of Psychiatric Disorders in Three Communities." *Archives of General Psychiatry* 41:959–67.

MILLS, C. WRIGHT. 1959. *The Sociological Imagination.* New York: Oxford University Press.

NEWMAN, JOY P. 1986. "Gender, Life Strains, and Depression." *Journal of Health and Social Behavior* 27: 161–78.

PARKES, COLIN MURRAY. 1971. "Psycho-Social Transitions: A Field for Study." *Social Science and Medicine* 5: 101–15.

PEARLIN, LEONARD I. 1975. "Sex Roles and Depression." In *Life Span Developmental Psychology: Normative Life Crises,* ed. Nancy Datan and Leon H. Ginsberg. New York: Academic Press, pp. 191–207.

PEARLIN, LEONARD I. 1982. "The Social Contexts of Stress." In *Handbook of Stress: Theoretical and Clinical Aspects,* ed. Leo Goldberger and Shlomo Breznitz. New York: The Free Press, pp. 367–79.

PEARLIN, LEONARD I. 1988. "Social Structure and Social Values: The Regulation of Structural Effects." In *Survey Social Life,* ed. H. O'Gorman. Conn: Wesleyan University Press, pp. 252–64.

PEARLIN, LEONARD I. 1989. "The Sociological Study of Stress." *Journal of Health and Social Behavior* 30:241–56.

PEARLIN, LEONARD I., and CARMI SCHOOLER. 1978. "The Structure of Coping." *Journal of Health and Social Behavior* 19: 2–21.

PEARLIN, LEONARD, and JOYCE S. JOHNSON. 1977. "Marital Status, Life Strains, and Depression." *American Sociological Review* 42:704–15.

PEARLIN, LEONARD, and MORTON A. LIEBERMAN. 1979. "Social Sources of Emotional Distress." In *Research in Community Mental Health,* ed. Roberta Simmons. Greenwich, CT: JAI Press, pp. 217–48.

RADLOFF, LENORE S. 1975. "Sex Differences in Depression: The Effects of Occupation and Marital Status." *Sex Roles* 1: 249–65.

RADLOFF, LENORE S. 1977. "The CES-D Scale: A Self-Reported Depression Scale for Research in the General Population." *Applied Psychological Measurement* 1: 385–401.

RIESSMAN, CATHERINE KOHLER. 1990. *Divorce Talk: Women and Men Make Sense of Personal Relationships.* New Brunswick: Rutgers University Press.

ROBINS, LEE N., JOHN E. HOLZER, MYRNA M. WEISSMAN, HELEN ORVASCHEL, ERNEST GRUENBERG, JACK D. BURKE, and DARREL A. REGIER. 1984. "Life-Time Prevalence of Specific Psychiatric Disorders in Three Sites." *Archives of General Psychiatry* 41: 949–58.

ROSS, CATHERINE E., and JOHN MIROWSKY. 1984. "Men Who Cry." *Social Psychology Quarterly* 47: 138–46.

SCHACTER, STANLEY, and JERMONE E. SINGER. 1962. "Cognitive, Social, and Physiological Determinants of Emotional State." *Psychological Review* 69: 379–99.

SHOTT, SUSAN. 1979. "Emotion and Social Life: A Symbolic Interactionist Analysis." *American Journal of Sociology* 84: 1317–34.

SHROUT, PATRICK E., BRUCE G. LINK, BRUCE P. DOHRENWEND, ANDREW E. SKODOL, ANN STUEVE, and JEROLD MIRITZNICK. 1989. "Characterizing Life Events as Risk Factors for Depression: The Role of Fateful Loss Events." *Journal of Abnormal Psychology* 98: 460–67.

SHWEDER, RICHARD A. 1985. "Menstrual Pollution, Soul Loss, and the Comparative Study of Emotions." In *Culture and Depression: Studies in the Anthropology and Cross-Cultural Psychiatry of Affect and Disorder,* ed. Arthur Kleinman and Byron Good. Berkeley, CA: University of California Press, pp. 182–215.

SILVER, ROXANNE L., and CAMILLE B. WORTMAN. 1980. "Coping with Undesirable Events." In *Human Helplessness: Theory and Applications,* ed. J. Garber and E.P. Seligman. New York: Academic, pp. 279–375.

SIMON, ROBIN W. 1992. "Parental Role Strains, Salience of Parental Identity, and Gender Differences in Psychological Distress." *Journal of Health and Social Behavior* 33: 2–35.

SIMON, ROBIN W. 1995. "Gender, Multiple Roles, Role Meaning, and Mental Health." *Journal of Health and Social Behavior* 36: 182–94.

SIMON, ROBIN W. 1997. "The Meanings Individuals Attach to Role Identities and Their Implications for Mental Health." *Journal of Health and Social Behavior* 38: 256–74.

SIMON, ROBIN W. 1998. "Assessing Sex Differences in Vulnerability Among Employed Parents: The Importance of Marital Status." *Journal of Health and Social Behavior* 39: 37–53.

SIMON, ROBIN W., and KRISTEN MARCUSSEN. 1999. "Marital Transitions, Marital Beliefs, and Mental Health." *Journal of Health and Social Behavior* 40: 111–25.

SIMON, ROBIN W., DONNA EDER, and CATHY EVANS. 1992. "The Development of Feeling Norms Underlying

Romantic Love Among Adolescent Females." *Social Psychology Quarterly* 52: 35–43.

SPIRO, MELFORD E. 1959. "Cultural Heritage, Personal Tensions, and Mental Illness in a South Sea Culture." In *Culture and Mental Health: Cross-Cultural Studies,* ed. Marvin K. Opler. New York: McMillan, pp. 141–71.

SPIRO, MELFORD E. 1965. *Context and Meaning in Cultural Anthropology.* New York: Free Press.

STEARNS, PETER N. 1992. "Gender and Emotion: A Twentieth-Century Transition." *Social Perspectives on Emotion* 1:127–60.

STEARNS, CAROL Z., and PETER N. STEARNS. 1986. *Anger: The Struggle for Emotional Control in America's History.* Chicago: University of Chicago Press.

STEARNS, PETER N., and CAROL Z. STEARNS. 1985. "Emotionology: Clarifying the History of Emotions and Emotional Standards." *American Historical Review* 90: 813–30.

THOITS, PEGGY A. 1983. "Dimensions of Life Events that Influence Psychological Distress: An Evaluation and Synthesis of the Literature." In *Psychosocial Stress: Trends in Theory and Research,* ed. H.B. Kaplan. New York: Academic, pp. 33–103.

THOITS, PEGGY A. 1984. "Explaining Distributions of Psychological Vulnerability: Lack of Social Support in the Face of Life Stress." *Social Forces* 63: 453–81.

THOITS, PEGGY A. 1989. "The Sociology of Emotions." *Annual Review of Sociology* 15: 317–42.

THOITS, PEGGY A. 1991. "On Merging Identity Theory and Stress Research." *Social Psychology Quarterly* 54: 101–12.

THOITS, PEGGY A. 1992. "Identity Structures and Psychological Well-Being: Gender and Marital Status Comparisons." *Social Psychology Quarterly* 55: 236–56.

THOITS, PEGGY A. 1995. "Stress, Coping, and Social Support Processes: Where Are We? What Next?" *Journal of Health and Social Behavior* (Extra Issue): 53–79.

TURNER, R. JAY, and WILLIAM R. AVISON. 1989. "Gender and Depression: Assessing Exposure and Vulnerability to Life Events in a Chronically Strained Population." *Journal of Nervous Mental Disorders* 177: 443–55.

TURNER, R. JAY, BLAIR WHEATON, and DONALD A. LLOYD. 1995. "The Epidemiology of Social Stress." *American Sociological Review* 60: 104–25.

UMBERSON, DEBORAH, CAMILLE B. WORTMAN, and RONALD C. KESSLER. 1992. "Widowhood and Depression: Explaining Long-Term Gender Differences in Vulnerability." *Journal of Health and Social Behavior* 33: 10–24.

UMBERSON, DEBORAH, MEICHU D. CHEN, JAMES S. HOUSE, KRISTINE HOPKINS, and ELLEN SLATEN. 1996. "The Effect of Social Relationships on Psychological Well-Being: Are Men and Women Really So Different?" *American Sociological Review* 61: 837–57.

WEST, CANDACE, and DON H. ZIMMERMAN. 1987. "Doing Gender." *Gender and Society* 1: 125–51.

WHEATON, BLAIR. 1990. "Life Transitions, Role Histories, and Mental Health." *American Sociological Review* 55: 209–23.

WORTMAN, CAMILLE B., ROXANNE C. SILVER, and RONALD C. KESSLER. 1993. "The Meaning of Loss and Adjustment to Bereavement." In *Handbook of Bereavement: Theory and Research Intervention,* ed. M.S. Stroebe and R.O. Hansson. New York: Cambridge University Press, pp. 349–66.

6 SOCIOECONOMIC INEQUALITIES IN HEALTH: AN ENDURING SOCIOLOGICAL PROBLEM

STEPHANIE A. ROBERT, *University of Wisconsin-Madison*

JAMES S. HOUSE, *University of Michigan*

The description and study of socioeconomic inequalities in health is one of the most enduring concerns of medical sociology. Using various methods, data, and measures of both socioeconomic position (e.g., education, income, occupation) and health, researchers from multiple disciplines have consistently found that persons of lower socioeconomic position have worse health and lower life expectancy than those with higher socioeconomic position (Adler et al. 1993, 1994; Antonovsky 1967; Black et al. 1982; Feinstein 1993; Marmot et al. 1987; Williams 1990; Williams and Collins 1995). For example, persons with incomes below the poverty level and even below the median in the United States have 2 to 3 times the risk of dying prematurely compared to individuals with incomes above the median, even after controls for age, race, gender, and even other behavioral and biomedical risk factors (Lantz et al. 1998).

For a time in the later 1960s and 1970s, many assumed that socioeconomic inequalities in health were gradually eroding, at least in the more developed societies, in the face of both the development of modern medicine and increasing economic affluence and equality. However, the late 1970s and early 1980s brought a growing recognition that neither population health nor economic equality was necessarily or evenly improving in the more developed societies. The persistence and even increase of socioeconomic inequalities in health were recognized first in the Black report in the United

Kingdom (Black et al. 1982), and then also in the United States (Pappas et al. 1993) and other countries (Evans et al. 1994; Marmot et al. 1987). Since then, the growth of interest in and research on these socioeconomic inequalities in health has been almost geometric (Kaplan and Lynch 1997), in part because socioeconomic inequalities in health are increasingly recognized as a major public health problem, arguably the greatest impediment to improving population health in developed societies. Hence, reducing socioeconomic and racial disparities in health will be central among the U.S. Public Health Service's goals for *Health People 2010.*

Biomedical and psychological scientists have played a more central role than sociologists in the recent revival of interest in socioeconomic inequalities in health (e.g., Adler et al. 1993, 1994). This has led to a major focus in the literature on understanding the biomedical and psychological pathways or mechanisms by which socioeconomic position may come to affect health (e.g., Adler et al. 1994; Anderson and Armstead 1995). However, this increasing focus on the "downstream" pathways or processes linking socioeconomic position to health needs to be supplemented and complemented by a more "upstream" sociological perspective (McKinlay 1974).

This chapter discusses three ways in which sociological approaches must continue to contribute to understanding and alleviating socioeconomic inequalities in health. First, socioeconomic inequalities in health constitute a problem of social stratification, requiring sociological (and also demographic and economic) theories and methods of stratification research. Second, a

This work was partially supported by the Scholars in Health Policy Research Program (Robert) and Investigator Awards in Health Policy Research Program (House), both supported by The Robert Wood Johnson Foundation.

sociological approach can provide both context and content to research on the social, psychological, behavioral, and even physiological pathways and mechanisms linking socioeconomic position to health. Finally, a sociological approach can provide a more "upstream" perspective on socioeconomic inequalities in health by emphasizing socioeconomic position as a *fundamental cause* of health—an emphasis that suggests looking not only at the more proximate psychological, behavioral, and physiological pathways to health that result from socioeconomic position, but also at the more macro societal factors that shape socioeconomic position and its distribution in society.

We focus our discussion on socioeconomic inequalities in health in more developed societies, although socioeconomic inequalities in health are substantial problems in less developed societies as well. In addition, our focus will be on indicators of physical rather than mental health, although we believe there is no sharp separation here, and much of what we say is relevant to mental health as well.

SOCIOECONOMIC INEQUALITIES IN HEALTH: A PROBLEM IN SOCIAL STRATIFICATION

The study of socioeconomic inequalities in health has benefited from the same kind of theoretical and methodological analyses as other problems in social stratification by paying careful attention to: (1) the nature and measurement of the stratification or socioeconomic variables; (2) the extent, form, and causal priorities in their relationships to health; and (3) whether and how these relationships vary across major sociodemographic subgroups of the population (e.g., by race, gender, and age).

Measuring the Socioeconomic Position of Individuals and Families

Investigations of socioeconomic inequalities in health have used various terms for socioeconomic circumstances including socioeconomic status, socioeconomic position, and social class. We use the term socioeconomic position in this chapter to represent the broad range of socioeconomic resources on which people and places are hierarchically stratified.

A good deal has been written on how to measure socioeconomic position, which are the best indicators of socioeconomic position, and whether some indicators of socioeconomic position are more predictive of health in different populations (e.g., Krieger et al.

1997; Liberatos et al. 1988). European research makes heavy usage of occupational indicators, while research in the United States relies more heavily on income and education, the last being the most widely used indicator in less developed nations. Wealth or permanent income is now being used more in health research in the United States and Canada (e.g., Kington and Smith 1997; Robert and House 1996; Schoenbaum and Waidmann 1997; Wolfson et al. 1993) while material circumstances (such as car ownership or housing tenure) have been additional indicators used especially in British research (e.g., Arber and Ginn 1993; Marmot et al. 1987).

We concur with Nancy Krieger and colleagues (1997) that composite indices of socioeconomic position are generally to be avoided in favor of using a variety of separate indicators. Education and income, if measured reasonably well, have the virtues of being applicable to all individuals and being relatively continuous in nature; the same is true of wealth and material possessions, which are, however, usually more difficult to measure. Occupation, in contrast, works well for employed populations but becomes increasingly difficult or even inappropriate to apply to those not or never in the labor force. Researchers should increasingly try to use multiple measures of socioeconomic position, as there is evidence that (1) different measures have both common and independent pathways linking them to health (e.g., education affects health through but also independent of its impact on income (Reynolds and Ross 1998)), and (2) some measures of socioeconomic position may be particularly salient for specific populations or subgroups (e.g., wealth may increasingly rival or surpass income as a measure of socioeconomic position among older adults (Robert and House 1996)).

In addition, rather than measuring socioeconomic position at one point in time and assessing its relationship to health and mortality, we need to understand how stability and change in socioeconomic position relate to health and mortality. For example, Peggy McDonough and colleagues (1997), using a longitudinal panel study of adults ages 45 and older in the United States, found that persistent low income was a particularly strong determinant of mortality, but that income instability was also an important predictor of mortality among middle-income adults (see also Lynch, Kaplan, and Shema 1997).

Similarly, research needs to clarify the complex relationships among childhood socioeconomic position, adult socioeconomic position, childhood health, and adult health. For example, do socioeconomic conditions of childhood have a substantial persisting effect on health in adulthood, or are socioeconomic conditions in adulthood the primary determinants of health in adulthood? Recent research by Chris Power and colleagues (Power et al. 1998; Power and Matthews 1997; Power et al. 1996) suggests that occupational class differences in self-rated health at age 33 in Great Britain result from the accumulation of conditions and experiences throughout both childhood and early adulthood. Other studies similarly conclude that childhood socioeconomic conditions are related to adult health and mortality both through and independent of adult socioeconomic conditions, but that childhood socioeconomic conditions are by no means fully responsible for the robust association between adult socioeconomic position and health (Blane et al. 1996; Brunner et al. 1996; Davey Smith et al. 1997, 1998; Elo and Preston 1992; Lynch et al. 1997; Reynolds and Ross 1998). Measuring socioeconomic position and health at different points in the life course can help us understand the pathways linking socioeconomic position to health and at what point in the life course different types of interventions might be most beneficial (Bartley et al. 1997; Kuh and Ben-Shlomo 1997).

Measuring the Socioeconomic Characteristics of Communities, Regions, and Societies

Whereas most research focuses on how the socioeconomic position of individuals and families affects the health of individuals, two types of studies consider how the socioeconomic context of one's community might also affect health. The first type investigates the health impact of the socioeconomic *level* of communities, regions, and societies; the other, the health impact of socioeconomic *inequality* within and between communities, regions, and societies.

Socioeconomic Level of Communities, Regions, and Societies One of the now best established empirical regularities seen in population health is the monotonic but nonlinear relation across societies between average levels of income and population health, at least as indexed by life expectancy. First demonstrated by Samuel Preston (1975), and more recently updated by Richard Wilkinson (1996), population life expectancy rises rapidly with per capita income up to a level of about $5,000 per capita (in current international dollars), with rapidly diminishing returns to per capita income above that level, and this relationship has been observed repeatedly across time (see Figure 6.1). Research within societies has also consistently shown that

FIGURE 6–1 Life Expectancy and Income Per Capita for Selected Countries and Periods

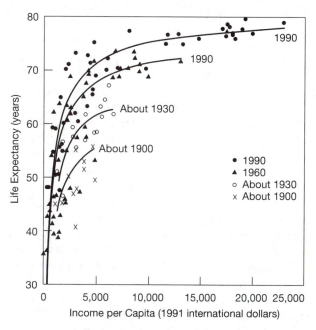

SOURCE: Published in Richard G. Wilkinson, *Unhealthy Societies: The Afflictions of Inequality* (New York: Routledge, 1996). Data from the World Bank, *1993 World Development Report.*

communities and regions with lower average levels of income, education, etc. have higher rates of morbidity and mortality than communities with higher socioeconomic levels (Crombie et al. 1989; Curtis 1990).

But since these findings at the community, regional, and societal levels derive primarily from ecological data, it is unclear to what extent communities, regions, and societies with lower socioeconomic levels have overall worse health because (1) residents with lower socioeconomic position have poor health, or (2) living in lower socioeconomic communities, regions, and societies is detrimental to the health of all residents, in addition to (or interacting with) their individual-level socioeconomic position. That is, is the aggregate relation at the community, regional, or societal level simply reflecting the relationship at the individual level, or is there an effect of community, regional, or societal socioeconomic level on individual health that is over and above the effect of individual-level socioeconomic position?

With some exceptions (Ecob 1996; Sloggett and Joshi 1994; Reijneveld 1998), studies using both individual-level and community-level socioeconomic information find that community socioeconomic level is associated with health (Diez-Roux et al. 1997; Hochstim et al. 1968; Jones and Duncan 1995; Krieger 1992; Morgan and Chinn 1983; O'Campo et al. 1997; Robert 1998; Sloggett and Joshi 1998) and mortality (Anderson et al. 1997; Haan et al. 1987; LeClere et al. 1997; Sloggett and Joshi 1998; Waitzman and Smith 1998a), over and above the impact of individual-level socioeconomic position, in both the United States and Great Britain. For example, early work by Mary Haan and colleagues (1987) showed that, in a population of adults age 35 and older living in Oakland, California, in 1965, the effects of residence in a poverty area on nine-year mortality persisted after controlling separately for individual-level measures of socioeconomic position, age, gender, and race, and even after adjusting for some mediating health behavior and social support factors. These findings have recently been confirmed in a study of urban areas of the United States as well (Waitzman and Smith 1998a). Focusing on health status rather than mortality in a national sample of adults in the United States in 1986, Stephanie Robert (1998) found that the percentage of families earning $30,000 or more and the percentage of adults who are unemployed in respondents' census tracts each had an independent association with individuals' reported number of chronic conditions, over and above the effects of respondents' own age, race, gender, education, income, and assets. Similarly, the percentage of households receiving public assistance had independent associations with self-rated health, after controlling for the same individual-level variables.

Although such multilevel studies indicate an independent role of community socioeconomic level in predicting health and mortality, most of the independent community effects have been relatively small in size, considerably smaller than effects of individual-level socioeconomic position on health.

Socioeconomic Inequality Within and Between Communities, Regions, and Societies Another line of research suggests that it is not only the average level of income or deprivation, but also the income inequality across communities, regions, or societies that is associated with health and mortality, with inequality perhaps more important than level of income (e.g., per capita income) for developed countries. As already indicated (see Figure 6–1), per capita income is strongly and linearly associated with health among less developed countries, but the relationship weakens and becomes almost nonexistent among more developed countries. However, across developed countries, the degree of income inequality is strongly and linearly

associated with differences in morbidity and mortality rates between countries, even after controlling for average level of income within each country (Rodgers 1979; Wilkinson 1996; van Doorslaer et al. 1997). Simply put, the bigger the gap in income between the rich and the poor in a country, the worse the health of the population. In addition, comparing areas within single countries rather than between countries, studies in England and the United States suggest that income inequality between local authorities in England (Ben-Shlomo et al. 1996) and between states (Kaplan et al. 1996; Kennedy et al. 1996, 1998), counties (Soobader and LeClere 1999), and metropolitan statistical areas (Waitzman and Smith 1998b) in the United States is strongly related to morbidity and mortality. However, recent studies assessing the effects of community or regional inequality on individual-level health and mortality net of both community or regional socioeconomic level and individual-level socioeconomic position generally indicate effects of community or regional inequality that are much smaller than, and largely mediated through, the effects of individual-level socioeconomic position (Soobader and LeClere 1999; Fiscella and Franks 1997).

Summary Beyond measuring socioeconomic position at the individual level and investigating its relationship to individual level health, recent research has examined whether socioeconomic characteristics of communities, regions, and societies may play an additional role in impacting health, over and above the effects of individual socioeconomic position. Later sections of this chapter will show how expanding our notions of socioeconomic position to include measures at the community, regional, and societal levels may help us better understand why and how socioeconomic inequalities in health are created and maintained, and thus how they may be addressed.

The Shape of the Relationship Between Socioeconomic Position and Health: Linear Gradient or Diminishing Returns?

Some research intriguingly finds that the relationship between socioeconomic position and health occurs at all levels of the socioeconomic hierarchy, with even those in the highest socioeconomic groups having better health than those just below them in the socioeconomic hierarchy (Adler et al. 1994; Marmot et al. 1991).

Despite this evidence for gradient effects of socioeconomic position on health, studies of broad national or community populations generally indicate that the relationship of income to health is monotonic but not a linear gradient. There are substantially diminishing returns of higher income to health, with decreasing and even nonexistent relationships between income and both mortality (Backlund et al. 1996; McDonough et al. 1997; Wolfson et al. 1993) and morbidity (House et al. 1990, 1994; Mirowsky and Hu 1996) at higher levels of income. This trend partially reflects a health "ceiling effect"; people in the upper socioeconomic strata maintain overall good health until quite late in life, leaving little opportunity for improvements in average health among these groups throughout much of adulthood (House et al. 1994). Thus, it is most important to understand what factors may explain or alleviate this relationship across lower levels of socioeconomic position, rather than across the gradient or at higher levels.

Causation Some debates about possible explanations for the robust socioeconomic inequalities in health have centered around issues of causation—whether people with low socioeconomic position are more likely to become unhealthy, or whether unhealthy people are more likely to remain in or move into lower socioeconomic strata. Evidence suggests that although poor health can certainly affect socioeconomic position (Fuchs 1983; Smith and Kington 1997), most of the relationship flows from socioeconomic position to health. Such conclusions are based on research that: (a) shows a prospective effect of socioeconomic position on health and mortality while adjusting for health at baseline (House et al. 1994; Lynch, Kaplan, and Shema 1997; Mirowsky and Hu 1996; Wolfson et al. 1993); (b) measures the relative weight of different explanations for the association between socioeconomic position and health and finds that the selection effect of health on socioeconomic position is not the major explanation (Blane et al. 1993; Fox et al. 1985; Power et al. 1996); and (c) indicates that actual patterns of downward and upward mobility work to constrain rather than cause overall patterns of socioeconomic inequalities in health (Bartley and Plewis 1997). Although we believe the evidence for the impact of socioeconomic position on health is strong, there is still a need for more careful analyses of the potential reciprocal effects, especially in data sets that have good and continuing measures of both socioeconomic position and health over time, preferably from as early in life as possible.

Moreover, research on the socioeconomic characteristics of communities, regions, and societies needs to better specify the causal relationships between individual socioeconomic position, community-level socioeconomic level and inequality, and health. As discussed above, some recent research has examined whether there are independent effects of community-level socioeconomic characteristics on individual health, over and above individual socioeconomic position. However, future research needs to examine the joint effects of individual- and community-level socioeconomic position on health as well. Individual socioeconomic position affects the types of communities people live in, but the socioeconomic characteristics of communities can in turn affect the socioeconomic position of individual residents. Changes in health can similarly affect changes both in individual socioeconomic position and in the types of communities in which one remains in or into which one moves. We discuss these complex causal pathways further below.

Race, Gender, and Age Variation

More general stratification research finds complex and variable relationships both among stratification variables (e.g., race, gender, age) and between them and their causes and consequences (e.g., Featherman and Hauser 1978). Thus it is important that research on race, gender, and age differentials in health consider the role of socioeconomic position and that research on socioeconomic inequalities in health consider the roles of race, gender, and age. Ideally, we should study the complex interactions among these stratification variables simultaneously, but because most research and theory do not yet do this, we review work here that considers how race, gender, and age each separately interact with socioeconomic position in affecting health.

Race, Socioeconomic Position, and Health A growing number of studies find that many, but not all, of the race differences in health in the United States are explained by socioeconomic factors (Krieger et al. 1993; Lillie-Blanton and LaVeist 1996; Mutchler and Burr 1991; Rogers et al. 1996; Schoenbaum and Waidmann 1997; Williams and Collins 1995). However, simply controlling for individual-level socioeconomic position when looking at race differences in health may overlook the significant race differences in the types of neighborhoods in which whites and nonwhites live and the other types of differential experience they have (e.g., of discrimination) even at similar individual-level socioeconomic positions (Anderson and Armstead 1995; Jargowsky 1997; Lillie-Blanton and LaVeist 1996), which may further explain race differences in health. For example, in metropolitan areas in 1990, only 6.3 percent of poor white people lived in high poverty areas, compared to 33.5 percent and 22.1 percent of poor black and poor Hispanic people, respectively.

Research focusing on socioeconomic inequalities in health often does not investigate whether this relationship differs by race, and what little research there is has found inconsistent results. Nancy Krieger and colleagues (1993) summarize work showing that education does not have the same economic return (e.g., actual salary, nonwage benefits, or occupational position) for blacks as it does for whites, raising the question about whether there might also be differential health returns by race. Some research does find that education has less of an effect on measures of self-rated health (Mutchler and Burr 1991; Reynolds and Ross 1998), coronary heart disease (Diez-Roux et al. 1995), and infant mortality (Din-Dzietham and Hertz-Picciotto 1998) among blacks compared to whites, whereas other research finds virtually no race differences in the effects of income (Diez-Roux et al. 1995; McDonough et al. 1997; Mutchler and Burr 1991) and occupation (Gregorio et al. 1997) on health and mortality.

In sum, race and socioeconomic position are inextricably related to each other and to health, and hence one cannot be considered without the other. Socioeconomic position is a major explanation of race differences, but not the full one. Other experiences associated with race in our society, such as discrimination (Hummer 1996; Krieger et al. 1993; Krieger and Sidney 1996; Williams 1997), residential segregation (Jargowsky 1997), and cultural differences (Lannin et al. 1998), may also account for some race effects on health. Finally, the relation of different indicators of socioeconomic position to health may vary across racial/ethnic populations due to the differential importance or sensitivity of different socioeconomic measures across these populations. These are major areas for current and future research.

Gender, Socioeconomic Position, and Health

Socioeconomic inequalities in health have often been found to be stronger in men than in women, resulting in much debate about whether standard measures of socioeconomic position are equally appropriate for men and women, especially whether married women should be classified according to their own socioeconomic position, that of their husbands, or both. Although some research finds that measuring socioeconomic position at the individual or family level makes little difference in patterns of socioeconomic inequalities in health for women (Arber and Ginn 1993), other research suggests that measuring socioeconomic position at both

the individual and family levels may be important in understanding the full association between socioeconomic position and health—for both women and men (Pugh and Moser 1990; McDonough et al. in press). Nancy Krieger and colleagues (1993) suggest that individual-level socioeconomic position may be most directly related to working conditions, whereas family-level socioeconomic position may be most directly related to overall standard of living. Community-level socioeconomic characteristics might be considered additional measures of a family's overall standard of living, one that may be particularly salient for women who do not work and may spend a substantial amount of time in their community environment.

The issue of gender differences in the relationship between socioeconomic position and health goes beyond determining how to classify the socioeconomic position of married women and homemakers. Gender differences in labor force participation and in the structure and quality of occupations themselves may play a role in explaining gender differences in socioeconomic inequalities in health (Arber 1991; Arber and Lahelma 1993; Stronks et al. 1995). For example, Sara Arber and Eero Lahelma (1993) compared Finland and Britain and found that socioeconomic inequalities in health are strong for both women and men in Finland, but only for men in Britain. However, housewives in Britain were found to have particularly poor health. The researchers suggest that in countries with a high degree of female labor force participation, socioeconomic position may be strongly related to health for both men and women, whereas in countries with less female labor force participation, women's family roles and housing characteristics may play more of a role than socioeconomic position in affecting women's health. Other research in the Netherlands suggests that the socioeconomic inequalities in health, more pronounced in men than in women, may partially reflect the poor working conditions of men with low socioeconomic position (Stronks et al. 1995).

In sum, research often finds a stronger relationship between socioeconomic position and health for men compared to women, which challenges us to consider: (1) whether *community* socioeconomic characteristics may play an additional role in affecting health, particularly for women who do not work outside the home; (2) how gender differences in labor force participation and in family roles affect health both directly and in interaction with socioeconomic position; and (3) what role gender differences in working conditions may play in explaining gender differences in socioeconomic inequalities in health.

Age, Socioeconomic Position, and Health
Socioeconomic inequalities are large in prenatal, neonatal, and infant health and mortality (Aber et al. 1997; Singh and Yu 1996) but are strikingly diminished by adolescence (West et al. 1990; Ford et al. 1994). With few exceptions, research indicates that socioeconomic inequalities in health and mortality are generally small in early adulthood, increasingly larger through middle and early old age, and then smaller again in later old age (Elo and Preston 1996; House et al. 1990, 1994; McDonough et al. 1997; Sorlie et al. 1995; Wilkins et al. 1989). Stephanie Robert and James House (1994) have described some of the potential explanations for this diminished relationship between socioeconomic position and health at older ages including: (1) health and social policies targeted to older people (such as Medicare and Social Security) might help equalize access to care and resources at older ages; (2) only the hardiest and healthiest people of low socioeconomic position may survive infancy and into older ages, making their health increasingly similar with age to that of people with high socioeconomic position; (3) there may be age variation in how socioeconomic position affects exposure to and impact of mediating psychosocial, behavioral, and environmental factors that are known to help explain socioeconomic inequalities in health; (4) standard measures of socioeconomic position may be less applicable to very young as well as older adults, thereby creating at these ages a diminished relationship between socioeconomic position and health that reflects poor measurement rather than true differences by age; (5) the biological robustness of late adolescence/early adulthood and the frailty of later old age may limit the ability of socioeconomic position or other factors to affect health at these ages. To date, we are still far from understanding the relative importance of these and other potential explanations. However, increasing our understanding of age variations in the relationship between socioeconomic position and health will ultimately improve our understanding of the overall relationship between socioeconomic position and health.

Summary In sum, issues such as the measurement of socioeconomic position, the nature and direction of relationships among measures of socioeconomic position and of these with various outcomes (including health), and the interplay of race, gender, and age with socioeconomic position in systems of social stratification are all issues that sociologists have studied extensively in analyzing social stratification, and that merit greater attention in research on the relationship between socioeconomic position and health.

EXPLAINING SOCIOECONOMIC INEQUALITIES IN HEALTH: SOCIAL CONTENT AND CONTEXT

As noted in the introduction, the burgeoning research literature on socioeconomic inequalities in health has tended to focus on the mechanisms or pathways, especially behavioral and psychophysiologic ones, by which socioeconomic inequalities "get under the skin" (Taylor et al. 1997). Much work has focused on discovering the one or several major pathways or mechanisms that account for socioeconomic inequalities in health, with the hope that intervening on these pathways can alleviate or significantly reduce these inequalities. The following sections describe how medical care, health behaviors, and psychosocial and environmental factors have each been examined for their abilities to explain socioeconomic inequalities in health, and how each has been rejected as the single "magic bullet" answer to reducing the inequalities. Sociological research, however, provides broader context and content for examining the mechanisms linking socioeconomic position to health. (See also Chapter 4 by Mirowsky, Ross, and Reynolds for a related discussion.)

The Role of Medical Care— Baby and Bath Water Failed

It has been widely assumed for most of this century that socioeconomic inequalities in health primarily reflect differentials in access to and utilization of modern medical care—the disease-preventive (e.g., vaccination) and curative powers of which have grown strikingly since the mid-nineteenth century. Thus, reduction or elimination of socioeconomic differences in access to and utilization of medical care was expected to more or less proportionately reduce socioeconomic inequalities in health. The failure of this expectation to be fulfilled has been a major impetus both to the current revival of research on socioeconomic inequalities in health and to a growing literature on the limitations of modern medical care.

The recognition of the limits of medical care in affecting both population health generally and socioeconomic inequalities in health in particular, at least in developing societies, has a long history (cf. Dubos 1959), but it has gained strength since the 1970s. Beginning in 1976, Thomas McKeown (1976) published a series of works showing that most of the increase in life expectancy in England and Wales between the mid-eighteenth and mid-twentieth century occurred prior to the formulation of the "germ theory" of disease in the later nineteenth century or its widespread application in the twentieth century. Subsequently, John McKinlay and Sonja McKinlay (1977) showed much the same for the United States, and most recently John Bunker and colleagues (1994) concluded that of the 30-year increase in life expectancy in the United States in this century, only about 5 years has been due to preventive or therapeutic medical care, with a potential of 1.5–2.0 years of further increase due to wider use of existing medical care.

At about the same time, the Black report (Black et al. 1982) showed that socioeconomic inequalities in mortality in England and Wales had not declined and even had increased in the three decades following the establishment of the British National Health Service; Michael Marmot and colleagues (1987) showed that the same continued to be true over the next decade. Subsequently, research indicated that the establishment of the Canadian National Health Insurance system in the early 1970s did little or nothing to reduce socioeconomic inequalities in mortality in Canada (Wilkins et al. 1989; Roos and Mustard 1997). Further, crossnational research also indicates that the percentage of GDP spent on health care is unrelated to population life expectancy across the United States and in other developed nations. In fact, as shown in Figure 6–2, although

the United States spends a greater percentage of gross domestic product on health than any does other OECD nation, overall life expectancy at birth in the United States is worse than average and is no better than that of other OECD nations that spend considerably less (e.g., United Kingdom, Greece, Spain). Finally, explicitly controlling at the individual level for indicators of access to or utilization of health care (such as health insurance status, number of visits to doctors) accounts for little of the association between socioeconomic position and health (Marmot et al. 1987; Williams 1990; Ross and Wu 1995). For all of these reasons, many scientists have increasingly concluded that improving access to and quality of medical care is not going to greatly reduce socioeconomic inequalities in health.

Although improving access to medical care may not be the magic bullet approach to eliminating socioeconomic inequalities in health, we need to be careful not to throw out the baby with the bath water. A growing body of research shows that medical care is a complex social system in which equality of gross access and utilization can mask wide variations in the nature, timeliness, and appropriateness of care (Dutton 1978). Residents of middle- and lower-income areas are more likely than residents of high-income areas to be hospitalized with conditions that wouldn't require hospitalization

FIGURE 6–2 Life Expectancy at Birth by Percentage of GDP Spent on Health, 1995–1996 (for Selected OECD Countries)

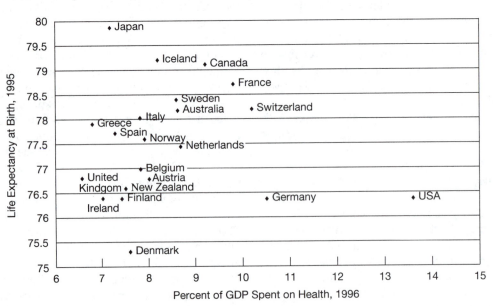

SOURCE: United Nations Development Program, *Human Development Report, 1998* (New York: Oxford University Press); OECD, *Health Data 98*. See http://www.oecd.org/els/health/fad_l.htm.

if timely, appropriate ambulatory care were available (Pappas et al. 1997). Even among people who share a particular disease or medical condition, subsequent recovery is affected by socioeconomic position. For example, among men ages 29–69 participating in a multicenter, randomized, double-blind clinical trial, Jeannette Ickovics and colleagues (1997) found that those with low socioeconomic position on a composite measure of education and occupation were almost twice as likely as those with high socioeconomic position to have no improvements in functional status one year after myocardial infarction. The odds ratio was reduced only to 1.51 after controlling for numerous clinical factors, age, race, life stress, social isolation, and depression. Additionally, women with lower socioeconomic position are less likely to receive breast and cervical cancer screening (Lantz et al. 1997) or to get medical care when their cancer is at an earlier and more treatable stage (Lannin et al. 1998). Even where access to health care has been equalized via national health insurance or health care systems, research finds that differential access to and quality of care still exist (Katz and Hofer 1994). For example, in the Medicare program in the United States, large racial inequalities in access to specific forms of health care exist among participants (Gornick et al. 1996).

Moreover, research that concludes that medical care plays a limited role in explaining socioeconomic inequalities in health has generally focused on mortality and not considered multiple dimensions of health—particularly concepts of health related to functional status and quality of life. Although access to health care may not be the most important factor explaining socioeconomic inequalities in *mortality,* access to medical care undoubtedly plays an important role in affecting people's *health-related quality of life*—particularly for people who experience chronic conditions (Bunker et al. 1994). Sol Levine, to whom this book is dedicated, gave an address titled "The Changing Terrain in Medical Sociology: Emergent Concern with Quality of Life," when he received the Leo G. Reeder Award for Distinguished Scholarship in Medical Sociology (Levine 1987). He emphasized that medical sociologists should increasingly address issues of health-related quality of life rather than just issues of morbidity and mortality, since one of the primary successes and functions of modern medical care is its ability to enhance quality of life. Yet research in medical sociology has not fully caught up with his idea.

In sum, although inequalities in medical care are not the primary factors explaining socioeconomic inequalities in health, future research should explore in more depth the role that different dimensions of access to and use of medical care play in explaining socioeconomic inequalities in health.

Health Behaviors—The New Magic Bullet That Failed?

After medical care, probably the most widely recognized determinant of health, and hence potential explanation for socioeconomic inequalities in health, is health behavior or lifestyle. Cigarette smoking, lack of exercise, excess (and also inadequate) weight due to unhealthful eating habits, and immoderate consumption of alcoholic beverages have been identified by the Department of Health and Human Services (1990) as perhaps the major threats to population health and hence the major avenues for health improvement or promotion in the United States. Although persons of lower socioeconomic position have riskier profiles on all of these health behaviors, research shows that these behavioral factors account for only a small proportion of socioeconomic inequalities in mortality (e.g., Lynch et al. 1996; Haan et al. 1987). Most recently, Paula Lantz and colleagues (1998) showed, in a nationally representative sample of adults age 25+ in the United States, that the hazard-rate ratio of mortality was 3.22 for those in the low-income group and 2.34 for those in the middle-income group compared to those in the upper-income group (essentially those above the median), after controlling for age, gender, race, urbanicity, and education. Controlling further for health behaviors (cigarette smoking, alcohol drinking, physical activity, weight relative to height), reduced the hazard-rate ratios only modestly to 2.77 for the low-income group and to 2.14 for the middle-income group.

Other Psychosocial and Environmental Factors— The Magic Bullet? Beyond medical care and health behaviors, many other psychosocial factors such as social relationships and support, stress, and lack of control or self-efficacy are associated with both health and socioeconomic position (cf. Chapter 4 by Mirowsky and colleagues). Again, however, any one or few of these variables can explain only a small part of the predictive association between socioeconomic position and health (House et al. 1994).

The Composite Explanation—There Is No Magic Bullet Beyond Socioeconomic Position Itself Although neither medical care nor health behavior nor any one or a few of the growing list of psychosocial and environmental risk factors for health constitute a "magic bullet" that mediates the impact of socioeconomic position on health, when sets of 10–20 of these various risk factors are considered simultaneously, 50–100 percent of the relationship between socioeconomic position and health or mortality can be explained among adults in the United States and other countries. For example, James House and colleagues (1994) found that education and income differences in health among adults in the United States are substantially explainable by differences in exposure to and impact of a number of health behaviors (smoking, weight, drinking) and psychosocial factors (social relationships and supports, acute and chronic stress, self-efficacy). Catherine Ross and Chia-Ling Wu (1995) similarly found that the relationship between education and health among adults was partially, though not entirely, explained by work and economic conditions (employment status, income, economic hardship, work fulfillment), social-psychological resources (sense of control, social support), and health behaviors (exercise, smoking, drinking). Among a sample of men ages 42–60 in Finland, John Lynch and colleagues (1996) found that an array of 23 biological, behavioral, psychological, and social risk factors accounted for much of the income differentials in mortality. For men in the lowest income quintile, adjusting for the set of risk factors reduced the excess relative risk of all-cause mortality by 85 percent, the risk of cardiovascular mortality by 118 percent, and the risk of acute myocardial infarction by 45 percent. Chris Power and colleagues (1998) showed that occupational class differences in self-rated health among adults age 33 in the 1958 British cohort were to a large extent explained by material, behavioral, and psychosocial characteristics in both childhood and adulthood—reducing the odds ratio of poor health at age 33 from 3.15 to 1.64 in men, and from 2.30 to 1.11 in women.

Though there is much speculation about the many aspects of the physical, social, and service environments of communities that may account for independent effects of community socioeconomic level on health (Robert 1998; MacIntyre et al. 1993), few studies have actually tested whether specific mediating factors account for this relationship. Mary Haan and colleagues (1987) found that respondents' health behaviors and social network characteristics explained little of the relationship between living in a poverty area and mortality, after controlling for age, gender, race, and baseline health, among a sample of people living in Oakland, California, in 1965. Norman Waitzman and Ken Smith (1998a) similarly found that the impact of living in a poverty area on mortality (age, race, and gender adjusted rate ratio of 2.01) was only somewhat attenuated after further controlling simultaneously for marital status, income, education, alcohol consumption, body mass index, smoking, exercise frequency, baseline health status, hypertension, and cholesterol level (rate ratio reduced to 1.78) among respondents age 25–54 in a United States national sample of people in the early 1970s who were followed up through 1987.

In order to explain the relationship between socioeconomic inequality or distribution and health between communities, regions, and societies, recent research has explored the potential mediating role of aggregate measures of social capital. This research suggests that communities or societies with low income inequality possess higher levels of social capital, such as strong feelings of community trust and social cohesion (Wilkinson 1996; Kawachi et al. 1997; Kawachi and Kennedy 1997) and/or high levels of social, educational, and medical investment and expenditures (Kaplan et al. 1996) that in turn affect health. However, others suggest that we still need to examine to what extent the impact of community or societal income inequality on individual mortality may operate primarily through individual socioeconomic position rather than via aggregate levels of social capital (Robert and House in press; Fiscella and Franks 1997; Gravelle 1998).

How and Why These Mediators Work: Areas for Future Research

Knowing which combination of psychosocial, behavioral, and environmental factors account for the relationship between individual socioeconomic position and health in statistical analyses does not answer questions about *how* and *why* these mediators work. Some research essentially looks "downstream" to determine the physiological processes that link behavioral, psychosocial, and environmental factors to health, while other research looks "upstream" to examine how and why behavioral, psychosocial, and environmental factors are distributed by socioeconomic position in the first place.

Research focusing on "downstream" processes essentially asks how biological processes mediate the relationship between psychosocial factors and health. For example, reviews by Seeman and McEwen (1996) and Uchino and colleagues (1996) suggest the specific biological responses to social support and social interactions that in turn affect health. Similarly, other research investigates the biological pathways linking health to other behavioral and psychosocial factors such as stress (Brunner 1997) and sense of control (Taylor et al. 1997). In addition, there has been some speculation that gradient effects of socioeconomic position on health may partially result from a direct physiological response to being lower in the socioeconomic hierarchy (Adler et al. 1994). These and other "downstream" approaches to examining the physiological mechanisms linking socioeconomic position to health will be important in helping us fully understand the processes through which socioeconomic position "gets under the skin" to affect health (Anderson and Armstead 1995; Evans et al. 1994).

In contrast, other more sociological research focuses "upstream" to investigate why and how psychosocial and behavioral factors come to be differentially distributed by socioeconomic position in the first place. Some of this research attempts to conceptualize the pathways through which different dimensions of socioeconomic position (e.g., income, education, occupation) may affect health both separately and in combination. For example, income may indirectly affect health by determining access to material conditions of life such as safe housing, health insurance, and nutritious food. Occupational position may affect health through physical and psychological conditions of the work environment. Education may indirectly affect health through its impact on income and occupation, but it may also have independent effects on health such as by shaping health beliefs and health behaviors (cf. Chapter 4 of this volume by Mirowsky and colleagues).

In the context of a society and health care system that focuses on trying to get individuals to change their own behaviors and lifestyles in order to improve individual and population health, sociologists play a particularly important role in showing the more "upstream" causes of unhealthy behaviors and lifestyles and illuminating other possibilities for intervention that may be more efficient, effective, and appropriate for improving health. Sociologists view health behaviors, for example, not solely as matters of individual choice, but as patterned responses to or products of the social environment.

Using smoking behavior as an example, we can see the different types of questions that are being asked and that need to be asked to better understand the relationship between socioeconomic position and health behavior. Evaluations of smoking cessation programs have found that they are less successful with smokers of lower socioeconomic position compared with those with higher socioeconomic position (Matheny and Weatherman 1998; Kaprio and Koskenvuo 1988), thus, paradoxically, perpetuating and even exacerbating socioeconomic differences in smoking behavior. These socioeconomic differences in smoking behavior raise questions as to whether people with lower socioeconomic position are more likely to have:

(a) less knowledge about the links between smoking and health, (b) different evaluations of the relative importance of smoking to the length and/or quality of their lives, (c) psychological dispositions (e.g., low sense of self-efficacy or control) that make them more likely to smoke and/or less likely to quit (such as using smoking as a coping strategy to deal with stress), (d) social support networks that encourage smoking but not quitting, (e) family, work, and community environments with a greater prevalence of smoking behavior, (f) more exposure to tobacco marketing strategies, and/or (g) a number of the characteristics listed above that combine to affect smoking behavior. Each of these different explanations for the prevalence and persistence of socioeconomic inequalities in smoking would require different types of interventions at different levels (e.g., at the individual, family, workplace, community, and national levels), making it important that we better understand how socioeconomic position is linked to smoking behavior.

Research on socioeconomic inequalities in health has only begun examining some of the particular conditions and experiences, arising and accumulating over the life course, that help to explain how socioeconomic position affects health. For example, John Lynch and colleagues (1997) studied 2,674 middle-aged Finnish men and found that physical activity and diet in adulthood were strongly associated with childhood socioeconomic conditions, whereas smoking behavior was more strongly associated with respondents' own level of education and occupation. Chris Power and Sharon Matthews (1997) suggest that conditions associated with low socioeconomic position in both childhood and adulthood may interact to produce worse health in adulthood. They provide and summarize evidence that having lower birth weight (associated with lower socioeconomic position of parents) combined with being overweight in adulthood (associated with lower socioeconomic position in adulthood) produces a higher probability of having noninsulin-dependent diabetes mellitus in adulthood than either risk factor alone.

Although a large number of studies suggest that fetal and infant physiological conditions (e.g., fetal and infant weight and growth) affect health in later life, such studies have been criticized for prematurely concluding the predominance of biological explanations for this association (review in Joseph and Kramer 1996). Sociologists are particularly well positioned to examine the complex web of causality between biological, socioeconomic, and social factors that accumulate and interact across the life course to affect health trajectories, and without appropriate sociological inquiry, some of the pieces of this web may not receive adequate attention.

Other research, ultimately requiring both "downstream" and "upstream" types of investigation, involves discovering how behavioral, psychosocial, and environmental factors work additively and interactively to mediate the relationship between socioeconomic position and health. For example, socioeconomic position might affect both *exposure* and *vulnerability* to mediating behavioral, psychosocial, and environmental factors. Those with lower socioeconomic position are more likely both to be exposed to negative life events and conditions that may lead to poor health and to be more vulnerable or susceptible to those exposures because of less effective social and psychological resources to deal with negative life events and conditions (Berkman and Syme 1979; McLeod and Kessler 1990).

Summary In sum, as an alternative and complement to the focus of biomedical and psychological science on identifying key behavioral, psychological, and physiological pathways by which socioeconomic position comes to affect health, we believe current evidence points to a broader and more complex sociological explanation, the unity and strength of which derives from the pervasive power of socioeconomic position to affect almost all aspects of a person's life experience and circumstances relevant to health—from medical care, to health behavior, to chronic and acute stress, to social relationships and supports, to major psychological dispositions, and to physical-chemical and biological exposures. There remains much to be learned about how and why various indicators of socioeconomic position influence each of these outcomes, and about which combinations are most consequential for health. However, the pervasive and powerful effects of socioeconomic position on these intervening variables, and ultimately on the broad array of health outcomes affected by these variables, suggest that socioeconomic position itself may be the "magic bullet" that provides the key to understanding and alleviating socioeconomic inequalities in health.

SOCIOECONOMIC POSITION AS A FUNDAMENTAL CAUSE, AND THE BROADER SOCIAL DETERMINANTS OF IT

Though the idea had been discussed previously (House et al. 1990, 1994; Williams 1990), Bruce Link and Jo Phelan (1995) have provided the central statement of the idea that socioeconomic position is a "fundamental cause" of disease, emphasizing that the association between socioeconomic position and health persists *even when the pathways that mediate this relationship change* (see Chapter 3 by Link and Phelan in this volume). Socioeconomic inequalities in health once primarily reflected the exposure of people with lower socioeconomic position to unhealthy living and working conditions such as inadequate sanitation and housing, unclean water, and lack of medical care. Although many of these living and working conditions, as well as access to medical care, have improved tremendously, socioeconomic inequalities in health remain and may even be increasing. But now these socioeconomic inequalities in health are "explained" by a combination of other factors discussed above, such as health behaviors, stress, low social supports, personal dispositions, and environmental exposures.

Bruce Link and Jo Phelan (1995) argue that the reason socioeconomic position continues to affect health, despite the amelioration of mediating factors at any given time, is that people with higher socioeconomic position always have more access to whatever resources can help them avoid health risks or promote health. For example, although smoking cigarettes used to be more prevalent among people with higher socioeconomic position, this relationship reversed as the damaging health effects of smoking become clear. Higher socioeconomic individuals began to quit smoking at greater rates than lower socioeconomic individuals, and also became less likely to begin smoking in the first place. Similarly, coronary heart disease and AIDS were both, in the initial stages of their respective epidemics, more incident and prevalent at higher socioeconomic levels. As their importance as sources of overall morbidity and mortality increased, however, they came to be more prevalent and incident at lower socioeconomic levels.

Therefore, a focus on socioeconomic position as a fundamental cause of disease moves the perspective on socioeconomic inequalities in health even further "upstream" than most lines of inquiry. Beyond focusing on how particular health behaviors and psychosocial factors are contextualized by socioeconomic position, viewing socioeconomic position as a fundamental cause suggests that the pathways linking socioeconomic position to health at any one time are arguably less important than the fact that socioeconomic position continues to affect health over time, despite the changing array of explanatory mediating factors.

This in turn leads to the need to understand how and why the socioeconomic position of individuals is determined by higher order social and economic processes. It is often assumed that little can be done to improve the socioeconomic conditions of individuals or populations, or that improving the socioeconomic position and hence health of some individuals and populations can only result in equal and opposite changes in the socioeconomic position and health of others. However, this has not and need not be the case.

As discussed above, much and probably most of the massive improvements in individual population health over the last two centuries have been due to the equally massive improvements in the average socioeconomic and living conditions of individuals and societies. Also as discussed above, current research across developed societies suggests that current variations and further improvements in population health are dependent less on the average socioeconomic conditions of societies, though improvements here are likely to still have salutary effects, and more on levels of socioeconomic inequality within and across societies. Most of this research has focused on determining what role socioeconomic inequality within and between communities, regions, and societies plays in affecting individual health, *over and above* the effects of individual socioeconomic position. Although this is a worthwhile question, it will also be particularly important for future research to investigate what role the socioeconomic conditions of communities, regions, and societies play in shaping individual socioeconomic positions that more directly affect health. Rather than investigating larger socioeconomic processes and conditions as *independent* of individual socioeconomic conditions, we need to understand how socioeconomic levels and inequalities in communities, regions, and societies affect the socioeconomic levels of individual residents.

Because persons of higher socioeconomic position in our and other developed societies may be approaching the biological limits of improvement in health and longevity, increases in their socioeconomic positions have diminishing returns for individual and population health (and conversely, even modest decreases in their socioeconomic levels would likely have little effect on their health and longevity). Hence, the greatest determinant of individual and population health is the absolute and relative socioeconomic position of those in the broader lower range (lower one-third to one-half) of the socioeconomic distributions. The major attribute of communities, regions, and societies with lower socioeconomic inequality and better population health is the better socioeconomic position and hence health of these broad lower socioeconomic strata, due to their better income and/or the more equal availability of social capital such as education, housing, medical care, etc., reflecting policies in both the private and public sectors. The mechanisms by which societies, communities, and regions sometimes achieve such improved socioeconomic conditions for lower socioeconomic strata, usually accompanied by lesser social inequality, deserve equal or more attention in research on socioeconomic inequalities in health as the mechanisms linking individual socioeconomic position to health (Kaplan et al. 1996; Robert and House in press; Wilkinson 1996). In short, we need to recognize that socioeconomic policy in both the public and private sectors may now be the major avenue for alleviating socioeconomic inequalities in health and hence improving individual and population health.

CONCLUSION

Despite everything we do know about socioeconomic inequalities in health, there is still much to learn. In order to increase our understanding of how and why socioeconomic inequalities in health exist and persist, research from different disciplines will be needed, as well as research that is interdisciplinary. In fact, there has been a recent surge of research on socioeconomic inequalities in health across and between disciplines (Kaplan and Lynch 1997). A sociological perspective is crucial at this time, not *in spite of* the increasing interest of other disciplines in this topic, but rather *because of* the increasing interest of researchers from other disciplines. Sociologists and some social epidemiologists are more likely to emphasize "upstream" questions and explanations regarding socioeconomic inequalities in health, at a time when more "downstream" approaches are proliferating. Although the knowledge obtained from more "downstream" approaches is important, such knowledge must be balanced by more "upstream" perspectives and approaches.

We have suggested three major ways that sociological perspectives and approaches can, have, and should continue to contribute to understanding and alleviating socioeconomic inequalities in health. The first is by bringing the sociological theories and methods regarding social stratification to bear on issues such as (1) the measurement of socioeconomic position, (2) the nature and directionality of its relationship to health, and (3) the ways in which socioeconomic position combines, directly and interactively, with other dimensions of stratification such as age, race, and gender, to affect individual and population health.

The second is by providing sociological content and context to discussions of the mechanisms or pathways linking socioeconomic position to health.

Particularly important is the recognition that the power and pervasiveness of the impact of socioeconomic position on health derives not from one or few mechanisms or pathways, but rather from the substantial influence that socioeconomic position has on exposure to almost all behavioral, psychological, social, and environmental risk factors for health, as well as on medical care, and hence on almost all health and disease outcomes. Sociological and social epidemiological researchers have a special role in developing our understanding of how and why these pervasive effects of socioeconomic position occur, complementing the focus of psychological and physiological scientists on the psychophysiological mechanisms and pathways by which socioeconomic inequality gets "under the skin."

Finally, sociological perspectives and approaches emphasize that socioeconomic position is itself a "fundamental cause" of health, due to its pervasive effects on a range of health risk factors. As such, increasing attention is being and must continue to be paid to the broader macro socioeconomic factors, such as overall average socioeconomic levels and socioeconomic inequality in communities, regions, and societies, which have major impacts on individuals' socioeconomic position, as well as affecting health over and above individual socioeconomic position.

Because individuals, communities, and societies of upper socioeconomic position are approaching the biological limits of longevity and other indicators of health, the major opportunity for improving population health lies in reducing the socioeconomic inequalities in health between and within nations. This, in turn, seems increasingly likely to require alleviating current levels of socioeconomic inequality within and between nations. Sociologists will continue to play an important role in keeping the problem of socioeconomic inequalities a major area for research and increasingly a focus for public policy as well.

REFERENCES

ABER, J. LAWRENCE, NEIL G. BENNETT, DALTON C. CONLEY, and JIALI LI. 1997. "The Effects of Poverty on Child Health and Development." *Annual Review of Public Health* 18: 463–83.

ADLER, NANCY E., THOMAS BOYCE, MARGARET A. CHESNEY, SHELDON COHEN, SUSAN FOLKMAN, ROBERT L. KAHN, and S. LEONARD SYME. 1994. "Socioeconomic Status and Health: The Challenge of the Gradient." *American Psychologist* 49: 15–24.

ADLER, NANCY E., W. THOMAS BOYCE, MARGARET A. CHESNEY, SUSAN FOLKMAN, and S. LEONARD SYME. 1993. "Socioeconomic Inequalities in Health: No Easy Solution." *Journal of the American Medical Association* 269: 3140–45.

ANDERSON, NORMAN B., and CHERYL A. ARMSTEAD. 1995. "Toward Understanding the Association of Socioeconomic Status and Health: A New Challenge for the Biophysical Approach." *Psychosomatic Medicine* 57: 213–25.

ANDERSON, ROGER T., PAUL SORLIE, ERIC BACKLUND, NORMAN JOHNSON, and GEORGE A. KAPLAN. 1997. "Mortality Effects of Community Socioeconomic Status." *Epidemiology* 8: 42–47.

ANTONOVSKY, AARON. 1967. "Social Class, Life Expectancy and Overall Mortality." *The Milbank Memorial Fund Quarterly* 45: 31–73.

ARBER, SARA. 1991. "Class, Paid Employment and Family Roles—Making Sense of Structural Disadvantage, Gender and Health Status." *Social Science and Medicine* 32: 425–36.

ARBER, SARA, and EERO LAHELMA. 1993. "Inequalities in Women's and Men's Ill-Health: Britain and Finland Compared." *Social Science and Medicine* 37: 1055–68.

ARBER, SARA, and JAY GINN. 1993. "Gender and Inequalities in Health in Later Life." *Social Sciences and Medicine* 36: 33–46.

BACKLUND, ERIC, PAUL D. SORLIE, and NORMAN J. JOHNSON. 1996. "The Shape of the Relationship Between Income and Mortality in the United States." *AEP* 6: 12–20.

BARTLEY, MEL, and IAN PLEWIS. 1997. "Does Health-Selective Mobility Account for Socioeconomic Differences in Health? Evidence From England and Wales, 1971 to 1991." *Journal of Health and Social Behavior* 38: 376–86.

BARTLEY, MEL, DAVID BLANE, and SCOTT MONTGOMERY. 1997. "Health and the Life Course: Why Safety Nets Matter." *British Medical Journal* 314: 1194–96.

BEN-SHLOMO, Y., I.R. WHITE, and M. MARMOT. 1996. "Does the Variation in the Socioeconomic Characteristics of an Area Affect Mortality?" *British Medical Journal* 312: 1013–14.

BERKMAN, LISA F., and LEONARD SYME. 1979. "Social Networks, Host Resistance, and Mortality: A Nine-Year Follow-up Study of Alameda County Residents." *American Journal of Epidemiology* 109: 186–204.

BERKMAN, LISA F., and SALLY MACINTYRE. 1997. "The Measurement of Social Class in Health Studies: Old Measures and New Formulations." In *Social Inequalities and Cancer,* ed. M. Kogevinas, N. Pearce, M. Susser, and P. Boffetta. Lyon: International Agency for Research on Cancer, pp. 51–63.

BLACK, DOUGLAS, J.N. MORRIS, CYRIL SMITH, and PETER TOWNSEND. 1982. *Inequalities in Health: The Black Report.* New York: Penguin.

BLANE, D., C. L. HART, G. D. SMITH, C. R. GILLIS, D. J. HOLE, and V. M. HAWTHORNE. 1996. "Association of Cardiovascular Disease Risk Factors With Socioeconomic Position During Childhood and During Adulthood." *British Medical Journal* 313: 1434–38.

BLANE, DAVID, GEORGE DAVEY SMITH, and MEL BARTLEY. 1993. "Social Selection: What Does It Contribute to Social Class Differences in Health?" *Sociology of Health and Illness* 15: 1–15.

BRUNNER, E., G. DAVEY SMITH, M. MARMOT, R. CANNER, M. BEKSINSKA, and J. O'BRIEN. 1996. "Childhood Social Circumstances and Psychosocial and Behavioural Factors as Determinants of Plasma Fibrinogen." *Lancet* 347: 1008–13.

BRUNNER, ERIC. 1997. "Stress and the Biology of Inequality." *British Medical Journal* 314: 1472–76.

BUNKER, JOHN P., HOWARD S. FRAZIER, and FREDERICK MOSTELLER. 1994. "Improving Health: Measuring Effects of Medical Care." *The Milbank Quarterly* 72: 225–58.

CASSEL, JOHN. 1976. "The Contribution of the Social Environment to Host Resistance." *American Journal of Epidemiology* 104: 107–23.

CHAPMAN, KENNETH S., and GOVIND HARIHARAN. 1996. "Do Poor People Have a Stronger Relationship Between Income and Mortality Than the Rich? Implications of Panel Data for Health-Health Analysis." *Journal of Risk and Uncertainty* 12: 51–63.

CLARK, DANIEL O., and GEORGE L. MADDOX. 1992. "Racial and Social Correlates of Age-Related Changes in Functioning." *The Journal of Gerontology* 47: S222–S232.

COHEN, SHELDON, GEORGE A. KAPLAN, and JUKKA T. SALONEN. In press. "The Role of Psychological Characteristics in the Relation Between Socioeconomic Status and Perceived Health." *Journal of Applied Social Psychology.*

CROMBIE, I.K., M.B. KENICER, W.C.S. SMITH, and H.D. TUNSTALL-PEDOE. 1989. "Unemployment, Socioenvironmental Factors, and Coronary Heart Disease in Scotland." *British Heart Journal* 61: 172–77.

CURTIS, SARAH E. 1990. "Use of Survey Data and Small Area Statistics to Assess the Link Between Individual Morbidity and Neighbourhood Deprivation." *Journal of Epidemiology and Community Health* 44: 62–68.

DAVEY SMITH, G., C. HART, D. BLANE, C. GILLIS, and V. HAWTHORNE. 1997. "Lifetime Socioeconomic Position and Mortality: Prospective Observational Study." *British Medical Journal* 314: 547–52.

DAVEY SMITH, G., C. HART, D. BLANE, and D. HOLE. 1998. "Adverse Socioeconomic Conditions in Childhood and Cause Specific Adult Mortality: Prospective Observational Study." *British Medical Journal* 316: 1631–51.

DEPARTMENT OF HEALTH AND HUMAN SERVICES. 1990. "Healthy People 2000: National Health Promotion and Disease Prevention Objectives Summary." Washington, D.C.: U.S. Government Printing Office.

DIEZ-ROUX, ANA V., F. JAVIER NIETO, C. MUNTANER, HERMAN A. TYROLER, G. W. COMSTOCK, E. SHAHAR, L. S. COOPER, R. L. WATSON, and MOYSES SZKLO. 1997. "Neighborhood Environments and Coronary Heart Disease: A Multilevel Analysis." *American Journal of Epidemiology* 146: 48–63.

DIEZ-ROUX, ANA V., F. JAVIER NIETO, HERMAN A. TYROLER, LARRY D. CRUM, and MOYSES SZKLO. 1995. "Social Inequalities and Atherosclerosis." *American Journal of Epidemiology* 141: 960–72.

DIN-DZIETHAM, REBECCA, and IRVA HERTZ-PICCIOTTO. 1998. "Infant Mortality Differences Between Whites and African Americans: The Effect of Maternal Education." *American Journal of Public Health* 88: 651–56.

DUBOS, RENÉ J. 1959. *Mirage of Health.* New York: Harper.

DUTTON, DIANA B. 1978. "Explaining the Low Use of Health Services by the Poor: Costs, Attitudes, or Delivery Systems?" *American Sociological Review* 43: 348–68.

ECOB, RUSSELL. 1996. "A Multilevel Modelling Approach to Examining the Effects of Area of Residence on Health and Functioning." *Journal of the Royal Statistical Society A* 159: 61–75.

ELO, IRMA T., and SAMUEL H. PRESTON. 1992. "Effects of Early-Life Conditions on Adult Mortality: A Review." *Population Index* 58: 186–212.

ELO, IRMA T., and SAMUEL H. PRESTON. 1996. "Educational Differentials in Mortality: United States, 1979–85." *Social Science and Medicine* 42: 47–57.

EVANS, ROBERT, G., MORRIS L. BARER, and THEODORE MARMOR (eds.). 1994. *Why Are Some People Healthy and Others Not?* New York: Aldine DeGruyter.

FEATHERMAN, DAVID L., and ROBERT M. HAUSER. 1978. *Opportunity and Change.* New York: Academic Press.

FEINSTEIN, JONATHAN S. 1993. "The Relationship Between Socioeconomic Status and Health: A Review of the Literature." *The Milbank Quarterly* 71: 279–322.

FIGUEROA, JANIS BARRY, and NANCY BREEN. 1995. "Significance of Underclass Residence on the Stage of Breast or Cervical Cancer Diagnosis." *AEA Papers and Proceedings* 85: 112–16.

FISCELLA, KEVIN, and PETER FRANKS. 1997. "Poverty or Income Inequality as a Predictor of Mortality: Longitudinal Cohort Study." *British Medical Journal* 314: 1724–27.

FORD, G., R. ECOB, K. HUNT, S. MACINTYRE, and P. WEST. 1994. "Patterns of Class Inequality in Health Through the Lifespan: Class Gradients at 15, 35 and 55 Years in the West of Scotland." *Social Science and Medicine* 39: 1037–50.

FOX, A.J., P.O. GOLDBLATT, and D.R. JONES. 1985. "Social Class Mortality Differentials: Artefact, Selection or Life Circumstances?" *Journal of Epidemiology and Community Health* 39: 1–8.

FUCHS, VICTOR R. 1983. *How We Live.* Cambridge, MA: Harvard University Press.

GILLUM, RICHARD F., MICHAEL E. MUSSOLINO, and JENNIFER H. MADANS. 1998. "Coronary Heart Disease Risk Factors and Attributable Risks in African-American Women and Men: NHANES I Epidemiologic Follow-up Study." *American Journal of Public Health* 88: 913–17.

GORNICK, M. E., P. W. EGGERS, T. W. REILLY, R. M. MENTNECH, L. K. FITTERMAN, L. E. KUCKEN, and B. C. VLADECK. 1996. "Effects of Race and Income on Mortality and Use of Services Among Medicare Beneficiaries." *New England Journal of Medicine* 335: 791–99.

GRAVELLE, HUGH. 1998. "How Much of the Relation Between Population Mortality and Unequal Distribution of Income Is a Statistical Artefact?" *British Medical Journal* 316: 382–85.

GREGORIO, DAVID I., STEPHEN J. WALSH, and DEBORAH PATURZO. 1997. "The Effects of Occupation-Based Social Position on Mortality in a Large American Cohort." *American Journal of Public Health* 87: 1472–75.

HAAN, MARY, GEORGE A. KAPLAN, and TERRY CAMACHO. 1987. "Poverty and Health: Prospective Evidence From the Alameda County Study." *American Journal of Epidemiology* 125: 989–98.

HAHN, ROBERT A., ELAINE D. EAKER, NANCY D. BARKER, STEVEN M. TEUTSCH, WALDEMAR A. SOSNIAK, and NANCY KRIEGER. 1996. "Poverty and Death in the United States." *International Journal of Health Services* 26: 673–90.

HOCHSTIM, JOSEPH R., DEMETRIOS A. ATHANASOPOULOS, and JOHN H. LARKINS. 1968. "Poverty Area Under the Microscope." *American Journal of Public Health* 58: 1815–27.

HOUSE, JAMES S., JAMES M. LEPKOWSKI, ANN M. KINNEY, RICHARD P. MERO, RONALD C. KESSLER, and A. REGULA HERZOG. 1994. "The Social Stratification of Aging and Health." *Journal of Health and Social Behavior* 35: 213–34.

HOUSE, JAMES S., RONALD C. KESSLER, A. REGULA HERZOG, RICHARD P. MERO, ANN M. KINNEY, and MARTHA J. BRESLOW. 1990. "Age, Socioeconomic Status, and Health." *The Milbank Quarterly* 68: 383–411.

HOUSE, JAMES S., RONALD C. KESSLER, A. REGULA HERZOG, RICHARD P. MERO, ANN M. KINNEY, and MARTHA J. BRESLOW. 1992. "Social Stratification, Age, and Health." In *Aging, Health Behaviors, and Health Outcomes,* ed. K.W. Schaie, D. Blazer, and J.S. House. Hillsdale, NJ: Lawrence Erlbaum Associates, pp. 1–32.

HUMMER, ROBERT A. 1996. "Black-white Differences in Health and Mortality: A Review and Conceptual Model." *The Sociological Quarterly* 37: 105–25.

ICKOVICS, JEANNETTE R., CATHERINE M. VISCOLI, and RALPH I. HORWITZ. 1997. "Functional Recovery After Myocardial Infarction in Men: The Independent Effects of Social Class." *Annals of Internal Medicine* 127: 578–25.

JARGOWSKY, PAUL A. 1997. *Poverty and Place: Ghettos, Barrios, and the American City.* New York: Russell Sage Foundation.

JONES, KELVYN, and CRAIG DUNCAN. 1995. "Individuals and Their Ecologies: Analysing the Geography of Chronic Illness Within a Multilevel Modelling Framework." *Health and Place* 1: 27–40.

JOSEPH, K.S., and M.S. KRAMER. 1996. "Review of the Evidence on Fetal and Early Childhood Antecedents of Adult Chronic Disease." *Epidemiologic Reviews* 18(2): 158–74.

KAPLAN, G. A. and J. T. SALONEN. 1990. "Socioeconomic Conditions in Childhood and Ischaemic Heart Disease During Middle Age." *British Medical Journal* 301: 1121–23.

KAPLAN, GEORGE A., and JOHN W. LYNCH. 1997. "Editorial: Whither Studies on the Socioeconomic Foundations of Population Health?" *American Journal of Public Health* 87: 1409–11.

KAPLAN, GEORGE A., ELSIE R. PAMUK, JOHN W. LYNCH, RICHARD D. COHEN, and JENNIFER L. BALFOUR. 1996. "Inequality in Income and Mortality in the United States: Analysis of Mortality and Potential Pathways." *British Medical Journal* 312: 999–1003.

KAPLAN, GEORGE A., S.J. SHEMA, JENNIFER L. BALFOUR, and IRENE H. YEN. In press. "Poverty Area Residence and Incidence of Disability." *American Journal of Public Health.*

KAPRIO, J., and M. KOSKENVUO. 1988. "A Prospective Study of Psychological and Socioeconomic Characteristics, Health Behavior, and Morbidity in Cigarette Smokers Prior to Quitting Compared to Persistent Smokers and Non-Smokers." *Journal of Clinical Epidemiology* 41(2): 139–50.

KATZ, S. J., and T. P. HOFER. 1994. "Socioeconomic Disparities in Preventive Care Persist Despite Universal Coverage: Breast and Cervical Cancer Screening in Ontario and the United States." *Journal of the American Medical Association* 272: 530–34.

KAWACHI, ICHIRO, and BRUCE P. KENNEDY. 1997. "Health and Social Cohesion: Why Care About Income Inequality?" *British Medical Journal* 314: 1037–40.

KAWACHI, ICHIRO, BRUCE P. KENNEDY, KIMBERLY LOCHNER, and DEBORAH PROTHROW-STITH. 1997. "Social Capital, Income Inequality, and Mortality." *American Journal of Public Health* 87: 1491–98.

KENNEDY, BRUCE P., ICHIRO KAWACHI, and DEBORAH PROTHROW-STITH. 1996. "Income Distribution and Mortality: Cross Sectional Ecological Study of the Robin Hood Index in the United States." *British Medical Journal* 312: 1004–1007.

KENNEDY, BRUCE P., ICHIRO KAWACHI, ROBERTA GLASS, and DEBORAH PROTHROW-STITH. 1998. "Income Distribution, Socioeconomic Status, and Self Rated Health in the United States: Multilevel Analysis." *British Medical Journal* 317: 917–21.

KINGTON, RAYNARD S., and JAMES P. SMITH. 1997. "Socioeconomic Status and Racial and Ethnic Differences in Functional Status Associated With Chronic Diseases." *American Journal of Public Health* 87: 805–10.

KITAGAWA, EVELYN M., and PHILIP M. HAUSER. 1973. *Differential Mortality in the United States: A Study in Socioeconomic Epidemiology.* Cambridge, MA: Harvard University Press.

KRIEGER, NANCY. 1992. "Overcoming the Absence of Socioeconomic Data in Medical Records: Validation and Application of a Census-Based Methodology." *American Journal of Public Health* 82: 703–10.

KRIEGER, N., D.L. ROWLEY, A.A. HERMAN, B. AVERY, and M.T. PHILLIPS. 1993. "Racism, Sexism, and Social Class: Implications for Studies of Health, Disease, and Well-Being." *American Journal of Preventive Medicine* 9(6): 82–122.

KRIEGER, NANCY, and ELIZABETH FEE. 1994. "Social Class: The Missing Link in U.S. Health Data." *International Journal of Health Services* 24: 25–44.

KRIEGER, NANCY, and STEPHEN SIDNEY. 1996. "Racial Discrimination and Blood Pressure: The CARDIA Study of Young Black and White Adults." *American Journal of Public Health* 86: 1370–78.

KRIEGER, NANCY, DAVID R. WILLIAMS, and NANCY E. MOSS. 1997. "Measuring Social Class in US Public Health Research: Concepts, Methodologies, and Guidelines." *Annual Review of Public Health* 18: 341–78.

KUH, D., and Y. BEN-SHLOMO. 1997. *A Lifecourse Approach to Chronic Disease Epidemiology.* Oxford: Oxford University Press.

LANNIN, D.R., H.F. MATHEWS, J. MITCHELL, M.S. SWANSON, F.H. SWANSON, and M.S. EDWARDS. 1998. "Influence of Socioeconomic and Cultural Factors on Racial Differences in Late-Stage Presentation of Breast Cancer." *Journal of the American Medical Association* 279(22): 1801–7.

LANTZ, PAULA M., JAMES S. HOUSE, JAMES M. LEPKOWSKI, DAVID R. WILLIAMS, RICHARD P. MERO, and JIEMING CHEN. 1998. "Socioeconomic Factors, Health Behaviors, and Mortality." *Journal of the American Medical Association* 279: 1703–1708.

LANTZ, PAULA M., MARGARET E. WEIGERS, and JAMES S. HOUSE. 1997. "Education and Income Differentials in Breast and Cervical Cancer Screening." *Medical Care* 35: 219–36.

LECLERE, FELICIA B., RICHARD G. ROGERS, and KIMBERLEY D. PETERS. 1997. "Ethnicity and Mortality in the United States: Individual and Community Correlates." *Social Forces* 76: 169–98.

LEVINE, SOL. 1987. "The Changing Terrains in Medical Sociology: Emergent Concern with Quality of Life." *Journal of Health and Social Behavior* 28(1): 1–6.

LIBERATOS, PENNY, BRUCE G. LINK, and JENNIFER L. KELSEY. 1988. "The Measurement of Social Class in Epidemiology." *Epidemiologic Reviews* 10: 87–121.

LICHTENSTEIN, PAUL, JENNIFER R. HARRIS, NANCY L. PEDERSEN, and G.E. MCCLEARN. 1993. "Socioeconomic Status and Physical Health, How Are They Related? An Empirical Study Based on Twins Reared Apart and Twins Reared Together." *Social Science and Medicine* 36: 441–50.

LILLIE-BLANTON, MARSHA, and THOMAS LAVEIST. 1996. "Race/ethnicity, the Social Environment, and Health." *Social Science and Medicine* 43: 83–91.

LINK, BRUCE G., and JO PHELAN. 1995. "Social Conditions as Fundamental Causes of Disease." *Journal of Health and Social Behavior* (Extra Issue): 80–94.

LUNDBERG, OLLE. 1991. "Causal Explanations for Class Inequality in Health—an Empirical Analysis." *Social Science and Medicine* 32: 385–93.

LYNCH, J. W., G. A. KAPLAN, and J. T. SALONEN. 1997. "Why Do Poor People Behave Poorly? Variation in Adult Health Behaviours and Psychosocial Characteristics by Stages of the Socioeconomic Lifecourse." *Social Science and Medicine* 44: 809–19.

LYNCH, J.W., G.A. KAPLAN, and S.J. SHEMA. 1997. "Cumulative Impact of Sustained Economic Hardship on Physical, Cognitive, Psychological, and Social Functioning." *New England Journal of Medicine* 337: 1889–95.

LYNCH, JOHN W., GEORGE A. KAPLAN, RICHARD D. COHEN, JAAKKO TUOMILEHTO, and JUKKA T. SALONEN. 1996. "Do Cardiovascular Risk Factors Explain the Relation Between Socioeconomic Status, Risk of All-Cause Mortality, Cardiovascular Mortality, and Acute Myocardial Infarction." *American Journal of Epidemiology* 144: 934–42.

LYNCH, JOHN W., GEORGE A. KAPLAN, RICHARD D. COHEN, JUSSI KAUHANEN, THOMAS W. WILSON, NICHOLAS L. SMITH, and JUKKA T. SALONEN. 1994. "Childhood and Adult Socioeconomic Status as Predictors of Mortality in Finland." *Lancet* 343: 524–27.

MACINTYRE, SALLY, SHEILA MACIVER, and ANNE SOOMAN. 1993. "Area, Class and Health: Should We Be Focusing on Places or People?" *Journal of Social Policy* 22: 213–34.

MARMOT, M. G., G. D. SMITH, S. STANSFELD, C. PATEL, F. NORTH, J. HEAD, I. WHITE, E. BRUNNER, and A. FEENEY. 1991. "Health Inequalities Among British Civil Servants: The Whitehall II Study." *Lancet* 337: 1387–93.

MARMOT, M.G., M.J. SHIPLEY, and GEOFFREY ROSE. 1984. "Inequalities in Death-Specific Explanations of a General Pattern?" *Lancet* 1: 1003–1006.

MARMOT, M.G., M. KOGEVINAS, and M.A. ELSTON. 1987. "Social/Economic Status and Disease." *Annual Review of Public Health* 8: 111–35.

MARMOT, MICHAEL, CAROL D. RYFF, LARRY L. BUMPASS, MARTIN SHIPLEY, and NADINE F. MARKS. 1997. "Social Inequalities in Health: Next Questions and Converging Evidence." *Social Science and Medicine* 44: 901–10.

MASSEY, DOUGLAS S., and NANCY A. DENTON. 1993. *American Apartheid: Segregation and the Making of the Underclass.* Cambridge, MA: Harvard University Press.

MATHENY, K.B., and K.E. WEATHERMAN. 1998. "Predictors of Smoking Cessation and Maintenance." *Journal of Clinical Psychology* 54(2): 223–35.

MCDONOUGH, PEGGY, DAVID WILLIAMS, JAMES HOUSE, and GREG J. DUNCAN. 1999. "Gender and the Socioeconomic Gradient in Mortality." *Journal of Health and Social Behavior* 40(1): 17–31.

McDonough, Peggy, Greg J. Duncan, David Williams, and James House. 1997. "Income Dynamics and Adult Mortality in the United States, 1972 Through 1989." *American Journal of Public Health* 87: 1476–83.

McKeown, T.J. 1976. *The Role of Medicine: Dream, Mirage, or Nemesis.* London: Nuffield Provincial Hospitals Trust.

McKinlay, John B. 1974. "A Case for Refocusing Upstream: The Political Economy of Illness." In *Applying Behavioral Science to Cardiovascular Risk.* American Heart Association.

McKinlay, John B., and Sonja J. McKinlay. 1977. "The Questionable Contribution of Medical Measures to the Decline of Mortality in the U.S. in the Twentieth Century." *Milbank Memorial Fund Quarterly* 55: 405–28.

McLeod, Jane D., and Ronald C. Kessler. 1990. "Socioeconomic Status Differences in Vulnerability to Undesirable Life Events." *Journal of Health and Social Behavior* 31: 162–72.

Mendes de Leon, Carlos F., Laurel A. Beckett, Gerda G. Fillenbaum, Dwight B. Brock, Laurence G. Branch, Denis A. Evans, and Lisa F. Berkman. 1997. "Black-White Differences in Risk of Becoming Disabled and Recovering From Disability in Old Age: A Longitudinal Analysis of Two EPESE Populations." *American Journal of Epidemiology* 145: 488–97.

Mirowsky, John, and Paul Nongzhuang Hu. 1996. "Physical Impairment and the Diminishing Effects of Income." *Social Forces* 74: 1073–96.

Morgan, Myfanwy, and Susan Chinn. 1983. "ACORN Group, Social Class, and Child Health." *Journal of Epidemiology and Community Health* 37: 196–203.

Mutchler, Jan E., and Jeffrey A. Burr. 1991. "Racial Differences in Health and Health Care Service Utilization in Later Life: The Effect of Socioeconomic Status." *Journal of Health and Social Behavior* 32: 342–56.

O'Campo, Patricia, Xiaonan Xue, Mei-Cheng Wang, and Margaret O'Brien Caughy. 1997. "Neighborhood Risk Factors for Low Birthweight in Baltimore: A Multilevel Analysis." *American Journal of Public Health* 87: 1113–18.

Pappas, Gregory, Susan Queen, Wilbur Hadden, and Gail Fisher. 1993. "The Increasing Disparity in Mortality Between Socioeconomic Groups in the United States, 1960 and 1986." *New England Journal of Medicine* 329: 103–109.

Pappas, G., W.C. Hadden, L.J. Kozak, and G.F. Fisher. 1997. "Potentially Avoidable Hospitalizations: Inequalities in Rates Between U.S. Socioeconomic Groups." *American Journal of Public Health* 87(5): 811–6.

Peck, Maria Nystrom. 1994. "The Importance of Childhood Socio-Economic Group for Adult Health." *Social Science and Medicine* 39: 553–62.

Power, C., and S. Matthews. 1997. "Origins of Health Inequalities in a National Population Sample." *Lancet* 350: 1584–89.

Power, C., S. Matthews, and O. Manor. 1996. "Inequalities in Self-Rated Health in the 1958 Birth Cohort: Lifetime Social Circumstances or Social Mobility?" *British Medical Journal* 313: 449–53.

Power, C., S. Matthews, and O. Manor. 1998. "Inequalities in Self-Rated Health: Explanations From Different Stages of Life." *Lancet* 351: 1009–14.

Preston, Samuel H. 1975. "The Changing Relation Between Mortality and Level of Economic Development." *Population Studies* 29(2): 231–48.

Pugh, Helena, and Kath Moser. 1990. "Measuring Women's Mortality Differences." In *Women's Health Counts,* ed. Helen Roberts. London: Routledge, pp. 93–112.

Reijneveld, S.A. 1998. "The Impact of Individual and Area Characteristics on Urban Socioeconomic Differences in Health and Smoking." *International Journal of Epidemiology* 27: 33–40.

Reynolds, John R., and Catherine E. Ross. 1998. "Social Stratification and Health: Education's Benefit Beyond Economic Status and Social Origin." *Social Problems* 45: 221–47.

Robert, Stephanie A. 1998. "Community-Level Socioeconomic Status Effects on Adult Health." *Journal of Health and Social Behavior* 39: 18–37.

Robert, Stephanie A., and James S. House. 1994. "Socioeconomic Status and Health Across the Life Course." In *Aging and Quality of Life,* ed. Ronald P. Abeles, Helen C. Gift, and Marcia G. Ory. New York: Springer, pp. 253–74.

Robert, Stephanie, and James S. House. 1996. "SES Differentials in Health by Age and Alternative Indicators of SES." *Journal of Aging and Health* 8: 359–88.

Robert, Stephanie A., and James S. House. In press. "Socioeconomic Inequalities In Health: Integrating Individual-, Community-, and Societal-Level Theory and Research." *Handbook of Social Studies in Health and Medicine,* ed. Gary L. Albrecht, Ray Fitzpatrick, and Susan C. Scrimshaw. London: Sage Publications.

Rodgers, G.B. 1979. "Income and Inequality as Determinants of Mortality: An International Cross-Section Analysis." *Population Studies* 33: 343–51.

Rogers, Richard G., Robert A. Hummer, Charles B. Nam, and Kimberly Peters. 1996. "Demographic, Socioeconomic, and Behavioral Factors Affecting Ethnic Mortality by Cause." *Social Forces* 74: 1419–38.

Roos, Noralou P., and Cameron A. Mustard. 1997. "Variation in Health and Health Care Use by Socioeconomic Status in Winnipeg, Canada: Does the System Work Well? Yes and No." *The Milbank Quarterly* 75: 89–111.

Ross, Catherine E., and Chia-Ling Wu. 1995. "The Links Between Education and Health." *American Sociological Review* 60: 719–45.

Ross, Catherine E., and Chia-Ling Wu. 1996. "Education, Age, and the Cumulative Advantage in Health." *Journal of Health and Social Behavior* 37: 104–20.

Sapolsky, R. M. 1989. "Hypercortisolism Among Socially Subordinate Wild Baboons Originates at the CNS Level." *Archives of General Psychiatry* 46: 1047–51.

Sapolsky, R. M., and G. E. Mott. 1987. "Social Subordinance in Wild Baboons Is Associated With Suppressed High Density Lipoprotein-Cholesterol Concentrations: The Possible Role of Chronic Social Stress." *Endocrinology* 121: 1605–10.

Schoenbaum, Michael, and Timothy Waidmann. 1997. "Race, Socioeconomic Status, and Health: Accounting for Race Differences in Health." *The Journal of Gerontology* 52B: 61–73.

Schoendorf, K. C., C. J. Hogue, J. C. Kleinman, and D. Rowley. 1992. "Mortality Among Infants of Black as Compared With White College-Educated Parents." *New England Journal of Medicine* 326: 1522–26.

Seeman, Teresa E., and Bruce S. McEwen. 1996. "Impact of Social Environment Characteristics on Neuroendocrine Regulation." *Psychosomatic Medicine* 58(5): 459–71.

Shaar, K.H., M. McCarthy, and G. Meshefedjian. 1994. "Disadvantage in Physically Disabled Adults: An Assessment of the Causation and Selection Hypotheses." *Social Science and Medicine* 39: 407–13.

Shahtahmasebi, Said, Richard Davies, and G. Clare Wenger. 1992. "A Longitudinal Analysis of Factors Related to Survival in Old Age." *The Gerontologist* 32: 404–13.

Singh, Gopal K., and Stella M. Yu. 1996. "US Childhood Mortality, 1950 Through 1993: Trends and Socioeconomic Differentials." *American Journal of Public Health* 86: 505–12.

Sloggett, A., and H. Joshi. 1998. "Deprivation Indicators as Predictors of Life Events 1981–1992 Based on the UK ONS Longitudinal Study." *Journal of Epidemiology and Community Health* 52: 228–33.

Sloggett, Andrew, and Heather Joshi. 1994. "Higher Mortality in Deprived Areas: Community or Personal Disadvantage?" *British Medical Journal* 309: 1470–74.

Smith, J.P., and R. Kington. 1997. "Demographic and Economic Correlates of Health in Old Age." *Demography* 34(1): 159–70.

Soobader, M.J., and F.B. LeClere. 1999. "Aggregation and the Measurement of Income Inequality: Effects on Morbidity." *Social Science and Medicine* 48(6): 733–44.

Sorlie, Paul D., Eric Backlund, and Jacob B. Keller. 1995. "U.S. Mortality by Economic, Demographic, and Social Characteristics: The National Longitudinal Mortality Study." *American Journal of Public Health* 85: 949–56.

Stronks, K., H. van de Mheen, J. van den Bos, and J. P. Mackenbach. 1995. "Smaller Socioeconomic Inequalities in Health Among Women: The Role of Employment Status." *International Journal of Epidemiology* 24: 559–68.

Taylor, Shelly E., Rena L. Repetti, and Teresa Seeman. 1997. "Health Psychology: What Is an Unhealthy Environment and How Does It Get Under the Skin?" *Annual Review of Psychology* 48: 411–47.

Uchino, B.N., J.T. Cacioppo, and J.K. Kiecolt-Glaser. 1996. "The Relationship Between Social Support and Physiological Processes: A Review with Emphasis on Underlying Mechanisms and Implications for Health." *Psychological Bulletin* 119(3): 488–531.

van Doorslaer, E., A. Wagstaff, H. Bleichrodt, S. Calonge, U.-G. Gerdtham, M. Gerfin, J. Geurts, L. Gross, U. Hakkinen, R.E. Leu, O. O'Donnell, C. Propper, F. Puffer, M. Rodriguez, G. Sundberg, and O. Winkelhake. 1997. "Income-Related Inequalities in Health: Some International Comparisons." *Journal of Health Economics* 16: 93–112.

Waitzman, Norman J., and Ken R. Smith. 1998a. "Phantom of the Area: Poverty-Area Residence and Mortality in the United States." *American Journal of Public Health* 88: 973–976.

Waitzman, Norman J., and Ken R. Smith. 1998b. "Separate But Lethal: The Effects of Economic Segregation on Mortality in Metropolitan America." *The Milbank Quarterly* 7(3): 341–73.

West, P., S. MacIntyre, E. Annandale, and K. Hunt. 1990. "Social Class and Health in Youth: Findings From the West of Scotland Twenty-07 Study." *Social Science and Medicine* 30: 665–73.

Wilkins, R., O. Adams, and A. Brancker. 1989. "Changes in Mortality by Income in Urban Canada from 1971 to 1986." *Health Reports (Statistics Canada catalogue 82-003)* 1: 137–74.

Wilkinson, Richard G. 1996. *Unhealthy Societies: The Afflictions of Inequality.* New York: Routledge.

Williams, D. R. 1997. "Race and Health: Basic Questions, Emerging Directions." *Annals of Epidemiology* 7: 322–33.

Williams, David R. 1990. "Socioeconomic Differentials in Health: A Review and Redirection." *Social Psychology Quarterly* 53: 81–99.

Williams, David R., and Chiquita Collins. 1995. "U.S. Socioeconomic and Racial Differences in Health: Patterns and Explanations." *Annual Review of Sociology* 21: 349–86.

Wolfson, Michael, Geoff Rowe, Jane F. Gentleman, and Monica Tomiak. 1993. "Career Earnings and Death: A Longitudinal Analysis of Older Canadian Men." *Journal of Gerontology* 48: S167–79.

World Bank. 1993. *World Development Report.* New York: Oxford University Press, published for the World Bank.

7 SOCIOLOGICAL EXPLANATIONS OF GENDER DIFFERENCES IN MENTAL AND PHYSICAL HEALTH

PATRICIA P. RIEKER, *Simmons College*

CHLOE E. BIRD, *Brown University*

INTRODUCTION

Socially constructed gender roles, identities, and inequality in opportunities and resources shape men's and women's lives and in turn affect their health. These gender differences arise through multiple pathways and have a wide range of health consequences. Sociologists have examined gender differences in exposure to particular stressors, vulnerability to stressors, access to care, type of treatment received, and responsiveness to particular social interventions and medical treatments. Sociological perspectives on gender differences in health proceed from the observation that social and economic inequality contributes to variations in health and well-being across individuals.

Although on average there are substantial gender differences in health, men and women do not represent two homogeneous groups. Socioeconomic position, race and ethnicity, and other aspects of social status interact with gender to produce variations in both gender inequality and its health consequences. Such subgroup differences in health effects highlight the fact that observed male social and health advantages do not accrue to all men, nor do female social and health disadvantages accrue to all women (MacIntyre, Hunt and Sweeting 1996).

In this chapter, we briefly review some of the major gender differences in physical and mental health. However, the main thrust of the chapter is on the unique sociological contributions to explicating gender differences in health. We discuss the strengths and limitations of the sociological models built on theories of inequality. In addition, we describe the evolution of particular sociological perspectives on gender and health. We also identify gaps in knowledge that occur as a result of the intellectual parochialism that discourages interdisciplinary research combining social and biological explanations of gender differences in health. Finally, we discuss new directions for research to improve our understanding of differences in men's and women's health.

GENDER DIFFERENCES IN HEALTH

Health status and rates of specific physical and mental health conditions vary by gender. In general, men report better physical health than do women but die younger. Lois Verbrugge and Deborah Wingard (1987) describe the gendered patterns of physical health as the "iceberg of morbidity" whereby male mortality makes up the smaller visible part of the iceberg and women's substantially higher rates of chronic nonfatal disease comprise the larger, less visible part. Overall, men's and women's mental health problems occur at similar rates; however, women experience higher rates of depressive disorders, whereas men experience higher rates of alcohol and substance abuse as well as antisocial behavior disorders (Robins et al. 1984; Kessler et al. 1994; Meltzer et al. 1995; Mirowsky and Ross 1995).

Physical Health

Although life expectancy at birth has been increasing for all demographic groups in the United States (from

The authors thank Alexandra Todd, Susan Gore, and Allen Fremont for their comments on earlier versions of this chapter.

an average of 70.8 years in 1970 to 76.1 years in 1996), gender differences in longevity rates vary substantially by race and income. Overall, women have a longer life expectancy than men (79.1 years vs. 73.1 years), but the gender difference is smaller for whites than for blacks (5.8 years vs. 8.1 years) (National Center for Health Statistics 1998, table 29). The discrepancy in life expectancy at birth is largest for white females compared to black males, a difference of almost 15 years. As shown in Figure 7–1, data from the National Longitudinal Mortality study for 1979 to 1989 show that life expectancy at age 45 increases with family income regardless of race or gender, but the difference between the highest and lowest income groups tends to be smaller for women than for men.

The three leading causes of death are the same for men and women: heart disease, cancer, and stroke. Despite the similarities, cause of death also varies substantially by gender and other social factors. Men are more likely to die at earlier ages from chronic diseases such as cardiovascular disease, lung cancer, communicable disease, and injuries (both accidents and homicide) than are women. For example, gender differences in mortality from heart disease vary by race and income (National Center for Health Statistics 1998). Within each income level, black women have higher mortality from heart disease than white women. However, regardless of income, black men have higher rates of mortality from heart disease than white men. Yet the poorest women of both races have death rates as low as those of the highest income men. Mortality from communicable diseases

also varies by gender and socioeconomic status. For example, the prevalence of AIDS is 3.5 times higher for men between the ages of 25–64 than for women, and 3.0 times higher among the least educated (less than high school) compared to the most educated (National Center for Health Statistics 1998). Moreover, many harmful health behaviors (such as smoking, drinking, poor diet, and risk taking) are themselves influenced by a variety of gender-related social processes (Walsh, Sorensen, and Leonard 1995).

Gender differences in risk of death from violence are larger for blacks than for whites. For the years 1994–96, the overall homicide rate per 100,000 population was 8.1 for white men compared to 2.7 for white women, and 58.8 for black men compared to 11.2 for black women (National Center for Health Statistics 1998). Differences in risk also vary substantially among subgroups of men and women. For example, compared to non-Hispanic white men, black and Hispanic men experience homicide rates 12 and 4 times higher, respectively. For black and Hispanic women the rates are 4 and 6 times higher than for non-Hispanic white women. Moreover, the homicide rate is lower for those with more education, but the education gradient is stronger for non-Hispanic white men and women than for other groups. However, in an analysis of data from 18 industrialized countries, Rosemary Gartner and colleagues (1990) show that the homicide rate from 1950 to 1980 for educated employed women was higher than for less educated men.

American women's life expectancy has exceeded men's since the turn of the century. However, since 1980 the gender gap in life expectancy has been closing in the United States as men's gains have begun to exceed women's (National Center for Health Statistics 1996). Moreover, while men are gaining healthy years, women's increased longevity reflects an increase in years of disability (Pope and Tarlov 1991).

The paradox of men's higher mortality and lower morbidity compared to women is often explained by gender differences in the patterns of disease (Verbrugge and Wingard 1987). Men have more life-threatening chronic diseases, including coronary heart disease, cancer, cerebrovascular disease, emphysema, cirrhosis of the liver, kidney disease, and atherosclerosis. In contrast, women face higher rates of chronic debilitating disorders as well as irritating but less serious diseases such as anemia, thyroid conditions, gall bladder conditions, migraines, arthritis, colitis, and eczema. Women also have more acute conditions such as upper respiratory infections, gastroenteritis, and other short-term infectious diseases (National Center for Health Statistics 1996).

FIGURE 7–1 Life Expectancy at Age 45 by Gender, Race, and Family Income

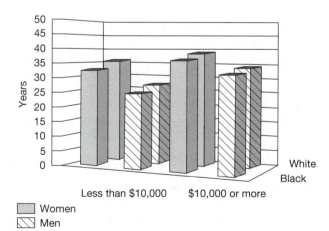

SOURCE: National Center for Health Statistics, *Health, United States, 1998* (Hyattsville, MD: U.S. Public Health Service, 1998), p. 152.

Mental Health

Although gender differences in mental health status are well established, for decades it was believed that women suffer from higher rates of mental illness than do men. However, findings from 1991 Epidemiological Catchment Area data (ECA) indicate that there are no large differences in men's and women's overall rates of major psychological disorders across all time frames (e.g., one month, six months, one year, lifetime)(Regier et al. 1993). These findings contradict earlier surveys (i.e., Dohrenwend and Dohrenwend 1976, 1977; Cleary et al. 1982; Gove and Tudor 1973), which showed higher rates of mental illness for women. The discrepancy is partly explained by the fact that previous studies focused on rates of depressive and anxiety disorders, which are higher among women, while the ECA included substance abuse, which is more common among men. The 1992 NIMH-sponsored National Comorbidity Survey of over 8,000 households also found no gender difference in overall rates of psychological disorder (Kessler et al. 1994). However, these general surveys and other studies have documented substantial differences in patterns of disorder by gender.

In the case of depressive disorders, women's rates are between 50 to 100 percent greater than men's (Gove and Tudor 1973; Kessler and McRae 1981; Mirowsky and Ross 1989). These differences occur in both treated and community samples (Nolen-Hoeksema 1990). For example, the U.S. National Comorbidity Survey and a similar psychiatric survey in Britain found that women are about two-thirds more likely than men to be depressed in both yearly and lifetime estimates (Kessler et al. 1994; Meltzer et al. 1995). Although the gender difference occurs at all ages, it appears to be greatest during the reproductive years (Bebbington 1996). In contrast, for substance abuse disorders, men have significantly higher rates of alcohol and drug abuse dependence and antisocial behavior disorders (Kessler et al. 1994; Regier et al. 1993). John Mirowsky and Catherine Ross (1995) demonstrate that the gender differences in rates of depression and substance abuse/antisocial behavior are real and not an artifact of reporting bias (see also Nazroo, Edwards, and Brown 1998).

SOCIOLOGICAL PERSPECTIVES ON THE BIOMEDICAL MODEL

By pointing out that diseases do not always have the same symptoms and outcomes across social circumstances, medical sociologists have contributed to a critique of purely biological explanations of differences in men's and women's health (Mishler 1981, 1986). For example, Judith Lorber (1997) examines how gender as a socially constructed category affects men's and women's risks and protections for physical illnesses, their behavior when ill, the responses they receive from health-care professionals, and how they influence the priorities of treatment, research, and financing. Sociologists argue that the biomedical model fails to fully recognize the contribution of social factors to disease patterns. A long line of sociological theory frames gender as a socially constructed set of societal norms, values, and sanctions that proscribe male and female behavior, roles, and life opportunities and in turn affect health (for a detailed review see Lorber 1997). By viewing gender as a social institution rooted in conflict over scarce resources and in social relationships of power, Robert Connell (1987) and Judith Lorber (1994) clarify the pervasive impact of gender stratification and demonstrate the many ways the complex concept of gender is itself misunderstood.

Critics of the biomedical model explicate the ways in which societal values and beliefs shape both what is studied in medical research and its results. Specifically, medical sociologists have illustrated the ways in which assumptions about men and women enter into conceptions of health and illness and affect medical research, doctor-patient encounters, and treatment protocols (e.g., Todd 1989; Fisher 1988). They also have identified patterns of gender bias in other assumptions of biomedical research and clinical practice. For example, until 1993, rigid protectionist Federal Food and Drug Administration policies encouraged the underrepresentation and frequent exclusion of women of child-bearing age from the majority of pharmaceutical trials. Initially intended to prevent the abuse of women as research subjects and to reduce the risk of fetal exposure to experimental treatments, these policies were based on the assumption that treatments developed by studying men were directly generalizable to women (Bell 1994; Mastroianni, Faden, and Federman 1994). The policies are effective only if fertility and fetal health are affected by women's health and exposure to toxic substances, but not men's. Underlying this perspective was the belief that damaged sperm could not impregnate and that any sperm that could impregnate would not lead to birth defects (Baranski 1993; Paul 1995). However, subsequent research indicates that men's fertility is vulnerable to the influence of toxic substances such as ionizing radiation, lead, inorganic mercury, and carbon disulfide, as well as chemotherapeutic agents (Baranski 1993; Paul 1995; Rieker et al. 1990).

Medical sociologists challenge the implicit assumption in biomedical research that differences in men's and women's health are primarily attributable to underlying sex differences in physiology; rather, they have theorized that gender inequality has consequences for men's and women's lives in terms of their physical and psychological well-being. Quantitative and qualitative sociological analysis of gender has elucidated the ways in which the social structure impinges on males and females, shaping their risks and opportunities and, in turn, their choices, actions, and behaviors (Doyal 1995; Rieker and Jankowski 1995). Gender differences in opportunities affect men's and women's choices and expectations regarding social roles and role-related activities (Reskin and Padavic 1994), which in turn affect their exposures to various risks (e.g., stress, role overload, occupational health risks such as carpal tunnel syndrome, exposure to toxic chemicals) and their access to protective resources (including income, wealth, health and disability insurance, and social support). Thus, *constrained choices* contribute to the reproduction of gender roles and gendered behavior whereby boys and girls (and men and women) make occupational, career, and family choices in the face of unequal opportunities and expectations for success. Under these circumstances, rational men and women differ on average in their choices regarding employment, careers, and health behaviors that cumulatively affect their health (Johnson and Hall 1995; Hertzman, Frank, and Evans 1994). Consequently, men's and women's health is the product not only of their biology, but also of their social experiences in a stratified society and the gendered roles that they enact (Bird and Rieker 1999).

In order to understand the broad effects of gender socialization on men's and women's health behaviors, their reporting styles, and their lifestyles in general, it is necessary to acknowledge that gender socialization does not end as one enters adulthood. Rather, the process evolves and in some ways becomes more subtle. Although adults increase support for their lifestyle and health behaviors through their selection of peer groups, both adults and children are subject to prevailing social norms regarding role expectations and health behaviors (both risky and preventive). Medical sociologists have concluded that the biomedical model underestimates the importance of the interplay between gender socialization, gender inequality, and patterns of health and illness. Therefore, medical sociologists tend to focus on the consequences of social and economic advantages and disadvantages for men's and women's health.

CONFUSION OVER TERMINOLOGY

The lack of clarity regarding the relative contribution of social and biological factors to differences in men's and women's health is reflected partly in the confusion over terminology. Whereas the term "sex" refers to the chromosomal structure determined at the moment of conception and is most appropriately reserved for reference to biological characteristics and their direct consequences, "gender" refers to what society and culture make of those biological differences and should be used when referring to social patterns. Sociological work demonstrates the profound influence that gender has on an individual's life experiences and why it is not reducible to his or her chromosomal structures. The meaning, status, and implications of gender result from socially structured access to resources and opportunities and associated attitudes, behaviors, and values. The term "gender" has rapidly replaced the term "sex" in medical research. Unfortunately, this change in terminology has not helped to clarify the contributions of social factors to men's and women's health. Instead, the term "gender differences" has frequently been misapplied to describe purely biological differences in human anatomy and to animal studies where the biological basis of such differences should be evident. In these studies gender is included as either an independent or a control variable, a practice Howard Taylor (1997) refers to as controlling for an "irritant" variable rather than conducting relevant subgroup analyses or testing for interaction effects.

In the following sections we examine sociological explanations of gender differences in mental and physical health. First we review stress and illness research; next we discuss gender differences in access to health care and treatment. We then critique the sociological model and offer an alternative conceptual framework for understanding the paradoxical differences in men's and women's health.

SOCIOLOGICAL EXPLANATIONS OF GENDER DIFFERENCES IN PSYCHOLOGICAL WELL-BEING

In general, mental health research is concerned with identifying both risk and protective processes. Psychological and biomedical approaches explain variation in mental health states on the basis of attributes of the individual. In contrast, sociologists focus on the distribution of social and economic resources and related variations in exposure to stress. Thus, sociological explanations of gender differences examine the ways in which inequities contribute to differences in men's and women's exposure to stressors, the meaning of particular stressful events and coping resources, and the psychological consequences of each of these factors.

Two sociological theories are used to explain gender differences in psychological well-being: *differential exposure theory* and *differential vulnerability theory*. Both theories attribute gender differences in psychological well-being to the social organization of men's and women's lives. The former emphasizes the extent to which men and women are exposed to particular stressors, whereas the latter focuses on men's and women's responses to those stressors. It is worth noting here that differential vulnerability theory as proposed by sociologists assumes a social, rather than a biological, basis for gender differences in stress response.

According to the *differential exposure theory*, women experience a heavier burden of hardship or constraint than men, which produces a higher prevalence of psychological distress among women, particularly those who are married. From this perspective, men's lower levels of psychological distress levels are attributed to their advantaged position relative to women in the labor force and in the division of roles and labor in the family (Hochschild with Machung 1989). In addition, sociologists have examined the impact of inequity in the division of labor in order to understand whether women are primarily burdened by doing relatively unrewarding work or overloaded by performing either the majority of household labor and caregiving in addition to employment or an inequitably large share of the housework and of total work hours. In particular, unrewarding work and the perception that the division of labor is inequitable decrease the sense of control over good and bad outcomes in one's life, which in turn increase depression (Mirowsky and Ross 1989). For example, compared to employment, household labor is associated with lower levels of perceived control and higher levels of psychological distress (Bird and Ross 1993; Brown and Harris 1978; Ross and Bird 1994; Thoits 1995a). Burdensome amounts and an inequitable share of household labor are therefore likely to reduce perceived control over one's life and, in turn, increase psychological distress (Bird 1999).

Differential vulnerability theory argues that the effects of particular stressors and role-related activities differ for men and women. Such differences could occur for a variety of reasons. In particular, work and

family roles may have different meanings for men and women, which in turn produce different psychological consequences (Simon 1995; Thoits 1991). Even if family roles such as spouse and parent have equal salience for men and women, they may have very different meanings in terms of the significance of employment and household labor as means of role fulfillment. Thus, Robin Simon (1995) argues that employment and household labor may affect men and women differently because their sociocultural beliefs regarding work and family roles affect both their feelings of guilt and their self-evaluations as parents and spouses. Men are more likely to experience their work and family roles as integral, whereas women are more likely to experience theirs as competing. In general, persons who perceive their roles as *competing* report more stress and role conflict than do those who perceive their roles as *integral*. In addition to the fact that women's gender roles may inherently involve greater role conflict, men and women also face different normative expectations regarding the significance of paid and unpaid work for their respective social roles (Simon 1995).

Thus, the meaning and identities associated with performing certain types of labor may differ for men and women. For example, women are generally expected to do more household labor than men, whether they are single or married. Mary Clare Lennon and Sarah Rosenfield (1994) found that on average, married men and women tend to report that the division of household labor is fair when women perform about two-thirds of the household labor. However, they found that women's perception of fairness of the division of household labor in their home is affected by the context of their lives. In particular, those women who had fewer alternatives to marriage and fewer economic resources were more likely to view performing a high percentage of the housework as fair, while women with more alternatives viewed the same division as unjust. Women who perceived an unequal situation as unfair were more psychologically distressed than those who did not. Therefore, the consequences of housework and employment can differ for men and women simply due to structural differences in their opportunities and options, such as men's higher incomes and greater chance of marrying a homemaker or a spouse who does not pursue a career (see Bellas 1992 on the "housewife bonus"). In other words, both the likelihood and the opportunity cost of doing a disproportionate share of household labor may differ for men and women, resulting in different thresholds for perceiving the division of labor as fair to themselves. Furthermore, given the norm that an unequal division of household labor is fair to both men and women, one would expect that performing a particular share of household labor would affect men and women differently.

Gender Differences in the Consequences of Stressors

Sociological research on the psychological effects of gender roles and exposure to role-related activities has focused primarily on depression and psychological distress. This emphasis has shaped our understanding of the consequences of differences in men's and women's paid and unpaid work. Whereas depression and milder forms of psychological distress are common particularly among women, alcohol abuse and alcoholism are more common among men (Aneshensel, Rutter, and Lachenbruch 1991; Kessler et al. 1994; Meltzer et al. 1995; Mirowsky 1996). Both have negative effects on one's work, finances, leisure, and fitness (Orford and Keddie 1985; Mirowsky and Ross 1989, 1995). Bruce Dohrenwend and Barbara Snell Dohrenwend (1976) argue that failure to examine a wide range of disorders that included those more prevalent among men had resulted in biased estimates of gender differences in mental illness rates. Similarly, Allan Horwitz and Helen Raskin White (1991) contend that gendered responses to frustration and hardship occur in different realms of disorder, producing, for example, emotional problems in women and behavioral problems in men. Carol Aneshensel and colleagues (1991) conclude that the failure of researchers to examine a range of disorders has resulted in drastic underestimates of gender differences in the impact of stressors.

Noting that stress researchers have virtually ignored men's higher rates of substance abuse, Peggy Thoits (1995b) argues that robust models of mental health should explain common outcomes for both men and women. "If depression and substance use are *alternative* ways of reacting to stress, then perhaps we should not be asking what it is about women's experience that makes them more depressed than men" (Thoits 1995b: 56). Rather, she asks whether specific stressors lead to one psychological response as opposed to another, to gendered responses, or to comorbidity. For example, in a study of depression and alcohol abuse, Robin Simon (1998) concluded that gender differences in psychological effects of strain are both stressor and outcome specific. Similarly, in an excellent review of the literature on family status and mental health, Debra Umberson (1998) argues that "Had researchers focused on alcohol

problems rather than depression, men would be labeled as more disturbed than women."

Sociological explanations of women's greater distress have typically focused on their restricted family roles, while the aspects of men's social roles that may contribute to excess rates of alcohol and drug dependence have not been well explicated. Therefore, to capture the cumulative effects of gender roles and role-related activities for both men and women, it is necessary to look at a broader range of psychological outcomes.

Why Did Sociologists Focus on Gender Differences in Depression?

Because both medical researchers and clinicians assumed that women's excess depression reflected inherent biological inferiority, in the 1970s and 1980s medical sociologists and others responded by developing theoretical and empirical explanations of the social causes of women's psychological disadvantage (Gove and Tudor 1973; Nathanson 1980). Walter Gove and colleagues (Gove 1972; Gove and Hughes 1979; Gove and Tudor 1973) theorized that women's higher rates of depression and mild physical illness were due to restricted gender roles and nurturant, caregiving tasks that negatively affected women's mental health, reduced their ability to care for themselves properly, and increased their risk of illness. As the gender differences in psychological distress were greatest among married people, traditional explanations focused on gender roles within the family (Rosenfield 1989). Consequently, rather than focusing broadly on social explanations of the gender variations in mental and physical health, medical sociologists focused on the health consequences of women's social and economic disadvantages and greater exposure to stressors associated with their work and family roles.

In 1977, Myrna Weissman and Gerald Klerman carried out a thorough review of the biomedical and sociological research on sex differences in depression because they were not convinced that there were any creditable data supporting Gove's argument that women's restricted social roles contributed to their excess rates of depression. However, they concluded that the most convincing evidence that social roles are important concerned the data that showed marriage had a protective effect on men's mental health but a detrimental effect on women. They also found, in experimental work on animals and humans, indirect support for the hypothesized disadvantage of female roles that demonstrated the negative effects of boredom—a central element of the restricted housewife role.

Because the model of the social determinants of depression was built on assessments of the impact of female disadvantage, it is not easily generalizable to men's excess rates of alcohol and drug dependence. In order to apply this type of explanation to men's mental health problems, it would be necessary to develop a conceptual model of male disadvantage. Therefore, recent work in this area has focused on stressors to which men are either more exposed or potentially more vulnerable (Sabo and Gordon 1995).

The female disadvantage field is so large that male disadvantages have long been overlooked and understudied (Cameron and Bernardes 1998). Because the majority of research has focused on the consequences of social inequality and injustice, it has been accepted as a "social fact" that women's greater depression was representative of greater emotional disturbance overall and that men did not experience excess mental health problems resulting from their work and family roles. Over time, these conclusions became accepted as unchallenged representations of reality. Because the question asked was "Why are women more emotionally disturbed than men?" empirical findings were not generalizable to or useful for understanding male excesses in particular psychological disorders. As with all research, conclusions are shaped by the research questions asked and by the definitions and measures of gender and health (Hubbard 1990).

The social construction of gender directly affects men's lives and in turn their health as well. Recent research in the area of men's feminism sheds light on the social construction of men's lives and identities. Just as it is necessary to avoid characterizing racial experiences as those of all minorities, gender experiences and socialization do not occur to women and a neutral sex. Sociologists confront the imbedded assumptions about men and women (Pleck and Brannon 1978; Harrison 1978; Pleck 1983; Kimmel and Messner 1993; Cameron and Bernardes 1998; Sabo and Gordon 1995). Their work involves recognizing that gendered roles disadvantage men in some ways as well as women and that not all men are equally advantaged. By exploring the ways in which gendered expectations shape men's lives, their choices, opportunities, and health-related lifestyles, these primarily qualitative studies offer a basis for a sociological model to explain male excesses in particular psychological health problems such as alcohol and substance abuse and other antisocial behaviors. As new models of male gender role stressors and sources of particular vulnerability are developed, they can be used to modify the existing models of women's gender-related exposures to stressors. Ultimately this work offers the possibility of generating theories that explain both male and female psychological health and illness and the ways these patterns might vary across race, class, or ethnicity.

SOCIOLOGICAL EXPLANATIONS OF GENDER DIFFERENCE IN PHYSICAL HEALTH

Most sociologists acknowledge that there are links between mental and physical health and that the social processes that contribute to poor mental health also negatively affect physical health. However, in practice most of the sociological work on gender differences in physical health focuses on issues of access and treatment. There is evidence that stressors contribute to increased hypertension and depressed immune function, which in turn lead to poor health outcomes. Because women have biological advantages that protect them from heart disease at earlier ages, the negative effects of gender inequality on risk of cardiovascular disease are not apparent. For example, research comparing male and female managers and female clerical workers indicates that whereas men's stress levels peak during the day and decline when they return home in the evening, women's stress hormones levels are sustained through the evening (Frankenhaeuser et al. 1989). Therefore, interdisciplinary research that examines both social and biological factors is necessary to capture the net health effects of women's biological advantages and their social economic disadvantages compared to men.

One interesting observation worth pursuing is the research that demonstrates a connection between psychological states and physical health. There is considerable evidence indicating a link between clinically diagnosed major depression and increased mortality. Although these studies do not show that depression is a predictor of mortality per se, symptoms of depression are associated with poor health and functional status, as well as increased disability, health care utilization, and cost of health services. For example, a recent prospective study of a large cohort of white women 67 years of age or older found that women with depressive symptoms, compared to those without such symptoms, had increased rates of cardiovascular and noncancer mortality (Whooley and Browner 1998). Thus gender differences in mental health may contribute in unknown ways to gendered patterns of physical health. Research in this area will help demonstrate the net effects of gendered patterns of depression.

Gender Differences in Access to Health Care and Treatment

Gender differences in health care are well established, and explanations for the disparities emphasize issues such as access and utilization, reporting bias, and differential treatment for the same condition. Access and utilization rates also vary by age, race, and income. Moreover, there are apparent contradictions; while women seek and receive more medical attention in general, there are still specific inequities in access to treatment. For example, excluding reproductive care, women use more physician services, are more likely than men to have a regular source of care, utilize more preventive care, are prescribed more medications, are more likely to visit outpatient clinics, and are more likely to be hospitalized (National Center for Health Statistics 1998; Verbrugge 1985; Nathanson 1980; Waldron 1995a, 1995b). Women have been shown to perceive more symptoms, to evaluate them as more serious, and to be more willing than men to seek medical care. According to Gregory Weiss and Lynne Lonquist (1997) it is unclear whether women's higher utilization rate represents an "overuse" or men's patterns represent an "underuse," or whether such a calculation is meaningful given the complexity of the differences in gender and disease patterns.

People below and just above the poverty line (a majority of whom are female) have difficulty gaining access to quality medical care across the life span. Women are less likely than men to have health insurance overall or pension coverage when they become old despite their greater utilization of health services and greater longevity (Meyer and Pavalko 1996). This pattern is especially pronounced in older women, poor women, and black women. In developing a framework for studying access to medical care, Ronald Anderson (1995) has identified primary determinants of health and illness behavior as the following: population characteristics, including those that may *predispose* one to use services (age, gender, and attitudes about health care); those that *enable* one to use health services (income and health insurance); and the *need* for health services. Although need is the most powerful predictor of use, David Mechanic (1992) and others caution that this should not be interpreted to mean that equity in access has been achieved or that utilization rates accurately reflect need. Moreover, differences in morbidity play a substantial role in men's and women's health care needs at the end of life because women are far more likely than men to suffer from debilitating chronic illnesses such as arthritis.

Less obvious are the related socioeconomic factors and health policy issues that may combine with these physical health differences to produce substantial differences in men's and women's end-of-life care. For example, Steven Miles and Kara Parker (1997: 219) made a compelling argument that Medicare serves men better than women because:

> [i]t covers hospital costs well, but provides less adequate coverage for nursing home care, community services, out-patient medications, preventive health examinations, and adaptive aids. . . . Even though the women covered by Medicare are older than men, Medicare distributes 12 percent more of its payments per beneficiary per year to men.

Under both Medicare and Medigap, the highest out-of-pocket costs for common illnesses are for diseases more common in women such as arthritis, whereas the lowest out-of-pocket costs are for diseases more common in men (Sofaer and Able 1990).

In regard to reporting bias, because men are less likely to report health problems than are women, differences in men's and women's styles of reporting were characterized in clinical practice as though men are more reliable reporters of their own health than are women. Consequently, women's health complaints have tended to receive relatively less attention than have men's. In fact, women were long considered unreliable reporters even in describing their own childbirth experiences (Kitzinger 1982; Oakley 1980). As a result of these assumptions as well as assumptions about the prevalence of particular diseases among men and women, some medical practices and treatment protocols have incorporated beliefs about essential differences between men and women. For example, women were long assumed to be less likely than men to suffer from cardiovascular disease, and consequently physicians were not trained to respond adequately to women's reports of symptoms now known to be indicative of a heart attack. Furthermore, although men are more likely than women to be hospitalized and to receive aggressive treatments, the psychosocial consequences of these treatments are studied in gender-specific ways (Nohria et al. 1998).

In the past decade, investigators have had a growing interest in determining how gender matters in treatment and outcomes for heart disease, in part because standard therapies were validated on primarily male populations. For example, in a review of 17 recent studies, V. Vaccarino and colleagues (1995) found that in 16, unadjusted in-hospital and one-month mortality rates after myocardial infarction (MI) for women exceeded those for men. There is some agreement among biomedical researchers that these mortality differences are largely attributable to women's older age and the presence of more unfavorable prognostic factors including greater number and severity of comorbidities (Malacrida et al. 1998). However, decreased efficacy of therapeutic modalities for women and a tendency to underuse invasive treatments also contribute to these differences (Nohria et al. 1998). For instance, in a study of cardiac procedures in four states, women were less likely than were men to have received coronary angiography, coronary artery bypass surgery, and thrombolytic therapy even after controlling for age, race, severity of MI, comorbidity, and geographic area (Weitzman et al. 1997). Furthermore, in spite of the improvements in success rates for angioplasty (PCTA), outcome studies still indicate that female sex remains a predictor of higher procedural mortality (Keelan et al. 1997). Although biomedical researchers attribute women's lower success rates to older age, greater comorbidity, and smaller body size, these factors are not easily translatable into strategies to improve women's outcomes. There is some evidence to suggest that intervention programs that focus on stress reduction as well as lifestyle change attract more women and have greater success (Ornish et al. 1990).

Gender Differences in Health-Related Quality of Life

In comparison to the biomedical literature, social scientists have explored nonclinical factors related to men's and women's cardiovascular disease outcomes while giving little or no attention to relevant biological factors (McKinlay 1996). These studies have tended to focus on sociodemographic risk factors, the role of social support, stress, and rehabilitation interventions. Social risk factors include low social class, low educational attainment, chronic troubling emotions, social isolation, and particularly for women, double loads of work and family responsibilities. Interestingly, much more attention has been paid to these social cardiovascular risk factors for women than to women's psychosocial adjustment after a heart attack. This is a serious gap because women fare worse after myocardial infarction than do men, return to

work at significantly lower rates, and have significantly less success staying in traditional rehabilitation programs. However, when women do stay in traditional rehabilitation programs, they generally recover as well as men, though the results vary substantially (for example, see Frasure-Smith et al. 1997).

Studies of men with testicular and prostate cancer provide an interesting example of how men are underserved and the ways that gender assumptions have affected both treatment and outcomes. For example, although numerous studies in the 1960s and 1970s documented the psychological and social consequences of breast cancer in women, there were no similar studies for men with either testicular or prostate cancer (Rieker et al. 1989). Moreover, while there was great concern and considerable research about the impact of anticancer therapies on women's reproductive capacity, much less attention has been paid to men's fertility and loss of fatherhood potential (Rieker et al. 1990). Such prerogatives were seen as essential to women's identity but not to men's. In the case of older men with prostate cancer, there are no published studies of the impact of support groups on quality of life outcomes following diagnosis and treatment despite the impressive research documenting the positive outcomes of such groups for women. There is some evidence to suggest that men do not join support groups for a variety of reasons, but there is little understanding of how to help men to overcome their cautiousness about talking to other men about their illness experience.

There is also some evidence that researchers and clinicians make different assumptions about men's and women's health-related quality-of-life concerns. For example, there is almost no research on sexual functioning and little physician counseling about sexual activity for women after MI, whereas there is an extensive literature on men (Brezinka and Kittel 1996). Moreover, although the pyschosocial data are suggestive about what factors might be critical to women's health outcomes, the use of single-sex samples and the lack of comparative physiological data limits the value and usefulness of these findings. Issues of gender equity continue to be important both in their own right and because they have consequences for men's and women's health.

RESEARCH COMBINING PHYSICAL AND MENTAL HEALTH OUTCOMES

Researchers rarely examine physical and mental health outcomes simultaneously. However, we argue that such research would better capture the net effects of acute and chronic stressors on men's and women's health and well-being. One example of gender-relevant research that examines both physical and mental health is research on exposure to and consequences of interpersonal violence.

Women are more likely than men to experience some form of interpersonal abuse (e.g., rape, incest, and domestic abuse) across the life span. Available data document that interpersonal violence results in acute injuries, chronic health problems, and disabling short- and long-term psychological effects (Falik and Collins 1996). Women with histories of abuse receive more psychiatric treatment and counseling, make more emergency room and physician visits, have more comorbidity (drug and alcohol problems), and represent a higher proportion of the chronic mentally ill than women without such histories (see, for example, Koss et al. 1994; Horton 1995). Men who have been abused, particularly as children, experience both similar and different physical and mental health consequences. Although the trauma men and women experience is the same, it is manifested in gender role-differentiated behaviors in adulthood (see, for example, Carmen and Rieker 1989).

Multiple aspects of health are examined in research on interpersonal abuse in part because both the mental and physical health effects may be direct and acute as well as indirect and chronic. The multilayered consequences of interpersonal violence demonstrate the need to examine a range of health-related quality-of-life outcomes. Moreover, in the case of abuse, psychological consequences can either precede or follow from physical health consequences. Therefore, a dynamic model of health is necessary to understand the outcomes of such traumatic experiences. Moreover, this research indicates the potential value of assessing the dynamic, immediate, and long-term mental and physical health effects of other types of stressors.

LIMITATIONS OF THE SOCIOLOGICAL MODEL

Research on gender and health is limited in several ways. Social scientists recognize the biological factors but fail to explore them fully in research designs, and biomedical researchers tend to ignore the social processes altogether. Unexamined assumptions regarding the sources of differences in men's and women's health affect the development of scientific knowledge. These underlying assumptions shape the questions that have been and are currently being asked in scientific research. In addition, they affect the range of hypotheses that are tested. In doing so, these often-unarticulated assumptions are reified as scientific knowledge accumulates in the artificially distinct areas of biological and social science research. Thus, individual studies rarely examine the independent and combined effects of social and medical interventions. Consequently, the relative impact of each type of intervention can only be estimated by comparing the results from separate studies, and the potential combined effects are uncertain. In contrast, an integrated approach would examine the effects of both social and medical interventions. For example, studies of hypertension could assess both stress reduction and pharmacological interventions in order to determine whether the independent and combined effects are the same for men and for women. Such an approach would also establish a dialogue across social and biological disciplines studying the same health outcome.

Sociological research on patterns of illness treats biology as socially neutral and builds on the assumption that inherent biological differences between men and women are either minimal or largely irrelevant. While this perspective may be appropriate for the study of gender differences in achievement and related socioeconomic outcomes, it is an inadequate premise for research on men's and women's health.

Because social and biomedical models describe different aspects of men's and women's health differences, interdisciplinary studies that combine these health risks are necessary to fully understand the determinants of women's and men's health and illness. However, disciplinary boundaries reinforce the separation of research into biomedical and sociological approaches and discourage a critical examination of alternative explanations. As long as research funding and practice create barriers to interdisciplinary research, it will be difficult to systematically examine the social and biological sources of gender differences in health.

One drawback of working toward a combined model is that in the effort to include sociological factors and perspectives in biomedical research, we may too readily accept all of the assumptions of Western allopathic medicine. Although sociologists have a long history of critiquing the biomedical model, Alexandra Dundas Todd (1994) argues that when sociologists do collaborate with medical researchers, they tend to overlook alternative models of health and illness from outside Western medicine. For example, despite offering a general critique of the biomedical model, sociologists tend to accept the Cartesian mind/body distinction between physical and mental health and illness. Rather than considering alternative paradigms such as those offered by Eastern medicine, sociologists primarily focus on their goal of incorporating social factors into existing biomedical explanations of disease processes.

AN EXPANDED CONCEPTUAL MODEL OF GENDER AND HEALTH

How one interprets the strengths and limitations of particular theories and models of gender and health depends in large part on one's perspective and goals. For example, the goal may be to document inequality and its health and social consequences, to develop theories about the mechanisms through which inequality affects health, or to reduce inequality and improve population health. Each approach applies a particular perspective in interpreting findings from social and biomedical research, which leads to different questions for future research. While there is considerable diversity among medical sociologists, for our purposes a general distinction can be made between those whose work on gender focuses primarily on understanding the social processes that have health consequences and those who are mainly interested in reducing the differences by affecting health outcomes, clinical practice, and health policy.

To the extent that medical sociologists intend to advance health, they need to develop a precise understanding of both inherent sex differences and acquired gender differences that contribute to men's and women's health. Although such research requires an integrated interdisciplinary framework, neither social nor biological health researchers have developed such a model. This predicament raises three questions: "Are differences in men's and women's health social, physiological, or both?"; "How do interactions between social factors and physiological processes contribute to men's and women's health?"; and "Do such interactions extend the net effects of gender?"

In practice, the social and biomedical sciences operate as distinct paradigms with different research questions and often apparently conflicting findings. As a result of the differences in theories and methods, as well as competition for scarce resources in the form of research funding, researchers from both fields tend to ignore and often even disparage the other's perspective and work. Consequently, sociological explanations often proceed from the assumption that differences in men's and women's health can be attributed exclusively to social causes. Such intellectual parochialism limits the range of questions that are asked, hypotheses that are tested, and outcomes that are considered (Levine 1995).

Undoubtedly some health differences between men and women could be purely biological in origin (for example hemophilia and sex-specific cancers). However, the social organization of men's and women's lives affects their relative exposure to certain risks and health behaviors through patterns in employment and social roles or to differences in social and economic burdens. Thus some differences may have purely social origins. Moreover, socialization may also enhance or even suppress a biological difference. For example, gender differences in lung cancer may be attributed to socially patterned health behaviors such as smoking and diet. In addition, men and women appear to metabolize nicotine differently, affecting their rates of addiction and ability to quit (Walsh, Sorenson, and Leonard 1995). Thus, the combined effects may be additive or interactive (for further explanation see Bird and Rieker 1999). Therefore, to address inequity in men's and women's health requires an understanding of sex and gender differences and the interaction of the two.

A health advantage for one sex may arise from differences in men's and women's biology or in their social circumstances or from a combination of the two. For example, prior to menopause women have a lower risk of cardiovascular disease than men because estrogen reduces women's risk of high low-density lipoprotein (LDL) and low high-density lipoprotein (HDL) levels and increases the flexibility of their circulatory system. Yet, compared to men, women experience more "silent heart attacks." A biological model alone does not fully explain the gendered pattern of cardiovascular disease, which includes differences in the development, disease course, and outcomes. Thus, it may be that women do not receive the full benefit of their biological advantage because of the cumulative effects of stress associated with their multiple roles.

Another example is the gender difference in risk of infection. Women are at higher risk of acute and chronic infections than are men. However, the biomedical model cannot explain the female excess in rates of infection because women have higher levels of immune response than men. Consequently, one would expect them to have lower rates of infection. An explanation for this contradictory pattern is that women's social roles expose them to multiple stressors, which in turn increase their vulnerability to infectious disease. Only by examining both biological and social factors simultaneously can we gain insight into the extent to which social factors have independent or interactive effects on health.

A clearer understanding of the combined effects of social and biological factors could provide the basis for a new agenda for interventions and policy to address differences in men's and women's health. The appropriate interventions might be either biomedical or social and either individual or societal depending on the nature of the disadvantage and its health consequences. In general, sociologists contend that social inequalities should be addressed with social rather than medical interventions even when the inequalities have health implications. For example, as many sociologists have argued for over two decades, rather than just medicating women who report high levels of psychological distress, we should reduce the social inequalities that produce gender differences in psychological well-being. Likewise, research on how social inequalities contribute to men's excess rates of alcohol and drug abuse would advance knowledge regarding male disadvantage and possibly facilitate prevention and treatment.

CONCLUSION

Sociological research on gender and health has focused on how the social organization of men's and women's lives contributes to differences in their physical and mental health. Sociologists have shown that gender inequities in the family and in the labor force produce differences in men's and women's exposure and vulnerability to particular stressors, which in turn affect psychological well-being. In contrast, sociological research on men's and women's physical health focused on equity in access to care, utilization, and medical treatment. Unfortunately, research examining both mental and physical health effects has largely been limited to studies of particular problems such as interpersonal abuse. The near-absolute separation between the study of mental and physical health exaggerates the distinction between the two. Yet psychological distress contributes to poor physical health. Thus, the consequences of gender differences in exposure to stressors extend beyond psychological outcomes to include many aspects of health and health-related quality of life.

Only by studying a broader range of health outcomes can we fully capture the *net consequences* of social inequality for men and women. Ultimately, such work will provide a more complete model of the pathways between social factors and gender differences in mental and physical health. Moreover, because gender issues are intertwined with other social factors and processes, greater efforts should be devoted to explaining the variability in health *among* men and *among* women.

As we have argued, inequality has cumulative adverse effects on health for individuals and their family members. Therefore, examining only individual outcomes is insufficient. Inequity within the home simultaneously affects all members of the household; studies should consider the impact on both spouses, as well as on other family members. Moreover, because specific stressors may lead to different mental and physical health consequences for men and women, it is necessary to examine a range of health outcomes to accurately assess the impact of gender inequality. Failure to do so may lead to gross underestimates of health consequences for either gender.

For over two decades, sociological research on stress and illness has focused primarily on explaining women's excess psychological distress, examining sources of female disadvantage in resources and exposure to particular stressors. Recent work on the social organization of men's lives reveals a lack of attention to the health consequences of men's exposure and vulnerability to particular stressors. Incorporating this work into stress and illness models would reveal the pathways through which gender shapes health outcomes for men as well as for women.

Finally, we contend that ignoring biomedical explanations of differences in men's and women's health limits sociological models of health and illness. The intellectual parochialism that characterizes social and biomedical research leaves both with incomplete models. Greater attention to the findings from biomedical research would improve our understanding of the independent and interactive effects of social factors and facilitate the development of models of the complex interaction of social and biological factors on men's and women's health.

REFERENCES

ANDERSON, RONALD M. 1995. "Revisiting the Behavioral Model and Access to Medical Care: Does it Matter?" *Journal of Health and Social Behavior* 36:1–10.

ANESHENSEL, CAROL S., CAROLYN M. RUTTER, and PETER A. LACHENBRUCH. 1991. "Social Structure, Stress, and Mental Health: Competing Conceptual and Analytic Models." *American Sociological Review* 56:166–78.

BARANSKI, B. 1993. "Effects of the Workplace on Fertility and Related Reproductive Outcomes." *Environmental Health Perspectives* 101(suppl. 2): 81–90.

BEBBINGTON, P. 1996. "The Origins of Sex Differences in Depressive Disorder: Bridging the Gap." *International Review of Psychiatry* 8: 295–332.

BELL, SUSAN E. 1994. "From Local to Global: Resolving Uncertainty About the Safety of DES in Menopause." *Research in Sociology of Health Care* 11: 41–56.

BELLAS, MARCIA. 1992. "The Effects of Marital Status and Wives' Employment on the Salaries of Faculty Men: The (House)wife Bonus." *Gender and Society* 6 (4): 609–22.

BIRD, CHLOE E. 1999. "Gender, Household Labor, and Psychological Distress: The Impact of the Amount and Division of Housework." *Journal of Health and Social Behavior* 40: 32–45.

BIRD, CHLOE E., and CATHERINE E. ROSS. 1993. "Houseworkers and Paid Workers: Qualities of the Work and Effects on Personal Control." *Journal of Marriage and the Family* 55: 913–25.

BIRD, CHLOE E., and PATRICIA P. RIEKER. 1999. "Gender Matters: An Integrated Model for Understanding Men's and Women's Health." *Social Science and Medicine* 48(6): 745–55.

BREZINKA, V., and F. KITTEL. 1996. "Psychosocial Factors of Coronary Heart Disease in Women: A Review." *Social Science and Medicine* 42: 1351–65.

BROWN, G.W., and T. HARRIS. 1978. *Social Origins of Depression: A Study of Psychiatric Disorder in Women.* New York: Free Press.

CAMERON, ELAINE, and JON BERNARDES. 1998. "Gender and Disadvantage in Health: Men's Health for a Change" *Sociology of Health and Illness* 20(5):673–93.

CARMEN, ELAINE (H.), and PATRICIA P. RIEKER. 1989. "A Psychosocial Model of the Victim-to-Patient Process" *Psychiatric Clinics of North America* 12(2) :431–43.

CLEARY, PAUL D., DAVID MECHANIC, and JAMES R. GREENLY. 1982. "Sex Differences in Medical Care Utilization: An Empirical Investigation." *Journal of Health and Social Behavior* 23:106–19.

CONNELL, ROBERT W. 1987. *Gender and Power.* Stanford, CA: Stanford University Press.

DOHRENWEND, BRUCE P., and BARBARA SNELL DOHRENWEND. 1976. "Sex Differences and Psychiatric Disorders." *American Journal of Sociology* 81: 1147–54.

DOHRENWEND, BRUCE P., and BARBARA SNELL DOHRENWEND. 1977. "Reply to Gove and Tudor's Comment on 'Sex Differences and Psychiatric Disorders.'" *American Journal of Sociology* 82: 1336–45.

DOYAL, LESLEY. 1995. *What Makes Women Sick: Gender and the Political Economy of Health.* London: Macmillan.

FALIK, MARILYN M., and KAREN SCOTT COLLINS, eds. 1996. *Women's Health: The Commonwealth Fund Survey.* Baltimore, MD: Johns Hopkins University Press.

FISHER, SUE. 1988. *In the Patient's Best Interest: Women and the Politics of Medical Decisions.* New Brunswick, NJ: Rutgers University Press.

FRANKENHAEUSER, MARIANNE, ULF LUNDBERT, MATS FREDRIKSON, BO MELIN, MARTTI TUOMISTO, ANNA-LISA MYRSTEN, MONICA HEDMAN, BODIL BERGMAN-LOSMAN, and LEIF WALLIN. 1989. "Stress On and Off the Job as Related to Sex and Occupational Status in White-collar Workers." *Journal of Organizational Behavior* 10:321–346.

FRASURE-SMITH, NANCY, F. LESPERANCE, et al. 1997. "Randomised Trial of Home-Based Psychosocial Nursing Intervention for Patients Recovering From Myocardial Infarction." *The Lancet* 350: 473–79.

GARTNER, ROSEMARY, KATHRYN BAKER, and FRED C. HAMPEL. 1990. "Gender Stratification and the Gender Gap in Homicide Victimization." *Social Problems* 37: 593–612.

GOVE, WALTER. 1972. "The Relationship Between Sex Roles, Mental Illness, and Marital Status." *Social Forces* 51(1) : 34–44.

GOVE, WALTER, and JEANETTE TUDOR. 1973. "Adult Sex Roles and Mental Illness." *American Journal of Sociology* 78: 812–35.

GOVE, WALTER, and MICHAEL HUGHES. 1979. "Possible Causes of the Apparent Sex Differences in Physical Health: An Empirical Investigation." *American Sociological Review* 44: 126–46.

HARRISON, JAMES. 1978. "Warning: The Male Sex Role May Be Dangerous to Your Health." *Journal of Social Issues* 34(1): 65–86.

HERTZMAN, CLYDE, JOHN FRANK, and ROBERT G. EVANS. 1994. "Heterogeneities in Health Status and the Determinants of Population Health." In *Why Are Some People Healthy and Others Not? The Determinants of Population Health,* ed. R.G. Evans, M.L. Barer, and T.R. Marmor. New York: Aldine De Gruyter, pp. 67–92.

HOCHSCHILD, ARLIE, with ANNE MACHUNG. 1989. *The Second Shift.* New York: Viking.

HORTON, JACQUELINE A., ed. 1995. *The Women's Health Data Book.* New York: Elsevier.

HORWITZ, ALLAN V., and HELEN RASKIN WHITE. 1991. "Becoming Married, Depression, and Alcohol Problems Among Young Adults." *Journal of Health and Social Behavior* 32: 221–37.

HUBBARD, RUTH. 1990. "The Political Nature of Human Nature." In *Theoretical Perspectives on Sexual*

Difference, ed. Deborah L. Rhode. New Haven, CT: Yale University Press, pp. 63–73.

JOHNSON, JEFFREY V., and ELLEN M. HALL. 1995. "Class, Work and Health." In *Society and Health,* ed. B.C. Amick III, S. Levine, A.R. Tarlov, and D.C. Walsh. New York: Oxford University Press.

KEELAN, E.T., B.D. NUNEZ, D.E. GRILL, P.B. BERGER, D.R. HOLMES, and M.R. BELL. 1997. "Comparison of Immediate and Long-Term Outcome of Coronary Angioplasty Performed for Unstable Angina and Rest Pain in Men and Women." *Mayo Clinic Proceedings* 72: 5–12.

KESSLER, RONALD C., and JAMES A. McRAE. 1981. "Trends in the Relationship Between Sex and Psychological Distress: 1957-1976." *American Sociological Review* 46: 443–52.

KESSLER, RONALD C., KATHERINE A. McGONAGLE, SHANYANG ZHAO, CHRISTOPHER B. NELSON, MICHAEL HUGHES, SUZANN ESHLEMAN, HANS-ULRICH WITTCHEN, and KENETH S. KENDLER. 1994. "Lifetime and 12-Month Prevalence of DSM-III-R Psychiatric Disorders in the United States: Results From the National Comorbidity Survey." *Archives of General Psychiatry* 51(1): 8–19.

KIMMEL, MICHAEL S., and M. MESSNER, eds. 1993. *Men's Lives.* New York: Macmillan.

KITZINGER, SHELIA. 1982. "Birth and Violence Against Women: Generating Hypotheses From Women's Accounts of Unhappiness Following Childbirth." In *Women's Health Matters,* ed. Helen Roberts. London: Routledge, pp. 63–80.

KOSS, MARY P., LISA A. GOODMAN, ANGELA BROWNE, LOUISE F. FITZGERALD, GWENDOLYN PURYEAR KEITA, and NANCY FELIPE RUSSO. 1994. *No Safe Haven: Male Violence Against Women at Home, at Work, and in the Community.* Washington, DC: American Psychological Association.

LENNON, MARY CLARE, and SARAH ROSENFIELD. 1994. "Relative Fairness and the Division of Housework: The Importance of Options." *American Journal of Sociology* 100(2):506–31.

LEVINE, SOL. 1995. "Time for Creative Integration in Medical Sociology." *Journal of Health and Social Behavior* (Extra Issue): 1–4.

LORBER, JUDITH. 1994. *Paradoxes of Gender.* New Haven, CT: Yale University Press.

LORBER, JUDITH. 1997. *Gender and the Social Construction of Illness.* Thousand Oaks, CA: Sage Publications.

MACINTYRE, SALLY, KATE HUNT, and HELEN SWEETING. 1996. "Gender Differences in Health: Are Things Really As Simple As They Seem?" *Social Science and Medicine* 42: 617–24.

MALACRIDA, R., M. GENONI, A.P. MAGGIONI, V. SPATARO, S. PARISH, A. PALMER, R. COLLINS, and T. MOCCETTI. 1998. "A Comparison of the Early Outcome of Acute Myocardial Infarction in Women and Men." *The New England Journal of Medicine* 338: 8–14.

MASTROIANNI, ANNA C., RUTH FADEN, and DANIEL FEDERMAN, eds. 1994. *Women and Health Research: Ethical and Legal Issues of Including Women in Clinical Studies.* Washington, DC: Institute of Medicine, National Academy Press.

MCKINLAY, J.B. 1996. "Some Contributions From the Social System to Gender Inequalities in Heart Disease." *Journal of Health and Social Behavior* 37: 1–26.

MECHANIC, DAVID. 1992. "Health and Illness Behavior and Patient Practitioner Relationships." *Social Science and Medicine* 34:1345–50.

MELTZER, H., G. BALJIT, M. PETTICREW, and K. HINDS. 1995. *Prevalence of Psychiatric Morbidity Among Adults Living in Private Households.* London: HMSO.

MEYER, MADONNA HARRINGTON, and ELIZA K. PAVALKO. 1996. "Family, Work, and Access to Health Insurance Among Mature Women." *Journal of Health and Social Behavior* 37(4):311–25.

MILES, STEVEN, and KARA PARKER. 1997. "Men, Women, and Health Insurance" *New England Journal of Medicine* 336(3):218–21.

MIROWSKY, JOHN. 1996. "Age and the Gender Gap in Depression." *Journal of Health and Social Behavior* 37: 362–80.

MIROWSKY, JOHN, and CATHERINE E. ROSS. 1989. *Social Causes of Psychological Distress.* New York: Aldine.

MIROWSKY, JOHN, and CATHERINE E. ROSS. 1995. "Sex Differences in Distress: Real or Artifact?" *American Sociological Review* 60: 449–68.

MISHLER, ELLIOT G. 1981. "Viewpoint: Critical Perspectives on the Biomedical Model." In *Social Contexts of Health, Illness, and Patient Care,* ed. Elliot Mishler et al. Cambridge, UK: Cambridge University Press, pp. 1–23.

MISHLER, ELLIOT G. 1986. *The Discourse of Medicine: Dialectics of Medical Interviews.* Norwood, NJ: Ablex Publishing Corporation.

NATHANSON, CONSTANCE A. 1980. "Social Roles and Health Status Among Women: The Significance of Employment." *Social Science and Medicine* 14: 463–71.

NATIONAL CENTER FOR HEALTH STATISTICS. 1996. *Health, United States, 1995.* Hyattsville, MD: U.S. Public Health Service.

NATIONAL CENTER FOR HEALTH STATISTICS. 1998. *Health, United States, 1998.* Hyattsville, MD: U.S. Public Health Service.

NAZROO, JAMES Y., ANGELA C. EDWARDS, and GEORGE BROWN. 1998. "Gender Differences in the Prevalence of Depression: Artefact, Alternative Disorders, Biology or Roles?" *Sociology of Health and Illness* 20(3):312–30.

NOHRIA, A., V. VACCARINO, and H. KRUMHOLZ. 1998. "Gender Differences in Mortality After Myocardial Infarction." *Cardiology Clinics* 16: 45–57.

NOLEN-HOEKSEMA, SUSAN. 1990. *Sex Differences in Depression.* Stanford, CA: Stanford University Press.

OAKLEY, ANN. 1980. *Women Confined: Toward a Sociology of Childbirth.* Oxford: Martin Robinson.

ORFORD, JIM, and ALISTAIR KEDDIE. 1985. "Gender Differences in the Functions and Effects of Moderate and Excessive Drinking." *British Journal of Clinical Psychology* 24: 265–79.

ORNISH, D., S.E. BROWN, L.W. SCHERWITZ, J.H. BILLINGS, W.T. ARMSTRONG, T.A. PORTS, S.M. MCLANAHAN, R.L. KIRKERIDE, R.J. BRAND, and K.L. GOULD. 1990. "Can Lifestyle Changes Reverse Coronary Disease?" *Lancet* 336:129–33.

PAUL, MAUREEN. 1995. "Reproductive Disorders." In *Occupational Health: Recognizing and Preventing Work-Related Disease,* ed. Barry S. Levy and David H. Wegman. Boston: Little, Brown and Company, pp. 543–62.

PLECK, JOSEPH H. 1983. *The Myth of Masculinity.* Cambridge: MIT Press.

PLECK, JOSEPH H., and ROBERT BRANNON, eds. 1978. "Male Roles and the Male Experience." *Journal of Social Issues* 34(1).

POPE, ANDREW M., and ALVIN R. TARLOV, eds. 1991. *Disability in America: Toward a National Agenda for Prevention.* Washington, DC: Institute of Medicine.

REGIER, D.A., W.E. NARROW, D.S. RAE, R.W. MANDERSCHEID, B.Z. LOCKE, F.K. GOODWIN 1993. "The De Facto US Mental and Addictive Disorders Service System: Epidemiological Catchment Area 1-Year Prevalence Rates of Disorders and Services." *Archives of General Psychiatry.* 50: 85–94.

RESKIN, BARBARA, and IRENE PADAVIC. 1994. *Women and Men at Work.* Thousand Oaks, CA: Pine Forge Press.

RIEKER, PATRICIA P., EILEEN M. FITZGERALD, LESLIE A. KALISH, JEROME P. RICHIE, GIL S. LEDERMAN, SUSAN B. EDBRIL, and MARC B. GARNICK. 1989. "Psychosocial Factors, Curative Therapies and Behavioral Outcomes: A Comparison of Testis Cancer Survivors and a Control Group of Healthy Men." *Cancer* 64 (11):2399–2407.

RIEKER, PATRICIA P., and M. KAY JANKOWSKI. 1995. "Sexism and Women's Psychological Status." In *Mental Health, Racism and Sexism,* ed. C.V. Willie, P.P. Rieker, B. Kramer, and B. Brown. Pittsburgh: University of Pittsburgh Press, pp. 27–50.

RIEKER, PATRICIA P., EILEEN M. FITZGERALD, and LESLIE A. KALISH. 1990. "Adaptive Behavioral Responses to Potential Infertility Among Survivors of Testis Cancer." *Journal of Clinical Oncology* 8(2): 347–55.

ROBINS, LEE N., JOHN E. HELZER, MYRNA M. WEISSMAN, HELEN ORVASCHEL, ERNEST GRUENBERG, JACK D. BURKE, and DARREL A. REIGER. 1984. "Lifetime Prevalence of Specific Psychiatric Disorders in Three Sites." *Archives of General Psychiatry* 41: 949–58.

ROSENFIELD, SARAH. 1989. "The Effects of Women's Employment: Personal Control and Sex Differences in Mental Health." *Journal of Health and Social Behavior* 30(March): 77–91.

ROSS, CATHERINE E., and CHLOE E. BIRD. 1994. "Sex Stratification and Health Behaviors: Consequences for Men's and Women's Perceived Health." *Journal of Health and Social Behavior,* 35: 161–78.

ROSS, CATHERINE E., and MARIEKE VAN WILLIGEN. 1996. "Gender, Parenthood and Anger." *Journal of Marriage and the Family* 58: 572–84.

SABO, DONALD, and DAVID F. GORDON. 1995. "Rethinking Men's Health and Illness." In *Men's Health and Illness: Gender, Power and the Body,* ed. D. Sabo and D.F. Gordon. Thousand Oaks, CA: Sage Publications, pp. 1–21.

SIMON, ROBIN W. 1995. "Gender, Multiple Roles, Role Meaning, and Mental Health." *Journal of Health and Social Behavior* 36(2): 182–94.

SIMON, ROBIN W. 1998. "Assessing Sex Differences in Vulnerability Among Employed Parents: The Importance of Marital Status." *Journal of Health and Social Behavior* 39(1): 38–54.

SOFAER, S., and E. ABLE. 1990. "Older Women's Health and Financial Vulnerability: Implications of the Medicare Benefit Structure." *Women and Health* 16: 47–67.

TAYLOR, HOWARD. 1997. Presidential Address. Annual Meetings of the Eastern Sociological Association. Baltimore, MD.

THOITS, PEGGY. 1991. "On Merging Identity Theory and Stress Research." *Social Psychology Quarterly* 54(12): 101–12.

THOITS, PEGGY. 1995a. "Identity-Relevant Events and Psychological Symptoms." *Journal of Health and Social Behavior* 36: 72–82

THOITS, PEGGY. 1995b. "Stress, Coping, and Social Support Processes: Where Are We? What Next?" *Journal of Health and Social Behavior* (extra issue): 53–79.

TODD, ALEXANDRA DUNDAS. 1989. *Intimate Adversaries: Cultural Conflict Between Doctors and Women Patients.* Philadelphia: University of Pennsylvania Press.

TODD, ALEXANDRA DUNDAS. 1994. *Double Vision: An East-West Collaboration for Coping With Cancer.* Hanover: Wesleyan University Press.

UMBERSON, DEBRA, and KRISTI WILLIAMS. 1999. "Family Status and Mental Health." In *Handbook on the Sociology of Mental Health,* ed. C.S. Aneshensel and J. Phelan. New York: Kluwer Academic/Plenum Publishers, pp. 225–53.

UMBERSON, DEBRA, MEICHE D. CHEN, JAMES HOUSE, KRISTIN HOPKINS, and ELLEN STATEN. 1996. "The Effects of Social Relationships on Psychological Well-Being: Are Men and Women Really So Different?" *American Sociological Review* 61:837–57.

VACCARINO, V., H.M. KRUMHOLZ, L.F. BERKMAN, and R.I. HORWITZ. 1995. "Sex Differences in Mortality After Myocardial Infarction: Is There Evidence for an Increased Risk for Women?" *Circulation* 91: 1861–71.

VERBRUGGE, LOIS. 1985. "Gender and Health: An Update on Hypotheses and Evidence." *Journal of Health and Social Behavior* 24: 16–30.

VERBRUGGE, LOIS, and DEBORAH L. WINGARD. 1987. "Sex Differentials in Health and Mortality." *Women and Health* 12(2):103–45.

WALDRON, INGRID. 1995a. "Gender and Health-Related Behavior." In *Health Behavior: Emerging Research*

Perspectives, ed. David S. Gochman. New York: Plenum Press, pp. 193–208.

WALDRON, INGRID. 1995b. "Contributions of Changing Gender Differences in Behavior and Social Roles to Changing Gender Differences in Mortality." In *Men's Health and Illness: Gender, Power, and the Body,* ed. D. Sabo and D.F. Gordon. Thousand Oaks, CA: Sage Publications, pp. 22–45.

WALSH, DIANA CHAPMAN, GLORIAN SORENSEN, and LORI LEONARD. 1995. "Gender, Health, and Cigarette Smoking." In *Society and Health,* ed. Benjamin Amick, Sol Levine, Alvin Tarlov, and Diana Chapman Walsh. New York: Oxford University Press, pp. 131–71.

WEISS, GREGORY L., and LYNNE E. LONQUIST. 1997. *The Sociology of Health and Illness.* Englewood Cliffs, NJ: Prentice Hall.

WEISSMAN, MYRA M., and GERALD L. KLERMAN. 1977. "Sex Differences in the Epidemiology of Depression." *Archives of General Psychiatry* 34:98–111.

WEITZMAN, S., L. COOPER, L. CHAMBLESS, W. ROSAMOND, L. CLEGG, G. MARCUCCI, F. ROMM, and A. WHITE. 1997. "Gender, Racial, and Geographic Differences in the Performance of Cardiac Diagnostic and Therapeutic Procedures for Hospitalized Acute Myocardial Infarction in Four States." *American Journal of Cardiology* 79: 722–26.

WHOOLEY, MARY A., and WARREN S. BROWNER. 1998. "Association Between Depressive Symptoms and Mortality in Older Women." *Archives of Internal Medicine* 158: 2129–35.

8 RACE, ETHNICITY, AND HEALTH

CHRIS SMAJE, *University of Surrey, England*

INTRODUCTION

As in others in this book, the aim of the present chapter is to give an overview of the main currents of research and thinking in a particular domain of medical sociology. However, when attention is focused upon the relationship between race or ethnicity and health, a complicating factor arises because there are strong currents of thought, both within the parent discipline and in the traditions of medical sociology, that suggest that this particular domain cannot or should not be detached from broader contexts, even if a good deal of research proceeds as if "race" were a self-evident entity. These currents of thought manifest themselves in different ways that accord with the distinctive intellectual strands comprising the subdiscipline.

First, the core theoretical traditions of sociology share a fundamental concern to provide a *critique of ideology.* In other words, they attempt to transcend and thereby throw into relief the modes of thought and action people deploy in everyday life. The concepts of race and—to a lesser extent—ethnicity have long been subjected to particularly forceful critiques of this kind, which suggest that they are ideological categories of everyday life that are explicable in terms of other factors and cannot be viewed as analytical concepts in themselves. Thus, to make *race* or *ethnicity* the focus of sociological analysis, it is argued, is to render these concepts as essential or *sui generis,* when in fact they are contingent or epiphenomenal. A powerful case can be made for the view that race and ethnicity are at root ideologies of collective exclusion, and therefore race only matters because racism matters. In other words, the fundamental "reality" of race

is that people are sorted according to socially defined criteria through a variety of explicitly and implicitly exclusionary processes that ultimately affect their life chances. To consider race as if it is some essential quality attached to individuals is therefore to risk reifying as a matter of social being something that fundamentally has to do with socio-structural forces that impinge upon people's lives.

Second, medical sociology draws upon the traditions of public health or social epidemiology that emphasize how social, economic, and political location within societies structures people's experience of health. Thus, in a parallel fashion, it can be argued that health is not affected by ethnic or racial identity so much as by the consequences entailed in these identities for social and economic position. In this sense, the topic becomes a sub-branch of a broader domain, focusing on the social causes of health and illness and emphasizing the association between inequalities of social status and inequalities in health.

Set somewhat against these traditions are approaches that take the everyday categories through which people understand their world as a point of departure. These include policy or health services research, which—often with little theoretical reflection—take common racial or ethnic designations to refer to identifiable population groups with distinctive profiles as clients in the health sector. Another core tradition of medical sociology has been concerned with the way that people define and understand health and illness as components of *social* experience over and above any strictly physiological referent. With a somewhat greater degree of theoretical reflection, part of this enterprise has entailed consideration of how people's self-identities as members of particular racial or ethnic groups and the socio-cultural resources that they are thereby able to mobilize affect this social experience of health.

The author thanks Chloe Bird, Sara Arber, and Helen Cooper for their comments on a previous version of this chapter.

The present chapter attempts to give a flavour of how these different and sometimes apparently competing traditions jointly both constitute and problematize race and ethnicity as social contexts of health and illness. The critique of racial and ethnic ideologies demands that we take a careful look at the meaning of race and ethnicity as variables in sociological research. The next section is therefore devoted to a consideration of this question. It will suggest that the concepts of race and ethnicity are *categories* that are the result of particular historical processes of social construction. At the same time, it will suggest that these categories can nevertheless come to be implicated in determinate ways with the identities, behaviours, and life chances of real people, that they can act as a basis for social *groups* that can properly be made the object of sociological enquiry. It will be argued that race in itself can never be invoked as a self-adequate explanation for patterns of health experience, although the underlying mechanisms that mediate the relationship between race and health can be complex and intractable, leading back toward a consideration of race as a dimension of social experience. Thus, the four substantive sections of this chapter examine racial or ethnic patterns in health and health care respectively, together with the range of underlying mechanisms that can account for them.

Race and ethnicity are categories with particular histories that have varied in their consequences and meaning in different places and times. The focus in this chapter is upon the contemporary situation in the United States and the United Kingdom. As we shall see, there are certain similarities between these two countries in terms of the nature of racial and ethnic categorisation and the concomitant implications for health and health care, but there are also important differences. The aim of the chapter is not to provide a systematic comparison between the two countries, so much as it is to use examples from them to illustrate relevant processes and theories and help identify points of convergence and divergence in the field.

RACE AND ETHNICITY AS SOCIAL AND EPIDEMIOLOGICAL VARIABLES

From a sociological standpoint, race and ethnicity describe the way that distinctive and often hierarchically ranked human collectivities are defined through processes that construct one or more dimensions of human difference—such as physical (somatic) characteristics, language and territorial, historical, religious or "cultural" identifications of various kinds—and invest them with social significance. It should be noted here that race as much as ethnicity is a *social* and not a *natural* or biological fact, a point that has now been so well established that no further justification should be necessary (see Montague 1972). A distinction is often made between race and ethnicity as the creation of social identities on the basis of respectively somatic and cultural characteristics. However, this is perhaps a less useful distinction than the recognition that race is a term with a specific history that has emerged particularly in the nexus of colonial relationships between Europe, Africa, and the Americas over the past several hundred years. Ethnicity, on the other hand, is a more recent term, popularized through intellectual circuits, and connoting broader processes of national and cultural identification whose very generality has led some scholars to question the utility of ethnicity as an analytical concept, while provoking sociological debates, which remain very much alive, about the relationship between race, ethnicity, and nationalism. For present purposes, however, two points emerge from these broader sociological approaches to the topic. First, that race and ethnicity refer to *social processes* with definite historical moorings, and second, that questions of *power*—of who gets to define collective identity, of who is defined, and of what this means in terms of social experience—are inseparably bound up in these processes.

This observation leads to another way of approaching the topic: ethnogenesis (and racialization) involve assertions of a (positive) group identity—an "us" statement—and thus also a (negative) categorisation of others—a "them" statement. To distinguish between an *us* and a *them* requires the definition of some more or less identifiable boundary between the two. An influential approach to this point was first set out by Fredrik Barth (1969), who argued that ethnicity, rather than reflecting any substantive socio-cultural differentiation between actual groups of people, was better conceived as a set of processes through which boundaries were defined and symbolized in context-specific ways. This useful observation enables us to understand an otherwise puzzling feature of ethnic processes, namely how both people and cultural practices can flow across apparently firm ethnic boundaries. Race or ethnicity denote *relations between* people and not substantial qualities *possessed by* them.

But what is the purpose of such boundary formation? To think relationally involves locating two or more entities within the same encompassing domain, and a preferred mode of sociological analysis has been to project ethnic relations from such familiar domains as the political or economic processes through which people are incorporated into the class structure of contemporary societies. This kind of approach is invaluable, but it courts the danger of representing race or ethnicity as hollow surfaces that conceal the real underlying mechanisms. An alternative suggestion is that racial and ethnic identities are forged over the long term in the context of particular repositories of historical meanings and that specific attention to their effects is therefore warranted.

The relevance of these points is in moving toward a more subtle appreciation of the way in which power is invested in racial or ethnic identity claims. Instead of differentiating prior groups, which are then subject to racialization or ethnogenesis—as in a sharp distinction between asserted "us" identities and ascribed "them" identities—we are better able to see ascription and assertion as moments of the same process in which racial or ethnic identities possess a certain irreducible or emergent character, even if what people understand that character to be may vary considerably. In this sense, race or ethnicity may be understood as a *scheme or model for experience embodied in social actors* that acts as a marker or center for the subtle processes of identification through which a sense of self and other is inculcated, but in historically determinate ways which may create hard (racial) boundaries over which people have no personal control. This point contrasts both with the tendency in biomedically oriented writings simply to assume that race and ethnicity are meaningful categories defining social or even biological homogeneity and with writings that rightly criticize these assumptions, but usually through recourse to a naive understanding of the sociological basis upon which categories can be defined as social constructs.

The theoretical discussion above helps to show how race and ethnicity can properly be regarded as dimensions of social experience that can be the basis of sociological analysis, without supposing that these dimensions have a *sui generis* character that transcends their grounding within particular socio-historical circumstances. This distinction is important insofar as there can be a tendency to confuse *etiological mechanisms* with *ontological propositions*. For example, there is an association in the United States between risk of death in a given time period and race. Using a rather crude racial taxonomy of black and white, death rates for blacks are around 1.5–2 times greater than for whites in all but the oldest age groups. Yet when adjustment is made for a range of socioeconomic indicators, this association is reduced and in some studies disappears altogether. What this tells us is that the most likely explanation for racial differentials in health has to do with socioeconomic factors. It does *not* tell us that race is a less significant social characteristic than socioeconomic status, or class as it is commonly described. The significance or otherwise of these characteristics depends upon *a priori* theoretical judgments, and the fact that health outcomes seem to be correlated most powerfully with things like income, employment status, educational attainment, and housing conditions carries no implication for the way that people conceive of themselves. People do not experience the world through a set of partial coefficients, but as embodied social actors.

Let us now turn more specifically to the way that race and ethnicity can be constructed as variables in empirical research by medical sociologists. As was suggested earlier, even if one can legitimately construct race or ethnicity as social identities, one cannot invoke them as concepts that *explain* differences in people's experience of the world, such as their experience of health or health care. The idea of embodied agency outlined above suggests instead that they act as a centering point for a potentially extremely complicated array of material, social, psychological, and occasionally biological factors that sometimes covary with—but are always distributed across—socially defined racial or ethnic groups, and it is at the level of these factors that the explanation for the racial patterning of health based upon empirical research must be mounted. In this move from the theoretical to the empirical, the blurred and contextual nature of ethnicity or race conceived as boundary processes easily gives way to a concretized notion of ethnic groups or populations, particularly in quantitative studies.

At this point, some comments on the character of racial and ethnic categories in the two countries that are the focus of this chapter are in order. The United States has been characterised by a peculiar disjunction. On the one hand, it has generally been supposed by both academic commentators and in popular ideology that the ethnic identities of migrants from various European countries diminish over time until—a few vestigial attachments aside—people are fully assimilated into the American "melting pot." Race, on the other hand, captures a fundamental dichotomy between black and white, which is a persisting feature of the American social landscape and which has served historically largely to distinguish Americans who can trace any part of their ancestry back to African-origin slaves from the rest of the population. This duality is complicated by other factors, however, and now appears increasingly problematic. The aboriginal inhabitants have generally been thought of as a separate race of Indians or Native Americans, while the black–white dichotomy has struggled to assimilate more recent migrants from Asia and Latin America, the latter combining European, African, and Indian elements. Official U.S. classifications now recognize four racial groups—Whites, African Americans, Asian Pacific Americans, and Native Americans—and one cultural group, Hispanic Americans. People with the latter designation can in principle identify themselves with any race.

In the United Kingdom, distinctions between race and ethnicity are less clear cut, with the term *ethnic minorities* widely understood to apply to post-war labour migrants (and their descendants) who came to Britain principally from its former colonies in the Caribbean and the Indian subcontinent, and also from West Africa and Hong Kong, although settlement in Britain from these areas has a much longer history. In this sense, contemporary ideas of ethnicity in the United Kingdom are fundamentally racialized. There is a tendency to assume that the rest of the population forms a homogenous white ethnic group; this largely reflects the success of forms of imperial nationalism, which were not really concretized until the nineteenth century. Thus, in both countries there is an idea of race that continues to be defined around migrant origins in colonial or neo-colonial contexts, even if the historical details of this process in each country are quite different.

The principle examples given in this chapter refer to this racialized context in both countries, although much of the argument could be extended more broadly. Hence, terms like *race* and *racialized minorities* are generally used, notwithstanding the preference of some writers to avoid the pseudo-biological connotations of such terms (and the need to bear in mind that the white population in both countries is also racialized). The main U.S. examples this chapter examines relate to differences between the white and black (or African American) populations, if the reader will permit this early slippage from relational categories to substantive groups. Although this is partly a result of the preponderance of research that takes this focus, a crude racial dichotomy of this sort flouts the increasing sensitivity to U.S. ethnic plurality in which other groups either contain members who might otherwise be separated across the black–white divide (e.g., Hispanics) or imply a conception of race that is orthogonal to it (e.g. Native Americans and Asian Americans who are not black but are not white either). The main rationale for the focus on African Americans is in relation to the U.K. literature, where a good deal of analysis is still focused, not without good reason, upon issues to do with migration, such as migrant selection effects, cultural or lifestyle differences, and language competence, even though

the racialized context within which subsequent generations experience British society has assumed ever greater importance. The same point can be made of Hispanics in the United States; overall, around a third of this group were foreign-born in 1990, with a very much higher figure for Hispanic subgroups such as Cubans and Dominicans. African Americans in the United States represent by contrast an indigenously racialized population. The distinction is tentative; large-scale internal migration of African Americans from the rural southeast to the urban north earlier this century remains salient to contemporary health, while in the United Kingdom the Irish offer certain parallels to the indigenous racialization of African Americans. Nevertheless, the balance of racial or ethnic meaning in the two countries is quite different and potentially illuminating in relation to studies in medical sociology.

RACIAL AND ETHNIC PATTERNS OF HEALTH AND ILLNESS

U.S. health indicators suggest that, in general, the health of racialized minorities is poorer than that of the population in general. For example, infant mortality rates among African Americans are nearly double that of whites and are also considerably higher among Native Americans and some Hispanic groups (NCHS 1995). Mortality rates are also higher at all ages for African Americans relative to the general population, except in the very oldest age groups where a "mortality crossover" occurs (NCHS 1996). A particularly troubling feature of the U.S. situation is that life expectancy for African Americans has *decreased* in absolute terms since the late 1980s. Mortality rates are also somewhat higher for Hispanics in younger age groups than for the general population.

The data are not quite so clear cut in the case of the United Kingdom, but there is still a tendency toward raised mortality among its racialized minorities, particularly in relation to perinatal mortality and mortality of younger and middle-aged adults from Ireland, South Asia, the Caribbean, and Africa, though Caribbean men and older migrants appear in general to have lower mortality rates (Balarajan and Bulusu 1990; Balarajan and Raleigh 1990; Harding 1997). It should be noted that these findings refer to *migrants* and not *racialized minorities* as such, because U.K. death certificates record only place of birth.

These gross patterns conceal substantial variations in mortality and morbidity associated with specific causes. For example, death rates for homicide in the

United States—at around 75 per 100,000 annually—are over 7 times greater for African-American males than for white males, and 3 times greater for African-American females than for white females (derived from NCHS 1996). This is indicative of an epidemic of violent death in the United States unparalleled in countries of a comparable political and economic structure, the principal victims of which are African-American men. Less dramatic examples of variation in mortality from medical causes include, in the United Kingdom, raised mortality from cardiovascular diseases relative to the white population in most racialized minority groups and, conversely, lowered cancer rates. An extensive biomedical literature exists that examines the racial patterning of specific diseases in relation to their proximal causes (for summaries of this literature see Cruickshank and Beevers 1989; Balarajan and Raleigh 1995; Smaje 1995a; Haynes 1997). Its findings are important, but its significance from a specifically sociological point of view is debatable. Until there is a better understanding of the relationship between the clinical presentation of specific diseases and the social factors associated with health, sociological enquiry would seem more appropriately directed at elucidating the latter and at examining the social correlates of health and illness. This is particularly true insofar as epidemiological studies have tended to draw the attention of researchers to diseases where the relative risk between racialized groups is large, to the exclusion of those with smaller disparities in relative risk but a greater absolute contribution to the burden of ill health (Bhopal 1988).

The emphasis on the aetiology of specific diseases has been supplemented more recently by the collection of data on self-reported measures of general health status. In Britain, a question to this effect was included in the 1991 Census. Analysis of these data shows higher levels of self-reported chronic illness relative to whites among all minority ethnic groups except the Chinese (Charlton et al. 1994), a finding that has generally been confirmed in other studies employing various health questions and administered to different age and ethnic groups (Smaje 1995a).

A concern with the way that people understand and manage chronic illness in daily life has been fundamental to the traditions of medical sociology, but the possibility that this may vary between racialized groups has received comparatively little attention. There is evidence both from the United Kingdom and from North America that some racialized minorities tend to define health functionally, in terms of its effect upon the activities of daily living, rather than

biologically: Other evidence has shown that some groups are more likely to think of health as a matter of luck rather than personal control, and less likely to strive toward normalizing chronic illness by attempting to minimize its visible manifestations (Donovan 1986; Anderson et al. 1989, 1995; Howlett et al. 1992). As some of these writers point out, these tendencies are also associated with objective socioeconomic circumstances and perceptions of self within wider social structures, and there is often little to be gained from disembedding them from these contexts in order to isolate an independent racial effect. This underlines the point made in the previous section about the sense in which race can be regarded as a point of social embodiment over which other kinds of experience of the social world are distributed.

Nevertheless, evidence does exist for systematic patterns of social organisation associated with particular racialized minorities that mediate objective circumstances, for example, in relation to social roles, social support, and social networks. These concepts refer respectively to the different kinds of role (e.g., worker, parent, carer) that people occupy, the nature of the support they receive from others in the fulfillment of social roles, and the context of the relationships through which that support is offered. U.S. studies have found differences between racial groups in the impact of particular combinations of social roles and in the character of social networks and social support that are associated with a range of outcomes in terms of mental and physical health and the ability of families to cope with them, although these differences do not always correspond to the assumption that racialized minorities can draw upon larger and more supportive social networks (Brown et al. 1992; Rushing et al. 1992; Williams 1993). Other studies have found interactions between socioeconomic status and negative life events in relation to psychological distress that have a particularly deleterious effect upon disadvantaged African Americans (Ulbrich et al. 1989).

The extent to which there is a racial patterning to subjective or psychological well-being has been researched more thoroughly and with clearer results in the United States than in the United Kingdom. U.S. studies have shown that African Americans report higher levels of depression, hopelessness, and life dissatisfaction than whites, although results for Hispanics and other groups are less clear cut (Vega and Rumbaut 1991). Raised reporting is also associated with lower socioeconomic status. Researchers are divided as to whether the racial pattern is explicable in terms of socioeconomic status

(Kessler and Neighbors 1986; Cockerham 1990; Ulbrich et al. 1989), although it has also been shown that *changes* of socioeconomic status in either direction may be associated with poorer psychological well-being, particularly for people from minority ethnic groups who perceive that their life chances are limited by racism (Dressler 1988). In terms of the association between mental well-being and physical health, research by K. Fiscella and P. Franks (1997) suggests that psychological distress does not explain race or income differentials in mortality. Although they did not examine the combined effect of mental well-being *and* income on the race differential, this is one among several studies that point to the complexity of the pathways between race and the experience of health or health care. In general, racial differences do not appear reducible to simple additive effects such as the combination of poor socioeconomic status and the psychosocial consequences of discrimination.

Research on racial patterns in mental health has been particularly controversial in relation to findings of apparently raised rates of serious psychotic illness relative to the general population among African Americans in the United States and among Irish and Caribbean populations in the United Kingdom. As we shall see, there has been considerable debate over the causes of this excess, and indeed over whether an excess exists.

CAUSAL PATHWAYS

How can the patterns described in the previous section be explained? Figure 8–1 provides a schematic illustration of some of the main causal pathways that will be discussed in this section, before we move on to consider some complexities that cannot be captured adequately in the diagram. Following the schema set out earlier, for the purpose of tracing social etiologies of health and illness (and not necessarily for other purposes) race is regarded as a personal characteristic that involves both ascribed social status *and* asserted personal identity, whether explicit or implicit. Although inseparably combined, for analytic purposes it is heuristically useful to conceive them as distinctive components of race.

The figure indicates that race has a determinate effect upon socioeconomic position in society. By this, it is meant that the socially ascribed status associated with racial categorisation shapes the racialized individual's life chances in terms of factors such as education, income, occupational status, employment opportunities, environmental quality, and so on, and that these

FIGURE 8–1 Causal Pathways and Health Status

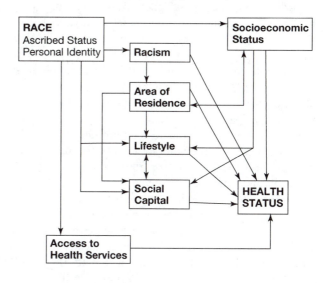

factors—as many studies throughout the world have consistently demonstrated—are associated in turn with poorer health outcomes of various kinds.

In addition to the direct relationship between race, socioeconomic status, and health, the figure indicates that this line of association is further mediated by racism. A useful summary to this postulated link is Wilson's (1987) distinction between past and present racism. The connection between racism and socioeconomic status indicated in the figure shows the effects of present racism—i.e., the systematic tendency of significant individuals or institutions (teachers, schools, employers, etc.) to disfavour people from racialized minorities—in preventing those people from accumulating the socioeconomic advantages that accrue to others. But there may be additional mechanisms resulting from the persisting effects of past racism that reproduce the association between race and socioeconomic status even in the absence of active contemporary discrimination. For example, black migrants from the U.S. south to northern cities (or from the British Commonwealth to Britain) found their options constrained by discriminatory practices of various kinds, which shaped where they were able to live and what work they were able to find. Even if these practices have now somewhat abated, they may have had a longer-term legacy in racializing the spatial and economic structure of opportunities in particular urban environments, a point for which there is considerable evidence in both countries (Smith 1989; Massey and Denton 1993). This particular mechanism is illustrated in the diagram through the associations between race, racism, area of residence, and socioeconomic status. Thus, part of the burden of ill health among racialized groups that is attributable to socioeconomic factors may be thought of as reflecting the effects of past racism. How useful this is as an explanatory factor in etiological studies is a moot point. It could, after all, be argued that the migrations mentioned above occurred in a neocolonial context that was itself a reflection of past racism, thus subsuming many of the specific circumstances of these migrations into an all-encompassing category of racism, but the point does provide a broader interpretive framework within which these circumstances can be located.

The extent to which adjustment for socioeconomic factors removes racial differences in health remains unclear. Until recently, the research literature in the United Kingdom has been divided between studies of class inequalities in health and studies of racial patterning, with little cross-fertilisation (Nazroo in press). In the United States, race has often been used as a proxy for class, and again it is only quite recently that attention has been paid to the joint effects of race *and* class in structuring health. Some U.S. studies have found that race differentials across various measures of health are accounted for by socioeconomic factors (Cockerham 1990; Logue and Jarjoura 1990; Rogers 1992), while others have found that a racial differential remains (Kessler and Neighbors 1986; Otten et al. 1990; Sorlie et al. 1992; Gornick et al. 1996). An important issue here is the nature of the adjustment for socioeconomic status, because evidence exists for racial disparities of socioeconomic status even *within* the broad categories of occupational class, income, wealth, or housing quality that are often employed, reflecting the weaker and historically shallower tenure of minorities among the middle classes, the salience of direct or indirect discrimination across all socioeconomic levels, and in some cases, problems of construct validity across ethnic groups in measures of socioeconomic status.

In view of the strong and finely grained associations between health and socioeconomic status at every level of the continuum, there is considerable potential for residual confounding of adjusted racial differentials by socioeconomic status; cautious methods and interpretations are warranted. But where independent racial effects are found, they might be taken as evidence that social life is structured and experienced in racialized ways that are not simply reducible to socioeconomic status. Parallel issues arise in relation to the "double jeopardy" hypothesis that a two-fold health disadvantage exists for older adults from minority ethnic groups through the interaction of old age with minority status.

In this instance, recent research suggests that such an effect is not operative, but that there is a steeper decline in health status for African Americans of all ages (Ferraro and Farmer 1996).

Ferraro and Farmer criticize the assumption implicit in the double jeopardy hypothesis that discrimination against racialized minorities operates equally on the health of *all* members of these groups, suggesting that intra-racial variation in perceived discrimination may be associated with the patterning of health. This has been a focus of research in both the United States and the United Kingdom (Krieger 1990; Benzeval et al. 1992), which has produced suggestive evidence that the experience of racism and the style of individual responses to it is associated with outcomes such as high blood pressure and poor self-reported general health. Thus, as Figure 8–1 indicates, in addition to the relationship between racism and health mediated by socioeconomic status, the everyday experience of racism can exert a direct influence upon health.

A rather different set of mediating factors between race and health relates to the two categories labelled "lifestyle" and "social capital" in the diagram. These separate out different dimensions of what are sometimes called "cultural factors." *Lifestyle factors* refer to specific kinds of behavior that are likely to affect health directly, such as the use of tobacco, alcohol, or other narcotics, the consumption of particular kinds of diet, or adherence to other health-damaging or health-promoting behaviours such as high-risk sexual or leisure activities or taking regular exercise (see also Chapter 11 by Cockerham, this volume). In some cases, there can be clear and obvious racial or ethnic patterns in relation to these factors. For example, since Pakistanis in Britain are overwhelmingly Muslim, alcohol use among British Pakistanis is at present very low. Here, asserted identity is associated with lifestyles that have particular health consequences.

However, lifestyles may also be associated with other factors. It is easier to take regular exercise if there is good access to sports facilities or open spaces, and this is associated with income and area of residence (MacIntyre et al. 1993). Use of open spaces may be limited by the fear or the reality of racist attack, and other lifestyle factors such as legal or illegal use of narcotics may also be affected both by the direct experience of racism or through the mediation of socioeconomic factors. Adherence to an ethnic diet—with either a negative or, the evidence would suggest, usually a positive effect upon health (Dowler and Calvert 1996)—may be easier if one lives in a community of "co-ethnics" that provides both the behavioral incentive and the practical means to do so, although the factors bearing upon dietary choice are likely to be complex. The preparation of proper ethnic food can symbolize powerfully the ability of the household to safeguard the well-being and identity of its members (Harbottle 1996), with potential health consequences over and above the nutritional qualities of the food itself.

Social capital refers to the various coping resources—networks of familial and extra-familial support, secular and religious community institutions, and so on—that are available to people, including particular social norms and institutions such as marriage. It is "the aggregate of the actual or potential resources which are linked to possession of a durable network of more or less institutionalized relationships of mutual acquaintance and recognition—or in other words, to membership in a group—which . . . entitles . . . [each of its members] to credit, in the various senses of the term" (Bourdieu 1986: 248–49). Thus, social capital may vary in extent, quality, and character between racial groups. To take the preceding example, marriage may tend to carry a different set of normative and practical meanings in different groups so that marital breakdown may, for individuals in some groups, constitute a more stressful life event, whereas for others it may be counterbalanced more easily through other sources of social support and through less stringent community norms being attached to its significance. This might also vary by age, class, and gender, so that inter-group variation in the outcomes of an event like marital breakdown may not be uniform across these other dimensions of social experience. These hypotheses are consistent with research on racial differences in psychological symptoms associated with marital dissolution (Williams et al. 1992). Social capital can therefore possess both a *mediating* and a *causal* association with health status.

The nature of the putative associations between race, socioeconomic status, and what has been termed here social capital has been a particularly controversial topic in the United States. A rather polarized debate has proceeded sporadically ever since the Moynihan Report notoriously suggested that modes of social (dis)organisation within African-American communities were the cause of their poverty, calling forth the counter-argument that these modes of social organisation were an adaptive *response* to poverty (Rainwater and Yancey 1967). That these forms of social organisation differ among people of equivalent socioeconomic status between racial groups would appear to suggest, however, that a simple adaptive theory is unlikely to be adequate. More recent studies have suggested that distinctive modes of social organisation among African-American

communities are in no sense pathological, but do have a historically embedded cultural component, even if features such as the extension of networks for child care and resource distribution reflect earlier adaptations to economic circumstances (Henry 1992; Stern 1993). It is worth pointing out that these features should not be thought of only as reactive adaptations to economic hardship, but also as attempts to realise distinctive visions of community and of freedom within the social and economic constraints faced by African Americans. The health consequences of this process are likely to be extremely complex and may differ depending upon the unit of analysis and the historical depth chosen by the researcher. Although there is some evidence to suggest that the ramification of demands for economic and social support impose burdens upon families and their members (particularly women), this needs to be offset against its historic role in community development (Stern 1993).

Turning to area of residence, we have already touched upon the importance of this factor for the association between race and health. A significant point here is that what may appear to be a *racial* effect may sometimes turn out to be an *area* effect. For example, there is evidence to suggest that the racial disparities in male homicide rates mentioned earlier disappear when area of residence is taken into account (Greenberg and Schneider 1994). The extent to which the quality of residential areas affects health over and above the characteristics of the people living in them has recently been a focus of debate (MacIntyre et al. 1993). It nevertheless also appears to be the case that ethnic residential concentration—perhaps mediated by racism—is associated both with socioeconomic status and with lifestyle and social capital factors. Research in both the United States (LaVeist 1993) and the United Kingdom (Smaje 1995b) suggests that the consequences for health are complex, but in essence it appears that while the concentration of minority ethnic groups in low-quality urban areas is associated with poorer outcomes, ethnic residential concentration may nevertheless be protective of health.

Finally, as the figure indicates, differences in access to health services may have some bearing upon ethnic patterns in health. This point will not be pursued in detail here as it forms the basis for the discussion in the following two sections, but as we shall see, in general the evidence points to less satisfactory access to health services among racialized minorities, which could be expected to result in poorer health outcomes.

Figure 8–1 by no means exhausts the factors bearing upon the association between race and health, or the ways of conceiving them. It may be worth commenting briefly upon three factors omitted from it. First, findings of specific associations between race and health may be methodological artefacts, reflecting biases of various kinds in the measurement, counting, and analysis of the relevant variables (see Smaje 1995a for further discussion). Second, inter- and intra-national migration complicates the picture, because where it is associated with racial status, as it is in both the United Kingdom and the United States, consideration must be given to etiological factors acting in the place of origin and in the migration process, as well as in the place of residence. On the other hand, these factors do not add further *conceptual* complexity since they can be fitted into the same broad framework proposed in the diagram. The complicating factor is principally a methodological one of separating out the effect of health selection from social causation. *Selection* refers to the circumstances in which health is causally antecedent to social position rather than vice versa, as is normally supposed. For example, international migrants are often positively selected for health, whereas the association between low socioeconomic status and poor health may reflect a process of negative selection or downward social mobility caused by poor health. Thus, one might reasonably reverse the direction of causality shown in the diagram from health to all of the mediating factors except racism, although on balance U.K. evidence suggests that selection is not the primary factor underlying socioeconomic patterns in health (Blane et al. 1993). It is, of course, possible that causality runs in *both* directions. Obviously, an individual's health state cannot affect his or her race, but selection does remain a possible factor underlying apparent associations between race and health found in research studies (e.g., racial differentials in rural/urban residential mobility of the seriously mentally ill (see Sashidharan and Francis 1993). With regard to this latter example, the U.K. evidence suggests that some combination of artefact and selection factors may be operative in different minority groups.

R. Williams (1992) argues that there is an "unhealthy migrant" effect among some migrants from Ireland to the United Kingdom in which the socially marginalized and mentally ill have a greater propensity to migrate, although it is offset by the more usual healthy migrant effect—a feature attributed to long-range historical factors. Thus, the high incidence of mental illness among the Irish population reflects the presence of this unhealthy subpopulation. However, there is no evidence for selection effects of this kind among Caribbean migrants. Debates over the etiology of psychotic illness in this population—and in African Americans in the United States—have been rather polarized between those who argue that a genuine epidemic exists and those who believe that it is an artefact of study design or diagnostic bias (Littlewood 1992; Smaje 1995a). No decisive evidence exists in support of either position, but the balance of the research literature suggests that if diagnostic bias is occurring, it manifests itself in subtle ways that transcend simple forms of discrimination.

Finally, biological factors may play some role in the association between race and health. We have seen that race is a social scheme for classification that corresponds to no underlying biological differentiation, but it does not follow that biological factors are of no relevance in accounting for the racial patterning of health. Genetic diversity associated with geographic distribution does exist within the human species, and although this diversity eludes any attempt to subdivide the species into discrete categories, the geographical referents of racial categories that have emerged historically through processes of colonial expansion are such that there are some associations between socially defined races and particular genetic characteristics. In the domain of health, there are specific genetic disorders whose prevalence varies widely across racial groups, although their contribution to the overall burden of ill health is small. However, there is some evidence to suggest that cardiovascular diseases of greater overall significance may also have a genetic component that varies by racial group, although the hypothesis remains somewhat controversial (Williams et al. 1994; Nazroo 1998).

Some final words of caution about the causal model implied in Figure 8–1 are appropriate. The model draws a relationship between two entities (race and health) mediated by six others. We have already examined the considerable complexities involved in defining race as a distinctive analytical entity, and as other chapters in this book show, similar problems attach to the definition of health. Moreover, the six intervening entities defined in the figure are themselves the result of a certain analytical abstraction. For example, it can be misleading to argue that some or all of the association between race and health is explained by socioeconomic status, because this reifies the latter—a category of spurious generality—as a causal factor, thereby neglecting the complexity of (and potential racial variation in) the actual mechanisms that act upon health. A superior approach, hinted at earlier, is to construct causal hypotheses for the efficacy of specific social characteristics that are distributed *across* racial groups in nonrandom ways.

PATTERNS OF UTILIZATION

We now turn to a consideration of ethnic patterns in the use of health services. Studies in the United States have consistently found that African Americans in all age groups are less likely to make physician visits and to receive preventive care than whites, whereas they are more likely to receive acute hospital care (Lozano et al. 1995; Gornick et al. 1996; Fichtenbaum and Gyimah-Brempong 1997). This result is generally preserved even when health status, insurance status, area of residence, and socioeconomic variables are held constant. Even though there is evidence to suggest that physician visits among racialized minorities in some age groups may be more closely associated with the need for health care (Wolinsky et al. 1989), this is not inconsistent with the more general suggestion that minority health-care needs are less likely to be met in primary and ambulatory care settings, resulting in the manifestation of more serious illness requiring hospitalization. However, it has also been shown that the quality and outcome of hospital care tends to be poorer. For example, there is evidence to suggest fewer clinical interventions for African-American patients where those interventions would appear to be indicated and poorer treatment outcomes (Escarce et al. 1993; Kahn et al. 1994; Peterson et al. 1994). There is also evidence of higher mortality from conditions such as cervical cancer, asthma, and appendicitis where appropriate medical intervention is life-preserving, suggesting that the obstacles to pathways through care are reflected in health outcomes. These findings would seem in general to warrant the suggestion by F. Wolinsky and colleagues (1989) that there is "conspicuous evidence of considerable inequalities."

The U.K. evidence points to a rather different situation. Use of general practitioner (GP) services (i.e., primary care physicians who act as the major point of initial contact for most users of health services) is roughly equivalent across all racial groups, and indeed several minority groups make heavier use of GP services than do whites. Use of preventive services also appears roughly equivalent. On the other hand, use of hospital ambulatory and acute care is generally much lower than among whites, at least for children and younger adults (Nazroo 1997; Smaje and Le Grand 1997; Cooper et al. 1999). These results are preserved even after controlling for health and socioeconomic status.

EXPLAINING PATTERNS OF UTILIZATION

Figure 8–2 outlines a conceptual model for explaining racial differences in the utilization of health-care services. It is based upon the behavioural model of utilization. At the broadest level, the model conceives utilization as a function of *need* (the [perceived] presence or potential presence of a clinical condition), *predisposing factors* (the social factors that intercede between perception of need and the decision to use

FIGURE 8–2 Causal Pathways and Health-Care Utilization

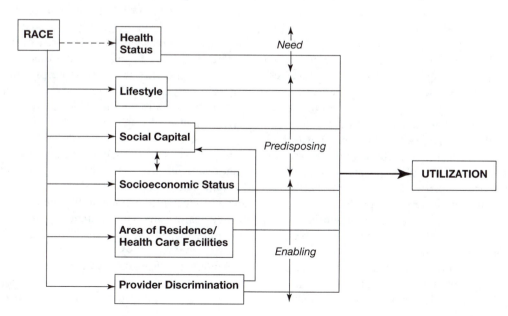

health services), and *enabling factors* (those features of social or health-care system organisation that enable people to translate the need and predisposition to use services into actual use).

As we have just seen, need can be regarded as an independent determinant of health care utilization, so we would expect a relationship between health status and use. The broken line from race to health status in the figure indicates the mediated relationship between these two factors, which was examined in previous sections. The figure also indicates the importance of the relationship between race and socioeconomic status. In the United States, there are strong associations between race, socioeconomic status, and insurance status that are likely to affect utilization. African Americans, Hispanics, and Asian-Americans are more likely to be uninsured, more likely to experience a lapse in insurance, and less likely to have employer-based insurance than whites (Browning 1993; Commonwealth Fund, 1995). As the figure indicates, this suggests racial differences in utilization mediated by the significance of socioeconomic status as an enabling factor. However, even where insurance status is held constant across racial groups—for example, by examining only participants in the Medicare or Medicaid schemes—there still appear to be racial differences in use consistent with poorer initial access to health-care services (e.g., Wolinsky et al. 1989; Lozano et al. 1995; Gornick et al. 1996).

In the publicly financed health-care system of the United Kingdom, there is no *prima facie* reason to expect socioeconomic differentials in health-care use. Empirical evidence for their existence, and for possible underlying mechanisms, is equivocal. The behavioural model would suggest a relationship between socioeconomic status and predisposing factors, the latter often subdivided into social-structural factors and health beliefs, but rendered in Figure 8–2 as lifestyle and social capital in keeping with the discussion in previous sections. Thus, it can be postulated that the network of familial and extra-familial relationships within which people are located and which co-varies with race affects the predisposition to use health care. Research in both the United Kingdom and the United States has suggested that the pattern of low physician use among racialized minorities relative to the white population is not readily explicable in terms of predisposing factors (Smaje 1995a; Fichtenbaum and Gyimah-Brempong 1997; Snowden et al. 1997), although in the United Kingdom there are some hints of different kinds of health belief among migrant groups, which may be associated with distinctive patterns of utilization. In addition, it may be that particular behaviours—which seem

explicable in terms of racialized differences in social capital such as the apparent propensity to prefer informal home care for the elderly over nursing home care in U.S. African-American families—in fact reflect a response to economic circumstances that is not captured in simple controls for socioeconomic status (Headen 1992). The association between social capital and socioeconomic status within particular racialized groups indicated in the diagram therefore involves considerable complexity and may have a differential effect upon men and women at different stages of the life course and at different points in the socioeconomic distribution.

Turning to enabling factors, the physical availability of appropriate health-care facilities locally is perhaps the most significant. In both the United Kingdom and the United States, there is a correspondence between the residential concentration of racialized minorities into particular kinds of urban area and the spatial patterning of health-care facilities. Typically, hospital facilities (and particularly prestige teaching hospitals) are predominantly urban in distribution, whereas urban primary health-care services are often of poorer quality. The U.S. patterns of utilization described above may be explicable in terms of substitution effects between primary and acute care in the context of these racialized geographies. Whether basic health care in higher quality facilities, if it is indeed significant, benefits racialized minorities is a moot point. There is evidence to suggest that disadvantaged groups including racialized minorities experience poorer quality care when the type of health-care facility is held constant, but higher use of prestige facilities in urban locations by these groups offsets the disadvantage (Kahn et al. 1994). In the United Kingdom, the dissonance between the quality of primary and hospital care in urban areas where the majority of racialized minorities live would seem to make reported racial patterns of health-care use even more puzzling, although possible geographic differences in GP treatment and referral behaviour may intercede in any hospital substitution effects.

Figure 8–2 also indicates that provider discrimination may act as an enabling (or, rather, a disabling) factor associated with racial patterns in health-care utilization. The term "provider discrimination" is used instead of racism to distinguish the specific ways through which health-care personnel may disfavour racialized minorities when they present for treatment from the broader context of societal racism within which that presentation is located. However, what provider discrimination might entail has rarely been a direct focus of research, not least because of the formidable conceptual and methodological problems involved. Neither can a particular patterning of health-care use be read off from the hypothesized existence of provider discrimination. The patterning of health-care use in the United Kingdom might suggest differences in the propensity of GPs to refer patients of different races on for secondary care, but the empirical evidence for this is not compelling (Smaje 1998). On the other hand, in relation to the specific example of acute presentation after myocardial infarction among U.K. South Asians, there is evidence of primary care referral delay that does not seem explicable in terms of need, predisposing factors, or the location of health facilities (Chaturvedi et al. 1997). In general, research in both countries tends to implicate enabling factors—and particularly provider discrimination—in the racial patterning of utilization, but the specific mechanisms through which this operates are unclear.

One potentially fruitful line of investigation may be to extend the conception of capital further through the suggestion that social capital and socioeconomic status are convertible into *cultural capital*—dispositions which are unconsciously embodied in providers and users of health-care and which structure expectations concerning their interaction in health-care settings. In these circumstances, cultural capital is likely "to be unrecognised as capital and recognised as legitimate competence" (Bourdieu 1986: 245), so that a dissonance arises between the provider's expectation of a "competent" patient and the patient's expectation of a "competent" provider, which is associated with the class and race positioning of both. The paradox of raised primary care consultation and reduced acute consultation among U.K. minorities may reflect this dissonance of expectations, manifested as mutual dissatisfaction within the primary care consultation (Cooper et al. 1999). This possibility is supported by findings in the United Kingdom of a tendency among GPs to regard patients from certain minority groups as presenting with "trivial complaints" (Smaje 1995a), while despite high levels of overall satisfaction with health services, patients from the same groups are more likely to regard physicians as insensitive to their needs (Donovan 1986; Judge and Solomon 1993). These kinds of experiences of health care themselves may contribute to the inculcation of dispositions toward health services over time, such that, as Figure 8–2 indicates, provider discrimination and user predisposition become mutually reinforcing elements of the racialized social capital associated with service use. Thus, the lower levels of satisfaction with health services among minorities reported in both the United States (Commonwealth Fund 1995) and the United Kingdom (Judge and Solomon 1993) may over time affect the predisposition to use them.

Figure 8–2 can also provide a structure for analyzing the use of mental health services, though in the case of acute psychiatric hospitalization some differences of emphasis are appropriate. As we have already seen, a significant debate exists over the nature of the links between race, psychiatric illness, and health-care use; some analysts view higher use of psychiatric services among racialized minorities as an artefact of societal racism rather than a reflection of genuine morbidity although it has not proved easy to elucidate the specific mechanisms through which that racism might operate. In relation to the use of health-care services, the matter is complicated by the fact that involuntary hospitalization through both the health-care and the criminal-justice system complements the usual factors that predispose and enable people to make their need for health care effective. In both countries, individuals from racialized minorities at all levels of psychiatric dysfunction appear to access health care disproportionately through forensic routes, and there have been disturbingly frequent reports of violent racism resulting in injury or death experienced therein (Thomas and Sillen 1979; Francis 1993). More generally, attention to the causes of the racial patterning of psychiatric hospitalization might profitably focus upon the relationship between provider discrimination and social capital. Community norms and networks of support together with patient expectations of treatment regimen in the broader context within which it operates may affect the propensity to seek care at specific junctures in the course of episodes of mental illness, with potentially complex consequences for the racial patterns in service use. Insofar as it has been possible to examine these issues empirically, once again the ill-defined operation of provider discrimination has been implicated (Rosenfield 1984).

A deficiency of much of the literature on racial patterns in utilization is its tendency to consider the episode of utilization as the end-point of the process. Equal utilization for equal need has generally been taken to indicate an equitable distribution of health services. But health care is better regarded as an intermediate good whose consumption is directed toward another end-point: maintenance or improvement of health state. It is therefore necessary to consider *health outcomes* as well as health-care utilization. There have been few systematic studies that consider racial patterns in health outcomes or even in the nature of clinical intervention, though of those U.S. studies available, there do appear to be racial differences in interventions—but not necessarily outcomes—not readily explicable in relation to other factors. The issue of outcomes is complicated by potential racial variations in the capacity to convert a given package of health care into improved health status as a result of the patterning of socioeconomic endowments that are socially distributed according to criteria including race. Health interventions that optimize the improvement of population health on an equitable basis in the light of these capacities is, ultimately, the broader goal for health policy in this area. However, whether either the base of research evidence or the political framework will develop sufficiently to make this goal realizable in either the United States or the United Kingdom remains an open question.

REFERENCES

ANDERSON, J., H. ELFERT, and M. LAI. 1989. "Ideology in the Clinical Context: Chronic Illness, Ethnicity and the Discourse on Normalisation." *Sociology of Health and Illness* 11: 253–78.

ANDERSON, J., S. WIGGINS, R. RAJWANI, A. HOLBROOK, C. BLUE, and M. NG. 1995. "Living With a Chronic Illness—Chinese-Canadian and Euro-Canadian Women with Diabetes—Exploring Factors That Influence Management." *Social Science and Medicine* 41: 181–95.

BALARAJAN, R., and L. BULUSU. 1990. "Mortality Among Immigrants in England and Wales, 1979–83." In *Mortality and Geography: A Review of the Mid-1980s,* ed. M. Britton. London: OPCS.

BALARAJAN, R., and V. RALEIGH. 1990. "Variations in Perinatal, Neonatal, Postneonatal and Infant Mortality by Mother's Country of Birth, 1982–85" In *Mortality and Geography: A Review of the Mid-1980s,* ed. M. Britton. London: OPCS.

BALARAJAN, R., and V. RALEIGH. 1995. *Ethnicity and Health in England.* London: HMSO.

BARTH, FREDRIK. 1969. "Introduction" In *Ethnic Groups and Boundaries,* ed. F. Barth. London: George Allen and Unwin.

BENZEVAL, M., K. JUDGE, and M. SOLOMON. 1992. *The Health Status of Londoners: A Comparative Perspective.* London: King's Fund.

BHOPAL, R. 1988. "Health Care for Asians: Conflict in Need, Demand and Provision." *Equity, A Pre-requisite for Health: Proceedings of the 1987 Summer Scientific Conference of the Faculty of Community Medicine.*

BLANE, D., G. DAVEY SMITH, and M. BARTLEY, 1993. "Social Selection: What Does It Contribute to Social Class Differences in Health?" *Sociology of Health and Illness,* 15 (1): 1–15.

BOURDIEU, P. 1986. "The Forms of Capital." In *Handbook of Theory and Research for the Sociology of Education,* ed. J. Richardson. New York: Greenwood Press.

BROWN, D., L. GARY, A. GREENE, and N. MILBURN. 1992. "Patterns of Social Affiliation as Predictors of Depressive Symptoms Among Urban Blacks." *Journal of Health and Social Behavior* 33: 242–53.

BROWNING, S. 1993. "Forces for Reforming the US Health Care System: A Review of the Cost and Access Issues." In *North American Health Care Policy in the 1990s,* ed. A. King, T. Hyclak, R. Thornton, and S. McMahon. Chichester: John Wiley & Sons.

CHARLTON, J., M. WALLACE, and I. WHITE. 1994. "Long-Term Illness: Results From the 1991 Census." *Population Trends* 75: 18–25.

CHATURVEDI, N., H. RAI, and Y. BEN-SHLOMO. 1997. "Lay Diagnosis and Health-Care-Seeking Behaviour for Chest Pain in South Asians and Europeans." *The Lancet* 350: 1578–83.

COCKERHAM, W. 1990. "A Test of the Relationship Between Race, Socioeconomic Status and Psychological Distress." *Social Science and Medicine* 31: 1321–26.

COMMONWEALTH FUND 1995. *National Comparative Survey of Minority Health Care.* New York: Commonwealth Fund.

COOPER, H., C. SMAJE, and S. ARBER. 1999. "Equity and Children's Use of Health Services: Examining the Ethnic Paradox." *Journal of Social Policy* 28.

CRUICKSHANK, J., and D. BEEVERS. 1989. *Ethnic Factors in Health and Disease.* Wright: Sevenoaks.

DONOVAN, J. 1986. *We Don't Buy Sickness, It Just Comes.* Aldershot: Gower.

DOWLER, E. and C. CALVERT. 1996. *Nutrition and Diet in Lone-Parent Families in London.* London: Family Policy Studies Centre.

DRESSLER, W. 1988. "Social Consistency and Psychological Distress." *Journal of Health and Social Behavior* 29: 79–91.

ESCARCE, J., K. EPSTEIN, D. COLBY, and J. SCHWARTZ. 1993. "Racial Differences in the Elderly's Use of Medical Procedures and Diagnostic Tests." *American Journal of Public Health* 83: 948–54.

FERRARO, K., and M. FARMER. 1996. "Double Jeopardy to Health Hypothesis for African Americans: Analysis and Critique." *Journal of Health and Social Behavior* 37: 27–43.

FICHTENBAUM, R. and K. GYIMAH-BREMPONG, 1997. "The Effects of Race on the Use of Physicians' Services." *International Journal of Health Services* 27: 139–56.

FISCELLA, K., and P. FRANKS. 1997. "Does Psychological Distress Contribute to Racial and Socioeconomic Disparities in Mortality?" *Social Science and Medicine* 45: 1805–1809.

FRANCIS, E. (1993). "Psychiatric Racism and Social Police: Black People and the Psychiatric Services." In *Inside Babylon: The Caribbean Diaspora in Britain,* ed. W. James and C. Harris. London: Verso.

GORNICK, M., P. EGGERS, T. REILLY, R. MENTNECH, L. FITTERMAN, L. KUCKEN, and B. VLADECK. 1996. "Effects of Race and Income on Mortality and Use of Services Among Medicare Beneficiaries." *New England Journal of Medicine* 335: 791–99.

GREENBERG, M., and D. SCHNEIDER, 1994. "Violence in American Cities—Young Black Males Is the Answer, but What Was the Question?" *Social Science and Medicine* 39: 179–87.

HARBOTTLE, L. 1996. "Bastard Chicken or Ghormeh-Sabzi?: Iranian Women Guarding the Health of the Migrant Family." In *Consumption Matters,* eds. S. Edgell, K. Hetherington, and A. Warde. Oxford: Blackwell.

HARDING, S., and R. MAXWELL. 1997. *Differences in Mortality of Migrants.* London: HMSO.

HAYNES, C. 1997. *Ethnic Minority Health: A Selected, Annotated Bibliography.* Lanham: Scarecrow Press.

HEADEN, A. 1992. "Time Costs and Informal Social Support as Determinants of Differences Between Black and White Families in the Provision of Long-Term Care." *Inquiry* 29: 440–50.

HENRY, C. 1992. "Understanding the Underclass: The Role of Culture and Economic Progress." In *Race, Politics and Economic Development,* ed. J. Jennings. London: Verso.

HOWLETT, B., W. AHMAD, and R. MURRAY. 1992. "An Exploration of White, Asian and Afro-Caribbean Peoples' Concepts of Health and Illness Causation." *New Community* 18: 281–92.

JUDGE, K., and M. SOLOMON. 1993. "Public Opinion and the National Health Service: Patterns and Perspectives in Consumer Satisfaction." *Journal of Social Policy* 22: 299–327.

KAHN, K., M. PEARSON, E. HARRISON, K. DESMOND, W. ROGERS, L. RUBENSTEIN, R. BROOK, and E. KEELER. 1994. "Health Care for Black and Poor Hospitalized Medicare Patients." *Journal of the American Medical Association* 271: 1169–74.

KESSLER, R., and H. NEIGHBORS. 1986. "A New Perspective on the Relationships Among Race, Social Class, and Psychological Distress." *Journal of Health and Social Behavior* 27: 107–15.

KLEINMAN, A. 1987. "Anthropology and Psychiatry: The Role of Culture in Cross-Cultural Research on Illness." *British Journal of Psychiatry,* 151: 447–54.

KRIEGER, N. 1990. "Racial and Gender Discrimination: Risk Factors for High Blood Pressure?" *Social Science and Medicine* 30: 1273–81.

LAVEIST, T. 1993. "Segregation, Poverty and Empowerment: Health Consequences for African Americans." *Milbank Quarterly* 71: 41–64.

LITTLEWOOD, R. 1992. "Psychiatric Diagnosis and Racial Bias: Empirical and Interpretive Approaches." *Social Science and Medicine* 34: 141–49.

LOGUE, E., and D. JARJOURA. 1990. "Modeling Heart Disease Mortality With Census Tract Rates and Social Class Mixtures." *Social Science and Medicine* 31: 545–50.

LOZANO, P., F. CONNELL, and T. KOEPSELL. 1995. "Use of Health-Services by African-American Children With Asthma on Medicaid."*Journal of the American Medical Association* 274: 469–73.

MACINTYRE, S., S. MACIVER, and A. SOOMAN. 1993. "Area, Class and Health: Should We Be Focusing on Places or People?" *Journal of Social Policy* 22: 213–34.

MASSEY, D., and N. DENTON. 1993. *American Apartheid.* Cambridge, MA: Harvard University Press.

MONTAGUE, A. 1972. *Statement on Race.* London: Oxford University Press.

NATIONAL CENTER FOR HEALTH STATISTICS (NCHS). 1995. *Health, United States 1995.* Hyattsville: Public Health Service.

NATIONAL CENTER FOR HEALTH STATISTICS (NCHS). 1996. *Leading Causes of Death by Age, Sex, Race and Hispanic Origin, United States 1992.* Monthly Vital Statistics Reports, Series 20, No.29. Hyattsville: Public Health Service.

NAZROO, J. 1997. *The Health of Britain's Ethnic Minorities.* London: Policy Studies Institute.

NAZROO, J. 1998. "Genetic, Cultural or Socioeconomic Vulnerability? Explaining Ethnic Inequalities in Health." In *The Sociology of Health Inequalities,* ed. M. Bartley, D. Blane, and G. Davey Smith. Oxford: Blackwell, 20(5): 710–30.

OTTEN, M., S. TEUTSCH, D. WILLIAMSON, and J. MARKS. 1990. "The Effect of Known Risk Factors on the Excess Mortality of Black Adults in the United States." *Journal of the American Medical Association* 263: 845–50.

PETERSON, E., S. WRIGHT, J. DALEY, and G. THIBAULT. 1994. "Racial Variation in Cardiac Procedure Use and Survival Following Acute Myocardial Infarction in the Department of Veteran's Affairs." *Journal of the American Medical Association* 271: 1175–80.

RAINWATER, L. and W. YANCEY. 1967. *The Moynihan Report and the Politics of Controversy.* Cambridge, MA: MIT Press.

ROGERS, R. 1992. "Living and Dying in the USA: Sociodemographic Determinants of Death Among Blacks and Whites." *Demography* 29: 287–303.

ROSENFIELD, S. 1984. "Race Differences in Involuntary Hospitalization: Psychiatric vs. Labelling Perspectives." *Journal of Health and Social Behavior* 25: 14–23.

RUSHING, B., C. RITTER, and R. BURTON. 1992. "Race Differences in the Effects of Multiple Roles on Health: Longitudinal Evidence From a National Sample of Older Men." *Journal of Health and Social Behavior* 33: 126–39.

SASHIDHARAN, S., and E. FRANCIS. 1993. "Epidemiology, Ethnicity and Schizophrenia." In *"Race" and Health in Contemporary Britain,* ed. W. Ahmad. Buckingham: Open University Press.

SMAJE, C. 1995a. *Health, "Race" and Ethnicity: Making Sense of the Evidence.* London: King's Fund.

Smaje, C. 1995b. "Ethnic Residential Concentration and Health: Evidence for a Positive Effect?" *Policy and Politics* 23: 251–69.

Smaje, C. 1998. "Equity and the Ethnic Patterning of GP Services in Britain." *Social Policy and Administration* 32: 116–31.

Smaje, C., and J. Le Grand. 1997. "Ethnicity, Equity and Health Care in the British National Health Service." *Social Science and Medicine* 45: 485–96.

Smith, S. 1989. *The Politics of "Race" and Residence.* Cambridge: Polity.

Snowden, L., A. Libby, and K. Thomas. 1997. "Health-Care-Related Attitudes and Utilization Among African American Women." *Women's Health* 3: 301–14.

Sorlie, P., E. Rogot, R. Anderson, N. Johnson, and E. Backlund. 1992. "Black-White Mortality Differences by Family Income." *Lancet* 340: 346–50.

Stern, M. 1993. "Poverty and Family Composition Since 1940." In *The "Underclass" Debate: Views from History,* ed. M. Katz. Princeton: Princeton University Press.

Thomas, A,. and S. Sillen. 1972. *Racism and Psychiatry.* New York: Bruner/Mazel.

Ulbrich, P., G. Warheit, and R. Zimmerman. 1989. "Race, Socioeconomic Status, and Psychological Distress: An Examination of Differential Vulnerability." *Journal of Health and Social Behavior* 30: 131–46.

Vega, W., and R. Rumbaut. 1991. "Ethnic Minorities and Mental Health." *Annual Review of Sociology* 17: 351–83.

Whittle, J., J. Conigliaro, C. Good, and R. Lofgren. 1993. "Racial Differences in the Use of Invasive Cardiovascular Procedures in the Department of Veteran's Affairs." *New England Journal of Medicine* 329: 621–27.

Williams, D., D. Takeuchi, and R. Adair. 1992. "Marital Status and Psychiatric Disorder Among Blacks and Whites." *Journal of Health and Social Behavior* 33: 140–57.

Williams, H. 1993. "A Comparison of Social Support and Social Networks of Black Parents and White Parents with Chronically Ill Children." *Social Science and Medicine* 37: 1509–20.

Williams, R. 1992. "The Health of the Irish in Britain." In *The Politics of "Race" and Health,* ed. W. Ahmad. Bradford: Race Relations Research Unit.

Williams, R., R. Bhopal, and K. Hunt. 1994. "Coronary Risk in a British Punjabi Population: Comparative Profile of Non-Biochemical Factors." *International Journal of Epidemiology* 23: 28–37.

Wilson, W. 1987. *The Truly Disadvantaged: The Inner City, the Underclass and Public Policy.* Chicago: University of Chicago Press.

Wolinsky, F., B. Aguirre, L. Fann, V. Keith, C. Arnold, J. Niederhauer, and K. Dietrich. 1989. "Ethnic Differences in the Demand for Physician and Hospital Utilization Among Older Adults in Major American Cities: Conspicuous Evidence of Considerable Inequalities." *The Milbank Quarterly* 67: 412–48.

Worobey, J., and R. Angel. 1990. "Poverty and Health: Older Minority Women and the Rise of the Female-Headed Household." *Journal of Health and Social Behavior* 31: 370–83.

9 POLITICAL ECONOMY OF HEALTH AND AGING

CARROLL L. ESTES, *University of California, San Francisco*

STEVEN WALLACE, *University of California, Los Angeles*

KAREN W. LINKINS, *University of California, San Francisco*

Age has become an increasingly important social category during the past century. At the beginning of the twentieth century, one's age was relatively unimportant. Ascribed statuses such as gender, race, class, and nationality had significant impacts on the life chances of Americans, but "old age" had not yet achieved a similar level of importance. Except for the issue of generational succession, aging was essentially ignored by classical sociological theory (Kohli 1988). Now, at the beginning of the twenty-first century, chronological age has become institutionalized as a determinative characteristic of individuals associated with access to a number of important social resources—both material and ideal. Yet medical sociology pays limited attention to older persons, just as general sociology pays limited attention to medical sociology (Pescosolido and Kronenfeld 1995). In this chapter we argue that both aging and health care have become increasingly determined by state actions in the latter half of the twentieth century. To understand health and aging, therefore, requires an understanding of the dynamics of the state of American society. We suggest that political economy theory, as informed by feminist theory and with attention to racial formation, provides the best means to understand the context that frames the changing patterns of health and aging as we move into the twenty-first century.

Old age has taken on the characteristic of a determinative status because of the use of age by the state and the economic system in allocating resources and positions. The clearest use of age began in the 1930s in the United States with the use of age 65 for regular eligibility for Social Security and Old Age Assistance (the latter of which was reorganized as Supplemental Security Income in the 1970s), and later Medicare and Medicaid. "Old age" has also been used in eligibility criteria for government-subsidized housing, social services, tax breaks, exemptions from some naturalization laws, and as a protected legal class (as in elder abuse and age discrimination laws). At the other end of the life course, age is used to categorize those who must attend school and those who are old enough to drink alcohol, smoke cigarettes, drive, vote, and otherwise be accorded the full privileges of membership in society. In short, chronological age has been used extensively during the past century as a criterion for distributing social rights and social resources, giving the state a key role in the creation and maintenance of the social category of "elderly" (Estes 1979; Mayer and Schoepflin 1989).

At the same time that the state has played a key role in the creation and maintenance of age as a criterion for the allocation of rights and resources, it has also come to take a central role in the organization and financing of medical care. For many years, starting in the mid-1800s, the role of the state was largely limited to providing the legal basis for physician dominance and self-regulation. Beginning with World War II, however, the state has become the primary actor in the development and financing of American medicine, through the purchase of services (such as Medicare and Medicaid), direct subsidies (such as construction grants through the

Hill-Burton program and funding for medical education), and indirect subsidies (such as through the tax deductibility of health insurance benefits) (Starr 1982). The United States now spends more than $1 trillion per year on medical care—14 percent of the GDP—making it one of the largest sectors of the economy. Medical care is the single largest category of personal consumption, exceeding food and tobacco, housing, and transportation and is twice as large as recreation (U.S. Bureau of the Census, 1997: table 702). This spending is projected to rise as high as $2.3 trillion by 2015, with the federal government financing as much as 50 percent of this bill (Pardes et al. 1999). The elderly are disproportionate users of medical care, accounting for 12 percent of the population and 28 percent of total medical expenditures (Rice 1996).

To better understand the interaction of the state, old age, and health, we will first provide a brief overview of the changing objective conditions of the older population. Next we will review the ways in which social theory and gerontology have traditionally approached understanding the situation of older persons in American society. We will then offer an alternative perspective based on a broader understanding of the state and its role in a capitalist society. We will conclude by outlining three challenges for the further growth and development of an analysis of the social and political context of health and aging in the United States.

DEMOGRAPHY AND POLITICS

There are two key demographic trends of the 1900s that affect the impact of aging on society. The first trend is the growth in the number and proportion of the population age 65 and older, due in part to the increased likelihood that persons will reach age 65 and in part to the lengthening life expectancy after age 65. The number of persons in the United States age 65 and over was 3.1 million in 1990 and 33.5 million in 1995 and is expected to grow to 78.8 million by 2050! At the beginning of the twentieth century older persons comprised 4.1 percent of the population; approaching the end of the century they account for 12.8 percent, and are expected to increase to over 20 percent of the total population by 2020 (U.S. Bureau of the Census 1996). In 1900, only 41 percent of those having born lived to see their 65th birthday, and those having reached age 65 had an additional life expectancy of 11.9 years. In 1991, 80 percent of those born lived to age 65, where they faced an average additional life expectancy of 17.4 years (U.S. Bureau of the Census 1996).

The second trend is the slower growth of the young population as a result of falling birth rates. Demographers call this the "squaring" of the (population) pyramid. The traditional age distribution has a wide base of children, a narrowing pillar of young and middle-aged adults, and the smallest group of persons at the top of the age pyramid. Now that most children born live to old age, and with a reduced birthrate, we are approaching an age distribution in most capitalist industrial countries of roughly similar numbers of persons at each age until very old age when most deaths occur (Friedland and Summer 1999), although substantial variations persist in survival rates by race, class, and gender (Wallace 1990, 1991; Markides and Black 1995).

Most of the attention to population aging has come from policy analysts and actuaries who have discussed the potential consequences of a ballooning number of older persons eligible for public programs (most notably Social Security and Medicare) under conditions of a relatively stable number of taxpayers. The concern that the United States will be overrun by "white haired greedy geezers" who will use so many public benefits that there are not sufficient funds for other worthwhile social purposes has been labeled "apocalyptic demography" (Robertson 1991). This image of an impending tidal wave of elderly was popularized in the early 1980s as federal budget deficits grew rapidly after major tax cuts were enacted. Yet those discussions failed to acknowledge the counter trends of fewer children in families, economic growth that provides more resources to distribute, and the possible reallocation of resources from other parts of the federal budget (e.g., military spending). Actuarial projections of shortfalls in both Social Security and Medicare also became topics of politically manufactured "crises" that were used to justify proposals to dramatically cut those programs (Estes 1983, 1998a). However, the large federal budget deficits of the 1980s and early 1990s unexpectedly turned into surpluses by the end of the 1990s. While the strong economic growth of the late 1990s took some of the impetus away from blaming the elderly for government budget problems (Kenen 1999), this demonizing of a distinguishable segment of the population parallels xenophobia, racism, and other divisive politics historically. Population aging is occurring in all industrial countries (in some already faster and further than in the United States), and different countries have adopted varying policy responses that do not necessarily weaken social programs for most older persons (Esping-Andersen 1996). This line of reasoning suggests that the social response to an aging population is politically and socially determined rather than demographically determined (Friedland and Summer 1999).

HEALTH AND THE SOCIAL CONSTRUCTION OF OLD AGE

Changing patterns of disease over the past century have concentrated life-threatening conditions into later ages. At the turn of the twentieth century, life-threatening diseases and conditions occurred throughout the life span, including infectious diseases such as typhoid, childhood killers such as diphtheria and whooping cough, high rates of maternal mortality and occupational injuries/deaths during adulthood, and high rates of death throughout older ages from infectious conditions such as the flu and pneumonia (McKinlay, McKinlay, and Beaglehole 1989). Most of these acute conditions are no longer major causes of death, thanks to a combination of improved housing, nutrition, and sanitation, along with immunizations and medical care. The primary causes of death and disability are now chronic conditions including heart disease, cancer, and stroke, all conditions that are more common among the old than the young. This shifting burden of disease has combined with the historical medical approach to aging as biological senescence to undergird a popular view of aging as an individual-level phenomenon that is decremental, unidirectional (inevitable loss of function and adaptability), and negative in terms of outcome. To the extent that aging is conceptualized as primarily a biological process, biomedical approaches to defining and treating aging take precedence over the social, economic, and political determinants of the well-being of older persons (Estes and Binney 1989).

As we enter the new millennium, the staying power of the medical engineering model (Renaud 1975) is increasingly evident in the support for molecular biology and genetics. Even as welfare and many other domestic social programs were cut in the 1990s, federal funding for the National Institutes of Health rose dramatically and consistently. In a 1999 *Science* magazine essay, the current scientific revolution in genetics and biology is touted as providing answers to multiple problems, not only to those of health and the costs of medical care, but also to problems of the U.S. economy and the demographics of aging. The article attacks the prevalent notion among health economists and policy makers that medical research, genetics, and technology generate higher (rather than lower) health costs. In contrast, the authors (Pardes et al. 1999) argue that lavish government

investment in biotechnology has the potential to solve the problems of financing the growing health care costs of an aging population by preventing disease and improving health. H. Pardes and colleagues. (1999) are virtually silent about the social and economic factors (what sociologists call "root causes") that are inextricably related to the health status, economic costs, individual outcomes, and health policy dimensions of H. Pardes and colleagues' called-for accelerated investment in science.

Recent gerontological work has identified the malleability and reversibility of various biological and behavioral phenomena previously thought to be inevitable (Rowe and Kahn 1998), while there has been an increasing recognition of the importance of social, behavioral, and environmental factors in the processes of aging and of health in old age (House, Kessler, and Herzog 1990; Robert 1998) and both individual and population health more generally (McKeown 1997; Adler et al. 1993; Navarro 1990; Hahn and Kaplan 1985). In particular, J.W. Rowe and R.L. Kahn (1998) and W.M. Bortz IV and W.M. Bortz II (1996) suggest a declining significance of medical and biological factors in health with advancing age and a rise in the importance of behavioral factors. M.W. Riley and J.W. Riley (1994) emphasize the interplay of social structures and structural change in explaining healthy and successful aging. Others calculate that more than 50 percent of health (mortality and morbidity) is accounted for by social, economic, and behavioral factors, while biological factors account for less than half (McGinnis and Foege 1993).

Despite the influence of social policy on retirement and income, the influence of social and economic factors on health, and a wide range of contextual factors on the well-being of older persons, gerontology has persisted in focusing primarily at the individual level in trying to solve problems faced by the aged. Drawing on A.D. Twaddle (1982), we consider this approach as equivalent to a sociology *in* medicine. Neither the construct of old age nor the clinical gaze on it is questioned. Gerontologists *in* medicine work to help older people be better patients and better adapt to their problems and to make social and health services better. Some gerontological research examines the medical and social service systems as topics worthy of study as examples of organizations and professions, similar to a sociology *of* medicine. We argue below that what needs the most development in the field is the further development of a *sociology of health* that refocuses on the political and economic conditions and context within which old age is defined, goods and services are distributed using age-specific criteria, and the aging process unfolds.

POLITY AND ECONOMY IN AGING AND HEALTH

As our society ages and disease and disability become increasingly concentrated in later years, we must understand the role of the state in society to have an adequate sociological understanding of health and aging. In mature capitalist countries the state has two inherently contradictory roles, that of fostering the private appropriation of profits (called *accumulation*) and that of fostering the ideology that the system is fair and worthy of popular support (called *legitimation*), to enhance social harmony (O'Connor 1973; Habermas 1975). The state has a stake in an expanding private economy because it relies on taxes from private profits and private economic activity. The conditions necessary for profit-making include not only establishing the rules and infrastructure necessary for business, but also assisting business to improve profits and open new fields for exploitation. In the field of health and aging, we can observe the shift of scientific medicine from a craft model of production with high levels of producer autonomy to an industrial model of production as part of a rationalizing process that provides the infrastructure necessary to maximize profits. The shift of these rationalized organizations from nonprofit to for-profit, including insurance companies from Blue Cross to HMO providers, opens new industries to profit-making. And as industries mature and profitable new markets are no longer available, the state facilitates the commodification of goods and services that had not previously been sold for profit as market goods (Estes 1991; Estes and Alford 1990). During the 1990s these trends have expanded to encompass global markets and involve international financial organizations such as the International Monetary Fund (IMF), which have become notorious for pushing nations to reduce social expenditures as a way of attracting multinational business investment.

At the same time, residents of the nation must believe that the state represents *their* interests and has a legitimate claim to power. Social programs, including Social Security and Medicare, are an important source of legitimacy for the nation-state. These types of programs have been successful in advanced capitalist states in promoting social integration, nation building, and the amelioration of class differences (Esping-Anderson 1996). The structure of social and health programs, however, also serves to reinforce existing social and economic relationships that have developed around a profit-oriented economy. Research on health and aging often reinforces and sustains those relationships, whether it focuses on how to help

employees "adjust" to retirement, how to get seniors to "comply" with medical recommendations, or how to better "coordinate" an inherently fragmented long-term care system. Seen in this perspective, the common "sociology in medicine and aging" approach fulfills a functionalist's role of helping the individual adapt to the environment without any question of whether the environment is appropriate or desirable.

The importance of the economic system in the health and well-being of older persons leads us to a theoretical framework that places the economic and political systems in the center of the analysis. In the United States it was not until the mid-1970s that a critical perspective surfaced in both medical sociology and gerontology. This occurred first with the critiques of classical medical sociology (and particularly of structural functionalist perspectives) by H. Waitzkin and B. Waterman (1974). This trenchant critique of the dominant theoretical approach in medical sociology followed shortly after the publication of two highly critical treatises on the commodification and profits in medical care: B. Ehrenreich and J. Ehrenreich (1971) on *The American Health Empire* and the report of the Medical Committee for Human Rights, *Billions for Band-Aids* (1972). V. Navarro's work on social class, medicine, and capitalism (1978) followed in this tradition. It was not until the mid- and late 1970s that critical perspectives on aging first surfaced in the United States (Estes 1978, 1979; Estes, Swan, and Gerard 1982; Olson 1982; Marshall and Tindale 1978). With few exceptions (Myles 1984; Navarro 1984; Quadagno 1988; Pampel 1994; Wallace and Villa 1997; Estes 1998b), gerontologists have not adequately focused on health and aging from a critical perspective engaging the macro-level debate on capitalism, the state, and old age.

Critical approaches to health and aging incorporate a variety of theoretical perspectives, including political economy, feminist theories, and theories of racial inequality (Estes and Linkins 1999; Minkler and Estes 1997; Estes 1998b; Phillipson 1998). Each of these perspectives offers the potential for revealing underlying ideological justifications of existing structural arrangements and resource distributions that affect health and aging. As such, these perspectives are open to multiple and alternative accounts of social structures and social processes. These perspectives also attempt to bridge issues of concern about many aging theories (Bengtson, Burgess, and Parrott 1997)—namely, fragmentation of the macro-micro problem—by considering the multi-level relationships among social structure, social processes, and the population. Issues of aging are not perceived as beginning with the individual, the generation, institutions or organizations, or society. Rather, all levels are viewed in terms of mutual dependency rather than opposition (Estes, Linkins, and Binney 1995).

The political economy approach offers an alternative and critical approach to understanding the condition of health and aging in society in contrast to classical social gerontological theory (see later sections of this chapter). Beginning with the work of C.L. Estes (1979), A.M. Guillemard (1977, 1983), C. Phillipson (1982), and A. Walker (1980, 1981), these theorists initiated the task of describing the role of ideology in systems of domination and marginalization of the aged. The political economy perspective can be distinguished from other political approaches in that it gives greater importance to social structures and social forces other than public opinion and the government as shaping and reproducing the prevailing power structure of society. Social policies pertaining to issues such as income, health, and social service benefits and entitlements are seen as resulting from economic, political, and sociocultural processes and forces interacting at any given sociohistorical period. As such, policy is considered an outcome of the social struggles, conflicts, and dominant power relations of the period (Estes 1998b). Public opinion is seen as a weapon used by conflicting elites, such as in the battles over the role of HMOs in Medicare. As described by R.R. Alford (1976) more than twenty years ago in a different setting, the major policy players are professional monopolists who are losing autonomy to HMOs and corporate rationalizers who want to make medicine more economically efficient (and profitable to financial capital). Patient desires are used by both sides to support their positions, while older persons have little direct say in the direction that the system is unfolding. The structure and culture of advantage and disadvantage as reflected in class, race, gender, and age relations is embedded in these policy struggles, and the stratification in the medical care system along these lines is reproduced (Wallace and Villa 1997). At the same time, policy can stimulate struggles over the distribution of resources such as medical care for the elderly, as occurred during the push to establish Medicare, which redistributed resources to the poorest and oldest members of society, but which also occurred when the Medicare Catastrophic Insurance Bill was repealed under pressure from middle-class elders (Wallace and Williamson 1992).

The political economy perspective draws heavily upon state theory. A central dynamic is the examination of the contradictions between the social needs of persons throughout the life course and of how the organization of work (capitalist modes of production and their transformations and struggles around them) and state actions around them interact and affect these social needs. New political-economy perspectives explain how the state is gendered (Acker 1988) and racialized (Omi and Winant 1994; Quadagno 1994), reproducing structures of gender and racial domination. There is debate and tension about whether and how gender and race are functional for and/or an inevitable result of capitalism. In particular, work in the political economy paradigm attends to how the state regulates and reproduces different life chances throughout the life course and how these ultimately affect the health status and health care of older persons. Feminist theory, for example, demonstrates how basing universal social programs such as Social Security on employment history works to reinforce male privilege and devalues women's care giving and other home-based work (Sainsbury 1996). At the same time, American social policy has often worked to reinforce rather than ameliorate racial inequality by allowing the local administration of many health and welfare programs in ways that enhanced the marginalization of African Americans (Quadagno 1994)

The most obvious link between older persons and the state is through older persons' reliance on the state for medical care through Medicare and Medicaid and retirement income through Social Security. J. Myles (1984) has argued that Social Security and Medicare represent an expansion of the family or citizen wage, which simultaneously socializes the costs of production. The way in which the state organizes and regulates medicine as a social institution is particularly consequential for older persons. The institutions affecting the life chances and experiences of persons vary by age group; younger persons are more often directly affected by the educational system, labor markets, and the criminal justice system, as well as being more residentially mobile and therefore more involved with housing markets. In contrast, health status and life stage of older persons make the social and political organization of health of paramount importance. Thus, when medical sociology studies the economy and polity, it almost unavoidably has implications for the older population.

When studying the economy and polity, sociological inquiry must also examine human agency and popular movements that may contest macro-social trends. To the extent that age is now an important social category, an analysis of social movements and grass roots organizing by and about older persons is important. The hospice movement had parallels to the women's health movement in its demedicalizing thrust (Abel 1986), and the "right to death" movement can be seen as a continuation of modernism's commodification and expansion of control over nature (O'Connor 1998; Hall et al. 1997). Much of the public policy attention that the elderly have garnered over the past fifty years has been the result of political movements and trends involving older persons as both subjects and actors. The Townsend Movement of older persons during the depression of the 1930s helped push the creation of Social Security, while national sympathy toward elders as a group and their legitimacy provided a focus for the establishment of Medicare in the 1960s. During the 1980s these two programs became known as the "third rail" of politics as politicians who tried to overtly "touch" program benefits were punished at election time (Wallace and Williamson 1992).

THE MEDICALIZATION, COMMODIFICATION, AND RATIONALIZATION OF AGING

Both the legitimization and accumulation imperatives of the modern capitalist state can be observed in its role in fostering the medicalization, commodification, and rationalization of aging. The dominance of the medical model in aging has already been discussed as a means of obscuring the extent to which illness and other problems of the elderly are determined by exogenous social structural or cultural causes. In the 1970s, counter movements emerged to reduce the medical dominance of health care for older persons. Home health care, provided largely through quasi-public nonprofit Visiting Nurses Associations grew in popularity as a way to assist persons who had left the hospital but needed ongoing professional services. Hospice care also evolved out of a social movement to demedicalize death built on the volunteer labor of laypersons in their own homes and communities (Abel 1986). The net effect of both trends was to shift a significant amount of medical care out of the hospital and away from physicians into the home. Also, both trends (1) disproportionately affected the elderly—although neither were "senior movements" per se—and (2) shifted substantial work from formal delivery systems to informal (unpaid) ones, and thus predominantly on to women. By the end of the 1980s, however, both of these demedicalizing movements had been commodified and rationalized, shifting the emphasis from fulfilling human needs to generating profits.

Commodification involves the shift in the mode of production of a good or service from an orientation to its immediate consumption in filling a human need (such as food, shelter, functional assistance for the disabled, etc.)

to a mode of production that is oriented toward exchange for the creation of private profits. The lives and health care of older persons have become increasingly commodified over the past century (Estes 1979). One of the central features of capitalism is that labor is treated as a commodity, and the development of the concept of retirement is a logical development of this concept. Retirement developed as a consequence of the changing methods of production in industry and the need for capital to replace older and more expensive members of the labor force as a means of maximizing profits (Graebner 1980). Medical care for the elderly has always been a commodity in the United States. Despite a tradition of charitable medical care, doctors and hospitals have always charged for their services (fee-for-service) when possible. The medical profession has been organized historically along a guild model, with physician control over the education, licensing, and practice of medicine (Starr 1982). While interested in their own pecuniary benefit, doctors did not organize as other businesses along rational-bureaucratic lines. Hospitals were mostly standalone facilities controlled primarily by doctors who saw the facilities as their personal workshops. Hospitals "sold" medical care, but their institutional interests were less in profits and more in providing conditions desirable for physician practice and in creating community good will for financial donations and patient referrals.

The passage of Medicare and Medicaid in 1965 created a "gold rush" for the modern hospital and medical care, characterized as a "medical-industrial complex" (Ehrenreich and Ehrenreich 1971) comprised of hospitals, drug companies, insurers, and suppliers. For-profit hospital chains grew in prominence, expanding in suburban and sun-belt areas where there was well-paying private insurance and little competition from or loyalty to nonprofit hospitals. With Medicare and "cost-based" reimbursement, there was little risk involved in guaranteeing hospital profits. For-profit nursing homes similarly grew in number dramatically during this time. Services were increasingly provided because of the revenues they generated, and there was increased concern over "provider-induced demand" for medical care. The net result was to reinforce a technological and institutional approach to the health care of older persons through hospital and physician services for elders under Medicare and for nursing home care for the poor elderly under Medicaid.

This medical care commodification defined the needs of older persons in terms of individual medical services that are "sold" for profit, rather than in terms of the right to health and health care (Estes and Binney 1989). Access to major health-care services (e.g., prescription drugs and long-term care) is limited by the ability of elders to individually pay out of pocket for them. Most important was the transformation of the health needs of the aging into commodities for specific economic markets supporting high technology, the manufacture of drugs, and specialization by experts who treat parts of the problem presented by "consumers" seeking goods and services in the medical marketplace. The concept of "health-care consumers" is developed and refined as part of the legitimating system of an individualistic, commodified form of health care (e.g., consumer report cards for HMOs in the 1990s). Treating health care as a commodity for consumption puts the onus of access, quality, and cost on atomized individuals who make decisions in a theoretically free market. In contrast, a "social rights" approach treats the elderly and others as citizens with an entitlement to health care independent of their "property rights" and ability to pay privately (Myles 1984).

By 1980 medical costs were rising rapidly, and the U.S. economy experienced both inflation and recession, putting strong pressures on corporate profits. This development generated pressures for cost containment and system rationalization. Arnold Relman (1980), editor of the *New England Journal of Medicine,* voiced the position of traditional craft-oriented physicians when he decried the "new medical industrial complex." Relman's concern was the shift of service delivery and control from nonprofit institutions and physicians to profit-making businesses. Corporate capital was expanding beyond the pharmaceutical and medical device industries (where Relman felt it belonged), weakening the "best kind of regulation of the health care market place. . . the informed judgments of physicians working in the interests of their patients" (Relman 1980: 967).

The 1980s and 1990s were a period of dramatic reorganization of American medicine toward a for-profit industrial model. Medicare legislation in 1981 promoted for-profit entry into the medical field, including the shift toward for-profit home health care (Estes et al. 1992), the establishment of a new Medicare hospice benefit that helped eliminate its community-based voluntary organization (Abel 1986), and the rationalization of hospital care through diagnosis-based rather than cost-based reimbursement (Estes, Swan, and Associates 1993). As the for-profit sector grew in size and power, nonprofits were forced by reimbursement and market practices to become part of chains and to operate increasingly like for-profits (Estes and Alford 1990). Health maintenance organizations (HMOs) grew in popularity, first with private employers, then the state, as a way to both contain costs and generate private profits.

Commodification and rationalization also extended into the insurance industry. Blue Cross was established as a nonprofit organization by hospitals to guarantee their payment during the depression, and Blue Shield followed as a medically controlled payer of physician care (Stevens 1983). Those nonprofits were slowly marginalized by for-profit insurance companies' entry into health insurance in the 1950s, the growing importance of public payers beginning in the 1960s, and corporate pressures for cost controls in the 1970s (Krause 1996). The rupture was complete as Blue Cross and Blue Shield converted nationally to for-profit businesses in the 1990s along with most nonprofit HMOs and many nonprofit hospitals.

Rationalization increased as big business formed purchaser alliances such as the Washington Business Group on Health (Bergthold 1990). These groups have advocated for health care to take a more businesslike approach as a way to reduce rising health-care costs. The pressure on provider organizations to restrain costs has opened many insurance companies, HMOs, hospitals, physician management groups, and others to both vertical and horizontal mergers. Increasingly, the key contests have large corporate and government payers on one side pushing for cost control and large corporate providers on the other side trying to rationalize their operations to increase economic efficiency. Meanwhile, doctors defensively try to retain some autonomy and control over the practice of medicine, while their control over the recruitment of patients, contract negotiations, and their own fees decreases (McKinlay and Stoekle 1988).

For the elderly Medicare policy has been an instrument to further these processes of rationalization, privatization, and commodification with state subsidies and deregulation. Examples are Medicare cost containment through prospective payment, increased beneficiary premiums and co-payments, managed care, and benefit reductions in home care. The privatization and commodification of nursing home care is extended via Medicaid.

DOMINANT AND CONTENDING THEORIES OF HEALTH AND AGING

In contrast to a political economy perspective, which can be classified as a conflict theory, most social gerontological theory has tended to look at age stratification as a functional basis for social differentiation and interdependence. The assumption that the distribution of roles in society tends toward a functional equilibrium informs disengagement and activity theory, and their more recent theoretical heirs. In these dominant perspectives, age is portrayed as a natural basis for social differentiation.

Disengagement theory (Cumming and Henry 1961) holds that old age is a period in which the aging person and society engage in mutual separation as the older person slowly reduces the number of roles he or she plays (e.g., via retirement) so that the impending death creates a minimal disruption in society. As such it could be seen as a functional adaptation for both the society and the individual to generational change. Although disengagement theory is no longer widely accepted among researchers in aging, its influence is still apparent in the policy arena and popular discourse.

Activity theory developed as an alternative to disengagement theory from within a functionalist paradigm. It asserts that as people age they continue the roles and activities they develop over the course of life into old age, including maintaining the same needs and values present at earlier points in their lives. Activity theory assumes that the more active people are (the more roles that they occupy), the more likely they are to be satisfied with their lives. Activity theory stimulated the development of several social-psychological theories of aging, including continuity theory (Costa and McCrae 1980; Atchley 1989) and more recent theories of successful aging (Baltes and Baltes 1990; Abeles, Gift, and Ory 1994). *Continuity theory* focuses on the tendency and need of older persons to maintain their same personalities, habits, and perspectives on life over their life course. Individuals are seen as adapting to their environment and adjusting their personalities to cope with environmental demands. Decreases in activity and social interaction are viewed as related to adaptive changes to health and physical declines.

Theories of successful aging expand the basic framework of activity and continuity theory to involve three components: low probability of disease and disease-related disability, high cognitive and physical functional capacity, and active engagement with life (Rowe and Kahn 1998). Successful aging is seen as involving more than the absence of disease and the maintenance of functional capacities. Rather, these two components combine and interact with the active engagement with life. One shortcoming of this work is that it largely ignores the necessity of having an adequate material and social base in order to foster and support the desired engagement and functioning. However, by moving beyond role occupancy to include physical function, this currently popular conceptualization is consistent with a biomedical emphasis in the social analysis of aging.

On the surface, activity theory and its later derivations belie ageist stereotypes of the elderly and are congenial to an emphasis on individual empowerment and quality of life in later years. Activity theory, in particular, underlies a large segment of social service policy that aims to provide older persons with activities and replacement roles through senior centers, congregate meals, and volunteer opportunities (Estes 1979). Continuity theory legitimates the efforts of the health and social service industries to work on making older persons adapt to their circumstances, rather than confront the inequities in economic and health resources and/or advocate for structural or policy changes in social institutions. Each of these functionalist-based conceptualizations suggests that "unsuccessful" aging is a result of the inability of the *individual* to meet the role obligations and opportunities of society. This perspective has also influenced a wide range of cross-national studies that have examined the relative status of older persons in different cultures.

Modernization theory, which draws on a functionalist evolutionary framework, posits that urbanization and industrialization are inevitable historical processes that decrease the resources of older people and create values that further socially marginalize the elderly (Silverstein et al. 1998). This approach takes a more sociohistorical view than the social-psychological theories just noted, but it is limited by its failure to take into account the influences of the global economy and of how political variations between countries result in different conceptualizations and policies.

Feminist theories correct the gender biases in social science research on health and aging and within social policy, particularly regarding inequality. Gender is seen as an organizing element of social life throughout the life course that influences and shapes the experience of aging (Ginn and Arber 1995; Calasanti 1996; Estes 1998b) and the distribution of resources in old age to men and women. Feminist approaches to aging offer an important angle for addressing differences in the health and aging experiences of the population as well as how social, cultural, and structural factors influence and shape social conditions (Calasanti 1996). Gender is a crucial organizing principle in economic and power relations and societal institutions. This perspective builds a more robust picture of the aging population (which is majority female) by identifying and challenging the dominant, male-centered biases in society (Calasanti 1996; Arber and Ginn 1991). When integrated into the political economy perspective, feminist approaches argue that there are fundamental, gender-based differences in the accessibility of material (e.g., income), health, and caring resources that influence the aging experience for men and women (Estes 1998c). When the state organizes social policy based on employment history, women are particularly disadvantaged, although benefits based on need may enhance the status of women *if* these benefits are accompanied by an ideology that recognizes the right to a basic minimum, and women fare best when citizenship is the basis of entitlement (Sainsbury 1996).

In spite of (and in some cases, because of) their longer life expectancy, older women suffer a number of disadvantages relative to older men: (1) Significantly, women comprise the majority of the aging population. A. O'Rand and the National Academy of Aging (1994: 4) identify this as "the feminization of the older population in the U.S." in which over half of those 65 and older and more than two-thirds of those 85 and older are women. (2) Women are more dependent upon the state than men, and this is true across the life course. If anything, the degree of women's dependency on the state grows with age and the loss of spouses and other means of economic and social support, just as health and functional status are declining. These factors enhance the vulnerability of millions of women, particularly those in advanced ages, to the larger political and economic forces as mediated by the state. These forces are particularly serious for women who live alone, who are in minorities, and who are poor and near poor. Instability in employment and marital status over the life course has been identified as a major factor in women's vulnerable economic situation. Marital status is a strong predictor of income and health security measured by health insurance coverage (Meyer 1996). Married older women fare significantly better than single older women. However, the rising instability in employment and marital status across the life course means that secure health insurance coverage will not be employment- or family-based. The work of Patricia Hill Collins (1990) draws our attention to the concept of interlocking systems of oppression and inequality of gender, social class, and racial and ethnic status over the life course (Quadagno 1990; Street and Quadagno 1993; Dressel, Minkler, and Yen 1998).

Theories of racial inequality are essential to the understanding of health inequalities in old age (Markides and Black 1995). M. Omi and H. Winant (1994) posit that basic rights associated with citizenship in the United States have been reserved for whites only, and they call this "racial dictatorship." They cite several important consequences, including the fact that the definition of American identity is as white; that the "color line" is the most important division of society; and that there is an essentializing of diverse communities into racial categories. While federal civil rights laws have addressed legal aspects of racial dictatorship, there remain substantial and increasing inequalities for minorities in terms of power, money, and health, which are reflected in old age and old-age policy (Quadagno 1994). Data consistently show African-American elderly to be disadvantaged compared to whites in life expectancy, chronic illness rates, and levels of disability. While the health disparity between African Americans and whites declines with advancing age on some health indicators including mortality rates, African-American elderly as a group are less healthy and more disabled than white elderly. Some suggest that the health gap between white and African-American elderly will widen due to increased rates of diabetes and hypertension (Wallace et al. 1998: 331). Older African Americans and older Latinos have two to three times the poverty rate of white elderly, and many do not have health insurance. Thus, access to care is a serious problem to many minority elders. Because minority elderly are projected to comprise over one-third of all persons age sixty-five and older in 2050 (U.S. Bureau of the Census 1996), racial disparities in health status and access of older minorities to health and long-term care will be a growing concern.

Overall, elders of color experience more health problems than whites because of high poverty rates, problems in accessing adequate medical care, and lower participation in Social Security. These factors contribute to morbidity and mortality differences across populations. For example, G. Pappas (1994) demonstrates that the most important factor contributing to the widening gap in life expectancy between whites and African Americans is the slower decline in heart disease mortality in the African-American population in recent decades.

In sum, theories based on functionalist and psychological paradigms continue to dominate much of social science on health and aging, although the literature includes critical theories of gender and race that can be fruitfully combined with a political economy of aging.

CONCLUSION

Robert Strauss (1957) described two types of sociological approaches to the field of medical sociology: first, "sociology *in* medicine," which characterized work that aims to advance the goals of clinicians and clinical practice; second, "sociology *of* medicine," in which medical institutions and providers are the focus of the study of basic sociological processes and structures. Andrew Twaddle (1982) contended that a paradigm shift had occurred in medical sociology, characterized by a move to the "sociology of health" that brought in both social science and humanistic perspectives. This shift was reflected in attention to environmental, social, and behavioral factors, in contrast to the biological science or psychological (role/personality) perspectives that earlier dominated medical sociology.

There are parallels between social gerontology and medical sociology. For example, the biological science models that have influenced sociological studies *in* medicine have also been dominant in gerontology, with parallel research on individual changes in the organism and physical failure designed to aid medical practitioners in treating older persons with failing bodies. Similarly, the psychological and micro-behavioral models that characterize the sociology *of* medicine are repeated in social gerontology in research on human development, psycho-behavioral patterns, and social roles throughout the life cycle. These studies accept the existence of the category of the "elderly" as an analytic category and generally take the social, political, and economic context as given.

Since the founding of social gerontology in the mid 1940s, sociological research has focused on both sociology *in* health and aging and sociology *of* health and aging. Health services and health policy research on aging reflect sociology *in* medicine and aging. This applied, social engineering approach is dominated by economic and econometric work that is concerned with the cost and efficacy of medical care and is federally funded through the Agency for Health Policy Research and the Health Care Financing Administration, and by private foundations. The National Institute on Aging (NIA) supports primarily biomedical research (basic and applied/disease focused) (Estes and Binney 1989) and a growing field of behavioral medicine in aging, all of which are strongly influenced by the scientific problems defined by medicine. Congress has designated substantial NIA funding for Alzheimer's Disease research and other studies focused on individual etiology and treatment (Adelman 1995). Basic research questions of genetics, biology, and biochemistry infuse NIA studies.

Unlike the paradigm shift described by Twaddle for medical sociology, there is no clear movement in gerontology away from the applied and toward a broader sociology *of* health and aging. However, there is substantial intellectual ferment in "critical gerontology" and "humanistic gerontology" resulting from a combination of, on the one hand, persistent problems with medicine under capitalism and growing concerns over state restructuring and the privatization of entitlements

such as Medicare and Social Security, and, on the other hand, the entry of post-modernist and cultural studies (Phillipson 1996; Moody 1998; Estes and Linkins 1999). Results are a rise in institutional social system analysis of welfare states and policy applications, as Twaddle predicted and a rise in work on meanings, identities, and knowledges.

With regard to the elderly, the dominant biomedical paradigm faces a number of challenges. The first challenge results from developments that have extended the life span *without resolving the problems* of an increased societal chronic illness burden with demographic aging. The problem stems from the continuing overemphasis by the medical industrial complex on the treatment of acute rather than chronic illness. The problem centers on how society will deal with the "longevity revolution" (Roszak 1998) without changing the basic premises underlying the hegemony of medicine, or producing a loss of faith in biomedicine itself as it fails to extend the life span as one of "active life expectancy" and "successful aging" (Rowe and Kahn 1998).

The second challenge is the inability of the biomedical model to address the root causes that are implicated in the etiology of ill health (e.g., economic, social, and environmental) in old age. The response of medicine, which also is consistent with the present political conservatism, has been twofold: (1) to focus attention on individual health behaviors and lifestyles, making the individual responsible for illness and for "unsuccessful" aging and "usual" aging (Estes and Mahakian 1998), thereby shifting the blame for the shortcomings of medicine and medical failures to those who are ill or suffer from them such as the elderly; and (2) the assertion that genetics and biotechnology offer the solution to the health problems of the elderly including chronic illness, as well as the solution to the problems of the U.S. economy in an aging society (Pardes et al. 1999).

The third challenge is the ideological commitment of American medicine and the media to the highly debatable notion that medicine is the source of nearly all major health improvements in the last century, despite the well-documented fact that public health improvements in the environment, sanitation, water, and nutrition are major causes of such improvements. A competing view is that medical care and medical procedures themselves are costly and often ineffective or unnecessary, and are not the major reasons for the health improvements or longevity gains (McKeown 1997; McKinlay, McKinlay, and Beaglehole 1989). The current field of health (medical) services research is today's version of sociology *in* medicine, with its application of cost effectiveness and outcomes-measurement techniques based on medical and econometric definitions. By not questioning the assumptions underlying the market—individual preferences and theorized consumer "choices"—or examining its opposing concept—the right to health care—these approaches serve economic interests by preserving and expanding the costly and highly profitable medical industrial complex.

On the one hand, there is an increasing theory-less empiricism and social engineering in gerontology where applied research on demographics, health, health care, and health economics of aging fails to problematize or measure the full effects of the surging for-profit and managed care medical industries. Here the "problem" of aging for the individual and society is defined as *technical* and capable of administrative correction under the continued dominance of medicine and its ever more powerful alliances (and power struggles) with and within profit-making corporations and the scientific disciplines of genetics and economics. Technical and statistical developments, including demographic, econometric, and actuarial modeling and the availability of national Medicare and Medicaid data, permit the production of what appear to be objective and precise value-neutral calculations of the cost/benefits of health policy changes. Such calculations are usually made at individual and aggregate levels and without consideration of other social costs that are shifted onto others in society (e.g., nonvalorized costs of women's unpaid labor whose work is increased with shortened lengths of hospital stays and ambulatory surgery).

On the other hand, research on the sociology of health and aging in 2000 continues to be dominated by a focus on individual behavior and, for some, the pursuit of "nirvana" via attempts to interrupt or reverse the aging process. Challenging these approaches are political-economy theories and critical and cultural theories. These latter theoretical developments have been energized by the political and economic threats of conservative governments and the socially constructed demographic and intergenerational "crises" of the aging of the Baby Boom that have become the rationale for cutting back entitlements. These events are occurring in the context of globalization aided by a revolution in telecommunications ("informationalism"), both of which reinforce control and power in the hands of major corporate concentrations around the globe (Castells 1989).

A critical sociological perspective on aging and health must embrace both a life-course perspective and a political-economy perspective that accords conceptual attention to "interlocking oppressions throughout life" (Pescosolido and Kronenfeld 1995; Meyer 1996; Dressel, Minkler, and Yen 1998) as they affect one's own and one's group's life chances. This type of analysis of health and aging can provide the insights necessary for a positive response to the three challenges to biomedicine noted above. The way that the biomedical paradigm is being used in combination with the commodification and rationalization of medical care contains inherent contradictions that will eventually bring its universal applicability into question. A crisis in the legitimacy of biomedicine could reverberate into a broader legitimacy crisis for the state, if it is seen to be putting most of its resources into profit-making treatments of individuals rather than into creating social and economic conditions under which people can be healthy. A critical sociological perspective on health and aging can provide an alternative paradigm that locates some of the key factors of "healthy aging" in the society and economy and prioritizes the production of health care as a social good for all, rather than as an economic good that is inequitably distributed.

REFERENCES

ABELES, R.P., H.G. GIFT, and M.G. ORY, eds. 1994. *Aging and Quality of Life.* New York: Springer.

ABEL, E.K. 1986. "The Hospice Movement." *International Journal of Health Services* 16 (1): 71–85.

ACKER, J. 1988. "Class, Gender and the Relations of Distribution." *Signs* 13 (3): 473–93.

ADELMAN, R. 1995. "The 'Alzheimerization' of Aging." *Gerontologist* 35 (4): 526–32.

ADLER, N.E., T. BOYCE, M.A. CHESNEY, S. FOLKMAN, and L. SYME. 1993. "Socioeconomic Inequalities in Health." *Journal of the American Medical Association* 269 (24): 3140–45.

ALFORD, R.R. 1976. *Health Care Politics.* Chicago: University of Chicago Press.

ARBER, S., and J. GINN. 1991. *Gender and Later Life.* London: Sage Publications.

ATCHLEY, R.C. 1989. "A Continuity Theory of Normal Aging." *Gerontologist* 29:183–90.

BALTES, P.B., and M.M. BALTES. 1990. "Psychological Perspectives on Successful Aging." In *Successful Aging,* ed. P.B. Baltes and M.M. Baltes. New York: Cambridge University Press, pp. 1–34.

BENGTSON, V.E., O. BURGESS, and T.M. PARROTT. 1997. "Theory, Explanation, and a Third Generation of

Theoretical Development in Social Gerontology." *Journal of Gerontology: Social Sciences* 52B (2): S72–88.

BERGTHOLD, LINDA. 1990. *Purchasing Power in Health.* New Brunswick, NJ: Rutgers University Press.

BORTZ, W.M., IV, and W.M. BORTZ II. 1996. "How Fast Do We Age?" *Journal of Gerontology: Medical Sciences* 51A (5): M223–M225.

CALASANTI, T. 1996. "Incorporating Diversity: Meaning, Levels of Research, and Implications for Theory." *Gerontologist* 36:147–56.

CASTELLS, M. 1989. *The Informational City.* Cambridge, MA: Blackwell.

COLLINS, P. HILL. 1990. *Black Feminist Thought.* New York: Routledge.

COSTA, P.T., and R.R. MCCRAE. 1980. "Still Stable After All These Years." In *Life-Span Development and Behavior* Vol. III, ed. P.B. Baltes and O.G. Brim. New York: Academic Press, pp. 65–102.

CUMMING, E., and W.E. HENRY. 1961. *Growing Old: The Process of Disengagement.* New York: Basic Books.

DRESSEL, P., M. MINKLER, and I. YEN. 1998. "Gender, Race, Class, and Aging: Advances and Opportunities." In *Critical Gerontology,* ed. M. Minkler and C.L. Estes. Amityville, NY: Baywood Publication Company, pp. 275–94.

EHRENREICH, B. and J. EHRENREICH. 1971. *The American Health Empire.* New York: Vintage.

ESPING-ANDERSON, GOSTA, ed. 1996. *Welfare States in Transition.* Thousand Oaks, CA: Sage.

ESTES, C.L. 1978. "Political Gerontology." *Transaction Society* 15, 43–49.

ESTES, C.L. 1979. *The Aging Enterprise.* San Francisco: Jossey Bass.

ESTES, C.L. 1983. "Social Security: The Social Construction of a Crisis." *Milbank Memorial Fund Quarterly/Health and Society* 61(3): 445–61.

ESTES, C.L. 1998a. "Crisis and the Welfare State in Aging." Paper presented to American Sociological Association. August. San Francisco, CA.

ESTES, C.L. 1998b. "Critical Gerontology and the New Political Economy of Aging." In *Critical Gerontology,* ed. M. Minkler and C.L. Estes. Amityville, NY: Baywood Publishing Company.

ESTES, C.L. 1998c. "Patriarchy and the Welfare State Revisited." Paper presented to The World Congress of Sociology. July 29. Montreal, Canada.

ESTES, C.L. 1991. "The Reagan Legacy: Privatization, The Welfare State, and Aging in the 1990s." In *States, Labor Markets and the Future of Old Age Policy,* ed. J. Myles and J. Quadagno. Philadelphia: Temple Univ. Press, pp. 59–83.

ESTES, C.L., and E.A. BINNEY. 1989. "The Biomedicalization of Aging." *Gerontologist* 29 (5): 587–96.

ESTES, C.L., and J. MAHAKIAN. 1998. "The Political and Moral Economy of Productive Aging." Paper presented to Productive Aging Conference, Washington University. December 4. Saint Louis, Missouri.

ESTES, C.L., and K.W. LINKINS. 1999. "Critical Health and Aging." In *Handbook of Social Science in Medicine and Health,* ed. G. Albrecht et al. Newbury Park: Sage.

ESTES, C.L., and R. ALFORD. 1990. "Systemic Crisis and the Nonprofit Sector." *Theory and Society* 19(2): 173–98.

ESTES, C.L., J.H. SWAN, and ASSOCIATES. 1993. *The Long Term Care Crisis.* Newbury Park: Sage.

ESTES, C.L., J.H. SWAN, and L. GERARD. 1982. "Dominant and Competing Paradigms: Toward a Political Economy of Aging." *Aging and Society* 2 (2): 151–64.

ESTES, C.L, K.W. LINKINS, and E.A. BINNEY. 1995. "The Political Economy of Aging." In *Handbook of Aging and the Social Sciences.* 4th ed., ed. L. George and R. Binstock. San Diego: Academic Press, pp. 346–61.

ESTES, C.L., J.H. SWAN, L.A. BERGTHOLD, and P. HANES-SPOHN. 1992. "Running as Fast as They Can: Organizational Changes in Home Health Care." *Home Health Care Services Quarterly* 13(1/2): 35–69.

FRIEDLAND, R.B., and L. SUMMER. 1999. *Demography Is Not Destiny.* Washington DC: National Academy on an Aging Society. Gerontological Society of America.

GINN, J., and S. ARBER. 1995. "Only Connect: Gender Relations and Aging." In *Connecting Gender and Aging,* ed. S. Arber and J. Ginn. Philadelphia: Open University Press.

GRAEBNER, W. 1980. *A History of Retirement.* New Haven CT: Yale University Press.

GUILLEMARD, A.M. 1977. *A Critical Analysis of Governmental Policies on Aging from a Marxist Sociological Perspective.* Paris: Center for Study of Social Movements.

GUILLEMARD, A.M. ed. 1983. *Old Age and the Welfare State.* New York: Sage.

HABERMAS, J. 1975. *Legitimation Crisis.* Boston: Beacon Press.

HAHN, M., and G.A. KAPLAN. 1985. "The Contribution of Socioeconomic Position to Minority Health." In *Report of the Secretary's Task Force on Black and Minority Health,* ed. M. Heckler. Washington DC: U.S. Department of Health and Human Services.

HALL, S., D. HELD, D. HUBERT. and K. THOMPSON. 1997. *Modernity.* Malden MA: Blackwell.

HARDING, E., S. CUMMINGS, and T. BODENHEIMER, eds. 1972. *Billions for Band-Aids.* San Francisco: Bay Area Medical Committee for Human Rights.

HOUSE, J., C. KESSLER, and A.R. HERZOG. 1990. "Age Socioeconomic Status, and Health." *Milbank Quarterly* 68: 383–411.

KENEN, JOANNE. 1999. "Social Security, Medicare Bankruptcy Delayed." *Los Angeles Times* March 31.

KOHLI, M. 1988. "Aging as a Challenge for Sociological Theory." *Aging and Society* 8:367–94.

KRAUSE, E.A. 1996. *Death of the Guilds.* New Haven, CT: Yale University Press.

MARKIDES, K.S., and S.A. BLACK. 1995. "Race, Ethnicity and Aging." In *Handbook of Aging and the Social Sciences.* 4th ed., ed. R. Binstock and L. George. New York: Academic Press, pp. 153–70.

MARSHALL, V., and J.A. TINDALE. 1978. "Notes for a Radical Gerontology." *International Journal of Aging and Human Development* 9: 163–75.

MAYER, K.U., and U. SCHOEPFLIN. 1989. "The State and the Life Course." *Annual Review of Sociology* 15:187–209.

McGINNIS, J.M., and W.H. FOEGE. 1993. "Actual Causes of Death in the US." *Journal of the American Medical Association* 270 (18): 2207–13.

McKINLAY, J., and J. STOEKLE. 1988. "Corporatization and the Social Transformation of Doctoring." *International Journal of Health Services* 18:191–205.

McKINLAY, J.B., S.M. McKINLAY, and R. BEAGLEHOLE. 1989. "Trends in Death and Disease and the Contribution of Medical Measures." In *Handbook of Medical Sociology,* 4th ed., ed. H.E. Freeman and S. Levine. Englewood Cliffs: Prentice Hall.

McKEOWN, T. 1997. "Determinants of Health." In *The Nation's Health,* 5th ed., ed. P.R. Lee and C.L. Estes. Sudbury, MA: Jones & Bartlett.

MEYER, M. HARRINGTON. 1996. "Making Claims as Workers or Wives." *American Sociological Review* 61 (June): 449–65.

MINKLER, M., and C.L. ESTES. 1997. *Critical Gerontology.* Amityville, NY: Baywood.

MOODY, H.R. 1998. *Aging.* 2nd ed. Thousand Oaks, CA: Pine Forge Press.

MYLES, J. 1984. *Old Age and the Welfare State.* Lawrence, KS: University of Kansas Press.

NAVARRO, V. 1978. *Class Struggle, the State, and Medicine.* Oxford: Martin Robertson.

NAVARRO, V. 1984. "Political Economy of Government Cuts for the Elderly." In *Readings in the Political Economy of Aging,* ed. M. Minkler and C.L. Estes. Amityville, NY: Baywood.

NAVARRO, V. 1990. "Race or Class versus Race and Class: Mortality Differentials in the US." *Lancet* 336: 1238–40.

O'CONNOR, J. 1973. *The Fiscal Crisis of the State.* New York: St. Martin's.

O'CONNOR, J. 1998. *Natural Causes.* New York: Guilford.

OLSON, L. 1982. *The Political Economy of Aging.* New York: Columbia University Press.

OMI, M., and H. WINANT. 1994. *Racial Formation in the United States.* New York: Routledge.

O'RAND, A., and NATIONAL ACADEMY ON AGING. 1994. *The Vulnerable Majority: Older Women in Transition.* Syracuse, NY: Syracuse University National Academy of Aging.

PAMPEL, F.C. 1994. "Population Aging: Class Context and Age Inequality in Public Spending." *American Journal of Sociology* 100 (1): 153–59.

PAPPAS, G. 1994. "Elucidating the Relationship Between Race, Socioeconomic Status, and Health." *American Journal of Public Health* 84: 892–93.

PARDES, H., K.G. MANTON, E.S. LANDER, H.D. TOLLEY, A.D. ULLIAN, and H. PALMER. 1999. "Effects of Medical Research on Health Care and the Economy." *Science* 283: 36–37.

PESCOSOLIDO, B.A., and J.J. KRONENFELD. 1995. "Health, Illness and Healing in an Uncertain Era." *Journal of Health and Social Behavior* (extra issue): 5–33.

PHILLIPSON, C. 1982. *Capitalism and the Construction of Old Age.* London: Macmillan.

PHILLIPSON, C. 1996. "Interpretations of Ageing." *Ageing and Society* 16: 359–69.

PHILLIPSON, C. 1998. *Reconstructing Old Age.* London: Sage.

QUADAGNO, J. 1988. *Transformation of Old Age Security.* Chicago: University of Chicago Press.

QUADAGNO, J. 1990. "Race, Class, and Gender in the U.S. Welfare State." *American Sociological Review* 55(1):11–29.

QUADAGNO, J. 1994. *The Color of Welfare.* New York: Oxford University Press.

RELMAN, A. 1980. "The New Medical Industrial Complex." *New England Journal of Medicine* 303: 963–70.

RENAUD, M. 1975. "On the Structural Constraints of State Intervention in Health." *International Journal of Health Services* 5 (4): 559–71.

RICE, D.P. 1996. "Medicare Beneficiary Profile." *Health Care Financing Review* 18 (18): 23–46.

RILEY, M.W., and J.W. RILEY. 1994. "Structural Lag." In *Age and Structural Lag,* ed. M.W. Riley, R.L. Kahn, and A. Foner. New York: Wiley, pp. 15–36.

ROBERT, S. 1998. "Community Level Socio-Economic Status Effect on Adult Health." *Journal of Health and Social Behavior* 39: 18–37.

ROBERTSON, A. 1991. "The Politics of Alzheimer's Disease." In *Critical Perspectives on Aging,* ed. M. Minkler and C. Estes. Amityville, NY: Baywood, pp. 135–50.

ROSZAK, T. 1998. *America the Wise: The Longevity Revolution and the True Wealth of Nations.* New York: Houghton Mifflin.

ROWE, J.W., and R.L. KAHN. 1998. *Successful Aging.* New York: Pantheon Random House.

SAINSBURY, D. 1996. *Gender, Equality, and Welfare States.* New York: Cambridge University Press.

SILVERSTEIN, M., V. BURHOLT, C. WENGER, and V.L. BENGTSON. 1998. "Parent-Child Relations Among Very Old Parents in Wales and The United States." *Journal of Aging Studies* 12(4): 387–409.

STARR, P. 1982. *The Social Transformation of American Medicine.* New York: Basic Books.

STEVENS, R. 1983. "Comparisons in Health Care: Britain as a Contrast to the US." In *Handbook of Health, Health Care and the Health Professions,* ed. D. Mechanic. New York: Free Press.

STRAUSS, R. 1957. "The Nature and Status of Medical Sociology." *American Sociological Review* 22: 200–204.

STREET, D., and J. QUADAGNO. 1993. "The State, the Elderly, and the Intergenerational Contract." In *Societal Impact on Aging,* ed. K.W. Schaie and W.A. Achenbaum. New York: Springer, pp. 130–50.

TWADDLE, A.D. 1982. "From Medical Sociology to the Sociology of Health" In *Sociology: The State of the Art,* ed. T. Bottomore, S. Nowak, and M. Sokolowska. Beverly Hills: Sage.

U.S. BUREAU OF THE CENSUS. 1996. *Population Projections of the US by Age, Race, Sex and Hispanic Origin: 1995-2050,* Series P25–1130, Table F. Washington DC: U.S. Government Printing Office.

U.S. BUREAU OF THE CENSUS. 1996. *65+ in the U.S.* Series P23–190, Table 2–1. Washington, DC: U.S. Government Printing Office.

U.S. BUREAU OF THE CENSUS. 1997. *Statistical Abstract of the United States 1997.* Washington, DC: U.S. Government Printing Office.

WAITZKIN, H., and B. WATERMAN. 1974. *The Exploitation of Illness in Capitalist Society.* Indianapolis: Bobbs-Merrill.

WALKER, A. 1980. "The Social Creation of Poverty and Dependency in Old Age." *Journal of Social Policy* 9: 49–75.

WALKER, A. 1981. "Towards a Political Economy of Old Age." *Ageing and Society* 1 (1): 73–94.

WALLACE, S. 1990. "Race Versus Class in Health Care of African-American Elderly." *Social Problems* 37 (4): 101–19.

WALLACE, S. 1991. "The Political Economy of Health Care for Elderly Blacks." In *Critical Perspectives on Aging,* ed. M. Minkler and C.L. Estes. Amityville, NY: Baywood, pp. 253–70.

WALLACE, S., V. ENRIQUEZ-HAASS, and K. MARKIDES. 1998. "The Consequences of Color-Blind Health Policy for Older Racial and Ethnic Minorities." *Stanford Law and Policy Review* 9 (2): 329–46.

WALLACE, S.P., and J.B. WILLIAMSON. 1992. "The Senior Movement in Historical Perspective." In *The Senior Movement,* ed. S.P. Wallace and J.B. Williamson. New York: G.K. Hall, pp. vii–xxxvi.

WALLACE, S.P., and V. VILLA. 1997 "Caught in Hostile Cross-Fire: Public Policy and Minority Elderly in the United States." In *Minorities, Aging, and Health,* ed. K. Markides and M. Miranda. Thousand Oaks: Sage, pp. 397–420.

10 ENVIRONMENT AND HEALTH

PHIL BROWN, *Brown University*

DEVELOPMENT OF SOCIAL CONCERN WITH ENVIRONMENTAL HEALTH

The Centrality of Environmental Factors on Health

Much disease is caused by substances and conditions in people's surrounding environment. Factory workers are made sicker by chemicals and air particles in their immediate work setting; farm workers become ill and even sterile from pesticides they apply to crops; people contract illnesses from toxic wastes long-buried in their neighborhood; melanoma (skin cancer) increases as ozone-depleting gases reduce the ozone layer and allow in ultraviolet rays; infectious diseases spread from bacteria in contaminated water supplies. These illnesses are the subject of considerable public discussion, as the public increasingly becomes aware of environmental causes of disease.

It would be impossible to consider thinking or writing about medical sociology, public health, or social medicine without placing the environment in a central position. When sociologists have examined the history and political economy of disease, they have always seen the environment as a source of disease. Early analysts of health and society viewed the conditions of the surrounding world as central to health. Friedrich Engels (1971) in *The Condition of the Working Class in England,* Rudolph Virchow in *Poverty in Spessart: Discussion of the Ongoing Typhus Epidemic in Oberschlesien, 1848* (cited in Waitzkin 1983), and George Orwell (1958) in *The Road to Wigan Pier* were among those who considered poor working conditions, crowded slums, polluted water, and contamination of the air as central to health status.

By observing such evidence, medical sociology has long understood the importance of the environment on health improvement. We commonly cite the perspective that attributes the largest part of mortality decline in the nineteenth century to improved housing and sanitation, modern sewage systems, cleaner water supply, and other public health measures, rather than to advances in medical technology and science (McKeown 1976). Medical sociologists have often used this perspective as a critique of the medical model.

But in another way, medical sociology has not put much effort into health and the environment. Most of the research and writing in this area comes from environmental sociology, environmental epidemiology, and public health. Environmental sociology, in particular, has been significant in providing community-based case studies, quantitative studies of inequalities in hazards exposure, and conflict-oriented analyses of the origins of environmental health effects that result from changes in the political economy. The absence of medical sociology is troubling, since so many of the issues dealt with by environmental sociologists are health related. Hence, it is now appropriate to also view the McKeown thesis on mortality decline as a positive statement that the environment is of central concern to the social scientific study of health and to make up for much lost ground.

In light of this approach, we may take as a jumping-off point John Snow's study of a cholera epidemic in London, a classic observational study that was the prototype of epidemiology. Snow hypothesized a connection with the water, specifically sewage, even though the cholera vibrium was not yet isolated. Snow conducted a health survey that showed him that mortality among people living further from the well occurred only when they specifically used that well. Other mortality away from the well area was equal to pre-epidemic rate. To account for cholera among persons who were believed to

143

have not drunk contaminated water, Snow tracked down the indirect sources of water intake. To account for lack of cholera among people who would be expected to be exposed due to their location, Snow found that workhouse residents had their own water supply, and that brewery workers were often drinking beer instead of water (Goldstein and Goldstein 1986).

Snow determined the source of the water as being one of two companies, identifiable by pipes and further confirmed by the concentration of chloride. The tabulation of cholera rate by water company provided proof of the source. Snow did not confront an intentional pollution episode but did come upon a seemingly natural environmental situation that caused disease, and he made a historic analysis of the cause. It is especially important that Snow had a very modern public health approach to the problem, as seen in his recommendation to prevent cholera: "The communicability of cholera ought not to be disguised from the people, under the idea that the knowledge of it would cause a panic, or occasion the sick to be deserted." Note also his public health and sociological prescriptions: sanitation, cleanliness, better living conditions, and even work breaks for miners to go home for lunch (Goldstein and Goldstein 1986). Snow's approach, often called "barefoot epidemiology," is quite similar to what citizens do at present in what Michael Edelstein (1988) terms "contaminated communities." Snow went beyond individual illness, and he integrated social context and physical environment in his analysis of cholera. Thus, from reading Snow's description of his foundational epidemiologic study, we learn about the social embeddedness of disease and the environment; we learn the importance of collective or aggregated, rather than individual, clinical data; we learn the need to use both survey methods and intense first-hand observation to attain adequate information; and we learn about medical and governmental inability and reluctance to face environmentally induced disease.

Defining the Scope of Environment and Health

What exactly do we mean by "environment," when we address environment and health? In the broadest sense, we could consider the totality of social surroundings. This would include at a minimum unhealthy living and working conditions; bacteria and viruses in human waste; animal vectors for infectious diseases (flies, mosquitos, rodents, birds); surface-water and groundwater pollution (ranging from nontoxic forms, such as road salt, to toxic chemicals); air pollution from fires, vehicle exhaust, and incineration; chemical and petroleum

product spills and explosions; and disasters, such as floods, hurricanes, and fires (which may be natural, human-caused, or human-exacerbated).

But that totality is so broad as to encompass virtually all disease-causing factors in the world. Moreover, it makes it difficult to assess the specifics of what we usually consider environmental health (for coverage of the broad approach, see basic environmental epidemiology or environmental health texts such as Goldsmith 1986; Greenberg 1987; Moeller 1992; National Research Council 1991). I choose to focus on the health effects caused by toxic substances in people's immediate or proximate surroundings (soil, air, water, food, household goods), a definition that resonates with the usual conception of environmental health. These are chemical-related, air pollution-related, and radiation-related diseases and symptoms that affect groups of people in neighborhoods and communities. There are many good reasons for focusing on toxic substances. It is an area that has engendered an enormous amount of conflict, policy-making, legislation, public awareness, media attention, and social movement activity. It puts into sharp relief a variety of disputes between laypeople and professionals, citizens and governments, and among professionals. It demonstrates an interesting and ongoing example of social-problems construction. These environmentally induced diseases (EIDs) are especially contested and thus represent an interesting challenge for medical sociology. Also, toxins are an enormous source of anxiety—Kai Erikson's (1994) notion of "a new species of trouble" and Ulrich Beck's (1992) conceptualization of a pervasive "risk society" touch on the widespread fears that contemporary society is saturated with technological hazards that are threatening to human survival.

Precisely because environmental diseases are so centered in the daily life and economy, the recognition of and action on these diseases is especially contested. The potency of these "contested diseases" is so great that these diseases have become highly politicized and have engendered a very significant social movement.

The Legacy of Occupational Disease in Defining and Detecting Environmental Disease

Despite attempts to narrow the definition, this "narrower" definition (health effects caused by toxic substances in people's immediate or proximate surroundings) requires some discussion of occupational health, which is frequently left out of both medical sociology and environmental sociology. Indeed, occupational and environmental medicine are linked in medical specialization (postgraduate training and board certification), even though there are far fewer practitioners of environmental medicine than of occupational medicine. Many harmful effects of chemicals and substances are first found in the work setting and then generalized to the community level, even though nonwork exposures are often smaller and harder to measure. The discovery of occupational health effects often provided impetus for the discovery of environmental health effects, because the same substances were causing disease both at the worksite and in the community. In addition, there was much corporate, governmental, and scientific opposition to detecting and remediating occupational causes of disease, setting a tone that carried through to environmental conditions.

Occupational diseases are often contested. Even as clear a condition as black lung disease was the source of great contention, with coal miners and their union pitted against mining corporations and the federal government (Smith 1981). Mesothelioma (cancer of the pleura) and asbestosis (a pulmonary disease) are now generally understood as caused by asbestos, though there was great conflict until quite recently (Brodeur 1985). These are examples of dramatic diseases that have specific, visible signs and symptoms, as well as clearer etiological links. Hence, these are more likely to result in medical and governmental disease recognition. But at present there is attention to other work-related conditions, such as the relationship of silicon chip production to miscarriages, repetitive stress injury (RSI), and sick building syndrome, where the signs and symptoms are vaguer and where etiological links are weaker (see Fox 1991; Robinson 1991; Rosner and Markowitz 1989). Despite many years of efforts to recognize these health effects, many occupational diseases are still contested.

Toxic Waste Crises and the Origins of Environmental Health Concern

Rachel Carson published *Silent Spring* in 1962, launching the first mass public attention to environmental health effects. Carson synthesized an enormous amount of observation and experimental data to demonstrate how pesticides, especially DDT, ubiquitous at that time, were serious hazards, causing morbidity and mortality in animals and humans (Carson 1962). Like many other pioneers in public health, Carson was sharply criticized for being unscientific and for attacking major economic sectors. Carson's powerful impact led to significant regulation of pesticides and other chemicals and eventually to the National Environmental Protection Act and establishment of the Environmental Protection Agency (EPA). As any reading of environmental history or policy tells

us, *Silent Spring* is credited with the growth of the new wave of the environmental movement (Hynes 1989; Steingraber 1996).

Although Carson's emphasis was on health, the modern environmental movement that cites her as a main founder is mostly a revival of an older environmentalism, based on conservation and preservation, with little or no concern for human health issues. Love Canal was the next major phenomenon in the development of the modern environmental movement, and the first time that human health was central in an environmental crisis, prompting the creation of the Superfund Program by EPA. Although only a small amount of all waste is hazardous, the EPA estimates that 90 percent of hazardous wastes are improperly disposed.

It was only after Love Canal that we realized the magnitude of this problem. In the Love Canal crisis, residents were warned by state health officials that toxic chemicals permeated their neighborhood in Niagara Falls, New York. This knowledge stemmed from the International Joint Commission on the Great Lakes, which traced the pesticide Mirex to the dumpsite that had been given free to the city as a school site. But the revelation meshed with residents' awareness of a history of seeing toxic substances and experiencing their effects. As residents organized to learn more, they discovered high rates of miscarriages, birth defects, cancer, and chromosome damage (Levine 1982).

Love Canal was very different from Rachel Carson's exposé. Carson's work was that of a committed scientist, working pretty much alone and attempting to reach people through persuasion. Love Canal was different not only for its emphasis on human health, but for its social movement nature. Rather than rely on lobbying and education, Love Canal activists took direct action by community organizing, demonstrating, organizing health studies, and demanding action by state and federal governments. Their approach to a toxic crisis soon became the rallying cry for thousands of neighborhoods and communities around the country that were faced with many forms of toxic contamination. As a result, it has become impossible to speak of environmental health issues without discussing related social movements.

TYPES OF ENVIRONMENTAL HEALTH EFFECTS

Lay Discovery of Environmental Health Effects

Much of the knowledge about environmental health effects has come from people actually or potentially affected by toxic contamination. In some instances, there were major contamination episodes with immediate health effects, such as the spreading of dioxin-laced fuel oil meant to contain road dust in Times Beach, Missouri. In other cases were contamination episodes without immediate health effects, but where such effects were expected to follow, as at Three Mile Island. In other cases there was the discovery of prior contamination episodes, such as both accidental and deliberate releases of radioactivity from the Hanford (Washington State) nuclear facility. Sometimes we find unexplained clusters of disease where people seek the cause, but do not yet have a specific release or emission to trace it to, as in the case of the Gulf War Syndrome. Perhaps the most extreme cases were official experimentation with radioactivity, which included exposing military personnel to nuclear explosions within a mile of ground zero and the injection or projection of radiation on prisoners, retarded facility residents, and others to examine the impact of such doses. Across a variety of situations, the lay discovery of environmental health effects—termed "popular epidemiology" by Phil Brown and Edwin J. H. Mikkelsen (1990/1997)—has been crucial. Lay efforts continue to play pioneering efforts in such areas as environmental causes of breast cancer, the effect of endocrine disruptors on reproduction, and the effects of air pollution on respiratory diseases. In many cases, scientific knowledge lags behind lay identification of diseases and their causes. As well, there is considerable governmental and corporate opposition to an expanded view of environmental causation of disease. This opposition requires lay efforts to become transformed into social movements in order to press for research, remediation, and regulatory prevention.

Environmental justice activism followed the initial burst of community toxic activism (Szasz 1994). Blacks, Latinos, and Native Americans discovered disproportionate placement of landfills, incinerators, and toxic waste sites in neighborhoods with high minority populations. In many cases there was also overexposure to hazards based on class. Superfund cleanups took longer to arrange and were less thorough in minority locations as well. There was also a disproportionate exposure to lead poisoning. Just as the toxic waste movement pushed the broader environmental movement to take on the issues of human health, the environmental justice movement pushed both the toxic waste movement and broader environmental movement to link environmental health with race and class stratification (Brown 1995; Bullard 1993; Hofrichter 1993; Mohai and Bryant 1992). Additionally, the dramatic growth in

women's involvement as leaders and members of toxic waste activist groups has heightened the importance of gender issues in environmental health (Blocker and Eckberg 1989; Brown and Ferguson 1995; Cable 1992; Krauss 1993). In addition, breast cancer activists began to target environmental causes, while exposing medical and governmental slowness in investigating that link. This revelation led to a further emphasis on gender issues in environmental health.

Sociologists often explain laypeople's discovery of and action on environmental hazards through the lens of "frame transformation." This stems from "frame analysis," which focuses on cognitive and ideological shifts in which people transform their value and belief systems and reinterpret causality and responsibility (Gamson et al. 1982; Snow et al. 1986). Louise Kaplan (1997) provides a useful example in her research on the lay discovery of Hanford health effects and citizen pressure for the government to release many documents. She traces a path of initial questioning, followed by extensive self-education through reading, talking with neighbors and others, querying officials, and analyzing primary sources. Ultimately, these citizen activists compelled the disclosure of massive numbers of documents, documented many accidental and planned radioactivity releases, identified thyroid disease among "downwinders," and were instrumental in Energy Secretary Hazel O'Leary's "openness" policy that brought to light many instances of faulty production and storage, extensive releases and accidents, and many unethical radioactivity experiments on captive populations.

Laypeople's sustained self-education, self-organization, and scientific success in identifying environmentally induced diseases and their likely causes is one of the most significant phenomena in the field of environmental health. A growing literature, especially ethnographic case study research, demonstrates the capacities of nonspecialists with little or no higher education to bring to public light the extensive problems of toxic substances on human health (Balshem 1993; Brown and Mikkelsen 1990/1997; Edelstein 1988; Fox 1991; Kaplan 1997; Reich 1991).

Physical Health Effects

As noted already, there are many health effects from toxic substances. In addition to the occupational exposures mentioned earlier, people are exposed through many routes: volatile organic compounds in the water supply, contamination of foodstuffs and animal feed, chemical factory and transportation leakages and explosions, trash incineration, contamination from abandoned toxic waste sites, and use of and exposure to household chemicals, fertilizers, and pesticides.

Toxic substances have been implicated in diseases of all organ systems. Physical health effects of toxics are not a separate category of symptoms and diseases, but are best understood as forms of *poisoning*. Disputes over environmental health effects are of two types. First, there is often actual doubt as to the physical reality of the symptoms themselves, especially multiple chemical sensitivity (Kroll-Smith and Floyd 1997). Second, when symptoms are "accepted," disputes arise about their etiology. Although a few toxins have "signature" diseases (e.g., asbestosis and mesothelioma), most do not. Hence, neither sufferers nor clinicians are likely to attribute individual cases to a toxic exposure. People usually notice environmentally induced diseases when they observe clusters of them, especially if there is a known source (e.g., abandoned toxic waste sites, operating incinerators, deep injection toxic disposal wells, and nearby chemical and other factories). At other times, people learn about excess cancer rates from annual cancer registry reports. Sometimes people notice health effects on animals and become concerned that humans too will be affected.

There is another category of toxic effects that has been the subject of intense debate: the presence of abnormalities that are not specific diseases. The chromosome damage at Love Canal is one example. Another is the presence among Woburn residents of eye blink reflexes attributable to trichloroethylene (Brown and Mikkelsen 1990/1997). Theo Colborne et al. (1996) discuss the high prevalence of reproductive abnormalities that may not necessarily be of immediate health concern. In these examples, we see concern with a range of abnormalities that may very well lead to morbidity in the future. Advocates for environmental health argue that such markers are important evidence that warrants immediate health care, site, remediation, and regulatory action. This makes particular sense if we look at lead. Lead poisoning is now defined at blood levels that do not necessarily show up as clinical morbidity but are likely to become clinically significant based on extensive experience.

This is not the place to catalog all types of health effects; the environmental health and environmental epidemiology texts mentioned earlier can provide finer degrees of detail. It is, rather, important to emphasize that the health effects of toxic substances are an increasingly common part of our landscape. As Steve Kroll-Smith and H. Hugh Floyd (1997) show in their study of "environmental illness" (often called multiple chemical sensitivity or MCS) the routine, ordinary materials of the society have many toxic effects. These MCS sufferers seem to be allergic to many chemicals and plastics that pervade building materials, personal care products, and foods. Colborne et al. (1996) amass a wealth of evidence that many chemically based products, ubiquitous in our daily surroundings, act as endocrine disruptors, affecting female and male reproductive development and capacities, including miscarriages and lowered sperm count. The "hormone havoc" of these chemicals also causes thyroid deficiency and neurological deficits, such as weaker reflexes and lowered IQ scores. The very pervasive polychlorinated biphenyls (PCBs) and dioxins are especially implicated.

Both medicine and epidemiology have difficulty in understanding the relations between toxic substances and morbidity and mortality. Measurement standards have often been very haphazard, and hazard exposure levels have been revised downward by purely experiential processes. This downward revising began with radiation, where the first rating of dangerous exposure was considered to be a visible lesion on the skin—usually by that time a fatal exposure (Caufield 1989). Lead poisoning, which continues to be a major problem, faced a similar problem, where allowable exposures have quite recently been lowered upon viewing the health effects. Although experts were often aware of the need for lower limits, they faced much opposition from skeptical scientists, reluctant government regulators, and corporations that feared the financial costs (Berney 1993). An important current debate on measurement issues involves air particles under 10 microns in diameter. Researchers estimate that these cause 50,000 to 60,000 deaths per year, yet regulatory practices deal only with larger particles (Dockery and Pope 1996).

Mental Health Effects

Researchers have paid much attention to mental health effects because toxic-contamination episodes leave a residue of fear and anxiety. Depression is often found among residents of toxic neighborhoods. Depression among the Woburn families was found to be so deep by a psychiatrist examining the families on behalf of the companies' defense attorneys that after reading his reports, the defense attorneys chose not to call him as an expert witness. Only an order from the judge enabled the plaintiffs to obtain copies of his notes, which referred to the widespread depression (Brown and Mikkelsen 1990/1997).

Psychological effects are amplified by lack of social support. Unlike in natural disasters, people have to fight to gain public recognition of the pollution in human-caused disasters. The litigation so common to toxic sites itself also contributes to the ongoing depression by forcing parents to relive the horrors of a child's illness through the seemingly endless process of depositions, testimony, and numerous consultations with independent experts for both defendants and litigants. This example points to one of the most disturbing aspects of community action on toxics: Remedies and recompense are available only at the cost of intense reliving and public display of the suffering. People lose privacy for their sorrow and are forced to grieve in public. People often can no longer distinguish their private feelings from what is the public record. They are compelled to justify their suffering by legal proof, lest it be diminished and discredited. At Love Canal, too, depression was common. Many residents threatened suicide and several attempted it (Gibbs 1982). Three Mile Island residents also experienced high levels of depression. During the year after the accident, mothers experienced new episodes of affective disorder at a rate three times higher than people in a nonexposed control group in another location (Bromet et al. 1982)

Hypervigilance is common in toxic waste sites, as residents become preoccupied with searching for causes of and responsibility for contamination and with protecting their future health. Ordinary minor health complaints provoke anxiety and concern. A woman at Three Mile Island kept her police scanner on day and night for four years, hoping to find out the reason for the frequent sirens heard in the TMI complex (Lifton ND).

Post-traumatic stress disorder (PTSD) has been found in many toxic waste sites. These people exhibit most characteristics of what Lifton calls the "general constellation of the survivor," a phenomenon he studied extensively in relation to atomic bomb survivors. They retain a "death imprint" of images and memories of the disaster and feel a strong "death anxiety." Many family members experienced "death guilt," based on the feeling that they could have done something to prevent a loved one's death. "Psychic numbing" was also common, with its diminished capacity for feelings, particularly involving apathy, withdrawal, depression, and overall constriction in living. People also suffer "impaired human relationships," sometimes manifested as an inability to comfort one another, even when family members knew that others needed mutual support (Lifton and Olson 1976).

The generalized distress that people who live near toxic waste sites experience can be understood as "demoralization," a feeling of being upset and out of control. Demoralization is widely used in psychiatric epidemiology to measure the emotional state of the general population (excluding those classified as mentally ill). Bruce Dohrenwend and his colleagues (1981) compared the demoralization of Three Mile Island area residents with the clientele of a community mental health center. With a higher score indicating more disorder, the overall mean score of the mental health center clients was 28.3, for TMI-area women 30, and for TMI-area men 25. Twenty-six percent of those interviewed directly after the accident showed severe demoralization. Although this figure declined over the next four months, the researchers calculated that 10 percent of the area population suffered extreme demoralization directly attributable to the accident. Such demoralization can be seen in Duane Gill and Steven Picou's (1995) study of three areas that experienced environmental disasters. Compared to a control group, environmental-disaster residents were more likely to want to move, to experience social disruption and stress, and to engage in avoidance behavior.

The mental health effects of disasters last a considerable time. In one study, researchers followed over time a group of people who experienced the 1972 Buffalo Creek, Kentucky, flood that Kai Erikson (1976) chronicled. That flood, caused by a coal company's poorly constructed, inappropriately used slag dam, was widely blamed on the company rather than nature. Two years after the flood, victims demonstrated more anxiety, depression, social isolation, somatic concerns, and disruption of daily activities than did a control group. Even after four years, victims suffered higher degrees of disturbance. At the site of the Three Mile Island nuclear plant leak, both at the time of the incident and two years after, residents had more symptoms, poorer task performance, higher risk for psychiatric problems, and higher levels of catecholamines (a reliable biochemical marker of stress) in their blood than did controls who lived near an undamaged nuclear facility (Baum et al. 1983).

Based on the planned restart of the TMI reactor, a research team looked at a sample of mothers of young children. A panel of 385 women who had been interviewed after the incident during 1981–1982 provided baseline information. Of these, 52 percent returned questionnaires that were mailed to them one month after the restart. A composite measure of subclinical symptoms of depression, anxiety, and hostility was used, and the researchers found that symptomatology did in fact increase after the restart (Dew et al. 1987).

Even the planned siting of a toxic hazard can cause distress, as found in a survey of a rural community near Phoenix, Arizona, where a hazardous waste facility was to be built. Using the mean demoralization data from Three Mile Island, investigators found that 36 percent of their sample scored higher on demoralization than the mean score of community mental health center clients (Bachrach and Zautra 1985).

In his study of Legler, New Jersey, Michael Edelstein (1988) found that contamination was inherently stigmatizing. People affected by water pollution were scorned by others, just as TMI residents were stigmatized even in distant locations. Victims' own fears were a form of self-stigmatization, as they worried about dreaded health impacts, such as cancers, threats to unborn children, and cross-generational genetic defects.

People in contaminated communities often reassess the environment, seeing it as a malevolent force. Even the home, typically a place of refuge and safety, becomes threatening. Residents lose faith that the world is just and may even think that they deserve what happened to them. (Edelstein 1988: 56–58). Victims lose trust in government and in the ordinary operations of the economy and polity, since the established institutions do not help them. This failure precipitates further emotional distress. Ultimately, as Brown and Mikkelsen (1990/1997) found, people come to believe that there is "no safe place," since contamination is so widespread. Such attitudes even occur in the midst of highly organized communities that are fighting corporations and government.

Community-Wide Effects

Environmental health effects are often community-type effects. Rather than only affecting individuals, contamination episodes harm communities, disrupting ordinary social relations as well as damaging health. Kai Erikson (1976) first pointed this phenomenon out in his groundbreaking work, *Everything in Its Path: The Destruction of Community in the Buffalo Creek Flood*. Subsequently, other sociologists analyzed case studies to further this line of work. Adeline Levine's (1982) study of Love Canal offered the first sociological case study that explained the conflict between lay discoverers of disease on the one hand, and government and corporate parties on the other. Michael Edelstein's (1988) book on "contaminated communities" introduced this term as a standard for research on toxic-affected communities. Stephen Couch and Steve Kroll-Smith's (1990) study of an underground mine fire in Centralia, Pennsylvania, added the emphasis on how internal divisions concerning health effects and corporate/governmental responsibility pitted groups of residents against each other, further

undermining the bonds of community. This problem of "corrosive communities" (Freudenburg and Jones 1991) leads to fundamental rifts in the social bonds of community, including rancorous disputes between individuals and between groups. Residents also face discrimination by bankers in terms of mortgages and insurance companies in terms of coverage (Couch et al. 1997).

Communities facing contamination episodes were often in the midst of "chronic technological disasters" (Couch and Kroll-Smith 1985), long-term, unfolding problems that often had no visible starting point, but which unravelled the social fabric. Henry Vyner (1988) pursued this idea with the concept of "invisible environmental contaminants," in his case mostly concerning ionizing radiation. Because they were unseen, Vyner termed them "occult," mysterious factors that people had a hard time seeing or identifying.

Health and environment research pushes us to reconceptualize our level of analysis and to take on a more community-oriented approach. Traditional epidemiology likes to differentiate itself from clinical medicine in that it takes into account *populations*. Hence it can see patterns, and even causes, that would be invisible to health professionals who look at individual cases. Such a population-based approach is clearly necessary, but is only partly sufficient. In fact, much of what epidemiology does is to examine *populations* while using *individual-level data,* for instance, studying personal risk factors and heart disease in a state. In some cases this approach is insufficient. For example, if one wanted to study race or class difference in toxic hazards, one could easily be stymied by small numbers. One alternative is to selectively study the toxic exposures of large numbers of minority populations in order to characterize their risks, and to compare the results with that from known populations that are more typically white.

Going beyond this, a more purposive examination of community-level characteristics might be much more fruitful. Researchers often fail to do this for four reasons:

1. Statistically, they want large random samples of individuals.

2. They are trained to think in terms of traditional medical and demographic variables at the individual level, rather than to think about community characteristics. Thomas LaVeist (1992) offers an example showing that black political power at the municipal level is highly related to infant mortality.

3. Epidemiologists lack the interest or ability to examine communities in depth, including their industrial, economic, geographic, and political histories. Social scientists and epidemiologists are beginning to do this sort of study, in which they find different hazard exposures depending on the history and location of geographic areas (c.f., Krieg 1995; Maxwell 1996).

4. Epidemiologists often fear the "ecological fallacy," in which erroneous estimates of individuals' behavior or risks are made on the basis of aggregate community-level characteristics. While such mis-estimation can occur, there is also the less recognized problem of the "individual fallacy," whereby researchers miss the larger social context by virtue of examining only individual cases, when in fact certain variables can only (or best) be defined at the level of community. Examples include the effect of social disorganization on newborn care, the intensity of neonatal care on infant mortality, and the effect of religious patterns on suicide (Maxwell 1996; Schwartz 1994; Susser 1994a, 1994b).

There are many aspects of community that need to be taken into account in studying the effects of toxins. These include people's ontological sense of security, provisions of personal security and social support, the security of the home, the structures and bonds of the family, sets of relationships, physical and geographic features, racial/ethnic distributions and cultures, class distributions and cultures, economic and industrial history, sharing and control of local resources, shared political beliefs, governmental structures, civic empowerment, shared goals for social change, and community health status. While this chapter is not the place to develop all of these elements, it is important to recognize the complexity that is involved. The following example indicates how this might be applied.

Martha Balshem (1993) offers an alternative view of community context in her study of how a Philadelphia cancer prevention project clashed with the white, working-class neighborhood's belief system. The project identified excess cancer in the urban Tannerstown area, a fact widely known by the residents and the media. The medicalized approach of the health educators focused on individual habits, especially smoking, drinking, and diet. Tannerstown residents countered this worldview with their belief that the local chemical plant and other sources of contamination were responsible for the increased cancer.

The professionals approached the working class as a monolithic mass of people with many unhealthy behaviors and nonscientific attitudes. What professionals call working-class "fatalism" appears more sensible as a response to economic insecurity in the face of Philadelphia's declining industrial workforce. The health educators medicalized working class fatalism as a "disease" that prevents people from complying with cancer prevention experts' prescriptions. To change lifestyles appeared to be merely what Balshem (1993: 57) notes is "to adapt to life in the 'cancer zone'." As one example of lay reframing of the problem, Balshem recounts one case of a woman having to get her husband's medical record rewritten, and having an autopsy to show that he didn't die of lung cancer, but of metastatic pancreatic cancer, so that he would not be blamed for smoking-induced cancer. This effort was made on an individual level of experience, as well as in a general sense of community aggrievement.

Like the above example, many of the major works dealing with health and the environment are community-based studies. Much of the survey and other quantitative research has centered on community-level effects as well. This centrality of community is useful for medical sociology overall to develop more community-based approaches.

Social Responsibility

Residents in Love Canal (Levine 1982), Woburn (Brown and Mikkelsen 1990/1997), and many other sites have emphasized how environmentally induced disease sufferers and their allies target the corporations they hold responsible for contamination episodes, as well as various levels of government for failing to do their job in recognition and remediation.

The sum of these social movement approaches to environmental health has been to firmly situate environmental health as tied to the fundamental social structure. In addition to seeing race, class, and gender differences in exposure and social action, we can link the health effects of substances to a larger political-economic view of the world. Chemicals provide one example. The post-World War II explosion of science and technology was based largely on the expansion of chemicals in the form of plastics and petroleum derivatives. This development was also central to much unparalleled economic growth. The rapid innovation in the chemical industry led to unchecked application of these substances in the environment, resulting in an as-yet-unknown scourge of disease. The powerful economic role of these substances has made it extremely difficult to examine their health effects.

Residents in contaminated communities have often expected local, state, and federal government support for their claims, at least in earlier years. The failure of many government bodies to support victims' claims has led to increased mistrust of government. Residents in many contaminated communities have become radicalized in response to governmental failure to respond to citizen complaints concerning corporate polluters (Cable and Cable 1995; Krauss 1989). In addition, federal regulatory failure has created a climate of mistrust toward the government (Szasz 1994). Corporate unwillingness to take responsibility, combined with government inaction, delays the appropriate understanding of environmental health effects, their causes, and their treatment.

Since environmental health effects are so widespread, it is perhaps surprising that we do not have more research, medical education, government effort, and social recognition. But if we add the other significant element I have just addressed—how environmental health effects are tied to fundamental societal structure—it is not surprising that we have seen so much resistance to dealing with environmental health. The next section examines difficulties and disputes in dealing with environmental health, including methodological issues, disputes over lay involvement, disputes among scientists, and opposition by government and corporate actors.

ISSUES AND CONFLICTS IN THE DEFINITION AND MEASUREMENT OF ENVIRONMENTAL HEALTH

Standards of Proof

There are often problems in studying environmental health, such as inadequate history of the site, the unclarity of the route of contaminants, determining appropriate sampling locations, small numbers of cases, bias in self-reporting of symptoms, getting appropriate control groups, people's movement in and out of exposed areas, lack of knowledge about the characteristics and effects of certain chemicals, and unknown or varying latency periods for carcinogens and other disease-causing agents. Given the many forms of cancer reported for all municipalities or counties in a state (e.g., on annual state cancer registry reports), it is likely that some elevations will be attributable to chance (National Research Council 1991). Raymond Neutra (1990) points out that environmental epidemiology studies usually have such small numbers of exposed persons that observed rates must often be 20 times that of expected rates in order to attain statistical significance. This presents many problems for people trying to determine if there is a disease cluster, prior to the daunting difficulty of linking the cluster to a purported cause (such as a local polluter). Some scientists argue that these problems make determining specific causes of environmental disease improbable. Others, including the National Research Council's (NRC) Committee on Environmental Epidemiology, argue that traditional approaches are not necessarily appropriate. The NRC argues that the same flaws in data can be understood in the opposite fashion: We cannot reject claims of environmental causation precisely because we don't have the right data. Further, small effect sizes should not be viewed as obstacles. Even low relative risks are very powerful if large numbers of people are affected. Along the same line, consistency across many studies should be acceptable as evidence of etiological linkages, even if some of those studies do not meet statistical significance (National Research Council 1991). Although it is not always easy to evaluate the effects of the removal of a hazard, researchers have shown such findings; no new cases of leukemia developed in Woburn once contaminated wells were shut, and birth weights returned to normal in Love Canal and the Lipari, New Jersey, landfill after exposure was decreased (National Research Council 1991: 31–42). David Ozonoff and Leslie Boden (1987) distinguish statistical significance from public health significance, since an increased disease rate may be of great public health significance even if statistical probabilities are not met. They believe that epidemiology should mirror clinical medicine more than laboratory science by erring on the safe side of false positives.

Even without statistical significance, we may find a clear association based on such factors as strength of association; consistency across persons, places, circumstances, and time; specificity of the exposure site and population; temporality of the exposure and effect; biological plausibility of the effect; coherence with known facts of the agent and disease; and analogy to past experience with related substances. Pointing to the above factors, as well as to more "provable" experimental models and dose-response curves, Austin Bradford Hill (1987) argues that there are no hard and fast rules for establishing causality. Given the potential dangers of many classes of materials, he believes it often wise to restrict a substance to avoid potential danger.

Residents in contaminated communities view traditionally oriented scientists as too concerned with having each element of scientific study as ideal as possible. From their point of view, there have been visible health effects and clear evidence of contamination, as well as strong indications that these two are related. Indeed, much of environmental epidemiology has been developed as a result of such lay input.

Despite the many shortcomings in environmental epidemiology data, reviews of the research show that most controlled studies find associations between hazardous waste sites and human health (Upton et al. 1989; National Research Council 1991). Indeed, lay disease discovery and social movement action have played tremendous roles in expanding the scientific base of environmental epidemiology.

Other Obstacles to Knowledge on Environmental Health

Environmental health has been inadequately studied both by epidemiology and by medicine. The previous section pointed to many such reasons. In addition, environmental epidemiologists have found it hard to gain federal and private grant support for research. In medical training, occupational and environmental medicine have been relegated to a minor position, and the environmental component gets less attention than the occupational (Castorina and Rosenstock 1990; IOM 1988). In one survey of all Massachusetts physicians, those whose practices were located within communities that have EPA National Priority List (NPL) sites (Superfund sites) within their borders were no more knowledgeable about environmental health hazards than those whose practices were not located in communities with NPL sites (Brown and Kelley 1996). Medical centers and research institutions are not necessarily interested, since environmental health has low prestige and little funding and can put medical facilities in conflict with local centers of power.

Corporations have fought against recognition of environmental health effects because of the financial cost involved in settlements, fines, production restructuring, and alternative forms of disposal. This opposition has involved resistance and deception to state and federal regulatory agencies (Szasz 1994), lobbying for environmental deregulation (Gelbspan 1997), and vigorously fighting citizens' complaints

about environmental health effects (Brown and Mikkelsen 1990/1997; Harr 1995).

Government agencies have been reluctant to affirm most relationships between contaminants and disease. Environmental activists argue that one reason is the fear that business will be harmed. Another stated reason is that governmental failures to regulate chemicals and other toxic substances are a source of public anger, and governments do not want to be criticized for their shortcomings (Bullard 1993; Clarke 1989; Gibbs 1995).

In terms of resource availability, laypeople generally don't have the ability to carry out the research necessary to make their cases. It is significant that the burden of proof is on the contaminated communities, rather than the parties who contaminated them or on the public health and regulatory agencies. As a result of these various obstacles, citizens have themselves had to be central actors in discovering and dealing with toxic contamination.

Lay Involvement

Dramatic environmental catastrophes shaped an alarmed public that brought environmental health to prominence. The contamination at Love Canal, the dioxin exposure at Times Beach, Missouri, the dioxin explosion in Seveso, Italy, the Union Carbide explosion of methyl isocyanate (MIC) in Bhopal, India, the Michigan feed contamination with polybrominated biphenyls (PBBs), and the leukemia cluster at Woburn, Massachusetts, were among the major incidents that made citizens consider the importance of environmental health. Lay involvement in contaminated communities has led to some of the most significant social legislation in recent decades. The Environmental Protection Agency was set up to attend to widespread public concern over the environment. The Love Canal episode led to the Superfund program in 1980. And, as mentioned above, lay-initiated health studies have been central to the development of environmental epidemiology.

Yet many epidemiologists and government officials have criticized lay involvement on the assumption that it must be biased. We can see a good example in the Woburn toxic waste crisis, where a major health survey was conducted by an alliance of Harvard School of Public Health biostatisticians and Woburn residents. This study was a massive source of information on adverse pregnancy outcomes and childhood disorders from 5,010 interviews, covering 57 percent of Woburn residences with telephones. The researchers trained 235 volunteers to conduct the survey, taking precautions to avoid bias. Other data included information on 20 cases of childhood leukemia (ages 19 and under), which were diagnosed between 1964 and 1983, and the state environmental agency's water model of the two contaminated wells. Childhood leukemia was found to be significantly associated with exposure to water from wells G and H. Children with leukemia received an average of 21.2 percent of their yearly water supply from the wells, compared to 9.5 percent for children without leukemia. Controlling for risk factors in pregnancy, the investigators found that access to contaminated water was associated with perinatal deaths since 1970, eye/ear anomalies, and CNS/chromosomal/oral cleft anomalies. With regard to childhood disorders, water exposure was associated with kidney/urinary tract and lung/respiratory diseases (Lagakos et al. 1986). Due to lack of resources, this study would not have been possible without community involvement. Yet precisely this lay involvement led professional and governmental groups—the Department of Public Health, the Centers for Disease Control, the American Cancer Society, and the EPA—to charge that the study was biased (Brown and Mikkelsen 1990/1997). Such charges erroneously assume that laypeople must have biases that will interfere with research and that scientists automatically have no biases. This kind of outdated perspective clearly fails to understand the drastic changes in how we now view the relationship between science and politics.

Oppositional Professionals

Lay discovery has prompted many scientists to reevaluate their traditional approaches. The expansion of the nation's toxic waste crisis has shaped the awareness of epidemiologists and other scientists in a more critical direction. "Oppositional professionals" (Brown 1998) come from two different backgrounds. The first group are veterans of the late '60s and early '70s—people already part of a larger social movement who find themselves past college, in professions, and faced with carrying out jobs and developing careers. The second type do not come from an activist background but find a large kinship with the activists, and seek to reform their professions and institutions in the process. Whether the oppositional professionals come from one path or the other, they play a major role in environmental health issues. Here, the popular epidemiology of the laypeople is joined to the critical epidemiology of the oppositional professionals.

Some scientists began with a traditional perspective and were simply won over to supporting contaminated communities. Beverly Paigen (1982), who worked with laypeople in Love Canal, spoke of her new awareness:

> Before Love Canal, I also needed a 95 percent certainty before I was convinced of a result. But seeing this rigorously applied in a situation where the consequences of an error meant that pregnancies were resulting in miscarriages, stillbirths, and children with medical problems, I realized I was making a value judgment...whether to make errors on the side of protecting human health or on the side of conserving state resources.

John Till, who heads the Dose Reconstruction Study at the Hanford Nuclear Facility, which is reconstructing historical dosages of radioactive iodine releases, recounted how he had been transformed by the process of being part of what he terms a "public study." He came to grasp the importance of openness to the public and of access to classified information. He found a great empathy for the Hanford downwinders and a special understanding of the concerns of Native Americans in the area, who viewed Hanford as an assault on their entire heritage (Till 1994).

As the number of critical epidemiologists grows, we may see a greater number of well-designed health studies in which laypeople play a central role. What can such scientists do? Steve Wing (1994) puts forth an alternative conceptualization of epidemiology that taps the concerns of both popular epidemiology activists and critical epidemiologists:

1. Ask not what is good or bad for health overall, but for what sectors of the population.

2. Look for connections between many diseases and exposures, rather than looking at merely single exposure-disease pairs.

3. Examine unintended consequences of interventions.

4. Utilize people's personal illness narratives.

5. Include in research reporting the explicit discussion of assumptions, values, and the social construction of scientific knowledge.

6. Recognize that the problem of controlling confounding factors comes from a reductionist

approach that looks only for individual relations rather than a larger set of social relations. Hence, what are nuisance factors in traditional epidemiology become essential context in a new ecological epidemiology.

7. Show humility about scientific research, combined with a commitment to supporting broad efforts to reform society and health.

NEW METHODS AND MEASURES NEEDED FOR IMPROVED KNOWLEDGE AND ACTION ON HEALTH AND THE ENVIRONMENT

Sociologists and others are really at an early stage in research on health and the environment, and their greatest challenge now is probably the methodology. We do have health studies from specific toxic waste sites and from occupational exposures, which offer us a good amount of knowledge. But these are often carried out in crisis situations and involve very small numbers of people, and they may involve very high concentrations of toxins. Further, they often take quite a long time and wind up being the subjects of endless debate.

What is really needed is more routine monitoring. One helpful feature would be the addition to regular national health surveys of questions on environmentally related illnesses. This would provide a larger picture of prevalence, which could be linked to databases of environmental variables. This would help shift the typical emphasis from mortality, since there are many environmental illnesses for which morbidity is a more significant measure. Another important innovation would be toxic disease registries. The Agency for Toxic Substances and Disease Registry now has one, but only for Superfund sites, and it requires individuals to specifically give permission to be included. These points on monitoring and registries are, of course, larger issues than individual researchers can deal with. They represent broader goals we should be pursuing for the future.

But at present there is much that can be accomplished. Researchers and activists need to spend more time thinking about how to make clear connections between community contexts, environmental variables, and health outcomes. They need to decide what are the best health outcomes, both in terms of data access and in terms of plausible connections to environmental quality.

Scholars need to decide what size geographical areas are most useful. Studies today range from census tracts to zip codes to cities to metropolitan statistical areas. They need to figure out how different area units are needed to best answer our questions. It is necessary to get better measures of the characteristics of various geographic areas. Existing data sources give an unbelievably wide array of units of measurement for such items as toxic releases, type of releasing facilities, water quality, and air quality. Data access is also difficult. Extracting data from the EPA is cumbersome, requiring tedious Freedom of Information Act requests and lengthy waits. It would also be helpful to link cross-state data, since scientists are unable to match exposure in one state with morbidity and mortality in another. In states without cancer registries, researchers lack necessary geographical levels of data. Even where there is a registry, a state may use county-level data rather than city- and town-level data.

Cancer incidence and mortality is not sufficient. Other less serious illness must also be studied. Among other things, this would generate larger numbers. Mortality from any one cause is not sufficient. Morbidity studies are widely done in occupational safety and health, where there is a longer history of knowledge about relationship of disease to exposure.

Researchers need to develop creative models that study health outcomes in relation to a variety of inputs, including political structure, public participation, access to health services, economic factors, population density, racial/ethnic proportions, environmental quality, and access to the natural environment. In addition to the quantification necessary for the above connections, the field needs more qualitative work on the illness experience of people living in toxic areas. In developing new, creative models, medical sociology can offer much to the study of health and the environment through its well-developed critique of the medical model, its literature on illness experience, and its contributions in health services research.

SUMMARY

In summary, I want to point out the common elements shared by medical sociology and environmental sociology, the field which has pioneered the study of environmental health. At the same time, I want to note areas of environmental health research that can inform other work throughout medical sociology. Citizens' environmental health concerns have been a prominent issue in American public life over the last two decades. It is striking that Jonathan Harr's (1995) *A Civil Action,* examining the legal issues of the Woburn toxic waste case, has been so popular; the paperback has been steadily on the *New York Times* best seller list for over two years as of this writing.

In studying toxic waste activism, we see the prominence of lay perceptions of health and illness, patient explanatory models, lay/professional differences in health knowledge, social movements in health care, and the conflictual nature of medical diagnosis. There are a number of common elements in these two areas of sociology that can help steer future research in environmental health and also provide general theoretical directions for medical sociology overall.

In medical sociology, the uncertainty theme is very common, dealing with the various uncertainties in medical knowledge. In environmental sociology, there is considerable uncertainty about hazard measurements and about causal relationships between environmental factors and health outcomes.

Both fields are very concerned with the nature of risks: Who decides what risks are acceptable, and what is the proper balance between risks of personal safety and risks of societal benefit. This brings up the additional issue of how a society, or parts of a society, decide on what science and technology developments are appropriate and beneficial.

The above elements of uncertainty and risk are clear examples of lay/professional differences. Other such differences involve the perception of the situation, what medical sociology would term illness experience as opposed to biomedical disease, and what environmental sociology would often see as the lay experience of hazards as opposed to the calculations of risk assessors. The "popular epidemiology" approach, taken by growing numbers of people and groups, motivates lay disease discovery and lay participation. This approach offers many opportunities for expanding lay involvement throughout health care. In related fashion, we can understand the reorientation of professionals, through "critical epidemiology," to take on a more public-based approach to environmental health.

Many forms of illness result in social stigma, including mental illness, AIDS, and cancer. Disabling conditions, which medical sociology often examines, likewise are often stigmatized. When we see how contaminated communities are the victims of stigma, we can apply the concept of stigma to the community level.

The importance of communities is central. In contextualizing health and illness, medical sociology moves away from a bare epidemiological concern with people as units of analysis and situates them in communities that are geographic, cultural, ethnic, and sometimes based on illness or condition. So much of the

meaning of illness and how to treat it stems from social networks and social support, as well as from community norms. In environmental sociology, the community has been central, since it is the focus of how people experience technological and natural disasters, as well as routine environmental conditions. Case studies of community response to these crises are central to the way environmental sociology views the world.

In studying the impact of social movements, the study of lay action on toxins has shown the importance of social movements in defining illness and suffering, in providing remediation, and in struggling with government, establishment science, and corporations over the responsibility for illness and suffering. Just as health social movements have expanded our knowledge base of reproductive concerns, drug side effects, unequal access, biased treatment, and unnecessary surgery, these movements have shaped the way our society knows about environmental health.

At the same time, there are examples of citizen reaction that are not well founded. Sheldon Krimsky and Alonzo Plough's (1988) discussion of the scare about Alar residue on apples demonstrates how rapidly a nonissue can become an issue. In all social movements, such overreaction occurs as an almost automatic reaction to the many cases in which real problems were denied. Overreaction to feared environmental threats also stems from the uncertainties of living in a world that is indeed full of risks, some of them new, and some that have recently come to public attention.

Health inequalities are an important overlap area as well. Environmental sociology has been profoundly influenced by the emphasis on environmental inequality, usually based on geographic areas. The recent growth in interest on inequalities on the part of medical sociology provides a solid source of new approaches, especially in terms of using aggregate data on people.

Both medical sociology and environmental sociology share an important intersection with the sociology of science. This intersection involves understanding the social biases of establishment science, biases inherent in scientific method as well as biases caused by social structures such as corporate control. These fields have employed both political economic analyses and science-in-action approaches. Medical sociology has focused widely on the critique of the biomedical model, something very important for any work on health and the environment.

Popular action on environmental concerns focuses extensively on prevention. Although the magnitude of direct morbidity and mortality from toxins is less than that of other causes of disease and death, the pervasiveness of environmental risks and the potential for long-term impacts is socially very significant. Action on environmental health already centers largely on prevention rather than on treatment and can offer important lessons for other arenas of social health.

REFERENCES

BACHRACH, KENNETH M., and ALEX J. ZAUTRA. 1985. "Coping With a Community Stressor: The Threat of a Hazardous Waste Facility." *Journal of Health and Social Behavior* 26: 127–41.

BALSHEM, MARTHA. 1993. *Cancer in the Community: Class and Medical Authority.* Washington D.C.: Smithsonian Institution Press.

BAUM, ANDREW, RAYMOND FLEMING, and JEROME E. SINGER. 1983. "Coping With Victimization by Technological Disaster." *Journal of Social Issues* 39: 117–38.

BECK, ULRICH. 1992. *Risk Society.* London: Sage.

BERNEY, BARBARA. 1993. "Round and Round It Goes: The Epidemiology of Childhood Lead Poisoning, 1950-1990." *Milbank Memorial Fund Quarterly* 71:3–39.

BLOCKER, JEAN, and DOUGLAS LEE ECKBERG. 1989. "Environmental Issues as Women's Issues: General Concerns and Local Hazards." *Social Science Quarterly* 70(3): 586–93

BRODEUR, PAUL. 1985. *Outrageous Misconduct: The Asbestos Industry on Trial.* New York: Pantheon.

BROMET, EVELYN J., D. K. PARKINSON, H.C. SCHULBERG, L.O. DUNN, and P.C. GONDEK. 1982. "Mental Health of Residents Near the Three Mile Island Reactor: A Comparative Study of Selected Groups." *Journal of Preventive Psychiatry* 1:225–76.

BROWN, PHIL. 1995. "Race, Class, and Environmental Health: A Review and Systematization of the Literature." *Environmental Research* 69:15–30.

BROWN, PHIL. 1998. "Contested illnesses: Lay, professional, and governmental perspectives on environmentally induced diseases." Lecture at Rensselaer Polytechnic Institute, March 4.

BROWN, PHIL, and EDWIN J. MIKKELSEN. 1990/1997. *No Safe Place: Toxic Waste, Leukemia, and Community Action.* Berkeley: University of California Press.

BROWN, PHIL, and FAITH FERGUSON. 1995. " 'Making a Big Stink': Women's Work, Women's Relationships, and Toxic Waste Activism." *Gender & Society* 9:145–72.

BROWN, PHIL, and JUDITH KELLEY. 1996. "Physicians' Knowledge of and Actions Concerning Environmental Health Hazards: Analysis of a Survey of Massachusetts Physicians." *Industrial and Environmental Crisis Quarterly* 9: 512–42.

BULLARD, ROBERT, ed. 1993. *Confronting Environmental Racism: Voices From the Grassroots.* Boston: South End Press.

CABLE, SHERRY. 1992. "Women's Social Movement Involvement: The Role of Structural Availability in Recruitment and Participation Processes." *Sociological Quarterly* 33: 35–47

CABLE, SHERRY, and CHARLES CABLE. 1995. *Environmental Problems, Grassroots Solutions: The Politics of Grassroots Environmental Conflict.* New York: St. Martin's Press.

CARSON, RACHEL. 1962. *Silent Spring.* New York: Houghton Mifflin.

CASTORINA, JOSEPH, and LINDA ROSENSTOCK. 1990. "Physician Shortage in Occupational and Environmental Medicine." *Annals of Internal Medicine.* 113: 983–86.

CAUFIELD, CATHERINE. 1989. *Multiple Exposures: Chronicles of the Radiation Age.* New York: Perennial Books.

CLARKE, LEE. 1989. *Acceptable Risk? Making Decisions in a Toxic Environment.* Berkeley: University of California Press.

COLBORNE, THEO, DIANE DUMANOSKI, and JOHN MEYER. 1996. *Our Stolen Future: Are We Threatening Our Fertility, Intelligence, and Survival? A Scientific Detective Story.* New York: Dutton.

COUCH, STEPHEN R., and J. STEPHEN KROLL-SMITH. 1985. "The Chronic Technical Disaster: Towards a Social Scientific Perspective." *Social Science Quarterly* 66:564–75.

COUCH, STEPHEN R., and J. STEPHEN KROLL-SMITH. 1990. *The Real Disaster Is Above Ground: A Mine Fire and Social Conflict.* Lexington, KY: University Press of Kentucky.

COUCH, STEPHEN R., and J. STEPHEN KROLL-SMITH, eds. 1992. *Communities at Risk: Collective Responses to Technological Hazards.* New York: Peter Lang.

COUCH, STEPHEN R., J. STEVE KROLL-SMITH, and JOHN P. WILSON. 1997. "Toxic Contamination and Alienation: Community Disorders and the Individual." *Research in Community Sociology* 17: 95–115.

DEW, MARY AMANDA, ET AL. 1987. "Mental Health Effects of the Three Mile Island Nuclear Reactor Restart." *American Journal of Psychiatry* 114:1074-77.

DOCKERY, DOUGLAS, and ARDEN POPE. 1996. "Epidemiology of Acute Health Effects: Summary of Times Series Studies" In *Particles in Our Air: Concentrations and Health Effects,* ed. Richard Wilson and John Spengler. Cambridge: Harvard University Press, pp. 123–147.

DOHRENWEND, BRUCE, BARBARA S. DOHRENWEND, GEORGE J. WARHEIT, GLENN S. BARTLETT, RAYMOND L. GOLDSTEEN, KAREN GOLDSTEEN, and JOHN L. MARTIN. 1981. "Stress in the Community: A Report to the President's Commission on the Accident at Three Mile Island." *Annals of the New York Academy of Sciences* 365: 159–74.

EDELSTEIN, MICHAEL. 1988. *Contaminated Communities: The Social and Psychological Impacts of Residential Toxic Exposure.* Boulder: Westview.

ENGELS, FRIEDRICH. 1971. *The Condition of the Working Class in England,* trans. and ed. W.O. Henderson and W.H. Chaloner. Oxford: Blackwell.

ERIKSON, KAI. 1976. *Everything in Its Path: The Destruction of Community in the Buffalo Creek Flood.* New York: Simon & Schuster.

ERIKSON, KAI. 1994. *A New Species of Trouble: Explorations in Disaster, Trauma, and Community.* New York: Norton.

FOX, STEVE. 1991. *Toxic Work: Women Workers at GTE Lenkurt.* Philadelphia: Temple University Press.

FREUDENBURG, WILLIAM, and THOMAS JONES. 1991. "Attitudes and Stress in the Presence of Technological Risk: A Test of the Supreme Court Hypothesis." *Social Forces* 69: 1143–68.

GAMSON, WILLIAM, BRUCE FIREMAN, and STEVEN RYTINA. 1982. *Encounters With Unjust Authority.* Homewood, IL: Dorsey.

GELBSPAN, ROSS. 1997. *The Heat is On: The High Stakes Battle Over Earth's Threatened Climate.* Reading, MA: Addison-Wesley.

GIBBS, LOIS. 1982. "Community response to an emergency situation: Psychological destruction and the Love Canal." Paper presented at the American Psychological Association. August 24.

GIBBS, LOIS. 1995. *Dying From Dioxin: A Citizen's Guide to Reclaiming Our Health and Rebuilding Democracy.* Boston: South End Press.

GILL, DUANE A., and J. STEVEN PICOU. 1995. "Environmental disaster and community stress." Paper presented at Third International Conference on Emergency Planning and Disaster Management, Lancaster, England.

GOLDSMITH, JOHN R., ed. 1986. *Environmental Epidemiology.* Boca Raton, FL: CRC Press.

GOLDSTEIN, INGE, and MARTIN GOLDSTEIN. 1986. "The Broad Street Pump." In *Environmental Epidemiology,* ed. John R. Goldsmith. Boca Raton, FL: CRC Press, pp. 37–48.

GREENBERG, MICHAEL R., ed. 1987. *Public Health and the Environment: The United States Experience.* New York: Guilford.

HARR, JONATHAN. 1995. *A Civil Action.* New York: Random House.

HILL, AUSTIN BRADFORD. 1987. "The Environment and Disease: Association or Causation." In *Evolution of Epidemiologic Ideas,* ed. Kenneth Rothman. Chestnut Hill, MA: Epidemiology Resources, Inc., pp. 15–20.

HOFRICHTER, RICHARD, ed. 1993. *Toxic Struggles: The Theory and Practice of Environmental Justice.* Philadelphia: New Society Publishers.

HYNES, H. PATRICIA. 1989. *The Recurring Silent Spring.* Elmsford, NY: Pergamon.

INSTITUTE OF MEDICINE (IOM). 1988. *Role of the Primary Care Physician in Occupational and Environmental Medicine.* Washington, D.C.: National Academy Press.

KAPLAN, LOUISE. 1997. "The Hanford Education Action League: An Informed Citizenry and Radiation Health Effects." *International Journal of Contemporary Sociology* 34: 255–66.

KRAUSS, CELENE. 1989. "Community Struggles and the Shaping of Democratic Consciousness." *Sociological Forum* 4: 227–39.

KRAUSS, CELENE. 1993. "Women and Toxic Waste Protests: Race, Class and Gender as Resources of Resistance." *Qualitative Sociology* 16: 247–62.

KRIEG, ERIC. 1995. "A Socio-Historical Interpretation of Toxic Waste Sites: The Case of Greater Boston." *American Journal of Economics and Sociology* 54: 1–14.

KRIMSKY, SHELDON, and ALONZO PLOUGH. 1988. *Environmental Hazards: Communicating Risks as a Social Process.* Dover, MA: Auburn House.

KROLL-SMITH, STEVE, and H. HUGH FLOYD. 1997. *Bodies in Protest: Environmental Illness and the Struggle Over Medical Knowledge.* New York: New York University Press.

LAGAKOS, STEVEN, BARBARA J. WESSEN, and MARVIN ZELEN. 1986. "An Analysis of Contaminated Well Water and Health Effects in Woburn, Massachusetts." *Journal of the American Statistical Association* 81: 583–96.

LaVEIST, THOMAS. 1992. "The Political Empowerment and Health Status of African-Americans: Mapping a New Territory." *American Journal of Sociology* 97:1080–95.

LEVINE, ADELINE. 1982. *Love Canal: Science, Politics, and People.* Lexington, MA: Heath.

LIFTON, ROBERT. "Psychological Report on Three Mile Island Litigation." Unpublished manuscript.

LIFTON, ROBERT, and ERIC OLSON. 1976. "The Human Meaning of Total Disaster: The Buffalo Creek Experience." *Psychiatry* 39: 1–18.

MAXWELL, NANCY. 1996. "Land use, demographics, and cancer incidence in Massachusetts communities." Sc.D. dissertation, Boston University School of Public Health.

McKEOWN, THOMAS. 1976. *The Modern Rise of Population.* New York: Academic Press.

MOELLER, DADE W. 1992. *Environmental Health.* Cambridge: Harvard University Press.

MOHAI, PAUL, and BUNYAN BRYANT, eds. 1992. *Race and the Incidence of Environmental Hazards.* Boulder: Westview.

NATIONAL RESEARCH COUNCIL. 1991. *Environmental Epidemiology,* Vol. I. Public Health and Hazardous Wastes. Washington D.C.: National Academy Press.

NEUTRA, RAYMOND R. 1990. "Counterpoint From a Cluster Buster." *American Journal of Epidemiology* 132: 1–8.

ORWELL, GEORGE. 1958. *The Road to Wigan Pier.* New York: Harcourt, Brace.

OZONOFF, DAVID, and LESLIE I. BODEN. 1987. "Truth and Consequences: Health Agency Responses to Environmental Health Problems." *Science, Technology, and Human Values* 12:70–77.

PAIGEN, BEVERLY. 1982. "Controversy at Love Canal." *Hastings Center Reports* 12(3):29–37.

POPE, ARDEN, and DOUGLAS DOCKERY. 1996. "Epidemiology of Chronic Health Effects: Cross-Sectional Studies." In *Particles in Our Air: Concentrations and Health Effects,* ed. Richard Wilson and John Spengler. Cambridge: Harvard University Press, pp. 149–67.

REICH, MICHAEL. 1991. *Toxic Politics: Responding to Chemical Disasters.* Ithaca, NY: Cornell University Press.

ROBINSON, JAMES G. 1991. *Toil and Toxics: Workplace Struggles and Political Strategies for Occupational Health.* Berkeley: University of California Press.

ROSNER, DAVID, and GERALD MARKOWITZ. 1989. *Dying for Work: Workers' Safety and Health in Twentieth-Century America.* Bloomington, IN: Indiana University Press.

SCHNAIBERG, ALLAN, and KENNETH ALAN GOULD. 1994. *Environment and Society: The Enduring Conflict.* New York: St. Martin's Press.

SCHWARTZ, SALLY. 1994. "The Fallacy of the Ecological Fallacy: The Potential Misuse of a Concept and the Consequences." *American Journal of Public Health* 84:819–24.

SMITH, BARBARA ELLEN. 1981. "Black Lung: The Social Production of Disease." *International Journal of Health Services* 11:343–59.

SNOW, DAVID A., E. BURKE ROCHEFORD, JR., STEVEN K. WORDERN, and ROBERT D. BENFORD. 1986. "Frame Alignment Processes, Micromobilization, and Movement Participation." *American Sociological Review* 51:464–81.

STEINGRABER, SANDRA. 1996. *Living Downstream: An Ecologist Looks at Cancer and the Environment.* Reading, MA: Addison-Wesley.

SUSSER, MERVYN. 1994a. "The Logic of Ecological: I. The Logic of Analysis." *American Journal of Public Health* 84:825–29.

SUSSER, MERVYN. 1994b. "The Logic of Ecological: II. The Logic of Design." *American Journal of Public Health* 84:830–35.

SZASZ, ANDREW. 1994. *Ecopopulism: Toxic Waste and the Movement for Environmental Justice.* Minneapolis: University of Minnesota Press.

TILL, JOHN. 1994. "Update from the Hanford Dose Reconstruction Project." Presentation at Radiation Health Effects and Hanford Conference. Saturday September 10. Spokane, Washington.

UPTON, ARTHUR C., THEODORE KNEIP, and PAOLO TONIOLO. 1989. "Public Health Aspects of Toxic Chemical Disposal Sites." *Annual Review of Public Health* 10:1–25.

VYNER, HENRY M. 1988. *Invisible Trauma: The Psychosocial Effects of the Invisible Environmental Contaminants.* Lexington, MA: Lexington Books.

WAITZKIN, HOWARD. 1983. *The Second Sickness: Contradictions of Capitalist Health Care.* New York: Macmillan.

WEED, D. L. 1995. "Epidemiology, the Humanities, and Public Health." *American Journal of Public Health* 85:914–18.

WING, STEVE. 1994. "Limits of Epidemiology." *Medicine and Global Survival* 1:74–86.

11 THE SOCIOLOGY OF HEALTH BEHAVIOR AND HEALTH LIFESTYLES

WILLIAM C. COCKERHAM, *University of Alabama at Birmingham*

The purpose of this chapter is to examine current research in medical sociology on health behavior and health lifestyles. In past historical periods, health was a given; that is, a person was either healthy or unhealthy and tended to take this situation more or less for granted (Hitzler and Koenen 1994). Today, however, in late or postmodern society, this view of "health" has changed. In advanced societies, health is no longer taken for granted; rather, it has become a condition to be achieved and maintained through personal effort (Cockerham 1998; Gallagher 1988; Kotarba and Bentley 1988). That is, people are healthy if they "work" at it, and risk disease and premature death if they do not. This circumstance has its origins in the public's recognition that medicine is limited in its capacity to cope with chronic diseases and the association of such diseases with unhealthy lifestyles (Crawford 1984). Consequently, the responsibility for one's own health ultimately falls on one's self, and it is this realization that is helping promote health behavior (Goldstein 1992). Although personal responsibility for health is more obvious in the United States, which lacks national health insurance, the perception is also common in developed societies with such insurance (Cockerham, Kunz, and Lueschen 1988; Herzlich and Pierret 1987; Lüschen et al. 1995).

Health behavior is defined as the activity undertaken by people for the purpose of maintaining or enhancing their health, preventing health problems, or achieving a positive body image. This definition goes beyond that provided in 1966 by Stanislav Kasl and Sidney Cobb, who depicted health behavior solely as the activity of healthy people to prevent illness. It does not limit participation in health behavior and health lifestyles to healthy people trying to stay healthy but also includes the physically handicapped and people with chronic illnesses like diabetes and heart disease,

who seek to control or contain their condition through diet, exercise, and other health-related activity. It likewise reflects contemporary modes of health-related practices primarily motivated by the desire of the individual to look and feel good. For example, we now know from studies of wellness programs in American business corporations that the health goals of some people are focused on enhancing their bodily appearance and physical condition so they can get more enjoyment out of life; becoming healthier in this circumstance is secondary to the desire to look and feel good (Conrad 1988a, 1988b, 1994; Kotarba and Bentley 1988). For many other people, however, their health behavior is primarily intended to prolong their lives and prevent sickness and injury (Cockerham 1998; Goldstein 1992). Yet regardless of the underlying motivation to behave in a healthy manner, it is clear that health-promoting behavior is becoming increasingly common (Cockerham et al. 1988; Conrad 1988a, 1988b, 1994; Goldstein 1992).

The significance of living as healthful a life as possible is not a new concept. Historical research by Harvey Green (1986) on health and physical fitness in the United States showed a long-term interest on the part of Americans to be healthy for a variety of reasons, including religious beliefs, patriotism, the potential of upward social mobility, the association of health with ideas about success, and the desire to be healthier. What is new is the reawakened interest in health behavior that originated in the fitness movements in the 1960s and is stimulated by the increased recognition within the general public that: (1) the major disease patterns have changed from infectious illnesses to chronic diseases that medicine cannot cure; (2) chronic diseases are often caused by unhealthy living; and (3) taking control over one's own health situation by adopting a health lifestyle is perhaps the only viable strategy an individual can pursue in preventing or coping with chronic disease

(Crawford 1984; Glassner 1989; Goldstein 1992). Health professionals and the mass media have also spread the message that people need to avoid certain behaviors and adopt others as part of their daily routines if they want to maximize their life expectancy and be as healthy as possible for as long as possible. These recommendations are supported by ample evidence that a lack of exercise, diets high in fats, stress, smoking, excess body weight, alcohol and drug abuse, unprotected sex, and exposure to chemical pollution promote disease and premature death.

The focus of research in medical sociology, however, is not on the discrete health practices of individuals, which are more appropriately defined as self-care behavior (Dean 1989), but rather on the transformation of this behavior into its aggregate form: health lifestyles. Health lifestyles are collective patterns of health-related behavior based on choices from options available to people according to their life chances (Cockerham and Ritchey 1997; Cockerham, Rütten, and Abel 1997). A person's life chances are the probabilities they have in life to find satisfaction and are largely determined by their socioeconomic status, age, gender, race, ethnicity, and other factors that shape lifestyle choices. The behaviors that are generated from these choices can have either positive or negative consequences on body and mind, but they nonetheless form an overall pattern of regular health practices that constitute a lifestyle. Health lifestyles include contact with the medical profession for preventive care and routine checkups, but the majority of activities take place outside of health-care delivery systems. They include decisions about diet, exercise, smoking, alcohol and drug abuse, coping with stress, relaxation and rest, using automobile seatbelts, personal hygiene, and other health-related actions.

The standard public health approach treats health behavior and lifestyles as matters of individual choice and targets the individual to change his or her harmful health practices largely through education. The theoretical models used in such programs, like the Health Belief Model and the Stages of Change Model, are typically based on individual psychology (Sweat and Denison 1995). The effects of social systems on health tend to be ignored, even though social situations and conditions may be ultimately responsible for causing the health problem (Lomas 1998; McKinlay 1995; Sweat and Denison 1995). A sociological perspective, however, allows us to analyze health lifestyles as a social phenomenon that goes beyond the psychology of the single person and uncovers the source of risk behavior in the norms, practices, and values of groups, social classes, and society at large that contour both individual and collective behavior. For example, some people smoke cigarettes even though it is well established that smoking is a major risk behavior for heart disease and lung cancer. Yet the observation that they smoke does not explain why they do so, or why smoking is embedded in the social context of their lives. Identification of the latter is necessary if the causes and reasons for the persistence of poor health practices are to be altered or eliminated.

Furthermore, a sociological perspective allows the researcher to address macro-level conditions like poverty, the stress of economic downturns, and environmental pollution, over which the individual has little or no control but must cope with as part of his or her social circumstances. These conditions not only engender unhealthy living situations in themselves, but also contribute to negative health lifestyles as individuals and groups respond to them with heavy drinking and smoking, disregard for personal and/or public safety, inattention to diet, and the like. Applying sociological forms of analysis to risk behavior patterns within lifestyles provides a more complete explanation of that behavior by accounting for both the individual and the social.

Sociology also has something unique to offer the study of health lifestyles in terms of theoretical understanding. Health lifestyles are not just matters of individual psychology, but rather a collective form of behavior grounded in social structure and societal influences. Sociology brings to the discussion of lifestyles a rich theoretical literature that takes these considerations into account. While this literature is in its infancy, it nonetheless draws on classical and contemporary sources involving some of the discipline's major theorists. We will begin our discussion, accordingly, by examining the theoretical discourses in sociology on lifestyles generally and then apply these theoretical considerations to the conceptualization of health lifestyles and the empirical research on the topic.

THEORETICAL PERSPECTIVES

One of the most important new developments in sociological theory is the increased attention given to lifestyles as a key concept in explaining human social behavior (Abel 1991; Chaney 1996; Giddens 1991). Lifestyles are adopted by individuals and are utilitarian social practices and ways of living that reflect personal, group, and socioeconomic identities (Giddens 1991). Stated simply, the study of lifestyles helps make sense of what people do, why they do it, and what doing it means to them and others (Chaney 1996). But a great deal of work needs to be done to understand why and how people adopt, maintain, and change their lifestyles not only in terms of more empirical elaboration, but also in regard to theoretical issues (Williams 1995). Aside from Max Weber's (1978) seminal insight, lifestyle theory has only recently begun to emerge. This is seen most prominently in the work of Giddens (1991) and Bourdieu (1984), yet little of this literature has been transferred to empirical research on health lifestyles (Cockerham, Abel, and Lüschen 1993; Cockerham 1997a, 1997b; Williams 1995). Health lifestyles are a lifestyle subtype, and the theoretical foundation underlying lifestyle research generally is appropriate for conceptualizing health lifestyles as well. In this section we will examine the theoretical perspectives of Weber, Giddens, and Bourdieu on lifestyles and apply them to health.

Max Weber

Weber (1978:932) links lifestyles to status by pointing out that a distinguishing characteristic of status is "status honor or prestige which is normally expressed by the fact that above all else a specific *style of life* is expected from all those who wish to belong to the circle." Status groups are aggregates of people with similar status, class backgrounds, and political influence, and they originate through a sharing of similar lifestyles or as a means to preserve a particular style of life. The lifestyles of status groups are based not so much on what they and the people within them produce but on what they consume. As Weber (1978:933) put it, "One might thus say that classes are stratified according to their relations to the production and acquisition of goods: whereas status groups are stratified according the principles of their *consumption* of goods as represented by special styles of life."

Consumption is, of course, not independent of production; rather lifestyle differences between status groups are based on their relationship to the means of consumption, not the means of production in a Marxist sense. The economic mode of production sets the basic parameters within which consumption occurs, but does not determine or even necessarily affect specific forms of it (Bocock 1993). This is because the consumption of goods and services conveys a social meaning that displays, at the time, the status and social identity of the consumer. Consumption can therefore be regarded as a set of social and cultural practices that *establish* differences between groups, not merely a means of *expressing* differences that are already in place because

of economic factors (Bocock 1993:64; Bourdieu 1984). It is the use of particular goods and services through distinct lifestyles that ultimately distinguishes status groups from one another.

Three terms in the original German are used by Weber to express his concept of lifestyles. These terms are *Stilisierung des Lebens* (stylization of life) or, more simply, *Lebensstil* (lifestyle), along with *Lebensführung* (life conduct), and *Lebenschancen* (life chances), which comprise the two basic components of lifestyles (Abel and Cockerham 1993; Cockerham, Abel, and Lüschen 1993). *Lebensführung* refers to the choices that people have in their selection of lifestyles, and *Lebenschancen* is the probability of actually realizing those choices. Ralf Dahrendorf (1979:73) notes that while Weber is vague about what he means by life chances, the best interpretation is that life chances are: "the crystallized probability of finding satisfaction for interests, wants and needs, thus the probability of the occurrence of events which bring about satisfaction." The probability of acquiring satisfaction is anchored in structural conditions that are largely socioeconomic, but Dahrendorf suggests the concept of life chances also involves rights, norms, and social relationships (the probability that others will respond in a certain manner). Weber does not consider life chances to be a matter of pure chance; rather, they are the chances people have in life because of their social situation. His overall thesis is that chance is socially determined, and social structure is an arrangement of chances. Hence, lifestyles are not random behaviors unrelated to structure but typically are deliberate choices influenced by life chances.

Consequently, Weber's most important contribution to conceptualizing lifestyles in sociological terms is to impose a dialectical capstone over the interplay of choice and chance in lifestyle determination (Cockerham et al. 1993). Choices and the constraints of life chances work off one another to determine a distinctive lifestyle for individuals and groups. The identification of life chances as the dialectic opposite of choice in Weber's lifestyle scheme provides the theoretical key to conceptualizing the manner in which lifestyles are operationalized in the empirical world. It can be said that individuals have a range of freedom, yet not complete freedom, in choosing a lifestyle. That is, people are constrained in determining their lifestyle but have the freedom to choose within the constraints that apply to their situation in life.

However, Weber did not view patterns of social action as the uncoordinated practices of individuals. Rather, he saw them as regularities and uniformities repeated by numerous actors over time. The ways in which individuals act in concert, not as single actors, are the focus of his attention (Kalberg 1994). For example, Weber suggests that the "spirit" of capitalism was not uniquely Western, and not particularly unusual if considered merely an attribute of individuals. He suggests that there have always been economically successful people who conducted their business on a systematic basis, had frugal personal habits, worked harder than their employees, and invested their earnings (Bendix 1960:54–55). But, as individuals, they could not establish a dominant economic system like capitalism. "In order that a manner of life so well adapted to the peculiarities of capitalism could be selected at all," states Weber (1958:55), "i.e. should come to dominate others, it had to originate somewhere, and not in isolated individuals alone, but as a way of life common to whole groups of men [and women]." It is the origin of this lifestyle that Weber insists requires attention, and he finds it in the Protestant Ethic of the early Calvinists, whom he credits for the expansion of modern capitalism.

Although Weber recognizes the constraining effects of structure, such as his warning of the potential for bureaucratic organizations to suppress freedom of action by the individual, he ultimately favors the capacity of the individual to assume control over his or her circumstances (Alexander 1987; Löwith 1982; Mommsen 1989; Roth 1987). Whereas the individual may not be capable of breaking the iron cage of bureaucratic submission for all, he or she can break it for himself or herself by finding ways to maneuver around its barriers (Löwith 1982). Weber (1949:124–25) observes, for instance, that people associate the strongest feelings of freedom with those actions in which they pursue and achieve a clear purpose rationally with the most adequate means at their disposal. All social action in Weber's view takes place in contexts that imply both constraints and opportunities, with the actor's interpretive understanding (*Verstehen*) of the situation guiding interaction (Kalberg 1994).

Weber's lifestyle concept can account for individual choice and structural constraints, thus merging the functions of both structure and agency. The structure–agency debate is one of the core issues in sociological theory. *Structure* refers to the rules and resources associated with societies, institutions, social classes, groups, and roles that both constrain and enable individuals to act, while *agency* is the freely chosen activities of individuals. Proponents of structure emphasize the power of structural conditions in determining social behavior, while advocates of agency favor the ability of actors to choose their behavior regardless of structural constraints. Weber recognizes

the importance of structure in his notion of life chances, but appears to favor agency in the form of choice. His overall contribution to our understanding of contemporary lifestyles is that lifestyles: (1) are associated with status groups, therefore they are principally a collective, rather than individual phenomenon; (2) represent patterns of consumption, not production; and (3) are shaped by the dialectical interplay between life choices and life chances, with choice playing the greater role.

Anthony Giddens

Anthony Giddens (1991) describes how modernity—the mode of social life resulting from the Industrial Revolution—influences contemporary lifestyles. He explains that modernity differs from all previous forms of social order because of its dynamism, global impact, and the degree to which it undercuts traditional customs and habits. The more tradition loses its hold, observes Giddens, the more individuals are forced to negotiate lifestyle choices among a variety of local and, increasingly, global options. Consequently, late modernity promotes a diversity of lifestyle choices, and even people in the lowest social classes have some choice because, in Giddens's view, no culture eliminates choice entirely, and survival at the bottom of society necessitates some degree of choice in daily matters.

However, Giddens does not overlook the influence of sources external to the individual on lifestyle choices and cites group pressures, role models, and socioeconomic conditions as examples. In conditions of late modernity, people are likely to be pushed by social situations into choosing a particular lifestyle, or as Giddens (1991:81) puts it, "we have no choice but to choose." That is, it is necessary to adopt the appropriate lifestyle of a specific group or stratum of society if one wishes to belong to it and move within it. Giddens (1991:82) therefore makes the pertinent observation that "a lifestyle involves a cluster of habits and orientations, and hence has a certain unity—important to a continuing sense of ontological security—that connects options to a more or less ordered pattern." As a result, the particular lifestyle choices an individual makes tend to fit a pattern that makes alternative choices "out of character." The basic message is that lifestyles not only fulfill utilitarian needs, but also provide material to form one's self-identity.

Giddens therefore takes the position that lifestyles occur within the constraints and opportunities provided by an individual's social class location, but everyone—to some extent—is forced to adopt reflexivity constructed lifestyles to sustain his or her self-identity. This reflexivity is grounded in a climate of change resulting from society's evolution into the next stage of modernity. Giddens's (1991) work provides an introduction to new conditions, noting how changing perceptions of time and space, combined with other developments like increasingly sophisticated and abstract money systems and the penetration of technical knowledge throughout society, promote constant change. As social life becomes more open, the contexts for action more plural, and authority more diverse, Giddens finds that lifestyle choices are increasingly more important in the construction of self-identity and daily activities.

Another area of Giddens's (1984) work having relevance for lifestyle theory is his notion of the duality of structure as the centerpiece of his structuration theory. Giddens explains that neither structure nor agency is independent of the other, rather, the two are codependent. Structure is not possible without action because action reproduces structure. Action is not possible without structure because action begins with a given structure resulting from prior actions. An agent is not the abstract or dependent subject of action, but rather an individual who constructs social behavior. That behavior, however, is embedded in a structure and contributes to that structure's continuation or change. Structures are therefore not predetermined but evolve through social interaction. Since structures are both the means and outcomes of action, they contain a dual dimension; that is, structures are both objective (constraining) and subjective (enabling) at the same time.

The logical appeal of Giddens's notion of the duality of structure is based on his recognition that structures empower agents as well as constrain them and, in the process, can be changed by the practices of those agents. This insight helps to overcome arguments that structures are rigid, impervious to agency, and impossible to change, while assigning agents the capacity for innovation and improvisation. Giddens does note that structures place limits on the range of options open to an actor or plurality of actors in particular circumstances. Moreover, he acknowledges that it is possible for the structured properties of social systems to stretch out, in time and space, to the point at which they are beyond the control of any individual actors. Nevertheless, he strongly favors agency over structure. Giddens (1984:129), in fact, claims that there is no such entity as a distinctive type of "structural explanation" in the social sciences and maintains that "all explanations will involve at least implicit reference both to the purposive, reasoning behavior of agents and to its intersection with constraining and enabling features of the social and material contexts of that behavior."

Giddens (1991) views lifestyles as structured patterns of behavior with norms, values, and boundaries, yet through the feedback processes of social agents, they are reproduced or transformed over time as people operationalize them. Whereas structure may hinder the creativity of agents in constructing or modifying lifestyles, agents have the capacity to change structures and are ultimately viewed as the stronger entity. What we primarily gain from Giddens's analysis is the recognition of: (1) late modernity's role in fostering a diversity of lifestyle choices, (2) the necessity of having to choose, (3) the tendency of choices to cluster into distinct patterns, (4) the role played by lifestyles in expressing self-identity for the individual, and (5) the dual nature of structure as empowering and constraining.

Pierre Bourdieu

Whereas Weber and Giddens favor agency in the structure–agency debate, Bourdieu favors structure. Bourdieu's principal focus is on the question of how routine practices of individuals are influenced by the external structure of their social world, and how these practices, conversely, contribute to the maintenance of that structure (Jenkins 1992). The key concept in this regard is that of "habitus," which Bourdieu (1990:53) defines as "systems of durable, transposable dispositions, structured structures predisposed to operate as structuring structures, that is, as principles which generate and organize practices and representations that can be objectively adapted to their outcomes without presupposing a conscious aiming at ends or an express mastery of the operations necessary in order to attain them." What Bourdieu is saying is that knowledge of social structures and conditions produces enduring orientations toward action that are more or less routine, and when these orientations are acted upon they tend to reproduce the structures from which they are derived.

The lasting nature of the orientations and control imposed by habitus on thought, perception, and action signals a dominant role for structure in guiding social behavior. As Bourdieu and Wacquant (1992) explain, the human mind is socially bounded and constructed within the limits of experience, upbringing, and training. People are able to assess their circumstances, but their perceptions are typically shaped by their particular social and economic situation. "The *habitus*," states Bourdieu (1990:54), ". . . ensures the active presence of past experiences, which, deposited in each organism in the form of schemes of perception, thought and action, tend to guarantee the 'correctness' of practices and their constancy over time, more reliably than all formal rules and explicit norms." Therefore, habitus provides a cognitive map of an individual's social world and channels behavior down paths that appear to be reasonable to the individual and society.

However, situations vary—so habitus can vary to fit the situation. Habitus is not, in Bourdieu's view, a mechanical response to all situations; rather, the dispositions it reflects are subject to change by the individual. The same habitus can generate different, even opposite outcomes, since people are not mechanically pushed about by external forces but are able to act on their own. Bourdieu (1977), in fact, calls for the abandonment of theories that explicitly or implicitly treat social practices as mechanical reactions to situations or roles. But he maintains that rejection of mechanistic theories does not imply that we should bestow on some creative free will the power to determine the meaning of situations and the intentions of actors. The dispositions generated by habitus tend to be compatible with constraints set by society through experience, socialization, and the realities of class circumstances; therefore, usual modes of behaving—not unpredictable novelty—typically prevail.

Bourdieu's conceptualization of habitus as a mind-set that operates more or less routinely—even unconsciously—to guide behavior has prompted critics like Jeffrey Alexander (1995) to argue that habitus has no independent power to direct action. Alexander (1995:136), calling habitus a "Trojan horse for determinism," claims it is a reflection and replication of exterior structures rather than a locus for voluntary action. The habitus, in Alexander's view, merely translates exterior social structures into subjective constraints in a noninterpretive way. This scenario places actors in a continuous adaptation to their external environment instead of in a state of discourse with it. What the habitus initiates, states Alexander (1995:138), "is an endless and circular account of objective structures structuring subjective structures that structure objective structures in turn." Because it does not have its own emergent properties, internal complexity, and logic, Alexander concludes that the habitus has no real independence and cannot be a means of establishing a true micro-macro link between the individual and society in accounting for social behavior.

Yet is this really the case? Certainly Bourdieu's concept of habitus can suggest an endless and circular routine of structure shaping structures and lacks the properties, complexity, and logical pathways seen in Sigmund Freud's notion of the personality or George Herbert Mead's concept of self. But the habitus does provide a relatively seamless blending of macro and micro processes by assimilating exterior structures into

the subjectivity of the individual and providing a general frame of reference, with boundaries and constraints, for the conduct of everyday life. The habitus generates perceptual schemes that promote consistent and routine forms of behavior; it also, as Bourdieu regularly insists, reorients the agent toward new or modified behaviors when social situations require change. The habitus accounts best for routine and day-to-day behaviors grounded in normative structures that require little thinking and adjustment, but it nevertheless has the capacity for creative direction. Habitus is also a strategy-generating entity that enables agents to cope with unforeseen and changing circumstances and, in Bourdieu's (1977) view, makes possible the achievement of an infinite diversity of tasks. As Bourdieu (Bourdieu and Wacquant 1992:133) explains: "habitus is not the fate that some people read into it." As a product of history, "it is an *open system of dispositions* that is constantly subjected to experiences and therefore constantly affected by them in a way that either reinforces or modifies its structures."

Bourdieu (Bourdieu and Wacquant 1992:135) therefore rejects the notion that his scheme is overly deterministic, but he assigns a strong preference to structure in influencing behavior. In his view, people can consciously inhibit or alter their dispositions, but categories of perception and appreciation—the basis for self-determination—are themselves largely determined by socialization and experience, which include recognition of the reality of their class situation. In Bourdieu's concept, social practices are based upon *both* the objective structures that define external constraints affecting interaction and the immediate lived experience of agents, which shape internal categories of perception and appreciation; however, while the two components are equally necessary, they are not equal (Wacquant 1992:11). When it comes to the extent to which dispositions to act are socially determined, Bourdieu (Bourdieu and Wacquant 1992:136) notes that "one could say that I am in a sense hyper-determinist."

Consequently, Bourdieu awards epistemological priority to objective conditions over subjectivist understanding (Wacquant 1992:11), even though he regards both as important. Structure is therefore dominant over the habitus mind-set from which perceptions and behavioral choices are derived. This view suggests that the selection of a course of social action is affected by life chances to a much greater extent than allowed by Weber or Giddens. Bourdieu's work indicates that life choices are not only constrained but largely determined by life chances. Although individuals choose their lifestyles, they do not do so with complete free will, as the habitus predisposes them toward certain choices. They have the option to reject or modify these choices, but Bourdieu maintains that an agent's choices are generally consistent with his or her habitus. Choices also tend to reflect class position because persons in a similar social class share the same general habitus. As Bourdieu (1990) explains, internalization of the same structures and common schemes of perception and appreciation produce the same or similar set of distinctive signs or tests; the result is a wide sharing of a class-based world view. The habitus ("a structured and structuring structure") is structured by an individual's class conditions and, in turn, structures social action thereby reproducing class differences.

When it comes to the operationalization of lifestyles, Bourdieu (1984:171) says the following sequence of action takes place: (1) objective conditions of existence combine with positions in the social structure to (2) produce the habitus, which consists of (3) a system of schemes generating classifiable practices and works, and (4) a system of schemes of perception and appreciation (taste), that, together, produce (5) specific classifiable practices and works that (6) result in a lifestyle. As systematic products of habitus, lifestyles become sign systems that are socially distinct and function as forms of cultural capital with symbolic values. This is seen in Bourdieu's view that the human body constitutes physical capital, which is transformed into cultural capital as a consequence of social practices like lifestyles (Shilling 1993; Turner 1992). For example, different classes have different styles of exercising, eating, and dressing that define their bodies in particular ways. According to Turner (1992:88), "weight lifting articulates working-class bodies, while jogging and tennis produce a body which is more at ease in the middle-class milieu or habitus." Thus, Turner (1992:90) concludes that the body is a site on which the cultural practices of the various social classes are inscribed.

It is therefore certain that structure is the dominant aspect of Bourdieu's concept of lifestyles. The notion of "structure" suggests persistence, repetition, and self-maintenance; hence, habitation, or the tendency of lifestyles to become habitual, is a key feature of his perspective. Lifestyles not only reflect social differences in ways of living, but reproduce them. Compared to Weber and Giddens, whose ideas emphasize the voluntary nature of lifestyles, Bourdieu's approach is grounded on the social parameters of lifestyle selection. For instance, class-based lifestyles, as unitary sets of tastes or distinctive preferences, are practices that are classified and supported not only by participants within a class, but also by other classes.

In sum, Bourdieu's contributions to our understanding of lifestyles fall into two major areas: (1) identifying the role of habitus in creating and reproducing lifestyles, and (2) emphasizing this role by showing how structure, or in Weberian terms, life chances, determines lifestyle choices. In Bourdieu's work, the gap between life chances and life choices in Weber's original analysis is significantly reduced through his concept of habitus, which incorporates both within a single entity. The importance of Bourdieu's perspective is that it presents a theoretical model of social practice that includes consideration of the powerful effects of structure (Jenkins 1992). His work serves as an important counter-weight to perspectives that view lifestyle decisions almost entirely in terms of personal choice and reflexive control (Williams 1995:601).

Health Lifestyles

The theoretical insight of Weber, Giddens, and Bourdieu concerning lifestyles generally helps us synthesize a concept of health lifestyles. As previously stated, health lifestyles can be considered "collective patterns of health-related behavior based on choices from options available to people according to their life chances" (Cockerham et al. 1997:338). This definition is obviously Weberian in orientation as seen in the depiction of health lifestyles as a collective form of health behavior resulting from the interplay of choice and chance. The general orientation reflected in Weber's writings points toward choice/agency being dominant over chance/structure in health lifestyle selection.

The form of rational thought that underlies individual and collective choices in participating in health lifestyles tends to be formal. Formal rationality (*Zweckrationalität*) is the purposeful calculation of the most efficient means and procedures to realize goals as compared to substantive rationality (*Wertrationalität*), which is the realization of values and ideals based on tradition, custom, piety, or personal devotion. In Western society, formal rationality dominates its substantive counterpart as people seek to achieve their objectives by employing the most efficient means and, in the process, tend to disregard or minimize substantive rationality because it may be ineffective, inefficient, time-consuming, cumbersome, and resistant to change.

Although some people pursue fitness activities because they believe health is good in itself and a moral obligation (Conrad 1994), the bulk of the literature shows that people do not participate in health lifestyles primarily because health is an idealized end state; rather, they adopt such lifestyles because they want to be healthy in order to use their health as a means to reach practical goals (d'Houtand and Field 1984; Cockerham 1998). This situation suggests, consistent with Weber's perspective, that while health lifestyles are oriented toward producing health, the aim of the activity is ultimately toward its consumption as people want to use their health for a practical end: living longer, avoiding disease, and feeling and looking good.

Giddens ties individual self-identity to lifestyle practices, thereby suggesting that participation in health lifestyles is intrinsically related to a person's sense of self. However, people could be motivated to engage in healthy activities not only because of their sense of who they are, but also because they are forced through group pressures and the social changes associated with the evolution of the next stage of modernity to take greater responsibility for their own health. As traditional centers of power and authority (i.e., the medical profession) decline in strength, the individual is left more on his or her own to secure a healthy life, and participation in a health lifestyle is the obvious strategy for accomplishing this goal. Structural conditions in society can both enable and constrain the individual with respect to health lifestyle participation, but the degree of participation suggested by Giddens's work would presumably be determined largely by agency.

Following Giddens, Ronald Hitzler and Elmar Koenen (1994) claim that people today have no choice but to choose whether or not they want to be healthy because health in contemporary society is something that requires activity. The question thus becomes how they deal with their choices. Hitzler and Koenen's analysis suggests three possibilities: (1) copying an existing health lifestyle connected to a particular pattern of behavior and following it, rather than making new choices all the time; (2) being so disorganized in one's life that one is unable to choose or follow a stable and consistent health lifestyle; or (3) seeing individuality itself as determining one's health lifestyle, as is the case when a person wants to show that he or she is different from others and chooses radically different health practices. Most people apparently choose the first option; they copy an existing health lifestyle and adopt it as their own. In doing so, they become connected to and part of a larger normative pattern of behavior characteristic of groups, social classes, and societies. Therefore, with the twenty-first century at hand, health lifestyles have become an activity that individuals are supposed to choose in a normative sense. They may not do so, but the normative and common sense expectation in contemporary society is that they will do something to promote their health.

Bourdieu (Bourdieu and Wacquant 1992) argues, however, that there is little empirical evidence to suggest that collective patterns of social behavior are merely a deliberate product of independent individuals; without the social conditions of autonomy, individuals, in his view, cannot be autonomous. It is the internalization of external structures in the habitus, including not just past experiences and socialization, but also the realization by the individual of his or her class circumstances, that largely determines perceptions. This is why Bourdieu depicts the habitus as a socialized subjectivity whose limits are set by society and embedded in individual perceptions of social reality. The outcome is a tendency on the part of the habitus to react to situations in a consistent fashion. When it comes to health lifestyles, the role of the habitus is to create and reproduce such lifestyles in a manner consistent with the structural parameters of social expectations and experience. Bourdieu is able to explain the pathways by which structure provides durable health lifestyles among the various social classes; thus, his work is particularly fruitful in accounting for the relationship between class-generated structures and health-related behavior (Williams 1995).

Bourdieu's emphasis on structure clearly sets him apart from Weber and Giddens. His project is to construct a model of social practice that recognizes the influence of external structures on the individual; but, in doing so, his work is subject to severe criticism that he underestimates the role of agency in shaping social behavior (Alexander 1995; Jenkins 1992; Williams 1995). "Choice," states Williams (1995:588), "is largely underplayed." Nevertheless, Bourdieu interjects the importance of structure back into the structure-agency debate and brings lifestyle theory to the discussion.

As Williams (1995) points out, how we theorize the structure–agency problem in relation to health and lifestyle is a key question in medical sociology that has yet to receive much attention. Among the few existing studies, Cockerham and his colleagues (1988, 1993) advanced a Weberian argument in their earlier research that participation in health lifestyles was largely a matter of choice. But they reversed themselves in their most recent work (Cockerham et al. 1997) and assigned priority to chance (structure) over choice. They found Bourdieu's assertion that structure determines the perceptual boundaries underlying choice to be the critical factor in health lifestyle selection.

In a subsequent study of the decline of life expectancy in the late twentieth century in the former socialist countries of Russia and Eastern Europe, Cockerham (1999) found that negative health lifestyles derived from structural conditions were the major social determinant of the downturn in longevity. In other research on corporate wellness programs, Peter Conrad and Diana Chapman Walsh (1992) observed that such programs represented the potential expansion of a corporation's social control from the workplace into the private lives of their workers. Although a worthy measure, the promotion of health lifestyles and the positive feedback provided to workers who exercised, lost weight, and quit smoking, allowed business corporations to promote worker productivity and extend their jurisdiction over their workers to leisure-time activities.

Of course, people in corporate wellness programs are not necessarily representative of participants in health lifestyles generally, nor are the structural conditions fostered by communism applicable to health lifestyles in the West. But these studies, in the absence of other evidence, demonstrate how structure can be more dominant than agency in special situations. The task for theory development is not to focus exclusively on either structure or agency, but rather to develop an integrated concept. Obviously, additional research is needed to determine the full relationship between structure and agency with respect to health lifestyles, but to date, studies emphasizing the role of agency in health lifestyles are particularly lacking. Also missing is research on health lifestyles as a form of social control. The work of Michel Foucault (1973) would seem to be especially relevant for theoretical insight in this area. Foucault details, for example, how elite groups use knowledge as power to impose their standards of normality on society, including norms for health. And, while there are Marxist critiques of the emphasis on health lifestyles as a means by which the state can evade direct accountability for health matters by displacing responsibility to the individual (Waitzkin 1983), research in this area is likewise absent. In conclusion, the study of health lifestyles is potentially rich in theoretical discourse, and even the limited amount of work accomplished negates charges that medical sociology is an atheoretical enterprise.

EMPIRICAL RESEARCH

The research literature on health lifestyles in sociology began to develop only in the 1980s as the extent and durability of participation in such lifestyles in Western society became apparent. The focus in most studies is on determining differences and similarities between social classes in health lifestyle participation, with one

body of research detailing variations between social classes and another noting growing similarities. The discussion has recently moved, however, from descriptive reports of social behavior, notable in leisure studies research, to a more analytical and theory-oriented debate (Lüschen et al. 1995). The concentration on the relationship between social class and health lifestyles, however, has not been matched by studies focusing on alternative statuses like gender, age, race, and ethnicity. In this section we will first review studies focused on social stratification and then examine the few sociological studies of variables other than class.

Social Class

Among the earliest and most influential lifestyle studies considering health practices is Bourdieu's (1984) book, *Distinction*. Based on survey data collected during the 1960s and not published until several years later, Bourdieu examined class competition and the role of culture in class reproduction in France. He constructed a general model of stratified lifestyles based on differing cultural tastes in art, music, food, dress, and the like. Although his focus was not on health lifestyles, he included an analysis of food and sports preferences in his study. He found that distinct class preferences existed in these areas. People in the professions, for example, preferred tennis, while the working class favored soccer. The working class was attentive to notions of masculinity and the physical strength of males and also tended to choose foods that were cheap, nutritious, and abundant. The professional class, in contrast, was more concerned about body image and opted more for food that was light, tasty, and lower in calories. Bourdieu's principal interest, however, was not in describing class differences, but, as previously discussed, in determining how the routine practices of individuals are influenced by the external structure of their social world, and how these practices, in turn, contribute to the maintenance of that structure (Jenkins 1992). But, in respect to eating and sports, Bourdieu had detailed how a class-oriented habitus shaped health lifestyles.

Another early study was that of Cockerham and his colleagues (1986a) who examined similarities in health lifestyles by seeking to determine whether such lifestyles spread across class boundaries. This research tested the Weberian notion that while lifestyles were specific to particular social classes, they could also expand within a class structure and encompass several classes instead of the one in which it originated. Utilizing data collected in Illinois, these researchers (Cockerham et al. 1986a) found that considerable similarity existed between socioeconomic groups in certain lifestyle practices involving appearance, food habits, physical exercise, smoking, and alcohol use. Exercise, for example, emerged as a behavioral pattern that people from all social classes accepted as something a person should do and that most people say they attempt in some form, ranging from short walks to sports participation. When it came to food, most people, regardless of their class position, attempted to obtain the best nutritional value in the food available.

In subsequent research comparing Americans and Germans (Cockerham et al. 1986b, 1988; Lüschen, Cockerham, and Kunz 1989), Cockerham found a distinct lack of difference between social classes, races, and occupational groups in health lifestyles. Although the quality and style of participation in health lifestyles varied by social class, a general form of participation had nonetheless spread across class boundaries in these studies. The fact that Germans had government-sponsored national health insurance and Americans were more on their own in securing medical care and health insurance did not have significant effects on health lifestyle participation in either nation. Other studies in the European Union also found few or no differences in health lifestyles between social classes in Germany, France, Belgium, and the Netherlands (Lüschen et al. 1995) or between the Dutch and Germans (Stevens et al. 1995). Although some respondents reported poor health behavior, such as above average alcoholic intake and heavy smoking, others were markedly health conscious, and this group represented sizable proportions of people from all social strata, which minimized class differences.

An important exception to claims that health lifestyles have penetrated class lines in Western Europe is found in Great Britain. In a major survey conducted by Mildred Blaxter (1990) in England, Wales, and Scotland, this study found that important differences in health lifestyles persisted between social classes, with the upper and upper-middle classes tending to take much better care of their health than the working class and the lower class. People who lived in the most disadvantaged social circumstances were the least likely to behave in a healthy manner, as were manual workers and those with low incomes and education. Blaxter's (1990) principal conclusion was that the social circumstances within which a person lives (which could be inferred as "structure") were more important for health than health-related behavior. Some behaviors, such as not smoking, were definitely relevant for health; but, on balance, healthy behavior was most effective in a positive social environment and least effective in adverse social conditions. Other research shows greater similarity in health lifestyles among socioeconomic lines in the south of England, the most affluent region of the country (Calnan 1989), but such lifestyles remain identified in Britain as a predominantly middle-class practice (Bunton and Burrows 1995). Much of the current British research is oriented toward identifying the health lifestyles of special population groups (i.e., working-class mothers, adolescents, menopausal women, the homeless and socially marginal, and gays and lesbians) or determining lay perceptions of the practices associated with such lifestyles (Calnan 1987; Backett and Davison 1995; O'Brien 1995).

Among the most recent studies of health lifestyles is the research of Cockerham (1999) on health practices in Russia and Eastern Europe, where a 30-year period of decline in life expectancy had accelerated with the collapse of communism in the early 1990s. The rise in mortality was primarily due to premature deaths among middle-aged, working-class males whose health behavior was characterized by heavy drinking and smoking, disregard for their diet, and rejection of exercise. These practices resulted in a lifestyle that promoted excessive rates of heart disease, accidents, alcohol poisoning, and other health problems leading to a shortened life. Dependence on a deteriorating state health-care delivery system also tended to produce a false sense of security, while the state, in turn, assumed responsibility for health and failed to promote the individual's role in maintaining his or her health. Poor health behaviors were lodged in the norms established through group interaction and structured by the limited opportunities to exercise individual choice in the former socialist countries. While the downturn in life expectancy was primarily a male phenomenon that affected all social categories, age and class were key variables.

It can therefore be concluded that the relationship between health lifestyles and social class remains significant. A person's class position provides structural boundaries to the options that he or she can successfully execute in life. Thus, the health lifestyles of the upper and upper-middle classes—featuring more healthy diets, greater opportunities for relaxation and coping with stress, higher levels of participation in sports and leisure-time exercise, more physical checkups by physicians, and other preventive-care activities—assist the affluent in living a healthier and longer life. The lower class, in turn, has choices and opportunities for health lifestyles that are much more limited and confronts lessened life expectancy than the classes above it.

Strategies on the part of individuals to live healthier lifestyles have gained in popularity, and participation has expanded out of the upper-middle class to all other strata, but participation appears to remain strongest among the upper and middle classes generally (Blaxter 1990; Cockerham 1998; Cockerham et al. 1988; d'Houtaud and Field 1984; Goldstein 1992). People in these higher social classes have experienced greater life chances and have likely acquired a stronger sense of control over life situations than individuals in the classes below them (Mirowsky and Ross 1989). A major outcome of these cumulative experiences and the perception derived from them is that planning and effort will have the desired result. While many lower-class persons undoubtedly try to live a healthy lifestyle, others may be less likely to expect that their efforts to maintain their health will succeed and be passive or less active in their health-promoting behavior. Overall, it would appear that when disadvantaged life chances reduce the opportunities for positive health behaviors or reduce their effectiveness, the impact of agency on the part of individuals is minimized despite educational campaigns to improve health by changing behavior.

Additionally, it should be noted that the strongest measures of socioeconomic status are those that combine income, level of education, and occupational prestige to determine a person's position in a class structure. Of these three variables, the single most important in relation to health lifestyles is education. While income and occupational status are important, well-educated people are generally the best informed about the merits of a healthy lifestyle; they are also more likely to have fulfilling, subjectively rewarding jobs, less economic hardship, and a greater sense of control over their lives and their health than the less educated; moreover, they are less likely to smoke and more likely to exercise and drink alcohol moderately (Ross and Wu 1995).

OTHER VARIABLES

Although the bulk of the research on health lifestyles has been focused on social stratification, other variables hold importance for our understanding as well. Health lifestyle decisions in some cases may be grounded in age, gender, race, religion, and sexual preference, and other factors like the effects of advertising and mass medical campaigns. For some individuals, the group whose norms are important to them in terms of lifestyle may have a more narrow orientation than their social class membership, such as teen peer

groups, lesbians, Orthodox Jews, and military officers. Members of these groups adopt norms and behaviors that constitute specific lifestyles and cannot be explained by class alone. Other variables, like age and gender, may, in fact, induce age-specific or gender-specific lifestyles that transcend social class. Consequently, socioeconomic status cannot be considered the sole determinant of lifestyles.

This appears to be particularly true of health lifestyles. Dietary, exercise, drinking, and smoking patterns can be characteristic of specific groups regardless of the class position of its members (Cockerham 1998; Dean 1989; Ross and Bird 1994). Strong religiosity, for example, has been found to consistently promote health lifestyle practices (Dwyer, Clarke, and Miller 1990; Green 1986). Religious groups typically discourage or prohibit smoking and drinking, while promoting diet, hygiene, and exercise. Age is also an important variable as health behavior and lifestyles tend to change over the life course (Backett and Davison 1995). There is evidence, for example, that people tend to take better care of themselves as they grow older by showing more careful food selection, more relaxation, and either abstinence or reduced use of tobacco and alcohol (Backett and Davision 1995; Cockerham et al. 1988; Lüschen et al. 1995). But exercise declines significantly at older ages, causing one major health lifestyle activity to be largely curtailed over the life span.

Gender is a critical variable in health lifestyle research because perhaps no other single characteristic influences perception, behavior, and position in society as much, and perhaps no characteristic is subject to the same degree of cultural learning and socialization (Dean 1989). "It may be," states Dean (1989:138), "that one of the most fruitful approaches to more meaningful knowledge regarding the health impact of lifestyle is to focus on gender differences in behavioral and attitudinal variables." It would be particularly interesting, for example, to map the structure–agency issue in health lifestyle research in relation to gender. The notion of a female versus male habitus is not a feature of Bourdieu's work but is clearly a promising line of inquiry for assessing the validity of his theoretical perspective. Yet despite its obvious significance, there is a paucity of research on gender differences in health lifestyles.

Existing studies show that females tend to have healthier lifestyles than males, with the general exception of exercise (Cockerham et al. 1988; Dean 1989; Dean, Colomer, and Pérez-Hoyos 1995; Ross and Bird 1994; Stevens et al. 1995). Power relations between genders, however, can intervene to modify the attempts by women to take care of themselves. Walsh, Sorensen, and Leonard (1995), for example, observed that negative male attitudes toward female smoking in the United States helped suppress cigarette use by women until females entered the labor force in large numbers during World War II. Empowered by the greater job equality that came with employment outside the home, rates of smoking among women increased dramatically.

Perhaps the leading study to date on the health lifestyles of men and women is the research of Ross and Bird (1994). They found that men are more likely than women to exercise strenuously and walk, but are also more likely to smoke and be overweight. Men are particularly at risk if their advantaged position in the marketplace (higher salaries and decision-making roles) is accompanied by smoking, high-fat foods, and passive leisure-time activities. Other research shows that men also consume more alcohol and women are more careful about their diet (Cockerham 1998; Dean 1989; Stevens et al. 1995). Gender shapes women's health behavior and lifestyles with respect to dieting and emphasis on appearance, and it shapes men's in promoting such activities as weight lifting and a similar emphasis on looks (Sabo and Gordon 1995). Consequently, gender can be regarded as one of the most important causal factors in health lifestyle selection. Women generally take better care of their health than men, and this is seen in their lifestyle practices including seeking medical attention. It is therefore clear that any concept of health lifestyles needs to go beyond considerations of class to consider other variables that also impact significantly on health practices.

CONCLUSION

This chapter has reviewed the current state of theory and research on health behavior and health lifestyles. This is a relatively new field within medical sociology and an area that is likely to attract increasing attention as lifestyle studies demonstrate their capability to explain the health practices of individuals and groups. A sociological approach to the study of health lifestyles brings an additional dimension to the topic by allowing researchers to go beyond concerns with individual psychology and account for the influence of social structure on health and health practices. With people becoming increasingly aware of health risks associated with unhealthy styles of living and medicine's limitations, participation in health lifestyles becomes the major option for those seeking good health and longevity. This means that health lifestyles will be a more important subject of scholarly inquiry for medical sociologists than ever before. As Abel (1991:899) points out: "Health lifestyle is currently perhaps the cross-cutting issue of social science and medical research and, as such, it provides an intriguing and fascinating topic for medical sociology."

REFERENCES

ABEL, THOMAS. 1991. "Measuring Health Lifestyles in a Comparative Analysis: Theoretical Issues and Empirical Findings." *Social Science and Medicine* 32:899–908.

ABEL, THOMAS, and WILLIAM C. COCKERHAM. 1993. "Lifestyle or Lebensführung? Critical Remarks on Mistranslation of Weber's 'Class, Status, Party'." *Sociological Quarterly* 34:551–56.

ALEXANDER, JEFFREY C. 1987. "The Dialectic of Individuation and Domination: Weber's Rationalization Theory and Beyond." In *Max Weber, Rationality and Modernism*, ed. S. Whimster and S. Lash. London: Allen & Unwin, pp. 185–206.

ALEXANDER, JEFFREY C. 1995. *Fin de siècle Social Theory.* London: Verso.

BACKETT, KATHRYN C., and CHARLIE DAVISON. 1995. "Lifecourse and Lifestyle: The Social and Cultural Locations of Health Behaviors." *Social Science and Medicine* 40: 629–38.

BENDIX, REINHARD. 1960. *Max Weber: An Intellectual Portrait.* New York: Doubleday.

BLAXTER, MILDRED. 1990. *Health and Lifestyles.* London: Routledge.

BOCOCK, ROBERT. 1993. *Consumption.* London: Routledge.

BOURDIEU, PIERRE. 1977. *Outline of a Theory of Practice.* Cambridge, UK: Cambridge University Press.

BOURDIEU, PIERRE. 1984. *Distinction,* trans. R. Nice. Cambridge, MA: Harvard University Press.

BOURDIEU, PIERRE. 1990. *The Logic of Practice,* trans. R. Nice. Stanford, CA: Stanford University Press.

BOURDIEU, PIERRE, and LOÏC J.D. WACQUANT. 1992. *An Invitation to Reflexive Sociology.* Chicago: University of Chicago Press.

BUNTON, ROBIN, and ROGER BURROWS. 1995. "Consumption and Health in the 'Epidemiological' Clinic of Late Modern Medicine." In *The Sociology of Health Promotion,* ed. R. Bunton, S. Nettleton, and R. Burrows. London: Routledge, pp. 206–22.

CALNAN, MICHAEL. 1987. *Health and Illness: The Lay Perspective.* London: Tavistock.

CALNAN, MICHAEL. 1989. "Control Over Health and Patterns of Health Related Behavior." *Social Science and Medicine* 29:131–36.

CHANEY, DAVID. 1996. *Lifestyles.* London: Routledge.

COCKERHAM, WILLIAM C. 1997a. "Lifestyles, Social Class, Demographic Characteristics, and Health Behavior." In *Handbook of Health Behavior Research.* Vol. I., ed. David S. Gochman. New York: Plenum, pp. 253–65.

COCKERHAM, WILLIAM C. 1997b. "The Social Determinants of the Decline in Life Expectancy in Russia and Eastern Europe." *Journal of Health and Social Behavior* 38:117–30.

COCKERHAM, WILLIAM C. 1998. *Medical Sociology,* 7th ed. Upper Saddle River, NJ: Prentice Hall.

COCKERHAM, WILLIAM C. 1999. *Health and Social Change in Russia and Eastern Europe.* London: Routledge.

COCKERHAM, WILLIAM C., and FERRIS J. RITCHEY. 1997. *Dictionary of Medical Sociology.* Westport, CT: Greenwood Press.

COCKERHAM, WILLIAM C., ALFRED RÜTTEN, and THOMAS ABEL. 1997. "Conceptualizing Contemporary Health Lifestyles: Moving Beyond Weber." *Sociological Quarterly* 38: 321–42.

COCKERHAM, WILLIAM C., GERHARD KUNZ, and GUENTHER LUESCHEN. 1988. "Social Stratification and Health Lifestyles in Two Systems of Health Care Delivery: A Comparison of the United States and West Germany." *Journal of Health and Social Behavior* 29:113–26.

COCKERHAM, WILLIAM C., GERHARD KUNZ, GUENTHER LUESCHEN, and JOE L. SPAETH. 1986a. "Social Stratification and Self-Management of Health." *Journal of Health and Social Behavior* 27: 1–14.

COCKERHAM, WILLIAM C., GERHARD KUNZ, GUENTHER LUESCHEN, and JOE L. SPAETH. 1986b. "Symptoms, Social Stratification, and Self-Responsibility for Health in the United States and West Germany." *Social Science and Medicine* 22:1263–71.

COCKERHAM, WILLIAM C., THOMAS ABEL, and GÜNTHER LÜSCHEN. 1993. "Max Weber, Formal Rationality, and Health Lifestyles." *Sociological Quarterly* 34:413–35.

CONRAD, PETER. 1988a. "Worksite Health Promotion: The Social Context." *Social Science and Medicine* 26: 485–89.

CONRAD, PETER. 1988b. "Health and Fitness at Work: A Participant's Perception." *Social Science and Medicine* 26: 545–50.

CONRAD, PETER. 1994. "Wellness as a Virtue: Morality and the Pursuit of Health." *Culture, Medicine, and Society* 18: 385–401.

CONRAD, PETER, and DIANA CHAPMAN WALSH. 1992. "The New Corporate Health Ethic: Lifestyle and the Social Control of Work." *International Journal of Health Services* 22: 89–111.

CRAWFORD, ROBERT. 1984. "A Cultural Account of Health: Control Release and the Social Body." In *Issues in the Political Economy of Health Care,* ed. John McKinley. New York: Tavistock, pp. 60–103.

D'HOUTAUD, A., and MARK G. FIELD. 1984. "The Image of Health: Variation in Perception by Social Class in a French Population." *Sociology of Health and Illness* 6:30–59.

DAHRENDORF, RALF. 1979. *Life Chances.* Chicago: University of Chicago Press.

DEAN, KATHRYN. 1989. "Self-Care Components of Lifestyle: The Importance of Gender, Attitudes, and the Social Situation." *Social Science and Medicine* 29:137–52.

DEAN, KATHRYN, CONCHA COLOMER, and SANTIAGO PÉREZ-HOYOS. 1995. "Research on Lifestyles and Health: Searching for Meaning." *Social Science and Medicine* 41:845–55.

DWYER, JEFFREY W., LESLIE L. CLARKE, and MICHAEL K. MILLER. 1990. "The Effect of Religious Concentration and Affiliation on County Cancer Rates." *Journal of Health and Social Behavior* 31:185–202.

FEATHERSTONE, MIKE. 1987. "Lifestyle and Consumer Culture." *Theory, Culture, & Society* 4:55–70.

FOUCAULT, MICHEL. 1973. *The Birth of the Clinic.* London: Tavistock.

GALLAGHER, EUGENE B. 1988. "Modernization and Medical Care." *Sociological Perspectives* 31:59–87.

GIDDENS, ANTHONY. 1984. *The Constitution of Society: Outline of the Theory of Structuration.* Cambridge: Polity Press.

GIDDENS, ANTHONY. 1991. *Modernity and Self-Identity.* Stanford, CA: Stanford University Press.

GLASSNER, BARRY. 1989. "Fitness and the Postmodern Self." *Journal of Health and Social Behavior* 30:180–91.

GOLDSTEIN, MICHAEL S. 1992. *The Health Movement: Promoting Fitness in America.* New York: Twayne.

GREEN, HARVEY. 1986. *Fit for America: Health, Fitness, Sport, and American Society.* New York: Pantheon.

HERZLICH, CLAUDINE, and JANINE PIERRET. 1987. *Illness and Self in Society,* trans. E. Forster. Baltimore: Johns Hopkins University Press.

HITZLER, RONALD, and ELMAR KOENEN. 1994. "Kehren die Individuen zurück? Zwei divergente Anrworten auf eine institutionentheoretische Frage"[Are Individuals Returning? Two Divergent Answers to Questions of Institutional Theory]. In *Riskante Freiheiten* [*Risky Freedom*], ed. Ulrich Beck and Elizabeth Beck-Gernsheim. Frankfurt am Main: Suhrkamp, pp. 447–65.

JENKINS, RICHARD. 1992. *Pierre Bourdieu.* London: Routledge.

KALBERG, STEPHEN. 1994. *Max Weber's Comparative-Historical Sociology.* Chicago: University of Chicago Press.

KASL, STANISLAV, and STANLEY COBB. 1966. "Health Behavior, Illness Behavior, and Sick Role Behavior." *Archives of Environmental Health.* 12: 246–66.

KOTARBA, JOSEPH A., and PAMELA BENTLEY. 1988. "Workplace Wellness Participation and the Becoming of Self." *Social Science and Medicine* 26:551–58.

LOMAS, JONATHAN. 1998. "Social Capital and Health: Implications for Public Health and Epidemiology." *Social Science and Medicine* 47:1181–88.

LÖWITH, KARL. 1982. *Max Weber and Karl Marx,* ed. T. Bottomore and W. Outhwaite. London: Allen and Uwin.

LÜSCHEN, GÜNTHER, WILLIAM C. COCKERHAM, and GERHARD KUNZ, eds. 1989. *Health and Illness in America and Germany: Comparative Sociology of Health Conduct and Public Policy.* Munich: Oldenbourg.

LÜSCHEN, GÜNTHER, WILLIAM COCKERHAM, JOUKE VAN DER ZEE, FRED STEVENS, JOE DIEDERIKS, MANUAL GARCIA FERRANDO, ALPHONSE D'HOUTAUD, RUUD PEETERS, THOMAS ABEL, and STEFFEN NIEMANN. 1995. *Health Systems in the European Union: Diversity Convergence, and Integration.* Munich: Oldenbourg.

McKINLAY, JOHN B. 1995. *Bringing the Social System Back: An Essay on the Epidemiological Imagination.* Boston: New England Research Institution.

MIROWSKY, JOHN, and CATHERINE E. ROSS. 1989. *Social Causes of Psychological Distress.* New York: Aldine de Gruyter.

MOMMSEN, WOLFGANG J. 1989. *The Political and Social Theory of Max Weber.* Cambridge: Polity.

O'BRIEN, MARTIN. 1995. "Health and Lifestyle: A Critical Myth? Notes on the Dedifferentation of Health." In *The Sociology of Health Promotion,* ed. R. Bunton, S. Nettleton, and R. Burrows. London: Routledge, pp. 191–205.

ROSS, CATHERINE E., and CHIA-LING WU. 1995. "The Links Between Education and Health." *American Sociological Review* 60: 719–45.

ROSS, CATHERINE E., and CHLOE E. BIRD. 1994. "Sex Stratification and Health Lifestyle: Consequences for Men's and Women's Perceived Health." *Journal of Health and Social Behavior* 35:161–78.

ROTH, GUENTHER. 1987. "Rationalization in Max Weber's Developmental History." In *Max Weber, Rationality and Modernism,* ed. S. Whimster and S. Lash. London: Allen & Unwin, pp. 75–91.

SABO, DONALD, and DAVID FREDERICK GORDON, eds. 1995. *Men's Health and Illness: Gender, Power, and the Body.* Thousand Oaks, CA: Sage.

SHILLING, CHRIS. 1993. *The Body and Social Theory.* London: Sage.

STEVENS, FRED, JOS DIEDERIKS, JOUKE VAN DER ZEE, and GÜNTHER LÜESCHEN. 1995. "Health Lifestyles, Health Concern and Social Position in the Netherlands and Germany." *European Journal of Public Health* 5: 46–47.

SWEAT, MICHAEL D., and JULIE A. DENISON. 1995. "Reducing HIV Incidence in Developing Countries With Structural and Environmental Interventions." *AIDS* 9: 5251–57.

TURNER, BRYAN S. 1992. *Regulating Bodies.* London: Routledge.

WACQUANT, LOÏC J.D. 1992. "Toward a Social Praxeology: The Structure and Logic of Bourdieu's Sociology." In *An Invitation to Reflexive Sociology,* ed. Pierre Bourdieu and Loïc Wacquant. Chicago: University of Chicago Press, pp. 1–61.

WAITZKIN, HOWARD. 1983. *The Second Sickness: Contradictions of Capitalist Health Care.* New York: The Free Press.

WALSH, DIANA CHAPMAN, GLORIAN SORENSEN, and LORI LEONARD. 1995. "Gender, Health, and Cigarette Smoking." In *Society and Health,* ed. B. Amick, S. Levine, A. Tarlov, and D. Walsh. New York: Oxford University Press, pp. 131–71.

WEBER, MAX. 1949. *The Methodology of the Social Sciences,* ed. and trans. E. Shils and H. Finch. New York: Free Press.

WEBER, MAX. 1958. *The Protestant Ethic and the Spirit of Capitalism,* trans. T. Parsons. New York: Scribner's.

WEBER, MAX. 1978. *Economy and Society,* 2 vols, ed. and trans. Guenther F. Roth and Claus Wittich. Berkeley: University of California Press.

WILLIAMS, SIMON J. 1995. "Theorizing Class, Health and Lifestyles: Can Bourdieu Help Us?" *Sociology of Health and Illness* 17: 577–604.

12 ON CHRONIC ILLNESS AND DISABILITY

MICHAEL BURY, *University of London*

INTRODUCTION

In a recent paper, A. Frank (1997) sets out a case for re-orienting the way in which medical sociology typically approaches illness, especially chronic disabling illness. In essence, Frank argues, most sociological analysis follows the lines laid down by Parsons in the 1950s. That is to say, illness is regarded, normatively, as an undesirable state, and the "enactment of illness," so to speak, is hedged about by strictures and limitations. Being ill (or "sick") is thus socially regulated in order to minimise its disruption to the social system, as well as to individual lives. As Frank puts it, in the Parsonian paradigm the ill person is transformed into "the patient, but the patient remains a suspicious character in Parsonian sociology: the physician is expected to treat the patient, without colluding in the patient's withdrawal into sickness" (Frank 1997:132). Patienthood therefore reduces the social threat of illness by rendering the patient passive and by insisting on a return to social functioning as quickly as possible. The negative experience of illness (and loss of "personhood") is as much a function of normative values as it is of its biological effects.

In arguing against this view, Frank seeks to highlight the "agency" of the patient, to move the emphasis from patient to person once again. Whereas medical sociology has often been preoccupied with how the ill person becomes a patient, through "illness behaviour," "help seeking behaviour" and the like, the task now is to uncover the way in which the ill or disabled retain or recover a sense of personhood. In arguing the case for an active and "moral" view of the patient, Frank seeks to follow other writers, including sociologists such as G. Williams (1984) and K. Charmaz (1991) and anthropologists such as A. Kleinman (1988) who begin from a very different vantage point to that of Parsons. In the new approach roles become almost reversed. Kleinman, for example, sees the physician now in a more supportive if not passive role, acting as a witness to the suffering of the patient, or offering guidance in practical coping in the everyday business of living with illness (Kleinman 1988:10). Regulating and limiting illness by the doctor is transformed into "witness" and acceptance. The religious (at least, Christian) overtones to this kind of approach have not gone unnoticed (G. Williams 1998).

However, as the shift in attention turns to the legitimate role of the active patient, so the concern with describing and focusing on the problems patients face diminishes (Bury 1991). Rather, the aim of the new research is to document the comeback of the patient (Corbin and Strauss 1991) and, in Frank's terms, the *moral dilemmas* of the person/patient as he or she makes active decisions about the strategies to be adopted in fashioning a meaningful life. In the end it may even be possible, Frank suggests, to shift attention from the undesirability of illness to "being successfully ill," in which people live with illnesses creatively and meaningfully (Frank 1997: 136). The general context in which this is occurring is what Frank terms the *remission society,* where substantial numbers of people are well, but who "could never be considered cured" (Frank 1995:10). Under such circumstances people achieve remarkable successes, especially where they "grasp suffering as moral opening, as occasion for witness and change" (Frank 1997: 141).

A similar if not always strictly comparable move is underway in the field of disability studies. Just as medical sociology is being urged to reverse the role of doctor and patient, so those researching and writing on disability are being enjoined to reject the implications of a Parsonian view of society for their activities. In a paper on language and identity, Zola, for example, makes the point that Parsons was not only concerned with the tying in of the sick person to the individualising world of medicine, but, by the same token, to a view of sickness which would not lead to *solidary collectivities*. Such collectivities and subcultures of the sick or disabled would, for Parsons, constitute a threat, if only because they might prove attractive to virtually anyone frustrated with the social system (Zola 1993a:168; Parsons 1951:477). Yet, as Zola notes, contemporary societies are now characterised by various groups of the disabled and chronically sick, challenging not only the language with which they are described, but the stigma and discrimination experienced. In the United Kingdom disability writers have set out a strong programme for research that rejects disability as a characteristic of individuals, and instead opts for a view of a disabling society that excludes and discriminates (Oliver 1990, 1996). A general move is thus afoot to raise consciousness and organise against earlier definitions and practices surrounding disability.

In the fields of chronic illness and disability, then, there are several strands of thought rejecting putative negative approaches and emphasising, in their place, human agency, moral worth, and political rights. These powerful impulses appear to contradict the functionalist view of modern life that Parsons delineated. Against Parsonian functionalism and a consensus view of professional–client relationships, postmodern voices speak of difference, subjective experience, and challenges to professional power. In doing so they build on the conflict perspectives of writers such as Freidson and Zola in the 1970s (Freidson 1970; Zola 1972, 1973) and Mishler in the 1980s (Mishler 1984) who, in rejecting Parsonian views, set out a case for regarding professional dominance as socially suspect, and patient views as central to the process of illness and patienthood. Subsequently, the conflict perspective has been broadened to take into account feminist views of the doctor-patient relationship, among other critical standpoints (for a fuller description of the doctor–patient relationship, see, Bury 1997, Chapter 3).

In contemporary writings on illness and disability, however, even conflict perspectives are downplayed, as attention increasingly focuses on individual and collective action, with professional care relegated to a more contingent place in the illness and disability experience. Expert discourse is now replaced by the moral career and personal narratives of the sufferer, and patienthood is replaced by the rights of personhood. It is true that some of the writers already mentioned here

recognise ambiguity in such reversals—especially Zola, who was alive to contradictions of current changes, but this only reinforced his view that there was a need for a closer appreciation of the changes underway (Zola 1993a).

The rest of this chapter attempts, therefore, to provide an analysis of the sociology of chronic illness and disability under conditions of considerable and rapid change. It does so through three main sections. The first provides a map for the changing definitions and terms that now abound in this field. Though there is little consensus on terminology, the main lines of argument can be identified, together with the different perspectives that underlie them. The second section involves a necessarily selective review of contemporary social research in chronic illness. This involves an examination of the relationship between a *problems* approach and one that starts with agency and lived experience. Third, the chapter offers an analysis of the often complex relationship between chronic illness and disability, in light of the foregoing discussion. Here, difficulties in arguing for a radical separation of disability from chronic illness and impairment (and, it will be noted, aging) are discussed. Finally, following these three main discussions, the chapter concludes by considering whether bringing different sociological perspectives on chronic illness and disability together can constitute an adequate basis for future research in the field.

DEFINING CHRONIC ILLNESS AND DISABILITY

It is clear that the distinction between acute and chronic illness may be more apparent than real. Many forms of illness contain elements of both and, indeed, include fluctuating episodes of exacerbation and remission. Some forms of illness may have acute onset, followed by long and progressive illness (for example, chronic renal failure, some forms of heart disease, and stroke). Others may have acute flare ups in an otherwise deteriorating or even relatively stable trajectory (for example, arthritis, multiple sclerosis, and diabetes). Moreover, whilst most forms of chronic illness are degenerative in character and associated with later life, many infectious diseases have been major sources of chronic illness in the past. The case of tuberculosis gave rise to one of the earliest sociological accounts of chronic illness (Roth 1963) as did polio, of the links between illness and disability (Davis 1963). In recent times, the most dramatic reminder of the power of the HIV/AIDS infections has also taken on features of chronicity and disability, as rapid death has been postponed by new forms of treatment (Carricaburu and Pierret 1995).

The transformation of many life-threatening illnesses into chronic ones, whether through the development of healthier environments or as the result of effective treatments, underlines their importance in contemporary society and the need to have a cogent view of their core features. In the main, and with necessary qualifications, we can define chronic illness from a sociological viewpoint in the following terms. First, such illness tends to have insidious onset and be characterised by early symptoms that make it difficult for the individual or social group to separate it from normal experience. Though some illnesses have dramatic onsets, typically people find it difficult to say exactly when the illness started, and encounters with medical practitioners may be characterised by uncertainty and failure to diagnose. Early diagnosis may be elusive, as evidence from those suffering from conditions such as multiple sclerosis testifies (Robinson 1988).

Second, chronic illness often has a fluctuating course. Again, contact with medical practitioners may prove frustrating when specialist care, based on advanced science and therapeutics, cannot, as in the case of leukemia, predict when remissions and exacerbations will occur in any given case. Such fluctuations provide moments of hope and despair by turns and frustrate life planning and normal social encounters. In the case of leukemia, J. Comaroff and P. Maguire have shown that uncertainty is a defining feature of the course of the illness (Comaroff and Maguire 1981).

Third, chronic illness is defined by uncertain outcome. In the case of life-threatening infections the (stereo)typical model of outcome has been one of death or recovery. Fever, in particular, has marked the cultural shaping of such experiences for generations, the result of which moves the person in one direction or the other. Fictional as well as real experience has testified over and again to the role of such crises in the natural history of infectious diseases. In chronic illness such natural histories are rarely to be found, and equivalents to a fever crisis are equally rare. Quoting R.G. Rothenberg and J.P. Koplan (1990), L.M. Verbrugge and A.M. Jette (1994) point out that "people mostly *live with* chronic conditions rather than *die from* them" (1994:1, emphasis in original). Today, Frank's remission society may be more characteristic, where large numbers of people live ostensibly normal lives, having emerged from a period of illness, but where the outcome is, as was noted earlier, likely to have fallen short of a cure, and where disability, to a lesser or greater extent, is frequently the result.

Though chronic illness is linked with disability in many ways, any discussion of the term "disability" shows why such links are likely to prove problematic and controversial. In essence this arises because disability is more relational in character, that is, rarely entirely present or absent, but present by a matter of degree. Moreover, though chronic illness often has disabling consequences, some forms of disability are not the result of illness. Disability is thus a heterogeneous category, covering the effects of illness, genetic disorders, injury, and some aspects of the aging process.

Until recently two main approaches to defining disability have been used in sociological thinking and in policy-oriented social research, especially in Europe and the United States, in grappling with these complexitites. Verbrugge and Jette's summary of these two definitional schemes is reproduced in Table 12–1. The upper part, by the World Health Organisation (WHO) shows the International Classification of Impairments, Disabilities, and Handicaps (ICIDH). The lower part shows the Institute of Medicine scheme.

The main difference between the two schemes, as will be seen, is that the WHO scheme draws a distinction between "disability" and "handicap," whilst the Nagi, or the Institute of Medicine scheme, substitutes "functional limitation" for the WHO's definition of disability and rejects the use of the term handicap. In the WHO scheme, the importance of handicap was to conceptualise social disadvantage consequent on impairment or disability, that is, social advantage related to disablement. It is important to note, in passing, as do Verbrugge and Jette, that the WHO scheme has been undergoing substantial revision. At the time of this writing the results are not yet clear, but it is likely that in the future the WHO scheme will not include the dimension or term "handicap." Some of its features will be incorporated into "disability."

In any event, the important point to note from these schemes is that they both suggest a sequence of events based on an initial causal mechanism of disease or active pathology. That is, health status (broadly defined in terms of impairment caused by disease, accident, or trauma) is seen as a central element in the disablement process. Controversy has arisen from attempts by some disability researchers and activists to redefine disability in such a way as to break the links between health status (or impairment) and disablement, as seen in these schemes, arguing that these links overemphasise characteristics of individuals, rather than focusing on the social environment.

One way of bringing about this change has been to argue for an alteration in the way language is used,

TABLE 12–1 Two Definitional Schemes

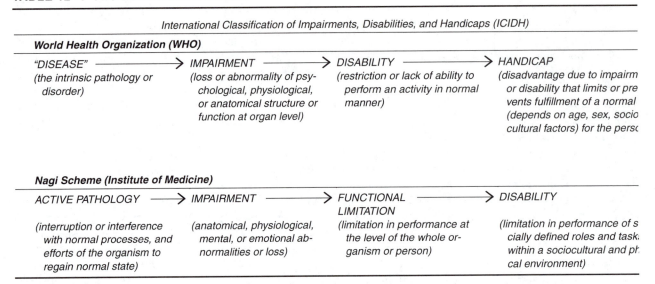

International Classification of Impairments, Disabilities, and Handicaps (ICIDH)

World Health Organization (WHO)

"DISEASE" ———————→ IMPAIRMENT ———————→ DISABILITY ———————→ HANDICAP

(the intrinsic pathology or disorder) | (loss or abnormality of psychological, physiological, or anatomical structure or function at organ level) | (restriction or lack of ability to perform an activity in normal manner) | (disadvantage due to impairm or disability that limits or pre vents fulfillment of a normal (depends on age, sex, socio cultural factors) for the perse

Nagi Scheme (Institute of Medicine)

ACTIVE PATHOLOGY ———→ IMPAIRMENT ———————→ FUNCTIONAL ———————→ DISABILITY
                                                LIMITATION

(interruption or interference with normal processes, and efforts of the organism to regain normal state) | (anatomical, physiological, mental, or emotional abnormalities or loss) | (limitation in performance at the level of the whole organism or person) | (limitation in performance of s cially defined roles and task within a sociocultural and ph cal environment)

SOURCE: L.M. Verbrugge and A.M. Jette, "The Disablement Process," *Social Science and Medicine* 38(1994).

in order to distance disability from the individual. Zola (1993a) expresses this well when he says: "Prepositions . . . imply both 'a relationship to' and 'a separation from. . . . ' At this juncture the awkwardness in phrasing may be all to the good, for it makes the user and hearer stop and think about what is meant as in 'persons *with* disabilities'" (Zola 1993a:170, emphasis in the original).

Though this particular change in the use of language suggests a change in outlook, it still retains the idea of disability as a functional limitation of the individual, even if it involves the idea that this is lived with rather than being a core aspect of personal identity. Verbrugge and Jette's model of the disablement process was also based on the idea of living with; it similarly contains a view that disability is to be defined in part as personal capability, though it goes on to highlight the gap between this individual component of the process and environmental demand (Verbrugge and Jette 1994:1; see also, Albrecht 1992:19–20).

Other, more radical definitions of disability have now come into play, however, especially in the United Kingdom, seeking to reject entirely any relationship between personal capability, or individual characteristics linked to health status and impairment, on the one hand, and the effects or demands of the environment, on the other. Oliver (1990) for example, drawing on the stance taken by an international group of disability activists, argues for a definition of disability as:

The disadvantage or restriction of activity caused by a contemporary social organisation which takes no or little account of people who have physical impairments and thus excludes them from the mainstream of social activities. (Oliver 1990:11)

In this *social model of disability,* impairment or disease is seen to have no prior or causal connection with disability. The latter is wholly social in origin and character. In a recent discussion Oliver has gone so far as to claim that disablement "has nothing to do with the body. It is a consequence of social oppression" (Oliver 1996:35). Illness or impairment may well be a characteristic of the individual, but restriction in activity and function or disability is held to be the result of exclusionary practices and discrimination. Even the interactional view of writers such as Verbrugge and Jette or Albrecht are eschewed in favour of a wholly social definition of the disablement process.

The results of the development and popularity of the social model of disability, among some activists and researchers, have been far reaching, spreading out from the United Kingdom, and connecting with movements such as those for "Independent Living," already well established in the United States (de Jong 1983). Although, as will be seen below, differences in emphasis exist amongst disability activists concerning the links between illness, impairment, and disability, the social model as espoused by Oliver and others sets up a potentially sharp tension with other approaches to social research on the consequences of chronic illness. These need to be explored as the discussion proceeds.

SOCIOLOGICAL RESEARCH ON CHRONIC ILLNESS

Sociological research and writing on chronic illness is now extensive. As mentioned in the introduction to this chapter, all that can be offered here in the space available is a selective view of the major trends, especially as they bear on disability questions. Insofar as medical sociologists have considered disability in the context of chronic illness, this has tended to be within the frames of reference explored by Verbrugge and Jette laid out in Table 12–1. That is to say, they have seen disability unfold with the impact of chronic conditions on "the functioning of specific body systems, and on people's abilities to act in necessary, usual, expected and personally desired ways in their society" (Verbrugge and Jette 1994:3). The development of chronic illness, or what writers such as J. Corbin and A. Strauss have preferred to call "illness trajectories" (Corbin and Strauss 1988:225) has, therefore, a causal link with some forms of disability. However, the use of terms such as "illness trajectories" serve to emphasise the social and temporal contexts in which these experiences and processes take place. Whilst illness is an intensely personal matter, its experience is inevitably social in character, as the individual interacts over time with the physical and social environment.

Thus, although there has been a preoccupation with the meaning of illness in sociological work, it extends from cognitive to cultural and social structural issues. Indeed, I have identified elsewhere at least two core senses in which meaning is used in the context of studying chronic illness (Bury 1988). The first concerns the meaning of illness in terms of its *consequences*. This sense falls squarely within the *problems approach,* in which the variety of material and practical difficulties that flow from the emerging disability and the surrounding social environment are documented (Bury 1988:91). These difficulties range from those at work and their attendant financial problems to practical difficulties in the home. Though much medical sociology research on the impact of chronic illness has been based on qualitative studies of small groups of people suffering from specific disorders (arthritis, diabetes, stroke, and so on), it has also been premised on the wider public health literature documenting the epidemiological

and policy dimensions of illness and disability (e.g., Zola 1993b; Bury 1997). The material difficulties people face have thus received attention, though sometimes indirectly; for example, through a focus on the experience of illness and disability in relation to maintaining paid employment (Pinder 1995).

In the middle range of "meaning as consequence" has been work on the family dynamics of chronic illness. Here, practical difficulties are negotiated within the limits of tolerance that specific family contexts create—a situation of "meanings at risk" (Bury 1988). With the onset of illness and emerging disability, individuals must negotiate a pathway between making demands that will lead to either acceptance or rejection. The effects of living with a chronic disorder cannot easily be predicted in advance. As K. Charmaz states:

> The meaning of disability, dysfunction, or impairment becomes real in daily life. Until put to the test in daily routines, someone cannot know what having an altered body is like. (Charmaz 1991:21).

Such tests involve finding out who your real friends are in a time of trouble, as attempts are made to mobilise social support. The presence or absence of wider supportive networks, and the consequences of chronic illness for such relationships, may be significant (Morgan 1989). As will be emphasised in more detail below, studies of younger adults with chronic disorders need to be set against the wider social distribution of chronic illness and disability, where the aging population comes to the fore (Albrecht and Levy 1991; Zola 1991, 1993b). In a study of older respondents with chronic respiratory disease (S. Williams 1993), participants reported little help from wider social networks, even when, in the pre-illness situation, they had been in existence (S. Williams 1993:18).

In making these points it becomes clear that the meaning of illness in terms of its consequences is intimately bound up with a second dimension, namely, meaning as *significance* (Bury 1988:91). Alterations in the body interact with the wider society in cultural and structural contexts that go beyond practical consequences to issues of appearance, social performance, and thus identity. In part this stems from the associations made in specific cultures with particular disorders. Being diagnosed as having arthritis, multiple sclerosis or epilepsy is likely to be profoundly significant for a person's identity, over and above any immediate disabling effects, that is, of changes in function and activity levels.

The combined effects of disabling symptoms and the cultural imagery surrounding particular disorders have been termed *biographical disruption* (Bury 1982, 1991), or alterations to the person's *biographical body conception* (*BBC*) (Corbin and Strauss 1988). These changes can have lasting implications for the person's outlook and life chances. The purpose of such concepts has been to point to the various ways in which the significance of an illness and its practical consequences combine to challenge taken-for-granted assumptions, both for individuals and for those with whom they come into contact. The biographical "interruption" of chronic illness, to use Charmaz's term (Charmaz 1991), may well, "rip apart taken for granted daily routines" forcing people to relate especially to time in new ways, such that "chronic illness often chrysalises vital lessons about living" (Charmaz 1991:vii).

Part of what is involved here is the ways in which people with chronic illness and disability need to attend to an altered body and its significance and effects on social interaction, as well as on physical functioning. In one of a number of calls to bring the body more closely into sociological analyses of illness, M. Kelly and D. Field (1996) state that in order "to be acknowledged as competent social performers we have to be able to give the impression of some degree of control, use and presentation of our bodies" (Kelly and Field 1996:246). In chronic illness this issue can take many forms, from the hidden effects of disorders such as diabetes, where self and body management may largely be concealed, to people in wheelchairs where "their public identity is always constrained by the wheelchair" (Kelly and Field 1996:249; for a longer discussion of the impact of using a wheelchair on identity and daily life, see Zola 1982).

The links between body, self, and identity bring out the active way in which people seek to respond or come back in the face of chronic illness (Corbin and Strauss 1991). In an earlier paper I summarised three of the processes that are involved here, namely, coping, strategy, and style (Bury 1991). I argued that these terms point to different planes of experience: *coping* concerns cognitive processes used in putting up with the effects of illness on identity and the efforts made by people to retain a sense of self-worth; *strategy* refers to the actions people take to mobilise resources, both material and social, such as help from family and wider networks; and *style* is a term covering the decisions people often make about the presentation of their illness in everyday settings as part of their lifestyle—what one might call the performance aspects of illness and disability (Radley 1994:152).

These aspects of chronic illness bring the discussion back to questions of agency and morality. The shift from a problems perspective to one that stresses the active engagement of the person with his or her illness and disability suggests potential positive aspects of such experiences. Through battling with illness and through suffering may come a sense of gain as well as loss. Illness and disability are then turned into moral narratives, in which the person is no longer the victim or sufferer but presents himself or herself as a "wounded storyteller," to use Frank's ringing phrase. Such a moral stance can both enhance a sense of positive identity and also help establish the person as a moral actor with respect to others (G. Williams 1984, Charmaz 1991). In both senses, the damaged self is repaired if not completely restored. As the chapter now goes on to show, this emphasis on resisting a passive or victim status has taken a particular form among some disability activists and theorists.

CHRONIC ILLNESS AND DISABILITY

The relationship between chronic illness and disability is a complex one. It will be clear by now that much depends on the definition of disability used, as well as how chronic illness is characterised. In order to explore the relationship in more detail, we therefore need to take each of these perspectives in turn.

It will be remembered that the first approach—the socio-medical model of chronic illness and disability—is closely associated with the ICD (Impairment, Disability, and Handicap) classification developed by the World Health Organisation (WHO). The Institute of Medicine schema, though differing in some respects, follows similar lines of reasoning. Although often characterised by adherents of the social model as offering a deterministic and medical conception of disability, these schemes seek to provide a consistent approach to the effects of medically related disorders, *and* their interaction with the social environment. Whilst some key features of disability are clearly the result of illness and impairment, both schemes recognise, albeit in different ways, that disability is also influenced by context and culture.

Studies of chronic illness show that symptoms may, at times, lead swiftly or inexorably to disability. The effects of conditions such as stroke, arthritis, or multiple sclerosis are likely to have a direct bearing on mobility and self-care, as well as on identity and social life, as we have seen. In the main, these restrictions in activity and function are what the vast majority of people in developed modern societies mean by disability. As I have pointed out elsewhere (Bury 1996), this is actually also what most disabled activists mean, in practice, when they used the term *the disabled,* if only because in referring to *the able bodied* and *the disabled,* adherents of any position are admitting the link between alterations to the body and disability. The denial of any causal relationship between illness, changes in the body, and disability comes up against the daily realities experienced by the chronically sick and those that care for them, whether in the community or in health-care systems. Chronic illness frequently, though not always, has effects that no social arrangement or supportive environment can entirely mitigate. The disabling effects of illness (and indeed, of impairments from other causes) can be reduced in some instances but not all. As Sally French argues, "Some of the most profound problems experienced by people with certain impairments are difficult, if not impossible to solve by social manipulation" (French 1993:17).

Most important here is the relationship between chronic illness, disability, and age. Just as the prevalence of chronic illness rises with age, so too does disability. In the largest national study of disability in Great Britain, carried out by the then Office of Population Censuses and Surveys (OPCS), based on a development of the WHO definition of disability, it was found that of the 6 million people estimated to be disabled, no less that 70 percent were age 60 and over, and more than 50 percent were age 70 and over (Martin et al. 1988:27). Whether one takes the milder forms of disability or those of a more severe kind, the elderly, and especially the very old, predominate. Sixty-three percent of women and 53 percent of men over the age of 75 were disabled (Martin et al. 1988). The difference between men and women is overwhelmingly the result of chronic illnesses such as arthritis.

But, the recognition of the causal connection between chronic illness, impairment, and disability does not mean that *all* forms or facets of impairment and disability result from illness. Clearly, as stated earlier, there are many other causes of impairment including trauma, accidents, injuries, and the results of genetic disorders. Moreover, whilst health care is frequently of paramount importance to some chronically ill and disabled people at various points of an illness trajectory or disability trajectory, medical responses will only be one of a number to be tackled across the life course. In any event, even when necessary, medical care may often be approached with a mixture of hope and trepidation. It is important to recognise that medical responses to disabling illness can be harmful as well as helpful; medicalising disability can have negative effects as well as positive ones (Conrad 1992; Zola 1991), particularly

when lay values are overshadowed by those of providers (Zola 1991:304). The point needs to be stressed, however, that in any overview of disability in modern society, chronic illness remains its most significant cause, and medical care an important site of lay/professional encounters.

Having said this, it is also important to underline that whilst socio-medical approaches stress the need for health-care systems and policy makers to take a wider view of impairment and chronic illness, this involves recognising that disability is often related to impairment in complex ways. Carrying out self-care tasks and other daily functions involves more than dealing with the direct effects of illness or impairment. Disability is clearly relational in the sense that much depends on social circumstance and social interactional issues, as well as individual or biomedical characteristics.

In summary, the socio-medical approaches of the WHO or Institute of Medicine type attempt to capture the impact of illness on everyday life, without reducing disability to impairment. Disability, from this vantage point, occupies a meeting point between the direct effects of chronic illness and impairment and the social contexts (micro and macro) in which people live. Disability may be seen, in this sense, as "the gap between personal capability and environmental demand" (Verbrugge and Jette 1994:1), a perspective that can only be worked out in detail by applying it to empirical social research. "Handicap" in the WHO scheme demands that attention be paid to the social disadvantage consequent on the interaction between impairment and disability, on the one hand, and the wider social and economic environment, on the other.

The second approach to disability identified in this chapter—the social model—rejects the personal tragedy imagery that is felt to surround chronic illness and disability in socio-medical approaches. Even though, as has been shown, sociological studies of chronic disabling illness now routinely highlight questions of agency and active response in everyday life, advocates of the social model relocate these issues to the plane of political struggle against discrimination and oppression. In this view, disability is nothing less than the effects of exclusion and oppression, perpetrated by the dividing practices of a capitalist society that wishes to separate the able bodied from the disabled bodied, for the purposes of maximising production and thus profit (Oliver 1990:28).

Even when medical sociologists emphasise the importance of social environments in the creation of disability or handicap, particularly under conditions of modern capitalism, advocates of the social model still often judge them to fall short of an adequate explanation. C. Barnes (1998), for example, in reviewing the arguments put forward by a series of recent medical sociologists, focuses critical attention on the formulation of disability in G. Albrecht's *The Disability Business* (1992). In that book Albrecht argues that not only does industrial capitalism play a part in the creation of inequalities in health and disability, but it also creates a multimillion-dollar business out of disability itself. Barnes, however, centres his critique on Albrecht's definition of disability. Albrecht argues that:

> Disability is constituted both by impairments and by the disabling environment. The concept of disabling environments, however, forces us to acknowledge that disabilities are physically based but socially constructed. Societies, then, produce disabilities differently from impairments. (Albrecht 1992:35, cited in Barnes 1998:72)

Though this formulation offers an attempt to bridge the socio-medical and social models of disability, recognising both the physical *and* social components of the disablement process, Barnes sees no merit in such a formulation. He comments, "disabled people are treated [in this argument] as an abstraction somehow distinct from the human race, and the crucial question of causality is fudged rather than clarified" (Barnes 1998).

From the viewpoint of some disability theorists, then, only the most radical separation of impairment from disability will do, resulting in a view of disability as entirely the function of social oppression and exclusion. Such a view rejects any notion of disability's containing elements of individual capacity or being physically based at all. In a mixture of Marxian materialism and labeling theory, writers such as Barnes argue that an "ideology of individualism" pervades medical sociological writings on chronic illness and disability, as well as health and welfare systems that deliver individualising care (Barnes 1998). Here, even individual action and human agency set in a social and cultural context, are eschewed in favour of collectivist politics, focusing "on those aspects of disabled people's lives which can and should be changed" (Barnes 1998:78).

But herein lies a major problem for the social model, for it is difficult to reject the evidence that some aspects of disabled people's lives are intimately affected by their illnesses or impairments. To speak as if any reference to personal attributes or bodily limitations immediately turns into negative individualising is to exclude whole areas of experience. In reality, the link between impairment and disability is not so easily broken; many significant aspects of disability *are* constituted by

impairments and illness, as we have seen. In fact, some disability theorists' views of impairment and illness are strangely disinterested. In arguing for a complete separation of impairment from disability, the social model is forced into portraying impairment and illness as if they are neutral states, with no consequences for personal or social functioning.

So when Barnes, for example, asserts that in separating impairment from disability he does not want to "deny the importance of impairment, appropriate medical intervention, or, indeed, discussions of these experiences" (Barnes 1998:78), these states are left without any apparent connection with everyday life and social functioning. Oliver, having argued that "the social model does not deny that impairment is closely related to the physical body," and that, "impairment is, in fact, nothing less than a description of the physical body" (Oliver 1996:35) simply leaves these issues on one side. The separation of a medical view of impairment and illness from a social view of disability fails, finally, to articulate the complex interplay between the two. In the understandable desire to resist the negative aspects of the medicalization of disability, the social model often produces an oversocialised perspective that denies the effects of impairments and illness on personal and social life and on the disablement process as a whole (Bury 1997:138).

WOUNDED STORYTELLER OR POLITICAL ACTIVIST?

Two contrasting images of chronic illness and disability have been explored in this chapter. Both speak to changes that have occurred in perception and experience in late modern cultures. Until recently, the chronically sick and disabled were largely hidden from view, being treated with a mixture of social control and care. Experts, whether medical or rehabilitative, dominated public responses to these areas of life, and patients or clients were expected to act with respect and gratitude for the services they received, even when these had deleterious effects on their life chances. Now, under conditions of greater pluralism and democracy (or at least populism), an emphasis on subjective experience and collective grass roots action has brought about a sea change in both public and private spheres.

The first of the new images of chronic illness and disability explored in this chapter has been that of "the wounded storyteller." Here the chronically sick or disabled person is no longer portrayed as a victim but as someone who comes back at illness and disability, finding strategies to deal with their effects and adopting lifestyles and narrative forms that refuse to accept these states as a defeat. In the language of A. Frank (1995) the individual can now strive to be "successfully ill," in the attempt to integrate long-standing illness into everyday life. Rather than illness and disability constituting failure in a person's life, this image suggests that pain and suffering do not mean the end of meaningful social life. Indeed, they may mean the opening of new doors to self-development, of providing "latent lessons that foreshadow a new concept of self" (Charmaz 1991:vii). Moreover, the actions of the chronically sick and disabled may contribute to the development of a more tolerant and pluralistic culture.

The second image is less personal and moral and more political in character. Here the disabled individual is a campaigner and activist, involved with others in collective action to maximise integration of the impaired and chronically ill into mainstream society. As I. Zola has put it, this approach suggests that "the fault is not in us, not in our diseases and disabilities, but in mythical denials, social arrangements, political priorities and procedures" (Zola 1993a:171). As we have seen, especially in the social model, material circumstances are regarded as paramount, through which the capitalist system effectively marginalises the disabled. Indeed, this marginalisation creates and constructs disability and thus the propensity to struggle and protest. As a result, it is argued, the overcoming of barriers to employment, public places and buildings, and social participation in general, can only be brought about by the self-activity of disabled people, not by experts in health and welfare, or through academic research.

These two images of chronic illness and disability have become pervasive in contemporary societies. For this reason alone they need to be taken seriously. Insofar as they point to the reduction in negative and oppressive responses to illness and disability, and inasmuch as they point to the need for positive policies and responsive services, they are difficult to resist. Few would argue that the chronically ill and disabled should not have an improved quality of life or full civil and political rights. The trend in legislation and courtroom decisions in most developed societies points in these directions; professional malpractice and incompetence, lack of compensation for injury, and discrimination are all now open to challenge. Despite arguments to the contrary, and despite the enormous efforts needed to do so, the chronically sick and disabled now knock at doors that have never been more capable of being opened. Though disability activists tend to claim that what positive changes have occurred are the result of the actions of radical groups, the success of these groups also reflects the growth of populism and wider democracy of which they are a part.

It will be clear by now that the present author regards these images of chronic illness and disability—the wounded storyteller and the political activist—as both significant and ambiguous. The ambiguity involved arises most obviously with respect to the range of experience they purport to cover. The tensions that these images create can be summarised in three final remarks.

First, both of these new images of chronic illness and disability seem to apply almost entirely to relatively young people. When writers such as Barnes speak of disabled people and their organisations (Barnes 1998:72) or Frank of the self-help movement (Frank 1995:138), they invariably have in mind highly self-selected groups of young and middle-aged individuals whose values are taken as generalisable. The idea of struggling to integrate illness or disability into working life or campaigning for the removal of barriers to employment make a good deal more sense to the young than to the old. As I have pointed out, however, the vast majority of people with chronic illness and disability are over retirement age. Though old age is not synonymous with disability, it is important to note that "people with a whole range of chronic diseases and disabilities are reaching old age, and more adults remain alive sufficiently long to experience age-associated chronic illness and disability" (Zola 1991:301).

The needs and aspirations of the older disabled will inevitably differ from those of younger people. This is not to say that quality of life and social integration do not matter in later life. Far from it; they matter a great deal. It is, however, important to document exactly what this means for different age groups. Older people may be less interested in work and environmental barriers than in good quality housing or in health and social services that meet their needs (see, for example, Arber and Ginn 1991). They may also be more concerned than younger people with the needs of carers and relatives. Aging and the elderly rarely feature in the new active images of chronic illness and disability.

Second, while it has arguably been a step forward for sociological research to move away from a purely problems perspective to one emphasising human agency and moral purpose, this, too can signal normative expectations that are difficult to meet. The tendency to emphasise activism and positive come back responses may themselves turn into oppressive cultural expectations. There is, especially perhaps in American writing at present, a tendency to play down the documentation of failure and defeat in the face of illness; sometimes the new imagery conveys the unfortunate side of a can-do culture. Only the successful or politically committed need apply for mainstream life. Yet sociological work must surely document variations in experience and values within representative social contexts. As with the question of age, the outlook of middle-class individuals and activists can easily be taken as representing experience as a whole. Despite the emphasis on materialism and Marxism in the social model, social class is often ignored in the disability and chronic illness literature. Sociological work on chronic illness and disability needs to recognise social variations in the range of handicaps associated with disability, in order to point to the public health implications of its research. Indeed there is now a great deal of social and epidemiological research on chronic illness and disability, which, despite objections from some disability activists to official sources, contains vital data on social disadvantage that can be integrated into sociological analysis.

Third, those advocating a wholly social approach to disability may, as has been argued, underestimate the impact that biological and bodily factors have on the development of disability. It is unfortunate that in the desire to stress structural and political influences on disability, advocates of the social model have often distanced themselves from the corporeal dimensions of illness and impairment. As Zola has stated, changing images and conceptions of disability (including changes in terminology) should be approached with caution. He argues, "We must seek a change in the connotations and pervasiveness of our names without denying the essential reality of our conditions. Thus biology may not determine our destiny; but . . . our physical, mental and biological differences are certainly part of that destiny" (Zola 1993a:170). The need to explore fully the interaction between chronic illness, impairment, and disability, within specific social contexts, remains a central challenge to medical sociology. The mid-range, between a wounded storyteller and an overly politicised conception would, as Zola suggests, seem to offer the best way forward.

REFERENCES

ALBRECHT, G. 1992. *The Disability Business.* London: Sage.

ALBRECHT, G., and J. LEVY. 1991. "Chronic Illness and Disability as Life Course Events." In *Advances in Medical Sociology,* Vol. 2, ed. G. Albrecht. Greenwich, CT: JAI Press.

ARBER, S., and J. GINN. 1991. *Gender and Later Life: A Sociological Analysis of Resources and Constraints.* London: Sage.

BARNES, C. 1998. "The Social Model of Disability: A Sociological Phenomenon Ignored by Sociologists?" In *The Disability Reader: Social Science Perspectives,* ed. T. Shakespeare. London: Cassell.

BURY, M.R. 1982. "Chronic Illness as Biographical Disruption." *Sociology of Health and Illness* 4 (2): 167–82.

BURY, M.R. 1988. "Meanings at Risk: The Experience of Arthritis." In *Living With Chronic Illness: The Experience of Patients and Their Families,* ed. R. Anderson and M. Bury. London: Unwin Hyman.

BURY, M.R. 1991. "The Sociology of Chronic Illness: A Review of Research and Prospects." *Sociology of Health and Illness* 13 (4): 451–68.

BURY, M.R. 1996. "Defining and Researching Disability: Challenges and Responses." In *Exploring the Divide: Illness and Disability,* ed. C. Barnes and G. Mercer. Leeds: The Disability Press.

BURY, M.R. 1997. *Health and Illness in a Changing Society.* London: Routledge.

CARRICABURU, D., and J. PIERRET 1995. "From Biographical Disruption to Biographical Reinforcement: The Case of HIV-Positive Men." *Sociology of Health and Illness* 17 (1): 65–88.

CHARMAZ, K. 1991. *Good Days, Bad Days: The Self in Chronic Illness and Time.* New Brunswick: Rutgers University Press.

COMAROFF, J., and P. MAGUIRE. 1981. "Ambiguity and the Search for Meaning: Childhood Leukaemia in the Modern Clinical Context." *Social Science and Medicine* 15b: 115–23.

CONRAD, P. 1992. "Medicalization and Social Control." *Annual Review of Sociology* 18: 209–32.

CONRAD, P. 1994. "Wellness as Virtue: Morality and the Pursuit of Health." *Culture, Medicine, and Psychiatry* 18: 385–401.

CORBIN, J. and A. STRAUSS. 1988. *Unending Work and Care: Managing Chronic Illness at Home.* San Francisco: Jossey Bass.

CORBIN, J., and A. STRAUSS. 1991. "Comeback: The Process of Overcoming Disability." In *Advances in Medical Sociology.* Vol. 2, ed. G.L. Albrecht and J.A. Levy. Greenwich, CT: JAI Press.

DAVIS, F. 1963. *Passage Through Crisis: Polio Victims and Their Families.* Indianapolis: Bobbs-Merril.

DE JONG, G. 1983. "Defining and Implementing the Independent Living Concept." In *Independent Living for Physically Disabled People,* ed. N.M. Crowe and I.K. Zola. San Francisco: Jossey Bass.

FRANK, A. 1995. *The Wounded Storyteller: Body, Illness and Ethics.* Chicago: University of Chicago Press.

FRANK, A. 1997. "Illness as Moral Occasion: Restoring Agency to Ill People." *Health* 1 (2): 131–48.

FREIDSON, E. 1970. *Profession of Medicine: A Study in the Sociology of Applied Knowledge.* Chicago: University of Chicago Press.

FRENCH, S. 1993. "Disability, Impairment or Something in Between?" In *Disabling Barriers—Enabling Environments,* ed. J. Swain, V. Finkelstein, S. French, M. Oliver, et al. London: Sage.

KELLY, M. and D. FIELD. 1996. "Medical Sociology, Chronic Illness and the Body." *Sociology of Health and Illness* 18 (2): 241–57.

KLEINMAN, A. 1988. *The Illness Narratives: Suffering, Healing and the Human Condition.* New York: Basic Books.

MARTIN, J., H. MELTZER, and D. ELLIOTT. 1988. *The Prevalence of Disability Among Adults.* London: HMSO.

MISHLER, E.G. 1984. *The Discourse of Medicine: Dialectics of Medical Interviews.* New Jersey: Ablex Publishing Co.

MORGAN, M. 1989. "Social Ties, Support and Well Being." In D. Patrick and M. Peach eds., *Disablement in the Community.* Oxford. Oxford Medical Publications.

OLIVER, M. 1990. *The Politics of Disablement.* London: Macmillan.

OLIVER, M. 1996. *Understanding Disability: From Theory to Practice.* London: Macmillan.

PARSONS, T. 1951. *The Social System.* New York: Free Press.

PINDER, R. 1995. "Bringing Back the Body without the Blame: The Experience of Ill and Disabled People at Work." *Sociology of Health and Illness* 17(5):605–631.

POUND, P., M. BURY, P. GOMPERTZ. and S. EBRAHIM. 1995. "Stroke Patients' Views on Their Admission to Hospital." *British Medical Journal* 311: 18–22.

RADLEY, A. 1994. *Making Sense of Illness.* London: Sage.

ROBINSON, I. 1988. *Multiple Sclerosis.* London: Routledge.

ROTH, J.A. 1963. *Timetables: Structuring the Passage of Time in Hospital Treatment and Other Careers.* Indianapolis: Bobbs Merrill.

ROTHENBERG, R.G., and J.P. KOPLAN. 1990. "Chronic Disease in the 1990s." In *Annual Review of Public Health.* Vol II, ed. L. Breslow et al. Palo Alto CA: Annula Reviews Inc.

STONE, D.A. 1984. *The Disabled State.* London: Macmillan.

STRAUSS, A., ed. 1975. *Chronic Illness and the Quality of Life.* St Louis: Mosby.

VERBRUGGE, L.M., and A.M. JETTE. 1994. "The Disablement Process." *Social Science and Medicine* 38 (1): 1–14.

WILLIAMS, G. 1984. "The Genesis of Chronic Illness: Narrative Reconstruction." *Sociology of Health and Illness* 6: 175–200.

WILLIAMS, G. 1998. "The Sociology of Disability: Towards a Materialist Phenomenology." In *The Disability Reader: Social Science Perspectives,* ed. T. Shakespeare. London: Cassell.

WILLIAMS, S. 1993. *Chronic Respiratory Illness.* London: Routledge.

WORLD HEALTH ORGANIZATION. 1980. *International Classification of Impairments, Disabilities and Handicaps.* Geneva: WHO.

ZOLA, I.K. 1972. "Medicine as an Institution of Social Control." *Sociological Review* 20, 497–504.

ZOLA, I.K. 1973. "Pathways to the Doctor—From Person to Patient." *Social Science and Medicine* 7: 677–89.

ZOLA, I.K. 1982. *Missing Pieces: A Chronicle of Living With a Disability.* Philadelphia: Temple University Press.

ZOLA, I.K. 1991. "The Medicalisation of Ageing and Disability." In *Advances in Medical Sociology.* Vol. 2, ed. G. Albrecht and J. Levy. Greenwich CT: JAI Press.

ZOLA, I.K. 1993a. "Self, Identity and the Naming Question: Reflections on the Language of Disability." *Social Science and Medicine* 36 (2): 167–73.

ZOLA, I.K. 1993b. "Disability Statisitcs, What We Count and What It Tells Us." *Journal of Disability Policy Studies* 4 (2): 9–39.

13 EXPERIENCING ILLNESS IN/AND NARRATIVE

SUSAN E. BELL, *Bowdoin College*

INTRODUCTION

This chapter reviews the literature about the experience of illness and narrative. First, it connects the emergence and growth of the field of illness studies and the "narrative turn" in it to transformations in social and academic life. Second, it reviews what is known about living with illness and some of the problems and questions for future research. It concentrates on topics of research about the experience of illness that are also of greatest interest to narrative analysis: how illness affects identity and ways in which "local" contexts shape experience and its analysis.[1] Studies about these two topics also address questions mirroring those of major importance within sociology as a whole and within the academy more generally: the familiar problems about the meaning of knowledge, the possibility of producing accurate knowledge about social life and about what constitutes a "self" (Seidman 1992; Smith 1987). Exploring the experience of illness and narrative, in other words, necessarily involves exploring problems in and of the discipline of sociology itself.

[1] Giving attention to these two topics and linking them to discussions within the discipline as a whole means that I have omitted huge areas of research about living with illness and downplayed problems already identified by researchers studying illness as a lived experience. Other domains of research on illness experience include uncertainty, careers, managing regimens, the role of information awareness and sharing, family relationships, and practitioner–patient encounters in the short and long term (Bury 1991; Conrad 1987; 1990; Charmaz and Olesen 1997). A new domain of illness studies also not covered in this essay is the illness experiences of physicians. This domain includes narratives of/by those caring for people with illnesses (Charon 1996; Verghese 1994) and living with illnesses (Sacks 1984; McKevitt and Morgan 1997). This review also gives less attention to the experiences of children and elderly people and to people living with a diagnosis of mental illness or substance abuse.

SOCIOLOGICAL CONTEXT

As will become clear in the course of this chapter, defining "experience of illness" and "narrative" is not an easy or straightforward process. I begin with fairly standard and oversimplified definitions by way of an introduction. I return to these definitions later in the chapter, complicating, reflecting on, and exploring intersections between them.

In the first serious attempt to establish a field of studies and define a sociology of illness experience, Peter Conrad (1987:4–5) wrote that it "must consider people's everyday lives living with and in spite of illness. . . . Such a perspective necessarily focuses on the meaning of illness, the social organization of the sufferer's world, and the strategies used in adaptation." This definition intentionally draws scholarly attention away from medical settings and medical perspectives on disease and toward the nonmedical settings and nonmedical perspectives of everyday life. Similarly, in its most general sense, "the narrative approach begins and ends with everyday life: the experiences, speech, purposes, and expectations of agents as they express them in their [written or spoken] stories about themselves" (Hinchman and Hinchman 1997:xvi). A widely used definition of narrative—a term used interchangeably with story in this chapter—is a discourse that consists of a sequence of temporally related events connected in a meaningful way for a particular audience in order to make sense of the world and/or people's experiences in it (Hinchman and Hinchman 1997:xvi). This definition of narrative includes everyday life and also draws attention to ways in which all knowledge—including scientific and nonscientific knowledge, medical and nonmedical knowledge—is produced, communicated, and sustained. Its intention is to counter traditional models of knowledge by stressing that there are multiple truths, constructed by knowers who are socially and historically located, about a world that is neither fixed nor independent of knowers. Narratives are produced in every imaginable setting, ranging from the dinner table to the doctor's office, from the playground or lecture hall to the research interview and journal article. People produce them for many reasons: remembering, engaging, entertaining, convincing, and even fooling their audiences (Bamberg and McCabe 1998:iii).

Approaches to the study of narrative and the experience of illness reflect and address general problems in sociology. The first problem concerns knowledge. Over the past twenty years, an increasing number and range of scholars have questioned the assumptions upon which modern social science is based. They argue that sociologists may want to tell the truth, but there is no Real, fixed world existing independently of any knower embodied in Facts that can be Truthfully (universally) known (Davis and Fisher 1993). Within the field of medical sociology, early ethnographers simultaneously provided the basis both for questioning the authority of medical knowledge about illness and for questioning the possibility of knowing the Truth about the experience at all, when they turned away from physician-centered and outsider knowledge of the experience of illness (Charmaz and Olesen 1997; Conrad and Bury 1997). These possibilities remained only implicit in their work, for, as Alan Radley (1993:7) puts it, they made the assumption that "there are subjective experiences, in this context a 'patient's view,' that needs to be accommodated." Although they questioned the adequacy of a biomedical model of disease on its own, early ethnographers did not question the existence or the adequacy of the opposite, subjectivist view. They assumed that a lifeworld exists, and that sociologists can know it if they turn their attention away from the medical world of doctors and toward the lifeworld of "sufferers."

Recent studies of the experience of illness have begun to challenge this oppositional way of thinking. It is not enough to turn away from a biomedical perspective to use a one-dimensional sociological model, such as one that emphasizes "isolation, stigma, or the 'master status' of illness and disability labels" (Bury 1991:463). To do so simply replaces one inadequate, unidimensional perspective with another. As Michael Kelly and David Field (1996:241) write "Illness, like life itself, is a multi-phenomenal experience and therefore a multilayered object of analysis." To understand the multilayered experience of illness, sociologists have begun to look at sick persons and their families and care givers outside of medical care; their experiences with care givers inside

medical care; their experiences beyond illness; and the experiences of medical care givers themselves (Weitz 1991; Fine and Asch 1988a).

Disenchantment with the "dominant 'Cartesian' paradigm of rationality" at the core of modern social science has led some scholars to narrative because narrative emphasizes the plurality of truths that cultures and subcultures claim about themselves, instead of assuming that there is one set of indisputable truths that can be known and told (Hinchman and Hinchman 1997:xiv). According to narrative theory, narratives are not merely representations or explanations of events that take place, or feelings that these events evoke in people going through them. Narratives, like the events they portray, take place in specific historical contexts and in shifting relations of power. Narratives "are constructed, creatively authored, rhetorical, replete with assumptions, and interpretive" (Riessman 1993:4–5). At any point in time there is a plurality of truthful narratives that differently positioned members of a culture can reasonably claim. Because narratives are constructed at particular moments in time and directed to particular audiences, they are about pasts of the moments in which they are told; a truthful narrative might be substantially different if told in other moments or to other audiences (Williams 1984:198).

Beyond plurality, narratives include rich and complex clues about why members of cultures act as they do because "people are guided to act by the relationships in which they are embedded and by the stories with which they identify" (Somers and Gibson 1994:67). Narratives enable people to explain the multiple projects in which they are always engaged and the multiple ways in which those projects are connected with one another (Ortner 1995:191).

Another problem for sociology concerns knowing. According to an increasing number of scholars, there is no objective, disembodied, value-free position from which the social scientist (knower) can know Truth (Riessman 1993). Both the knower and the world(s) she studies are "historically and culturally variable . . . firmly situated within and helping to construct the context of inquiry itself" (Davis and Fisher 1993:6–7). Together, the problems of knowledge and knowing suggest that knowledge of the social world is partial, not universal, constructed by knowers who are themselves socially and historically positioned.

According to modernist sociology, the particular identity of the researcher and relationship between researcher and subject was (is) unproblematic. As long as the researcher adhered to the ethics and scientific standards of research, the work would be unbiased and generalizable, and the rights of the subject would be protected through informed consent. However, in recent years, these assumptions have been questioned, and the identity of the researcher as well as the relationship between researcher and subject have become matters of scholarly concern (Mishler 1986; Smith 1987; Reinharz 1992).

There are different ways researchers have brought themselves into the domain of study in the field of illness experience. The first is a recognition that, as in all human research, who the researcher is and the framework of understanding she brings to the research are significant parts of the research process and have an effect on the production of knowledge. This has led some sociologists to argue in favor of making the researcher a visible part of the analysis (Smith 1987; Paget 1993; DeVault 1996). The second is that understanding the experience of illness involves more than "simply" the experiences of others; it also involves the experiences of sociologists attempting to understand the experiences of others (Weitz 1991). Finally, the researcher has entered the domain of study by turning his or her sociological "eye" toward his or her own experiences, reflecting on these experiences sociologically. This is exemplified in autobiographical accounts by sociologists and anthropologists about their experiences of having illnesses (Zola 1982; Murphy 1987; Frank 1991; Butler and Rosenblum 1991; Paget 1993) or caring for family members who are ill (Butler and Rosenblum 1991; Todd 1994; Ellis 1995). Whereas earlier studies were sometimes conducted by sociologists and anthropologists who happened to have chronic illnesses but did not address those illness experiences in their research (Talcott Parsons had diabetes; Renée Fox had polio; Arthur Kleinman suffers from asthma), in recent years, the field of illness studies has reflected more generally the turn in social sciences to bring the "self" of the researcher back in.

One of the common denominators in narrative studies is researchers' "awareness of subjectivity and reflectivity in their means of knowing" (Lieblich 1994:xi). Narrative approaches to studying social life bring researchers into the investigative process. Catherine Kohler Riessman (1993:1) puts the argument simply: "Story telling . . . is what we do with our research materials and what informants do with us. The story metaphor emphasizes that we create order, construct texts in particular contexts." Story telling is a two-fold process. At first, informants and researchers are co-authors during an interview, and then they are co-authors after an interview when a researcher re-presents and transforms the interview texts and discourses. Yet these co-authors are not equal participants in the process. Instead, they are social actors whose production of a story is embedded in social relations of gender, class, race, sexuality, professional status, and so forth (Langellier 1989, forthcoming). This approach encourages scholars to reflect on how "research strategies, data samples, transcription procedures, specifications of narrative units and structures, and interpretive perspectives" produce social science narratives (Mishler 1995:117). It also encourages them to consider not only the epistemological, but also the social and political, consequences for scholars and their respondents of the narratives that are produced (Estroff 1995; Langellier forthcoming).

A third problem for sociology concerns notions of self and identity. According to modern social science, one of the distinguishing features of modern society is the differentiation of individuals from one another and the rise of autonomous "selves" (Seidman 1994:60). The predominant (reigning) conception of the modern self defines it as individualistic, unitary, rational, and active. This view of the (adult) self maximizes characteristics associated with masculinity and minimizes characteristics associated with femininity (i.e., interpersonal commitments, including friendship, love, and care-giving relationships). It downplays the difficulty of resolving conflicts that arise between these commitments and personal aims (Meyers 1997:2). In addition, this view of the self assumes that the individual is a "stabilized entity," one that "is generally imbued with a structure of self-descriptions (concepts, schemata, prototypes) that remains stabilized until subjected to external influences from the social surroundings" (Gergen and Gergen [1983] 1997:162). This view of a stable self "ignores the multiple, sometimes fractious sources of social identity constituted by one's gender, race, class, ethnicity, sexual orientation, and so forth" (Meyers 1997:2), as well as the capacity of individuals to shape the configuration of this structure (Gergen and Gergen [1983] 1997:162).

Even the earliest studies of the experience of illness have adopted an alternative view of the self, building on the ideas of George Herbert Mead and William James. According to this symbolic, interactionist view of the self, a "self" is both process and product. It is product because it is a "relatively stable, coherent, organization of characteristics, attributes, attitudes, and sentiments that a person holds about himself or herself" (Charmaz 1991:279, note 2). In this respect, a self is an organized entity, with boundaries, parts, and elements that are integrated through memory and habit (Charmaz 1999:73). A self is also a process, a reflexive phenomenon that changes in response to emergent events. These events include interactions with others, feelings of cultural constraints and imperatives, and evaluations of self in relation to experiences, situations, others, and society generally (Charmaz 1991:279, note 2). A self develops from, but is not determined by, past discourses of meaning, present social identifications, and future motivations and goals (Charmaz 1987, 1995).

Disenchantment with modern views of the self has led some scholars to narrative, because it emphasizes the active, self-shaping quality of human thought and the power of stories to create and refashion personal identity (Hinchman and Hinchman 1997:xiv). Through narratives, people construct identities by locating themselves or being located within what Margaret Somers and Gloria Gibson call "a repertoire of emplotted stories" (1994:38–39) and Catherine Kohler Riessman calls "a community of life stories" or " 'deep structures' about the nature of life itself" (1993:2). People are especially likely to construct narratives in order to make meaning of unanticipated or apparently unrelated events. Through narratives, people create order, coherence, and connection between events that are not obviously connected to one another and thereby create "important reference points in the interface between self and society" (Williams 1984:198).

EXPERIENCING ILLNESS

There is a fairly standard history of the development of the field of study of the experience of illness (Conrad 1987, 1990; Gerhardt 1990; Bury 1997). According to this history, several books appeared as early as the 1960s, but the field itself did not take off until the 1970s. Reviews of the field separated by less than a decade reflect the consequence of this surge of attention. Whereas in 1987 Peter Conrad (1987) bemoaned the lack of theoretical grounding in the field, four years later Mike Bury (1991) wrote in a review essay that there had been a more theoretically informed approach to studying chronic illness, especially in the qualitative interpretive tradition of sociology (see also Kleinman et al. 1995).

The standard history tells us that there are multiple interrelated reasons the field of experience of illness studies took off in the 1970s. The first concerns the distribution of disease. Although chronic illness began to replace infectious diseases as "the dominant health care challenge" by the 1920s, not until the 1970s was it recognized as the predominant type of medical "problem." When the first National Health Survey was conducted in 1935, 22 percent of the U.S. population

had a chronic disease, orthopedic impairment, or deficit in vision or hearing. By 1987, the proportion had more than doubled, to over 45 percent of the U.S. population (Hoffman, Rice, and Sung 1996:1473).

A second reason for the emergence of this field of study stems from changes in medical practice that directed attention to the "whole person" as opposed to "the part," signaled by physician Leon Eisenberg (1977:10–11) in his now classic, if admittedly "somewhat overstated contrast" that "patients suffer 'illnesses'; physicians diagnose and treat 'diseases.' " Disease is an abnormality "in the *structure and function* of body organs and systems," whereas illness is an experience of "disvalued changes in states of being and in social function" (Eisenberg 1977:11). That is, "illness refers to how the sick person and the members of the family or wider social network perceive, live with, and respond to symptoms and disability" (Kleinman 1988:3). Making a distinction between disease and illness made it possible to turn the focus of analysis from the perspective of the physician to that of the patient and to explore the ways in which physicians reconfigured patients' and families' problems into "narrow technical issues." This shift of focus also created the possibility of exploring the consequences of this reconfiguration: "Treatment assessed solely through the rhetoric of improvement in disease processes may confound the patient's (and family's) assessments of care in the rhetoric of illness problems," leading to conflict between people who are sick and people who are medical practitioners (Kleinman 1988:6). These problems can arise in all episodes of disease and illness, but they are exacerbated when the diseases never entirely disappear: "Chronic illness persists over time; it does not go away. It is, therefore, not simply a discrete episode in the course of a life narrative but rather a permanent feature of that narrative" (Toombs, Barnard, and Carson 1995:xi; see also Radley 1993).

Simultaneous with these calls in the 1970s within medicine for more patient-centered care were calls outside of it for empowering patients in medical encounters and in the institution of medicine more generally (Boston Women's Health Book Collective 1971). According to women's health movement activists who were subsequently joined by disability rights activists (Fine and Asch 1988b), medicine's focus on disease not only systematically silences patients' viewpoints but reproduces unequal relations of power.

A third reason for the emergence of this field is medical sociologists' turn from a study of sociology *in* medicine to a study of sociology *of* medicine, primarily in the tradition of symbolic interaction (Conrad 1987:3–4). Whereas in a sociology in medicine, the institution of medicine defines sociologists' research problems, a sociology of medicine takes "the institution of medicine itself as a problematic focus of inquiry" (Charmaz and Olesen 1997:457). In the late 1950s, a few University of Chicago-trained sociologists began to examine illness from the patient's perspective, even though at the time the field was dominated by sociology in medicine. This early ethnographic work about illness contributed to the development of a sociology of medicine (Charmaz and Olesen 1997:457). "Implicitly at least" it challenged "the then dominant 'sick role' conception, that assumed the centrality of the medical perspective and the functionality and complementarity of the doctor–patient relationship" (Conrad and Bury 1997:374).

From its inception, study of the experience of illness has for all practical purposes meant study of the experience of chronic illness. To some extent, the attention to chronic illness reflects the rise in the sheer numbers of people living with chronic illnesses in comparison with those living with acute illnesses. To some extent it reflects differences in expectations and experiences of those diagnosed with chronic, as opposed to acute, illness. As Kleinman notes, some acute illnesses "are brief, minimally disruptive of our life activities," while others "are more distressing; they take longer to run their course." But chronic illnesses, by definition, never entirely disappear (Kleinman 1988:7). That is, chronic illnesses have a trajectory, or temporal dimension. Beyond this, however, they are more likely than acute illnesses to disturb seriously a person's "essential relationships and very sense of self" (Freund and McGuire 1991:168).

To some extent the attention to studying the experiences of people with chronic illness in order to understand the experience of illness reflects unexamined assumptions by researchers. Arthur Frank (1991:57) writes that with acute critical illnesses, the body may be restored to health, but life "does not go back to where it was before." Scholars need to examine this assumption about boundaries between the experiences of acute and chronic illness in order to illuminate more richly the array of experiences that living with illness entails. There has been more attention in this field to the distinction between chronic illness and disability (Conrad 1987; Bury 1997). Irving Zola (1982, 1989) and others in the field of disability studies (Fine and Asch 1988a, 1988b) argue that the boundaries between them are not only artificial but problematic for understanding the range of experiences for people living with illness.

At first, the field turned to subjective ("insider") accounts, in opposition to the objective ("outsider") accounts of illness. It looked to the "sufferers" of illness and gave them "voice" (but left the medical care giver and the sociologist out of the picture). Early work on identity produced the concepts of "stigma" (Goffman 1963), "biographical disruption" (Bury 1982), and "identity levels" (Charmaz 1987). Subsequent work in the field has developed and critically assessed these concepts, while simultaneously enlarging our understanding of the relationship between illness and identity.

To date, studies of the experience of illness have been dominated by British and U.S. sociologists whose focus of attention has primarily been on western culture. The effect of this western bias on the development of concepts and theories (for example, stigma) has been explored in recent studies of epilepsy in China (Kleinman et al. 1995) and infertility in India (Riessman forthcoming). Peter Conrad's (1987:20) statement that "the connection between social structure and the illness experience is still poorly understood," is less true today than it was a decade ago. There has been consistent attention to ways in which class differences have affected people's experiences of illness, notably in their access to and use of material resources and their construction of meanings (Bury 1982; Williams 1984; Corbin and Strauss 1988; Blair 1993; Blaxter 1993). Recently, more attention has been given to ways that racial/ethnic and gender identities and locations in the social structure have shaped illness experiences (Anderson, Blue, and Lau 1991; Charmaz 1994; Hill 1994; Castro 1995; Dyk 1995; Bell and Apfel 1995; Langellier forthcoming). Most of the research has either focused on the experiences of adults or taken an adult-centered view of the experiences of children (for exceptions see Blueblond-Langner 1980; Bearison 1991).

NARRATIVE

In the social sciences generally, there is an outpouring of narrative research today. The analysis of written and spoken narrative discourse has become a central topic for scholars. Indeed, the word "narrative" has become ubiquitous throughout the academic community, crossing disciplines, theoretical frameworks, methodological perspectives, and national borders (Josselson 1993; Mishler 1995). This general outpouring has spilled over into the field of medical sociology. Whereas Gareth

Williams (1984:177) cautioned in 1982 that "the concept of 'narrative' does not hold an established theoretical place in any sociological school or tradition," by 1996, Paul Atkinson (1997:325) stated firmly that "an appreciation of narrative forms and functions represents one of the most significant analytic perspectives for contemporary qualitative research on health and medicine" (see also Hyden 1997).[2] Interest in narratives and narrative analysis reflects attempts in medical sociology to extend the theoretical and methodological frameworks linking illness with self-identity, critical features of the life course, social interaction, and elements of the social structure (Bury 1997:136).

Apart from continuing this tendency in social sciences generally, narrative approaches to understanding the experience of illness emerged alongside and as a response to criticisms of biomedicine's traditional focus on disease as opposed to illness (see above). According to the biomedical model (Mishler 1981), health and disease are universal to the human species. Diseases have specific etiologies and can be diagnosed in individuals on the basis of objective signs and symptoms. References to individual life experiences that do not specify objective indications of disease are superfluous to a biomedical understanding of disease. Critics of the biomedical way of knowing argue that it strips away the social context of health and disease and ignores patients' experiences and self-understandings of their problems (Mishler 1984, 1986). When they turned their attention to the patients' experiences within and beyond medical encounters, some social scientists turned to the study of narratives because of narratives' capacity to "represent and reflect illness experience in everyday life" (Hyden 1997:52) and because they place the person with the disease (instead of just the disease) at the center of the analysis (Mattingly 1994). Narrative, simply, gives people "triumph over the alienation created by the institutional appropriation of the body through an official, medical discourse that interpellates that body in an exquisite physiological detail but denies the voice of the person who is the *lived* body" (Frank 1996:62).

At first, as with the field of illness studies more generally, narrative studies of illness dichotomized the distinction between everyday and medical ways of knowing and telling. They equated everyday understandings of illness with narrative, and biomedical "truths" about disease with nonnarrative discourse. Almost immediately this dichotomization gave way to a more complex understanding of illness narratives, when scholars began to recognize that narratives are also central aspects of medical culture, especially in (late) modern medical clinics (Mishler 1986, 1995; Atkinson 1997; Hyden 1997). At times, "in the modern clinic the patient is but a pretext for a round of orations, narratives, and disputations" (Atkinson 1997:328). Arthur Frank (1995:5) writes that "the modern experience of illness begins when popular experience is overtaken by technical expertise." When people become patients, they "accumulate entries on medical charts which . . . become the official story of the illness." As patients, ill people simply repeat "what has been said elsewhere—boring second-hand medical talk" (Frank 1991:4; see also Estroff 1995).

In addition to exploring the ways narrative creates and sustains the cultural authority of medicine, scholars have also explored intersections between medical and lay narratives of illness (Williams 1984; Atkinson 1997). Although narrative studies, like the sociology of health and illness more generally, are dominated by investigations about physicians and medical culture, a few scholars have explored the construction of illness narratives by and about other health-care providers (Gray 1993; Mattingly 1994).

Though the word "narrative" is now used widely in the social sciences generally and in the sociology of illness experience particularly, there is considerable disagreement about its precise definition (Riessman 1993). At one end of the continuum, the definition is so broad that it includes "just about anything" concerning people's lives and excludes systematic methods of transcription and formal analysis (Riessman 1993:17). At the other end of the continuum, the definition has been restricted to only those narratives that are stories about a specific past event, and that are composed of a set of particular structural elements (Riessman 1993:17). There is also disagreement about what constitutes narrative analysis. For some (Riessman 1993; Mishler 1995; Atkinson 1997), the structural and linguistic details of a narrative are crucial resources for its interpretation. How people talk about and present events conveys something important about a narrative's meaning. Scholars differ on how to make use of these details. Byron Good and Mary-Jo Del Vecchio Good (1994:837), for example, caution that

---

[2] Two social science journals are entirely devoted to the publication of narrative studies. The *Journal of Narrative and Life History* (renamed *Narrative Inquiry* in 1998) began publication in 1991. *The Narrative Study of Lives* (Sage) is an annual series, now in its fifth year of publication. Studies of narrative and the experience of illness also regularly appear in *Sociology of Health & Illness, Social Science and Medicine, Culture, Medicine and Society,* and *Health.*

"focusing attention on the *structure* of illness narratives . . . may leave an impression of coherence and completeness that is lacking in such accounts, a coherence that is lacking in the experience of illness as well." At the other end of the spectrum are those (Kleinman 1988; Mathieson and Stam 1995; Charles et al. 1998) for whom these formal details are less consequential for interpretation than the content of a narrative.

In addition to disagreement about the meaning of narrative and narrative analysis, there is disagreement within the field of illness studies about the place of narrative. Many social scientists have found that narrative richly illuminates the complicated and transformative experience of illness. One reason they find this approach productive is that narrative formats are among the cultural resources available for understanding "life in time" (Mattingly and Garro 1994:771). When a person's life is interrupted by an illness, narrative offers "an opportunity to knit together the split ends of time, to construct a new context," and to fit the disruption caused by illness "into a temporal framework" (Hyden 1997:53). Narratives organize experience through "unfolding of events and evaluations" (Atkinson 1997:340).[3]

Beyond accounting for the connection between events in time, narratives also have the "capacity to describe a world through the evocation of sensory images, to interweave even contradictory pictures and symbols and thus offer contradictory explanations in the very same story" (Mattingly and Garro 1994:771). Narratives of illness draw upon culturally shared images and conventions to present and interpret experience and draw connections between individual and society (Hyden 1997; Mattingly and Garo 1994). In this way, they have the potential of connecting the personal experiences of individuals to public issues of social structure (Williams 1984; Carricaburu and Pierret 1995; Bell 1999).

Another reason given to support the fit between narrative and illness is that listening to and analyzing narrative accounts of illness enable researchers to understand the experiences of sick people that simply cannot be "captured" by other qualitative or quantitative methods (Conrad 1990). According to Arthur Kleinman, the experience of illness and narrative are connected to one another through suffering (1988:49). Kleinman (1988:29, 30) argues that suffering "remains central to the experience of illness" and that narrative methods (including ethnography, biography, history, and psychotherapy) are ways of creating knowledge about suffering, of grasping "the complex inner language of hurt, desperation, and moral pain (and also triumph) of living an illness." This is a form of knowledge that is foreign to the modern medical bureaucracy and the helping professions that work within it, as well as to clinical and behavioral science research. The institution of medicine arranges "for therapeutic manipulation of disease problems in place of meaningful moral or spiritual response to illness problems" (Kleinman 1988:28). Similarly, clinical and behavioral science research typically uses symptom scales and survey questionnaires and behavioral checklists to quantify functional impairment and disability, but this is a "thinned-out image of patients and families [and] has statistical, not epistemological, significance; it is a dangerous distortion" (Kleinman 1988:28). For Kleinman, thus, there are medical and social scientific reasons to study/listen for illness narratives because this form of knowing provides knowledge of the experience of illness that ordinarily is missed by the clinical and behavioral sciences.[4]

Narratives of illness, like narratives more generally, are not simply reports of experiences. Instead, they

[3] This approach assumes, to put it simply, that "life itself has an implicit narrative structure" (Hinchman and Hinchman 1997:xx). However, there is another current of thought about the relationship between what might be called "brute data" and narrative: that these data "are not inherently sequential, developmental, or meaningful" (Hinchman and Hinchman 1997:xx). Accordingly, narrative imposes order and meaning on chaotic, recalcitrant material. These two currents of thought represent unresolved philosophical difficulties about the relationship between events and representations for narrative scholars: "Is self-narrative nothing but an elaborate, wholly contingent creation of the self, or does it manifest the underlying character of the object (human experience qua temporality) that it strives to encompass?" (Hinchman and Hinchman 1997:xx). It is beyond the scope of this essay to explore in detail the potential consequences of these difficulties for narrative analysis of illness experiences. For more on this topic generally, see Mishler (1995), Hinchman and Hinchman (1997), and Riessman (1993). For a beginning discussion about narrative and illness, see Mattingly (1994).

[4] The term "suffering" is widely used in studies of the experience of illness. In his classic discussion of recent and new directions in the experience of illness, Conrad (1987:5) suggests that "we self-consciously reconceptualize our respondents as *sufferers* or 'people with . . .' rather than patients." Although replacing "patient" with "sufferer" functions to distinguish experiences in the world of medicine from those in everyday life, it is not without problems. According to the dictionary definition of the word, a person who suffers is one who receives chiefly negative experiences. Thus, changing from "patient" to "sufferer" does not change the association of "illness" with "passivity," even though this is a change in meaning sought by most scholars in the field. In addition, the word "suffer" equates "illness" with loss, pain, and damage. Although these are accompaniments of illness, they are qualities that do not encapsulate the experience of illness. See Fine and Asch (1988a) for an extended critique of the use of the metaphor of "suffering victim" to describe people with disabilities generally.

"formulate reality and an attitude toward it. They shape experience and organize behavior..." (Good and Good 1994:841). According to Arthur Frank (1996:56), when people are ill, their bodies are affected by exterior inscriptions (diagnoses, surgery, social attitudes and so forth), as well as by interior "reality," such as "the pain of tumors creating pressure on organs." Narrative gives a person critical distance and thereby allows him/her the capacity to reflect on pain, "fragmented griefs and unresolved angers" about a disease and its treatment (Frank 1996:57). In this process, "illness becomes *experience,* which [is] the perpetually shifting synthesis of this perpetually spiraling dialectic of flesh, inscription and intention" (Frank 1996:58). Narrative is constantly engaged in the work of interrogating inscriptions, and that interrogation can become resistant and responsible, just as it has the capacity to become docile and appropriated.

Finally, joining together narrative and the experience of illness has enabled some scholars to explore the ways in which narratives connect selves to one another (Ellis 1995). Narratives about illness are collaboratively performed events (Langellier 1989:forthcoming). They emerge in the relationship between a teller and audience when a person represents his or her experience of illness to others who are present during the telling and present in the teller's imagination (Riessman forthcoming). In addition, they are created within clinical interactions, during "existential negotiations between clinicians and patients, ones that concern the meaning of illness, the place of therapy within an unfolding illness story, and the meaning of a life which must be remade in the face of serious illness" (Mattingly 1994:821). Written narratives of illness, like all written narratives, also connect narrators with readers, who can even imaginatively rewrite them (Riessman forthcoming:23).

To date, narrative analysts have focused their attention on establishing the credibility and possibilities of narrative approaches as a whole. As the number and range of narrative projects has grown, so has a more nuanced awareness of potential weaknesses and limitations of these approaches to studying the experiences of illness. Even though narrative analysts have consistently examined the ways in which location in the social structure affects experiences and narratives, they have given less attention to ways that narratives vary for people of different ages, for those with different diseases, or for those located within different cultures (Hyden 1997; Bury 1997). Related to this is the question of which dimensions of illness experience are likely to evoke narratives, and which are better understood

through other, non-narrative, forms of knowing (Atkinson 1997). From the beginnings of this approach, some analysts have also explored the ways in which "a" narrative is "evidence for or against the proposition that [the] image of the past would have been substantially different in other presents" (Williams 1984:198). That is, some narrative analysts are concerned about the possibility of falling into what Paul Atkinson (1997:335) calls "the trap of Romanticism":depicting "a" story told by a person about her illness experiences to another person as "the" story of her illness.

IDENTITY

The scholarly literature on narrative and the experience of illness overlaps primarily in two topics of research:identity and ways in which "local" contexts shape experience and its analysis. I now turn from a discussion of the emergence and growth of the field of illness studies and the narrative turn in it as a whole to a review of empirical studies of illness and identity. The discussion begins with the concept of stigma (Goffman 1963) and moves on to the concepts of biographical disruption (Bury 1982), preferred identity (Charmaz 1987), and biographical reinforcement (Carricaburu and Pierret 1995). Studies about identity are dominated by what Conrad (1990:1258) calls "categorical" as opposed to "narrative" data. Because of this disparity, I point out narrative approaches to the study of illness and identity in my summaries of them, but do not do the same for categorical approaches.

Categorical data are characteristically used in grounded theory analysis. Grounded theory starts with "research participants' meanings, intentions, and actions" (Charmaz 1995:51). Observers seek to achieve "intimate familiarity" with research participants in their everyday lives (Charmaz 1995:49). They collect data during interviews, through participant observation, or from existing documents; code data by theme or category; use these coded data as the basis of an analysis; and include excerpts from the coded data to illustrate the interpretation (Conrad 1990). As a result of investigators' search for causal patterns, a potential weakness in categorical data is a tendency to explain away rather than explain connections between living with illness and identity (Ellis 1995). Additionally, coding by theme or category fragments or disembodies experience (Mishler 1986; Riessman 1993). Narrative analysis is similar to grounded theory in its attempt to become intimately familiar with subjects' experience but different in significant respects:Observers preserve and attend to the discourse of research participants by focusing on how a narrative unfolds and makes sense in the process of collection, transformation, and interpretation of data. Observers using categorical data seek to be attentive to the particulars of experience and simultaneously to arrive at analytic generalizations. Observers using narrative data are cautious about the possibility of meeting both goals, notably of the modernist assumptions embedded in the quest for generalization.

The concept of stigma, an attribute that is deeply discrediting, was brought into sociological usage by Erving Goffman (1963). According to Goffman, the construction of self and self-identity through interactions with others is a central life activity. The stigmatized self is fundamentally an alienated self, even if others do not know about someone's shameful condition. People who are discreditable (whose different attribute is unknown or not immediately apparent) or discredited (whose different attribute is evident or known) interfere with everyday social interactions by introducing tension into these interactions. Goffman was interested in the sociological features common to different types of stigma: the process of stigmatization, the management of information about discreditable/discredited attributes, the feelings people have about their stigma and its management. The link between the experience of illness and stigma has been explored since the publication of his book because, as Rose Weitz writes, for all illnesses, "subjective, moral judgments . . . declare ill persons less socially worthy than healthy persons and somehow responsible for their illnesses" (1991:34). Furthermore, Goffman was especially interested in the problems of managing stigma in everyday life, and for this reason his analysis has had important ramifications for understanding the socially stigmatizing consequences of illness and the ways people manage and adapt in everyday life (Williams 1987:161). Following Goffman, sociologists have asked "What are the experiences of people with a particular stigma?" and "How does this particular case 'fit with' the general conceptual web spun by Goffman?"

The discussion that follows is limited to a summary of studies that highlight the most important conceptual material in the field. It is also contained within a stigma framework, because this framework remains a predominant framework in illness studies, even though it is a unidimensional one. This unidimensionality leads the stigma framework to view obstacles faced by people with illness and disabilities as being solely the consequence of their biological limitations, rather than the human-made barriers of architecture, discriminatory work practices, or other elements of social structure (Fine and Asch 1988a).

Whereas Goffman depicted people who are stigmatized as recipients of a spoiled identity, that is as relatively passive participants in the process of stigmatization, subsequent research has demonstrated that people actively engage in quite complex and creative strategies to manage and at times even resist discrediting information. These strategies include selectively concealing, disguising, or revealing information to others; revelations can include apologies or acts of bravado (Schneider and Conrad 1980; Weitz 1991; Kleinman et al. 1995). The "self" depicted in this work is a more active one than in Goffman's original formulation of the stigma framework. Riessman's (forthcoming) narrative analysis of a South Indian woman's experiences with infertility is particularly attentive to the details of the woman's creative strategies of resistance in collaboration with her husband and family.[5]

Nonetheless, people's perceptions about discredited attributes do influence their strategies for controlling information in interactions with others (Schneider and Conrad 1980). "Felt stigma" is the product of coaching by key individuals, and leads people to try to reduce "opportunities for, and hence rate of, enacted stigma" (Scambler 1984:217). Graham Scambler argues that felt stigma, "especially the fear of enacted stigma, [is] typically the source of more personal anguish and unhappiness than . . . enacted stigma" (Scambler 1984:217). What the influence of these perceptions, and the interactions resulting from them, mean for the development of "identity" is an unresolved matter. For Schneider and Conrad (1980:38), they may have much less to do with identity "than with the more practical matter of preventing others from applying limiting and restrictive rules that disqualify one from normal social roles." By contrast, for Scambler (1984), the "self" is tightly connected to anticipated interactions.

Whether or not people who become stigmatized remain stigmatized, as Goffman believed, is another matter of dispute. Although some have found a permanent quality to it (Scambler 1984; Link et al. 1997), others have found evidence to challenge Goffman's "contention that stigma is an ineradicable phenomenon and the notion of the spoiled identity as permanently spoiled" (Jacoby 1994:273). There is also evidence that people who become stigmatized at one point in their lives can subsequently develop enhanced selves by

---

[5] To include "infertility" in a review of the literature about living with illness is problematic. In her essay, Riessman cautions that infertility is not a disease. Just where to draw the lines between "chronic illness" and "disability" or between "health" and "disease" no longer seems as clear as it once was. I discuss the problem of blurred boundaries later in this essay.

developing new values that allowed them "to define their current selves and lives as equal to or more valuable than their previous ones" (Weitz 1991:146).

Goffman (1963:4) identified different types of stigma (abominations of the body, blemishes of individual character, and tribal stigmas), but he did not consider different degrees of stigma. Studies of illness have found that some illnesses are more stigmatized than others (Frank 1991). In her study of living with HIV disease, which is stigmatized to a greater extent than any other contemporary illness, Weitz proposes the metaphor of "continuum" for understanding the relationship between stigma and illness. The illnesses that will result in the greatest stigma are those evoking the strongest blame (the idea that ill persons are responsible for their illnesses) and dread (fear of and revulsion against an illness and those who have it) (Weitz 1991:34).

Following Goffman, most stigma research has had a Eurocentric bias, leading scholars to assume privacy and mass society, and to explore the experiences of individual selves in relation to others. A few studies have begun to question these Eurocentric assumptions. In some cultures, stigma is a moral category encompassing families as well as individuals. In their study of epilepsy in China, Kleinman and his colleagues (1995:1328) found that a moral crisis "occurs because of the delegitimation of the person and family in a structure of social relationships that affects marriage, livelihood, and all aspects of social intercourse." In India, selective disclosure is not an individual strategy; village life means that hiding an "invisible" and potentially stigmatizing attribute (such as infertility) is rarely possible (Riessman forthcoming). Beyond stigma, these studies of experiencing illness in China and India display how social science knowledge is constructed by actors who are embedded in social, cultural, and historical settings.

The line of work begun by Goffman concerns ways that illness stigmatizes—or spoils—self identity. Another line of work concerns how illness interrupts a person's taken-for-granted assumptions about himself or herself, and a person's attempts to reorder his or her self-understanding. In a now-classic paper in which he proposed the concept of "biographical disruption," Mike Bury (1982) examines the disruptive effect of the onset and early development of chronic illness on a person's identity. With "biographical disruption," Bury links the process of self-transformation in response to illness both to social structural conditions and to specific cultural and familial contexts in modern society. In this type of society, "the relationship between self and others is a precarious enterprise, characterized . . . by high degrees of self-reflection, individualism, and the manipulation of appearances" (Bury 1982:178). Individuals hold this precariousness "in check by a wide range of 'cognitive packages,'" predominantly those resonating strongly with the imperatives of modern science and medicine (Bury 1982:178). When these cognitive packages, or logics, of scientific and medical discourse cannot explain radically altered, threatening, or seemingly arbitrary circumstances in a person's everyday life—such as the onset of illness—people need to develop new packages. People establish new cognitive packages by drawing from both professional and everyday knowledge as well as their own biographical experience (Bury 1982:174–75). The new packages enable them to impose meaning and to re-establish points of reference between body, self, and society (Williams 1984:177). They accomplish this connection by turning to what Gareth Williams (1984) calls "narrative reconstruction," an act of interpretation that reconnects profound discontinuities in a person's daily life.

Bury emphasized the cognitive dimensions and consequences of biographical disruption. Subsequent research has explored different dimensions of biographical work (Corbin and Strauss 1987, 1988) and given attention to the causes of biographical disruption (Williams 1984). In connection with this work is a further exploration of the kind of identities people establish after the onset of illness to attain, maintain, or recreate valued selves (Charmaz 1987, 1991, 1994). Over time, people choose different types of what Kathy Charmaz calls "preferred identities," ranging hierarchically from a "supernormal social identity, an identity demanding extraordinary achievement in conventional worlds" to a "salvaged self, retaining a past identity based on a valued activity or attribute while becoming physically dependent" (Charmaz 1987:285). The experience of progressive illness often means reducing identity goals and aiming for a lower or less preferred identity level in the identity hierarchy. Movement up and down the identity hierarchy is influenced by changes in physical status and by others' "strategies of assistance, intervention, or even abandonment" (Charmaz 1987:297).

All of the studies on interruption demonstrate how illness profoundly disrupts people's lives and identities, their responses to this disruption, and connections between individual responses and the social and historical settings of their lives. Adding further complexity to this work is a recent study of asymptomatic HIV-positive men; some men were gay and had been infected through sexual practices, and other men had been infected through medical products used to treat hemophilia. The authors of this study found evidence of what they call "biographical reinforcement," that is, "reinforcement of the components of identity that, prior to HIV-infection, had already been built around hemophilia or homosexuality" (Carricaburu and Pierret 1995:85). In addition to reinforcement (as opposed to disruption) of identity, findings from this study suggest that sometimes identity has a collective dimension to it; being HIV-positive is not just a matter of being individually infected but also being affected as part of a group having its own history that includes decimation by AIDS (Carricaburu and Pierret 1995:86). The collective dimension of illness identity has also been explored by Bell (1988, 1999) in her narrative analysis of accounts by DES daughters, women exposed prenatally to a synthetic estrogen prescribed to their mothers to prevent miscarriage that later caused cancer and reproductive tract problems in DES daughters.

Identifying and exploring tensions between categorical and narrative knowing, as well as the consequences of each approach for understanding illness, identity, and the self, offer potentially rich rewards to sociologists interested in this line of research. As sociologists develop further our understanding of the biographical and life course dimensions of living with illness and place these dimensions within the changing contexts of physical status and cultural and structural settings, we should also attend to the intellectual benefits and limitations of each approach (see Charmaz 1995; Bury 1997).

KNOWING IN CONTEXT

A recognition that "there is no observer-free science, and that accounts of objects are never independent of the observer" (Josselson 1996:xii) has led sociologists to argue in favor of making the researcher part of the analysis. In studies of illness, scholars have taken different approaches to using and locating themselves in the research process and the resulting "product." For some, this has involved an exploration of the developing relationship between themselves and the people whose life experiences they are attempting to understand. This exploration includes ethical tensions and dilemmas that emerge during the course of the study. For others, it has meant exploring their own life experiences, becoming both the observer and observed. In the discussion that follows I begin by giving some examples of ethical tensions and dilemmas and then some examples of personal narratives of illness experiences by sociologists.

Whereas the literature on identity is dominated by categorical approaches, the literature about location is dominated by narrative approaches to understanding illness experiences.

A prerequisite for understanding the lives of people with illness is attending to the details of everyday life in the collection, interpretation, and presentation of this material (Charmaz 1995; Kleinman et al. 1995). Although there are ethical dilemmas in all social science research, these dilemmas are exacerbated when the research involves understanding in exquisite detail the experiences of people living with illness who may be "vulnerable, impaired, pained, and lonely" (Estroff 1995:96). First, this knowledge, even those details not appearing publicly, can turn researchers into witnesses, reducing the distance between them and their subjects and connecting them in unanticipated and complex ways (Weitz 1991; Frank 1995). A second dilemma arising for researchers concerns a tension between presenting details and placing lives in contexts, while simultaneously protecting the privacy of respondents (Davis 1991; Estroff 1995). Researchers typically mask the identities of their respondents, and respondents usually (Charmaz 1995), but not always (Langellier forthcoming), want their identities hidden. Connected to the second dilemma is a third: the meaning of informed consent. It is difficult to translate the principles of informed consent into action, and the most difficult part of the process may not even begin until a consent form is signed (Weitz 1991; Bamberg and Budwig 1992). Sue Estroff (1995:97) argues that scholars have not sufficiently explored "how far our responsibilities go and what they are, what authority we do and do not rightly claim, and how we give proper voice to what we know and what informants tell us" even long after a consent form has been signed.

These three sorts of ethical dilemmas for studies of illness are connected to the general problems in sociology of knowledge and knowing discussed in the first part of this chapter. Modern social science aims to split "facts" from "values" (Seidman 1994). A typical strategy for including a discussion of values in a sociological study of illness is to relegate it to appendices, footnotes, prefaces, and acknowledgments (Estroff 1995; Weitz 1991). It is in these margins of a standard social science text that scholars appear to be able to provide accounts of the ethical dilemmas in their work, splitting attention to facts from attention to values.

For scholars who take the position that there is a plurality of truths and that knowers are always positioned in the world they study, the relationship between facts and values is no longer taken to be oppositional. In sociology as a whole, a major problem for proponents of this point of view is "to reconcile their moral advocacy with their claims to knowledge" (Seidman 1994:9). Scholars whose focus is the experience of illness have this same problem. To put it simply, even though "ethical language and principles have seldom been invoked or applied explicitly to the production of knowledge in ethnographic and qualitative study of illness" (Estroff 1995:86), some scholars see a connection and are exploring it. In line with this approach to connecting facts and values, perhaps the marginalizing strategies described above can be seen as hinting at a solution: that an exploration of possible links between the ethical and analytical dimensions of research at the center of a text is more compatible with narrative than other forms of knowing and representing knowledge (Riessman 1993: forthcoming; Estroff 1995; Bell 1997; Langellier forthcoming).

First-person narratives have become an increasingly popular genre within and outside of the academy for understanding experiences generally, including illness experiences. It is within this general tendency that the turn to personal narratives of illness by sociologists must be placed. Like other narrative studies, they contest traditional social science approaches by collapsing the distinction between the knower and the known and questioning the possibility of producing accurate knowledge about social life. Irving Kenneth Zola (1982) was the first to turn his illness experiences, and himself, into the subject of an investigation. Zola (1982:7) produced what he called "a socio-autobiography, a personal and social odyssey" to chronicle his beginning acknowledgment of the impact on his life of polio and the use of a leg brace and canes after a severe automobile accident. Zola interweaves his individual experiences with an ethnography of a village designed to house four hundred severely disabled adult Netherlanders. His account, organized in the form of a story, ends with a moral claim: Anything separating and negating those with a chronic condition will ultimately invalidate all members of society (Zola 1982:238).

Whereas Zola began his career by taking the stance of a detached observer and became connected through his illness experiences, Marianne (Tracy) Paget (1993:7) had always located herself in her work as "an experiencing subject, methodically attempting to understand other subjects and a subject matter." After her diagnosis with cancer, she simply turned herself into the subject both experienced and understood. Misdiagnoses made in Paget's own life mirrored and gave support to her earlier work in which she argued that error is endemic to medicine.

Arthur Frank (1991:5) went further than Zola and Paget in his collapse of the knower/known distinction, shedding his sociological identity and taking on the identity of "fellow sufferer, trying to make sense of" a heart attack at age 39 and cancer a year later. Based on this identity, he began to develop the concept of a "remission society," a post-modern world in which people must learn to tell their own stories "not just to work out their changing identities, but also to guide others who will follow them" (Frank 1995:17). Not in spite of, but as a result of collapsing the distinction between knower and known, Irving Zola (1982), Marianne Paget (1993), and Arthur Frank (1991, 1995) draw sociological insights from their personal experiences of illness (see also Todd 1994). These include re-examining the meaning of health and illness, the ways boundaries between them are blurred, and the consequences for knowledge and practice of either separating or blurring these boundaries.

A second topic of sociological narratives of illness concerns the meaning of the body and the possibility of constructing accurate knowledge about it. When Barbara Rosenblum (Butler and Rosenblum 1991:54) was diagnosed with breast cancer, she "went inside [herself] and wrote about [her] life and feelings," instead of using a traditional social science approach to build an interpretation of her experiences. Rosenblum's experiences of illness led her to question the stability and "truth" of the body, and to search for a new language and vocabulary of meaning (see also Frank 1996). In a sustained reflection about embodiment, Barbara Rosenblum and her lover Sandra Butler explore the consequences of having a body that gives different signals every month, becoming a "language of symptoms, not sexuality," and ultimately becoming the only body in both of their lives, delineating their day with its stamina, vitality, and appetites (Butler and Rosenblum 1991:132, 141). Rosenblum and Butler's narrative accounts, written in the form of successive chapters, about a body's instability and the lack of boundaries between their bodies, communicate the ways in which illness is a multilayered experience about which more than one truthful narrative can be claimed.

CONCLUSION

I return to the theme introduced at the start of this chapter. Studies of living with illness address questions mirroring those of major importance within sociology as a whole and within the academy more generally: How can we "know" about the social world if all knowledge and all knowers are situated? How can we understand the lives and selves of people with illnesses in context? I have explored how scholars interested in understanding the experiences of people who live with illness have engaged in systematic study, positioning themselves and their respondents in local settings, developing the field substantively and conceptually. My focus has been on how two fields of work have emerged and contributed to the development of this understanding. I have downplayed antagonisms between the two fields, preferring instead to reformulate into unresolved questions charges that narrative analysis is reductionist, romantic, and guilty of making misguided assumptions about grounded theory, and that grounded theory is insufficiently sensitive to the details of subjects' experiences and naively tied to modernist assumptions about social research. In my discussion throughout the chapter, I have also indicated directions that researchers might profitably take.

There are persistent, underlying assumptions in all of this work that I have not yet highlighted. The first is that both approaches take subjective reality seriously and recognize its importance to understanding illness experiences. A prerequisite for understanding the experience of illness is systematically and rigorously collecting observations about people's lived experience in their social worlds. Researchers in this field of sociology, that is, do not fall at the end of the postmodern continuum that claims there are no bodies but only social practices. Beyond this, there are disputes about this assumption. Scholars disagree about how bodies and people are "real," and what constitutes "systematic" and "rigorous" research.

A second shared assumption is that all knowledge, knowers, and selves are situated. Situating knowledge, knowers, and selves can lead to the view that all knowledge is relative and that there is not necessarily any relationship between knowledge and reality. However, studies of living with illness do not take this extreme position. Instead, this assumption is taken to mean that we need to locate research in its cultural, temporal, spatial, political, and economic contexts. Even though the assumption is shared, scholars disagree about its consequences for doing social science research into the experiences of living with illness. Some argue that stories are the units of analysis most likely to encourage researchers to explore the complex relation between illness and culture, to enable social policy to address the local and collective dimensions of the experiences of illness, and to raise awareness of the complicated ways researchers are implicated in the production of knowledge. Others warn that narrative analysis is a limited approach to studying social life. Because social life is enacted through a complex variety of forms, we need multiple approaches to studying it.

Finally, a third shared assumption is that there are (and should be) social consequences of knowledge about living with illness. A sociological understanding of the experiences of illness provides a way of linking the feelings, ideas, and relationships of individuals with their social settings, and of linking bodies and social structures. This understanding opens up possibilities for making transformations in the lives of our subjects, our disciplines, and our social and political worlds.

REFERENCES

ANDERSON, JOAN M., CONNIE BLUE, and ANNIE LAU. 1991. "Women's Perspectives on Chronic Illness: Ethnicity, Ideology and Restructuring of Life." *Social Science and Medicine* 33(2):101–13.

ATKINSON, PAUL. 1997. "Narrative Turn or Blind Alley?" *Qualitative Health Research* 7(3): 325–44.

BAMBERG, MICHAEL, and ALLYSSA MCCABE. 1998. "Editorial." *Narrative Inquiry* 8(1):iii–v.

BAMBERG, MICHAEL, and NANCY BUDWIG. 1992. "Therapeutic Misconceptions: When the Voices of Caring and Research Are Misconstrued as the Voice of Curing." *Ethics & Behavior* 2(3):165–84.

BEARISON, DAVID J. 1991. *"They Never Want to Tell You." Children Talk About Cancer.* Cambridge: Harvard.

BELL, SUSAN E. 1988. " 'Becoming a Political Woman' The Reconstruction and Interpretation of Experience Through Stories." In *Gender and Discourse: The Power of Talk,* ed. A. D. Todd and S. Fisher. Norwood, N.J.: Ablex, pp. 97–123.

BELL, SUSAN E. 1999. "Narrative and Lives: Women's Health Politics and the Diagnosis of Cancer for DES Daughters." *Narrative Inquiry* 9(2):1–43.

BELL, SUSAN E., and ROBERTA J. APFEL. 1995. "Looking at Bodies: Insights and Inquiries about DES-Related Cancer." *Qualitative Sociology* 18(1):3–19.

BLAIR, ALAN. 1993. "Social Class and the Contextualization of Illness Experience." In *Worlds of Illness,* ed. A. Radley. New York and London: Routledge, pp. 27–48.

BLAXTER, MILDRED. 1993. "Why Do the Victims Blame Themselves?" In *Worlds of Illness,* ed. A. Radley. New York and London: Routledge, pp. 124–42.

BLUEBOND-LANGNER, MYRA. 1980. *The Private Worlds of Dying Children.* Princeton, N.J.: Princeton.

BOSTON WOMEN'S HEALTH BOOK COLLECTIVE, eds. 1971. *Our Bodies, Ourselves.* Boston: Free Press.

BURY, MICHAEL. 1982. "Chronic Illness as Biographical Disruption." *Sociology of Health & Illness* 4(2):167–82.

BURY, MICHAEL. 1991. "The Sociology of Chronic Illness: A Review of Research and Prospects." *Sociology of Health & Illness* 13(4): 451–68.

BURY, MICHAEL. 1997. *Health and Illness in a Changing Society.* London and New York: Routledge.

BUTLER, SANDRA, and BARBARA ROSENBLUM. 1991. *Cancer in Two Voices.* San Francisco: Spinsters Book Company.

CARRICABURU, DANIELE, and JANINE PIERRET. 1995. "From Biographical Disruption to Biographical Reinforcement: The Case of HIV-Positive Men." *Sociology of Health & Illness* 17(1): 65–88.

CASTRO, ROBERTO. 1995. "The Subjective Experience of Health and Illness in Ocuituco: A Case Study." *Social Science and Medicine* 41(7):1005–21.

CHARLES, CATHY, CRISTINA REDKO, TIM WHELAN, AMIRAM GAFNI, and LEONARD REYNO. 1998. "Doing Nothing is No Choice: Lay Constructions of Treatment Decision-Making Among Women With Early-Stage Breast Cancer." *Sociology of Health & Illness* 20(1): 71–95.

CHARMAZ, KATHY. 1987. "Struggling for a Self: Identity Levels of the Chronically Ill." *Research in the Sociology of Health Care* 6: 283–321.

CHARMAZ, KATHY. 1991. *Good Days, Bad Days: The Self in Chronic Illness and Time.* New Brunswick, NJ: Rutgers.

CHARMAZ, KATHY. 1994. "Identity Dilemmas of Chronically Ill Men." *The Sociological Quarterly* 35(2): 269–88.

CHARMAZ, KATHY. 1995. "Between Positivism and Postmodernism: Implications for Methods." *Studies in Symbolic Interaction* 17: 43–72.

CHARMAZ, KATHY. 1999. "'Discoveries' of Self in Illness." In *Health, Illness, and Healing: Society, Social Context, and Self,* ed. K. Charmaz and D. A. Paterniti. Los Angeles, CA: Roxbury, pp. 72–82.

CHARMAZ, KATHY, and VIRGINIA OLESEN. 1997. "Ethnographic Research in Medical Sociology: Its Foci and Distinctive Contributions." *Sociological Methods & Research* 25(4): 452–94.

CHARON, RITA. 1996. "To Listen, To Recognize." In *Perspectives in Medical Sociology,* ed. P. Brown. Prospect Heights, Ill.: Waveland Press, pp. 310–317.

CONRAD, PETER. 1987. "The Experience of Illness: Recent and New Directions." *Research in the Sociology of Health Care* 6:1–31.

CONRAD, PETER. 1990. "Qualitative Research on Chronic Illness: A Commentary on Method and Conceptual Development." *Social Science and Medicine* 30(11): 1257–63.

CONRAD, PETER, and MIKE BURY. 1997. "Anselm Strauss and the Sociological Study of Chronic Illness: A Reflection and Appreciation." *Sociology of Health & Illness* 19(3): 373–76.

CORBIN, JULIET M., and ANSELM STRAUSS. 1987. "Accompaniments of Chronic Illness: Changes in Body, Self, Biography and Biographical Time." *Research in the Sociology of Health Care* 6:249–81.

CORBIN, JULIET M., and ANSELM STRAUSS. 1988. *Unending Work and Care: Managing Chronic Illness at Home.* San Francisco and London: Jossey-Bass Publishers.

DAVIS, DENA S. 1991. "Rich Cases: The Ethics of Thick Description." *Hastings Center Report* 21(4):12–16.

DAVIS, KATHY, and SUE FISHER. 1993. "Power and the Female Subject." In *Negotiating and the Margins: The Gendered Discourses of Power and Resistance,* ed. S. Fisher and K. Davis. New Brunswick, N.J.: Rutgers, pp. 3–20.

DEVAULT, MARJORIE L. 1996. "Talking Back to Sociology: Distinctive Contributions of Feminist Methodology." *Annual Review of Sociology* 22: 29–50.

DYK, ISABEL. 1995. "Hidden Geographies: The Changing Lifeworlds of Women With Multiple Sclerosis." *Social Science and Medicine* 40(3): 307–20.

EISENBERG, LEON. 1977. "Disease and Illness: Distinctions Between Professional and Popular Ideas of Sickness." *Culture, Medicine and Psychiatry* 1: 9–23.

ELLIS, CAROLYN. 1995. *Final Negotiations: A Story of Love, Loss, and Chronic Illness.* Philadelphia, PA: Temple.

ESTROFF, SUE E. 1995. "Whose Story Is It Anyway? Authority, Voice, and Responsibility in Narratives of Chronic Illness." In *Chronic Illness: From Experience to Policy,* ed. S. K. Toombs, D. Barnard, and R. A. Carson. Bloomington and Indianapolis: Indiana University Press, pp. 77–102.

FINE, MICHELLE, and ADRIENNE ASCH. 1988a. "Disability Beyond Stigma: Social Interaction, Discrimination, and Activism." *Journal of Social Issues* 44(1): 3–21.

FINE, MICHELLE, and ADRIENNE ASCH. 1988b. *Women With Disabilities: Essays in Psychology, Culture, and Politics.* Philadelphia: Temple.

FRANK, ARTHUR W. 1991. *At the Will of the Body: Reflections on Illness.* Boston: Houghton Mifflin.

FRANK, ARTHUR W. 1995. *The Wounded Storyteller: Body, Illness, and Ethics.* Chicago: University of Chicago.

FRANK, ARTHUR W. 1996. "Reconciliatory Alchemy: Bodies, Narratives and Power." *Body & Society* 2(3):53–71.

FREUND, PETER E.S., and MEREDITH B. McGUIRE. 1991. *Health, Illness, and the Social Body: A Critical Sociology.* Englewood Cliffs, NJ: Prentice Hall.

GERGEN, KENNETH J., and MARY M. GERGEN. [1983] 1997. "Narratives of the Self." In *Memory, Identity, Community,* ed. L. P. Hinchman and S. K. Hinchman. Albany: State University of New York Press, pp. 161–84.

GERHARDT, UTA. 1990. "Qualitative Research on Chronic Illness: The Issue and the Story." *Social Science and Medicine* 30(11): 1149–2259.

GOFFMAN, ERVING. 1963. *Stigma: Notes on the Management of Spoiled Identity.* Englewood Cliffs, NJ: Prentice Hall.

GOOD, BYRON J., and MARY-JO DELVECCHIO GOOD. 1994. "In the Subjunctive Mode: Epilepsy Narratives in Turkey." In collaboration with Isenbike Togan, Zafer Ilbars, A. Guvener, and Ilker Gelisen. *Social Science and Medicine* 38(6):835–42.

GRAY, DAVID E. 1993. "Negotiating Autism: Relations Between Parents and Treatment Staff." *Social Science and Medicine* 36(8):1037–46.

HILL, SHIRLEY A. 1994. *Managing Sickle Cell Disease in Low-Income Families.* Philadelphia, PA: Temple.

HINCHMAN, LEWIS P., and SANDRA K. HINCHMAN. 1997. "Introduction." In *Memory, Identity, Community: The Idea of Narrative in the Human Sciences,* ed. L. P. Hinchman and S. K. Hinchman. Albany: State University of New York Press, pp. vii–xxxii.

HOFFMAN, CATHERINE, DOROTHY RICE, and HAI-YEN SUNG. 1996. "Persons With Chronic Conditions: Their Prevalence and Costs." *Journal of the American Medical Association* 276(18):1473–79.

HYDEN, LARS-CHRISTER. 1997. "Illness and Narrative." *Sociology of Health & Illness* 19(1): 48–69.

JACOBY, ANN. 1994. "Felt Versus Enacted Stigma: A Concept Revisited. Evidence From a Study of People With Epilepsy in Remission." *Social Science and Medicine* 38(2):269–74.

JOSSELSON, RUTHELLEN. 1993. "A Narrative Introduction." In *The Narrative Study of Lives.* Vol. 1, ed. R. Josselson and A. Lieblich. Newbury Park, CA: Sage, pp.ix–xv.

JOSSELSON, RUTHELLEN. 1996. "Introduction." In *Ethics and Process in the Narrative Study of Lives.* Vol. 4, ed. R. Josselson. Newbury Park, CA: Sage, pp. xi–xvii.

KELLY, MICHAEL P., and DAVID FIELD. 1996. "Medical Sociology, Chronic Illness, and the Body." *Sociology of Health & Illness* 18(2) :241–57.

KLEINMAN, ARTHUR. 1988. *The Illness Narratives: Suffering, Healing & The Human Condition.* New York: Basic.

KLEINMAN, ARTHUR, WEN-ZHI WANG, SHI-CHUO LI, XUE-MING CHENG, XIU-YING DAI, KUN-TUN LI, and JOAN KLEINMAN. 1995. "The Social Course of Epilepsy: Chronic Illness as Social Experience in Interior China." *Social Science and Medicine* 40(10):1319–30.

LANGELLIER, KRISTIN M. 1989. "Personal Narratives: Perspectives on Theory and Research." *Text and Performance Quarterly* 9: 243–76.

LANGELLIER, KRISTIN M. Forthcoming. " 'You're Marked': Breast Cancer, Tattoo and the Narrative Performance of Identity." In *Narrative and Identity,* ed. D. Carlbaugh and J. Brockmeier.

LIEBLICH, AMIA. 1994. "Introduction." In *The Narrative Study of Lives.* Vol. 2, ed. A. Lieblich and R. Josselson. Newbury Park, CA: Sage, pp. ix–xiv.

LINK, BRUCE G., ELMER L. STRUENING, MICHAEL RAHAV, JO C. PHELAN, and LARRY NUTTBROCK. 1997. "On Stigma and Its Consequences: Evidence From a Longitudinal Study of Men With Dual Diagnoses of Mental Illness and Substance Abuse." *Journal of Health and Social Behavior* 38(June):177–90.

MATHIESON, CYNTHIA M., and HENDERIKUS J. STAM. 1995. "Renegotiating Identity: Cancer Narratives." *Sociology of Health & Illness* 17(3): 283–306.

MATTINGLY, CHERYL. 1994. "The Concept of Therapeutic 'Emplotment.' " *Social Science and Medicine* 38(6):811–22.

MATTINGLY, CHERYL, and LINDA C. GARRO. 1994. "Introduction." *Social Science and Medicine* 38(6): 771–74.

MCKEVITT, CHRISTOPHER, and MYFANWY MORGAN. 1997. "Anomalous Patients: The Experiences of Doctors With an Illness." *Sociology of Health & Illness* 19(5):644–67.

MEYERS, DIANA TIETJENS. 1997. "Introduction." In *Feminists Rethink the Self,* ed. D. T. Meyers. Boulder, CO: Westview Press, Inc., pp. 1–11.

MISHLER, ELLIOT G. 1981. "Viewpoint: Critical Perspectives on the Biomedical Model." In *Social Contexts of Health, Illness, and Patient Care,* ed. E.G. Mishler, L.R. Amara Singham, S.T. Hauser, R. Liem, S.D. Osherson, and N.E. Waxler. New York: Cambridge, pp. 1–23.

MISHLER, ELLIOT G. 1984. *The Discourse of Medicine: Dialectics of Medical Interviews.* Norwood, N.J.: Ablex.

MISHLER, ELLIOT G. 1986. *Research Interviewing: Context and Narrative.* Cambridge: Harvard.

MISHLER, ELLIOT G. 1995. "Models of Narrative Analysis: A Typology." *Journal of Narrative and Life History* 5(2): 87–123.

MURPHY, ROBERT F. 1987. *The Body Silent.* New York: H. Holt.

ORTNER, SHERRY. 1995. "Resistance and the Problem of Ethnographic Refusal." *Comparative Studies in Society and History* 37(1): 173–93.

PAGET, MARIANNE A. 1993. *A Complex Sorrow: Reflections on Cancer and an Abbreviated Life,* ed. Marjorie L. DeVault. Philadelphia, PA: Temple.

RADLEY, ALAN. 1993. "Introduction." In *Worlds of Illness: Biographical and Cultural Perspectives on Health and Disease,* ed. A. Radley. London and New York: Routledge, pp. 1–8.

REINHARZ, SHULAMIT. 1992. *Feminist Methods in Social Research.* New York: Oxford.

RIESSMAN, CATHERINE KOHLER. 1993. *Narrative Analysis.* Newbury Park: Sage.

RIESSMAN, CATHERINE KOHLER. Forthcoming. " 'Even if We Don't Have Children [We] Can Live': Stigma and Infertility in South India." In *Narrative and Cultural Construction of Illness and Healing,* ed. C. Mattingly and L. C. Garro. Berkeley: University of California.

SACKS, OLIVER. 1984. *A Leg To Stand On.* New York: Harper & Row.

SCAMBLER, GRAHAM. 1984. "Perceiving and Coping With Stigmatizing Illness." In *The Experience of Illness,* ed. R. Fitzpatrick, J. Hinton, S. Newman, G. Scambler, and J. Thompson. London and New York: Tavistock, pp. 203–26.

SCHNEIDER, JOSEPH W., and PETER CONRAD. 1980. "In the Closet With Illness: Epilepsy, Stigma Potential and Information Control." *Social Problems* 28(1): 32–43.

SEIDMAN, STEVEN. 1992. "Postmodern Social Theory as Narrative With a Moral Intent." In *Postmodernism and Social Theory,* ed. S. Seidman and D. Wagner. Oxford, U.K. and Cambridge, MA: Blackwell, pp. 47–81.

SEIDMAN, STEVEN. 1994. *Contested Knowledge: Social Theory in the Postmodern Era.* Oxford, U.K. and Cambridge, MA: Blackwell.

SMITH, DOROTHY E. 1987. *The Everyday World as Problematic: A Feminist Sociology.* Boston: Northeastern.

SOMERS, MARGARET R., and GLORIA D. GIBSON. 1994. "Reclaiming the Epistemological 'Other': Narrative and the Social Constitution of Identity." In *Social Theory and the Politics of Identity,* ed. C. Calhoun. Cambridge: Blackwell, pp. 36–99.

TODD, ALEXANDRA DUNDAS. 1994. *Double Vision: An East-West Collaboration for Coping with Cancer.* Hanover: Wesleyan University Press (published by University Press of New England).

TOOMBS, S. KAY, DAVID BARNARD, and RONALD A. CARSON. 1995. "Preface." In *Chronic Illness: From Experience to Policy,* ed. S. K. Toombs, D. Barnard, and R. A. Carson. Bloomington: Indiana University Press, pp. ix–xiv.

VERGHESE, ABRAHAM. 1994. *My Own Country: A Doctor's Story of a Town and Its People in the Age of AIDS.* New York: Simon & Schuster.

WEITZ, ROSE. 1991. *Life with AIDS.* New Brunswick, NJ: Rutgers.

WILLIAMS, GARETH. 1984. "The Genesis of Chronic Illness: Narrative Re-Construction." *Sociology of Health & Illness* 6(2):175–200.

WILLIAMS, GARETH. 1993. "Chronic Illness and the Pursuit of Virtue in Everyday Life." In *Worlds of Illness,* ed. A. Radley. New York and London: Routledge, pp. 92–108.

WILLIAMS, SIMON. 1987. "Goffman, Interactionism, and the Management of Stigma in Everyday Life." In *Sociological Theory and Medical Sociology,* ed. Graham Scambler. New York and London: Tavistock.

ZOLA, IRVING KENNETH. 1982. *Missing Pieces: A Chronicle of Living With a Disability.* Philadelphia: Temple.

ZOLA, IRVING KENNETH. 1989. "Toward the Necessary Universalizing of a Disability Policy." *The Milbank Quarterly* 67(Suppl.2, Pt.2): 401–28.

14 THE MEDICAL PROFESSION AND ORGANIZATIONAL CHANGE: FROM PROFESSIONAL DOMINANCE TO COUNTERVAILING POWER

DONALD W. LIGHT, *University of Medicine and Dentistry of New Jersey*
Rutgers University

Professions are both a special kind of occupation, with elements of a collective social movement, and a population of organizations. They are memic by intent, by professional policy (DiMaggio and Powell 1983), yet located in and interdependent with one or more clustered networks of organizations that form the client base (Flood and Fennell 1995). They are also strongly tied to the state, both exploiting and being subject to its regulatory and financial powers. Finally, they usually have clients who care very much about services and can be both dependent and very critical. In these ways, professions operate within a field force of countervailing powers (Light 1993).

This essay provides a historical overview of how the American medical profession has interacted with its interdependent partners and countervailing powers during the twentieth century. It explains the paradigm shift from professional dominance to managed care and reconceptualizes the concept of autonomy. It then takes up the question of what distinguishes professionals from businessmen by revisiting a classic theoretical article on that question by Talcott Parsons and closes by examining briefly the issue of trust and professionalism. Building on previous reviews (Light 1993; Hafferty and Light, 1995), the essay is selective rather than comprehensive. While it focuses on the United States, international materials will be used to show both what the United States shares in these developments with other advanced health care systems and how it differs.

THE PROFESSION AND MANAGED CARE

In the sociology of occupations and organizations, few groups have undergone such extensive and important changes as the American medical profession has in the organizational transformation of its work known as *corporate managed care*. These changes cannot accurately be characterized as the corporatization of a once-autonomous profession (McKinlay and Stoeckle 1988), because the profession itself played such a central and active role in developing large medical bureaucracies and a medical-industrial complex well before managed care began. Paul Starr (1982) provided the historical account missing in Eliot Freidson (1970a, 1970b), of how the medical profession fought to establish legal, occupational, organizational, and economic dominance, and how this led to an increasingly specialized, hospital-based, and bureaucratic complex. Andrew Abbott (1988) has further examined the key role of technological advances and the changing nature of work in these developments. The consequences of technology for the profession's clients and for the large-scale organizational changes that resulted were only partly worked out by Abbott, though he wryly noted that oligarchy in a profession leads toward bureaucratization, which then tends to undermine the basis of expert judgment on which individual autonomy rests (Abbott 1988: 172–73)! Another irony of technological advances has been to rescue millions of patients from death but leave them with chronic conditions, so that the very successes of modern medicine have slowly refocused its work around what it cannot cure. This sociological recomposition of patients has, in turn, led patients to seek alternative therapies to address their enduring problems. The prevalence of chronic disorders has profound organizational and policy implications (Fox 1996). Albrecht (1992) has described the corporatization of care for those with disabilities and the active participation of clinicians.

In a historical analysis of how professional dominance transmogrified into corporate managed care, Light (1989, 1997a) has emphasized how the medical profession's creation of protected markets for professional autonomy created ideal markets for corporations as well. This is one of several "ironies of success" that any sociological history must take into account to avoid the trap of regarding managed care as the invasion of barbarians from the hills of corporate America who have destroyed the social advantages of professionalism. To wistfully remember "the Golden Age of Doctoring" (McKinlay 1999) is to forget that it was also the age of gold (Rodwin 1993), the age of unjustified large variations of hospitalization and surgery caused by autonomy and lack of accountable standards (Wennberg and Gittelsohn 1973), the age of large portions of tests, prescriptions, operations, and hospitalizations judged to be unnecessary by clinical researchers (Greenberg 1971), the age of medicalizing social problems (Conrad and Schneider 1992), the age of irresponsibly fragmented care in the name of "autonomy," the age of escalating prices and overcharging to a degree unknown anywhere else in the West (Navarro 1976; Waitzkin 1983; White 1991), the age of provider-structured insurance that paid for almost any mistake or poor investment anyone happened to make, and the age of corporations moving in to reap the no-lose profits of such a world by exploiting the profession on its own terms. The cultural authority of the profession, emphasized by Starr (1982), Freidson (1986), and Abbott (1988), was shaken by the early 1970s, when a spate of books and articles appeared about the social pathologies of professional dominance just mentioned, as well as the neglect of the poor, of those with chronic conditions, and of public health issues (e.g., Greenberg 1971; Ehrenreich and Ehrenreich 1971; Kennedy 1972; Nixon 1971).

Today, managed care is widely considered by its advocates to be the "rational" solution to the social and economic excesses and pathologies of "the Golden Age of Doctoring." The best managed care aims to create clinical services that are coordinated and based on scientific evidence and to combine them with a systematic approach to prevention and patient education, so that people stay healthy and get better care at lower cost when they become ill. The worst managed care aims to wrest deep discounts out of what is paid to doctors, hospitals, and all other sectors, reap huge profits as a result, and actually not get around to developing good clinically managed care and prevention. Recent assessments by independent and even sympathetic observers have concluded that so far it is the latter scenario that has happened (Zelman and Berenson 1998, Ch 8; Kilborn 1998; Ginsberg 1998). The best managed care has inspired models for integrated health-care delivery systems and even for community-based health-care management systems (Shortell, Gillies, Anderson, et al. 1996). But the dynamics of competition constantly break down the potential for integrated clinical care, as plans switch providers and employers switch plans (Zelman and Berenson 1998, Ch 8; Light 1999a). And the foundations for community-based care are less present in the United States than in almost any other Western country. A comparative analysis of corporate versus community paradigms of health care shows how different they are and how little basis exists for the current revival of community health care as a policy fashion (Light 1997b).

The tendency to regard managed care as "rational" is sociologically interesting. Frank Dobbin (1994) has shown how "rationality" is itself a cultural construct, and how different countries develop quite different industrial policies that are regarded by each as "rational." Likewise, American policy makers for the health-care industry are so entrenched in their own constructed reality of how "rational" managed care is that they do not realize that none of the other first-rate health-care systems in the world have used anything remotely like corporate managed care to hold their costs down to a flat percent of GNP over the past twenty years (White 1991).

THE CONCEPT OF THE PROFESSION AS A COUNTERVAILING POWER

The concept of professional dominance refers to the ways in which a profession uses legal and clinical autonomy to gain control over other competing professional groups, over the profession's institutional domain, and over its financing. The history of how the American medical profession mounted campaigns against several competing forces in the early 1900s in order to achieve organizational, institutional, and financial control has been described elsewhere (Light 1989). But the theoretical problem with the concept of professional dominance is that decline is not possible.

Dominance begets still more dominance, making a profession still more impregnable. Moreover, Freidson's account (1970a, 1970b) contained little history and, as Elliott Krause (1996) observes, dealt with one country at one point in time.

Throughout the 1980s, the perception grew that the profession's dominance was experiencing decline. In a review addressing the "paradox of medical advances and professional decline," Donald Light and Sol Levine (1988) assessed the major concepts of the medical profession: dominance, deprofessionalization (Haug 1988), proletarianization (McKinlay and Arches 1985), and its de-Marxed variation, corporatization (Oppenheimer 1973; McKinlay and Stoeckle 1988). They concluded that each concept characterized parts of the profession's changing relationships with patients and corporations, but each had serious limitations. All are limited to one historical period. Each is named for a given contemporary feature or process, (e.g., "deprofessionalization" or "corporatization"), but theoretically and historically these concepts are not very useful. David Coburn (1993) concluded that Freidson's continued insistence on the profession's dominance is "fatally weakened by his slide from a defense of the notion of medical dominance (control over others) to a defense of the more restricted idea of medical autonomy (freedom from control by others)." David Frankford (1993) concluded that the contending theorists constructed self-referent arguments, talking past one another so that no resolution was possible. Marjorie Weiss and Ray Fitzpatrick (1997) have pointed out more recently that deprofessionalization and corporatization represent quite different challenges from different parties. These later assessments support the earlier conclusion that "a new framework is needed, one that incorporates historical trends and current features" of medical practice (Light and Levine 1988).

One framework that is more historical, dynamic, and comparative is that of countervailing powers. The central idea is to regard the medical and other health professions as one of several major countervailing powers in society, consisting of the state and employers as payers of health care, patient groups and enrollees as consumers of health care, the medical-industrial complex as producers of products and services for profit, alternate modalities or schools of healing and wellness, and perhaps other parties depending on the country and its sociological character (Light 1995). These parties have different interests, cultures, and goals that are in tension with each other, though significant alignments are possible. Each seeks, to a greater degree or less, in a more organized way or less, and with greater resources or less, to fulfill its interests. These too change over long periods of time. Thus, the rise to dominance of the American medical profession can be analyzed in terms of its alignment with cultural and institutional development in American society and with other major parties' interests. It can be compared to the development of professional dominance in other countries that have quite different field forces of countervailing powers, like Germany (Light and Schuller 1986; Light, Liebfried, and Tennstedt 1986).

The countervailing model provides an analytic framework that puts into a comparative, historical context a development such as "professional dominance" or "deprofessionalization" or "corporatization." These trends may span decades, but with an enlarged sociological imagination one realizes that they produce their own imbalances, excesses, and neglects, which in time will elicit countervailing powers to assert themselves. This macro picture can be refined in any of its parts to analyze the field force of countervailing powers among any one of them, such as among the health professions. Thus studies like Abbott's (1988) or Stevens's (1984) focus on contending occupational and professional groups for control over techniques, kinds of clients, organizational resources and complexes, prestige, and finance. These struggles may lead to new organizational forms, as they have among payers trying to hold costs down (Light 1988a).

The concept of countervailing powers builds on the work of Terrance Johnson (1972) and Magali Larson (1977), who emphasized professionalization as a concerted effort to gain market control and lock in monopoly powers by recruiting the state to its cause. Navarro (1976) emphasized how the medical profession, medical practice, and the state were shaped by capitalism. The model of countervailing powers also takes into account the central roles of the state in forming, training, institutionalizing, and employing professions (Freddi 1989; Rueschemeyer 1986; Burrage and Torstendahl 1990; Torstendahl and Burrage 1990; Frenk and Duran-Arenas 1993). This model is also framed by the values and culture of health care, by technological developments (Frenk and Duran-Arenas 1993), and by the state as reflected in Julio Frenk and Luis Duran-Arenas's (1993) insightful taxonomy of state-professional relations. Countervailing powers as a model combines such thematic studies and focuses attention on the interactions of powerful actors in a field where they are inherently interdependent yet distinct.

This kind of model has received considerable enrichment and extension by the comparative historical research of Elliott Krause (1996), who begins by writing, "Visualize a triangle, with the state, capitalism, and the professions at the corners" (p. 1). Each influences the other two. Which of these eventually gains or loses power depends on the time, the place, and what the parties are doing. There are four dimensions of power and control, Krause concludes from his comparative study: the association, the workplace, the market, and the state. Krause encourages researchers to trace over time the relations among the three parties and their degree of control over these four dimensions. The comparative work of Andrew Twaddle (1996) has also led him to a similar depiction of three models for medical care; he has particularly focused on competing values and priorities, such as the trade-offs between quality and efficiency, profit and equity.

The sociological concept of countervailing powers recognizes several parties, not just buyers and sellers. For example, alliances with dominant political parties or governments can lead to the profession being isolated and weakened (Harrison 1998), or co-opted (Jones 1991; Krause 1988, 1996). Governmental dependency can lead to controlling professionalism's excesses and to structuring professional work around wellness, health education, occupational health, and prevention, as happened in post-war East Germany (Light and Schuller 1986). But such harnessing of professional work to the state's goals can also lead to underfunding, perfunctory medical services, delays and bureaucratic hassles, demoralization, and the eventual deterioration of medical practice, as happened in later decades (Jones 1991). One is struck by how similar the complaints are now, as U.S. employers and government programs contract with managed-care companies and use corporate forms of what is usually called "socialism" to achieve similar ends. A fundamental change in the balance of power has come from the ability now of employers or government to analyze the practice patterns of providers more systematically than they can themselves (Bjorkman 1989; Whitman and Fishman 1997).

Analytically similar but substantively quite different are the medical profession's relationships to the corporations that supply it with equipment, tools, and information technology. They can both benefit the profession and make it dependent in uneasy ways. These corporations make up the medical-industrial complex and want to maximize growth and profits by constantly refining and upgrading products, creating market niches, expanding current markets, creating new markets, and rewarding doctors for generating new revenues (Waitzkin 1983, Ch.4). Their products significantly enhance professional power and income, and when they do not strengthen the profession's scientific base, they enhance its scientistic image. But in return, medical corporations support the profession's meetings, journals, continuing medical education, clinical research, and even professional careers, until the profession is deeply dependent on their interests. Government as a countervailing power seems conflicted. It wants the economic growth of biomedical industries, but also lower health-care costs.

Time and Dimensions of Change

The time frame for shifts in countervailing powers can be years or decades. Dominance slowly produces imbalances, excesses, and neglects that offend or threaten other countervailing powers and alienate the larger public. Relations can be affected by:

1. Internal elaboration and expansion that weaken the dominant institution from within

2. The changing technological base of its expertise

3. Tendencies to drain more and more wealth or power from other parties

4. A self-regarding importance that ignores the concerns of clients and institutional partners

5. An expansion of control that threatens the interests of other parties

6. Relations with adjacent occupations or professions

7. The changing demographic composition of members.

Governmentality and the Interdependence of "Autonomy"

Countervailing powers are to some degree separate and distinct, but as Johnson (1995) emphasizes, they also define and shape each other over time. Drawing on Foucault's concept of *governmentality,* Johnson argues that both the state and professions are "the outcome of governing" (p. 12). Indeed, the professions were created or developed, he argues, as tools for governing. Although somewhat true, this thesis leaves out the degree to which both the state and the professions are shaped by their own ambitions and by the priorities of corporations. But health care also neutralizes the moral content of social problems and holds out the promise of scientific, rational cures.

Theoretically, this perspective puts the profession's coveted autonomy into a different light, for professional autonomy arises from and depends on state support and intervention and on agreement by other powers, especially corporations and governments as the institutions that pay most of the bills. Is autonomy then not grounded in interdependence? If so, Freidson's (1970b: 42) argument, that a profession remains autonomous as long as it controls (or has autonomy over) its own technical core of work, even if countervailing powers control external resources, is untenable. For the effects of external resources and powers on clinical work belie this distinction both in theory (Abbott 1988) and in reality (Field 1988). Attempting to keep internal forms of control distinct from external relations is often not realistic or helpful (Frenk and Duran-Arenas 1993). Budgets and institutions deeply affect the character of the technical core of professional work, as evidenced by the effects of stringent budgets and access barriers in nations with paltry funds, or by the effects of some managed care organizations on clinical services in the United States (Ware et al. 1996; Anders 1996; Manian 1998; Schlesinger et al. 1997). This symbiotic relationship between micro and macro controls over the conditions of work reframes autonomy as part of a continuum of control.

HISTORY OF PROFESSIONAL DOMINANCE AND ITS IRONIES

Within this conceptual framework, let us turn to the ironic history of how the American medical profession rose to dominance and brought managed care upon itself. The connections between the two are missing in Starr's excellent history (1982), which depicts a profession muscling its way into dominance as it assaults or suppresses all challengers in the first half of the twentieth century but then depicts a noble profession being attacked from all sides thereafter. The missing ingredient is the ironies of professional dominance that lead to such imbalances that the countervailing powers react.

Much of the early history appeared in the last edition of this handbook and so will not be repeated here (Light 1989). Suffice it to say that at the turn of the century, the medical profession faced competitors on several fronts, including institutional buyers contracting on a discount or capitated basis for services to a population of employees or members. It would be inaccurate to call these "managed care," but they do ring familiar to contemporary ears. In response, medical societies organized a series of campaigns, and by 1920, organized medicine controlled the institutional, financial, legal, educational, and clinical nature of most medical work. The campaigns shut down medical schools for women and for blacks and blocked efforts to make medical services widely accessible to the poor, except by acts of charity. They stopped the highly successful public

health movement from expanding into clinical services for the working poor (Waitzkin 1983). Part of this history supports Johnson's (1995) thesis that the state and the profession have a symbiotic relationship in which each shapes the other as both pursue issues of governance. In Europe, the state often played a central role in developing different professions and institutionalizing them; in the United States, state inaction led professions to take the initiative (Larson 1990).

The medical profession fought against any health insurance for patients as long as it could. But when mounting unpaid bills during the Depression made insurance necessary for doctors, the profession carefully chose a form that minimized any incursions on its autonomy (Light 1997a). When the organized profession's relentless opposition to any kind of government insurance, even for the elderly and poor who could not afford medical services or private insurance, seemed finally on the brink of failure, it successfully insisted that Medicare and Medicaid also reimburse fees and not alter the practice of medicine.

The ironies of professional dominance are multiple. All innovations reinforced specialization and the emphasis on providing the best clinical medicine for every sick patient. Prevention and public health had low status. Expenditures rose rapidly in the 1940s, 1950s, and '60s, as well as the '70s and '80s. Specifically, total spending increased by 315 percent during the 1940s, from $3.9 billion to $12.3 billion by 1950. It doubled again (unadjusted for inflation) during the 1950s, to $25.2 billion by 1960 (Somers and Somers 1960, Table A-1). Total spending tripled during the 1960s, to $75.0 billion in 1970. Physicians' incomes during this period started much higher than the other 90 percent of health workers and rose many times faster (Navarro 1976: 136–45). Doctors became the lynchpins for a booming medical–industrial complex far larger than themselves, and the specialization they had pursued required large buildings and medical complexes that spawned new centers of organizational power and a new profession, hospital administration.

By the early 1970s both patients and doctors were complaining about "bureaucratic medicine" and impersonal care (Greenberg 1971). The only part of medicine not yet corporatized was direct services. Thus, protected markets were created in which specialty corporations could hardly lose. Costs escalated and a medical–industrial complex arose. But the more medicine elaborated itself, the more marginal its contributions to the general health needs of a population became, and the more those needs got neglected. In time, payers (be they employers or governments) rebelled against escalating costs for diminishing returns. When Arnold Relman (1980) protested against this new medical-industrial complex of for-profit health services, he missed the point, for-profit services were simply the last step in a process of corporatization that the profession had nurtured for decades.

The Revolt of Payers as Countervailing Powers

Just about the time that Freidson published his treatise on professional dominance in 1970, countervailing powers started to dismantle it.

Richard Nixon's (1971) historic speech before both houses of Congress, the first on health care, envisioned a nation of "HMOs," the newly coined employer's dream of a private, self-regulating delivery system based on capitation, the opposite of reimbursed fees. Nixon's bill for national health insurance promised to reverse the pathologies of professional dominance and transform American health care into a system focused on prevention and primary care, an end to fragmented specialty care and impersonal bureaucracy, an emphasis on personal care and continuity coordinated by your own personal physician, and an end to spiraling costs and personal medical debt. Nixon's bill deeply threatened doctors and hospitals. They made sure it did not pass, and thirty years later the nation has yet to fulfill the vision of universal, equitable, well-managed health care in Nixon's speech.

The oil crisis and an international recession made cost containment urgent for governments as well as for all payers (Coburn 1993). Meanwhile, total costs more than tripled again during the 1970s, to \$248.0 billion in 1980, despite extensive federal and state efforts to partner with the profession to contain costs (Bruner et al. 1992). By the early 1980s both employers and Congress (as the largest payer of all) took concerted action in what I call the Buyers' Revolt. Its dimensions are outlined in Table 14–1, and they characterize the main lines of change since then. Perhaps most basic was a growing distrust of doctors' values, decisions, and even competence, as evidence mounted of overtreatment, medical errors and uneven quality, and large variations in practice style. This has led to a profoundly threatening shift, from granting physicians exclusive control over how they practiced medicine, to close monitoring of their practices.

Economically, the buyers' revolt has taken control by degrees of the old system in which physicians set their fees and replaced it with various kinds of fixed prepayments or budgets with requirements to account for how money is spent. Fixed budgets, in turn, have reversed the incentives, from rewarding more costly specialized procedures after patients get sick, to rewarding prevention and primary care so that costly specialized procedures can be kept to a minimum. Fixed budgets and contracts have also eliminated the informally arranged cross subsidies, from high-fee, high-profit

TABLE 14–1 The Buyer's Revolt: Axes of Change in the 1980s

From	To
Provider dominance (a system run and shaped by doctors)	Buyer dominance (an effort to dismantle and reshape the laws, customs, and institutions established by organized medicine to allow buyer choice and competition)
Sacred trust in doctors	Distrust of doctors' values, decisions, even competence
Quality assumed by medical profession as high (but uneven and unattended)	Quality a major focus of systematic review
"Nonprofit" guild monopoly	Competition for profit (even among nonprofit organizations)
Cottage industry structure	Corporate industry structure
Specialization and subspecialization	Primary care and prevention, with minimal referrals to specialists
Hospital as the "temple of healing"	Home and office as equal centers of care
Fragmentation of services as a byproduct of preserving physicians' autonomy	Coordination of services to minimize error and reduce unnecessary and inappropriate services and costs (slow in coming)
Payment of costs incurred by doctors' decisions	Fixed prepayment, with demand for a detailed account of decisions and of their efficacy
Cross-subsidization of the poor by the more affluent, of low-tech and service departments by hi-tech departments	Cross-subsidization seen as "cost shifting," a suspect maneuver that imposes hidden charges on buyers

Source: Donald W. Light, "Toward a New Sociology of Medical Education," *Journal of Health and Social Behavior* 29(1988), pp. 307–22.

departments like surgery to money-losing activities such as clinical teaching and research, charity care, and community services. Parallel to this removal of economic buffers has been a political shift toward minimizing the legal and administrative protections the profession long enjoyed from competition and outside corporations. These changes also alter the environment for developing medical technologies.

Organizationally, the buyers' revolt has transformed a cottage industry of physicians' practices, nonprofit community hospitals, and thousands of local health-care agencies and organizations into an increasingly for-profit corporate structure in which these units have been amalgamated. But just as the provider-driven system had its disadvantages and liabilities, so does the new buyer-driven one. Table 14–1 ends by listing them for each system.

From Autonomy to Accountability

At the heart of this paradigm change lies the displacement of autonomy by accountability and a disillusionment in the trust given to physicians (Rodwin 1993; Sulmasy 1992). A theoretical inference of this paradigm shift is that professional autonomy, both at the collective level (Freidson 1994) and the individual level (McKinlay and Stoeckle 1988), is not autonomous but rather a socially constructed reality (Atkinson 1995; Frankford 1997), a conviction that has its liabilities as well as it assets. Further, autonomy is a secondary rather than fundamental characteristic of professionalism. Theoretically, this radically recasts the role of autonomy in the sociology of the professions (Light 1988b). Rather than being the irreducible core of professionalism, autonomy is a second-best substitute for accountability, long used because one could not look inside the black box of clinical judgment and therefore had to grant the profession autonomy and trust that members would use it to maximize patients' well-being.

Rhetorically, autonomy is that claim and posture of a countervailing power that ironically weakens it from the inside out, as individual professionals confidently practice as they wish in ways of dubious quality or value. Physician autonomy led to well-documented excesses and unprofessional practices that became known as computers created a revolution of information that leveled hierarchies throughout society (Fukuyama 1999). During the 1970s and '80s, too many physicians were found to be making "gang visits" to hospitalized patients, upcoding procedures, and investing in facilities to which they referred their patients. Too many reports appeared documenting significant proportions of tests, operations, and prescriptions judged unnecessary by their clinical peers, or large variations in surgery and hospitalization in the same small areas for patients with the same diagnoses (Wennberg and Gittelsohn 1973; McPherson et al. 1982). Too many times, researchers found that doctors were continuing to use obsolete or even contraindicated practices. The sacred core of professionalism—autonomy—turned out to result in widely different clinical judgments and practice styles, with no assurances of quality for patients or cost-effectiveness for payers (Mayor 1998; Smith 1998; Matheson 1999). Looked at in light of this evidence, autonomy seemed like the last thing one would want in good professional care.

In cutting back sharp rises in utilization, insurers and managed-care plans have largely used crude and unscientific criteria to deny payment of bed days and procedures, in effect deciding what is "medically necessary" (Rosenbaum et al. 1999). But state and federal governments, and some health plans, have set about to measure performance and quality with increasing precision. To take one of many examples, the state of New Jersey, as the largest payer of surgery and as a promoter of increased quality and accountability, collects data on every patient who had bypass surgery, calculates the risk-adjusted mortality rate of different hospitals and surgeons, and publishes the results *by name* (Whitman and Fishman 1997). Thus, citizens, other payers, and medical staffs can read that UMDNJ/University Hospital did only 123 CABG surgeries in 1996, while Robert Wood Johnson University Hospital did 1,400. Further, they can read that among the staff at RWJ Hospital, Dr. Peter Scholz had a risk-adjusted mortality rate of 2.1 per 100 for his operations, well below the state average for surgeons, while Dr. Gregory Scott had a very high mortality rate of 5.6. Measures of comparative performance like this, inside autonomy's black box, are increasingly carried out and distributed.

The sociological paradox is that the critics of "professionalism" are helping the medical profession overcome its own weaknesses, even as they seem to be weakening it. They have taken over the core professional responsibility of assessing what is effective and being sure that members practice accordingly. For example, Congress, as the largest buyer, has undertaken many of what should be professional responsibilities (McCormick, Cummings, and Kovner 1997). They include:

- The PORTS (comparative analysis of outcomes for different interventions)
- Pharmaceutical outcomes research

- Clinical practice guidelines, evidence-based practice centers
- Development of computerized information systems
- "Gold standard" clinical practice guidelines
- Assessment of new technologies
- Development of computerized quality assessment systems
- Development of health plan report cards for consumers.

Patient groups and deprofessionalized knowledge on the Internet are challenging professional powers (Haug 1988). One might say, as Freidson (1986, 1994) has emphasized, that professionalism is being reborn by responding to the demands of payers for evidence-based procedures and better outcomes. Physician-led research teams, academic medical centers, and specialists societies are now dedicating themselves to identifying which interventions and protocols are most effective. Further, institutional bridges are being built between medical schools and the profession and the communities they serve (Frankford and Konrad 1998). Theoretically then, if the discourses and control over the application of medical knowledge stem from the actions of countervailing powers outside the profession, what does it mean for medicine to be a "profession"? (Larson 1990).

Professionalism and Countervailing Powers Abroad

American readers should not assume that the historic dynamic of professional dominance, its excesses and ironies, and the reassertion of countervailing powers are not taking place outside the United States in "socialist" systems that have government-directed or government-run national health insurance or services. In nearly all those countries, the medical profession captured the national system from within and built in rules and prohibitions to protect their dominance (Immergut 1992; Wilsford 1991; Larkin 1983; Willis 1989; Coburn, Torrance, and Kaufert 1983; Light and Schuller 1986). But this dominance has been secured within systems that have far better levers for modulating cost increases than does the United States (White 1991). These include long-term planning of hospital construction and other capital investments, long-term regulation of the workforce size, composition and distribution, macro budgetary control, and firm price controls. Commercialization and for-profit services are minimal in other Western

countries. Compared to the United States, professional dominance has been more balanced by government controls over supply and cost, providing foreign corporations with an essential service at significantly lower cost (Anderson 1997). This has meant that America's international competitors, such as Finland's Nokia against Motorola for cell phones, or Germany's Volkswagen against Ford, or Holland's Unilever against Colgate-Palmolive, get high quality comprehensive health care for their employees at considerably lower cost and without the hassle of running a complex and costly health-benefits department.

In all these countries, countervailing powers work to weaken the profession's grip and to address the excesses or pathologies of professional dominance. This has proven to be more difficult in several countries than in the United States because the profession is so deeply entrenched within those systems (Saltman and Figueras 1997; Powell and Wessen 1999). A good example is a recent treatise advocating managed care for the German system (Seitz, Konig, and Jelastopulu 1998). At every critical point, the authors in their frustration acknowledge that some institutional or legal entrenchment established by the medical profession long ago blocks the managed-care reforms.

MANAGED CARE: WHAT DOES "PROFESSIONAL" MEAN?

In revolting against the spiraling costs, waste, and a focus on state-of-the-art medicine, buyers by degrees have moved toward what is now called "managed care." They started with utilization review, which became quite elaborated, and spawned a secondary industry (Gray and Field 1989). Practice variation and utilization review naturally led to the idea of selecting more efficient or cheaper doctors and creating networks out of them. Insurers and new independents offered to put these networks together and monitor them. In these ways, the managed-care industry in the United States was formed piece by piece throughout the 1980s to carry out the mission of employers and government programs of reducing the unnecessary services and prices that the professionally driven health-care system had generated over the preceding 20 years.

Despite these get-tough cost-containment efforts in the 1980s, providers found ways to drive up costs another 269 percent, to $666.0 billion by 1990 (Bruner et al. 1992). In particular, specialists won the first round of the buyers' revolt (Light 1993). They rapidly organized into larger and larger groups, invested more as partners in profit-making services to which they referred their patients, and maximized revenues through the loopholes in DRGs and other cost-containment measures. As a result, they gained a greater share of total health-care expenditures, and their personal incomes rose briskly, moving still further ahead of primary care physicians. By the early 1990s, the countervailing powers of Congress, state legislatures, and corporate buyers redoubled their efforts.

Meantime, a profound organizational change occurred when investors realized that HMOs had two functions that could be separated: the insurance function and the professional function of treating patients. That is, investors could form an HMO that took in premium revenues and contracted out for services, without having any clinical staff or facilities itself, a "virtual" HMO. This meant not only that an HMO (not a full-service organization like the traditional HMOs) could be started quickly, but also that it could sign up hundreds of doctors along with hospitals and clinics, to broaden its appeal to more employees. These providers could be "taught" to practice cost-effective medicine through incentives, disincentives, close monitoring, and in-house treatment protocols. Even more threatening to medicine as a profession was the further step of contracting out the financial risk as well as the clinical services, so that the fewer tests and procedures doctors ordered, the more they made. The traditional HMO was by these steps being transformed from a full-service organization to a contracting and marketing office that made providers bear the financial risk and take care of all the patients' problems (Anders 1996).

The term *managed care* has traditionally referred to what doctors and nurses do when they coordinate or clinically manage the various services that patients with complicated problems need. The term was adopted by investors packaging the new provider networks, to convey a sense of enlightened responsible coordination (Light 1994). Most managed-care corporations, however, so far have principally managed contracts and costs through deep discounting, rather than the more complex task of managing patient care ("Managed Care Woes" 1998; Ginsberg 1998; Kilborn 1998; Winslow 1998; Abelson 1999). The public holds a similar view as the experts: "Few people feel there is a health care 'system' in any positive sense of the word. If they see any 'system' at all, it is one devoted to maximizing profits by blocking access, reducing quality, and limited spending, all at the expense of the patient" (Edgman-Levitan 1998).

Still, the pursuit of high quality, accountable professionalism continues at a minority of stable, serious, managed care organizations. For example, the Lovelace managed-care system in Albuquerque surveyed how often its cardiologists used highly effective beta blockers for MI (myocardial infarction) patients, found disappointing variability, developed managed-care protocols, implemented them, changed clinical behavior, and showed high, uniform use afterwards (Friedman 1998). In such an example, board-certified specialists are made more professional than they otherwise would be by a managed-care corporation acting as the buyers' agent.

A leading edge of managed care centers around physician-owned systems that hold the full budget and contracts for hospitals and other services (Robinson 1994, 1997). Here the physicians are the captains of managed care, not its victims. Ironically, evidence shows they cut specialty and hospital use as much as do investor-run managed care organizations. Services are organized through contracts, creating a virtual organization through a modified network structure. These developments represent a new paradigm for the medical profession in which doctors own and run the entire delivery system as investors. Now the theoretical shoe is on the other foot, with doctors in control of everything, but at full risk. To many this feels "unprofessional," but physicians have owned and run their practices for years. It seems our traditional Anglo-American concept of a profession has been idiosyncratic and logically garbled for decades.

THE PROFESSIONAL AND THE BUSINESSMAN—PARSONS REVISITED

Are doctors businessmen, and if not, what are the critical differences? An important early attempt to answer this question was made by Talcott Parsons (1939) during the Depression, and surprising insights result from revisiting his answers. The first surprise is that Parsons did not press for an answer by comparing professions with a more analogous and challenging group like craftsmen. He did not ask himself, for example, how a certified electrician or bricklayer differs from a certified cardiologist. Rather, he asked how professionals differ from businessmen, because his larger purpose was to explain the altruism of the professions in light of the assumption in economic theory and utilitarianism that self-interest motivates all behavior. The differences between professionals and businessmen may seem so obvious and great as to be not worth the asking. Parsons, however, instead emphasized how *similar* businessmen are to professionals like physicians. In an era today when a great many physicians own or operate their businesses, including physician-owned managed-care companies, Parsons's essay gains compelling salience.

Parsons (1939: 185) begins by stating that "professions occupy a position of importance in our society which is . . . unique in history" because they pursue and apply the fruits of science and liberal learning to societal needs. But Parsons immediately takes away what he has given by observing that businessmen also do this. Next, he turns to the common argument that businessmen pursue self-interest, while "the professions are marked by 'disinterestedness'" (1939: 186). But are the motives of businessmen and professionals really so different, he asks? Do not businessmen sometimes act altruistically and professionals pursue their self-interests? "Perhaps even it is not mainly a difference of typical motive at all, but one of the different situations in which much the same commonly human motives operate. Perhaps the acquisitiveness of modern business is institutional rather than motivational" (1939: 187). More broadly, Parsons points out (in the 1930s) that the professionals have flourished in a capitalist society, and professional work is interpenetrated with capitalism.

Business and the professions are both rational, and Parsons points out that rationality is primarily institutional and cultural, not "natural." Both are contractually specific. Both are functionally specific around a certain task or transaction. Relations in both are segmented around that functional specificity and universal criteria. The professional has a "case," the businessman a "customer." Even when a heart specialist decides whether a given person "is eligible for a relatively permanent relationship to him as his patient," it is done on technical, universal criteria. Both professionals and businessmen seek success. You may think that professionals differ in seeking honor and respect, but so do businessmen, Parsons argues. In sum, professionals such as physicians are similar to businessmen in many ways.

What distinguishes the professions, Parsons concludes, is an *institutional* pattern or context of disinterestedness versus self-interest. Elements of both motivations are found in the professional and business institutional pattern, Parsons argues. Doctors are not necessarily more altruistic, he writes, and "the doctor could, if he did these things according to the business pattern, gain financial advantages which conformity with his own professional pattern denies him" (Parsons 1939: 192). It is the institutional structure, norms, rules, and roles (supported by state laws and regulations) that define and reward a collective orientation and the dedicated application of medical science to patients' needs. This answer is surprisingly compatible with Dobbin's (1994) research, with the new institutionalism in sociology (Brinton and Nee 1998), and with the call for a revival of professionalism today (MAP 1999).

The theoretical implication of Parsons's analysis is that if the institutional context changes so that medicine becomes a for-profit business, then doctors will be no different from businessmen. The usual arguments about personal altruism and fiduciary obligations to patients are absent here. In fact, as Parsons was writing, the medical profession was responding to the Depression by setting up a financing scheme for its work that would make any businessman envious: deciding what to charge and then having it reimbursed (Starr 1982; Light 1997a). In time, group practices, professional incorporation, and investing in equipment or facilities became routine, and the AMA code of ethics was amended to accommodate these changes so that they would not be regarded as commercial violations of the "professional institutional pattern."

By 1951, as medicine was entering its "Golden Age" (and age of gold), Parsons painted a much more ambiguous picture of professional practice. Influenced by his training in psychoanalysis, Parsons (1951: 429) emphasized how patients are helpless, anxious, vulnerable, and lacking technical competence. He emphasized their anxieties, even about a needle being inserted in their body, and their "very complex non- and irrational reactions."

Again, the profession is seen as rationally applying science, but this time with difficulty. Often, Parsons now pointed out, there is no clear treatment or no treatment at all, a theme familiar in advanced medicine today (Fox 1996, 1999). There are also significant areas of uncertainty. Yet American culture and expectations demand action and results, leading to magical thinking and wish fulfillment through surgery. Lynn Payer (1988) has nicely described this American culture, and Peter Conrad (1999) describes its latest manifestation in the visions of genetic engineering to prevent or cure mankind's ills. Parsons reported that unnecessary operations were much discussed (a notable historical observation in 1951, long before volumes of unnecessary operations are believed to have arisen), and they are too easily attributed to the "direct financial incentive to be biased in favor of operating" (Parsons 1951: 467). More important are cultural expectations that press to "Do *something*," even though one is uncertain what, if anything, will help. "The primary definition of the physician's responsibility is to 'do everything possible' to forward the complete, early and painless recovery of patients" (Parsons 1951: 450). But this is not often possible. Magical thinking and beliefs are found in both patients and physicians, Parsons emphasized.

This sensitivity by Parsons to ambiguity and magical thinking, however, contrasts sharply with his firmly normative solutions. Universalism, he asserted, will protect the doctor from identifying with patients or being personally drawn into their anxieties. Technical competence, together with functional specificity, will allow a focused intrusion into the patient's life and body by providing assurance to the patient that she or he can trust the doctor's intrusiveness. But most important is a "collectivity orientation" for the "protection of the patient against the exploitation of his helplessness, his technical incompetence and his irrationality . . . " (Parsons 1951: 463). "[The doctor] cannot advertise. . . . He cannot bargain over fees. . . . He cannot refuse patients on the grounds that they are poor 'credit risks'. . . . The general picture is one of sharp segregation from the market and price practices of the business world . . . "(p. 464). A psychoanalytically trained observer might suspect denial in such puristic insistence, for what Parsons did not see was that the profession had constructed a monopoly market in which it set its own prices. In a market like that, who needs to bother with the practices of businessmen? At one point, Parsons (1951: 436) acknowledges that the physician must take responsibility for the "settlement of the terms of exchange" with patients. This genteel reference to fees and bills reminds one of a Henry James character who cannot bring himself to talk about money.

The institutional framework set up by the organized profession between 1906 and 1940, however, did not lead physicians to act differently from businessmen. Ironically, it was in the post-war years that the commercialization of medicine took off, and costs were much discussed. Long forgotten today, the founders of medical sociology documented that health-care costs increased by 60 percent from just 1952–53 to 1957–58 (Anderson, Collette, and Feldman 1960, Table 1). Construction increased the assets of American hospitals by 57 percent from 1935 to 1947 and then by another 122 percent from 1947 to 1956 (Lerner and Anderson 1963, Chart 22.1). Doctors' admissions of patients per thousand more than doubled from 1935 to 1956 (Lerner and Anderson 1963: 246). " . . . health and its costs have become a major issue in this country," a major study concluded (Lerner and Anderson 1963: 285–86). "An indication of the current state of affairs is the amount of consideration currently being given to health care programs by the United States Congress. . . . Critics of the hospitals contend that 'overuse' or 'abuse' of their facilities, unnecessary admission of patients [by physicians], is widespread."

Driven by the fee-for-service system they fought tirelessly to retain, doctors worked "too long and too hard for their own good or for that of their patients" (Mean 1953: 66), but earned nearly four times the income of factory workers. Harvard professor of health economics Seymour Harris said " . . . there is a serious question whether there is any justification for such a discrepancy" (Mean 1953: 66).

Discrimination against the most vulnerable, poor, sick patients, showed up in many pioneering sociological studies (Freidson and Feldman 1960; Roth 1969; Sussman 1969). The poor had much greater need for medical care than the middle class but received much less care, evidence that "poor credit risks" were turned away as patients on a widespread basis (Falk 1933). The first study of "medical indigence," or poverty caused by high medical bills, was done by Anderson and Alksne in 1960. Although the profession's design for voluntary pass-through health insurance had spread to three-quarters of the population by the end of the 1950s, it covered only 25 percent of medical expenditures on average and was much less available to the working poor and unaffordable to those on welfare (Anderson, Collette, and Feldman 1963, Figure 12; Freidson and Feldman 1960). Thus, while total family medical expenses used up 3.9 percent of upper-middle family incomes, it consumed 13.0 percent of average lower-class family incomes (Anderson, Collette, and Feldman 1963, Table 6), forcing serious trade-offs with food, clothing, education, and other essentials.

In sum, the profession itself did not establish an institutional framework of disinterestedness and protection of the patient, but many other countries did establish institutional structures that professionalized rather than commercialized the profession.

THE STUBBORN PROBLEM OF (DIS)TRUST

A core attribute and sociological function of professions is trustworthiness. To be "a professional" implies that you have mastered a field and can be trusted to apply it honestly, reliably, fairly, and for the benefit of your client. Echoing Everett Hughes (1958), Robert Dingwall and Paul Fenn (1987:61) wrote, "The judgement of the professional stabilizes the unpredictable into a basis sufficiently reliable for human action." Many of the institutional features of professions and professional practices bolster this sense of trust. But can we trust professionals to be trustworthy? This is a key question for other countervailing powers about professional dominance, for trustworthiness is the silent ingredient for sustaining control over one's domain.

In a valuable review of economic and sociological analysis of the professions, Dingwall and Fenn (1987) point out that Adam Smith's hostility to occupational monopolies did not extend to the professions, because uncertainties and complexities created the need for a natural monopoly of expertise. This, however, creates a problem of poor market information, Smith argued, so that the seller knows much more than the buyer. Quality is so hard to measure that profit-seeking physicians could compromise quality without the patient or payer knowing it, what G. A. Akerlof (1970) called a "market for lemons." Like shiny used cars' hidden defects, in a "market for lemons" high-quality products or services will not be recognized and will have to compete against cheaper alternatives, even as distrust grows among disappointed consumers. Adam Smith's solution, to pay professionals well, might secure high-quality services. Or the professionals might just take the money and skimp on quality anyway. Kenneth Arrow (1963) likewise argued during the era of fee-for-service that "Delegation and trust are the social institutions designed to obviate the problem of informational inequality." But capitation and fixed-sum contracts change this argument profoundly because the historic alignment of pay and trust is reversed; the less one does the more one makes. Given the large gray area of medical care that is neither clearly necessary nor unnecessary, a market for lemons will prevail. Such markets are a problem for competition and economics as well. Sociologists from Talcott Parsons to Amitai Etzioni (1988) and a number of important economists

have noted that norms of honest dealing and shared values are the foundations upon which most markets rest. They are also reflected in laws and regulations. Competition is not anarchy. Markets are not "free" (Light 1999b). But the problem is more complex and subtle in medical work where uncertainty, variability, and interactions increase as medicine progresses (Fox 1999). And the problem of (dis)trust did not arise with managed care but during the golden age of fee-for-service.

What shall we do? Adam Smith's strategy did not work. Neither, seemingly, did Parsons's solution of institutionalizing strong norms and practices aimed at getting clinicians themselves to protect clients from having their vulnerabilities exploited. The resulting forms of clinical and economic distrust during the golden age of medicine compelled payers to revolt as a countervailing power, but hiring managed-care companies to clean up these problems has engendered new forms of distrust that undermine efforts to ration needed care or even to reduce unnecessary services. David Mechanic (1996) and Bradford Gray (1997) have provided insightful sociological analyses of trust and a number of recommendations. Most critical for Gray is to "build institutional settings that allow the fiduciary ethic of health professionals to exist and flourish." Once again we are back to Parsons's 1939 emphasis on institutional context, implying that if we want health care we can trust when we are sick and vulnerable, the body politic has to help the profession be as trustworthy as it would like to be, but cannot be on its own. In fact, a number of countries have built such institutional settings and financial arrangements, underscoring the importance of comparative sociological analysis.

REFERENCES

Abbott, Andrew. 1988. *The System of Professions.* Chicago: University of Chicago Press.

Abelson, Reed. 1999. "For Managed Care, Free-Market Shock." *The New York Times* 3 Jan.: 4WK.

Akerlof, G.A. 1970. "The Market for Lemons: Qualitative Uncertainty and the Market Mechanism." *Quarterly Journal of Economics* 84:488–500.

Albrecht, Gary L. 1992. *The Disability Business.* Newbury Park, CA: Sage.

Anders, George. 1996. *Health Against Wealth.* New York: Houghton Mifflin.

Anderson, Gerald. 1997. "In Search of Value: An International Comparison of Cost, Access and Outcomes." *Health Affairs* 16 (6): 163–71.

Anderson, Odin W., and Harold Alksne. 1960. *An Examination of the Concept of Medical Indigence.* New York: Health Information Foundation Research Series No. 2.

Anderson, Odin W., Patricia Collette, and Jacob J. Feldman. 1960. *Family Expenditure Patterns for Personal Health Services.* New York: Health Information Foundation Research Series No. 14.

Anderson, Odin W., Patricia Collette, and Jacob J. Feldman. 1963. *Changes in Family Medical Care Expenditures and Voluntary Health Insurance: A Five-Year Resurvey.* Cambridge: Harvard University Press.

Arrow, Kenneth J. 1963. "Uncertainty and the Welfare Economics of Medical Care." *American Economic Review* 53: 941–73.

ATKINSON, PAUL. 1995. *Medical Talk and Medical Work: The Liturgy of the Clinic.* Thousand Oaks, CA: Sage.

BJORKMAN, JAMES WARNER. 1989. "Politicizing Medicine and Medicalizing Politics: Physician Power in the United States. In *Controlling Medical Professionals: The Comparative Politics of Health Governance,* ed. G. Freddi and J.W. Bjorkman. London: Sage, pp. 28–73.

BRINTON, MARY V., and VICTOR NEE, eds. 1998. *The New Institutionalism in Sociology.* New York: Russell Sage Foundation.

BRUNER, SALLY T., DANIEL R. WALDO, and DAVID R. MCKUSICK. 1992. "National Health Expenditures Projections Through 2030." *Health Care Financing Review* 14:1–29.

BURRAGE, MICHAEL, and ROLF TORSTENDAHL, eds. 1990. *Professions in Theory and History: Rethinking the Study of the Professions.* London: Sage.

COBURN, DAVID. 1993. "Professional Powers in Decline: Medicine in a Changing Canada." In *The Changing Medical Profession: An International Perspective,* ed. F.W. Hafferty and J.B. McKinlay. New York: Oxford University Press, pp. 92–103.

COBURN, DAVID, G.M. TORRANCE, and J. KAUFERT. 1983. "Medical Dominance in Canada in Historical Perspective: The Rise and Fall of Medicine?" *International Journal of Health Services* 13: 407–32.

CONRAD, PETER. 1999. "A Mirage of Genes." *Sociology of Health and Illness* 21: 228–41.

CONRAD, PETER, and JOSEPH W. SCHNEIDER. 1992. *Deviance and Medicalization: From Badness to Sickness.* Philadelphia: Temple University Press.

DIMAGGIO, PAUL, and WALTER W. POWELL. 1983. "The Iron Cage Revisited: Institutional Isomorphism and Collective Rationality in Organizational Fields." *American Sociological Review* 48: 147–60.

DINGWALL, ROBERT, and PAUL FENN. 1987. " 'A Respectable Profession?' Sociological and Economic Perspectives on the Regulation of Professional Services." *International Review of Law and Economics* 7: 51–64.

DOBBIN, FRANK. 1994. *Forging Industrial Policy.* New York: Cambridge University Press.

EDGMAN-LEVITAN, SUSAN. 1998. "Patient Confidence in the Health Care System." *Quality Connection: News From the Institute for Healthcare Improvement* 7(1): 1.

EHRENREICH, JOHN, and BARBARA EHRENREICH. 1971. *The American Health Empire: Power, Profits and Politics.* New York: Vintage.

ETZIONI, AMITAI. 1988. *The Moral Dimension: Toward a New Economics.* New York: Free Press.

FALK, I.S. 1933. *The Incidence of Illness and the Receipt of Costs of Medical Care Among Representative Families.* Committee on the Costs of Medical Care Publication No. 26. Chicago: University of Chicago Press.

FIELD, MARK G. 1988. "The Position of the Soviet Physicians: The Bureaucratic Professional." *The Milbank Quarterly* 66 (Suppl. 2): 182–201.

FLOOD, ANN BARRY, and MARY L. FENNELL. 1995. "Through the Lenses of Organizational Sociology: The Role of Organizational Theory and Research in Conceptualizing and Examining Our Health Care System." *Journal of Health and Social Behavior* (extra issue): 154–69.

FOX, DANIEL M. 1996. *Power and Illness: The Failure and Future of American Health Policy.* Berkeley: University of California Press.

FOX, RENÉE C. 1999. "Medical Uncertainty Revisited." In *Handbook of Social Studies in Health and Medicine,* ed. G.L. Albrecht, R. Fitzpatrick and S.C. Scrimshaw. London: Sage.

FRANKFORD, DAVID M. 1993. "Professions and the Law." In *The Changing Medical Profession: An International Perspective,* ed. F.W. Hafferty and J.B. McKinlay. New York: Oxford University Press, pp. 43–53.

FRANKFORD, DAVID M. 1997. "Institutions of Reflective Practice." *Journal of Health Politics, Policy and Law* 22:1295–1308.

FRANKFORD, DAVID M. and THOMAS R. KONRAD. 1998. "Responsive Medical Professionalism: Integrating Education, Practice, and Community in a Market-Driven Era." *Academic Medicine* 73: 138–44.

FREDDI, GIOGIO. 1989. "Problems of Organizational Rationality in Health Systems." In *Controlling Medical Professionals: The Comparative Politics of Health Governance,* ed. G. Freddi and J.W. Bjorkman. London: Sage, pp. 1–27.

FREIDSON, ELIOT. 1970a. *Professional Dominance: The Social Structure of Medical Care.* Chicago: Aldine.

FREIDSON, ELIOT. 1970b. *Profession of Medicine: A Study of the Sociology of Applied Knowledge.* New York: Dodd, Mead.

FREIDSON, ELIOT. 1986. *Professional Powers: A Study of the Institutionalization of Formal Knowledge.* Chicago: University of Chicago Press.

FREIDSON, ELIOT. 1994. *Professionalism Reborn: Theory, Prophecy and Policy.* Chicago: University of Chicago Press.

FREIDSON, ELIOT, and JACOB J. FELDMAN. 1960. *Public Attitudes Toward Health Insurance.* New York: Health Information Foundation Research Series No. 5.

FRENK, JULIO, and LUIS DURAN-ARENAS. 1993. "The Medical Profession and the State." In *The Changing Medical Profession: An International Perspective,* ed. F.W. Hafferty and J.B. McKinlay. New York: Oxford University Press, pp. 25–42.

FRIEDMAN, NEAL. 1998. *Building a Disease Management Program.* Albuquerque: Lovelace Healthcare Innovations.

FUKUYAMA, FRANCIS. 1999. *The Great Disruption: Human Nature and the Reconstruction of Social Order.* New York: Free Press.

GINSBERG, PAUL B. 1998. "A Perspective on Health System Change 1997." In *Charting Change: A Longitudinal Look at the American Health System.* Washington, D.C.: Center for Studying Health System Change, 1997 Annual Report, pp. 3–9.

GRAY, BRADFORD H. 1997. "Trust and Trustworthy Care in the Managed Care Era." *Health Affairs* 16: 34–49.

GRAY, BRADFORD H., and MARILYN J. FIELD, eds. 1989. *Controlling Costs and Changing Patient Care: The Role of Utilization Management*. Washington, D.C.: National Academy Press.

GREENBERG, SELIG. 1971. *The Quality of Mercy: A Report on the Critical Condition of Hospital and Medical Care in America*. New York: Atheneum.

HAFFERTY, FREDERIC W., and DONALD W. LIGHT. 1995. "Professional Dynamics and the Changing Nature of Medical Work." *Journal of Health and Social Behavior* (extra issue): 132–53.

HARRISON, MICHAEL. 1998. "Professional Power and Health System Reform: Physicians in Germany and the Netherlands." Paper presented at the International Sociological Association meetings. July 1998.

HARRISON, STEPHEN, and CHRISTOPHER POLLITT. 1994. *Controlling Health Professionals*. Philadelphia: Open University Press.

HAUG, MARIE R. 1988. "A Reexamination of the Hypothesis of Physician Deprofessionalization." *The Milbank Quarterly* 66 (Suppl. 2): 48–56.

HUGHES, EVERETT CHERRINGTON. 1958. *Men and Their Work*. Glencoe, Ill: The Free Press.

IMMERGUT, ELLEN M. 1992. *Health Politics: Interests and Institutions in Western Europe*. New York: Cambridge University Press.

JOHNSON, TERRANCE. 1972. *Professions and Power*. London: Macmillan.

JOHNSON, TERRANCE. 1995. "Governmentality and the Institutionalization of Expertise." In *Health Professions and the State in Europe*, ed. T. Johnson, G. Larkin, and M. Saks. London: Routledge, pp. 7–24.

JONES, ANTHONY, ed. 1991. *Professions and the State: Expertise and Autonomy in the Soviet Union and Eastern Europe*. Philadelphia: Temple University Press.

KENNEDY, EDWARD M. 1972. *In Critical Condition*. New York: Simon & Schuster.

KILBORN, PETER T. 1998. "Reality of the H.M.O. System Doesn't Live Up to the Dream." *The New York Times* 5 October: A1,A16.

KRAUSE, ELLIOTT A. 1988. "Doctors, Partitocrazia, and the Italian State." *The Milbank Quarterly* 66 (Suppl. 2): 76–91.

KRAUSE, ELLIOTT A. 1996. *Death of the Guilds: Professions, States, and the Advance of Capitalism, 1930 to the Present*. New Haven: Yale University Press.

LARKIN, GERALD V. 1983. *Occupational Monopoly and Modern Medicine*. London: Tavistock.

LARSON, MAGALI SARFATTI. 1977. *The Rise of Professionalism: A Sociological Analysis*. Berkeley: University of California Press.

LARSON, MAGALI SARFATTI. 1990. "In the Matter of Experts and Professionals, or How Impossible It Is To Leave Nothing Unsaid." In *The Formation of Professions: Knowledge, State and Strategy*, ed. Rolf Torstendahl and Michael Burrage. London: Sage, pp. 24–50.

LERNER, MONROE, and ODIN W. ANDERSON. 1963. *Health Progress in the United States 1900-1960*. Chicago: University of Chicago Press.

LIGHT, DONALD W. 1988a. "Toward a New Sociology of Medical Education." *Journal of Health and Social Behavior* 29:307–22.

LIGHT, DONALD W. 1988b. "Turf Battles and the Theory of Professional Dominance." *Research in the Sociology of Health Care* 7:203–25.

LIGHT, DONALD W. 1989. "Social Control and the American Health Care System." In *Handbook of Medical Sociology,* 4th ed., ed. Howard E. Freeman and Sol Levine. Englewood Cliffs: Prentice Hall, pp. 456–74.

LIGHT, DONALD W. 1993. "Countervailing Power: The Changing Character of the Medical Profession in the United States." In *The Changing Medical Profession: An International Perspective,* ed. F.W. Hafferty and J.B. McKinlay. New York: Oxford University Press, pp. 69–80.

LIGHT, DONALD W. 1994. "Managed Care: False and Real Solutions." *The Lancet* 344: 1197–99.

LIGHT, DONALD W. 1995. "Countervailing Powers: A Framework for Professions in Transition." In *Health Professions and the State in Europe,* ed. T. Johnson, G. Larkin, and M. Saks. London: Routledge, pp. 24–41.

LIGHT, DONALD W. 1997a. "The Restructuring of the American Health Care System." In *Health Politics and Policy,* eds. T. J. Litman and L. S. Robbins. Albany: Delmar, pp. 46–63.

LIGHT, DONALD W. 1997b. "The Rhetorics of Realities of Community Health Care: Limits of Countervailing Powers to Meet the Health Care Needs of the 21st Century." *Journal of Health Politics, Policy and Law* 22:105–45.

LIGHT, DONALD W. 1999a. "Good Managed Care Needs National Health Insurance." *Annals of Internal Medicine* 130: 686–89.

LIGHT, DONALD W. 1999b. "The Sociological Character of Markets in Health Care." In *Handbook of Social Studies in Health and Medicine,* ed. G. L. Albrecht, R. Fitzpatrick, and S.C. Scrimshaw. London: Sage.

LIGHT, DONALD W., and ALEXANDER SCHULLER, eds. 1986. *Political Values and Health Care: The German Experience*. Boston: MIT Press.

LIGHT, DONALD W., and SOL LEVINE. 1988. "The Changing Character of the Medical Profession: A Theoretical Overview." *The Milbank Quarterly* 66 (Suppl. 2): 10–32.

LIGHT, DONALD W., STEPHAN LIEBFRIED, and FLORIAN TENNSTEDT. 1986. "Social Medicine vs. Professional Dominance: The German Experience." *American Journal of Public Health* 76:78–83.

"MANAGED CARE WOES: INDUSTRY TRENDS AND CONFLICTS." 1998. *Health System Change Issue Brief Number 13, May 1998*. Washington, D.C.: Center for Studying Health System Change.

MANIAN, FARRIN A. 1998. "Should We Accept Mediocrity?" *New England Journal of Medicine* 338:1067–69.

MAP (Medicine as a Profession). 1999. *Program Statement.* New York: Open Society Institute.

Marmor, Theodore R., and Jon B. Christianson. 1982. *Health Care Policy: A Political Economy Approach.* Beverly Hills: Sage.

Matheson, Norman A. 1999. "A Career Challenge for Consultants." *Journal of the Royal Society of Medicine* 92:55–57.

Mayor, S. 1998. "UK Surgeons May Undergo Performance Review Every Five Years." *BMJ (British Medical Journal)* 317:1173.

McCormick, Kathleen A., Mary A. Cummings, and Chris Kovner. 1997. "The Role of the Agency for Health Care Policy and Research in Improving Outcomes of Care." *Nursing Clinics of North America* 32:521–42.

McKinlay, John B. 1999. "The End of the Golden Age of Doctoring." *New England Research Institutes Network* (Summer): 1,3.

McKinlay, John B., and Joan Arches. 1985. "Toward the Proletarianization of Physicians." *International Journal of Health Services* 15: 161–95.

McKinlay, John B., and John D. Stoeckle. 1988. "Corporatization and the Social Transformation of Doctoring." *International Journal of Health Services* 18: 191–205.

McPherson, Klim, John E. Wennberg, Ole B. Havind, and Peter Clifford. 1982. "Small-Area Variations in the Use of Common Surgical Procedures: An International Comparison of New England, England, and Norway." *New England Journal of Medicine* 307:1310–14.

Mean, James Howard. 1953. *Doctors, People, and Government.* Boston: Little, Brown and Company.

Mechanic, David. 1996. "Changing Medical Organization and the Erosion of Trust." *The Milbank Quarterly* 74:171–89.

Navarro, Vincent. 1976. *Medicine Under Capitalism.* New York: Prodist.

Nixon, Richard M. 1972. *Public Papers of the Presidents of the United States: Richard Nixon 1971,* item 63. Washington, D.C.: U.S. Government Printing Office.

Oppenheimer, Martin. 1973. "The Proletarianization of the Professional." *Sociological Review Monograph* 20:213–27.

Parsons, Talcott. 1939. "The Professions and Social Structure." In *Essays in Sociological Theory.* Glencoe, IL: The Free Press, pp. 185–99.

Parsons, Talcott. 1951. *The Social System.* Glencoe, IL: The Free Press.

Payer, Lynn. 1988. *Medicine and Culture.* New York: Penguin.

Powell, Francis D., and Albert F. Wessen, eds. 1999. *Health Care Systems in Transition.* Thousand Oaks, CA: Sage.

Relman, Arnold S. 1980. "The New Medical-Industrial Complex." *New England Journal of Medicine* 303:963–70.

Robinson, James C. 1994. "The Changing Boundaries of the American Hospital." *Milbank Quarterly* 72:259–75.

Robinson, James C. 1997. "Physician–Hospital Integration and the Economic Theory of the Firm." *Medical Care Research and Review* 54: 3–24.

Rodwin, Marc A. 1993. *Medicine, Money & Morals.* New York: Oxford University Press.

Rosenbaum, Sara, David M. Frankford, Brad Moore, and Phyllis Borzi. 1999. "Who Should Determine When Health Care Is Medically Necessary?" *New England Journal of Medicine* 340: 229–32.

Roth, Julius A. 1969. "The Treatment of the Sick." In *Poverty and Health,* ed. John Kosa, Aaron Antonovsky, and Irving Kenneth Zola. Cambridge: Harvard University Press, pp. 168–90.

Rueschemeyer, Dietrich. 1986. "Comparing Legal Professions Cross-Nationally: From a Professions-Centered to a State-Centered Approach." *American Bar Foundation Research Journal,* pp. 415–46.

Saltman, Richard B., and Josep Figueras. 1997. *European Health Care Reform: Analysis of Current Strategies.* Copenhagen: World Health Organization Regional Office for Europe.

Saltman, Richard B., Josep Figueras, and Constantino Sakellarides, eds. 1998. *Critical Challenges for Health Care Reform in Europe.* Philadelphia: Open University Press.

Schlesinger, Mark, Robert Dorwart, Claudia Hoover, and Sherrie Epstein. 1997. "The Determinants of Dumping." *Health Services Research* 32: 561–90.

Seitz, Robert, Hans-Helmut Konig, and Eleni Jelastopulu. 1998. *Managed Care—An Option for the German Health Care System?* London: Office of Health Economics.

Shortell, Stephen M., Robin R. Gillies, David A. Anderson, et al. 1996. *Remaking Health Care in America: Building Organized Delivery Systems.* San Francisco: Jossey-Bass.

Smith, Richard. 1998. "All Changed, Changed Utterly." *BMJ (British Medical Journal)* 316:1917–18.

Somers, Herman M., and Anne Ramsey Somers. 1960. *Doctors, Patients and Health Insurance.* Washington, D.C.: The Brookings Institution.

Starr, Paul. 1982. *The Social Transformation of American Medicine.* New York: Basic.

Stevens, Rosemary A. 1984. "Defining and Certifying the Specialists." In *The Coming Physicians Surplus,* ed. Eli Ginzberg and Mariam Ostow. Totowa, NJ: Rowman and Allanheld, pp. 83–98.

Sulmasy, Daniel P. 1992. "Physicians, Cost Control, and Ethics." *Annals of Internal Medicine* 116: 920–26.

Sussman, Marvin B. 1969. "Readjustment and Rehabilitation of Patients. In *Poverty and Health,* ed. John Kosa, Aaron Antonovsky, and Irving Kenneth Zola. Cambridge, MA: Harvard University Press, pp. 244–64.

TORSTENDAHL, ROLF, and MICHAEL BURRAGE, eds. 1990. *The Formation of Professions: Knowledge, State and Strategy.* London: Sage.

TWADDLE, ANDREW C. 1996. "Health System Reforms—Toward a Framework for International Comparisons." *Social Science and Medicine* 43:637–54.

WAITZKIN, HOWARD. 1983. *The Second Sickness: Contradictions of Capitalist Health Care.* New York: Free Press.

WARE, JOHN E. JR., ET AL. 1996. "Differences in 4-Year Health Outcomes for Elderly and Poor, Chronically Ill Patients Treated in HMO and Fee-for-Service Systems." *Journal of the American Medical Association* 276:1039–47.

WEISS, MARJORIE, and RAY FITZPATRICK. 1997. "Challenges to Medicine: The Case of Prescribing." *Sociology of Health and Illness* 19: 297–327.

WENNBERG, JOHN E., and A. GITTELSOHN. 1973. "Small Area Variations in Health Care Delivery." *Science* 182:1102–1108.

WHITE, JOSEPH. 1991. *Competitive Solutions: American Health Care Proposals and International Experience.* Washington, D.C.: The Brookings Institution.

WHITMAN, CHRISTINE TODD, and LEN FISHMAN. 1997. *Coronary Artery Bypass Graft Surgery in New Jersey 1994-1995.* Trenton: New Jersey Department of Health and Senior Services.

WILLIS, EVAN. 1989. *Medical Dominance: The Division of Labour in Australian Health Care,* 2nd ed. Sydney: Allen and Unwin.

WILSFORD, DAVID. 1991. *Doctors and the State: The Politics of Health Care in France and the United States.* Durham, NC: Duke University Press.

WINSLOW, RON. 1998. "Health-Care Inflation Revives in Minneapolis Despite Cost-Cutting." *Wall Street Journal* 19 May: A1, A15.

ZELMAN, WALTER A., and ROBERT A. BERENSON. 1998. *The Managed Care Blues and How to Cure Them.* Washington, D.C.: Georgetown University Press.

15 TIDES OF CHANGE: THE EVOLUTION OF MANAGED CARE IN THE UNITED STATES

DOUGLAS R. WHOLEY, *University of Minnesota*

LAWTON R. BURNS, *University of Pennsylvania*

In 1965, Stinchcombe called our attention to the historical formation of new forms and types of organizations (Stinchcombe 1965). Since 1965, tidal waves of organizational change have swept over the health-care system in the United States. In response to high health-care costs, new forms of managed care organizations (MCOs), incentive arrangements, and organizational monitoring and reporting structures have appeared on a continuing basis. Concomitantly, health services researchers have developed a wide array of quality assessment, provider profiling, and risk-adjustment tools; patients have become increasingly informed and participative in medical decision-making; and technological changes have provided new possibilities for treating patients and managing providers. The commingling of these trends is rationalizing the organization of health care and the practice of medicine.

We examine the role of managed care in this transformation. The effects of MCOs are intertwined with a shift in health care from hospital to ambulatory settings, the development of health services research (e.g., quality measurement, guidelines, risk adjustment), societal and employer efforts to contain health-care costs, technological change, and the redefinition of individuals as consumers rather than patients. While such trends are transforming health-care delivery in many countries, MCOs operating within a market ideology of managed competition is the form that health-care restructuring takes in the United States.

The evolution of the MCO industry is a story of the development of new organizational forms, creating an alphabet soup of names. Early forms included *Health Maintenance Organizations* (HMOs), an umbrella term

that covered two distinct forms, Group HMOs based on physicians in multispecialty group practices and *Independent Practice Associations* (IPAs) based on physicians in solo or single-specialty practice. New forms, such as *Preferred Provider Organizations* (PPOs), *Integrated Delivery Systems* (IDSs), and *Physician Practice Management Companies* (PPMCs) quickly followed. The flux in organizational forms has been matched with a similar flux in organizational arrangements designed to measure, monitor, and manage providers. These structures include utilization management, new incentive structures, bureaucratic structures such as clinical guidelines, and information systems. These structures are transforming physician and patient roles in the health-care system and the context of medical work.

The continual flux in organizational forms and structures has created the opportunity for the invention of new, and possibly better, ways of organizing health care. But the flux has imposed significant costs on patients and providers. The continuity of the patient-provider relationship, which is key to developing relational trust and high-quality health care, is threatened by changes in relationships among patient, employer or health purchaser, MCO, and providers. Employers switching MCOs, MCOs switching providers, and providers developing new MCO contracting vehicles can all disrupt the patient–provider relationship. While these disruptions may not be burdensome for healthy patients, they may be costly to those with chronic conditions who are dependent on comprehensive, continuous care.

At their best, MCOs organize and improve health care in a stable, reliable, and less costly manner. Patients in need of services are identified and treated, preventive health care programs are implemented, and quality improvement is pursued. Health-care costs and the rate of their increase are decreased. At their worst, MCOs earn profits by skimming favorable risks, taking advantage of market imperfections, and disrupting the patient–physician relationship. In the middle are a large number of MCOs muddling along, locally rational actors in a garbage can environment in which decisions arise out of the intermingling of problems, solutions, and decision-makers (Cohen et al. 1972). Solutions in the form of consultants and bureaucrats seek or create problems for which their services are needed. Problematic, unintended consequences from these solutions are managed by new satisficing solutions found in the problem's locale.

The first section of this chapter defines MCOs, distinguishing them from related concepts such as managed competition. The second section describes the context for the development of MCOs, with a particular attention to correlated trends that are a cause of MCO development or that have rationalizing effects similar to those of MCOs. The third section describes the evolution of MCO organizational populations. The fourth and fifth sections describe MCO managerial structures and performance. The final section projects the future of managed care.

DEFINING MANAGED CARE

In the United States, purchasers, plans, providers, and patients are involved in organizing health care. Purchasers pay plans for the health care delivered by providers to a defined population of individuals. The main purchasers are private-sector employers, public-sector employers, and public-sector programs such as Medicare and Medicaid, which purchase health services for the elderly and poor, respectively. Providers are organizations and individuals who provide health-care services, such as physicians, hospitals, pharmaceutical firms, and home-health agencies. Patients are individuals who use health-care services.

An iron triangle of competing interests is reconciled in the organizing process (Kissick 1994). Purchasers are interested in minimizing cost, subject to a quality constraint. Patients are interested in maximizing health outcomes, often through having access to providers of their choice, subject to a cost constraint. Providers are interested in either maximizing patient outcomes subject to an income constraint or maximizing

provider income subject to a patient-outcomes constraint (Eisenberg 1986). The trade-off among the three interests can be characterized as an iron triangle of trade-offs among cost, quality, and access.

Immediately prior to the development of MCOs, the health-care system emphasized quality and access at the expense of cost. Most plans provided indemnity health insurance. Under indemnity insurance, purchasers paid plans a premium to reimburse patients for the financial expenses they incurred in obtaining a defined set of health benefits, and patients were financially responsible for reimbursing providers for the health services they used. This indemnity insurance-based system emphasized quality and access at the expense of cost. Since insurance lowered a patient's cost of obtaining health services at the point of use, patients had an incentive to use more health services than they would if they had been paying full production cost. Since providers maximized income by providing more services, they had an incentive to increase service provision.

MCOs are plans that developed to increase the emphasis on cost in the iron triangle. The initial type of MCO, the HMO, was based on prepaid medical practices in which purchasers paid a premium to the HMO plan in exchange for the delivery of a defined set of benefits over a defined period of time (typically one year) (Starr 1982). While some HMOs existed prior to 1973, the start of MCOs as an industry can be dated to the passage of the Health Maintenance Organization (HMO) Act of 1973 and its subsequent amendments in 1976. This federal legislation was designed to encourage the formation of HMOs, which policy analysts believed would help contain health-care costs. Since HMOs delivered health services in exchange for a premium, HMOs would place a greater emphasis on cost-containment than did indemnity insurers. Further, it was believed that HMOs could develop the organizational structures necessary to manage costs more effectively.

Because of the early emphasis on the health insurance function among HMOs, many definitions of MCOs include both risk-bearing and care-management components. Luft, in an early definition, stated that HMOs were distinguished by their promise to deliver health services to a specified population for a given period of time in exchange for a fixed, prepaid premium (Luft, 1981: 3). Over time, though, there has been a growing emphasis on the care management function rather than the insurance function. The American Medical Association (AMA), for example, currently defines managed care as "processes or techniques used by any entity that delivers, administers and/or assumes risk for health services in order to control or influence the quality, accessibility, utilization, costs and prices, or outcomes of such services provided to a defined population" (American Medical Association 1998).

The rapid evolution of the MCO industry since the early 1980s has made the definitional linkage of MCOs and risk bearing inappropriate. Many indemnity plans began including such managed-care features as utilization review and second opinions in their products. And employers began to carry the health insurance risk themselves and contract with MCOs to manage health-service delivery under the umbrella of the Employee Retirement Income Security Act (ERISA), a 1974 federal law (Acs et al. 1996; Mariner 1996). Thus, identifying risk bearing as a key characteristic of MCOs excessively limits the applicability of a definition of managed care.

Building from the AMA definition and taking into account the qualifications above, we define MCOs as *organizations using administrative processes or techniques to influence the quality, accessibility, utilization, costs, and prices or outcomes of health services provided to a defined population by a defined set of providers.* This definition is consistent with viewing managed care as "a process of rationing in which demands of patients and their advocates are balanced against the price purchasers are willing to pay. Managers presumably try to allocate care as cost-effectively as they can within the financial constraints established by payers and the political process" (Mechanic 1998: 95).

The restricted set of providers who are the focus of MCO managerial efforts discriminates MCOs from the use of managed care techniques in indemnity insurance and federal programs such as Medicare. Restricted networks make freedom of provider choice conditional on a patient's choice of MCO. In some MCOs, consumer choice is limited to a relatively small set of providers. In other MCOs, consumers can choose from a broad range of physicians but are guided to selected, preferred providers through the use of financial incentives. Selective contracting is not necessary for using many features of managed care such as utilization review, guidelines and pathways, provider profiling, prevention, service bundling, service carve-outs, gatekeeping, and limitations on prices and volume. However, selective contracting and serving a defined population are essential for structuring consumer health-plan choices in which MCOs compete on the basis of their ability to manage health-care quality and costs.

There are three corollaries to our MCO definition. First, providers in MCOs are accountable for the health care of enrollees who have and those who have not presented themselves to a provider. This corollary strongly contrasts MCOs with indemnity coverage, in which providers are accountable only for care delivered to individuals who have presented themselves. Second, as soon as provider organizations contract to manage the delivery of health-care services to a defined population, they become an MCO. Third, the organizational boundary of an MCO is the set of providers with whom the MCO contracts.

There are three corollaries for what MCOs are not. First, MCOs are not managed competition. Managed competition "is the use of available tools (by sponsors or purchasers) to structure cost-conscious consumer choice among health plans in the pursuit of equity and efficiency in health-care financing and delivery" (Enthoven 1988:307). Second, MCOs are not designed to provide access to the uninsured. MCOs are designed to manage care for a defined population. The empirical result is that the presence of MCOs in a community and in a physician's practice reduces the physicians' provision of charity care (Cunningham et al. 1999) and lowers access for the uninsured indigent (Cunningham 1999). Third, MCOs are not accountable for producing research as a public good. MCOs are accountable for supporting research that improves their quality subject to a cost constraint or that reduces cost subject to a quality constraint.

THE INSTITUTIONAL CONTEXT OF MANAGED CARE

Three trends have strongly influenced the development of MCOs: increasing health care costs, the development of health services research, and technological change. Because these trends have also influenced other developments, such as the provision of charity care, support of academic research, and uninsurance, these latter may be spuriously related to MCO development.

Health Care Costs and Purchaser Activism

The past thirty years have witnessed dramatic increases in health-care costs. In the 1960s, 1970s, and 1980s the average annual percentage changes in per capita health-care expenditures were 8.7 percent, 11.3 percent, and 9.4 percent (Levit et al. 1980). In 1960, overall health expenditures were 5.1 percent of GDP. By 1990, health expenditures were 13.6 percent of GDP. The rising cost of health care has been increasingly financed by the public sector. In 1960, 1970, 1980, 1990, and 1995 public funding accounted for 25 percent, 38 percent, 42 percent, 40 percent, and 46 percent of all health care expenditures (Levit et al. 1998). The large jump between 1960 and 1970 is attributable to the implementation of Medicare in the mid-1960s.

There are several reasons underlying this increase with professional dominance only one, and possibly a relatively minor, source of cost increases. Technology and technological change is an oft-mentioned source of cost increases (Newhouse 1993; Weisbrod 1991). Weisbrod argues that technological increases are influenced by the structure of health insurance. In a fee-for-service indemnity insurance system, consumers pay a relatively small proportion of technology and health services cost at time of consumption because their insurance covers much of the expenses. This causes a moral hazard problem and higher consumption than would occur without the insurance. In turn, this encourages the development of technology (Weisbrod 1991), particularly cost-increasing technology. This implies that much of the growth in medical spending can be attributed to declining coinsurance levels and technology development (Peden and Freeland 1998).

Policy decisions by the federal government have also led to cost increases. First, federal policy has structured health insurance so that it is purchased with before-tax dollars. This subsidy increases the amount of health insurance purchased. Employers who take advantage of the untaxed nature of health insurance to structure health insurance plans with low co-insurance and few restrictions to attract employees have exacerbated this policy. Second, the shift to public funding caused by the implementation of Medicare played a major role in decreasing co-insurance. Medicare and Medicaid were implemented in 1966. To gain the support of organized medicine (e.g., the American Medical Association), the programs were designed to pay providers usual, customary, and reasonable rates (UCR). The consequence was predictable: Health care costs increased rapidly, and the federal government began to look for ways to manage them.

The federal government introduced new payment systems designed to restrain spending. A diagnosis related group (DRG) payment paid one fee to a hospital for the bundle of services used to produce the discharge of a patient with a given DRG. This practice shifted the risk associated with overuse of inpatient services to hospitals, encouraging them to manage costs. Since outpatient services were still paid on a fee-for-service basis, DRGs accelerated the shift from inpatient treatment to outpatient settings. The expansion of ambulatory costs led Medicare to explore and develop new ways of managing ambulatory costs, such

as the resource-based relative-value system (RBRVS) and the more recent ambulatory care cost groups (ACGs) (Starfield et al. 1991). These tools and ideas have migrated to MCOs.

Very active and powerful employers have also acted as catalysts to restructure markets to contain health-care costs by emphasizing "value-based purchasing" (Christianson 1998; Ellwood et al. 1971; Enthoven 1988). Employees are given financial incentives for selecting least-cost health plans; quality information is demanded from health plans; and competitive bidding is used for health insurance providers. In other communities, purchaser coalitions actively structure and define the market. In Minneapolis, for example, the Buyers Health Care Action Group (BHCAG) has developed a strategy for the direct purchasing of health services from medical groups, with third party administrators used to process discounted fee-for-service claims (Christianson et al. 1995; Knutson, 1998). Corporate purchasers (e.g., Xerox) and MCOs (e.g., Kaiser) have played significant roles in the National Committee for Quality Assurance's (NCQA) development of quality performance measures and accreditation programs.

Health Services Research

The tools used by purchasers and plans to measure, monitor, and manage providers have been largely developed by health-services researchers. Health services research is "a multi-disciplinary field of inquiry, both basic and applied, that examines the use, costs, quality, accessibility, delivery, organization, financing, and outcomes of health care services to increase knowledge and understanding of the structure, processes, and effects of health services for individuals and populations" (Field et al. 1995: 3). Health services research in the United States can be traced to Ernest Codman's work in the early 1900s relating success and failure of surgeons to both controllable (e.g., surgeon skill) and uncontrollable factors (Millenson 1997: 142–47).

Widespread adoption of health-services research techniques began in 1973, with Wennberg and Gittelsohn's finding that health services use varied dramatically across small areas (Wennberg and Gittelsohn 1973). One area in Vermont, for example, had a tonsillectomy rate of 13 per 10,000 persons, while neighboring areas had rates hovering around 30 percent. The highest rate in Vermont was 151. A person living in the highest-rate area had a 66 percent chance of having a tonsillectomy by age 20, while people living in adjacent areas had a 20 percent chance. These differences did not appear to be due to chance or health status alone and were correlated with provider availability and types of providers. Noncomplex surgery rates were higher in areas with more general practitioners, while complex surgery rates were higher in areas with more surgeons. Wennberg and Gittelsohn (1973: 1006) concluded that "given the magnitude of these variations, the possibility of too much medical care and the attendant likelihood of iatrogenic illness is presumably as strong as the possibility of not enough service and unattended morbidity and mortality."

Health-services researchers began to show that some of the small area variations were attributable to procedures being done inappropriately (Brook et al. 1984; Chassin et al. 1987) or unnecessarily (Leape 1989). Outcomes research, which "evaluates the impact of health care (including discrete interventions such as particular drugs, medical devices, and procedures as well as broader program of system interventions) on the health outcomes of patients and populations" (Mendelson et al. 1998: 77), was identified as a federal research priority and became a key focus for the new Agency for Health Policy and Research formed in 1989. Outcomes and evidence-based practice has led to the development and use of clinical guidelines and disease-management protocols (Grimshaw and Russell 1993). By 1999, for example, many sets of guidelines were being made available to professional and laypersons on the World Wide Web (Agency for Health Care Policy and Research 1999). Other health-services researchers have focused on implementing quality improvement practices and new ways of organizing care that will reduce adverse events (Leape 1997). Ironically, medical professionals are among the leaders in these rationalization processes.

Although evidence-based practice and outcomes research can identify appropriate practice, they do not provide a technology to measure, monitor, and manage health-care delivery. Medical insurance claims analysis addresses these issues. The health-insurance process generates insurance claims showing diagnoses and treatments provided to patients. More sophisticated systems include pharmacy and laboratory data. Enabled by rapid increases in information technology cost-effectiveness and power, major purchasers, such as Medicare, began using medical claims data in the 1990s to measure quality-of-care profiles, case mix, complications of care, episodes of care, and physician care (Garnick et al. 1994; Iezzoni 1997; Weiner et al. 1990). Use of these tools to compare provider performance led to the development of sophisticated risk-adjustment technologies (Iezzoni 1997). When combined, medical claims and risk adjustment can be used to monitor some aspects of

care quality, screen individuals in need of treatment, measure provider performance, and identify effective treatments.

Claims-based tools provide only one, rather rough, view of the process of care. Health-service researchers have developed sophisticated survey measurement techniques to assess health status and outcomes. Health status is measured with tools such as the SF-36, a 36-item questionnaire that was used extensively in the Medical Outcomes Study to compare performance across health insurance organizations (Ware et al. 1996; Ware and Sherbourne 1992). The first article using the SF-36 was published in 1988; in 1997, 179 articles using the SF-36 were published (Manocchia et al. 1997). The SF-36 was adopted in 1999 by the National Council on Quality Assurance (NCQA) as a measure of the performance of MCOs providing services to Medicare enrollees. The Consumer Assessment of Health Plans (CAHPs) is similarly used to monitor consumer experiences with health plans (Cleary 1998). The SF-36 and CAHPs were rapidly institutionalized, becoming standard performance measures.

Health services research has supplied a major component to the rationalization process underlying the transformation of health services. Health-services researchers are now among the occupational groups "with authority to speak to the collective good in the name of truths about nature: the nature of the physical world, of human individuals and their psyches, and of the natural workings of the social system itself" (Meyer 1994: 39). The demonstration of substantial small-area variations and inappropriate health-care delivery provides the rationale that quality can be improved and cost decreased by managing health care. Health-services research provides tools such as guidelines and clinical pathways that define appropriate care processes, as well as tools to measure, monitor, and manage health-care delivery. The health-services research community has developed as an institutional actor with its own agenda.

The rationalization of health care associated with health-services research would have occurred, and would continue occurring, without MCOs. There is an inherent interest in addressing quality shortcomings in all forms of health-care organization (Bodenheimer 1999; Brook 1997). A roundtable examining quality in health care concluded "that quality is the problem, not managed care" (Chassin and Galvin 1998:1002). Nevertheless, MCOs and health services research enjoy a symbiotic relationship. The development of new MCO forms and structures spurs health-services research on to study the structure's effect on cost and quality and the development of quality and outcomes measurement tools. Health-services research provides MCOs legitimated tools to measure, monitor, and manage medical practice.

Technological Change

Technological change influences both treatment possibilities and health-care organization. As suggested above, technological change affecting treatment possibilities and outcomes is a major driver of cost increases (Newhouse 1993; Weisbrod 1991). Technological change may also underlie the development of MCOs. Technological changes such as minimally invasive surgical techniques have increasingly made possible the provision of services in ambulatory, rather than inpatient, settings. This shift provides a fundamental niche in which MCOs can operate.

Information technology has emerged as a powerful motor behind MCO organizational change. Declining computational costs enabled the development of health-services research tools. The availability of newly developed minicomputers, for example, enabled Wennberg and Gittelsohn's work on small-area variations. The presence of substantial computing power and availability of claims allowed the Health Care Financing Administration and Medicare to begin developing sophisticated health-services research tools to measure quality and profile providers. Provider profiling also required the development of tools such as ambulatory care groups (Starfield et al. 1991), which require significant computational capacity. Information technology and its greater computational power increase information channel capacity allowing greater measuring, monitoring, and managing. The declining cost of computation, the routinization of the analytic procedures, and the proliferation of consulting and management firms that supply these services increase the availability of information tools that manage health care.

The continuing decline in computational costs, through the development of powerful, inexpensive microcomputers and low-cost connectivity through the Internet, threatens to make information technology the key driver of change. As C. Everett Koop comments (Skolnick 1996), "I have implied that health care reform is going to force us to change the way we exchange information in the health care system. But now we are going to see that role reversed: Changes in the way we exchange information are going to dictate reform." The evidence for such a change is readily available. Consumers have access through the web to a wide array of health information that describe symptoms,

how to do self-examinations, and the appropriate treatments (Blumenthal 1997). Drug interactions can easily be checked. Clinical guidelines are readily available. One consequence is that providers are increasingly losing their monopolistic hold on information, a key source of professional power (Abbott 1988).

Summary

MCO evolution has occurred within a context of significant institutional changes that are also restructuring and rationalizing health care. Similar to societal trends (Meyer 1994), health-care organization is increasingly bureaucratized, with both MCOs and individual consumers making rational choices. One event signifying this change in health care was Paul Ellwood's deliberate choice of the term "consumer," rather than "patient," in discussions leading up to the initial legislation that developed MCOs (Millenson 1997).

More broadly, the health-care system is being transformed from a medical model to a market and bureaucratic model. The individual as patient subject to the authority of the medical profession has been replaced by the rational, informed consumer who makes the market function by trading off cost and quality and who is an active participant in the health-care process. Formalized clinical guidelines and pathways are replacing the localized individual, physician-practice signatures. While managed care has played a role in this transformation, it is itself an outcome of significant institutional changes. The methodological implication for researchers is that focusing on the effects of managed care is likely to be subject to specification bias unless other causal institutional processes are incorporated in models.

MCOS: ORGANIZATIONAL FORMS AND EVOLUTIONARY PROCESSES

MCO organization has evolved rapidly. Initially, Group HMOs represented MCOs. These plans date back to the mid-1930s to mid-1940s, which saw the formation of plans like Ross-Loos and Kaiser Foundation Health Plans (Starr 1982), which were sponsored by employer or consumer groups that provided them access to a patient population. The group practice structure and the link to a patient population allowed these MCOs to weather resistance to prepaid medical care from organized medicine.

The 1954 formation of the San Joaquin Medical Care Foundation in California marked a recurring event throughout the development of MCOs—actors based on a different organizational form than multispecialty groups responded to the competitive pressure from prior MCO types (Starr 1982; Wholey et al. 1993). The San Joaquin Medical Care Foundation was based on physicians who were predominantly in solo or small single-specialty practice. MCOs of its type would eventually become known as Independent Practice Associations HMOs (IPA HMOs).

In response to rapidly increasing health-care costs following the passage of Medicare, the federal government adopted managed care as a cost-containment strategy in 1973. Interestingly, this cost-containment strategy was the consequence of a garbage-can model of decision making (Kingdon 1995: 6). Paul Ellwood, one of the proponents of managed care, sat next to a senior White House administrative assistant on an airplane flight, during which he suggested managed care as a solution to the Nixon administration's problem of rapidly increasing health-care costs. To make it attractive to a Republican administration, managed care was packaged as a component of a market-based managed competition approach. The resulting HMO Act of 1973 and its amendment in 1976 encouraged HMO formation. Drawing from the available institutional building blocks—prepaid medical group practices (such as Kaiser) and IPAs (such as the San Joaquin Medical Care Foundation)—the act specified two different HMO forms.

Beginning with IPA HMOs in the mid-1980s, there have been regular waves of MCO formation (Christianson et al. 1991a). In the late 1980s, health insurers responded to HMOs by developing preferred provider organizations (PPOs) and point-of-service (POS) organizations, which provided more choice of providers. In the early 1990s, hospitals began developing MCOs and MCO contracting vehicles (Burns and Thorpe 1993). Loosely coupled forms included alliances of medical staff-organized independent practitioner associations (IPAs) and physician-hospital organizations (PHOs). Moderately coupled forms included management services organizations (MSOs) that provide physicians administrative support and equity or foundation models in which the hospital takes an ownership interest in physician practices. Tightly coupled forms included integrated salary models (ISMs), in which the hospital purchases physician practices and employs physicians and integrated health organizations (IHOs), in which a single parent organization owns a hospital, group practice, and a health plan. The mid-1990s saw physicians sponsoring their own contracting vehicles, including group practices without walls (GPWWs), single specialty networks, and physician practice management companies (PPMCs)

(Burns 1997). The newest provider model is the provider sponsored organization (PSO) authorized under the Balanced Budget Amendments of 1997.

A central theme of MCO development has been purchaser demand for MCOs as a cost-containment vehicle. MCOs are most likely to form in communities where corporate interests dominate, as reflected in high health-care costs and business health-care coalition activity, and where physicians are less able to resist HMOs (Wholey et al. 1993). A second theme is that of providers responding to competitive pressure by each developing their own type of MCO based on their self-proclaimed expertise.

The development of each MCO form disrupts existing relationships between purchasers, plans, providers, and patients. Each MCO form has encountered problems similar to those experienced by earlier populations (Burns 1999), with productivity low until new organizational arrangements are learned. The biggest problem faced by providers is integrating health-care delivery, health insurance, and business functions. The failure to perform insurance functions, such as underwriting, and determine adequate reserve levels has caused failures in the early stages of each MCO population (Christianson et al. 1991b). Providers have little experience in marketing their services to healthy populations, who are critical for a balanced risk mix. Providers also have little expertise in claims and physician-management systems. Even by the mid-1990s, HMOs were the only form of MCOs that had implemented extensive provider-management capabilities (Gold et al. 1995). Even among HMOs, it was not until 1993 that IPA HMO productivity matched the productivity of Group HMOs (Wholey et al. 1999a). PHOs lack most of the mechanisms found in HMOs, including provider selection, medical management, and provider economic incentives (Burns and Thorpe 1997). The development difficulties are exacerbated in later MCO forms because of the competitive environment created by the success of earlier forms.

These MCO evolutionary processes, reflected in the formation and failure of MCO forms, are both a strength and weakness of MCO development. Their strength is testing innovative ways of organizing. But, the evolutionary processes disrupt patient, provider, and purchaser relationships, which may affect the quality and productivity of health-care delivery. If these new organizational forms have HMOs as their limiting case (Greaney 1994), then it is unclear what is gained by the proliferation of new MCO forms. And federal policies defining new MCO forms may exacerbate these problems.

MCO Organization

MCOs sell health-services coverage measured in member months of coverage. Revenues come from a premium charged for a member month of coverage. Eighty-five percent of MCO costs derive from medical costs associated with assembling the inputs of hospital days, ambulatory visits, and other medical resources to provide health-services coverage, while 15 percent of costs come from administrative functions (Wholey et al. 1996b). Major MCO functions typically include health insurance and medical management (Kongstvedt 1996). MCOs manage risk and providers in network organizations that link providers in an incredibly complex array of organizational arrangements.

MCO Structures

The two basic provider building blocks that MCOs assemble are multispecialty physician group practices and physicians in solo/single-specialty practice. These two building blocks pose substantially different organizing problems (Wholey and Burns 1993; Wolinsky and Marder 1985). In multispecialty physician groups, spatial contiguity of diverse physicians allows them to coordinate and control their activities by direct interaction, curbside consulting, shared medical records, and mutual adjustment (Freidson 1975). These coordination and control devices are not available for physicians in solo or single-specialty practice. Research on HMOs consistently shows a significant difference between HMO forms based on these two types of organizing physicians (Wholey and Burns 1993; Wholey et al. 1992, 1993) and research on provider organization also shows consistent differences (Wolinsky and Marder 1985).

Understanding how provider organization mediates the effect of MCO structures is a central research issue. E. Freidson (1975) and T. Hoff and D.P. McCaffrey (1996) show that physician embeddedness in social networks affects physician social control. While a medical group may be capitated as a whole, for example, individual physicians within the group are typically paid on a salary, and the effect of the shared risk due to capitation is likely to be mediated by social interaction patterns within the provider group. Research on how different types of social embeddedness mediate the effect of MCO incentives and structures on outcomes is required to understand the performance of various MCO structures.

As well as assembling provider networks, MCOs choose how to segment patient populations and health care services among provider organizations. Patient populations can be segmented by common health condition, such as being HIV positive or diabetic, while specialty or episode of care can be used to segment health-care services. Contracting with a provider group to provide all services to all patients is the most inclusive form of bundling. Carve-outs for specific conditions or populations are increasingly used, although little is known about their performance (Blumenthal and Buntin 1998; Frank and McGuire 1998). An MCO carves out a particular service, such as behavioral-health services or cancer, by contracting with one provider group for all medical services required for a patient population and with a specialist provider group for behavioral-health services (Feldman 1998; Kurowski 1998). An MCO carves out a particular patient population, such as HIV-positive patients, by contracting with a provider group to provide all services to that population. Pooling relatively rare demand allows specialist providers to provide more cost-effective care through scale economies. Since volume is positively correlated with quality, pooling may improve quality. Carve-outs are useful when specialists, such as cardiologists caring for congestive heart failure, can coordinate all of a patient's care. The organizational design issue in service carve-outs is balancing the integration loss caused by a carve-out with the development of specialized expertise and economies by providers across all of a patient's providers (Christianson et al. 1997; Wholey et al. 1996a). Carve-outs provide an opportunity to organizational researchers for detailed analyses of the determinants of make–buy decisions and of the effects of those decisions on cost and quality.

Once patient populations and services have been bundled, MCOs face a choice in what functions, such as utilization management and quality assurance, the provider group will provide. MCOs appear to be increasingly subcontracting functions such as quality assurance and improvement, utilization management, credentialing and selecting providers (Kerr et al. 1995).

The fact that many providers contract with multiple MCOs exacerbates the fragmentation of the MCO environment. Each MCO a provider contracts with has its own structures and policies for bundling patient populations, health-care services, drug formulary rules, laboratories, information systems, and provider management. The fragmentation results in confusion and administrative overhead. Each level of complexity and interface difference is an opportunity for normal errors to occur, and patients are put at risk (Leape et al. 1995; Perrow 1984). The fragmentation can result in ambiguous and conflicting performance evaluations, which means that providers have difficulty in determining actions to take to improve quality. The fragmentation of the contractual environment means that the potential gains due to integrated health care will be difficult to attain.

MANAGING HEALTH SERVICES USE

Medical management focuses on managing the demand of medical services. Figure 15–1 is a simplified model of how MCOs manage this demand with structures directly aimed at decisions about health-services use such as utilization review and structures designed to influence consumer and physician behavior (Landon et al. 1996).

Consumer-oriented structures include product design, demand management, and network structure. Product design and network structure affect use by influencing consumers attracted to the MCO. Benefits for expectant mothers and children may attract relatively young, healthy populations, while generous mental health benefits may attract relatively costly populations. The openness of provider networks and the availability of specialists for a chronic condition may also attract relatively costly patient populations. Patient financial incentives, such as co-payments and deductibles, influence consumer demand for services (Newhouse 1994). Demand management, such as nurse call centers to triage patient problems and educating hypertensive consumers about healthy lifestyles, uses educational strategies and preventive health care to help consumers make health-care use decisions that will optimize their health status (MacStravic and Montrose 1998).

There are three central themes in MCO provider management. First, MCOs emphasize primary care, substituting ambulatory care for hospitalization (Wholey

Figure 15–1 Managed Medical Care

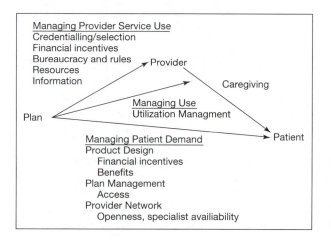

Managing Provider Service Use
Credentialling/selection
Financial incentives
Bureaucracy and rules
Resources
Information

Provider

Caregiving

Managing Use
Utilization Managment

Plan

Managing Patient Demand
Product Design
    Financial incentives
    Benefits
Plan Management
    Access
Provider Network
    Openness, specialist availiability

Patient

et al. 1999a) and primary care for specialist care (Flood et al. 1998). Second, managing providers and health-services use is similar to squeezing a balloon. Third, MCOs influence use by structuring the context of physician decision-making.

Primary Care

Primary care is "the provision of integrated, accessible health care services by clinicians who are accountable for addressing a large majority of personal health care needs, developing a sustained partnership with patients, and practicing in the context of family and community" (Donaldson et al. 1996: 1). Primary care providers (PCPs) are often the initial contact points for health-care patients. As initial contacts, PCPs perform a gatekeeper role, managing a patient's access to the health-care system. This can be interpreted as either containing costs by limiting access (e.g., denying requests for specialist referrals) or as managing appropriate health care (e.g., by guiding patients to the correct specialists). Primary care practice occurs within social contexts. Providers are embedded in relationships with other providers, and patients are embedded in social support groups. These social contexts influence demand and supply of health-care services.

A PCP's position as initial contact leads him or her to observe a wide range of conditions for a particular patient over an extended period of time. Starfield (1992) refers to these dimensions as comprehensiveness, longitudinality, and continuity. Comprehensiveness refers to the variance in types of problems a PCP observes in a patient. Longitudinality refers to the ongoing personal relationship between a PCP and a patient (Starfield 1992: 41); it is considered an important component in a patient's perceptions of caring and trust (Scott et al. 1995; Starfield 1992), and it is associated with continuity of care (Starfield 1992: 79), which is the integration of information necessary to treat a patient across time and across health-care problems.

Research suggests that organizing around primary care is efficacious. Health-care costs are lower for an episode of care when primary care physicians are a patient's first contact with the health-care system (Forrest and Starfield 1996). Lower costs do not imply lower quality, because no consistent relationship between cost efficiency and quality of care was found in primary care (Starfield et al. 1994).

Comprehensive care, longitudinal relationships, and continuity of care generate a substantial amount of information. This implies a need for coordination of care by combining diverse pieces of information. MCOs have the opportunity to address the fragmentation and localization of this information by their organizational structures and policies. But the fragmentation caused by MCO bundling of services and populations, providers contracting with multiple health plans, and consumers switching between providers works against MCOs providing the support necessary to provide effectively integrated primary care.

Squeezing Balloons

Managing providers is most aptly described by a balloon analogy—whenever one part of the balloon is pushed down, another part of the balloon tends to expand. Reducing hospital utilization is associated with greater use of primary care visits, specialist visits, and laboratory use. Research shows that ambulatory visits are substituted for hospital days in all types of HMOs (Wholey et al. 1999a). Physicians respond to moving from a fee-for-service setting to an HMO setting by reducing hospital admissions while increasing ambulatory visits, especially specialist referrals (Stearns et al. 1992). Pushing physicians to be more productive in their office visits through higher patient loads may cause pharmaceutical use and specialist referral to increase. Primary care physicians paid a salary and faced with a heavy patient load have a tendency to refer patients to specialists, order laboratory tests, and schedule patients for a return visit (Freidson 1975). Physicians respond to managed care in IPA settings by devising "ways to circumvent insurers or the government and maintain some degree of economic control" (Hoff and McCaffrey 1996: 173).

Structuring the Context of Physician Decision-Making

Decision behavior can be viewed from either a rational or institutional perspective. The perspective understands decision behavior as a choice among a set of alternatives to obtain positive utility. Individual behavior can be modified by structuring the set of alternatives that providers consider by modifying the estimated probability of an outcome occurring by choosing a specific alternative and by influencing the utility derived from the outcome. The institutional perspective understands decision behavior as the application of bureaucratic rules and social identities to particular problems.

Managing Utility through Incentives There are three basic ways of compensating providers: fee-for-service payment, capitation, and salary (Pauly et al. 1992).

Fee-for-service is a fixed payment per service, salary is a payment per unit of time, and capitation is a fixed fee per patient per unit of time for some bundle of services to be provided to the patient. Three common capitation bundles include primary care only, primary care and specialty care, and global capitation of primary, specialty, and hospital care. Withholds and bonuses are wrapped around these basic forms. Withholds reserve some percentage of a provider's revenues, which is paid to the provider if MCO performance targets are reached. Bonuses pay a provider if MCO performance targets are reached. Coupling three different payment structures (fee-for-service, capitation, salary), wrap-around incentives (withholds, bonuses), different service bundles and carve-outs, multiple MCO contracts result in a dizzying array of potential incentive structures for providers. Not surprisingly, while there is extensive discourse about incentive structure effects, there is little research.

Capitation provides an incentive to provide fewer services (Pauly et al. 1992). Bundling all services together in a global capitation structure allows providers to determine the best way to organize services. Bundling at lower levels is extremely difficult to manage. Capitating a primary care gatekeeper for primary and specialty care, for example, may lead to too few referrals to specialists. Addressing this problem by developing administrative systems for monitoring provider use of specialists contradicts one of the major reasons for capitating—simplifying MCO administrative structures—and introduces costs that offset savings due to capitation. MCOs also deal with the problem of restructuring capitation, paying primary care physicians on a fee-for-service basis, which encourages primary care visits, and then capitating specialists for all the care necessary for a specific condition. The elaboration of incentive structures can be best described as searching in the location of a problem for some perhaps satisfactory solution to the unintended consequence of the last decision about incentive structures. Perhaps the main consequence is a continual flux that contributes to administrative overhead and confusion.

Capitation appears to reduce costs. J.E. Kralewski and his colleagues found that capitation is associated with lower patient-care costs, while salary compensation is associated with higher costs (Kralewski et al. 1999). Conversely, Conrad and his colleagues found no effect of capitation on resource use in medical groups (Conrad et al. 1998). Kralewski and his colleagues found that being capitated was endogenous, with high-cost clinics more likely to be capitated. Flood and her colleagues found that patients covered by an HMO had lower costs than those receiving fee-for-service care (Flood et al.

1998). A strength of the analysis was controlling for clinic differences by comparing fee-for-service and HMO patients receiving care in the same clinic. Cost savings were due to which physicians were seen and what services were used, rather than due to influencing the behavior of particular physicians. Capitated physician groups are more likely to review costly services that may be overused (such as cesareans) than to review less costly areas of underuse such as preventive services and follow-up services for patients with chronic conditions (Kerr et al. 1996).

Capitation may discourage MCOs or providers from developing expertise in treating conditions that may attract a less healthy population. Because capitation payments for patients with chronic conditions are consistently low (Fowles et al. 1996), attracting chronically ill patients is argued to be a money-losing proposition for MCOs. So MCOs may avoid a primary care physician with expertise in treating AIDS because of the patient population that provider would attract. Similarly, provider organizations or IDSs that are based on prestigious tertiary care referral centers may perform poorly because they attract a costly enrollment mix. Risk-adjusting provider payments so that providers with healthier patients are reimbursed less and providers with less healthy patients are reimbursed more provides the promise of ameliorating some of these problems (Smith and Weiner 1992; Weiner et al. 1998).

There is very little direct evidence on the effects of capitation on patient outcomes, although there are some hints that chronically ill individuals under capitation may be at greater risk. Lurie et al. (Lurie et al. 1994) found that among patients with chronic mental illness, there was greater decline over time in health status in MCOs than in fee-for-service (FFS) settings. Among the elderly with chronic illnesses, Ware et al. (Ware et al. 1996) report a greater health status decline among patients in MCOs than in FFS settings. But, Ware et al. also reported that patients with mental illness improved more in one MCO than in any FFS arrangements they studied.

Overall, Berwick aptly summarizes the evidence: "What can be said with certainty is that the empirical literature as a whole so far does not make capitation out to be the villain that some believe it is. Dire predictions are common, but they are based more on theoretical issues than on systematic data. If anything, the data suggest hazards and ethical problems in the overuse of services in fee-for-service settings, rather than its underuse in capitated care" (Berwick 1996: 1228). While there is little negative evidence, positive evidence is just as difficult to find.

The relative absence of a sociological voice in the current literature on physician payment structures is striking. There is a scarcity of, and a tremendous opportunity for, research on physician incentive structures that takes advantage of the sociological foundation in medical sociology and research in the sociology of work that examines the effects of incentive structures.

Structuring Alternatives MCOs can influence resources by structuring the alternative resources that can be used. Some of these tools include structuring the network of specialists and hospitals that primary care physicians may refer patients to, structuring the laboratory network, and using drug formularies. Because of an MCO's ability to channel volume to particular providers and laboratories, the better the MCO's ability to obtain a lower unit price, monitor performance on a statistically reliable basis, and cause laboratories and specialists to respond to quality improvement suggestions. The cost of structuring alternatives is reducing choice for providers and patients and making access more difficult.

Bureaucracy and Guidelines Bureaucracy includes structures targeted directly at modifying the decisions providers make, such as utilization review and reminder systems, and indirect structures designed to change physician decision-making parameters.

Reviewing Physician Decisions Utilization review (UR) includes prospective, concurrent, and retrospective review of provider decision making (Kongstvedt 1996). Prospective review includes precertification and second-opinion, preadmission testing. Concurrent review includes activities such as the MCO reviewing the status of hospitalized patients on a regular basis. Retrospective includes monitoring sentinel events (e.g., unexpected death) and reviewing them. Prospective and concurrent review can alter decisions about patient care. UR reduces health-service use (Feldstein et al. 1988).

Gatekeeper physicians are another mechanism for reviewing decisions by requiring that all specialist and laboratory referral decisions be approved by the patient's primary care physician.

Modifying Provider Decision-Making by Supporting Decision-Making Continuing education and computer-based clinical reminder systems are examples of organizational processes designed to influence provider behavior by changing alternatives considered or the estimated probability of an outcome for a given alternative. These systems typically provide physicians with information about alternative treatments, activities that should be performed, or potential adverse events.

These systems are effective in modifying physician behavior (Yano et al. 1995), reducing adverse drug events (Bates et al. 1998), and improving preventive care (Shea et al. 1996) such as vaccinations, cardiovascular risk reduction, and breast and colorectal cancer screening. These systems appear to work better the more specifically they are tailored to a physician. Educational systems such as continuing medical-education conferences and less tailored interventions are less effective (Davis et al. 1995; Oxman et al. 1995).

Clinical guidelines are an example of institutional rules and procedures that define appropriate practices given a condition. Guideline use improves processes of care, such as increasing preventive health counseling and decreasing inappropriate use of antibiotics, and outcomes of care, such as decreases in blood pressure among hypertensives treated by physicians following guidelines (Grimshaw and Russell 1993).

Case-management services support decision making by assisting patients with catastrophic, expensive cases and their providers in managing the diverse range of services the patients require. Research suggests that case management may be effective in managing resource use (Burns et al. 1996). Case management includes the activities of screening, locating enrollees who are most likely to benefit from case management, assessment, gathering information about and evaluating screened enrollees for inclusion in the case management program, and care management.

Modifying Provider Decision-Making by Bundling Conditions and Tasks An organizational response to conditions of high uncertainty and reciprocal interdependence is integrating the personnel and programs necessary for performing a task so that mutual adjustment can be used as a coordinative device (Thompson 1967). One such integrative device is disease management, which has the goal of integrating provider and patient references, best available evidence-based medicine, and clinical guidelines across health-care settings (Christianson et al. 1998; Von Korff et al. 1997; Wagner et al. 1996). These programs seek to understand and improve the processes of care for particular chronic conditions (e.g., asthma, diabetes, cardiovascular disease, etc.) and focus on the entire course of a disease and provide multidisciplinary patient management that cuts across care settings (lateral perspective) and time (longitudinal perspective).

Information Technology to Measure, Monitor, and Manage MCOs are responsible for the health of a population of individuals delivered through a defined provider network. Since a health insurance claim necessarily involves patients and providers, claims can be used to manage the health of individuals in the population and to measure, monitor, and manage physician performance (Wholey et al. 1999b). An example of the former is physicians being assisted in identifying hypertensive patients who are not being provided appropriate drugs such as beta blockers (Brand et al. 1995). An example of the latter is that physicians who are caring for diabetics can be shown their rate of providing eye examinations to diabetic patients relative to that of other providers (Hanchak et al. 1996).

Physician profiling has also been targeted at managing utilization. A review of the effect of physicians on resource utilization found that while profiling did reduce health-care use, the savings were modest, perhaps less than the cost of the profiling program (Balas et al. 1996). Similarly, while profiling reduces clinic costs, the magnitude of the savings is not large (Kralewski et al. 1999).

MCO Organization—Summary

There are many managed care structures that appear to be useful for improving health care quality and reducing health care costs. MCOs and providers have a choice of the hierarchical level for locating these structures. Some activities, such as disease management and clinical decision support systems, are most appropriately implemented at the clinical level because the structures can be adjusted to the particular providers and patient population of a clinic (Berg 1997). In contrast, other activities are more appropriately allocated at the MCO level. Developing information systems and reviewing medical literature to develop guidelines have high fixed costs that would be costly to replicate across provider groups. Statistical analysis of claims for case-mix adjustment, population monitoring, and physician profiling are also more appropriately done at the MCO level because of the need for large, nonfragmented sets of data.

MCO PERFORMANCE

This section first summarizes research on MCO performance, then discusses common research issues in examining MCO performance, and finally discusses the role of selection as a determinant of MCO performance. There has been a variety of reviews of MCO performance (Berwick 1996; Hellinger 1998; Luft 1981; Miller and Luft 1994, 1997; Wholey et al. 1998). Much of the research on MCO performance has focused on

HMOs, possibly because HMOs were established earlier than other MCO forms or because HMOs have better-developed managerial structures than do other forms of MCOs for managing health-care use (Gold et al. 1995).

Compared to FFS, HMOs have higher rates of physician office visits, preventive tests, and health counseling and lower rates of hospital admissions, shorter hospital stays, less use of costly technology, and lower rates of referral to specialists. Differences between HMOs and FFS in utilization rates may have attenuated from the 1980s to the 1990s, possibly because of increased use of utilization management structures among indemnity insurers.

Access to primary care providers is better in MCOs, but access to specialists and hospitals is lower in MCOs than in FFS. It is not clear how to interpret lower access to specialists and the lower rate of performing some procedures in MCOs relative to FFS. One interpretation is that MCOs are skimping and not providing appropriate care. An alternative view is that some procedures are being over-performed in the fee-for-service sector, perhaps due to over-referral or greater self-referral to specialists among indemnity. Given access, a number of studies report no differences between MCOs and FFSs in processes of care, with some studies reporting more attentiveness to processes of care in MCOs than in FFSs. Patient satisfaction results mirror access results. MCO enrollees are more satisfied with financial aspects of a health plan and less satisfied with access to specialists, hospitals, prescriptions, obtaining information, and quality of care.

MCOs have lower total expenditures and premiums, with competition among MCOs lowering premiums (Wholey et al. 1995). The movement of individuals from traditional indemnity insurance into managed care plans during the 1990s was associated with a strong moderation in premium increases (Jensen et al. 1997). These cost savings appear to be due to substituting less costly primary care services for hospital use, by using specialists and costly technology less, and by using primary care gatekeepers.

A significant source of lower MCO costs is lower prices paid to providers (Melnick et al. 1989; Robinson 1996; Simon and Born 1996; Wholey et al. 1996b; Zwanziger et al. 1994). The result is that MCOs have caused income for hospitals and physicians to increase more slowly or caused median incomes to decline. Associated with the decline in income and the restructuring of the context of medical work, MCOs also may have decreased provider satisfaction (Hadley and Mitchell 1997; Hadley et al. 1999); but see (Burdi and Baker 1997).

As well as directly influencing quality and cost of care for MCO enrollees, MCO development is associated with a lower rate of technology adoption in communities (Chernew et al. 1998), with lower fee-for-service expenditures for Medicare enrollees (Baker 1999), with adoption of managed care structures by fee-for-service providers (Joesch et al. 1998), with lower provision of charity care by physicians (Cunningham et al. 1999), with lower access to care for the indigent (Cunningham 1999), and with less support for academic research.

Evaluation of MCO Research

There are several common methodological problems in the research literature on MCO performance and the effect of MCO structures on performance. Most studies usually suffer from at least a few. Generalizability is a limitation, particularly among major research projects that have the strongest controls for case mix and strongest array of outcome measures (e.g., the Rand Health Insurance Experiment (Newhouse 1994); the Medical Outcomes Study (Tarlov et al. 1989)). Because of the number of substudies embedded in a major project, these studies are represented very heavily in the research literature. But each study had very few MCOs participating. It is not clear that participating MCOs are not systematically different than MCOs that choose not to participate; and, the information in each published research report is not an independent observation.

When studying MCOs, care must be taken to select appropriate subpopulations to study (Angell and Kassirer 1996). Satisfaction measures or health-status-change measures for the population of all MCO enrollees are likely to be relatively high because most enrollees are healthy. The preponderance of healthy individuals masks important differences within subpopulations. Since the chronically ill may be the canary in the mine, special care must be taken to measure the effect of managed care on their satisfaction and outcomes.

The balloon nature of health care input use is often ignored (Wholey et al. 1999a). Although an MCO structure may reduce specialty visits, it may also cause providers to substitute drugs. While studies of total resource use, as measured by total cost of care for a patient, capture the overall effect of an MCO structure, they often do not measure substitution effects. This causes the total effects of MCO structures to be poorly understood.

Accurately modeling the effect of MCO structures requires controlling for endogeneity, case mix, and benefit design. MCO structures such as capitation and gatekeeping are endogenous, being adopted because an

MCO is having difficulty managing the associated problem. For example, MCOs capitate more costly groups (Kralewski et al. 1999), or productive provider groups may choose to seek a capitated contract. Inadequate controls for endogeneity will bias estimates of the effect of MCO structures. Controls for case mix are often rudimentary, particularly in studies incorporating larger numbers of MCOs. New risk-adjustment technologies based in claims data, such as ACGs (Starfield et al. 1991; Weiner et al. 1991), episodes of care (Wingert et al. 1995), or diagnostic cost groups (Ellis and Ash 1995) provide a foundation for building accurate case-mix controls. Benefit structures are another strong alternative explanation. In the early research, differences in preventive health care may have been due to MCOs' being more likely to cover preventive health care than were indemnity plans.

Efficiency in Production and Selection

Patient selection effects are a standard alternative explanation of observed MCO and provider-performance differences. There are substantial profits to be made from exploiting temporarily advantageous positions, and methods to exploit these transitory positions may be difficult to observe. An MCO, for example, could avoid recruiting physicians who provide care to HIV-positive individuals to make its network unattractive to them. Or, an MCO could choose specialists who are difficult for members with chronic conditions to access. The most obvious examples are irregularities in premium payments.

MCOs profit from attracting relatively healthy individuals for whom they receive a premium that is higher than care will cost and by avoiding chronically ill patients for whom they will be underreimbursed (Fowles et al. 1996). Weiner and Starfield explored the magnitude of this difference in a comparison of community rating, age-gender adjusted community rating, and ambulatory care group (ACG) risk-adjusted methods for setting provider payments. In pure community rating, providers are paid the average amount of cost incurred by an individual enrolled in a health plan. Age-gender adjusted rating calculates average costs by age-gender combination. ACGs risk adjust rates, taking into account an enrollee's diagnoses in the prior year as well age and gender. Comparison of age-gender rating to ACG rating in a Medicaid population showed that age-gender adjustment overpaid providers by 19.2 percent for relatively healthy individuals, −.2 percent for average individuals, and −11.7 percent for relatively unhealthy individuals (Weiner et al. 1998). Comparable

percentage differences for ACG-adjusted payments were 3.8 percent, −.5 percent, and −1.8 percent. Under age-gender rate determination methodology, which is by far the most common methodology used in the United States, health-care organizations and providers profit from enrolling the healthy and avoiding the ill.

Medicare's implementation of risk contracting with MCOs provides an example of the selection effects. Medicare set the price it paid MCOs as 95 percent of the average cost per Medicare enrollee in fee-for-service arrangements in a geographic area. Early evidence from enrollment patterns suggested that MCOs attracted relatively healthy individuals with low costs (Hill and Brown 1990). Inpatient services for individuals in the year prior to enrolling in Medicare MCOs was 66 percent of the rate of individuals not enrolling in Medicare MCOs, and the inpatient use rate of those disenrolling from Medicare risk MCOs was 180 percent of the use rate of a comparable fee-for-service group (Morgan et al. 1997). Many disenrollees returned to MCOs once their hospital-use rate became comparable to those of fee-for-service enrollees. This enrollment-disenrollment-reenrollment process can be interpreted as a signal that MCOs are seeking favorable selection, seeking the healthy, and encouraging the ill to disenroll.

Profiting through taking advantage of temporary opportunities is not solely an MCO phenomena. The enrollment-disenrollment-reenrollment process among Medicare beneficiaries in MCOs can be interpreted as beneficiary "gaming" of an institutional structure. If Medicare beneficiaries disenroll because quality of care is extremely poor, then they would not be expected to re-enroll when they obtained desired procedures. Other research shows that Medicare patients with cancer are no more likely to disenroll from Medicare MCOs than are other individuals (Riley et al. 1996) and that MCOs do not skim relatively healthy Medicare patients in some markets (Dowd et al. 1994).

Taking advantage of selection is a systemic issue in health care. The appropriate object that inferences are drawn about may be the consumer as well as the MCO. Providers also have an opportunity to take advantage of selection advantages. Physician groups with relatively healthy patients or with relatively productive organizations may actively seek capitated contracts. Or providers may try to block some benefits from being covered. The fluid definition of what constitutes a medical condition (Conrad 1992), a treatment, and a covered benefit allows actors at all levels, from physicians to MCOs, to compete to control profitable market spaces and occupational arenas (Abbott 1988). Physicians providing radial keratomy, for example, may resist making it a covered benefit because of the anticipated MCO-sponsored reduction in their fees. When an individual's statement of benefits says that mental health and substance abuse treatment are covered benefits, purchasers, providers, and MCOs must define what actually constitutes a mental health condition and its appropriate treatment. While MCOs contribute to this debate, they are not the sole determinant of the debate's outcome.

Selection effects appear to attenuate over time (Hellinger 1995). While MCOs may attract enrollees who are relatively healthy, the health conditions of these enrollees comes to resemble the remainder of the population over time. This attenuation effect may also occur at the community level. No selection effects in Medicare enrollment were found in Minneapolis, a well-developed Medicare market (Dowd et al. 1994).

The development of risk-adjusted premiums may reduce some of the gains to be obtained from playing the selection game. Until these gains are limited, however, some MCOs and providers may be more interested in profiting from selection games rather than from improving the production of health care.

THE FUTURE OF MANAGED CARE

MCOs are under increasing scrutiny and are suffering from a managed care backlash (Blendon et al. 1998). Patients worry about MCOs interfering in their relationship with their provider and disrupting the trust necessary for high-quality health care. Utilization management could counteract a decision jointly arrived at by patient and provider. Gatekeeping, the requirement that a patient receive approval from his or her primary care physician before seeing a specialist, interferes with the relationship with a specialist. Explicit rationing policies call attention to denial of access to resources (Mechanic 1995). Capitation is an incentive system designed to reduce the volume of services physicians provide to patients. All of these lead patients to worry that MCOs will interfere in the care their provider recommends for them (Blendon et al. 1998; Sleeper et al. 1998) and encourage policy makers to micromanage MCOs through regulatory processes.

Some MCOs appear to be moving toward less directly obtrusive control of the medical-delivery process for a number of reasons. Less obtrusive control reduces the limit on MCO growth caused by the backlash and reduces the possibility of regulatory micromanagement of MCOs. Less obtrusive controls also reduce the liability that MCOs face from malpractice suits. The benefits

from these obtrusive controls may have dissipated so that the structures are not as useful as they once were. Many of the early medical-management techniques were best suited to an environment with "low hanging fruit," which could be easily picked off. Utilization management (UM), for example, functioned well in environments with relatively low MCO penetration because reducing utilization from the levels observed among indemnity insurers was not difficult. As physician practice styles change and as evidence based medicine is implemented, UM may be less useful. Physician profiling can be used to identify the providers a patient normally goes to, and those providers can become de facto primary care gatekeepers who replace explicit gatekeepers. Disinterested third parties can be used to adjudicate patient grievances. Advances in the ability to use information technology to measure, monitor, and manage care may provide new ways of organizing medical practice. While old-line prepaid medical groups such as Kaiser argue that they do managed care right, newer MCOs based on physicians in solo or single-specialty practice, such as United HealthCare and U.S. HealthCare, may have extensively developed information systems that allow them to do managed care right in a new way.

CONCLUSION

MCOs have contained costs associated with delivering health care to a defined population and have moderated premium increases. They have done this by: (1) reducing utilization, particularly of hospitals, specialists, and costly procedures; (2) skimming favorable risks early in the MCO development cycle; (3) reducing prices paid to providers, such as hospitals, physicians, and pharmaceutical firms; and (4) making sure that only covered benefits are paid. Some of these effects may be due to favorable selection and may result in only single-time savings. But the continued moderation of health-care premium increases in the late 1990s suggests that as well as a single-time shift, the expansion of MCOs may be associated with a moderation in the rate of increase of health-care costs (Ginsburg and Gabel 1998). The externalities of MCO development include: (1) decreasing growth rates in indemnity insurance premiums; (2) decreasing growth in technology; (3) decreasing provision of charity care by providers; and (4) lowering access to care for the indigent. The latter three are a consequence of MCOs containing health care costs for the defined population they serve.

In terms of quality, MCOs increase provision of preventive care and health behavior counseling.

Research does not show any adverse effects on quality compared to fee-for-service health insurance. But there are some worrisome signals about care for the chronically ill, and there is no strong evidence that MCOs integrate and coordinate care better than do fee-for-service settings.

Rather than describing MCOs as the source of the changes occurring in health care, MCOs are perhaps best described as an institutional structure that mediates purchaser pressure to contain costs and health-services research pressure to improve quality. Information technology is a catalyst that enables new ways of measuring, monitoring, and managing care. Health care is increasingly rationalized with exchange. "Exchange is governed by rules of rational calculation and bookkeeping, rules constituting a market, and includes such related processes as monetarization, commercialization, and bureaucratic planning; cultural accounts increasingly reduce society to the smallest rational units—the individual" (Meyer 1994: 20). Patients have become informed consumers and purchasers of health care who are expected to be active participants in the health-care process. While MCOs are affected by this rationalization and contribute to the particular form it takes, the forces underlying the rationalization would be present without MCOs.

MCOs and this rationalization both have had adverse consequences for patient–provider relations, particularly trust between patient and provider (Kao et al. 1998), and for trust in health-care institutions. The decline in trust can be decomposed into the societal trends of rationalization and commodification, the rapid development of MCOs, which has disrupted the relationships between organizations, providers, and patients upon which relational trust is built, and MCO structures. These declines are worrisome because trust in provider is critical for implicit rationing, and trust in social institutions is important for explicit rationing. The portion that is due to federal- and state-induced changes in market structures is addressable by stabilizing institutional definitions of MCOs and markets. The portion that is due to MCO structures and actions is an institutional design issue, possibly addressable by policies encouraging a more corporatist governance structure (Wholey et al., 1999a).

MCOs have not resolved the fragmentation problems that plagued fee-for-service health-care systems. In fact, the rapid evolution of managed care may have exacerbated the fragmentation. New structures, such as carve-outs, and incentive mechanisms are legitimated as structures that will reduce selection problems and allow providers to better integrate care. New organizational forms, such as integrated delivery systems, are legitimated by their sponsors, physicians and hospitals, who claim their unique expertise allows them to do managed care right. But these advantages are difficult to observe in the performance of the new forms. The formation and failure of MCO organizations disrupt relationships between patient and provider, which are particularly important for the chronically ill. The difficulty in implementing these structures provides ample opportunity for MCOs, providers, and consumers to profit by taking advantage of selection. New ways of segmenting patients and services and ways of paying providers create interest and incentive boundaries that impede coordination. In part because of worries about the performance of these organizations in terms of quality, costly administrative structures elaborate to meet demands for quality information and to measure, monitor, and manage providers. It is unclear how well, or how poorly, MCOs will perform in a stable environment.

While MCOs are undoubtedly an important institutional change, it must not be forgotten that MCOs exist in a wider policy context. In fact, MCOs may have served as a red herring in distracting health-services researchers and the country from more important policy issues. MCOs have attracted substantial research and policy attention and effort over the past few years. The effort to test dire predictions about MCO performance may have distracted us from studying and addressing more fundamental policy issues, such as the level of health uninsurance in the United States.

REFERENCES

ABBOTT, A. 1988. *The System of Professions: An Essay on the Division of Labor.* Chicago: The University of Chicago Press.

ACS, G., S.H. LONG, M.S. MARQUIS, and P.F. SHORT. 1996. "Self-insured Employer Health Plans: Prevalence, Profile, Provisions, and Premiums." *Health Affairs* 15(2): 266–78.

AGENCY FOR HEALTH CARE POLICY AND RESEARCH. 1999. "National Guideline Clearinghouse." *http://www.guideline.gov.*

AMERICAN MEDICAL ASSOCIATION. 1998. "Principles of Managed Care." *http://www.ama-assn.org/advocacy/principl.htm.*

ANGELL, M., and J.P. KASSIRER. 1996. "Quality and the Medical Marketplace—Following Elephants." *New England Journal of Medicine* 335(12): 883–85.

BAKER, L.C. 1999. "Association of Managed Care Market Share and Health Expenditures for Fee-For-Service Medicare Patients." *Journal of the American Medical Association* 281(5): 432–37.

BALAS, E.A., S.A. BOREN, G.D. BROWN, B.G. EWIGMAN, J.A. MITCHELL, and G.T. PERKOFF. 1996. "Effect of Physician Profiling on Utilization. Meta-Analysis of Randomized Clinical Trials." *Journal of General Internal Medicine* 11(10): 584–90.

BATES, D.W., L.L. LEAPE, D.J. CULLEN, N. LAIRD, L.A. PETERSEN, J.M. TEICH, E. BURDICK, M. HICKEY, S. KLEEFIELD, B. SHEA, M. VANDER VLIET, and D.L. SEGER. 1998. "Effect of Computerized Physician Order Entry and a Team Intervention on Prevention of Serious Medication Errors." *Journal of the American Medical Association* 280(15): 1311–16.

BERG, M. 1997. *Rationalizing Medical Work: Decision-Support Techniques and Medical Practices.* Cambridge, MA: The Massachusetts Institute of Technology Press.

BERWICK, D.M. 1996. "Quality of Health Care. Part 5: Payment by Capitation and the Quality of Care." *New England Journal of Medicine* 335(16): 1227–31.

BLENDON, R.J., M. BRODIE, J.M. BENSON, D.E. ALTMAN, L. LEVITT, T. HOFF, and L. HUGICK. 1998. "Understanding the Managed Care Backlash." *Health Affairs* 17(4): 80–94.

BLUMENTHAL, D. 1997. "The Future of Quality Measurement and Management in a Transforming Health Care System." *Journal of the American Medical Association* 278(19): 1622-25.

BLUMENTHAL, D., and M.B. BUNTIN. 1998. "Carve Outs: Definition, Experience, and Choice Among Candidate Conditions." *American Journal of Managed Care* 4 (Suppl.): SP45–57.

BODENHEIMER, T. 1999. "The American Health Care System—The Movement for Improved Quality in Health Care." *New England Journal of Medicine* 340(6): 488–492.

BRAND, D.A., L.N. NEWCOMER, A. FREIBURGER, and H. TIAN. 1995. "Cardiologists' Practices Compared With Practice Guidelines: Use of Beta-Blockade After Acute Myocardial Infarction." *Journal of the American College of Cardiology* 26(6): 1432-36.

BROOK, R.H. 1997. "Managed Care Is Not the Problem, Quality Is." *Journal of the American Medical Association* 278(19): 1612–14.

BROOK, R.H., K. LOHR, M. CHASSIN, J. KOSECOFF, A. FINK, and D. SOLOMON. 1984. "Geographic Variations in the Use of Services: Do They Have Any Clinical Significance?" *Health Affairs* 3(2): 63–73.

BURDI, M.D., and L.C. BAKER. 1997. "Market-Level Health Maintenance Organization Activity and Physician Autonomy and Satisfaction." *The American Journal of Managed Care* 3(9): 1357-66.

BURNS, L.R. 1997. "Physician Practice Management Companies." *Health Care Management Review* 22(4): 32–46.

BURNS, L.R. 1999. "Why Provider Sponsored Organizations Don't Work." *Integrated Healthcare 2000.*

BURNS, L.R., and D.P. THORPE. 1993. "Trends and Models in Physician-Hospital Organization." *Health Care Management Review* 18(4): 7–20.

BURNS, L.R., and D.P. THORPE. 1997. "Physician Hospital Organizations: Strategy, Structure, and Conduct." In *Integrating the Practice of Medicine,* ed. R. Conners. Chicago, IL: American Hospital Association Publishing.

BURNS, L.R., G.S. LAMB, and D.R. WHOLEY. 1996. "Impact of Integrated Community Nursing Services on Hospital Utilization and Costs in a Medicare Risk Plan." *Inquiry* 33(1): 30–41.

CHASSIN, M.R., and R.W. GALVIN. 1998. "The Urgent Need to Improve Health Care Quality: Institute of Medicine National Roundtable on Health Care Quality." *Journal of the American Medical Association* 280(11): 1000–1005.

CHASSIN, M.R., J. KOSECOFF, R.E. PARK, C.M. WINSLOW, K.L. KAHN, N.J. MERRICK, J. KEESEY, A. FINK, D.H. SOLOMON, and R.H. BROOK. 1987. "Does Inappropriate Use Explain Geographic Variations in the Use of Health Care Services? A Study of Three Procedures." *Journal of the American Medical Association* 258(18): 2533–37.

CHERNEW, M.E., R.A. HIRTH, S.S. SONNAD, R. ERMANN, and A.M. FENDRICK. 1998. "Managed Care, Medical Technology, and Health Care Cost Growth: A Review of the Evidence." *Medical Care Research and Review* 55(3): 259–88; discussion 289–97.

CHRISTIANSON, J.B. 1998. "The Role of Employers in Community Health Care Systems." *Health Affairs* 17(4): 158–64.

CHRISTIANSON, J., B. DOWD, J. KRALEWSKI, S. HAYES, and C. WISNER. 1995. "Managed Care in the Twin Cities: What Can We Learn?" *Health Affairs* 14(2): 114–30.

CHRISTIANSON, J.B., D. WHOLEY, and M.S. PETERSON. 1997. "Strategies for Managing Service Delivery in HMOs: An Application to Mental Health Care." *Medical Care Research and Review* 54(2): 200–22.

CHRISTIANSON, J.B., R.A. TAYLOR, and D.J. KNUTSON. 1998. *Restructuring Chronic Illness Management.* San Francisco, CA: Jossey-Bass.

CHRISTIANSON, J.B., S. SANCHEZ, D.R. WHOLEY, and M. SHADLE. 1991a. "The HMO Industry: Evolution in Population Demographics and Market Structure." *Medical Care Review* 48(1): 3–46.

CHRISTIANSON, J.B., D.R. WHOLEY, and S.M. SANCHEZ. 1991b. "State Responses to HMO Failures." *Health Affairs* 10(4): 78–92.

CLEARY, P.D. 1998. "Satisfaction May Not Suffice! A Commentary on a Patient's Perspective." *International Journal of Technology Assessment in Health Care* 14(1): 35–37.

COHEN, M.D., J.G. MARCH, and J.P. OLSEN. 1972. "A Garbage Can Model of Organizational Choice." *Administrative Science Quarterly* 17: 1–25.

CONRAD, D.A., C. MAYNARD, A. CHEADLE, S. RAMSEY, M. MARCUS-SMITH, H. KIRZ, C.A. MADDEN, D. MARTIN, E.B. PERRIN, T. WICKIZER, B. ZIERLER, A. ROSS, J. NOREN, and S.Y. LIANG. 1998. "Primary Care Physician Compensation Method in Medical Groups: Does It Influence the Use and Cost of Health Services for Enrollees in Managed Care Organizations?" *Journal of the American Medical Association* 279(11): 853–58.

CONRAD, P. 1992. "Medicalization and Social Control." *Annual Review of Sociology*. Palo Alto, CA: Annual Reviews.

CUNNINGHAM, P.J. 1999. "Pressures on Safety Net Access: The Level of Managed Care Penetration and Uninsurance Rate in a Community." *Health Services Research* 34(1, Pt 2): 255–70.

CUNNINGHAM, P.J., J.M. GROSSMAN, R.F. ST. PETER, and C.S. LESSER. 1999. "Managed Care and Physicians' Provision of Charity Care." *Journal of the American Medical Association* 281: 1087–92.

DAVIS, D.A., M.A. THOMSON, A.D. OXMAN, and R.B. HAYNES. 1995. "Changing Physician Performance: A Systematic Review of the Effect of Continuing Medical Education Strategies." *Journal of the American Medical Association* 274(9): 700–705.

DONALDSON, M.S., K.D. YORDY, K.N. LOHR, and N.A. VANSELOW. 1996. "Primary Care: America's Health in a New Era." Washington, D.C.: National Academy Press.

DOWD, B., I. MOSCOVICE, R. FELDMAN, M. FINCH, C. WISNER, and S. HILLSON. 1994. "Health Plan Choice in the Twin Cities Medicare Market." *Medical Care* 32(10): 1019–39.

EISENBERG, J.M. 1986. *Doctors' Decisions and the Cost of Medical Care: The Reasons for Doctors' Practice Patterns and Ways To Change Them*. Ann Arbor, MI: Health Administration Press.

ELLIS, R.P., and A. ASH. 1995. "Refinements to the Diagnostic Cost Group (DCG) Model." *Inquiry* 32(4): 418–29.

ELLWOOD, P.M., JR., N.N. ANDERSON, J.E. BILLINGS, R.J. CARLSON, E.J. HOAGBERG, and W. MCCLURE. 1971. "Health Maintenance Strategy." *Medical Care* 9(3): 291–98.

ENTHOVEN, A. 1988. "Managed Competition of Alternative Delivery Systems." *Journal of Health Politics, Policy and Law* 13(2): 305–21.

FELDMAN, S. 1998. "Behavioral Health Services: Carved Out and Managed." *American Journal of Managed Care* 4(Suppl.): SP59–67.

FELDSTEIN, P.J., T.M. WICKIZER, and J.R. WHEELER 1988. "Private Cost Containment: The Effects of Utilization Review Programs on Health Care Use and Expenditures." *New England Journal of Medicine* 318: 1310–1314.

FIELD, M.J., R.R. TRANQUADA, and J.C. FEASLEY. 1995. *Health Services Research: Work Force and Educational Issues*. Washington, D.C.: National Academy Press.

FLOOD, A.B., A.M. FREMONT, K. JIN, D.M. BOTT, J. DING, and R.C. PARKER, JR. 1998. "How Do HMOs Achieve Savings? The Effectiveness of One Organization's Strategies." *Health Services Research* 33(1): 79–99.

FORREST, C.B., and B. STARFIELD. 1996. "The Effect of First-Contact Care with Primary Care Clinicians on Ambulatory Health Care Expenditures." *Journal of Family Practice* 43(1): 40–48.

FOWLES, J.B., J.P. WEINER, D. KNUTSON, E. FOWLER, A.M. TUCKER, and M. IRELAND. 1996. "Taking Health Status into Account When Setting Capitation Rates: A Comparison of Risk-Adjustment Methods." *Journal of the American Medical Association* 276(16): 1316–21.

FRANK, R.G., and T.G. MCGUIRE. 1998. "The Economic Functions of Carve Outs in Managed Care." *American Journal of Managed Care* 4(Suppl.): SP31–39.

FREIDSON, E. 1975. *Doctoring Together: A Study of Professional Social Control*. Chicago: The University of Chicago Press.

GARNICK, D.W., A.M. HENDRICKS, and C.B. COMSTOCK. 1994. "Measuring Quality of Care: Fundamental Information From Administrative Datasets." *International Journal of Quality Health Care* 6(2): 163–77.

GINSBURG, P.B., and J.R. GABEL. 1998. "Tracking Health Care Costs: What's New in 1998?" *Health Affairs* 17(5): 141–46.

GOLD, M.R., R. HURLEY, T. LAKE, T. ENSOR, and R. BERENSON. 1995. "A National Survey of the Arrangements Managed-Care Plans Make With Physicians." *New England Journal of Medicine* 333(25): 1678–83.

GREANEY, T.L. 1994. "Managed Competition, Integrated Delivery Systems and Antitrust." *Cornell Law Review* 79(September): 1507–45.

GRIMSHAW, J.M., and I.T. RUSSELL. 1993. "Effect of Clinical Guidelines on Medical Practice: A Systematic Review of Rigorous Evaluations." *Lancet* 342(8883): 1317–22.

HADLEY, J., and J.M. MITCHELL. 1997. "Effects of HMO Market Penetration on Physicians' Work Effort and Satisfaction." *Health Affairs* 16(6): 99–111.

HADLEY, J., J.M. MITCHELL, D.P. SULMASY, and M.G. BLOCHE. 1999. "Perceived Financial Incentives, HMO Market Penetration, and Physicians' Practice Styles and Satisfaction." *Health Services Research* 34(1 Pt 2): 307–21.

HANCHAK, N.A., J.F. MURRAY, A. HIRSCH, P.D. MCDERMOTT, and N. SCHLACKMAN. 1996. "USQA Health Profile Database as a Tool for Health Plan Quality Improvement." *Managed Care Quarterly* 4(2,Spring): 58–69.

HELLINGER, F.J. 1995. "Selection Bias in HMOs and PPOs: A Review of the Evidence." *Inquiry* 32(2): 135–42.

HELLINGER, F.J. 1998. "The Effect of Managed Care on Quality: A Review of Recent Evidence." *Archives of Internal Medicine* 158(8): 833–41.

HILL, J., and R. BROWN. 1990. "Biased Selection in the TEFRA HMO/CMP Program." Princeton, NJ: Mathematica Policy Research.

HOFF, T., and D.P. McCAFFREY. 1996. "Resisting, Adapting, and Negotiating: How Physicians Cope With Organizational and Economic Change." *Work and Occupations* 23: 165–89.

IEZZONI, L. 1997. *Risk Adjustment for Measuring Healthcare Outcomes.* Ann Arbor, MI: Health Administration Press.

JENSEN, G.A., M.A. MORRISEY, S. GAFFNEY, and D. LISTON. 1997. "The New Dominance of Managed Care: Insurance Trends in the 1990s." *Health Affairs* 16(1,January/February): 125–36.

JOESCH, J.M., T.M. WICKIZER, and P.J. FELDSTEIN. 1998. "Does Competition by Health Maintenance Organizations Affect the Adoption of Cost-Containment Measures by Fee-For-Service Plans?" *American Journal of Managed Care* 4(6): 832–38.

KAO, A.C., D.C. GREEN, A.M. ZASLAVSKY, J.P. KOPLAN, and P.D. CLEARY. 1998. "The Relationship Between Method of Physician Payment and Patient Trust." *Journal of the American Medical Association* 280(19): 1708–14.

KERR, E.A., B.S. MITTMAN, R.D. HAYS, A.L. SIU, B. LEAKE, and R.H. BROOK. 1995. "Managed Care and Capitation in California: How Do Physicians at Financial Risk Control Their Own Utilization?" *Annals of Internal Medicine* 123(7): 500–504.

KERR, E.A., B.S. MITTMAN, R.D. HAYS, B. LEAKE, and R.H. BROOK. 1996. "Quality Assurance in Capitated Physician Groups. Where Is the Emphasis?" *Journal of the American Medical Association* 276(15): 1236–39.

KINGDON, J.W. 1995. *Agendas, Alternatives, and Public Policies.* New York: Harper Collins College Publishers.

KISSICK, W.L. 1994. *Medicine's Dilemmas.* New Haven: Yale University Press.

KNUTSON, D. 1998. *Case Study: The Minneapolis Buyers Health Care Action Group. Inquiry* 35(2): 171–77.

KONGSTVEDT, P.R. 1996. *The Managed Health Care Handbook,* 3rd ed. Gaithersburg, MD: Aspen Publishers.

KRALEWSKI, J.E., E.C. RICH, R. FELDMAN, B.E. DOWD, T. BERNHARDT, C. JOHNSON, and W. GOLD. 1999. "The effects of medical group practice and physician payment methods on costs of care." Working Paper, Division of Health Services Research and Policy, School of Public Health, University of Minnesota.

KUROWSKI, B. 1998. "Cancer Carve Outs, Specialty Networks, and Disease Management: A Review of Their Evolution, Effectiveness, and Prognosis." *American Journal of Managed Care* 4(Suppl.): SP71–89.

LANDON, B., L.I. IEZZONI, A.S. ASH, M. SHWARTZ, J. DALEY, J.S. HUGHES, and Y.D. MACKIERNAN. 1996. "Judging Hospitals by Severity-Adjusted Mortality Rates: The Case of CABG Surgery." *Inquiry* 33(2): 155–66.

LEAPE, L.L. 1989. "Unnecessary Surgery." *Health Services Research* 24(3): 351–407.

LEAPE, L.L. 1997. "A Systems Analysis Approach to Medical Error." *Journal of Evaluation of Clinical Practice* 3(3): 213–22.

LEAPE, L.L., D.W. BATES, D.J. CULLEN, J. COOPER, H.J. DEMONACO, T. GALLIVAN, R. HALLISEY, J. IVES, N. LAIRD, G. LAFFEL, ET AL. 1995. "Systems Analysis of Adverse Drug Events. ADE Prevention Study Group." *Journal of the American Medical Association* 274(1): 35–43.

LEVIT, K., C. COWAN, B. BRADEN, J. STILLER, A. SENSENIG, and H. LAZENBY. 1998. "National Health Expenditures in 1997: More Slow Growth." *Health Affairs* 17(6, November/December): 99–110.

LUFT, H.S. 1981. *Health Maintenance Organizations: Dimensions of Peformance.* New York: John Wiley & Sons.

LURIE, N., J. CHRISTIANSON, M. FINCH, and I. MOSCOVICE. 1994. "The Effects of Capitation on Health and Functional Status of the Medicaid Elderly. A randomized Trial." *Annals of Internal Medicine* 120(6): 506–11.

MacSTRAVIC, S., and G. MONTROSE. 1998. *Managing Health Care Demand.* Gaithersburgh, MD: Aspen Publishers, Inc.

MANOCCHIA, M., M.S. BAYLISS, and J. CONNER. 1997. *SF-36 Health Survey Annotated Bibliography.* 2nd ed. (1988-1996). Lincoln, RI: Qualitymetric Inc.

MARINER, W.K. 1996. "Liability for Managed Care Decisions: The Employee Retirement Income Security Act (ERISA) and the Uneven Playing Field." *American Journal of Public Health* 86(6): 863–69.

MECHANIC, D. 1995. "Dilemmas in Rationing Health Care Services: The Case for Implicit Rationing." *British Medical Journal* 310(6995): 1655–59.

MECHANIC, D. 1998. "Emerging Trends in Mental Health Policy and Practice." *Health Affairs* 17(6, November/December): 82–98.

MELNICK, G.A., J. ZWANZIGER, and T. BRADLEY. 1989. "Competition and Cost Containment in California: 1980-1987." *Health Affairs* 8(2): 129–36.

MENDELSON, D.N., C.S. GOODMAN, R. AHN, and R.J. RUBIN. 1998. "Outcomes and Effectiveness Research in the Private Sector." *Health Affairs* 17(5): 75–90.

MEYER, J.W. 1994. "Rationalized Environments." In *Institutional Environments and Organizations,* ed. W.R. Scott and J.W. Meyer. Thousand Oaks, CA: Sage Publications.

MILLENSON, M.L. 1997. *Demanding Medical Excellence.* Chicago, IL: University of Chicago Press.

MILLER, R.H., and H.S. LUFT. 1994. "Managed Care Plan Performance Since 1980. A Literature Analysis." *Journal of the American Medical Association* 271(19): 1512–19.

MILLER, R.H., and H.S. LUFT. 1997. "Does Managed Care Lead to Better or Worse Quality of Care?" *Health Affairs* 16(5): 7–25.

MORGAN, R.O., B.A. VIRNIG, C.A. DeVITO, and N.A. PERSILY. 1997. "The Medicare-HMO Revolving Door—The Healthy Go In and the Sick Go Out." *New England Journal of Medicine* 337(3): 169–75.

NEWHOUSE, J. 1994. *Free for All?: Lessons From the Rand Health Insurance Experiment.* Cambridge, MA: Harvard University Press.

NEWHOUSE, J.P. 1993. "An Iconoclastic View of Health Cost Containment." *Health Affairs* 12(Suppl.): 152–71.

OXMAN, A.D., M.A. THOMSON, D.A. DAVIS, and R.B. HAYNES. 1995. "No Magic Bullets: A Systematic Review of 102 Trials of Interventions To Improve Professional Practice." *California Medical Association Journal* 153(10): 1423–31.

PAULY, M.V., J.M. EISENBERG, M.H. RADANY, M.H. ERDER, R. FELDMAN, and J.S. SCHWARTZ. 1992. *Paying Physicians: Options for Controlling Cost, Volume, and Intensity of Services.* Ann Arbor, MI: Health Administration Press.

PEDEN, E.A., and M.S. FREELAND. 1998. "Insurance Effects on US Medical Spending (1960–1993)." *Health Economics* 7: 671–87.

PERROW, C. 1984. *Normal Accidents: Living With High Risk Technologies.* New York: Basic Books.

RILEY, G.F., E.J. FEUER, and J.D. LUBITZ. 1996. "Disenrollment of Medicare Cancer Patients From Health Maintenance Organizations." *Medical Care* 34(8): 826–36.

ROBINSON, J.C. 1996. "Decline in Hospital Utilization and Cost Inflation Under Managed Care in California." *Journal of the American Medical Association* 276(13): 1060–64.

SCOTT, R.A., L.H. AIKEN, D. MECHANIC, and J. MORAVCSIK. 1995. "Organizational Aspects of Caring." *Milbank Quarterly* 73(1): 77–95.

SHEA, S., W. DUMOUCHEL, and L. BAHAMONDE. 1996. "A Meta-Analysis of 16 Randomized Controlled Trials To Evaluate Computer-Based Clinical Reminder Systems for Preventive Care in the Ambulatory Setting." *Journal of the American Medical Informatics Association* 3(6): 399–409.

SIMON, C.J., and P.H. BORN. 1996. "Physicians' Earnings in a Changing Managed Care Environment." *Health Affairs* 15(3): 124–33.

SKOLNICK, A.A. 1996. "Experts Explore Emerging Information Technologies' Effects on Medicine." *Journal of the American Medical Association* 275(9): 669–70.

SLEEPER, S., D.R. WHOLEY, R. HAMER, S. SCHWARTZ, and V. INOFERIO. 1998. "Trust Me: Technical and Institutional Determinants of Health Maintenance Organizations Shifting Risk to Physicians." *Journal of Health and Social Behavior* 39(3): 189–200.

SMITH, N.S., and J.P. WEINER. 1992. "Applying Population-Based Case Mix Adjustment in Managed Care: The Johns Hopkins Ambulatory Care Group System." *Managed Care Quarterly* 2(3): 21–34.

STARFIELD, B. 1992. *Primary Care: Concept, Evaluation, and Policy.* New York: Oxford University Press.

STARFIELD, B., J. WEINER, L. MUMFORD, and D. STEINWACHS. 1991. "Ambulatory Care Groups: A Categorization of Diagnoses for Research and Management." *Health Services Research* 26(1): 53–74.

STARFIELD, B., N.R. POWE, J.R. WEINER, M. STUART, D. STEINWACHS, S.H. SCHOLLE, and A. GERSTENBERGER.

1994. "Costs vs. Quality in Different Types of Primary Care Settings." *Journal of the American Medical Association* 272(24): 1903–1908.

STARR, P. 1982. *The Social Transformation of American Medicine.* New York: Basic Books, Inc.

STEARNS, S.C., B.L. WOLFE, and D.A. KINDIG. 1992. "Physician Responses to Fee-For-Service and Capitation Payment." *Inquiry* 29(4): 416–25.

STINCHCOMBE, A.L. 1965. "Social Structure and Organizations." *Handbook of Organizations,* ed. J.G. Marsh. Chicago: Rand McNally.

TARLOV, A.R., J.E. WARE, JR., S. GREENFIELD, E.C. NELSON, E. PERRIN, and M. ZUBKOFF. 1989. "The Medical Outcomes Study. An Application of Methods for Monitoring the Results of Medical Care." *Journal of the American Medical Association* 262(7): 925–30.

THOMPSON, J.D. 1967. *Organizations in Action.* New York: McGraw-Hill.

VON KORFF, M., J. GRUMAN, J. SCHAEFER, S.J. CURRY, and E.H. WAGNER. 1997. "Collaborative Management of Chronic Illness." *Annals of Internal Medicine* 127(12): 1097–1102.

WAGNER, E.H., B.T. AUSTIN, and M. VON KORFF. 1996. "Organizing care for patients with chronic illness." *Milbank Quarterly* 74(4): 511–44.

WARE, J.E., JR., and C.D. SHERBOURNE. 1992. "The MOS 36-Item Short-Form Health Survey (SF-36). I. Conceptual Framework and Item Selection." *Medical Care* 30(6): 473–83.

WARE, J.E., JR., M.S. BAYLISS, W.H. ROGERS, M. KOSINSKI, and A.R. TARLOV. 1996. "Differences in 4-Year Health Outcomes for Elderly and Poor, Chronically Ill Patients Treated in HMO and Fee-For-Service Systems. Results From the Medical Outcomes Study." *Journal of the American Medical Association* 276(13): 1039–47.

WEINER, J.P., A.M. TUCKER, A.M. COLLINS, H. FAKHRAEI, R. LIEBERMAN, C. ABRAMS, G.R. TRAPNELL, and J.G. FOLKEMER. 1998. "The Development of a Risk-Adjusted Capitation Payment System: The Maryland Medicaid Model." *Journal of Ambulatory Care Management* 21(4): 29–52.

WEINER, J.P., B.H. STARFIELD, D.M. STEINWACHS, and L.M. MUMFORD. 1991. "Development and Application of a Population-Oriented Measure of Ambulatory Care Case-Mix." *Medical Care* 29(5): 452–72.

WEINER, J.P., N.R. POWE, D.M. STEINWACHS, and G. DENT. 1990. "Applying Insurance Claims Data to Assess Quality of Care: A Compilation of Potential Indicators." *Quality Review Bulletin* 16(12): 424–38.

WEISBROD, B.A. 1991. "The Health Care Quadrilemma: An Essay on Technological Change, Insurance, Quality of Care, and Cost Containment." *Journal of Economic Literature* 29: 523–52.

WENNBERG, J., and A. GITTELSOHN. 1973. "Small Area Variations in Health Care Delivery." *Science* 182: 1102-1108.

WHOLEY, D.R., and L.R. BURNS. 1993. "Organizational Transitions: Form Changes by Health Maintenance

Organizations." In *Research in the Sociology of Organizations,* ed. S. Bacharach. Greenwich, CT: JAI Press.

WHOLEY, D.R., J.B. CHRISTIANSON, and M. PETERSON. 1996a. "Organizing the Delivery of Mental Health Services: Contracting for Mental Health Care by Health Maintenance Organizations." *Administration and Policy in Mental Health* 23(4): 307–28.

WHOLEY, D.R., J.B. CHRISTIANSON, and S. SANCHEZ. 1992. "Organizational Size and Failure Among Health Maintenance Organizations." *American Sociological Review* 57(December): 829–42.

WHOLEY, D.R., J.B. CHRISTIANSON, and S. SANCHEZ. 1993. "Professional Reorganization: The Effect of Physician and Corporate Interests on the Formation of Health Maintenance Organizations." *American Journal of Sociology* 99(July): 175–211.

WHOLEY, D.R., J. ENGBERG, and C. BRYCE. 1999a. "The Evolution of Productivity among Health Maintenance Organizations, 1985 to 1995." Working Paper, Division of Health Services Research and Policy, School of Public Health, University of Minnesota.

WHOLEY, D.R., L.R. BURNS, and R. LAVIZZO-MOUREY. 1998. "Managed Care and the Delivery of Primary Care to the Elderly and the Chronically Ill." *Health Services Research* 33(2 Pt II): 322–53.

WHOLEY, D.R., R. FELDMAN, and J.B. CHRISTIANSON. 1995. "The Effect of Market Structure on HMO Premiums." *Journal of Health Economics* 14(May): 81–105.

WHOLEY, D.R., R. FELDMAN, J.B. CHRISTIANSON, and J. ENGBERG. 1996b. "Scale and Scope Economies Among HMOs." *Journal of Health Economics* 15: 657–84.

WHOLEY, D.R., R.M. PADMAN, R.E. HAMER, and S. SCHWARTZ. 1999b. "The Diffusion of Information Technology Among Health Maintenance Organizations." *Health Care Management Review* 25: 2.

WINGERT, T.D., J.E. KRALEWSKI, T.J. LINDQUIST, and D.J. KNUTSON. 1995. "Constructing Episodes of Care From Encounter and Claims Data: Some Methodological Issues." *Inquiry* 32(4): 430–43.

WOLINSKY, F.D., and W.D. MARDER. 1985. *The Organization of Medical Practice and the Practice of Medicine.* Ann Arbor, MI: Health Administration Press.

YANO, E.M., A. FINK, S.H. HIRSCH, A.S. ROBBINS, and L.V. RUBENSTEIN. 1995. "Helping Practices Reach Primary Care Goals. Lessons From the Literature." *Archives of Internal Medicine* 155(11): 1146–56.

ZWANZIGER, J., G.A. MELNICK, and A. BAMEZAI. 1994. "Costs and Price Competition in California Hospitals, 1980–1990." *Health Affairs* 13(4): 118–26.

16 RECONFIGURING THE SOCIOLOGY OF MEDICAL EDUCATION: EMERGING TOPICS AND PRESSING ISSUES

FREDERIC W. HAFFERTY, *University of Minnesota, Duluth, School of Medicine*

INTRODUCTION

The sociological study of medical education, like many other academic endeavors, is a dynamic, contentious, and sometimes unruly beast. Ways of seeing and knowing are "discovered," disappear, and are resurrected across endless waves of understandings. Previously, *Handbook* chapters functioned to bring a measure of order to this noise. Literature was summarized and core findings placed within a broader interpretive framework. But as a field expands, so does its knowledge base. Boundaries become blurred as knowledge is stacked like so much firewood. Core themes, in turn, become more cryptic. The arrival of bibliographic databases intensified these problems. Today, thousands of references can be retrieved instantaneously, rendering the promise of a "comprehensive" literature review both pretentious and suspect. For all of these reasons, I am neither inclined to organize this chapter around "major concepts" or "key research findings," nor will I spend much time discussing the conceptual legacies of prominent scholars. There are a number of readily available publications that do an excellent job in these regards.[1] Instead, I want to

tackle six issues that touch upon the evolving story of medical education. First, I will reappraise briefly the relationship between early sociological studies of medical education and the evolution of medical sociology as a discipline. Second, I will examine the topic of medical socialization, stress the need for theory building in this area, and close with a summary of recent work on medicine's "hidden curriculum." Third, I will examine three issues that I believe represent new ways of thinking about medical education; (1) the funding and policy base of medical education; (2) the "discovery" of medical student abuse; and (3) the growth of for-profit medical education. Finally, I will close by examining some of the recent trends within organized medical education and offer some suggestions about how the sociological study of medical training might serve as a remedial source of light in what has become an increasingly troubled domain.

---

[1] Readers who are unfamiliar with this literature might want to begin their "studies" with some background reading in the evolution of medicine as a profession: Paul Starr's *The Social Transformation of American Medicine* (1982), Rosemary Stevens' *American Medicine and the Public Interest* (1971), and Lawrence Henderson's *Physician and Patient as a Social System* (1935), followed by a more focused look at the history of medical education: Steven Jonas's *Medical Mystery: The Training of Doctors in the United States* (1978) and Kenneth Ludmerer's *Learning to Heal: The Development of American Medical Education* (1985). From here, readers can focus on more specific issues such as the organization and structure of medical education (see Bloom 1988, 1990, 1992), medical socialization (see Fox 1979, 1989; Light 1979, 1980,

1988), the development of medical discourse during training (B. J. Good 1994; M-J. Good, 1995; Anspach 1993), and the form and function of medical slang (Coombs et al. 1993). Other excellent resources include previous *Handbook* chapters on medical education (see Becker and Geer 1963; Becker, Geer, and Miller 1972; Gallagher and Searle 1989). Forthcoming books include Sam Bloom's long-awaited history of medical sociology, *The Word as a Scalpel: A History of Medical Sociology* and Kenneth Ludmerer's newest volume on medical education, *The Development of American Medical Education* (1999). If I were to restrict my list to only four authors (or author teams), I would recommend reading: (1) David Stern's finely rendered dissertation on the transmission of values in medical education; (2) Dimitri Christakis and Chris Feudtner's (1997) wonderfully crafted analysis of time, interpersonal interactions, and medical training; (3) Donald Light's (1988) prophetic and brilliant essay on new directions in medical sociology; and (4) Charles Bosk's (1979) classic sociological study of surgery training; this latter volume is suggested as much for its beauty and soul as for its elegant sociological analysis.

Hovering over all of these issues is the presence of managed care. Efforts to rationalize health-care services have generated tremendous changes not only in the delivery of services but also in the structure, process, and content of medical education. These changes stand as a monumental challenge to—and opportunity for—medical sociologists interested in the study of medical education. Much of what we have come to "know" about medical training is now suspect, at least until we can re-examine our traditional tools and concepts under the harsh light of what has become medicine's penultimate oxymoron—managed "care."

THE EARLY YEARS

Medical sociology emerged as a distinct field of study in the 1950s. Studies of medical education, in turn, appeared to occupy a seminal position in its growth. Following Talcott Parsons's (1951) famous Chapter 10 (Social Structure and Dynamic Process: The Case of Modern Medical Practice) in *The Social System,* two of the most enduring beacons during medical sociology's early years in the 1950s were studies of medical education: Robert Merton's *The Student Physician* (Merton et al. 1957) and Howard Becker's *Boys in White* (Becker et al. 1961). The cast of players involved in these studies was a veritable sociological "who's who" (or at least who's about-to-become who). Besides Robert K. Merton, the Columbia-based/Cornell-focused/*Student Physician* team included Sam Bloom, Renée Fox, Mary Goss, Patricia Kendall, and George Reader. The *Boys in White*/University of Chicago/Kansas team included Everett Hughes, Howard Becker, Blanche Geer, and Anselm Strauss. Furthermore, these were not the only studies of medical education taking place at this time (see Bloom 1965; Fox 1979).[2] Nursing education was represented as

well during this period with the tabloid-sounding *Twenty Thousand Nurses Tell Their Story* (Hughes, Hughes, and Deutscher 1958), and with publications by Fred Davis (1968) and Virginia Olesen (Olesen and Whittaker 1968).

In addition, organizations such as the Association of American Medical Colleges (AAMC) began to sponsor meetings to assess medical school admissions along with basic science and clinical training. At one of these conferences (The Ecology of the Medical Student; see Gee and Glaser 1958), the AAMC invited Merton, Hughes, Kendall, and Bloom to meet with physician leaders and medical educators. It was a grand moment for sociology, but a gathering that would, over time, represent a high-water mark rather than some first step in an overall rise of sociology to the status of "important player" in the policy hallways of medical education. Although dozens of national commissions and forums on medical education would be convened in the ensuing decades, sociology never again would occupy so many seats so close to the center of the table. In fact, sociology's disappearance was so pronounced that in 1973, Renée Fox would lament the current "paucity of work on medical socialization." Ten years later, she would reiterate these concerns and join with Sam Bloom (1979) in noting a shift toward studies involving "economic, political, technological, organizational, and social stratification variables" (Fox 1979: 73). In short, Eliot Freidson had arrived.

As Dante Alighieri came to discover, any fall from grace is a complicated affair and any redemption fragmentary at best. With respect to *Boys in White* and *The Student Physician,* part of its amorphous history can be traced to the discipline itself. In contrast to the accolades often accorded these two studies in contemporary medical sociology textbooks, the fact is that neither study was reviewed favorably when first published. Furthermore, the selection of reviewers suggests that there were considerable tensions within the broader sociology community around issues of power, prestige, and accommodation.

The Student Physician, for example, was reviewed in the *American Sociological Review (ASR)* by none other than Howard Becker, the lead investigator of the *Boys in White* study. At the time of his review, Becker was in the final stages of bringing his fieldwork

[2] In point of fact, the Merton and Becker studies were less about medical education than they were about highlighting the relative merits of a structural versus a symbolic interactionist approach to the analysis of social phenomenon (Light 1980; Cockerham 1988; Fox 1989; Hafferty 1991). The research teams backing these two projects represented different—and differing—analytical traditions with the study of medical students acting merely as a backdrop. It was Parsons versus Homans, with the principles, Merton and Hughes, heavyweights in their own right. The emphasis on structure in the Merton study represented the more traditional sociological approach to the study of social phenomenon. *Boys in White,* on the other hand, sought to establish an interactionist approach as the chief pretender to this throne. For the most part, the principals in these studies had no preceding—or subsequent—commitment to the study of medical training. None of the "big three" (Merton, Hughes, and Becker) have ever been considered "medical sociologists." In an edited reappraisal of Robert

Merton's intellectual career, Clark, Modgil, and Modgil (1990), did not include a single chapter (out of twenty-five) or section covering Merton's contributions to the study of medical education. A similar volume (Ben-Yehuda et al. 1989) devoted to the work of Howard Becker, however, did acknowledge this aspect of Becker's career.

to a close.[3] The first review of *Boys in White* appeared in 1962 in *ASR* and was written by George G. Reeder, a physician and second author for *The Student Physician*. Neither review was flattering.[4,5,6] Fred Kern Jr.'s *Journal of Health and Human Behavior* review of *Boys in White* was similarly unenthusiastic. Kern, a physician, found the Merton study "often loose," the interpretive framework "at times . . . obscure," and the book "excessively long."[7]

Skirmishing did not end here. When Howard Freeman, Sol Levine, and Leo G. Reeder sought to include a chapter on medical education in their inaugural issue of this *Handbook* (1963), they selected Becker and Geer of *Boys in White* fame.[8] Although reviews of the *Handbook* as a whole were quite positive (Robert Straus in *AJS* and Sam Bloom in *ASR*), the Bloom review criticized the volume's lack of a catholic approach to issues of medical training and socialization, along with the missed opportunity to establish a "natural dialogue" between Becker's own work and that of the Merton team (which included Bloom).

In summary, although studies of medical student training in the 1950s and early 1960s appeared to have burst upon the sociological landscape with great radiance and impact, the fact is that these studies played to a critical sociological audience and did not generate any appreciable follow-up work by the principals (see Light and Levine 1988).[9] Merton continued with his work on middle-range theory and the sociology of science, Hughes on the organization of work, and Becker on issues of deviance and later the sociology of art. The more junior members of these two teams, such as Fox and Bloom, did pursue work on medical training and did so with appreciable success, but without the level of support lavished on Merton and Hughes by private foundations. Finally, and as noted by Fox (1989) and Bloom (1979), the conjoint publication of Freidson's *Profession of Medicine* and *Professional Dominance*, helped to orchestrate a shift in the sociological agenda toward studies with an organizational focus. There would be no *Men in White* or *Student Physician II* waiting in the wings.

MEDICAL SOCIALIZATION AND THE HIDDEN CURRICULUM OF MEDICAL TRAINING

Over the past four decades, a considerable (although waning), amount of attention has been devoted to the study of physician socialization by medical sociologists.[10,11] Although a number of these studies have generated important insights into the content (the "what") and the context (the "where") of this process, relatively

---

[3] Although *Boys in White* was published in 1962, fieldwork for the study began in 1955 with data collection virtually completed by 1958 (Becker, personal communication).

[4] In his review, Becker characterized *The Student Physician* as an "interesting appetizer" and "fragmentary" (given its ten chapters by eleven authors). He criticized the study for "seldom [dealing] with conflict or tension" and therefore missing an important source of data on the "understanding of social structure and process." In his comments, Becker cited an earlier review by James A. Davis in *AJS,* that focused more on methodological issues. Although Davis did point out that "the major significance of this book may be in the area of research methodology," he too was unimpressed with the methodological approaches taken by Merton and colleagues. Davis criticized the absence of "any formal criterion for arriving at a conclusion" along with its "intuitive interpretations of heavily partialed tables." He referred to the study's "new survey methodology" as an "art form" and characterized it as "dangerous" because the authors (whom Davis refers to as "performers") were "talented, sophisticated, and probably correct." The chapter by Renée Fox on "Training for Uncertainty," is separately noted by Davis as being more qualitative in nature, which, given the overall critical tone of Davis' review, may have been a blessing or complement in disguise.

[5] In his review, Reeder wasted no time in informing the reader that the Becker study ignored social structure while identifying "almost entirely with the student." As might be expected from this quote, Reeder particularly was critical of the methodological approach used by Becker, Hughes, and colleagues. While complimenting the study's identification of an "autonomous student culture," including how students came to define issues of "responsibility" and "experience," Reeder closed his review with the backhanded compliment that although the book might be of interest to those curious about participant observation as a fieldwork method, it failed to provide "insights into the daily life of medical students."

[6] Curiously, *Boys in White* was not reviewed in *AJS,* although it did appear in a listing of "Current Books." This omission is all the more notable because *AJS,* then and now, is published through Chicago's Department of Sociology. Everett C. Hughes had been both an editor and associate editor of *AJS* while both studies were being conducted, although by 1962 he had become an "advisory editor" with his move to Brandeis. As noted in Footnote 4, *The Student Physician* was reviewed, and critically so, in *AJS,* by James A. Davis.

[7] *The Student Physician* (1957) was published three years before the *Journal of Health and Human Behavior* was founded (1960) and therefore was not reviewed in this journal.

[8] In the second edition of the *Handbook,* Stephen J. Miller was added as a third author.

[9] Much of the data collected by the Columbia's team remains unpublished, although there have been scattered references to these data in the sociological literature of medical training (see Light 1988).

[10] Rather than identify particular studies, readers are directed to Renée Fox's (1989) excellent review of the physician socialization literature covering undergraduate, graduate/residency, and practice settings. Perhaps the most well-developed subfield in the study of medical training is work on social control and the management of error in medical work. See Hughes (1951), Scheff (1963), Stelling and Bucher (1973), Millman (1977), and Bosk (1979) as examples.

[11] The basic definition of socialization used in this chapter is the collection of "processes by which people acquire the values and attitudes, the interests, skills, and knowledge—in short, the culture—current in the groups of which they are, or seek to become a member" (see Merton et al. 1957:287).

little progress has been made in translating these findings into an overall model of professional socialization (the "how"). The result has been an analytical schism between data largely gathered from individuals about their experiences in a process that, by definition, transforms the self and the largely unexplored impact of structural, cultural, economic, and political factors on the training of physicians.

Donald Light (1979, 1980, 1983) was one of the first medical sociologists to develop a model of physician socialization. Based on his study of psychiatric residents, Light sought to construct a model of "secondary socialization" that would be valid for a wide variety of occupations.[12] Although Light posited that all socialization requires active participation and emotional involvement by the participants, he explicitly rejected the notion of socialization as a case of "negotiated order," an interpretive framework that had been popularized by the *Boys in White* study. Light rejected "adult socialization" as an explanatory tool, drew a key distinction between "training" ("learning certain skills or knowledge") and "socialization" ("internalizing values and attitudes"), and labeled the process of medical education as a "moral career." Light identified five stages in his model of moral transformation, with students moving from feelings of disquietude and the threat of being discredited to the acquisition of a new set of values for judging oneself and others.[13]

Another effort, directed more toward exploring the underlying structure of socialization per se as opposed to model building, can be found in Hafferty (1988, 1991). Beginning with Renée Fox's (1957) observations about the important role of anatomy lab in the socialization of medical students, Hafferty examined different types of exposure to death encountered by one class of first-year medical students. Among other things, Hafferty concluded that student reactions to these exposures are governed neither by a psychologically based "fear of death" (a dominant interpretive model at the time data were being collected),[14] nor by idiosyncratically generated and individually manifested "coping strategies," but by a series of socially anchored, normative processes within which students internalize rules about the appropriateness of certain feelings, behaviors, and rationales within the lifeworld of medicine.[15] Similar to Light, Hafferty documented the fundamental role played by student peers in the socialization process (see also Shuval 1975; Mizrahi 1986). Hafferty also joined Light in concluding that his data best fit the interpretive model advanced by *The Student Physician* (the internalization of shared values) rather than the general model advanced in *Boys in White* (situational adjustment).[16] Finally, both drew upon the concept of anticipatory socialization and framed the process of socialization as an example of moral transformation.

Hafferty's efforts to dissect the structure of medical socialization extend Light's work in several respects. Based upon an analysis of cadaver stories as oral culture,[17, 18] Hafferty detailed how the process of medical socialization involves movement along two concurrently operating dimensions: (1) the shedding of lay norms and values, and (2) the adoption of a new, medical-value system, thus framing socialization not as a "simple" process of replacing one value system with another but rather as an ongoing and tension-ridden series of encounters during which lay values and attitudes become labeled as "suspect," "dysfunctional,"

---

[12] Light's model, for example, nicely captures later work on the socialization and moral transformation of Marine recruits during boot camp (see Ricks 1997, Perry 1998).

[13] Light's five stages are: (1) feeling different and being discredited, (2) moral confusion, (3) numbness and exhaustion, (4) moral transition, and (5) self-affirmation. Light identified "personal anxiety" (generated by "involvement or responsibility plus uncertainty") as key to his model of socialization. In turn, Light saw uncertainty as having two additional conditions ("lack of definition and irrelevance of past experience"). Overall, Light's model begins with the presence of moral ambiguity and disquietude, followed by a process of "resocialization," and finally, a "growing sense of mastery" in which students assimilate "new moral precepts in a coherent world view."

[14] See the writings of Elizabeth Kubler-Ross (1969, 1974, 1975), Ernest Becker (1973), Edwin Schneidman (1973), and Robert Kastenbaum (Kastenbaum and Aisenberg 1972). During this time period, a more sociological look at death and dying was being offered by Barney Glaser and Anselm Strauss (1965, 1968, Strauss and Glaser 1970) and Orville Brim, Howard Freeman, Sol Levine, and Norman Scotch (1970).

[15] Other studies of anatomy lab and its impact include Segal (1987), Smith and Kleinman (1989), and William (1992). Also see a parallel examination of a cardiovascular dog lab by Arluke and Hafferty (1996).

[16] In addition to Light (1980) and Hafferty (1991), see Simpson (1979) and Fox (1989) for an extended discussion of the relative merits of *Boys in White* and *The Student Physician*.

[17] Cadaver stories are narratives describing "jokes" played by medical student protagonists on unsuspecting and emotionally vulnerable victims by manipulating whole bodies or particular body parts for the dual purpose of shocking their intended victims and deriving humor from their victim's distress.

[18] The existence of "horror stories" within occupational subcultures serves as an important tool in the study of organizational culture and related areas of organizational and institutional socialization. Besides Hafferty's (1988, 1991) study of cadaver stories, Conrad (1986) has done a similar study of stories that circulate among pre-meds about medical school interview. On a broader level still, the study of medical student and physician slang offers a wealth of information about the process and structure of medical training (see Coombs et al. 1993).

and ultimately "inferior," while newly encountered, medical "ways of seeing and feeling" become internalized as "desirable," "functional," and "superior."[19] Hafferty concluded that the contentious dynamics of moving "away from" and "towards" were better captured by the concept of remedial socialization than was Light's preference for "secondary socialization" as a conceptual fulcrum.

Based on his analysis of the cadaver as "ambiguous man," Hafferty argued for the concepts of structural ambiguity and sociological ambivalence (see Merton and Barber 1976) rather than "uncertainty" as being the key force driving this process of transforming the self. Most important, Hafferty's dissection of the socialization process identified the presence of secondary or structural norms that function to "protect" the socialization process itself rather than to advance some independent end or goal. Examples of subsidiary norms are (1) the transformation of time, (2) the characterization of personal reflection as a "waste of time" and "dysfunctional," and (3) the privatization of personal feelings and emotional behaviors.[20, 21]

By exploring the rich normative underbelly of the socialization process itself, Hafferty sought to highlight this process as something fundamentally social—rather than psychological—in nature. In particular, Hafferty pointed out that while the concepts of induration and acclimation ("You just get used to it") were invoked almost ritualistically by students as *the* explanation for their adjustment to the medical school experience, the notion of "getting used to it" actually functions as a socially sanctioned "second order" norm that functions to "protect" this process of personal transformation from the critical gaze of those being transformed. All of this, in turn, maximizes socialization's short-term impact along with its long-term prospects for "success."

When viewed together, the model-building of Light and the deconstruction of Hafferty allow us to differentiate between social practices more appropriately characterized as "indoctrination" (as in military or religious training, where the enculturation of values is a more formal and explicit part of the training process) and professional socialization as something that operates at a more latent level and is accompanied by normative ambiguities and structural inconsistencies. As we will soon see, much of the socialization of medical students takes place not within the formal medical training but within what has been termed medicine's "hidden curriculum."

The Hidden Curriculum

Over the past forty years, studies of medical education have tended to highlight social psychological processes and attitude change "rather than how the impact of structural factors of the schools, their politics, and their economics may fundamentally affect the education of health professionals" (Light 1983; see also 1979, 1980).[22] In what would be his last formal article on medical training, (see Light and Levine 1988) Light called for a "new sociology of medical education" to examine the "changing locus of medical education in the matrix of economic, cultural, and organizational forces exhibited by the health care system." Given that in 1987, managed care had yet to spawn for-profit behemoths such as Columbia/HCA and Oxford Health Plans, Light's now decade-old essay stands as an eerily brilliant anticipation of a new health-care order. But Light's basic message, like that of Sam Bloom before him, has gone largely unheeded as medical educators continue to focus on the development of new coursework and on integrating various aspects of pre-existing formal curricula. In the meantime, economic, cultural, and organizational forces have continued to exert their largely invisible toll on successive generations of new physicians.

More recent work by Hafferty (1998), Hafferty and Franks (1994), Hundert (1997), Hundert, Douglas-Steele, and Bickel (1996), and others (Coles and Grant 1985; Stern unpublished; Wear 1997) have attempted to draw attention to the structural and cultural underpinnings of medical education by identifying the presence of a "hidden curriculum" within the process of medical training. Although the use of particular concept labels (i.e., "hidden" versus "informal") vary by author, the basic theme is that medical education is a multidimensional learning environment composed of at least three interrelated spheres of influence: (1) the "formal curriculum," which is the stated, intended, and formally offered curriculum (e.g., those courses and course content formally identified by the school and faculty); (2) an "informal curriculum" composed of unscripted, frequently ad hoc, and highly interpersonal forms of teaching and learning that take place among and

---

[19] See Hughes (1966) and Haas and Shaffir (1987) about distinctions between lay and medical views.

[20] The theme of medical education as a process of "instant repression" (Shem 1978:30) or as a "deadening experience" can be found in a number of autobiographical accounts of medical training (see LeBarron 1981:241 as an example).

[21] As noted by Mary J. Good in 1995, one's perceived ability to endure and to "just get used to" the traumas of medical training, including the things that happen to patients, can be seen as a marker of competence within the culture of medicine.

[22] Light identifies Kendall (1961), Mumford (1970), Bloom (1973), and Mizrahi (1986) as exceptions to this generalization.

between faculty and students in the hallways, hospital cafeterias, elevators, on-call rooms, etc.; and (3) a set of influences that function as the level of organizational structure and culture (the hidden curriculum).

The concept of the hidden curriculum has its roots in educational circles and in studies of how the K-12 experience functions as a conduit for broader societal values around issues of social control, class stratification, and the (re)production of gender, ethnic, and racial hierarchies (see Jackson 1968). Although sociologists have been peripheral players in this literature, the general concept of the hidden curriculum has strong roots in conflict theory, critical theory, feminist theory, and the sociology of knowledge (Shah 1997). Within health care, the concept has been used sporadically in writings on residency training (Anderson 1992), general medical education (Marinker 1997), dental education (DeSchepper 1987), and nursing education (Partridge 1983; Mayson and Hayward 1997). Efforts to reform medical education dating back to the 1950s, most notably at Case Western (Horowitz 1964), were framed around the distinction between what students are taught and what they learn (a core theme in the hidden curriculum literature). Although the term has made only the briefest of appearances in the medical socialization literature[23], sociologists such as Renée Fox (1989), Donald Light (1983), and others have long drawn a distinction between the formal /manifest and the informal/ latent aspects of medical training.

Several themes or points of focus distinguish this body of more recent writings on the hidden curriculum from these earlier references. First, there is an explicit attempt to move beyond simple dichotomies in which the formal curriculum is identified, for example, as the site of "knowledge transmission" while the hidden curriculum is relegated to the enculturation of "values."[24]

Second, these more recent writings have tended to highlight the impact of social structure and organizational culture versus interpersonal interactions in exploring the internalization of core cultural values. Capital funding drives, building dedications, award ceremonies, and even the allocation of classroom space and floor plans not only structure opportunities for learning but send rather compelling messages of their own to community members about what "really" is—and should be—valued.

By drawing distinctions among the formal, the informal, and the hidden curriculums, we can begin to explore how a particular theme or issue can be addressed across the various dimensions (rather than "stages" or "levels") of the training process. For example, we might examine how the basic science curriculum conveys important messages to students about the nature of science and the fundamental presence of uncertainty in scientific evidence. In turn, we can move into the informal curriculum and explore how faculty "teach" and students "learn" about the relative value of scientific evidence versus "personal experience" during student preceptorship, clerkship, or residency rotations. Finally, we can traverse into the domain of organizational culture and scrutinize how award ceremonies can function as expressions of core organizational values and thereby "teach" students about the relative value of scientific research and the studied detachment of the scientific gaze versus practicing medicine in an underserved community or the place of humanism in the physician–patient relationship.[25]

By creating a series of socially based distinctions among the formal, the informal, and the hidden curricula, those interested in understanding the structure, process, and impact of medical education can begin to explore the "space" that exists between what students are taught formally and what they learn during training. With an eye toward organizational structure and culture,

[23] Haas and Shaffir (1982), for example, used the term "hidden curriculum" to identify the source of interaction skills developed by students as they learn to take on a "cloak of competence" during their medical training. The authors, however, did not attempt to develop the concept.

[24] Also, while certain settings are more likely to "house" one type of curriculum over another, settings are not "curriculum specific." For example, there can be a latent aspect to all formal teaching as students attempt to "read into" what is being presented. Similarly, faculty "teach" a great deal more than what is contained in their course descriptions or class handouts. Anatomy lab is not just about identifying anatomical structures. It also is about death and about drawing important distinctions between what is human versus "not human" in the culture of medicine. Similarly, a course on physical diagnosis includes much more than teaching students to use a stethoscope, percuss, or draw blood. It also is infused with issues of sexuality, and this remains true whether or not students are called upon to function as "patients." Physical diagnosis courses also posit core definitions about the

relative power of physicians vis-à-vis "their" patients. Even basic science courses such as biochemistry have a great deal to say about the nature of science and uncertainty—and this remains true even if faculty and/or students believe that they are being taught "nothing more" than details about pathways and cycles.

[25] The University of Pittsburgh School of Medicine recently announced that it had established the nation's first medical school endowed chair in the "patient doctor relationship and patient-centered care" (see AAMC-STAT, July 5, 1998; contact gshaw@aamc.org). In this announcement, the donor specified: "We established this chair to address the deterioration of the doctor-patient relationship in today's technology-based, bottom-line oriented health care system." One need only count the number of endowed chairs in basic science and clinical research and compare this to the number of chairs in patient-centered care to gain a rather clear picture of which is held in higher regard by medical schools.

we can begin to understand how the content and process of accreditation review, for example, can send important messages throughout the medical community about what should and should not be valued in carrying out the work of medical education. For too long, reform in medical education has been defined in terms of curricula change, with issues of organizational culture marginalized or excluded from consideration altogether. As noted by Light (1983) "If curricular changes lack organizational underpinnings, they are unlikely to succeed."

Before leaving this section, I also want to touch upon recent work by Byron Good and Mary-Jo DelVecchio Good, working independently (B. Good 1995; M-J. Good 1995) and as a team (Good and Good 1989), along with work by Renée Anspach (1988, 1993) and Howard Waitzkin (Maynard and Waitzkin 1993). Earlier writings on socialization tended to emphasize the role of "signal events" or "milestone happenings" (see Fox 1989). In contrast, these more recent studies, with their particular focus on residency training, document how the almost invisible routines of medical work, such as learning to construct proper progress notes and "write-ups," how to "present" on rounds, and how to deliver succinct case presentations transmit important messages to students and faculty alike about what is core versus what is superfluous within the practice of medicine.

At the level of structure, Dimitri Christakis and Chris Feudtner (1997) document how the timing and scheduling of residency rotations, the physical space of the hospital, and the organization of medical work creates transient social relations among physicians and between physicians and patients. Within all of these routines, acceptable definitions of reality are constructed, power relationships reproduced, and the nature, content, and pace of work imbrued with moral meaning. This body of work also provides us with an opportunity to reappraise Light's distinction between medical training (skills and knowledge) and medical socialization (values and attitudes). As noted above, even the transmissions of basic science "factoids" contain latent messages about the nature of science and scientific evidence. The realms of knowledge and values, it appears, are not as distinct as we might wish to believe.[26]

SPECIAL ISSUES

Money and Policy

Educating medical students costs money.[27, 28] This expense, coupled with the perception of medical training as a somewhat unresponsive "social good," has subjected medical education to a variety of regulatory inducements and constraints. Policies are generated by a host of players, including the federal government, state legislatures, corporate interests, and private

---

[26] Efforts to differentiate between things that are labeled "factual/objective/hard/scientific" and things considered to be "subjective/soft/value-laden" has long been a part of medical culture. Most basic science faculty, for example, earnestly believe that their teaching involves nothing more than the transmission of scientific

facts (along with a funny anecdote or two), and therefore they are engaged in a "simple" process of knowledge transmission. It certainly is in their interest to do so since such a framing delimits the nature of their work along with related issues of responsibility and accountability. The realm of skills, particularly during clinical training, is slightly more difficult to disentangle as faculty and students alike draw distinctions between skills that are "technical" (e.g., inserting a sigmoidascope) and more people-oriented realms such as "communication skills." As a behavioral science preceptor in a family practice residency program (where precepting is carried out by M.D.-behavioral scientist teams) I have found it personally fascinating to watch residents learn how to strip a case presentation of behavioral-psychosocial/ethical elements, thereby marginalizing the behavioral half of the precepting team, reinforcing the distinction between "science" and "art," and most important (as far as their intentions go), making the "precept" much more time efficient. Furthermore, by stripping the precept of behavioral and social references, any subsequent interaction with the patient also become more "streamlined," now that certain lines of inquiry and action "officially" have been excluded from the case (including the additional time consuming need to write up psychosocial aspects of the case in the patient's chart).

[27] Revenues supporting medical school programs and activities in 1995–96 exceeded $31 billion (Ganem and Krakower 1997). Jones and Korn (1998) differentiate between the "instructional cost" of educating a medical student (costs that can be tied directly to the teaching program and its support), which they estimate is between $40,000 and $50,000 per student per year, versus the "total educational resource costs" (defined as "those costs supporting all faculty deemed necessary to conduct undergraduate medical education in all their activities of teaching, research, scholarship, and patient care"), which runs approximately $72,000 to $93,000 per year. The difference between these two "costs" and the tuition set by an individual school represents the moneys that need to be generated in some other fashion. The total federal funding for GME health professions education in FY 1995 was $8.98 billion (see Young and Coffman 1998).

[28] Examining the types of funding made available to students by their schools can serve as an important source of information about core organizational values, and thus it functions as one aspect of a medical school's hidden curriculum. For example, my own medical school (University of Minnesota–Duluth School of Medicine) is strongly identified with the training of rural family practitioners and Native American physicians. Of the different scholarship (N = 38) and loan (N = 15) programs listed in the school's "Financial Aid Information 1998," 11 are identified as having something to do with "ruralness" (e.g., coming from a rural community). An additional 13 identify American Indians either directly or indirectly (minority, low income, disadvantaged) as a target population. In contrast, "academic excellence" or "academic performance" rarely is mentioned as a criterion.

foundations—acting alone or within some form of partnership.[29] To disentangle these various sets of influences is a formidable task, made all the more difficult by the fact that not all regulations are clear in their intent, have their desired impact, or can escape the clutches of unanticipated consequences. Furthermore, not all funding streams can be traced once they enter the bookkeeping labyrinths employed by universities, academic health centers, and medical schools.[30] It is impossible to have an adequate understanding of the structure, content, process, product, and social impact of our system of medical education without some appreciation for the variety of environmental factors—policies and funding being two—that influence its current operation and its future directions.[31]

From its very inception, and as but one example, managed care has been supported, as well as buffeted, by a host of policies and regulations. Laws designed to encourage the growth of a nascent health-maintenance industry, state and federal laws designed to regulate the current menagerie of managed-care companies, and internal decisions by managed-care corporations about issues of capital accumulation, revenue streams, and profits all have implications for medical education—at least when such strategizing impacts on patient care. In an education system that has remained essentially unchanged since the 1920s (see Ludmerer 1985), shifts in patient mix, reduced lengths of hospital stays, and the

transfer of many services from tertiary care to outpatient settings have generated basic challenges to the traditional content and process of medical training. Many teaching programs, long accustomed to a privileged status, are finding themselves shackled by the cost of their training programs as they seek to compete for patient care contracts with companies not so "encumbered." In turn, managed-care companies, competing furiously among each other to capture "covered lives," are not inclined to support either medical education or clinical research. Not only does managed care view these two realms of activity as points of cost (as opposed to sources of revenue), but managed care also views the product of medical education—the physician—as needing considerable "retooling" in order that new hires can function productively in managed-care settings (see Shine 1996). In short, and irrespective of any future investments in medical education, managed care already feels that it is underwriting a rather substantial remedial effort.

Given these circumstances, it is not surprising to find managed care advocating (and in some instances demanding) that medical schools add a variety of coursework (e.g., courses in the organization and financing of health care, resources allocation and risk management, quantitative methods related to the health of populations, such as epidemiology, biostatistics and decision analysis, health services research skills, computer applications and medical informatics, social and behavioral sciences, and medical ethics) to what already is an exceedingly dense curriculum (see Group Health Association of America 1994).

All of this organizational change—and chaos—has generated a variety of issues and questions that can benefit from a sociological perspective. Although not necessarily the most important (readers can develop their own list), I offer two examples: (1) interdisciplinary/professional training, and (2) the role of diversity in medical education and the need to train a physician workforce that reflects the racial, ethnic, and socioeconomic characteristics of our population.

Creating multi-professional training programs is not simply a matter of cross-listing courses or of scheduling lectures to be attended by some combination of nursing, physical therapy, pharmacy, and medical students. Such an approach may appear efficient (a core value in managed care), but it fails to recognize the history of strained professional relations, power discrepancies, and deeply ingrained value differences that exist among these groups. Medical sociology, however, has long understood the relative professional status of

[29] Examples of nationally based initiatives include: (1) The Health of the Public (supported by The Pew Charitable Trusts and The Robert Wood Johnson Foundation, in collaboration with The Rockefeller Foundation); (2) the Interdisciplinary Generalist Curriculum Project (funded by the Health Resources and Services Administration); (3) the Kellogg Community Partnerships with Health Professions Education (W. K. Kellogg Foundation); (4) the Robert Wood Johnson Foundation's Generalists Physician Initiative; and (5) Health Professions Schools in Service to the Nation Program (supported by the Pew Charitable Trusts, the Corporation for National Service, and the Health Resources and Services Administration).

[30] Medical schools, much like their clinical department brethren, employ cost-shifting strategies by using "excess" money, often from research and clinical activities, to subsidize the "underfunded cost" of training medical students.

[31] Efforts to disentangle the effects of policy initiatives, regulatory efforts, and revenue streams are not limited to the United States. See Thorne (1997), Gray and Ruedy (1998), and Hollenberg (1996) for details about similar issues and efforts in Canada. The United Kingdom, interestingly, represents a somewhat different set of contingencies in that the U.K. defines its core problem as one of undersupply rather than oversupply. Correspondingly, the U.K. has embarked on a program to increase the number of students entering medical training by 20 percent per year over the next five years. The goal is to admit 6,000 students per year (versus the current 2,005) by the year 2005 (see *http://www.oopen.gov.uk/doh/dhhome .htm*).

different health occupations along with their different cultural underpinnings and thus has much to say about how best to approach intraprofessional training. Medical sociology can also contribute to how medical schools might approach the creation of a new "managed care curriculum." As noted above, organized managed care has suggested extensive revisions in the core curriculum of medical training. But if medical educators are to develop new learning environments, then medical schools must direct their attention and efforts not only to the formal curriculum but to the informal and hidden curricula as well.

In training students to practice in a new managed-care world, medical schools can adopt one of two general strategies. They can define managed-care companies as their "principal customer" and therefore seek to train students who will be attractive to and employable in these new practice settings and value systems. Alternatively, schools may identify the broader community or general public as their point of focus and commitment and thus seek to train physicians who will be responsive to the needs of patients rather than to the needs of "systems." In the first case, students will be trained to be "good employees." In the second case, issues of employability will be kept distinct from issues of good doctoring. The issue of advocacy is but one example of who (or what) physicians will define as the appropriate object of their service efforts.

We also have the challenge of creating a physician workforce that is both able and willing to serve a racially, ethnically, and socioeconomically diverse patient population (see AAMC 1999; Jeffrey 1995). We know that underrepresented minority students are more likely to work in underserved areas than nonminority students (Association of American Medical College [AAMC] 1996). We also know that medical schools have not been successful in generating necessary increases in the enrollment and education of minority students (Association of American Medical College 1998). Finally, in light of the recent Hopwood decision, the AAMC estimates that without affirmative action, minority acceptances to medical school will drop by 80 percent (http://www.aamc.org/newsroom/preerel/960522b.htm, AAMC-STAT 1998).[32]

Medical sociology can shed important light on this complicated issue. By exploring the current organizational culture of medical training, for example, it can identify those factors and forces that serve as barriers to the acceptance and matriculation of minority students. Relatedly, sociologists can explore how premedical course requirements, virtually unchanged since 1975, may function as a pre-emptive barrier to potential minority applicants (see AAMC 1998). From a somewhat different vantage point, sociologists can explore how medicine's hidden and informal curricula function to minimize the value of "serving the underserved" as students move through their training. For an occupational group that holds itself up as placing caring, altruism, and a fiduciary orientation at the core of its professional value system, the abandonment of minority and other socioeconomically disenfranchised populations by generations of physicians is as telling an indictment of American medical education as one can find.

Medical Education as Abuse

One of the most remarkable transformations quietly unfolding over the past fifteen years is the recasting of medical training from something that is "stressful," "rigorous," "intimidating," "overwhelming," and even "dehumanizing" to something that is "abusive." This transliteration has been fueled by a number of research articles, several of which have appeared in "high profile" medical journals such as the *Journal of the American Medical Association* (Rosenberg and Silver 1984; Clark and Zeldow 1988; Sheehan et al. 1990; Silver and Glicken 1990; Kleinerman 1992; Richman et al. 1992; Uhari et al. 1994; Lubitz 1994; Daugherty, Baldwin, and Rowley 1998), and *Academic Medicine* (Baldwin, Daugherty, and Eckenfels 1996). These articles detail a litany of contumelious actions by faculty and student superiors toward trainees at both the undergraduate and graduate/residency training levels, along with related symptomatologies such as depression. Based largely on survey data, the behaviors and social actions labeled as "abusive" include: (1) being belittled or humiliated by more senior residents or attending physicians; (2) being the object of sexual harassment or discrimination; (3) having others, usually

---

[32] If minority students were required to have the same level of MCAT scores and grades as white students, the AAMC calculates that there would have been 397 minority students accepted in 1996 rather than the 1,890 that were. Graduation rates for minorities, while lower than whites, are still quite high. In 1997, 87 percent of the minorities (Black, Mexican American, Chicano, Mainland Puerto Rican, Native Hawaiians or American Indian) who matriculated in 1990 had graduated versus 95 percent of whites and 94 percent of Asians (see AAMC-STAT 1998).

superiors, taking credit for someone else's work; (4) being assigned tasks ("scut-work") as punishment, being physically abused; (5) being sleep deprived; (6) being exposed to "abusive" on-call schedules; (7) having one's career threatened by a superior; and (8) being given inappropriate or unfair evaluations or grades. Data have been gathered from American, Canadian (Margittai, Moscarello, and Rossi 1994), and other international sites (Uhari et al. 1994). In their review of this literature, Edward Eckenfels, Steven Daugherty, and DeWitt Baldwin (1997) concluded that the most frequent type of abuse is "psychological mistreatment (yelling and humiliation)," followed by "academic mistreatment (work for punishment, lack of credit for work, an unfair grade)."

Although the social sciences could never be accused of being "soft" on medical training, the language of abuse renders training in a far different light than the depictions and characterizations offered in Merton's *The Student Physician,* Becker's *Boys in White,* or in Terry Mizrahi's often cited—and damning—*Getting Rid of Patients* (1986). Under the paradigmatic eyes of the social scientist, medical training has been cast as something infused with rituals and built around ceremonies of status degradation and rights of passage (Fox 1989) but not as awash with criminal acts of a highly offensive and immoral nature. Medical students, we learned, were establishing their "professional identity," something quite different from being morally and criminally assaulted.[33] The oral culture of medicine, long associated with war metaphors, gallows humor, and derogatory depictions of patients (Doctor X 1965; Coombs et al. 1993) has become the site of moral carnage. Analogies to child abuse have been advanced (Silver 1982; Rosenberg and Silver 1984), debated (Daugherty, Baldwin, and Rowley 1998), and rejected (Eckenfels, Daugherty, and Baldwin 1997), but the fact remains that medical educators and students have begun to acquire a new set of moral identities. In turn, the public has been offered a new moral yardstick by which they can assess the process, impact, and meaning of faculty–student interactions.[34, 35]

Issues of conceptual validity aside, it is the moral recasting of medical training that concerns us here. In what may stand as a fundamental irony in an era of medicalization (see Conrad and Schneider 1992), medical training is being criminalized and infused with a new moral significance. By drawing upon child abuse as an interpretive framework (with abused children/medical students becoming abusive parents/doctors), the abuse literature extends greater explanatory weight to psychological explanations than to social-structural interpretations. In addition, by positing that medical-student abuse is pervasive, systemic, and enduring (at least in terms of its effects), the abuse literature aligns itself more within the Mertonean tradition of socialization as a transformation of the self rather than the view of medical education as situational adaptation.

Meanwhile, medical sociology has been invisibly silent on these issues. One exception is Eckenfels, Daugherty, and Baldwin (1997) who argue that the "battered child" analogy fails as an explanatory tool because "there is no evidence that there is anything inherent in the 'medical student personality' that makes them particularly susceptible to a cycle of abuse" (14). Instead, they propose a sociocultural model in which structure is provided by a system of highly defined roles, a stratified division of labor, and a "tradition of hierarchy" within which operates a series of cultural values, beliefs, and accompanying rationales, all of which serve to perpetuate a system of privilege and power based on position. A key concept in their model is medicine's hidden curriculum with its more covert yet powerful set of expectations and sanctions regarding physician behavior and values.

[33] The propensity to recast certain types of interactions between teacher/supervisor and students as "abusive" is not limited to medical education. Other educational/training arenas, particularly the military (see Ricks 1997) and military academies (Dornbusch 1955), have redefined "hazing" and other "privileges of seniority" as instances of abuse and therefore practices that no longer are to be tolerated. On an even broader plane, parallels can be seen in the general workplace with respect to issues of gender equity and sexual harassment.

[34] In addition to compiling a rather extensive list of "abusive" behaviors, this literature documents the presence of unethical or illegal behavior on the part of students and faculty, including the falsification of patient records, abuse of drugs and alcohol while on duty, physical mistreatment of patients, billing for services not provided by the individual of record, and general disappearance of attendings and physician superiors from teaching services. Taken as a whole, these studies deliver a sorry tale of morally corrupt and incompetent providers, compromised patient care, provider fraud, a decrease in provider humanism, a deteriorating provider–patient relationship, and an increase in conflicts among staff.

[35] The redefinition of a variety of different kinds of faculty–student interactions as "abusive" creates a rather interesting vantage point from which to review the large number of autobiographical and quasi-autobiographical accounts of medical training and practice that have been published over the past 30 years (see Stoeckle 1987; Conrad 1988; Pollock 1996 for an overview of some of these materials). Although this literature often conveys a romanticized, and even nostalgic, view of the training experience, many of the authors are quite critical of their experiences during medical training.

Nonetheless, the interpretive framework offered by Eckenfels and colleagues represents a rather solitary sociological voice in what has become an interpretive minefield dominated by psychological explanations and nomenclatures of crime and denigration. The literature on abuse, now over fifteen years old, is redefining the meaning of medical education, with nary a sociological squeak in response.

CME, Medical Publishing, and Other Domains of For-Profit Medical Education

The sociological literature on medical education, in large part, has tended to mimic the formal organization of medical training. Studies often are classified by whether they focus on undergraduate medical education, residency training, or post-graduate work settings such as the clinic or hospital (see Fox 1989). But these settings in no way exhaust the range of activities that can be subsumed under the appellation "medical education." In the spirit of broadening this approach, I want to examine briefly several different—but interrelated—types of medical education that have, to date, escaped sociological scrutiny. They include: (1) companies that provide MCAT preparation and USMLE National Board review coursework; (2) medical publishers; and (3) continuing medical education (CME).[36, 37] In some instances, (e.g., MCAT, board review, and test-preparation courses) these companies operate entirely outside the influence of organized medical education. In other instances (e.g., CME), they represent a mix of sponsors, including medical associations, medical schools, medical special-interest groups, and private for-profit corporations (see Lewis 1998).[38]

Overall, what once used to take place much more informally within teaching rounds and hospital-based case presentations has grown into an international, multimillion dollar industry. The evolution of a for-profit medical education industry has been encouraged by several factors, including the unrelenting growth in medical knowledge (along with the inability of medical education to integrate this knowledge rather than simply add it on), the hierarchical and competitive nature of medical school and residency training (including, but not limited to, admissions), the perception/suspicion/recognition (by students and employers) that the instruction being offered by medical schools and residencies is inadequate/faulty, and the existence of requirements by state licensing boards and medical specialty organizations that physicians demonstrate "life-long learning" and a "current" knowledge base by meeting some minimum level of learning activities. All of these "needs," in turn, are being identified and pursued much more aggressively within the for-profit medical education sector than within academic health centers, medical schools, and residency training programs.

While it would be impossible in these few paragraphs to outline a complete sociological agenda on this topic, several issues should be highlighted. First, "for-profit" medical education needs to be studied with the same intensity as has been devoted to the study of "traditional/not-for-profit" medical education. Second, this focus needs to include an understanding of how for-profit medical education "plays off" and "feeds into" organized medical education. In other words, in what ways do for-profit enterprises provide services that are deemed "missing" or otherwise "inadequate" by those within the system? Similarly, how does the current structure, content, and process of organized medical education create the need/demand for these auxiliary/complementary services? Are they alternative in the same way that homeopathy, acupuncture, and other therapeutic modalities function as alternatives to organized medicine? Turning to CME, what percentage of CME credits is consumed by what percentage of the physician population? Are there differences among physicians (e.g., race, age, ethnicity, practice setting, etc.) in the type and amount of CME consumed? Are physicians who take more hours of CME "better" doctors? If so, what is the direction of this association?

---

[36] There are, of course, many other domains of medical education, including the explosion of medical information on the World Wide Web and internally organized "remedial" training offered by HMOs for their physicians. There are a large number of Internet sites targeting physicians (e.g., www. medscape.com; www.plgroup.com/docguide.htl), many of which offer technical information, CME credit, and services such as bookstores devoted entirely to medical publications and related products (see www.lb.com, which can be accessed from both of the medical websites listed above). Readers may find it interesting that the American Medical Student Association website (www.amsa.org) features the sociologically intriguing slogan: "It takes more than medical school to make a physician."

[37] CME comes in many forms, including home study, web-based sites, subprograms within national association meetings, and stand-alone programs. In this chapter, I focus largely on meeting-based CME.

[38] Although most CME programs are offered by a single sponsor, it is not infrequent to find a medical school and a for-profit CME company team up as sponsors. See *Physician Travel and*

Meeting Guide: The CME Planner, published by Quadrant HealthCom Inc. This is a monthly publication that contains (along with drug and related medical advertising) a complete listing of upcoming CME programs.

In a similar fashion, we can study the MCAT, Board preparation, and test review services being offered by companies such as Princeton Review and Stanley Kaplan. In particular, we might want to focus on what these companies do *not* offer as a window into organized medical education. For example, these companies do not offer medical school hopefuls training in physician–patient communication skills or in medical ethics. They do not arrange for applicants to become engaged in community service activities. Why? Because in the best tradition of market forces and the spirit of capitalism, these companies link their products and services to what medical schools themselves indicate are important—reflected not in what schools *say* but in what they *do* during the process of admitting, educating, and evaluating medical students. By examining the actual work of medical education, these companies match products to "need" and therefore stress things like: (1) test-taking skills; (2) the promise of information mastery; and (3) the prospects of constructing a "pleasing" presentation of self during the interview process. Anything else is (and would be) superfluous. If for-profit companies like Princeton Review thought that admissions programs or matriculation committees used evidence about altruism or dutifulness in their evaluations, these companies would offer such training, with customers enthusiastically (or fearfully) paying quite handsomely for that "edge." In a lesson that appears to have been lost on medical educators and sociologists alike, the real "pudding of proof" about what medical education "truly" values is not to be found in medical school mission statements or in announcements by the AAMC about a new set of "core competencies" (AAMC 1998), but rather in the marketplace of medical education and in what these companies—and their customers—define as worth the extra expense of time—and money.

We can approach the medical publishing industry from a similar vantage point. Over the past twenty years, this industry has undergone a dramatic transformation, driven not only by new technologies (e.g., CD-ROMs, WWW-based information resources) but also by a profound shift in how medical students and residents view and approach medical information. The traditional king of medical publishing, the textbook, has been dethroned by a new monarch, board review and test preparation "mini-books." Entire sections of medical school bookstores have been taken over by Lippincott's "Board Review Series" (behavioral science, clinical medicine, biochemistry, cell biology and histology, gross anatomy, microbiology and immunology, neuroanatomy, pathology, and physiology), the "Pretest Series" (covering many of the same topics and published by McGraw-Hill), the "High Yield Series" (Williams & Wilkins), and the "Ridiculously Simple Series" (MedMaster Inc.). Often, these books are used by students not as a quick reference or as an auxiliary resource but as "first order" reading. Residents, in turn, covet publications with the prefix "Pocket" (e.g., "Pocket Manual . . . ," "Pocket Guide . . . ," and "Pocket Reference . . . ,"). In a world where small fonts predominate, *Maxwell Quick Medical Reference* ($7.95) stands as the epitome of reductionism. All you need to know (but can't remember) about clinical medicine is reduced to eleven double-sided, index-card-sized pages. In my home town, all the residents I know carry *Tarascon Pocket Pharmacopoeia* ($6.95). This compendium of information requires 20/40 vision to read its cataloging of drug names and drug dosages—but nothing on drug interactions. Williams & Wilkins (now Lippincott Williams & Wilkins) holds a trademark on the phrase "The Science of Review." It now appears, at least in medicine, that science can come in many—mainly condensed—forms.

One outgrowth of this mania for condensation is that medical bookstores "stock what sells" and therefore are less likely to carry textbooks. Students meanwhile vote with their wallets by demanding ever shorter (and what they consider to be "more useful") booklets of information. In a publishing empire where products range from multivolume, thousand page, hundred dollar tomes to 3X5 laminated cards, the following question goes begging: "In a field that has taken reductionism to a high art, what exactly is a 'medical fact' and how much can it be reduced before it ceases to be factual?"

The language of medical publishing reflects these trends. In contrast to the field of sociology, for example, something labeled a "Handbook" lies midway between the multivolume compendiums and the 3X5 epitomes of portability. The largest books often come with the prefix *Textbook of . . .* or *Principles of . . .* or simply are emblazoned with the title of the subject area (e.g., *Surgery* or *Internal Medicine*). If the title contains the prefix *Essentials . . . ,* then the book is recognized as a condensed version of some larger body of medical knowledge. The prefixes *Practical Guide* or *Guide to . . .* send a similar message of "usefulness" in a world where the terms "comprehensiveness" and "usefulness" are often considered antithetical. In medical publishing, a "Handbook" is literally that; something in paperback that can be held in one's hand or jammed into the side pocket of one's whites. Handbooks often are underwritten by drug companies. Finally, we have the above-mentioned "pocket" publications.

Although the following list is by no means exhaustive, two broad issues come to mind when considering the network of interrelationships that exist between the medical publishing industry and organized medical education. All forms of medical text, but particularly those considered as "authoritative" (e.g., *New England Journal of Medicine*) versus "throwaways" function as vehicles for the transmission of core medical values and therefore function as a site of medicine's hidden curriculum. Furthermore, trends within the medical publishing industry, such as the growth of "crib books," have much to tell us about the values that underscore organized medical education. Medical educators may bemoan the tendency of their students to be consumed by "minutia," but nothing stands as a greater testimony to medical education's success in enculturating just such an approach to knowledge than the social fact that there is a billion-dollar industry devoted to "making medicine simple." Don't have time to read the literature? Fine. There are many services that will evaluate methods and summarize study findings for you (see www.medscape.com/Medscape/features/ JournalScan/public/index-JournalScan.html for one on-line example).

Finally, I believe there are fundamental ironies that reside within the fact that while organized medical education seeks to promote the value of "life-long learning" and the skills of "self-directed learning," it overlooks that its own system actively supports an industry that sells "remedial" and "supplemental" products to students and physicians who must first define the "primary" educational system as lacking and who are, by their very participation in this auxiliary marketplace supposedly "self-directed."

SOME CLOSING THOUGHTS

Many of the chapters in this *Handbook,* including those on the doctor–patient relationship (Howard Waitzkin), medical technology (Stefan Timmermans), managed care (Douglas Wholey and Robert Burns), professional dynamics (Donald Light), and chapters that address issues of race, gender, aging, and ethnicity are tied intimately to issues of medical education, medical training, and medical socialization. As noted earlier in this chapter, medicine is a somewhat unique profession in that it fuses training with the delivery (usually billable) of medical services. From this vantage point, there is very little that happens within medicine that does not have at least the potential of shaping the content and/or the process of medical training.

Even so, there remains a lot that is "missing" in this chapter. Material on medical education in other countries was dropped for space considerations. In particular, I had hoped to take a comparative look at medical training in Canada (see Gray and Ruedy 1998; Hollenberg 1996) and Mexico (see Cordova et al. 1996; Nigenda and Solorzano 1997; Spitzer 1994), given their status as bordering countries. I wanted to explore how broader social values, the relation between state and professional organizations, and differences in health-care policies and delivery systems might be reflected in the training of physicians. In addition, this chapter contains very few references to nursing education and none at all to the training of other types of health-care providers, such as physician assistants and nurse practitioners, dentists, pharmacists, physical therapists, and chiropractors, to name but a few. Readers also have received an embarrassingly truncated look at the issues of race and ethnicity as well as the funding and policy decisions that underscore medical education. Similarly, issues of language, medical slang, and oral culture, along with a sociological analysis of time and of bioethics have made an all too brief appearance.[39] Finally, sociology has only begun to scratch the surface of how for-profit companies—drug companies being the most notable example—directly and purposefully attempt to influence the value structure (and ordering preferences) of medical providers with company-sponsored theater events, conferences, product samples, general "favors," and the ubiquitous flow of donuts, bagels, pizza, and other culinary enticements designed to satiate (and ingratiate) generations of ravenous housestaff (Fremont 1998).

At the outset of this chapter, I stated that the arrival of managed care has rendered suspect much of what we know—sociologically speaking—about medical education. During my work on this chapter, I found no reason to retreat from this claim. At the same time, I do not believe that this conceptual conundrum leaves us directionless with respect to identifying issues that

---

[39] Readers who have an interest in the topics of time and bioethics are urged to acquaint themselves with the recent work of three sociologists-posing-as-physicians (Dimitri Christakis, Nicholas Christakis, and Chris Feudtner) and a body of work that ranges from the erosion of ethical principles during medical training (Feudtner, Christakis, and Christakis 1994), the critical impact of "everyday" ethical dilemmas on the moral socialization of physicians (Feudtner and Christakis 1993), the evanescent nature of relationships in medicine and how the physical space of the hospital and the organization of work creates transient social relationships among physicians and between physicians and patients (Christakis and Feudtner 1997), and how the process of constructing and conducting national reviews of medical education serve to undermine the manifest goal of reform (Christakis 1995).

would greatly benefit from a concerted dose of sociological inquiry. Three issues command my attention list. The first involves shifts currently under way in the evaluation of medical training with a focus on content's (e.g., courses, credits, hours, and settings) being replaced by an emphasis on outcomes and "core competencies." The second issue involves the proliferation of practice guidelines, clinical protocols, and related efforts to rationalize and standardize the clinical practice of medicine. The third is the growing popularity within medical circles of "evidence-based medicine."

The recent focus on having outcomes defined in terms of competencies (as opposed to the percentage of graduates going into, for example, primary care) (see Shugars et al. 1991; O'Neil 1993; AAMC 1998) represents a fundamental shift in the way that medical school faculty, administrators, and even students are being asked to think about and value all that takes place under the rubric of medical education. The language of competencies involves a different set of verbs (e.g., " . . . has mastery of . . . ," " . . . demonstrates an ability to . . . ") than does the language of content (" . . . provide students with . . . ," " . . . increase hours in . . . "). The language of competencies is more active and more focused on social factors than is the language of content. It also is more rational. An evaluation system based on competencies requires that more explicit linkages be established between means (coursework, clinical rotations, etc.) and ends (the ability to perform in a certain manner). This is vastly different from a system in which means and ends had become indistinguishable. A focus on competencies also requires at least a passing acquaintance with the notion of organizational culture and latent learning processes.

A shift to a competencies-based evaluation system also requires a corresponding change in how medical schools are reviewed and accredited. Traditionally, the Liaison Committee of Medical Education (LCME), the body responsible for accrediting this country's 125 medical schools, has chosen to focus its evaluative eye on content rather than outcomes. Not surprisingly, medical schools have followed suit. However, reconfiguring the LCME's *Medical Education Database* (the primary data-gathering tool used by the LCME) and related operating guidelines will be a contentious undertaking. Sociologists can facilitate this transition by providing medical educators with measurement tools and conceptual frameworks to better understand the relevance of organizational culture and medicine's hidden curriculum to the assessment of outcomes. Moreover, the outcomes/competency movement affords social sciences yet one more chance to establish the realms of attitudes and values as

something that should be kept on par with knowledge and skills. The recent release of the AAMC's MSOP Report (*Medical School Objectives Project*) with "altruism" and "dutifulness" as two of the four core attributes all medical students should possess upon graduation (the other two being "knowledge" and "skill") is one specific example (AAMC 1998). In some very important respects, the current environment of change represents the most favorable opportunity for sociology to return to the policy table it was banished from almost 40 years ago.

The rationalization of medical work under managed care moves us into the second of my three areas. First, we need to differentiate between the deployment of practice guidelines, protocols, and drug formularies (i.e., practice standardization) and the "normalization" of health-care practices by employing physician report cards and other forms of "practice averaging." In the latter instance, data about patterns of practice are collected, measures of central tendency are calculated, and reports are generated comparing how individual physicians compare in their use of diagnostic tests and other resources with some group of "peers" (e.g., co-workers, a target comparison group, national norms). Within the world of corporate managed care, rank and file physicians are viewed by management as being extremely sensitive to the threat of being "different." The use of modes, medians, and averages, by definition, creates outliers and thus a new class of deviants within the culture of medicine. With the attempt by managed care to measure anything that moves, physicians are being socialized within their current work settings to "covet the mean" as outliers (at both ends) fleeing to the safety of "central tendencies." Meanwhile, although some have equated the arrival of managed care with the death of physician autonomy, it would be advisable to take a "sociological pause" and examine to how clinicians (and students) will respond to these new tools and value systems and how they will seek to transform them on the factory floor.

Guidelines, protocols, and formularies are of a different ilk, although they serve a similar end. Often developed by consensus panels or based on randomized clinical trials, these tools are generated in the thousands (AMA 1994) by medical associations (national and state), government-funded programs (e.g., PORT programs funded by AHCPR), third-party payers, managed-care companies, for-profit entities that specialize in just such a product (e.g., Health Risk Management), and individual hospitals and clinics. In comparison to conformity by normalization, the use of algorithms and related "best practice" tools represent standardization by fiat as physicians are given proscriptions (masquerading as "guidelines") to be followed along with an ever-shorter list of procedures that will be reimbursed.

Taken as a whole, techniques of standardization are not simply new tools in the war against disease, but also new norms of clinical practice. Today more so than yesterday, and tomorrow more than today, medical students and residents are being exposed to new definitions of "good medicine" and all within a value system that emphasizes either standardization or uniformity or some combination of the two. The fact that new management techniques and standards of practice have reduced the length of hospital stays and shifted more procedures to outpatient settings has important implications for the training of medical students and residents already has been mentioned. But there are other transformations underway as well, more subtle in presence but potentially more profound in consequence. For example, we might wish to revisit the writings of Renée Fox, Donald Light, Jack Haas and William Shaffir, and others on the nature and impact of uncertainty in medical work and question whether the deployment of protocols and the use of report cards is generating a new definition of uncertainty in medical practice. Moving to the work of Charles Bosk (1979, 1980, 1986) we might consider re-exploring his classic distinction between normative and technical errors and whether they are being altered within this new value system. Will there be new interaction rituals and a new cloak of competence within clinical training (see Haas and Shaffir 1982)? Furthermore, and perhaps most importantly, how will the value of firsthand experience and the long-standing belief within medicine that general knowledge is inadequate for dealing with specific cases (see Freidson 1970) be altered in a world of protocols and guidelines? What will happen to the importance of "personal experience" in a medical world ruled by "evidence" of EBM? Relatedly, what is to become of role models in a system where the protocol has become king?

The rise of evidence-based medicine (EBM) can be traced to a similar host of concerns about rising health-care costs, along with the work of John Wennberg on variations in physician practice styles ("local area analysis") and the perception that much of American medicine has been awash in "unnecessary" (and therefore inappropriately costly) medical procedures (Gray 1991; Wennberg 1973, 1985). The appearance of EBM, like the growth of standardization and normalization techniques, represents a shift within the culture of medicine regarding what is and what is not to be considered "science" within the arena of clinical practice.

On one level, EBM poses as a methodology, a set of rules and guidelines for approaching and interpreting the medical literature. For example, the Evidence-Based Medicine Working Group at McMaster University defines EBM as "an approach to healthcare practice in which the clinician is aware of the evidence in support of her clinical practice and the strength of that evidence" (http://bagel.aecom.yu.edu /evidence.htm). But EBM also is a social movement complete with slogans, a new liturgy, a priesthood, devoted followers, centers of "worship," and a core of moral entrepreneurship (Hafferty 1998). Proponents of EBM seek to shift the locus of power in clinical decision-making from "personal experience," "textbooks," "experts," "continuing medical education," "pharmaceutical reps," "academic or 'throw-away' reviews," and "original research" in favor of "the use of rules of logic and science." Proponents of EBM define it as a "new paradigm" and unabashedly announce that its use will change the way physicians practice medicine by replacing "experts" with "evidence" (http://bagel.aecom.yu.edu/evidence.htm). There is CME coursework on EBM, as well as postdoctoral training programs. Meanwhile, medical schools are being encouraged to develop formally labeled coursework in EBM. The growing influence of EBM not only offers sociologists important opportunities to examine medicine's changing value system but also for collaboration across a wide variety of areas in sociology, including technology, social movements, the sociology of religion, and medical education.

But these are not the only issues. The proliferation of guidelines, many of which cover the same diseases or sets of clinical circumstances, guarantees that there will be "winners" and "losers," as guidelines (along with their producers or sponsors) jockey for legitimacy and power within the arena of medicine. There also is a potential for conflict between guidelines and EBM. That the language of EBM currently disavows experts and "expertise" in favor of something that must be both "evidence" and "applicable" appears to place individual physicians at the moral hub of clinical decision-making, something quite antithetical, at first blush, to the value underpinnings and locus of control being promulgated by protocols and guidelines. Similarly, the notion of "responsibility" may undergo a shift in meaning as the locus of clinical expertise, but perhaps not responsibility, shifts from the physician to the organization. According to EBM, the practice of medicine is supposed to be driven by data, not anecdotes, but the fact that all groups possess an oral culture makes me eagerly await the emergence of evidence-based allegories before too long.

Finally, I believe that it is both fitting and important to end this chapter by revisiting an issue I see as one of the most important threats to the social legitimacy of medical education as presently configured. Despite a plethora of programs, promises, and money, medical educators have not been able to increase appreciably the number of minority physicians. Meanwhile, managed care is actively courting minority customers and, in turn, seeking minority providers (see Jeffrey 1995). If medical schools cannot meet this need, then managed care will turn to other provider types (advanced practice nurses or mid-level providers such as physician assistants and nurse practitioners) to deliver first-line care to its burgeoning ranks of minority customers. As this happens, managed-care companies will escalate their efforts to ensure that certification requirements and state-based medical practice acts are rewritten to reflect these new social and corporate exigencies. Meanwhile, medical school deans, the AAMC,

the AMA, and legions of national commissions continue to identify physician oversupply as one of the most pressing problems facing medical education. But oversupply is a socially constructed reality (Hafferty 1986) and one that is closely tied to ever-changing sets of definitions about what does and does not constitute a "medical" need along with the resources required (including workforce) to meet those needs. From this vantage point, the problem is not one of oversupply so much as it is one of maldistribution, where maldistribution is defined in terms of needs that are not being met. But organized medical education continues to resist this message in much the same way that organized medicine continues to accept the notion that we are moving toward a multitiered delivery system in which innumerable lines are being drawn between different types of haves and have-nots. Unless medical education is able to initiate some fundamental changes in the way it selects and educates future physicians, these problems will only continue to escalate.

REFERENCES

AMERICAN MEDICAL ASSOCIATION, M.C. TOEPP, and N. KUZNETS. 1994. *Directory of Practice Parameters: Titles, Sources and Updates.* Chicago: American Medical Association.

AMERICAN JOURNAL OF SOCIOLOGY. 1962. "Current Books." *American Journal of Sociology* 67: 477–78.

ANDERSON, D.J. 1992. "The Hidden Curriculum." *American Journal of Roentgenology* 159: 21–22.

ANSPACH, R.R. 1988. "Notes on the Sociology of Medical Discourse: The Language of Case Presentation." *Journal of Health and Social Behavior* 29: 357–75.

ANSPACH, R.R. 1993. *Deciding Who Lives: Fateful Choices in the Intensive Care Nursery.* Berkeley: University of California Press.

ARLUKE, A.B., and F.W. HAFFERTY. 1996. "From Apprehension to Fascination with 'Dog Lab'." *Journal of Contemporary Ethnography* 25: 201–05.

ASSOCIATION OF AMERICAN MEDICAL COLLEGES. 1996. *AAMC-STAT: Underrepresented Minorities More Likely to Work in Underserved Areas.* Washington, DC: Association of American Medical Colleges.

ASSOCIATION OF AMERICAN MEDICAL COLLEGES. 1998a. *AAMC Data Book: Statistical Information Related to Medical Education.* Washington, DC: Association of American Medical Colleges.

ASSOCIATION OF AMERICAN MEDICAL COLLEGES. 1998b. *Report 1. Learning Objectives for Medical Student Education: Guidelines for Medical Schools.* Medical School Objectives Project (MSOP). Washington, DC: Association of American Medical Colleges.

ASSOCIATION OF AMERICAN MEDICAL COLLEGES. 1998c. *AAMC-STAT: Short, Topical and Timely News from the Association of American Medical Colleges.* Washington, DC: Association of American Medical Colleges.

ASSOCIATION OF AMERICAN MEDICAL COLLEGES. 1998d. *AAMC-STAT: Short, Topical and Timely News from the Association of American Medical Colleges.* Washington, DC: Association of American Medical Colleges.

BALDWIN, D.W.C., S.R. DAUGHERTY, E.J. ECKENFELS. 1996. "Cheating in Medical School: A Survey of Second-Year Students at 31 Schools." *Academic Medicine* 71: 267–73.

BECKER, E. 1973. *The Denial of Death.* New York: The Free Press.

BECKER, H. 1998. Personal communication.

BECKER, H., B. GEER, E.C. HUGHES, and A.L. STRAUSS. 1961. *Boys in White: Student Culture in Medical School.* Chicago: University of Chicago Press.

BECKER, H., and B. GEER. 1963. "Medical Education." In *Handbook of Medical Education,* ed. H. Freeman, S. Levine, and L. Reeder. Englewood Cliffs, NJ: Prentice Hall, pp. 169–86.

BECKER, H., B. GEER, and S. MILLER. 1972. "Medical Education." In *Handbook of Medical Education,* ed. H. Freeman, S. Levine, and L. Reeder. Englewood Cliffs, NJ: Prentice Hall, pp. 191–205.

BEN-YUHUDA, N., R. BRYMER, S.C. DUBIN, D. HARPER, R. HERTZ, and W. SHAFFIR. 1989. "Howard Becker: A

Portrait of an Individual's Sociological Imagination." *Sociological Imagination* 59: 467–89.

BLOOM, S. 1964. "Book Review: Handbook of Medical Sociology Volume 1." *American Sociological Review* 29: 616–17.

BLOOM, S. 1965. "The Sociology of Medical Education: Some Comments on the State of a Field." *Milbank Memorial Fund Quarterly/Health and Society* 43: 143–84.

BLOOM, S. 1973. *Power and Dissent in the Medical School.* New York: Free Press.

BLOOM, S. 1979. "Socialization for the Physician's Role: A Review of Some Contributions of Research to Theory." In *Becoming a Physician: Development of Values and Attitudes in Medicine,* ed. E. Shapiro and L. Lowenstein. Cambridge, UK: Ballinger Publishing Company, pp. 3–52.

BLOOM, S. 1988. "Structure and Ideology in Medical Education: An Analysis of Resistance to Change." *Journal of Health and Social Behavior* 29: 294–306.

BLOOM, S. 1990. "Episodes in the Institutionalization of Medical Sociology: A Personal View." *Journal of Health and Social Behavior* 31: 1–10.

BLOOM, S. 1992. "Medical Education in Transition: Paradigm Change and Organizational Stasis." In *Medical Education in Transition,* ed. R. Marston and R. Jones. Princeton: The Robert Wood Johnson Foundation, pp. 15–25.

BOSK, C.L. 1979. *Forgive and Remember.* Chicago: University of Chicago Press.

BOSK, C.L. 1980. "Occupational Rituals in Patient Management." *New England Journal of Medicine* 303: 71–76.

BOSK, C.L. 1986. "Professional Responsibility and Medical Error." In *Applications of Social Science and Health Policy,* ed. L. Aiken and D. Mechanic. New Brunswick, NJ: Rutgers University Press, 460–77.

BRIM, O., H. FREEMAN, S. LEVINE, and N. SCOTCH. 1970. *The Dying Patient.* New York: Russell Sage Foundation.

CHRISTAKIS, N.A. 1995. "The Similarity and Frequency of Proposals to Reform U.S. Medical Education: Constant Concerns. *Journal of the American Medical Association* 274: 706–11.

CHRISTAKIS, D.A., and C. FEUDTNER. 1997. "Temporary Matters: The Ethical Consequences of Transient Social Relationships in Medical Training." *Journal of the American Medical Association* 278: 739–43.

CLARK, D.C., and P.B. ZELDOW. 1988. "Vicissitudes of Depressed Mood During Four Years of Medical School." *Journal of the American Medical Association* 260: 2521–28.

CLARK, J., C. MODGIL, and S. MODGIL. 1990. *Robert K. Merton: Consensus and Controversy.* Bristol, PA: Falmer Press.

COCKERHAM, W. 1988. "Medical Sociology." In *Handbook of Sociology,* ed. N. Smelser. Newbury Park, CA: Sage Publications, pp. 575–99.

COLES, C.R., and J.G. GRANT. 1985. "Curriculum Evaluation in Medical and Health-Care Education." *Medical Education* 19: 405–22.

CONRAD, P. 1986. "The Myth of Cut-Throats Among Premedical Students: On the Role of Stereotypes in Justifying Failure and Success." *Journal of Health and Social Behavior* 27: 150–60.

CONRAD, P. 1988. "Learning to Doctor: Reflections on Recent Accounts of the Medical School Years." *Journal of Health and Social Behavior* 29: 323–32.

CONRAD, P., and J. SCHNEIDER. 1992. *Deviance and Medicalization: From Baldness to Sickness.* Philadelphia: Temple University Press.

COOMBS, R.H., S. CHOPRA, D. SCHENK, and E. YUTAN. 1993. "Medical Slang and Its Functions." *Social Science and Medicine* 36: 987–98.

CORDOVA, J.A., E. AQUIRRE, A. HERNANDEZ, V. HIDALGO, and F. DOMINQUEZ. 1996. "Assessment and Accreditation of Mexican Medical Schools." *Medical Education* 5: 319–21.

DAUGHERTY, S.R., D.W.C. BALDWIN, and B.D. ROWLEY. 1988. "Learning, Satisfaction, and Mistreatment During Medical Internship: A National Survey of Working Conditions." *Journal of the American Medical Association* 279: 1194–99.

DAVIS, J. 1958. "Book Review: The Student Physician." *American Journal of Sociology* 63: 445–46.

DAVIS, F. 1968. "Professional Socialization as a Subjective Experience: The Process of Doctrinal Conversion Among Student Nurses." In *Institutions and the Person,* ed. H.S. Becker, B. Geer, D. Reisman, and R.S. Weiss. Chicago: Aldine, pp. 235–41.

DESCHEPPER, E.J. 1987. "The Hidden Curriculum in Dental Education." *Journal of Dental Education* 51: 575–77.

DOCTOR, X. 1965. *Intern.* New York: Harper and Row.

DORNBUSCH, S.1955. "The Military Academy as an Assimilating Institution." *Social Forces* 33: 316–21.

ECKENFELS, E.J., S.R. DAUGHERTY, and D.W.C. BALDWIN. 1997. "A Socio-Cultural Framework for Explaining Perceptions of Mistreatment and Abuse in the Professional Socialization of Future Physicians." *Annals of Behavioral Science and Medical Education* 4: 11–18.

FEUDTNER, C., and D.A. CHRISTAKIS. 1993. "Ethics in a Short White Coat: The Ethical Dilemmas that Medical Students Confront." *Academic Medicine* 68: 249–54.

FEUDTNER, C., D.A. CHRISTAKIS, and N.A. CHRISTAKIS. 1994. "Do Clinical Clerks Suffer Ethical Erosion? Students' Perceptions of Their Clinical Environment and Personal Development." *Academic Medicine* 69: 670–79.

FOX, R. 1957. "Training for Uncertainty." In *The Student Physician: Introductory Studies in the Sociology of Medical Education,* ed. R. Merton, G. Reader, and P. Kendall. Cambridge, MA: Harvard University Press, pp. 204–41.

FOX, R. 1979. "The Autopsy: Its Place in the Attitude-Learning of Second-Year Medical Students." In *Essays in*

Medical Sociology: Journeys Into the Field, ed. R. Fox. New York: John Wiley and Sons, pp. 51–77.

Fox, R. 1989. *Sociology of Medicine: A Participant Observer's View.* Englewood Cliffs, NJ: Prentice Hall.

Fremont, A. 1998. Personal communication.

Freidson, E. 1970. *Profession of Medicine: A Study of the Sociology of Applied Knowledge.* New York: Harper & Row.

Gallagher, E., and M. Searle. 1989. "Content and Context in Health Professional Education." In *Handbook of Medical Education,* ed. H.E. Freeman and S. Levine. Englewood Cliffs, NJ: Prentice Hall, pp. 437–55.

Ganem, J.L., and J. Krakower. 1997. "Review of U.S. Medical School Finances, 1995–1996." *Journal of the American Medical Association* 278: 755–60

Gee, H.H., and R.J. Glaser. 1958. "The Ecology of the Medical Student: Report of the Fifth Teaching Institute, Association of American Medical Colleges, Atlantic City, New Jersey, October 15–19, 1957." *Journal of Medical Education* 33(10): part 2.

Glaser, B.G., and A.L. Strauss. 1965. *Awareness of Dying.* Chicago: Aldine.

Glaser, B.G., and A.L. Strauss. 1968. *Time for Dying.* Chicago: Aldine.

Good, B. J. 1994. *Medicine, Rationality, and Experience: An Anthropological Perspective.* The Lewis Henry Morgan Lectures. Cambridge, UK: Cambridge University Press.

Good, M.-J.D.V. 1995. *American Medicine: The Quest for Competence.* Berkeley: University of California Press.

Good, M.-J.D.V. and B. Good. 1989. "Disabling Practitioners: Hazards of Learning to Be a Doctor in American Medical Education." *Journal of Orthopsychiatry* 59: 303–09.

Gray, B. 1991. "The Legislative Battle Over Health Services Research." *Health Affairs* 11: 38–66.

Gray, J.D., and J. Ruedy. 1998. "Undergraduate and Postgraduate Medical Education in Canada." *Canadian Medical Association Journal* 158: 1047–50.

Group Health Association of America. 1994. *Group Health Association of America. Primary Care Physicians: Recommendations to Reform Medical Education. Competencies Needed to Practice in HMOs.* Washington, DC: Group Health Association of America.

Haas, J., and W. Shaffir. 1982. "Ritual Evaluation of Competence: The Hidden Curriculum of Professionalization in an Innovative Medical School Program." *Work and Occupations* 9: 131–54.

Haas, J., and W. Shaffir. 1987. *Becoming Doctors: The Adoption of a Cloak of Competence.* Greenwich, CT: JAI Press.

Hafferty, F.W. 1986. "Physician Oversupply as a Socially Created Reality." *Journal of Health and Social Behavior* 27: 358–69.

Hafferty, F.W. 1988. "Theories at the Crossroads: A Discussion of Evolving Views on Medicine as a Profession." *Milbank Quarterly* 66(Suppl. 2): 202–25.

Hafferty, F.W. 1991. *Into the Valley: Death and the Socialization of Medical Students.* New Haven, CT: Yale University Press.

Hafferty, F.W. 1998. "Beyond Curriculum Reform: Confronting Medicine's Hidden Curriculum." *Academic Medicine* 73: 403–07.

Hafferty, F.W., and R. Franks. 1994. "The Hidden Curriculum, Ethics Teaching, and the Structure of Medical Education." *Academic Medicine* 69: 861–71.

Henderson, L.J. 1935. "Physician and Patient as a Social System." *New England Journal of Medicine* 212: 819–23.

Hollenberg, C.H. 1996. "The Effect of Health Care Reform on Academic Medicine in Canada: Editorial Committee of the Canadian Institute for Academic Medicine." *Canadian Medical Association Journal* 154: 1483–89.

Horowitz, M.J. 1964. *Educating Tomorrow's Doctors.* New York: Appleton-Century-Crofts.

Hughes, E. 1951. "Mistakes at Work." *Canadian Journal of Economics and Political Science* 17: 320–27.

Hughes, E. 1966. "The Making of a Physician—General Statement of Ideas and Problems." In *Medical Care,* ed. W.R. Scott and E.H. Volkart. New York: John Wiley, pp. 86–96.

Hughes, E., H.M. Hughes, and I. Deutscher. 1958. *Twenty Thousand Nurses Tell Their Story.* Philadelphia: Lippincott.

Hundert, E. 1997. "The role of the hidden curriculum in the professional development of medical students." Paper Presented at the 27th Annual Meeting of Association for Behavioral Sciences and Medical Education, October 18–21, Brewster, Massachusetts.

Hundert, E.M., D. Douglas-Steele, and J. Bickel. 1996. "Context in Medical Education: The Informal Ethics Curriculum." *Medical Education* 30: 353–64.

Jackson, P. 1968. *Life in Classrooms.* New York: Holt, Rinehart and Winston.

Jeffrey, N.A. 1995. "HMOs Say 'Hola' To Potential Customers." *Wall Street Journal:* B1,B6.

Jonas, S. 1978. *Medical Mystery: The Training of Doctors in the United States.* New York: W.W. Norton and Company.

Jones, R.F., and D. Korn. 1998. "On the Cost of Educating Medical Students." *Academic Medicine* 72: 200–10.

Kastenbaum, R., and R. Aisenberg. 1972. *The Psychology of Death.* New York: Springer.

Kendall, P. 1961. "Impact of Training Programs on the Young Physician's Attitudes and Experiences." *Journal of American Medical Association* 176: 992–97.

Kern, F. 1962. "Book Review: Boys in White." *Journal of Health and Human Behavior* 3: 295–96.

Kleinerman, M.J. 1992. "Elucidating and Eradicating Medical Student Abuse." *Journal of the American Medical Association* 267: 738, 742.

Kubler-Ross, E. 1969. *On Death and Dying.* New York: Macmillan.

KUBLER-ROSS, E. 1974. *Questions and Answers on Death and Dying.* New York: Collier.

KUBLER-ROSS, E. 1975. *The Final Stage of Growth.* Englewood Cliffs, NJ: Prentice Hall.

LEBARRON, C. 1981. *Gentle Vengeance.* New York: Richard Marek Publishers.

LEWIS, C.E. 1998. "Continuing Medical Education: Past, Present, Future." *Western Journal of Medicine* 168: 334–40.

LIGHT, D. 1979. "Uncertainty and Control in Professional Training." *Journal of Health and Social Behavior* 20: 310–22.

LIGHT, D. 1980. *Becoming Psychiatrists.* New York: W.W. Norton.

LIGHT, D. 1983. "Medical and Nursing Education: Surface Behavior and Deep Structure." In *Handbook of Health, Health Care and the Health Professions,* ed. D. Mechanic. New York: Free Press, pp. 455–78.

LIGHT, D. 1988. "Toward a New Sociology of Medical Education." *Journal of Health and Social Behavior* 29: 307–22.

LIGHT, D., and S. LEVINE. 1988. "The Changing Character of the Medical Profession: A Theoretical Overview." *Milbank Quarterly* 66: 10–32.

LUBITZ, R.M. 1994. "Medical Student Abuse During Third-Year Clerkships." *Journal of the American Medical Association* 275: 414–16.

LUDMERER, K.M. 1985. *Learning to Heal: The Development of American Medical Education.* New York: Basic Books.

LUDMERER, K.M. 1999. *The Development of American Medical Education.* New York: Oxford University Press.

MARGITTAI, K.J., R. MOSCARELLO, and M.F. ROSSI. 1994. "Medical Students' Experiences of Abuse: A Canadian Perspective." *Annals of the Royal Canadian Physician Society* 27: 199–204.

MARINKER, M. 1997. "Myth, Paradox and the Hidden Curriculum." *Medical Education* 31: 293–98.

MAYNARD, D., and H. WAITZKIN. 1993. "The Politics of Medical Encounters: How Patients and Doctors Deal With Social Problems." *American Journal of Sociology* 98: 976–79.

MAYSON, J., and W. HAYWARD. 1997. "Learning to Be a Nurse: The Contribution of the Hidden Curriculum in the Clinical Setting." *Nurse Practitioner New Zealand* 12: 16–22.

MERTON, R.K., and E. BARBER. 1976. "Sociological Ambivalence." In *Social Ambivalence and Other Essays,* ed. R.K. Merton. New York: Free Press, pp. 3–31.

MERTON, R.K., L.G. READER, and P.L. KENDALL, eds. 1957. *The Student Physician: Introductory Studies in the Sociology of Medical Education.* Cambridge, MA: Harvard University Press.

MILLMAN, M. 1977. *The Unkindest Cut: Life in the Backrooms of Medicine.* New York: William-Morrow.

MIZRAHI, T. 1986. *Getting Rid of Patients: Contradictions in the Socialization of Physicians.* New Brunswick: Rutgers University Press.

MUMFORD, E. 1970. *Interns: From Students to Physicians.* Cambridge, MA: Harvard University Press.

NIGENDA, G., and A. SOLORZANO. 1997. "Doctors and Corporatist Politics: The Case of the Mexican Medical Profession." *Journal of Health Politics, Policy and Law* 22: 73–100.

O'NEIL, E.H. 1993. *Health Professions Education for the Future: Schools in Service to the Nation.* San Francisco: Pew Health Professions Commission.

OLESEN, V.L., and E.W. WHITTAKER. 1968. *The Silent Dialogue: A Study in the Social Psychology of Professional Socialization.* San Francisco: Jossey-Bass.

PARSONS, T. 1951. "Social Structure and Dynamic Process: The Case of Modern Medical Practice." In *The Social Structure,* ed. T. Parsons. New York: Free Press, pp. 428–79.

PARTRIDGE, B. 1983. "The Hidden Curriculum of Nursing Education." *Lamp* 40: 30.

PERRY, T. 1998. "Putting Marines Through a 'Crucible'." *Los Angeles Times On-Line* (WWW.latimes.com) March 7.

POLLOCK, D. 1996. "Training Tales: U.S. Medical Autobiography." *Cultural Anthropology* 11: 339–61.

REEDER, G. 1962. "Book Review: Boys in White." *American Sociological Review* 27: 418–19.

RICHMAN, J.A., J.A. FLAHERTY, J.M. ROSPENDA, and M.L. CHRISTENSEN. 1992. "Mental Health Consequences and Correlates of Reported Medical Student Abuse." *Journal of the American Medical Association* 267: 692–94.

RICKS, T.E. 1997. *Making the Corps.* New York: Scribner.

ROSENBERG, D.A., and H.K. SILVER. 1984. "Medical Student Abuse: An Unnecessary and Preventable Cause of Stress." *Journal of the American Medical Association* 251: 739–42.

SCHEFF, T. 1963. "Decisions Rules, Types of Error, and Their Consequences in Medical Diagnosis." *Behavioral Science* 8: 97–107.

SCHNEIDMAN, E. 1973. *Deaths of Man.* New York: Quadrangle.

SEGAL, D.A. 1987. "A Patient So Dead: American Medical Students and Their Cadavers." *Anthropology Quarterly* 61: 17–25.

SHAH, L.J. 1997. *International Encyclopedia of the Sociology of Education.* New York: Pergamon.

SHEEHAN, K.H., D.V. SHEEHAN, K. WHITE, A. LEIBOVITZ, and D.C. BALDWIN. 1990. "A Pilot Study of Medical Student 'Abuse': Student Perceptions of Mistreatment and Misconduct in Medical School." *Journal of the American Medical Association* 263: 533–37.

SHEM, S. 1978. *The House of God.* New York: Dell.

SHINE, K.I. 1996. "Educating Physicians for the Real World." In *Urban Medical Centers: Balancing Academic and Patient Care Functions,* ed. E. Ginsberg. Boulder, CO: Westview Press.

SHUGARS, D.A., E.H. O'NEAL, and J.D. BACKER, eds. 1991. *Healthy America: Practitioners for 2005, an Agenda for Action for U.S. Health Professional Schools.* Durham, NC: The Pew Health Professions Commission.

SHUVAL, J.T. 1975. "From 'Boy' to 'Colleague': Processes of Role Transformation in Professional Socialization." *Social Science and Medicine* 9: 413–20.

SILVER, H.K. 1982. "Medical Students and Medical School." *Journal of the American Medical Association* 247: 309–10.

SILVER, H.K., and A.D. GLICKEN. 1990. "Medical Student Abuse: Incidence, Severity, and Significance." *Journal of the American Medical Association* 263: 527–32.

SIMPSON, I. 1979. *From Student to Nurse.* Cambridge, UK: Cambridge University Press.

SMITH, A.C., and S. KLEINMAN. 1989. "Managing Emotions in Medical School: Students' Contacts with the Living and the Dead." *Social Psychology Quarterly* 52: 56–69.

SPITZER, T.C. 1994. "The Hidden Curriculum in a Mexican University: The Case of the Universidad Autonoma Chapingo." Paper presented at the International Sociological Association, Spain.

STARR, P.E. 1982. *The Social Transformation of American Medicine: The Rise of a Sovereign Profession and the Making of a Vast Industry.* New York: Basic Books.

STELLING, J., and R. BUCHER. 1973. "Vocabularies of Realism in Professional Socialization." *Social Science and Medicine* 7: 661–75.

STERN, D.T. Hanging Out: Teaching Values in Medical Education. Unpublished.

STEVENS, R. 1971. *American Medicine and the Public Interest.* New Haven: Yale University Press.

STOECKLE, J. 1987. "Physicians Train and Tell." *Harvard Medical Alumni Bulletin* 61: 9–11.

STRAUSS, A.L., and B.G. GLASER. 1970. *Anguish: A Case History of a Dying Trajectory.* Mill Valley, CA: Sociology Press.

THORNES, S. 1997. "Medical Schools Seeking New Ways to Cope with Funding Cutbacks." *Canadian Medical Association Journal* 156: 1611–13.

UHARI, M., J. KODDONEN, M. NUUTINEN, H. RANTALA, and P. LAUTALA. 1994. "Medical Student Abuse: An International Phenomenon." *Journal of the American Medical Association* 271: 1049–51.

WEAR, D. 1997. "Professional Development of Medical Students: Problems and Promises." *Academic Medicine* 72: 1056–62.

WENNBERG, J.E. 1973. "Small Area Variations in Health Care Delivery." *Science* 182: 1102–08.

WENNBERG, J.E. 1985. "Variations in Medical Practice and Hospital Costs." *Connecticut Medicine* 49: 444–53.

WILLIAM, J.L. 1992. "Don't Discuss It: Reconciling Illness, Dying and Death in a Medical School Anatomy Laboratory." *Family Systems Medicine* 10: 65–78.

YOUNG, J.Q., and J.M. COFFMAN. 1998. "Overview of Graduate Medical Education: Funding Streams, Policy Problems, and Options for Reform." *Western Journal of Medicine* 168: 428–36.

17 THE EVOLVING RELATIONSHIP BETWEEN MEDICAL SOCIOLOGY AND HEALTH POLICY

BRADFORD H. GRAY, *New York Academy of Medicine*

JAMES O'LEARY, *Blue Cross/Blue Shield Association*

People's health and the medical care they receive are affected in countless ways by the complex and diverse set of rules (or their absence) and incentives that compose health policy.[1] A variety of levers can be used by policy makers to affect health and medical care—creating entitlements to benefits, funding programs to provide services, using taxes and tax exemptions to create incentives and disincentives, and establishing programs to protect the public's health. In addition, many governmental actions whose primary purpose is unrelated to health may nevertheless have significant health-related effects. This includes such policy areas as social welfare, drug enforcement, antitrust, labor, and regulation of the economy itself. The details within programmatic areas and the relationships among them can be numbingly complex, and the thousands of pages of regulations connected with large governmental programs provide careers for analysts, consultants, and legal technicians who develop expertise in arcane areas.

The venues of governmental policy making in the United States are numerous, as are the forms. At the federal level, policy can be seen in the President's budget and legislative proposals (and vetoes), in legislation, in Congressional oversight activities and the annual appropriations process, in judicial decisions, and in various forms of administrative rule making, including regulations, decisions by administrative law judges, conditions of participation for federal programs, and manuals of procedure for all kinds of governmental funding and regulatory programs.

The federal agencies that make and execute health policy form a long list indeed, including not only numerous components of the Department of Health and Human Services (e.g., the Health Care Financing Agency that administers the Medicare and Medicaid programs, the Social Security Administration, the Food and Drug Administration, the Health Resources and Services Administration, the Agency for Health Care Policy and Research, the National Institutes of Health, and the Centers for Disease Control, which includes the Occupational Safety and Health Administration), but also the Department of Justice, which prosecutes a growing volume of health care fraud; the Federal Trade Commission, which shares the increasingly important antitrust arena with Justice; the Securities and Exchange Commission, which regulates publicly traded companies in the increasingly for-profit health-care field; the Department of Veterans Affairs and the hospitals it operates; the Department of Agriculture (inspection of meat and other agricultural products); the Department of Labor, which has oversight over self-insured corporate health plans; the Office of Personnel Management, which operates the Federal Employees Health Benefit Plan, which is held out by some advocates as a model consumer-choice plan; the Environmental Protection Agency and Atomic Energy Commission; the

---

[1] Although health policy is usually thought of as the product of governmental action (or inaction), health policy is also made by private entities, as when employers decide whether to provide health benefits for their employees or when private bodies establish criteria for accreditation of health-care organizations. However, we concentrate on *public* policy in this chapter. Our focus is also limited to the American context.

Department of Defense, which buys or provides medical care for members of the armed services and their families; the Drug Enforcement Agency; the Internal Revenue Service, which sets criteria for tax exemption of nonprofit health care organizations; and the Congressional agencies—the General Accounting Office, the Congressional Budget Office, and the Congressional Research Service. This list is far from complete at the federal level and ignores the state and local entities that make or administer health policy.

The Medicare and Medicaid programs affect the health-care system in countless ways through the incentives established by their payment methods and through the conditions that they establish for the participation of providers of health services and of patients. Because of the size of these programs—Medicare, which covers the elderly and disabled, is the nation's largest purchaser of medical services, and the state-administered Medicaid program is the largest single purchaser in most states—substantial changes in these programs have far-reaching and often unexpected effects on health-care organizations and professionals and on patients and their families. Even seemingly minor features of these programs can have major effects. For example, the rise of investor-owned hospital companies was an unintended consequence of obscure provisions regarding capital payments in the original Medicare legislation (Gray 1991).

How does medical sociology relate to health policy in the United States? In this chapter, we will argue that the relationship has changed over time and that the relationship has become increasingly close, today taking two different forms, which we call *policy-relevant* and *policy-oriented* research. We will examine the evolving relationship between medical sociology and health policy through the lens of the various editions of the *Handbook of Medical Sociology* (1963, 1972, 1979, and 1989) up to the fifth edition, in which this chapter appears. We focus primarily on governmental policy that affects the financing and organization of medical services, recognizing that there are many other large areas of policy-relevant activity that we are not considering. Our focus is primarily on health policy rather than health politics—that is, on the effects rather than the causes of governmental actions.

THE EMERGENCE OF MEDICAL SOCIOLOGY IN THE UNITED STATES

The establishment of the Section on Medical Sociology within the American Sociological Association in 1955 signaled that a coherent new field of interest had developed within the discipline. The Section grew to become the largest section within the American Sociological Association before being surpassed in recent years. In 1998, it was the third largest section of the ASA, with some 1002 members.

As the field grew, it incorporated researchers from a broad spectrum of theoretical orientations and methodological approaches from the parent discipline. The growing diversity of subjects and theoretical and methodological approaches was a discipline-wide phenomenon, but the growth of medical sociology also received major external stimulus from private foundation and federal support for research and graduate training, particularly from the National Institute of Mental Health. The growth of medical sociology was also influenced by other developments outside the discipline, including the growing importance of medical care in economic terms and the increasing influence of public policy on the health-care system.

Certain types of work by medical sociologists brought them face to face with health policy topics. This is true of historically oriented sociologists (from Bernard J. Stern to Paul Starr) and sociologists interested in cross-national comparisons of health systems (for example, Odin Anderson and William Glaser), and health-policy actions provided subject matter for some political sociologists (such as Robert Alford and Theda Skocpol). But as medical sociology developed, health policy was a background factor that was largely taken for granted. Most work in the first decade of the field's emergence was concerned either with health care as a closed system that involved doctors, patients, nurses, and hospitals or with epidemiological research.

HEALTH POLICY AND THE *HANDBOOK OF MEDICAL SOCIOLOGY*

The publication of the *Handbook of Medical Sociology* in 1963 was the first major codification of sociological work in the field, and a broad array of topics was covered. What is particularly striking from today's perspective is the virtual absence of any explicit attention to health policy or its influence. The topic was not addressed either in a separate chapter or in chapter sections on policy relevance. The index contains no reference to such terms as policy, legislation, regulation, or government.

The absence of health policy in the 1963 *Handbook* accurately reflects the field at that time. In his later review of the institutional development of medical sociology, Samuel Bloom (1986) noted that it had closely followed larger developments in the parent discipline. The early classic works of medical sociology, such as Talcott Parsons's (1951) theoretical analysis of medicine as a social system, the professional socialization studies of Robert Merton and colleagues (1957) at the Bureau of Applied Social Research and of Howard Becker and his colleagues (1961), and the social stratification perspective on mental illness in the work of August Hollingshead and Frederick Redlich (1958) all arose from central sociological areas of inquiry. The extraordinary organizational research of Erving Goffman (1961) was also as much mainstream sociology as medical sociology.

Bloom's account also implicitly identifies another reason for the previous lack of a policy focus in medical sociology. Medical sociology was influenced from its inception by the tension between applied and basic approaches to sociological research. Applied work had a second-class status. Because some medical sociologists worked in medical schools to help medical practitioners better understand how social factors affect medical care (e.g., influencing whether patients seek care, communicate health problems, and comply with medical regimens) medical sociology seemed to be part of the social amelioration tradition from which scientific sociology sought to escape. Bloom also noted tensions between social scientists who were attempting to conduct research from an external (disciplinary) perspective and researchers drawn from the medical profession itself. Sociologists struggled with the choice of being either insiders with good access to research material or outsiders in both perspective and ability to conduct research.

Notably, Bloom did not identify developments in health policy as an influence on the emergence of the field. From a present-day perspective, when health policy has an obvious and extensive influence over much of the subject matter with which medical sociologists are concerned, the relative lack of interest in the early years is notable.

HEALTH POLICY BEFORE THE *HANDBOOK*

The mainstream work by the founders of American medical sociology took place at a time in which the health-policy environment was stable and government was, by today's standards, unobtrusive. As Paul Starr later described the policy environment of the period, the federal government left health and welfare matters to state and local government, where "the general rule was to leave as much to private and voluntary action as

possible" (Starr 1982: 240). Medical care was not among the constitutionally enumerated responsibilities of the federal government. The structure of the health-care system was largely set at the state level, where state medical societies had won the battles that consolidated the medical profession's control over mechanisms for licensing, hospital privileges, and medical school accreditation (Freidson 1970; Starr 1982). Medical care consisted in the main of a fee-for-service system characterized by solo practice, locally controlled nonprofit hospitals, and private insurers who wrote checks and asked few questions.

Although the federal role in health policy was quite limited in the period in which medical sociology emerged, antecedents for a future, much broader role existed. Federal regulation of pharmaceuticals and food safety had been established, though in much more limited form than today's regulatory framework. In an important case that involved the Group Health Association, a prepaid group practice that was an antecedent of the modern HMO, the federal government challenged policies of the medical society of the District of Columbia and successfully applied anti-trust laws to the health-care field. Through the combination of regulatory statutes and common law precedents, federal authority to regulate in the interest of the public health grew slowly in the twentieth century.

The federal government has also long had at least a limited role in directly purchasing health-care services, going back to a 1798 law that provided for the financing of medical services for sick and disabled U.S. seamen (Straus 1950). The first federal grant-in-aid program for direct health services for a population other than seamen and military personnel dates back to the Maternal and Infancy Act of 1921 (Wallace et al. 1982). Despite these early examples of direct purchasing of medical services, unlike most other Western Countries, the United States has never expanded them into a universal health-care program and had only a peripheral role as a direct purchaser until the mid-1960s, after the field of medical sociology had developed.

Until then, medical care had been almost exclusively privately financed and was regulated at the state level, as was health insurance. Although the widespread lack of health insurance among the neediest portions of the population—the elderly and the poor—was clearly a major problem, medical care was not yet an important concern of the federal government. By the 1950s, the structure of private employment-based insurance was set, having expanded during the war. The most serious attempt to pass national health insurance was soundly defeated in the late 1940s and did not arise as a serious topic of policy activity during the Eisenhower administration.

Where the federal government had developed a role during the pre-Medicare period was as a financier of hospital construction and biomedical research. With the economic depression of the 1930s having been followed by severe restrictions on civilian construction during the war years, hospital availability had not kept pace with the nation's need. Congress passed the Hill-Burton Act in 1946 to finance hospital construction, particularly in rural and underpopulated areas. This became the first of many federal efforts to enhance the availability of medical services to the population at large. The federal government also expanded the Veterans Administration by building new hospitals in urban areas and, wherever possible, establishing close affiliations with medical schools.

At the war's end, Congress increased federal support of biomedical research, consolidating the effort in the National Institutes of Health (NIH), whose research budget grew steadily and rapidly over the next decades (Strickland 1972). The federal research funds were predominantly for studying specific diseases, and medical schools became increasingly dependent upon research funds for revenues. This encouraged an emphasis in medical education toward biological processes in disease and treatment, with little attention to the social environment in which people lived and worked (Ginzberg 1977). Federal payments in support of medical education began in the early 1960s and only reinforced this pattern.

An important exception to the exclusively biological focus in the federal medical research efforts was the establishment of the National Institute of Mental Health (NIMH), which saw the behavioral and social sciences as central to the development of its mission. NIMH (and, earlier, several private foundations) funded the training programs, fellowships, and grants that launched the careers of many of the first generation of medical sociologists (Freeman et al. 1975).

In sum, at the time the Medical Sociology Section was being formed, the flow of federal funds and influence into the health-care field was limited and mostly directed to areas that were not primary sociological concerns. By the mid-1960s, federal expenditures accounted for 86 percent of all research in health care and 18.5 percent of all construction costs, but only 13.2 percent of national expenditures for medical services—almost all of which was targeted to current and past military personnel (Rice and Cooper 1968: 4).

It is not surprising, therefore, that the 1963 *Handbook* gave almost no explicit attention to health policy. The orientation of existing federal health policy was implicitly criticized, however, in one of the book's important themes—the inadequacies of the biological paradigm that lay beneath the biomedical research effort and the tertiary care orientation of the dominant institutions. In the Introduction to the *Handbook,* Hugh Leavell (1963: xiv) observed that "the early optimism about specific causation of and specific treatment for all man's ills has to be tempered. . . . The importance of the environment in all its aspects, of genetic factors, and of the mental and emotional aspects of illness has to be recognized once more." He noted the contribution that sociology could make to an understanding of how organizational issues and environmental influences impact the practice of medicine and the spread of disease. The *Handbook*'s chapters were organized around specific illnesses, medical settings and practitioners, and public health and patterns of health-care utilization. An unstated policy implication in many chapters was that research funding should recognize and attempt to understand the contributions to health and disease of social factors as well as biological ones.

A stable policy environment is not fertile ground for the emergence of a policy-sensitive cadre of researchers. Changes and variations in health policy supply variables whose possible effects can attract the interest of researchers, and an active public policy arena stimulates the imagination regarding how research findings might be used to address real problems. But in a field that became coherent during the Eisenhower years, this sense of the possibilities of policy was largely missing in medical sociology.

HEALTH POLICY AND THE SECOND EDITION OF THE *HANDBOOK*

Health policy in the United States experienced its greatest transforming event—the passage in 1965 of the legislation that created Medicare and Medicaid—between the publication of the original *Handbook* and its second edition nine years later, in 1972. The direction of federal health policy changed dramatically with the passage of this legislation with impacts that are difficult to overstate. In extending medical insurance to the elderly, disabled, and large segments of the poor population, these programs made the federal government the most powerful force in the American health-care system. Medicare and Medicaid account for more than half of the revenues of the average hospital, for example, and Medicaid (with shared federal and state funding) has become the largest budgetary item in state budgets, as well as the most important source of funding for patients requiring long-term care.

The expanded federal role of the Great Society period was not limited to these two major programs, however. The combination of civil rights legislation and Medicare resulted in the end of racially segregated health facilities in the South. Other federal legislation also addressed concerns about access and equity, including funding for clinics for migrant workers, neighborhood health centers in low-income areas, and special services for low-income mothers, children, and youth (Kronenfeld and Whicker 1984). Not only did health-service differentials within the population decline over the next decade (Davis and Schoen 1978), but federal funding and associated regulations became a vehicle for many future changes in the health-care system.

By the late 1960s the emphasis on access and equity in federal programs was starting to be balanced by growing concern about cost containment, as the cost of both the Medicare and Medicaid programs far exceeded the cost projections that had been offered at the time they were passed. Health-care costs became a major concern of the federal government, and policy debates began to focus on innovative approaches to the problem, such as the idea for something called a "health maintenance organization" that was implanted into the policy world in early 1970s (Brown 1983). These debates increased awareness of existing but seldom emulated alternative delivery forms such as prepaid group practices (e.g., Kaiser-Permanente) and foundations for medical care (the forerunner of the modern independent practice association).

Although the world of health policy and medical care underwent a sea change after 1965, the influence of these developments can barely be discerned in the second (1972) edition of the *Handbook*. The same editors oversaw the preparation of the second edition, and the book's organization was largely unchanged. The subject matter and chapter headings were almost identical to the first edition, and "policy" and "government" continued to be absent from the subject index.

Still, the second edition had a somewhat new flavor. The Introduction, written by the physician John Knowles, reaffirmed the important contribution medical sociology could make to the understanding of the causation and course of disease, but Knowles also placed the field's potential contribution into a larger policy context. Citing how the rising expectations of health professionals are matched by rising costs and greater medical indigence, he stated that medicine ". . . needs the social sciences and the effects of their study as never before in the history of man" (Knowles 1972: xviii). Knowles clearly envisioned a practical, policy-influencing potential in the work of medical sociologists that went beyond informing clinical decision making.

Various chapter authors drew more explicit attention to the policy implications in their areas. New federal programs were mentioned in some chapters, although in a glancing manner that suggests that for sociologists, public policy was still more part of the background than an active concern. For example, Saxon Graham, in his first edition chapter on "Social Factors in Relation to the Chronic Illnesses," had suggested that chronic diseases have high social and economic costs that cannot be met through reliance on either private savings or charity care, but he had not discussed policy options for addressing the problem (Graham 1963: 92). In the second edition, with Leo Reeder as a co-author, the chapter makes direct reference to federal policy in the discussion of the costs of chronic disease, but the reference is remarkably oblique: "Even though Medicare lessens the burden on the older patient, the burden on society remains considerable" (Graham and Reader 1972: 70).

To cite another example, Eliot Freidson's chapter on the organization of medical practice in the first edition discussed what types of physician organizations should be encouraged by public policy. He concluded (1963: 312) that, "In theory, formal and cooperative rather than informal arrangements are more likely to provide good medical care." He acknowledged that scant empirical evidence was available to back up this claim and suggested the need for more comparative organizational studies on solo versus bureaucratic medical practice. Writing nine years later on the same subject for the *Handbook*'s second edition, Freidson made only passing reference to the two new federal programs, stating that Medicare and Medicaid, ". . . are developing new third-party relationships" (1972: 351). He then suggested that the development of these third-party arrangements did not appear to impinge upon the physician's freedom and judgment and repeated his call for more research on the practice of medicine within a bureaucratic setting. Although it was written at about the same time the HMO Act was being introduced and debated in Congress, Freidson's second edition chapter offered no policy recommendations.

Interestingly, some other authors in the second edition picked up on policy issues raised by Freidson's writings. In the chapter on "Contribution of Sociology to Medicine," Patricia Kendall and George Reader (1972: 24) observed prophetically that, "The question of what type of arrangement will be least costly and most efficient and satisfying to the consumer as well as acceptable to the powerful professional interest groups, . . . will be grist for sociological research for some time to come."

The most direct acknowledgment of the change wrought by the new federal programs of the 1960s was less about the *effects* of health policy than about the *politics* of health policy. In his chapter on "The Politics of Health," Bert Swanson (a professor of political science, not of sociology, incidentally) observed that the health-care policies of the 1960s had moved the federal government beyond its previous commitment to construct health facilities and into the direct purchase of services. Noting that these programs had widened the boundaries of government activity and made health care a major policy issue, he urged medical sociologists to pay more attention to the politics of policy decisions: "The question is no longer whether there is a 'politics of health' but how better to understand the political process" (1972: 455). Still, the sparse attention to policy issues in the second edition of the *Handbook* is striking and revelatory of the detachment of the field's leaders from public policy concerns.

POLICY DEVELOPMENTS AND THE THIRD EDITION

Even as the second edition of the *Handbook* was going to press in 1972, federal health-care policy making was taking an increasingly activist turn. A large expansion took place in the Medicare program with the passage of a new entitlement for patients with end-stage renal disease. However, most health policy activity in the 1970s was concerned with the cost problem. Three major approaches were embodied in legislation and regulation: The HMO Act of 1973, Professional Standards Review Organizations (PSROs) in the 1972 amendments to the Medicare Act, and the National Health Planning and Resources Development Act of 1974. Although none of these initiatives had much success stemming the cost problem created by Medicare's fee-for-service payment methods based on costs incurred (for hospitals) or on billed charges (for doctors), these new programs nevertheless had large, far-reaching effects on the health-care system and on matters with which sociologists had been concerned.

The Health Planning Act extended the Hill-Burton program's aspirations to link decisions to add new hospital beds to measures of need for such beds, thereby theoretically rationalizing hospital construction. Using the regulatory device of "certificates of need," the Act created state and local agencies whose job was to assess local needs and base approval of major new capital investments by hospitals on those assessments. The hope was that those planning agencies would combat the evident tendency toward excess investment in new hospital beds (the operant aphorism being " a bed built is a bed filled") and expensive new technologies (CAT scans being the prime concern of the day). For several reasons, including flawed institutional design (too little power in an intensely political arena), the planning program did not work very well and was repealed in the early 1980s. The planning program provided grist for students of health policy making at the local level (Marmor and Morone 1980), but its major legacy for the health-care system concerned its unintended consequences. By creating a barrier for major capital spending by hospitals (compliance with the planning program was a condition for maintaining hospitals' eligibility for the Medicare program), the program opened the way for numerous entrepreneurs who created a wide variety of ambulatory care centers that provided high-tech services.

The Professional Standards Review Organization (PSRO) program created new entities to review the medical necessity of hospital admissions and continued stays for determining whether Medicare payments would be made. Although PSROs were organizations of physicians, the program nevertheless involved an extraordinary change in the autonomy of individual physicians. An important byproduct of the program was the drawing of attention to regional differences in medical practice (e.g., hospital stays averaged two days longer on the East Coast than on the West Coast). This in turn led to the idea that standards of appropriate utilization of medical services might be developed and implemented independent of the judgment of the patient's physician. Although the program was ultimately viewed as a failure because of controversial but politically potent evidence that it cost more money than it saved, new inroads to limit physicians' prerogatives had been established and provided a key step in the development of utilization management and managed care.

The HMO program, the third of the major cost-containment programs of the 1970s, provided financial support for the development of HMOs (a then-nascent form of medical care organization), set standards of social responsibility (e.g., requirements for "community rating" of premiums), and helped create a market for HMO services by requiring large employers to offer available HMOs as an option in health-benefit programs. Although the most rapid growth of managed care actually took place after federal HMO funding was ended in the early 1980s, the program provided vitally important legitimacy and support for HMOs at a crucial time and helped create the market for managed care. The rise of managed care in its various forms led in turn to increased demand for evidence-based tools to define the appropriate use of medical services, thereby stimulating the field of outcomes research and the development of practice guidelines, both staples of medical care in the 1990s.

Although seven years again separated the publication of new editions of the *Handbook,* there is a much greater difference in subject matter and tone between the second (1972) and third (1979) editions than between the first two editions. In the third edition, the impact of health policy issues became explicit for the first time in the *Handbook*'s contents. Not only were topics covered in earlier editions reworked and updated, but three new chapters reflecting new policy issues were added. These chapters dealt respectively with the relationship of community variables to health, the relationship between technology and medical care, and the abuse of psychoactive substances. (The chapter on health politics had a different nonsociologist author, the historian Daniel Fox.) For the first time, the book's concluding bibliography included a lengthy section on "health policy and politics." Clearly, a new emphasis had developed in the field. Even so, the strategies in and implications of the battle over cost containment in the Medicare program received little attention.

HEALTH POLICY IN THE 1980S AND THE FOURTH EDITION

Health policy in the United States took a new direction soon after the publication of the third edition with the election in 1980 of Ronald Reagan and a conservative Congress. President Reagan came to office with a broad agenda of cutting federal programs, eliminating "unnecessary" regulation, transferring responsibilities to the states, and unleashing the power of the private sector. This agenda manifested itself in budget cuts of categorical health programs (Dallek 1993), reductions in research funding in the social sciences, and the slowing or ending of various regulatory programs.

An ideology that extolled competition rather than regulation as the "solution" to health-care problems came to the fore. Not only was this ideology powerful enough to sweep aside the regulatory cost-containment programs of the 1970s, it even provided cover for a new and comparatively effective Medicare cost-containment strategy—the replacement of the cost-based reimbursement methods of hospital payment with per-case payment methods based on prospectively set, diagnosis-specific rates. (The new approach was commonly called the *prospective payment system,* though only the rates, not the payments, were set prospectively.) Being paid per case rather than per unit of service created cost-containment incentives for hospitals that did not exist under cost-based reimbursement. Moreover, hospitals were allowed to keep any profits generated by achieving shorter stays and providing fewer services.

Although governmental rate-setting for hospital services might have been expected to be anathema to a conservative political regime that was opposed to government regulation, the new system's emphasis on creating economic incentives that rewarded "efficiency" had considerable political appeal. Besides, every other cost-containment method had failed. A new program—with the acronym PRO (for peer review organization)—was created to focus on potential abuses that the new incentives created, particularly unnecessary admissions and premature discharges ("quicker and sicker"). This new program replaced the PSRO program. Because patients' physicians, who actually made the care decisions that affected hospitals' costs, continued to be paid fee for service, there was much speculation that hospitals would be unable to make the changes in patient care needed to control their costs and succeed under the new system. However, average lengths of stay fell rapidly (a trend that actually began before the prospective payment system), and Medicare became a very profitable payer for most hospitals in the mid-1980s.

The changes in patterns of patient care that followed Medicare's switch from cost-based reimbursement for hospitals were but one of a growing body of indications that physicians were strongly influenced not only by patients' needs and preferences but also by economic incentives. A growing body of health services research in the 1970s and 1980s provided evidence of great geographic variations in patterns of care, large amounts of unnecessary and inappropriate care, and physician responsiveness to economic incentives (see Chapter 10 of Gray 1991 for a summary).

Outside the hospital context, the fee-for-service system—in which highly autonomous physicians or other providers of ambulatory services received payments for billed charges from third-party payers for whatever services physicians provided or ordered—attracted entrepreneurs from both within and outside the profession. The number and variety of services that could be provided to patients outside the inpatient setting grew rapidly in the past two decades. The system became increasingly unsatisfactory to governmental and corporate purchasers in the 1980s because of rapidly increasing costs. The eventual bankruptcy of the Medicare program began to be predicted; the costs of the Medicaid program became a major budgetary problem in state after state; and corporate employers complained that the costs of their health-benefits program for employees and retirees (and their families) were out of control and threatening their ability to compete in an increasingly global economy.

Public and private purchasers grew increasingly certain in the 1980s that their health-care cost problems were caused in substantial part by their own policies in the purchase of services. The resulting initiatives continue to shake the system at the century's end. Private employers began to drop or narrow coverage of their health-benefit programs, and the numbers of the uninsured grew accordingly. Both private and public purchasers turned increasingly to rate-setting and managed care. The use of competitive strategies was facilitated by the excessive supply of hospital beds and physicians.

In Medicare and Medicaid in the 1980s, the involvement with managed care took the form of HMO experiments and demonstration programs, and concurrent and retrospective utilization review programs in Medicare, with payment denials used when services were deemed to have been unnecessary or inappropriate. Employers tried all forms of managed care. HMO enrollment grew rapidly in the mid-1980s. (The federal government, incidentally, had stopped providing seed money for HMOs and had begun an active campaign of encouraging private investment in HMOs; by the mid-1980s, most HMOs were for-profit.) Indemnity insurance was transformed by the addition of utilization management programs involving prior authorization of hospital admissions, case management of high-cost cases, and profile analyses of patterns of care (Gray and Field 1989). The era of unchallenged physician autonomy had ended, and complaints were increasingly heard that purchasers were now running the system.

These and other developments of the 1980s changed the orientation of medical sociology toward health policy. Cuts in social programs coupled with a sluggish economy pushed the level of poverty up, along with the number of uninsured Americans. Access to care became an important policy issue, with important expansions to Medicaid passed in the late 1980s. A federal insurance program for catastrophic health care costs was passed and then repealed. Access and its measurement, already an important topic of sociological research (Aday, Anderson, and Fleming 1980), became a core concern of health policy.

The research environment itself was changed by Reagan administration policies. By the 1980s, the ideas developed by medical sociologists had slowly worked their way into the curriculum of medical schools and the research agendas of NIH and other government research institutes. But in the early Reagan years, the social sciences came under broad attack by conservatives, who attributed costly and failed social programs to their influence. The Reagan administration attempted to eliminate social research at the National Science Foundation and substantially reduced funding for broad social and theoretical studies at NIMH. Just as funding the development of medical sociology had been influenced by expanding federal funding in an earlier era, the field now began to be influenced by decreasing spending on social research and training. As funding for medical sociology training programs disappeared, so did the number of medical sociologists on sociology department faculties.

The shifting federal policies toward both the poor and social science research had a dual impact on strengthening the link between medical sociology and policy studies. First, cutbacks for theoretical social research led some researchers to increase their attention to the policy implications of their work in their grant applications, since the policy world had its own grant-making structure. Second, perhaps because of the growing numbers of uninsured and the growing body of research on the problem, sociologists increasingly wrote on public policy issues, including such topics as unintended consequences of social policies and the challenge of balancing access and cost containment.

Medical sociologists increasingly examined the relevance of their work to policy formulation and change. In their introduction to the fourth edition of the *Handbook* in 1989, Freeman and Levine (1989: 6) stated that "the effort to improve health care for the poor and the otherwise disfranchised is one of the impetuses for medical sociologists to move into policy research, policy development, macro-planning, and managerial activities." In a departure from previous editions of the *Handbook,* the editors of the fourth edition asked contributors to emphasize health-policy issues in the subject matter of their chapters. New policy-relevant chapters were added on quality of life, ethical issues, and social control.

HEALTH POLICY SINCE THE FOURTH EDITION

Health policy has become a topic of high public attention in the years since the publication of the fourth edition. The degree of public interest in health policy was foreshadowed by the passage and rapid repeal of catastrophic health insurance in 1988 and 1989 and by the creation of the Agency for Health Care Policy and Research in 1989 (Gray 1992). The early part of the period featured a presidential election in which, for the first time in memory, health policy was discussed seriously by the candidates, and then the public agenda was captured by the Clinton administration's unsuccessful attempt at legislation to assure universal health insurance and comprehensive reform of the health-care system. Sociologists were very much involved in the process. In particular, Paul Starr moved from intellectual historian to policy analyst to policy designer and helped provide the intellectual underpinnings of the Clinton proposal for an approach to foster competition within a budget plan (Starr 1994). At least seven other sociologists served along with Starr on the large task force that put the President's Health Reform Act together (Gray and Phillips 1995: 180). Later, sociologists were prominent in tracing the trajectory of the Clinton Health Plan and putting it into a historical context (Starr 1995; Skocpol 1996).

In the wake of the failure of comprehensive health reform, much of the health-policy action has been devolved to the states and to the activities of private employers. The continuation of, and responses to, some trends of the 1980s have also characterized the period, but the organizational structure of the health-care delivery system has arguably undergone a greater change than ever before.

The numbers of the uninsured continued to grow (42 million people or about 16 percent of the population were without insurance at some point during the year in 1996), and welfare reform introduced time limits on eligibility for welfare. Because federal legislation of the late 1980s had made children's eligibility for Medicare a matter of income level rather than being linked to coverage under Aid to Families with Dependent Children, the impact of welfare reform on Medicaid coverage for children was less than it would otherwise have been, but the "de-linking" of Medicaid and welfare led to growing levels of uninsured among children who were actually eligible for Medicaid. The problem of the uninsured was also addressed in some other federal government reforms in the 1990s involving insurance "portability" and coverage of children, and some states addressed the problem through new programs and charity-care pools. Although it has become clear that the problem of the uninsured and underinsured cannot be fully addressed without comprehensive reform, the 1990s remained a period of incremental change regarding governmental policy.

Managed care continued to grow, in a proliferating array of forms—not only HMOs, but also "point of service" plans, preferred provider arrangements, so-called managed fee for service, and, most recently, provider-sponsored plans. Managed care became standard in employer health-benefit plans; virtually all states adopted Medicaid managed care; and managed care options and enrollment substantially increased in Medicare. Total enrollment in HMOs and preferred provider organizations (PPOs) grew from about 75 million in 1990 to 165 million in 1996, according to the trade association, the American Association of Health Plans. The operation and effects of managed-care plans became the dominant health policy topic of the 1990s. Although numerous aspects of managed care attracted attention, four stand out.

First, managed care plans achieved sufficient scale and power to actually, if only temporarily, slow or, in some cases, halt the double-digit annual health-cost increases that had come to be seen as the norm. The share of the national wealth that went to health care actually stopped its inexorable increase in the mid-1990s. The economic pressures that managed care organizations could bring to bear on provider organizations, it was frequently noted, would make it difficult for them to continue to cross-subsidize public goods (e.g., care of the uninsured) using revenues generated from insured patients. Academic health centers, with their multiple missions of care, research, and education, saw threats in the competitive environment because of their high costs. It became increasingly clear that direct ways of funding public goods would eventually have to be found.

Second, the growing economic power of managed care organizations, when added to the cost-containment efforts of Medicare and Medicaid, led to rapid changes among providers of health services. The dominant trend was aggregation. Hospitals were characterized by growing numbers of mergers and multi-institutional arrangements, networks, and affiliations. Physicians too found ways to aggregate their strength in a variety of arrangements—group practices, physician-hospital organizations, practice-management organizations, and even unions. Rapid change became characteristic of an industry that had once seemed impervious to change.

Third, the managed-care industry, working with large purchasers through the National Committee on Quality Assurance (NCQA), adopted unprecedented new forms of accountability. HEDIS—the Health Plan Employer Data and Information Set—was adopted and provided a standardized set of dimensions, which have subsequently undergone regular revision and augmentation, on which to measure the performance of health plans. NCQA also developed and implemented an accreditation system for HMOs and released information on plans' performance on the various dimensions of accreditation. Although many important aspects of the performance of health plans remain beyond the reach of measurement tools, HEDIS and NCQA accreditation were important steps in increasing the public accountability of health plans.

Fourth, managed care experienced an enormous public backlash, which centered on: (a) restrictions on patients' choice of providers, (b) limitations on what services would be covered, and (c) the kinds of incentives that health plans used with physicians. Feeding all of these concerns was the perception that the HMO industry was being driven by economic goals that had little to do with providing good medical care. This perception strengthened as the industry came to be increasingly dominated by for-profit organizations, and tales of denials of services to enrollees came to be juxtaposed in the media with accounts of senior HMO executives receiving incomes and stock options worth tens of millions of dollars. By the late 1990s reforming managed care became an attractive issue for politicians. Trust was a theme that attracted medical sociologists (Mechanic and Schlesinger 1996; Gray 1997).

THE POLICY EVOLUTION OF MEDICAL SOCIOLOGY

This brief history of medical sociology has covered a period of enormous change in the American health-care system. At the time the original edition of the *Handbook* was under preparation, health care accounted for about 5 percent of national spending, and the federal government's role was minimal. Federal spending accounted for 11 percent of national health expenditures in 1960, less than was spent by state and local governments (13.9 percent); private spending accounted for the other 75 percent. Now, health care accounts for 14 percent of the gross domestic product (50 percent more than any other industrialized country), with federal spending accounting for one-third of the total. (State and local spending accounted for 13 percent, with private spending accounting for just over half.)

With the heavy influence of government on medical care, and with disease prevention having become a more significant concern, health policy has gone from a virtually invisible topic in medical sociology in the early 1960s, not mentioned at all in the original *Handbook* of 1963, to an important theme in medical sociology at the millennium. This seems most appropriate, since the near tripling of medical care as a share of national wealth, although influenced by an older population with more chronic conditions, is substantially attributable to changes in the societal response to disease. The change has been partly technological (organ transplantation, dialysis, artificial joints, proliferating diagnostic testing, genetically engineered drugs), partly attitudinal (symptoms should be addressed, not lived with), and partly a matter of the organization and financing of medical care (particularly third-party payment systems based on providers' reported costs or on billed charges). All of these factors have existed in a complicated interaction with public policy.

In tracing the relationship of medical sociology and health policy through the lens of succeeding editions of the *Handbook,* we have seen great change. At the outset, health policy was essentially taken for granted by all but the historically oriented sociologists, those who made cross-national comparisons of health-care systems, and those who studied health politics. By the 1980s, discussions of policy implications of research had become common in medical sociology, and contributors to the *Handbook* were asked to address the policy implications of their respective topics. Now, in this the fifth edition, health policy is not only dealt with in numerous chapters but has also become a separate chapter. Other signs of the growing sociological interest in and contribution to health policy have also been seen along the way (for example, Aiken and Mechanic 1986; *Journal of Health and Social Behavior* Extra Issue 1995).

How does medical sociology relate to health policy today? With health care accounting for one out of seven dollars in the American economy, health care is of interest to any discipline that has societal concerns. Robert Straus's (1957) distinction of forty years ago between sociology *in* and sociology *of* medicine has a new analogue in the relationship of medical sociology and health policy. We characterize the distinction in terms of *policy-relevant* and *policy-oriented* medical sociology.

POLICY-RELEVANT MEDICAL SOCIOLOGY

In much of today's research in medical sociology, at least one variable is of potential policy significance.

Such *policy-relevant* research, though not necessarily designed to do so, can shed light on matters that could influence or be addressed by imaginable policy options. For example, a typical issue of the *Journal of Health and Social Behavior* in the late 1990s (Vol. 38, December 1997) contains articles on racial differences in heart-disease mortality, influences on sexual behavior of adolescents, determinants of mental health of young married people, sources of social support for care givers of people with AIDS, and determinants of physician's choice of a specialty. Relevance to policy concerns is quite apparent. Managed care and medical professionalism have even reached the pages of the *American Sociological Review* (Boyd 1998).

As official publications of the American Sociological Association, the *Journal of Health and Social Behavior* and *American Sociological Review* publish mainstream medical sociology that is addressed to the important themes and concerns of the field. The fact that these concerns also pertain to health policy is largely incidental, a reflection of the breadth of matters that are potentially relevant to health policy. The policy-relevant work of discipline-oriented medical sociologists may actually enter into the policy process if it bears directly on an issue of policy importance, as did some ethnographic work during the early years of the AIDS epidemic, or when sociologists achieve a degree of prominence that reaches far beyond the field, as with David Mechanic, Eliot Freidson, Paul Starr, Linda Aiken, Stephen Shortell, Carroll Estes, or Ronald Kessler, or when sociologists publish in outlets that are not read primarily by disciplining specialists and in sources covered by online electronic health-related data bases such as MEDLINE and HEALTHStar.

POLICY-ORIENTED MEDICAL SOCIOLOGY

In contrast to policy-relevant medical sociology, *policy-oriented* research is driven by questions that arise from the policy environment itself and may be conducted by researchers from a variety of disciplines—most notably economics, medicine, and public health, as well as sociology. Policy-oriented research is focused on assessing the effects of existing policy, predicting the potential effects of policy alternatives, or putting policy actions or alternatives into a broader analytic context. The audience for policy-oriented research is not only (or not necessarily even primarily) policy makers. As with research in any field, the main audience for most policy-oriented research is other policy-oriented researchers, some of whom work for policy-making agencies.

POLICY-RESEARCH AS A FIELD

Although sociologists may conduct both policy-relevant and policy-oriented research, health policy as a *field* can be distinguished from medical sociology. This field, which is in part an outgrowth of the increased federal role in the financing of health services, has its own funding sources (including the Agency for Health Care Policy and Research and other government agencies, along with several foundations), journals, and professional associations (Gray and Phillips 1995: 176–77). The field of health policy research is interdisciplinary, and medical sociologists who are oriented to it tend to be members of policy-oriented professional associations, such as the Association for Health Services Research (AHSR). For the most part, this membership is *instead of* rather than *in addition to* membership in the American Sociological Association's Section on Medical Sociology. In 1994, fewer than 50 of the 1,160 members of the ASA's Section were members of the Association for Health Services Research (Gray and Phillips 1995). The most recent data (1998) from the Association for Health Services Research shows that 149 of its 2,850 members identify themselves as sociologists, suggesting many of the sociologists working in this field are more apt to professionally align themselves with health-service research (a field that has become so imbued with policy as to be indistinguishable from health-policy research) than with their own home discipline.

Health policy provides a career alternative for sociologists. Because their orientation is toward policy questions rather than disciplinary questions, policy-oriented sociologists tend not to hold positions in sociology departments (although they may have appointments in schools of public health or public policy). They may be employed in a broad array of nonacademic settings—particularly governmental agencies, research organizations, and trade and professional associations. Their professional association membership preferences suggest they gravitate more toward presenting their work at health-policy conferences rather than the annual meetings of the American Sociological Association. They also tend to publish in reports issued by their organizations or in interdisciplinary journals such as *Health Affairs, The Milbank Quarterly, Health Services Research,* or *Inquiry.* Thus, while researchers trained as medical sociologists are making active contributions to the dialogue on health policy, the discussion itself occurs primarily outside the discipline. On the other hand, medical sociologists working *within* academic sociology departments are generating important work with potential to inform health policy debates, although much of this potential is not fully realized due to its form and channels of publication.

CONCLUSION

Health policy has moved from a matter of little notice to medical sociologists to a field in which sociological work is often pertinent. But as health policy has become a distinctive area of research activity, the work of many medical sociologists has become oriented more to policy concerns than disciplinary concerns. We believe that the fact that medical sociologists can pursue research careers oriented primarily either to sociological or to policy concerns is a sign of health of the discipline. But we also believe that the choice of doing policy-relevant research or policy-oriented research involves substantially different career paths—the one in academic sociology and the other in a wide variety of research contexts.

Although a few sociologists have been able to contribute to both policy-oriented and sociological publishing channels, orienting one's work to policy concerns is a risky endeavor for discipline-oriented scholars who are not already established. The alternative of policy-oriented research careers has grown in the past two decades as government and foundations have supported research into policy-relevant problems and programs. Although this has produced a continual source of research support during a period of reduced federal expenditures on basic social science, it means that much research is driven by practical concerns rather than theory—an approach that had contributed to a view within the discipline that medical sociology is the prototype of "theoryless empiricism" (Gouldner 1970). Or as Donald Light (1992) more generously framed the issue, an analysis that is sociologically useless can be "worth its weight in policy gold."

During the first two decades during which the *Handbook* was being published, American medical sociologists could focus their policy pronouncements on criticisms of strictly biomedical explanations of the origins of disease and draw attention to the social determinants of health. The development of the field of health-policy research has created an alternative set of research questions, funding sources, and potential audiences for sociologists who choose to focus on policy. Medical sociologists who decide to participate actively in policy debates must devote a considerable amount of time and energy to policy issues if they are to be treated as credible in that arena. But, without question, the sociologist's knowledge and skills have application to the great and small policy problems that exist in the expensive and inequitable American health-care system.

REFERENCES

ADAY, LUANN, RONALD ANDERSON, and GRETCHEN V. FLEMING. 1980. *Health Care in the U.S.: Equitable for Whom?* Beverly Hills: Sage.

AIKEN, LINDA, and DAVID MECHANIC, eds. 1986. *Applications of Social Science to Clinical Medicine and Health Policy.* New Brunswick, NJ: Rutgers University Press.

ASSOCIATION FOR HEALTH SERVICES RESEARCH. 1998. Personal communication.

BECKER, HOWARD, BLANCHE GEER, EVERETT HUGHES, and ANSELM STRAUSS. 1961. *Boys in White: Student Culture in Medical School.* Chicago: University of Chicago Press.

BLOOM, SAMUEL. 1986. "Institutional Trends in Medical Sociology." *Journal of Health and Human Behavior* 27(September): 265–76.

BOYD, ELIZABETH. 1998. "Bureaucratic Authority in the 'Company of Equals': The Interactional Management of Medical Peer Review." *American Sociological Review* 63 (April): 200–24.

BROWN, LAWRENCE. 1983. *Politics and Health Care Organizations: HMOs as Federal Policy.* Washington, D.C.: Brookings Institution.

DALLEK, GERALDINE. 1993. "Frozen in Ice: Federal Health Policy During the Reagan Years." In *Beyond Crisis: Confronting Health Care in the United States,* ed. Nancy McKenzie. New York: Meridian, pp. 154–66.

DAVIS, KAREN, and CATHY SCHOEN. 1978. *Health and the War on Poverty.* Washington: Brookings Institution.

FREEMAN, HOWARD, and SOL LEVINE. 1989. "The Present Status of Medical Sociology." In *Handbook of Medical Sociology,* ed. Howard Freeman and Sol Levine. Englewood Cliffs, NJ: Prentice Hall, pp. 1–13.

FREEMAN, HOWARD E., and SOL LEVINE, eds. 1989. *Handbook of Medical Sociology.* 4th ed. Englewood Cliffs, NJ: Prentice Hall.

FREEMAN, HOWARD, EDGAR BORGATTA, and NATHANIEL SIEGAL. 1975. "Remarks on the Changing Relationship Between Government Support and Graduate Training." In *Social Policy and Sociology,* ed. N.J. Demerath, K. F. Schuessler, and O. Larsen. New York: Academic Press, pp. 297–305.

FREEMAN, HOWARD E., SOL LEVINE, and LEO G. REEDER, eds. 1963. *Handbook of Medical Sociology.* Englewood Cliffs, NJ: Prentice Hall.

FREEMAN, HOWARD E., SOL LEVINE, and LEO G. REEDER, eds. 1972. *Handbook of Medical Sociology.* 2nd ed. Englewood Cliffs, NJ: Prentice Hall.

FREEMAN, HOWARD E., SOL LEVINE, and LEO G. REEDER, eds. 1979. *Handbook of Medical Sociology.* 3rd ed. Englewood Cliffs, NJ: Prentice Hall.

FREIDSON, ELIOT. 1963. "The Organization of Medical Practice." In *Handbook of Medical Sociology,* ed. Howard Freeman, Sol Levine, and Leo Reeder. Englewood Cliffs: Prentice Hall, pp. 299–319.

FREIDSON, ELIOT. 1970. *The Profession of Medicine.* New York: Dodd, Mead.

FREIDSON, ELIOT. 1972. "The Organization of Medical Practice." In *Handbook of Medical Sociology.* 2nd ed., ed. Howard Freeman, Sol Levine, and Leo Reeder. Englewood Cliffs: Prentice Hall, pp. 343–58.

GINZBERG, ELI. 1977. *The Limits of Health Reform: The Search for Realism.* New York: Basic Books.

GOFFMAN, ERVING. 1961. *Asylums.* New York: Doubleday & Co.

GOULDNER, ALVIN. 1970. *The Coming Crisis of Western Sociology.* New York: Basic Books, Inc.

GRAHAM, SAXON. 1963. "Social Factors in Chronic Illnesses." In *Handbook of Medical Sociology,* ed. Howard Freeman, Sol Levine, and Leo Reeder. Englewood Cliffs: Prentice Hall, pp. 65–98.

GRAHAM, SAXON, and LEO REEDER. 1972. "Social Factors in Chronic Illnesses," In *Handbook of Medical Sociology,* ed. Howard Freeman, Sol Levine, and Leo Reeder. Englewood Cliffs: Prentice Hall, pp. 63-107.

GRAY, BRADFORD H. 1991. *The Profit Motive and Patient Care: The Changing Accountability of Doctors and Hospitals.* Cambridge: Harvard University Press.

GRAY, BRADFORD H. 1992. "The Legislative Battle Over Health Services Research." *Health Affairs* 11:4 (Winter): 38–66.

GRAY, BRADFORD H. 1997. "Trust and Trustworthy Care in the Managed Care Era." *Health Affairs* 16:1 (January/February): 34–49.

GRAY, BRADFORD H., and MARILYN J. FIELD, eds. 1989. *Controlling Costs and Changing Patient Care? The Role of Utilization Management.* A Report of the Institute of Medicine. Washington, D.C.: National Academy Press.

GRAY, BRADFORD H., and SARAH R. PHILLIPS. 1995. "Medical Sociology and Health Policy: Where Are the Connections?" *Journal of Health and Social Behavior* (Extra Issue): 170–81.

HOLLINGSHEAD, AUGUST, and FREDRICK REDLICH. 1958. *Social Class and Mental Illness.* New York: Wiley.

Journal of Health and Social Behavior. 1995. Extra Issue: Forty Years of Medical Sociology: The State of the Art and Directions for the Future.

KENDALL, PATRICIA, and GEORGE READER. 1972. "The Contribution of Sociology to Medicine." In *Handbook of Medical Sociology,* 2nd ed., ed. Howard Freeman, Sol Levine, and Leo Reeder. Englewood Cliffs: Prentice Hall, pp. 1–22.

KNOWLES, JOHN. 1972. "Introduction to the Second Edition." In *Handbook of Medical Sociology.* 2nd ed., ed. Howard Freeman, Sol Levine, and Leo Reeder. Englewood Cliffs: Prentice Hall, pp. xvii–xxi.

KRONENFELD, JENNIE, and MARCIA WHICKER. 1984. *U.S. National Health Policy: An Analysis of the Federal Role.* New York: Praeger.

LEAVELL, HUGH. 1963. "Introduction." In *Handbook of Medical Sociology,* ed. Howard Freeman, Sol Levine, and Leo Reeder. Englewood Cliffs: Prentice Hall, pp. xiii–xv.

LEVINE, SOL. 1995. "Time for Creative Integration in Medical Sociology." *Journal of Health and Social Behavior* (Extra Issue): 1–4.

LIGHT, DONALD. 1992. "Introduction: Strengthening Ties Between Specialties and the Discipline." *American Journal of Sociology* 97(4): 909–18.

MARMOR, THEODORE R., and JAMES A. MORONE. 1980. "Representing Consumer Interests: Imbalanced Markets, Health Planning, and the HSAs." *Milbank Memorial Fund Quarterly-Health & Society* 58(1): 125–65.

MECHANIC, DAVID, and MARK SCHLESINGER. 1996. "The Impact of Managed Care on Patients' Trust in Medical Care and Their Physicians." *Journal of the American Medical Association* 275 (21): 1693–97.

MERTON, ROBERT, GEORGE READER, and PATRICIA KENDALL, eds. 1957. *The Student-Physician.* Cambridge, MA.: Harvard University Press.

PARSONS, TALCOTT. 1951. *The Social System.* Glencoe, IL: Free Press.

RICE, DOROTHY, and BARBARA COOPER. 1968. "National Health Expenditures, 1950–66." *Social Security Bulletin,* U.S. Department of Health, Education and Welfare (April): 6.

SKOCPOL, THEDA. 1996. *Boomerang.* New York: W.W. Norton.

STARR, PAUL. 1982. *The Social Transformation of American Medicine.* New York: Basic Books.

STARR, PAUL. 1994. *The Logic of Health Care Reform: Why and How the President's Plan Will Work.* New York: Whittle Books.

STARR, PAUL. 1995. "What Happened to Health Care Reform?" *The American Prospect* (Winter):20.

STRAUS, ROBERT. 1950. *Medical Care for Seamen: The Origin of Public Medical Service in the United States.* New Haven: Yale University Press.

STRAUS, ROBERT. 1957. "The Nature and Status of Medical Sociology." *American Sociological Review* 22: 200–204.

STRICKLAND, STEPHEN. 1972. *Politics, Science, and Dread Disease.* Cambridge: Harvard University Press.

SWANSON, BERT. 1972. "The Politics of Health." In *Handbook of Medical Sociology,* 2nd ed., ed. Howard Freeman, Sol Levine, and Leo Reeder. Englewood Cliffs: Prentice Hall, pp. 447–60.

WALLACE, HELEN, EDWIN GOLD, and ALLAN OGLESBY. 1982. *Maternal and Child Health Practices: Problems, Resources and Methods of Delivery,* 2nd ed. New York: John Wiley and Sons.

18 CHANGING PATIENT–PHYSICIAN RELATIONSHIPS IN THE CHANGING HEALTH–POLICY ENVIRONMENT

HOWARD WAITZKIN, *University of New Mexico*

As managed care proliferates in the United States and other countries, it transforms the nature of the patient–physician relationship in very fundamental ways. This transformation has occurred rapidly, with little preparation by either clinicians or patients. In any assessment of managed care's impact, the effects on patient–physician relationships deserve attention. The debate so far has raised many potential problems, few of which have received serious enough analysis to exert an impact on health-care policy, either within or outside the managed-care industry.

The impact of managed care illustrates a more general principle: Changes in the health-policy environment pattern changes experience in patient–physician relationships. Important constraints emerge from the economic structure of the health–policy environment. Such constraints currently include the financial and contractual arrangements that physicians and patients make with managed care organizations (MCOs).

Although problems in patient–physician relationships of course antedated the recent growth of managed care, the characteristics of managed care both exacerbate old problems and create new ones. There is no reason to idealize with nostalgia the patient–physician relationships of the past. Managed care, however, is leading to rapid changes in these relationships that are raising wide concern. Also, while the characteristics of MCOs differ (for instance, see the categories that Wholey and Burns set forth in Chapter 15 of this book), structural features of managed care introduce strains in patient–physician relationships that cut across different types of MCOs. The connections between these structural features of managed care and the changes that are occurring in patient–physician relationships will be a central focus of this chapter.

One other cautionary point at the start: By exploring some of the structural problems of managed care that constrain the patient–physician relationship, I am not implying that increased organization of medical practice is necessarily undesirable. Patients' relationships with physicians comprise only one of many relationships with health-care providers in professional, paraprofessional, and nonprofessional roles. Improved coordination of physician and nonphysician providers compromises a worthy goal in new health policies. Some MCOs have, in fact, achieved improvements in the coordination of physician and nonphysician providers. On the other hand, the perverse incentives that I discuss later have affected MCOs' motivations to take advantage of the opportunities offered by new forms of organization in health care.

To point ahead, I address these connections by developing a series of themes, with examples of how managed care is affecting patient–physician relationships. First, I argue that managed care has created a structural conflict involving two relatively new roles, both adopted by primary care physicians who work for MCOs: the role of gatekeeper and the role of double agent. Then I present two clinical case summaries of actual patient–physician interactions that illustrate how this role conflict plays itself out in practice. Subsequently, I focus on the emerging financial and organizational issues that constrain patient–physician communication in the managed-care setting. This analysis leads to an attempt to clarify barriers to information sharing and motivations that support information withholding in managed care, including the issue of lawsuits and the observation of variation in MCO policies concerning these problems. After considering how difficulties in the social context of primary care arise in primary care encounters, I conclude the chapter with some suggestions for medico-political struggle that will address the problems raised here.

GATEKEEPER VERSUS DOUBLE AGENT

Advocates of managed care often claim that this method of organizing services can and should actually improve the patient–physician relationship. For instance, since MCOs generally assign patients to a single primary care physician, that person presumably can provide continuity and can help improve the coordination of services. The primary care provider can communicate about preventive services and encourage their utilization. Since managed-care services are mostly paid in advance through monthly capitation payments, the predictability of copayments required for each outpatient visit may also reduce financial barriers to access for some patients.

To my knowledge, however, not a single research project has conclusively demonstrated improved patient–physician communication processes or patient satisfaction in managed-care systems. The limited studies comparing communication and satisfaction in managed-care versus fee-for-service sectors have found either no difference or observations disfavoring managed care (Davies et al. 1986; Consumer Reports 1992; Rubin 1993). The adverse impact of managed care on communication processes and the patient–physician relationship has also received attention in several influential editorials and position papers (Angell 1993; Emanuel 1995; Balint and Shelton 1996). Further, the claimed advantages of managed care in the arenas of communication and interpersonal relationships have not been assessed in detail for growing subgroups of enrollees, including minorities, the poor, non-English speakers, the elderly, and the chronically ill.

Meanwhile, managed care refers to primary care practitioners as "gatekeepers." That is, such physicians tend the gate, keeping it closed for expensive procedures or referrals to specialists or emergency visits, and open the gate only when it is absolutely necessary for preservation of life or limb. The reason for tending the gate carefully is very clear: That is how physicians and their bosses keep enough of patients' capitation payments to break even or maybe come out a little ahead.

Double agent, as Marcia Angell (1993) and others have pointed out, has probably become a more cogent way to think about the physicians' role as gatekeeper under managed care. In essence, while continuing to pose as advocates for patients, physicians in actuality work as double agents for both patients and MCOs. The latter organizations hold interests that structurally are often diametrically opposed to patients'.

Perhaps "continuing to pose" as patient advocates does not convey the conflict adequately. Recently I spent nearly a day advocating for a single patient, a 58-year-old psychologist with a displaced fracture of her elbow, to various Health Net bureaucrats in order to convince them that she really did need an orthopedic appointment today rather than in three weeks, and also really needed surgery in three days rather than possibly in the indefinite future. Many clinician colleagues are burning out at the energy such maneuvering takes, with little apparent benefit for either patients or the physician gatekeepers. At the very least, doctors find that such activities lead to rationing of services by inconvenience (Grumet 1989). That is, when obtaining services for patients entails such inconvenience, an incentive arises not to pursue the matter vigorously, thus decreasing the probability that the patient will receive the services, even though needed.

More often, clinicians feel an inherent conflict—either ethical or financial or both—between patients' interests and those of the managed-care systems that physicians represent as gatekeepers. This is the essence of physicians' work as double agents. Clinicians experience this conflict even when they supposedly benefit financially by keeping the gate closed.

ILLUSTRATIVE CASE SUMMARIES

These structural constraints of course also affect patients' experience of medicine in general and managed care in particular. The following encounters illustrate some generic issues that increasingly manifest themselves as managed care proliferates.

> The first patient was a 58-year-old male engineering professor, insured by UC Care, the University of California's new self-insured managed-care program. This patient developed severe substernal chest pain at 1 A.M. one morning during a Thanksgiving holiday weekend. The patient called the on-call primary care internist to approve a visit to an emergency room, as he had been instructed to do when he signed up for the plan. The on-call physician had covered more than thirty patients on the inpatient wards, in the intensive care units, and by phone that day for his colleagues. He was sleeping soundly when the patient called. He also was a little hard of hearing and did not wake up until a half hour after the patient called, when the answering service again tried to reach him. By that time, the patient had left for the emergency room because of continuing pain. The physician then called the emergency room to

approve the visit. As soon as the patient arrived, his electrocardiogram revealed a large myocardial infarction. If the patient had waited for approval, as he was supposed to do, he would have arrived too late for treatment with streptokinase to help lyse the clot in his coronary artery, which was the standard of care for a patient with this type of heart attack.

* * *

The second patient, a 25-year-old, Spanish-speaking woman who worked as a hospital maintenance worker, was insured by Health Net, the health maintenance organization that workers for the University of California can join for the cheapest rate. She presented to the emergency room during her shift at 3 A.M. with a sore throat and a fever of 101 degrees. Because she had not realized that she was supposed to call the on-call physician for permission, the emergency room staff called the physician and woke him up. Groggy and mad at being awakened for this bureaucratic reason, he asked to speak with the patient (fortunately, he could speak Spanish), realized the problem could wait until the daytime, and did not approve the emergency room visit. The patient complained that it would be difficult to come during the day because of her child-care responsibilities, but she could not persuade the physician to approve the emergency room visit, since he had been instructed not to approve such visits for minor outpatient problems.

In dealing with these cases, the physician experienced several feelings:

- Guilt that he had not heard or responded quickly to the initial phone call from the patient having a heart attack

- Anger that the nature of managed care led to a critical delay in this patient's evaluation and treatment

- Sympathy for the patient whose visit he refused to approve because a later visit would prove inconvenient and because she hadn't understood the rules

- Annoyance that he had to perform mainly a gatekeeper role in both cases, using essentially none of his clinical skills

- Awareness that financial considerations underlay all these decisions: that he and his colleagues would receive a bonus at the end of the year if they could hold down emergency room utilization; that the paltry $7 per month two of his colleagues received to cover all outpatient care for each of these patients would decrease even further if utilization became much higher; and that his own motivation to provide services subtly

decreased with such managed-care patients, since doing more work was not associated with more income. He also thought of Health Net's chief executive officer at the time, Roger Greaves, who reportedly received a salary of almost $3 million, plus bonuses and stock options, in 1994, and who seemed the main beneficiary of physicians' good work as gatekeepers (Coyle 1996).

- Frustration that all these emotions deviated enormously from those he had expected to have in medicine, a career he selected with the assumption that he would mainly have the opportunity to serve those in need and receive an adequate salary for doing so, not linked to patients' ability to pay or insurance coverage.

- Most of all, awareness that his communication with managed-care patients was becoming distorted by the structural nature of these payment arrangements, and that the openness and honesty he valued were becoming ever more tenuous.

Although the above situations were uniquely experienced by the author of this chapter, many clinicians have had similar experiences under managed care. That is why some clinicians have struggled for suitable policies that would not require such conflictual activities.

The two patients in the above case summaries directly confronted the limitations that managed care imposes on individual discretion. In the first case, the patient—though knowledgeable about the rule that emergency room visits must be pre-approved to be paid for by the managed care plan—overrode that constraint through a judgment decision about the urgency of his symptoms. As it later became clear, his sophistication as a scientist and educator contributed to his choice to take action without the gatekeeper's permission—a decision that may have saved his life. The second patient acted from a position of ignorance about the structural constraints of the plan in which she had enrolled and could not present a convincing enough argument to accomplish her own preferences to be seen sooner rather than later. In neither case did the structural constraints imposed by managed care's gatekeeping principle conform with a close and trusting patient–physician encounter in which the patient's preferences could guide the course of care in a predictable way.

FINANCIAL AND ORGANIZATIONAL ISSUES

From the patient's viewpoint, the structure of managed care constrains the very nature of the communicative process. Here, instead of exploring possible options with full participation by patients in decision-making, the patient must make a case strong enough to be accepted by the gatekeeping physician. Financial interests, by which up to 80 percent of physicians' annual income may be at risk if they do not adequately restrict services under managed-care contracts (Kuttner 1998), reinforce the physician's skeptical appraisal. Under these conditions, especially as patients become more aware of these financial relationships, patients' trust of their physicians may seriously erode.

Further, the communicative process increasingly occurs under constraints of time. The on-call physician, unpaid for time spent on the phone in the middle of the night, is not disposed to lengthy and supportive conversation, especially with a patient who is a stranger. For more routine encounters during daylight hours, additional constraints on communication arise, as the productivity expectations of MCOs create standards that require physicians to see greater numbers of patients per unit of time. From the organizational viewpoint, the fixed capitation received per patient exerts pressure to maximize the number of patients seen by each salaried practitioner in each patient-care session. Since MCOs strive to fill physicians' schedules, patients may have to see other practitioners than their own, including physician substitutes like nurse practitioners and physician assistants; such organizations frequently employ mid-level practitioners to handle overflow from physicians' full schedules. Physicians employed by MCOs therefore enjoy little discretion in determining how much time to spend with each patient.

On the other hand, we also want to make clear our position that structural constraints in the patient–physician relationship did not begin with managed care. Under the prior fee-for-service system, communication between patients and physicians suffered from a variety of problems, some tied to the financial underpinnings of that particular form of practice organization (Waitzkin 1984, 1991; Roter and Hall 1992). For instance, encounters between primary care practitioners and patients tended to be hurried, and little time was spent communicating information. Interruptions and dominance gestures by physicians commonly cut off patients' concerns. Further, exploration of issues in the social context of medical encounters, which patients experienced as important components of their lived experience of illness, tended to become marginalized in patient–physician encounters.

The financial structure of fee-for-service medicine created an incentive to maximize patients seen per unit of time and to decrease the time devoted to in-depth exploration of patients' concerns. In contrast to managed care, this productivity constraint usually permitted the practitioners substantial discretion in choosing how much time to spend with a given patient. Patients' dissatisfaction with communication under the fee-for-service system nevertheless continued to rank among their most frequently voiced complaints about U.S. medical practice (Waitzkin 1984). In recent years, even before the advent of managed care, many calls for improvements in physicians' communicative practices came to the surface (Roter and Hall 1992; Lipkin et al. 1995; Smith 1996).

It therefore would be an error to see the fee-for-service structure as necessarily more conducive to favorable communication and relationships than managed care. The financial incentives of fee-for-service medicine created their own adverse effects. Yet the structure of managed care does little to improve those earlier problems and also introduces a new set of constraints that may prove even more contradictory and discouraging for patient–physician relationships.

PREVIOUS BARRIERS TO INFORMATION SHARING

Although organizational and financial conflicts of interest are changing the fabric of patient–physician communication and relationships, several research projects documented many barriers to communication between patients and physicians even before the ascendance of managed care. These barriers derive from differences in social class, education, gender, ethnicity, cultural background, language, and age. In particular, physicians have tended to perform poorly in responding to patients' desire for information about their medical problems, diagnostic testing, treatments, and other aspects of care (Roter and Hall 1992).

Our own research group constructed a random sample of practicing internists in Massachusetts and California and tape-recorded 336 encounters in several clinical settings, including private practice and hospital outpatient departments (Waitzkin 1984, 1985). Regarding information giving and withholding, we asked the physicians to rate each patient's desire for information and the helpfulness of giving the information; patients completed a self-rating based on the same seven-point scale. According to their responses, patients wanted to know almost everything and thought that the information would be helpful, but physicians underestimated the patients' desire for information and, when compared with the patients, underrated the clinical usefulness of information giving. In 65 percent of the encounters, physicians underestimated their patients' desire for information; in 6 percent, they overestimated; and in 29 percent, they estimated correctly.

One way that we looked at the transmittal of information was simply the amount of time devoted to the process. We found that physicians spent very little time giving information to their patients—a mean time of 1 minute and 18 seconds, in encounters lasting a mean time of 16.5 minutes. After the recorded encounters, we asked the physicians how much time they thought they devoted to information giving, and then we compared this perception to the actual time that we measured from the tape recordings. On average, physicians overestimated the time they spent giving information by a factor of nine. Physicians thought that they spent much more time informing their patients than they actually did.

We tried to relate physicians' information giving to other variables that we thought might be important. In this analysis, we looked at the time physicians spent informing patients. We also studied the number of explanations and the level of technicality of the explanations. Considering the clinical process of information transmittal, we thought that an effective type of communication might involve the physician's giving a technical explanation and then translating it into simpler terms. This is what we meant by "multilevel" explanations. "Nondiscrepant" responses were answers at the same level of technicality as patients' questions; we thought that this measure would reflect physicians' tendency to respond at a similar linguistic level, rather than "talking up" or "talking down" to patients. The following paragraphs present some highlights of our multivariate analysis.

First, we assessed the relationships between information transmittal and patients' characteristics. We expected an association between information and patients' gender. Based on feminist critiques of medicine, we thought that physicians might give less information to women patients. The findings were just the reverse. Women received more physician time, more total explanations, and more nondiscrepant responses. This finding may reflect gender differences in language use, as described in the sociolinguistic literature (Tannen 1993; Fisher 1995). Women also tended to ask more questions and generally to engage in more verbal behavior within the encounters we studied.

Patients' education and social class (measured by occupation) also were predictors of physicians' tendency to give them information. College-educated patients tended to receive more information than patients who did not go to college. Patients from upper- or upper-middle-class positions received more physician time, more total explanations, more multilevel explanations, and more nondiscrepant responses than did patients from lower-middle-class or lower-class backgrounds. There was no difference between poorly educated, lower-class patients and better educated, upper-class patients in their desire for information. However, physicians misperceived this desire much more commonly for poorly educated or lower-class patients. This observation confirmed what other researchers already had observed: lower-class patients tend to be diffident; that is, they usually ask fewer questions. Partly as a result, physicians tend to misperceive these patients' desire for information and generally believe that they want or could use less information. This finding is clinically important; lower-class patients want more information than physicians may think, and their diffidence reinforces a structural barrier to communication in patient–physician communication.

In addition to gender and social class, various studies have revealed the importance of ethnicity and language as barriers to information giving (Castillo et al. 1995). Regarding verbal communication, interpreting spoken language poses a challenge in primary care encounters. Lay interpreters who accompany monolingual patients often are family members or friends who lack training in procedures of accurate interpretation. In addition to limited knowledge of medical terminology, lay interpreters may experience cultural inhibition or embarrassment in explaining patients' symptoms or in conveying requests for information. Because of these difficulties, the participation of trained, professional interpreters is highly desirable but frequently is not feasible to obtain in primary care settings (Putsch 1985; Hardt 1991; Haffner 1992; Baker et al. 1996; Hornberger et al. 1996).

Such difficulties in communication may have begun to improve somewhat, partly as patients and physicians gained greater awareness of barriers to information giving. We also believe that the changing gender and ethnic composition of the profession is contributing to these improvements. For instance, female physicians tend to spend more time with patients, both giving information and listening to their patients (Roter and Hall 1991). In addition, female physicians tend to interrupt less and devote more attention to socioemotional aspects of care (Roter and Hall 1991; Hall, 1994). Although not well studied, it is felt that practitioners who themselves derive from ethnic minorities may prove better able to provide information and other components of communication that patients in their communities desire.

INFORMATION WITHHOLDING
IN MANAGED CARE

Beyond such barriers to communication under prior practice arrangements, a new source of information withholding by physicians now pertains to the structure of managed care. This barrier to the sharing of information adds to the other barriers already considered. Physicians participating in managed care rarely if ever explain to patients that physicians' own financial earnings under capitated arrangements improve to the extent that they can limit services such as diagnostic tests, expensive treatments, and specialty consultations. In other words, physicians tend not to reveal the financial conflict of interest inherent in managed care.

Of course, MCOs do not communicate this conflict of interest explicitly to patients whom they seek to enroll. In fact, an increasing source of contention involves "gag rules" that many MCOs require their physician employees to follow. These rules explicitly prohibit physicians under contract from disclosing a range of diagnostic or treatment options to patients when they are different from those approved by the administrators of the organization (Woolhandler 1995; Olmos 1996). The gag rules that restrict physicians in managed care from sharing information that they believe may prove important for patients' health and well-being imposes a basic conflict with physicians' responsibilities under the Hippocratic oath and current ethical norms, which call for prioritization of the patient's welfare over all other concerns (American College of Physicians 1993).

While physicians find themselves in an ethical bind from the imposition of these gag rules, patients are caught in an even more precarious situation. Seen from a patient's viewpoint, contracts that forbid a physician to reveal the full range of treatment options or diagnostic techniques to patients violate patients' rights, particularly the right to informed consent (Brennan 1993; Rodwin 1995). The legal doctrine of informed consent requires that physicians explain to patients the choices available, the risks and benefits of the proposed treatment, and any alternatives (Rodwin 1995). Because a patient's access to this information is restricted as a result of managed-care gag rules, informed consent is not achieved, and subsequently, the patient is put at risk. Most often, patients are unaware that such a gag rule exists, and therefore falsely assume that they are receiving all relevant information to give informed consent for the procedure chosen. Not recognizing physicians' conflict of interest, patients predictably assume that they can trust the physician's advice and recommendations because of the ethical responsibility to act in the patient's best interests. In such a scenario, informed consent may not be obtained because the patient is in essence not given all necessary information to make a consensual decision. In addition, the consent is obtained under false pretenses; the patient believes that the physician has given all necessary information because it is the physician's responsibility to do so.

These constraints lead to a strange and ethically difficult situation in which patients remain naive about the financial motivations that underlie many clinical decisions. In some ways, this naivete becomes reminiscent of the ignorance and lack of information that physicians paternalistically formerly maintained for patients who developed cancer or other fatal illnesses. Physicians in the United States used to assume that revealing a professional inability to cure would prove deleterious to patients' morale, and so patients very often remained in the dark, even when they strongly wanted to know (Waitzkin and Stoeckle 1972). The paternalistic atmosphere has changed in the United States over the last two decades, partly in response to the demands of the consumer movement and parallel struggles for full information within the women's movement and civil rights movement (Novack et al. 1979).

In recognition of the ethical dilemmas that gag rules impose, many consumer rights organizations have advocated their abolition. As a response, the federal government has banned explicit gag rules for MCOs participating in the national Medicare and Medicaid programs. In addition, patients' rights laws in many state legislatures have extended this ban to private managed-care plans. However, even when formal gag clauses are eliminated from physicians' contracts with MCOs, the financial risk that MCOs frequently impose on physicians to limit their services (Kuttner 1998) maintains a more subtle pressure that restricts the communication of diagnostic and therapeutic options. Under these circumstances, although formal gag clauses may appear less frequently in MCOs' contracts with physicians, the financial conditions that encourage less than full communication will continue.

INFORMATION CONTROL, LAWSUITS,
AND VARIATION IN MCO POLICIES

When physicians work as double agents in managed care, one can expect trouble in this litigious society, and trouble is what is going to arise. Some beneficial results probably will come from this trouble, at least for patients and those physicians who vaguely remember why they went into health care in the first place.

For several years now, lawyers who work the malpractice circuit have been turning to managed care because of its lucrative potential for big settlements. The reason is precisely the financial conflict of interest imposed by managed care on practitioners. If physicians make mistakes, or if it can be alleged that they have made mistakes, it is very easy to make the case that they erred because a financial conflict of interest caused them to limit care to the injured patient. A malpractice case in Southern California, for instance, sought damages from an MCO whose practitioners refused to approve a gastroenterology consultation for vague abdominal pain in a 36-year-old woman who later died from metastatic colon cancer (Olmos and Roan 1996). Similar malpractice cases have been initiated against other MCOs for limiting needed services due to financial conflicts of interest.

Nowadays, physicians, or the organizations for which they work, may assume that to reveal the true financial structure of managed care to the patients whose care they manage would lead to major problems in patients' morale, and certainly in their acquiescence to professionals' decisions to limit services. Therefore, physicians tend to withhold that critical piece of information. To maintain the advances of the last twenty years in patients' rights, there remains an ethical obligation to obtain informed consent through full disclosure to patients about physicians' financial and ethical conflicts of interest within the managed-care system. From this perspective, it can be argued that disclosure should be a requirement not only for physicians to their patients, but also for managed-care institutions to their patients.

Recently a public interest law firm in Arizona asked me to consult on a monumental lawsuit based on the conflict of interest that causes physicians and MCOs to withhold the financial components of clinical decisions from patients. In recruiting patients and their employers, this particular company, like most, promised comprehensive, easy-to-obtain services but provided no information about the financial structure of managed care. After several malpractice cases based on the ill effects of decisions to limit services, the law firm initiated a class action suit against the managed-care firm; a successful outcome, of course, could be used as a precedent in suits against other firms.

Some of the physicians working with this firm responded to the suit with an interesting argument, which creates a sense of déjà vu: If physicians told patients that they or their companies make more money when they limit tests and referrals, patients would lose morale and confidence in the patient–physician relationship (Kilgore 1996). Paternalism thus has moved from protecting the patient's ignorance about death and dying, to protecting the patient's ignorance about the financial motivations in restricting services to the living and otherwise healthy.

The structural constraints on communication may vary across different types of MCOs. For instance, such variation might pattern the restrictions on time spent in communication and on openness about the financial underpinnings of managed care. From this perspective, not-for-profit health maintenance organizations, where physicians work as members of a professional partnership (such as Kaiser-Permanente) might exert less pressure on physicians to shape their communication in certain ways than would for-profit HMOs where physicians participate as salaried staff (such as FHP, Aetna, or CIGNA). For-profit HMOs contracting with independent physician groups (such as Foundation or Health Net) might represent intermediate positions on this hierarchy of institutionalized control over information sharing (see Sleeper et al. 1998).

However, we know of no research that as yet has compared communication, or policies about communication, in different types of MCOs. Predictions that organizations with somewhat different financial structures would pattern communication differently remain almost entirely hypothetical at this point. Further knowledge about such variability may come from research but more likely from a spate of litigation that will address gag rules and other restrictions on communication in MCOs.

SOCIAL CONTEXT AND PATIENT–PHYSICIAN COMMUNICATION

One of our research group's interests over the last few years has focused on the question of how patients and physicians deal with social problems in medical encounters (Waitzkin 1991; Waitzkin et al. 1994). The following encounter, which conveys an elderly woman's loss of home, community, and autonomy, illustrates this problem.

An elderly woman visits her physician for follow-up of her heart disease. During the encounter she expresses concerns about decreased vision, her ability to continue driving, lack of stamina and strength, weight loss and diet, and financial problems. She discusses her recent move to a new home and her relationships with family and friends. Her physician assures her that her health is improving; he recommends that she continue her current medical regimen and that she see an ophthalmologist.

From the questionnaires that the patient and physician completed after their interaction, some pertinent information is available: The patient is an 81-year-old white high school graduate. She is Protestant, Scottish-American, and widowed, with five living children whose ages range from 45 to 59 years; she describes her occupation as "homemaker." Her physician is a 44-year-old white male who is a general internist. The physician has known the patient for about one year and believes that her primary diagnoses are atherosclerotic heart disease and prior congestive heart failure. The encounter takes place in a suburban private practice near Boston.

The patient recently has moved from a home that she occupied for 59 years. The reasons for giving up her home remain unclear, but they seem to involve a combination of financial factors and difficulties in maintaining it.

During silent periods in the physical examination of the patient's heart and lungs, the patient spontaneously narrates more details about the loss of possessions and relationships with previous neighbors, along with satisfaction about certain conveniences of her new living situation. Further, as the patient speaks, the physician asks clarifying questions about the move and gives several pleasant fillers, before he cuts off this discussion by helping the patient from the examination table:

P: Yeah . . . (moving around noises) Well, I sold a lot of my stuff.
D: Yeah, how did the moving go, as long as [words inaudible]

* * *

P: And y'know take forty ni- fifty nine years accumulation. Boy, and I've got cartons in my closet it'll take me till doomsday to, ouch.
D: Gotcha.
P: But I've been kept out of mischief by doing it. But I've got a lot to do, I sold my rugs 'cause they wouldn't fit where I am. I just got a piece of plain cloth at home.
D: Mm hmm.
P: Sometimes I think I'm foolish at 81. I don't know how long I'll live. Isn't much point in putting money into stuff, and then, why not enjoy a little bit of life?
D: Mm hmm, (words).
P: And I've got to have draperies made.
D: Now, then, you're (words).
P: But that'll come. I'm not worrying. I got an awfully cute place. It's very very comfortable. All electric kitchen. It's got a better bathroom than I ever had in my life.
D: Great. . . . Met any of your neighbors there yet?
P: Oh, I met two or three.
D: Mm hmm.

P: And my, some of my neighbors from Belmont here, there's Mrs. F_____ and her two sisters are up to see me, spent the afternoon with me day before yesterday. And all my neighbors um holler down the hall (words) . . . years ago. They're comin', so they say. So, I'm hopin' they will. I hated to move, cause I loved, um I liked my neighbors very much.
D: Now, we'll let you down. You watch your step.
P: You're not gonna let me, uh, unrobe, disrobe today.
D: Don't have to, I think.
P: Well!
D: Your heart sounds good.
P: It does?
D: Yep.

After the physician mentions briefly that the patient's heart "sounds good," he and the patient go on to other topics. The physician's cutoff and a return to technical assessment of cardiac function (he previously has treated her congestive heart failure) have the effect of marginalizing a contextual problem that involves loss of home and community.

From the patient's perspective, the move holds several meanings. First, in the realm of inanimate objects, her new living situation, an apartment (one line mentions a hallway), contains several physical features that she views as more convenient, or at least "cute." On the other hand, she apparently has sold many of her possessions, which carry the memories of 59 years in the same house. Further, she feels the need to decorate her new home but doubts the wisdom of investing financial resources in such items as rugs and draperies at her advanced age.

Aside from physical objects, the patient confronts a loss of community. In response to the physician's question about meeting new neighbors, the patient says that she has met "two or three." Yet she "hated" to move, because of the affection that she held for her prior neighbors. Describing her attachment, she first mentions that she "loved" them and then modulates her feelings by saying that she "liked them very much." Whatever pain this loss has created, the full impact remains unexplored, as the physician cuts off the line of discussion by terminating the physical exam and returning to a technical comment about her heart.

Throughout these passages, the physician listens supportively. He offers no specific suggestions to help the patient in these arenas, nor does he guide the dialogue toward deeper exploration of her feelings. Despite his supportive demeanor, the physician here functions within the traditional constraints of the medical role. When tension mounts with the patient's mourning a much-loved community, the physician returns to the realm of medical technique.

DEALING WITH SOCIAL CONTEXT UNDER MANAGED CARE

Even before managed care made its inroads into clinical practice, many practitioners felt reluctant to get involved in helping to improve the contextual problems that patients face—no matter how important such problems may be. Physicians may rationalize that there is not time or that intervening in social problems goes beyond the medical role. The answers have never been simple, but the productivity expectations and financial structure of managed care discourage even further efforts to deal with such problems. Several years ago, members of our research group and I worked out some preliminary criteria to guide practitioners in addressing contextual concerns.

These criteria try to address the question: To what extent *should* physicians intervene in the social context? The answer to this question depends partly on clarification of the practitioner's role, especially the degree to which intervention in the social context comes to be seen as appropriate and desirable. Practitioners reasonably may respond to this analysis by referring to the time constraints of current practice arrangements, the need to deal with challenging technical problems, and a lack of support facilities and personnel to improve social conditions. How physicians should involve themselves in contextual difficulties, without increasing professional control in areas where physicians claim no special expertise, therefore, takes on a certain complexity.

On the other hand, our research suggests that the presence of social problems in medical encounters warrants more critical attention. Elsewhere, we and others have spelled out suggestions for improving medical discourse by dealing with contextual difficulties more directly (Mishler et al. 1989; Waitzkin 1991). Briefly, on the most limited level, we have argued that physicians should let patients tell their stories with far fewer interruptions, cutoffs, or returns to technical matters. Patients should have the chance to present their narratives in an open-ended way. When patients refer to personal troubles that derive from contextual issues, physicians should try not to marginalize these connections by reverting to a technical track.

Although such suggestions encourage more "attentive patient care" (Mishler et al. 1989) and more acknowledgment of patients' contextual stories within medical encounters (Smith 1996), some preliminary criteria may prove helpful for physicians in deciding when and under what circumstances they could initiate, extend, or limit discussions about contextual matters.

First, it is important to recognize that patients differ in their openness and desire for contextual discussion; physicians should take their cues here from the initiative that patients themselves show in raising contextual concerns. For instance, in the above encounter, the patient introduces extensive contextual material concerning loss of home and community, social isolation, transportation problems, financial insecurity, and nutritional concerns. Rather than supportive listening alone, the physician here might respond more directly to these patient-initiated concerns by mentioning contextual interventions that could prove fairly easy to arrange: referral to seniors' organizations in the patient's new neighborhood, home-care services including nursing and nutritional assistance, social work support to help with financial issues, information about transportation services, and efforts to coordinate care with the patient's family members and friends.

Second, under other circumstances, physicians should remain sensitive to patients' differing desires and needs. Some patients may prefer no contextual interventions. Physicians' inquiry about contextual concerns requires tactful recognition of patients' autonomy to limit contextual discussion and to refuse such interventions.

In considering the time and costs devoted to contextual discussion and intervention, a point of concern especially to MCOs, a third criterion suggests that physicians and patients consider effects of contextual conditions on outcomes of care, such as prognosis, functional capacity, and satisfaction. Regarding the above encounter, for instance, the geriatric literature provides extensive evidence that social isolation, lack of convenient transportation, financial insecurity, and inadequate nutritional support all worsen the functional capacity of older people (for example, Reuben et al. 1992). Contextual concerns like isolation and related social psychological problems can also affect morbidity and mortality. For instance, there is now a large literature showing that social isolation and psychological distress are associated with higher rates of adverse cardiac events after myocardial infarction and that these effects may be equal or greater in magnitude than previously established cardiac risk factors (Allison et al. 1995; Brezinka and Kittel 1996). Current productivity standards in managed care are leading to tighter scheduling of shorter appointments, which do not encourage the exploration of contextual concerns. When constraints of time and costs require prioritization, existing evidence about the importance of specific contextual problems for health outcomes can help guide physicians and patients in targeting contextual issues for discussion and intervention. Likewise, a reasonable hypothesis for future research is that the marginalization of contextual issues may be inversely related to patient satisfaction, an important outcome of care (see Roter and Hall 1992), and that for many patients more explicit attention to contextual problems would enhance satisfaction.

As a fourth criterion, practitioners should consider referral to social workers, psychologists, or psychiatrists but should also evaluate whether specific patients would benefit more from dealing with contextual issues exclusively in the primary care setting. In managed care, the primary care practitioner usually initiates such referrals, but administrative reviewers, often through utilization review committees, must approve the referrals for reimbursement. For some patients, experiences with mental health professionals prove unsatisfactory or financially prohibitive. In addition, mental health professionals' role in mediating socially caused distress has received criticism both outside and inside the psychiatric profession (for example, Laing and Esterson 1970; Kupers 1981; Davis 1986, 1988). Even aside from utilization review, because many patients do not feel comfortable in seeking help from mental health professionals, primary care practitioners rather than psychiatrists probably will continue to see the majority of patients with emotional problems who present to physicians for care (Depression Guideline Panel 1993). While referrals to mental health professionals sometimes may prove necessary or appropriate, a broad mandate encouraging such care for people suffering from contextually based distress is not a solution.

As a fifth criterion, physicians and managed-care organizations should try to avoid the "medicalization" of social problems that require long-term reforms in social policy, and medicalization itself requires further critical attention (Waitzkin et al. 1994). At the individual level, medicalization can become a subtle process. For instance, there is a fine line between physicians' discussing contextual interventions and assuming professional control over broad arenas of patients' lives. It is important that physicians not imply that the solution of contextual difficulties is ultimately an individual's responsibility.

Even from the standpoint of utilization and cost, it can be argued that attention to contextual concerns in many instances can improve functional status, decrease unnecessary utilization, and possibly reduce the costs of care, especially for at-risk people like the elderly and those affected by poverty. Aiming toward a more supportive and humanistic encounter, one that can address contextual concerns rather than simply marginalizing them, may emerge as a goal that even some enlightened MCOs could support.

Clearly, it would be helpful if patients and physicians could turn to more readily available forms of assistance outside the medical arena to help in the solution of social problems; current conditions do not evoke optimism about broader changes in medicine's social context. Such changes would require time and financial resources, although not necessarily more than those now consumed in inefficient conversations that marginalize contextual issues. From our study, we are convinced that contextual problems warrant social policies to address unmet needs like those expressed in the encounters we studied. Of course, these suggestions are not new. Yet it is evident that meaningful improvements in medical discourse between physicians and older patients will depend partly on such wider reforms that go beyond the changes inherent in managed care.

MEDICO-POLITICAL STRUGGLE

As managed care works its transformation of the patient–physician relationship, questions of consent and acquiescence present themselves. Why do patients and physicians put up with such a fundamental shift in the historical basis of their relationships? Do patients see little space to resist a new system of care in which physicians—the professionals with whom they previously valued close and trusting relationships (even if those relationships sometimes became flawed)—have become double agents, gatekeepers who purportedly represent the interests of both patients and corporations, whose revenues depend in large part on restricting services? Have physicians' quest to maintain their livelihoods really become so desperate that they have become, as some have argued whimsically, like lemmings marching into the ocean of managed care?

Resistance among patients has mounted, although slowly. In many states, consumers' organizations have initiated major campaigns to resist some of the observed excesses of managed care. These efforts have led to state-level lobbying activities for protective legislation prohibiting unreasonable limitations and delays in services. Some advocacy groups have heavily criticized the gag rules and similar restrictions on information, by which physicians either formally or informally feel restrained from advising patients about the full range of diagnostic and therapeutic options available. As noted earlier, some of this advocacy work has culminated in class action lawsuits and similar forms of legal action that may lead to reforms in some of the constraining policies that managed care has imposed on the patient–physician relationship.

Physicians' resistance is gradually increasing, despite the surprising acquiescence shown so far in accepting administrative control and micromanagement of the everyday conditions of practice. State medical associations and the American Medical Association have supported legislative efforts to curb gag rules and other constraints on free communication between patients and physicians. Such efforts, however, so far have proven surprisingly mild, with little criticism of the underlying structural features of managed care, especially related to its corporatization, that impinge on the patient–physician relationship.

An important exception to passivity in the community of U.S. physicians involves an organization that has worked to achieve a national health program for the United States. Physicians for a National Health Program (PNHP), with chapters in all fifty states, initiated a series of proposals between 1989 and 1994 that called for a national health policy based on a single-payer national approach (Himmelstein et al. 1989; Grumbach et al. 1991; Harrington et al. 1991; Schiff et al. 1994). Modeled on the Canadian system but advocating policies to correct problems that have arisen in Canada, PNHP's proposals led to the most widely supported alternative to the managed-care-oriented proposal of the Clinton administration. Although Congressional legislative measures based on the single-payer model failed along with those of the Clinton plan, PHNP has continued to work actively at the national and state levels to maintain the vision of a well-organized national program as a viable policy option.

One component of PNHP's work since the failure of the Clinton proposal has involved a continuing, sharp critique of managed care's impact on the patient–physician relationship. PNHP leaders have called attention in many forums to the deleterious effects of gag rules and other restrictions on free communication between patients and physicians (Woolhandler and Himmelstein 1995). These efforts have contributed to movement in state legislatures and gradually in the national Congress toward reforms that will modify such practices. Further, PNHP has called attention to the adverse impact of corporate policies on access to appropriate care.

A major part of this critical work has focused on administrative waste and the erroneous view that physicians' practice patterns account for much of the problem of high costs in health care. Although uncontrolled costs comprise a multifaceted problem, administrative waste deserves special emphasis from this viewpoint (Woolhandler and Himmelstein 1991; Shulkin et al. 1993). Many of the structural problems that affect the patient–physician relationship under managed care, analyzed earlier in this chapter, are connected to intensive administrative practices that encourage micromanagement of clinical decisions by nonclinical managers within MCOs.

Administrators represent the fastest growing sector of the health-care labor force, expanding at three times the rate of physicians and other clinical personnel. Even before the latest proliferation of managed care, the United States spent more on administration than any other economically developed country; currently, administration consumes approximately 24 percent of health-care costs. This figure compares unfavorably to all countries with national health programs, which spend between 6 and 14 percent of health-care costs on administration. If the United States could reduce administrative spending to a proportion comparable to that of countries with national health programs, the savings (approximately 10 percent of $1 trillion, or about $100 billion) would be adequate to provide universal access to health services without additional spending (U.S. General Accounting Office 1991).

Part of the savings achieved through a national health program could be used to address problems in the patient–physician relationship, such as the development of systems to help deal with the contextual issues that impinge on medical encounters, as described previously in this chapter. Yet because managed care is administratively intensive, it tends to increase the proportion of health-care expenditures devoted to administrative activities as opposed to clinical services well beyond the prior 24 percent figure. Administrative practices that curtail services and constrain communication in the patient–physician relationship under managed care themselves are costly. The evidence that these added administrative costs can be justified by appropriate reductions in clinical costs has been quite limited (Langwell et al. 1992; Gabel and Rice 1993; Waitzkin 1994).

Inappropriate physician practices account for a small part of this country's cost crisis—in comparison with unnecessary administrative waste (Woolhandler and Himmelstein 1991, 1995). Overall expenditures on unnecessary procedures ordered or performed by physicians are currently unknown. Even generous estimates, however, put this figure at no more than about 10 percent of total spending on health care (National Leadership Commission on Health Care 1989). Under the circumstances of managed care's unproven effects in improving efficacy or reducing overall costs, the micromanagement policies that restrict clinical decisions and physicians' open explanations of them deserve greater critical attention than they have received thus far.

CONCLUSION

This chapter has spelled out some of the troubling contradictions that managed care has created in day-to-day patient–physician encounters and relationships. Under the constraints of managed care, practitioners' role as double agents and the financial structures that constrain open communication have thoroughly changed the nature of patient–physician interactions. Managed care has created enduring legal and ethical dilemmas in interpersonal relationships that warrant attention in health policy.

Toward this end, the chapter has touched on the unresolved question of what kind of patient–physician encounter we should be striving to create and has outlined some of the struggles that have emerged and will continue to emerge as managed care continues to flower. In these struggles, the very future of the patient–physician relationship as we have known it is at stake. The era that preceded managed care obviously was not free of problems in this relationship, but the conflicts of interest and mixed loyalties inherent in managed-care arrangements have further clouded patients' and health professionals' relationships with one another. A loss of trust and open communication, linked to the structure of managed care, will continue to generate conflict and policy debate. Without such conflict and debate, medicine will have lost some of its most basic qualities of interpersonal caring and compassion.

REFERENCES

ALLISON, THOMAS. G., DONALD E. WILLIAMS, TODD D. MILLER, CHRISTI A. PATTEN, KENT R. BAILEY, RAY SQUIRES, and GERALD T. GAU. 1995. "Medical and Economic Costs of Psychologic Distress in Patients with Coronary Artery Disease." *Mayo Clinic Proceedings* 70(8): 734–42.

AMERICAN COLLEGE OF PHYSICIANS. 1993. *Ethics Manual* 3rd ed. Philadelphia: The College.

ANGELL, M. "The Doctor as Double Agent." *Kennedy Institute for Ethics Journal,* 3:279–86.

BAKER, D.W. ET AL. 1996. "Use and Effectiveness of Interpreters in an Emergency Department." *Journal of the American Medical Association* 275: 783–88.

BALINT, J., and W. SHELTON. 1996. "Regaining the Initiative: Forging a New Model of the Patient-Physician Relationship." *Journal of the American Medical Association* 275(11): 887–91.

BRENNAN, T. A. 1993. "An Ethical Perspective on Health Care Insurance Reform." *American Journal of Law and Medicine* 19(1–2), 37–74.

BREZINKA, V., and F. KITTEL. 1996. "Psychosocial Factors of Coronary Heart Disease in Women: A Review." *Social Science & Medicine* 42:1351–65.

CASTILLO, R., H. WAITZKIN, Y. VILLASEÑOR, and J.I. ESCOBAR. 1995. "Mental Health Disorders and Somatoform Symptoms Among Immigrants and Refugees Who Seek Primary Care Services." *Archives of Family Medicine* 4:637–46.

CONSUMER REPORTS. 1992. "Health Care in Crisis: Are HMOs the Answer?" *Consumer Reports* 57 (August): 519–31.

COYLE, W., and G. HOSTETTER. 1996. "Kaiser Leader in Care Payout." *Fresno Bee* February 13:E1.

DAVIES, A. R. ET AL. 1986. "Consumer Acceptance of Prepaid and Fee-For-Service Medical Care: Results From a Randomized Controlled Trial." *Health Services Research* 21:429–52.

DAVIS, K. 1986. "The Process of Problem (Re)formulation in Psychotherapy." *Sociology of Health and Illness* 8:44–74.

DAVIS, K. 1998. *Power Under the Microscope: Toward a Grounded Theory of Gender Relations in Medical Encounters.* Dortrecht, Holland: Foris.

DEPRESSION GUIDELINE PANEL. 1993. *Depression in Primary Care.* Rockville, MD: Agency for Health Care Policy and Research (AHCPR Publication No. 93–0550).

EMANUEL, E. J., and N. N. DUBLER. 1995. "Preserving the Physician-Patient Relationship in the Era of Managed Care." *Journal of the American Medical Association* 273(4):323–29.

FISHER, S. 1995. *Nursing Wounds: Nurse Practitioners, Doctors, Women Patients and the Negotiation of Meaning.* New Brunswick, NJ: Rutgers University Press.

GABEL, J. R., and T. RICE. 1993. "Is Managed Competition a Field of Dreams?" *Journal of American Health Policy* 3:19–24.

GRUMBACH, K., ET AL. 1991. "Liberal Benefits, Conservative Spending: The Physicians for a National Health Program Proposal." *Journal of the American Medical Association* 265:2549–54.

GRUMET, G. W. 1989. "Health Care Rationing Through Inconvenience." *New England Journal of Medicine* 321(9): 607–11.

HAFFNER, L. 1992. "Translation Is Not Enough: Interpreting in a Medical Setting." *Western Journal of Medicine* 157:255–59.

HALL, J. A., ET AL. 1994. "Satisfaction, Gender, and Communication in Medical Visits." *Medical Care* 32(12): 1216–31.

HARDT, E. J. 1991. *The Bilingual Medical Interview.* Boston, MA: Boston Department of Health and Hospitals and Boston Area Health Education Center.

HARRINGTON, C., ET AL. 1991. "A National Long-term Care Program for the United States: A Caring Vision." *Journal of the American Medical Association* 266:3023–29.

HIMMELSTEIN, D.U., ET AL. 1989. "A National Health Program for the United States: A Physicians' Proposal." *New England Journal of Medicine,* 320:102–108.

HORNBERGER, J.C., ET AL. 1996. "Eliminating Language Barriers for Non-English-Speaking Patients." *Medical Care,* 34:845–56.

KILGORE, R. 1996. Personal communication on class action litigation on the effects of conflicts of interest on patient-doctor communication in managed care organizations. Phoenix, AZ.

KUPERS, T. A. 1981. *Public Therapy.* New York: Free Press.

KUTTNER, R. 1998. "Must Good HMOs Go Bad?" *New England Journal of Medicine* 338:1558–63, 1635–39.

LAING, R.D., and A. ESTERSON. 1970. *Sanity, Madness and the Family.* Baltimore: Penguin.

LANGWELL, K.M., V.S. STAINES, and N. GORDON. 1992. *The Effects of Managed Care on Use and Costs of Health Services.* Washington, D.C.: Congressional Budget Office.

LIPKIN, M., JR., S.M. PUTNAM, and A. LAZARE, eds. 1995. *The Medical Interview: Clinical Care, Education, and Research.* New York: Springer.

MISHLER, E. G., ET AL. 1989. "The Language of Attentive Patient Care: A Comparison of Two Medical Interviews." *Journal of General Internal Medicine* 4:325–35.

NATIONAL LEADERSHIP COMMISSION ON HEALTH CARE. 1989. *For the Health of a Nation.* Technical Appendix III. Washington, D.C.: The Commission.

NOVACK, D. H., ET AL. 1979. "Changes in Physicians' Attitudes Toward Telling the Cancer Patient." *Journal of the American Medical Association* 241:897–900.

OLMOS, D. R., and S. ROAN. 1996. "HMO Curbs Prompt Rising Doctor Protest." *Los Angeles Times* April 14: A1.

PEAR, R. 1992. "The 1992 Elections: Disappointment—The Turnout." *New York Times* November 5: B4.

PUTSCH, R. W. 1985. "Cross-Cultural Communication: The Special Case of Interpreters in Health Care." *Journal of the American Medical Association* 254(23):3344–48.

REUBEN, D. B., ET AL. 1992. "The Use of Targeting Criteria in Hospitalized HMO Patients: Results From the Demonstration Phase of the Hospitalized Older Persons Evaluation (HOPE) Study." *Journal of the American Geriatrics Society* 40: 482–88.

RODWIN, M. A. 1995. "Conflicts in Managed Care." *The New England Journal of Medicine* 332(9):604–605.

ROTER, D. L., and J. A. HALL. 1992. *Doctors Talking with Patients/ Patients Talking with Doctors.* Westport, CT: Auburn House.

ROTER, D., M. LIPKIN, JR., and A. KORSGAARD. 1991. "Sex Differences in Patients' and Physicians' Communication During Primary Care Visits." *Medical Care* 29(11): 1083–93.

RUBIN, H. R., ET AL. 1993. "Patients' Ratings of Outpatients Visits in Different Practice Settings." *Journal of the American Medical Association* 270: 835–40.

SCHIFF, G. D., A. B. BINDMAN, and T. A. BRENNAN. 1994. "A Better-Quality Alternative: Single-Payer National Health System Reform." *Journal of the American Medical Association* 272: 803–808.

SHULKIN, D. J., A. L. HILLMAN, and W. M. COOPER. 1993. "Reasons for Increasing Administrative Costs in Hospitals." *Annals of Internal Medicine* 119: 74–78.

SLEEPER, SALLY, DOUGLAS R. WHOLEY, RICHARD HAMER, SHAWN SCHWARTZ, and VITO INOFERIO. 1998. "Trust Me: Technical and Institutional Determinants of Health Maintenance Organizations Shifting Risk To Physicians." *Journal of Health and Social Behavior* 39(3): 189–200.

SMITH, R. C. 1996. *The Patient's Story.* Boston, MA: Little, Brown and Company.

TANNEN, D., ed. 1993. *Gender and Conversational Interaction.* New York: Oxford University Press.

U.S. GENERAL ACCOUNTING OFFICE. 1991. *Canadian Health Insurance: Lessons for the United States.* Washington, D.C.: Government Printing Office.

WAITZKIN, H. 1984. "Doctor-patient Communication: Clinical Implications of Social Scientific Research. *Journal of the American Medical Association* 252: 2441–46.

WAITZKIN, H. 1985. "Information Giving in Medical Care." *Journal of Health and Social Behavior* 26: 81–101.

WAITZKIN, H. 1991. *The Politics of Medical Encounters: How Patients and Doctors Deal With Social Problems.* New Haven, CT: Yale University Press.

WAITZKIN, H. 1994. "The Strange Career of Managed Competition: From Military Failure to Medical Success?" *American Journal of Public Health* 84: 482–89.

WAITZKIN, H., and J. D. STOECKLE. 1972. "The Communication of Information About Illness: Clinical, Sociological, and Methodological Considerations." *Advances in Psychosomatic Medicine* 8:180–215.

WAITZKIN, H., T. BRITT, and C. WILLIAMS. 1994. "Narratives of Aging and Social Problems in Medical Encounters With Older Persons." *Journal of Health and Social Behavior* 35:322–48.

WOOLHANDLER, S., and D. U. HIMMELSTEIN. 1991. "The Deteriorating Administrative Efficiency of the U.S. Health Care System." *The New England Journal of Medicine* 324: 1253–58.

WOOLHANDLER, S., and D. U. HIMMELSTEIN. 1995. "Extreme Risk—The New Corporate Proposition for Physicians." *New England Journal of Medicine* 333: 1706–1708.

19 THE GROWING ACCEPTANCE OF COMPLEMENTARY AND ALTERNATIVE MEDICINE

MICHAEL S. GOLDSTEIN, *University of California*

There is little doubt that "complementary and alternative medicine" (CAM) is increasingly accepted in the United States. David Eisenberg et al. (1993) found that about one-third of the American adult population had used what he called "unconventional medicine" to treat a problem in the past year. Extrapolating from his national sample, Eisenberg estimated that in 1993 Americans made 425 million visits to unconventional providers that year, well more than the 388 million visits made to all primary care physicians. In making these visits, clients spent over $13.7 billion more that they spent out of pocket on conventional care that same year. As these figures exclude visits for maintaining health in the absence of symptoms, they are likely a considerable underestimate of the phenomena.

Over the past few years *Time, Life,* the *New York Times Magazine, Newsweek,* and many other national magazines have each done multiple cover stories on this topic. Bookstores are overflowing with titles on Chinese Medicine, Ayurveda, homeopathy, herbalism, and dozens of other modes of care, along with scores of more general guides to the area. Just one of Deepak Chopra's books, *Ageless Body, Timeless Mind,* has sold more than seven million copies since it was first published in 1993. Disease-specific information published for the public or available on the Internet now routinely includes CAM as part of what it assumes an informed individual should know. Physicians are hurrying to catch up. In 1997 the editors of the *Journal of the American Medical Association* ranked alternative medicine as the third most important topic out of 86 for the Journal to cover. Their readership survey found alternative medicine ranked seventh most important on a list of 73 topics the Journal should be addressing (Fontarosa and Lundberg 1997).

These developments have been a surprise to many medical sociologists. For example, to the extent that the topic appeared at all in the second edition of *The Handbook of Medical Sociology,* it occupied a small portion of chapters with titles like "Limited, Marginal, and Quasi Practitioners" (Wardwell 1972), in which most of the material dealt with the struggles of groups of conventional providers like pharmacists, optometrists, and psychologists for power and autonomy. Osteopaths and chiropractors were discussed as occupations that had achieved a measure of success by moving toward accommodation with the medical mainstream. Everything else was considered either "quackery," "faith healing," or "primitive and magical." Anything accomplished through the use of these techniques was assumed to be a result of suggestion or the acumen of the practitioners as psychotherapists. By the fourth edition, published in 1989, when clients were visiting alternative providers more frequently than primary care physicians, the topic had disappeared completely from the *Handbook.*

This chapter first presents an overview of the major points which, in my view, distinguish alternative medicine from conventional care. Next, the chapter evaluates the evidence that CAM is beginning to take on the quality of a distinct entity with its own institutions and recognized by the government, the media, and the public. The ability of CAM to transcend traditional liberal–conservative differences is one of its strengths. An example of this is the formation and growth of the Office of Alternative Medicine within the National Institutes of Health. This section of the chapter is followed by a discussion of CAM's transformation from a marginal economic activity into a commodity promoted and distributed by the corporate economy. The popular, political, and economic acceptance of CAM has led to its increased integration into conventional medical care. The chapter concludes with a discussion of the forces acting upon all of medical care that are likely to lead to even greater acceptability and integration of CAM in the future, and a brief coda on the relationship of alternative medicine and medical sociology.

THE CORE OF ALTERNATIVE MEDICINE

A residual definition of alternative medicine is commonly employed (Eisenberg et al. 1993). Alternative medicine is what is *not* taught in most medical schools. The Office of Alternative Medicine (OAM) calls it an "unrelated group of therapeutic practices that do not follow conventional biomedical explanations" (Office of Alternative Medicine 1992). But from a sociological perspective, the wide array of techniques and approaches that comprise CAM do seem to be informed by a relatively coherent and synergistic set of core beliefs (Alster 1989; Lowenberg 1989; Mattson 1982). The cohesiveness of these core beliefs and their ability to offer a response to concerns about the shortcomings of conventional care foster the growing acceptance of alternative medicine. I see five significant points distinguishing alternative medicine from conventional care (Goldstein 1999).

Holism The belief that individuals are more than the sum of their parts permeates alternative medicine. The entire physical, mental, spiritual, and social make-up of the person must be considered in understanding the origins of illness and the healing process. Thus, pathology and treatment are often unique to the individual. Alternative medicine asks why the disease or symptom is taking the specific form it has in a specific individual. Deepak Chopra put it this way, "An Ayurvedic physician is more interested in the patient he sees before him than in his disease. He recognizes that what makes up the person is experience—sorrows, joys, fleeting seconds of trauma, long hours of nothing special at all. The minutes of life silently accumulate, and like grains of sand deposited by a river, the minutes can eventually pile up into a hidden formation that crops above the surface as disease" (1989: 142).

Holism is the most commonly held premise among all alternative medical healing systems, and it is a view that resonates with the value American society places on the importance and uniqueness of the individual. Thus, the emphasis on holism heightens the potential acceptability of alternative medicine to many people.

The Interpenetration of Mind, Body, and Spirit

While almost any conventional physician would agree that the body and the mind are intimately related, alternative medicine is distinctive in the emphasis it places on this connection. This is the heart of traditional Chinese medicine, Ayurveda, yoga (which literally means "union" of body and mind) and every alternative healing system and technique that derives from them (meditation, biofeedback, guided imagery, massage, Rolfing, Feldenkrais, etc.). The history of chiropractic, Bach flower remedies, homeopathy, and many others reveals a strikingly similar set of beliefs.

This focus on the interpenetration of body, mind, and spirit has been expressed in social movements around health from William Alcott's Christian Physiology Movement in the 1850s through Seventh Day Adventism and scores more (Goldstein 1992). Public opinion polls consistently show the vast majority of the population, regardless of religion or religiosity, hold these beliefs as fundamental and fault conventional medicine for not doing so.

Alternative medicine often includes the interaction of the "spirit" along with the body and mind. For example, almost every one of the conventionally trained physicians who have become the most prominent in the media as spokespersons for alternative medicine (Deepak Chopra, Bernie Siegel, Larry Dossey, Dean Ornish, and Andrew Weil) emphasize the importance of spirituality as a source of health and healing. This emphasis on spirituality contributes to the acceptability of alternative medicine for many people. The annual Gallup Poll finds about 90 percent of the adult population consider themselves "believers"—a figure that has remained constant for about fifty years. About 60 percent of the populace consider religion "very important" in their lives (Pew Research Center 1996). A 1996 TIME/CNN poll found 82 percent of adults believe personal prayer can have healing power, 77 percent believe that god sometimes intervenes to cure a serious illness, and 73 percent believe that praying for someone else can help bring about a cure (Wallis 1996:62). Thus, American society is suffused with beliefs that are congruent with the spiritual outlook of alternative medicine.

In a society where the belief in god is so pervasive, it should not be a surprise that there is a great desire to find a way of integrating spirituality into health care. The medical mainstream has been deficient in this arena, a defect heightened by the recent rise of managed care. For many, the ability of alternative medicine to offer a nonsectarian, "dereligicized" spirituality is a great attraction. Religious meditation has become "the Relaxation

Response," and the laying on of hands is now "Therapeutic Touch." As Andrew Weil put it in his *Eight Weeks to Optimum Health,* ". . . it is possible to lead a spiritual life and explore the influence of spirituality on health whether you are religious or not" (Weil 1997a: 24–25).

The acceptability of alternative medicine's views regarding spirituality have been enhanced by recent social science research. A large number of studies have reported that religious beliefs and practices are associated with positive health status and outcomes (Levin 1994). Whether these consistent findings are due to religiosity's association with better health behavior, a positive state of mind that instills optimism and calmness, greater social support, or a supernatural force is unclear. But regardless of which mechanisms eventually prove to be correct, it is clear that the spiritual dimension of alternative medicine is one of its great strengths and attractive qualities for many people. These same qualities make alternative medicine highly problematic for many conventional medical practitioners, institutions, and payers.

The Possibility of High Level Wellness For much of conventional medicine, health is the absence of symptoms. For most alternative approaches, health is something more than the lack of a diagnosable disease. Health is something positive that can only be attained through effort, striving, and eventually, transcendence. Everyone, from the championship athlete to the severely ill, can always be healthier. In this emphasis on striving and the possibility of attaining personal goals, CAM has an affinity with core beliefs in American culture. This convergence serves to heighten its appeal and acceptability.

Vitalism: Life Suffused by the Flow of Energy In most forms of alternative medicine, life is viewed as an ecosystem, with the various elements of mind, body and spirit tied together by the flow of energy. Chinese medicine, where the energy flow is called "chi" or "qi," is one commonly known example. In Ayurveda, the body is seen as a river, defined by its ever-changing flow. When energy flow is blocked, illness or symptoms appear. Chiropractic is based on manipulations to remove blockages and allow the flow of "Universal Intelligence." Herbalists use the substances found in plants to cure illness by enhancing the body's own energies. Other modes of healing, such as acupuncture, allow the possibility of the healer's own energy to be transmitted to the one being healed. These beliefs are distinctive to alternative medicine and have little presence in conventional biomedicine. Neither do they resonate or amplify any important values in American society.

The Healing Process A final distinctive belief common to most forms of alternative healing, and one which most consistently differentiates it from conventional medicine, concerns the nature of healing itself. In alternative medicine, healing is a cooperative, active process, entailing a commitment on the part of the individual. Whatever the cause of the problem, the sufferer must accept the reality of the illness and the responsibility for doing something about it. Illness is not always the "enemy" to be destroyed by a stronger medicine, surgical invasion, or radioactive bombardment. A changed consciousness about what is possible is the essence of healing. In alternative medicine, this change in consciousness is usually brought about indirectly, through imagery or an altered state of consciousness, as opposed to a simple act of will.

In CAM caring and nurturance are considered extremely important. Larry Dossey quotes Paracelsus, "The main reason for healing is love" (1993: 109). This is not a point of view that lends itself to being learned in the classroom, and many alternative healers base what they do, in part, on their own personal experiences with health and illness. My own studies of physicians who have redefined themselves as "holistic" found that they were quite similar to other primary care MDs, except for their own personal experiences with illness and spirituality (Goldstein et al. 1985, 1987).

Alternative medicine does have a set of core beliefs that underlie its practices. It is not merely a residual category or an arbitrary classification. Of course, just as not all conventional physicians adhere equally to the core beliefs of biomedicine, alternative providers vary considerably in their commitment to the elements described above. The various beliefs I have set out are mutually reinforcing, and they act in synergy to point out a range of paradoxes, confusions, and inconsistencies that afflict the dominant biomedical model. Taken together, these core beliefs offer a response of sorts to the growing litany of complaints about the dominant world of medicine, with its lack of emphasis on the individual, prevention, and caring. The strength of the core beliefs lies not so much in what they can explain as in the sense of possibility they provide. In many respects the core beliefs are not radically at odds with elements of the dominant biomedical view. What differentiates the two is the centrality and emphasis placed upon them by alternative medicine.

Thus, for the most part, the core beliefs of alternative medicine are a potent force in enhancing its acceptability. They build on strong, traditional American values such as individualism, personal responsibility, and a belief in god and the possibility of transcending one's problems. These views are not solely found among conservatives. They have much in common with the values held by those who identify with feminism, gay liberation, and an array of other progressive social movements, all of which are very comfortable questioning the style and substance of mainstream medicine.

ALTERNATIVE MEDICINE AS A PROFESSIONAL ENTITY

Today it is common to find practitioners who explicitly describe themselves as "alternative" or "holistic," as opposed to viewing themselves solely as homeopaths, herbalists, or some other more specific type of healer. An example is the work of Deepak Chopra. His earlier writings are open attempts to advocate and foster Ayurvedic medicine to Americans. Chopra claims Ayurvedic medicine is "better than any alternative" (1989: 13). But, when Chopra presented the same ideas a few years later (1993), Ayurveda was barely mentioned. Instead Chopra now explicitly talks about "chi," Sufism, Christianity, and many other traditions to show how they all support the introduction of "a new paradigm" where, as "In all religious traditions the breath of life is spirit"(1993: 21). A number of new and successful publications such as *Alternative Therapies* refuse "to endorse any particular therapy," seeking instead to "encourage the development of a lingua franca, a common language . . . ." (Dossey 1995: 7).

While the development of alternative medicine as a profession in the sense that sociologists use this term has barely begun, the process is further along than it was a short while ago. Twenty-five years ago there were no organized groupings of alternative, "holistic," or "complementary" health care providers in the United States. Today there are a number of such groups, ranging from the American Holistic Medical Association, which restricts its full membership to physicians and medical students, and the 4,000-member American Holistic Nursing Association, to scores of organizations like Professional Association of Traditional Healers that are open to anyone. Numerous medical, nursing, and other health-science schools sponsor symposia and continuing-education courses around inclusive categories such as alternative, holistic, integrative, or mind-body medicine.

Recognition by the government, an important indicator of acceptability, is also growing. Chiropractic and osteopathy are recognized in all states, and there are provider practice acts for acupuncture, homeopathy, massage therapy, and scores of other modalities in varying numbers of states and jurisdictions. Increasingly, the pattern in many areas is that better-known forms of care such as naturopathy or chiropractic have their licenses expanded to include less widely known forms of care. Intended or not, the effect of this inclusiveness (or professional imperialism), is to create practitioners who can (and increasingly do) practice many different modes of care. Eight states have expanded the licenses of MDs to include the full array of alternative therapies. David Sale terms these developments a "convergence" in the forms of alternative practice, and suggests it fosters "a multidisciplinary orientation and fluidity in practice boundaries" (Sale 1995:50). Legislation on the national level, most notably the formation of the Office of Alternative Medicine (OAM), has also been inclusive of many forms of care under a single rubric. The use of the term "alternative medicine" in the agency's name is a reflection of its acceptability and a bestowal of even greater legitimacy.

Acceptance of the term "alternative medicine" or CAM by conventional practitioners, while increasing, is minimal. Until quite recently groups like the American Medical Association did consider the vast array of alternative techniques and approaches as a singular phenomenon: quackery. In 1993 an AMA guidebook for consumers called alternative methods "unproven, disproven, controversial, fraudulent, quack, and/or otherwise questionable approaches to solving health problems" (Zwicky 1993). Although the response of some elements in mainstream medicine has shifted since then, it is unclear to what extent this represents genuine acceptance. Conventional providers seldom recognize alternative medicine as a comprehensive approach to care or a coherent set of assumptions. For example, in 1998 *The New England Journal of Medicine* published a number of articles, case reports, and letters about specific alternative treatments. All were found useless and/or harmful. The editors defined alternative medicine as medicine "that has not been scientifically tested and (whose) advocates largely deny the need for such testing" (Angell and Kassirer 1998). Insurers such as Blue Cross and managed-care plans like Oxford have been considerably more accepting of some alternative techniques. Mainstream providers affiliated with such plans have had little choice but to accept the presence of alternative providers. Thus, many conventional providers are more exposed to alternative medicine, and this has led to heightened interest, and at least a pragmatic or situational familiarity, if not acceptance.

One of the factors driving the acceptance of alternative medicine among physicians and other professional groups is that the general public is increasingly familiar and comfortable with the term. The terms CAM, "alternative medicine," and to a lesser extent, "holistic medicine" frequently appear in the mass media in a context that either explicitly or implicitly recognizes that various approaches are linked by a common set of assumptions or beliefs. For example, a 1996 special issue of *Time* magazine on "The Frontiers of Medicine" described a wide range of alternative techniques as similar because they all "emphasize human contact" in their relations between healers and clients. The Internet and the World Wide Web have become important sources for information about alternative medicine (as well as health care in general). Sites such as "Ask Dr. Weil" (over 90,000 hits a day) provide abundant information and hundreds of relevant links to other sites. Almost all the major sources of general health information on the Internet and in other mass media now offer information on alternative medicine along with conventional care. This both reflects and enhances CAM's acceptance.

Another dimension of alternative medicine's growing acceptance is taking place on the level of "rights." Personal freedom is a deeply held and cherished American value. From colonial times, through the emergence of religious groups such as Christian Scientists, to the current debates about "the right to die" or "the right to reject medical treatment," the idea that the individual her- or himself should decide on what course of therapy to follow has been an accepted notion in American life. Today ideas about the individual's right to control his or her own body and to associate with whom he or she pleases are widely recognized. Advocates of alternative medicine frequently promote the idea of personal freedom as a basic element of what they offer and as a means of unifying a vast array of techniques and approaches. Practitioners from the widest range of backgrounds can agree that clients should have the right to choose freely between them. Very conservative groups like The National Health Federation promote the freedom "to choose a natural healer or allopathic doctor as we see fit" as a first amendment right, using language that is not that different from that used by feminist, disability rights, or gay liberation activists (National Health Federation 1995; Boston Women's Health Collective 1992).

The rise of movements advocating feminism, gay liberation, and disability rights, with their use of "consciousness raising groups," along with the proliferation of "12-step programs" for scores of personal problems, has created a tremendous pool of individuals who are likely to find many of the underlying values and

assumptions of alternative medicine very familiar and comfortable. Each of these settings places a strong emphasis on taking personal responsibility for bringing about both personal and social change. This affinity between "progressive" groups and the values of alternative medicine offers an additional indicator of the growing acceptability of some of alternative medicine's basic premises and also indicates that an emphasis on personal responsibility is not inevitably associated with a conservative political outlook.

The assumption that alternative medicine's stress on personal responsibility has an intrinsic affinity with conservatism reflects a culture-bound perspective. Traditional Chinese medicine and many other alternative modalities view the human body as reflecting or embodying the larger environment. The forces of nature—fire, wood, earth, metal, and water—are the bridge between the outside ecology and the internal organs. What joins the inside and the outside is energy, in this case "chi." Thus, a disease inside the body doesn't mean that it was caused by the individual. Still, the individual is responsible for acknowledging that the disease exists, and for dealing with it insofar as that is possible. Healing consists of being better able to mobilize one's own chi, as well as receiving the chi from the outside through dietary change, physical stimulation, or directly from a healer. These ideas are not really so different from a consciousness-raising or 12-step group where the individual specifies in great detail how the problem, be it sexism or some sort of addiction, is connected to the environment but must be first addressed through taking some individual responsibility for change.

Another source of the growing acceptability of alternative medicine comes from its association with the "counter-culture." This phrase, while indisputably vague, does have value in describing groups following a certain lifestyle marked by distinctive music, dress, the use of psychoactive drugs, and an antipathy toward conventional institutions, bureaucracies, expertise, and high technology. Those who identify with the counter-culture share a number of values with the advocates of alternative medicine in that they seek low technological solutions to problems, greater personal responsibility for their lives, and altered states of consciousness. Since the late 1960s the counter-culture has been largely trivialized by commercialization, but in two ways it has continued to have an influence on the broader society's acceptance of alternative medicine. The first is through its emphasis on the use of "mind expanding" or psychoactive drugs. Timothy Leary, Richard Alpert, and others who originally popularized the use of drugs like LSD described the experience in terms of Buddhist and Taoist concepts that were much like those that were basic to alternative medicine. By 1970 Alpert had changed his name to Baba Ram Dass and was teaching nutrition along with the best ways to get high. He remains involved with institutions like the Omega Institute, which are heavily involved in promoting many forms of CAM. The creation of an altered state of consciousness, by drugs or another technique such as meditation or self-hypnosis, is central to both the counter-culture's view of what is desirable and the view of alternative medicine about what people need to do to assume control over their health (Weil and Rosen 1993).

The second way in which the counter-culture has fostered the acceptance of alternative medicine is through the development of "free clinics," which used alternative techniques for dealing with problems such as drug abuse; some clinics integrated alternative techniques more pervasively in their activities (Nebelkopf 1995).

THE POLITICAL ACCEPTANCE OF ALTERNATIVE MEDICINE

The recognition of alternative medicine by the government and other quasi-official bodies through laws, licensure, and regulations reflects acceptance by political elites. They frequently lead to even greater levels of general acceptability for CAM because of how they are interpreted by the public, or because of legal requirements that demand a certain degree of societal acceptance of legally sanctioned activities. While the political acceptance of alternative medicine remains chaotic, varying considerably according to the jurisdiction and the specific therapeutic approach, it is clear that there has been considerable progress toward greater acceptance over the past several years.

Acquiring and maintaining power and autonomy are almost always the underlying issues when licensure and certification are at issue. Typically, "new" practitioners seek to maximize their professional status and authority, while those that have already achieved higher status tend to resist the demands in favor of granting more limited "paraprofessional" rights or no rights at all. The situation with regard to CAM is complicated by the fact that the different groups involved have very different needs. For a profession that already has full licensure, a broad certification like "holistic doctor" or dentist might be desirable. Groups like massage therapists or reflexologists need a much more limited

mandate, while other groups, like chiropractors, may wish to expand upon an existing license. The fact that alternative practitioners are increasingly using more than one mode of care (for example, many chiropractors have begun to use homeopathic remedies) has made the situation even more confusing.

The situation is much like what allopathic physicians faced at the turn of the century. Their progress in gaining professional autonomy was not based on the validity of their theories or the utility of their therapies; rather, it was the consolidation of professional leadership to create internal cohesion that led to political acceptance (Starr 1982). A consensus must be forged among the existing practitioners, many of whom do not have the formal training or systematic experience to qualify for licensure. Typically, they agree to the new higher standards because they are "grandfathered" into licensure or certification, which has the effect of raising their incomes and often leads to their becoming the gatekeepers for new recruits (Freidson 1970; Berlant 1975; Larson 1977; Starr 1982). Among MDs there has been some effort to establish "holistic" or "integrative" medicine as a specialty (American Holistic Medical Association 1997, Weil 1997b). Thus far this effort has met with little success, largely because it has not been possible to form an internal consensus on the meaning of these terms.

The American political system, where licensure and certification are the responsibility of the states, has led to a maze of inconsistency. Over 1,100 different health-related occupations are regulated in the nation, over 600 by full licensure. Yet some states regulate fewer than 60 different job titles. Chiropractors are the only alternative providers licensed in all fifty states. They, along with acupuncturists and naturopaths, are the only groups whose training is accredited by organizations recognized by the U.S. Department of Education. There is no consistency between the states in how to handle alternative therapists beyond an overall increase in attention to the problem (Sale 1995; Milbank Memorial Fund 1998). Most states allow those professionals who are already best established, like MDs, naturopaths, and acupuncturists, to consolidate their power by adding other modes of practice, such as homeopathy, to their mandate, regardless of any training they may have. Often state regulations are contradictory. For example, over twenty states regulate acupuncture, but some define it as needle insertion, others as an attempt to control energy flows in the body. Almost all of the twenty some states that define "massage" do it differently. Some will include techniques such as "reflexology" as part of massage, while others will specifically exclude them.

Despite the chaos, it is clear that all this activity is indicative of heightened political acceptability for alternative medicine throughout the nation.

Another indication of alternative medicine's growing acceptance is the chorus of calls for more "objective" evaluation of particular treatments. The desire for more and better data typically arises from the heightened attention that some form of alterative therapy has received in the media or from growing client demands to include it as part of a health-care plan. For example, all sorts of claims have been made about the value of various herbs such as ginseng or ginkgo biloba. But the claims are almost impossible to evaluate if these herbs are not available in standardized dosages and strengths. In this country, as opposed to Europe, none exist. It has been repeatedly demonstrated that commercial products are extremely uneven and sometimes contain none of the substance in question at all (Seligman and Cowley 1995). Thus, both advocates and critics of these substances now typically call for more standardization and certification in order that some sort of conclusions about their validity be made. Regardless of the motives for their establishment, creating legally binding standards for CAM training and substances is likely to facilitate their overall acceptance in society.

The extent to which political acceptance of alternative therapies in the United States trails behind that in other industrialized nations such as those of western Europe is striking. These countries have long-standing mechanisms for conducting research on herbs and other alternative approaches, along with centralized official or quasi-official bodies for accrediting training programs and certifying practitioners. For example, in Germany, "Commission E," an official government agency, routinely informs all physicians about research outcomes using herbal remedies. The twenty-five nations that make up the European Commission have been cooperating on standardizing various alternative practices since 1992. Not only are Americans far behind their European counterparts, they are generally ignorant of how far behind they are. The differences between Europe and the United States may be partially explained by the greater power of organized medicine in the United States and the corresponding hesitancy of the government to challenge the traditional prerogatives of physicians to control all aspects of clinical practice.

In the United States there is minimal national legislation dealing with alternative medicine. But what is most striking is that those legislators who have shown most interest in the topic transcend the typical divisions between Democrat and Republican. Some, like Orin Hatch, who sponsored the 1994 Dietary Supplement Health and Education Act that removed FDA oversight from nutritional supplements, are well-known conservatives whose support for "freedom of choice" in therapy is congruous with a general antipathy toward most regulation. Conservatives are also likely to favor alternative approaches because of the emphasis they place on personal responsibility, and the fact that they may be a less costly drain on the public purse. But others, like Tom Harkin or Peter DeFazio, are liberal Democrats. In many cases the politicians who have become involved trace their interest to their own personal experiences, which convinced them of the need to go beyond the conventional medicine. Harkin, whose severe allergies were finally brought under control by bee pollen, has written of the need to bring alternative therapies into the medical mainstream without the use of standard randomized clinical trials. "Did I need someone to show me exactly how that (the control of his allergies) was accomplished in order to experience the results I did? Of course not! And it is not necessary for the scientific community to understand the process before the American people can benefit from these therapies" (Harkin 1995).

Some "liberals" may also be attracted to alternative medicine because of its orientation toward "the whole person" as well as its openness toward "empowerment" and healing traditions from other cultures. Similarly, both right and left have reasons to be skeptical or hesitant about alterative medicine. Conservatives have generally drawn support from organized medicine and groups like the AMA who have generally opposed alternative approaches. Liberals have been concerned about the possibility of "victim blaming," given CAM's emphasis on personal responsibility, and the unchecked growth of its entrepreneurial dimension.

All this means that alternative medicine has drawn its political support from across the political spectrum. As Larry Dossey, editor of *Alternative Therapies,* told an interviewer, "Newt loves it, Bill and Hillary love it. Who would have thought!" (Chowka 1996:157).

THE OFFICE OF ALTERNATIVE MEDICINE (OAM)

Berkeley Bedell, an ex-Congressman who believed both his Lyme disease and prostate cancer had been cured by alternative therapies, had long championed the idea that the National Institutes of Health (NIH) should be actively involved with alternative medicine. After Bedell's good friend Tom Harkin, who headed the

Senate committee that controlled the NIH budget, attributed the cure of his allergies to bee pollen, Bedell convinced him to have the committee declare it was dissatisfied with NIH's approach to alternative care and appropriate two million dollars for a special office to "fully investigate and validate these practices" (Tractman 1994). Since its founding in 1992, OAM has had a stormy history, going through three directors and attracting the wrath of many in conventional medicine as well as in NIH itself.

Despite this turmoil, there is no question that the creation of OAM represents a major landmark in the growing acceptability of alternative medicine. The very existence of the agency implies an overall stamp of approval about what knowledge is to be officially accepted as legitimate or "real." The ability of OAM to survive and grow (its budget has grown 600 percent during a period when the overall NIH budget remained the same) indicates at least a preliminary acceptance by the federal government of a set of ideas that the established health professions have long resisted. As OAM grows, the nature of what is "rational" and "irrational" with regard to health and illness is brought into question; the monopoly of conventional medicine on defining these terms has weakened. OAM also offers a direct political channel for the needs of alternative medicine's providers and institutions to be addressed. But it can only address these concerns effectively if a consensus can emerge within the alternative community on such issues as certification, licensure, the role of research, and relationships with mainstream providers. Thus OAM not only reflects the growing acceptability of alternative medicine, but also acts as a vehicle to further that very acceptability among politicians, the larger medical establishment, and the broader society.

THE COMMODIFICATION
OF ALTERNATIVE MEDICINE

The most significant indicator of alternative medicine's growing acceptance within the larger society is its transformation from a marginal entrepreneurial activity into part of the corporate economy. This shift reflects the growing acceptability of alternative medicine throughout the population and acts as a major factor in furthering its acceptability even more.

Until fairly recently almost all money spent on alternative medicine was paid to individual practitioners or relatively small entrepreneurial businesses (Young 1961; Gevitz 1988; Armstrong and Armstrong 1991). There is no question that the eclectic mix of alternative medicine continues to encompass what has traditionally been viewed as "quack" or fraudulent practices and therapies. Examining the alphabetical listings in the *1998 Healthy Yellow Pages* for Los Angeles under A, one finds: acupressure, acupuncture, addiction recovery-treatment services, AIDS and HIV services, air purifiers and filtering, Alexander technique, alien-UFO abduct support, allergy treatment, alternative energy, angel artwork and gifts, animal healers, animal: humane and ethical treatment organizations, anti-aging products and services, appliance and metal recycling, applied kinesiology, aromatherapy, artists, astrology, attorneys, aura and chakra services, and Ayurvedic medicine.

Today any large city has scores of such providers, along with various referral services, directories, and Internet information pages that promote their services and products. Independent of their skill, training, or ethical standards, these individuals and concerns operate self-consciously as business people. In many cases their methods and honesty are above reproach, while in other instances they might best be described as "hucksters" or charlatans whose only goal is the maximization of their incomes. Local health "expos" are filled with sellers of "miracle" drugs and herbs that are purported to cure scores of ailments. For example, one manufacturer of aloe vera gel offers it as a cure for so many problems that they are just listed alphabetically in the firm's literature ("C: cancer, candida, corneal ulcers, contusions, canker sores, cold sores, cuts, cataracts, chapped and chafed skin and lips, coughs, colds, colitis, carbuncles, colic, cradle cap, cystitis, chemotherapy, constipation (R Pure Aloe International nd). Cell Tech, a producer of "super green algae," offers its product as a cure for a similar array of problems along with the promise that it will increase one's I.Q. by up to twenty points (Cell Tech 1992).

It is easy to find information about, and practitioners of, all sorts of therapies for cancer and other serious illnesses that make extravagant claims for success, such as Hoxsey therapy, shark cartilage, laetrile, Gerson's therapy, and many others. Regardless of their therapeutic efficacy, these sorts of treatments and practitioners are representative of one aspect of alternative medicine's economic and organizational reality: independent, fee-for-service capitalism. The aims and desires of these individuals and clinics are identical to those of all small business people: to be left alone. They are the embodiment of *laissez faire* capitalism. Regulation by the government, oversight by state boards or other regulatory groups, and meddling by third-party payors are all anathema to them (Burton-Goldberg Group 1993: 17–32). Twenty or thirty years ago almost all of alternative medicine could be described as part of this world. But now, they are only a small part of the picture. The barriers between alternative medicine and the larger corporate economy have begun to crumble.

Alternative medicine is becoming "big business." Sales of homeopathic remedies reached 100 million dollars a year in 1991 and have grown at a 20 percent annual rate since then. Medicinal herb sales were $1.3 billion in 1991 and have almost tripled to $3.6 billion by 1997 (Canedy 1998). As in the broader market for conventional medical services, mergers and the growing dominance of a few large firms have been rapidly occurring. These changes have both reflected and facilitated the acceptability of alternative approaches. Now, the growth of the homeopathic market has led some national drug chains, such as Savon and Thrifty, to stock homeopathic remedies. The amount of the product such huge chains require, along with their need for consistent access to a standardized product, is something that large firms are better able to provide. For example, until the late 1980s homeopathic remedies were difficult to find in most American communities. They were formulated by practitioners themselves or a small number of homeopathic pharmacies and small firms. Two large European homeopathic firms have bought out many of the American firms and invested heavily in expansion. Now they and two California companies dominate the market and routinely sell their products to mainstream retailers.

The identical pattern is evident in the sale of "natural" foods, where about 20 percent of all such products are now sold in mass-market food stores. A few years ago the percentage was almost nil (Brooks 1996). Just as conventional supermarkets now stock herbs and homeopathic remedies, the large health food chains, such as Whole Foods and Wild Oats, now promote themselves as "complete" markets and sell products like Haagen Daz and Cheerios. These chains are themselves the product of many mergers and takeovers of smaller chains. The growing similarity of health food stores and regular supermarkets is driven from both sides by a need to maximize profit, match competition, and increase market share. One effect of all this is a mainstreaming of alternative therapies, which heightens their general level of acceptance.

At one time large corporations were hesitant to produce and market things like vitamins and herbal remedies because the market was small, and as naturally occurring substances, they could not be patented. But now the market has become so large that major drug companies like Warner-Lambert and American Home Products are bringing out lines of herbal supplements. One of their strategies has been to sell various combinations that they can target to specific problems or give descriptive names like "Tranquility," "Super Charge," "Skeletal Support," or "Balanced Woman" (Equinox 1995). The companies then charge about three to four times what the individual ingredients would cost if purchased separately. As no clear standards exist for dosages of herbs, compared to vitamins, firms have tried to create a sense of brand identification that can be promoted to consumers as a mark of credibility.

Media conglomerates have realized that information about CAM is a highly sought after and profitable commodity. Books by authors like Deepak Chopra and Andrew Weil sell in the millions of copies. Works by authors like these have become important for publishers and "megastores" like Barnes and Noble or Borders. Weil's website, "Ask Dr. Weil" gets over 90,000 hits a day. In 1997 the website, which had long carried ads, became part of the Pathfinder Network, which is owned by Time Warner. Weil's advice now comes wrapped in a listing of other Time Warner websites, with links to Barnes and Noble to buy the books Weil recommends, and sponsorship by a vitamin supply house that sells what he suggests. *Time* magazine ran a cover story on Weil a few weeks before its parent company took over his website.

The convergence between the alternative and mainstream consumer can be seen by examining an issue of *Prevention* magazine. This flagship publication of the Rodale Press has probably done more to encourage the consumption of natural food and the use of herbal remedies than any other single source in the United States. In 1997 a typical issue had full-page ads from Lever Brothers, Dupont, Mars Candy Company (Three Musketeers Bars), and Ford.

Alternative medicine's acceptability to the corporate world is both a reflection of its acceptance in the larger community and a harbinger of still-greater acceptance to come as the forces of corporate advertising, marketing, and distribution are brought into play.

THE INTEGRATION OF CAM AND CONVENTIONAL CARE

The most significant indication of CAM's growing acceptability is its increasing assimilation into conventional medical-care organizations. Although this development can be ascribed in some significant part to expediency and marketing considerations on the part of HMOs and other managed-care groups, the affinity of managed care and alternative medicine has a more fundamental basis as well. Despite the fact that managed care has come to be highly criticized by many consumers, policy makers, and politicians for its profit-driven approach to care, its original appeal stems, in part, from some of the same factors that have facilitated the growing acceptability of alternative medicine: dissatisfaction with conventional medicine's ability to deal with chronic illness, its lack of attention to prevention, and the high cost of (often ineffective) care. Thus, it tends to be relatively open to innovations, including the integration of alternative therapies.

Many leaders in alternative medicine have been quick to note the supposed financial benefits that may accrue to managed-care plans that integrate their approaches (Jacobs 1995:48; Burton-Goldberg Group 1993: 431). An article in the 25th Anniversary issue of *Natural Health* magazine entitled "The Medical Revolution" put it this way: "Perhaps the biggest momentum carrying the country toward a new system of health care is coming from the people who pick up the tab for much of the nearly one trillion dollars spent on health care services and products . . . bluntly . . . if a patient has back pain that he [a primary care provider] believes would improve with movement therapy, he'll say to the insurance representative, 'look do you want me to order an MRI for $1,200 and refer the patient to a neurosurgeon for a $20,000 laminectomy? Or do you want to pay for $350 worth of Alexander Technique?' " (Thomson 1996:102). The growth of managed care has heightened the recognition of conventional medicine's limitations in dealing cost effectively with many chronic illnesses. If equally (in)effective but less costly therapy could be substituted for all or part of treatment, might not some patients at least be more satisfied and overall expenditures be reduced? This reasoning, combined with the realization that conventional care has little to offer those who wish to change their behavior or attitudes, as well as the desire to limit the side effects of many conventional treatments, has given the administrators of many managed-care organizations little reason to be hostile to alternative forms of treatment.

Insurance companies, such as Mutual of Omaha and Blue Cross, have begun to offer coverage for some forms of alternative care either separately or in combination with their normal coverage, and HMOs (beginning in 1996 with Oxford Health Care) have started to include coverage for some forms of alternative care. There have been two major stumbling blocks to this integration. The first is the lack of good data on the cost-effectiveness of many of those alternative interventions

that would be most acceptable to managed-care plans. Managed care accepts alternative medicine in the same way that it accepts conventional care: as something that can be delivered in standardized units and measured using standard outcomes. For this reason managed-care plans have been much more interested in techniques like acupuncture than in systems like Chinese Medicine or Ayurveda. For example, the use of St. Johns wort to treat moderate depression is likely to be less costly and have fewer side effects than conventional psychoactive medications. But all the research supporting the herb has been done in Europe. It was only in 1998 that NIH/OAM began to organize large-scale trials of the herb in the United States. Part of the impetus for these trials came from managed-care companies and health-services researchers who see their primary audience as health plan administrators.

The second major barrier to the integration of alternative techniques into managed-care plans is that there are no agreed-upon credentials for many alternative providers, and the standardization that does exist is a geographic hodgepodge. Health planners, think tanks, and managed-care leaders have begun to seek remedies for this situation as well. The point is that the rise in alternative medicine's acceptability to the public has placed conventional medical institutions, planners, and researchers in a position where they must act in a way that both reinforces and extends the acceptability of these approaches.

The growing acceptability of alternative medicine has brought with it greatly enhanced economic value and clout. This connection to huge corporations, insurance companies, and media conglomerates in turn helps bring about an even greater level of acceptability in the eyes of the public. The nature of alternative medicine may be reshaped by this commodification. For example, about twenty-five years ago the AMA was still calling chiropractic a "pseudomedical cult" and asking its members to boycott all interaction with chiropractors (American Medical Association 1973). Today almost every state requires that comprehensive health insurance include chiropractic, and all major insurers and HMOs have lists of "preferred chiropractors" whose fees they reimburse. But this inclusion of chiropractic as part of the medical mainstream encompasses only limited treatment for a specific list of conditions. Many chiropractors had long been unwilling to abandon chiropractic's claims to be a system for treating a full range of illnesses and accept its new status as an "allied health profession." But the economic incentives and disincentives of managed care have made it a reality.

The generally favorable coverage that alternative medicine receives in *Time, Newsweek,* and many other publications offers the constant message that alternative therapies are being used by educated, middle-class people, and that an informed, intelligent consumerism should prevail in assessing them. The implicit, if not explicit, message is: "This is something our readers or viewers should know about and consider using themselves." In 1998 *Newsweek* ran a full page story on "How to find the right doctor for alternative care" that concluded, "The days when alternative medicine meant quackery are waning—with good reason. It's where many people find solutions that conventional doctoring couldn't give them. But, . . . you'd better keep your eyes open." (Spragins 1998:73).

Advocates of alternative medicine traditionally assumed that their approaches would triumph and become a part of the mainstream due to their underlying validity and therapeutic utility. The reality is that the integration of the alternative and conventional worlds of medicine is taking place largely because the same standards of cost saving, and the generation of economic surpluses are being applied to both. The acceptability of alternative medicine to the corporations that control the media and managed care is one of the driving forces behind its growing acceptability to the population at large.

WILL THE ACCEPTABILITY OF ALTERNATIVE MEDICINE CONTINUE TO GROW?

It is highly likely that what we call "alternative medicine" will continue to gain acceptance in the United States over the coming years. The boundaries of "mainstream" medicine have always been permeable and highly pragmatic in what is included. Approaches like osteopathy and chiropractic are now well-accepted, if restricted, modes of care. The groundswell of consumer demand is the greatest force promoting the acceptance of alternative approaches. People who are ill seek not to validate some particular approach to medicine, but to get well, or at least feel better. They want to know, "Does it work?" not "Is it mainstream or alternative?" As Merrijoy Kelner and Beverly Wellman found in their study of Canadians, "Patients chose specific kinds of practitioners for particular problems, and some use a mixture . . . the choice is multidimensional and cannot be explained . . . by an 'alternative ideology'" (1997:203). In his national sample of 1,035 respondents, John Astin (1998) found

that using alternative therapies over the past year was associated with being in poor health, suffering from a chronic problem, being highly educated, and identifying with the values of feminism, environmentalism, and spiritual or personal growth. Dissatisfaction with one's own physician was not related to use. Although Astin did find that using alternative medicine was associated with having a "holistic philosophy," this was based on a "yes/no" response to a single vaguely worded item.

Almost every study has found that the chronically ill use both conventional and alternative care. For example, over 90 percent of those suffering from arthritis use alternative medicine at some point. About half of them don't disclose this to their conventional doctor (Himmel, Schulte, and Kochen 1993; Eisenberg 1997). In Astin's study fewer than 5 percent of respondents relied "primarily" on alternative therapies. The recognition by patients, their advocates, and many conventional providers that a rational consumerism can encompass both alternative and conventional approaches will likely be a major factor in heightening the acceptability of alternative medicine. The fact that many conventional medical institutions such as hospitals, managed care plans, and groups like the AMA have already changed their attitude toward at least some aspects of alternative medicine will also heighten its acceptability in the future. The AMA no longer refers to alternative medicine as "quackery" and has an official position calling for its members to learn more about CAM (American Medical Association 1995: 410).

As more biomedical and technical advances are made, the "critical distancing" toward conventional medicine experienced by many people in the society will continue to increase. The commodification of all health care will advance through the expansion of managed care and the corporate-based health-care industry. Ongoing debates about the cost of health care, the lack of continuity and caring in medicine, and the neglect of prevention and mind–body interactions will all serve to make people see health and medicine, not as something "special," but as more like any other commodity or service that requires vigilance and skepticism. This process will be abetted by the rising proportion of the population suffering from chronic illness or at risk for such conditions. As the population ages, this proportion can only increase. Yet it is these conditions for which conventional medicine and managed care are often judged least satisfactory. Knowledge about "risk factors" for such conditions, as well as information about how to limit their impact and severity, are becoming widely known. The "at-risk" population is growing rapidly and highly motivated to change. Yet conventional medicine often downplays the importance of some risk factors or is not very helpful in fostering and maintaining the necessary behavioral changes (Angell 1997). Increasingly, this population (consisting of those already diagnosed, diagnosed as "at-risk," and self-diagnosed or self-defined at risk) will avail themselves of alternative approaches, particularly as the media make them more widely known and acceptable.

Ironically, many of the most dramatic advances of conventional medicine, such as the use of artificial organs, gene therapy, and transplants, may heighten the distance from medicine many people feel by widening the gulf between how scientists and physicians understand who we "are," and how we understand ourselves (Williams 1997). In this context the integration of our bodies and minds offered by alternative medicine, and reinforced by developments in other fields such as psychoneuroimmunology, may become more appealing. Those who are ill, or who feel themselves at risk to become ill, are increasingly desirous of playing a more active role in their own healing. Whether CAM is a truly new paradigm depends, in part, on its ability to point up and respond to the gaps and failures in the existing dominant biomedical model. To the extent that CAM offers a sense that the current situation is riddled with contradictions and that a new and better "framing" for ideas about health and illness is possible, it does represent a new paradigm (Wolpe 1990).

The identity offered by alternative medicine offers a way to transcend the misfortune of illness and the day-to-day drudgery of maintaining health. The acceptability of the idea that people can and should be doing something about their health creates the need for an identity that can foster our ability to act in this way. To the extent that alternative medicine can turn pathology into opportunity, it will continue to gain acceptance in society.

ALTERNATIVE MEDICINE AND MEDICAL SOCIOLOGY

Most of what sociologists have written about alternative medicine over the past few decades has portrayed it as something deviant or foreign. Alternative medicine often represented the irrational, and its use was explained either by the absence of opportunities to use "real" medicine or as part of a residual commitment to some other collectivity such as an ethnic or religious group. Over time, alternative medicine would surely wither away. But reality doesn't appear to have been reading sociology. As I've shown, the population, the media, and even some people in conventional medicine have been busy increasing and enhancing the presence of alternative medicine, at times even integrating it into the mainstream. In this sense one might be justified in citing the growing acceptability of alternative medicine as a good example of sociology's inability to understand, let alone make predictions, about society.

Yet from another point of view, the growing acceptability of alternative medicine reflects the success of medical sociology. More than most other academic fields, sociology has stressed themes that are essential parts of the alternative worldview: the importance of the "self" and the "self-concept" in determining how people feel and what they are capable of achieving; the power of social support and social ties to bring about well-being and prevent illness or social breakdown; and the notion of the individual as a reflection of the community. These concepts, along with sociological critiques of mainstream medicine for its dysfunctional levels of professional autonomy and dominance, as well as its bureaucracy and the way it reinforces the unequal distribution of societal resources, are ideas that are common to *both* sociology and alternative medicine. From this vantage point, the growing acceptability of alternative medicine reflects and reinforces the utility of sociology and the acceptance of a sociological view of the nature of health and illness.

REFERENCES

ALSTER, KRISTINE B. 1989. *The Holistic Health Movement.* Tuscaloosa, AL: The University of Alabama Press.

AMERICAN HOLISTIC MEDICAL ASSOCIATION. 1997. Homepage. URL *http://www.ahma.org.*

AMERICAN MEDICAL ASSOCIATION. 1973. "Proceedings of the House of Delegates." New York, NY.

AMERICAN MEDICAL ASSOCIATION. 1995. "Proceedings of the House of Delegates." Chicago, IL.

ANGELL, MARCIA. 1997. "Overdosing on Health Risks." *New York Times Magazine* May 4: 44–45.

ANGELL, MARCIA, and JEROME P. KASSIRER. 1998. "Alternative Medicine—The Risks of Untested and Unregulated Remedies." *New England Journal of Medicine* 339: 839–41.

ARMSTRONG, DAVID, and ELIZABETH M. ARMSTRONG. 1991. *The Great American Medicine Show.* New York, NY: Prentice Hall.

Astin, John. 1998. "Why Patients Use Alternative Medicine." *JAMA* 279:1548–53.

Berlant, Jeffery L. 1975. *Profession and Monopoly*. Berkeley, CA: University of California Press.

Boston Women's Health Collective. 1992. *The New Our Bodies Ourselves*. New York: Simon and Schuster.

Brooks, Nancy R. 1996. "From Gooch to High Gloss: Change Signals Shift for Natural Foods Industry." *Los Angeles Times* July 24: D1,7.

Burton-Goldberg Group. 1993. *Alternative Medicine: The Definitive Guide*. Puyallup, WA: Future Medical Publishing.

Canedy, Dana. 1998. "Real Medicine or Medicine Show?" *New York Times* July 23: C1,4.

Cell Tech. 1992. "Super Blue-Green Algae: The Key." *Newsletter* (December).

Chopra, Deepak. 1989. *Quantum Healing: Exploring the Frontiers of Mind-Body Medicine*. New York: Bantam Books.

Chopra, Deepak. 1993. *Ageless Body, Timeless Mind: The Quantum Alternative to Growing Old*. New York: Harmony Books.

Chowka, Peter B. 1996. "Prayer Is Good Medicine." *Yoga Journal* July/August: 61–67, 156–58.

Dossey, Larry. 1993. *Healing Words: The Power of Prayer and the Practice of Medicine*. San Francisco, CA: Harper-Collins.

Dossey, Larry. 1995. "A Journal and a Journey." *Alternative Therapies* 1(1):6–9.

Eisenberg, David M. 1997. "Advising Patients Who Use Alternative Medical Therapies." *Annals of Internal Medicine* 127:61–69.

Eisenberg, David M., Ronald C. Kessler, Cindy Foster, Francis E. Norlock, David Calkins, and Thomas L. Delbanco. 1993. "Unconventional Medicine in the United States: Prevalence, Costs, and Patterns of Use." *New England Journal of Medicine* 328:246–52.

Equinox. 1995. Catalog.

Fontanarosa, Phill B., and George D. Lundberg. 1997. "Complementary, Alternative and Unconventional and Integrative Medicine." *JAMA* 278: 2111–12.

Freidson, Eliot. 1970. *Profession of Medicine*. New York: Dodd, Mead.

Gevitz, Norman, ed. 1988. *Other Healers: Unorthodox Healers in America*. Baltimore, MD: Johns Hopkins University Press.

Goldstein, Michael S. 1992. *The Health Movement: Promoting Fitness in America*. New York: Twayne/Macmillan.

Goldstein, Michael S. 1999. *Alternative Health Care: Medicine, Miracle, or Mirage?* Philadelphia, PA: Temple University Press.

Goldstein, Michael, Dennis T. Jaffe, Carol Sutherland, and Josie Wilson. 1987. "Holistic Physicians: Implications for the Study of the Medical Profession." *Journal of Health and Social Behavior* 28:103–19.

Goldstein, Michael S., Dennis T. Jaffe, Dale Garrell, and Ruth Ellen Berk. 1985. "Holistic Doctors: Becoming a Nontraditional Medical Practitioner." *Urban Life* 14:317–44.

Harkin, Tom. 1995. "The Third Approach." *Alternative Therapies* 1(1):71.

Himmel, Wolfgang, Miriam Schulte, and Michael M. Kochen. 1993. "Complementary Medicine: Are Patients Expectations Being Met by Their General Practitioners?" *British Journal of General Practice* 43: 232–35.

Jacobs, Jennifer. 1995. "Homeopathy Should Be Integrated Into Mainstream Medicine." *Alternative Therapies* 1(4): 48–53.

Kelner, Merrijoy, and Beverly Wellman. 1997. "Health Care and Consumers' Choice: Medical and Alternative Therapies." *Social Science and Medicine* 45: 203–12.

Larson, Magali S. 1977. *The Rise of Professionalism: A Sociological Analysis*. Berkeley, CA: University of California Press.

Levin, Jeffery S. 1994. "Religion and Health: Is There an Association, Is It Valid, Is It Causal?" *Social Science and Medicine* 28: 1475–82.

Lowenberg, June S. 1989. *Caring and Responsibility*. Philadelphia, PA: University of Pennsylvania Press.

Mattson, Phyllis H. 1982. *Holistic Health in Perspective*. Palo Alto, CA: Mayfield Publishing Co.

Milbank Memorial Fund. 1998. *Enhancing the Accountability of Alternative Medicine*. New York: Milbank Memorial Fund.

National Health Federation. 1995. *Health Freedom News*. Monrovia, CA.

Nebelkopf, Ethan. 1995. "Psychedelic and Shamanistic Influences in the Human Services in the U.S." *Yearbook of Cross Cultural Medicine and Psychotherapy*.

Office of Alternative Medicine. 1992. *Alternative Medicine: Expanding Medical Horizons: A Report to the National Institutes of Health on Alternative Medical Systems and Practices in the United States*. Washington, DC: U.S. Government Printing Office.

Pew Research Center for the People and the Press. 1996. "The Diminishing Divide . . . American Churches, American Politics." URL *http://www.people-press.org*.

R Pure Aloe International. nd. "A-Z: Why Aloe Vera?"(pamphlet) Northglen, CO.

Sale, David M. 1995. *Overview of Legislative Developments Concerning Alternative Health Care in the United States*. Kalamazoo, MI: The Fetzer Institute.

Seligman, Jean, and Geoffrey Cowley. 1995. "Sex, Lies, and Garlic." *Newsweek* November 6:65–68.

Spragins, Ellyn E. 1998. "Frontier Medicine: How to Find the Right Doctor for Alternative Care." *Newsweek* June 29:73.

Starr, Paul. 1982. *The Social Transformation of American Medicine*. New York: Basic Books.

Thomson, Bill. 1996. "The Medical Revolution." *Natural Health* March/April: 98–103.

Tractman, Paul. 1994. "NIH Looks at the Implausible and the Inexplicable." *Smithsonian* September: 110–24.

Wallis, Claudia. 1996. "Faith and Healing." *Time Magazine,* June 24: 58–64.

Wardwell, Walter, I. 1972. "Limited, Marginal, and Quasi-Practitioners." In *Handbook of Medical Sociology,* 2nd ed., ed. Howard E. Freeman, Sol Levine, and Leo G. Reeder. Englewood Cliffs, NJ: Prentice Hall, pp. 250–73.

Weil, Andrew. 1997a. *Eight Weeks to Optimum Health: A Proven Program for Taking Full Advantage of Your Body's Natural Healing Power.* New York: Knopf.

Weil, Andrew. 1997b. "Ask Dr. Weil." Homepage of Andrew Weil. URL *http://cgi.pathfinder.com/drweil/home.*

Weil, Andrew, and Winifred Rosen. 1993. *Chocolate to Morphine: Understanding Drugs.* Boston, MA: Houghton Mifflin.

Williams, Simon J. 1997. "Modern Medicine and the Uncertain Body: From Corporeality to Hyperreality." *Social Science and Medicine* 45: 1041–49.

Wolpe, Paul R. 1990. "The Holistic Heresy: Strategies of Ideological Challenge." *Social Science and Medicine* 31:913–23.

Young, James H. 1961. *The Toadstool Millionaires: A Social History of Patent Medicine in America.* Princeton, NJ: Princeton University Press.

Zwicky, John F. 1993. *Reader's Guide to Alternative Methods.* Chicago, IL: American Medical Association.

20 QUALITY OF LIFE IN HEALTH, ILLNESS, AND MEDICAL CARE

DEBRA LERNER, *New England Medical Center, Boston*

CAROLYN E. SCHWARTZ, *Harvard Medical School*

Historic changes in population health and medical care within the United States have stimulated interest in "health-related quality of life" (QOL). This term has been difficult to define precisely, but there is increasing agreement that "health-related QOL" refers to the degree to which valued aspects of a person's life have been influenced, positively or negatively, by health and/or health-related interventions such as medical care.

Health-related QOL is related to the more general concept "quality of life," which social scientists have used to reflect how "good" life is within specific communities, states, or nations. In the 1960s and 1970s, QOL variables were used as social indicators to describe the level of progress or social well-being reached within the United States (Andrews and Withey 1976; Campbell, Converse, and Rodgers 1976). Environments in which certain features were present according to objective indicators, or perceived by members of the community as satisfactory (e.g., good schools), were rated as having a good QOL. In contrast, "health-related QOL" entered the popular and scientific parlance as a term for describing the consequences, for individuals or groups, of having a chronic and/or life-threatening health problem or undergoing a particular treatment. A variety of different criteria have been used to decide who has a relatively good or poor health-related QOL. Some of the indicators that are considered relevant are an individual's (or patient's) level of functional independence, psychological well-being, perceived health status, disease symptoms, and the quantity and quality of social participation.

The principle aim of this chapter is to present a comprehensive review of health-related QOL. It will begin with a discussion of the social, political, and economic conditions that have contributed to the emergence of the concept and its importance within medical sociology. It will identify important developments in its definition and assessment. It will discuss the constituencies that have emerged for information concerning health-related QOL and the uses of this information. Finally, this chapter will focus on the application of health-related QOL assessment to the care of individual patients. Specifically, it will examine why health-related QOL considerations and assessment methods are not well integrated with the care of people with chronic or life-threatening illnesses and/or impairments. These are among the groups that tend to be vulnerable to losses in health-related QOL and, conceivably, may benefit most from increased attention to this issue.

A second and equally important aim is to encourage more sociologists to become interested in this topic. Only a small number have been active in this area of inquiry despite the fact that it is highly compatible with and relevant to the discipline. For example, health-related QOL studies are concerned with the "person" and, thus, differ from biomedical research, which tends to be "disease-focused." Consequently, attention to this topic can contribute to a medical sociology that is more independent of medical categories (e.g., diagnoses and symptoms) and assumptions. Additionally, health-related QOL is assessed by patients according to criteria that are important to their health. Historically, physicians have had the primary role in assessing health and the success of intervention. Thus, the topic is a fertile one for exploring questions concerning doctor–patient communication and examining the discontinuities between normative or so-called "objective" measures of health and health outcomes and those defined and/or valued by the patient or layperson (Albrecht and Fitz-patrick 1994). Finally, because a variety of different constituencies advocate for specific definitions of health-related QOL, which may be used to make claims about the benefits and risks of specific treatments, there are many opportunities to study the social construction of health, illness, and medical progress.

CURRENT CONTEXT

Many individuals within the health-care industry, academia, government agencies, and patient and consumer advocacy groups have become interested in health-related QOL. This interest reflects both the high degree of value that many in the United States and elsewhere place on health, as well as rising expectations regarding the performance of health professionals (Thier 1992).

A steadily increasing number of efforts have been made within the past two decades to integrate health-related QOL considerations into clinical research, medical practice, and health-policy deliberations. By far, health-related QOL considerations have been most successfully integrated into clinical research. Currently, patient health-related QOL is used as an endpoint in many illness and treatment studies (Gill and Feinstein 1994; O'Boyle 1992). Additionally, health-related QOL ratings have acquired an important role in cost-effectiveness and cost-utility analyses. These methods, which are used primarily for resource allocation purposes, compare the cost of an illness and its treatment(s) to the outcomes achieved (Russell et al. 1996).

This relatively new emphasis on health-related QOL is an important development in the history of western medicine and health care. For most of this century, physicians, scientists, and policy makers have measured morbidity and mortality to determine the degree of success or failure achieved in coping with health problems. Morbidity and mortality are considered objective and, therefore, correct. In contrast, health-related QOL assessment relies on information that is reported directly by the patient (or other subject of interest) or, in some cases, by a surrogate, such as a family member. Physicians, scientists, and policy makers have tended to avoid using self-reported information on the grounds that it is subjective and, thus, unreliable. However, methodological developments in health-related QOL assessment and the widespread availability of information systems in medical organizations have weakened such criticisms and facilitated acceptance and use of this information. Efforts to enhance the clarity of the concept have contributed as well.

BACKGROUND

Medical sociologists had an important role in drawing attention to health-related QOL, providing the intellectual rationale for including it as a criterion for determining the outcome of illness and treatment. Sol Levine, to whom this book is dedicated, was a pioneer in this regard. Levine (1987), with Sydney Croog (Croog and Levine 1989), J. Najman (Najman and Levine 1981), and others (Lerner and Levine 1994) indicated that three conditions made it increasingly necessary to focus on health-related QOL. These were: the epidemiological transition in population health, advances in medical technology, and increased concerns about medical care expenditures. Each represented an important and dramatic change that altered prevailing patterns of illness and the structure of medical care.

The Epidemiological Transition Since the turn of the century, rates of many acute infectious diseases within the United States and other industrialized nations have declined while life expectancies and rates of chronic health problems have increased (Wilkinson 1994). Life-threatening illnesses, such as coronary heart disease and certain cancers, were on the rise as were conditions such as arthritis and major depression, which were not necessarily fatal but often caused substantial impairment and disability. The epidemiological transition raised important questions about the meaning of "health" and the appropriate role of medical care.

For most of this century, "health" had been defined within the parameters specified by biomedicine. Health professionals in general and physicians in particular have tended to regard "health" as the absence of disease and the role of medical care to be to provide a cure. According to the model, the appropriate yardsticks for measuring the success or failure of medical intervention, for an individual or a social system, were morbidity and mortality. Critics of the biomedical model regarded it as too narrow, as not fully encompassing issues that were of importance to an older, chronically ill and disabled population. For example, the biomedical model gave insufficient consideration to issues such as how an illness or medical treatment might affect life satisfaction or a person's ability to carry out important activities, such as working. In 1947, the World Health Organization published a document defining "health" as "a state of complete physical, mental and social well-being and not merely the absence of infirmity" (World Health Organization 1947). This event marked the beginning of intensified interest in adopting a vision of population health, which encompassed both the quality as well as the quantity of life .

Advances in Medical Technology New technologies were having a profound impact on medical practice, in some cases bringing physicians' life-saving capabilities to new heights (Elkinton 1966). However, ethicists and others began to question whether the emphasis on life-saving technologies was overshadowing the importance of innovations that were life enhancing and, in effect, shifting medical attention from the "person" to the "disease." For example, "heroic" procedures such as kidney dialysis and organ transplantation, while enabling physicians to extend the lives of very ill or impaired individuals, did not necessarily free patients from pain, discomfort, distress, and/or a loss of functional independence. Additionally, new prescription medications offered improved control of serious illness; however, some had serious side effects. Thus, awareness and interest in health-related QOL emerged partially as a reaction to technology-driven medical care, which some regarded as dehumanizing and risky.

Concerns About Medical Care Expenditure In the 1980s, the U.S. health-care system was perceived as being in a state of economic crisis as medical inflation spiraled out of control. In a little more than a decade, medical-care costs as a percent of gross domestic product rose from 9 percent to 13 percent. Many cost-control measures were being instituted in an effort to reshape medical care delivery and financing. Service cutbacks and the specter of medical-care rationing supported the need for increased attention to the human consequences of economic policies (Gellert 1993).

Thus, to a certain degree, the emergence of health-related QOL as a public health and medical issue evolved from an awareness within different sectors of society that the winds of technological and economic change were moving the U.S. health-care system in an undesirable direction. An emphasis on health-related QOL was perceived as contributing to preserving and enhancing its more humane and holistic features.

Health-related QOL continues to be an important and highly relevant topic of inquiry for medical sociologists. The conditions that instigated interest in health-related QOL remain deeply in effect today. The baby boom generation born between the 1940s and the early 1960s has entered middle age (Fullerton 1997) and is likely to have a dramatic impact on the incidence and prevalence of chronic disease and disability during the next two decades. Internationally, the burden of chronic disease has intensified in industrialized and developing nations

(Murray and Lopez 1996). By the year 2020, noncommunicable diseases are projected to account for seven out of ten deaths in developing countries. Currently, they account for about half. Technological developments continue to occur at a rapid pace. Health-related QOL issues not only persist but have become increasingly more complicated. Technologies such as genetic testing and sophisticated fertility treatments have implications for individuals as well as their offspring. Certain pharmaceutical treatments require patients and their physicians to make complicated treatment choices, weighing several health risks simultaneously. For example, tamoxifen has been found to reduce the risk of breast cancer and, thus, has been recommended for certain groups of high-risk women. However, women who use tamoxifen also increase their risk of developing other cancers. Finally, the trend toward managed care continues. While more U.S. citizens than ever are enrolled in such plans, a swarm of criticism and distrust has enveloped the industry, prompting a new wave of consumer activism and physician dissatisfaction as well as increased demands for accountability (Donelan et al. 1997).

EMERGENT FORCES

Two relatively recent developments are likely to further propel health-related QOL considerations into the social and health-policy arena: persistent ferment surrounding the question of national health insurance in the United States and other nations and the quality-improvement movement within medicine.

Ferment Around National Health Insurance National health-policy debates in the United States, Canada, Great Britain, and elsewhere are ongoing. There is a lack of resolution regarding the structure of health care and the nature of reforms necessary to reduce perceived health and fiscal problems. Questions concerning the appropriate aims of health care and the degree to which current and future policies meet these aims are far from settled. It is unlikely that any major health-policy alternative will be adopted without consideration of both its projected and actual economic impact and its impact on the health and health-related QOL of the population.

The Quality Improvement Movement The widespread adoption of quality-management programs within health-care plans and clinical practice settings has invigorated interest in health-related QOL assessment. Quality-management programs have been established in medical-care settings to study patterns of care, health outcomes, and costs, and to attempt to resolve lapses in quality (McGlynn 1997). Quality management programs became popular as a result of several influences, which include: increased competition for patient revenues on behalf of health plans, physicians, and hospitals; administrative efforts to manage medical professionals and limit variability in their practices; and pressures from consumer groups as well as from employers, who want evidence of "value" for their health-care investment. Health-related QOL assessment is becoming one piece of a larger effort to find an acceptable balance between cost and quality.

NORMATIVE AND IDIOGRAPHIC APPROACHES TO DEFINING HEALTH-RELATED QOL

As several constituencies attempt to measure health-related QOL and use the information generated by assessment, it becomes ever-more important to determine what is meant by declaring that a person has a relatively good or poor health-related QOL. There is a political and ideological dimension to defining health-related QOL because it involves asserting which aspects of health (e.g., physical functioning, fatigue, and mental health) have value to whom. For example, a pharmaceutical firm testing a new compound could claim success on the basis of one set of health-related QOL criteria, but these may differ from those criteria patients employ. Health-related QOL also has a philosophical dimension. Definitions are deeply rooted in personal and cultural values and ideas about personal fulfillment. Many have attempted to tackle the definitional problem, but this task has proved to be difficult. Despite progress, the appropriate definition of health-related QOL remains an issue of some debate.

Initially, academicians who were interested in the topic attempted to define the term by enumerating aspects of a person's life that presumably were *normative* or valued among individuals within the population and thus contributed to quality of life. Alternatively, some have defined the term by indicating that it is *idiographic,* that is, entirely dependent on personal values. Therefore, health-related QOL would not be compatible with attempts to define it objectively.

Both the normative and idiographic perspectives tend to agree that health-related QOL is influenced by the ability to function and perceived health status. Where the perspectives disagree is on which specific components should be included in a definition of health-related QOL and how these should be identified. Despite disagreements, both perspectives have survived and continue to dominate in the research literature.

It is not surprising that definitions vary when one considers the range of different disciplines represented in this field, the variety of uses of health-related QOL information, and the number of actual and potential consumers of the information. For example, the topic has been addressed by sociologists, health-services researchers, health economists, philosophers, and physicians representing a wide range of specialties and often with different purposes in mind. While some cross-fertilization among disciplines inevitably has occurred, research concerning health-related QOL has not been especially interdisciplinary or synergistic (Lerner and Levine 1994). This situation is unfortunate considering the extent to which interests are shared.

The normative approach to defining health-related QOL assumes that the degree to which an individual has achieved a good health-related QOL is determined by a person's status on a number of criteria, which are presumed to be important. Proponents of this approach suggest that a "good" health-related QOL is signified by the degree to which one is able to function physically, cognitively, emotionally, and socially. Ability to participate in valued social roles (e.g., employment and household roles) is also considered important. Additionally, some consider health-related QOL to be related to the degree to which a person is free of pain and is able to maintain a high level of vitality or energy (Levine and Croog 1984; Ware 1991; McDowell, Martini, and Waugh 1978). More comprehensive concepts suggest that health-related QOL is influenced by resiliency, social opportunity, and spirituality (Patrick and Erickson 1993). While there is a great deal of consistency in the formulations, it is also recognized that the relative importance of certain criteria will vary according to the characteristics of the subjects who are being assessed (e.g., their demographics, illnesses, or treatments) (Croog and Levine 1989).

The normative approach, therefore, focuses on criteria that are regarded as "objectively" of value. In contrast, the idiographic approach assumes that health-related QOL is a subjective phenomenon because it describes only those elements of a person's life that are important to that individual. According to Cleary and colleagues, health-related QOL consists of aspects of a person's life that are "affected strongly by health status (health-related) and that are important to the person (QOL)" (Cleary, Wilson, and Fowler 1994). It has also been described as a summary of the manner in which people perceive and evaluate the impact of their own health status on their lives. Thus, in principle, the idiographic perspective differs markedly from the normative one.

Another conceptual framework, which is an extension of the idiographic approach, was developed by Donald Patrick and Pennifer Erickson. They regard health-related QOL as "the value assigned to the duration of life as modified by impairments, functional states, perceptions, and social opportunities that are influenced by disease, injury, treatment or policy" (1993). Thus, health-related QOL refers to the value ascribed to the years of life remaining after an illness or treatment has begun. Methods to estimate the value of remaining life years are used in cost-effectiveness and cost-utility analyses of diagnostic and therapeutic modalities.

While certain criteria are typically considered important to determining a person's health-related QOL in the United States and other industrialized nations, advocates of either the normative or idiographic approach indicate that they will vary according to a number of sociodemographic, disease-specific, and cultural variables. For example, elderly people being treated in a long-term care facility will have different health-related QOL concerns than will the parents of school-aged children. Similarly, physical health problems such as arthritis will affect different aspects of QOL than mental health problems such as schizophrenia, though there may be some overlapping issues. Cultural considerations, such as the role of spirituality in people's lives or one's expectation for independence, may be important for determining a person's health-related QOL.

The World Health Organization has significantly advanced this perspective in the course of developing its QOL survey instrument, the WHOQOL. It has defined QOL (which encompasses but is not limited to health-related QOL) as "an individual's perception of their position in life in the context of the culture and value systems in which they live and in relation to their goals, expectations, standards and concerns. It is a broad ranging concept affected in a complex way by the person's physical health, psychological state, level of independence, social relationships and their relationship to salient features of the environment" (WHOQOL Group 1993).

The different permutations and shades of meaning given to health-related QOL are both necessary and appropriate, since the concept and methods of measurement must remain open to the variability in values and expectations regarding health and health-related matters. Thus, it may be more appropriate to regard health-related QOL as an umbrella term for a particular category of considerations rather than as a concept that adheres to any single definition or set of criteria.

MEASUREMENT OF HEALTH-RELATED QOL

In certain respects, health-related QOL is like happiness. It cannot be measured directly like taking a temperature with a thermometer. It can only be assessed indirectly on the basis of a set of variables that are surrogates for the concept, and it must be evaluated to the degree possible from the person's perspective.

Typically, the approach has been to ask people to rate certain health-related QOL criteria on the basis of their responses to questionnaires or interviews. Many measurement tools have been designed with a particular primary application in mind, such as to assess knee-replacement surgery or medication for migraine headaches. These are known as "condition-specific" instruments. Many tools are regarded as serving multiple purposes and as being broadly applicable to different populations. These are referred to as "generic" instruments.

In the United States, financial support for the development of health-related QOL questionnaires frequently has come from the pharmaceutical industry and, to a lesser extent, from private foundations and federal agencies such as the National Institutes of Health. The large role of commercial entities in questionnaire development and research has raised issues about the influence of sponsorship on measurement and intellectual property (Berzon et al. 1994). Access to health-related QOL data and measurement tools may be considered proprietary or subject to user fees.

The demand for practical solutions to health-care system problems has undoubtedly been a force driving the development and dissemination of assessment methodologies. However, perhaps too frequently, the tail has been wagging the dog. Methodology has determined meaning, not vice versa. Thomas Gill and Alvan Feinstein (1994) report the detrimental effect on the quality of research. In many of the clinical studies they reviewed, there was little consistency in the manner in which the concept was defined. Additionally, indicators were employed frequently without justification. To some degree, this problem has been remedied by greater standardization of approaches to assessing health-related QOL. However, standardization will be useful only as long as the methods are meaningful.

Measurement methods have developed along two distinct lines, which are related to the two perspectives discussed previously. Questionnaires are used to generate either descriptive "profiles" of health-related QOL (consistent with the normative approach) or reports that are preference-based or weighted—sometimes, but not always, consistent with the idiographic approach (Berzon, Mauskopf, and Simeon 1996).

Descriptive profiles are obtained by questionnaires that ask respondents to rate their status (e.g., level of limitation or frequency of problem) on a set of indicators. One of these indicators might be the degree to which health limits one's ability to climb stairs. Ratings on these indicators are organized into different health-related QOL "domains," such as physical functioning, mental health, and social role limitation (Spilker 1996), and scored. The resultant scores signify the level of health-related QOL. According to this method, the individual who completes the questionnaire doesn't determine which indicators are used and how they should be weighted to generate a final health-related QOL score. Thus, individual values and preferences do not "intrude" in an obvious manner. However, the failure to explore the importance of domains to individual respondents has led some to reject this approach.

In an attempt to enable individuals to indicate which outcomes are most important to their lives, the preference-weighting approach was developed. It defines a set of plausible health outcomes (e.g., inability to walk without assistance) that are associated with one or more health problems and/or treatments and obtains information about how individuals rate their relative importance (i.e., value).

Some rating systems attempt to determine a person's preference or "utility" for a defined health state (Drummond, Stoddard, and Torrance 1995). The concept of utility is derived from economics and rational choice theory (Coleman 1992). Essentially, this framework assumes that people assign different utilities to different outcomes and act on the basis of these choices. To establish preferences for certain health outcomes, one of three methods is used: the standard gamble, the time trade-off approach, and willingness-to-pay techniques.

The time trade-off approach asks people to indicate how many years of life they would be willing to spend in a certain state of ill health. In contrast, willingness-to-pay methods attempt to determine the investment people are willing to make to achieve or avoid certain states. Preference-rating approaches have been subjected to methodological criticisms (lack of reliability) and substantive ones as well; the individual is portrayed as acting completely out of self-interest, and health is treated as a commodity. Further, the foundational work in some preference-based approaches assumes a community standard

is the best approximation of the real value assigned to health states. Thus, the weights for different health-related QOL variables are average scores obtained from community samples or other aggregations (Kind 1996). Averaging ignores the perspective that individuals have on their own health states.

The advantages and disadvantages of these two broad measurement methods have led to some tension to combine information that is both normative and idiographic (e.g., to evaluate outcomes in any way that integrates comprehensive descriptions of function with individual-level values-based assessment that illustrates the impact on important aspects of life). This movement toward "patient-centered" outcomes assessment emphasizes the need to combine normative and idiographic measurement into methods that can be used for medical decision-making and health-policy applications.

One example is the Extended Q-TWiST methodology (Schwartz, Cole, and Gelber 1995; Schwartz, Cole, Vickrey, and Gelber 1995). It was built on the quality-adjusted time without symptoms and toxicity (Q-TWiST) methodology developed for use in clinical trials for cancer and AIDS (Gelber and Goldhirsch 1986; Gelber, Cole, Gelber, and Goldhirsch 1995). The original approach was aimed at estimating how useful a treatment was by subtracting from the estimated amount of survival time the total time patients spent with treatment-related toxicities and disease progression. Time spent in these other states was weighted to determine under what combination of utility values the treatment in question was better than the comparison treatment. The Extended Q-TWiST was designed to integrate individual patient values over time (assuming that values may change) and to integrate the perspectives of the provider and social cost into a single analysis. Thus, the impact of the experience of disease and treatment toxicities would explicitly be considered in the treatment evaluation. Besides making the patient's perspective central, the method integrates information from the provider as well as social cost, so that all three perspectives are considered in the estimate of treatment gain. The method reflects a perceived need to have the patient's perspective play a lead but not solo role in determining the impact of an intervention.

THE APPLICATION OF HEALTH-RELATED QOL INFORMATION

The availability of assessment techniques has eliminated some of the barriers to obtaining health-related QOL information. However, in practice, health-related QOL is formally and/or routinely included in a small fraction of the decision-making activities of health-care professionals, including physicians and nurses, and policy makers.

Conceivably, health-policy development, population health assessment, public health improvement, clinical research, and individual patient care could all benefit from incorporating information about the impact of health problems and treatments on health-related QOL. H. J. Sutherland and J. E. Till (1993) suggest that the information could have an important and potentially beneficial role on three distinct levels of decision-making concerning health and health-related matters: the macro, meso, and micro levels. At the macro level, policy decisions must be made by legislators and other officials who will need to consider the value of various strategies and proposals and their impact on large segments of the population. At the meso level, the health professions and health-care delivery organizations, such as hospitals and health plans, must determine how best to care for defined populations (e.g., patients or community residents). These decisions require information concerning the effectiveness of specific interventions. A chief concern at the meso level is influencing physician practice patterns by assembling evidence concerning the effectiveness of different treatments. At the micro level, physicians and other health professionals must decide on the appropriate course of treatment for individual patients. An important assumption underlying the application of health-related QOL assessment at the individual patient-care level is that the information yielded by assessment and, potentially, the act of performing an assessment will have therapeutic value for the person.

Currently, health-related QOL assessments have become used mainly as a gatekeeping device—a mechanism for the evaluation and control of patient-care resources. For example, regulators and insurers are beginning to incorporate findings from clinical research to decide whether certain treatments should be covered. Far less common is the purposive use of health-related QOL assessment as a tool to enhance the lives of individual patients or groups of patients.

Macro Level Applications The federal Health Care Financing Administration, in partnership with the National Committee for Quality Assurance, has initiated the Health of Seniors program. This program will evaluate the outcomes of elderly people who are enrolled in the Medicare program and receiving care through managed care organizations. It is an important effort because Medicare enrollees will be surveyed to determine the impact of managed care on aspects of their health-related QOL.

The state of Oregon recently employed a preference rating procedure to establish health-care funding priorities. A telephone survey was administered to assess residents' preferences for particular health states. Results were incorporated into a cost-benefit analysis and used to rank the relative value of specific conditions and associated treatments. However, the results were rejected by the federal government because they were perceived to be biased against people with disabilities; disabled states received lower rankings (Patrick and Erickson 1993: 338–52).

Additionally, the federal Food and Drug Administration's (FDA) Division of Drug Marketing, Advertising, and Communications has had significant involvement in matters pertaining to health-related QOL. The FDA regulates the use of health-related QOL information in the marketing and sales promotion of prescription drugs by pharmaceutical firms. It has a large role in evaluating methods for measuring health-related QOL, evaluating the accuracy of the information and controlling its use. However, the FDA does not require the use of QOL endpoints in clinical drug trials, even for products that have health-related QOL implications (Burke 1998).

Meso Level Applications Health-related QOL considerations have become relatively well integrated in research and meso level decision making in the health professions and health-care delivery organizations such as hospitals and health plans. For example, pharmacoeconomic research has employed health-related QOL criteria to assess the cost-effectiveness of various medications (Revicki 1996). Additionally, many health-services research investigations have included health-related QOL criteria. The federal Agency for Health Care Policy and Research has been a major proponent and sponsor of treatment-effectiveness studies and clinical-practice guideline development efforts that incorporate health-related QOL criteria.

The growth of research has been so great that, at present, there are more than one hundred published measurement tools available (Berzon et al. 1995). An entire industry has been spawned consisting of national and international measurement registries and data archives and firms specializing in the development and administration of these assessments.

Micro Level Applications Though individual patients are the primary intended beneficiaries of health-related QOL measurement and research, little has been done to integrate health-related QOL considerations into the care of individual patients. It is still rare for a physician or other health professional to take the time to perform a formal assessment of health-related QOL or to find systematic use of such information in the process of developing a treatment plan. Moreover, while the intent of most treatment-effectiveness studies is to improve patient care, it is not at all clear that patients have been the beneficiaries of the gains in knowledge that have been made in research. There is little evidence to indicate that much of what is currently known about the impact of illness or treatment on health-related QOL is either communicated directly to patients by their physicians or used by physicians in deciding about the course of treatment. The impact of research is largely indirect. Research results may lead to measures that restrict physician access to certain treatments (e.g., by excluding a drug from a hospital formulary) or provide disincentives to discourage their use (e.g., higher reimbursement rates for some treatments instead of others).

BARRIERS TO INTEGRATING HEALTH-RELATED QOL ASSESSMENT INTO PATIENT CARE

Why has the process of health-related QOL assessment, widely regarded as largely having benefit to individual patients, not been widely employed at the individual level? There are multiple possible reasons. One is that physicians may think that they are adept at assessing health-related QOL and, therefore, do not need special approaches to enable them to find out how patients are doing and what is important to them. However, some studies suggest this is not the case. In a national survey conducted by Edward Schor and colleagues, the majority of respondents reported that their physicians never or rarely asked them about how their health was affecting their daily functioning (Schor, Lerner, and Malspeis 1995). David Nerenz and colleagues compared physician and patient assessments of functional status and found that physicians frequently didn't perceive patient functioning accurately (Nerenz et al. 1992).

Additionally, physicians may not feel that the information they obtain from assessments is valuable. One study found that even when information about the functional status of patients with rheumatoid arthritis was given to their physicians, it had no influence on treatment (Kazis et al. 1990). However, other studies have suggested that physicians perceive that the information has value (Nelson et al. 1990). Nevertheless, in one study, the information was regarded as valuable but still had no impact on treatment (Rubenstein et al. 1989). The perceived lack of value may be related to the fact

that physicians lack familiarity with some of the methods used. E. Lydick and R. S. Epstein (1993) suggest that physicians have not yet developed an intuitive basis for interpreting what scores mean. The scores vary with the instrument and are not calibrated according to a universal standard of measurement as are many clinical laboratory tests. Moreover, there is not enough information available to physicians to tell them how different therapies correspond to scores. Thus, some physicians feel that even if they have the information, they may not be able to improve a patient's health-related QOL. Finally, the perceived lack of value may also be related to biases concerning the use of self-reported information, which is regarded as "soft."

Another barrier to integrating QOL assessments into clinical practice has been the striking lack of congruence between subjective assessments of QOL and objective assessments of functional status. This disagreement is caused by a variety of factors, including the different domains typically assessed by QOL assessments (e.g., limitations in daily activities) and clinical exam (e.g., walking 20 feet down a hallway outside of the waiting room) (Schwartz, Kozora, and Zeng 1996). It is clear that humans evidence a remarkable resilience and ingenuity for identifying alternative methods for achieving desired goals. Thus, they might find other ways of implementing important daily activities despite ambulation limitations.

Another reason for this disparity between subjective and objective assessments may be the "response shift" phenomenon. This evolving concept in QOL assessment refers to the idea that when individuals experience changes in health status, they may change their internal standards, their values, or their conceptualization of health (Schwartz and Sprangers under review). These changes are currently below the surface of measurement, although methodological work is being done to develop sensitive tools and approaches for assessing response shift (see Schwartz and Sprangers, under review). As an example of how response shift leads to an apparent lack of congruence between subjective and objective estimates of health-related QOL, consider a chronically ill patient whose disease is characterized by recurrent flare-ups and periods of remission (e.g., multiple sclerosis). This patient might rate her current level of fatigue as "moderate" since she feels tired at the end of each day when she returns from work. Imagine that this patient has a flare-up in her disease and is forced to stay home from work for a week due to extreme fatigue that restricts her to her bed. If one were to ask her about her fatigue as she is recovering from the flare-up, she might consider that now she is able to work half the day without resting so her fatigue is "moderate." Comparing the patient's answers on the QOL questionnaire would suggest a stability in her QOL despite the flare-up. A closer consideration suggests, however, that her internal standards may have changed. There is some empirical evidence that response shift may explain some of the incongruity between subjective and objective assessments of function (Daltroy, et al. in press).

Significant structural barriers also limit the physician's propensity to explicitly address a patient's health-related QOL. Cost controls and managed care have significantly limited the duration of hospital stays and the amount of time physicians spend with patients during office visits. Thus, physicians and patients have little opportunity to discuss QOL issues. Additionally, physicians may perceive health-related QOL assessment to be an additional burden on an already heavy workload. Also, physicians may be unwilling to take on more responsibilities without additional payment. At present, there are no mechanisms for rewarding physicians for addressing health-related QOL. Croog and Levine (1989) indicate that physician willingness to take a patient's QOL into account in determining the course of a patient's treatment and ability to do so are complicated by the fact that medical practice involves a range of other important considerations. For example, there are ethical and legal considerations as well as cost-benefit issues, which cannot be ignored. Additionally, most physicians feel they have a responsibility to sustain life.

CONCLUSIONS

The pioneering work of Sol Levine and other sociologists has been instrumental in establishing the intellectual basis for the large number of subsequent efforts to reduce the consequences of illness and ensure that life enhancement remains a fundamental goal of medicine and public health. In a few short years, concern about the health-related QOL of many groups has become firmly entrenched in research. Simultaneously, assessment has become increasingly more technical and highly commercialized. Assessments are playing an important part in resource-allocation formulas and decisions, but barriers to their integration in patient care remain rather formidable.

Within this context, there are many opportunities for sociologists to both enrich knowledge within their own discipline and contribute to a variety of other fields, such as medicine, public health, nursing, health-services research, psychology, philosophy, and economics. Health-related QOL research has been characterized by a high degree of involvement of individuals from many different disciplines. Thus, it is an area in which sociologists can become valuable contributors and forge interdisciplinary relationships. Health-related QOL research has been a vibrant area of intellectual activity and will continue along this path well into the future.

REFERENCES

ALBRECHT, GARY, and RAY FITZPATRICK, eds. 1994. *Advances in Medical Sociology.* Vol. 5. Greenwich, CT: JAI Press, Inc.

ANDREWS, F. M., and S. B. WITHY. 1976. *Social Indicators of Well-Being: America's Perception of Life Quality.* New York: Plenum.

BERZON, R. A., M. A. DONNELLY, R. L. SIMPSON, JR., G. P. SIMEON, and H. H. TILSON. 1995. "Quality of Life Bibliography and Indexes: 1994 Update." *Journal of Quality of Life Research* 4:547–69.

BERZON, R., DONALD PATRICK, G. GUYATT, and J. M. CONLEY. 1994. "Intellectual Property Considerations in the Development and Use of HRQL Measures for Clinical Trial Research." *Journal of Quality of Life Research* 3:273–78.

BERZON, RICHARD A., JOSEPHINE A. MAUSKOPF, and GEORGE P. SIMEON. 1996. "Choosing a Health Profile (Descriptive) and/or a Patient-Preference (Utility) Measure for a Clinical Trial." In *Quality of Life and Pharmacoeconomics in Clinical Trials.* 2nd ed., ed. Bert Spilker. Philadelphia: Lippincott-Raven, pp. 375-79.

BURKE, LAURIE B. 1998. "Quality of Life Evaluation: The FDA Experience." *Quality of Life Newsletter* March:8–9.

CAMPBELL, A. 1981. *The Sense of Well-Being in America: Recent Patterns and Trends.* New York: McGraw-Hill.

CAMPBELL, ANGUS, PHILIP E. CONVERSE, and WILLARD L. ROGERS. 1976. *The Quality of American Life: Perceptions, Evaluations and Satisfactions.* New York: Russell Sage Foundation.

CLEARY, PAUL D., IRA B. WILSON, and FLOYD J. FOWLER. 1994. "A Theoretical Framework for Assessing and Analyzing Health-Related Quality of Life." In *Advances in Medical Sociology,* ed. Gary L. Albrecht and Ray Fitzpatrick. Greenwich, CT: JAI Press, Inc., p. 24.

COLEMAN, JAMES S. 1992. "Rational Choice Theory." In *Encyclopedia of Sociology.* Vol. 3, ed. Edgar F. Borgatta and Marie L. Borgatta. New York: MacMillan Publishing Company, pp. 1619–24.

CROOG, SYDNEY H., and SOL LEVINE. 1989. "Quality of Life and Health Care Interventions." In *Handbook of*

Medical Sociology. 4th ed., ed. Howard E. Freeman and Sol Levine. Englewood Cliffs, NJ: Prentice Hall, pp. 508–28.

DALTROY, L. H., MARTY G. LARSON, HOLLY M. EATON, CHARLOTTE H. PHILLIPS, and MATTHEW. H. LIANG. In Press. "Discrepancies Between Self-Reported and Observed Patient Function in the Elderly: The Influence of Response Shift and Other factors." *Social Science and Medicine.*

DONELAN, KAREN, ROBERT J. BLENDON, GEORGE D. LUNDBERG, DAVID R. CALKINS, JOSEPH P. NEWHOUSE, LUCIAN L. LEAPE, and CAHLIA K. REMLER HUMPHREY TAYLOR. 1997. "The New Medical Marketplace: Physicians' Views." *Health Affairs* 16 (5):139–48.

DRUMMOND, MICHAEL F., GREG L. STODDART, and GEORGE W. TORRANCE. 1995. *Methods for the Economic Evaluation of Health Care Programmes.* New York: Oxford University Press.

ELKINTON, J. R. 1966. "Medicine and the Quality of Life." *Annals of Internal Medicine* 64 (3):711–14.

FULLERTON, HOWARD N., JR. 1997. "Labor Force 2006: Slowing Down and Changing Composition." *Monthly Labor Review* November: 23–34.

GELBER, RICHARD. D., and AARON GOLDHIRSCH. 1986. "A New Endpoint for Assessment of Adjuvant Therapy in Postmenopausal Women with Operable Breast Cancer." *Journal of Clinical Oncology* 4:1772–79.

GELBER, RICHARD. D., BERNARD F. COLE, SHERRIE GELBER, and AARON GOLDHIRSCH. 1995. "Comparing Treatments Using Quality-Adjusted Survival: The Q-TWiST Method." *American Statistician* 49:161–69.

GELLERT, G. A. 1993. "The Importance of Quality of Life Research for Health Care Reform in the USA and the Future of Public Health." *Journal of Quality of Life Research* 2: 357–61.

GILL, THOMAS M., and ALVAN R. FEINSTEIN. 1994. "A Critical Appraisal of the Quality of Quality-of-Life Measurements." *Journal of the American Medical Association* 272 (8): 619–26.

KAZIS, LEWIS E., L. F. CALLAHAN, R. F. MEENAN, and T. PINCUS. 1990. "Health Status Reports in the Care of Patients With Rheumatoid Arthritis." *Journal of Clinical Epidemiology* 43:1243–53.

KIND, PAUL. 1996. "The EuroQol Instrument: An Index of Health-Related Quality of Life." In *Quality of Life and Pharmacoeconomics in Clinical Trials.* 2nd ed., ed. Bert Spilker. Philadelphia: Lippincott-Raven, pp. 191–201.

LERNER, DEBRA J., and SOL LEVINE. 1994. "Health-Related Quality of Life: Origins, Gaps, and Directions." In *Advances in Medical Sociology.* Vol. 5, ed. Gary Albrecht and Ray Fitzpatrick. Greenwich, CT: JAI Press, Inc, pp. 43–65.

LEVINE, SOL. 1987. "The Changing Terrains in Medical Sociology: Emergent Concern With Quality of Life." *Journal of Health and Social Behavior* 28 (March): 1–6.

LEVINE, SOL, and SYDNEY H. CROOG. 1984. "What Constitutes Quality of Life? A Conceptualization of the Dimensions of Life Quality in Healthy Populations and Patients With Cardiovascular Disease." In *Assessment of Quality of Life in Clinical Trials of Cardiovascular Therapies,* ed. Nanette K. Wenger, Margaret E. Mattson, Curt D. Furberg, and Jack Elinson. Greenwich, CT: LeJacq Communications, pp. 46–66.

LYDICK, E., and R. S. EPSTEIN. 1993. "Interpretation of Quality of Life Changes." *Journal of Quality of Life Research* 2: 221–26.

McDOWELL, I. W., C. J. M. MARTINI, and W. WAUGH. 1978. "A Method for Self-Assessment of Disability Before and After Hip Replacement Operations." *British Medical Journal* 2: 857–59.

McGLYNN, ELIZABETH A. 1997. "Six Challenges in Measuring the Quality of Health Care." *Health Affairs* 16 (3): 7–25.

MURRAY, CHRISTOPHER J. L., and ALAN D. LOPEZ. 1996. *The Global Burden of Disease: Summary.* Boston, MA: Harvard School of Public Health.

NAJMAN, J., and SOL LEVINE. 1981. "Evaluating the Impact of Medical Care and Technologies on the Quality of Life: A Review & Critique." *Social Science and Medicine* 15F: 107–15.

NELSON, E. D., JEANNE M. LANDGRAF, R. D. HAYS, J. H. WASSON, and J. W. KIRK. 1990. "The Functional Status of Patients: How Can It Be Measured in Physicians' Offices?" *Medical Care* 28:1111–26.

NERENZ, DAVID R., DENISE P. REPASKY, FRED W. WHITEHOUSE, and DOROTHY M. KAHKONEN. 1992. "Ongoing Assessment of Health Status in Patients With Diabetes Mellitus." *Medical Care* 30 (5): MS112–24.

O'BOYLE, C. A. 1992. "Assessment of Quality of Life in Surgery." *British Journal of Surgery* 79: 395–98.

PATRICK, DONALD L., and PENNIFER ERICKSON. 1993. *Health Status and Health Policy: Allocating Resources to Health Care.* New York: Oxford University Press, pp. 22, 338–52.

REVICKI, DENNIS A. 1996. "Relationship of Pharmacoeconomics and Health-Related Quality of Life." In *Quality of Life and Pharmacoeconomics in Clinical Trials.* 2nd ed., ed. Bert Spilker. Philadelphia: Lippincott-Raven, pp. 1007–83.

RUBENSTEIN, L. V., D. R. CALKINS, R. T. YOUNG, ET AL. 1989. "Improving Patient Function: A Randomized Trial of Functional Disability Screening." *Annals of Internal Medicine* 111: 836–42.

RUSSELL, LOUISE B., MARTHE R. GOLD, JOANNA E. SIEGEL, NORMAN DANIELS, MILTON C. WEINSTEIN, and the Panel on Cost-Effectiveness in Health and Medicine. 1996. "The Role of Cost-Effectiveness Analysis in Health and Medicine." *Journal of the American Medical Association* 276 (14): 1172–77.

SCHOR, EDWARD L., DEBRA J. LERNER, and SUSAN MALSPEIS. 1995. "Physicians' Assessment of Functional Health Status and Well-Being: The Patients' Perspective." *Archives of Internal Medicine* 155: 309–14.

SCHWARTZ, CAROLYN E., and MIRJAM A. G. SPRANGERS. 1999. "Methodological Approaches for Assessing

Response Shift in Longitudinal Quality of Life Research." *Social Science and Medicine* 48 (June): 1531–48.

Schwartz, Carolyn. E., Bernard F. Cole, and Richard D. Gelber. 1995a. "Measuring Patient-Centered Outcomes in Neurologic Disease: Extending the Q-TWiST Methodology." *Archives of Neurology* 52:754–62.

Schwartz, Carolyn E., Bernard F. Cole, Barbara Vickrey, and Richard Gelber. 1995b. "The Q-TWiST Approach for Assessing Health-Related Quality of Life in Epilepsy." *Quality of Life Research* 4 (2): 135–41.

Schwartz, Carolyn E., Elizabeth Kozora, and Qui Zeng. 1996. "Towards Patient Collaboration in Cognitive Assessment: Specificity, Sensitivity, and Incremental Validity of Self-Report." *Annals of Behavioral Medicine* 1996:18 (3): 177–84.

Spilker, Bert. 1996. "Introduction." In *Quality of Life and Pharmacoeconomics in Clinical Trials.* 2nd ed., ed. Bert Spilker. Philadelphia: Lippincott-Raven, pp. 1–10.

Sprangers, Mirjam A. G., and Carolyn E. Schwartz. 1999. "Integrating Response Shift into Health-Related Quality of Life Research: A Theoretical Model." *Social Science and Medicine* 48 (June): 1507–15.

Sutherland, H. J., and J. E. Till. 1993. "Quality of Life Assessments and Levels of Decision Making: Differentiating Objectives." *Journal of Quality of Life Research* 2: 297–303.

Thier, Samuel O. 1992. "Forces Motivating the Use of Health Status Assessment Measures in Clinical Settings and Related Clinical Research." *Medical Care* 30 (5): MS15–22.

Ware, John E., Jr. 1991. "Conceptualizing and Measuring Generic Health Outcomes." *Cancer* 67(3): 774–79.

WHOQOL Group. 1993. "Study Protocol for the World Health Organization Project to Develop a Quality of Life Assessment Instrument (WHOQOL)." *Quality of Life Research* 2:153–59.

Wilkinson, Richard G. 1994. "The Epidemiological Transition: From Material Scarcity to Social Disadvantage?" *Daedalus* 123 (4): 61–77.

World Health Organization. 1947. *The World Health Organization Constitution.* Geneva: World Health Organization.

21 TECHNOLOGY AND MEDICAL PRACTICE

STEFAN TIMMERMANS, *Brandeis University*

Medical technology is an exciting and rapidly developing research area for sociologists. Consider organ donation. Once immuno-suppressant drugs were available and Medicare funds were allocated for kidney transplants, the number of transplants increased tremendously. Social scientists probed the development of the technology (Fox and Swazey 1974, 1992), the social inequalities of both supply and demand (Kutner 1987), the discrepancy between support for organ donation and actual rate of consent for organ retrieval (Schutt, Smit, and Duncker 1995), the commodification of body parts (Prottas 1993), the exchange relationship between donor and recipient (Simmons and Simmons 1971), the high cost of organ transplant and medication in light of an overall increase of health-care expenses (Kutner 1987), the tyranny of the gift of life (Murray 1996), the definition of death (Lock 1989), the procurement of organs at the brain-dead patient's bedside (Hogle 1995), kinship relations arising among donor and recipients, and long-term outcomes for survivors (Sharp 1995). And organ transplantation is only one example of the ever-expanding list of medical technologies that have entered the medicine cabinet during the last decades. Medical technologies intersect with multiple social, ethical, and corporeal boundaries and form a fertile microcosm for the study of everything from the gendered conversation analysis of patient–physician interaction around cosmetic surgery (Dull and West 1991) to the exacerbation of financial and access problems in the U.S. health-care system following the introduction of new imaging technologies (Kevles 1998).

Medicine forms a geology of layer upon layer of technology, from sophisticated devices like artificial hearts and ultrasound machines to mundane tools (pencils, thermometers, and tongue depressors) and highly symbolic artefacts (Viagra, speculum, stethoscope). What qualifies as medical technology? Because of the enormous variety and omnipresence of medical technology, most authors defer to the broad definition provided by the Office of Technology Assessment. Medical technology consists of "the drugs, devices, and medical and surgical procedures used in medical care, and the organizational and supportive systems within which such care is provided" (Behney 1989: 759), including diagnostic, preventive, therapeutic, rehabilitative, organizational, information, educational, and supportive technologies.

Examining the tools that make up this broad definition, the writings of sociological pioneers Renée Fox (Fox and Swazey 1974) and Anselm Strauss (Strauss et al. 1985) remain an inspiration because of their detailed ethnographic analysis of technology as part of hospital culture.[1] Most of the early medical technology studies originated from within medical sociology and incorporated medical technology en route to understanding medical professionalization. For example, sociologists studied how advanced new technologies interacted with the prevalent "sanctity of life" ethic and created ethical dilemmas that required "detached concern" from nurses and physicians (Fox and Lief 1963), or how tools such as blood pressure instruments led to increased medicalization (Kawichi and Conrad 1996). As social critics, sociologists participated in debates about the social and psychological costs of allocating scarce resources to often terminally ill patients (Fox 1976). New technologies were also analyzed for their role in the socialization of medical students (Mizrahi 1985), hospital work (Strauss et al. 1985), medical

I thank Peter Conrad, Claire Cummins, Valerie Leiter, Debi Osnowitz, Reya Stevens, and Joanne Southwell for their helpful comments.

[1] For an earlier review, see Fox 1976.

decision-making (Anspach 1993), and social inequality (Kutner 1987).

In these early studies, the specific technological content and uses of medical technology were subservient to the study of the social negotiations and financial consequences prompted by the technology. As Casper and Berg (1995: 47) noted rather harshly, "The investigator stood with his or her back to the heart of medicine and studied the 'social phenomena' surrounding it." Since the mid-eighties, a new generation of scholars have drawn from developments in the interdisciplinary field of science and technology studies to investigate the "technology" part of medical technology. These authors usually focus on one technology or technological practice and follow it from its conception to practical application in medical settings. They retrace the origins of the technology in laboratories, computer sites, and engineering facilities (e.g., Fujimura 1996) and map the different ways in which technology transforms care-giving and how, in turn, the medical activities transform the medical technology.

Unfortunately, social scientists have also continued to misunderstand and misrepresent the role of new medical technologies in the contemporary health-care field. The first fallacy is to exempt medical technology from sociological analysis, assigning it to the realm of instrumental reason, clinical therapy, or experimental science (Franklin 1996). Medical technologies are viewed as "mere tools." The human-related aspects of health care belong to the social sciences, but the technoscientific aspects are the domain of biomedical scientists and engineers. The second fallacy is to cast technology in the role of scapegoat in the current health-care crisis. Social scientists often assume that technology directly or indirectly exacerbates all problems in health care; technologies ratchet up costs and dehumanize care.

These fallacies—two variations on the same theme—reflect social scientists' unease with the double-edged sword of technology: How can something that has the potential to do so much good also be so harmful? Many social researchers either over- or underestimate the way technology affects care-giving and fail to investigate how medical technology in particular instances modifies the relationship between care giver and patient. The purpose of this overview is to spell out the common misconceptions and to review recent alternatives from within the borderland of science and technology studies and sociology of health and illness.[2]

THE "MERE TOOLS" ARGUMENT

According to the "mere tools" argument, medical technology is somehow exempt from sociological analysis because these devices and practices are grounded in the realm of scientific truth and biological fact, or the new tools descended unproblematically and linearly from previously established technologies. Their nonhuman character renders them objective and irrelevant for sociological scrutiny. According to this essentialist–reductionist argument, "technical attributes derive from the internal characteristics of the technology" (Grint and Woolgar 1995). A variation of this argument is what David Bloor ([1976] 1991) called "the sociology of error." If a new medical device fails to materialize, or the FDA pulls it from distribution with dead bodies in its wake, social factors explain what went wrong. Sociologists may point to diverging interests, power differences, and social inequality that contributed to the error of awarding the Nobel prize for medicine to the Italian Moniz for his "psychosurgical" bilateral frontal lobotomies or the mistakes that led the producers of Thalidomide[3] to promote their teratogenic drug as a sleeping pill and as a treatment for morning sickness during pregnancy in the sixties, resulting in more than 10,000 infants worldwide born with major congenital malformations. But if a drug regimen is credited with curtailing the spread of syphilis in the United States, if the pictures generated by an MRI reduce the need for invasive surgery, or if nurses routinely auscultate a patient's congested chest with a stethoscope, medical technologies have not been grist for the sociologist's mill because they reflect the realm of nature instead of culture. Somewhere an invisible line is drawn, and functioning medical technology is a technoscientific fact reflecting biomedical knowledge instead of a social construction.

Sociologists have indirectly contributed to the "mere tools" rhetoric by bracketing the technological content of technology and instead focusing on its sociological context, questioning the biomedical model while taking technology's efficacy for granted (Nettleton 1995). For example, in the studies analyzing the diffusion of medical technology, social scientists track the dissemination of new technologies as black-boxes[4]

---

[2] For other reviews of the merger between sociology of science and technology and sociology of health and illness, see Casper and Berg (1995); Elston (1997).

[3] Thalidomide was first synthesized in 1954 by Kunz in Germany as an antihistamine but introduced as a sedative in 1956 by the West German company Chemie Grunenthal. The drug was marketed in 46 countries, particularly in Europe, Canada, Australia, South America, and Japan, under 51 brand names (e.g., Contegan, Distaval, Softenon) as a sedative and mild hypnotic.

[4] "Black-box" is an engineering term referring to a piece of technology or set of commands for which the engineers need only

traveling through medicine and a particular social context, fueled by an inherent technological rationality (Press and Browner 1997). For example, in Susan Bell's (1989) "interactive" diffusion model of medical technology, the artificial hormone DES remains an undisputed, factual chemical substance. Interactions occur in the social context around and outside the medical technology, but the drug itself remains immutable.

The "mere tools" argument threatens a sociological exploration of medical technology, and over the last decades, several social scientists have demonstrated that even in the "hardest cases" (Collins 1983) social factors permeate medical technology. For example, Diana Forsythe (1996) studied the creation of an automated computer system that takes the history of migraine patients before the patient enters the doctor's office. She convincingly demonstrated that the questions asked and even the assumptions behind the computer programming language reflected the lifeworld of physicians and program designers rather than the lifeworld of the patients. For example, implicit in the automated system was the assumption that patients were passive information providers, while physicians possessed the necessary migraine knowledge. Patients could only choose from options pre-given by physicians and needed to be told the "right" diagnosis. And although 75 percent of migraine sufferers are women and migraine has been associated with battering, domestic violence was not an option in the computer system. Social scientists have also shown that simple mechanical tools reflect the values and norms of the wider social context in which they are used. Historians, for example, have studied how in the eighteenth century male doctors monopolized the use of forceps to wrest the jurisdiction over childbirth from educated middle-class female midwives (Wertz and Wertz 1989). The use of forceps was presented as an improvement over nature and as a way to speed up delivery.[5]

MEDICAL TECHNOLOGY AS SCAPEGOAT

Where the first fallacy denies a role to sociology, the medical-technology-as-scapegoat misconception reflects sociologists' unreflective analytical pigeonholing of medical technology. Because sociologists have made a science out of debunking and demystification, they have uncritically represented technology as the source of problems in the current health-care situation and relied on medical technology as the preferred residual explanatory variable.[6] Because of the omnipresence and recent surge of advanced technologies, technology *must* have caused all the recent changes in patient care. Medical technology is said to inevitably and unilaterally lead to the deskilling of workers and a de-personalization of patient care. This line of reasoning is particularly prevalent in the field of death and dying. Sociologist David Wendell Moller, for example, is a fervent believer in the power of technology to spoil contemporary dying:

> Clearly, technology is the driving force in medical education. Clearly, technological activism is the dominant factor which shapes the world view of physicians. Clearly, the technological orientation of the medical profession is the major force which shapes physician interaction with dying patients. Thus, despite the realities of normlessness and the appearance of differences in the approach of doctors to the treatment of the dying patient, technology is the pre-eminent tool used in the management of the terminally ill. (Moller 1990, p. 37)

Moller labeled this "technological force" "the save-at-all costs orientation" that led to "aggressive," "dehumanizing," and "depersonalized" treatment (Moller 1990:32–34). In his latest book, Moller (1996) repeated the main thesis of his earlier work: "The social status of the dying person is diminished. The dying person is at mercy of technology and their (sic) worth as human beings becomes less and less important" (Moller 1996: 22). Many authors clearly agreed with Moller. They explained that "technological death" (Illich 1975: 206) facilitated "the loss of the dignity of the individual" (Mannes 1973: 31), "loss of self possession and conscious integrity" (Fletcher 1977:355), "depersonalization" (Cassell 1976: 459; Benoliel 1987:174), "psychological mutilation and scars for unprepared family members" (Thompson 1984:227), "avoidance and distancing" (Campbell 1979:47), and ultimately turned health-care workers into "technocrats" (Illich 1975: 205) or "plumbers making repairs, connecting tubes and flushing out clogged systems, with no questions

---

to consider inputs and outputs. The working of the black-box can be taken for granted (Latour 1987).

[5] Some of these social constructivists' studies have in turn been criticized for reifying a social realm. They succeeded in mapping the social dimensions of medical technology but lost sight of how technological and social aspects interrelate.

[6] Few social scientists inhabit the opposite camp of technology worshiping. Health-care providers themselves seem to pin their hopes on technological innovations as the miraculous devices that will help solve the problems of aging, illness, and death (there exists a journal titled *Medical Progress Through Technology).* Still, pockets of disability scholars have embraced technology as the solution for true adaption, rehabilitation, or integration, while some social scholars have argued that life prolonging and sustaining technologies help suppress health-care costs or lower mortality rates because they introduce a better kind of rationality and fiscal accountability.

asked" (Veatch 1991:52). In a primer on the sociology of death and dying, Michel Kearl (1989:428) summarized modern dying: "Technology prolongs the dying process in sterile, alien environments. It requires the presence of paid, impersonal professionals, instead of family and friends, to conduct the modern death watch." The diagnosis of technology as the source of depersonalization in death and dying is further documented with anthropological and historical studies that provide narratives of past or exotic Durkheimian community dying characterized by an organic solidarity (Ariès 1977; Walker 1994). Those narratives rely on reified and idealized tropes of the "natural" dignified death spoiled by modern medical technology, a technology that unburdens us from social and bodily engagement with dying.

On a more macro level, sociologists and others have cast technology in a similar villain role when they explain the current health-care crisis. The explosion of health-care costs and continuing access problems in the U.S. health-care system can—according to this argument—largely be explained by the increased reliance on "advanced medical technology." Technology is often one of a short list of variables thought to explain the increase in health-care spending. For example, when discussing health-care reform, P.R. Lee, D.S. Soffel, and H.S. Luft (1992) listed market failure, technology, administrative costs, unnecessary care, patient complexity, excess capacity, and productivity as the major factors leading to more expensive health care. Conrad and Brown (1993) listed population growth, hospital costs, medical technologies, and third-party payers as major explanatory variables for the increase in health-care costs. But estimates of the impact of new technologies on health-care costs vary widely. Researchers at the Office of Technology Assessment, for example, estimated that new technologies account for anywhere between one-third to three-quarters of the cost of hospital care—a range of several hundred million dollars (Banta, Behney, and Willems 1981).

Similar to the "mere tools" argument, the technology-as-scapegoat reasoning suffers from a bad case of technological essentialism and reductionism. This outbreak can be specifically diagnosed as technological determinism: the notion that technology is the driving force in post-industrial societies. This perspective attributes great explanatory power to technology by isolating it and assuming that technology's effect is negative. Technological determinism comes in different strengths (Smith and Marx 1994; Winner 1980). Strong technological determinists believe that technology develops as the sole result of an internal dynamic; it molds society to fit its patterns. In a weaker version, medical technology is viewed as a political phenomenon in itself. Technology as politics occurs when a particular techological device or system becomes a way of settling an issue in a particular community, or when technologies require particular kinds of political relationships. In both versions, the focus is on what has been lost after the introduction of medical technologies. The purpose of these critiques is to warn of overtechnologization and to recapture a (mystified) technology-impoverished past.

The strong version of technological determinism rests upon a romanticized neoluddism, which seems rather naive at the dawn of the twenty-first century. Would these critics of modern dying really want to return to a passing on without the option of barbiturates, pharmacies without antibiotics, and hospitals without imaging technologies, computers, or stethoscopes? Or how does a health economist cut technology from the U.S. health-care budget? The problem is that—with the possible exception of faith healing—a technology-free medicine has never existed. Any medicine that rests upon a clinical, material, corporeal base involves technology. But in the condemnation process, the justifiable critical reflections about the increased reliance on medical technologies are lost in an analysis from the extremes. Often, the sweeping dismissals of medical technologies hide a reality that is more complex and interesting than a wholesale condemnation of the technology would suggest.

Medical technology is only part of the problem of modern dying. For example, ethicists have turned CPR into the poster child of all that is wrong in contemporary dying; the technology prolongs lives unnecessarily and robs the dying experience of dignity and compassion. With a survival rate of 1 to 3 percent (Cummins, Ornato, and Thies 1991), CPR is mostly an exercise in futility, another instance of the needless medicalization of sudden death. Still, the negative effects of CPR are not as much a characteristic of the technology as they are symptomatic of the entire emergency medical system (Timmermans 1999). Most of the problems of CPR can be traced back to indiscriminate, universal use of the life-saving techniques. Although medical researchers are aware that CPR is only successful under exceptional circumstances, they recommend CPR for all situations in which breathing and heartbeat cease. In addition, emergency system directors in most U.S. counties do not allow paramedics to declare patients dead in the field. Instead, paramedics work under standard orders to start a reviving effort and transport the patient to an emergency department. There a physician cannot just stop a resuscitation attempt, because interrupting CPR before the protocols are exhausted would open the physician to legal liability. Finally, the staff in the emergency department would rather not continue a clinically hopeless unnecessary resuscitation attempt but is required to do so because the patient failed to sign an advance directive. The resuscitation technology is thus only one element of a dense network of social, ethical, and professional interactions, which cumulatively explains how people die suddenly.

And if the problem of contemporary dying is an inhumane passing, it is important to point out that the same resuscitation technology can also be part of the solution. Resuscitation technologies have altered the way Westerners think about the finality of life (Timmermans 1999). From an absolute endpoint of life, any sudden death has become a malleable boundary guarded by emergency professionals trained in CPR. While resuscitation techniques keep a person temporarily between life and death, relatives and friends have a unique opportunity—unavailable without resuscitation technologies—to prepare for impending death. In some hospitals, relatives and friends are invited during the resuscitative attempt to say goodbye to their loved one; the notice that everything medically possible has been done to save a human life might be a source of comfort.

Sociologist Paul Starr also criticized the notion that new technologies are the major cost drivers in the current health-care crisis. Big-ticket technologies such as new imaging technologies, organ transplantation, intensive care units, and renal dialysis have undoubtedly brought higher costs. "But, only about a third of the higher levels of spending, compared with Canada, reflects the expense of hospital care—and of that, only a portion is due to greater use of technology" (Starr 1994:22). Starr instead suggested that we adopt a systemic view to explain the raising health-care costs in the United States. He located expanding costs in the historical development of a number of incentives for private decision makers to expand and intensify medical services. The consequence of these incentives is that more medical technology actually leads to less care because of underuse.

> Consider the case of early detection of breast cancer through the use of mammography. With fully utilized mammography machines, a screening mammography examination should cost no more than $55. . . . But because machines are typically used far beneath capacity, prices run double that amount. With prices so high, many women cannot afford a mammogram. . . . In other words, *because we have too many mammography machines, we have too little breast cancer screening.* (Starr 1994: 25, emphasis in original)

Technology indeed increases costs in the United States, not because technology is inherently expensive but because of the way technology is configured in American health care.

A particularly persistent variation of technological determinism rampant among social scientists discussing life-prolonging technologies is the "technological imperative" argument (see Fuchs 1968; Koenig 1988). The technological imperative refers to "an attitude that stimulates the development and use of medical technology at a rapid rate. This occurs when both health-care providers and the public feel a compulsion to use the latest techniques, the newest drugs, and the most complex devices. This takes place regardless of the technology's improved ability to combat a particular condition or disease" (Spiegel 1981:35). Fuchs (1968) summarized the technological imperative as the "can do, should do" ethic. With regard to organ transplantation, a social researcher echoed the widespread belief that once the technology is available, "there can be no decision not to transplant." (Nightingale in Kutner 1987:23). Somehow, the technological rationality inherent in advanced medical technology propels the public to use it, physicians to order it, and hospitals to install it in a move to remain competitive.

Again, this line of reasoning ascribes more power to technology than is warranted because it decontextualizes medical tools and interventions. The list of "functioning" technologies that do not fit the technological imperative profile is long. Anthropologist Margaret Lock (1989) explained that organ transplants did not become a standard procedure in Japan because of a variety of cultural and structural differences. Although Japanese physicians and scientists possess all the technical know-how and skills to implement organ transplants, Japanese people have chosen not to take the transplant route but instead focus on the development of artificial organs. The reason for Japan's reluctance to jump on the organ-transplant bandwagon is that brain death is not accepted as a sufficient criterion of death for religious reasons, and because Japanese families nurse their terminally ill and would be reluctant to accept that a breathing body with a heartbeat is "dead." In addition, Japanese have a different concept of the self and feel reluctant to just emulate every technological innovation from the West.[7] For a similar example on

---

[7] In 1997, Japan recognized brain death after all. Still, as Lock points out, this change comes after a lengthy debate over the merits of organ transplants and brain death. The Japanese example does not fit the "anything goes in medical technology" assumption.

the refusal of amniocentesis for prenatal testing, see R. Rapp (1998), or the activism of the deaf community against the "oralist society's" cochlear implants, see S.S. Blume (1997).[8]

MEDICAL TECHNOLOGY AS PRACTICE

The "mere tools" and the "technology-as-scapegoat" arguments are two variations of a similar theme that ascribes an overpowering technological rationality to medical devices and gadgets. The problem that emerges is how to conceptually balance the social and the technological in medical technologies. To answer that question, sociologists from the science and technology community developed SCOT—the social construction of technology—program to study the creation and acceptance of new technologies (Pinch and Bijker 1987). A social constructivist researcher maps the diverse groups that support or contest a piece of technology and analyzes whether and how a consensus about the technology's interpretation is reached. The difference between a working and a failing artifact resides in an interest group's power to have its definition of the situation prevail. For example, E. Yoxen (1987) discussed how the diagnostic use of ultrasound rested on a consensus of representation to render three-dimensional forms as two-dimensional images. He explained the stability of the scanning technology in the ability of divergent medical groups to convince each other about the value of their representation for clinical decision making. The SCOT program spawned a number of empirical case studies (see Bijker, Hughes, and Pinch 1987; Bijker and Law 1992), but critics quickly pointed to the epistemological conundrum: SCOT had traded technological essentialism for social essentialism by assuming that social interests can be distinguished a priori from the technical (Grint and Woolgar 1995; Pickering 1995; Latour 1987). SCOT researchers wrote that the social "shaped" the technological, the technology "embodied" the social, or at least that the social was "constitutive" of the technological (see Grint and Woolgar 1995). Lost in the SCOT case studies were the material and corporeal differences of technology. Only a reified social realm remained.

Drawing from pragmatism, ethnomethodology, and symbolic interactionism, the works of the French philosopher Michel Serres, and feminist and post-structuralist theory, a diverse group of technology scholars agreed that every project aimed at establishing the dominance of either the social or technological realm over the other was doomed, and they instead refused to make a priori assumptions about technology and social factors (Akrich 1992; Haraway 1991; Latour 1987; Pickering 1992; Star 1991a). Although important differences among these scholars remained, they offered a new analytical vantage point: technology ought to be studied in practice. In Bruno Latour's words, researchers should study technoscience "in action" and investigate how all actors—human and nonhuman—manage to produce factual science and working technology. Agency was thus extended from people to things.[9] According to Latour (1987), this ontological extension of human agency occurs through the *delegation* of agency from humans to nonhumans. Machines and instruments, such as thermostats and tape recorders, perform as agents because they substitute for—stand in for and hold the place of—the actions of people. As Stefan Hirschauer (1991) has shown, during surgery pumps and monitors become a patient's "externalized organs," taking over vital functions. Because a malfunctioning ventilator might mean the end of life, there is no easy distinction between the human and the technical realm. This does not mean that humans and nonhumans are equal. Andrew Pickering (1995), for example, draws the line at intentionality; scientists might act intentionally, but those intentions would still only emerge in practice. Intentions cannot be attributed to nonhumans (but see Law 1993).

Around the same time, feminist scholar Donna Haraway (1991) reached similar conclusions about nonhuman agency when she argued that pure nature–culture–human–technology divisions do not exist. According to Haraway, engineering and science have blurred these modernist ideal types: we are hybrids, cyborgs surrounded by cyborgs.[10] She invited scholars to study the new configurations and particularly the consolidation of new race, class, and gender

[9] The extension of agency from humans to things is heavily contested (see, for example, Collins and Yearley 1992).

[10] True to her theoretical insights, Donna Haraway writes as a poet/social-observer/scientist and refuses to provide clear, consistent, conceptual definitions (which, I would add, is part of the evocative strength of her writing). In her latest book, Haraway comes close to a definition when she writes that "The cyborg is a cybernetic organism, a fusion of the organic and the technical forged in particular, historical, cultural practices. Cyborgs are not about the Machine and the Humans, as if such Things and Subjects universally existed. Instead, cyborgs are about specific historical machines and people in interaction that often turns out to be painfully counterintuitive for the analyst of technoscience" (Haraway 1997: 51). The concept first gained prominence in Haraway's "Cyborg Manifesto" (1985) and spurred a cottage industry of cyborg studies (see Gray 1995).

[8] Many disability activists are hostile to medical technologies that promise an increased "normalization."

differences spawned by the creation of biomedical technologies and research instruments (Haraway 1997). Sociologists working in the symbolic-interactionist tradition of Anselm Strauss, Howard Becker, and Everett Hughes (Star 1991b; Clarke and Fujimura 1992) welcomed this renewed attention to the ecologies of knowledge in medical practice and raised the *cui bono* (who benefits?) question to emphasize the importance of including the viewpoints of marginalized groups (Star 1991a, b). These sociologists emphasized the interpretive flexibility of technoscience across different social worlds when they analyzed the standardization of new technologies as "boundary objects." According to S.L. Star and J.R. Griesemer (1989), a boundary object such as the automated uniform patient record is both adaptable to different viewpoints (diagnostic requirements for nurses and billing purposes for health insurers) and robust enough to maintain a common identity as, in this case, a computerized representation of the medical encounter across the different social worlds. The key issue becomes to investigate under which circumstances and with what kind of consequences tools function as boundary objects.

Seeing medical technology as practice, the multiple trajectories leading to the construction and use of technology are traced. Social scientists map how the social and material mutually shape and co-produce each other. The purpose is to look at how power differentiations emerge or are re-established in medicine (Timmermans and Berg 1997; Berg and Mol 1998). As a prime example of this approach, sociologist Marc Berg (1997) addressed whether medicine has become more rational and scientific since World War II because of its reliance on formal tools such as standardized protocols, expert systems, clinical decision analysis, and automated decision systems. Berg neither supported the luddite camp, which argues that such technologies primarily lead to de-skilling, nor bolstered the pro-technology argument that the formal tools necessarily reduce the staff's work load, but instead showed how technologies have shifted medicine's understanding of rationality. Rationality was not a pre-given quality but achieved in tandem with the production and implementation of formal tools. Berg analyzed how the designers of the clinical decision analysis systems and protocols obtained a smooth fit between their tools and practice by redescribing medical practice in the tools. As proto-ethnographers, the designers of formal tools studied the work activities and places in which their tools needed to function and made assumptions about users, environment, input, and expected output. At the same time,

designers of automated decision-making systems—systems in which the physician enters diagnostic data in a computer (for example about chest pain), the computer calculates a diagnosis (indigestion, muscle pain, or heart attack) and suggests further treatment (admit to intensive care or treat as outpatient)—tried to discipline medical practice with guidelines, prerequisites, and a reshuffling of existing professional relationships to make their devices work. In the end, the automated decision-making system provided a diagnosis and the tool worked, but not like their designers intended it because the tool's purpose is just one element in the management of patients' medical conditions and needs to be weighted with the other tasks at hand. For example, nurses quickly learned to enter the "right" data based on the availability of beds in the intensive care unit. Medical practice and tools emerged simultaneously to constitute new forms of knowledge, new challenges, and problems to keep both the tools and the users on track, and ultimately new opportunities for diagnosing and curing.

Interestingly, some researchers have taken the move toward practice one step further and have become partners in technology—particularly informatics—development. These social scientists have teamed up with medical informaticians (Forsythe 1996), library-system developers (Star 1995), and even copier manufacturers (Suchman 1987) to study the work practices of the potential users of the new technologies. Based on the Scandinavian approach of participatory design and the burgeoning field of computer-supported cooperative work (CSCW), the social scientists attempted to study the tacit skills of future users, map their interests, and fortify them in the design of new technologies. These political incentives have merged with epistemological and sociological critiques of practice and systems design (Berg 1998). Currently, several social scientists are working with informaticians and physicians to implement prototypes of the uniform computerized patient record.

The "technology as practice" camp has focused its attention on a wide variety of medical technologies. In particular, technologies prodding and probing women's bodies and fertility—the new reproductive technologies—have been well researched (Clarke 1998). Social scientists have analyzed infertility (Cussins 1998), fetal surgery (Casper 1998), RU486 (Clarke and Montini 1993), the representation of female bodies in medical textbooks (Martin 1987), sex hormones (Oudshoorn 1994), sex tools (Moore 1997), and transsexualism (Hirschauer 1991). Other researchers turned to an analysis of visual and imaging medical technologies (Dumit

1995; Pasveer 1989), genetics (see Chapter 22 by Conrad in this volume), drugs (Gomart 1998), adaptation technologies (Croissant 1994), organ transplants (Hogle 1995), sudden death (Timmermans 1998), cancer (Hess 1996), AIDS science (Epstein 1996), classification systems (Bowker and Star 1993), and medical informatics (Berg 1997; Forsythe 1996). Rather than chart the topography of all these different technologies, I will examine the relationship between medical technology, the body, and identity to explore the strengths and weaknesses of this approach.

MEDICAL TECHNOLOGY, BODY, AND IDENTITY

Drawing upon Michel Foucault's writings on the extension of the clinical gaze and the prevalence of biopower through medical technologies (Foucault 1963, 1978), a major theme running through the technology as practice perspective has been how new technologies reconfigure bodies and identities. Sociologists have looked at how the fetus became a work object in fetal surgery (Casper 1998), the diagnostic and cognitive paradigm shift that occurred when x-ray technologies provided an inside view of the body (Pasveer 1989), and the redefinition of self prompted by genetic technologies (Nelkin and Lindee 1996). These studies remained close to Foucault's views of how medical technologies shift and restructure power relationships rather than the more limited examination of medical technologies as tools of surveillance and disciplining (but see Cartwright 1995). For example, Nelly Oudshoorn (1994) studied the process whereby scientific concepts such as the hormonal body assume the appearance of natural phenomena by virtue of the activities of scientists. She explained how scientists managed to set the parameters for the "natural" body when they created the context in which their knowledge claims could be accepted as facts and then rendered these contexts invisible as human constructions. The result is to view "natural" male and female bodies distinguished by specific hormones, reflected in the vocabulary we use to describe our bodies, and changes in medical practices and power relations.

Oudshoorn's analysis brought together a heterogeneous universe of hormones, laboratories, anti-conception scientists, funding policies, the Food and Drug Administration (FDA), clinics, pregnant mares' urine, and women's health advocates and therefore bridged the sociological divide between the micro and macro levels of analysis. Initially, sociologists exploring the practices emerging around new technologies studied either the technology's conception in the laboratory until these technologies became standard practice or they focused on the clinics where the technologies were used. But gradually the laboratory–clinic divide has become blurred and new medical technologies are traced from designers to users. A benefit of studying both the places of origin and the sites of use is that researchers found similar dynamics of defining and shaping technologies at work (Berg 1997; Epstein 1996; Latour 1987; Oudshoorn 1997; Timmermans 1999). For example, the management of uncertainty faced by scientists in the laboratory to turn observations, clinical trials, and test results into factual knowledge about, for example, a drug's safety and efficiency is similar to the uncertainty medical practitioners confront when basing a diagnosis and treatment plan on test results (Timmermans and Berg 1997).

Studies that focus directly on technology have been slow to address the interrelationship between medical technology and the welfare state, globalization processes, government policies, corporate capitalism, third-party payers, or even managed care (Butter 1993; Singleton and Michael 1993). Although Latour (1988) wrote that "science [and technology] is politics by other means," his refusal to make a priori assumptions about the social world and his focus on emergence made it conceptually more difficult to link new technologies to broader political themes (but see Haraway 1997). A related point of contention has been which actors and technologies to study. Critics have noted that the sociological gaze is more likely to rest upon doctors than nurses and patients, upon scientists than technicians, and upon engineers than secretaries (Elston 1997; Layne 1998). More attention has been paid to the creators of new technoscience than the recipients of technological care or the undervalued health-care workers. While this is a justifiable criticism of many works, some scholars have examined the activities of those performing the articulation work in technoscience (Barley 1986; Shapin 1989). Articulation work refers to "the work that gets things back 'on track' in the face of the unexpected, and modifies action to accommodate unanticipated contingencies" (Star 1991a: 275). In medical settings, nurses are the prime articulation agents; they do the preparatory work that makes the surgery possible and perform the unaccounted emotional support work for relatives and friends when a patient dies. Nurses seem to do everything, but their work is quintessentially invisible. S. Timmermans, G. Bowker, and S.L. Star (1998) have looked at the construction of a nursing interventions classification system aimed at making nurses' invisible work visible in billing systems, international medical classification systems, education, and record keeping.

When studying technoscience in action, social observers documented that the distinction between scientists–engineers–physicians and others is itself contested and shifting. Steven Epstein's important study (1996, 1997) of how AIDS activism influenced science and, vice versa, how the participation in science regulation and clinical trials shaped AIDS activism exemplified the contested dispersion of scientific agency. Epstein showed how AIDS activists in an alliance with community-based physicians were not only able to informally adopt promising drugs via buyer's clubs but were also able to change the measures of drug efficacy used in FDA trials from "body count" measures (how many patients died in each arm of the clinical trial) to surrogate markers. Lay AIDS activists of the East and West coasts consolidated alliances with different scientific and pharmaceutical interests to rebalance the tension between access to drugs and "good" science and in the process affected the credibility of antiviral drugs. The activists' participation altered not only the process and outcome of drug testing and clinical trials but reshuffled the division of scientific labor.

On the issue of how not only professional but personal identities are reconfigured in medical practice, Charis Cussins's (1998) work on infertility clinics is exemplary because it attempted to address the political implications of the technology. Cussins analyzed how undergoing infertility treatments figures in women's self-making and transforms their body conceptions. She located the fertility treatment in women's biography. Before entering the infertility clinic, many women already had a history of trying not to get pregnant using anticonceptiva, followed by a period of increased awareness of what could have gone wrong while trying to conceive. Cussins showed that the objectification, naturalization, and bureaucratization of the women's bodies during pelvic exams, ultrasound, explanatory surgery, and a work-up in the embryology laboratory is, paradoxically, associated with particular forms of agency. For example, the agency that followed bureaucratization "exists to the extent to which the patient is interacting as a unique individual as opposed to interacting merely as a generic patient" (Cussins 1998: 184). If the activities in the infertility clinic lead to pregnancy, the patient exercises agency in her active participation of the different forms of objectification. If the treatment cycle has been unsuccessful, women reported their lack of agency or insufficient attention to the specificity of the patient. In unsuccessful treatments, "The oppositional tension between objectification and agency alienates us from technology: operationalization renders us as mechanistic discrete body parts, naturalization turns us into objects of experimentation and manipulation, bureaucratization turns us into institutional cogs, and we are hoodwinked by our epistemic disciplining" (Cussins 1998: 187). The consequence of the process in which women render themselves compatible with instruments, drugs, and material surroundings is what Cussins called an "ontological choreography" with the potential of transforming the women's long-term self-perceptions as potential mothers.

Although empirically and theoretically rich, critics could argue that Cussins's analysis of the different agencies women use in their interactions with infertility clinics did not indicate a clear avenue of social change. Cussins's message to women's health advocates might seem to be that women willingly submit to infertility treatment in order to get pregnant, and that in case of unsuccessful treatment, they internalize and individualize the failures as lack of personal agency. But Amy Agigian (1998) analyzed artificial insemination (AI) practices by lesbians for lesbians. Lesbian AI also led to ontological change for long-term self-perceptions but generated different associations in terms of medical power, families, and legal implications of parenting. In the same way that technology might foster a diversity of political identities and change, its effect on power relationships varies from conservative to more subversive.

According to critics of the medical technology in practice perspective, there is a more fundamental political problem when agency is extended to things. Even when social researchers treat technology and humans symmetrically, only humans can claim responsibility and be held accountable. Analyzing tools as agents when new medical technologies are introduced sweeps political accountability under an epistemological rug and unnecessarily obfuscates important power differences. British sociologist Harry Collins made this point forcefully when, at a conference, he allegedly broke a pencil and dared the audience to throw him in jail for destroying a technological agent.[11] But as others have pointed out, studying technology in practice needs not lead to conformist or powerless sociology. Indeed, Leigh Star (1991a: 53) encouraged us to put power central and investigate how the human–technological configurations "might have been otherwise." Such a perspective means that instead of putting technology on trial and condemning it, social researchers

[11] Andy Pickering, personal communication.

analyze how technology configures, reflects, and shifts power relationships.

CONCLUSION

During the last decade, scholars have been taking the technological aspects of medical technology seriously. This shift has resulted in a rich body of work that emphasizes how technology reconfigures care-giving relationships, bodies, identities, and to a lesser extent, the more structural aspects of the health-care system. Medical technology allows health-care providers and consumers to obtain diagnostic precision and treatment options previously inconceivable. But because technology interacts on so many different levels with human users, the technology often also operates in ways that were not intended by designers or policy makers. Unintended consequences of human-technology interactions redefine previously taken-for-granted assumptions about nature, culture, health, body, professional authority, life, and death.

Focusing attention on technology implies a move away from traditional sociological concerns toward a more symmetric investigation of the interactions between technological and human actors. Instead of looking primarily at how technology fosters medical professionalization, the new generation of technology scholars have investigated how new technologies reframe bodies *and* how these technologies have become routine interventions. A nuanced view of how technologies operate in practice means that a condemnation of technology's negative consequences or a glamorization of technology's benefits is no longer adequate. Instead, studying medical technology often requires a revision of sociology's humanist assumptions. The question is not only how technology affects the agency of medical practitioners but how, in turn, medical practice impacts technology's agency.

Where do we go from here? Medical technologies create a perpetually shifting target for sociologists of health and illness, and the potential for substantial and theoretical contributions abounds. The establishment of a genetic paradigm offers a new kaleidoscope through which to view life in all its aspects, including heredity, human behavior, sexuality, race, risk, and mortality. Neonatal intensive care units are currently experimenting with innovations in telemedicine in an attempt to free beds, cut costs, and "outsource" some of the intensive medical surveillance. Revamped established technologies such as scanning electron microscopes are allowing ultrastructural investigations in forensic medicine, and thus redefine the concept of precision in the search for the cause of death. Also previously discarded technologies such as the drug thalidomide—which in the 1960s caused a wave of congenital malformations—are recycled in light of countless applications for new immunological conditions. Each of those technological innovations will require a revision of what it means to be a health-care provider or consumer at the turn of the twenty-first century and raise issues about equity, safety, efficiency, financial cost, and social benefits. Medical technology offers the sociologist of health and illness a compass with which to chart the opportunities and challenges of the coming health-care infrastructure.

REFERENCES

AGIGIAN, A. 1998. "Lesbian artificial insemination." Ph.D. diss., Department of Sociology, Brandeis University.

AKRICH, M. 1992. "The De-Scription of Technical Objects." In *Shaping Technology/Building Society: Studies in Sociotechnical Change,* ed. W.E. Bijker and J. Law. Cambridge: MIT Press, pp. 205–224.

ANSPACH, R.R. 1993. *Deciding Who Lives: Fateful Choices in the Intensive-Care Nursery.* Berkeley, CA: University of California Press.

ARIÈS, P. 1977. *L'homme devant la mort.* Paris: Editions du Seuil.

BANTA, H.D., C.J. BEHNEY, and J.S. WILLEMS. 1981. *Toward Rational Technology in Medicine: Considerations for Health Policy.* New York: Springer.

BARLEY, S. 1986. "Technology as an Occasion for Structuring: Evidence From Observations of CT Scanners and the Social Order of Radiology Departments." *Administrative Science Quarterly* 31: 78–108.

BEHNEY, C. 1989. "Medical Technology—Contributions to Health Care." In *The Future of Health in America.* Washington DC: U.S. Government Printing Office.

BELL, S. 1989. "Technology in Medicine: Development, Diffusion, and Health Policy." In *Handbook of Medical Sociology.* 4th ed.

BENOLIEL, J.Q. 1987. "Institutional Dying: A Convergence of Cultural Values, Technology, and Social Organization." In *Dying: Facing the Facts,* ed. H. Wass, F.H. Berardo, R.A. Neimeyer. Washington, DC: Hemisphere Publishing Corporation.

BERG, M. 1997. *Rationalizing Medical Work: A Study of Decision Support Techniques and Medical Practices.* Cambridge: MIT Press.

BERG, M. 1998. "The Politics of Technology: On Bringing Social Theory Into Technological Design." *Science, Technology and Human Values* 23. 330–364

BERG, M., and A. MOL. 1998. *Differences in Medicine.* Durham: Duke University Press.

BIJKER, W.E., and J. LAW. 1992. *Shaping Technology-Building Society. Studies in Sociotechnical Change.* Cambridge: MIT Press.

BIJKER, W.E., T.P. HUGHES, and T.J. PINCH. 1987. *The Social Construction of Technological Systems: New Directions in the Sociology and History of Technology.* Cambridge: MIT Press.

BLOOR, D. [1976] 1991. *Knowledge and Social Imagery.* 2nd ed. Chicago: University of Chicago Press.

BLUME, S.S. 1997. "The Rhetoric and Counter-Rhetoric of a 'Bionic' Technology." *Science, Technology, and Human Values* 22 (1): 3–57.

BOWKER, G., and S.L. STAR. 1993. "Knowledge and Infrastructure in International Information Management: Problems of Classification and Coding." In *Information Acumen: The Understanding and Use of Knowledge in Modern Business,* ed. L. Bud. London: Routledge.

BUTTER, I. 1993. "Premature Adoption and Routinization of Medical Technology: Illustrations from Childbirth Technology." *Journal of Social Issues* 49 (2): 11–35.

CAMPBELL, T. 1979. "Do Death Attitudes of Nurses and Physicians Differ?" *Omega* 9 (4): 43–49.

CARTWRIGHT, L. 1995. *Screening the Body: Tracing Medicine's Visual Culture.* Minneapolis: University of Minnesota Press.

CASPER, M. 1998. *The Making of the Unborn Patient: A Social Anatomy of Fetal Surgery.* New Brunswick, NJ: Rutgers University Press.

CASPER, M., and M. BERG. 1995. "Constructivist Perspectives on Medical Work: Medical Practices and Science and Technology Studies." *Science, Technology, and Human Values* 18: 42–78.

CASSELL, E. 1976. "Dying in a Technological Society." In *Death Inside Out,* ed. P. Steinfels and R. Veatch. New York: Harper and Row.

CLARKE, A. 1998. *Disciplining Reproduction: Modernity, American Life Sciences and "the Problem of Sex."* Berkeley: University of California Press.

CLARKE, A., and J. FUJIMURA. 1992. *The Right Tools for the Job.* Princeton, NJ: Princeton University Press.

CLARKE, A., and T. MONTINI. 1993. "The Many Faces of RU486: Tales of Situated Knowledges and Technological Contestations." *Science, Technology, and Human Values* 18 (1): 42–78.

COLLINS, H.M. 1983. *Changing Order: Replication and Induction in Practice.* London, Sage.

COLLINS, H.M., and S. YEARLEY. 1992. "Epistemological Chicken." In *Science as Practice and Culture,* ed. Andrew Pickering. Chicago: University of Chicago Press, pp. 301–27.

CONRAD, P., AND P. BROWN. 1993. "Rationing Medical Care: A Sociological Reflection." *Research in the Sociology of Health Care* 10: 3–32.

CROISSANT, J. 1994. "Disability Activism and Technology Choice." Paper presented at the American Sociological Association Meeting, Los Angeles, CA.

CUMMINS, R., J.P. ORNATO, and W.H. THIES. 1991. "Improving Survival From Sudden Cardiac Arrest: The 'Chain of Survival' Concept." *Circulation* 83:1832–47.

CUSSINS, C. 1998. "Ontological Choreography: Agency for Women in an Infertility Clinic." In *Differences in Medicine: Unraveling Practices, Techniques and Bodies,* ed. M. Berg and A. Mol. Durham: Duke University Press, pp. 164–201.

DULL, D., and C. WEST. 1991. "Accounting for Cosmetic Surgery: The Accomplishment of Gender." *Social Problems* 38 (1): 54–70.

DUMIT, J. 1995. "Brain-Mind Machines and American Technological Dream Marketing: Toward an Anthropology of Cyborg Envy." In *The Cyborg Handbook,* ed. C. Gray. New York: Routledge.

ELSTON, M.A. 1997. "Introduction: The Sociology of Medical Science and Technology." *The Sociology of Medical Science and Technology.* London: Blackwell Publishers.

EPSTEIN, S. 1996. *Impure Science: AIDS, Activism, and the Politics of Knowledge.* Berkeley, CA: University of California Press.

EPSTEIN, S. 1997. "Activism, Drug Regulation, and the Politics of Therapeutic Evaluation in the AIDS Era: A Case Study of ddC and the 'Surrogate Markers' Debate." *Social Studies of Science* 27, 691–726.

FLETCHER, J. 1977. "Elective Death." In *Understanding Death and Dying: An Interdisciplinary Approach,* ed. R. Fulton. New York: McGraw-Hill.

FORSYTHE, D. 1996. "New Bottles, Old Wine: Hidden Cultural Assumptions in a Computerized Explanation System for Migraine Sufferers," *Medical Anthropology Quarterly* 10 (4).

FOUCAULT, M. 1963. *Birth of the Clinic.* New York: Random House.

FOUCAULT, M. 1978. *The History of Sexuality: An Introduction.* Vol. 1. New York: Vintage Books.

FOX, R. 1976. "Advanced Medical Technology: Social and Ethical Implications." *Annual Review of Sociology* 231–68.

FOX, R., and H.I. LIEF. 1963. "Training for Detached Concern in Medical Students." In *The Psychological Basis of Medical Practice,* ed. H.I. Lief et al. New York: Harper and Row, pp. 12–35n.

FOX, R.C., and J.P. SWAZEY. 1974. *The Courage to Fail: A Social View of Organ Transplants and Dyalisis.* Chicago: University of Chicago Press.

FOX, R.C., and J.P. SWAZEY. 1992. *Spare Parts: Organ Replacement in American Society.* New York: Oxford University Press.

FRANKLIN, S. 1996. "An Excellent Prognosis." *Medical Anthropology Quarterly* 10 (4): 683–90.

FUCHS, V.R. 1968. *The Growing Demand for Medical Care.* New York: National Bureau for Economic Research.

FUJIMURA, J. 1987. "Constructing 'Do-able' Problems in Cancer Research: Articulating Alignment." *Social Studies of Science* 17: 257–93.

FUJIMURA, J. 1996. *Crafting Science: A Sociohistory of the Quest for the Genetics of Cancer.* Cambridge, MA: Harvard University Press.

GOMART, E. 1998. "Seized by methadone: An experimentation on freedom and causes at the Blue Clinic." Paper presented at Society for Social Study of Science conference. Halifax, Canada.

GRAY, C.H. 1995. *The Cyborg Handbook.* New York: Routledge.

GRINT, K., and S. WOOLGAR. 1995. *Deus ex Machina: Technology, Work, and Society.* Cambridge, UK: Polity.

HARAWAY, D.J. 1989. *Primate Visions: Gender, Race, and Nature in the World of Modern Science.* New York: Routledge.

HARAWAY, D.J. 1991. *Simians, Cyborgs, and Women.* New York: Routledge.

HARAWAY, D.J. 1997. *Modest_Witness@Second_Millennium.FemaleMan©_Meets_Oncomouse™.* New York: Routledge.

HESS, D. 1996. "Technology and Alternative Cancer Therapies: An Analysis of Heterodoxy and Constructivism." *Medical Anthropology Quarterly* 10 (4): 657–74.

HIRSCHAUER, S. 1991. "The Manufacture of Bodies in Surgery." *Social Studies of Science* 21: 279–319.

HOGLE, L. 1995. "Standardization Across Non-Standard Domains: The Case of Organ Procurement." *Science, Technology, and Human Values* 20 (4): 482–501.

ILLICH, I. 1975. *Medical Nemesis.* London: Calder and Boyars.

KAWACHI, I., and P. CONRAD. 1996. "Medicalization and the Pharmacological Treatment of Blood Pressure." In *Contested Ground: Public Purpose and Private Interest in the Regulation of Prescription Drugs.* Oxford University Press, pp. 26–41.

KEARL, M.C. 1989. *Endings: A Sociology of Death and Dying.* New York: Oxford University Press.

KEVLES, B.H. 1998. *Naked to the Bone.* New Brunswick, NJ: Rutgers Univesity Press.

KOENIG, B.A. 1988. "The Technological Imperative in Medical Practice: The Social Creation of a 'Routine' Treatment." In *Biomedicine Examined,* ed. M. Lock and D.R. Gordon. Dordrecht: Kluwer Academic Publishers, pp. 465–97.

KUTNER, N.G. 1987. "Issues in the Application of High Cost Medical Technology: The Case of Organ Transplantation." *Journal of Health and Social Behavior* 28: 23–36.

LATOUR, B. 1987. *Science in Action: How To Follow Scientists and Engineers Through Society* Milton Keynes, UK: Open University Press.

LATOUR, B. 1988. *The Pasteurization of France.* Cambridge, MA: Harvard University Press.

LATOUR, B. 1993. *We Have Never Been Modern.* Cambridge, MA: Harvard University Press.

LAW, J. 1993. *Modernity, Myth, and Materialism.* Oxford: Blackwell.

LAYNE, L.L. 1998. "Introduction: Anthropological Approaches in Science and Technology Studies." *Science, Technology and Human Values* 23 (1): 4–24.

LEE, P.R., D.S. SOFFEL, and H.S. LUFT. 1992. "Costs and Coverage: Pressures Toward Health Reform." *Western Journal of Medicine* 157: 576–83.

LOCK, M., 1989, "Reaching Consensus About Death: Heart Transplants and Cultural Identity in Japan," *Society-Societe* 13 (1): 15–26.

MANNES, M. 1973. *Last Rights: A Case for the Good Death.* New York: Signet.

MARTIN, E. 1987. *The Woman in the Body: A Cultural Analysis of Reproduction.* Boston: Beacon Press.

MIZRAHI, T. 1985. "Getting Rid of Patients: Contradiction in the Socialization of Internists to the Doctor–Patient Relationship." *Sociology of Health and Illness* 7: 214–35.

MOLLER, D.W. 1990. *On Death Without Dignity: The Human Impact of Technological Dying.* New York: Baywood Publishing Company.

MOLLER, D.W. 1996. *Confronting Death: Values, Institutions, and Human Mortality.* New York: Oxford University Press.

MOORE, L.J. 1997. "'It's Like You Use Pots and Pans to Cook. It's the Tool': The Technologies of Safer Sex." *Science, Technology and Human Values* 22 (4): 434–71.

MURRAY, T.M. 1996. "Organ Vendors, Families, and the Gift of Life." In *Organ Transplantation: Meanings and Relities,* ed. S.J. Younger, R.C. Fox, L.J. O' Connell. Madison, WI: The University of Wisconsin Press, pp. 101–26.

NELKIN, D., and S. LINDEE. 1996. *The DNA Mystique: The Gene as Cultural Icon.* New York: Freeman.

NETTLETON, S. 1995. *The Sociology of Health and Illness.* Cambridge: Polity.

OUDSHOORN, N. 1994. *Beyond the Natural Body: An Archeology of Sex Hormones.* New York: Routledge.

OUDSHOORN, N. 1997. "From Population Control Politics to Chemicals: The WHO as an Intermediary Organization in Contraceptive Development." *Social Studies of Science* 27: 41–72.

PASVEER, B. 1989. "Knowledge of Shadows: The Introduction of X-Ray Images in Medicine." *Sociology of Health and Illness* 11 (4): 360–81.

PICKERING, A., ed. 1992. *Science as Practice and Culture.* Chicago: University of Chicago Press.

PICKERING, A. 1995. *The Mangle of Practice: Time, Agency, and Science.* Chicago: University of Chicago Press.

PINCH, T., and W.E. BIJKER, 1987. "The Social Construction of Facts and Artifacts: Or How the Sociology of Science and the Sociology of Technology Might Benefit Each Other." In *The Social Construction of Technological Systems: New Directions in the Sociology and*

History of Technology, ed. W.E. Bijker, T.P. Hughes, and T.J. Pinch. Cambridge: MIT Press, pp. 17–51.

PRESS, N., and C.H. BROWNER. 1997. "Why Women Say Yes to Prenatal Diagnosis." *Social Science and Medicine* 45: 979–90.

PROTTAS, J.M. 1993. "Altruisim, Motivation, and Allocation: Giving and Using Human Organs." *Journal of Social Issues* 49 (2): 127–51.

RAPP, R. 1998. "Refusing Prenatal Diagnosis: The Meanings of Bioscience in a Multicultural World." *Science, Technology, and Human Values* 23 (1): 45–70.

SCHUTT, G., H. SMIT, and G. DUNCKER. 1995. "Huge Discrepancy Between Declared Support for Organ Donation and Actual Rate of Consent for Organ Retrieval." *Transplantation Proceedings* 27 (1): 1450–51.

SHAPIN, S. 1989. "The Invisible Technician." *American Scientist* 77: 554–63.

SHARP, L. 1995. "Organ Transplantation as a Transformative Experience: Anthropological Insights in to the Restructuring of the Self." *Medical Anthropology Quarterly* 9: 356–89.

SIMMONS, R.G., and R.L. SIMMONS. 1971. "Organ Transplantation: A Societal Problem." *Social Problems* 19: 36–57.

SINGLETON, V., and M. MICHAEL. 1993. "Actor-Networks and Ambivalence: General Practitioners in the UK Cervical Screening Programme." *Social Studies of Science* 23 (2): 227–65.

SMITH, M.R., and L. MARX, 1994. *Does Technology Drive History? The Dilemma of Technological Determinism.* Cambridge, MA: MIT Press.

SPIEGEL, A.D. 1981. "A Consumer's Primer on Medical Technology." In *Medical Technology, Health Care and the Consumer,* ed. A.D. Spiegel, D. Rubin, and S.B. Frost. New York: Human Sciences Press, pp. 25–83.

STAR, S.L. 1991a. "Power, Technologies and the Phenomenology of Conventions: On Being Allergic to Onions." In *A Sociology of Monsters: Essays on Power, Technology and Domination,* ed. J. Law. London: Routledge.

STAR, S.L., 1991b. "The Sociology of the Invisible: The Primacy of Work in the Writings of Anselm Strauss." In *Social Organization and Social Process: Essays in Honor of Anselm Strauss,* ed. D. Maines. New York: Aldine de Gruyter, pp. 265–85.

STAR, S.L. 1995. *The Cultures of Computing.* Oxford: Blackwell.

STAR, S.L., and J.R. GRIESEMER. 1989. "Institutional Ecology, 'Translations' and Boundary Objects: Amateurs and Professionals in Berkeley's Museum of Vertebrate Zoology, 1907–39." *Social Studies of Science* 19: 387–420.

STARR, P. 1994. *The Logic of Health Care Reform: Why and How the President's Plan Will Work.* New York: Whittle Books.

STRAUSS, A., S. FAGERHAUGH, B. SUCZEK, and C. WIENER. 1985. *Social Organization of Medical Work.* Chicago: The University of Chicago Press.

SUCHMAN, L. 1987. *Plans and Situated Actions. The Problems of Human–Machine Communication.* Cambridge: Cambridge University Press.

THOMPSON, L. 1984. "Cultural and Institutional Restrictions on Dying Styles in a Technological Society." *Death Education* 8: 223–29.

TIMMERMANS, S. 1998. "Resuscitation Technology in the Emergency Department: Toward a Dignified Death." *Sociology of Health and Illness* 20 (2): 144–67.

TIMMERMANS, S. 1999. *Sudden Death and the Myth of CPR.* Philadelphia: Temple University Press.

TIMMERMANS, S., and M. BERG. 1997. "Standardization in Action: Achieving Local Universality Through Medical Protocols." *Social Studies of Science* 27 (2): 273–305.

TIMMERMANS, S., G. BOWKER, and S.L. STAR. 1998. "The Architecture of Difference: Visibility, Controllability, and Comparability in Building a Nursing Intervention Classification." In *Differences in Medicine: Unraveling Practices, Techniques and Bodies,* ed. M. Berg and A. Mol. Durham: Duke University Press.

VEATCH, R.M. 1991. "Models for Ethical Medicine in a Revolutionary Age." In *Biomedical Ethics,* ed. T.A. Mappes and J.S. Zembaty. New York: McGraw-Hill, Inc.

WALKER, T. 1994. "Natural Death and the Noble Savage." *Omega* 20 (4): 237–48.

WERTZ, R.W., and D.C. WERTZ. 1989. *Lying In: A History of Childbirth in America.* exp. ed. New Haven, CT: Yale University Press.

WINNER, L. 1980. "Do Artifacts have Politics?" *Daedalus* 109: 121–26.

YOXEN, E. 1987. "Seeing With Sound: A Study of the Development of Medical Images." In *The Social Construction of Technological Systems,* ed. W.E. Bijker, T.P. Hughes, and T. Pinch. Cambridge, MA: MIT Press.

22 MEDICALIZATION, GENETICS, AND HUMAN PROBLEMS

PETER CONRAD, *Brandeis University*

Medicalization has interested sociologists for more than three decades. The earliest mention focused on the medicalization of deviance (Pitts 1968), but analysts soon saw its applicability to a wide range of human problems that had entered into medical jurisdiction (Freidson 1970; Zola 1972; Illich 1976). In the ensuing decades, a considerable literature on medicalization has developed in sociology (see Conrad and Schneider 1992; Conrad 1992) and other disciplines (Conrad 1997b). This chapter first reviews some general issues concerning medicalization, then discusses some controversies that have emerged in recent years, and, finally, examines the impact of the new genetics on medicalization.[1] The primary emphasis here is on the medicalization of deviance and the potential impact of behavioral genetics on the medicalization process; the issues discussed, however, have wide applicability in terms of the influence of genetics on human problems.

DEFINING MEDICALIZATION AND DEMEDICALIZATION

Medicalization describes a process by which nonmedical problems become defined and treated as medical problems, usually in terms of illnesses or disorders. While it literally means "to make medical," it has most frequently been used in the context of a critique of medicalization (or overmedicalization). While researchers tend to agree that medicalization refers to the process of problems entering the medical jurisdiction, they have offered different definitions. Irving K. Zola

(1972:495) saw it as a "process whereby more and more of everyday life has come under medical dominion, influence, and supervision." Peter Conrad (1975:12) conceived of it as "defining behavior as a medical problem or illness and mandating or licensing the medical profession to provide some type of treatment for it." Ivan Illich (1976) termed medicalization "social iatrogenesis" and depicted it as resulting from medical imperialism. But as several studies have pointed out, in particular instances (e.g., alcoholism) the medical profession or even individual doctors may be only marginally involved, and actual medical treatments are not a requisite for medicalization (e.g., Conrad and Schneider 1992; Appleton 1995).

It is by now clear that the key to medicalization is the definitional issue. Medicalization consists of defining a problem in medical terms, using medical language to describe a problem, adopting a medical framework to understand a problem, or using a medical intervention to "treat" it. Medicalization occurs when a medical frame or definition has been applied in an attempt to understand or manage a problem; this is as true for epilepsy as for "gender dysphoria" or transexualism (Conrad 1992).

In our society, medicalization of human problems has occurred primarily with deviance and "natural life processes," encompassing broad areas of human life. Medicalization of deviance includes alcoholism, mental disorders, opiate addictions, eating disorders, sexual and gender difference, sexual dysfunction, learning disabilities, child and sexual abuse among others, and has spurred numerous new categories from attention deficit-hyperactivity disorder (ADHD) to premenstrual syndrome (PMS) to post-traumatic stress disorder (PTSD) to chronic fatigue syndrome (CFS). Behaviors that were once defined as immoral, sinful, or criminal have been

My thanks to Chloe Bird, Phil Brown, Allen Fremont, and Stefan Timmermans for comments on an earlier draft of this chapter.
[1] For a more complete review of the literature and issues around medicalization, see Conrad 1992.

322

given medical meaning, moving from badness to sickness. Certain common life processes have been medicalized as well, including childbirth, aging, menstruation, menopause, birth control, infertility, anxiety and mood, and death. The growth in medicalized categories suggests an increase in medicalization, although we have little quantitative data on the actual amount of medicalization. To the extent that medicalization is increasing, it is not simply a result of medical colonization or moral entrepreneurship. Arthur Barsky and Jonathan Borus (1995: 1931) point out that the public's tolerance for mild symptoms and benign problems has decreased, spurring a "progressive medicalization of physical distress in which uncomfortable body states and isolated symptoms are reclassified as diseases. . . . " The growth of medicalization can occur due to an increase in supply or demand for medical categorization.

Medicalization need not be total. There are degrees of medicalization; some cases of a condition may not be medicalized, competing definitions may exist, or remnants of a previous definition may cloud the picture. Certain conditions are almost fully medicalized (e.g., death, childbirth), others are partly medicalized (e.g., opiate addiction, menopause), and still others are minimally medicalized (e.g., sexual addiction, spouse abuse). While we do not know specifically which factors affect the degrees of medicalization, it is likely that support of the medical profession, availability of treatments, discoveries of new etiologies, coverage by medical insurance, and the presence of individuals or groups promoting or challenging medical definitions may all be significant in particular cases.[2]

While the trend in the past century has been toward the expansion of medical jurisdiction, there have been cases of demedicalization as well. Demedicalization means that a problem no longer retains its medical definition. A classic example is masturbation. In the nineteenth century masturbation was considered a disease and a cause for medical intervention (Engelhardt 1974). By the mid-twentieth century it was no longer defined as a medical problem, nor was it the subject of medical treatment. To take another example, in 1973 the American Psychiatric Association officially voted to no longer define homosexuality as an illness, representing at least a symbolic demedicalization of homosexuality (Conrad and Schneider 1992; Bayer 1981). Childbirth, on the other hand, has been radically reformed in recent years with "natural childbirth,"

birthing rooms, nurse midwives, and a host of other reforms, but it has not been demedicalized. Childbirth is still defined as a medical event, and medical professionals still attend it. Birthing with lay midwives at home approaches demedicalization. For demedicalization to occur, problems are no longer defined in medical terms, and medical personnel are not deemed appropriate or necessary for intervention.

While numerous common features inhere to all types of medicalization, most of the examples in this chapter focus on the medicalization of deviance. Many issues discussed here may be equally applicable to medicalized natural life processes.

CONTROVERSIES AND CRITIQUES

The earliest critiques argued that the medicalization case has been overstated and that significant constraints limit rampant medicalization (Fox 1977; Strong 1979). Some of these critiques conflate deprofessionalization with demedicalization (Fox 1977), while others fail to recognize that most medicalization studies adopt a historical, social-constructionist perspective, which focuses on the emergence of medical categories and how problems entered the medical domain, bracketing whether a phenomena is "really" a medical problem (Bury 1986; see Conrad 1992: 212). From a sociological perspective, case studies of medicalization create new understandings about the social processes involved in the cultural production of medical categories or knowledge but don't necessarily contain a mandate as to how the categories and knowledge are to be evaluated. While the analytical emphasis has been on overmedicalization, this evaluation is not inherent in the perspective.

Recent commentators have suggested ways of "rethinking" or "reconsidering" medicalization. For example, some have noted how changes in society and medicine may place new constraints on medicalization. Simon Williams and Michael Calnan (1996) contend that most medicalization studies view individuals or the lay public as largely passive or uncritical of medicine's expansion. They point out that lay perspectives of medicine have become more critical, with an increased disillusionment with medicine and a decline in trust of the medical profession. A better informed public will create a "challenge of the articulate consumer." Barsky and Barus (1995) suggest that despite a growing medicalization of bodily distress (e.g., somatization), managed care creates great incentives to reduce utilization, therefore placing new constraints on medicalization. While it is questionable whether most medicalization studies see

[2] There are, of course, constraints on medicalization, including competing definitions, costs of medical care, lack of support in the medical profession, and the like (see Strong 1979; Barsky and Borus 1995).

the public as passive ("medical dupes," as Navarro [1976] put it many years ago), it seems clear that changes in the culture and medicine may limit medicalization. But it is important to recognize that problems can still be medicalized, even in the face of a skeptical public or a medical system that resists treating them. For example, the fact that insurance companies won't pay for certain medical diagnoses limits medicalization, but doesn't necessarily undermine it, as long as medical categories are accepted and applied to the problems. It may, however, affect the degree of medicalization. Much of what we call self-care involves the use of medical approaches by lay people, in the absence of professional medical treatment.

Most analysts of medicalization write in a critical mode, either emphasizing the problems of overmedicalization or its consequences. Using the case of chronic fatigue syndrome (CFS), Dorothy H. Broom and Roslyn V. Woodward (1996) maintain that some writers have overemphasized the downsides of medicalization and that medicalization can be both helpful and unhelpful to patients. They suggest with CFS that medical explanations can provide coherence to patients' symptoms, validation and legitimation for their troubles, and support for self-management for their problems. Broom and Woodward distinguish medicalization from medical dominance, which they see as problematic for patients, and call for a collaborative approach between the physician and patient. They suggest that this "constructive medicalization" can improve individual well-being. In a sense, they echo Catherine Kohler Reissman's (1983) point that medicalization can be a "two-edged sword" and Peter Conrad's (1975) notion of a brighter and darker side of medicalization but give more credence to the benefits. It seems likely that certain benefits of medicalization will be more apparent with controversial illnesses like CFS, although as Talcott Parsons (1951) pointed out in his classic formulation of the sick role, medical diagnosis can legitimate a range of human troubles. Broom and Woodward (1996) depart from Parsons by suggesting that legitimation can occur with collaboration rather than through professional dominance.

The medicalization of alcoholism has been well documented; while several factors in and out of the medical profession facilitated medicalization, all analysts agreed that the rise of Alcoholics Anonymous was crucial to the increased acceptance of alcoholism as a disease (Schneider 1978; Roman 1988; Conrad and Schneider 1992). Conrad and Schneider present it as an exemplar of how nonmedical advocates can be central to the medicalization process (see also Oinas 1998). In a recent article, Lynn Appleton (1995) suggests we see AA as a form of alternative medicine, rather than primarily as a lay self-help group and argues for a modification of the conceptualization of medicine to include alternative and folk medicine. But it is problematic to include AA in a broader framing of medicine since recovery groups explicitly don't see themselves as part of any "medicine." The relationship of nonmedical healing groups to medicalization has yet to be articulated. But it is important to recognize that advocates outside of medicine may play significant roles in medicalizing problems.

Holistic health approaches are typically deemed alternative medicine and often are taken as a step toward demedicalization. After all, holistic approaches move away from the traditional medical model and frequently bypass the medical profession. June Lowenberg and Fred Davis (1994), using a broad conceptualization of medicalization, found that adaptation of holistic health does not by itself constitute evidence for either demedicalization or medicalization. Some aspects support medicalization (e.g., broadening the pathological sphere, maintaining a reshaped medical model), others support demedicalization (e.g., reduction of technology, reduction of status difference between providers and clients). Holistic health is frequently a form of deprofessionalization without demedicalization. Lowenberg and Davis found no unilateral movement in either the direction of medicalization or demedicalization and rightly caution against simplistic generalizations.

Medicalization studies are not limited to sociologists. In recent years anthropologists (see Conrad 1997b), physicians (Barsky and Burus 1995), and psychologists (Zuriff 1996) have written on the topic. Foucault did not use the term medicalization but "tends to present a consonant vision" that shows the impact of medical discourses and practices on people's lives (Lupton 1997: 94). At this point, issues around medicalization have been widely disseminated and have even moved into the public discourse.

But the situation with medicalization remains dynamic. There is no question that changes in the medical-care system will place new constraints on medicalization. While the insurance-driven managed care direction may reduce the amount of medicalized treatment, new diagnoses and categories may emerge that strain managed care. It is just as likely that informed patients will come to their physicians and providers seeking medical definitions of their troubles as it is that they will question medical diagnoses and the authority of physicians. It is important to keep in mind that medicalization is centered on the definitional issue and that medicalization can occur on the conceptual, organizational, or interactional level (Conrad 1992). Whether medicalization is expanding or contracting is an empirical question and depends in part on what is measured as medicalization (e.g., number of new medical categories or number of people medicalized); regrettably we do not have adequate data to address this question.

At the end of the century, one yet unexamined factor that is likely to influence medicalization is the rise of the new genetics. The remainder of the chapter will discuss old and new genetics and their relationships to medicalization.

GENETICS AND MEDICALIZATION

Scientific discoveries in themselves do not produce medicalization, but they can be a significant piece of the picture. New paradigms can affect the way in which problems are defined and what we do about them. The development of psychoanalytic theory engendered new categories of deviants such as psychopathy, kleptomania, and pyromania. In the late twentieth century, genetics and neuroscience are the rising paradigms to explain illness and behavior and could have considerable impact on medicalization. Up to this point, genetic findings have played only minor roles in medicalization, but it is likely that researchers now will need to attend more carefully to the impact of genetic research and claims on the medicalization process.

The Rise of the Genetic Paradigm[3]

In the wake of the discovery of the structure of DNA and innovations in identifying and cloning genes, a new genetics has emerged in recent decades that now stands on the cutting edge of science. Significant discoveries include genes for cystic fibrosis, Huntington's disease, Fragile X Syndrome, Duchenne muscular dystrophy, and types of breast and colon cancer. The advent of the Human Genome Project in 1989, the largest biological project in history (Kevles and Hood 1992), further fuels genetic research. The genome project is a 15-year, international research initiative with the goal of mapping all of the 3 billion base pairs of the human genetic structure. The genome project aims to find the chemical or genetic basis for the 4,000 or so genetic diseases that affect humans, as well as identify genetic linkages with other diseases,

with the ultimate hope of producing new preventions and cures. As the project proceeds, new claims about genetic associations and linkages with diseases, conditions, and behaviors will likely be announced at an accelerated pace over the next decade.

The mapping of the human genome has been the object of several provocative metaphors, including the search for the "holy grail" (Gilbert 1992), investigating "the essence of human life," and decoding "the book of life." James Watson, co-discoverer of the double helix structure of DNA and former head of the genome project, declared, "We used to think our fate was in our stars. Now we know, in large part, it is in our genes." (cited in Horgan 1993: 123) Critics contend that the "geneticization" of human problems has expanded beyond scientific knowledge (Lippman 1992) and that a kind of "genetic fatalism"—the assumption that a genetic association is deterministic, implying that such a trait or behavior is unchangeable—underlies much public discourse about genetics (Alper and Beckwith 1993).

Fueled by tangible successes and scientific hope, genetics is a rising paradigm in science and medicine and has become an explanatory frame for a wide range of human problems. This paradigm posits that genes are a key component in producing particular diseases or behaviors. The assumption is that some anomaly in the genes (i.e., a mutation) is a primary cause of the problem. Genetics as an explanation often has been privileged in the public discourse, implying that genes are *the* main cause of a problem (Conrad 1997a).

The genetic paradigm has considerable appeal. It promises primary causes, located on a basic level of biological reality. Genes are often depicted as an essence, the material that one is really made of. This gives genetic thinking almost a mystical quality. While the older genetics relied on correlations and twin studies, we now can be tempted by the lure of specificity, associating specific genes with particular problems (see Conrad 1999). Identifying specific genes seems so much neater than complex, messy epidemiological and social analyses. This specificity feeds hopes for genetic "magic bullets" to alleviate human problems. A growing amount of genetic research is being reported in the news, often highlighted in front-page stories (Nelkin and Lindee 1995; Conrad 1997a).

While the genetics of behavioral and social problems is not a central concern of the genome project or molecular biology, it seems clear that with the huge scientific industry searching for differences in the DNA, we are likely to continue to see more genetic explanations for human problems.

---

[3] Parts of the section are taken from Conrad 1997a.

Genetic Discoveries and Social Deviance

In this section I will briefly review the fate of some recent genetic findings related to deviance. There is no attempt to be comprehensive here, but rather to highlight some of the most significant research that has entered the public discourse. It is important to keep in mind that behavioral genetics investigates the genetic associations with behaviors that are often already defined as deviant or problematic. This is precisely why scientists are researching the genetic links to these behaviors. If the behavior was not deemed problematic, it is unlikely that much research energy (or grant money) would be expended in searching out its origins. At the risk of stating the obvious, society, rather than geneticists, has defined these behaviors, traits, or conditions as deviant.

Until the last decade or so, genetic heritability was measured by sibling, twin, and adoption studies. Using statistical calculations, scientists now ascertain a heritability score, for example, suggesting that a trait is 60 percent genetic. Behavioral geneticists have measured heritability for well-known areas like intelligence, depression, homosexuality, and shyness, and also for divorce, political conservatism, and racial prejudice. Presenting heritability as a single figure gives the impression of clear-cut measurement, but heritability is notoriously imprecise (Peele 1995). While heritability affects scientists' and the public's view of genetic contribution in the era of molecular biology, locating genetic markers (strips of DNA that designate a chromosomal neighborhood where a gene is suspected) or actual genes should be considered the "gold standard" (Billings et al. 1992).

Mental Illness Researchers have had a long interest in the role of inheritance in mental disorders, making claims relating biology or genetics to mental illness. With the maturation of molecular biology in the 1980s, the pace and specificity of discoveries and claims relating to genetics and mental illness accelerated. But some of the most promising claims couldn't be replicated or were retracted in short order. In 1987 a genetic marker for manic-depressive disorder was identified by research among the Old Order Amish (Egeland et al. 1987). While the actual gene was not isolated, the research depicted it as a dominant gene (i.e., it could be inherited from either parent) and pointed to its location (on the tip of the short arm of chromosome 11). A month later an Israeli study of three large families identified a second genetic marker (this time on the X chromosome) linked with the development of manic-depressive illness. These

discoveries made front-page news. Both of these studies were soon disconfirmed: the Amish study in 1989 and the Israeli study two years later. In 1988 two studies linking genes (on chromosome 5) to schizophrenia were published and also widely reported in the news (Sherrington et al. 1988). These, too, were disconfirmed in short order. More recently other studies have claimed associations with genetics and mental illness; in 1996 researchers found an association suggesting a predisposing gene for manic-depressive illness on the long arm of chromosome 18. But, to date, no specific genes for mental disorders have been isolated; to the extent that there are associations between genetics and mental disorders, they are likely to be polygenetic and expressed in interaction with particular environments or conditions. James Watson (1997: 18) is convinced that genes are implicated in schizophrenia yet notes that "the new statistical tricks for analyzing polymorphic inheritance patterns have not yet led to the unambiguous mapping of even one major schizophrenic gene to a defined chromosomal site."

Given that mental illness has been medicalized for over a century (Conrad and Schneider 1992), any new genetic discoveries are unlikely to change its medical status. Perhaps new genetic associations with more marginal psychiatric disorders like obsessive compulsive disorder or attention deficit-hyperactivity disorder could provide evidence for claims of further medicalization, although it would depend on how the evidence was used. Recent discussion of "shadow syndromes" (Ratey and Johnson 1997) contend that quirky behaviors may actually be mild mental illnesses that are tied to genes. Here illness and behaviors are seen on a continuum: one or two altered genes give you a little disorder; perhaps three or four create a serious personality problem; and seven give you a full-blown illness. If geneticists found actual evidence to support the "shadow syndromes" conception, it is possible that the psychiatric net would widen and medicalization increase.

Homosexuality For at least a century, scientists have offered theories about the hereditary predisposition or congenital nature of homosexuality. Such theories produced little evidence. In the 1970s, with the rise of the gay liberation movement, homosexuality was at least symbolically demedicalized (Conrad and Schneider 1992; Bayer 1981). Throughout the 1970s and 1980s, with the emergence of open homosexual and lesbian "lifestyles" (later called sexual "orientations"), there was little research and public discussion on the heritability of homosexuality.

While a few important twin studies conducted in the 1980s found a higher concordance of homosexual orientation among identical twins than among other sibling pairs (Bailey and Pilliard 1991), suggesting a genetic association with homosexuality, it wasn't until nearly a decade later that an actual genetic marker was discovered. In 1993 Dean Hamer published an article using family pedigree and DNA analysis that reported a genetic marker associated with homosexuality located on the Xq28 region of the X chromosome (Hamer et al. 1993). This research received worldwide publicity. Before long the news media and Hamer himself began referring to the finding with the term "gay gene" (although no gene has be identified, only a marker). Two years later Hamer and his colleagues published a replication of the study with a different sample (Hu et al. 1995). Neither Hamer nor anyone else claims that this or another other gene is likely to be *the* cause of homosexuality, but Hamer's claims and the wide attention his study was given has moved heredity back into the central public discourse of homosexual origins.

The lesbian and gay community is divided about the implications of finding genetic links to homosexuality. One faction suggests that genetic evidence may be beneficial to gays, in that it demonstrates that homosexuality is a natural variation (like left-handedness) and should not be deviantized or discriminated against. Another faction is concerned that identifying genetic markers could lead to a remedicalization of homosexuality, testing and aborting fetuses with implicated genes, potential "treatments" for the "defect," and new forms of discrimination against gays and lesbians. There are some, however, who caution that genetics is irrelevant to justice (Nardi 1993).

If we were to measure the degrees of medicalization from 1973 (the APA vote to demedicalize) to now, we would probably see some movement toward remedicalization. Several factors were involved with this change, most beyond our discussion here. Few gays and lesbians completely adopt the "lifestyle" paradigm that was dominant in the 1980s. The HIV/AIDS epidemic has more deeply involved the medical profession with the male gay community and has led to some use of HIV testing of gay men. The discovery of a genetic marker for male homosexuality is an additional factor that could spur medicalization.

The homosexuality example raises some interesting issues about genetics. Even if the discovery of a "gay gene" is eventually validated (it has not yet been replicated by another research group), it is not clear how it will affect medicalization. If it is interpreted as evidence for the "naturalness" of homosexuality, as Hamer and others claim, then it may actually support demedicalization. If, however, it is taken as evidence that there is a genetic defect that could be medically treated or prevented with prenatal testing, then it could contribute to a remedicalization of homosexuality. The lesson here is that it is not the genetic discovery itself that could engender medicalization, but rather the way it is interpreted and what meanings are attributed to it. At least in this case, genetic association does not necessarily mean medicalization.

Alcoholism It has long been observed that alcoholism "runs in families." In recent years, scientists have reported twin and adoption studies that provided suggestive evidence of a component of biological heredity (Goodwin 1991), but it wasn't until 1990 that an actual genetic link was reported.

Blum and Noble's (Blum et al. 1990) study for the first time reported a specific genetic associated with alcoholism. Using cadaver brain research, they found that the gene for the dopamine D_2 receptor (DRD_2) discriminated significantly between alcoholics and nonalcoholics. The authors concluded that they had found a marker for a specific gene at a specifically located (q22-q23) region of chromosome 11 that "confers susceptibility to at least one form of alcoholism" (Blum et al. 1990: 2055). Like many others, the finding was widely reported in the news (Conrad and Weinberg 1996), announcing that "alcoholism was linked to a gene." Eight months later, the same journal *(JAMA)* published an article that essentially found no significant differences between alcoholics and controls (Bolos et al. 1990) and hence the DRD_2 gene for alcoholism was not confirmed.

Some geneticists believe that genes may differentially affect the ability to metabolize alcohol and thus play a role in the onset of alcoholism. For example, there is evidence that some groups of people (e.g., those of North American Indian and Japanese ancestry) have a reduced ability to break down alcohol due to a lower level of an enzyme called alcohol dehydrogenase, which may increase their susceptibility to alcoholism (Jones 1993). Increased genetic susceptibility does not, however, indicate who will become alcoholic. If such susceptibility genes exist, most people who inherit them do not become alcoholic, suggesting there are other factors at work.

As mentioned earlier, virtually all analysts agree that the emergence of AA and its ideology were key to the medicalization of alcoholism. The medical response, alcoholism hospital, and insurance coverage for treatment are more recent developments. It seems that alcoholism's place among the pantheon of illnesses is for the moment set. Perhaps identifying genes could be used by the alcoholism industry (those organizations that treat alcoholism) to give further credence to the disease model, but it is unlikely that not finding genes will have any effect on its medical status. Since the origins of the disease of alcoholism reside outside of medicine, the relevance of genetics to the definition of alcoholism is minimal.

Other Categories of Deviance Genetic associations to behavior have been reported for other categories of deviance. I will briefly mention a few here.

Obesity has been increasingly medicalized in our society (Sobal 1995). The incidence of obesity has grown as well; a recent NIH report suggested 55 percent of Americans are overweight or obese, up from 43 percent in 1960. (*Boston Globe* 1998). In recent years there have been several different reports claiming discovery of "obesity genes," although all of the identified genes thus far are only in mice. While obese mice may have processes in common with obese people, no genes in humans have yet been identified. It seems likely, however, since obesity is already partially medicalized, that the discovery of genes that increase the susceptibility of obesity, particularly if they lead to some kind of medical treatment, could well lead to an increased medicalization of obesity.

For nearly a century, various studies have claimed that some crime and violence results from a hereditary taint (Rafter 1997). In the late 1960s claims that the males with a XYY chromosome were more likely to be criminals received wide publicity. While this has since been scientifically discredited, the idea that biology can cause crime still has its proponents (Wilson and Herrnstein 1985). Based on the study of several generations of a Dutch kindred, researchers in 1993 published an article in *Science* (Brunner et al. 1993) that reported linking an apparently rare mutation on the X chromosome to deviant behavior, including "arson, attempted rape and exhibitionism." When the affected gene does not work properly, it causes a deficiency in monoamine oxidase A (MAOA), a compound associated with the metabolization of serotonin and adrenaline, which researchers suggest can increase aggressive behavior. While some of the researchers have emphasized that an MAOA deficiency doesn't automatically lead to violence (Mann 1994), the media reported it as a "violence gene" whose unlucky possessors were "born bad." The search for the born criminal is an old

one, and it is not surprising that the new techniques of genetics are now brought to bear on this quest. Crime has only been marginally medicalized—largely through the "insanity defense"—but if strong genetic associations for violence were found, we could hear new calls for a medicalization of some types of criminal behavior. How successful these would be would be more of a political than a scientific question.

The possibility also exists that genetic research could lead to the expansion of the categories of deviance. There have already been widely publicized reports of genes for shyness and "thrill seeking." If these findings become accepted by medicine and the public, they could create new medicalized categories of deviance. For example, while scientists see their research on the gene for "thrill seeking" as the first instance of discovering a common and "normal" behavioral trait, one could imagine the creation of a new disorder based on genetics, a "thrill seeking disorder." Similarly, we know genetics plays a role in human height. We now have growth hormone therapy, which can treat childhood short stature. At the moment most children treated have a growth hormone deficiency, a certified medical problem (Cutler et al. 1996). But what happens when we can isolate genes for shortness, a deviance in height? Will this create a new "shortness disorder" and require medical treatments to alleviate it and bring everyone up to normal height? In these cases, genetic evidence could be used not only to medicalize the problem but to create new categories of deviance.

Geneticization and Medicalization

Lippman (1991) coined the term "geneticization" to describe how genetic explanations for human problems have expanded beyond scientific knowledge.[4] She explains that the problems are old but the genetic framing is new:

> Only their categorization has changed, so that common conditions (cancer, alcoholism, schizophrenia, etc.) that could be categorized in many other ways are now (re)constructed by the application of biomedical information to be labeled as genetic diseases. (Lippman 1992: 1471)

Although the geneticization of disease might have profound implications for established diseases that were

---

[4] While *medicalization* has become a common term in both the sociological and medical literature, the term *geneticization* has not taken hold. A search of several computerized indices showed hundreds of references to medicalization with less than a handful for geneticization, and most of these were by Lippman. Nonetheless, geneticization describes a phenomenon relevant to this chapter.

not previously seen as genetic (e.g., breast or ovarian cancer), such as creating new categories of people at risk for certain disorders or shifting stigma, genetic explanations by themselves do not engender medicalization. As noted above, geneticization of homosexuality can be used to argue for or against medicalization. While Herrnstein and Murray's *The Bell Curve* geneticizes intelligence, this does not necessarily make lower intelligence a medical problem.

For medicalization to occur, lay or professional champions need to take genetic evidence and use it to make claims of illness or disability. Following social constructionist notions (Schneider 1985; Best 1995), genetics can be used to make medical claims, but for medicalization to occur there must be a change in the social definition and response to a problem. Ultimately, there needs to be some type of legitimation of the new designation (Conrad and Schneider 1992). Simply, genetic findings by themselves will not medicalize a problem, but they may be a piece in the medicalization process. Medicalization doesn't require specific claims about cause, although the assumption is often biological; certain medicalized problems like child abuse make no biological claims whatsoever. Geneticization, on the other hand, is very specific about where at least part of the cause lies.

Critics have pointed to the pitfalls and dangers of geneticization. Nelkin and Lindee (1995) contend that the gene has become something of an icon in American society, invested with mythical powers. This development has reinforced a genetic essentialism, where the DNA is seen as the essence of life and its problems. Many have noted that reductionist interpretations of genetics ignore the importance of the social environment and lead to a naive and misinformed genetic determinism (Rose 1995). Like medicalization, this determinism represents an individualization of social problems but adds a misplaced specificity about causality. A major concern is that genetics becomes the privileged cause and makes the problem into a genetic problem, relegating other causal factors to secondary status.

While most geneticists recognize that the links between genes and behavior are likely to be complex, in the public discourse the issues are often oversimplified. There is talk of a "gay gene," "obesity gene," or "breast cancer gene," when the issues are more complex. The scientific reality is not represented in these catch phrases. For homosexuality only a genetic marker has been discovered; for obesity we only know about genes that produce fat mice; and with breast cancer, while a specific gene has been identified, it is not "the" breast cancer gene, since only 10 percent of breast cancer is hereditary. "Genestalk"—talking as if genes are causal of behavior or problems—is common in everyday conversation, news media constructions, and policy debates (Kitcher 1996). Such depictions are ubiquitous in the public discourse and, for the moment at least, outstrip scientific knowledge.

Genetic explanations of behavior have a rather sordid history in the United States and Europe. Beginning in the late nineteenth century, many scientists, intellectuals, and politicians supported *eugenics,* what founder Frances Galton called "the science of improvement of the human race germplasm through better breeding" (cited in Haller 1963:3). The eugenics movement embodied the faulty "science" of the era, identifying genetic "defectives" and attempting to control their procreation and/or assimilation into society (Kevles 1985; Paul 1995). This control was accomplished through intelligence testing, selective immigration laws, and sterilization. Between the 1920s and 1970, 60,000 genetic "defectives" (mostly mentally retarded) were sterilized (Reilly 1991). Under the Nazis, eugenics reached its greatest horror, beginning with the 1933 Eugenics Law that resulted in the compulsory sterilization of 400,000 individuals diagnosed with schizophrenia, manic depression, hereditary epilepsy, and severe deformity and ending with the murder of six million people defined as genetically inferior (Muller-Hill 1988).

Numerous analysts have written sober and cautionary tales about the potentials of a "new eugenics" (Kevles 1985) or a "backdoor" to eugenics (Duster 1990). However, with current geneticization, the situation seems rather different. As Diane Paul (1992) notes, the old genetics focused on populations and was political and manifestly coercive, while the new genetics focuses on individuals and emphasizes genetic counseling and individual choice. Yet social anxieties over genetic potentials remain. This may be especially true among racial and ethnic minorities and the disability community, who see the potential of prenatal genetic screening and subsequent selective abortion as a threat to their community.

While the new genetics is not a state-mandated eugenics by intent, there are more subtle eugenic pressures that could affect individual decisions and social outcomes. The ability to "deselect" genetically impaired fetuses may lead to new cultural norms that make screening obligatory and pressure women to terminate their "disabled" fetus. Those who resist these social and medical admonitions may become defined as deviant. Moreover, societal responses may "blame" parents for having disabled or deviant offspring (they could have avoided it), and social institutions, such as medical insurance, could refuse to support services for disabilities that could have been prevented. These social pressures could well promote a eugenics by outcome, if not by specific policy.

Geneticization creates concerns that go beyond those raised about medicalization (see Conrad and Schneider 1992, chapter 9) and by eugenics. These include genetic screening and testing, gene therapy, and genetic discrimination in insurance and employment. Prenatal screening for several disorders (e.g., Down's syndrome) has become a routine part of medicine. As scientists begin to isolate genes or markers for specific traits or disorders, it becomes more feasible to identify them through prenatal screening and develop some type of intervention (which currently is limited to abortion). We might soon be faced with the possibility of screening for certain behavioral traits (e.g., susceptibility to alcoholism or homosexuality), which will raise uncomfortable issues. At this point medicine can test individuals to see if they are carriers of known genes (e.g., cystic fibrosis) or if they have a particular gene that makes them highly susceptible to a disease (e.g., BRCA1 with breast cancer) or virtually assured to contract a genetic disease (e.g., Huntington's disease). The number of traits for which medicine has the capability to test is growing quickly, although the results may not be as clear or positive as some claim (Hubbard and Lewontin 1996). But analysts have raised concerns that such testing may lead to new forms of stigmatization (Miringoff 1989) or genetic discrimination (Geller et al. 1996). Gene therapy—knocking out "bad" genes and inserting "good" ones—is only in its infancy, but it is likely to exacerbate the current issues and raise new ones. It could provide great hope for preventing some terrible genetic diseases, but it also presents the possibility of germline (reproductive) interventions with the potential to alter the genetic structure for future generations (see Kitcher 1996). While these concerns are beyond the scope of this chapter, they reflect some of the implications of geneticization on society.

A FEW ISSUES TO CONSIDER

How widely are genetic explanations accepted by the public? The sparse data that exist suggest a growing acceptance. A 1987 Gallup poll found that over 60 percent of Americans see alcoholism as inherited (cited in Peele 1990), and a *New York Times/CBS News Poll* reported that Americans were evenly split on homosexuality's cause (Schmalz 1993). While some claim that genetic determinism is increasing (Nelkin and Lindee 1995), others contend that it has decreased in the last eighty years (Condit, Ofulue, and Sheedy 1998). What seems evident, however, is that scientific associations between genetics and particular behaviors have received wide coverage in the press. What impact this coverage has on the public's acceptance of genetic explanations is still an empirical question.

With the completion of the Human Genome Project in the first years of the twenty-first century, scientists are likely to find subtle genetic differences among individuals or groups of people. What impact identifying genetic differences will have on amount and degree of medicalization is not yet known. Will small genetic differences become evidence for the creation of new biomedical categories? If, for example, genetic differences were found in people who have trouble remembering names, could that lead to the medicalization of "memory disorders"? Does genetic difference mean disease or disorder? Although medicalization still turns on how the research is interpreted and what people do about it, genetic findings could fuel new calls for biomedical responses and treatments. Is medicalization then different for new or previously unestablished categories?

Historically, medicalization has typically consisted of human troubles that become defined and treated as medical problems. But genetics raises the specter of human enhancement. There are already medicalized forms of enhancement such as cosmetic surgery for modifying breasts or altering racial features (Kaw 1993), but genetics could vault enhancement into the mainstream of medicine. For example, if genes for tallness, intelligence, or athletic ability were identified, would these discoveries spur a genetic medicalization of height or performance or, more broadly, the medicalization of offspring choice? (Wertz and Sorenson 1989). How might public demand align with medical capability in the context of constrained health-care resources? Would medicalization be necessary for genetic enhancement, and if so, how would it play out in society?

The social consequences of medicalization have been frequently articulated (Zola 1972; Reissman 1983; Conrad and Schneider 1992). Does genetic medicalization modify any of these consequences or produce new ones? Does geneticization shift the burdens of blame and responsibility? The privacy of genetic information has become a contested issue; does genetic medicalization raise new and troubling privacy concerns? What impact do genetic definitions have on stigma potential and discrimination? While the implications of the new genetics have been outlined by many analysts (e.g., Kitcher, Jones), the specific impacts of genetic medicalization need to be more clearly differentiated.

How much genetics will influence the direction and degree of medicalization is not yet known. To the extent that scientific research and new paradigms influence the definition and treatment of human problems, genetics, along with neuroscience and psychopharmacology, will be a significant factor. While genetic evidence for many human traits is not yet compelling, we are only at the dawn of the genetic age. Constraints such as health-care costs and bioethical issues will affect the shape and pace of genetic influence. Genetics' effect on medicalization is by no means ordained, but their futures will remain intertwined and perhaps increasingly interdependent.

REFERENCES

ALPER, JOSEPH S., and JONATHAN BECKWITH. 1993. "Genetic Fatalism and Social Policy: The Implications of Behavior Genetics Research." *Yale Journal of Biology and Medicine* 66: 511–24.

APPLETON, LYNN M. 1995. "Rethinking Medicalization: Alcoholism and Anomalies. In *Images of Issues.* 2nd ed., ed. Joel Best. New York: Aldine de Gruyter, pp. 59–80.

BAILEY, J. MICHAEL, and RICHARD C. PILLARD. 1991. "A Genetic Study of Male Sexual Orientation." *Archives of General Psychiatry* 48: 1089–96.

BARSKY, ARTHUR J., and JONATHAN F. BORUS. 1995. "Somatization and Medicalization in the Era of Managed Care." *Journal of the American Medical Association* 274: 1931–34.

BAYER, RONALD. 1981. Homosexuality and American Psychiatry: The Politics of Diagnosis." New York: *Basic.*

BEST, JOEL, ed. 1995. *Images of Issues.* 2nd ed. New York: Aldine de Gruyter.

BILLINGS, PAUL R, JONATHAN BECKWITH, and JOSEPH S. ALPER. 1992. "The Genetic Analysis of Human Behavior: A New Era?" *Social Science and Medicine* 35: 227–38.

BLUM, KENNETH, ERNEST P. NOBLE, PETER J. SHERIDAN, ANNE MONTGOMERY, TERRY RITCHIE, PADUR JAGADEESWARAN, HAROU NOGAMI, ARTH H. BRIGGS, and JAY B. COHEN. 1990. "Allelic Association of Human Dopamine D_2 Receptor Gene and Alcoholism." *Journal of the American Medical Association* 263: 2055–60.

BOLOS, A.M., M. DEAN, S. LUCAS-DERSE, M. RAMSBURY, G.L. BROWN, and D. GOLDMAN. 1990. "Population and Pedigree Studies Reveal Lack of Association Between the Dopamine D_2 Receptor Gene and Alcoholism." *Journal of the American Medical Association* 264: 3156–60.

BOSTON GLOBE. 1998. "NIH Offers Doctors Rx on Obesity." June 18: A9.

BROOM, DOROTHY H., and ROSLYN V. WOODWARD. 1996. "Medicalization Reconsidered: Toward a Collaborative Approach to Care." *Sociology of Health and Illness* 18: 357–78.

BRUNNER, H.G., M. NELEN, X.O. BREAKEFIELD, H.H. ROPERS, and B.A. VON OOST. 1993. "Abnormal Behavior Associated With a Point Mutation in the Structural Gene for Monoamine Oxidase A." *Science* 261: 578–80.

BURY, MICHAEL. 1986. "Social Constructionism and the Development of Medical Sociology." *Sociology of Health and Illness* 8: 137–69.

CONDIT, CELESTE M., and MELANIE WILLIAMS. 1997. "Audience Responses to the Discourse of Medical Genetics: Evidence Against the Critique of Medicalization." *Health Communication* 9: 219–35.

CONDIT, CELESTE M., NNEKA OFULUE, and KRISTIN M. SHEEDY. 1998. "Determinism and Mass Media Portrayals of Genetics." *American Journal of Human Genetics* 62: 679–91.

CONRAD, PETER. 1975. "The Discovery of Hyperkinesis: Notes on the Medicalization of Deviant Behavior." *Social Problems* 23: 12–21.

CONRAD, PETER. 1992. "Medicalization and Social Control." *Annual Review of Sociology* 18: 209–32.

CONRAD, PETER. 1997a. "Public Eyes and Private Genes: Historical Frames, News Constructions, and Social Problems." *Social Problems* 44: 139–54.

CONRAD, PETER. 1997b. "Parallel Play in Medical Anthropology and Medical Sociology." *The American Sociologist* 28: 90–100.

CONRAD, PETER. 1999. "A Mirage of Genes." *Sociology of Health and Illness* 21: 228–41.

CONRAD, PETER, and JOSEPH W. SCHNEIDER. 1980/1992. *Deviance and Medicalization: From Badness to Sickness.* exp. ed. Philadelphia: Temple University Press.

CONRAD, PETER, and DANA WEINBERG. 1996. "Has the Gene for Alcoholism Been Discovered Three Times Since 1980? A News Media Analysis." *Perspectives on Social Problems* 8: 3–24.

CUTTLER, LEONA, J. B. SILVERS, JAGDIP SINGH, URSULA MARRERO, BETH FINKELSTEIN, GRACE TANNIN, and DUNCAN NEUHAUSER. 1996. "Short Stature and Growth Hormone Therapy: A National Study of Physician Recommendation Patterns." *Journal of the American Medical Association* 276: 531–37.

DUSTER, TROY. 1990. *Backdoor to Eugenics.* New York: Routledge.

EGELAND, JANICE A., DANIELA S. GERHARD, DAVID L. PAULS, ET AL. 1987. "Bipolar Affective Disorders Linked to DNA Markers on Chromosome 11." *Nature* 325: 783–87.

ENGLEHARDT, H. T. 1974. "The Disease of Masturbation: Values and the Concept of Disease." *Bulletin of the History of Medicine* 48: 234–48.

Fox, Renée C. 1977. "The Medicalization and Demedicalization of American Society." *Daedalus* 106: 9–22.

Freidson, Eliot. 1970. *Profession of Medicine.* New York: Dodd, Mead.

Geller, Lisa N., Joseph S. Alper, Paul R. Billings, Carol I. Barash, Jonathan Beckwith, and Marvin R. Natowicz. 1996. "Individual, Family, and Societal Dimensions of Genetic Discrimination: A Case Study Analysis." *Science and Engineering Ethics* 2: 71–88.

Gilbert, Walter. 1992. "A Vision of the Grail." In *The Code of Codes,* ed. Daniel Kevles and Leroy Hood. Cambridge: Harvard University Press, pp. 83–97.

Goodwin, Donald W. 1991. "The Genetics of Alcoholism." In *Genes, Brain and Behavior,* ed. Paul R. McHugh and Victor McKusic. New York: Raven Press, pp. 219–29.

Haller, Mark H. 1963. *Eugenics: Hereditarian Attitudes in American Thought.* New Brunswick, NJ: Rutgers University Press.

Hamer, Dean, Stella Hu, Victoria L. Magnuson, Nan Hu, and Angela M.L. Pattatucci. 1993. "A Linkage Between DNA Markers on the X Chromosome and Male Sexual Orientation." *Science* 261: 321–27.

Herrnstein, Richard J., and Charles Murray. 1994. *The Bell Curve: Intelligence and Class Structure in American Life.* New York: Free Press.

Horgan, John. 1993. "Eugenics Revisited." *Scientific American* 269 (June): 122–31.

Hu, S., A.M.L. Pattucci, C. Patterson, L. Li, W. Fulker, S. Cherny, L. Kruglyak, and D. Hamer. 1995. "Linkage Between Sexual Orientation and Chromosome Xq28 in Males but Not in Females." *Nature Genetics* 11L: 248–56.

Hubbard, Ruth, and R.C. Lewontin. 1996. "Pitfalls of Genetic Testing." *New England Journal of Medicine* 334: 1192–94.

Illich, Ivan. 1976. *Medical Nemesis.* New York: Pantheon.

Jones, Steve. 1993. *The Language of Genes.* London: Flamingo.

Kaw, Eugenia. 1993. "Medicalization of Racial Features: Asian American Women and Cosmetic Surgery." *Medical Anthropology Quarterly* (n.s.) 7: 74–89.

Kevles, Daniel J. 1985. *In the Name of Eugenics: Genetics and the Uses of Human Heredity.* Berkeley: University of California Press.

Kevles, Daniel J., and Leroy Hood, eds. 1992. *The Code of Codes.* Cambridge: Harvard University Press.

Kitcher, Philip. 1996. *The Lives to Come: The Genetic Revolution and Human Possibilities.* New York: Simon and Schuster.

Lippman, Abby. 1991. "Prenatal Genetic Testing and Screening: Constructing Needs and Reinforcing Tendencies." *American Journal of Law and Society* 17: 15–50.

Lippman, Abby. 1992. "Led (Astray) by Genetic Maps: The Cartography of the Human Genome and Health Care." *Social Science and Medicine* 35: 1469–96

Lowenberg, June S., and Fred Davis. 1994. "Beyond Medicalization-Demedicalization: The Case of Holistic Health." *Sociology of Health and Illness* 16: 579–99.

Lupton, Deborah. 1997. "Foucault and the Medicalization Critique." In *Foucault: Health and Medicine,* ed. Alan Peterson and Robin Bunton. London: Routledge, pp. 94–112.

Mann, Charles. 1994. "Behavioral Genetics in Transition." *Science* 264: 1686–89.

Miringoff, Marque. 1989. "Genetic Intervention and Problem of Stigma." *Policy Studies Review* 8: 389–404.

Muller-Hill, Benno. 1988. *Murderous Science: Elimination by Scientific Selection of Jews, Gypsies and Others, Germany 1933–45.* New York: Oxford University Press.

Oinas, Elina. 1998. "Medicalization by Whom? Accounts of Menstruation Conveyed by Young Women and Medical Experts in Medical Advisory Columns." *Sociology of Health and Illness* 20: 52–70.

Nardi, Peter. 1993. "Gays Should Lean on Justice, not Science." *Los Angeles Times* August 6: B7.

Navarro, Vicente. 1976. *Medicine Under Capitalism.* New York: Prodist.

Nelkin, Dorothy, and M. Susan Lindee. 1995. *The DNA Mystique: The Gene as a Cultural Icon.* New York: W.H. Freeman.

Parsons, Talcott. 1951. *The Social System.* Glencoe: The Free Press.

Paul, Diane B. 1992. "Eugenic Anxieties, Social Realities, and Political Choices." *Social Research* 59: 663–83.

Paul, Diane B. 1995. *Controlling Human Heredity: 1865 to the Present.* Atlantic Highlands, NJ: Humanities Press.

Peele, Stanton. 1990. "Second Thoughts About a Gene for Alcoholism." *Atlantic Monthly* 269 (August): 52–58.

Peele, Stanton. 1995. "My Genes Made Me Do It." *Psychology Today* (July-August): 50–68.

Pitts, Jesse. 1968. "Social Control: The Concept." *International Encyclopedia of Social Sciences.* Vol. 14. New York: Macmillan.

Rafter, Nicole Hahn. 1997. *Creating Born Criminals.* Urbana: University of Illinois Press.

Ratey, John, and Catherine Johnson. 1997. *Shadow Syndromes.* New York: Pantheon.

Reilly, Phillip. 1991. *The Surgical Solution.* Baltimore: Johns Hopkins University Press.

Reissman, Cathrine Kohler. 1983. "Women and Medicalization: A New Perspective." *Social Policy* 14 (Summer): 3–18.

Roman, Paul. 1988. "The Disease Concept of Alcoholism: Sociocultural and Organizational Bases of Support." *Drugs and Society* 2: 5–32.

Rose, Steven. 1995. "The Rise of Neurogenetic Determinism." *Nature* 373: 380–82.

Schmalz, Jeffrey. 1993. "Poll Finds an Even Split on Homosexuality's Cause." *The New York Times* March 5: 14.

Schneider, Joseph W. 1978. "Deviant Drinking as a Disease: Alcoholism as a Social Accomplishment." *Social Problems* 25: 361–72.

Schneider, Joseph W. 1985. "Social Problems Theory: The Constructionist View." *Annual Review of Sociology* 11: 209–29.

SHERRINGTON R., J. BRYNJOLFSSON, H. PETURSSON, M. POTTER, K. DUDLESTON, B. BARRACLOUGH, J. WASMUTH, M. DOBBS, and H. GURLING. 1988. "Localization of a Susceptibility Locus for Schizophrenia on Chromosome 5." *Nature* 336: 164–67.

SOBAL, JEFFERY. 1995. "The Medicalization and Demedicalization of Obesity." In *Eating Agendas: Food and Nutrition as Social Problems,* ed. Donna Maurer and Jeffery Sobal. Hawthorne, NY: Aldine, pp. 67–90.

STRONG, PHIL. 1979. "Sociological Imperialism and the Profession of Medicine: A Critical Examination of the Thesis of Medical Imperialism." *Social Science and Medicine* 13A: 199–215.

WATSON, JAMES. 1997. "President's Essay." *Annual Report.* Maine: Cold Spring Harbor.

WERTZ, DOROTHY C., and JAMES R. SORENSON. 1989. "Sociologic Implications." In *Fetal Diagnosis and Therapy: Science, Ethics and the Law,* ed. M.I. Evans, J.C. Fletcher, A.O. Dixler, and J.D. Shulman. Philadelphia: Lippincott, pp. 545–54.

WILLIAMS, SIMON J., and MICHAEL CALNAN. 1996. "The 'Limits' of Medicalization?: Modern Medicine and the Lay Populace in 'Late' Modernity." *Social Science and Medicine* 42: 1609–20.

WILSON, JAMES Q., and RICHARD HERRNSTEIN. 1985. *Crime and Human Nature.* New York: Simon and Schuster.

ZOLA, IRVING KENNETH. 1972. "Medicine as an Institution of Social Control." *Sociological Review* 20: 487–504.

ZURIFF, G.E. 1996. "Medicalizing Character." *Public Interest* (Spring): 94–99.

23 SOCIAL AND PSYCHOLOGICAL FACTORS, PHYSIOLOGICAL PROCESSES, AND PHYSICAL HEALTH

ALLEN M. FREMONT, *Harvard Medical School*

CHLOE E. BIRD, *Brown University*

INTRODUCTION

Associations between social and psychological factors such as socioeconomic status or social support and health are now well established, yet precisely how these psychosocial factors alter health remains unclear and a source of ongoing debate (see Chapter 4 by Mirowsky, Ross, and Reynolds; Chapter 6 by Robert and House; and Chapter 25 by Syme and Yen). The robustness of these relationships and the uncertainty about underlying mechanisms is attracting an increasingly diverse range of researchers who emphasize different parts of the causal chain. In this chapter we consider evidence from a variety of other disciplines about one possible pathway—physiological links between psychosocial processes and health.

Since Selye's (1936, 1956) pioneering work on the General Adaptation Syndrome (GAS), research linking social and psychological factors to physiologic processes and disease has grown rapidly, particularly within the past two decades. Advances in this area of research are challenging dominant models of human physiology by revealing multiple ways in which social and psychological phenomena can directly influence physiologic processes. For example, until recently biomedical scientists viewed the immune system as a completely autonomous system. Compelling new findings have led to

recognition that the immune system is actually intricately linked to, and in constant communication with, the brain and other physiologic systems (Ader, Cohen, and Felten 1995). Although physiological mechanisms are far "downstream" from those sociologists typically examine, evidence from this area provides support for sociologists' long-held assumption that socially patterned stressors, coping resources, and psychological distress can directly affect health by impairing physiologic responses, which in turn predispose individuals to disease. This area of research also provides unprecedented opportunities to refine and strengthen our theoretical and empirical models (Coe 1997; Levine 1995). In addition to revealing multiple causal pathways with complex interactions between social, psychological, behavioral, and biological factors, this research suggest that the effects are compounded over the life course.

Evidence of links between psychosocial factors, physiologic processes, and disease is contributing to a wider paradigm shift in medical research and practice from a biomedical model—which sociologists have long critiqued for its reductionist approach, tendency to treat the mind and body as separate entities, and failure to examine the larger social context—to a broader "biopsychosocial" model, which includes social and psychological factors (Engel 1977; Watkins 1997). However, narrower biological models still dominate most allopathic medical research. Although social factors are increasingly considered, most mainstream researchers continue to view them as confounders of minor importance, or as individual risk

This work was supported in part by the Harvard Faculty Development and Fellowship Program in General Internal Medicine, Brigham and Women's Hospital, and the Department of Health Care Policy, Harvard Medical School. We thank Paul Cleary, Peter Conrad, and Patricia Rieker for their helpful comments.

factors (Kaplan 1995). Even in the more progressive, mind–body literature, the impact of social structure and processes are often ignored (Antonovsky 1994; Dreher 1995; Schafer 1998).

These limitations are matched by those of our own discipline. We tend to treat physiological pathways as a black box. Mental health effects of psychosocial stress are often assumed to be generalizable to physical health or to be part of a causal chain that, in turn, affects physical health. Yet sociological models generally examine only mental health outcomes and rarely include biological measures necessary to test physiological mechanisms (Fremont and Bird 1999; Thoits 1995). The possibility of interactions between psychosocial factors such as chronic psychological stress or social support and biological factors such as a genetic predisposition for premature atherosclerosis or the pathophysiology of specific diseases such as Type I versus Type II diabetes mellitus is also often ignored (Peyrot, McMurry, and Kruger 1999). By failing to recognize either the multiple pathways to specific health outcomes (Thoits 1995) or that a particular stressor may lead to multiple outcomes, we risk oversimplifying and underestimating relationships between psychosocial factors and health (Aneshensel, Rutter, and Lanchenbruch 1991).

We have two major goals in this chapter. First, we seek to briefly summarize current knowledge and unanswered questions regarding interactions between social and psychological factors, physiological processes, and health. We do not intend this chapter to be comprehensive, as numerous excellent reviews are available (Adler 1994; Biondi and Zannino 1997; Brezinka and Kittel 1996; Cohen and Herbert 1996; Hemingway and Marmot 1999; Lovallo 1997; Rozanski, Blumenthal, and Kaplan 1999). Rather, we aim to increase sociologists' familiarity with this body of research by presenting representative findings from two of the most well-developed areas: the immune system and the cardiovascular system.

We begin with a brief "primer" on traditional and emerging views on physiologic responses to stress. We assume this material will be a review for some readers and an introduction for others. In the next two sections, we describe typical findings from research linking psychosocial factors to functioning and pathophysiology of the immune and cardiovascular systems, respectively. We conclude our discussion of these two areas by highlighting new directions in research of particular relevance to sociology.

Our second major goal is to delineate and discuss implications of this rapidly developing area for medical sociology. We argue that this area of research has implications not only for those interested in stress research but also for a much wider range of medical sociologists. Simply put, societal values and beliefs about why people get sick and how we should care for them once they are sick not only shape the way health care is structured and provided, they also influence virtually every major societal institution as well as individuals' everyday lives. To demonstrate the potential value of incorporating knowledge about physiological mechanisms into sociological research, we consider two examples: Socioeconomic Status (SES) and the health gradient and gender differences in health. We conclude with a discussion of the potential impact of research on the physiologic pathways between psychosocial factors and health.

A BRIEF PRIMER ON PHYSIOLOGICAL RESPONSES TO STRESS

The vast majority of work linking psychosocial factors and health examines the impact of various types of psychological distress. Therefore, in this section we focus on current and emerging conceptions about physiologic responses to acute and chronic stress. We assume that many readers do not have extensive backgrounds in current knowledge regarding human physiology and intend this section as an introduction. Nevertheless, readers may find this section particularly challenging compared to the remainder of the chapter. For interested readers, a more extended discussion of key concepts is included in an appendix on the *Handbook* web page.

The human body has an elaborate, remarkably complex hierarchy of physiologic control and feedback systems. Thus, though various organ systems (e.g., cardiovascular system) and physiological processes (e.g., pumping action of the heart) can function autonomously, their activities are also regulated and coordinated by higher-level control systems. For our purposes, the major control systems are the sympathetic nervous system (part of the autonomic nervous system and capable of stimulating release of epinephrine, which is commonly referred to as adrenaline, from the adrenal gland) and the Hypothalamic Pituitary Adrenal (HPA) axis (a neuroendocrine pathway that produces cortisol, a key stress hormone). The sympathetic nervous system and HPA axis are, in turn, heavily influenced by other control centers within the brain. During periods of stress, activity of the sympathetic nervous system and the HPA axis increase dramatically, resulting in increased levels of stress hormones (e.g., cortisol and epinephrine) and numerous physiological changes (e.g., increased heart rate, muscle tone, and glucose and fatty acid levels) that prepare the body for action (Lovallo 1997).

Until fairly recently, the basic conceptualization of the stress response stopped here. Although it was generally agreed that prolonged exposure to stress and stress hormones could be damaging by "exhausting" organs and physiologic systems, very little was understood about the specifics of this process. Moreover, Selye's original conception assumed that the stress response was nonspecific, uniformly activating the sympathetic nervous system and the HPA axis regardless of the type of stress, the circumstances, or the individual in which it occurs. Because these models were based on animal experiments using relatively severe physical and psychosocial stressors, it was also generally assumed that only severe and prolonged psychological distress could lead to pathology in humans.

In the last twenty years, this basic conceptualization has changed considerably, as it has become clear that different types of stress and circumstances can elicit different physiological responses and that even subtle forms of stress or emotional changes can produce significant short- and long-term changes in physiologic processes (Herbert and Cohen 1993b). Moreover, it is now apparent that severe or chronic stress does not simply exhaust physiologic systems but may fundamentally alter the physiological responses to additional stressors (McEwan 1998). For example, chronically high levels of one stress hormone (e.g., cortisol) can alter the number and sensitivity of tissue receptors throughout the body to other stress hormones, including catecholamines such as epinephrine (Lovallo 1997).

Finally, conventional wisdom regarding the extent of independence of various organ systems from the brain and from other organ systems has been shown to be largely incorrect. One of the clearest examples is the changing understanding of the immune system and its close communication with the brain. In contrast to the previously held view that the immune system operated completely autonomously, it is now known that the brain, autonomic nervous system (including the sympathetic nervous system), endocrine system, and the immune system are intimately intertwined (Ader, Cohen, and Felten 1995). For example, not only do immune cells have receptors for and responses to most known neurotransmitters and hormones, but certain immune tissues (e.g., lymph nodes) also are directly connected to nerves from the sympathetic nervous system, which can influence "trafficking" of immune cells residing there into and out of the bloodstream as well as their degree of activation or suppression (Glaser and Kiecolt-Glaser 1994).

Immune cells are not simply passive recipients of commands from higher-level control centers in the brain. Rather, they communicate with each other via dozens (perhaps hundreds) of chemical messengers (e.g., cytokines). For example, certain immune cells (e.g., T-helper cells) can signal other immune cells to become more or less active, migrate to specific locations, rapidly proliferate clones of themselves, or make more antibodies. Immune cells are also capable of producing a variety of chemical neurotransmitters, hormones (identical to those produced by the nervous and endocrine systems), and certain cytokines that are both perceived by and acted upon by the brain (Ader, Cohen, and Felten 1995; Schindler 1993).

For instance, macrophages and T-helper cells produce interlukin 6, a cytokine that not only has local effects such as increasing inflammation, but also activates the HPA axis resulting in increased cortisol production. Like many cytokines, interlukin 6 can induce mood changes (e.g., irritability or depressed mood), physical symptoms (e.g., fatigue), and behavioral changes (e.g., social withdrawal)(Lovallo 1997). Indeed, some researchers contend that the action of various cytokines may explain certain types of depression and other psychiatric disorders (Miller 1998). Other researchers have argued that the brain and the endocrine and immune systems are all part of the same integrated information and control system with a universal set of chemical messengers. Hence, emotions are manifested in the body as much as in the brain (Pert 1986).

SOCIAL AND PSYCHOLOGICAL FACTORS AND THE IMMUNE SYSTEM

In this section, we briefly present typical studies showing physiological effects of social and psychological factors on immune function. Psychologists and other researchers with training in the biological sciences dominate this body of work. Studies typically involve relatively small samples and use experimental designs based in laboratory or naturalistic settings; large, community-based prospective studies are uncommon in this literature. Most studies focus on the impact of various types of psychological stress and coping resources. Few studies examine different patterns across social groups such as by socioeconomic status or gender. Finally, though we discuss only human studies, there is a large and intriguing literature involving animal studies (Glaser and Kiecolt-Glaser 1994).

Examples of Studies Linking Psychosocial Factors to Immune Function

Research on humans provides substantial evidence of a relationship between psychological stress and decreases in functional immune measures such as proliferation of lymphocytes (a type of white blood cell) in response to an antigen (e.g., a foreign material). Stress also is associated with changes in the number and percentage of different types of lymphocytes and antibodies (Herbert and Cohen 1993b). The specific effects appear to vary somewhat depending on the type of stressor. For example, stressors involving social interaction (e.g., public speaking) consistently show larger and longer lasting effects than nonsocial stressors (e.g., solving a math problem). The configuration of immune changes and the likely physiological pathways also vary with the duration of a given stressor (Herbert and Cohen 1993b; Lovallo 1997). As we discuss later, the effects of a specific stressor may also vary depending on individuals' inherent or acquired biological vulnerabilities and physiological reactiveness.

Short-term naturalistic studies focus on the impact of transient stressors (lasting from days to weeks) and generally use young adults as subjects. Perhaps most well known is a year-long prospective study of medical students during and between major exam periods. Compared to relatively low-stress periods between or after exams, students reported higher levels of distress leading up to major exams and showed changes in a variety of immune markers (e.g., decreased lymphocyte proliferation) that are consistent with immunosuppression (Glaser, Rice, Sheridan, et al. 1987). In a more recent study, exam stress was associated with dysregulation in the amount and type of cytokines (e.g., interferon) in ways that could predispose students to increased viral infections, herpes recurrence, and allergic reactions (Marshall, Agarwal, Lloyd, et al. 1998).

Other studies have demonstrated that daily hassles can affect immune function. For instance, on days subjects reported more hassles (e.g., losing keys, having an argument), they had decreased antibody response (Stone, Neale, Cox, et al. 1994). Interestingly, subjects reporting more positive events (e.g., accomplishing a goal, good interaction with the boss) on a given day tended to have higher antibody response. Few studies have assessed the impact of positive events.

Longer-term stress, lasting months or years, also has been shown to affect immune function. In contrast to the transient neuroendocrine and immune changes with brief stressors, more sustained stress may produce relatively stable changes, shifting the baseline levels

and functioning of various immune cells (Herbert and Cohen 1993b). For example, compared to people living in other areas, those living near the Three Mile Island (TMI) nuclear power plant had higher levels of psychological distress and immune changes that could increase risk of infection as long as ten years after the TMI disaster (McKinnon, Weisse, Reynolds, et al. 1989). Similarly, acting as the primary caregiver to a spouse with Alzheimer's Disease (AD) was associated with increased psychological distress and decreased immune functioning including slowed wound healing, which is dependent on proper immune functioning (Kiecolt-Glaser, Dura, et al. 1991; Kiecolt-Glaser, Marucha, Malarkey, et al. 1995).

Numerous studies have also shown that depression can reduce immune function (Herbert and Cohen 1993a). However, the effects of depression may be conditional on other psychosocial and biological factors. For example, depressed smokers had lower Natural Killer (NK) cell activity than depressed nonsmokers even though smoking did not affect NK cell activity in nondepressed individuals (Jung and Irwin 1999). Similarly, several studies have shown that individuals who are severely depressed, older, male, and hospitalized were much more likely to show significant immune changes than others (Miller 1998). Moreover, though much of the attention on the link between depression and the immune system has focused on the effects of depression on immune function, there is growing evidence that the causal direction is sometimes reversed. For example, cytokines produced by immune cells have been shown to induce many symptoms associated with depression, including social withdrawal, decreased appetite, altered sleep patterns, and lack of pleasure in enjoyable tasks (Connor and Leonard 1998; Miller 1998).

As in the broader stress literature, the effects of stress on immune function appear to be mediated by coping resources. Most work on coping resources has examined the impact of social support (i.e., network size, network diversity, or level of support). Social support and isolation have proven to be robust predictors of immune function that, at least partly, mediate the impact of both acute and chronic stress. Thus, medical students who reported more loneliness or less social support had larger declines in immune function both during and between testing periods (Kiecolt-Glaser, Garner, Speicher, et al. 1984). Similarly, caregivers to spouses with Alzheimer's who were the most psychologically distressed by their partner's dementia and had the least social support also had the lowest levels of cellular immunity (Kiecolt-Glaser et al. 1991). Furthermore, those with little support in caring for their spouse had higher resting epinephrine levels and significant decreases in cellular adhesion molecules on lymphocytes, which are crucial to lymphocytes' ability to migrate to a site of active infection (Mills, Yu, Ziegler, et al. 1999). In addition to acting as a buffer against stress on immune function, social support may have direct effects on immune function (Uchino, Cacioppo, and Kiecolt-Glaser 1996).

Evidence Linking Psychosocial Factors to Immune Function and Disease

Despite evidence that certain social psychological processes can suppress immune function, it remains unclear whether such changes actually lead to disease. For example, most studies measure only a few markers of immune function in the peripheral blood system (i.e., from a venous blood draw). These markers may not reflect activity in key immune tissues (e.g., spleen and lymph nodes), where the most active and effective immune response may occur. Perhaps more important, it is unclear whether the relatively small changes in immune functions that have been demonstrated are sufficient to significantly increase vulnerability to disease particularly in otherwise healthy adults (Cohen and Herbert 1996).

Thus far, research attempting to link social psychological factors to the development or progression of actual disease has been much less consistent than that showing changes in immune markers. This has been disappointing for many researchers and advocates of mind–body interactions because it stands to reason that if psychosocial factors affect immune function, then they should also affect the development and course of diseases that involve the immune function, such as HIV/AIDS, rheumatoid arthritis, and cancers.

Although animal studies have provided compelling evidence in support of this hypothesis, human studies on a variety of conditions have been much less consistent (Fife, Beasley, and Fertig 1996; Kiecolt-Glaser and Glaser 1995; Nott, Vedhara, and Spickett 1995; Rogers and Fozdar 1996). The mixed findings in human studies are not surprising, considering that studies of disease onset and progression must circumvent numerous difficulties. For example, attempts to link psychosocial factors with cancer development and progression are confounded by difficulty in determining the severity and stage of the cancer, accounting for differences in the biology of different tumors, assessing and controlling medication effects and compliance, and the possibility that either comorbidities or the cancer itself may influence both psychological well-being and prognosis. Moreover, even if psychosocial factors affect survival, their contribution may be small and overshadowed by biological factors in the late stages of many cancers (Cohen and Herbert 1996).

Some of these methodological problems can be overcome by well-designed intervention studies (Biondi and Zannino 1997). Indeed, some of the most intriguing work to date on cancer progression comes from a series of interventional studies of patients from whom a stage 1 or 2 malignant melanoma had been surgically removed. The patients were randomly assigned to either a no-treatment control group or an intervention group that combined education about the disease, stress management, coping skills, and support groups that met for 6 weeks. Compared to the control group, the intervention group showed better psychological coping, as well as increased numbers and activity of Natural Killer cells, which are crucial in the immune system's defense against cancer. These effects persisted for 6 months after the intervention, though to a lesser magnitude. Nevertheless, in a 6-year follow-up study, the intervention group had a significantly lower mortality rate and a trend toward less recurrence (Fawzy, Fawzy, Hyun, et al. 1993; Fawzy, Kemeny, Fawzy, et al. 1990).

Though seemingly mundane compared to cancer, studies of colds and the flu provide useful insights into the complex ways social and psychological factors affect immune function and predispose to illness. Because these two conditions have rapid onset and generally benign outcomes, it is practical and ethical to expose volunteers to standardized doses of cold and flu viruses in studies that control for many of the confounding factors mentioned above. For example, one series of studies demonstrated that individuals with a greater number of stressful life events and higher levels of acute psychological distress had greater incidence and severity of colds (Cohen, Frank, Doyle, et al. 1998). Individuals with a greater variety of social ties also developed fewer and less severe colds (Cohen, Doyle, Skoner, et al. 1997)

However, although virtually all volunteers became infected with the virus in these studies, not all volunteers developed signs and symptoms of a cold, nor, was there a consistent association between the immune markers typically studied and developing a cold. As expected, individuals reporting more psychological distress prior to infection tended to report the worst symptoms. However, in contradiction to the widely held assumption that their greater symptoms simply reflected reporting bias due to psychological distress, objective measures of severity of infection such as viral shedding and mucus production confirmed their reports. The apparent physiological pathway in this instance was greater production of interlukin 6 (a chemical messenger used by immune cells) in the nasal tissues of those reporting high levels of distress (Cohen, Doyle, and Skoner 1999). As previously noted, ongoing distress can increase cortisol levels, which in turn influence the production of interlukin 6.

Summary and Critique— Psychosocial Factors and the Immune System

Taken as a whole, this literature offers compelling evidence that psychosocial factors, particularly acute and chronic stress, can have direct effects on immune function in ways that may make individuals more susceptible to disease. In addition, other factors such as social support may buffer immune function against the effects of stress and may perhaps enhance immune function directly. Although less consistent and weakened by methodological problems, there is also increasing evidence that the immune changes are sufficient in some cases to increase the chance of developing immune-related disease or increase its severity once it develops.

This area of research is still quite new, and the methods and measures used are in rapid flux. For example, earlier studies assessed the number and responsiveness of a few types of immune cells. More recent studies also examine an increasingly wide array of chemical messengers crucial to effective immune functioning. Research involving immune measures has, of necessity, been dominated by laboratory and naturalistic studies with small sample sizes. However, this is likely to change as less expensive and invasive and more sensitive bioassays become readily available. It is also becoming clear that changes in some immune markers are more robust than others, depending on the type of psychosocial factors considered. For example, decreases in Natural Killer cell activity in response to depression is more reproducible than is lymphocyte proliferation, typically seen in response to acute laboratory stressors (Miller 1998). This suggests subtle, but significant differences in the physiological pathways linking different types of stressors and emotions to immune function and disease.

Finally, most of this research has been conducted on healthy populations. It seems likely that the relatively small immune effects of psychosocial factors have greater consequences for more biologically vulnerable persons, such as the elderly or individuals with existing conditions that make them more susceptible to infection (e.g., diabetics) and other immune-mediated diseases. Indeed, initial speculation that psychosocial factors frequently play a major role in the causation of immune-mediated diseases is being replaced by a view in which damaging effects of psychosocial factors occur mainly through interactions with other disease determinants, including inherited or acquired biological vulnerabilities and pathogen exposure, and are most apparent in effects on disease course and outcome (Miller 1998).

Thus far, the range of psychosocial factors considered in this literature has focused primarily on acute and chronic psychological stress and social support. With some exceptions, conceptual models and measures used in many studies have lacked the sophistication of the broader stress and coping literature. For example, the mediating effects of coping resources such as perceived control or meaning of a given stressor for different individuals is rarely considered. This literature, particularly the earlier studies, has also been inconsistent in controlling for alternative explanations for the association between psychosocial factors and immune changes, such as the effects of stress on sleep or health behavior (e.g., nutrition, smoking, and alcohol use), which can affect immune function (Keller, Shiflett, Schleifer, et al. 1994). Perhaps most striking from a sociologic perspective is the scarcity of human studies that explicitly test whether immune effects differ across social groups, and whether the effects of stress and coping on immune function are moderated by other psychosocial variables (e.g., social status). Greater participation by sociologists in discourse and research design could substantially strengthen this literature by encouraging greater emphasis on social context and the linkages with more "upstream" social factors.

More collaboration with researchers in this area could also enhance sociological models. Although this literature should provide solace for sociologists who have assumed that psychosocial factors can directly affect physiological processes, it also indicates the need for caution and reflection. Though still in its infancy, this literature has already exposed numerous anomalies in conventional ideas about how stress affects immune function. As has been shown in the cold studies, it is likely that the processes through which psychosocial stress affects immune function and disease are far more complex than commonly assumed. This literature also suggests that sociological models that either assume identical physiological pathways between different social stressors and different diseases or ignore interactions with inherent or acquired biological vulnerabilities will yield inconsistent results that underestimate the impact of social factors. Although it may be reasonable to assume that some inherited biological vulnerabilities are randomly distributed across the social groupings that sociologists typically consider, it seems contradictory to also assume that acquired biological vulnerabilities are randomly distributed since we argue that social factors such as race, class, and gender can pattern health behaviors (e.g., alcohol use) and exposure to environmental stressors (e.g., carcinogens) that in turn have pathophysiologic effects. Moreover, as we discuss later, socially patterned exposure to psychosocial stressors and availability of coping resources can temporarily, or perhaps permanently, alter physiological responses to subsequent stressors.

SOCIAL AND PSYCHOLOGICAL FACTORS AND THE CARDIOVASCULAR SYSTEM

We now turn to examples of evidence linking various psychosocial factors to cardiovascular function and disease. In contrast to the immune literature discussed above, which has its origins in experimental psychology and the biological sciences, the cardiovascular literature also draws extensively from the work of social and clinical epidemiologists and includes numerous large, prospective studies. In addition, the range of psychosocial variables considered is more diverse, and with the exception of hostility and anger, the psychosocial factors typically considered are often those commonly studied by medical sociologists.

As in the immune and sociological literature linking psychosocial factors to health, most studies in the cardiovascular literature do not simultaneously test for an overall association between psychosocial factors and disease and the underlying physiological mechanism. However, in contrast, many studies in the cardiovascular literature do control for a variety of biological risk factors (e.g., high cholesterol, known heart disease or diabetes) and behavioral factors (e.g., diet, smoking, alcohol use, or sedentary lifestyle) as possible confounders (or mechanisms). Though numerous biological and behavioral variables are typically controlled, most study designs and models are based on previously established empirical associations rather than well-developed theoretical models. Moreover, measures of "upstream" social factors (e.g., measures of socioeconomic status)

are often viewed as proxies for more "downstream" variables (e.g., smoking).

Evidence Linking Psychosocial Factors to Cardiovascular Function: Physiological Mechanisms

A variety of laboratory and naturalistic studies indicate that both transient and chronic psychological stressors can induce cardiovascular effects that predispose individuals to life-threatening cardiac events such as myocardial infarctions (i.e., heart attacks) and arrhythmias (i.e., abnormal rate and rhythm of heart beat) (Rozanski, Blumenthal, and Kaplan 1999). For example, myocardial ischemia refers to the situation in which portions of the heart receive insufficient blood flow and become oxygen deprived. It is associated with angina (i.e., chest pain), heart attacks, and arrhythmias. In the laboratory setting, mental stress (e.g., simulated public speaking) can induce myocardial ischemia (Rozanski, Bairey, Krantz, et al. 1988). Similarly, studies using ambulatory electrocardiographic (ECG) monitors have demonstrated that mental stress and negative emotions can produce ischemia (often without symptoms) in everyday life (Gullette, Blumenthal, Babyak, et al. 1997).

In fact, a given psychosocial stressor can contribute to cardiovascular disease through a wide variety of pathophysiological mechanisms. The most well-studied stressor, in this respect, is acute psychological stress (including transient mental stress). Established effects of acute stress (particularly if stress is recurrent) include: (1) increased heart rate and blood pressure (which increase the work of the heart and its need for oxygen); (2) dysfunction of the normal function of coronary arteries so that they paradoxically constrict (thus reducing blood supply to the heart muscle) at a time when more oxygen is needed; (3) increased electrical excitability and lowered threshold for arrhythmias (a common cause of sudden death); (4) damage to the highly complex lining of coronary arteries (i.e., endothelium) in ways that increase the likelihood of plaque formation and rupture (which can cause a heart attack); and (5) increased "stickiness" of platelets and other clotting factors resulting in increased likelihood of a clot that could occlude a coronary artery (Rozanski, Blumenthal, and Kaplan 1999).

These effects are thought to be mediated primarily by increased activity of the sympathetic nervous system. Though other types of psychological distress such as depression or chronic stress may also involve increased sympathetic activity, their effects are thought to occur via other physiological pathways, such as chronically increased cortisol levels, which can increase cholesterol and glucose levels and accelerate atherosclerosis (Lovallo 1997; Nixon and King 1997).

Examples of Studies Linking Psychosocial Factors to Cardiovascular Disease

Large community studies consistently show a strong association between acute social stress and cardiac events such as heart attacks (Hemingway and Marmot 1999). For example, the risk of cardiac-related mortality doubles in men and triples in women during the first month of bereavement for their spouse. However, after one month the risk is the same as in the general population (Kaprio, Koskenvuo, and Rita 1987). Studies of the immediate aftermath of natural or manmade disasters also show substantial short-term increases in the number of cardiac-related deaths (Rozanski, Blumenthal, and Kaplan 1999). Episodes of anger are also associated with cardiac events. For example, among individuals with preexisting coronary heart disease, those who had an episode of anger were two times more likely to have a heart attack within the next two hours (Mittleman, Maclure, Sherwood, et al. 1995).

Chronic stress has also been linked to cardiovascular disease. The most active area of research is on work-related stress. For example, numerous studies have shown that the combination of high psychological demand and low control over decisions (i.e., job strain) increases cardiac risk factors (e.g., smoking, high blood pressure, and high cholesterol) and is predictive of greater cardiac-related morbidity and mortality (Theorell and Kareseck 1996). Similarly, high demand and low reward work is associated with increasing atherosclerosis (Lynch, Krause, Kaplan, et al. 1997). Social conflict and instability on a societal scale have also been shown to increase cardiovascular morbidity and mortality. For instance, life expectancy in Russia fell sharply during the 4-year period immediately following the collapse of communism. Cardiovascular disease accounted for more than 75 percent of the decline in life expectancy (Notzon, Komarov, Ermakov, et al. 1998).

Major depression predicts development of heart disease in healthy populations and increased mortality in patients with existing coronary artery disease (particularly after a heart attack) (Rozanski, Blumenthal, and Kaplan 1999). Even mild depressive symptoms

appear to be associated with the development and progression of cardiac disease. For instance, a recent prospective study of elderly white women found that those with six or more depressive symptoms were almost twice as likely to die from a cardiac cause than those with fewer depressive symptoms (Whooley and Browner 1998). Other chronic troubling emotions and stable emotional traits have been associated with cardiovascular disease. For instance, a two-year prospective study found a six-fold increase in the risk of sudden cardiac death (which often involves an arrhythmia such as ventricular fibrillation) among those men who were anxious (Kawachi, Colditz, Ascherio, et al. 1994). In another prospective study, male veterans with the most anger had more than double the risk of cardiac morbidity and mortality of those reporting the least anger (Kawachi, Sparrow, Spiro, et al. 1996b).

Social isolation and social support have been particularly powerful predictors of the development and progression of cardiovascular disease (Uchino, Cacioppo, and Kiecolt-Glaser 1996). The magnitude of these associations is substantial and often equals or exceeds that of well-established cardiovacular risk factors (Rozanski, Blumenthal, and Kaplan 1999). For example, in a prospective study of male health professionals, socially isolated men had double the mortality from cardiovascular disease compared to those with the largest and most varied social networks (Kawachi, Colditz, Ascherio, et al. 1996a). Similarly, in a cohort study of men and women following a myocardial infarction, those living alone had nearly double the rates of recurrent cardiac events (e.g., another heart attack or death from cardiac arrhythmia) within six months compared to those living with others (Case, Moss, Case, et al. 1992). In another prospective study of heart attack patients, lack of emotional support was related to both in-hospital mortality and cardiac-related mortality during the subsequent six months. Compared to men or women with one or more sources of emotional support, individuals with no emotional support were almost three times (odds ratio 2.9) as likely to die in the first six months. Interestingly, the unadjusted relationship (i.e., not taking clinical factors into account) was actually less (odds ratio 2.2) than the adjusted relationship noted above, indicating that clinical factors tended to mask, rather than reduce, the size of this relationship (Berkman, Leo-Summers, and Horowitz 1992).

Regardless of the specific measure used, socioeconomic status (SES) has also proven to be a remarkably robust predictor of cardiovascular health. For instance, both income and education have been shown to vary inversely, in a graded fashion, with progression of atherosclerosis in a general population (Lynch, Kaplan, Salonen, et al. 1997b). Lower social class (measured as a composite of education and occupation) is also associated with less improvement in functional status in individuals after a heart attack (Ickovics, Viscoli, and Horwitz 1997). Similarly, among adults with documented heart disease, the chance of a subsequent cardiac event decreases with higher income levels (Williams, Barefoot, Califf, et al. 1992). Some aspects of SES may partly mediate the effects of other psychosocial variables on cardiovascular disease. For example, in a follow-up study to their study that established that an episode of anger can increase risk of heart attack, Murray A. Mittleman and his colleagues (1997) showed that angered individuals with less than a high school education had double the risk of a heart attack within the next two hours of individuals with at least some college education. Precisely how more education buffered the effects of anger (e.g., greater perceived control or more coping resources) was not assessed.

Research on the effects of race and ethnicity on cardiovascular disease has focused primarily on differences in treatments and outcomes (Philbin and Desalvo 1998), as well as on the consistent finding of higher blood pressures among African Americans (Anderson, Myers, Pickering, et al. 1989). Some of the most intriguing work examines the impact of John Henryism on blood pressure and its interactions with gender. John Henryism refers to the folklore about John Henry, a black steel driver, who, in the face of seemingly insurmountable odds, refused to be deterred in his aspirations. In a cross-sectional study of African Americans in the rural South, William W. Dressler and his colleagues (1998) found that increasing levels of John Henryism were associated with higher blood pressure levels; however, this effect was seen only in men. For women, increasing John Henryism was associated with decreasing risk of hypertension. The authors speculated that these different effects reflected differing cultural expectations and social constraints for men and women in the community studied. This study not only highlights the importance of cultural meaning when considering social stressors (e.g., discrimination), but also suggests that the effects of gender, race, and coping style on physiological processes interact in complex ways rather than being simply additive. Research on gender and cardiovascular disease is further discussed in Chapter 7 by Rieker and Bird (also see Brezinka and Kittel 1996).

Summary and Critique: Psychosocial Factors and the Cardiovascular System

This literature provides strong evidence for the impact of social and psychological factors on both cardiovascular function and the development and trajectory of cardiovascular disease. Most studies do not actually demonstrate the entire causal chain from psychosocial factors to specific physiological processes to disease. Consequently, as in the sociological literature, causation is often inferred. However, many studies use large prospective samples and control for a wide array of biological, behavioral, and other psychosocial factors that make spurious associations less likely. Moreover, related studies provide ample evidence of many plausible physiological pathways between specific psychosocial factors and disease.

Although impressive, from a sociological perspective this literature is undermined by several major conceptual and methodological problems that likely lead to an underestimation of the impact of social factors. Most studies treat psychosocial variables as individual risk factors and assess their independent effects with regression analysis. In this way, the overall effect of a given variable (e.g., SES) on a given health outcome (e.g., risk of heart attacks) is parceled out among other variables that also are associated with SES and heart attacks. This approach may lead to underestimation of total impact because a given psychosocial risk factor often "clusters" with many other social and/or biological risk factors (see Chapter 4 by Mirowsky, Ross, and Reynolds; see also Rozanski, Blumenthal, and Kaplan 1999). For example, SES is inversely associated with a variety of risk factors for coronary artery disease (including hypertension, hyperlipidemia, diabetes, obesity, cigarette smoking, less exercise, and higher levels of anger) and worse post-heart attack outcomes (Anderson and Armstead 1995). This problem is exacerbated by the fact that relatively few researchers explicitly test for interactions among psychosocial and biological factors, even though there is ample evidence that psychosocial factors can either ameliorate or exacerbate the impact of conventional risk factors. Moreover, it is plausible that many factors frequently viewed in the medical literature as primarily biological, such as age, gender, and race, also reflect the accumulated impact of social factors over the life course.

Finally, a subtler problem is the increasing use of medications for common conditions (e.g., hypertension) that can affect physiological pathways through which social and psychological variables operate. For example, as noted above, increased sympathetic nervous system activation and its various physiologic effects are a common pathway through which different psychosocial variables exert their influence. These effects can be blocked, at least in part, by the administration of beta-blockers (a commonly prescribed medication for high blood pressure) (Cacioppo 1994). Consequently, the increasing use of these and other medications may make it more difficult to demonstrate the potential impact of psychosocial factors, Thus, a recent randomized study on the effects of a psychosocial intervention to reduce patients' stress and isolation in the year after their heart attack failed to find any beneficial effect on mortality despite the fact that the same researcher found a large beneficial effect in a similar study ten years earlier (Frasure-Smith 1991; Frasure-Smith, Lesperance, Prince, et al. 1997). This inconsistent finding may, in part, reflect more widespread use of beta-blockers and other new medical treatments in patients in the later study that increased their survival.

NEW DIRECTIONS IN CARDIAC AND IMMUNE RESEARCH

Stress Reactivity: Cardiac and Immune Interactions

Do all individuals share a similar physiologic response to a given type of stress? Although there appear to be some common pathways, there is increasing evidence that individuals differ substantially in their physiologic response to a given stressor. Degree of physiologic reactivity is one example. It is now well-established that certain individuals consistently respond to brief, mild stressors (typically mental stressors in a laboratory setting) with greater increases in blood pressure, heart rate, and catecholamine levels (e.g., epinephrine). Individuals with high cardiac reactivity also show greater ischemia (i.e., inadequate oxygen supply to heart muscle tissues) in response to brief stressors (Krantz, Helmers, Bairey, et al. 1991) and accelerated development of atherosclerosis and increased risk of subsequent heart disease (Rozanski, Blumenthal, and Kaplan 1999). A relative hyperreactivity of the sympathetic nervous system response to stressors is thought to be the underlying physiological cause of cardiac reactivity (Bachen, Manuck, Cohen, et al. 1995; Cacioppo 1994).

Cardiac reactivity to stress interacts with other psychosocial and biological factors. For example, two small experimental studies of women suggest that social support attenuates cardiovascular reactivity (Christenfeld, Gerin, Linden, et al. 1997; Kamarck, Manuck, and Jennings 1990). Similarly, in a study of job stress in men, the effect of job demand on the progression of atherosclerosis depended on individuals' cardiac reactivity. Those with high cardiac reactivity and job demands showed the most advanced atherosclerosis (Everson, Lynch, Chesney, et al. 1997). Finally, among young men without hypertension, cardiac reactivity was predictive of the development of hypertension ten years later only if one or both parents also had hypertension (assumed to mainly reflect genetic susceptibility) (Light, Girdler, Sherwood, et al. 1999).

Interestingly, those individuals showing the greatest sympathetically mediated cardiovascular reactivity also tend to have the greatest immune reactivity. That is, individuals who have the largest increases in blood pressure and heart rate also show the greatest declines in immune function in response to brief stressors. Though this research is still preliminary (Cohen and Manuck 1995), it suggests that individuals with high sympathetic reactivity are at greater risk not only for cardiovascular disease, but also for infections and other immune related disorders as well. This view is supported by a prospective study of respiratory infections in children (Boyce, Chesney, Alkon, et al. 1995). Boyce and colleagues found that psychosocial stressors (e.g., beginning school, family stressors, life events) were associated with more illness only in those children with high physiologic reactivity to a brief stressor.

The extent to which cardiovascular and immune reactivity is inherent rather than acquired is not yet clear. There is evidence that some individuals are born with greater behavioral and physiological reactivity than others and that these differences may persist to some degree (Kagan 1997). However, there is also increasing evidence that individuals may acquire physiological reactivity as a consequence of social and psychological factors.

Several studies suggest that individuals experiencing chronic stress, such as care givers to Alzheimer's patients, not only develop greater physiologic reactivity including greater immune decrements to minor stressors, but also take a significantly longer time to return to baseline after a brief stressor (Kiecolt-Glaser and Glaser 1995; Pike, Smith, Hauger, et al. 1997). Thus, for chronically stressed individuals at least, the effects on immune function can be amplified by an acquired increase in immune suppression in response to relatively minor or brief stressors including daily hassles. Moreover, the effects can be further compounded by the fact that chronically stressed individuals tend to already have other biological and social vulnerabilities. For instance, immune and cardiovascular function decreases with age. Caregivers to relatives with Alzheimer's tend to be elderly and to have less social support and resources, both of which can increase vulnerability to stress (Kiecolt-Glaser and Glaser 1995).

IMPLICATIONS FOR MEDICAL SOCIOLOGY

Some sociologists have raised concerns that focusing on physiologic pathways encourages biological reductionism and draws attention away from the larger social context and fundamental social causes such as socioeconomic stratification (Link and Phelan 1995). However, in our estimation the benefits of further involvement in this area of research outweigh the risks. Through this work, sociologists can help to clarify the full impact of social and psychological factors on health, demonstrate causal links between physiologic and sociological processes, and provide a contextual framework for interpreting results. Moreover, integrated conceptual models have the potential to significantly alter the nature of the debate on how resources are allocated and how health care is structured.

In this section we briefly consider the relevance of new knowledge about physiological pathways related to social determinants of health to two broad areas of interest to sociologists: the SES health gradient and gender differences in health.

Social Inequalities, the Health Gradient, and the Life Course

The possibility that repeated or chronic exposure to negative psychosocial factors can significantly alter physiological responses to social stressors in ways that over time increase an individual's biologic vulnerability to similar psychosocial factors represents a challenge to the way most of us think and talk about psychosocial factors and health. It implies not only that there are additive and interactive effects of psychosocial and biological factors on health at a given time, but also that there may be a compounding or amplification of effects over time as well (see the Mirowsky, Ross, and Reynolds discussion of "structural amplification" in Chapter 4).

Such a view is complementary to a life course perspective (Giele and Elder 1998; Gotlib and Wheaton 1997) and has the potential to provide new insights into well-established associations between social factors and health. One such association is the graded, inverse relationship between socioeconomic status and health (Adler, Boyce, Chesney, et al. 1993; see also Chapter 6 by Robert and House). Proponents of a life course perspective argue that the impact of social status can only be fully appreciated if one considers structured inequalities at different stages of life (Wadsworth 1997). A basic assumption of this perspective is that the roots of the health gradient seen in adult life begin much earlier in life.

There are two major explanations of how poor conditions in infancy and childhood can predispose individuals to poor adult health (Dahl and Birkelund 1997; Wadsworth 1997). The biological programming hypothesis asserts that adverse conditions associated with poverty can influence the development of organ systems (e.g., respiratory and cardiovascular systems) during crucial developmental stages in utero and infancy that render individuals more susceptible to illness as children and throughout life (Barker 1990). An alternative, albeit not mutually exclusive, explanation is a social hypothesis. According to this perspective, the social position of parents and living conditions during childhood and adolescence foster an individual's health behaviors and primary coping styles, and influence opportunities for and expectations about education and occupational attainment. These factors, particularly lower educational and occupational attainment, are, in turn, strongly associated with health later in life. In contrast to the biological programming hypothesis, the social hypothesis does not assume that effects operate solely or mainly at critical developmental periods (Wadsworth 1997).

A third explanation that relates to a life course perspective and may be useful in understanding the health gradient is the allostatic load model (McEwen 1998). This hypothesis emphasizes both acquired biological vulnerability over time from pathological effects of chronic stress (e.g., atherosclerosis) and changes in a wide range of physiological responses to chronic or recurrent stress that further increase individuals' vulnerability to disease. Allostatic load is essentially the acquired physiological dysfunction and damage that results from chronic overactivity or underactivity of the body's allostatic (i.e., adaptive) systems (McEwen 1998).

Although these three hypotheses have yet to be thoroughly tested, there is some evidence in support of each of them. Consistent with the biological programming hypothesis, parental smoking, maternal alcohol consumption, and poor nutrition in utero and during the first year of life have been shown to decrease respiratory capacity in children and are associated with higher incidence of chronic lung diseases later in life. Similar processes are thought to affect the development of coronary heart disease (Barker and Martyn 1992).

Similarly, several recent longitudinal studies provide support that social inequalities early in life may, at least to some extent, influence health in mid and later life. For instance, John W. Lynch and colleagues (1996, 1997b, 1997c) have shown that the association between low SES and poor health could be explained by a combination of biological, behavioral, and psychosocial factors, and that many of these factors were related to poor childhood conditions, low levels of education, and blue-collar occupation. Similarly, Espen Dahl and Gunn E. Birkeland (1997) have shown that lower childhood SES influences health in later life even in countries such as Norway, which has a welfare system designed to minimize economic inequalities later in life. However, other studies have shown that social status of parents, family context, and other aspects of early life do not account for much of the health gradient seen among adults and the elderly (Marmot, Ryff, Bumpass, et al. 1997).

Although a measure of allostatic load has been shown to predict cardiovascular disease in a cross-sectional and three-year prospective study (McEwen 1998), no studies have yet explicitly tested the model as an explanation for the relationship between social inequalities and the health gradient.

In our view, research on the SES gradient in health begs for additional research from a life course perspective, including physiological measures. Until recently, with the exception of studies linking higher blood pressure or accelerated atherosclerosis to lower SES, little research has been done directly linking SES and physiologic processes. Most large epidemiological data sets with good measures of SES do not contain physiologic data. Conversely, laboratory studies typically do not include adequate measures of SES and rarely test for interactions such as between SES and race or ethnicity and/or physiological reactivity (Anderson and Armstead 1995).

The few studies that have been done are intriguing and persuasive. For example, Thomas Wilson and colleagues (Wilson, Kaplan, Kauhanen, et al. 1993) showed that despite controls for an impressive number of behavioral and biological covariates, several measures of lower SES were associated with higher blood fibrinogen levels (a clotting factor that can increase the risk of heart attack). Interestingly, the effect of low SES was greatest for those adults who had low SES in childhood as well. However, low childhood SES did not significantly affect fibrinogen levels for those who achieved high SES in adulthood. A more recent study demonstrated that the effect of cardiac reactivity in middle-aged men on atherosclerosis progression depended on their SES at different points on the life course. Individuals who showed high cardiovascular reactivity to stress (either inherited or acquired) and were born into poor families, received little education, or had low current incomes had the greatest progression of atherosclerosis over a four-year period. These effects were essentially unchanged when history of heart disease and other cardiac risk factors were taken into account (Lynch, Everson, Kaplan, et al. 1998).

The possibility that individual physiological responses to social stressors may be, in part, acquired through a lifetime of exposures is consistent with a long line of sociological research and new directions in our field. But without more research that explicitly tests for this hypothesis, this hypothesis will remain in the realm of conjecture.

Gender and Health

The possibilities that social factors interact with biological vulnerabilities and that exposure to negative social factors can alter individual vulnerability have substantial implications for the ways in which we study differences in men's and women's health (see Chapter 7 by Rieker and Bird). Although the differences in men's and women's health are the cumulative result of both their innate sex differences and a lifetime of health-related behaviors and exposures, research on the social patterns of illness typically proceeds from the assumption that innate biological differences between men and women are either minimal or largely irrelevant. While this perspective may be appropriate for the study of gender differences in achievement and related socioeconomic outcomes, it is an inadequate premise for research on men's and women's health (Bird and Rieker 1999).

Sociological research has focused on the contribution of social factors to differences in men's and women's health; for example, sociologists have demonstrated effects of gender inequality in the labor force and in the home on psychological distress. However, relatively few studies have assessed physical health consequences and even fewer studies have incorporated biological measures, yet the results of this research are revealing. For instance, several studies help clarify "carry-over" effects of stressors across different role domains (Thoits 1995). Among those working in white-collar jobs, multiple roles were associated with sustained high levels of stress hormones for women well into the evening, whereas men's stress hormone levels peaked during the day and declined when they returned home in the evening (Frankenhaeuser, Lundberg, Fredrikson, et al. 1989). In a related study of blood pressure among white-collar workers, those women with heavy family responsibilities (based on an index of number of children and share of domestic work) showed higher average blood pressure during a 24-hour period. Interestingly, having both heavy family responsibilities and high job strain produced higher blood pressure than either alone but only in women with university education (Brisson, Laflamme, Moisan, et al. 1999). Taken together, these studies indicate that role-related stressors have physiological effects.

Including physiological measures of stress responses can also make differential effects of psychosocial factors on men's and women's health clearer. For instance, marital status has been shown to have different effects for men and women. Among women, those with low marital satisfaction or the perception that their marriage was at high risk of dissolution experienced greater physiological changes (e.g., increased cortisol and poorer immune response) during a negative interaction with their spouse (Kiecolt-Glaser, Glaser, Cacioppo, et al. 1997). Men did not show significant changes irrespective of their perceptions of risk of divorce. Studies such as this beg for a systematic assessment of the ways in which social and biological factors interact to produce or exacerbate differences in men's and women's health.

A new area of research demonstrates that social exposures may reduce women's physiological advantage over men in risk of developing cardiovascular disease. The conventional wisdom has been that women are protected against atherosclerosis by the effects of estrogen. Thus, beginning after menopause the incidence of heart disease increases. However, the development of atherosclerosis takes place over decades, and recent evidence indicates that many premenopausal women have significant atherosclerosis (Sutton-Tyrell et al. 1998). An emerging hypothesis is that recurrent or chronic stress in premenopausal women may decrease their estrogen production and therefore accelerate their development of atherosclerosis, thereby increasing their risk of significant heart disease in later years. It is well established that stress can cause irregular menstrual periods because of effects on ovarian function. Even when women do not clearly have irregular menstrual periods, stress has been shown to decrease estrogen levels. Several studies provide compelling evidence for this hypothesis, but much more work needs to be done (Rozanski, Blumenthal, and Kaplan 1999). Related research suggests that stress in premenopausal women may also contribute to lower bone density later in life because of decreased estrogen levels. Depression in women also appears to accelerate bone loss, though in this case the primary mechanism is thought to be high cortisol levels (Michelson, Stratakis, Hill, et al. 1996).

Thus, physiological differences in adult men and women may be socially acquired or attenuated. Consequently, the integration of social and biomedical research has the potential to improve our understanding of the total effect of socially organized differences in men's and women's lives on differences in their health. Moreover, studies incorporating both social and biological measures would yield new insights into the relative impact of social and biological differences with greater precision than can be achieved by comparing the results of separate studies.

CONCLUSION: POTENTIAL IMPACT

Why do some people get sick while others do not? The research highlighted in this chapter provides compelling evidence that at least a partial explanation is physiological pathways between the social organization of individuals' lives and their health. Much of this research, particularly in the immune literature, is quite preliminary and undermined by methodological problems. However, taken as a whole, it indicates that social and psychological factors, particularly stressors and coping resources, can alter physiological processes of both the immune and cardiovascular system in ways that affect individual risk of disease and subsequent prognosis. This relationship may be especially strong in socially disadvantaged groups whose members tend to have acquired over the life course other social and biological vulnerabilities that increase their susceptibility to the physiological effects of psychosocial stressors. Consequently, current conceptual and empirical models that emphasize independent effects of psychosocial factors or cross-sectional analyses likely underestimate the full impact of social factors.

Precisely how new and emerging knowledge from this research will be interpreted and applied is not a foregone conclusion. On the one hand, this research has the potential to facilitate the types of changes in social institutions that sociologists often advocate. For example, growing evidence that job-related stress is associated with cardiovascular disease (Theorell and Karesek 1996) and other health problems is prompting significant changes in the organization of the workplace in order to reduce work-related stress (National Occupational Research Aganda (NORA) 1999; Quick, Quick, Nelson, et al. 1997). In this instance, factors such as decreased productivity and rapidly escalating medical, legal, and worker's compensation costs are undoubtedly playing a role.

On the other hand, there are many reasons to suspect either that little will change or that this knowledge may paradoxically result in further marginalization of psychosocial factors in health care and social policy. As alluded to in the introduction to this chapter, a biomedical model still dominates, and structural barriers to meaningfully addressing psychosocial factors remain. For example, though physicians increasingly acknowledge the importance of psychosocial factors, the literature and conventional medical training typically offer little practical information on how to address them. Recommended interventions are invariably individually oriented and designed to improve coping abilities without addressing the underlying sources of stress (Lazar 1996). Moreover, the current organization of care provides numerous organizational, professional, and financial disincentives for attempting to address psychosocial issues (Rozanski, Blumenthal, and Kaplan 1999; Waitzkin 1991). Indeed, for most physicians the simplest solution is to prescribe a medication. That reality, coupled with new evidence that certain medications may partly block the physiological pathways between various psychosocial factors and disease, may ensure further medicalization of social problems.

Finally, it is worth asking how health care organizations will interpret and apply the types of findings considered in this chapter. For instance, it is likely that research demonstrating the clinical impact and economic costs of psychosocial factors and cost savings associated with psychosocial interventions has caught the attention of at least some managed care organizations (Allison, Williams, Miller, et al. 1995; Sobel 1995). Undoubtedly, health care organizations will continue to take an increasing role in determining the types of preventive services and medical care patients receive (see Chapter 15 by Wholey and Burn). Thus, the impact of how they interpret this search may be substantial and worthy of further sociological attention.

At a time when some sociologists are increasingly concerned about the apparent fragmentation of the field and are calling for a return to our roots with greater focus on "upstream" or fundamental causes, the notion of extending sociologic discourse and research further "downstream" to focus on physiologic processes may seem unwise (see Chapter 3 by Link and Phelan). Indeed, we agree that the ultimate concern of sociologists should be the overall impact of social factors on individual well-being regardless of the causal mechanisms. However, we believe that in a society in which a biomedical, individually oriented model still dominates how health care providers, researchers, policy makers, and lay persons think about health and illness, it is crucial to demonstrate the plausibility of clinically significant physiological pathways between the social organizations of life and health. Furthermore, by demonstrating links and interactions of upstream social factors with factors at multiple levels along the causal chain and over the life course, the amplification of socially patterned vulnerabilities and exposures to stressors, and consequently the full impact of social inequalities, will be more clearly shown. Along these lines, we would also encourage researchers to include some reference to the practical translation of such knowledge and the cost effectiveness of an appropriate intervention, since without this reference, change is even less likely.

Although it would be simpler for sociologists to continue traditional lines of research on the determinants of health and illness, we argue that a better strategy would be to expand and increase creative collaboration with other disciplines (Levine 1995). As an inherently interdisciplinary field, sociology is in an excellent position to embark on such collaboration. This approach offers the opportunity to refine theoretical and empirical models and strengthen sociology's standing as a meaningful participant in the development of new knowledge regarding the contribution of social factors to health. Although there are barriers to interdisciplinary work, researchers from a wide range of disciplines are interested in collaboration (see Chapter 24 by Umberson, Williams, and Sharp). In addition, funding agencies such as the National Institutes of Health have expressed growing interest in supporting this type of multilevel, interdisciplinary research between social, behavioral, and biomedical researchers (Anderson 1998, see also http://www1.od.nih .gov/obssr/sciinfo.htm).

Regardless of whether sociologists become more involved in this discourse, it will continue to develop. Researchers from a diverse range of disciplines will consider the impact of social and psychological factors and devise sophisticated conceptual and empirical models. However, if other disciplines continue to fill the void, sociological perspectives are likely to receive less emphasis, and this work is less likely to build on existing sociological knowledge. We hope that sociologists will not forego the opportunity to contribute further to this area, which is ripe for sociological analysis.

REFERENCES

ADER, ROBERT, NICHOLAS COHEN, and DAVID FELTEN. 1995. "Psychoneuroimmunology: Interactions Between the Nervous System and the Immune System." *Lancet* 345: 99–103.

ADLER, NANCY E., W. THOMAS BOYCE, MARGARET A. CHESNEY, SUSAN FOLKMAN, and S. LEONARD SYME. 1993. "Socioeconomic Inequalities in Health: No Easy Solution." *Journal of the American Medical Association* 269: 3140–45.

ADLER, NANCY. 1994. "Health Psychology: Why Do Some People Get Sick and Some Stay Well?" *Annual Review of Psychology* 45:229–59.

ALLISON, THOMAS G., DONALD E. WILLIAMS, TODD D. MILLER, CHRISTI A. PATTEN, KENT R. BAILEY, RAY W. SQUIRES, and GERALD T. GAU. 1995. "Medical and Economic Costs of Psychologic Distress in Patients With Coronary Artery Disease." *Mayo Clinic Proceedings* 70: 734–42.

ANDERSON, NORMAN B., HECTOR F. MYERS, THOMAS PICKERING, and JAMES S. JACKSON. 1989. "Hypertension in Blacks: Psychosocial and Biological Perspectives." *Journal of Hypertension* 7:161–72.

ANDERSON, NORMAN B. and CHERYL A. ARMSTEAD. 1995. "Toward Understanding the Association of Socioeconomic Status and Health: A New Challenge for the Biopsychosocial Approach." *Psychosomatic Medicine* 57:213–25.

ANDERSON, NORMAN B. 1998. "Levels of Analysis in Health Science: A Framework for Integrating Sociobehavioral and Biomedical Research." *Annals of New York Academy of Science* 840: 563–76.

ANESHENSEL, CAROL S., CAROLYN M. RUTTER, and PETER A. LANCHENBRUCH. 1991. "Social Structure, Stress, and Mental Health: Competent Conceptual and Analytic Models." *American Sociological Review* 56:166–78.

ANTONOVSKY, AARON. 1994. "A Sociologic Critique of the 'Well-Being' Movement." *Advances: The Journal of Mind-Body Health* 10: 6–12.

BACHEN, ELIZABETH A., STEPHEN B. MANUCK, SHELDON COHEN, MATTHEW F. MULDOON, ROBERT RAIBLE, TRACY B. HERBERT, and BRUCE S. RABIN. 1995. "Adrenergic Blockade Ameliorates Cellular Immune Responses to Mental Stress in Humans." *Psychosomatic Medicine* 57: 366–72.

BARKER, DAVID J. 1990. "The Fetal and Infant Origins of Adult Disease." *British Medical Journal* 301:1111.

BARKER, DAVID J. and CHRISTOPHER N. MARTYN. 1992. "The Maternal and Fetal Origins of Cardiovascular Disease." *Journal of Epidemiology & Community Health* 46: 8–11.

BERKMAN, LISA F., LINDA LEO-SUMMERS, and RALPH HOROWITZ. 1992. "Emotional Support and Survival after Myocardial Infarction: A Prospective Population-based Study of the Elderly." *Annals of Internal Medicine* 117: 1003–09.

BIONDI, MASSIMO, and LUCA-GIONATA ZANNINO. 1997. "Psychological Stress, Neuroimmunomodulation, and Susceptibility to Infectious Diseases in Animals and Man: A Review." *Psychotherapy and Psychosomatics* 66:3–26.

BIRD, CHLOE E., and PATRICIA P. REIKER. 1999. "Gender Matters: An Integrated Model for Understanding Men's and Women's Health." *Social Science and Medicine* 48: 745–55.

BOYCE, W.THOMAS, MARGARET CHESNEY, ABBEY ALKON, JEANNE M. TSCHANN, SALLY ADAMS, BETH CHESTERMAN, FRANCES COHEN, PAMELA KAISER, SUSAN FOLKMAN, and DIANE WARA. 1995. "Psychobiologic Reactivity to Stress and Childhood Respiratory Illnesses: Results of Two Prospective Studies." *Psychosomatic Medicine* 57: 411–22.

BREZINKA, VERONIKA, and FRANCE KITTEL. 1996. "Psychosocial Factors of Coronary Heart Disease in Women: A Review." *Social Science Medicine* 42: 1351–65.

BRISSON, CHANTAL, NATHALIE LAFLAMME, JOCELYNE MOISAN, ALAIN MILOT, BENOIT MASSE, and MICHEL VEZINA. 1999. "Effect of Family Responsibilities and Job Strain on Ambulatory Blood Pressure Among White-Collar Women." *Psychosomatic Medicine* 61: 205–13.

CACIOPPO, JOHN T. 1994. "Social Neuroscience: Autonomic, Neuroendocrine, and Immune Responses to Stress." *Psychophysiology* 31: 113–28.

CASE, ROBERT B., ARTHUR J. MOSS, NAN CASE, MICHAEL McDERMOTT, and SHIRLEY EBERLY. 1992. "Living Alone After Myocardial Infarction. Impact on Prognosis." *Journal of the American Medical Association* 267: 515–59.

CHRISTENFELD, NICHOLAS, WILLIAM GERIN, WOLFGANG LINDEN, MARA SANDERS, JENNIFER MATHUR, JAMES D. DEICH, and THOMAS G. PICKERING. 1997. "Social Support Effects on Cardiovascular Reactivity: Is a Stranger as Effective as a Friend?" *Psychosomatic Medicine* 59: 388–98.

COE, RODNEY M. 1997. "The Magic of Science and the Science of Magic: An Essay on the Process of Healing." *Journal of Health and Social Behavior* 38: 1–8.

COHEN, SHELDON, and STEPHEN B. MANUCK. 1995. "Stress, Reactivity, and Disease." *Psychosomatic Medicine* 57:423–23.

COHEN, SHELDON, and T.B. HERBERT. 1996. "Health Psychology: Psychological Factors and Physical Disease From the Perspective of Human Psychoneuroimmunology." *Annual Review of Psychology* 47: 113–42.

COHEN, SHELDON, E. FRANK, WILLIAM J. DOYLE, DAVID P. SKONER, BRUCE S. RABIN, and JACK M. GWALTNEY.

1998. "Types of Stressors That Increase Susceptibility to the Common Cold in Healthy Adults." *Health Psychology* 17: 214–23.

COHEN, SHELDON, WILLIAM J. DOYLE, and DAVID P. SKONER. 1999. "Psychological Stress, Cytokine Production, and Severity of Upper Respiratory Illness." *Psychosomatic Medicine* 61: 175–80.

COHEN, SHELDON, WILLIAM J. DOYLE, DAVID P. SKONER, BRUCE S. RABIN, and JACK M. GWALTNEY, JR. 1997. "Social Ties and Susceptibility to the Common Cold." *Journal of the American Medical Association* 277: 1940–44.

CONNOR, THOMAS J., and BRIAN E. LEONARD. 1998. "Depression, Stress and Immunological Activation: The Role of Cytokines in Depressive Disorders." *Life Sciences* 62: 583–606.

DAHL, ESPEN, and GUNN E. BIRKELUND. 1997. "Health Inequalities in Later Life in a Social Democratic Welfare State." *Social Science & Medicine* 44: 871–81.

DREHER, HENRY. 1995. "The Social Perspective in Mind-Body Studies: Missing in Action?" *Advances: The Journal of Mind-Body Health* 11: 39–54.

DRESSLER, WILLIAM W., JAMES R. BINDON, and YASMIN H. NEGGERS. 1998. "John Henryism, Gender, and Arterial Blood Pressure in an African American Community." *Psychosomatic Medicine* 60:620–24.

ENGEL, G. L. 1977. "The Need for a New Medical Model: A Challenge for Biomedicine." *Science* 196: 129–36.

EVERSON, SUSAN A., JOHN W. LYNCH, MARGARET A. CHESNEY, GEORGE A. KAPLAN, DEBBIE E. GOLDBERG, STARLEY B. SHADE, RICHARD D. COHEN, RITA SALONEN, and JUKKA T. SALONEN. 1997. "Interaction of Workplace Demands and Cardiovascular Reactivity in Progression of Carotid Atherosclerosis: Population-based Study." *British Medical Journal* 314: 553–58.

FAWZY, FAWZY I., MARGARET E. KEMENY, NANCY W. FAWZY, ROBERT ELASHOFF, D. MORTON, N. COUSINS, and J. L. FAHEY. 1990. "A Structured Psychiatric Intervention for Cancer Patients. II. Changes Over Time in Immunological Measures." *Archives of General Psychiatry* 47: 729–35.

FAWZY, FAWZY I., NANCY W. FAWZY, CHRISTINE S. HYUN, ROBERT ELASHOFF, D. GUTHRIE, J. L. FAHEY, and D. L. MORTON. 1993. "Malignant Melanoma. Effects of an Early Structured Psychiatric Intervention, Coping, and Affective State on Recurrence and Survival 6 Years Later." *Archives of General Psychiatry* 50: 681–89.

FIFE, ALISON, PAMELA J. BEASLEY, and DEBRA L. FERTIG. 1996. "Psychoneuroimmunology and Cancer: Historical Perspectives and Current Research." *Advances in Neuroimmunology* 6: 179–90.

FRANKENHAEUSER, MARIANNE, ULF LUNDBERG, MATS FREDRIKSON, BO MELIN, MARTTI TUOMISTO, ANNA-LISA MYRSTEN, MONICA HEDMAN, BODIL BERGMAN-LOSMAN, and LEIF WALLIN. 1989. "Stress On and Off the Job as Related to Sex and Occupational Status in White-Collar Workers." *Journal of Organizational Behavior* 10: 321–346.

FRASURE-SMITH, NANCY. 1991. "In-Hospital Symptoms of Psychological Stress as Predictors of Long-Term Outcome After Acute Myocardial Infarction in Men." *American Journal of Cardiology* 67: 121–17.

FRASURE-SMITH, NANCY, FRANCOIS LESPERANCE, RAYMOND PRINCE, PIERRE VERRIER, RACHEL GARBER, MARTIN JUNEAU, CHRISTINA WOLFSON, MARITAL BOURASSA. 1997. "Randomised Trial of Home-Based Psychosocial Intervention for Patients Recovering From Myocardial Infarction." *Lancet* 350: 473–79.

FREMONT, ALLEN M., and CHLOE E. BIRD. 1999. "Integrating Sociological and Biological Models: An Editorial." *Journal of Health and Social Behavior* 40:126–29.

GIELE, JANET Z., and GLEN J. ELDER, JR. 1998. *Methods of Life Course Research: Qualitative and Quantitative Approaches.* Thousand Oaks, CA: Sage Publications.

GLASER, RONALD, JOHN RICE, JOHN SHERIDAN, RICHARD FERTEL, J. STOUT, C. SPEICHER, D. PINSKY, M. KOTUR, A. POST, M. BECK, ET AL. 1987. "Stress-Related Immune Suppression: Health Implications." *Brain, Behavior, & Immunity* 1: 7–20.

GLASER, RONALD, and JANICE KIECOLT-GLASER. 1994. *Handbook of Human Stress and Immunity.* San Diego: Academic Press.

GOLEMAN, DANIEL, and JOEL GURIN. 1993. *Mind Body Medicine: How to Use Your Mind for Better Health.* Yonkers: Consumer Reports Books.

GOTLIB, IAN H., and BLAIR WHEATON. 1997. *Stress and Adversity Over the Life Course: Trajectories and Turning Points.* New York: Cambridge University Press.

GULLETTE, ELIZABETH C., JAMES A. BLUMENTHAL, MICHAEL BABYAK, WEI JIANG, ROBERT A. WAUGH, DAVID J. FRID, CHRISTOPHER M. O'CONNOR, JAMES J. MORRIS, and DAVID S. KRANTZ. 1997. "Effects of Mental Stress on Myocardial Ischemia During Daily Life." *Journal of the American Medical Association* 277: 1521–26.

HEMINGWAY, HARRY, and MICHAEL MARMOT. 1999. "Psychosocial Factors in the Aetiology and Prognosis of Coronary Heart Disease: Systematic Review of Prospective Cohort Studies." *British Medical Journal* 318: 1460–67.

HERBERT, TRACY B., and SHELDON COHEN. 1993a. "Depression and Immunity: A Meta-Analytic Review." *Psychological Bulletin* 113: 472–86.

HERBERT, TRACY B., and SHELDON COHEN. 1993b. "Stress and Immunity in Humans: A Meta-Analytic Review." *Psychosomatic Medicine* 55: 364–79.

ICKOVICS, JEANNETTE R., CATHERINE M. VISCOLI, and RALPH I. HORWITZ. 1997. "Functional Recovery after Myocardial Infarction in Men: The Independent Effects of Social Class." *Annals of Internal Medicine* 127:518–25.

JUNG, WAYMOND, and MICHAEL IRWIN. 1999. "Reduction of Natural Killer Cytotoxic Activity in Major Depression: Interaction Between Depression and Cigarette Smoking." *Psychosomatic Medicine* 61: 263–70.

KAGAN, JEROME. 1997. "Temperament and the Reactions to Unfamiliarity." *Child Development* 68: 139–43.

KAMARCK, THOMAS W., STEPHEN B. MANUCK, and J. RICHARD JENNINGS. 1990. "Social Support Reduces Cardiovascular Reactivity to Psychological Challenge: A Laboratory Model." *Psychosomatic Medicine* 52: 42–58.

KAPLAN, GEORGE A. 1995. "Where Do Shared Pathways Lead? Some Reflections on a Research Agenda." *Psychosomatic Medicine* 57: 208–12.

KAPRIO, JAAKKO, MARKKU KOSKENVUO, and HELI RITA. 1987. "Mortality After Bereavement: A Prospective Study of 95,647 Widowed Persons." *American Journal of Public Health* 77: 283–87.

KAWACHI, ICHIRO, GRAHAM A. COLDITZ, ALBERTO ASCHERIO, ERIC B. RIMM, EDWARD GIOVANNUCCI, MEIR J. STAMPFER, and WALTER C. WILLETT. 1994. "Prospective Study of Phobic Anxiety and Risk of Coronary Heart Disease in Men." *Circulation* 89: 1992–97.

KAWACHI, ICHIRO, GRAHAM A. COLDITZ, ALBERTO ASCHERIO, ERIC B. RIMM, EDWARD GIOVANNUCCI, MEIR J. STAMPFER, and WALTER C. WILLETT. 1996a. "A Prospective Study of Social Networks in Relation to Total Mortality and Cardiovascular Disease in Men in the USA." *Journal of Epidemiology & Community Health* 50:245–51.

KAWACHI, ICHIRO, DAVID SPARROW, A. SPIRO, III, PANTEL VOKONAS, and SCOTT T. WEISS. 1996b. "A Prospective Study of Anger and Coronary Heart Disease. The Normative Aging Study." *Circulation* 94: 2090–95.

KELLER, STEVEN E., SAMUAL C. SHIFLETT, STEVEN J. SCHLEIFER, and JACQUELINE A. BARTLETT 1994. "Stress, Immunity, and Health" In *Handbook of Human Stress and Immunity,* ed. Ronald Glaser and Janice Kiecolt-Glaser. San Diego: Academic Press.

KIECOLT-GLASER, JANICE K., and RONALD GLASER. 1995. "Psychoneuroimmunology and Health Consequences: Data and Shared Mechanisms." *Psychosomatic Medicine* 57: 269–74.

KIECOLT-GLASER, JANICE K., J. R. DURA, C. E. SPEICHER, O. J. TRASK, and RONALD GLASER. 1991. "Spousal Caregivers of Dementia Victims: Longitudinal Changes in Immunity and Health." *Psychosomatic Medicine* 53: 345–62.

KIECOLT-GLASER, JANICE K., PHILLIP T. MARUCHA, WILLIAM B. MALARKEY, ANA M. MERCADO, and RONALD GLASER. 1995. "Slowing of Wound Healing by Psychological Stress." *Lancet* 346: 1194–96.

KIECOLT-GLASER, JANICE K., RONALD GLASER, JOHN T. CACIOPPO, ROBERT C. MACCALLUM, MARY SNYDER-SMITH, CHEONGTAO KIM, and WILLIAM B. MALARKEY. 1997. "Marital Conflict in Older Adults: Endocrinological and Immunological Correlates." *Psychosomatic Medicine* 59: 339–49.

KIECOLT-GLASER, JANICE K., WARREN GARNER, CARL SPEICHER, GERALD M. PENN, JANE HOLLIDAY, and RONALD GLASER. 1984. "Psychosocial Modifiers of Immunocompetence in Medical Students." *Psychosomatic Medicine* 46: 7–14.

KRANTZ, DAVID S., KARIN F. HELMERS, C. NOEL BAIREY, LINDA E. NEBEL, SUSAN M. HEDGES, and ALAN ROZANSKI. 1991. "Cardiovascular Reactivity and Mental Stress-Induced Myocardial Ischemia in Patients With Coronary Artery Disease." *Psychosomatic Medicine* 53: 1–12.

LAZAR, JOEL S. 1996. "Mind-Body Medicine in Primary Care. Implications and Applications." *Primary Care* 23: 169–82.

LEVINE, SOL. 1995. "Time for Creative Integration in Medical Sociology." *Journal of Health and Social Behavior* Spec:1–4.

LIGHT, KATHLEEN C., SUSAN S. GIRDLER, ANDREW SHERWOOK, EDITH E. BRAGDON, KIMBERLY A. BROWNLEY, SHEILA G. WEST, and ALAN L. HINDERLITER. 1999. "High Stress Responsivity Predicts Later Blood Pressure Only in Combination with Positive Family History and High Life Stress." *Hypertension* 33: 1458–64.

LINK, BRUCE G., and JO PHELAN. 1995. "Social Conditions as Fundamental Causes of Disease." *Journal of Health and Social Behavior* Spec: 80–94.

LOVALLO, WILLIAM R. 1997. *Stress & Health: Biological and Psychological Interactions.* Thousand Oaks: Sage Publications.

LYNCH, JOHN, NIKLAS KRAUSE, GEORGE A. KAPLAN, RIITTA SALONEN, and JUKKA T. SALONEN. 1999. "Workplace Demands, Economic Reward, and Progression of Carotid Atherosclerosis." *Circulation* 96: 302–307.

LYNCH, JOHN, GEORGE A. KAPLAN, RIITTA SALONEN, and JUKKA T. SALONEN. 1997b. "Socioeconomic Status and Progression of Carotid Atherosclerosis. Prospective Evidence From the Kuopio Ischemic Heart Disease Risk Factor Study." *Arteriosclerosis, Thrombosis & Vascular Biology* 17: 513–19.

LYNCH, JOHN W., GEORGE A. KAPLAN, and JUKKA T. SALONEN. 1997c. "Why Do Poor People Behave Poorly? Variation in Adult Health Behaviours and Psychosocial Characteristics by Stages of the Socioeconomic Lifecourse." *Social Science & Medicine* 44: 809–19.

LYNCH, JOHN W., GEORGE A. KAPLAN, RICHARD D. COHEN, JAAKKO TUOMILEHTO, and JUKKA T. SALONEN. 1996. "Do Cardiovascular Risk Factors Explain the Relation Between Socioeconomic Status, Risk of All-Cause Mortality, Cardiovascular Mortality, and Acute Myocardial Infarction?" *American Journal of Epidemiology* 144: 934–42.

MARMOT, MICHAEL, CAROL D. RYFF, LARRY L. BUMPASS, MARTIN SHIPLEY, and NADINE F. MARKS. 1997. "Social Inequalities in Health: Next Questions and Converging Evidence." *Social Science & Medicine* 44:901–10.

MARSHALL, GAILEN D., SANDEEP K. AGARWAL, CAMILLE LLOYD, LORENZO COHEN, EVELYN M. HENNINGER, and GLORIA J. MORRIS. 1998. "Cytokine Dysregulation Associated with Exam Stress in Healthy Medical Students." *Brain Behavior and Immunity* 12: 297–307.

MCEWEN, BRUCE S. 1998. "Protective and Damaging Effects of Stress Mediators." *New England Journal of Medicine* 338: 171–79.

MCKINNON, WILLIAM, CAROL S. WEISSE, C. PATRICK REYNOLDS, CHARLES A. BOWLES, and ANDREW BAUM.

1989. "Chronic Stress, Leukocyte Subpopulations, and Humoral Response to Latent Viruses." *Health Psychology* 8: 389–402.

MICHELSON, DAVID, CONSTANTINE STRATAKIS, LAUREN HILL, JAMES REYNOLDS, ELISE GALLIVEN, GEORGE CHROUSOS, and PHILIP GOLD. 1996. "Bone Mineral Density in Women with Depression." *The New England Journal of Medicine* 335: 1176–80.

MILLER, ANDREW H. 1998. "Neuroendocrine and Immune System Interactions in Stress and Depression." *Psychiatric Clinics of North America* 21: 443–63.

MILLS, PAUL J., HENRY YU, MICHAEL G. ZIEGLER, THOMAS PATTERSON, and IGOR GRANT. 1999. "Vulnerable Caregivers of Patients with Alzheimers' Disease Have a Deficit in Circulating CD62L- T Lymphocytes." *Psychosomatic Medicine* 61: 168–74.

MITTLEMAN, MURRAY A., MALCOLM MACLURE, JANE B. SHERWOOD, RICHARD P. MULRY, GEOFFREY H. TOFLER, SUE C. JACOBS, RICHARD FRIEDMAN, HERBERT BENSON, and JAMES E. MULLER. 1995. "Triggering of Acute Myocardial Infarction Onset by Episodes of Anger. Determinants of Myocardial Infarction Onset Study Investigators." *Circulation* 92: 1720–25.

MITTLEMAN, MURRAY A., MALCOLM MACLURE, MANESH NACHNANI, JANE B. SHERWOOD, and JAMES E. MULLER. 1997. "Educational Attainment, Anger, and the Risk of Triggering Myocardial Infarction Onset. The Determinants of Myocardial Infarction Onset Study Investigators." *Archives of Internal Medicine* 157: 769–75.

NATIONAL OCCUPATIONAL RESEARCH AGENDA (NORA). 1999. "Organization of Work." *http://www.cdc.gov/niosh/nrworg.html.*

NIXON, PETER, and JENNY KING. 1997. "Ischemic Heart Desease: Homeostasis and the Heart." In *Mind-Body Medicine: A Clinician's Guide to Psychoneuroimmunology,* ed. Alan Watkins. San Francisco: Churchill Livingstone.

NOTT, KENNETH H., KAVITA VEDHARA, and GAVIN P. SPICKETT. 1995. "Psychology, Immunology, and HIV." *Psychoneuroendocrinology* 20: 451–74.

NOTZON, FRANCIS C., YURI M. KOMAROV, SERGEI P. ERMAKOV, CHRISTOPHER T. SEMPOS, JAMES S. MARKS, and ELENA V. SEMPOS. 1998. "Causes of Declining Life Expectancy in Russia." *Journal of the American Medical Association* 279: 793–800.

PERT, CANDACE B. 1986. "The Wisdom of the Receptors: Neuropeptides, the Emotions, and the Bodymind." *Advances: Institute for the Advancement of Health* 3: 8–16.

PEYROT, MARK, JAMES F. McMURRY, and DAVID KRUGER. 1999. "A Biopsychosocial Model of Glycemic Control in Diabetes: Stress, Coping, and Regimen Adherence." *Journal of Health and Social Behavior* 40: 141–58.

PHILBIN, EDWARD F., and THOMAS G. DiSALVO. 1998. "Influence of Race and Gender on Care Process, Resource Use, and Hospital-based Outcomes in Congestive Heart Failure." *The American Journal of Cardiology* 82: 76–81.

PIKE, JENNIFER L., TOM L. SMITH, RICHARD L. HAUGER, PERRY M. NICASSIO, THOMAS L. PATTERSON, JOHN McCLINTICK, CAROLYN COSTLOW, and MICHAEL R. IRWIN. 1997. "Chronic Life Stress Alters Sympathetic, Neuroendocrine, and Immune Responsivity to an Acute Psychological Stressor in Humans." *Psychosomatic Medicine* 59: 447–57.

QUICK, JAMES CAMPBELL, JONATHAN D. QUICK, DEBRA L. NELSON, and JOSEPH J. HURRELL. 1997. *Preventive Stress Management in Organizations.* Washington, DC: American Psychological Association.

ROGERS, MALCOLM P., and MANISH FOZDAR. 1996. "Psychoneuroimmunology of Autoimmune Disorders." *Advances in Neuroimmunology* 6: 169–77.

ROZANSKI, ALAN, C. NOEL BAIREY, DAVID S. KRANTZ, JOHN FRIEDMAN, KENNETH J. RESSER, MARIE MORELL, SALLY HILTON-CHALFEN, LISA HESTRIN, JAMES BIETENDORF, and DANIEL S. BERMAN. 1988. "Mental Stress and the Induction of Silent Myocardial Ischemia in Patients With Coronary Artery Disease." *New England Journal of Medicine* 318: 1005–12.

ROZANSKI, ALAN, JAMES A. BLUMENTHAL, and JAY KAPLAN. 1999. "Impact of Psychological Factors on the Pathogenesis of Cardiovascular Disease and Implications for Therapy." *Circulation* 99: 2192–217.

SCHAFER, WALT. 1998. "Incorporating Social Factors Into the Mind-Body and Wellness Fields." *Advances in Mind-Body Medicine* 14: 43–51.

SCHINDLER, LYDIA WOODS. 1993. "Understanding the Immune System." National Institutes of Health. NIH Publication No. 93–529.

SELYE, HANS. 1936. "Syndrome Produced by Diverse Nocuous Agents." *Nature* 138: 32.

SELYE, HANS. 1956. *The Stress of Life.* New York: McGraw-Hill.

SOBEL, DAVID S. 1995. "Rethinking Medicine: Improving Health Outcomes With Cost-Effective Psychosocial Interventions." *Psychosomatic Medicine* 57: 234–44.

STONE, ARTHUR A., JOHN M. NEALE, DONALD S. COX, ANTHONY NAPOLI, HEIDDIS VALDIMARSDOTTIR, and EILEEN KENNEDY-MOORE. 1994. "Daily Events are Associated with a Secretory Immune Response to an Oral Antigen in Men." *Health Psychology* 13: 440–46.

SUTTON-TYRRELL, KIM, HOLLY C. LASSILA, ELAINE MEILAHN, CLAREANN BUNKER, KAREN A. MATTHEWS, and LEWIS H. KULLER. 1998. "Carotid Atherosclerosis in Premenopausal and Postmenopausal Women and Its Association with Risk Factors Measured after Menopause." *Stroke* 29: 1116–21.

THEORELL, TOERES, and ROBERT A. KARESECK. 1996. "Current Issues in Relating Psychosocial Job Strain and Cardiovascular Disease Research." *Journal of Occupational Health Psychology* 1: 9–26.

THOITS, PEGGY A. 1995. "Stress, Coping, and Social Support Processes: Where Are We? What Next?" *Journal of Health and Social Behavior* Spec: 53–79.

UCHINO, BERT N., JOHN T. CACIOPPO, and JANICE K. KIECOLT-GLASER. 1996. "The Relationship Between Social Support and Physiological Processes: A Review with Emphasis on Underlying Mechanisms and Implications for Health." *Psychological Bulletin* 119: 488–531.

WADSWORTH, M. E. 1997. "Health Inequalities in the Life Course Perspective." *Social Science & Medicine* 44: 859–69.

WAITZKIN, HOWARD. 1991. *The Politics of Medical Encounters: How Patients and Doctors Deal With Social Problems.* New Haven, CT: Yale University Press.

WATKINS, ALAN. 1997. "Mind-Body Medicine: A Clinican's Guide to Psychoneuroimmunology." San Francisco: Churchill Livingstone.

WHOOLEY, MARY A. and WARREN S. BROWNER. 1998. "Association Between Depressive Symptoms and Mortality in Older Women. Study of Osteoporotic Fractures Research Group." *Archives of Internal Medicine* 158: 2129–35.

WILLIAMS, REDFORD B., JOHN C. BAREFOOT, ROBERT M. CALIFF, THOMAS L. HANEY, WILLIAM B. SAUNDERS, DAVID B. PRYOR, MARK A. HLATKY, ILENE C. SIEGLER, and DANIEL B. MARK. 1992. "Prognostic Importance of Social and Economic Resources Among Medically Treated Patients With Angiographically Documented Coronary Artery Disease." *Journal of the American Medical Association* 267: 520–24.

WILSON, THOMAS W., GEORGE A. KAPLAN, JUSSI KAUHANEN, RICHARD D. COHEN, MELIEN WU, RIITTA SALONEN, and JUKKA T. SALONEN. 1993. "Association Between Plasma Fibrinogen Concentration and Five Socioeconomic Indices in the Kuopio Ischemic Heart Disease Risk Factor Study." *American Journal of Epidemiology* 137:292–300.

24 MEDICAL SOCIOLOGY AND HEALTH PSYCHOLOGY

DEBRA UMBERSON, *University of Texas*

KRISTI WILLIAMS, *University of Texas*

SUSAN SHARP, *University of Oklahoma*

Health psychology is sister to the field of medical sociology. Our fields differ in fundamental ways, yet we study many of the same topics. For example, the following broad definition of health psychology, which could easily stand as a definition of medical sociology, is offered in Shelly Taylor's (1995) leading undergraduate textbook of health psychology:

> Putting it all together, health psychology represents the educational, scientific, and professional contributions of psychology to the promotion and maintenance of health, the prevention and treatment of illness, the identification of causes and correlates of health, illness and related dysfunction, the improvement of the health care system, and health policy formation. (Matarazzo 1980)

Sociology and psychology differ in their theoretical underpinnings, and this affects their orientation to empirical research. Medical sociologists emphasize how social structures shape health and illness in socially patterned ways. Health psychologists, on the other hand, emphasize individual differences in health and illness. For example, medical sociologists are more interested in explaining social causes of group variation in health, whereas health psychologists are more interested in explaining personal factors that contribute to health (Thoits 1995). The fields also diverge in that health psychology is oriented toward clinical application and intervention.

Sol Levine (1995) argued that medical sociology must have an interdisciplinary focus if it is to move forward. This chapter reviews the most significant areas of health psychology that have relevance for the current and future research agendas of medical sociologists. This chapter is about what health psychologists and medical sociologists might learn from one another. The insights from each field can further the theoretical and methodological work of the sister field. These insights may help to infuse the field of medical sociology with some of the energy and foresight needed to insure the viability of medical sociology in the future.

PSYCHOSOCIAL EPIDEMIOLOGY

Arguably, the greatest degree of overlap in the interests of medical sociologists and health psychologists lies in the field of psychosocial epidemiology. Both health psychologists and medical sociologists have demonstrated decades of success in identifying psychosocial correlates of health and illness. Health psychology and medical sociology share an early rejection of the biomedical model in the study of health and illness. Both fields also advance the view, now commonly accepted among social scientists, the public, and most physicians, that health and illness are the result of a complex interplay of biological, social, and psychological factors. A key difference, however, is the extent to which the two fields acknowledge this complex interplay in theoretical and empirical work. The centerpiece of psychosocial epidemiology is stress research. In this area, the more interdisciplinary approach of psychologists is apparent.

The Stress Model

Stress is defined as "a process in which environmental demands tax or exceed the adaptive capacity of an organism, resulting in psychological and biological changes that may place persons at risk for disease" (Cohen, Kessler, and Gordon 1995:3). Stress is associated with an increased risk for depression and alcohol problems, cardiovascular disease, cancer, autoimmune disease (e.g., rheumatoid arthritis, multiple sclerosis, insulin-dependent diabetes), and infectious disease (Cohen 1996; Cohen and Williamson 1991; Seeman and McEwan 1996; Taylor 1995). These conclusions are drawn from both sociology and psychology and from various research designs, including prospective studies of community samples and intervention studies with clinical and healthy subjects.

Health psychologists and medical sociologists work along parallel lines, and often in direct collaboration, on stress research. Traditionally, medical sociologists have focused more on identifying social group differences in exposure to stress and, to a lesser degree, group differences in vulnerability to stress. Sociological research on differential vulnerability to stress generally identifies certain individuals or groups as more vulnerable to a stressor on the basis of the degree of distress they exhibit in association with the stressor. For example, men exhibit more psychological distress than do women in response to widowhood. This apparent greater vulnerability may then be explained in terms of exposure to certain chronic strains that occur as a result of widowhood (e.g., greater social isolation of men) (Umberson, Wortman, and Kessler 1992). Although sociologists consider that the individual's unique assessment of the stressor is important, they do not typically study the nature or process of the assessment itself. This, however, is the primary focus of psychologists who study stress.

Psychologists strongly emphasize the evaluative role of the individual in assessing an environmental stimulus as stressful. Although medical sociologists recognize that the individual's subjective perception of a stimulus plays an important role in determining the consequences of exposure to the stimulus (Wethington and Kessler 1986), sociologists devote considerably less time to assessing how individuals come to perceive a stimulus as stressful or not stressful. In fact, most sociological research simply identifies some social environmental feature (e.g., poverty) or life event (e.g., divorce) as stressful. It is assumed that individuals exposed to the stressful stimulus are exposed to more stress than are individuals without such exposure. The individual's perception of the stimulus receives minimal attention. Where it does receive attention, it is typically only to allow the individual to rate how much stress is associated with the stimulus rather than to focus on the cognitive or social processes inherent in this subjective designation.

The issue of greatest importance in psychological research on stress is how stress is perceived by the individual. That is, the impact of a stressful event or situation on health is thought to be mediated by the individual's perception of the stressor. The process through which the individual evaluates the stressor in relation to stress is referred to as *appraisal* (Lazarus and Folkman 1984). *Primary appraisal* refers to the initial appraisal of an environmental stimulus as threatening or benign. A stress reaction occurs when the stimulus is appraised as threatening to the individual. *Secondary appraisal* refers to the individual's evaluation of his or her ability to cope with the stressful stimulus. The appraisal process is central to the stress model in health psychology. In fact, Scott Monroe and John Kelley argue that appraisal is "what many regard as the conceptual core of the stress process" (1995: 123). They contend that the perception of stress is "at least as important as, if not more so than, the events themselves" (1995: 124). The perception of stress then explains individual differences in the response to a stressful event or situation. A significant literature in health psychology concerns the factors that lead one individual to appraise an event as stressful while another individual appraises the same event as benign.

Determinants of Appraisal

Psychologists identify a number of factors to explain individual differences in the appraisal of stress. Certain personality characteristics are associated with stress appraisal. In particular, dispositional optimism, an internal locus of control, self-esteem, and hardiness are associated with a decreased propensity to label situations and events as stressful (Taylor and Aspinwall 1996). An individual's appraisal of a potential stressor also depends on the existence of personal psychopathology and mood state (Monroe and Kelley 1995). For example, anxiety and neuroticism are associated with increased stress appraisals (see a review in Kaplan 1996). Sociologists recognize that individual perceptions of stress are important in predicting individual responses to potentially stressful stimuli, yet little research attention is directed toward appraisal processes. However, medical sociologists are by training uniquely suited to extending the research on appraisal to focus on *environmental* antecedents of cognitive appraisal:

Without an understanding of the antecedents of appraisal, the investigator cannot make very penetrating statements about the etiologic mechanisms or role of appraisal in the stress process. (Monroe and Kelley 1995: 133)

In fact, medical sociologists are currently conducting research in several areas that are directly relevant to the appraisal process, most notably on the topics of meaning and identity, personal control, and social support. Although these research areas are highly relevant to the stress-appraisal process, they are not integrated with psychological work on appraisal. If these links were established, sociologists could create a more comprehensive multilevel assessment of the stress/health connection.

Meaning and Identity   Psychologists Monroe and Kelley (1995) argue that an environmental stimulus must be perceived as psychologically meaningful to the individual if it is to have any impact on the individual. Psychologists focus on cognitive appraisal as the process of determining the personal meaning of a potential stressor. Psychologists identify a number of factors that shape the personal meaning of potential stressors. For example, stimuli that are perceived as less controllable and less predictable are more likely to be perceived as threatening to the individual (Lerner 1980; Wortman, Silver, and Kessler 1993). Environmental stimuli that are contrary to the individual's worldviews—for example, a view of the world as a just or safe place—are also more likely to be viewed as stressful (Lerner 1980; Wortman et al. 1993). However, psychologists do not consider that perceptions of controllability and predictability, as well as worldviews, are strongly influenced by the individual's social context. Therein lies a principal role for sociologists to fill.

Sociological work often focuses on the social context of potential stressors. Sociologists recognize that contextual factors shape the meaning of a stressor (as well as the probability of exposure to the stressor) for the individual. For example, Leonard Pearlin (1989; also see a review in Simon 1997) argues that social position (e.g., defined by race, gender, socioeconomic status) shapes individuals' values and beliefs. In turn, these values and beliefs shape the meaning of a potential stressor for the individual. For example, gender shapes values and beliefs about work and family in ways that influence the perception of work and family stress (Simon 1995). In addition, the experience of work and family roles is associated with different costs and opportunities for men and women. Gender differences in the value attached to empathy, as well as gender differences in relationship experiences, may lead women to attach more

significance to strains experienced by close friends. In turn, women may experience more distress as a result of greater empathy and involvement in relationships that shape the meaning of their roles and relationships (Kessler and McLeod 1984). Sociologists explain that divorce and widowhood affect men and women differently because marital dissolution is an experience that carries distinctly different meanings for men and women (Reissman 1990; Umberson et al. 1992). For example, widowhood is characterized by a greater reduction in emotional support for men but greater reduction in financial resources for women. Several studies suggest that the loss of relationships typically associated with an increase in distress (e.g., divorce, widowhood) may actually be associated with a *reduction* in distress if those relationships were characterized by negative meaning (e.g., strain, conflict, and burden) (Umberson and Chen 1994; Wheaton 1990).

An additional sociological approach to meaning in stress research recognizes that contextual factors may shape individual role identities—self-conceptions that are linked to an individual's position in the social structure. According to the identity-relevance perspective, the meaning of a stressor and its psychological impact depend upon the salience of the role domain in which it occurs (Thoits 1995; also see a review in Simon 1997). More specifically, stressors that occur in role domains that are highly salient to the individual should be appraised as more threatening than those that occur in domains that are less important to one's self-concept or identity. For example, Simon (1992) finds that parents who are highly committed to the parental role are more vulnerable to parental role strains than those for whom the parental role is less salient.

Most sociological work imputes the meaning of a particular stressor based on the consequences of the stressor. For example, because women exhibit less psychological distress in response to widowhood, and because widowhood creates a different set of chronic strains for men and women, it is assumed that widowhood has a different meaning for men and women (Umberson et al. 1992). Psychologists, on the other hand, focus more specifically on the individual's perception of an event as threatening or benign. It is rare for sociologists to go to the source (i.e., the individual) to ascertain the meaning of a particular event. A recent exception is Robin Simon's work (1997) that directly asks individuals about the meaning of their social roles and considers these meanings in relation to mental health.

Another line of sociological research focuses on a sense of global meaning as mediating the impact of potential stressors on health (Antonovsky 1979). This research follows a lengthy sociological tradition suggesting that involvement in key social roles (i.e., social context) may imbue the individual with a strong sense of meaning and purpose that, in turn, has a salutary effect on health (Antonovsky 1979; Burton 1998; Durkheim, 1897[1951]). This research literature, however, does not suggest the cognitive process through which social roles may convey a sense of meaning and purpose to the individual.

In sum, sociologists focus more on social contextual factors that shape the meaning of a potential stressor, while psychologists focus more on cognitive processes through which an environmental stimulus is perceived as meaningful. Certainly, both levels are operative. The social context influences the values and beliefs of individuals in socially patterned ways. Yet the impact of the social context on individual health and well-being must be mediated by some cognitive process. How the social context and cognitive processes intersect is not addressed by either discipline. Sociological research on cultural differences in views of health and illness suggests that the social context does translate into different ways of dealing with health concerns (Angel and Cleary 1984). We should consider the cognitive process through which this translation occurs in addition to group differences in perceptions and reports of health/illness. In this way, sociologists can help to explain social-group variation in health as a consequence of social context in relation to stress-appraisal processes.

Personal Control The association of personal control and health is a prolific and exciting research topic in both medical sociology and health psychology, although its origins clearly lie in the field of psychology. Many different constructs have been used to refer to the notion of personal control. These constructs include mastery, self-efficacy, and internal locus of control. The obverse of personal control is seen in the constructs of external locus of control, fatalism, and helplessness. These constructs share a basic premise that individuals who are higher on personal control have a:

> . . . perception of effective personal agency: of being the cause of that which happens in one's own life, the means by which it occurs, the authority with power to act, and the author of intended effects. (Mirowsky 1997: S125)

What is the evidence for a link of personal control to health? Personal control is positively associated with health behaviors that protect health (Lefcourt and Davidson-Katz 1991). Personal control is inversely associated with depressed mood, and depressed mood is inversely associated with health status (Lefcourt and Davidson-Katz 1991). Finally, personal control is inversely associated with mortality risk in prospective study designs (Seeman and Lewis 1995).

The initial push to study personal control stems from the early 1960s, when personality psychologists became interested in "locus of control." In fact, Lefcourt and Davidson-Katz argue that "by 1975 . . . the locus of control construct had come to be the central preoccupation in personality research" (1991: 246). Research evidence suggests that individuals with a greater internal locus of control behave more adaptively when faced with health concerns, that these individuals are more likely to engage in preventive health behaviors and to seek appropriate medical care (Lefcourt and Davidson-Katz 1991). Early research suggested that an internal locus of control served to buffer individuals from the adverse consequences of stress. This occurs, in part, because individuals with a greater internal locus of control are less likely to see events as threatening (primary appraisal) and more likely to choose adaptive strategies (secondary appraisal) for dealing with the stressor (Cohen and Edwards 1989).

Personality psychologists have traditionally viewed locus of control as a characteristic of the individual. Locus of control, like any personality characteristic, may influence appraisal processes, ultimately affecting health behavior and health. Many health psychologists recognize the importance of the social environment in contributing to individual perceptions of personal control as well as to stress and health (e.g., Taylor 1995). However, health psychology, as a whole, is much more focused on how individuals' perceptions of personal control affect health outcomes than on how these perceptions are established in the first place. Medical sociologists have devoted more effort to identifying environmental correlates of personal control: Older age, lower socioeconomic status, minority status, and female gender are associated with a lower sense of personal control (Umberson 1993). Sociological research should focus on the mechanisms through which the environment affects perceptions of control. For example, many studies indicate that women score lower on personal control than men, but few studies offer empirical investigation of how these gender differences arise, nor do they consider how these differences might contribute to the health status of different groups. Instead, researchers assume that the social environment of women is less conducive to personal control than is men's. Sociologists should draw from and build on the considerable psychological research that focuses on identifying the mechanisms through which personal control affects health.

What are the mechanisms through which personal control affects health? First, personal control influences the primary appraisal of stress as less threatening and influences coping in an adaptive way (i.e., a psychological mechanism). Second, personal control triggers a physiological mechanism that benefits health:

> Perceived control over aversive events decreases autonomic reactivity in animals and humans, and reduces gastric ulceration and weight loss in animals exposed to severe stress. (Rodin 1986: 1274)

Third, individuals who are higher on personal control engage in more health-protective behaviors, recognize and react appropriately to symptoms of illness, and better comply with medical regimens (Grembowsky et al. 1993).

John Mirowsky argues that "the sense of control seems to act as a pivot of social, psychological, and biological processes" (1997: S126). The social environment affects individual perceptions of control. These perceptions influence how individuals appraise and react to stress, health behavior, and, ultimately, health outcomes. The sense of control positively affects health outcomes, in part by enacting psychological and physiological mechanisms that affect physical health. Certainly, research on personal control represents great opportunities for the cross-fertilization of ideas and research across disciplines. Sociologists can extend their study of personal control by considering the psychological and physiological mechanisms through which the social environment affects personal control and through which personal control affects health behavior.

Social Support The study of social support has its origins in sociology. At least dating to Durkheim (1897 [1951]), sociologists have argued that involvement in social relationships serves to protect the health of individuals. Durkheim argued that social involvement characterized by more social control and social integration deterred suicidal behavior. Subsequent to this seminal work, numerous sociological studies document the apparent salutary effect of social involvement on health (House et al. 1988). Two basic dimensions of social involvement are typically considered: social integration and social support. Social integration refers to the existence or quantity of significant social ties, while social support refers to the emotionally sustaining quality of one's social relationships. Both social integration and social support are inversely associated with morbidity and mortality risk (see House et al. 1988; Uchino et al. 1996). James House et al. (1988) argue that the evidence linking social relationships to health is as persuasive as the evidence in the 1960 Surgeon General's report linking cigarette smoking to lung cancer. Although the interest in social involvement and health may have originated in sociology, psychologists have been at least as enthusiastic and productive on this topic as have sociologists.

Sociologists view social relationships as a key feature of the individual's social environment. While some health psychologists adopt this same view, other psychologists tend to see social support as a stable personality characteristic of the individual (Sarason, Sarason, and Shearin 1986). That is, social support is seen as resulting from an individual's propensity and ability to seek out and sustain supportive relationships. For example, Sheldon Cohen and J. R. Edwards (1989) conclude that individuals who have more social competence, lower social anxiety, and better self-disclosure skills are able to make more friends and obtain more effective support from others. They do not, however, consider that social context (e.g., as defined by socioeconomic status) may foster social competence, social anxiety, and self-disclosure skills.

Psychologists and sociologists have shared a common interest in identifying the antecedents and consequences of social support. While psychologists focus more on individual-level antecedents of social support (e.g., personality), sociologists focus more on environmental-level or structural antecedents (e.g., socioeconomic status). Both fields recognize the need to move beyond identifying antecedents and consequences of social support to identifying the key mechanisms through which social support affects health:

> We must further understand the psychological and biological processes or mechanisms linking social relationships to health, either as extensions of the social processes just discussed [for example, processes of cognitive appraisal and coping] or as independent mechanisms. (House et al. 1988: 543–44)

Although this call for further understanding was made by three sociologists a decade ago, sociologists have conducted few studies in this area. Health psychologists, however, have made great gains in two areas: (1) considering how social support affects cognitive appraisal, and (2) considering the physiological mechanisms through which social support affects health.

Cognitive Appraisal Social support from others may affect the appraisal of stress in several basic ways. First, supportive others may alter the individual's perception of the severity of a stressor by helping the individual understand the event and develop strategies for coping with the stressor. Supportive others may offer financial support or instrumental assistance to help the individual cope with the stressor. Emotional support may make the individual feel loved and cared for. In turn, social support may reduce the degree to which the individual appraises a potential stressor as threatening:

> . . . social support may operate proactively to offset or minimize stressful events before they become major stressors; they may operate to help reduce the impact of an existing stressor; or they may act as buffers against high levels of stress. (Taylor and Aspinwall 1996:92)

Taylor and Aspinwall (1996) suggest that social support may even influence behaviors that serve to prevent stress from occurring. For example, social support may serve to deter negative health behaviors that could create illness or injury. Perhaps more important is the psychological research showing that social support has beneficial effects on physiological processes that, in turn, positively affect health. This significant research is discussed in detail in the section on physiological mechanisms.

BEHAVIORAL AND PHYSIOLOGICAL MECHANISMS LINKING THE SOCIAL ENVIRONMENT TO HEALTH

Personal control, social support, and symbolic meaning—constructs currently studied by sociologists—may affect the appraisal of potential environmental stressors. Sociologists may draw on the work of psychologists who study the psychological mechanisms (i.e., cognitive-appraisal processes) through which the social environment affects health. Sociologists may build on the study of social environment and health by considering social structural variation in cognitive appraisal, as well as how structured variation in cognitive appraisal ultimately affects social variation in health and illness outcomes. A particular strength of health psychology is its focus, not just on psychological mechanisms linking stress to health, but also on behavioral and physiological mechanisms through which stressors—once they are appraised as stressful—adversely affect health. Behavioral and physiological mechanisms may present medical sociologists with

their greatest opportunities for advancing sociological research on the social environment and health.

Behavioral Mechanisms

Health Behavior Health behavior includes preventive health behaviors such as seat belt use, health-compromising behaviors such as smoking, compliance with medical regimens such as drug therapy for an ongoing disorder, and rehabilitation regimens such as physical therapy following a stroke. Numerous health behaviors are clearly linked to morbidity and mortality (Berkman and Breslow 1983).

Health psychologists, much more often than medical sociologists, conduct research on health behavior. Much of the psychological research on health behavior has an applied focus, concerned with health promotion through behavioral change—through reducing risk behaviors, improving adherence to a healthy lifestyle, and improving compliance with medical regimens (Gochman 1997). Health psychologists, by virtue of their close connection to clinical psychologists, are impelled to consider how basic research may be translated into effective intervention strategies. Behavioral medicine, a field closely related to health psychology, is more directly concerned with the actual application of research to health promotion, illness and injury prevention, and rehabilitation. Medical sociologists seldom stray from an interest in basic research to application. In part, this is because sociologists interested in health behavior are concerned almost entirely with epidemiological questions about health behavior. In particular, most sociological research on health behavior considers how various facets of the social environment (e.g., stress, social integration, and socioeconomic status) contribute to or deter certain health behaviors. Sociologists sometimes attempt to identify the social mechanisms through which these features of the social environment might affect health behavior (e.g., social control and social support) (see House et al. 1988). This work is typically used to describe how certain facets of the environment affect health behavior but rarely to suggest how future behavior might be altered, and it does not consider psychological mechanisms through which the social environment affects health behavior.

Psychologists emphasize intraindividual factors (e.g., personality) that affect the propensity to engage in various health behaviors. For example, psychologists consider how locus of control, anxiety, depression, and appraisal processes are associated with health behavior. Health psychologists have conducted considerable research on the impact of two central features of the social environment on health behavior: stress and social support. A significant body of psychological research clearly establishes that stress adversely affects health behavior. Individuals may attempt to alleviate their stress by engaging in health-compromising behavior such as smoking or drinking excessively (Cohen and Williamson 1991). Furthermore, health-compromising behavior may impair immune competence (Cohen and Williamson 1991). Psychological research suggests that social support may affect health behavior in a positive direction (Cohen 1988). For example, social support is associated with more health-protective behavior that, in turn, has a direct and positive effect on health. In addition, social support's beneficial effect on health behavior may indirectly benefit overall health by positively affecting immune competence (Cohen 1988).

Psychologists seldom consider how the social environment might affect individual-level variables that, in turn, affect health behavior. Medical sociologists can build on this substantial body of work in psychology by considering how the social context shapes these individual-level variables. In particular, sociologists can assess how social contexts affect appraisal processes that, in turn, affect health behavior. Some sociological research indirectly addresses appraisal processes. For example, Joseph Schneider and Peter Conrad (1983) find that individuals who perceive their illness as highly stigmatized (e.g., epileptics) sometimes fail to engage in behavior (e.g., taking prescription drugs) that might actually help to control their illness. This failure to act is, in part, a result of the social stigma attached to the medical condition. Sociological work on cultural determinants of the meaning of health and illness shows that Hispanic and white Americans define illness in different ways, ways that reflect their cultural context (Angel and Cleary 1984). If different groups of individuals perceive health and illness in different ways, this may influence individual propensity to engage in various health behaviors. Furthermore, different cultural groups are characterized by different levels of personal control that may influence health behavior. For example, minorities report less personal control than do whites (Umberson 1993). Individuals who perceive little control over their own health, illness, and timing of mortality, may see little reason to engage in preventive health behavior with its time-deferred benefits—thus partly explaining racial differences in health-compromising behavior.

It is remarkable that sociologists do not study health behavior to a greater extent than they do. Health behavior is a social behavior that reflects social circumstances and that affects health in socially patterned ways. Sociologists can draw on the substantial psychological literature on health behavior research to build a multilevel approach to the study of health behavior. Sociologists are uniquely poised to consider the social structural determinants of health behavior, something they have done to some degree. However, they can provide a more comprehensive understanding of this social behavior by considering how psychological mechanisms mediate the impact of the social environment on health and how the social environment affects those psychological mechanisms. For example, social conditions associated with socioeconomic context may affect psychological mechanisms (e.g., locus of control, cognitive images of illness) in different ways for individuals in different social classes. In turn, those mechanisms may help to explain social group differences in health behavior. In this multilayered study of health behavior, sociologists should also consider the physiological mechanisms (described more fully below) that may mediate the impact of health behavior on health.

Sociological research on health behavior will be limited without an appreciation for the application of research findings. Sociologists have emphasized the social determinants of health behavior. The rationale for conducting such research is that health behavior affects physical health and even mortality. Sociologists should take the next step and suggest how our research findings might be used to enhance physical health, particularly the health of social groups that we know to be relatively disadvantaged.

Physiological Mechanisms

Psychoneuroimmunology The most striking difference in epidemiologic research based in psychology as compared to sociology is the emphasis that psychologists place on physiological processes. While sociologists and psychologists recognize that stress affects health via physiological pathways, psychologists directly incorporate this recognition into their theoretical formulations and research designs. As a result, health psychology is characterized by a much stronger interdisciplinary approach than is medical sociology. Health psychologists recognize that the social environment (i.e., particularly sources of stress and support in that environment) affects health. This reflects a recognition of social structural influences on the individual (although stress and social support are sometimes viewed as individual difference variables rather than structural conditions imposed upon individuals). They emphasize that individual differences in reactions to environmental influences exist and explain these individual differences primarily through differences in appraisal and coping processes. This emphasis reflects a recognition of psychological mechanisms linking the social environment to health. Finally, they recognize that social and psychological influences on health must be mediated by biological or physiological processes. This reflects a further recognition of physiological mechanisms linking the social environment to health. In sum, health psychologists adopt a model that incorporates social, psychological, and physiological components, although the social components are least well developed:

> Historically, the environmental, psychological, and biological traditions have each focused on a specific part of the [stress] model, thus often ignoring other parts. For example, sociologists and epidemiologists have addressed the question of whether life events increase disease risk but usually ignore the psychological and biological pathway through which this influence might occur. Psychologists have focused on the role of appraisal and emotional response in disease risk, with less emphasis on the environmental causes of these states and the biological pathways responsible for links between psychological states and disease. . . . (Cohen et al. 1995: 11)

Many health psychologists have a good understanding of the interplay of psychological, neurological, and immunological systems. Psychologists are much more likely than sociologists to have an interest in and understanding of these systems, in part because their training typically includes at least a rudimentary exposure to them. Sociology has, at its origin, a rejection of biological determinism and a belief in the power of the social environment to shape the attitudes, behaviors, and mental and physical life chances of individuals in socially patterned ways. To this end, sociologists-in-training are rarely exposed to biological models. The emerging expertise of psychologists in the area of psychoneuroimmunology represents not a focus on biological processes in a social vacuum, but rather an emphasis on the interplay of social, psychological, and physiological processes. This emphasis places psychologists on the cutting edge of research that emphasizes the impact of the social environment on the individual. Sociologists are largely excluded from this new frontier.

Psychoneuroimmunology is a field of research that "focuses on the relationships between psychosocial processes and the activities of the nervous, endocrine, and immune systems" (Sarafino 1998: 120).

Research over the past fifteen years shows that two key features of the social environment—stress and social support—affect immune functioning. The psychoneuroimmunology model suggests the biological mechanisms through which stress and social support affect health. The basic premise of research on stress is that stress activates the sympathetic nervous system—that is, triggering large increases in blood pressure, heart rate, and hormonal responses (epinephrine and norepinephrine). This physiological arousal then affects the onset and progression of disease. Health psychologists have recognized for many decades that stress adversely affects cardiovascular health because of the negative physiological effect of stress on cardioreactivity. More recent research shows that stress may increase susceptibility to infectious disease by:

> (a) altering biologic susceptibility and hence *predisposing* persons exposed to a pathogen to infection, (b) *initiating* or triggering a process that allows a pathogen that is already in the body (e.g., a latent virus) to reproduce, or (c) contributing to *maintenance* of an ongoing pathogenic process. (Cohen and Williamson 1991: 7)

Cohen and Williamson conclude that the adverse effect of stress on less serious infectious disease (e.g., colds, influenza) is "consistent and convincing" (1991). Though less conclusive, evidence also suggests that stress contributes to or triggers autoimmune disease (e.g., rheumatoid arthritis).

The social environment may also affect immune competence through the psychological pathway of depressed mood. Depressed mood, clinical depression, and anxiety are associated with lower immune functioning (Schleifer et al. 1989). On the other hand, positive mood states are associated with better immune functioning (Cohen 1996). Certain personality characteristics, particularly an optimistic orientation, are also associated with better immune competence (Segerstrom et al. 1998). Sociologists should consider the environmental precursors of mood in combination with interactions of mood and the environment in their impact on immune competence.

Supportive relationships are also associated with increased immune competence (Seeman and McEwan 1996), presumably because social support has direct beneficial effects on physiological functioning:

> . . . there is relatively strong evidence linking social support to aspects of the cardiovascular, endocrine, and immune systems. These data are consistent with research suggesting that the formation and disruption of social relationships have important immunological

and endocrinological sequalae in nonhuman primates and humans . . . More important, the physiological systems reviewed may play important roles in the leading causes of death in the United States. (Uchino, Cacioppo, and Kiecolt-Glaser 1996: 521)

Emotional support seems to be the most important dimension of social support, in terms of affecting physiological processes. Once a situation is perceived as stressful, the presence of supportive others may also reduce physiological arousal in response to the stressor (Uchino et al. 1996). This is an example of the stress-buffering effect of social support.

Psychologists' focus on the social environment is largely limited to social support and stress. These two facets of the environment are not considered in structural terms—that is, psychologists tend to view social support and stress as conditions to which any individual might be exposed and as being mediated by characteristics of the individual. For example, psychologists often view social support as a function of the individual's personality characteristics, so that an individual who is more extroverted elicits more support from the environment. Psychologists rarely consider how social structures systematically expose certain groups of individuals to more or less social support and stress or how social structures contribute to personality characteristics. The failure to consider these basic social processes results in an incomplete picture of the impact of the social environment on health. In fact, social, psychological, and biological processes should be incorporated into a single model (Cohen et al. 1995). For example, numerous studies suggest gender differences in exposure and vulnerability to stress and social support. A few studies indicate the possibility of gender differences in the effect of social support on immune functioning. For example, Teresa Seeman and colleagues (1994) find a significant and inverse association of emotional support with endocrine activity only among men. This finding is consistent with the evidence that social ties are more beneficial in reducing mortality risk for men than for women (House, Umberson, and Landis 1988). Research that considers the impact of social-structural variables (e.g., sex, race, socioeconomic status) along with cognitive and physiologic processes in their impact on health is virtually nonexistent and represents an important area of future research for medical sociologists:

> Much remains to be specified regarding relationships between social environment characteristics and neuroendocrine regulation and how any such relationships ultimately influence patterns of morbidity and

mortality. However, available evidence does support the conclusion that the positive and supportive aspects of social relationships can attenuate patterns of neuroendocrine reactivity and this apparent link between the social and biological realms may have important positive consequences for health and longevity. (Seeman and McEwan 1996: 467)

Measurement and Methods

Sociologists who are not familiar with the psychoneuroimmunology literature may feel ill-equipped to study physiological processes. Certainly, our training does not make us experts in this area. However, psychologists who study psychoneuroimmunology pay keen attention to measurement concerns. Several key markers of immunological functioning are easily accessible via simple blood tests. Kiecolt-Glaser and Glaser (1995) provide a good overview of key measures of immune competence as well as measurement concerns. They emphasize that behavioral scientists should collaborate with an immunologist when they begin to conduct psychoneuroimmunological research:

> The immunologist will help design studies with an eye to methodological and logistical constraints . . . , choose assays that are appropriate to the study population . . . , review immunological data from the study to ensure both reliability and validity, and provide immunological expertise for the interpretation of results. (Kiecolt-Glaser and Glaser 1995: 220)

Research that considers psychological, social environmental, and physiological factors is, by definition, interdisciplinary. Consultation and direct collaboration with psychologists will also contribute to the quality of sociological research on health and illness.

Sociologists have not been completely absent in the study of physiological processes. Several interdisciplinary projects of the past few years combine survey methodology—the most significant tool used by sociologists to study psychosocial issues and health—with biomedical assessments. For example, the MacArthur studies on successful aging rely on an interdisciplinary team that includes sociologists. This project provides some of the state-of-the-art research on physiological mechanisms through which the social environment affects health (e.g., the 1994 Seeman et al. study on social ties and neuroendocrine functioning). Alan Booth and his colleagues' work on the role of testosterone in affecting marriage, social behavior, and depression represents some of the most important new sociological work that integrates biological and sociological frameworks

(Booth, Johnson, and Granger 1999; Booth and Mazur 1998; Booth and Dabbs 1993; Booth and Osgood 1993). Peyrot, McMurry, and Kruger (1999) consider how stress and coping styles affect blood sugar control for Type 1 and Type 2 diabetes.

Sociologists can also learn from the keen attention that psychologists have devoted to measurement concerns. Psychologists, more than sociologists, are concerned with consistency in measurement of key constructs, establishing the reliability and validity of measurement, and considering multidimensional measures of key constructs such as social support and immunological function (Uchino et al. 1996). Much of the work in health psychology also addresses the importance of timing in the stress process. For example, the importance and precise roles of various mechanisms in linking appraisal processes and stress reaction may depend on when these mechanisms are assessed during the stress process. Certain mechanisms may be important early, but not late, in the stress process (Cohen et al. 1995).

CONCLUSION

Health psychologists have made a conscious effort to ensure their own viability through the application of their findings (Taylor 1995). Psychologists, in part because of their link to clinical colleagues, strive to conduct research that has some intervention utility. The goal is to improve or protect the health of individuals. Sociologists, although sometimes nodding to policy and clinical application, seldom make a serious effort to extend their research findings to the level of application. Sociologists would be well-advised to rethink the relevance of application to sociology. It is difficult to rationalize our role in the study of health if we make no contribution to the production of health. Certainly, our utility and relevance is easier to defend when we offer solutions to social problems. Health psychologists tend to emphasize the individual as the point for intervention. For example,

psychologists consider how an individual's perception of personal control might be enhanced through intervention strategies (Rodin 1986). Sociologists can provide specific ways to change not only the subjective perceptions of individuals but also the objective social environment in ways that affect how people perceive the world. For example, John Mirowsky suggests:

> . . . the key to improving the sense of control that older Americans feel over their own lives lies in improving their circumstances and effectiveness. In the long run this apparently requires rising levels of education and longer preservation of physical function. In the short run the best adaptive strategy may lie in keeping shocks to subjective life expectancy and the sense of control from creating intractable consequences that further undermine morale. (1997: S133)

Sociologists may have a greater potential to contribute to intervention and policy by considering psychological and physiological processes. Health and illness are shaped by a complex interplay of sociological, psychological, behavioral, and physiological factors. In addressing the "how" question, we must adopt a broader interdisciplinary focus. Health psychologists are far ahead of us in identifying the linkages of psychosocial variables to physiological mechanisms. We can learn from their substantial knowledge base as well as build on it by emphasizing the important influence of social-structural variables on psychological and physiological processes:

> . . . many of us are becoming more hospitable to the contributions of other disciplines to our own subject matter. Those of us who work on the social determinants of health, for example, find that analyses are sometimes more fruitful when we understand, or at least inquire into, the psychological and biological mechanisms through which social factors influence health status. We must discard lingering reservations that making use of the concepts and findings of other disciplines represents faltering allegiance to our sociological discipline." (Levine 1995: 3)

REFERENCES

ANGEL, RONALD, and PAUL CLEARY. 1984. "The Effects of Social Structure and Culture on Reported Health." *Social Science Quarterly* 65:814–28.

ANTONOVSKY, AARON. 1979. *Health, Stress, and Coping.* San Francisco: Jossey-Bass Publishers.

BERKMAN, LISA F., and LESTER BRESLOW. 1983. *Health and Ways of Living: The Alameda County Study.* New York: Oxford University Press.

BOOTH, ALAN, and JAMES DABBS. 1993. "Testosterone and Men's Marriages." *Social Forces* 72:463–77.

BOOTH, ALAN, DAVID R. JOHNSON, and DOUGLAS A. GRANGER. 1999. "Testosterone and Men's Depression: The Role of Social Behavior." *Journal of Health and Social Behavior* 40: 130–40.

BOOTH, ALAN, and ALLAN MAZUR. 1998. "Testosterone and Dominance in Men: Old Issues and New Perspectives." *Behavioral and Brain Sciences* 21:386–97.

BOOTH, ALAN, and WAYNE OSGOOD. 1993. "The Influence of Testosterone on Deviance in Adulthood: Assessing and Explaining the Relationship." *Criminology* 31:93–117.

BURTON, RUSSELL D. 1998. "Global Integrative Meaning as a Mediating Factor in the Relationship Between Social Roles and Psychological Distress." *Journal of Health and Social Behavior* 39:201–15.

COHEN, SHELDON. 1988. "Psychosocial Models of the Role of Social Support in the Etiology of Physical Disease." *Health Psychology* 7: 269–97.

COHEN, SHELDON. 1996. "Health Psychology: Psychological Factors and Physical Disease From the Perspective of Human Psychoneuroimmunology." *Annual Review of Psychology* 47:113–42.

COHEN, SHELDON, and GAIL M. WILLIAMSON. 1991. "Stress and Infectious Disease in Humans." *Psychological Bulletin* 109:5–24.

COHEN, SHELDON, and J.R. EDWARDS. 1989. "Personality Characteristics as Moderators of the Relationship Between Stress and Disorder." In *Advances in the Investigation of Psychological Stress,* ed. R. W. J. Neufeld. New York: Wiley, pp. 235–283.

COHEN, SHELDON, RONALD C. KESSLER, and LYNN UNDERWOOD GORDON. 1995. "Strategies for Measuring Stress in Studies of Psychiatric and Physical Disorders." In *Measuring Stress,* ed. S. Cohen, R.C. Kessler, and L.U. Gordon. New York: Oxford University Press, pp. 3–26.

DURKHEIM, EMILE. 1897[1951]. *Suicide.* New York: Free Press.

GOCHMAN, DAVID S. 1997. "Relevance of Health Behavior Research: An Integration of Applications." In *Handbook of Health Behavior Research IV: Relevance for Professionals and Issues for the Future,* ed. D.S. Gochman. New York: Plenum Press, pp. 377–425.

GREMBOWSKY, DAVID, DONALD PATRICK, PAUL DIEHR, MARY DURHAM, SHIRLEY BERESFORD, ERICA KAY, and JULIA HECHT. 1993. "Self-Efficacy and Health Behavior Among Older Adults." *Journal of Health and Social Behavior* 34: 89–104.

HOUSE, JAMES S., DEBRA UMBERSON, and KARL LANDIS. 1988. "Social Relationships and Health." *Science* 241: 540–55.

KAPLAN, HOWARD B. 1996. *Psychosocial Stress: Perspectives on Structure, Theory, Life-Course, and Methods.* New York: Academic Press.

KESSLER, RONALD C., and JANE D. MCLEOD. 1984. "Sex Differences in Vulnerability to Undesirable Life Events." *Journal of Health and Social Behavior* 28: 51–59.

KIECOLT-GLASER, JANICE K., and RONALD GLASER. 1995. "Measurement of Immune Response." In *Measuring Stress,* S. Cohen, R.C. Kessler, and L.U. Gordon. New York: Oxford University Press.

LAZARUS, RICHARD, and SUSAN FOLKMAN. 1984. *Stress, Appraisal, and Coping.* New York: Springer.

LEFCOURT, HERBERT M., and KARINA DAVIDSON-KATZ. 1991. "Locus of Control and Health." In *Handbook of Social and Clinical Psychology: The Health Perspective,* ed. C.R. Snyder and R.R. Forsyth. New York: Pergamon, pp. 246–66.

LERNER, MELVIN J. 1980. *The Belief in a Just World: A Fundamental Delusion.* New York: Plenum.

LEVINE, SOL. 1995. "Time for Creative Integration in Medical Sociology." *Journal of Health and Social Behavior* (Extra Issue): 1–4.

MATARUZZO, J.D. 1980. "Behavioral Health and Behavioral Medicine: Frontiers for a New Health Psychology." *American Psychologist* 35: 805–17.

MIROWSKY, JOHN. 1997. "Age, Subjective Life Expectancy, and the Sense of Control: The Horizon Hypothesis." *Journal of Gerontology: Social Sciences* 52B: S125–S134.

MIROWSKY, JOHN, and CATHERINE E. ROSS. 1994. "Social Patterns of Distress." *Annual Review of Sociology* 12: 23–45.

MONROE, SCOTT M., and JOHN M. KELLEY. 1995. "Measurement of Stress Appraisal." In *Measuring Stress,* ed. S. Cohen, R.C. Kessler, and L.U. Gordon, New York: Oxford University Press.

PEARLIN, LEONARD I. 1989. "The Sociological Study of Stress." *Journal of Health and Social Behavior* 30:241–56.

PEYROT, MARK, JAMES F. MCMURRY, JR., and DAVIDA F. KRUGER. 1999. "A Biopsychosocial Model of Glycemic Control in Diabetes: Stress, Coping and Regimen Adherence." *Journal of Health and Social Behavior* 40: 141–58.

RIESSMAN, CATHERINE KOHLER. 1990. *Divorce Talk: Women and Men Make Sense of Personal Relationships.* New Brunswick, NJ: Rutgers University Press.

RODIN, JUDITH. 1986. "Aging and Health: Effects of the Sense of Control." *Science* 233:1271–76.

SARAFINO, EDWARD P. 1998. *Health Psychology: Biopsychosocial Interactions.* New York: Wiley.

SARASON, I.G., B.R. SARASON, and E.N. SHEARIN. 1986. "Social Support as an Individual Difference Variable: Its Stability, Origins, and Relational Aspects." *Journal of Personality and Social Psychology* 50:845–50.

SCHLEIFER, S.J., S.E. KELLER, R.N. BOND, J. COHEN, and M. STEIN. 1989. "Major Depressive Disorder and Immunity: Role of Age, Sex, Severity, and Hospitalization." *Archives of General Psychiatry* 46: 81–87.

SCHNEIDER, JOSEPH W., and PETER CONRAD. 1983. *Having Epilepsy: The Experience and Control of Illness.* Philadelphia: Temple University Press.

SEEMAN, M., and S. LEWIS. 1995. "Powerlessness, Health and Mortality." *Social Science and Medicine* 41: 517–25.

SEEMAN, TERESA E., and BRUCE S. MCEWEN. 1996. "Impact of Social Environment Characteristics on Neuroendocrine Regulation." *Psychosomatic Medicine* 58: 459–71.

SEEMAN, TERESA E., LISA F. BERKMAN, DAN BLAZER, JOHN W. ROWE. 1994. "Social Ties and Support and Neuroendocrine Function: The MacArthur Studies of Successful Aging." *Annals of Behavioral Medicine* 16: 95–106.

SEGERSTROM, SUZANNE C., SHELLEY E. TAYLOR, MARGARET E. KEMENY, and JOHN L. FAHEY. 1998. "Optimism Is Associated With Mood, Coping, and Immune Change in Response to Stress." *Journal of Personality and Social Psychology* 74:1646–55.

SIMON, ROBIN W. 1992. "Parental Role Strains, Salience of Parental Identity and Gender Differences in Psychological Distress." *Journal of Health and Social Behavior* 33: 25–35.

SIMON, ROBIN W. 1995. "Gender, Multiple Roles, Role Meaning, and Mental Health." *Journal of Health and Social Behavior* 36: 182–94.

SIMON, ROBIN W. 1997. "The Meanings Individuals Attach to Role Identities and Their Implications for Mental Health." *Journal of Health and Social Behavior* 38: 256–74.

TAYLOR, SHELLEY E. 1995. *Health Psychology,* 3rd ed. New York: McGraw-Hill.

TAYLOR, SHELLEY E. 1996. "Mediating and Moderating Processes in Psychosocial Stress: Appraisal, Coping, Resistance, and Vulnerability." In *Psychosocial Stress: Perspectives on Structure, Theory, Life Course, and Methods,* ed. Howard B. Kaplan. New York: Academic Press.

TAYLOR, SHELLEY E., and LISA G. ASPINWALL. 1996. "Mediating and Moderating Processes in Psychosocial Stress: Appraisal, Coping, Resistance, and Vulnerability." In *Psychosocial Stress: Perspectives on Structure, Theory, Life-Course, and Methods,* ed. Howard B. Kaplan. New York, Academic Press, pp. 71–110.

TAYLOR, SHELLEY E., and RENA L. REPETTI. 1997. "Health Psychology: What Is an Unhealthy Environment and How Does It Get Under the Skin?" *Annual Review of Psychology* 48: 411–47.

THOITS, PEGGY A. 1995. "Social Psychology: The Interplay Between Sociology and Psychology." *Social Forces* 1231–42.

UCHINO, BERT N., JOHN T. CACIOPPO, and JANICE K. KIECOLT-GLASER. 1996. "The Relationship Between Social Support and Physiological Processes: A Review With Emphasis on Underlying Mechanisms and Implications for Health." *Psychological Bulletin* 119: 488–531.

UMBERSON, DEBRA. 1993. "Sociodemographic Position, World Views, and Psychological Distress." *Social Science Quarterly* 74: 575–89.

UMBERSON, DEBRA, and MEICHU D. CHEN. 1994. "Effects of a Parent's Death on Adult Children: Relationship Salience and Reaction to Loss." *American Sociological Review* 59:152–68.

UMBERSON, DEBRA, CAMILLE B. WORTMAN, and RONALD C. KESSLER. 1992. "Widowhood and Depression: Explaining Long-Term Gender Differences in Vulnerability." *Journal of Health and Social Behavior* 33:10–24.

WETHINGTON, ELAIN, and RONALD C. KESSLER. 1986. "Perceived Support, Received Support, and Adjustment to Stressful Life Events." *Journal of Health and Social Behavior* 27: 78–89.

WHEATON, BLAIR. 1990. "Life Transitions, Role Histories, and Mental Health." *American Sociological Review* 55: 209–23.

WORTMAN, CAMILLE B., ROXANNE C. SILVER, and RONALD C. KESSLER. 1993. "The Meaning of Loss and Adjustment to Bereavement." In *Handbook of Bereavement: Theory and Research Intervention,* ed. M.S. Stroebe, W.S. Stroebe, and R.O. Hansson. New York: Cambridge University Press, pp. 349–66.

25 SOCIAL EPIDEMIOLOGY AND MEDICAL SOCIOLOGY: DIFFERENT APPROACHES TO THE SAME PROBLEM

S. LEONARD SYME, *University of California, Berkeley*

IRENE H. YEN, *University of California, San Francisco*

INTRODUCTION

The field of public health encompasses disease prevention, health promotion, and the protection of human populations. The subject matter of public health ranges from infectious and communicable diseases such as AIDS and tuberculosis to noninfectious disease and problems such as coronary heart disease and violence. Epidemiology is the basic science of public health; it focuses on the distribution of disease in populations and on the factors that explain that distribution. The field of *social* epidemiology is a subfield of epidemiology that deals with social factors as explanatory variables.

In this chapter, we review some research that is now being done by social epidemiologists to explain disease distributions. We have divided this review into eight areas of research: social class, social support, work, children, gender, family, social areas, and racial discrimination. As will be evident, the research in some of these areas is fairly extensive, while in others, work is in the very early stages. In all areas, however, we emphasize gaps in knowledge and the issues that need to be studied in the future. Our argument is that this future research would benefit enormously by a closer collaboration between social epidemiologists and medical sociologists.

Both social epidemiologists and medical sociologists study many of the very same concepts—but from different perspectives and for different reasons. There are gaps in knowledge in both fields. It is our view that the work of both disciplines would be enhanced by

collaboration. The purpose of this chapter is to facilitate this process.

SOCIAL CLASS

People in lower social class positions have higher rates of virtually every disease. In 1967, Aaron Antonovsky reviewed this topic and found it to be a consistent observation dating from the twelfth century. In a massive report published in 1973, Kitagawa and Hauser found that mortality rates in the United States varied dramatically by social class for both men and women, whether social class was studied in terms of education, income, or occupation. Those in lower class positions had higher death rates for virtually every cause of death and higher morbidity rates for a wide range of conditions, including mental illness, depression, unhappiness, worry, anxiety and hopelessness. This observation has been made by many other investigators and is one of the most persistent and well-recognized facts in public health.

Based on this observation, many have concluded that poverty is a major risk factor for disease. Poverty can be seen to lead to inaccessible medical care, inadequate nutrition, unsafe housing, low levels of education, and other problems that can affect health. It is of course difficult to disentangle the relative importance of these various factors, and it is therefore difficult to decide which of them should be the target of intervention efforts. As a result, most epidemiologists pay little attention to social class except to hold it constant in statistical analysis: If there is little that can be done to "fix" the problem, they see little reason to study it.

Michael Marmot and his associates (1978) took a different approach. They studied disease in British civil servants and found that those in the lowest occupational grades (mainly unskilled manual workers) had rates of coronary heart disease (CHD) four times higher than those in the highest grade (heads of agencies). After they took account of such CHD risk factors as serum cholesterol, cigarette smoking, blood pressure, physical activity, glucose intolerance, and social support, the difference in rates between those at the top and bottom of the civil service hierarchy was reduced to three times. However, about 60 percent of the difference in CHD rates remained after this adjustment. The most interesting thing about these findings was that workers in civil service grade 2 (professionals and executives) and grade 3 (clerical workers) had CHD rates 2 and 3.2 times as high as heads of agencies. People in grades 2 and 3 did not have inadequate medical care, low income, poor nutrition, substandard housing, or low levels of education, and yet they had higher CHD rates than people in grade 1. What would explain this gradient?

The social class gradient is not unique to British civil servants. It has been observed in a wide variety of populations in many different countries for many body systems, including the digestive, genito-urinary, respiratory, circulatory, nervous, blood, and endocrine systems. It also has been documented for most malignancies, congenital anomalies, infectious and parasitic diseases, injury, poisoning and violence, perinatal mortality, diabetes, and musculoskeletal impairments (Adler et al. 1994). David Barker (1996) has suggested that the origins of this gradient can be seen in-utero. John L. Lynch and colleagues (1997) have shown that a large number of health behaviors and psychological orientations also are graded in adulthood, according to social class position in childhood, adolescence, and adulthood.

For social epidemiologists the importance of this research on the gradient is that it may allow us to identify risk factors that are amenable to intervention. Thus, while those in the lowest social class may have many risk factors inextricably intertwined with each other, this is not true for people in higher social classes. If we can identify factors that explain the higher rates of disease among people in higher social classes, we may be able to develop practical interventions to prevent these higher rates. For example, it may be that as one moves down the social class hierarchy, one has less control of the events that influence life (Syme 1990). Robert Karasek and Tores Theorell (1990) have found higher rates of disease among workers who have heavy job demands and little latitude and discretion for dealing with those demands. If this idea is supported by further research, it would be possible to develop interventions in children (Berrueta-Clement et al. 1984) and adults (Syme 1997) that could increase their ability to deal with life challenges and thereby lower the risk of disease. In any case, social class is a major risk factor for disease, and we need to learn more about the ways in which it influences health and about ways to deal with it in intervention programs.

A new area of research related to social class is that of income inequality. In this work, higher rates of disease have been observed in populations where there exists greater inequality in income compared to those with more egalitarian distributions (Wilkinson 1992; Kaplan et al. 1996; Wolff 1995). This finding suggests that low income in itself may not be a problem, but that relative deprivation may be the issue. This work raises interesting new questions that need to be considered by both medical sociologists and social epidemiologists.

SOCIAL SUPPORT

In 1897, Emile Durkheim (1951) suggested that social integration was an important factor in determining the rate of suicide in various groups. By this term, Durkheim was referring to the extent to which individuals were integrated into social life. Epidemiologists have long recognized that married people have better health than those single, widowed, or divorced, even after adjustments are made for such risk factors as age, smoking, blood pressure, and obesity. John Cassel (1976) suggested that the lack of social connection (such as disruption of marriage or moving to a new social setting) was associated with a wide range of disease outcomes. One of the first empirical studies on the effects of social support on health was a study by Katherine Nuckulls and colleagues (1972) on complications of pregnancy and delivery among 107 women with a similar demographic background. Among women who experienced many life changes before or during pregnancy and who also reported poor social support, 90 percent had one or more complications of pregnancy, while the other groups had much lower rates.

Social support subsequently was studied in a much larger community sample in Alameda County, California (Berkman and Syme 1979). In that study, an increased mortality rate was seen among persons previously identified as having fewer friends and social relationships. This study was done on a random sample of 6,928 adults whose mortality experience was monitored for nine years following a baseline interview. Those with fewer ties had mortality rates 2 to 3 times higher than those with strong ties, even after account had been taken of such other risk factors as weight, smoking, alcohol consumption, physical activity, health practices, and health status at the baseline interview. Following the Alameda County study, many other studies have been done that generally, but not consistently, support the hypothesis that weakened social ties are related to higher rates of disease (House et al. 1982; Cohen and Syme 1985). In most of these studies, lack of social support was found to be a risk factor for men; in several studies in small towns, however, it was not a risk factor for women. In a study done among Japanese men and women in Hawaii, lack of social support was not a risk factor for either group. One of the conclusions reached in a review of this mixed pattern of results is that something of importance clearly is going on but that the precise elements of this "something" are not yet clear.

For example, it may be that a few simple questions about relationships (e.g., about marriage, clubs, or number of friends) may be enough in a large, urban area like Alameda County, California, to separate those with ties from those without ties, but they may not be precise enough in smaller, more rural communities. This may be especially true for women. It may be that more sensitive, detailed, and culturally appropriate questions about relationships may be necessary in small towns and in close-knit groups such as Japanese Americans in Hawaii. In addition, it will be important to consider the idea of mutual support. Thus, a person not only receives support from others, but gives support to them as well.

Further research will be necessary to better define the relative importance of various dimensions of social networks and social support for health, and this work would be strengthened if medical sociologists and social epidemiologists collaborated more than is now the case.

WORK

Bertil Gardell (1980), a Swedish sociologist, argued that work is one of the most important sources of social and psychological well-being and that it provides much of the meaning and structure in adult life. He urged that researchers study both the ways in which work can kill the human spirit and the ways in which it can encourage the development of full human potential. While this view may seem obvious, it has been very difficult to do high-quality research to demonstrate that Gardell is right. Many different approaches to the study of work have yielded confusing and contradictory findings. Some early studies found "stressful" work to be a risk factor for disease, but others were unable to confirm this finding. However, in 1983 Melvin Kohn and Carmi Schooler suggested that "occupational self-direction" was an important concept in psychological functioning, and in 1979, Robert Karasek began an important research program supporting that idea. Over the succeeding years, Karasek and his colleague, Tores Theorell, (1990) have shown that disease rates and quality of life are negatively affected when workers experience high job demands coupled with low authority and little flexibility in dealing with those demands. Their early studies on this concept were done on machine-paced auto workers, lumber mill employees, and later, among 23 other blue-collar and white-collar occupations. In an interesting addition to the work of Karasek and Theorell, Jeffrey Johnson and Ellen Hall (1988) found that social support is an important moderating force in the demand-latitude process. Current work in this area now deals with demand, latitude, and social support.

As noted in the discussion of social class in this chapter, there is some thought that the idea of demand and latitude may be central in explaining some of the gradients of disease we see according to social class. In their study of British civil servants, Marmot and his group (1978) attempted to explain the gradient by taking account of several dozen important risk factors, but none of these adjustments diminished the gradient. For example, even after information on such risk factors as smoking, blood pressure, and physical activity were taken into account, the gradient in disease remained. A possible explanation for the gradient might be that of *control* (Syme 1990). Thus, the lower one is in the occupational hierarchy, the less control one has of events that impinge on life. Marmot and his associates (1997) recently added the concept of control to their analyses, with the result that the gradient disappeared. This finding suggests that differences in disease rates between job grades and social class groups may be due to differences in the ability, opportunity, or training that people have in controlling the events that impinge on their lives.

This research on demand-latitude and control is in a very early stage, and there is considerable opportunity for innovative thinking. A network now exists to bring researchers from various disciplines in contact with one another to study these issues. This network can be found on the Internet at www.workhealth.org.

Johannes Siegrist (1996) has recently proposed another way to look at work stress: an effort-reward imbalance model. This model hypothesizes that higher rates of disease will be seen when there is an imbalance between personal effort (competitiveness, overcommitment to work, and hostility) and rewards (promotions and blocked careers). In his six-and-a-half-year prospective study of 416 male, blue-collar workers, Siegrist has shown a six-fold increase in cardiovascular events among workers with an effort-reward imbalance.

It is clear that work is of central importance for health and well-being and that further research is warranted on it. From this increased understanding will come new ideas for interventions so that, as Gardell hoped, work can better nourish the human spirit.

CHILDHOOD

In spite of the fact that we have made important progress in understanding risk factors for disease, there are major gaps in our knowledge. For example, the risk for the most aggressively and successfully studied disease, coronary heart disease, clearly is raised by such factors as high serum cholesterol, hypertension, cigarette smoking, physical inactivity, and obesity. In spite of this knowledge, 60 percent of people who develop this disease have none of the known risk factors (Marmot and Winkelstein 1975). This situation is roughly similar for most other major diseases. And even when we have identified important risk factors, we have substantial difficulty in helping people change behavior to lower their risk (Syme 1997). Part of the explanation for these problems is that we are dealing with complex issues that are difficult to define and measure. But part of the difficulty may be that we typically study adults, when we should perhaps be studying infants and children.

Many risk factors can be identified early in life. These include blood pressure (Kuller et al. 1980; Rosner et al. 1977), obesity (Clarke et al. 1986), cholesterol (Venters 1986), respiratory function (Samet et al. 1983), and even temperament (Kagan 1994). It may be that by the time we study adults 40 or 50 years later, the impact of these risk factors is blurred and can no longer be clearly seen. Thus, it may be that the major impact of risk factors takes place early in life, and that the risk factors we study in adults represent only a rough measure of that early impact. More important is the fact that if we intervene on risk factors early in life, we may be able to lower disease risk in a much more effective way than we are able to do later in life.

One of the most intriguing findings in this area involves a follow-up study of children enrolled in an early education program (Berrueta-Clement et al. 1984). This study reported a twenty-two-year follow-up of low-income children three and four years of age, from Ypsilanti, Michigan. These children had been randomly assigned either to a special program offering education prior to enrollment in regular school or to no program. Children who had one or two years of early education were more likely than those in the control group to complete high school and be employed and were less likely to have been arrested or have been on public assistance; for girls, they were less likely to have had a teenage pregnancy. Since these children were assigned at random to the program, these reported differences are probably attributable to the program itself and not to such other factors as motivated parents or differences in baseline intellectual level. It is interesting that one or two years of exposure to an early-education program would, at age 19, make such a difference in life circumstances. We have no direct evidence from the Ypsilanti study that these life changes have any effect on risk of heart or other diseases. The study of British civil servants, however, clearly demonstrates that heart disease rates are lower among people with more control over their lives; the data from Ypsilanti suggest that early education can enhance control.

It is hardly original to suggest that experiences in early life are important for later life. In spite of the fact that this relationship is well-known, it is difficult to find solid research evidence demonstrating this phenomenon. Many pediatricians and child-development experts feel that early experiences are important but base their view on personal experience and on intuition. They have so little data to rely on because it is difficult to do follow-up research covering 40 or 50 years. Nevertheless, if one could review the data already available in many long-term data sets, it might be possible to document more precisely how much tracking really occurs and with what strength. If certain physical or psychological traits are established early in life and continue to be present later in life, are we doomed as adults? What other factors modify the impact of early experiences? One interesting study of high-risk children in Kauai, Hawaii (Werner 1989), for example, suggests that subsequent life events can buffer or ameliorate earlier experiences and that childhood "high-risk" status can in fact be modified.

If it could be established more clearly that certain risk factors are initiated early in life, it might be more appropriate to initiate interventions at that time instead of many years later. While it might make intuitive sense that interventions early in life will result in better health later in life, we have little solid research to demonstrate this because of the long follow-up effort needed. For this reason, it is difficult to shift the financial and organizational resources necessary to do this kind of follow-up without a sound body of research evidence to support it. In any case, given our difficulty in making sense of risk factors in the adult years and of developing effective intervention programs in adults, it may be useful now to at least raise this issue for debate and study.

GENDER AND HEALTH: SEX DIFFERENTIALS VERSUS SOCIAL ROLES

Examining the role of gender on health requires understanding of two different dimensions of the problem: (1) sex differences in disease, and (2) the influence of social roles on health and disease. While it is a commonly recognized distinction in sociology, not all epidemiologists pay attention to the difference between *sex* and *gender*. The importance of this distinction is illustrated by reference to research on sex differentials in disease (Wingard 1984; Macintyre et al. 1996). A large body of literature shows that women live longer but that they also report more illness than men. Most of the epidemiologic literature on sex explores the biological basis for these differences. On the other hand, consideration of gender would lead to an exploration of social roles in the production of differences in disease rate. By ignoring the distinction between sex and gender, research proceeds along very different paths with dramatically different results.

In a classic epidemiologic study examining sex differences in mortality risk, Wingard (1982) analyzed data from the Alameda County Study. Without adjusting for potential confounders, men had a 50 percent increased risk of mortality compared to women. One might think that this difference in mortality rates would be eliminated if account was taken of a series of risk factors that men are exposed to more often than women. Wingard adjusted for age, race, socioeconomic status, occupation, physical health status, use of health services, smoking, alcohol consumption, physical activity, weight, sleeping patterns, marital status, social contacts, church and group membership, and life satisfaction. Instead of observing the elimination of the higher rate among men, she reported that men then had a 70 percent increased mortality risk. Wingard (1984) wrote an extensive literature review that examined the possible biological, social, and behavioral explanations for the observed morbidity and mortality differentials. She concluded that reporting does not explain the observed health differential. She found that even after adjusting for social characteristics and differences (marriage, parenthood, employment, and behavior, e.g., smoking, type A behavior), a sex differential remained in morbidity and mortality. Clearly, there is more to learn about why men and women have different disease rates. And certainly much remains to be uncovered about social definitions of roles and the social construction of gender as it relates to health behaviors and health status.

More recently, health researchers have studied HIV infection as a way to explore the intersection of ethnicity, social class, and sexuality (Farmer et al. 1996). They argue that understanding HIV infection in women cannot be done with only biological information, noting that the women who are infected are exposed to a wide variety of economic, political, social, and biologic circumstances that affect disease circumstances. The numbers are telling. In the United States, by the end of 1995, 75 percent of the AIDS cases among women were among black or Latina women (Centers for Disease Control and Prevention 1996). In 1994, AIDS was the leading cause of death for African-American women age 25 to 44, and the death rate for them was nine times higher than for white women (Centers for Disease Control and Prevention 1994). These differences in rates among groups of women suggest that powerful social and cultural forces are involved in the cause of this disease.

Sally Zierler and Nancy Krieger (1997) contrast individual-level and structural-level frameworks for studies of occurrence of HIV infection in women. For example, a biomedical framework assumes that disease occurrence is based on individual susceptibility to biologic, chemical, or physical exposures. A behavioral framework assumes that individuals can voluntarily alter their ways of living. A feminist framework assumes that "women's position and experiences in society are determined by social roles and conventions, not by biology."

Standard epidemiologic studies have documented sex differences from a variety of health outcomes but have been unable to identify the underlying causes for the differences. Social factors such as social networks and marital status have been included in the explanatory models with little to no effect on the observed risk differences. And with little explicit guidance by social theory, we are not clear about exactly what we are adjusting for in these models. By incorporating sociological perspectives on gender and social roles, we might be able to uncover the important factors that cause differences in rates of particular diseases in men and women.

FAMILY AND HEALTH

Increasingly, social epidemiologists are recognizing the family as an important factor influencing individual health status. The family can be viewed as the most proximal social environment to the individual, influencing important health-related behaviors such as diet, exercise, and smoking. Very little epidemiologic research has been conducted to investigate the relationship between the family and an individual's health. Here are examples of a few studies that have been done.

Lawrence Fisher and colleagues (1992a) recruited families and measured four family domains: (1) worldview—spectrum of beliefs, values, sentiments, and expectations; (2) emotion management—how emotion is expressed, acknowledged, and managed by the family; (3) structure/organization—the style and pattern of family organization, the architecture of the family, and the structural frame within which the family operates; and (4) problem solving—ways in which the family conducts itself to resolve a shared problem. Health was assessed with self-report scales of previous health, functional capacity, illness, current health, and expectations for future (Fisher 1992a, 1992b; Ransom 1992a, 1992b; The California Family Health Project 1992). They found that levels of "aggressive emotional distancing, active guilt induction, and overt hostility" were negatively associated with the husband's general well-being and positively associated with husband's depression, and that an organized cohesive family pattern was positively correlated with general well-being and negatively correlated with depression and problem drinking.

In a very different approach to family and health, William Dressler (1994) has studied lifestyle incongruity and health. By lifestyle incongruity, he means a situation in which one attempts to maintain a high status lifestyle in the context of low occupational or educational status (Dressler 1993). Lifestyle is measured by ownership of consumer durables (e.g., refrigerators, microwave ovens), technological items (e.g., televisions and cameras), and self-reported behaviors (e.g., watching television, going to the movies, traveling for leisure). Dressler reported that family job stressors and lifestyle incongruity were the most important variables that distinguish families with and without chronically ill members.

W. Thomas Boyce and colleagues (1977) hypothesized that: (1) intensity of life change would be associated with more frequent or more severe respiratory illness in children; and (2) family routines would buffer negative intense life changes. They tested their hypothesis by investigating the incidence of respiratory infections in a sample of children in day care. From interviews with nonstudy families, the researchers devised a list of common daily or weekly routines. Children's life events score correlated with the severity, but not the frequency, of respiratory illnesses. And contrary to the authors' hypothesis, family routines contributed to illness severity, especially in the presence of high stress. They considered that children in more routinized families may be more stressed than protected by the routines when major life changes occur.

Annette Beautrais and colleagues (1982) in New Zealand conducted a large-scale study on family life events and overall childhood morbidity. They followed a group of one-year-olds for three years, asking their mothers to report family life events that were not likely to have been influenced by illness in the child. Morbidity was strongly associated with life events. Children from families with the highest number of life events had six times as many hospitalizations as children from the families with the lowest number of life events.

Research on the topic of family and health provides a good example of both the tensions between epidemiology and sociology and the possibilities for important collaboration. There are tensions between the methods we use. As epidemiologists, we tend to assign or assume directionality to our research questions. So, we argue, families affect individuals and lead to changes in health. As a result, our methods have directionality. Most commonly, we use linear and logistic regression or standardized ratios. Statistical methods such as latent variable analysis, path analysis, and structural equation modeling—common to sociology—are just beginning to be used by epidemiologists. These methods do not assume directionality and can accommodate a model like the following: Families affect and are affected by individuals; this in turn, affects and is affected by health.

As in other topics discussed in this chapter, the field of epidemiology is lacking in theory to assess family. Epidemiologists will need to clarify what we mean by "family." Is it the biological family? The extended family? The household regardless of biological relationship? Obviously, research on this issue will benefit from better collaboration between epidemiologists and sociologists.

SOCIAL AREAS AND SOCIAL ENVIRONMENT

There is a distinguished tradition in sociology that has developed theories about how the social environment is important for health. This tradition can be traced back to the 1920s and 1930s when the Chicago School of Sociology was being established. At that time, Robert Park and Ernest Burgess (1925), and later, Louis Wirth (1938) developed ecologic models for urban areas describing patterns and consequences for the growth of cities. Other researchers associated with this group developed concepts of social disorganization and social control to understand life in these areas. Robert Faris and H. Warren Dunham (1939) examined the relationship between social disorganization and rates of hospitalization for mental disorders. They measured social disorganization with several indices, including percentage of foreign-born residents in the community, number of restaurants, infant mortality rate, percentage of families living in multiple-family dwellings, percentage of persons living in hotels, and percentage of adults who completed less than nine grades in school. In the 1940s, Clifford Shaw and Henry McKay (1942) further developed the concept of social disorganization by examining data from cities all over the United States. They demonstrated a consistent pattern of association between juvenile-delinquency rates and poor housing, poverty, concentration of foreign born, prevalence of tuberculosis, and prevalence of mental disorders. Later, Eshref Shevky, Marilyn Williams, and Wendell Bell proposed a form of "social area analysis" (Shevky and Williams 1949; Shevky and Bell 1955). A social area contained persons with similar social positions in the larger society. Social areas were created by classifying census tracts based on social urbanization.

Social epidemiologists have recognized the importance of area characteristics for disease prevention and health promotion, and some important research has been done on this topic. In 1987, Mary Haan, George Kaplan, and Terry Camacho presented findings from the Alameda County Study demonstrating that residence in a federally designated poverty area was associated with an approximately 50 percent increased risk of all-cause mortality over nine years, even after adjusting for individual-level confounders. More recently, Irene H. Yen and George A. Kaplan (1998, 1999) found that residing in a poverty area also predicted a decline in physical activity levels, an increased risk of developing depressive symptoms, and a decline in perceived health status, adjusting for individual-level confounders. In these studies, poverty area was defined by combining the proportion of families with low income, of substandard housing, of adults with low educational attainment, of unemployed, of unskilled male laborers, and of children in homes with a single parent.

In other studies, Patricia O'Campo and colleagues (1997) examined the relationship between neighborhood-level variables and risk of low birthweight. To describe the neighborhood, they used data on the ratio of home owners to renters, number of community groups, unemployment rate, rate of housing violations, per capita crime rate, average wealth, and per capita income. They found that residents of census tracts with lower per capita income had a significantly higher risk of low birth weight than women living in census tracts with higher per capita income. They also found that as the unemployment rate increased, the protective effect of early prenatal care initiation diminished. Ana V. Diez-Roux and colleagues (1997) reported that living in more disadvantaged neighborhoods was associated with increased odds of smoking, increased blood pressure, and increased serum cholesterol after adjusting for individual-level factors.

The epidemiologic research linking disease to social areas and the social environment has drawn extensively from early research in sociology. However, many questions remain to be answered, and continued collaboration between investigators in the two disciplines would be productive. For example, all the research mentioned above defined neighborhoods using census-tract boundaries. While it is a practical definition, it is not a realistic one. Most people do not know where their census tract begins and ends. People's concept of, activity within, and exposure to their neighborhood depends on a number of factors, such as their age, their household (e.g., people with young children will tend to interact with other people with young children in a neighborhood), and the physical characteristics of the area (e.g., street lighting, traffic, open space). If these ideas are pursued, we will be better able to clarify the roles of "neighborhood" and "area" on health promotion and disease causation, and this clarification can lead to better programs to prevent disease.

HEALTH EFFECTS OF RACIAL DISCRIMINATION

A large body of epidemiologic literature is available showing racial differences in disease occurrence. Social epidemiologists have argued that while race has a physical manifestation, it is not a discrete biological characteristic, but rather a socially constructed concept. Indeed, it may be that the health-relevant aspects of race are the consequences of discrimination. James Jackson and co-authors (1996) have suggested three causal pathways whereby discrimination on the basis on race could affect the health status of African Americans. First, discrimination can lead to differences in the quality and quantity of medical care. Second, discrimination can contribute to different life chances and living conditions, such as housing, employment, and education. Poorer life chances are associated with low socioeconomic status, which is a strong predictor of poor health. Third, the experience of unfair treatment based on one's race may cause psychological distress and accompanying physiological injury. A few studies have examined the relationship between discrimination and mental health or psychological outcomes (Salgado de Snyder 1987; Amaro et al. 1987; Williams and Chung 1996). Only a handful of epidemiologic studies that examine the relationship between discrimination and physical-health outcomes have been conducted.

Nancy Krieger (1990) studied black and white women and found that racial discrimination was associated with hypertension. Black women who responded passively to discrimination were four times more likely to have high blood pressure than those who coped actively. In another study, Krieger and Stephen Sidney (1996) investigated the association between experiences with racial discrimination and blood pressure in a population of black men and women age 25 to 37 years old. They found that experiences with discrimination affected blood pressure differently depending on the individual's social-class level. Among working-class black men and women, blood pressure was highest among those who reported no experiences of racial discrimination.

Jackson and co-authors (1996) investigated the independent effects of racism on physical health status over a 13-year period, adjusting for poverty status, education, sex, age, region, and previous health status. Two measures of racism were used: (1) a perception of whites' intentions (choose from: whites want to keep blacks down; whites want to see blacks get a better break; whites just don't care one way or the other about blacks); and (2) whether in the past month they or their family had been treated badly because of their race. In cross-sectional analyses, respondents who reported that whites want to keep blacks down had more physical health problems. However, the longitudinal results did not show strong health effects.

Even though only a few epidemiologic studies have been done on the health effects of racial discrimination, the findings are already compelling. There is evidence that racial discrimination does have adverse health consequences. There is also evidence that individual reaction to discrimination differs, and types of reactions are related to health consequences. Racial discrimination is a complex concept with social, economic, and psychological meaning. Racial discrimination can manifest at different levels: (1) *interpersonal:* between co-workers, in public with service workers, between neighbors; (2) *institutional:* company hiring and promotion policies, criminal justice-system practices; and (3) *social:* from popular media images, news stories. Advancing this line of inquiry will be served well by a collaboration between epidemiologists and sociologists to address measurement and interpretation issues.

DISCUSSION

As noted in the introduction to this chapter, both social epidemiologists and medical sociologists are concerned with social factors and health. Social epidemiologists are interested in studying the distribution of disease in populations and in understanding the role of social factors in explaining that distribution. The topics reviewed in this chapter reveal many gaps in the knowledge that social epidemiologists have developed. These gaps have seriously compromised our understanding of the causes of disease, and they have made it difficult for social epidemiologists to develop effective interventions to prevent disease. A closer collaboration between social epidemiologists and medical sociologists would go a long way toward solving some of these problems.

As was evident in the studies reviewed in the chapter, the major focus of research in social epidemiology is on disease; the social epidemiologist makes use of as many social concepts as possible to help explain disease distributions. The social epidemiologist's choice of social factors is typically heuristic: If a social factor predicts disease occurrence, use it; if it does not, exclude it. In this use, little attention is paid to the theory underpinning the concept or to its relationship with other concepts. As a consequence, social epidemiologists have accumulated a substantial amount of information about a large number of social factors without knowing much about how these factors are interrelated. For the most part, social epidemiology is a field driven by empirical observations and not by theory.

On the other hand, medical sociologists typically are more interested in social concepts per se. For example, the medical sociologist might study the relationship between social class and coronary heart disease. If an interesting relationship is found, the inquiry may be broadened to include the study of other diseases. In any case, interest typically is focused on better understanding of the concept of social class; the diseases being studied are merely useful and convenient means of achieving such understanding. The results from such work are directed more to the enrichment of social theory than to understanding the causes of disease.

In brief, the social epidemiologist is fundamentally interested in learning about the nature of human disease by studying social characteristics, while the medical sociologist seeks to learn about the social characteristics of human populations by studying the occurrence of disease. The social epidemiologist typically focuses on one disease in order to determine all the relevant "causes" of it; the sociologist typically seeks to uncover all of the relevant disease consequences of a social condition.

There are two problems faced by epidemiologists that would especially benefit from a sociological perspective. One of these problems is that epidemiology, and the field of public health in general, focuses much of its attention and energy on the individual. There is in epidemiology much work on such individual risk factors as serum cholesterol levels, blood pressure, smoking behavior, physical activity, diet, and obesity. Accordingly, most intervention efforts in public health are designed to get people to lower their risk by changing behavior. These programs are not nearly as successful as one might hope, and one of the reasons for this ineffectiveness is that the social dimension surrounding these issues is largely ignored. Individuals, of course, live in social groups, and these groups exert powerful pressures on individuals to initiate and maintain behaviors. Without taking these forces into account, we tend to fail to recognize that social and community factors are involved in disease etiology and are of crucial importance in behavior change. The central thesis of Durkheim's work on suicide a century ago needs to be emphasized in public health today. The rates of disease in a community are a *social* fact, and the prevention of disease must be seen as a *social* issue. To do this work, epidemiologists will need to learn how to study groups and communities as topics in their own right and not simply as collections of individuals. Closer collaboration between epidemiologists and medical sociologists could be of great importance in this work.

The second problem is that most research in epidemiology is tightly focused on such diseases as coronary heart disease, cancer, and arthritis. While this is reasonable for some purposes, it is not a useful perspective for most of the health problems we face today. For example, the importance of studying children has been emphasized in this chapter. Epidemiologists have not studied children, in part because children do not have *enough* disease. Until 10 to 20 years ago, epidemiologists did not study the elderly because older people have *too many* diseases, and this pattern did not fit well into the usual clinical model. As noted in the discussion of the eight topics presented in this chapter, a disease focus does not help social epidemiologists or in developing interventions. Epidemiologists need to move away from a disease focus and concentrate instead on such issues as appropriate child development for children and effective functioning for the elderly. A sociological perspective that is not so firmly rooted in a disease model could be of great value in helping epidemiologists and others in public health to develop a more appropriate perspective on outcomes. This would allow us to much more effectively study the health consequences associated with gender, discrimination, social support, social class, family, work, social areas, and children.

Medical sociologists would benefit from a closer collaboration with social epidemiologists. In studying the health consequences of social factors, medical sociologists would find useful a review of the extensive epidemiologic data that has been collected in studies of particular diseases. These data would provide a solid empirical grounding for the development of social theory. When contrasting conceptual models are being considered, it often is useful to test their relative value in predicting specific disease outcomes. In addition, several longitudinal sets that would be of value to sociologists interested in studying the life course and the intergenerational transmission of values, attitudes, and beliefs have been developed by epidemiologists.

The time is ripe for such collaboration. Epidemiologists increasingly are turning their attention to such nontypical topics as violence, injury, and levels of functioning among the elderly. Instead of studying coronary heart disease only in men, much research in now being done in women. Instead of doing research primarily among middle-class people, investigations increasingly are being done in other populations, especially among the poor and ethnic minorities. Input from medical sociologists regarding social theory would benefit enormously this epidemiologic work. Medical sociologists would benefit from such collaboration by more closely linking their theoretical work to outcome variables that we all care about. This is a good time to begin thinking about joining forces.

REFERENCES

ADLER, NANCY E., W. THOMAS BOYCE, MARGARET A. CHESNEY, SHELDON COHEN, SUSAN FOLKMAN, ROBERT L. KAHN, and S. LEONARD SYME. 1994. "Socioeconomic Status and Health: The Challenge of the Gradient." *American Psychologist* 49:15–24.

AMARO, HORTENSIA, NANCY F. RUSSO, and JULIE JOHNSON. 1987. "Family and Work Predictors of Psychological Well-Being Among Hispanic Women Professionals." *Psychology of Women Quarterly* 11: 505–21.

ANTONOVSKY, AARON. 1967. "Social Class, Life Expectancy and Overall Mortality." *Milbank Memorial Fund Quarterly* 45:31–73.

BARKER, DAVID. 1996. "Growth in Utero and Coronary Heart Disease." *Nutrition Reviews* 54: S1–7.

BEAUTRAIS, ANNETTE L., DAVID M. FERGUSSON, and FREDERICK T. SHANNON. 1982. "Life Events and Childhood Morbidity: A Prospective Study." *Pediatrics* 70: 935–40.

BERKMAN, LISA F., and S. LEONARD SYME. 1979. "Social Networks, Host Resistance, and Mortality: A Nine Year Follow-up Study of Alameda County Residents." *American Journal of Epidemiology* 109: 186–204.

BERRUETA-CLEMENT, JOHN R., LAWRENCE J. SCHWEINHART, W. STEVEN BARRET, ANN S. EPSTEIN, and DAVID P. WEIKART. 1984. *Changed Lives: The Effects of the Perry Preschool Program on Youths Through Age 19.* Ypsilanti, MI: High/Scope Press.

BOYCE, W. THOMAS, ERIC W. JENSEN, JOHN C. CASSEL, ALBERT M. COLLIER, ALLAN H. SMITH, and CRAIG T. RAMEY. 1977. "Influence of Life Events and Family Routines on Childhood Respiratory Illness." *Pediatrics* 60: 609–15.

CASSEL, JOHN. 1976. "The Contribution of the Social Environment to Host Resistance." *American Journal of Epidemiology* 104:107–23.

CENTERS FOR DISEASE CONTROL AND PREVENTION. 1994. "Update: Mortality Attributable to HIV Infection Among Persons Aged 25–44 years—United States." *Morbidity and Mortality Weekly Report* 45(6): 121–24.

CENTERS FOR DISEASE CONTROL AND PREVENTION. 1996. *1995 HIV/AIDS Surveillance Report.* Atlanta: U.S. Department of Health and Human Services, Public Health Service, 7 (no.2).

CLARKE, WILLIAM R., ROBERT F. WOOLSON, and RONALD M. LAUER. 1986. "Changes in Ponderosity and Blood Pressure in Childhood: The Muscatine Study." *American Journal of Epidemiology* 124: 195–206.

COHEN, SHELDON, and S. LEONARD SYME. 1985. *Social Support and Health.* New York: Academic Press.

DIEZ-ROUX, ANA V., JAVIER NIETO, CARLES MUNTANER, HERMAN A. TYROLER, GEORGE W. COMSTOCK, EYAL SHAHAR, LAWTON S. COOPER, ROBERT L. WATSON, and MOYSES SZKLO. 1997. "Neighborhood Environments and Coronary Heart Disease: A Multilevel Analysis." *American Journal of Epidemiology* 146: 48–63.

DRESSLER, WILLIAM W. 1993. "Social and Cultural Dimensions of Hypertension in Blacks: Underlying Mechanisms." In *Pathophysiology of Hypertension in Blacks,* ed. J. Douglas and J. Fray. New York: Oxford University Press, pp. 69–89.

DRESSLER, WILLIAM W. 1994. "Social Status and the Health of Families: A Model." *Social Science and Medicine* 39:1605–13.

DURKHEIM, EMILE. 1951. *Suicide: A Study in Sociology,* ed. and trans. G. Simpson. Glencoe, IL: Free Press.

FARIS, ROBERT E.L., and H. WARREN DUNHAM. 1960 (original 1939). *Mental Disorders in Urban Areas: An Ecological Study of Schizophrenia and Other Psychoses,* 2nd ed. New York: Hafner Publishing Company.

FARMER, PAUL, MARGARET CONNORS, and JANIE SIMMONS. 1996. *Women, Poverty, and AIDS: Sex, Drugs and Structural Violence.* Monroe, ME: Common Courage Press.

FISHER, LAWRENCE, DONALD C. RANSOM, HOWARD E. TERRY, MACK LIPKIN, and RICHARD WEISS. 1992a. "The California Family Health Project: I. Introduction and a Description of Adult Health." *Family Process* 31: 231–50.

FISHER, LAWRENCE, LINDA C. NAKELL, HOWARD E. TERRY, and DONALD C. RANSOM. 1992b. "The California Family Health Project: III. Family Emotion Management and Adult Health." *Family Process* 31: 269–87.

GARDELL, BERTIL. 1980. "Psychosocial Aspects of Industrial Product Methods." In *Society, Stress and Disease, Volume IV, Working Life,* ed. L. Levi. London: Oxford University Press, pp. 65–75.

HAAN, MARY, GEORGE A. KAPLAN, and TERRY CAMACHO. 1987. "Poverty and Health: Prospective Evidence From the Alameda County Study." *American Journal of Epidemiology* 125: 989–98.

HOUSE, JAMES S., CYNTHIA ROBBINS, HELEN L. METZNER. 1982. "The Association of Social Relationships and Activities With Mortality: Prospective Evidence From the Tecumseh Health Study." *American Journal of Epidemiology* 116: 123–40.

JACKSON, JAMES S., TONY N. BROWN, DAVID R. WILLIAMS, MYRIAM TORRES, SHERILL L. SELLERS, and KENDRICK BROWN. 1996. "Racism and the Physical and Mental Health Status of African Americans: A Thirteen Year National Panel Study." *Ethnicity and Disease* 6: 132–47.

JOHNSON, JEFFREY V., and ELLEN M. HALL. 1988. "Job Strain, Workplace Social Support and Cardiovascular Disease: A Cross-Sectional Study of a Random Sample of the Swedish Working Population." *American Journal of Public Health* 78:1336–42.

KAGAN, JEROLD. 1994. *Galen's Prophecy: Temperament in Human Nature.* New York: Basic Books.

KAPLAN, GEORGE A., ELSIE R. PAMUK, JOHN W. LYNCH, RICHARD D. COHEN, and JENNIFER L. BALFOUR. 1996. "Inequality in Income and Mortality in the United States: Analysis of Mortality and Potential Pathways." *British Medical Journal* 312:999–1003.

KARASEK, ROBERT, and TORES THEORELL. 1990. *Healthy Work: Stress, Productivity, and the Reconstruction of Working Life.* New York: Basic Books.

KARASEK, ROBERT A. 1979. "Job Demands, Job Decision Latitude and Mental Strain: Implications for Job Re-Design." *Administrative Science Quarterly* 24: 285–307.

KITAGAWA, EVELYN M., and PHILLIP M. HAUSER. 1973. *Differential Mortality in the United States.* Cambridge, MA: Harvard University Press.

KOHN, MELVIN L., and CARMI SCHOOLER. 1983. *Work and Personality: An Inquiry Into the Impact of Social Stratification.* Norwood, NJ: Ablex.

KRIEGER, NANCY. 1990. "Racial and Gender Discrimination: Risk Factors for High Blood Pressure?" *Social Science and Medicine* 30:1273–81.

KRIEGER, NANCY, and STEPHEN SIDNEY. 1996. "Racial Discrimination and Blood Pressure: The CARDIA Study of Young Black and White Adults." *American Journal of Public Health* 86:1370–78.

KULLER, LEWIS H., MARIE CROOK, and MARY J. ALMES. 1980. "Dormont High School (Pittsburgh, PA) Blood Pressure Study." *Hypertension* (Supplement I) 2:109–16.

LYNCH, JOHN L., GEORGE A. KAPLAN, and JUKKA T. SALONEN. 1997. "Why Do Poor People Behave Poorly? Variation in Adult Health Behaviors and Psychosocial Characteristics by Stages of the Socio-Economic Lifecourse." *Social Science and Medicine* 44(6): 809–19.

MACINTYRE, SALLY, KATE HUNT, and HELEN SWEETING. 1996. "Gender Differences in Health: Are Things Really As Simple As They Seem?" *Social Science and Medicine* 42: 617–24.

MARMOT, MICHAEL, and WARREN WINKELSTEIN, JR. 1975. "Epidemiologic Observations on Intervention Trials for Prevention of Coronary Heart Disease." *American Journal of Epidemiology* 101:177–81.

MARMOT, MICHAEL G., GEOFFREY ROSE, MARTIN SHIPLEY, and PATRICK J.S. HAMILTON. 1978. "Employment Grade and Coronary Heart Disease in British Civil Servants." *Journal of Epidemiology and Community Health* 3:244–49.

MARMOT, MICHAEL G., HANS BOSMA, HARRY HEMINGWAY, ERIC BRUNNER, and STEPHEN A. STANSFELD. 1997. "Contribution of Job Control and Other Risk Factors to Social Variations in Coronary Heart Disease Incidence." *The Lancet* 350: 235–39.

NUCKOLLS, KATHERINE B., JOHN CASSEL, and BERTON H. KAPLAN. 1972. "Psychosocial Assets, Life Crises, and the Prognosis of Pregnancy." *American Journal of Epidemiology* 95:431–41.

O'CAMPO, PATRICIA, XIAONAN XUE, MEI-CHENG WANG, and MARGARET O'BRIEN CAUGHY. 1997. "Neighborhood Risk Factors for Low Birthweight in Baltimore: A Multilevel Analysis." *American Journal of Public Health* 87:1113–18.

PARK, ROBERT E., and ERNEST W. BURGESS. 1925. *The City.* Chicago: University of Chicago Press.

RANSOM, DONALD C., ELIZABETH LOCKE, HOWARD E. TERRY, and LAWRENCE FISHER. 1992a. "The California Family Health Project: V. Family Problem Solving and Adult Health." *Family Process* 31: 421–31.

RANSOM, DONALD C., LAWRENCE FISHER, and HOWARD E. TERRY. 1992b. "The California Family Health Project: II. Family World View and Adult Health." *Family Process* 31: 251–67.

ROSNER, BERNARD, CHARLES H. HENNEKENS, EDWARD H. KASS, and WILLIAM E. MIALL. 1977. "Age-Specific Correlation Analysis of Longitudinal Blood Pressure Data." *American Journal of Epidemiology* 106: 306–13.

SALGADO DE SNYDER, NELLY V. 1987. "Factors Associated With Acculturative Stress and Depressive Symptomatology Among Married Mexican Immigrant Women." *Psychology of Women Quarterly* 11: 475–88.

SAMET, JONATHAN M., IRA B. TAGER, and FRANK E. SPEIZER. 1983. "The Relationship Between Respiratory Illness in Childhood and Chronic Air-Flow Obstruction in Adulthood." *American Review of Respiratory Disease* 127: 508–23.

SHAW, CLIFFORD R., and HENRY D. McKAY. 1942. *Juvenile Delinquency and Urban Areas: A Study of the Rates of Delinquents in Relation to Differential Characteristics of Local Communities in American Cities.* Chicago: University of Chicago Press.

SHEVKY, ESHREF, and MARILYN WILLIAMS. 1949. *The Social Areas of Los Angeles.* Berkeley, CA: University of California Press.

SHEVKY, ESHREF, and WENDELL BELL. 1955. *Social Area Analysis: Theory, Illustrative Application and Computational Procedures.* Westport, CT: Greenwood Press.

SIEGREST, JOHANNES. 1996. "Adverse Health Effects of High Effort/Low Reward Conditions." *Journal of Occupational Health Psychology* 1: 27–41.

SYME, S. LEONARD. 1990. "Control and Health: An Epidemiological Perspective." In *Self-Directedness: Cause and Effects Throughout the Life Course,* ed. J. Rodin, C. Schooler and K.W. Schaie. Hillsdale, NJ: Erlbaum Associates, pp. 213–29.

SYME, S. LEONARD. 1997. "Community Participation, Empowerment, and Health: Development of a Wellness Guide for California." In *The California Wellness Foundation and the University of California 1997 Wellness Lectures.* Berkeley, CA: The Regents of the University of California, pp. 147–67.

THE CALIFORNIA FAMILY HEALTH PROJECT: IV. 1992. "Family Structure/Organization and Adult Health." *Family Process* 31: 399–419.

VENTERS, MAURINE H. 1986. "Family Life and Cardiovascular Risk: Implications for the Prevention of Chronic Disease." *Social Science and Medicine* 22: 1067–74.

WERNER, EMMY. 1989. "High-Risk Children in Young Adulthood: A Longitudinal Study from Birth to 32 Years." *American Journal of Orthopsychiatry* 59: 72–81.

WILKINSON, RICHARD G. 1992. "Income Distribution and Life Expectancy." *British Medical Journal* 6820:165–68.

WILLIAMS, DAVID R., and AN-ME CHUNG. 1996. "Racism and Health." In *Health in Black America,* ed. R. Gibson and J. Jackson. Newbury Park, CA: Sage Publications.

WINGARD, DEBORAH L. 1982. "The Sex Differential in Mortality Rates: Demographic and Behavioral Factors." *American Journal of Epidemiology* 115: 205–16.

WINGARD, DEBORAH L. 1984. "The Sex Differential in Morbidity, Mortality, and Lifestyle." *Annual Review of Public Health* 5:433–58.

WIRTH, LOUIS. 1939. "Urbanism as a Way of Life." *American Journal of Sociology* 44: 3–24.

WOLFF, EDWARD N. 1995. *Top Heavy: A Study of the Increasing Inequality of Wealth in America.* New York: Twentieth Century Fund.

YEN, IRENE H., and GEORGE A. KAPLAN. 1998. "Poverty Area Residence and Change in Physical Activity Level: Prospective Evidence From the Alameda County Study." *American Journal of Public Health* 88:1709–12.

YEN, IRENE H., and GEORGE A. KAPLAN. 1999. "Poverty Area Residence and Change in Depression and Perceived Health Status." *International Journal of Epidemiology* 28: 90–94.

ZIERLER, SALLY, and NANCY KRIEGER. 1997. "Reframing Women's Risk: Social Inequalities and HIV Infection." *Annual Review of Public Health* 18:401–36.

26

"PARALLEL SISTERS": MEDICAL ANTHROPOLOGY AND MEDICAL SOCIOLOGY

MARY-JO DELVECCHIO GOOD, *Harvard Medical School*

BYRON J. GOOD, *Harvard Medical School*

In the introductory essay to the 1995 special edition of the *Journal of Health and Social Behavior* marking forty years of medical sociology, Sol Levine challenged scholars in the field to overcome "intellectual parochialism that splinters medical sociology and impedes productive discourse and the creative integration of our subject matter" (1995: 1). Levine, citing Pearlin, noted the divide between "structure seekers" and "meaning seekers," between causal and meaning-oriented theoretical models, and the concomitant divide between quantitative and qualitative methods. Levine not only pleaded with sociologists to enhance creative integration within the field, he also lauded recent efforts to draw on sister disciplines such as psychology and biology to enrich investigations, foster methodological creativity, and enliven research paradigms.

One curious disciplinary divide noted by the editors of this volume is what Peter Conrad (1997) has aptly labeled "Parallel Play in Medical Anthropology and Medical Sociology." Although scholars in the two fields often explore similar topics and utilize similar methods, there is limited cross-conversation and cross-referencing. What at times may appear to be purposive avoidance of sister disciplines arises from the social boundaries that distinguish scientific communities, differentiating outsiders from those joined in what anthropologist Paul Rabinow, following Aristotle, refers to as *philia* or friendship (1997). Among communities of medical sociologists and medical anthropologists, as among the molecular biologists studied by Rabinow (1996), "the daily life of the sciences is saturated with personal ties that serve diverse functions" (Rabinow 1997: 200): professional self-interest, the accumulation of symbolic capital, and the weaving of dense networks of scientific/epistemological practices. In the spirit of *philia* and responding to Sol Levine's challenge to bridge disciplinary chasms, this paper is intended to provide a modest account of literature in medical anthropology that addresses several themes of central concern to medical sociologists.

We begin with a brief historical overview of medical anthropology, noting ways in which this history differs from that of medical sociology. We then elaborate three conceptual and methodological areas that intersect with and have relevance for medical sociology: (1) anthropological studies of biomedicine, the biosciences, and biotechnology, (2) studies of illness narratives and "clinical narratives" emergent in clinical conversations; and (3) comparative studies of culture, mental illness, and mental health services. Although these are only examples of domains of medical anthropology of special interest to medical sociologists, we conclude by noting the importance of convergent themes and analytic approaches in these fields and by speculating on reasons for the distance that continues to separate them.

A BRIEF HISTORICAL OVERVIEW OF MEDICAL ANTHROPOLOGY

Medical anthropology has origins quite different from those of medical sociology, and while the two fields overlap far more today than in their earlier years, a brief account of medical anthropology's history helps orient the following review of several specific domains.

Although its theoretical lineage can be traced to the beginning of this century, medical anthropology as we know it today began in the 1950s, when a group of anthropologists associated with the Smithsonian Museum, headed by George Foster, began collaborating with international public health specialists. Arguing that members of societies are not "empty vessels" waiting to be filled with medical knowledge from health educators (Polgar 1963), anthropologists asserted that medical "habits and beliefs" constitute elements in an elaborate "cultural system" (Paul 1955), which public health specialists need to address. Medical anthropology thus had its origins in cultural analysis applied to practical public-health problems, situating it firmly as an applied practice. As such, it was marginal to the great theoretical debates that emerged at the heart of anthropology in the 1960s.

In the 1970s, a group of anthropologists, led by Charles Leslie and Arthur Kleinman, turned their attention to the "great traditions" of Indian and Chinese classical medicine and the local or "little traditions" of medicine in Asian societies. Drawing together anthropologists, historians, sociologists, and public-health specialists, Leslie's *Asian Medical Systems* (1976), followed by Kleinman's collection on China (Kleinman et al. 1976), moved the center of medical anthropology from a focus on small-scale, pre-literate societies and applied public health to the *comparative study of medical systems* in complex, literate civilizations and nation states. "Medical pluralism" problematized a set of phenomena and indicated issues to be addressed: relations among diverse, competing healing systems within a given society; the forms of social organization of such systems—professional, popular, and folk systems, in Kleinman's (1980) terms—and their transformation through professionalization, indigenization, and modernization; the plurality of "semantic networks" (B. Good 1977), "idioms of distress" (Nichter 1981), and "care-seeking" strategies employed by individuals, families, and "therapy management groups" (Janzen 1978); and the complexity of clinical transactions across plural cultural systems. In this perspective, biomedicine was investigated as one of a plurality of medical subsystems; Leslie proposed the term "cosmopolitan" be used, rather than "Western," "modern," or "scientific" medicine, in order to acknowledge and problematize the transnational fluidity of knowledge and practices that are unbounded but appropriated locally and regionally and integrated into local cultures (Leslie 1976: 6). Today, the plurality of medical systems is largely assumed rather than explicitly theorized in anthropological studies, but Asian medical systems continue to be the source of interdisciplinary research (e.g. Leslie and Young 1992; Cohen 1998).

While the Asian medical systems model reoriented medical anthropology toward the comparative study of medical systems, an orientation that continues to frame much of the discipline to the present, a set of critical writings and debates in the late 1970s and early 1980s established medical anthropology as a domain of intense and explicit theorizing, as well as ethnographic research and writing, political activism, and engagement with "medicine"—with physicians, public health specialists, and policy makers. Medical anthropology shifted to a central position within anthropology, and some of the most interesting theoretical issues concerning the body, suffering, scientific cultures, and institutionalized knowledge/power complexes were debated within medical anthropology.

Efforts to theorize medical anthropology began with a set of critiques of the medical social sciences, challenging their implicit acceptance of the empiricist or positivist/reductionist epistemologies of medicine and the biological sciences, and elaborating a fundamental claim that "medicine is a cultural system" (Kleinman 1980), that "illness realities are fundamentally semantic—that is, culturally or meaningfully constituted" (Good and Good 1981: 188), and that comparative studies of medical knowledge and medical practices must therefore begin as cultural analyses. Drawing on classic social constructivism combined with Geertzian interpretive anthropology, as well as semiotics, hermeneutics, phenomenology, and narrative analysis, medical anthropologists working in the interpretive tradition carried out research on the cultural shaping of illnesses, on the symbolic processes associated with diverse popular and professional medical systems, and on "embodied experience" (for a review, see B. Good 1994: 52–56; examples of key texts include Kleinman's seminal *Patients and Healers in the Context of Culture* 1980; Kleinman 1986, 1988b; B. Good 1977; Csordas 1994; Desjarlais 1992; Janzen 1978; Jenkins 1988; Pandolfi 1990). This work included ethnographic research, conducted in a wide range of societies and among special populations and clinical settings in the United States, as well as "clinically relevant" translations of anthropological concepts addressing medical educators and practitioners (e.g., Kleinman, Eisenberg, and Good 1978; Eisenberg and Kleinman 1981).

One response to the development of this explicitly "meaning-centered" (interpretive, constructivist) medical anthropology was the emergence of a self-labeled "critical" medical anthropology, aimed at investigating "health issues in light of the larger political and economic forces that pattern interpersonal relationships, shape social behavior, generate social meanings, and condition collective experience" (Singer 1990: 181). This work, linked to that of sociologists Howard Waitzkin and John McKinlay, criticized the focus on illness meanings and experience (Young 1982) and set out to study how larger social forces and political economy shape the distribution of disease and care within and among societies (see Morsy 1990 for a review). "Power" replaced "meaning" as the key term in such analysis, and special attention was given to culture as "ideologies, disguising human political and economic realities" (Keesing 1987: 161). From this perspective, cultures are analyzed as "webs of mystification as well as significance," in Keesing's phrase. Foucault's studies, Gramsci's work on hegemony, and James Scott's analyses of resistance were all drawn on for analyzing how medical meanings mystify social relations and naturalize inequalities (e.g., Frankenberg 1988; Scheper-Hughes 1992).

In the early 1980s, debates over "interpretive" and "critical" theory, ecological and empiricist models, and cognitivist research on illness representations led to the development of explicitly theorized positions in medical anthropology and sharp exchanges over the implications of particular positions (see B. Good 1994, ch. 2). By the late 1980s and the 1990s, however, several changes in the field made such neat theoretical distinctions seem less relevant. First, the field of medical anthropology had grown enormously and had become extremely specialized. In 1957, Benjamin Paul, an anthropologist at the Harvard School of Public Health, assembled the names of 49 American anthropologists with experience in public health; by the 1990s, there were more than 1,700 members of the Society for Medical Anthropology. Medical anthropologists today are often highly specialized—by region and culture area, as well as by area of research interest. Anthropologists specializing in infectious diseases and international health, AIDS/HIV, drugs and street ethnography, reproductive technologies, disabilities, high technology medicine and medical ethics, and many other topics form special-interest groups, which are often more significant than theoretical divisions.

Second, the boundaries of "medical anthropology" have been blurred by cross-cutting exchanges with other subdisciplines within anthropology. Much of the initial work on reproductive technologies and medicine was carried out by feminist anthropologists with little explicit interest in medical anthropology (e.g., Martin 1987; Rapp 1988; Ginsburg and Rapp 1995); however, this became a highly productive meeting ground between medical anthropologists and feminists, expanding and blurring the field. Much the same could be said for discussions of "the body" and recent exchanges between anthropologists interested in science studies and medical anthropologists, as we will describe below.

Third, by the 1990s, theoretical debates had shifted within anthropology at large. Debates between "symbolic anthropology" and critical theory were largely passé. The whole field had been affected by critical theory, and debates about post-structuralism, post-colonialism, experimental ethnographic writing, and transnationalism, which dominated the field at large (key examples include Marcus and Fischer 1986; Clifford 1988; Appadurai 1996), had vigorous counterparts within medical anthropology. Thus, while many of the debates of the early 1980s have lost their force, medical anthropology has continued to be a site of central debates in the field.

Rather than spell them out in general terms, we will turn to brief examinations of several subfields of medical anthropology with special interest for medical sociologists. It is, however, already possible to make several observations. Theoretical writings in medical anthropology and medical sociology share similarities in their broad historical trajectory, despite the lack of cross-referencing—with debates emerging between social constructivists or phenomenologically oriented writers and those interested in Marxism, critical theory, and political economy and then giving way to newer configurations of social theorizing. Many of the substantive areas of the fields are increasingly shared, with studies of high-technology medicine becoming increasingly important within medical anthropology, and issues of race and ethnicity becoming increasingly important within medical sociology. No neat lines between macro and micro analyses divide sociology and anthropology, as both are present in both fields. However, medical anthropology continues its clear focus on ethnographic research and ethnographic writing, and "culture" as an analytic construct and cross-cultural research continue to frame the discipline in a way that distinguishes it from most of medical sociology. These distinctions will become more apparent as we review recent work in several subfields of medical anthropology.

ANTHROPOLOGICAL STUDIES OF BIOMEDICINE, THE BIOSCIENCES, AND BIOTECHNOLOGY

As the field of medical anthropology flourished in the late 1970s and 1980s, and as a market for medical anthropologists in medical schools, public-health projects, and anthropology departments began to expand, many anthropologists who had conducted their formative field research on non-Western healing traditions turned their attention to diverse aspects of biomedicine. Some who had conducted research in societies and cultures outside North America brought their cross-cultural and comparative experience to investigations of American medicine. Others focused new attention on diverse aspects of biomedicine in Asian or African or Latin-American contexts: the production, prescription, and utilization of pharmaceuticals (e.g., Van der Geest and Whyte 1988); public-health programs (Turshen 1989; Nichter 1989; Yoder 1997); or "local" forms of "cosmopolitan" medicine (Good 1995b; Lock 1993; Ohnuki-Tierney 1994). Yet others launched a new generation of studies of health, illness, and healing activities among American ethnic groups (e.g., Harwood 1981; Gaines 1989; Guarnaccia, Good, and Kleinman 1990).

Major innovations in medical anthropology resulted from the shift in focus to the clinical culture of North American medicine and psychiatry. A collection of research-based essays, edited by Hahn and Gaines (1985) and published as *Physicians of Western Medicine,* marked a new beginning. Papers in this collection explored the culture and work of American surgeons (Katz); psychiatrists and their practices (Gaines; Rittenburg and Simons; Good et al.; Johnson); internal medicine (Hahn); medical politics, physician competence, and error (M. Good); and medical models of practice and knowledge (Maretzki; Lock; Gaines and Hahn). This book represented a serious entry of medical anthropologists into a domain long studied by medical sociologists. It legitimized anthropological work on North American and European biomedicine and launched wide-ranging studies of biomedicine by these authors and their students (e.g., Lindenbaum and Lock 1993; Lock and Gordon 1988), as well as a new generation of comparative studies in non-Western societies focusing on "local" biomedicines as a site of "traffic" in transnational knowledge forms, practices, and therapeutics (Good 1995b; cf. Brodwin 1996; Adams 1998). The rise to dominance on the 1990s of the for-profit managed-care sector of the health-care system, particularly in the United States, and the continued disparities between rich and poor nations forced anthropologists to combine cultural analysis with examinations of how political economy influences institutional structures, clinical transactions, and social trust. The transnational production and exchange of medical knowledge,

standards of care, and therapeutics have added global dimensions to medicine and medical practice seldom imagined by previous scholars.

Research on contemporary biomedicine led medical anthropologists to seriously address emergent biosciences and biotechnologies and thus to engage the larger field of social studies of science. The move from studies of biomedicine to studies of science and technology was inevitable, given the magnitude of changes in contemporary biomedicine. Advances in molecular biology, investigations of the human genome and its role in disease, and the development of space-age biotechnologies—reproductive technologies, imaging devices, routinized organ transplantation, and constantly changing therapeutic technologies—raise issues hardly conceived of as recently as a decade ago. Anthropologists studying biomedicine in the 1990s have thus explored what Marcus and Fischer (1986) referred to as "multiple regimes of truth," providing critical analyses of power/knowledge complexes embedded in technoscience, and have conducted "multi-sited" comparative ethnographic research (Marcus 1995a), drawing together in single projects divergent areas of science, technology, and clinical practice. Such research has intersected with parallel developments in both the sociology and anthropology of science and technology. A special issue of the journal *Culture, Medicine and Psychiatry—Bio-Politics: The Anthropology of the New Genetics and Immunology,* edited by Heath and Rabinow (1993), was among the initial crossings of medical anthropological inquiry with studies of the human genome and biotechnologies. Subsequent publications explicitly linking science studies and medical anthropology include Martin's innovative study of immunology (1994), papers in Marcus's collection on the "technoscientific imaginaries" (1995b), Rabinow's ethnography of a biotechnology firm and the "making of PCR" (1996), M. Good's work on oncology in diverse settings (Good 1995a, 1996; Good et al. 1990, 1993), Dumit's analysis of new medical imaging technologies (in Downey and Dumit 1997), Taussig's research on medical genetics in the Netherlands (1997), research on organ transplantation and organ sales (Ohnuki-Tierney 1994; Lock 1995), and the Downey and Dumit collection on "cyborgs and citadels" (1997). Much research by anthropologists on contemporary biomedicine explores these issues in multiple sites and locales, acknowledging transnational political economies and the cultural traffic of the biosciences across national boundaries.

This formulation, echoing recent trends in anthropological studies of "transnationality" (Appadurai

1996) and "technoscience" (Haraway 1997), highlights the dynamic relationship between the local worlds in which medicine is taught, practiced, organized, and consumed and the global worlds of the production of knowledge, technologies, markets, and clinical standards. Although anthropologists speak about a plurality of biomedicines that are socially and culturally situated rather than a single unified body of knowledge and practice, such local worlds are nevertheless "transnational" in character—neither cultural isolates nor biomedical versions of indigenous healing traditions. Local meanings and social arrangements are overlaid by global standards and technologies in nearly all aspects of local biomedicine (M. Good 1995a, 1995b).

Such a perspective continues to generate comparative questions for anthropologists. How do local and international political economies of medical research and biotechnology shape medicine's scientific imagination, the medical imaginary? Its cultural, moral, and ethical worlds? The structure of inequalities of use, access, and distribution of medicine's cultural and material "goods"? How do local and international ideologies, politics, and policies influence professional and institutional responses to specific health problems of particular societies—from the contemporary plagues of HIV or tuberculosis, to scarcity and poverty, trauma and civil strife, or to public health and profit-driven health-service markets? What form does the "political economy of hope" take? How does the culture of medicine and the production of bioscience and biotechnology "live" in respective societies and influence clinical culture? These are the questions being addressed by many medical anthropologists today, questions that are sociological as well as anthropological. They reflect, however, anthropology's continued interest in cross-national research and its current formulations of theories of culture.

NARRATIVE ANALYSIS, ILLNESS EXPERIENCE, AND THE CULTURE OF CLINICAL MEDICINE

Narrative analysis, one of the fundamental interpretive approaches of anthropologists (Ochs and Capps 1996), has increasingly become an explicit theoretical and methodological component of ethnographic research on illness experience, clinical culture, and clinician–patient transactions. Phenomenologically oriented anthropologists, such as Hallowell and Geertz, have long argued that experience is deeply cultural, organized through language and symbolic forms as well as through social

and institutional relations and practical activities in the world. Access to experience is thus mediated by cultural forms, and anthropologists argue that we often learn most about experience through *stories* people tell about things that have happened to or around them.

Narrative is a form in which experience is represented and recounted, in which events are presented as having meaningful and coherent order, and in which activities and experiences associated with events are described along with the significance that lends them their sense for the persons involved. Narratives not only report and recount experiences or events, describing them from the limited and positioned perspective of the present, they also project into the future, organizing desires and strategies, directing them toward imagined ends. Lived experience and social activities thus have a complex relationship to the stories that recount them (see Good 1994, ch. 6; cf. Mattingly 1998).

Narratives of Illness

For over a decade, a growing literature on narrative dimensions of illness, care-seeking, and therapeutic process has emerged. One stream, from literary-minded clinicians, provides detailed stories and reflections on what disease tells us about suffering and the human condition (e.g., Brody 1987). These are not unlike personal accounts of illness, an important genre that serves as primary source material for thinking about narrative structuring of illness (see Murphy 1987 for an anthropologists' reflections on his own illness experience).

A second stream of writing on narrative from qualitative sociology has had significant influence on anthropologists and is a prime example of disciplinary "cross-talk." Gareth Williams's (1984) analysis of "narrative reconstruction" and Gerhardt's conversational analysis (1990) examine the experience of chronic illness in North America and Europe. Mishler, who conducted detailed conversational analyses of clinical dialogue, exploring the "lifeworlds" of doctors and patients (1986), provided a classic analysis of physicians' interruptions of patients' stories. These works are often cited by anthropologists.

Anthropological studies of illness narratives have focused special attention on the role of culture in shaping plots, narration, and moral reasoning. Evelyn Early's work on "therapeutic narratives" in Cairo was among the first by an anthropologist to focus explicit attention on the stories told about illness and care-seeking, showing how stories embed illness and therapeutic efforts within local moral norms (Early 1982). Laurie Price (1987) and

Linda Garro (1994), cognitive anthropologists working in Ecuador and North America, respectively, demonstrated how cultural knowledge and "scripts" for care-seeking are encoded in illness narratives, whether naturally occurring or elicted through interviews.

In *The Illness Narratives,* Kleinman (1988b) combined anthropological and clinical traditions, moving comparatively between North American and Chinese cases. He demonstrated the importance of the social and cultural frames within which narratives emerge, showing how "meaning is created in illness." Narrative provided the methodological frame for an anthropological volume investigating the experience of sufferers of chronic pain (Good et al. 1992). Narratives in Kleinman were analyzed as ambiguous cultural performances (Garro, Brodwin), as modes of reconstructing lifeworlds (M. Good, B. Good), and as means of resisting disconfirming messages from clinicians (Jackson). Byron Good (1994; cf. Good and Good 1994), investigating the narrative representation of seizure disorders by patients and their families in Turkey, explored the value of reader-response theory, as well as more standard literary approaches, for analyzing temporality, the social positioning of suffering, and "subjunctivity" in illness narratives. And Cheryl Mattingly and Linda Garro (1999) have recently edited a cross-cultural collection of anthropological accounts of illness narratives.

Clinical Narratives

Within anthropology there has also been a turn toward analyzing narrative dimensions of clinical practice—the stories doctors tell each other in the construction of cases and disease entities, and the "clinical narratives" clinicians create in conversation with patients to give sense to the illness and order to the treatment. Mattingly (1998) has made extensive and explicit use of narrative theory to explore the story/experience relationship and the use of what she terms "therapeutic narratives" by American occupational therapists to organize their practice and the experiences of those they treat.

In our own research on how Harvard medical students come to enter the lifeworld of medicine and gain competence in medical practices, we found that students learn a distinctive set of narrative practices—"writing" in charts, presenting patients to other doctors, and interviewing patients in a way that will provide data for these distinctive medical narratives (Good 1994; Good 1995a; Good and Good 1999). Although clinical clerkship presentations vary by type of rounds, and oral presentations and written cases differ in structure, format, and detail, medical students discover that to be considered competent they must "edit" the common-sense "stories" of patients. Throughout clinical rotations, students are encouraged to create medically meaningful narrative arguments and plots with therapeutic consequences for patients. In these narrations, the lifeworld of patients is often regarded as "inadmissible evidence." Narrative strategies are learned—forms of argument, emplotting patients as medical mysteries or inconclusive cases—that enable students to produce distinctive stories about patients, tailored for their attending physicians, residents, and peers.

We have also drawn on narrative analysis in our ethnographic studies of high-technology medicine and the worlds of oncology to make sense of how the culture of clinical practice and patient–physician encounters are shaped by clinical science, therapeutic innovations, and "the political economy of hope" central to much of biomedicine's research enterprise (Good et al. 1990; Good 1995a, 1995b, 1996). American physicians are expected to provide patients with explicit diagnoses and to offer explanations of treatment options from oncology's vast array of treatment weapons. The expectation is cultural, one that has evolved over the past three decades in American medicine and has subsequently been institutionalized in legislative directives confirming patients' rights "to know" and "to decide" among treatment options. The conveying of hope is tied to providing information, to therapeutic action, and to a commitment to provide access to all available biotechnologies, even in an era of restrictions on health-care costs. Americans expect that societal investment in basic research and anti-cancer therapeutics will nurture breakthroughs in clinical oncology, that a master narrative of progress frames the fight against disease. Thus, medical research has broad popular support, and efforts to create a biotechnical fix are felt to justify the high investment of public funds and private monies in the National Cancer Institute, in experimental chemotherapies and clinical trials, and even in "fee-for-service" research and personally tailored oncogenetic therapies. Standards of practice in American oncology are defined in the context of this larger political economy of hope, defined as the joining of medicine's worlds of science and therapeutics by the skilled use and knowledge of the latest anti-cancer therapeutics and the artful engagement of patients in often toxic and arduous treatments journeys.

We chose the term "clinical narratives" to identify the clinical stories basic to the practice of oncology and the clinical sciences upon which the specialty is founded (Good 1995a; Good et al. 1994). Such narratives are created by physicians for and with patients over time and are about the progression of therapeutic activities and their impact on patient experience. There are multiple domains in which physicians are creators as well as "readers" or interpreters of clinical stories. They establish a therapeutic plot for patients, as a course of treatment is set in action, and they "read" the unfolding "medical plot" determined by disease process and patient response. Physicians, even within the same subspecialty, hold a variety of opinions about how best to devise appropriate clinical narratives that are therapeutic and caring. For example, the extent of disclosure of prognosis, the "aesthetics of statistics," and ways to convey realistic hope are frequently debated by oncologists.

As creators of clinical narratives, physicians also develop multiple and parallel subplots, each tailored to specific actors. These subplots include not only patients and patients' families, professional colleagues, and the treatment team, but also the research groups and scientific communities to which clinicians belong. Narratives of time, outcome, and endings may differ for each subplot, for each alternative form of the clinical story. A singular plot line or theme seldom characterizes a clinical narrative; multiple subplots and alternative readings, contributing to "subjunctivity" and an openness to unexpected sources of healing, are the norm in high-technology medicine.

As in much specialty medicine, in oncology the physician is nodal, directing the story, plotting the action, shaping the patient's experience of treatment and response, and managing the treatment team. In the worlds of clinical practice, this role is an ideal of professional power. However, institutional forces and system irrationalities, health system and economic constraints, adverse events, and fraud in clinical research (such as the scandals in the breast cancer trials) can disrupt and fragment the progression of a clinical story and wreak havoc with professional intent. In addition, patients may choose to step out of a professionally devised "plot" and seek alternative medical care. However, most patients collaborate with their physicians in creating a common story of combating disease and engaging in treatment.

Physicians are readers not only of the stories of their patients and the unfolding course of disease as clinically manifest, but also of the cultural flow from the biosciences. Bioscience narratives are brought into clinical practice not only through rank and file clinicians, but especially through the clinician investigators and teachers who set standards for competence in specialty medicine. Narratives of bioscience and technological expertise parallel even as they inform "standardized" clinical narratives, introducing "facts," ambiguities, and

uncertainties that are selectively employed by clinicians, depending on the clinical culture in which they work. Thus, physicians often integrate local cultural values with the science and therapeutics that are the foundation for standard specialty narratives. This integration is particularly evident in cross-national studies of medical culture, disclosure practices, and interactions between physicians and their patients; for example, the disclosure of diagnosis and details of treatments are usually reserved for kin in societies such as Japan and Italy (Good et al. 1993; Gordon and Paci 1997).

These anthropological studies of illness stories and clinical narratives have run parallel with sociological writing, particularly qualitative studies of illness experience and discourse analysis applied to clinical interactions. However, anthropologists have placed their writing in the context of larger cultural (or civilizational), national, and transnational analyses of medicine and medical "soteriologies," and have drawn on a variety of theoretical traditions—from hermeneutics to literary theory to post-structuralism—to frame their investigations.

CULTURE, MENTAL ILLNESS, AND CONTEMPORARY MENTAL HEALTH SERVICES

Studies of mental illness and mental-health services are also domains of overlapping interests among sociologists and anthropologists. We can only briefly sketch out areas where increased conversations would benefit both disciplines.

Anthropological studies of psychopathology are rooted historically in discussions of how culture shapes "normality" and what is considered abnormal, deviant, or illness in diverse societies (see Good 1992, 1994: 31–36, 1997; Kleinman 1988a). Edward Sapir, a founding figure in American anthropology who worked with Harry Stack Sullivan in Chicago, called for cross-ethnic and cross-cultural research "to discover what maladjustment means in the remoter cultures" (quoted in Darnell 1986: 166), and Ruth Benedict argued extensively that "those organizations of behavior that seem to us most incontrovertibly abnormal have been used by different civilizations in the very foundations of their institutional lives" (Benedict 1934: 73). Since "categories of borderline behavior which we derive from the study of the neuroses and psychoses of our civilization are categories of prevailing local types of instability," Benedict (1934: 79) argued, cross-cultural research is needed to determine whether categories of disorder are universal or culture specific. If similar arguments set sociologists off on a productive line of theorizing about the effects of social labeling on deviant experience and behavior (see Waxler 1974 for a cultural interpretation of labeling theory), these formulations led anthropologists to investigate whether mental disorders are similar or different across cultures, with special attention to the so-called "culture-bound disorders" (e.g., Simons and Hughes 1985).

In the 1980s, anthropologists turned their attention more explicitly toward investigations of specific psychiatric illnesses. This turn reflected a paradigm shift in psychiatry itself—from psychoanalytic dominance to medicalized conceptions of mental illnesses, defined operationally through diagnostic criteria—and resulting changes in psychiatric epidemiology (see Good 1992 for a critical analysis). As epidemiologists and sociologists turned from symptom levels to diagnostic entities in studies of psychopathology, anthropologists turned increasingly to studies of disorders such as depression, schizophrenia, and dissociative disorders. *Depression* was first submitted to critical, cross-cultural inquiry with Arthur Kleinman's research in China (1977, 1986) and an edited collection of anthropological studies (Kleinman and Good 1985). This work has been followed by a body of research investigating grief, depressive affect, and depression in several societies (see Jenkins, Kleinman, and Good 1991 for a review). The best full-length study to date is Theresa O'Nell's (1996) monograph on depression in an American-Indian society. Anthropological studies of *schizophrenia* have been influenced by the extraordinary findings of the World Health Organization (WHO). International Pilot Study of Schizophrenia, which demonstrated that there are great variations in course and outcome of schizophrenia cross-culturally, with higher than expected levels of "recovery" generally, and better outcomes in less highly industrialized societies (Jablenski et al. 1992; see Hopper 1991, Cohen 1992; Good 1997 for reviews). Studies seeking explanations for cross-cultural differences in levels of recovery from schizophrenia have focused on the influence of cultural interpretations and social response to illness (Waxler 1974), in particular on family responses (as represented by "expressed emotion," Jenkins 1991), on subjective experience across cultures (Jenkins 1997; Estroff et al. 1991), and on the role of the industrial organization of labor (Warner 1985). Ethnographic research continues to seek explanations for these findings. Finally, anthropologists have more recently turned to studies of *trauma and dissociative disorders,* providing anthropological studies of the rise of PTSD and multiple personality disorder in North America (Young 1995; Hacking 1995; Antze & Lambek 1996; Jenkins 1996), as well as studies of spirit possession as dissociation (e.g., Castillo 1994).

These anthropological studies of mental illness have addressed issues of interest to medical sociologists as well. Are diagnostic criteria valid across cultures and ethnic groups, or are there significant variations in symptom formation that should be reflected in epidemiological instruments? (Kleinman 1988a; Mezzich et al. 1996). What are the differences in care-seeking practices and mental health treatment for minority persons in the American mental healthcare system, and what are the sources of bias in diagnostic practice for minority patients (Good 1992, 1997)? What social and cultural factors account for significant differences in course and outcome of various forms of psychopathology, leading to differential rates of recovery and chronicity by culture, ethnic group, social class, and gender? How prevalent are mental health problems globally, and how are they related to broad processes of economic development and social change (Desjarlais et al. 1995)? These and other related questions are of critical importance for both anthropologists and sociologists interested in studies of mental illness.

Anthropologists have also carried out research on contemporary mental-health institutions both cross-culturally and in the United States. From Goffman's (1961) classic *Asylums* to current works influenced by Foucault and other post-structuralists, anthropological studies provide critical analyses of institutional ideologies and therapeutic practice. Studies reflect emerging forms of mental-health services and treatment ideologies. Estroff's classic *Making It Crazy* (1981) was a study of a day-care program for persons with schizophrenia and launched a new generation of anthropological studies of mental-health services. Rhodes' monograph *Emptying Beds* (1991) described a psychiatric emergency unit and the struggle to keep patients out of the hospital during the early stages of the transition to managed care. Barrett (1996) provides an account of a schizophrenia unit in an Australian psychiatric hospital, highlighting how schizophrenia is constituted from diverse professional perspectives in a contemporary 'biopsychosocial' treatment environment. Young (1995) gives a vivid ethnographic description of a PTSD inpatient unit for Vietnam vets and how PTSD has been "invented." Desjarlais's *Shelter Blues* (1997) provides a rich and troubling account of a shelter for homeless mentally ill men and women, an institutional form that has come to serve as the de facto mental health system for many Americans suffering mental illness. When combined with studies of colonial and post-colonial psychiatric institutions (e.g., Fisher 1985; Saris 1995; Nunley 1998), these ethnographic accounts provide critical analyses of diverse forms of mental-health services today. They share basic theoretical orientations with much contemporary sociological and historical research, addressing overlapping questions in ways that have led to increasingly significant conversations across disciplines.

CONCLUSION

We have provided examples of anthropological research and writing that illustrate broad historical similarities, as well as differences, between medical anthropology and medical sociology. It is obvious that medical anthropologists and many medical sociologists share an analytic vocabulary, often refer to a common corpus of social theory, and increasingly address common substantive problems. The fields cannot be distinguished, today, by any simple dichotomies—as providing macro versus micro accounts, focusing on North America and Europe versus non-Western societies, or as focusing on traditional healing versus biomedicine. It is even true that qualitative and quantitative research, and ethnographic and epidemiological writing proceed in parallel ways and address common problems. At the same time, citations make it apparent that the fields often remain quite divided. The reasons are partly substantive. Anthropologists are doggedly ethnographic, are interested in particular cultures and societies, and see illness and medical systems as lenses for understanding the particularities of a society. But the reasons are also more practical. Anthropologists and sociologists subscribe to and read a limited number of journals, fail to attend one another's professional meetings, and maintain separate networks. We can only conclude by acknowledging the importance of Sol Levine's exhortation to overcome "intellectual parochialism," to read and appreciate work across these fields, and to find new ways to enhance the creative integration of the disciplines.

REFERENCES

ADAMS, VINCANNE. 1998. *Doctors for Democracy: Health Professionals in the Nepal Revolution.* Cambridge: Cambridge University Press.

ANTZE, PAUL, and MICHAEL LAMBEK. 1996. *Tense Past: Cultural Essays in Trauma and Memory.* New York: Routledge.

APPADURAI, ARJUN. 1996. *Modernity at Large. Cultural Dimensions of Globalization.* Minneapolis, MN: University of Minnesota Press.

BARRETT, ROB. 1996. *The Psychiatric Team and the Social Definition of Schizophrenia.* Cambridge: Cambridge University Press.

BENEDICT, RUTH. 1934. "Anthropology and the Abnormal." *Journal of General Psychology* 10: 59–82.

BRODWIN, PAUL. 1996. *Medicine and Morality in Haiti. The Contest for Healing Power.* Cambridge: Cambridge University Press.

BRODY, HOWARD. 1987. *Stories of Sickness.* New Haven: Yale University Press.

CASTILLO, RICHARD. 1994. *Spirit Possession in South Asia, Dissociation or Hysteria? Part 1: Theoretical Background. Part 2: Case Histories. Culture, Medicine and Psychiatry* 18: 1–21, 141–62.

CLIFFORD, JAMES. 1988. *The Predicament of Culture.* Cambridge, MA: Harvard University Press.

COHEN, ALEX. 1992. "Prognosis for Schizophrenia in the Third World: A Reevaluation of Cross-Cultural Research." *Culture, Medicine and Psychiatry* 16: 53–75.

COHEN, LAWRENCE. 1998. *No Aging in India. Alzheimer's, the Bad Family, and Other Modern Things.* Berkeley: University of California Press.

CONRAD, PETER. 1997. "Parallel Play in Medical Sociology and Medical Anthropology." *The American Sociologist* 28: 90–100.

CSORDAS, THOMAS J. 1994. *The Sacred Self: A Cultural Phenomenology of Charismatic Healing.* Berkeley: University of California Press.

DARNELL, REGNA. 1986. "Personality and Culture: The Fate of the Sapirian Alternative." In *Malinowski, Rivers, Benedict and Others: Essays on Culture and Personality,* ed. G. W. Stocking. Madison: University of Wisconsin Press, pp. 156–83.

DESJARLAIS, ROBERT. 1992. *Body and Emotion: The Aesthetics of Illness and Healing in the Nepal Himalayas.* Philadelphia: University of Pennsylvania Press.

DESJARLAIS, ROBERT. 1997. *Shelter Blues: Sanity and Selfhood Among the Homeless.* Philadelphia: University of Pennsylvania Press.

DESJARLAIS, ROBERT, LEON EISENBERG, BYRON GOOD, and ARTHUR KLEINMAN. 1995. *World Mental Health: Problems and Priorities in Low-Income Countries.* Oxford: Oxford University Press.

DOWNEY, GARY LEE, and JOSEPH DUMIT. 1997. *Cyborgs & Citadels: Anthropological Interventions in Emerging Sciences and Technologies.* Seattle, WA: School of American Research Press.

EARLY, EVELYN ALEENE. 1982. "The Logic of Well-Being: Therapeutic Narratives in Cairo, Egypt." *Social Science and Medicine* 16:1491–97.

EISENBERG, LEON, and ARTHUR KLEINMAN. eds. 1981. *The Relevance of Social Science for Medicine.* Dordrecht, Holland: D. Reidel Publishing Co.

ESTROFF, SUE. 1981. *Making It Crazy.* Berkeley: University of California Press.

ESTROFF, SUE, ET AL. 1991. "Everybody's Got a Little Mental Illness: Accounts of Illness and Self Among People With Severe, Persistent Mental Illnesses." *Medical Anthropology Quarterly* 5: 331–69.

FISHER, LAWRENCE. 1985. *Colonial Madness: Mental Health in the Barbadian Social Order.* New Brunswick, NJ: Rutgers University Press.

FRANKENBERG, RONALD. 1988. "Gramsci, Marxism, and Phenomenology: Essays for the Development of Critical Medical Anthropology." *Special Issue of Medical Anthropology Quarterly,* R. Frankenberg ed. 2(4): 324–459.

GAINES, ATWOOD. 1989. "Alzheimer's Disease in the Context of Black (Southern) Culture." *Health Matrix* 6(4): 33–38.

GARRO, LINDA. 1994. "Narrative Representations of Chronic Illness Experience: Cultural Models of Illness, Mind, and Body in Stories Concerning the Temporomandibular Joint (TMJ)." *Social Science & Medicine* 38(6): 775–88.

GERHARDT, UTA, ed. 1990. "Qualitative Research on Chronic Illness." *Social Science and Medicine* 30 (special issue): 1149–1263.

GINSBURG, FAYE D., and RAYNA RAPP, eds. 1995. *Conceiving the New World Order: The Global Politics of Reproduction.* Berkeley: University of California Press.

GOFFMAN, ERVING. 1961. *Asylum: Essays on the Social Situation of Mental Patients and Other Inmates.* New York: Doubleday.

GOOD, BYRON. 1977. "The Heart of What's the Matter: The Semantics of Illness in Iran." *Culture, Medicine and Psychiatry* 1: 25–58.

GOOD, BYRON. 1992. "Culture and Psychopathology: Directions for Psychiatric Anthropology." In *New Directions in Psychological Anthropology,* ed. Theodore Schwartz, Geoffrey White, and Catherine A. Lutz. Cambridge: Cambridge University Press. See also P. Brodwin, "Symptoms and Social Performances: The Case of Diane Reden," pp. 77–99; L. Garro, "Chronic Illness and the Construction of Narratives," pp. 100–37; B. Good, "A Body in Pain—The Making of a World of Chronic Pain," pp. 29–48; M. Good, "Work as a Haven from Pain," pp. 49–77; J. Jackson, "After a While No One Believes You: Real and Unreal Pain," pp. 138–68."

GOOD, BYRON. 1994. *Medicine, Rationality and Experience.* Cambridge, England: Cambridge University Press.

GOOD, BYRON. 1997. "Studying Mental Illness in Context: Local, Global, or Universal?" *Ethos* 25(2): 1–19.

GOOD, BYRON J., and MARY-JO DELVECCHIO GOOD. 1981. "The Semantics of Medical Discourse." In *Sciences and Cultures. Sociology of the Sciences.* Vol. V., ed. Everett Mendelsohn and Yehuda Elkana. Dordrecht, Holland: D. Reidel Publishing Company, pp. 177–212.

GOOD, BYRON J., and MARY-JO DELVECCHIO GOOD. 1994. "In the Subjunctive Mode: Epilepsy Narratives in Turkey." *Social Science and Medicine* 38(6): 835–42.

GOOD, BYRON J., and MARY-JO DELVECCHIO GOOD. 1999. "'Fiction' and 'Historicity' in Doctors' Stories: Social and Narrative Dimensions of Learning Medicine." In *Narrative and the Cultural Construction of Illness and Healing,* ed. Cheryl Mattingly and Linda Garro. Berkeley: University of California Press.

GOOD, MARY-JO DELVECCHIO. 1995a. *American Medicine: The Quest for Competence.* Berkeley, CA: University of California Press.

GOOD, MARY-JO DELVECCHIO. 1995b. "Cultural Studies of Biomedicine: An Agenda for Research." *Social Science & Medicine* 41(4): 461–73.

GOOD, MARY-JO DELVECCHIO. 1996. "L'Abbraccio Biotecnico: Un Invito al trattamento sperimentale." In *Il sapere della guarigione,* ed. Pino Donghi. Spoletto: Laterza.

GOOD, MARY-JO DELVECCHIO, BYRON J. GOOD, CYNTHIA SCHAFFER, and STUART E. LIND. 1990. "American Oncology and the Discourse on Hope." *Culture, Medicine and Psychiatry* 14: 59–79.

GOOD, MARY-JO DELVECCHIO, BYRON J. GOOD, TSEUNETSUGU MUNAKATA, YASUKI KOBAYASHI, and CHERYL MATTINGLY. 1994. "Oncology and Narrative Time." *Social Science and Medicine* 38(6): 855–62.

GOOD, MARY-JO DELVECCHIO, IRENE KUTER, SIMON POWELL, HERBERT C. HOOVER, JR., MARIA E. CARSON, and RITA LINGGOOD. 1995. "Medicine on the Edge: Conversations With Oncologists." In *Technoscientific Imaginaries: Conversations, Profiles and Memoirs,* ed. George Marcus. Chicago: University of Chicago Press, pp. 129–52.

GOOD, MARY-JO DELVECCHIO, LINDA HUNT, TSEUNETSUGU MUNAKATA, and YASUKI KOBAYASHI. 1993. "A Comparative Analysis of the Culture of Biomedicine: Disclosure and Consequences for Treatment in the Practice of Oncology." In *Sociological Perspectives in International Health,* ed. Peter Conrad and Eugene Gallagher. Philadelphia: Temple University Press.

GOOD, MARY-JO DELVECCHIO, PAUL BRODWIN, BYRON GOOD, and ARTHUR KLEINMAN, eds. 1992. *Pain as Human Experience: An Anthropological Perspective.* Berkeley: University of California Press.

GORDON, DEBORAH R., and EUGENIO PACI. 1997. "Disclosure Practices and Cultural Narratives: Understanding Concealment and Silence Around Cancer in Tuscany, Italy." *Social Science and Medicine* 44(10): 1433–52.

GUARNACCIA, PETER J., BYRON J. GOOD, and ARTHUR KLEINMAN. 1990. "A Critical Review of Epidemiological Studies of Puerto Rican Mental Health." *American Journal of Psychiatry* 147: 1149–56.

HACKING, IAN. 1995. *Rewriting the Soul: Multiple Personality and the Sciences of Memory.* Princeton: Princeton University Press.

HAHN, ROBERT A., and ATWOOD GAINES eds. 1985. *Physicians of Western Medicine.* Dordrecht: D. Reidel Publishing Company. See A. Gaines, "The Once- and the Twice-Born: Self and Practice among Psychiatrists and Christian Psychiatrists," pp. 223–46; A. Gaines and R. Hahn, "Among the Physicians: Encounter, Exchange and Transformation," pp. 3–22; B. Good et al., "Reflexivity, Countertransference and Clinical Ethnography: A Case from a Psychiatric Cultural Consultation Clinic," pp. 193–222; M. Good, "Discourses on Physician Competence," pp. 247–68; R. Hahn, "A World of Internal Medicine: Portrait of an Internist," pp. 51–114; T. Johnson, "Consultation-Liaison Psychiatry: Medicine as Patient, Marginality as Practice," pp 269–92; M. Lock, "Models and Practice in Medicine: Menopause as Syndrome or Life Transition?" pp. 115–40; T. Maretzki, "Including the Physician in Healer-Centered Research: Retrospect and Prospect," pp. 23–50; W. Rittenberg and R. Simons, "Gentle Interogation: Inquiry and Interaction in Brief Initial Psychiatric Evaluations," pp. 177–92.

HARAWAY, DONNA. 1997. "Mice Into Wormholes/ A Comment on the Nature of No Nature." In *Cyborgs and Citadels,* ed. Gary Lee Downey and Joseph Dumit. Santa Fe, NM: School of American Research Press.

HARWOOD, ALLAN. 1981. *Ethnicity and Medical Care.* Cambridge: Harvard University Press.

HEATH, DEBORAH, and PAUL RABINOW, eds. 1993. "Bio-Politics: The Anthropology of the New Genetics and Immunology." *Culture, Medicine and Psychiatry* 17(1, Special Issue).

HOPPER, KIM. 1991. "Some Old Questions for the New Cross-Cultural Psychiatry." *Medical Anthropology Quarterly* 5:299–330.

JABLENSKY, ASSEN, ET AL. 1992. *Schizophrenia: Manifestations, Incidence and Course in Different Cultures. A W.H.O. Ten-Country Study.* Psychological Medicine Monograph Supplement 20. Cambridge: Cambridge University Press.

JANZEN, JOHN. 1978. *The Quest for Therapy in Lower Zaire.* Berkeley: University of California Press.

JENKINS, JANIS H. 1988. "Ethnopsychiatric Interpretations of Schizophrenic Illness: The Problem of *Nervios* Within Mexican-American Families." *Culture, Medicine and Psychiatry* 12: 301–29.

JENKINS, JANIS H. 1991. "Anthropology, Expressed Emotion, and Schizophrenia." *Ethos* 19: 387–431.

JENKINS, JANIS H. 1996. "Culture, Emotion and Post-Traumatic Stress Disorder." In *Ethnocultural Aspects of Post-Traumatic Stress Disorder,* ed. A. Marsella and N. Freedman. Washington DC: American Psychological Association Press.

JENKINS, JANIS H. 1997. "Subjective Experience of Persistent Psychiatric Disorder: Schizophrenia and Depression Among U.S. Latinos and Euro-Americans." *British Journal of Psychiatry* 170: 20–25.

JENKINS, JANIS H., ARTHUR KLEINMAN, and BYRON J. GOOD. 1991. "Cross-Cultural Aspects of Depression." In *Advances in Affective Disorders,* ed. J. Becker and Arthur Kleinman. Hillsdale, NJ: Lawrence Erlbaum Association Publishers, pp. 67–99.

KEESING, ROGER M. 1987. "Models, 'Folk' and 'Cultural': Paradigms Regained?" In *Cultural Models in Language & Thought,* ed. D. Holland and N. Quinn. New York: Cambridge University Press, pp. 369–93.

KLEINMAN, ARTHUR. 1977. "Depression, Somatization and the New Cross-Cultural Psychiatry." *Social Science and Medicine* 11: 3–10.

KLEINMAN, ARTHUR. 1980. *Patients and Healers in the Context of Culture. An Exploration of the Borderland Between Anthropology, Medicine, and Psychiatry.* Berkeley: University of California Press.

KLEINMAN, ARTHUR. 1986. *Social Origins of Distress and Disease: Depression, Neurasthenia, and Pain in Modern China.* New Haven: Yale University Press.

KLEINMAN, ARTHUR. 1988a. *Rethinking Psychiatry: From Cultural Category to Personal Experience.* New York: The Free Press.

KLEINMAN, ARTHUR. 1988b. *The Illness Narratives: Suffering, Healing and the Human Condition.* New York: Basic Books.

KLEINMAN, ARTHUR, and BYRON GOOD, eds. 1985. *Culture and Depression.* Berkeley: University of California Press.

KLEINMAN, ARTHUR, LEON EISENBERG, and BYRON GOOD. 1978. "Culture, Illness and Care: Clinical Lessons From Anthropologic and Cross-Cultural Research." *Annals of Internal Medicine* 88: 251–58.

KLEINMAN, ARTHUR, PETER KUNSTADTER, E. ALEXANDER, and JAMES GALE, eds. 1976. *Medicine in Chinese Cultures: Comparative Studies of Health Care in Chinese and Other Societies.* Washington, DC: U.S. Government Printing Office for Fogarty International Center, N.I.H.

LESLIE, CHARLES, ed. 1976. *Asian Medical Systems: A Comparative Study.* Los Angeles: University of California Press.

LESLIE, CHARLES, and ALLAN YOUNG, eds. 1992. *Paths to Asian Medical Knowledge.* Berkeley: University of California Press.

LEVINE, SOL. 1995. "Time for Creative Integration in Medical Sociology." *Journal of Health and Social Behavior* (extra issue): 1–4.

LINDENBAUM, SHIRLEY, and MARGARET LOCK, eds. 1993. *Knowledge, Power & Practice. The Anthropology of Medicine and Everyday Life.* Berkeley: University of California Press.

LOCK, MARGARET. 1993. *Encounters With Aging: Mythologies of Menopause in Japan and North America.* Berkeley: University of California Press.

LOCK, MARGARET. 1995. "Contesting the Natural in Japan: Moral Dilemmas and Technologies of Dying." *Culture, Medicine and Psychiatry* 19(1): 1–38.

LOCK, MARGARET, and DEBORAH GORDON. 1988. *Biomedicine Examined.* Dordrecht: Kluwer Academic Publishers.

MARCUS, GEORGE. 1995a. "Ethnography in/of the World System: The Emergence of Multisited Ethnography." *Annual Review of Anthropology* 24: 95–117.

MARCUS, GEORGE, ed. 1995b. *Technoscientific Imaginaries: Conversations, Profiles and Memoirs.* Chicago: University of Chicago Press.

Marcus, George, and Michael Fischer. 1986. *Anthropology as Cultural Critique. An Experimental Moment in the Human Sciences.* Chicago: University of Chicago Press.

Martin, Emily. 1987. *The Woman in the Body. A Cultural Analysis of Reproduction.* Boston: Beacon Press.

Martin, Emily. 1994. *Flexible Bodies: Tracking Immunity in American Culture from the Days of Polio to the Days of AIDS.* Boston: Beacon Press.

Mattingly, Cheryl. 1998. *Healing Dramas and Clinical Plots: The Narrative Structure of Experience.* Cambridge: Cambridge University Press.

Mattingly, Cheryl, and Linda Garro, eds. 1999. *Narrative and the Cultural Construction of Illness and Healing.* Berkeley: University of California Press.

Mezzich, Juan, et al. 1996. *Culture and Psychiatric Diagnosis: A DSM-IV Perspective.* Washington, D.C.: American Psychiatric Association Press.

Mishler, Elliot. 1986. *The Discourse of Medicine: Dialectics of Medical Interviews.* Norwood, NJ: Ablex.

Morsy, Soheir. 1990. "Political Economy in Medical Anthropology." In *Medical Anthropology: A Handbook of Theory and Method,* ed. Thomas M. Johnson and Carolyn F. Sargent. New York: Greenwood Press, pp. 26–46.

Murphy, Robert F. 1987. *The Body Silent.* New York: Henry Holt and Co.

Nichter, Mark. 1981. "Idioms of Distress: Alternatives in the Expression of Psychosocial Distress. A Case Study From South India." *Culture, Medicine and Psychiatry* 5: 5–24.

Nichter, Mark. 1989. *Anthropology and International Health: South Asian Case Studies.* Dordrecht: Kluwer Academic Publishers.

Nunley, Michael. 1998. "The Involvement of Families in Indian Psychiatry." *Culture, Medicine and Psychiatry* 22: 317–53.

O'Nell, Theresa. 1996. *Disciplined Hearts: Depression and Moral Imagination on the Flathead Reservation.* Berkeley: University of California Press.

Ochs, Elinor, and Lisa Capps. 1996. "Narrating the Self." *Annual Review of Anthropology* 25:19–43.

Ohnuki-Tierney, Emiko. 1994. "Brain Death and Organ Transplantation: Culture Bases of Medical Technology." *Current Anthropology* 35: 233–54.

Pandolfi, Mariella. 1990. "Boundaries Inside the Body: Women's Sufferings in Southern Peasant Italy." *Culture, Medicine and Psychiatry* 14: 255–73.

Paul, Benjamin. 1955. *Health, Culture, and Community: Case Studies of Public Reactions to Health Programs.* New York: Russell Sage Foundation.

Polgar, Steven. 1963. "Health Action in Cross-Cultural Perspective." In *Handbook of Medical Sociology,* ed. H. E. Freeman, Sol Levine, and L. G. Reeder. Englewood Cliffs, NJ: Prentice Hall.

Price, Laurie. 1987. "Ecuadorian Illness Stories: Cultural Knowledge in Natural Discourse." In *Cultural Models in Language and Thought,* ed. Dorothy Holland and Naomi Quinn. Cambridge: Cambridge University Press, pp. 313–42.

Rabinow, Paul. 1996. *Making PCR: A Story of Biotechnology.* Chicago: University of Chicago Press.

Rabinow, Paul. 1997. "Science as Practice: The Higher Indifference and Mediated Curiosity." In *Cyborgs and Citadels: Anthropological Interventions in Emerging Sciences and Technologies,* ed. Gary Lee Downey and Joseph Dumit. Santa Fe, NM: School of American Research Press.

Rapp, Rayna. 1988. "Chromosomes and Communication: The Discourse of Genetic Counseling." *Medical Anthropology Quarterly* 2:143–57.

Rhodes, Lorna. 1991. *Emptying Beds: The Work of an Emergency Psychiatric Unit.* Berkeley: University of California Press.

Saris, Jamie. 1995. "Telling Stories: Life Histories, Illness Narratives, and Institutional Landscapes." *Culture, Medicine and Psychiatry* 19: 39–72.

Scheper-Hughes, Nancy. 1992. *Death Without Weeping: The Violence of Everyday Life in Brazil.* Berkeley: University of California Press.

Simons, Ronald C., and Charles C. Hughes. 1985. *The Culture-Bound Syndromes: Folk Illnesses of Psychiatric and Anthropological Interest.* Dordrecht, Holland: Reidel.

Singer, Merrill. 1990. "Reinventing Medical Anthropology: Toward a Critical Realignment." *Social Science and Medicine* 30: 179–87.

Taussig, Karen Sue. 1997. "Calvinism and Chromosomes: Religion, the Geographical Imaginary and Medical Genetics in the Netherlands." *Science as Culture* 6 (part 4, no. 29): 495–524.

Turshen, Meredeth. 1989. *The Politics of Public Health.* New Brunswick, NJ: Rutgers University Press.

Van der Geest, Sjaak, and Susan Reynolds Whyte, eds. 1988. *The Context of Medicines in Developing Countries: Studies in Pharmaceutical Anthropology.* Dordrecht: Kluwer Academic Publishers.

Warner, Richard. 1985. *Recovery From Schizophrenia: Psychiatry and Political Economy.* London: Routledge and Kegan Paul.

Waxler, Nancy E. 1974. "Culture and Mental Illness: A Social Labeling Perspective." *Journal of Nervous and Mental Disease* 159: 379–95.

Williams, Gareth. 1984. "The Genesis of Chronic Illness: Narrative Reconstruction." *Sociology of Health and Illness* 6: 175–200.

Yoder, P. Stanley. 1997. "Knowledge and Practice in International Health." *Medical Anthropology Quarterly* 11(2, Special Issue).

Young, Allan. 1982. "The Anthropologies of Illness and Sickness." *Annual Review of Anthropology* 11: 257–85.

Young, Allan. 1995. *The Harmony of Illusions: Inventing Post-Traumatic Stress Disorder.* Princeton: Princeton University Press.

27 THE SOCIOLOGY OF HEALTH IN DEVELOPING COUNTRIES

EUGENE B. GALLAGHER, *University of Kentucky*

THOMAS J. STEWART, *United Arab Emirates University*

TERRY D. STRATTON, *University of Kentucky*

INTRODUCTION

Why should medical sociologists concern themselves with the developing world? There are several reasons. First, demographically, the developing world holds 80 percent of the world's population, a figure that will increase to 84 percent within two decades (U.S. Bureau of the Census 1996). Second, in economic terms, it is closely connected by trade to the industrial world; it is the major source for raw materials and increasingly, given its low labor costs, it is a source for manufactured products exported to the industrial world. Reciprocally, under the aegis of economic globalization, the developing world has become an indispensable market for goods and services exported from the industrial world (Evans and Stephans 1988). Third, in political terms, the developing world is the scene of political/ethnic/religious conflicts that have repeatedly endangered world peace during the Cold War and the current post-Cold War periods. Fourth, environmentally, the developing world embraces land, water, and atmosphere that are crucial to the future of the planet; if it follows the industrial world in patterns of energy utilization, resource extraction, land use, and pollution, widespread environmental deterioration will ensue.

The study of health and illness in the developing world holds great interest for sociology. Some beginnings have been made. The *Journal of Health and Social Behavior* (1989) devoted a special issue ("Sociological Studies of Third World Health and Health Care") to this topic in 1989. Representative books include Zeichner's edited collection (1988) and Peter Conrad and Eugene B. Gallagher's edited collection (1993).

The immediately previous edition of the *Handbook of Medical Sociology* (Freeman and Levine 1989) was the first in the *Handbook* series to contain a chapter on health care in developing countries, contributed by Jackob M. Najman. Although our approach to the topic in this fifth edition is different from Professor Najman's, we heartily recommend it for further reading (Chapter 16, *Handbook of Medical Sociology*).

We also note that the fourth edition contains no other chapter dealing entirely with health care outside of the American context. This is not to say that the other chapters are consciously focused on the United States, but rather that they deal in concepts, programs, and health goals that are familiar primarily within the American context. Aside from Najman's chapter on developing countries, the only other chapter with an "extra-American" section is Howard Waitzkin's chapter, "Health Policy in the United States: Problems and Alternatives." In it the author sketches important features of health care in Canada, England, and several European nations for sharp contrast with the highly decentralized, individualistic, profit-oriented structure of American health care.

The sociology of health in the developing world can be seen analytically as the intersection of two dimensions: geographic and disciplinary. The geographic dimension is the domain within which the developing world is delineated in contrast to the industrial world. The disciplinary (or academic) dimension is the domain within which the distinctive perspectives of medical sociology are laid out in relation to other behavioral/social sciences. We will discuss these two dimensions separately.

THE GEOGRAPHIC DIMENSION— THE "DEVELOPING" WORLD LOCATED IN THE GLOBAL CONTEXT

No one can point to a geographically bounded or contiguous part of earth and say "This is the developing world," as if it were a continent. The dispersed spatial character of the developing world means that it must be conceived abstractly. "Developed/developing" is a widely used dichotomy for grouping and placing nations on a scale of societal development. In earlier decades, it was styled "developed/underdeveloped." However, realization that the so-called "underdeveloped nations" are undergoing forward social and economic changes led to a shift in their designation from "underdeveloped" to "developing" nations.

A second widely used dichotomy is by Northern and Southern hemispheres. While it makes a better geographic fit to align North/South with developed/developing than the reverse, the fit is rough. India and China, with some 40 percent of the world's population, lie in the Northern hemisphere, while the Southern hemisphere contains Australia, New Zealand, Chile, Argentina, and Brazil, all of which are important industrial nations.

A third scheme of reference is that of First, Second, and Third Worlds (Goldthorpe 1984). This scheme dates back to the end of World War II, when nations at the low end of development were called the Third World, to set them off from the two hegemonic power blocs of the First World and the Second World. The First World consisted of democratic-capitalist nations dominated by the United States. The Second World consisted of communist–socialist nations dominated by the Soviet Union. With the demise of the Soviet Union, the Second World vanished as a category. Moreover, once shorn of military power, many nations of the Second World stand revealed as virtually "Third World" in their low level of economic development.

In this chapter we use the dichotomy industrial/developing (or equivalently, Third World) nations. As the counter- or contrast-term to "developing" we prefer to use "industrial" rather than "developed." This preference is not a mere semantic nicety; rather, it is based in the consideration that, literally, all nations are developing; all are changing. To call some nations "developed" implies misleadingly that they have reached an end-point. However, to call them "industrial" points realistically to a crucial feature—industry—of their economy and social structure while also distinguishing them from the "developing" nations.

THE DISCIPLINARY DIMENSION— "MEDICAL SOCIOLOGY" LOCATED WITHIN ITS PARENT DISCIPLINE

Where does medical sociology lie within the academic discipline of sociology? Should medical sociology function as an interdisciplinary field through lateral connections with other fields of study that do not reach down vertically through the fundamental concepts of sociology as a whole? Within medical sociology, how does one study health in particular countries? Most apposite to our topic, what special considerations apply to the study of health in developing countries? We offer these questions not to answer them directly (which would be beyond the scope of this chapter), but to indicate a broader framework within which our topic falls, and also to identify emerging connections within this framework. Among these connections are the following:

First, sociology as a discipline is expanding its focus beyond the United States. At various levels, increasing attention is being paid to foreign trends and events. International sociology and the internationalization of sociology are evident at the organizational level in publications such as *Footnotes,* which has a periodic section, "International News and Notes" as well as occasional articles in this vein (Clawson 1997). Also "introductory" textbooks are beginning to give prominent attention to social trends and events in foreign countries (Macionis 1999; Ferrante 1995).

Second, medical sociology has, in the past twenty years, developed a strong macro perspective on health, which contrasts with its earlier, and still-important micro perspective (e.g., on illness behavior, experience of illness, doctor–patient relationship and interaction, and health-professional socialization). The macro perspective is most-often cast upon, and confined to, the United States—the health status of its population (including various subgroups and categories) and its health-care system. Lacking explicit comparison with other nations, the macro perspective is inchoate. However, like the parent discipline of sociology, medical sociology is becoming more explicitly international in scope. This trend can be observed in several directions: in books (Lassey et al. 1997); in edited compilations (Elling 1980; Albrecht 1981; Field 1989; Gallagher and Subedi 1995; Subedi and Gallagher 1996); and in the penetration of the topic (i.e., health in foreign nations) in medical sociology texts and anthologies (Charmaz and Paterniti 1999; Cockerham 1998; Conrad 1997; Kurtz and Chalfant 1991). It should be noted that almost all of the foreign content deals with health in industrial nations. Much of that content is presented to illuminate health-care reform in the United States. It is concerned with finding out what "lessons" the United States can learn from the experience of other industrial nations and which analytic frameworks are best suited to the cross-national comparison of health care.

Third, as a corollary of the second point, very little of medical sociology's foreign content has dealt with Third World health. Further, what little there is, is presented in an informative or analytic fashion to expand sociological information, not with concern for the values or lessons that might apply to industrial nations.

Fourth, other academic disciplines border on medical sociology's knowledge of Third World health. Anthropology—especially anthropology's own subfield of medical anthropology—contains much of interest to medical sociology. A relatively distinct line between medical anthropology and medical sociology can, however, be drawn as follows: Medical anthropology concerns itself primarily with symbolic systems of meaning for health, illness, and therapeutic intervention, while medical sociology is more attuned to the social structures and social relationships through which illness is identified and through which health care is delivered. However, this distinction may be regarded as a "second order" classification in relation to the dominating fact that the discipline of sociology, sweeping medical sociology along with it, has focused overwhelmingly on industrial society. It is, indeed, not a great oversimplification to state that sociology emerged in the nineteenth century as a distinct field of thought in the attempt to understand the transition from pre-industrial society to industrial society. While anthropology, as the generic "study of man," has no inherent or logical preference for pre-industrial societies, it has in fact dealt overwhelmingly with such societies, sweeping its medical branch in the same direction. It is not surprising that the scope of work on developing societies is far greater in medical anthropology than in medical sociology. Thus the consequences of the basic originating thrusts for anthropology and sociology are still important today.

Public health is another field that borders medical sociology in its "Third World gaze." Public health arose in the industrializing world during the era when infectious disease predominated. Its success in measuring disease through epidemiology gives us a fairly accurate picture of the balance of health and disease in total populations. It has also enjoyed tremendous success in interventions that prevent disease, through the devising of effective vaccines, better control of the safety of food

and water, and improved waste disposal. Infectious and parasitic diseases have been considerably reduced, notwithstanding the recent rise of AIDS and the resurgence of tuberculosis. However, in the developing nations infectious and parasitic diseases remain a very potent threat.

Being closely tied to public funding and government, public-health workers and officials have objectives and resources that are sharply circumscribed by their political boundaries. Those in industrial nations have no mandate to concern themselves with the Third World. International health organizations, however, have by their mission a wider vision and a strong Third World focus. In particular, the World Health Organization has through its annual reports and its agenda *Health for All by the Year 2000* fostered an awareness of health and population trends in the Third World (World Health Organization 1981) that have global consequences.

Thus far in this chapter we have shown how sociological concern with Third World health has evolved and how this domain of study is defined by its geographic basis and its position within the discipline of sociology. Now we turn to two questions that, rather than bounding the domain, lie in the center of it. We deal first with the doctor-patient relationship in Third World settings. Then we deal with approaches to global assessments of disease and health status. Being truly "global," these approaches encompass the industrial as well as the developing countries. They are valuable for showing the contrasts between the two groups of countries.

THE DOCTOR-PATIENT RELATIONSHIP IN DEVELOPING COUNTRIES

Not surprisingly, the phenomena and problems that inspired the creation of medical sociology have been studied only in the industrial societies. This certainly holds for the doctor–patient relationship, which has been a central focus of medical sociology. We deal with it here to suggest the kinds of contextual alteration that medical processes may undergo when translated from the industrial society setting to the Third World setting.

A fundamental parameter of the doctor–patient relationship is that the two parties do not possess equal status; rather, the doctor dominates the relationship with his superior knowledge, access to resources, formal authority, and obligation of clinical responsibility. Sociological research has found that in interaction with the patient, the doctor typically exerts strong control over the extent, timing, and content of their communications, both verbal and nonverbal. Outside the scene of their direct encounter, only the doctor, and not the patient, is a recognized agent in medical hierarchies and health-care organizations, which status enables him to reach beyond his own skill and specialization. While the doctor works on behalf of the patient, and in that sense represents the latter, the patient himself cannot move as an active independent agent in the medical world.

The foregoing sketch of the doctor–patient relationship in industrial society is not presented to suggest that every important structural parameter of it is already well understood. More research is necessary to clarify it, even as it is used as the base from which to interpret and understand the doctor–patient relationship outside the context of industrial society.

We believe that the effort to characterize the doctor–patient relationship in developing societies must take into account variable yet widespread additional features of their cultural milieu, namely the important role played by respect for tradition and authority, and by the sway of patriarchalism. Given that these forces work their way into the functioning of the family, educational processes, and market/economic phenomena, we believe that they affect medical/health phenomena as well. Though the question has been little studied, there are preliminary indications that such is the case. For example, Nuria Homedes and Antonio Ugalde (1994) conclude that obstacles to patient compliance and understanding of treatment are increased because of "relatively great socioeconomic, educational, cultural, and linguistic differences" between patient and doctor, and because of the "health care provider's inability to translate scientific concepts into the culture of their patients."

Maureen Searle and Eugene Gallagher (1983) found that patriarchalism in Saudi Arabia had a profound effect in shaping the gender composition of the medical profession—though many of the primary care doctors are female, specialists are overwhelmingly male. Physician dominance of the doctor–patient relationship is moving toward status parity between the two parties in industrial society. The conventional higher status of the doctor is being altered by several factors of change in medical care, as follows:

1. New generations of patients are more knowledgeable about medical diagnoses and procedures than older generations.

2. Social expectations as well as formal/legal requirements are leading doctors to give patients more information about diagnosis and treatment and then to obtain their informed consent for treatment. Though the actual implementation of these requirements may often have a mechanical superficiality, it nevertheless does exert some pressure on doctors for accountable communication with patients (Wolpe 1998).

3. There is a growing prevalence of chronic, long-term disease, such as diabetes, through which the patient perforce becomes an "expert" and looks for guidance from the doctor.

4. A substantial increase has occurred in payment for medical care by third parties (including government). While third-party payment may not directly increase the standing of the patient, it does diminish the discretion and authority of the doctor.

The prevailing cultural patterns of developing countries (such as patriarchalism) do not insulate their medical care from similar kinds of change. For example, South Korea has adopted a national program of health insurance in response to the growth of a more urbanized labor force (Cho 1989). In Mexico, Mary-Jo DelVecchio Good (1993) and colleagues found increasing public discussion and agitation about doctors' ways of communicating with patients. Much discussion revolved around the question of whether doctors should be more open about cancer diagnoses to afflicted patients or remain in their traditional stance of nondisclosure. In a teaching hospital in the United Arab Emirates, Gallagher (1998) learned that doctors (or paramedicals representing the doctor) were routinely required to obtain informed consent from surgery patients prior to their surgery.

These changes in medical care may lead toward a somewhat more egalitarian doctor-patient relationship in developing countries, even against their entrenched culture patterns. The effects of the changes in medical care thus appear to be moving in a similar direction in both industrial and Third World countries.

THE GLOBAL ASSESSMENT OF DISEASE AND HEALTH STATUS

Sociologists are familiar with the idea, coming out of historical demography, of the *demographic transition.* It asserts that in the "pre-industrial" stage of development, nations have a steady-state population size that reflects a balancing of high death rates (including infant deaths) and high birth rates. At a later, "industrial" phase of development, when the demographic transition has been completed, a nation's population is once again in equilibrium, stability being achieved once again by a balancing of birth and death rates, both of which have greatly decreased. During the intermediate or active phase of the transition, birth and death rates change concurrently with the broad and complex process of industrialization (many other changes occur, most notably urbanization).

The lead/lag relationship between the decline in the death rate and that in the birth rate is critical for population size. During the greater part of the last two centuries, a slow but steady decline in birth rates has lagged behind the decline in death rates, leading cumulatively to a large population increase. Within recent decades, the developing world has seen a precipitous decline in death rates followed by a slower decline in birth rates, which leads to the "world population explosion." Nevertheless the decline in births appears to be coming about more rapidly than it did in the preceding two centuries, which will moderate the explosion.

The demographic transition says nothing about disease or causes of death; it deals only with birth and death rates. Another concept, the *epidemiological transition* (Omran 1971) can be regarded as the disease analogue of the demographic transition. It deals with the mix of diseases that afflict a population, causing death and lowering the quality of life. It states that in the pre-industrial era, the major diseases are infectious and parasitic in nature. Their causes are immediately "biological" or vector-borne rather than "biochemical." Infants, lacking a competent immune system, are particularly susceptible. Whole communities fall prey to epidemics. Famine and malnourishment also prepare the way for diseases such as cholera and tuberculosis that more robust, better-nourished populations might resist. Gradually, concurrent with industrialization, these causes of death are replaced by degenerative diseases of complex, often ambiguous etiology, long latency, and extended duration.

The quickening pace of the epidemiological transition has a particular effect that deserves emphasis in discourse on the health situation of developing countries, namely, the "double burden." This effect means that while developing countries continue to deal with infection/parasitic disease, they must at the same time face a mounting challenge from the chronic diseases that predominate in industrial countries. A 1994 statement by WHO (World Health Organization 1994: 9) puts it thus: ". . . in developing countries, the growing prevalence of chronic conditions—particularly cancer, cardiovascular diseases, diabetes and mental disorders—added to the longstanding communicable diseases such as cholera, viral hepatitis, malaria and tuberculosis, creates a 'double burden'."

Illustrative instances of the "modern," chronic-disease half of the burden are offered by investigators in the Caribbean (Nicholls et al. 1993), who report on a cardiovascular epidemic there, and by others in Africa who show that cardiovascular age-specific rates in many Sub-Saharan countries are similar to those in Western Europe and North America (Muna 1993). As various interrelations within the epidemiological transition have become better understood, a broad program for research and empowerment known as the *health transition (HT)* has emerged (Caldwell 1993). Its agenda has been carried out in the developing countries, especially South Asia and Sub-Saharan Africa. It can be summarized in the following three elements. First, HT argues that the decline of the death rate in developing countries is due much less to clinical medicine than to extra-medical measures such as improvements in food supply and hygiene for the general population. Working from this premise, Caldwell and others in the program advocate national social and health policies that favor primary health care and preventive medicine (rather than hospital-based specialization), community development, and greater opportunity for women to achieve educational, social, and economic parity with men. Concerning the specifically "health" part of their agenda, they deplore a trend that seems to occur in many Third World countries, namely the build-up of clinical and technological medicine under laissez-faire market economics, to the neglect of public and community health.

This part of the HT doctrine can be seen as a fresh confirmation, in the Third World, of findings by Thomas McKeown (1976), the McKinlays (1977), and others going back as far as the nineteenth-century German pathologist Rudolf Virchow (Rosen 1979). These studies were conducted on European and North American populations—that is, the industrial world rather than the Third World. They converged on the general idea that nonmedical improvements in sanitation, housing, and diet were of vital importance for health and for the reduction of mortality.

The second element in HT thinking is this: Although health progress in general occurs concomitantly with industrialization and rising living standards, it comes more rapidly in countries where there is a more equitable distribution of income and wealth. Several relatively poor countries have made health progress, such as the reduction of death rates including especially infant mortality, well beyond what would be expected only on the basis of their per capita income. These exceptional countries are Kerala (a state in South India), Sri Lanka, China, Jamaica, and Costa Rica. At the opposite extreme are wealthier countries, which despite their high income, nevertheless have lagged in health progress; this group includes Oman, Saudi Arabia, Iran, Libya, and Iraq (Caldwell 1993).

Third, the HT agenda emphasizes lifestyle and behavioral factors. Medical sociologists looking at the industrial world (Ostfeld 1986; Kessler and Wortman 1989; Gallagher and Stratton 1997) typically discuss behavioral factors in chronic disease. Lifestyle and personal choice come into view: diet; exercise; tobacco, alcohol, and substance use; seatbelt safety; sexual patterns; and sleep. Instead of dealing with *behavioral links to chronic disease in the industrial world,* HT researchers focus on *behavioral links to infectious disease in the Third World.* In their focus on behavioral factors, they often place a strong emphasis on infant health and on environmental hazards. Also, regarding a person's formal education as an aspect of lifestyle, they have discovered that educated parents are more likely to opt for family-size limitation. Another effect of education is that educated women, compared with less-educated women, are more likely to seek out and to properly utilize modern health services (Halstead et al. 1985; Caldwell 1979).

To illustrate the role of behavioral factors in health and also the double burden of disease, we compare diarrheal disease with tobacco-related disease. Diarrheal disease typically stems from drinking water containing bacteria; the user is thus exposed to the risk of infectious disease. In contrast, the risk that tobacco smokers face is from degenerative disease: chest diseases such as lung cancer and cardiovascular disease.

Obtaining potable water is another behavioral factor. It is scarce in the Third World because of the weak environmental infrastructure; to obtain it, one must travel, often by foot, considerable distances. Tradition in many developing societies defines as "women's work" the fetching of water for the household. If potable water is distant and hard to obtain, the female members must balance the time, energy, and difficulty of obtaining it against their other household tasks (Gallagher 1994).

Tobacco smoking is also a behavioral pattern, but cigarettes and cigars are of relatively recent derivation, not a part of the traditional culture of developing societies. Smoking in developing countries has increased dramatically within the past thirty years, fostered in part by the search by tobacco companies in the United States and other industrial countries for new, foreign markets as domestic restrictions on the sale of cigarettes increase and domestic demand decreases (Barry 1991).

The *global burden of disease (GBD),* like the HT, is a comprehensive concept for defining and assessing the global scope of health deficit (Murray and Lopez 1996; Brown 1996). Being of global reach, the GBD inevitably engages in an extensive analysis of conditions in the Third World. We have already noted that the great preponderance of the world's population lives in the Third World. It is notable that contemporary discourse on many topics—social security systems, educational reform, information technology, and employment policy—can proceed without reference to Third World conditions. Yet no overall conceptualization of health can ignore the Third World. Another feature of global conceptualization is that it immediately invites comparison between the industrial countries and the developing countries. This latter feature is evident in work carried out under the general mandate of the GBD.

The GBD builds upon the HT. However, its empirical and conceptual reach is strategically enlarged by *the inclusion of disability and premature death as well as disease in the GBD measure.* The GBD methodology yields the following representative findings:

- The peoples of Sub-Saharan Africa and India comprise only 26 percent of the world's population, but together they bear more than 40 percent of the worldwide GBD.

- China stands out as the healthiest of the seven designated regions of the developing world, with 20 percent of the world's population but only 15 percent of the GBD.

- "Despite the epidemiological transition, deaths from communicable diseases, maternal and perinatal conditions, and nutritional deficiencies continue to take a heavy, and largely avoidable, toll. . . . Fully 17.3 million deaths in 1990 were due to this group of causes, and more than 16.5 million of these were in developing regions, mainly India and Sub-Saharan Africa" (Brown 1996: 18). Almost all diarrheal deaths—2.9 million—occurred in developing countries.

- Five of the ten leading causes of disability worldwide in 1990 consisted of mental illness or substance abuse, as follows: unipolar depression, alcohol use, bipolar disorder, schizophrenia, and obsessive-compulsive disorders. They were the most important cause of years lived with a disability (YLD) in every part of the world except Sub-Saharan Africa. That is, the "mental" part of YLD was more important than disabilities rising from somatic problems and physical injuries.

The GBD broadens the debate on issues in health policy. Take, for example, the issue posed by this question: Does the increasing length of life in industrial societies simply expose their populations to a longer period of debility? Or, alternatively, can they look forward to a longer period of good health?

The same questions can be raised for the developing societies. These questions are particularly apposite because, within the past 30 years, the Third World has experienced a decline in death rates that came about more rapidly than in the historical record of the industrial world.

GBD projections in this regard are revealing. They show that, age for age, adults in developing societies face: (1) a shorter period of remaining life than those in industrial societies, and (2) a larger proportion of that period in disabled condition. For example, the 60-year-old in India will have a life expectancy of approximately 16 years, of which 10 will be disability-free. This can be compared with the 60-year-old in industrial countries, who will have a life expectancy of approximately 19 years, of which 15 will be disability-free.

CONCLUSION

From the foregoing account of illness and medicine in the Third World it might appear that the sociologists who study it will be merely looking at "catch-up" events and trends—that the health situation of the Third World will sooner or later be like the industrial world's, and that the road ahead for it is too well understood and well charted to warrant full sociological engagement.

Such a view would be, we think, wrong for two reasons. First, the industrial world—the target or model—is itself in flux. It is at the very least a moving target; the Third World, with its own diversity, will perforce wobble unpredictably to catch up.

The flux in the industrial world has several ingredients. Within medicine itself, the pace of biomedical research and application is hectic. Among the various age strata, the elderly in particular have high needs and expectations for the alleviation of their illnesses, with concomitant demands for broadened access to treatment. There is also a great need for smoother connections between home/family resources and medical treatment in chronic illness. At the same time, because of the strong orientation toward major illness, the system of medical/health care misses many opportunities for earlier intervention and primary prevention of illness.

The second reason smacks more of history, and less of the geometry of pursuit and catch-up. The Third World is laying its foundations for modern health care in an epoch that is historically quite different from the late nineteenth and early twentieth centuries, when the now-industrialized world established its own basic institutions for health care. Along with the well-known technological advances in communication, industry, and transportation is a less frequently recognized difference: namely, that the positive attitudes and expectations of medicine that now prevail in the industrial world grew gradually along with the effectiveness and scope of modern medicine over the past century. Now, however, the same expectations have arrived, full-blown, in the Third World. Along with an automobile, television, and telephone for daily use, people in the Third World when they are sick hope for modern medical care (perhaps also for traditional medicine along with, but not in place of, modern medicine).

The low economic level of the Third World is an obstacle to the development of modern medicine on a wide scale. Given the economic constraints, Third World countries will be led to devise less expensive modes of medical care that may, in a reverse direction, attract the interest of industrial nations. Such modes, though faithfully implementing biomedical knowledge, might also be less physician-centered than those in the industrial world. Further, they might draw to a greater extent upon the family solidarity that remains strong in the Third World. As a numerically small but strategically strong conduit from medicine to society, medical sociologists can convey outward what they learn from the developing health situation of the Third World.

REFERENCES

ALBRECHT, GARY L., ed. 1981. *Cross National Rehabilitation Policies—A Sociological Perspective.* Beverly Hills, CA: Sage Publications.

BARRY, MICHELE. 1991. "The Influence of the U.S. Tobacco Industry on the Health, Economy, and Environment of Developing Countries." *New England Journal of Medicine* 324 (13, March 28): 917–20.

BROWN, PHYLLIDA. 1996. *Summary—The Global Burden of Disease.* Cambridge, MA: Harvard University Press.

CALDWELL, JOHN C. 1979. "Education as a Factor in Mortality Decline: An Examination of Nigerian Data." *Population Studies,* 33, 395–413.

CALDWELL, JOHN C. 1993. "Health Transition: The Cultural, Social and Behavioural Determinants of Health in the

Third World." *Social Science and Medicine* 36 (2): 125–35.

CHARMAZ, KATHY, and DEBORA A. PATERNITI. 1999. *Health, Illness, and Healing—Society, Social Context, and Self.* Los Angeles: Roxbury Publishing Company

CHO, SUNGNAM. 1989. "The Emergence of a Health Insurance System in a Developing Country: The Case of South Korea." *Journal of Health and Social Behavior* 30 (4): 467–71.

CLAWSON, DAN. 1997. "A Bridge to International Sociology." *Footnotes* (April): 7.

COCKERHAM, WILLIAM C. 1998. *Medical Sociology.* 7th ed. Upper Saddle River, NJ: Prentice Hall.

CONRAD, PETER. 1997. *The Sociology of Health and Illness.* 5th ed. New York: St. Martin's Press.

CONRAD, PETER, and EUGENE B. GALLAGHER, eds. 1993. *Health and Health Care in Developing Countries— Sociological Perspectives.* Philadelphia, PA: Temple University Press.

ELLING, RAY H. 1980. *Cross-National Study of Health Systems—Political Economies and Health Care.* New Brunswick, NJ: Transaction Books.

EVANS, PETER B., and JOHN D. STEPHANS. 1988. "Development and the World Economy." In *Handbook of Sociology,* ed. Neil Smelser. Newbury Park, CA: Sage Publications, pp. 739–73 (Ch. 22).

FERRANTE, JOAN. 1995. *Sociology—A Global Perspective.* 2nd ed. Belmont, CA: Wadsworth.

FIELD, MARK G., ed. 1989. *Success and Crisis in National Health Systems—A Comparative Approach.* New York: Routledge.

FREEMAN, HOWARD E., and SOL LEVINE. 1989. *Handbook of Medical Sociology.* 4th ed. Englewood Cliffs, NJ: Prentice Hall.

GALLAGHER, EUGENE B. 1994. "A Typology of Health Rationality Applied to Third World Health." In *Advances in Medical Sociology,* ed. Gary L. Albrecht. Vol. 4. Greenwich, CT: JAI Press, pp. 257–80.

GALLAGHER, EUGENE B. 1998. "Advanced medical care in a wealthy Arab society—The hospital–family nexus of Zahira Qeteb, a Spina Bifida girl who developed chronic renal failure." Paper presented at meeting of the American Sociological Association.

GALLAGHER, EUGENE B., and C.M. SEARLE. 1983. "Women's Health Care: A Study of Islamic Society." In *Third World Medicine and Social Change: A Reader in Social Science and Medicine.* Lanham, MD: University Press of America, pp. 85–96 (Ch 7).

GALLAGHER, EUGENE B., and JANARDAN SUBEDI, eds. 1995. *Global Perspectives on Health Care.* Englewood Cliffs, NJ: Prentice Hall.

GALLAGHER, EUGENE B., and TERRY D. STRATTON. 1997. "Health Behavior in Persons Living with Chronic Conditions" In *Handbook of Health Behavior Research III: Demography, Development, and Diversity,* ed. David S. Gochman. New York: Plenum Press, pp. 229–45 (Ch 11).

GOLDTHORPE, JOHN E. 1984. *The Sociology of the Third World—Disparity and Development.* Cambridge, England: Cambridge University Press.

GOOD, MARY-JO DELVECCHIO, LINDA HUNT, TSUNETSUGU MUNAKATA, and YASUKI KOBAYASHI. 1993. "A Comparative Analysis of the Culture of Biomedicine: Disclosure and Consequences for Treatment in the Practice of Oncology," In *Health and Health Care in Developing Countries,* ed. Peter Conrad and Eugene B. Gallagher. Philadelphia: Temple University Press, pp. 180–210 (Ch 9).

HALSTEAD, S.B., J.A. WALSH, and K.S. WARREN, eds. 1985. *Good Health at Low Cost.* New York: Rockefeller Foundation.

HOMEDES, NURIA, and ANTONIO UGALDE. 1994. "Research on Patient Compliance in Developing Countries." *Bulletin of PAHO* 28 (1): 17–33.

Journal of Health and Social Behavior. "Sociological Studies of Third World Health and Health Care." 30 (4, December 1989): Issue theme.

KESSLER, RONALD C., and CAMILLE B. WORTMAN. 1989. "Social and Psychological Factors in Health and Illness." In *Handbook of Medical Sociology.* 4th ed., ed. Howard E. Freeman and Sol Levine. Englewood Cliffs, NJ: Prentice Hall, pp. 69–86 (Ch 4).

KURTZ, RICHARD A., and H. PAUL CHALFANT. 1991. *The Sociology of Medicine and Illness.* 2nd ed. Boston: Allyn and Bacon.

LASSEY, MARIE L., WILLIAM R. LASSEY, and MARTIN JINKS. 1997. *Health Care Systems Around the World—Characteristics, Issues, Reforms.* Upper Saddle River, NJ: Prentice Hall.

MACIONIS, JOHN J. 1999. *Society.* 4th ed. Upper Saddle River, NJ: Prentice Hall.

MCKEOWN, THOMAS. 1976. *The Role of Medicine: Dream, Mirage, or Nemesis?* London: Nuffield Provincial Hospitals Trust.

MCKINLAY, JOHN B., and SONJA M. MCKINLAY. 1977. "The Questionable Contribution of Medical Measures to the Decline of Mortality in the United States in the Twentieth Century." *Milbank Memorial Quarterly* 55 (3, Summer): 405–28.

MUNA, WALINJOM. 1993. "Cardiovascular Disorders in Africa." *World Health Statistical Quarterly* 46: 134–50.

MURRAY, CHRISTOPHER J.L., and ALAN LOPEZ, eds. 1996. *The Global Burden of Disease—A Comprehensive Assessment of Mortality and Disability From Disease, Injuries, and Risk Factors in 1990 and Projected to 2020.* Cambridge, MA: Harvard University Press.

NICHOLLS, ERIC, ARMANDO PERUGA, and HELENA RESTROPO. 1993. "Cardiovascular Disease Mortality in the Americas." *World Health Statistical Quarterly* 46: 134–50.

OMRAN, ABDEL R. 1971. "The Epidemiologic Transition." *Milbank Memorial Quarterly* (4, Part 1): 509–38.

OSTFELD, ADRIAN M. 1986. "Cardiovascular Disease." In *Applications of Social Science to Clinical Medicine and Health Policy,* ed. Linda H. Aiken and David

Mechanic. New Brunswick, NJ: Rutgers University Press, pp. 129–56 (Ch 8).

ROSEN, GEORGE. 1979. "The Evolution of Social Medicine" In *Handbook of Medical Sociology* 2nd ed., ed. Howard E. Freeman, Sol Levine, and Leo G. Reeder. Englewood Cliffs, NJ: Prentice Hall, pp. 30–60 (Ch 2).

SEARLE, C. MAUREEN, and EUGENE B. GALLAGHER. 1983. "Manpower Issues in Saudi Health Development." *Milbank Memorial Quarterly* 61 (4, Fall): 659–86.

SUBEDI, JANARDAN, and EUGENE B. GALLAGHER, eds. 1996. *Culture, Society, and Illness: Transcultural Perspectives.* Englewood Cliffs, NJ: Prentice Hall.

U.S. BUREAU OF THE CENSUS. 1996. *World Population Profile: 1996.* Washington, DC: U.S. Government Printing Office.

WEISS, GREGORY L., and LYNNE E. LONNQUIST. 1996. *The Sociology of Health, Healing, and Illness.* 2nd ed. Upper Saddle River, NJ: Prentice Hall.

WOLPE, PAUL ROOT. 1998. "The Triumph of Autonomy in American Bioethics: A Sociological View." In *Bioethics and Society—Constructing the Ethical Enterprise,* ed. Raymond DeVries and Janardan Subedi. Upper Saddle River, NJ: Prentice Hall.

WORLD HEALTH ORGANIZATION. 1981. *Global Strategy for Health for All by the Year 2000.* Geneva, Switzerland: World Health Organization.

WORLD HEALTH ORGANIZATION. 1994. *Ninth General Programme of Work, 1996–2001.* Geneva, Switzerland: WHO.

ZEICHNER, CHRISTIANE I., ed. 1988. *Modern and Traditional Health Care in Developing Societies—Conflict and Cooperation.* Lanham, MD: University Press of America.

28 THE SOCIOLOGICAL IMAGINATION AND BIOETHICS

CHARLES L. BOSK, *University of Pennsylvania*

The emergence, growth, and increased institutional legitimacy of bioethics in the last quarter of the twentieth century appears to be matched only by the inattention of sociologists to this phenomenon. This, at least, is the prevailing interpretation, the conventional wisdom, explaining the relationship of empirical sociology and normative bioethics. It is hard to state which is more peculiar in an intellectual climate marked by what Geertz (1983) calls "genre blurring": that such a state of affairs exists or that such a description of the relation of bioethics and sociology stands unchallenged.

In this chapter, I show that the conventional wisdom describing the relation of sociology and bioethics is incorrect. In place of the conventional wisdom, I provide an interpretation that holds that when it comes to bioethics, sociologists are a bit like Moliere's *Bourgeois Gentilhomme,* who spoke prose without ever realizing it. To state my conclusion first, the contribution of sociologists to topics bioethical is as remarkable as it is unappreciated. To understand how such an odd state of intellectual affairs came to be, I will: (1) provide a brief introductory sketch of bioethics; (2) develop a reappraisal of medical sociology that allows us to both appreciate the sociological involvement with those substantive issues that engage bioethicists and to see that the sociological involvement with these issues predates bioethics as either an organized domain of inquiry or an emergent professional occupation; and (3) recapitulate the conventional understanding of the gulf that separates the intellectual domain of sociology from bioethics. Finally, I will highlight those features of sociological work that cause sociologists simultaneously to deny involvement with bioethics and to contribute to its literature, as well as suggest inherent limitations to any rapprochement of bioethics and sociology.

BIOETHICS: AN INTRODUCTORY SKETCH

Any attempt to provide a capsule description of an intellectual movement and organizational development with a history that is longer than thirty years runs the risk of becoming a parody, as complex events are compressed into a tidy, coherent narrative. That risk, however, needs to be taken here since it helps us understand how sociological work was read out of bioethics and why sociologists did not object to this as it occurred. To ask the question: "How and why did bioethics develop within medicine as it did?" is, of course, to pose a question of origins. Such questions have multiple dimensions. We need to concern ourselves with simple facts: Who did what, when, with what intentions, and with what consequences? Yet which simple facts one chooses to arrange, how they are weighted, and what consequences they are assigned encode judgments about the goals, utility, and place of bioethics. It is impossible to describe the origins of bioethics without signaling as well the larger purposes of the enterprise, the individuals who might legitimately claim to be members of this professional community, the problems that belong to their domain, and the solutions to these problems that are likely to receive a friendly reception.

There are three different ways to understand the emergence of bioethics. These three narratives are not incompatible, but each stresses a different aspect of the field's emergence. The first, least influential and most sociological version of bioethics' emergence links a concern with ethics in medical arenas to an increased concern with ethics in other domains of public life: government, business, education, sports, and entertainment. In the post-Watergate era, trust in legitimate authority had eroded. An increased inspection of the ethics of public action was a natural consequence. In this version of events, there is nothing unique about bioethics; parallel developments can be identified in every other public institution. Not surprisingly, this first narrative, which effaces the unique subject matter and struggles of bioethicists, has no currency within bioethics. I refer to this narrative here only to highlight the inattention of bioethicists to the social context of their activities. I shall make no further reference to this sociological meta-narrative of the origins of bioethics. Instead I shall concentrate on the two other narratives that animate bioethicists' understanding of their own practices.

One narrative with currency among bioethicists sees bioethics as a reform movement within medicine. This is a narrative that stresses the "enlightened steward" role of the medical profession. In this view, the rise of bioethics is a response to problems that surfaced as a byproduct of medical progress. These problems existed at multiple levels. At the clinical level, progress had transformed the doctor–patient relationship—and not for the better. Clinicians recognized that while medical science as marked by diagnostic technique, bedside monitoring, clinical pharmacology, and surgical intervention waxed, medical art as marked by the humane and spiritual side of the doctor–patient relationship waned.

With the advent of new organizational forms, professionally public arenas with public-action adult and neonatal intensive-care units in particular, the opportunity to treat ultimate decisions of life and death as private matters among physician, patient, and family was seriously eroded, if not lost. The quasi-public, open space of intensive-care units made quasi-public surveillance of private decisions unavoidable. Much writing by clinicians in the early years of what we now understand as bioethics was a plaint about technological change and a plea for more humane and spiritual approaches. R. Duff and A. Campbell's (1973) classic New England Journal of Medicine article on the withdrawal of life support for severely compromised neonates after consultation with parents at Yale-New Haven Hospital is a good example. The authors frame their discussion as an illustration of "new" dilemmas and one approach to them. The authors' intent is to share their experience as an aid to those who are just beginning to experience similar tensions in their own institutions. Elite academic physicians writing in American medicine's most prestigious journal confess their ethical confusion. The center is warning the periphery and in prose more rhetorically impassioned than what is normally found on the staid pages of The New England Journal of Medicine.

Moreover, it was not just rare clinical problems that were paraded through the august pages of The New England Journal of Medicine. Henry Beecher (1966) published an exposé of physicians' conduct of scientific research. Deliberate deception, a lack of even a minimal concern with consent, sloppily designed trials unlikely to yield interpretable data, and overly risky protocols were among the faults that concerned Beecher. Like his Yale colleagues, the Harvard physician had an innate faith that if problems were made public, then they would be addressed. As David Rothman (1991) points out in his informative account of both the extent of and the limits to Beecher's whistle-blowing, Beecher recommended no remedy for the problems he uncovered other than the reawakening of ethical concern in well-intended, if careless, researchers. In Beecher's and Duff and Hollingshead's responses to the problems they spotlighted, there is something particularly American about the melioristic faith that open communications lead to solutions. There is little to no recognition by the authors of either article that problems may be intractable; values, discordant; goals, divergent; and decisions, difficult.

The second narrative with currency among bioethicists emphasizes the same criticisms that were made within medicine but stresses the role of outsiders to medicine in identifying problems and in resolving them. The end-of-life questions posed in The New England Journal of Medicine by Duff and Campbell (1973) were posed by E. Kubler-Ross (1969) in her trade publication On Death and Dying. The University of Chicago psychiatrist criticizes medical practice for its emphasis on managing death through a dehumanizing technological regime, while ignoring death's inevitability as well as its spiritual and emotional dimensions. While Kubler-Ross is a physician, she chose to make her critique largely outside of professional arenas, and her appeals are directed as much at patients and families who should demand better as at health professionals who should know better. Her account emphasizes the obstacles medical staff place on her work with the dying and the hostility of medical staff toward any changes in technologically based regimes of care. Media accounts of Kubler-Ross's work highlight her outsider, "maverick" status within the medical profession.

In addition, the first media-intensive right-to-die case, that of Karen Anne Quinlan, emerged in the mid-1970s. Besides the enormous amount of media coverage, and hence collective awareness of the ethical dilemmas in modern medicine the case generated, there are two features of it worth noting. First, this was not a conflict that could be resolved within the confines of the normal doctor–patient relationship. Karen Anne Quinlan's parents and her physicians were adversaries. This very fact pointed out nothing so much as how inadequate existing social means were for mediating such disputes. As the case unfolded, a considerable amount of commentary centered on this fact. Second, this fact did not escape the New Jersey Supreme Court, which while seeing the right to die as a privacy issue, nonetheless recommends that hospitals form and use ethics committees to resolve such problems. Such a policy, when followed, makes private decisions more public and requires individuals who are willing to claim expertise in ethical decision making. At the same time, it legitimates health-care organizations internalizing the ethics functions in some combination of committees and professional roles.

There were also critiques of research ethics from sources outside of medicine. Two particular well-publicized research projects received much media attention. Both involved the exploitation of vulnerable populations in federally sponsored research. The first was the infamous Tuskegee Syphilis Study (Jones 1981; Brandt 1978). This "natural history" of untreated syphilis in black males involved researchers actively preventing subjects who were poor black sharecroppers from receiving medical treatment. The research subjects were never informed that they were in a research project that forbade treatment. The second project involved the injecting of retarded children at Willowbrook, a residential treatment center operated by the State of New York, with hepatitis B in order to test a vaccine. As with Tuskegee, consent was foregone. The ordinary social controls of the medical profession did not discover, report, or correct these research abuses. Rather, the fact that journalists uncovered them and then legislators made them the subject of hearings was taken as evidence of the failure of internal self-regulation. In fact, the revelations of these research abuses helped create a national consensus that if ethical dilemmas were to be faced, they would be faced only because of pressures and resources brought from the outside. Through greater public surveillance, medicine as a public institution would be made more accountable.

Pressure and resources to allow the ethical dilemmas of medicine to be faced were forthcoming. The United States Public Health Service promulgated regulations protecting human research subjects. These regulations required that all institutions receiving federal funds have institutional review boards in place to monitor research protocols for the adequacy of consent procedures and the appropriateness of risk-benefit ratios. Next, a wide range of ethical dilemmas was attacked

through a Presidential Commission. Whatever may be said of the work of that Presidential Commission, at a very minimum it legitimated public discourse by nonmedical experts on clinical problems. The doctor–patient relationship and its attendant ethical problems were now very much a public concern.

Another signal event in an account of external forces driving the growth and development of bioethics was the formation of The Hastings Center for Ethics, Life Sciences, and Society. The Hastings Center provided an organizational locus for bioethical concerns, united scholars across disciplines within a single framework, and produced a journal, which kept debate alive. But perhaps most important, the Hastings Center allowed what had been seen as disparate issues to be linked by their similar unifying themes. Having a dominant central organization allowed for coherent growth; both legitimate problems and legitimate experts were now identifiable. In addition, the very fact that the Hastings Center was *outside* the academy—and, in part, hostile to it—meant that its focus could be more sharply resolved on substantive issues without a concern for the formalism of departments and disciplinary boundaries. This fact allowed for both a more public role and more cooperation among interested parties than would have been the case had this center been located in a university with its pre-existing structures of status and power, as well as its ceaseless competition for scarce resources.

From these humble beginnings in the 1970s, the institutional growth of bioethics has been breathtaking. Over fifty of this country's 126 medical schools have established centers or departments of bioethics. Many of these offer master's-level degree programs. There has been even more furious growth in ethics consultation services, which are provided by individual clinical ethicists or institutional ethics committees (Bosk and Frader 1997). In part, these committees are a response to a mandate of the Joint Commission on the Accreditation of Health Care Organizations, which recently required that institutions seeking its approval have in place a mechanism for resolving problems in clinical ethics. Finally, President Clinton has appointed a National Advisory Bioethics Commission, as sure a sign as any that bioethics has achieved a more than nominal legitimacy.

With all of this institutional growth, there has been some indication that the original interdisciplinary character of bioethics has weakened. Postgraduate educational programs require curricula and staffing. Philosophy is now the core discipline of bioethics. Beyond that, with the publication of Beauchamp and Childress's (1979) *Principles of Bioethics,* now in its fourth edition, the field even has a dominant approach:

principlism. This approach holds that four different principles or values of equal moral weight—autonomy, beneficence, nonmaleficence, and justice—need to be applied differentially, according to the demands of particular cases, in order to resolve conflicts. For clinicians beset with the quotidian conflicts of clinical care, principlism had the immediate appeal of offering a moral methodology to resolve conflict. This approach has its critics, who find the principle of principlism too abstract to be easily applied to the concrete empirical problems of clinical care (Hoffmaster 1990, 1992). Nor is principlism the only approach available to the bioethicist. To name but a few, other approaches include casuistry (Jonsen and Toulmin 1988), phenomenological ethics (Zaner 1993), narrative ethics (Charon 1994), and virtue ethics (MacIntyre 1981). While bioethics has more to offer than a principlist approach, the growth of a set of alternatives to principlism, all of which stress the liabilities of the principlist approach, speaks to the central position of principlism.

In either the internalist or the externalist narrative of bioethics' rise to prominence, sociologists had little to add to the emerging enterprise. Both narratives diagnose modern medicine's problems as a set of moral and/or spiritual failings. Since the problem is one of values, it is experts in values who are called upon to treat the problem. Theologians and, in our secular social order, philosophers are those experts. From the reformer's perspective, the problem was to inject humanism into an overly scientific and technologic regime of care. Given that there was already too much science in medicine, turning to a discipline increasingly reliant on scientific legitimations was not an attractive alternative. Beyond that, the critique of both narratives, however choleric it sounded, was actually quite limited. The problem was not one of structural arrangements—the distribution of power, privilege, and authority—which would have called for the expertise of the sociologist. Rather, the problem was one of values in the doctor–patient relationship. Both narratives seemed to argue that if we, as a society, placed the right values in that relationship, the problems of modern medicine would disappear. It was as if everything was right with medicine except what was said and done and how it was said and done in certain very exceptional circumstances of the doctor–patient relationship. Further, those circumstances—the problematic beginnings and endings of life—were areas where theologians, once, and philosophers, currently, have both practical experience and cultural authority.

In the zero-sum world that is both the medical school curriculum and the medical profession's tolerance of nonbasic science discourse, as the place of bioethics grew, the place of social science approaches to medical problems shrank. Courses on community medicine or the impact of social and cultural variables in health care were quickly replaced with courses on professional values and ethics. Bioethics did not simply rise to prominence; it paved over what inroads social scientists had made in getting physicians to appreciate how social context influences care.

WHERE ARE THE SOCIOLOGISTS?

Whichever narrative favored by bioethicists one chooses to explain the rise of bioethics, or however one combines the two dominant narratives, the major substantive theme was the same: patients and research subjects had difficulty exercising their will, largely because the control of information by physicians precluded any autonomy. The fact that both the internal and external narratives shared this sentiment makes it all the more remarkable that sociologists were not prominent actors in the coming of bioethics to American medicine. For when one looks at the medical sociology of the period, what one finds is an empirical analysis and critique that parallels many of the same sentiments that accompany the rise of bioethics.

Part of the problem is that much of the sociological writing on medicine does not self-consciously identify itself as such. The sociology of medicine was not at that time the robust, well-organized specialty that it is today. As a consequence, research is cast in rhetoric that appears unfamiliar to those whose interest is primarily in medicine. Much of this research is part of an intellectual tradition that borrows heavily on Marshallian ([1939] 1965) extensions of citizenship rights, on Weberian concerns about the growth of formal rationality, or on Marxian illustrations of domination by a ruling class that controls productive resources. Formally, studies are identified as contributions to studies of the professions, work and occupations, or organizations. These studies are presented as examples of how power asymmetries are created, managed, and sustained as legitimate and necessary. The lack of theoretical self-consciousness in the early years of the sociology of medicine is matched by a similar phenomenon in bioethics. Much of the early writing on ethical dilemmas in medicine does not announce itself as bioethics. That self-identification awaits emerging organizational forms. So with neither group of scholars yet clear about its identity, it becomes easier to see why the two groups did not pay more attention to one another.

Nonetheless, the topics that early researchers in the sociology of medicine focus on are precisely those topics that were so important in the formation of bioethics: namely, death and dying, information control and autonomy, and informed consent. Good examples are found in the studies of death and dying of the late 1960s. B. Glaser and A. Strauss provide two detailed empirical accounts, *Awareness of Dying* (1965) and *Time for Dying* (1968). The usefulness of these works to nonsociologists is no doubt blunted by the fact that these texts are self-consciously crafted as illustrations of the methodical use of "grounded theory" (Glaser and Strauss 1967), and the theory so grounded is one about "status passages" (Glaser and Strauss 1971). For the nonsociologist and perhaps even for some sociologists, to talk of death this way, even with rather gripping descriptions from first-hand observational data, appears overly abstract and distant from the phenomenological experience of death itself.

Nonetheless, there is much in Glaser and Strauss's accounts that parallels Kubler-Ross's work and echoes Duff and Campbell's concerns about communication. A major theme is the effect of "awareness contexts" on the patient's "dying trajectory." Glaser and Strauss (1964) define "awareness context" as follows: "By the term awareness context we mean the total combination of what each interactant in a situation knows about the identity of the other and his own identity in the eyes of the other." Glaser and Strauss identify four types of "awareness contexts" for dying patients: open, closed, pretense, and suspicion. They then discuss the factors that cause contexts to be transformed and deal with the tensions created by closedness, pretense, and suspicion. Glaser and Strauss have had a great influence on nursing practice. This influence makes sense: the tensions of awareness contexts fell most directly on nurses with their continual interactional responsibilities. Their work did not receive much attention from bioethicists, despite the fact that much of the need for bioethics is created out of the tensions of unstable or unshared "awareness contexts," and that much of the work of clinical bioethicists is an attempt to create "awareness contexts" that are shared.

Another classic piece of sociology from the same period is also on death and dying, David Sudnow's (1967) *Passing On: The Social Organization of Dying.* Like Glaser and Strauss, Sudnow uses a rhetoric with which the nonsociologist will have difficulty. His study is one of the ethnomethodology of dying. Sudnow's main concern is to document how death—recognized, organized, created, and accounted for as a "natural" fact—is, in reality, an ongoing, contingent, and fragile accomplishment of hospital workers. But, again, as in Glaser and Strauss, there is much in Sudnow that is useful and instructive to the bioethicist if one but pays attention to the empirical detail. There is, for example, a wonderfully drawn contrast between the social organization of dying in a private hospital with a middle-class clientele and of dying in a public one with a largely indigent one.

Most important is Sudnow's observation that the organization of effort over a dying body is directly related to physicians' evaluation of the social worth of the patient. "Social worth" is determined by such factors as age, race, gender, occupation, and visible evidence of class standing. Sudnow goes so far as to observe that "if one anticipates having a critical heart attack, he had best keep himself well-dressed and his breath clean . . ." (p. 105). Sudnow's observation has been challenged by Diana Crane (1975) in her *The Sanctity of Social Life: Physicians' Treatment of Critically Ill Patients.* Crane found no evidence that social worth influenced effort. Crane's analysis of what physicians said they did, in precisely those situations in which bioethicists claimed to be most interested, was no more warmly received than was Glaser and Strauss' or Sudnow's. The concept of "social worth" and its use has been imported into bioethics, but little credit for its development is given to Sudnow. Further, the bioethics community has largely ignored Sudnow's emphasis on the difference between class and the organization of dying; the community often writes as if the bioethical dilemmas surrounding death and dying have no social context, or, more sharply, as if social context does not affect the exercise of autonomy.

A second thread that runs through early medical sociology concerns the interrelationship of patient autonomy and the flow of information. In part a Weberian, in part a Marxian, theme, the general thrust of empirical observation is that by controlling, manipulating, and shaping information, physicians and other health-care workers control patients, maintain order and efficiency, and prevent patients and their families from "flooding out" and thereby creating "scenes" (Goffman 1961, 1967). A concern for death and dying is a topical linkage of sociology to bioethics; a concern with autonomy is a substantive one.

There are multiple studies that document that the flow of information to patients is highly imperfect and calculated to make the physician's exercise of authority easier. We have already seen how "awareness contexts" allow physicians to control dying patients. Emerson (1969) makes this analysis even more fine grained by showing how nurses manipulate the flow of humor to determine how aware patients are of their condition. Patients who are aware that they may be dying but have not been formally told so often probe nurses with remarks that can be seen as serious or as jokes. Nurses then have the option of hearing the remark in whatever way they want. If a nurse hears a remark as humor, then the patient's feelings are dismissed, ignored, or trivialized. However, if the nurse hears the "humorous" remark as "serious," then there is an opportunity to inform the patient, validate his/her concerns, and explore his/her feelings. Organizational pressures, such as deference to physicians as the legitimate passers of such fateful information or to a family's stated wishes, constrain the opportunities of nurses to hear remarks as "serious." Nonetheless, there are situations in which they do, especially when nurses make the judgment that a patient already "knows" and nothing is gained by further deception.

Information management is further discussed in contexts other than those that involve death and dying. Jeanne Quint's study (1972) of information control and cancer patients is one example. Quint details how "both consciously and unconsciously the staff makes use of strategies which limit patients' opportunity to negotiate for information" (Quint 1972: 232). Such strategies include a preoccupation with technical work, frequent rotation, and deliberate ignorance regarding patients' prognoses.

Yet another theme in the early sociology of medicine concerns uncertainty (Parsons 1951; Hughes 1953). Both Fred Davis (1960, 1963) and Julius Roth (1963) discuss how physicians manipulate uncertainty regarding time to recovery to control patients. Davis looks at uncertainty in predicting the extent of and the time to recovery in paralytic poliomyelitis. Davis (1960: 41–42) seeks:

> To distinguish between "real" uncertainty as a clinical scientific phenomenon and the uses to which uncertainty—real or "pretended," functional uncertainty— lends itself in the management of patients and their families by hospital physicians and other treatment personnel.

Davis demonstrates that physicians and other treatment personnel feign uncertainty about the extent of and time to recovery long after such uncertainty has been resolved. By feigning uncertainty, physicians sustain an atmosphere of buoyant optimism, motivate patients and their families to cooperate with demanding programs of physical therapy, and prevent (or at least stall) patients and their families from dropping out of conventional therapy in favor of unconventional alterna-

tives that physicians view as forms of quackery. In Julius Roth's (1963) analysis is of a tuberculosis sanitarium, like Davis, Roth focuses on how control of information serves organizational needs and quiets patient resistance.

Both Davis's and Roth's treatments of uncertainty contrast sharply with Renée Fox's treatment (1957, 1959) of the same topic. Fox studies uncertainty in two contexts: undergraduate medical education and the development of renal dialysis and transplantation. In both contexts, uncertainty is an irreducible part of medical practice. Medical students develop ways to cope with this uncertainty, as do clinician–researchers on medical frontiers. Where uncertainty assumes an interactional dimension in Fox's writing, it is shared with patients, who cooperate in the research project as if they were junior collaborators. In Fox's analysis, the physician never uses uncertainty as a tool for advantage. Davis and Roth emphasize the potential divergence of self-interest between patient and physician; Fox emphasizes convergence. It is Fox's analysis that has had the most influence among bioethicists.

These studies at the level of micro interaction emphasize how a lack of information inhibits patient autonomy. At a macro level, there is a concern with how the information monopoly of physicians runs counter to democratic values in modern American society. This critique finds its fullest elaboration in the work of Eliot Freidson (1970). Borrowing the concepts of substantive and formal or technical rationality from Weber, Freidson argues that physicians are prime examples of professional experts who usurp lay authority. Substantive rationality concerns a society's values and goals; technical rationality, the most efficient means to attain these goals. It is Freidson's contention that as scientific knowledge grows, so does the authority of technical rationality. Substantive rationality has, in Freidson's view, a zero-sum relation to technical rationality. As one grows, the other shrinks.

As this happens, there are cleavages between professional and lay interests. It is these that most disturb Freidson:

> The medical system, like many other professional systems, is one predicated on the view that the layman is unable to evaluate his own problem and the proper way which it may be managed: this justifies the imposition by the profession of its own conception of problem and management. The client's rights are specified simply as the right to choose or to refuse professional ministrations. And, as in the ballot in totalitarian countries, the client is sometimes not even free to choose. Once engaged in a service, its terms are largely not a matter of

choice, the client's position being similar to a child in juvenile court, considered incapable of managing himself, neither responsible nor competent, protected by none of the rules protecting the rights of adults in the legal system, essentially at the mercy of the good intentions and professional beneficence of court officials. This, I believe, is improper. (1970: 351–52)

In a footnote, Freidson suggests that the spirit of the juvenile court—and one would expect, by extension, medicine—is one of a deplorable "humanistic tyranny." This tyranny results from the fact that decisions that at their base are moral and evaluative, decisions such as "Is this a disease?" are seen as technical and scientific. Each time such a decision is made, expert authority grows, reducing lay authority and impoverishing, as a result, democratic values, beliefs, and processes.

Under such conditions, it is hard to imagine an ethical doctor–patient relationship, no matter what the interest, motives, and behaviors of the physician or the desires, consent, and cooperation of the patient. Ethicality in a democratic society requires a more level playing field. The issue, for Freidson, is not whether patients get better. Rather, the issue is the price paid for medical services in terms of autonomy, dignity, and adult capacities. If all illnesses were transient, perhaps, then the price is acceptable. But with the shift toward more and more patients becoming ill with chronic conditions, a democratic society slides into humanistic tyranny largely unaware that such a change is taking place. Like those voters in totalitarian societies, our own choices about what is a healthy life cease to have much meaning.

WHY NOT MORE CONVERGENCE OF BIOETHICS AND SOCIOLOGY?

So, on the one hand, we have a bioethics spurred by some combination of factors internal to medicine (new problems created by new technologies and organizational innovations) and factors external to medicine (the erosion of paternalism, the demands for an increased accountability associated with it, and several well-documented, dramatic abuses of power and privilege). On the other hand, we have a sociology that is empirically active looking at death and dying and the exercise of power and authority within the doctor–patient relationship. At the same time, that sociology is theoretically articulating a concern for internalized, elaborate, and rationalized forms of social control (Durkheim 1933, 1961, 1965; Janowitz 1975; Foucault 1965, 1973) and, as a kind of *gedanken* experiment, a concern for the relationship among individual autonomy, expert authority,

and democratic values (Weber 1919 [1922]; Simmel 1978; Durkheim 1933, 1961, 1965; Hughes 1953; Parsons 1951; Marshall 1939; Freidson 1970). We have had as well, until most recently, an almost complete silence on the relationship between the practice of medical ethics—its sociology—and the ideals of ethical practice—its philosophy.

There are, of course, a number of explanations offered by sociologists to explain the lack of interchange. The two with the most surface plausibility posit versions of what might be called the fundamentally different worldview hypothesis. P. Conrad (1994) has clearly presented one version. Conrad sees the initial mutual indifference as a product of fundamentally different intellectual agendas or professional projects. Put in its baldest form, this explanation holds that philosophers, when concerned with ethical action, are concerned with what ought to be, while sociologists explore what is. Neither group is much concerned with the fit between the two. This difference in focus is an outcome of the core mission of each of the two disciplines and of professional socialization to that mission.

The problem with this characterization is that it adequately describes neither the activities of bioethicists, on the one hand, or sociologists, on the other. To begin with bioethicists, especially those of a casuistic or narrative stripe, take as their starting point cases, what is. It is true that these cases are a starting point for discussion, as opposed to the object of discussion themselves, that their construction is largely left unexplored, and that the level of detail sociological analysis requires is missing (Davis 1991). But the empirical world is not entirely disregarded. Further, some ethicists have recognized from the relative beginnings of bioethics the importance of adequate description. Hauerwaus (1977), for example, has suggested that those involved in ethical analysis dispense with the question, What should we do? and concern themselves instead with the question, How do we know we are defining the situation correctly? Hauerwaus writes:

> Unlike mud puddles, situations are not something we simply fall into. Situations and the decisions we make about them are what they are because of the presumptions we hold and how we have come to see them.

While we recognize this as a clarion call for a more sociological, more contextual, more interactional view of ethical analysis, it is fair to say that few ethicists responded. But the reasoning about clinical cases cannot fairly be said to be a topic in which philosophers universally eschewed interest.

Moreover, it is not fair to describe the sociological research of the '60s and early '70 as uninterested in social oughts. After all, this was a period when the methodological doctrine of value-neutrality was facing a rigorous challenge. The very sociologists who were producing the medical sociology that one would have thought bioethicists would have been most interested in were among those most energetically questioning or abandoning value-neutrality. Advocacy sociology began to have a certain cachet, and medical sociologists began to play a prominent role in the patient-rights' movement. For example, consider Goffman's (1961) prefatory remarks in *Asylums*:

> To describe the patient's situation faithfully is necessarily to present a partisan view. (For this last bias I partly excuse myself by arguing that the imbalance is at least on the right side of the scale, since almost all of the literature on mental patients is written from the point of the psychiatrist, and he, socially speaking, is on the other side.) . . . Finally, unlike some patients, I came to the hospital with no great respect for the discipline of psychiatry nor for agencies content with its current practice.

Put another way, Becker (1967), in his Presidential Address to the Society for the Study of Social Problems, had asked, "Whose Side Are We On?" Many agreed with his answer to his own query. We were on the side of those who are low on the hierarchy of credibility and trust. We were for those who would otherwise be voiceless in public. We were on the side of patients. The problem with Conrad's version of the *different intellectual worlds* hypothesis is that there are too many exceptions to it, both among bioethicists and sociologists.

Anspach (1993; see also Chambliss 1993, 1996) presents a different version of the incompatible worldview hypothesis, this one bottomed on different views of medical decision-making. The reasoning here is that the bioethical and the sociological views of decision-making create models that emphasize complementary, but fundamentally incompatible, aspects of decision-making. The bioethics model is focused on a critical moment, locates responsibility and authority as residing in individuals, and sees internalized values as the dispositive component of decisions. In contrast, the sociological version of decision-making focuses on shared understandings that emerge over time, locates authority and responsibility in collectivities, and sees external factors and social context as critical to decision-making.

There is a great deal of truth to this version of the incompatible worldviews hypothesis. There are certainly disciplinary differences in valuing values. Even if we sociologists wished to make values the ultimate source of behavior, we have no epistemological way of seeing values independent of the components of the situation—purposes at hand, organizational roles, definitions of the situation, and the like. Sociologists, in general, see values as speaking about how situations are constructed. Rarely do sociologists see values as an independent feature of the situation. As a result, we constantly fold values back into the analysis. Those values that sociologists treat so lightly as idealistic epiphenomena of more solid material forces are the very subject of bioethical discussion.

Even granting their mutual differences on the place of values, a number of puzzles still remain in explaining the mutual disregard of sociologists and bioethicists of each others' work. First, one of the basic approaches to ethical decision-making is "situationalism" (Fletcher 1966), usually dressed up and obscured so as not to be saddled with all the disabilities of extreme relativism. One would assume that a "situational" approach to ethics could use and would appreciate the highly contextualized descriptions of the situation that sociological researchers provide. Another approach to ethical decision-making is "utilitarianism," the moral accounting system that requires the balancing of pleasures and pains, benefits and costs, and profits and losses. Again, one would think this is a moral calculus that could use and would appreciate the input of sociologists. After all, utilitarianism is best applied when all the actors in a situation have their interests most fully analyzed. This is precisely what the sociological research described above has done.

For its part, the neglect of sociological attention to the emergence of bioethics is likewise puzzling. First, the emergence of a new professional segment (Bucher and Strauss 1961), the inevitable battles over turf (Goode 1960, Hughes 1953; Bucher 1961), and the impact of these battles on medical authority (Haug 1976) are the sorts of phenomena that one would think sociologists research. If not, one might think that the use and deployment of new rhetorics, legitimations, and structures for exercising professional authority would be the kind of phenomena sociologists study. Failing that, even if sociologists of medicine chose not to pay attention to the emergence of bioethics, it hardly explains why there is so little attention from students of social movements.

Perhaps the fundamental disregard of the two disciplines for each other is best explained as a consequence of their different professional projects and missions, social identities, and formal organization. In this explanation, the differing worldviews are a necessary but not a sufficient condition for explaining mutual neglect. Rather than denying the reality of differing worldviews, this explanation places them in a social context. In its intellectual infancy, bioethics displayed all the egocentricity associated with that stage of development. The professional interests of bioethicists were closely linked with displaying their intellectual potency and usefulness, and thus it was necessary to identify and stress what unique features a philosophical approach brought to the discussion. To look outward and incorporate social science perspectives risked diffusing an identity and message at precisely that moment at which they had to be most concentrated. Bioethics, as it emerged, was not well-enough established to incorporate sociology or any other of the social sciences. Law was accepted but only because it could not be excluded.

By the same token, sociology was not well positioned to pay much attention to bioethics. Our models of the medical profession stressed the "professional dominance" of physicians in such a way that we would have had to be very flexible indeed to recognize challenges to that dominance. At the same time, our concerns as a discipline were shifting away from the individualized doctor–patient relationship to the more corporate and collective dimensions of medical practice. We had neither the inclination to attend to the rise in bioethical questions nor the theoretical tools to make sense of those questions. Moreover the rise of gender studies made it difficult to see questions of birth and reproduction so central to bioethics in any frame other than one that stressed power and politics.

STEPS TOWARD CONVERGENCE

There are movements toward ending the mutual noninvolvement of sociology and bioethics. Bioethicists (Brody 1987; Hoffmaster 1990, 1992) have identified the beginnings of disaffection with the tools philosophers possess for resolving clinical issues. General statements of value are too vague and contentless to apply in specific situations. For values to apply in the world in action, behavior must be precisely described. Articulating values that underlie action is one task of ethicists. Identifying which values apply in which situations is another. Moreover, the articulation of a casuistic approach along with narrative and descriptive ethics requires case material. Now that bioethics is a securely organized subspecialty in the academy, and the ethics function has been legitimated at the bedside (Rothman

1991), its practitioners are secure enough to look to other disciplines for aid in accomplishing their mission.

More than intellectual maturation is involved here; there are some rather formidable social forces at work as well. Chief among these is the success of bioethics at institutionalizing itself. Now that more than fifty medical schools have departments or centers of bioethics, and now that all accredited health-care organizations need a mechanism for resolving ethical conflicts, administrative requirements create useful roles for sociologists. After all, departments need to document their performance by analyzing outcomes, to identify their client needs, to lobby for organizational resources, and to plan strategically for the future. At the same time, changes in health-care organization, as well as in the larger culture that contains it, militate for tools far more sociological than most ethicists possess. As we saw earlier, bioethicists lean heavily on an individualistic and utilitarian tradition of philosophy. As health care grows more corporate, as responsibility is collectivized in organizations, as priority-setting and rationing mechanisms become more explicit, bioethicists need to develop a richer language for speaking about community and community values.

For their part, sociologists have begun to pay more attention in their research to bioethics. In the past few years, a number of volumes that take bioethics seriously from a social science perspective have appeared (Devries and Subedi 1997; Fox and Swazey 1992; Anspach 1993; Bosk 1992; Chambliss 1996; Guillemin and Holmstrom 1986; Weisz 1990; Zusssman 1992). Each of these works takes an ethnographic approach to explain how ethical problems are identified, classified, debated, managed, resolved, or stalemated in clinical situations. As the ethics function acquires a formal organization, it becomes easier for ethnographers to see it as the sort of "bounded whole" that is favored as an object of study.

Further, it is surely something of a stretch to suggest that this interest in matters ethical appears *de novo*. In a certain sense, as the literature review above suggests, interest has always existed in a muted form. In recent years, two Reeder prize winners of the ASA's medical sociology section have urged sociologists to pay more attention to ethical issues in medicine (Fox 1985; Olesen 1989). Charles Lidz (Lidz et al. 1984) has long been associated with empirical research on informed consent, continuing a research tradition initiated over a decade earlier by Bernard Barber (Barber et al. 1973; Grey 1975.) Renée C. Fox's involvement (Fox 1959; Fox and Swazey 1974, 1992) with the transplant community is a chronicle of continuity and change in research ethics over nearly half a century. My own *Forgive and Remember* (Bosk 1979) is explicitly framed as a study of occupational ethics. Here, however, my intent was to be self-consciously Durkheimian rather than bioethical. Finally, Everett C. Hughes, who remains a steadfast guide of mine in matters sociological, closes his classic essay "Mistakes at Work" ([1951] 1971) with these words: ". . . and it is precisely all the processes involved in the definition and enforcement of moral rule that form the core problems of sociology."

So as bioethics grows, it discovers sociology at the same time that sociologists grow curious about it. Bioethicists, while not eschewing survey research, seem most intrigued by research utilizing ethnographic methods. Thick description (Geertz 1974) is a goal—all the better to understand social process. At the same time, many ethnographers appear fascinated by the study of ethical questions in medicine. How values apply in the world is a question well suited to ethnographic analysis. The rhetorics, rationales, tacit understandings, maxims, aphorisms, rough rules of theme, and general principles that are socially structured and shared and that guide action have long been the object of ethnographic understanding. The "essentially contestable" (Gallie 1962) value terms of bioethics are a field in which those involved in the study or practice of ethics and those involved in group life meet.

CONCLUSION

So it would seem that bioethicists and sociologists are at the dawn of a bright new day of inter-, trans-, and multidisciplinary research. Philosophers will conduct surveys and become participant observers. Sociologists will speak without blushing about deontology and casuistry. Philosophers will footnote Weber and Goffman. Sociologists will footnote Kant and Callahan. Our conference tables will be the academic equivalent of the utopian community Marx (1964) described in *The Economic and Philosophic Manuscripts of 1844*. Instead of hunters, fisherpersons, farmers, poets, and artists, we will be sociologists in the morning, philosophers in the afternoon, and clinical experts in the evening. But some basic problems must be faced lest this utopia be as difficult for bioethicists and sociologists to achieve as Marx's was for him and his contemporaries.

The first problem is overcoming an incompatibility between bioethical and sociological inquiry. The purpose of bioethical inquiry, I assume, is to clarify which principles or values should guide action when decision is difficult. In bioethics, descriptions of motives, intent,

and purposes need to be fairly one-dimensional or the balancing of values gets too complex for application. The goal of sociology, especially as practiced by ethnographers (again this is my assumption) is how actors shape and trim their actions to fit their principles and how these same actors shape and trim their values and principles to fit their actions. Where bioethicists seek clarity, sociologists look for ambiguity and complexity. Sociologists seek to show that our subjects are not slavish followers of rules, that they are not in principle or action "judgmental dopes" (Garfinkel 1967), but that they have great flexibility in deciding which rules to apply and when to apply them. If one thinks about this, it is a message at odds with the goal of bioethical analysis—identify a situation correctly, decide what principle applies, and ethical behavior will follow. These are all premises that are implicitly challenged by ethnographic accounts. Clarity about values for the sociologist is very seldom reassurance that any specific behavior will occur in the next instant. Sociologists are more sensitive than bioethicists to the well-known lag between values and behavior. So, at the least, bioethicists need to recognize that this barrier needs to be overcome before sociological work is successfully embraced.

Second, it is not clear that the sociologist's skills or training are up to the tasks that engagement with bioethics demands. Sociology is, after all, a generalizing science. We discover what happens on average, typically, in a randomly drawn, or some other way representative sample. Sociological expertise is in drawing the scatterplot rather than placing the point. The problem here is that the kind of cases that engage the bioethicist are individual clinical dilemmas, the points in the plot, the discrete events. Cases present themselves one at a time. Another voice might prove useful, but this is not necessarily so. Nor is there any particular necessity for that voice to be either ethnographic or sociological.

As a sociologist, I am very comfortable looking at a series of cases; finding similarities and differences between them; abstracting the rationales actors use to explain, justify, and legitimate their actions; and analyzing the intended and unintended consequences of action. This is what I do; it is what I have been trained to do. I may be flattered when asked to help in specific cases. I may even make reasonable and sensitive judgments and suggestions. But they have nothing to do with my expertise, training, or skill as a sociologist. As a sociological ethnographer, I am expert at commenting on the processes by which action emerged, cataloguing the understandings actors employed, and comparing these to rationales in other domains where power and expertise produce decisions. What I have no particular skill or training in is determining in any particular situation what should be done and why.

As sociologists enter the realm of bioethics, we will all need to be clear about what we are interested in, what we can do, and, without fail, what we cannot do. We also face the difficult task of balancing intimacy and distance with our informants, the social worlds we study, and the problems we study. To do any less is to risk going native in ways that compromise our professional identity and intellectual autonomy.

This brings us to our third problem: bioethicists will ask us to go native. For them the problem is how the health-care system responds to what they believe are ethical problems. Bioethicists will ask us to assume their definition of what an ethical problem is and to contribute to its solutions. By training, this is a very foreign concept to us. Rather than rolling up our sleeves and joining bioethicists in their quest for health care that meets whatever ethical tests bioethicists set for it, we sociologists are more likely to problematize the actions of bioethicists: Why do they define this as an ethical problem? On what is their social authority legitimated? How does their definition serve their own self-interested ends? What ethical problems escape their notice? And so on and on. Bioethicists, if they are like other professional subjects of sociological research, are not likely to appreciate such a skeptical, debunking examination.

Yet there is much sociological work to be done. We know little of how ethics consultants, committees, networks, and professional associations operate. How are agendas set? How is authority legitimated? How consistent is the professionalization of the role of the ethics expert with the principles of pluralistic democracy? How is consensus in bioethics established? How are dissident opinions managed? Whose interests are served? Does bioethics extend patient autonomy? If so, do patients welcome this? If autonomy is extended, are physicians and others accomplishing this by simply shucking the moral responsibilities of their roles? Yes, there is much for the sociologist to do in the world of bioethics. Whether we are interested in doing it, whether bioethicists will allow us to do it is another question. For while there have been calls from bioethics for a greater involvement in bioethics, it is clear that these calls mean something different for the sociologist that they do for the bioethicist.

REFERENCES

ANSPACH, R. 1993. *Deciding Who Lives: Fateful Choices in the Intensive-Care Nursery.* New York: University of California Press.

BARBER, B., J. LALLY, J. MAKARUSHKA, and D. SULLIVAN. 1973. *Research on Human Subjects: Problems of Social Control in Medical Experiments.* New York: Russell Sage.

BEAUCHAMP, T., and J. CHILDRESS. 1979. *Principles of Biomedical Ethics.* New York: Oxford University Press.

BECKER, H.C. 1967. "Whose Side Are We On?" *Social Problems* 14: 239–47.

BEECHER, H. 1966. "Ethics in Clinical Research." *New England Journal of Medicine* 274: 1354–60.

BOSK, C.L. 1979. *Forgive and Remember: Managing Medical Failure.* Chicago: University of Chicago Press.

BOSK, C.L. 1992. *All God's Mistakes: Genetic Counseling in a Pediatric Hospital.* Chicago: University of Chicago Press.

BOSK, C., and J. FRADER. 1997. "Institutional Ethics Committees: Sociological Oxymoron, Theoretical Black Box," In *Constructing the Bioethics Enterprise,* ed. R. Devries and J. Subedi. Upper Saddle River, NJ: Prentice Hall, pp. 94–116.

BRANDT, A. 1978. "Racism and Research: The Case of the Tuskegee Syphilis Study." *Hastings Center Review.* 6: 21–29.

BRODY, H. 1987. *Stories of Sickness.* New Haven: Yale University Press.

BUCHER, R. 1962. "Pathology: A Study of Social Movements Within a Profession." *Social Problems* 10:40–51.

BUCHER, R. and A. STRAUSS 1961. "Professions in Process," *American Journal of Sociology* 66: 325–34.

CHAMBLISS, D. 1993. "Is Bioethics Irrelevant?" *Contemporary Sociology* 22 (5):649–52.

CHAMBLISS, D. 1996. *Beyond Caring: Hospitals, Nursing, and the Social Organization of Ethics.* Chicago: University of Chicago Press.

CHARON, R. 1994. "Narrative Contributions to Medical Ethics: Recognition, Formulation, Interpretation, and Validation in the Practice of the Ethicist." In *A Matter of Principles? Ferment in U.S. Bioethics,* ed. E. Dubose, R. Hamel, and L. O'Connell. Valley Forge, PA: Trinity Press, pp. 260–83.

CONRAD, P. 1994. "How Ethnography Can Help Bioethics." *Bulletin of Medical Ethics:* 13–18.

CRANE, D. 1975. *The Sanctity of Social Life: Physicians' Treatment of Critically Ill Patients.* New York: Russell Sage.

DAVIS, D. 1991. "Rich Cases: The Ethics of Thick Description." *Hastings Center Review* 21: 12–17.

DAVIS, F. 1960. "Uncertainty in Medical Diagnosis: Clinical and Functional." *American Journal of Sociology* 66:259–67.

DAVIS, F. 1963. *Passage Through Crisis.* Indianapolis: Bobbs-Merrill.

DEVRIES, R., and J. SUBEDI. 1998. *Bioethics and Society.* Upper Saddle River, NJ: Prentice Hall.

DUFF, R., and A. CAMPBELL. 1973. "Moral and Ethical Dilemmas in the Special Care Nursery." *New England Journal of Medicine* 289: 885–90.

DURKHEIM, E. 1933. *The Division of Labor in Society.* New York: Macmillan.

DURKHEIM, E. 1961. *Moral Education: A Study in the Theory and Application of the Sociology of Education.* New York: Free Press.

DURKHEIM, E. 1965. *The Elementary Forms of Religious Life.* New York: The Free Press.

EMERSON, J. 1969. "Negotiating the Serious Import of Humor." *Sociometry* 32: 169–81.

FISCHER, S. 1986. *In the Patient's Best Interest.* New Brunswick: Rutgers University Press.

FLETCHER, J. 1966. *Situation Ethics.* Philadelphia: Westminster Press.

FOUCAULT, M. 1965. *Madness and Civilization: A History of Insanity in the Age of Reason.* New York: Pantheon.

FOUCAULT, M. 1973. *The Birth of the Clinic: An Archaelogy of Medical Perception.* New York: Pantheon.

FOX, R.C. 1957. "Training for Uncertainty." In *The Student Physician,* ed. R.K. Merton, G, Reader, and P. Kendall. Cambridge MA: Harvard University Press, pp. 207–41.

FOX, R.C. 1959. *Experiment Perilous.* New York: Free Press.

FOX, R.C. 1985. "Reflections and Opportunities in the Sociology of Medicine," *Journal of Health and Social Behavior* 36: 6–14.

FOX, R.C., and J. SWAZEY. 1974. *The Courage to Fail.* Chicago: University of Chicago Press.

FOX, R.C., and J. SWAZEY. 1992. *Spare Parts.* Oxford and New York: Oxford University Press.

FREIDSON, E. 1970. *The Profession of Medicine: A Study in the Sociology of Applied Knowledge.* New York: Harper and Row.

GALLIE, W.B. 1962. "Essentially Contested Concepts." *Proceedings of the Aristotelian Society* 56: 139, 169.

GARFINKEL, H. 1967. *Studies in Ethnomethodology.* Englewood Cliffs, NJ: Prentice Hall.

GEERTZ, C. 1974. *The Interpretation of Cultures.* New York: Basic Books.

GEERTZ, C. 1983. *Local Knowledge: Further Essays in Interpretive Anthropology.* New York: Basic Books.

GINSBURG, F. 1989. *Contested Lives.* Berkeley: University of California Press.

GLASER, B., and A. STRAUSS. 1964. "Awareness Contexts and Social Interaction." *American Sociological Review* 29:669–79.

GLASER, B., and A. STRAUSS. 1965. *Awareness of Dying.* Chicago: Aldine.

GLASER, B., and A. STRAUSS. 1967. *The Discovery of Grounded Theory.* Chicago: Aldine.

GLASER, B., and A. STRAUSS. 1968. *Time for Dying.* Chicago: Aldine.

GLASER, B., and A. STRAUSS. 1971. *Status Passages.* Chicago: Aldine, Atherton.

GOFFMAN, E. 1961. *Asylums.* New York: Doubleday.

GOFFMAN, E. 1967. *Interaction Ritual.* New York: Pantheon.

GOODE, W.J. 1960. "Encroachment, Charlatanism, and the Emergent Profession: Psychology, Medicine, and Sociology." *American Sociological Review* 25: 902–14.

GRAY, B. 1975. *Human Subjects in Medical Experimentation: A Sociological Study of the Conduct and Regulation of Research.* New York: John Wiley.

GUILLEMIN, J., and L. HOLMSTROM. 1986. *Mixed Blessings: Intensive Care for Newborns.* Oxford and New York: Oxford University Press.

HAUERWAUS, S. 1977. "The Demands and Limits of Care: On the Moral Dilemmas of Neonatal Intensive Care." In *Truthfulness and Tragedy,* ed. S. Hauerwaus and R. Bondt. Notre Dame: Notre Dame University Press.

HAUG, M. 1976. "The Erosion of Professional Authority: A Cross-Cultural Inquiry in the Case of the Physician." *Millbank Memorial Fund Quarterly*: 83–106.

HOFFMASTER, B. 1990. "Can Ethnography Save the Life of Medical Ethics?" *Social Science and Medicine* 35: 1421–31

HOFFMASTER, B. 1992. "Can Ethnography Save the Life of Medical Ethics?" *Social Science and Medicine* 35: 1421–31.

HUGHES, E.C. 1951 [1971]. *Men and Their Work.* Glencoe and New York: Free Press.

IMBER, J. 1986. *Abortion and the Private Practice of Medicine.* New Haven: Yale Univerity Prcss.

JANOWITZ, M. 1975. "Sociological Theory and Social Control." *American Journal of Sociology,* 81: 82–109.

JENNINGS, B. 1990. "Ethics and Ethnography in Intensive Care." In *Social Science Perspectives on Medical Ethics,* ed. G. Weisz. Dordrecht: Kluwer.

JONES, J. 1981. *Bad Blood: The Tuskegee Syphilis Experiment.* New York: The Free Press.

JONSEN, A. and S. TOULMIN. 1988. *The Abuse of Casuistry.* Berkeley: The University of California Press.

KATZ-ROTHMAN, B. 1987. *The Tentative Pregnancy: Prenatal Diagnosis and the Future of Medicine.* New York: Viking.

KUBLER-ROSS, E. 1969. *On Death and Dying.* New York: Macmillan.

LIDZ, C., A. MEISEL, E. ZERUBAVEL, M. CASTER, R. SESTAK, and L. ROTH. 1984. *Informed Consent: A Study of Decision Making in Psychiatry.* New York: Guilford Press.

LUKER, K. 1984. *Abortion and the Politics of Motherhood.* Berkeley: University of California Press.

MACINTYRE, A. 1981. *After Virtue: A Study in Moral Theory.* Notre Dame, IN: University of Notre Dame Press.

MARSHALL, T.H. [1939] 1965. *Class, Citizenship, and Social Development.* Garden City: Doubleday.

MARX, K. 1964. *The Economic and Philosophic Manuscripts of 1844.* New York: International Publishers.

OLESEN, V. 1989. "Caregiving, Ethical and Informal: Emergent Challenges in the Sociology of Health and Illness." *Journal of Health and Social Behavior:* 1–10.

PARSONS, T. 1951. *The Social System.* Glencoe and New York: The Free Press.

QUINT, J. 1965. "Institutionalized Practices of Information Control." *Psychiatry:* 119–32.

QUINT, J. 1972. "Institutionalized Practices of Information Control." In *Medical Men and Their Work,* ed., E. Freidson and J. Lorber. Chicago: Aldine-Atherton, pp. 220–39.

ROTH, J. 1963. *Time Tables.* Indianapolis: Bobbs-Merrill.

ROTHMAN, D. 1991. *Strangers at the Bedside: A History of How Law and Bioethics Transformed Medical Decision Making.* New York: Basic Books.

SCULLY, D. 1980. *Men Who Control Women's Health.* Boston: Houghton Mifflin.

SIMMEL, G. 1978. *The Philosophy of Money.* London and Boston: Routledge and Kegan Paul.

SUDNOW, D. 1967. *Passing On: The Social Organization of Dying.* Englewood Cliffs, NJ: Prentice-Hall.

TOULMIN, S. 1982. "How Medicine Saved the Life of Ethics." *Perspectives in Biology and Medicine* 25: 736–50.

WEBER, M. 1919 [1922]. "Politics as a Vocation." In *From Max Weber,* ed. H.C. Gerth and C.W. Mills. Glencoe and New York: Free Press.

WEISZ, G., ed. 1990. *Social Science Perspectives on Medical Ethics.* Dordrecht: Kluwer.

ZANER, R. 1993. *Troubled Voices: Stories of Ethics and Illness.* Cleveland: Pilgrim Press.

ZUSSMAN, R. 1992. *Intensive Care: Medical Ethics and the Medical Profession.* Chicago: University of Chicago Press.

29 CONFRONTING THE SECOND SOCIAL CONTRACT: THE PLACE OF MEDICAL SOCIOLOGY IN RESEARCH AND POLICY FOR THE TWENTY-FIRST CENTURY

BERNICE A. PESCOSOLIDO, *Indiana University, Bloomington*

JANE MCLEOD, *Indiana University, Bloomington*

MARGARITA ALEGRÍA, *The University of Puerto Rico*

INTRODUCTION

In *Shifts in the Social Contract* Beth Rubin (1996) argues that modern capitalism's golden age became tarnished when post-war expansion ended in the 1970s, and the economy began the long decline that culminated in the 1980s with downsizing and deindustrialization. As a result, major social institutions no longer held the powerful cultural authority based on scientific and managerial expertise that marked the industrial age. The 1970s heralded the beginning of the "health-care crisis" and discussions of the declining power, prestige, and monopolistic practices of physicians (Hafferty and Light 1995; Pescosolido and Kronenfeld 1995). The first social contract between modern medicine and society—characterized by fee-for-service reimbursement, physician dominance as direct providers of care, and limited government intervention—was rejected in favor of a new contract—involving third-party reimbursement, the reassertion of nonphysician providers, and government

We would like to thank Chloe E. Bird, Peter Conrad, and Jack Martin for insightful comments on earlier versions of this paper. We also acknowledge financial assistance from the ConCEPT I Program in Health and Medicine, funded by the President's Strategic Directions Charter Initiative at Indiana University; Mort Lowengrub, Dean, College of Arts and Sciences; George Walker, Vice President for Research; and J. Scott Long, Chair of the Department of Sociology and the National Institute of Mental Health.

investment in medical effectiveness research (Hafferty and Light 1995).

According to Rubin, these economic changes were accompanied by a shift in cultural and social perspectives. Global economies and rapid increases in immigration flows globalized not only markets but also culture, creating both awareness and concern about global interdependence, on the one hand, and culturally marginalized groups, on the other. In the health and health-care arena, these globalization processes were reflected in the rise of "pandemics"; the "return" of "alternative" medical systems outside the formal canopy of "modern," "scientific" medicine; and critiques of medicine's approach to persons with disabilities, persons from minority cultures, and women (Figert 1996; Garrett 1994; Pescosolido and Kronenfeld 1995).

In essence, the shift that Rubin chronicles (referred to by some as the advent of post-modernism) signaled a transformation in the character of power, and with it, a change in the nature of social stratification for individuals and groups. The transformation of the economy to flexible accumulation, with its reliance on short-term employment contracts and labor-displacing and deskilling technologies, dramatically altered the potential for control over the conditions of work, not only for physicians, but for a diverse set of workers. In short, the "social contract" as it was understood during much of the twentieth century is being renegotiated.

411

From a sociology-of-knowledge perspective, it is no surprise that coincident with this shift came critiques of the theories and methods we use to understand the natural and social world. The post-modern critique reminded sociologists that even our theories and methods reflect the times and the ideologies in which they were created. They also suggested—in notions that organizations, classes, groups, and political parties are simply reifications—that we return to a focus on the real lives of real people and to an analysis of how (mechanisms) and why (effects) larger contexts matter for individual lives (Calavita and Seron 1992; Hutchinson 1992: 779).

On the one hand, post-modern critiques of sociology and of society force us away from a "business as usual" complacence about our research. On the other hand, they have failed to offer an equally compelling set of images and agendas in response (Pescosolido and Rubin 1999). By emphasizing chaos, ambiguity, and the failure of modern social and political agendas, post-modernism has challenged us to question the nature of contemporary society but has failed to offer a productive, alternative vision of society to guide our work. Our goal here is to begin to reassess the traditions of medical sociology in the light of post-modern challenges, and to consider the ways in which medical sociology might contribute to a broader sociological project concerned with describing and understanding the post-modern world.

In this paper, we consider the future role of medical sociology as a contributor both to our understandings of health, illness, and healing and to core issues in the discipline of sociology. We re-examine one of the basic, influential projects of medical sociology, the study of the rise of the "scientific" profession of medicine and the construction of the first social contract between modern medicine and society, to: (1) provide a heuristic device to illustrate the need to re-examine theories in light of the socio-historical context in which they were fashioned, and (2) highlight the basic elements that will shape the second social contract. To foreshadow what follows, we argue that, because they have focused only on "successful" American and Western European cases, most theories about the first social contract overestimate the contribution of science and the belief structures of the public to the rise of professional medicine, while underestimating the role of economic resources and the "holders of wealth." The illness challenges faced by industrializing society, coupled with the class-based alliance between physicians and the philanthropic managers of the wealth of the

new economic elite, shaped the profession of medicine at least as much as (and perhaps more than) the public's faith in scientific medicine.

As a result, it is not a surprise, though many social observers have expressed consternation at the fact, that cost has become predominant in debates about contemporary health care. Capital continues to shape the profession of medicine, but because the basic arrangements of stratification, wealth, work, and power have changed, there has been a renegotiation of the terms of the power and authority of professions. This renegotiation has had profound implications not only for the profession of medicine, but also for the field of medical sociology, inasmuch as it signals a broad change in the context within which medicine is practiced and knowledge about health, illness, and healing is produced.

Following our analysis of the profession of medicine, we highlight two key issues within research on health, illness, and healing that are intertwined with the future of the profession and that illustrate both where sociologists have been successful in their efforts to understand the second social contract, and where there is work that remains to be done: the search for the causes of current disease profiles, and the movement toward evidence-based medicine and accountability in managed care.

TRACING THE CONTOURS OF THE CENTRAL DEBATES IN SOCIOLOGY

If, as some contend, old forms of social organization, including social institutions such as medicine, are being replaced, the concerns of medical sociologists should be centered on the extent and nature of these metamorphoses, the role that individuals play in shaping new forms, and the effects of those changes and forms on the real lives of real people. The agenda of medical sociology is, thus, inextricably linked with the broader agenda of sociology as it struggles to understand the new institutional and personal structures that characterize contemporary, "post-modern," social forms. Sociology currently offers nothing like the grand-scale work of Marx, Comte, Weber, and Durkheim, who first focused on the contours, meaning, and human markers of the social change they experienced. They described, documented, and offered explanations for the new challenges that society faced and the new arrangements that linked people together. August Hollingshead (1949), Peter Blau and Otis D. Duncan (1967), and William

Domhoff (1974), among others, described, theorized about, and attempted to measure the basic nature of the stratification system in post-World War II America. The first generation of medical sociologists contributed to this effort by documenting the nature of medical beliefs and behaviors, the nature of medical professions, the overarching role sets involved in medical care, and the basic role of stratification in life and death (see, for example, Koos 1954; Parsons 1951; Merton, Reader, and Kendall 1957).

If, as some sociologists assert, we stand at a similar historical juncture in the shift of social forms, this raises a series of questions that call for a return to examining the basic landscape of society and, for medical sociologists, the roots of illness, disease, and sickness as well as the social arrangements constructed to confront them. For example, what is the nature of social life, the character of social interactions, and the operation of social institutions? What are the effects of new social forms on the way individuals understand, maneuver through, construct, and give meaning to their lives? Specifically, what is the profile of health problems, and how are they defined and responded to by both professionals and the public? Who is legitimated to "treat" them, and what are the outcomes for different social groups? These questions are not new; they can be traced back to Mills's (1959) central theme in sociology—how history shapes and is shaped by biography—but they have renewed relevance when seen against the backdrop of contemporary changes in medicine (Pescosolido and Rubin 1999).

If we are to understand and examine the causes of the second social contract of medicine and its effects on the real lives of those concerned with health problems—both those who provide care and those who access services across different medical systems—we must immerse ourselves in a broader sociological project concerned with the contours, meaning, and human markers of the social changes we observe. While this requires an engagement with specific substantive literatures (e.g., research on the uncoupling of class from lifestyles and consumption patterns; Grusky 1994), it also urges us to attend to four current (and perhaps perennial) disciplinary debates that transcend substantive specialties.

First, the *structure-agency debate* asks: "To what extent are individuals constrained by social context, and how do they enact agency in the face of social constraints?" Questions about structure and agency are central to understanding socially patterned risk factors for illness, whether and how labels of health and illness are imposed on others, and how people respond to medical treatments.

Second, the *macro-micro question* focuses on how macro structures affect individuals and how individuals, in turn, affect those structures. How are the predictors of health and illness shaped by the social context? How does social inequality affect individual health, and what are the intervening mechanisms? How are people's perceptions of themselves as healthy or sick shaped by the historical, social, and cultural context in which they live? These questions, although they flow from a concern with the relationship between macro and micro experiences, also raise questions about our understandings of causality. What are the conditions under which we observe an effect of one condition on another? How do we understand the various combinations of events that must occur in order for us to observe a certain outcome? How do we conceptualize and operationalize the various pathways that can lead to a given health or illness outcome?

Third, what is the *relationship between positive and reflexive science* and the requirements of a dynamic, multilevel sociology? Positive science, in Jack Katz's (1983) terms, is characterized by a concern with reliability, representativeness, replicability, and lack of reactivity. We standardize our procedures, we control bias, we seek generalizable laws. What do we gain and lose by discarding those criteria, and their implied procedures, in favor of intersubjectivity—the recognition that we are part of the world that we are studying, and that our biases cannot simply be erased? This approach focuses on the study of life as it is experienced by those who are living it, rather than as we represent it. It recognizes the contingencies inherent in social process, considers the futility of broad generalizations, and promotes the reconstruction of theory based on critical case studies rather than on hypothesis testing (Burawoy 1991). Can we fashion a better and stronger set of theories, methods, and techniques if we aim for integration of the best aspects of different methods, a partnership among different methodological experts, rather than an endless battle for intradisciplinary methodological supremacy? (Levine 1995).

Fourth, what is *the relationship between theory, research, and policy?* Does research have to test theories in order to be valid? What role do case studies play in theoretical development? What are the challenges that medical sociologists face as managed care, without the provisions of universal coverage, becomes a major feature of the sociocultural landscape? How do changes in social policy create new theoretical opportunities for medical sociologists? Can—and should—medical sociologists play a central role in policy formation? How can sociologists contribute to the evaluation of evidence-based medicine without losing our capacity to stand outside of medicine and offer critical commentary? (Brown 1995). Bradford H. Gray and Sarah R. Phillips (1995) argue that the desires of medical sociologists to become more closely aligned with the discipline of sociology and to become more closely aligned with health-policy makers are in conflict. Our allegiance to the big questions of sociology pulls us away from the very specific, substance-driven questions that are of interest to policy makers. Policy makers want us to take a side, which many academics are reluctant to do. Thus, many of us just wait, hoping that someone out there will read our work and find policy relevance, but our passivity is unlikely to result in a real policy impact; rather, we need to tailor the message of our perspective and research to that audience.

In sum, the challenges that medical sociologists confront in the next century reflect more general issues facing the discipline of sociology about the changing nature of our social world, but also about how sociology should study those changes and to what effect. The opportunity of medical sociologists to shape our basic understanding of society, as those before us have done, depends on a constant interchange between the general and the specific, between the arena of health, illness, and healing and the collective contours of society. Perhaps nowhere is the interchange between medical sociology and the broader discipline more evident than in research on the medical profession. Accordingly, we turn now to a discussion of medical sociologists' contributions to our understanding of modern professions.

REVISITING THE FIRST SOCIAL CONTRACT: UNDERSTANDING THE CONTEXT AND DYNAMICS OF THE RISE OF THE PROFESSION OF MEDICINE[1]

Societies organize the choices for medical care from which individuals draw. As theorists from very different ideological positions have maintained, this organization shapes what medical systems look like, affects what individuals believe, and constrains how they respond to the problems of illness and disease (e.g., Parsons 1951;

[1] We do not intend that this section provide a comprehensive review of research on the medical profession. Our goal here, rather, is more narrow: to illustrate the contextually specific nature of theories about the rise of the medical profession and to highlight what we see as some of the key issues facing the medical profession today.

Freidson 1970a; Waitzkin 1983). Eliot Freidson (1970b) argued that, in modern societies, the medical profession itself, through its links to the state, stands as the most critical determinant of the social structure of medical care. The profession convinces "elite" segments of society to provide a competitive edge for scientific medical practice through political incorporation. In this institutional approach, state-granted licensing privileges create successful monopolies (Berlant 1975; Collins 1979; Starr 1982). As such, the medical profession's role looms heavily in the history of the "scientific capture" of the medical marketplace, particularly in the western world. Although more-recent theories have elaborated the context of medicine's efforts to attain and maintain professional dominance (e.g., Light's (1993) web of institutional and cultural forces and Abbott's (1988) field of competing professions), they have continued to emphasize medicine's efforts to achieve public legitimation and state-supported institutionalization of medical control as key determinants of the profession's success.

As Larson (1977: xiii) observes, for all its strengths, this institutional perspective underestimates the critical part that scientific medicine's "allies" played in establishing its control over the definition and treatment of illness. While it considers both politics and culture in historical context, it neglects the fact that political legitimation can be secured only by translating it into *market resources* through the adequate financial backing of some societal group. The attempt by the medical profession at political incorporation succeeded, unlike earlier attempts, in western nations when "regular" physicians cornered a good deal of the medical marketplace for two reasons. First, the *ideology of scientific medicine* on which modern medical practice is based (i.e., the reductionist germ theory) provided a new "hook" for separating "regular" physicians from homeopaths, osteopaths, granny midwives, and itinerant medicine peddlers, and it matched the views and interests of the emerging middle class, a class that embraced rationality, objectivity, and the scientific resolution of society's problems (Brown 1979). Second, and more importantly, the new *holders of wealth* in modern society provided the political clout and financial backing to institutionalize the dominance of scientific medicine, respectively, by licensing laws that favored the legitimation of certain potential providers over others and by building a new medical marketplace (i.e., hospitals and medical schools) that created a set of institutions that virtually ensured its use by the public.

The lack of attention to the central role of the capital requirements of the emerging medical profession is partially attributable to the subtlety with which middle-class interests, corporate interests, and the profession's own interests merged. Although corporate interests backed the large infusion of wealth into the emerging system of modern medicine, they did not do it directly nor did they do so for profit reasons. They did it through the urging of the middle-class men who ran their philanthropic foundations and were tied socially and ideologically to other members of the emerging middle class of regular physicians (see Brown 1979 on Gates and the Rockefeller Foundation). The influence that flowed through these middle-class networks served as the "agency" by which the medical marketplace was created.

Our inattention to capital is also attributable to our reliance on empirical evidence from countries with "success" (i.e., the firm establishment of near monopoly for the medical profession, or quantitatively speaking, the "1s" in a professional-dominance variable) in which charitable or public capital played a major role.[2] In much the same way that sociological theory has often neglected the experiences of marginalized groups, theories of medical dominance have typically neglected the experiences of nonwestern and less-developed countries. Looking to countries where professional dominance is not as firmly set (i.e., counties where medical pluralism dominates or, the "0s" in a professional-dominance variable) reinforces the importance of capital requirements for medicine. It is not just hearts and minds but pocketbooks that must be won over (see Johnson 1972). The continuing scarcity of financial resources in countries outside the First World has failed to translate scientific medical expertise into adequate numbers of facilities, practitioners, and support personnel, limiting the growth of a marketplace characterized by professional dominance.

In this regard, Judith Lasker's (1977) detailed case study of the Ivory Coast is instructive. When provided for the indigenous people by colonial powers, medical services were disproportionately directed at the urban, working, and powerful segments of the population. Any desire the medical profession may have had to attain dominance in the broader medical marketplace was subordinated to the larger political interests of the colonial government. With independence, the control of medicine came under the purview of the new, independent nation's government. This new government was forced to address the wide discrepancies in medical care left by the colonial powers, since they represented very visible signs of former political domination. Often with foreign aid from governments in the industrial world and philanthropic foundations funded by industrial capital (another way to direct resources to the scientific, modern profession), the government became the major financier of medical care. However, although the scientific medical profession achieved state-supported licensing, it has not yet mustered adequate backing from financial sectors to build a medical marketplace that is favored by the public over and above other sources of care. The great proportion of surplus wealth in the Ivory Coast, as in many other countries, lies in the hands of a small group of Ivorians and foreign investors, not the government, and the holders of this wealth have not been convinced to underwrite the provision of modern medical services on a broad basis. As a result, traditional, indigenous practitioners continue to fill an important gap in the medical "workforce," and the medical profession has not achieved dominance. This case supports Frederic Hafferty and Donald Light's (1995) claim that research on the medical profession would be considerably enriched by studies of the dynamics of professionalization outside of the western world.

Theories of the rise of the medical profession also contend that the ability to convince the public of the value of modern medical care (i.e., "consulting status") cements the special status of scientific medical practice (Freidson 1970a; Starr 1982). There can be no doubt that science provided a "hook" to gain both political and capital backing. Germ theory offered a new and promising solution to infectious and parasitic diseases, the major scourges of the day. Further, scientific ideology was very much in line with the middle class's new ideas about the organization of work (i.e., Taylorism). However, there is little evidence to support the claim that public support for medicine was a rational response to "successes" that "brought the average man's ideas, knowledge and norms closer to that of the profession" at the turn of the last century (Freidson 1970a: 75). The historical record now clearly shows that the public was "captured" before the introduction of most of the important vaccines, and certainly before enough time had passed for such rationally guided shifts to take place (McKinlay and McKinlay 1981; McKeown 1976).

[2] In the United States philanthropic donations from the capitalist class and patient fees underwrote the medical marketplace during its critical, early years. In Britain and Germany, as in much of Europe, the government as a major holder of wealth (compared to either the U.S. or colonized countries of the time) played an early and active role in directing general and employer taxes to scientific medical practice (Berlant 1975; Rosen 1983). In those countries that were colonized by European nations, scientific medical care was not introduced for the purpose of advancing the profession; rather it blatantly served the interests of religion, politics, and economics with a deliberate inequality and a pattern of spread that closely marked the expansion of colonial interests (Johnson 1972; Lesson 1974; Banerji 1979).

Further, even if we concede that public support for scientific medicine was constructed on the basis of its promise to eradicate disease, there is little evidence that the general public shared the middle-class enthusiasm for scientific methods of vaccination, surgery, or hospital-based care. Even J.D. Rockefeller's personal physician came from the more noninvasive homeopathic system (Brown 1979). Studies of speciality care such as obstetrics show quite clearly that support for scientific medicine was class based (Reissman 1983).

Once the state and the holders of society's wealth were convinced of the superiority of scientific medicine, public and private resources were channeled exclusively into this avenue of care. In essence, with an infusion of capital, the medical profession was able to create a new medical marketplace in which the visibility and nature of services overshadowed competition from any and all alternatives. So, while monopoly requires licensing, it is not established by it, as the classic theories of professional dominance contend (e.g., Freidson 1970a; Berlant 1975). Rather, monopolies are established by the building of institutions that crystallize and reinforce power differences among competing providers and place limits on individual behavior (Berger and Luckmann 1966). Under these conditions, a new social reality of medicine is constructed by shaping a market that persuades individuals to consult it. If we consider "enabling factors" (Andersen 1995) to be crucial to the public's use of services, then the profession's ability to create a marketplace of services that overshadows or prohibits the use of other systems of medicine virtually predetermines the public choice and guarantees public support. Thus, the social organization of medical care both precedes and produces the shift in values that influence individuals' choices and decisions.

In sum, emphasizing the importance of class-based ideologies and the distribution of capital to the rise of the profession of medicine does not require that we dismiss interprofessional conflicts (Abbott 1988) and the balance of "countervailing powers" (Light 1993) in the history of the medical profession. Neither does it require that we ignore public faith in scientific medicine as it legitimated medical dominance. Rather, we suggest that a unique combination of the illness and disease profile, the developing stratification system, and state support produced a social organization of healing and, with it, an ideological structure that "primed the pump" for the development of professions seen to be removed from the cash nexus and concerns of capital accumulation.

Given this history, it should be no surprise that capital—particularly as it is held by corporate purchasers and providers of care—has come to play such a critical role in the transformation of the medical-care system. The second social contract that is being written for medical care, spurred on by the state's desire to control costs and by the recognition that medical interventions have not solved many of our most pressing health problems, involves a direct corporate presence, the increased use of nonphysician providers, and a movement toward evidence-based, standardized medicine. While much has been written about the implications of this transformation for the medical profession, less has been written about the implications of this transformation for medical sociology and about what changes in medicine and health care can teach us about the social changes we are experiencing. We consider two key issues facing the medical profession and medical sociology in this regard: our changing understanding of the causes of disease and evidence-based medicine and accountability in managed care.

CASE 1: THE "DEATH" OF RISK FACTOR EPIDEMIOLOGY

One important pathway through which social inequality affects the members of society is through its effect on their health and access to care. Although we are periodically reminded that we need to look beyond proximal causes of mental and physical health problems (e.g., stress) to the social structures that create them (e.g., Pearlin 1989, 1992), most epidemiological research focuses on precursors that can be measured, understood, and controlled at the individual level. "Risk factors"—high cholesterol, lack of exercise, smoking, and the like—have become the centerpiece of research and the focus of government health policies. What is missing from most of this research is an understanding of where these risk factors come from and how they reflect the nature, opportunities, and limitations embedded in social life.

We are starting to see a new generation of writings in medical sociology that has been identified with calls for the "death" of risk-factor epidemiology.[3] These writings follow a variety of traditions, but they share a concern with redirecting attention back to the

[3] However, we have to acknowledge that for John McKinlay, the call for "refocusing upstream" to the "manufacturers of illness" has been a consistent theme (McKinlay 1981).

real causes of disease. These writings were motivated, in part, by the recognition that individual-level interventions based on medical models of illness have not proved effective in altering the distribution of disease in western societies. Not only have individual-level behaviors proved stubborn in the face of medical logic (e.g., the disappointing results from the Multiple Risk Factor Intervention Trial in the United States; Syme 1996), but also new intervening mechanisms have emerged to re-establish familiar patterns of health disadvantage in lower-status groups.

To understand the tenacity of the socioeconomic distribution of disease, Link and Phelan (1995) introduce the notion of a "fundamental cause" of disease, a slight renaming of the concept of "basic cause" drawn from Lieberson's (1985) *Making It Count*. For Lieberson, a basic cause is the condition that *really* causes a particular outcome, in contrast to a superficial cause that *appears* to cause the condition. Basic and superficial causes can only be distinguished with data from more than one point in time or more than one place because a basic cause will show a robust effect across times and places, but a superficial cause will not. With respect to health, we interpret the persistence of the link between SES and mortality, from the city of Mulhouse, France, in the early 1800s to the United States in the late 1900s (Link, Northridge, Phelan, and Ganz 1998) as evidence for the fundamental nature of stratification as a determinant of health.

The distinction between basic and superficial causes raises the question of how we can best conceptualize and study the role of social factors in health and illness. Social epidemiologists, like Link and Phelan (1995), Waitzkin (1983), and McKinlay (1981), argue for a greater recognition of the fundamental importance of social conditions for the origins of disease, and they urge us to guard against the reductionism of biomedical and epidemiological models. These ideas, while not new, have historically held little sway in the field of epidemiology. At the end of the 1800s, germ theory came onto the scene and changed the way that people thought about disease. Unifactorial, biological models of disease became more popular, and interest in social conditions waned. The 1910 Flexner Report on American medical education promoted laboratory-based scientific medicine as the ideal, rejecting the tenets of holistic medicine and other alternative approaches, a position that solidified the hold that what we think of as modern medicine had on medical education, research, and practice. There were clearly exceptions (e.g., Allende's health policy in Chile), but analyses of the social determinants of health virtually disappeared from writings on health, particularly in western societies, until the 1960s.

In contrast, the "fundamental cause" approach to epidemiology focuses on social conditions that generate illness and early death. More specifically, it relates patterns of death and disease to the political, economic, and social structures of society. Researchers within this tradition emphasize themes related to: (1) the structural contradictions within societies (e.g., ideologies of equality that contradict the realities of inequities); (2) the necessity of seeing problems within medicine as linked inextricably to these contradictions; (3) conflict and exploitation as structural sources of disease (not conspiracies at the level of individuals but exploitation of certain groups as built into the social structure); and (4) historical specificity (the importance of understanding social problems with reference to the specific material realities of the case). For example, studies in occupational health emphasize the contradiction between profit and safety; studies of stress look not at the stressors experienced by particular individuals but at the ways in which particular forms of social organization lead to stress. They target a concern with structures of medical oppression that include both the social organization of medicine and the social conditions that generate disease but that are beyond the reach of medicine alone. Fundamental social causes (e.g., stratification) predict multiple risk factors and multiple outcomes.

A shift of interest away from behavioral and biological risk factors (e.g., cockroaches and childhood asthma, cholesterol and CHD) to social-structural causes raises a basic question. How far back do we need to go in the logical chain of causes to identify the cause that is truly fundamental? According to Waitzkin (1983), Engels looked to the organization of economic production and the fundamental contradiction between profit and safety (i.e., capitalism forces people to live and work under conditions that inevitably cause disease); Virchow concentrated on inequities in the distribution and consumption of social resources (i.e., some people live in poor conditions and cannot afford medical care); and Allende pointed to the exploitation of the Third World by advanced capitalist nations. More recently, Wilkinson (1996, 1997) targets the extent of social inequality in a political unit and the effect of that inequality on social cohesion, and LaVeist (1992) documents the role that African-American participation in the political power structure of cities plays in infant mortality. Which of these is a fundamental cause of disease, or are they inextricably bound both conceptually and empirically? While Lieberson (1985) argues that some fundamental causes cannot be observed and we can only infer their existence, medical sociologists must struggle with how to conceptualize, identify, and document fundamental causes and how to realize the potential to change them through health and social policies.

If we accept the existence of fundamental social causes, we accept implicitly the conclusion that explanatory models that posit intervening variables for risk factors (e.g., access to health care to explain the SES-mortality link) cannot tell us why certain conditions are related to disease because the mechanisms linking the conditions to the disease will change over time. For example, models tracing the effects of SES on health outcomes through health behaviors, health knowledge, or other proximal conditions have their uses. They confirm that the condition causes disease inasmuch as the identification of mechanism supports claims of causality. Particularly when coupled with subgroup analyses, they can also illuminate the ways in which the fundamental cause becomes manifest in the lives of persons living in particularly historical and geographic contexts—a contribution that tells us as much about the nature of stratification as it does about health per se. What they cannot do, however, is identify the "true" mechanisms responsible for the fundamental cause's effects. As Bruce Link and his colleagues (1998) demonstrate, risk-factor mechanisms can change while the SES-health association persists, a finding that parallels post-modernism's contention that many of our theories and explanations are historically and geographically bound.

In sum, the fundamental-cause approach leads to a general blueprint for sociologists engaged in epidemiology: We must develop theoretical frameworks, adequate study designs and measures, and appropriate analytic techniques to examine the macro/micro link between social conditions and life chances. Such an effort will require the epidemiologists among us to attend to historical context in a way that we have not always done. We are challenged to transcend the boundaries of ahistorical theorizing about health processes to discover the fundamental laws that underlie them. As such, this is an effort that exposes the enduring relevance of power, even as it recognized the historically grounded nature of power's expression. While it would be wise to draw upon work in the core of the discipline of sociology that is also struggling with this challenge, the health arena represents a critical window for the development of general social theory as many, if not most, of the founders of the discipline understood (e.g., Durkheim's *Suicide* 1951 [1897]; see Pescosolido and Kronenfeld 1995 on this point).

The Other Side of the Coin: The Need to Integrate the Biological and the Social— The Case of Psychiatric Disorders.

Even as we elaborate our understandings of fundamental social causes of disease, we must remain attentive to the expanding knowledge base of biomedical research. The best of the social epidemiologists among us have a deep understanding of relevant literatures on genetics, biology, pharmacology, and other medical treatments. There is no question that the multifactorial models of disease causation currently in vogue argue for the importance of interdisciplinary research (e.g., see Schwartz 1999, on "active participation" in the biomedical revolution in psychiatry). However, the role of the "social" often appears to be eclipsed by the most seemingly basic of genetic and biological research.

The biomedical model, taken to the extreme, would seem to eliminate all physical illness and many mental illnesses (e.g., schizophrenia) from medical sociology's purview. But there are four critical assumptions implicit in this claim that can and have been challenged by the work of medical sociologists. First, the exclusion of the social sciences in favor of the biological ones presumes that the state of knowledge is sufficient and rigorous enough to dismiss the role of environment in health and illness. Second, it suggests that there is no interaction between environment and biology, a fact that is not supported by biological research (e.g., the effect of toxins on genes). Third, it infers that the diagnosis of disease and the determination of causes of death are without systematic error, unshaded by social factors. Fourth, it supports the idea that the focus of biological research, on the "tail of the distribution," represents the best way to improve the health of the population as a whole (e.g., the arbitrary, dichotomous translation of a gradient of blood pressure into high or low categories, with medical focus only on the former; McKinlay and DiGruttolo 1997).

Although we reject these assumptions, we nevertheless believe that sociologists must make peace with the "biological" in two important ways. We must understand how the biological and the social work together (Levine 1987), and, perhaps more important, we must understand when "biological facts" mask important social processes. Beginning with the former, the idea that sociologists (or the general public for that matter) should accept all biological evidence as "truth" is belied both by the mounds of contradictory evidence reported and by the way that some research attains the status of "truth" without meeting scientific standards. McKinlay and his colleagues offer an exemplar for this type of research in a series of studies done at NERI on sex differences in coronary heart disease (CHD) (McKinlay 1996). The common medical wisdom reported in most medical textbooks of a biological theory that explains women's lower rate of CHD (i.e., estrogenic cardioprotectivity) is confronted by a social alternative. A combination of diagnostic (i.e., physicians' seeing women's CHD symptoms as gastrointestinal or psychiatric problems), medical-treatment (i.e., women with CHD symptoms not being referred for testing or treatment), and technological (i.e., EKG and even gamma-camera tests producing less accurate results for women than men) problems and biases shaped a medical belief about CHD as a men's problem. However, both the rate of "silent" heart attacks (i.e., undiagnosed myocardial infarctions [MI] in the 40 percent range) among pre-menopausal women in the Framingham Heart Study and the disappointing results of the Estrogen Replacement trials suggest both that the difference between men and women in CHD is more of a medical construction than a medical reality and that the theory of estrogenic cardioprotectivity plays, at best, a minor role in sex differences. Importantly, this body of sociological research has changed medical reality resulting in an increasing emphasis in the media and in medical schools on CHD for women. This case, which Schwartz (1999) would recognize as "counterrevolution," shows where sociological information challenges the biomedical model itself.

Turning to our claim that sociologists must understand how the biological and the social work together, we recognize the concern that sociologists' voices may be lost in interdisciplinary research (Schwartz 1999). Nevertheless, we contend that sociological critiques of the biomedical model lose their edge when they fail to acknowledge the possibility of biological causation. We take as an example the labeling theory of mental illness. For all of the insights it has allowed into the stigma of mental illness (Link and Cullen 1990), labeling theory has failed as an etiological argument. We believe that its failure can be directly linked to its inability (or unwillingness) to confront biomedical knowledge about mental illness.

As best laid out by Thomas Scheff (1966), labeling theory makes two key claims: (1) most chronic mental illness is, at least, in part a social role; and (2) society's reaction to a person's behavior is the most important determinant of entry into that role. The focus of the theory is on rule breaking—behavior that stands in clear violation of the agreed-upon norms of the group. According to Scheff's argument, rule breaking (i.e.,

primary deviance) is routine, and society has a well-established set of interpretational categories that are used to classify most of its various forms (e.g., criminal behavior, drunkenness). There are certain types of rule breaking, however, that fall outside of these categories. This residual rule breaking (which typically involves the violation of assumptive norms of interactional behavior) is typically denied or ignored and is, therefore, of transitory significance. However, when a set of contingencies describing the behavior, the rule breaker, and the observers (e.g., visibility, severity, social power, and social distance) coincide to result in a severe societal reaction, the reaction sets in motion a process of crystallization of the "crazy" behavior (i.e., secondary deviance) where both the person and others accept the label of mental illness and act in ways consistent with it.

There is no doubt that the label of mental illness becomes a lens through which all behavior is seen. From the classic D. L. Rosenhan (1973) study, to the experiences of persons with mental illness (Estroff 1981), to the most recent studies on public attitudes toward mental illness (Link and Cullen 1990; Link, Phelan, Bresnahan, Stueve, and Pescosolido 1999; Pescosolido, Monahan, Link, Stueve, and Kikuzawa 1999), the stigma carried by the label discredits the social identity of those labeled. But to what extent can sociologists embrace labeling theory as a theory of the etiology of mental illness? At this point in the development of research on mental illness, it would appear to be naïve either to dismiss the impact of inheritance *or* to dismiss the role of social factors in affecting prevalence and incidence rates.

One way to think about the possibility of merging social and biological approaches lies in examining Scheff's assumption of the distribution of rule breaking in society. Figure 29–1, Panel A, depicts a uniform statistical distribution of residual deviance, the distribution that implicitly underlies Scheff's contention that rule breaking is ubiquitous. In this distribution, more and less frequent acts of deviance are equally likely to occur. The theory suggests that social factors condition whether an incidence of residual rule breaking is observed, whether it is defined as problematic, and whether it engenders a severe societal reaction and a label of mental illness (see the "person" circled in Panel A). However, if we accept, at least in part, that some mental illnesses fit a disease model (e.g., schizophrenia), we may be better off to reconceptualize the distribution as shown in Figure 29–1, Panel B. That is, the majority of the population does engage in residual deviance, but the underlying distribution

Figure 29–1 Assumptions of Original Labelling Theory (A) and a Proposed Revision (B)

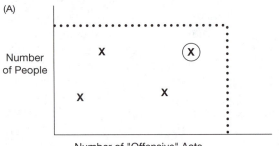

(A)

Number of People

Number of "Offensive" Acts

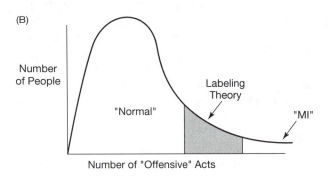

(B)

Number of People

"Normal"

Labeling Theory

"MI"

Number of "Offensive" Acts

that describes the frequency of deviant acts resembles more of a chi-square than a uniform distribution. In the tail, there are individuals whose behavior results in a special categorization across times and places, even if that is in "alternative roles" as prophet, healer, or guru. Where labeling theory may show its greatest power is in the "gray" area (shaded portion of Figure 29–1, Panel B) where the frequency of "odd" behavior can be considered neither to fit our agreed-upon "standard" for mental health problems nor to appear to be within societal norms. Not only are the "contingencies" that affect the fate of those caught in the gray area of classic sociological interest and general importance, but also, sociologists have played, and will continue to play, an important role in documenting how societies mark and push the limits of the gray area, in part, as a result of the role of reported biological research, whether replicated and validated or not (e.g., see the medical debates over PMS; Figert 1996; current discussion of "road rage" as a new disorder).

In sum, what this second distribution suggests is threefold. First, it supports recommendations that we consider the full range of mental-health problems as targets for social and health-care policy as we realize that the dichtomous point at which a "disease" is acknowledged represents a social construction (McKinlay and DiGruttolo 1997; Mirowsky and Ross 1989). Second,

even if we focus only on the tail of the distribution, at those behaviors defined as "serious" and "persistent" mental illness (e.g., the 1 percent population prevalence of schizophrenia), social epidemiologists should continue to evaluate the contribution of social factors, like social class, to the onset, course, and treatment of those behaviors. Third, sociologists and other social scientists can uniquely monitor the diagnostic practices and other aspects of medical culture that turn social problems in the gray area into disease categories subject to medicalization and individuals in socially powerless groups into medical cases.

CASE 2: THE TRANSFORMATION OF THE MEDICAL MARKETPLACE—THE MEANING AND MEASUREMENT OF "OUTCOMES" IN MANAGED CARE

McKinlay and Marceau (1998) argue that the state has moved from a "pluralist empire" to an "antileviathan." The state, because it is more interested in private rather than public interests, has lost its ability to protect the public's health or to influence the medical system in any major, meaningful way (e.g., the failure of the Clinton Reform Plan; Domhoff 1996; Skocpol 1997). Following B. Jessop (1990), they see this as part of a state process of "hollowing out," divesting certain functions and turning them over to private institutions. As a result, "[H]ealth care has been historically transformed—from a predominantly fee-for-service system controlled by dominant professionals to a corporatized system dominated by increasingly concentrated financial and industrial interests" (McKinlay and Marceau 1998: 4). While the medical profession, as a major interest group supported by the public, thrived under a pluralist state, its interests have been subjugated to those of financial organizations under the more laissez-fare approach. The predominance of financial interests in medical care was compounded by the profession's own decision to accept third-party reimbursement as a viable funding scheme. Initially strengthening the economic position of the medical profession (i.e., fee-for-service billing with little oversight), this eventually opened the door for profit-oriented interests to control the underlying financial structure of medical care and for the reassertation of less expensive, nonphysician clinicians into medical-care delivery.

The transfer of control over medical-care financing from physicians to purchasers has led to two related strands of research on the content and quality of health care: evidence-based medicine and health-outcomes research. The push for evidence-based medicine can be traced, in part, to insurers' motivations and authority to tie reimbursement to proof of treatment efficacy. Expert panels, such as the U.S. Preventive Services Task Force (Woolf, DiGuiseppi, Atkins, and Kamerow 1996) were established to review scientific evidence for the efficacy of specific interventions. Evaluations of treatment efficacy have typically relied on clinical trials that evaluate the outcomes of treatment under ideal conditions (e.g., close monitoring of regimens, homogeneous groups of patients, and highly skilled and motivated providers). Because clinical trials do not mimic medical care as it is practiced, they cannot tell us what will happen when treatments are made widely available and used by a diverse sample of providers and patients. Equally important, trials that rely exclusively on clinical outcomes fail to take into account the extent to which the results of the treatment meet patients' needs and expectations.

Health-outcomes research incorporates a broader definition of health status and, therefore, of the outcomes that might be reasonably expected from health care. Sociologists have made tremendous progress in promoting interest in health-related quality of life (HRQL) (Levine 1987; Stewart and Ware 1992), a concept that encompasses functional limitations, perceived health status, and patient preferences (although there is some debate about its specific components; Cleary, Wilson, and Fowler 1994). However, the advances that have been made in the conceptualization and measurement of HRQL are embedded in narrow conceptual models that fail to acknowledge the broader context within which patients understand and interpret their health status, and within which treatments are enacted. In short, although the measurement of health outcomes has become more comprehensive, models of HRQL continue to rely on the linear conceptualization of treatment efficacy that underlies clinical research.

Sociology's Basic Challenge to the Focus on Outcomes, Data-Based Policy Making, and Managed Care.

In keeping with the broader theoretical and methodological shifts with which we began this chapter, and in response to the narrow focus of treatment efficacy trials on clinical indicators, medical sociologists have promoted a patient-centered view of health outcomes. There is now widespread recognition that the conceptual focus of outcomes has been too narrow in the past (Attkisson et al. 1992; Krupnick 1999). As Cleary and his colleagues note, "[i]t has become almost axiomatic among researchers and policymakers that traditional outcome measures . . . do not adequately reflect the variations in health that are important to individuals" (1994: 24).

Despite the success that sociologists have had in elaborating the concept of health outcomes, our efforts have fallen short in two key ways. First, we have not adequately addressed the socially structured nature of health assessments. Whereas patient perceptions and preferences are now considered standard components of health-related quality of life, these perceptions and preferences have been treated as purely individual and unique. In much the same way that post-modernists have lost sight of the relevance of social structure, health-outcomes researchers have lost sight of the "binding power of common experiences" (Calavita and Seron 1992: 766) as they relate to health. Second, the conceptual models within which health-outcomes research is embedded maintain the assumptions from clinical trials that treatment directly and linearly influences health status and that all patients will respond in the same ways to the treatment.

The lack of attention to the socially structured nature of health outcomes is particularly evident in the general lack of attention given to the question of whether categories of outcome measures (simple or tailored to individuals' needs) represent meaningful constructs or are interpreted in the same way across culturally, socially, and economically diverse groups of the population (Levine 1995). As Bernal and colleagues (1995) note, theoretical and empirical research has focused on designing interventions for ethnic minorities but in the absence of an underlying theory of how culture raises the salience of certain domains, changes the connotation of standard items, or otherwise affects the suitability of outcome measures. The common *assumption* is that all ethnic/racial and socioeconomic groups both embrace and respond similarly to a common set of outcome measures. This assumption implies that the same underlying values and beliefs are held by those receiving services, despite sometimes gross dissimilarities in economic, cultural, and social circumstances and larger contexts. Yet the meaning and value attached to each of the components of health outcomes and each of the "domains" of role functioning may vary across cultural and socioeconomic subgroups. For example, evaluations of mental-health treatment often incorporate assessments of social skills and functional independence, but sociocultural expectations can affect which social skills are considered important and the level of independence or privacy considered acceptable and desirable. For example, many outcome instruments used in studies of mental health define independent living as a positive outcome, yet for some cultural groups (e.g.,

Hispanics), such independence may be considered undesirable (Canino and Bravo 1994).

These types of concerns go far beyond the narrow concern with semantic equivalence that has been emphasized in much cross-cultural research on health. Instruments that have the same technical meaning across racial and ethnic groups may nevertheless evoke different responses (e.g., a lower willingness of racial minorities to report sensitive health problems) or differentially represent outcomes that are valued within that group. Further, as sociologists point out, it is not enough to know simply if someone is "white" or "black"; one must know whether he or she is "incorporated" into mainstream society, enmeshed in ethnic enclaves, or isolated culturally and economically (Portes and Manning 1994).

With respect to the second point, the conceptual models that drive research on HRQL implicitly assume that the reasons why people enter treatment, their treatment goals, their interpretations and understandings of treatment, and their locations in the social structure are largely irrelevant to understanding their outcomes (Hohmann 1996). The limitations of these assumptions are clearly evident in the failure of two major demonstration projects that were designed to improve clinical, functional, and social outcomes by providing coordinated, integrated services for adults with serious mental illnessses and for children and adolescents with serious emotional disturbances (The Robert Wood Johnson Foundation Program on Chronic Mental Illness, Goldman et al. 1990; Ft. Bragg Demonstration, Bickman 1996). Both demonstrations failed—the changes in the systems were not related to better outcomes. Ann Hohmann (1996) argues that the failure of these demonstrations is attributable to their failure to take into account the social context within which the system changes were implemented and the ways in which the changes were experienced by the individuals who were enrolled. Their goals, needs, and desires, understood both as individual constructs and as constructs negotiated in interaction with social networks and broader cultures, were involved in their responses to the system changes but were not considered in those projects.

The limited evidence that exists supports Hohmann's claim. Conceptions and beliefs about physical and mental illness and treatment utilization vary across socioeconomic and racial/ethnic groups (Lefley 1998; Millstein, Guarnaccia, and Midlarsky 1995). For example, Osmond and colleagues (1996) found that, among African Americans and Spanish-speaking Latinos, use of health care was more strongly associated with chronic need for health care, while for European Americans, use of health services appeared as more discretionary and/or tied to preventive services.

In addition, individuals' health-care choices are socially structured in ways that are not yet adequately understood. For example, African Americans are generally reluctant to accept pharmacotherapy for the treatment of major depression, whereas Latinos are not, but the reasons for the difference are not known (Miranda 1998). These racial and ethnic differences echo classic anthropological findings from the 1950s, findings of clear differences in the willingness to take medications among Italians, Jews, and Irish in the Northeast (Zborowski 1952). However, medical sociologists have not pursued similar research on health and illness attitudes or beliefs for current immigrant groups (e.g., Chinese, Vietnamese, Puerto Ricans, and Eastern Europeans), ceding this area of research to medical anthropologists who tend to offer rich, but rarely empirical, comparisons across groups.

We have focused on health outcomes research in the context of evaluations of specific treatments, but a comparable set of questions and concerns can be raised about efforts to evaluate the quality of care provided by managed care organizations (Galvin 1998; Their and Gelings 1998; Mechanic 1998). Given the social, political, and financial interests involved, the specific outcome indicators that are used in these evaluations have tremendous implications. Ideally, outcome measures would be simple, practical, and inexpensive to collect in the real world, while reflecting important aspects of clients' thinking about treatment and offering a comparison among providers with respect to client outcomes, quality care, and accessibility of services. In reality, there is a growing tension between health plans desire for easy outcome measures and growing consumer demand for quality care tailored to their individual needs. The complications that we have identified in research on individual health outcomes are heightened in an environment where performance measurement fosters incentives to "dump" sicker clients so that the average performance of treated clients remains at an optimal level.

In sum, medical sociologists have made progress toward incorporating patients' understandings into health-outcomes research, but we have not yet adequately captured the process of treatment as it is enacted in the real lives of real individuals. Treatment success is to some degree dependent on the fit between the intervention and the fulfillment of the individual's most salient needs, goals, expectations, and preferences, as well as community and cultural norms of physical or mental illness and economic or environmental factors

(Hohmann 1996). Thus, we argue that the future progress on research on health outcomes requires a sophisticated reformulation that draws on the strengths of the post-modern challenge to bring the experiences of marginalized groups back into the mainstream, but one that does so with an eye toward understanding the socially structured and culturally bound nature of those experiences. In this effort, we can and must draw on sociological research concerned with the changing nature of social stratification and cultural identity. This work often comes from researchers who have not traditionally been interested in health-care issues per se but who have turned their attention to more general shifts in the basic reconstruction of social institutions of which health-care reform is only one example. If health-outcomes research and policy are an inevitable part of the second social contract, the sociologists must bring issues of social class, social networks, income, social capital, and race/ethnicity to the forefront of research and policy debates.

CONCLUSION

Most medical sociologists have substantive interests in other subfields of society, whether it be in occupations and professions for those who study changes in the medical profession, stratification for those interested in the distribution of health and illness in the population, or family for those who study the role of families in responses to treatment. In order to do medical sociology well, we contend, traditional divisions within the discipline of sociology must be transcended. Confronting the second social contract means that sociologists need to be familiar with literatures from diverse theoretical orientations and substantive foci, integrating them in ways that remain true to the phenomenon of interest but contributing to broader developments within sociology.

In addition, the work of medical sociologists and sociologists of mental health is embedded within interdisciplinary literatures that bring together the work of sociologists, economists, psychologists, policy analysts, and medical researchers who seek to understand fundamental questions about why some people get sick while others don't and how society can address their needs. We must negotiate our way into these literatures carefully and strategically. For example, in the area of outcomes assessment, sociologists' interests in elaborating the role of individual (and socially structured) preferences in treatment stands in direct conflict to evidence-based medicine's interest in developing a standardized set of treatment protocols. Given the context within which medicine is practiced today, we will need to demonstrate that it is in the best interest of purchasers, as well as patients, to understand for whom certain treatments work, why, and under what circumstances (Hohmann 1996).

We are living through a time of tremendous social change—the fashioning of the second social contract represents only part of this change. Social inequality is increasing, ethnicity has come to the fore in ways that are unprecedented in some of our lifetimes, and the health-care system is being reshaped and reconfigured. As sociologists, we are uniquely poised to offer the big picture view that is so important as these changes unfold (Pescosolido and Kronenfeld 1995). Our contributions do not lie only in discussing those big changes at the macro level; after all, individual lives are at stake in all of these changes. Even if we aim at micro level phenomena, we must place our considerations in larger social context. We have examined how revisiting and revising theories suggest new approaches, and we have called to task "business as usual" in epidemiology (risk factors), mental health (labeling theory), and social policy (outcomes). This is far easier than constructing the theories and protocols to understand and change the new social landscape of the twenty-first century. Sociologists must simultaneously reach across disciplines to integrate ideas and draw from the larger discipline of sociology to link micro and macro change. There is no question, in light of these circumstances, that the sociological imagination brought by medical sociologists offers a critical part of understanding health, illness, and healing.

REFERENCES

ABBOTT, ANDREW. 1988. *The System of Professions.* Chicago: University of Chicago Press.

ANDERSEN, RONALD. 1995. "Revisiting the Behavioral Model and Access to Care: Does It Matter?" *Journal of Health and Social Behavior* 36: 1–10.

ATTKISSON, C., J. COOK, M. KARNO, A. LEHMAN, ET AL. 1992. "Clinical Service Research." *Schizophrenia Bulletin* 18: 561–626.

BANERJI, DEBABAR. 1979. "The Place of the Indigenous and the Western Systems of Medicine in the Health

Services of India." *International Journal of Health Services* 9: 511–19.

BERGER, PETER, and THOMAS LUCKMANN. 1966. *The Social Construction of Reality.* New York: Doubleday and Company.

BERLANT, JEFFREY. 1975. *Profession and Monopoly: A Study of Medicine in the United States and Great Britain.* Berkeley, CA: University of California Press.

BERNAL, G., J. BONILLA, and C. BELLIDO. 1995 "Ecological Validity and Cultural Sensitivity for Outcomes Research." *Journal of Abnormal Child Psychology* 23: 67–82.

BICKMAN, L. 1996. "A Continuum of Care: More Is Not Always Better." *American Psychologist* 51: 689–701.

BLAU, PETER, and OTIS DUDLEY DUNCAN. 1967. *The American Occupational Structure.* New York: Wiley.

BROWN, E. RICHARD. 1979. *Rockefeller Medicine Men: Medicine and Capitalism in America.* Berkeley, CA: University of California Press.

BROWN, PHIL. 1995. "Naming and Framing: The Social Construction of Diagnosis and Illness." *Journal of Health and Social Behavior* (Extra Issue): 34–52.

BURAWOY, MICHAIL. 1991. *Ethnography Unbound: Power and Resistance in the Modern Metropolis.* Berkeley: University of California Press.

CALAVITA, KITTY, and CARROLL SERON. 1992. "Postmodernism and Protest: Recovering the Sociological Imagination." *Law and Society Review* 26: 765–71.

CANINO, G., and M. BRAVO. 1994. "The Adaptation and Testing of Diagnostic and Outcome Measures for Cross-Cultural Research." *International Review of Psychiatry* 6: 281–86.

CLEARY, PAUL D., IRA B. WILSON, and FLOYD J. FOWLER. 1994. "A Theoretical Framework for Assessing and Analyzing Health-Related Quality of Life." *Advances in Medical Sociology* 5: 23–41.

COLLINS, RANDALL. 1979. *The Credential Society.* New York: Academic Press.

DOMHOFF, WILLIAM G. 1974. *The Bohemian Grove and Other Retreats.* New York: Harper and Row.

DOMHOFF, WILLIAM G. 1996. *State Autonomy or Class Dominance? Case Studies on Policy Making in America.* New York: Aldine.

DURKHEIM, EMILE. 1951 [original 1897]. *Suicide.* New York: Free Press.

ESTROFF, SUSAN E. 1981. *Making It Crazy.* Berkeley: University of California Press.

FIGERT, ANNE E. 1996. *Women and the Ownership of PMS: The Professional, Gendered and Scientific Structuring of a Psychiatric Disorder.* New York: Aldine De Gruyter.

FREIDSON, ELIOT. 1970a. *Profession of Medicine.* New York: Free Press.

FREIDSON, ELIOT. 1970b. *Professional Dominance.* New York: Atherton Press.

GALVIN, R.S. 1998. "Are Performance Measures Relevant?" *Health Affairs* 17: 29–31.

GARRETT, LAURIE. 1994. *The Coming Plague: Newly Emerging Diseases in a World Out of Balance.* New York: Farrar, Straus and Giroux.

GOLDMAN, H.H., A.F. LEHMAN, J.P. MORRISSEY, S.J. NEWMAN, R.G. FRANK, and D.M. STEINWACHS. 1990. "Design for the National Evaluation of the Robert Wood Johnson Foundation Program on Chronic Mental Illness." *Hospital and Community Psychiatry* 41: 1217–21.

GRAY, BRADFORD H., and SARAH R. PHILLIPS. 1995. "Medical Sociology and Health Policy: What Are the Connections?" *Journal of Health and Social Behavior* (Extra Issue): 170–82.

GRUSKY, DAVID. 1994. "The Contours of Social Stratification." In *Social Stratification in Sociological Perspective,* ed. D. Grusky. Boulder: Westview Press, pp. 3–31.

HAFFERTY, FREDERIC W., and DONALD W. LIGHT. 1995. "Professional Dynamics and the Changing Nature of Medical Work." *Journal of Health and Social Behavior* (Extra Issue): 132–53.

HOHMANN, ANN A. 1996. "Measurement Sensitivity in Clinical Mental Health Services Research: Recommendation for the Future." In *Outcomes Assessment in Clinical Practice,* ed. L.I. Sederer and B. Dickey. Baltimore: Williams and Wilkins, pp. 161–67.

HOLLINGSHEAD, AUGUST. 1949. *Elmtown's Youth.* New York: Wiley.

HUTCHINSON, ALLAN C. 1992. "Doing the Right Thing? Toward a Postmodern Politics." *Law and Society Review* 26: 773–87.

JESSOP, B. 1990. *State Theory: Putting Capitalist States in Their Place.* Oxford: Polity Press.

JOHNSON, TERANCE. 1972. *Professions and Power.* London: Macmillan.

KATZ, JACK. 1983. "A Theory of Qualitative Methodology: The Social System of Analytic Fieldwork." In *Contemporary Field Research,* ed. Robert Emerson. Prospect Heights, IL: Waveland Press, pp. 127–48.

KOOS, E.L. 1954. *The Health of Regionville.* New York: Basic Books.

KRUPNICK, J.L. 1999. "The Assessment of Functional Outcomes in Cost-Effectiveness of Psychotherapy Studies." In *The Cost-Effectiveness of Psychotherapy: Developing Clinical and Services Research Models in An Era of Health Care Reform,* ed. E. Miller and K. Magruder. London: Oxford University Press.

LARSON, MAGALI. 1977. *The Rise of Professionalism.* Berkeley: University of California Press.

LASKER, JUDITH. 1977. "The Role of Health Services in Colonial Rule: The Case of the Ivory Coast." *Culture, Medicine, and Psychiatry* 3: 277–97.

LAVEIST, THOMAS. 1992. "The Political Empowerment and Health Status of African-Americans: Mapping A New Territory." *American Journal of Sociology* 97: 1080–95.

LEESON, JOYCE. 1974. "Social Science and Health Policy in Preindustrial Society." *International Journal of Health Services* 4: 429–40.

LEFLEY, H. 1998. "Culture and Chronic Mental Illness." *Hospital and Community Psychiatry* 41:277–86.

LEVINE, SOL. 1987. "The Changing Terrains in Medical Sociology: Emergent Concern With Quality of Life." *Journal of Health and Social Behavior* 28: 1–6.

LEVINE, SOL. 1995. "Time for Creative Integration in Medical Sociology." *Journal of Health and Social Behavior* (Extra Issue): 1–4.

LIEBERSON, STANLEY. 1985. *Making It Count: The Improvement of Social Research and Theory.* Berkeley: University of California Press.

LIGHT, DONALD W. 1993. "Countervailing Power: The Changing Character of the Medical Profession in the United States." In *The Changing Medical Profession: An International Perspective,* ed. F.W. Hafferty and J.B. McKinlay. New York: Oxford University Press, pp. 69–79.

LINK, BRUCE G., and FRANCES T. CULLEN. 1990. "The Labeling Theory of Mental Disorder: A Review of the Evidence." *Research in Community and Mental Health* 6: 75–105.

LINK, BRUCE G., and JO PHELAN. 1995. "Social Conditions as Fundamental Causes of Disease." *Journal of Health and Social Behavior* (Extra Issue): 80–94.

LINK, BRUCE G., JO C. PHELAN, MICHAELINE BRESNAHAN, ANN STUEVE, and BERNICE A. PESCOSOLIDO. 1999. "Public Conceptions of Mental Illness: Labels, Causes, Dangerousness and Social Distance." *American Journal of Public Health* 89(9): 1326–1333.

LINK, BRUCE G., MARY E. NORTHRIDGE, JO C. PHELAN, and MICHAEL L. GANZ. 1998. "Social Epidemiology and the Fundamental Cause Concept: On the Structuring of Effective Cancer Screens by Socioeconomic Status." *Milbank Quarterly* 76: 375–402.

McKEOWN, THOMAS. 1976. *The Rise of Modern Populations.* New York: Academic Press.

McKINLAY, JOHN B. 1981. "Refocusing Upstream." In *The Sociology of Health and Illness: Critical Perspectives,* ed. Peter Conrad and Rochelle Kern. New York: St. Martin's Press.

McKINLAY, JOHN B. 1996. "Some Contributions From the Social System to Gender Inequalities in Heart Disease." *Journal of Health and Social Behavior* 36: 1–26.

McKINLAY, JOHN B., and LISA D. MARCEAU. 1998. "The end of the golden age of doctoring." Presented at the American Public Health Association. Washington, DC. November.

McKINLAY, JOHN B., and LISA DiGRUTTOLO. 1997. "A tale of three tails." Presented at the Prevention: Contributions From Basic and Applied Research Conference. Chicago, IL.

McKINLAY, JOHN B., and SONJA M. McKINLAY. 1981. "Medical Measures and the Decline of Mortality." In *The Sociology of Health and Illness: Critical Perspectives,* ed. P. Conrad and R. Kern. New York: St. Martin's Press, pp. 12–30.

MECHANIC, D. 1998. "The Changing Face of Mental Health Managed Care." In *Managed Behavioral Health Care: Current Realities and Future Potential,* ed. D. Mechanic. San Francisco: Jossey-Bass, pp. 7–14.

MERTON, ROBERT K., GEORGE D. READER, and PATRICIA L. KENDALL, eds. 1957. *The Student Physician: Introductory Studies in the Sociology of Medical Education.* Cambridge: Harvard University Press.

MILLS, C. WRIGHT. 1959. *The Sociological Imagination.* Oxford: Oxford University Press.

MILLSTEIN, G, P. GUARNACCIA, and E. MIDLARSKY. 1995. "Ethnic Differences in the Interpretation of Mental Illness: Perspectives of Caregivers." *Research in Community and Mental Health* 8: 155–78.

MIRANDA, J. 1998. "Preliminary Findings of the Effectiveness Study With Three Ethnic Populations." Personal communication.

MIROWSKY, JOHN, and CATHERINE E. ROSS. 1989. "Psychiatric Diagnosis as Reified Measurement." *Journal of Health and Social Behavior* 30: 11–25.

OSMOND, D.H., K. VRARUZAN, D. SCHILLINGER, ET AL. 1996. "Measuring the Need for Medical Care in Ethnically Diverse Populations." *Health Services Research* 31: 551–71.

PARSONS, TALCOTT. 1951. *The Social System.* Glencoe, IL: Free Press.

PEARLIN, LEONARD I. 1989. "The Sociological Study of Stress." *Journal of Health and Social Behavior* 30: 241–56.

PEARLIN, LEONARD I. 1992. "Structure and Meaning in Medical Sociology." *Journal of Health and Social Behavior* 33: 1–9.

PESCOSOLIDO, BERNICE A., and BETH A. RUBIN. 1999. "The web of group affiliations revisited: Social life, postmodernism and sociology." Unpublished manuscript. Indiana University.

PESCOSOLIDO, BERNICE A., and JENNIE J. KRONENFELD. 1995. "Sociological Understandings of Health, Illness and Healing: The Challenge From and For Medical Sociology." *Journal of Health and Social Behavior* (Extra Issue):5–33.

PESCOSOLIDO, BERNICE A., JOHN MONAHAN, BRUCE G. LINK, ANN STUEVE, and SAEKO KIKUZAWA. 1999. "The Public's View of the Competence, Dangerousness and Need for Legal Coercion among Persons with Mental Illness." *American Journal of Public Health* 89(9): 1339–1345.

PORTES, ALEJANDRO, and R.D. MANNING. 1994. "The Immigrant Enclave: Theory and Empirical Examples." In *Social Stratification in Sociological Perspective,* ed. D. Grusky. Boulder: Westview Press, pp. 509–19.

RIESSMAN, CATHERINE KOHLER. 1983. "Women and Medicalization: A New Perspective." *Social Policy* Summer: 3–18.

ROSEN, GEORGE. 1983. *The Structure of American Medical Practice.* Philadelphia: University of Pennsylvania Press.

ROSENHAN, D.L. 1973. "On Being Sane in Insane Places." *Science* 179: 250–58.

RUBIN, BETH A. 1996. *Shifts in the Social Contract.* Thousand Oaks, CA: Pine Forge Press.

SCHEFF, THOMAS. 1966. *Being Mentally Ill: A Sociological Theory.* Chicago: Aldine Publishing Co.

SCHWARTZ, SHARON. 1999. "Biological Theories of Psychiatric Disorders: A Sociological Approach." In *The Sociology of Mental Health and Illness,* ed. Alan V. Horowitz and Teresa A. Scheid. Cambridge: Cambridge University Press.

SKOCPOL, THEDA. 1997. *Boomerang—Health Care Reform and the Turn Against Government.* New York: North and Co.

STARR, PAUL. 1982. *The Social Transformation of American Medicine.* New York: Basic Books.

STEWART, ABIGAIL L., and JOHN E. WARE, eds. 1992. *Measuring Functioning and Well-Being: The Medical Outcomes Study Approach.* Durham, NC: Duke University Press.

SYME, S. LEONARD. 1996. "To Prevent Disease: The Need for a New Approach." In *Health and Social Organization,* ed. D. Blane, E. Brunner, and R.G. Wilkinson. London: Routledge.

THEIR, S.O., and A.C. GELINGS. 1998. "Improving Health: The Reason Why Performance Measurement Matters." *Health Affairs* 17: 26–28.

WAITZKIN, HOWARD. 1983. *The Second Sickness: Contradictions of Capitalist Health Care.* New York: Free Press.

WARE, JOHN E. JR. 1995. "The Status of Health Assessment 1994." *Annual Review of Public Health* 16: 327–54.

WILKINSON, RICHARD G. 1966. *Unhealthy Societies: The Affliction of Inequality.* London: Routledge.

WILKINSON, RICHARD G. 1997. "Comment: Income, Inequality and Social Cohesion." *American Journal of Public Health* 87:1504–06.

WOOLF, STEVEN H., CAROLYN G. DiGUISEPPI, DAVID ATKINS, and DOUGLAS B. KAMEROW. 1996. "Developing Evidence-Based Clinical Practice Guidelines: Lessons Learned by the U.S. Preventive Services Task Force." *Annual Review of Public Health* 17: 511–38.

ZBOROWSKI, MARK. 1952. "Cultural Components in Responses to Pain." *Journal of Social Issues* 8: 16-30.

INDEX

Haney, C.A., 27
Hansell, Stephen, 48
Haraway, D.J., 314, 315, 316, 381
Harbottle, L., 121
Harding, S., 117
Hardt, E.J., 275
Harkin, Tom, 290
Harr, Jonathan, 152, 154
Harrington, C., 281
Harris, Tirril O., 70, 71, 102
Harrison, James, 104
Harrison, Michael, 204
Harwood, Allan, 380
Hauerwaus, S., 404
Haug, Marie R., 3, 203, 208, 405
Hauger, Richard L., 343
Hauser, Philip M., 36, 50, 51, 83, 365
Hayes, Diane, 55
Haynes, C., 118
Hayward, Mark D., 52
Hayward, W., 243
Headen, A., 124
Heath, Deborah, 380
Heck, Katherine, 43
Hellinger, F.J., 228, 231
Helmers, Karin F., 343
Helmert, U., 55
Hemingway, Harry, 335, 341
Henderson, Lawrence J., 12, 15
Hennekens, Charles H., 55
Henry, C., 121
Henry, W.E., 136
Herbert, Tracy B., 335, 336, 337, 338
Herold, Joan, 51
Herrnstein, Richard J., 328
Hertzman, Clyde, 101
Hertz-Picciotto, Irva, 84
Herzlich, Claudine, 159
Herzog, A.R., 131
Hess, D., 316
Hibbard, Judith H., 52
Hill, Austin B., 151
Hill, J., 230
Hill, Lauren, 346
Hill, Shirley A., 188
Himmel, Wolfgang, 294
Himmelstein, D.U., 281
Himsworth, H., 36
Hinchman, Lewis P., 184, 185, 187
Hinchman, Sandra K., 184, 185, 187
Hirdes, J.P., 34
Hirschauer, S., 314, 315
Hitzler, Ronald, 159, 166
Hochschild, Arlie R., 74
Hochstim, Joseph R., 82
Hofer, T.P., 87
Hoff, T., 224, 226
Hoffman, Catherine, 187
Hoffmaster, B., 401, 406
Hofrichter, Richard, 146
Hogan, Dennis P., 69
Hogle, L., 309, 316
Hohmann, Ann A., 422, 423
Holden, Constance, 23
Hollenberg, C.H., 250
Hollingshead, August B., 2, 8, 19, 260, 412
Hollingsworth, J. Rogers, 56
Holmstrom, L., 406
Homedes, Nuria, 392

Hood, Leroy, 325
Hopper, Kim, 384
Horgan, John, 325
Hornberger, J.C., 275
Horowitz, M.J., 243
Horowitz, Ralph I., 341, 342
Horwitz, Allan V., 103
House, James S., 33, 35, 38, 51, 52, 60, 80, 83, 85, 88, 90, 91, 131, 357, 358, 361, 367
Howlett, B., 118
Hu, Dale, 43
Hu, Paul N., 50, 52, 58, 59, 60, 83
Hubbard, Ruth, 104, 330
Huber, Joan, 50, 51, 52, 53, 59
Hughes, Charles C., 23, 384
Hughes, Everett C., 211, 255, 403, 405, 407
Hughes, H.M., 239
Hughes, Michael, 103
Hughes, T.P., 319
Hummer, Robert A., 57, 58, 84
Hundert, E., 242
Hunt, Kate, 98
Hurd, Michael D., 57
Hyden, Lars-Christer, 189, 190, 191
Hynes, H. Patricia, 145
Hyun, Christine S., 338

Ickovics, Jeannette R., 87, 342
Iezzoni, L., 221
Illich, Ivan, 311, 322
Illsley, R., 36
Immergut, Ellen M., 208
Institute for Scientific Information, 57
Institute of Medicine (IOM), 152
Irwin, Michael, 337

Jablensky, Assen, 384
Jackson, James S., 372
Jackson, Pamela B., 69, 243
Jacobs, Jennifer, 293
Jacobs, Jerry A., 48, 51
Jacobsen, Bjarne K., 55
Jacobson, David, 70–71
Jacoby, Ann, 192
Jankowski, M. Kay, 101
Janowitz, M., 404
Janzen, John, 378
Jargowsky, Paul A., 83, 84
Jarjoura, D., 120
Jasso, Guillermina, 37
Jeffrey, N.A., 246, 253
Jelastopulu, Eleni, 208
Jenkins, Janis H., 384
Jenkins, Richard, 163, 165, 166, 167
Jennings, J. Richard, 343
Jennings, Susan, 51
Jensen, G.A., 229
Jessop, B., 420
Jette, A.M., 175, 176, 177, 179
Joesch, J.M., 229
Johansson, Jan-Erik, 58
Johnson, Catherine, 326
Johnson, David R., 362
Johnson, Jeffrey V., 101
Johnson, Joyce M., 69
Johnson, Terrance, 203, 204, 415
Jones, Anthony, 204
Jones, D.R., 50, 51

Jones, J., 400
Jones, Kelvyn, 82
Jones, Maxwell, 14
Jones, Steve, 327
Jones, Thomas, 149
Jonsen, A., 401
Joseph, K.S., 89
Joshi, H., 81, 82
Josselson, Ruthellen, 188, 194
Journal of Health and Social Behavior, 267, 268, 389
Journal of the American Medical Association, 27–28
Judge, K., 125
Jung, Waymond, 337

Kagan, Jerold, 368
Kagan, Jerome, 343
Kahn, K., 123, 124
Kahn, R.L., 131, 136, 138
Kalberg, Stephen, 162
Kamarck, Thomas W., 343
Kamerow, Douglas B., 421
Kantor, Glenda K., 55
Kao, A.C., 232
Kapiro, J., 89
Kaplan, George A., 35, 37, 50, 55, 59, 82, 83, 88, 91, 131, 335, 340, 341, 342, 343, 345, 346, 347, 366, 371
Kaplan, Louise, 146
Kaprio, Jaakko, 341
Karasek, Robert A., 52, 341, 347, 366, 367
Kasl, Stanislav V., 51, 159
Kassirer, Jerome P., 229, 287
Katz, Jack, 413
Katz, S.J., 87
Kaufert, J., 208
Kauhanen, Jussi, 345
Kaw, Eugenia, 330
Kawachi, Ichiro, 35, 56, 88, 309, 341
Kazis, Lewis E., 305
Kearl, M.C., 312
Keelan, E.T., 106
Keesing, Roger M., 379
Keller, Steven E., 339
Kelley, John M., 354, 355
Kelley, Judith, 152
Kelly, M., 178
Kelly, Michael P., 185
Kelner, Merrijoy, 294
Kemeny, Margaret E., 338
Kendall, Patricia L., 2, 21, 262, 413
Kenen, Joanne, 130
Kennedy, Bruce P., 35, 37, 56, 82, 88
Kennedy, Donald, 23
Kennedy, Edward M., 202
Kerckhoff, Alan C., 60
Kern, Fred, 240
Kerr, E.A., 224, 227
Kessler, Ronald C., 50, 51, 52, 59, 69, 70, 72, 73, 90, 98, 100, 103, 119, 120, 131, 354, 355, 394
Kevles, B.H., 309, 325, 329
Kiecolt-Glaser, Janice, 336, 337, 338, 341, 343, 344, 346, 361
Kikuzawa, Saeko, 419
Kilborn, Peter T., 202, 209
Kilgore, R., 277
Kim, K.K., 56

Salonen, J.T., 59, 342
Saltman, Richard B., 208
Samet, Jonathan M., 368
Sandifer, W. Richard, 51
Sandvik, Leiv, 55
Sapolsky, R.M., 37
Sarachek, Deborah, 57, 58
Sarafino, Edward P., 360
Sarason, B.R., 357
Sarason, I.G., 357
Saris, Jamie, 385
Sashidharan, S., 122
Scambler, Graham, 192
Schacter, Stanley, 71
Schafer, Walt, 335
Scheff, Thomas, 419
Scheper-Hughes, Nancy, 379
Schiff, G.D., 281
Schindler, Lydia W., 336
Schleifer, Steven J., 339, 360
Schlesinger, Mark, 205, 267
Schmalz, Jeffrey, 330
Schneider, Joseph W., 4, 192, 202, 247,
    322, 323, 324, 326, 329, 330, 359
Schoen, Cathy, 262
Schoenbaum, Michael, 80, 83
Schoepflin, U., 129
Schooler, Carmi, 54, 70, 367
Schor, Edward L., 305
Schuller, Alexander, 203, 204, 208
Schulte, Miriam, 294
Schutt, G., 309
Schwartz, Carolyn, 298, 303, 305
Schwartz, Morris S., 2, 14
Schwartz, Sally, 150
Schwartz, Sharon, 418, 419
Scott, Chris B., 55
Searle, C. Maureen, 392
Seeman, Alice Z., 51, 54
Seeman, Melvin, 53, 54, 356
Seeman, Teresa, 54, 88, 354, 360, 361
Segal, Julius, 17, 19, 26
Segerstrom,Suzanne C., 360
Segovia, Jorge, 55
Seidman, Steven, 184, 186, 194, 195
Seitz, Robert, 208
Seligman, Jean, 290
Selye, Hans, 334
Seron, Carroll, 421
Sewell, William H., 18, 19
Shafir, W., 252
Shah, L.J., 243
Shapin, S., 316
Sharp, Kimberly, 57
Sharp, L., 309
Sharp, Susan, 353
Shaw, Clifford R., 371
Shea, Denis, 55, 60
Shea, Steven, 228
Shearin, E.N., 357
Sheedy, Kristin M., 330
Sheehan, K.H., 246
Shelton, W., 272
Shema, S.J., 80, 83
Sherbourne, C.D., 221
Sheridan, John, 337
Sherrington R., 326
Sherwood, Andrew, 343
Sherwood, Jane B., 341

Shevsky, Eshref, 371
Shiflett, Samuel C., 339
Shilling, Chris, 165
Shils, Edward, 11
Shine, K.I., 244
Shively, C., 37
Shore, Elsie R., 55
Shortell, Stephen, 5, 202
Shrout, Patrick E., 69
Shugars, D.A., 251
Shulkin, D.J., 281
Shuval, J.T., 241
Sidney, Stephen, 84, 372
Siegrest, Johannes, 368
Sillen, S., 125
Silver, H.K., 246, 247
Silver, Roxanne L., 70, 355
Silverstein, M., 136
Simeon, George P., 303
Simmel, G., 404
Simmons, Leo W., 21
Simmons, R.G., 309
Simmons, R.L., 309
Simon, C.J., 229
Simon, Robin W., 68, 70, 72, 73, 74, 75,
    102, 103, 355
Simons, Ronald C., 384
Simpson, O., 42
Singer, Jerome E., 71
Singer, Merrill, 379
Singh, G.K., 34, 85
Singleton, V., 316
Skocpol, Theda, 266, 420
Skodol, Andrew E., 50, 52
Skolnick, A.A., 222
Skoner, David P., 338, 339
Sleeper, Sally, 231, 277
Sloggett, A., 81, 82
Slomczynski, Kazimierz M., 52
Smaje, Chris, 114, 118, 122, 123, 124, 125
Smit, H., 309
Smith, Barbara E., 145
Smith, Dorothy E., 184, 186
Smith, Elaine M., 58
Smith, James P., 80, 83
Smith, Ken, 82, 88
Smith, M.R., 312
Smith, N.S., 227
Smith, R.C., 279
Smith, Richard, 207
Smith, S., 119
Smith, Tom L., 36, 343
Snow, David, 146
Snowden, L., 124
Sobal, Jeffrey, 328
Sobel, David S., 347
Sofaer, S., 105
Soffel, D.S., 312
Soloman, M., 125
Solorzano, A., 250
Somers, Anne R., 205
Somers, Herman M., 205
Somers, Margaret R., 185
Soobader, M.J., 82
Sorenson, Glorian, 99, 108, 170
Sorenson, James R., 330
Sorlie, Paul D., 34, 36, 38, 57, 85, 120
Sparrow, David, 341
Speicher, Carl, 337

Speizer, Frank E., 55
Spickett, Gavin P., 338
Spiegel, A.D., 313
Spilker, Bert, 303
Spitze, Glenna, 52
Spitzer, T.C., 250
Spragins, Ellyn E., 294
Sprangers, Miriam, 305
Stam, Henderikus J., 190
Stampfer, Meir J., 55
Stanton, Albert H., 2
Stanton, Alfred H., 14
Star, S.L., 314, 315, 316, 317
Starfield, B., 220, 222, 225, 230
Starr, Paul, 3, 17, 130, 134, 201, 202, 210,
    218, 223, 260, 266, 289, 313, 414,
    415
Stearns, S.C., 226
Stein, Shayna, 51
Steingraber, Sandra, 145
Stephans, John D., 389
Stern, Bernard J., 1, 13
Stern, D.T., 242
Stern, J., 36
Stern, M., 121
Stevens, Fred, 169, 170
Stevens, Rosemary A., 16, 135, 203
Stewart, Abigail, 421
Stinchcombe, A.L., 217
Stoddard, Greg L., 303
Stoekle, J., 135, 201, 203, 207, 276
Stokes, C. Shannon, 57, 58
Stokes, John, III, 27
Stone, Arthur A., 337
Stone, D.A.
Stone, George, 23
Stouffer, Samuel, 36
Strackee, J., 55
Stratakis, Constantine, 346
Stratton, Terry D., 394
Straus, Robert, 2, 13, 22, 23, 260, 267
Strauss, Anselm, 173, 177, 178, 188, 193,
    309, 315, 402, 405
Street, D., 137
Strickland, Stephen, 261
Strong, Phil, 323
Stronks, K., 84
Stueve, Ann, 419
Subedi, Janardan, 390, 406
Suchman, L., 315
Sudnow, David, 402
Sullivan, Harry S., 14
Sulmasy, Daniel P., 207
Summer, L., 130, 131
Sung, Hai-Yen, 187
Surgeon General, 55
Susser, Mervyn, 33, 150
Sussman, Marvin B., 211
Sutherland, H.J., 304
Sutton-Tyrell, Kim, 346
Swan, J.H., 132, 135
Swanson, Bert, 263
Swazey, Judith P., 8, 309, 406
Sweat, Michael D., 160
Sweeting, Helen, 98
Syme, Leonard S., 35, 36, 37, 50, 52, 55,
    90, 366, 367, 368, 417
Syverson, C.J., 57
Szasz, Andrew, 146, 151, 152

Zautra, Alex J., 148
Zborowski, Mark, 422
Zeichner, Christiane I., 389
Zeldow, P.B., 246
Zelman, Walter A., 202

Ziegler, Michael G., 338
Zierler, Sally, 369
Zimmerman, Don H., 74
Zola, Irving K., 170, 174, 176, 177, 178, 179, 181, 182, 186, 188, 195, 322, 330

Zuriff, G.E., 324
Zussman, R., 406
Zwanziger, J., 229
Zwicky, John F., 287

SUBJECT INDEX